Text and Materials in Commercial Law

Text and Materials in Commercial Law

L S Sealy
S J Berwin Professor of Corporate Law,
University of Cambridge;
Barrister and Solicitor (New Zealand)

R J A Hooley
Fellow of Fitzwilliam College, Cambridge;
of the Middle Temple, Barrister

Butterworths
London, Dublin and Edinburgh
1994

United Kingdom	Butterworth & Co (Publishers) Ltd, Halsbury House, 35 Chancery Lane, LONDON WC2A 1EL and 4 Hill Street, EDINBURGH EH2 3JZ
Australia	Butterworths, SYDNEY, MELBOURNE, BRISBANE, ADELAIDE, PERTH, CANBERRA and HOBART
Canada	Butterworths Canada Ltd, TORONTO and VANCOUVER
Ireland	Butterworth (Ireland) Ltd, DUBLIN
Malaysia	Malayan Law Journal Sdn Bhd, KUALA LUMPUR
New Zealand	Butterworths of New Zealand Ltd, WELLINGTON and AUCKLAND
Puerto Rico	Butterworth of Puerto Rico, Inc, SAN JUAN
Singapore	Butterworths Asia, SINGAPORE
South Africa	Butterworth Publishers (Pty) Ltd, DURBAN
USA	Butterworth Legal Publishers, CARLSBAD, California; and SALEM, New Hampshire

A CIP Catalogue record for this book is available from the British Library.

ISBN 0 406 01619 4

Typeset by Columns Design and Production Services Ltd, Reading
Printed and bound in Great Britain by Mackays of Chatham Plc, Kent

∞ This text paper meets the requirements of ISO 9706/1994.
Information and Documentation – paper for documents – requirements for permanence.

For my parents

RH

Preface

The aim of this book is to provide students of commercial law with a coursebook which combines the best features of a textbook and a casebook. We hope that they will benefit from the convenience of having an explanatory text and supporting materials available in one volume.

If there is one branch of English law of which we can be justly proud, it is its commercial law. This is the law chosen by a large proportion of the world's merchants to govern their contracts – far more than that of any other jurisdiction – and it is to English arbitrators and the English Commercial Court that they come to resolve their disputes. Very often, *all* the parties to these proceedings are foreign. Part of the explanation for this remarkable state of affairs may be historical, but businessmen are first and foremost practical people, and it is reasonable enough to suppose that if English law was not giving them what they wanted from a system of commercial law, they would long ago have sought satisfaction elsewhere.

This phenomenon may seem all the more surprising when it is realised that most of the other leading legal systems have a Commercial Code, specifically designed and intended to meet the particular needs of the mercantile community, while English commercial law has its sources almost entirely in case law and mercantile custom. Even the few statutes of major importance, such as the Bills of Exchange Act and the Sale of Goods Act, are no more than codifications of the law which had evolved through the cases prior to their enactment.

It is because the commercial law which we have inherited has been developed and refined through constant exposure to the demands of business and the marketplace that it serves its users so well. It is also because the essential features of this law have long been well settled that traders and their associations have been able to develop standard forms of contract, based on English law, on which they can do business with each other with confidence.

What better subject could there be, then, to be studied and taught from the cases themselves and from the documents which are typically used in everyday commerce? It is because we believe strongly that this is so that we have brought together the materials which are to be found in this book, and supplemented them with our own commentary which will, we hope, go some way to reveal the unique genius that underlies the commercial law of England and of those Commonwealth countries which have adopted it.

There is bound to be some controversy over the precise contents of a book such as this. It appears that no two commercial law courses are the same. However, our task in deciding which areas of the subject to include, and which to exclude, was made easier thanks to the assistance of those Law Schools which were kind enough to send us details of their commercial/mercantile law courses. Suggestions for changing the contents of future editions will always be gratefully received.

We both, of course, accept responsibility for the text as a whole. More particularly, Richard Hooley has written Chapters 1–6 and 15–25, while Len Sealy wrote Chapters 7–14 and 26–27. We gratefully acknowledge help on all sides from our colleagues in the Cambridge Law Faculty, and especially Michael Prichard and Malcolm Clarke. It is with pleasure and gratitude also that we record the help which we have received from the editorial staff of Butterworths throughout all stages of the planning and production of the work.

Finally, but most importantly, Richard Hooley would like to thank his wife, Elizabeth, for her encouragement and constant support throughout the preparation of this book.

The law is stated as it stood from sources available to us on 31 December 1993, save that the Companies Act 1989 is assumed to be fully in force; but the publishers have kindly allowed us to incorporate some changes and new material at proof stage.

Len Sealy
Richard Hooley
Cambridge
May 1994

Acknowledgments

We are grateful to the following for kindly allowing the reproduction of extract material:

Blackwell Publishers: Dowrick 'The Relationship of Principal and Agent' (1954) 17 MLR 24, 36–38; Battersby and Preston 'The Concept of "Property", "Title" and "Owner" used in the Sale of Goods Act 1893' (1972) MLR 268, 268–272, 288.

British Bankers' Association: *Good Banking* (2nd ed, 1994).

Butterworth & Co (Publishers) Ltd: Butterworths Company Law Cases; All England Law Reports; English Reports; Law Journal Reports; Law Times Reports; Commercial Cases; Gray *Elements of Land Law* (1st ed, 1987) pp 8–14 and Jack *Documentary Credits* (2nd ed, 1993), para 1.3.

Cambridge Law Journal and Authors: Sealy [1972B] CLJ 225, 226–227; Gray [1991] CLJ 252, 292–295.

Canadian Bar Review and Author: Fridman 'Agent – Agent acting beyond actual authority – Liability of undisclosed principal – The demise of *Watteau v Fenwick: Sign-O-Lite Plastics Ltd v Metropolitan Life Insurance Co*' (1991) 70 Can B Rev 329, 329–333.

Canada Law Book Inc: Geva 'The Evolving Law of Payment by Wire Transfer – An Outsider's View of Draft UCC Article 4A' (1988) 14 CBLJ 186, 187–188.

CCH Editions Ltd: British Company Cases.

Council of Law Reporting for New South Wales: New South Wales Law Reports.

ICC Publishing SA: *Uniform Customs and Practice for Documentary Credits* (No 500, 1993 Revision), arts 2, 3, 4, 13. Copyright © 1993. This publication is available from ICC Publishing SA, 38 Cours Albert 1er, 75008 Paris, France and from ICC United Kingdom, 14/15 Belgrave Square, London SW1X 8PS.

Incorporated Council of Law Reporting: Law Reports and Weekly Law Reports.

Institute of Bankers: Goode (ed) *Electronic Banking, the Legal Implications*, pp v–vi, 40–41.

Israel Law Review Association and Author: Barak 'The Nature of the Negotiable Instrument' (1983) 18 Is LR 49, 53–55, 60–63, 65, 69–70.

Juta & Co Ltd: Cowen *The Law of Negotiable Instruments in South Africa* (5th ed, 1985), Vol 1, p 52.

Law Book Company: Commonwealth Law Reports.

Lloyd's of London Press Ltd: Lloyd's Law Reports.

Longman Group UK Ltd: 'Commercial Equity' (1993) 14 Company Lawyer 41 (editorial comment).

J C B Mohr and Author: Weir 'The Common Law System' in *International Encyclopedia of Comparative Law*, Vol II, Ch 2, Part III, para 146.

Harvard Law Review Association: Holdsworth 'The History of the Treatment of Choses in Action by the Common Law' (1920) 33 Harvard LR 967, 967–968.

Her Majesty's Stationery Office: Law Commission, Report on Sale of Goods Forming Part of a Bulk (No 215, 1993), recs 6.1–6.10; Contributory Negligence as a Defence in Contract (No 219, 1993), para 5.20; Diamond, A Review of Security Interests in Property (1989), paras 3.1–3.3, 8.2.1–8.2.11, 18.2.3–18.2.4, 23.9.22, 23.9.25; Banking Services Law and Practice: Report by the Review Committee (Cmnd 622, 1989), p x and paras 2.07–2.08, 2.13–2.14, 6.11, 6.13, 6.14, 6.23–6.25, 7.74–7.76, 9.03, 9.11; Report of the Crowther Committee on Consumer Credit (Cmnd 4596, 1971), Vol 2, p 579; and statutes.

Monash University Law Review and Author: Goode 'The Codification of Commercial Law' (1988) 14 Mon LR 135, 141–143, 147–155.

Office of Official Publications of the European Community: EC Directive 86/653 of 18 December 1986, arts 1(2)–(3), 2(1)–(2).

Oxford University Press and Authors: Ellinger 'Bank's Liability for Paying Fraudulently Issued Cheques' (1985) 5 Ox JLS 293, 293–294 and Honoré 'Ownership' in *Oxford Essays in Jurisprudence* (ed AG Guest) (1961), pp 107–108, 112–123, 126–128: a revised version of which also appears in Honoré *Making Law Bind* (OUP, 1987).

Sweet & Maxwell Ltd and authors: Samuel 'Civil and Commercial Law: A Distinction Worth Making' (1986) 102 LQR 569, 577–578; Schmitthoff 'The Concept of Economic Law in England' [1966] JBL 309, 315, 318–319; Schmitthoff 'The Codification of the Law of International Trade' [1985] JBL 34, 41–43; Goode 'Ownership and Obligation in Commercial Transactions' (1987) 103 LQR 433, 433–435, 436–438; Goode 'Some Aspects of Factoring Law 1 – The Acquisition of Rights in Receivables' [1982] JBL 240, 240–241; Oditah 'Lightweight Floating Charges' [1991] JBL 49, 49–50; Palmer *Bailment* (2nd ed, 1991), pp 124–125; *Bowstead on Agency* (15th ed, 1985), arts 1(1), 20 and 112(1); Oditah *Legal Aspects of Receivables Financing* (1991), p 2; *Snell's Equity* (29th ed, 1990), p 79; and *Palmer's Company Cases*.

Times Newspapers Ltd: Times Law Reports.

UNIDROIT: Ottawa Convention on International Factoring 1988, arts 5–12, 17.

Most extracts have been reproduced without footnotes.

We are also grateful to the following for kindly allowing the reproduction of commercial documents: Standen Engineering Ltd; Transworld Freight Services Ltd; Trans Cargo International UK Ltd; British International Freight Association; Fédération Internationale des Associations de Transitaires et Assimilés; Midland Bank plc; The Thomas Cook Group Ltd; Venture Factors plc; 3i plc; Butterworth & Co (Publishers) Ltd (Encyclopaedia of Forms and Precedents (5th ed), Vol 12, Form 81 (Master block discounting agreement) and Vol 28, Form 304 (Trust receipt)); and the various officers of these companies and firms.

LSS
RH

Contents

PART II THE LAW OF AGENCY

PART III DOMESTIC SALES LAW

Table of statutes

References in this Table to *Statutes* are to Halsbury's Statutes of England (Fourth Edition) showing the volume and page at which the annotated text of the Act may be found.

Page references printed in **bold** type indicate where the section of the Act is set out in part or in full.

List of cases

Page references printed in **bold** type indicate where a case is set out.

B

P

Part I
Introduction

CHAPTER 1

An introduction to commercial law

1 The nature of commercial law

What is commercial law? In the absence of any established legal definition of commercial law, writers on the subject have put forward various definitions of their own. These include the following:

> 'Commercial law' is an expression incapable of strict definition, but it is used to comprehend all that portion of the law of England which is more especially concerned with commerce, trade and business.
> (H W Disney *The Elements of Commercial Law* (1931), p 1)

> The object of commerce is to deal in mechandise and, if we adopt this criterion, commercial law can be defined as the special rules which apply to contracts for the sale of goods and to such contracts as are ancillary thereto, namely, contracts for the carriage and insurance of goods and contracts the main purpose of which is to finance the carrying out of contracts of sale.
> (H C Gutteridge 'Contract and Commercial Law' (1935) 51 LQR 117)

> Commercial Law is that branch of law which is concerned with rights and duties arising from the supply of goods and services in the way of trade.
> (R M Goode *Commercial Law* (1982), p 35)

> 'Commercial Law' can . . . be defined as the law relating to commercial activity and transactions.
> (R Bradgate and N Savage *Commercial Law* (1991), p 4)

All four definitions emphasise the mercantile nature of the subject. Commercial law is the law of commerce. It is concerned with commercial transactions, ie transactions in which both parties deal with each other in the course of business (Goode, op cit, p 38). The paradigm commercial transaction is the sale and supply of goods by one merchant to another. But there are many other types of commercial transaction, eg contracts for the carriage of goods, contracts for the insurance of goods, contracts for the finance of sale transactions, equipment leasing agreements, receivables financing arrangements and so on.

Many different spheres of commercial activity fall within the ambit of commercial law. It is not possible, nor desirable, to draw up an exhaustive list of the contents of the subject. Commercial law is a pragmatic and responsive subject which looks to facilitate the commercial practices of the business community. As those practices change and develop, often to accommodate new technology, the contents of commercial law may change and develop with them. A rigid definition of the scope of the subject would only inhibit this process. By way of comparison, see Order 72, r 1(2) of the Rules of the Supreme Court 1965 (below, p 9) which defines a 'commercial action', suitable to be heard by the Commercial Court, in a similarly broad manner.

'The Codification of Commercial Law' by R Goode (1988) 14 Mon LR 135, pp 141–143

III WHAT SHOULD GO INTO A COMMERCIAL CODE?

On one view, this is simply another way of posing the question: what is commercial law? Some would even ask: does commercial law exist? Having taught the subject for nearly two decades I desperately hope it does! But what goes into it is another matter. For my purposes I shall treat commercial law as that body of law which governs commercial transactions, that is, agreements and arrangements between professionals for the provision and acquisition of goods, services and facilities in the way of trade. Commercial law as thus defined possesses four characteristics. It is based on transactions, not on institutions; it is concerned primarily with dealings between merchants, in the broad sense of professionals as opposed to consumers; it is centred on contract and on the usages of the market; and it is concerned with a large mass of transactions in which each participant is a regular player, so that the transactions are typical and in large measure repetitive and lend themselves to a substantial measure of standardised treatment. On this basis we would expect commercial law in the sense in which I have used it to exclude consumer law as a *lex specialis* involving non-professionals; to exclude for the most part obligations of a kind normally derived from non-contractual sources of law such as tort, equity, bankruptcy and trusts; and to exclude the law governing institutional structures such as partnerships, corporations, banks, insurance companies, and the like. This is not to say that these are unsuitable subjects for codification, merely that they do not belong in a *commercial* code, which is concerned with contracts and with the dynamics of goods and services moving in the stream of trade rather than with the general law of obligations and the statics of institutional structure and organisation . . . .

(i) Types of transaction to be covered

Central to commercial law is that most common of contracts, the contract of sale, with its associated contracts of carriage, warehousing, insurance and finance. But the modern view of commercial law embodies a wider perspective, embracing equipment leasing, receivables financing, payment systems, personal property security, rights to investment securities, and a range of other commercial transactions not derived from a contract of sale. It is also necessary for a modern commercial code to accommodate new technology, in particular the teletransmission of trade and financial data, and new systems for clearing dealings in money, commodities and securities.

In deciding what items from a shopping list should be included in a commercial code, two points must be borne in mind. First, commercial law is not an abstraction, it is a tool for its users, whose needs will vary from place to place according to national practices, tradition and the level of sophistication of its business and financial institutions. No country should slavishly copy the sophisticated model represented by the American *Uniform Commercial Code*, which is designed for a country of fifty jurisdictions and some two hundred million inhabitants addicted to lawyers and litigation. Secondly, where the business community has codified trade usage this may make legislation both unnecessary and unhelpful. For example, there would seem little need to codify the law relating to documentary credits in view of the adoption around the world of the Uniform Customs and Practice.

(ii) The application of a commercial code to non-commercial transactions

While the emphasis of the *Uniform Commercial Code* is on commercial transactions, the draftsmen, preserving the common law tradition, made no attempt to exclude non-commercial contracts from its ambit. The formal separation of civil and commercial transactions to be found in some civil law systems has never been adopted by the common law and even those civil law jurisdictions that have it are said to have experienced difficulties. What the *Uniform Commercial Code* does do is to identify certain rules which apply solely to dealings between merchants and others which are restricted to transactions involving consumers. This is a sensible approach, for many of the Code rules are equally appropriate for commercial and non-commercial transactions, and little purpose is served by leaving the latter to remain governed by the vagaries of the common law.

(iii) Transactions omitted from the *Uniform Commercial Code*

Of some interest is the omission from the *Uniform Commercial Code* of major types of commercial transaction which one might expect to find covered in a code of this kind. Examples are guarantees, commercial agency, banking transactions (other than those relating to cheques) and insurance contracts. One explanation of the omission of these is that the function of the *Uniform Commercial Code* was seen not so much as codifying the commercial law in general but rather as bringing together in revised and integrated form those branches of commercial law which had already been codified in uniform laws prepared under the aegis of the National Conference of Commissions on Uniform State Laws. It may also be noted that, whether by accident or by design, the types of contract selected for inclusion in the code and its statutory predecessors are those which had been allowed to develop with the minimum interference of equity, whereas guarantees, agency, duties of bankers to customers and third parties and contracts of insurance are heavily underpinned by concepts of equitable obligation, reflecting the fact that the parties are involved not merely in a contract but in a continuing relationship and, moreover, a relationship attracting fiduciary duties. The Code, on the other hand, is concerned primarily with short-term, discrete contracts; it is not directed to on-going relationships, nor has it anything to say about the special problems of long-term contracts, problems which are relational, not purely contractual.

There is in my view no necessary reason why the rights and duties of the various parties arising from contracts of guarantee, commercial agency and the like should not be dealt with in a commercial code; indeed, their inclusion would do much to dispel the widespread ignorance of these matters prevailing among lawyers as well as laymen. . . .

NOTES

1. Although written with the specific purpose of stating what should go into a commercial code, this extract offers a sharp insight into the nature of commercial law generally. Unlike most civil law systems, and unlike the United States with its Uniform Commercial Code, English law has no comprehensive commercial code. Professor Goode advocates that there should be one. The issue is considered further below at pp 30–31.

2. The American Uniform Commercial Code is a model statute sponsored by the National Conference of Commissioners on Uniform State Laws and the American Law Institute. The first official text of the UCC was approved by its sponsors and the American Bar Association in 1952 and it has since been fully adopted by all the United States except Louisiana (which has a civil law tradition). The stated purpose of the UCC is 'to simplify, clarify and modernize the law governing commercial transactions; to permit the continued expansion of commercial practices through custom usage and agreement of the parties; to make uniform the law among the various jurisdictions' (s 1–102(2)). It covers a wide range of commercial activity: sales (art 2); commercial paper (art 3); bank deposits and collections (art 4); letters of credit (art 5); bulk transfers (art 6); warehouse receipts, bills of lading and other documents of title (art 7); investment securities (art 8); secured transactions, sales accounts and chattel paper (art 9). The UCC has been a great success. Much of the credit for this must go to the Code's chief architect, Professor Karl N Llewellyn. Professor Llewellyn's desire to avoid unnecessary theorisation and keep the Code as close to business reality as possible has made the UCC extremely workable.

3. Professor Goode asks: does commercial law exist? His entertaining answer disguises the importance of the question. It is sometimes argued that commercial law consists of no more than a collection of distinct subjects (eg agency, sales, negotiable instruments, security) each possessing its own rules but with no common thread of principle running through them. If true, 'commercial law' is merely a label which is useful for gathering together diverse material with no obvious home of its own, so as to aid exposition on a lecture course or in a textbook, or for the better organisation of the business of the High Court of Justice, but no more. On the other hand, if there are common principles running through the law's response to those spheres of commercial activity which fall within the ambit of 'commercial law', the subject gains an existence of its own. Those common principles may then be used for the better understanding of the subject and as important guides when facing new problems not previously the subject of judicial decisions. Professor Goode firmly believes that such unifying principles do exist (Goode, op cit, pp 36–37, 984–985: see below, pp 23–28). We would agree with him. But those principles are not so easy to identify. There is no neat body of uniform rules unique to commercial transactions. Unlike most civil law systems, English common law does not make any formal distinction between commercial and non-commercial transactions (but statute may do so, see, eg, the Unfair Contract Terms Act 1977, ss 3, 6 and 7).

The question whether the English common lawyer recognises the distinction between civil and commercial law has exercised the minds of comparative lawyers for some time. Compare the following extracts.

'The Common Law System' by Tony Weir in *International Encyclopedia of Comparative Law*, Vol II, Ch 2, Part III, para 146

Resistance of judges and jurists.—Holdsworth (History V 147) said that 'the distinctive character of the rules of commercial law, and their adaptability to the ever changing needs of new commercial conditions, have caused them to preserve many characteristic features unknown in other departments of the common law'. This statement is, however, open to doubt. It has already been seen that the common law adapted increasingly slowly, when at all, to the changing needs and practices of commerce. Legislation was frequently called for and 'the necessity of such recourse . . . seems to argue a failure on the part of the lawyers to adjust to the views of commerce'. Furthermore, it is not at all clear that the rules of commercial law are really very different in substance from the rules of civil law. Some transactions, of course, will be entered only by merchants as, for example, marine insurance. But the rules of marine insurance, though different from those of land insurance, are surprisingly little different. Other transactions, such as sale of goods, are entered by merchants and private citizens alike. In such cases the common law studiously avoids making different rules for the two cases, although it may well be that the same rules are applied somewhat differently.

Indicative of the dislike of the judges for treating commercial law as special is their readiness to analogise from the commercial to the private sphere. The liability of the shipowner to the cargo-owner for damage to the goods is compared with the liability of the employer to the employee injured at work; whether a stevedore can claim the sea carrier's limitation of liability for damaging the cargo is related to whether a bus driver can claim his employer's immunity in a question with a passenger who falls off a bus.

In a difficult case concerning a time-voyage charterparty the House of Lords were pressed with the analogy of the consumer taking a car on hire-purchase; and of deviation from the contract by sea-carrier and dry-cleaner one judge said 'both are governed by and *only* by the general law relating to contracts' (judicial emphasis). The judges do not think of commercial law as a separate part of the law or they would not analogise so widely.

The same is true of jurists. Textbooks on the law of contract juxtapose, almost without comment, contracts in restraint of marriage and contracts in restraint of trade; both are treated simply as promises which are unenforceable on the grounds of public policy, and the distinction between civil law and commercial law is simply not perceived or, by not being mentioned, is actually obscured. More particularly, a decision of the Court of Appeal in 1906 has met with almost unanimous condemnation from academic writers. The Court decided that whereas a person was bound who carelessly permitted himself to be deceived into signing a negotiable instrument, subsequently negotiated, a person was not bound who similarly signed a non-negotiable instrument, it being supposed in both cases that the person signing the document believed himself to be signing a document of a quite different kind.

Writers think that the distinction between a negotiable instrument and a non-negotiable instrument is unsound. Yet almost any lawyer with a sense of the needs of commerce would find the distinction worth considering. Most significant of all indications that common lawyers do not consider commercial law as distinct from civil law is the fact that in English law the general part of contract is huge, and the differences between the specific types of contract always underplayed.

'Civil and Commercial Law: A Distinction Worth Making' by G Samuel (1986) 102 LQR 569, pp 577–578

At first sight it is very easy to answer the question whether the common lawyer recognises the distinction between civil and commercial law. As Weir has observed, the 'phrase "commercial law" is by no means unknown to English lawyers or unused by them,' but 'if asked what it contrasted with rather than what it contained [the English lawyer] would have no answer at all.' No doubt, then, the academic could write a monograph on the topic and the practitioner would see an important procedural significance in cases which attracted the label; yet if either the academic or the practitioner was asked whether it would be of significance that the parties, or a party, to a property or contractual transaction fall(s) into the class of *commerçant* the likely response would be in the negative. However such a response might well have to be qualified on reflection. Despite Maine, it is not beneath the dignity of a modern court to link ownership with mercantile status nor to measure liability by reference to the 'commercial man' or 'men of business or professional men'; and legislation for some time now has been prepared to place a litigant (including the state) into a business class if his activities are of a certain kind. The status of a party, whether it is defined directly or indirectly, can have a bearing on the application and interpretation of private law rules.

Moreover the status test is, as the Continental lawyer will testify, only one approach. If one looks at the other test, that of the type of transaction, then the problem for the English lawyer becomes more acute: for although topics like contract and tort do not on the whole like formally to distinguish between the status of the parties, the fact that the relationship or transaction is a commercial one can be of great significance. This transaction approach is, not surprisingly, of relevance in legislation, particularly in legislation recognising consumer interests; yet the common law must by no means be overlooked. Thus in bailment relationships the fact that the bailment is a 'commercial one' can be of importance in the determination of a restitution claim for the bailee's expenses; and in the law of contract not only must 'commercial reality' be on occasions openly recognised as an aid to the interpretation and application of a rule like consideration but the fact that the contract itself is a mercantile one can have important implications with regard to implied terms or agency. Furthermore in the tort relationship of duty of care a business context is to be differentiated from the social gathering when the focus is upon advice given or statements made; and in deciding upon the validity of an assignment of a cause of action much will depend upon whether the assignee has 'a genuine commercial interest' in enforcing the claim. The fact, then, that the act or transaction is a 'commercial' or 'business' one in that it involves, say, a mercantile contract, a commercial interest or a business context may well have a direct bearing upon the outcome of some contract, tort and property cases.

NOTE

In *Re State of Norway's Application (No 1 & 2)* [1990] 1 AC 723, the House of Lords had to decide whether a Norwegian court's request for the oral examination of witnesses in England related to 'proceedings in any civil or commercial matter' under s 9(1) of the Evidence (Proceedings in Other Jurisdictions) Act 1975. Lord Goff, with whom all their Lordships agreed, had no doubt that the words in s 9(1) should be given their ordinary meaning, so that proceedings in any civil matter should include all proceedings other than criminal proceedings, and proceedings in any commercial matter should be treated as falling within proceedings in civil matters. This means that the distinction between commercial and non-commercial civil matters is meaningless for the purposes of interpreting s 9(1) of the 1975 Act. The case does not decide that the distinction is necessarily meaningless in any other context.

2 The function of commercial law

In *Kum v Wah Tat Bank Ltd* [1971] 1 Lloyd's Rep 439 at 444, Lord Devlin stated that:

> The function of the commercial law is to allow, so far as it can, commercial men to do business in the way they want to do it and not to require them to stick to forms that they may think to be outmoded. The common law is not bureaucratic.

This statement captures the fundamental purpose of commercial law: the facilitation of commercial transactions, ie transactions between parties dealing with each other in the course of business. This purpose generally underlies the reasoning of the judges in cases involving commercial disputes. As Lord Goff once wrote in an article analysing the objectives of the judges when interpreting commercial contracts ([1984] LMCLQ 382 at p 391):

> Our only desire is to give sensible commercial effect to the transaction. We are there to help businessmen, not to hinder them: we are there to give effect to their transactions, not to frustrate them: we are there to oil the wheels of commerce, not to put a spanner in the works, or even grit in the oil.

Businessmen have special needs. First, they demand that their agreements be upheld. Secondly, they require the decisions of the courts on commercial issues to be predictable so that they know where they stand. Thirdly, they need the law to be flexible enough to take account of their latest business practices. Fourthly, they want their disputes resolved quickly, inexpensively and effectively. Both in its substance and in its procedure commercial law attempts to facilitate commercial transactions by endeavouring to meet the special needs of the business community.

As to the first need (upholding commercial bargains), the courts adopt a non-interventionist approach with regard to commercial contracts. The judges work on the assumption that there is equality of bargaining power between commercial men. This assumption underpins two basic principles of commercial law: freedom of contract and sanctity of contract. As Professor Schmitthoff has written ([1966] JBL 309 at p 315):

The basis of commercial law is the contractual principle of autonomy of the parties' will. Subject to the ultimate reservation of public policy, the parties are free to arrange their affairs as they like.

As to the second need (predictability of legal decisions on commercial issues), the courts have consistently promoted considerations of 'certainty' of outcome over those of fairness and justice. In *Vallejo v Wheeler* (1774) 1 Cowp 143 at 153 Lord Mansfield said: 'In all mercantile transactions the great object should be certainty: and therefore, it is of more consequence that a rule be certain, than whether the rule is established one way or the other. Because speculators in trade then know what ground to go upon.' More recently, in *Mardorf Peach & Co Ltd v Attica Sea Carriers Corpn of Liberia, The Laconia* [1977] AC 850 at 878, Lord Salmon stated tersely that: 'Certainty is of primary importance in all commercial transactions.'

Traditionally, the third need (flexibility to accommodate new commercial practices) has been met by judicial recognition of mercantile custom and usage thereby incorporating it within the common law (see below, p 475). But direct incorporation of custom and usage by judicial recognition is now rare (P Devlin (1951) 14 MLR 249 at p 251). Today, the courts tend to take mercantile custom and usage into account when interpreting a commercial contract (see below, p 16). Where the courts are unable to take account of mercantile practice, so that the smooth operation of commercial transactions is being frustrated by the courts, Parliament may intervene to remedy the situation (for a recent example, see the Carriage of Goods by Sea Act 1992: below, pp 444–445).

The fourth need (speedy, inexpensive and efficient dispute resolution) is met, to a greater or lesser degree, by the practice and procedures of the Commercial Court and the availability of commercial arbitration. The Commercial Court is a separate court of the Queen's Bench Division staffed by judges who are experienced arbiters of commercial disputes. The rules of the Commercial Court are flexible and operate with the minimum of formality. The judges of the Commercial Court have been willing to develop procedures which meet the needs of the Court users: eg injunctions to prevent defendants from disposing of their assets (the *Mareva* injunction) and orders allowing seizure of evidence which might otherwise be destroyed (the *Anton Piller* order): see generally R Ough and W Fenley *The Mareva Injunction and Anton Piller Order* (2nd ed, 1993). The Commercial Court has jurisdiction to try 'commercial actions'. Order 72, r 1(2) of the Rules of the Supreme Court 1965 defines 'commercial action' to include:

> . . . any cause arising out of the ordinary transactions of merchants and traders and, without prejudice to the generality of the foregoing words, any cause relating to the construction of a mercantile document, the export or import of merchandise, affreightment, insurance, banking, mercantile agency and mercantile usage.

For detailed discussion of workings of the Commercial Court, see A D Coleman *The Practice and Procedure of the Commercial Court* (3rd ed, 1990).

But litigation can prove costly and it is generally thought that arbitration provides a cheaper alternative. There are a number of other reasons why the parties to a commercial dispute may opt for arbitration as opposed to litigation: these include speed, more flexible procedures, privacy, the availability of arbitrators who have personal experience of the trade in which the dispute has arisen, and the fact that there is only a limited right of appeal against arbitration awards thus ensuring that the dispute is not prolonged by a long appeal process (there can only be an appeal to the High Court on a question of law and then only if both parties agree or the court grants leave to appeal: Arbitration Act 1979, s 1; *Pioneer Shipping Ltd v*

BTP Tioxide Ltd, The Nema [1982] AC 724; *Antaios Cia Naviera SA v Salen Rederierna AB, The Antaios* [1985] AC 191).

Sir John Donaldson MR (later Lord Donaldson) once described the courts and the arbitrators respectively as the public and private sectors of the administration of justice industry (*Bremer Vulkan Schiffbau und Maschinenfabrik v South India Shipping Corpn Ltd* [1981] AC 909 at 921). Both sectors of the industry have striven to meet the needs of the business community and in doing so have attracted many foreign litigants and arbitrants to have their disputes resolved in this jurisdiction (see R Goff [1984] LMCLQ 382 at p 387). This has brought much needed revenue into the United Kingdom. It has been estimated that the contribution of the legal profession of the City of London to the balance of payments of the UK amounts to not less than £200 million per year (D Liston and N Reeves *The Invisible Economy: A Profile of Britain's Invisible Exports* (1988), p 237, cited by M J Bonell in 'National Interests and Rules on Jurisdiction: The Partisan Attitude of English Courts viewed from the Continent' in R Cranston and R Goode (eds) *Commercial and Consumer Law* (1993), Ch 7). However, potential litigants and arbitrants now have an array of alternative dispute resolution procedures available to them (eg conciliation, mediation, mini-trials). If the established sectors of the administration of justice industry are to maintain their share of the lucrative dispute resolution market they must be innovative and continue to meet the needs of the business community, and the law also must be astute to adapt to these needs.

QUESTION

Why do you think that English commercial law has been so accommodating to the needs of the business community?

3 The historical development of commercial law[1]

(a) The *lex mercatoria*

Modern commercial law has its roots in the *lex mercatoria* (law merchant) of the Middle Ages. During that period merchants would travel with their goods to fairs and markets across Europe. Their disputes would be settled by special local courts, such as the courts of the fairs and boroughs and the staple courts, where judge and jury would be merchants themselves. These merchant courts would decide cases quickly and apply the *lex mercatoria* as opposed to the local law.

The *lex mercatoria* was an international law of commerce. It was based on the general customs and practices of merchants which were common throughout Europe and was applied almost uniformly by the merchant courts in different countries. In England the *lex mercatoria* developed outside the common law and many of its principles differed from those of the common law (eg while the common law required that consideration for a promise should not be past

---

1 For an excellent summary of the historical development of commercial law, see C M Schmitthoff *Commercial Law in a Changing Economic Climate* (2nd ed, 1981), Chs 1 and 2. For a detailed survey, see W S Holdsworth *A History of English Law*, Vol 1, pp 526–573; Vol 5, pp 60–154; Vol 8, pp 99–300.

consideration, this was not the case under the *lex mercatoria*). The *lex mercatoria* derived its authority from voluntary acceptance by the merchants whose conduct it sought to regulate. The *lex mercatoria* suited their needs. It emphasised freedom of contract and freedom of alienability of movable property. It was flexible enough to adapt to new mercantile practices. Most significantly of all, it was speedily administered by merchant courts which shunned legal technicalities and often decided cases *ex aequo et bono*. It was during this period that some of the most important features of modern commercial law were developed: the bill of exchange, the charterparty and the bill of lading, the concept of assignability and negotiability, the acceptance of stoppage *in transitu* and general average (per Schmitthoff, op cit, pp 2–3).

(b) Incorporation of the *lex mercatoria* into the common law

In the fifteenth and sixteenth centuries most of the business of the merchant courts was taken over by the Court of Admiralty, which continued to recognise the *lex mercatoria*. But in the seventeenth century the commercial jurisdiction of the Admiralty Court was itself taken over by the common law courts. This was mainly due to the work of Sir Edward Coke. As the merchant courts were by then defunct, the common law courts captured most of the nation's mercantile litigation. In an attempt to keep that business the common law courts adopted some of the rules of the *lex mercatoria*. But it was not until the late seventeenth and eighteenth centuries that the *lex mercatoria* was fully incorporated into the common law. This was largely done through the work of Sir John Holt (Chief Justice from 1689 to 1710) and Lord Mansfield (Chief Justice from 1756 to 1788). Holt CJ was responsible for important developments in the law relating to negotiable instruments, bailment and agency. But he was too conservative in outlook to complete the process of incorporation of the *lex mercatoria* into the common law (eg see his judgment in *Clerke v Martin* (1702) 2 Ld Raym 757: below, p 475). It was left to Lord Mansfield to complete this task and earn himself the accolade of 'founder of the commercial law of this country' (*Lickbarrow v Mason* (1787) 2 Term Rep 63 at 73, per Buller J). As Professor Schmitthoff has written:

> . . . the reform which Lord Mansfield carried out when sitting with his special jurymen at Guildhall in London was ostensibly aimed at the simplification of commercial procedure but was, in fact, much more: its purpose was the creation of a body of substantive commercial law, logical, just, modern in character and at the same time in harmony with the principles of the common law. It was due to Lord Mansfield's genius that the harmonisation of commercial custom and the common law was carried out with an almost complete understanding of the requirements of the commercial community, and the fundamental principles of the old law and that that marriage of ideas proved acceptable to both merchants and lawyers.
>
> (C M Schmitthoff 'International Business Law, A New Law Merchant' in *Current Law and Social Problems* (1961), p 137)

(c) The age of commercial codification[2]

The development of commercial law through the common law led to a complex, and sometimes conflicting, mass of case law. In the nineteenth century there was a

---

2   H C Gutteridge (1935) 51 LQR 91 at p 117.

call for rationalisation of the law through codification. This process was achieved not by an all-embracing commercial code but through the codification of certain defined areas of commercial law. It resulted from the work of some exceptional draftsmen. Sir Mackenzie Chalmers drafted the Bills of Exchange Act 1882, the Sale of Goods Act 1893 and the Marine Insurance Act 1906. Sir Frederick Pollock drafted the Partnership Act 1890. All of these statutes remain in force today – though the Sale of Goods Act 1893 has been re-enacted with minor amendments as the Sale of Goods Act 1979. A fine testimony to the work of these great draftsmen. For an historical account of the codification of commercial law in Victorian Britain, see A Rodgers (1992) 109 LQR 570.

(d) The rise of consumerism

The next great era of change came with the development of the welfare state after the Second World War. During this period there has been a move away from the principles of freedom and sanctity of contract (and the laissez-faire economics upon which those principles were based) which had dominated Victorian thinking,[3] towards those of social responsibility and the protection of the economically weaker against the economically stronger.[4] This change is reflected in the expansion of consumer protection legislation in recent years: eg the Trade Descriptions Acts 1968 and 1972, the Unsolicited Goods and Services Act 1971, the Fair Trading Act 1973, the Supply of Goods (Implied Terms) Act 1973, the Consumer Credit Act 1974, the Unfair Contract Terms Act 1977, the Consumer Protection Act 1987, the Consumer Arbitration Agreements Act 1988 and the Food Safety Act 1990.

It is important to get some idea of the relationship between consumer law and commercial law (as defined at the start of this chapter). Whereas commercial law is concerned with transactions in which both parties deal with each other in the course of business, consumer law is primarily concerned with transactions between ordinary individuals (consumers) and those who provide goods and services on a commercial basis. Whereas commercial law is based on the premise that businessmen are of roughly equal bargaining power, consumer law assumes that the consumer and business enterprise are economically unequal. Whilst commercial law is happy for businessmen to regulate their own affairs through mercantile usage, usage has no place in consumer transactions. These fundamental differences in philosophy mean that whereas commercial law is non-interventionist and essentially pragmatic in nature, consumer law intrudes into contracts made between consumer and business supplier and is essentially an instrument of social policy.

To allow the principles of consumer law to intervene in commercial transactions would undermine the level of certainty that such transactions demand. The legislature has tried to keep the two separate. For example, the code of regulation for the provision of credit, introduced by the Consumer Credit Act 1974, only applies when the debtors are individuals (not companies) and the credit supplied is under £15,000 (ss 8(1)–(2), 189(1)).

Similarly, the statutory control of exemption clauses, under the Unfair Contract

---

3 See generally, P S Atiyah *The Rise and Fall of Freedom of Contract* (1979).
4 However, Atiyah believes that the pendulum may have swung back towards freedom of contract during the 1980s as a result of the dominant political philosophy of successive Conservative Governments: see his *Introduction to the Law of Contract* (4th ed, 1989), pp 30–39 and his *Essays on Contract* (1990, reprint), Ch 12.

Terms Act 1977, does not apply to contracts of insurance, contracts of marine salvage or towage, charterparties, contracts for the carriage of goods by sea, and international supply contracts (ss 1(2), 26; Sch 1).

It is certainly true to say that consumer law and international trade law have been kept separate. However, the same cannot always be said with regard to the relationship between consumer law and commercial law on the domestic level. Despite some legislative attempts to keep the two separate, and the fact that the courts generally appear to keep the commercial or consumer nature of a dispute in mind when applying rules which do not formally distinguish between the two types of transaction (see above, p 6), there is evidence that the ambit of consumer law is expanding and threatening to draw within it some transactions which previously fell within the commercial domain.

Three examples illustrate this trend. First, the courts have shown a willingness to expand the notion of what is a 'consumer' to include within it a corporate business enterprise (see *R & B Customs Brokers Co Ltd v United Dominions Trust Ltd* [1988] 1 WLR 321). Secondly, proposed legislation threatens to weaken the mercantile nature of the paradigm commercial transaction, the sale of goods, by replacing the statutory implicition that goods be 'merchantable' with the consumer orientated requirement that they be 'acceptable' (see Law Commission Report No 160, 'Sale and Supply of Goods' (1987), paras 3.19–3.22 – although the Report does not wholly ignore the distinction between consumer and non-consumer sales, for it recommends additional restrictions on the buyer's right of rejection in cases of non-consumer sales, paras 4.21 and 6.20). Thirdly, the Department of Trade and Industry has recently put forward proposals to amend the Sale of Goods Act 1979 to make the manufacturer contractually liable with the retailer for the satisfactory quality of goods sold to a consumer. The DTI is also considering whether to extend that liability to goods supplied in small transactions to traders (*Consumer Guarantees, A Consultation Document* (1992), DTI). There must be some cause for concern as to how far consumer protection principles should be allowed to intervene in purely mercantile arrangements. The interventionist approach of consumer protection legislation appears to be at odds with the essential needs of the business community.

Consumer protection law has developed into a subject worthy of study in its own right. We do not intend to deal with the subject in any detail in this book, although we shall refer to certain consumer protection measures which are covered in some commercial law textbooks and on certain commercial law courses: eg consumer credit and product liability. Those students who would like to study consumer protection law further are referred to the following books: R Cranston *Consumers and the Law* (2nd ed, 1984); I Ramsay *Consumer Protection, Text and Materials* (1989); D Oughton *Consumer Law: Text, Cases and Materials* (1991); B Harvey and D Parry *The Law of Consumer Protection and Fair Trading* (4th ed, 1992).

(e) A new *lex mercatoria*

In the seventeenth and eighteenth centuries the *lex mercatoria* was incorporated into the national laws of Europe. This meant that the *lex mercatoria* lost its international character. It only started to regain that character in the second half of the twentieth century. This has mainly been due to the work of organisations such as the Hague Conference on Private International Law, the International Institute for the Unification of Private Law (UNIDROIT), the United Nations Commission on Uniform Trade Law (UNCITRAL), the International Chamber of Commerce

(ICC), the Council of Europe and the European Community. These organisations have sought to harmonise national laws relating to specific areas of international trade. Such areas include the international sale of goods, international factoring and financial leasing, international payment mechanisms, international shipping laws and international commercial arbitration. The techniques used to achieve harmonisation are considered below (see p 19).

The late Professor Schmitthoff was a forceful proponent of a new *lex mercatoria* by means of a world code on international trade law (see below, pp 30–31). Although such a code is probably some way off, he could point to the harmonisation of specific areas of trade law, and the recent trend towards broader harmonisation projects (eg the ongoing UNIDROIT project to draw up a set of principles of contract law relating to international transactions), as marking significant progress towards that goal (C M Schmitthoff *Commercial Law in a Changing Economic Climate* (2nd ed, 1981), pp 30–31).

4 The sources of commercial law

(a) Contracts

The law of contract lies at the heart of commercial law. In the world of commerce, goods and services are supplied pursuant to the terms of contracts made between businessmen. Sometimes each term of the contract will have been individually negotiated by the parties. But in many cases there will have been little or no negotiation as to the precise terms of the agreement beyond those terms relating to subject matter and price. In such cases the parties prefer to use standard form contracts to embody their bargain and thereby save time and money that would otherwise have been spent on the negotiation of each term. So long as the standard form contract is made between businessmen, and not between an ordinary person and the business provider of goods and services, the courts are reluctant to interfere with the principles of freedom and sanctity of contract. This is particularly true of those standard form contracts drawn up by trade associations and adopted by their members, eg bills of lading, charterparties, policies of insurance and contracts of sale in the commodity markets. As Lord Diplock said in *Schroeder Music Publishing Co Ltd v Macaulay* [1974] 1 WLR 1308 at 1316: 'The standard clauses in these contracts have been settled over the years by negotiation by representatives of the commercial interests involved and have been widely adopted because experience has shown that they facilitate the conduct of trade.'

Some types of standard form contract have been the subject of detailed legal analysis. A jurisprudence has grown up around them giving many of their terms legally predictable meanings. Lord Goff has even gone so far as to suggest that those standard form contracts which are widely used throughout the world (eg the Lloyd's standard marine policy, the various forms of charterparty and commodity trade contracts) each form the basis of their own separate commercial code ([1993] JCL 1 at p 3). See also C M Schmitthoff (1968) 17 ICLQ 551 discussing the harmonisation of international trade law by means of standard form contracts.

The courts are often called upon to construe the terms of commercial contracts. Most cases before the Commercial Court turn on points of construction of such contracts. How do the courts, and particularly the Commercial Court, set about construing them? The issue was addressed by Sir Robert Goff (now Lord Goff) in a paper entitled 'Commercial Contracts and the Commercial Courts' published in [1984] LMCLQ 382. His Lordship states that (p 388):

> . . . there is only one principle of construction so far as commercial documents are concerned: and that is to make, so far as possible, commercial sense of the provision in question, having regard to the words used, the remainder of the document in which they are set, the nature of the transaction, and the legal and factual matrix.

He continues (p 391):

> . . . In commercial transactions, the duty of the court is simply to give effect to the contract, and not to dictate to the parties what the court thinks they ought to have agreed, or what a person (reasonable or otherwise) might have agreed if he had read the contract and addressed his mind to the problem which, in the outcome, has arisen.

A similar approach to the construction of commercial contracts was taken by Lord Diplock in *Antaios Cia Naviera SA v Salen Rederierna AB, The Antaios* [1985] AC 191. The case concerned the construction of a particular clause (a withdrawal clause) of a standard form of charter party. Lord Diplock addressed the issue of construction in the following terms (at 200–201):

> To the semantic analysis, buttressed by generous citation of judicial authority, which led the arbitrators to the conclusions as to the interpretation of the wording of the withdrawal clause that I have summarised, the arbitrators added an uncomplicated reason based simply upon business commonsense:
>
> > We always return to the point that the owners' construction is wholly unreasonable, totally uncommercial and in total contradiction to the whole purpose of the NYPE time charter form. The owners relied on what they said was 'the literal meaning of the words in the clause.' We would say that if necessary, in a situation such as this, a purposive construction should be given to the clause so as not to defeat the commercial purpose of the contract.
>
> This passage in the award anticipates the approach to questions of construction of commercial documents that was voiced by this House in the very recent case, *Miramar Maritime Corpn v Holborn Oil Trading Ltd* [1984] AC 676, which dealt with a bill of lading issued under a charterparty in Exxonvoy 1969 form. There, after referring to various situations which might arise if the construction for which the shipowners in that case contended were correct, I added, at p 682, in a speech concurred in by my fellow Law Lords:
>
> > There must be ascribed to the words a meaning that would make good commercial sense if the Exxonvoy bill of lading were issued in *any* of these situations, and not some meaning that imposed upon a transferee to whom the bill of lading for goods afloat was negotiated, a financial liability of unknown extent that no business man in his senses would be willing to incur.
>
> While deprecating the extension of the use of the expression 'purposive construction' from the interpretation of statutes to the interpretation of private contracts, I agree with the passage I have cited from the arbitrators' award and I take this opportunity of re-stating that if detailed semantic and syntactical analysis of words in a commercial contract is going to lead to a conclusion that flouts business commonsense, it must be made to yield to business commonsense.

The other members of the House of Lords agreed with Lord Diplock's reasoning.

(b) Custom and usage

A custom is a rule which has obtained the force of law in a particular locality and a usage is the settled practice of a particular trade or profession (see generally

Halsbury's Laws of England (4th ed, 1975), Vol 12, para 401 ff). In fact, the courts often pay scant regard to the technical distinctions between custom and usage and use the terms interchangeably (but see Halsbury, op cit, para 405 as to the main points of distinction).

A court may admit evidence of a trade custom or usage to imply a term into a commercial contract or as an aid to construction of the contract. For these purposes the custom or usage must be one recognised by the courts. As Ungoed-Thomas J stated in *Cunliffe-Owen v Teather and Greenwood* [1967] 1 WLR 1421 at 1438–1439:

> 'Usage' is apt to be used confusingly in the authorities, in two senses, (1) a practice, and (2) a practice which the court will recognise. 'Usage' as a practice which the court will recognise is a mixed question of fact and law. For the practice to amount to such a recognised usage, it must be certain, in the sense that the practice is clearly established; it must be notorious, in the sense that it is so well known, in the market in which it is alleged to exist, that those who conduct business in that market contract with the usage as an implied term; and it must be reasonable.
>
> The burden lies on those alleging 'usage' to establish it . . . .
>
> A party to a contract is bound by usages applicable to it as certain, notorious and reasonable, although not known to him. If the practice, though certain and notorious, is unreasonable, it of course follows that it cannot constitute a usage which the court will enforce as a usage. Nevertheless if a party knows of such a practice and agrees to it, then though unreasonable, he is bound by it . . . .

A custom or usage is not reasonable unless it is fair and proper and such as reasonable, honest, and right-minded men would adopt (*Paxton v Courtnay* (1860) 2 F & F 131, per Keating J). For example, in *North and South Trust Co v Berkeley* [1971] 1 WLR 470 Donaldson J held that the practice of Lloyd's underwriters to use Lloyd's insurance brokers, who placed business with them, as their agents in communications with claims assessors was wholly unreasonable and incapable of being a legal usage. The practice was held to be unreasonable because it conflicted with a basic principle of the law of agency that an agent (the broker) cannot act at the same time for two opposing principals (the assured and the underwriters) without their consent (see below, p 171). See also *Anglo–African Merchants Ltd v Bayley* [1970] 1 QB 311.

The custom or usage must not be inconsistent with the express or implied terms of the contract (*Kum v Wah Tat Bank Ltd* [1971] 1 Lloyd's Rep 439), nor with the nature of the contract as a whole (*London Export Corpn Ltd v Jubilee Coffee Roasting Co* [1958] 1 WLR 661 at 675, per Jenkins LJ). Furthermore, the custom or usage must not be unlawful (*Daun v City of London Brewery Co* (1869) LR 8 Eq 155 at 161).

Trade custom and usage may be incorporated into the law both directly and indirectly. So far we have considered indirect incorporation via contract. For discussion of direct incorporation by judicial recognition of general custom and usage, see *Goodwin v Robarts* (1875) LR 10 Exch 337; affd (1876) 1 App Cas 476 (below, p 475). Statutory codification of custom and usage is also a form of direct incorporation (but in most cases the custom and usage will have already been recognised by the courts before codification, as occurred with major codifying statutes of the late nineteenth century, referred to above at p 12; cf the Promissory Notes Act 1704, referred to below at pp 474–475).

(c) National legislation

Primary and secondary legislation plays an important role in the regulation of commercial transactions.

Traditionally, commercial legislation has been designed to give effect to the free will of the parties to a commercial transaction and thereby promote the free flow of trade. The codifying statutes of the second half of the nineteenth and early party of the twentieth centuries were designed to do this (see above, p 12). But other, more recent, legislation has been of a much more intrusive character, designed to promote social and economic policies of the State rather than the free will of the parties to a commercial transaction.

Examples of such interventionist legislation include recent consumer protection legislation (see above, p 12) and those statutes regulating monopolies, restrictive trade practices and mergers (eg the Fair Trading Act 1973, the Restrictive Trade Practices Act 1976 and 1977, the Resale Prices Act 1976 and the Competition Act 1980; see also Arts 85 and 86 of the Treaty of Rome). Professor Schmitthoff has described interventionist legislation of this type as forming a body of 'economic law'.

'The Concept of Economic Law in England' by C M Schmitthoff [1966] JBL 309, pp 315, 318–319

An English lawyer, if pressed for a definition, would state that economic law comprises the regulation of state interference with the affairs of commerce, industry and finance. He would see the distinction between commercial law and economic law in their fundamental attitude to commerce. The basis of commercial law is the contractual principle of autonomy of the parties' will. Subject to the ultimate reservation of public policy, the parties are free to arrange their affairs as they like. The underlying philosophy of economic law is economic *dirigism*, ie, the idea that the paternalistic state may limit the autonomy of the parties' will in the public interest. Economic law should thus be placed between commercial law and administrative law; it shares with the former its concern with economic affairs and with the latter its governmental technique.

From this point of view, England has its fair share of economic law. Indeed, as state planning asserts itself in a constantly more consistent pattern, economic law develops into the discipline which reflects the transition to a planned and directed free market economy. Its importance is growing and full academic recognition cannot be withheld from it indefinitely.

What are the divisions of English economic law? This subject can be arranged into the law relating to:

1. financial regulation,
2. competitive economic regulation,
3. prices and incomes regulation, and
4. consumer protection regulation. . . .

The Characteristics of English Economic Law

English economic law shows two characteristics. First, it has evolved the central concept of public interest and, secondly, its fabric is very different from that of other branches of law.

It has been pointed out elsewhere that, unlike public policy, the term 'public interest' does not carry an inherent element of opprobrium. 'The new concept of public interest is used to indicate the wide – and growing – area in which Parliament has regulated certain activities of private persons in the social and economic sphere because it considers such regulation to be desirable for the common weal.' The concept of public interest is thus a socio-political concept. In the legislation relating to restrictive trade practices and resale price maintenance the notion of public interest is clearly defined; it operates in this manner that certain restrictive trade arrangements are generally declared to be prohibited by Parliament as being contrary to the public interest but that the relevant enactments establish closely defined grounds on which those arrangements can be justified; these grounds are known as the 'gateways' to legality. . . .

Secondly, the fabric of economic law is different from that of other branches of law. The normal technique of the legislator in commercial law is to place at the disposal of the parties certain legal institutions, to regulate their effect and to leave it to the parties to adopt the statutory scheme or to modify it as desired. Enactments pertaining to economic law are constructed differently. They are of mandatory rather than permissive character. They embody Governmental policy, and do so in considerable detail. . . . The detailed incorporation of Government policy into statutes gives English economic law its peculiar flavour.

NOTE

The term 'economic law', as used by Professor Schmitthoff, must not be confused with what is called the law and economics movement which has become prominent in American and Canadian law schools. This movement focuses on the application of economic theory to matters of legal concern. It uses economic concepts of market incentives, utility maximisation and allocative efficiency to analyse legal institutions, concepts and rules, including those relevant to commercial law: see J S Ziegel 'What Can the Economic Analysis of Law Teach Commercial and Consumer Law Scholars?' in R Cranston and R Goode (eds) *Commercial and Consumer Law* (1993), Ch 12 and the literature footnoted therein.

(d) European Community law

The European Community (the EC) was established by the 1957 Treaty of Rome (the 'EC Treaty'), as amended most recently by the Maastricht Treaty on European Union 1992. The EC is currently made up of twelve member states including the United Kingdom (which acceded to the Treaty of Rome in 1973). There are four 'Institutions' of the EC: the Commission, the Parliament, the Council of Ministers and the European Court of Justice. The Commission proposes laws which are ultimately adopted or rejected by the Council of Ministers after the latter has taken advice from the elected Parliament. There are two kinds of EC legislation: Regulations and Directives (see art 189 of the EC Treaty). Regulations apply to member states generally and are binding and enforceable without further action on their part. Directives, while binding on the member states, leave it to the states themselves to enact national legislation to implement them. However, if the terms of a Directive are sufficiently clear and precise the European Court of Justice may hold them to have direct effect even though not implemented by a member state. The European Court of Justice has a broad jurisdiction over actions involving the interpretation and application of the EC Treaty, Regulations, Directives and other activities of the Institutions of the EC (see arts 164–188 of the EC Treaty).

The importance of EC law as a source of law, including commercial law, applicable in the United Kingdom cannot be over-emphasised. As Lord Denning MR once said in his typically eloquent prose (*Shields v E Coomes (Holdings) Ltd* [1978] 1 WLR 1408 at 1416):

> . . . the flowing tide of Community Law is coming in fast. It has not stopped at the high water mark. It has broken the dykes and the banks. It has submerged the surrounding land. So much so that we have to learn to become amphibious if we wish to keep heads above water.

The supremacy of directly effective EC law over conflicting national law (including Acts of Parliament) is now clearly established: *R v Secretary of State for*

Transport, ex p Factortame Ltd (No 2) [1991] 1 AC 603, ECJ and HL (noted by HWR Wade (1991) 107 LQR 1). There are a number of excellent textbooks on EC law: these include T C Hartley *The Foundations of European Community Law* (2nd ed, 1988); L Collins *European Community Law and the United Kingdom* (4th ed, 1990); J Steiner *EEC Law* (3rd ed, 1992); D Wyatt and A Dashwood *The Substantive Law of the EEC* (3rd ed, 1993).

(e) International legislation

The harmonisation of international trade law has usually been carried out by two methods: international conventions and model codes (sometimes collectively, though inaccurately, referred to as 'international legislation': see C M Schmitthoff, *Commercial Law in a Changing Economic Climate* (2nd ed, 1981), p 22). Examples of recent harmonising conventions include the Vienna Convention on Contracts for the International Sale of Goods (1980) (see below, p 443), the Geneva Convention on Agency in the International Sale of Goods (1983) (see below, p 83), the UN Convention on International Bills of Exchange and International Promissory Notes (1988) (see below, p 521) and the Ottawa Conventions on International Factoring and International Financial Leasing (1988) (see below, p 783 and p 688). Examples of recent harmonising model codes include the Uniform Rules for Collections (1978 Revision) (see below, p 640), Incoterms (1990 Revision) (see below, p 443), the Uniform Rules for Demand Guarantees (1992) (see below, p 687), the Uniform Customs and Practice for Documentary Credits (1993 Revision) (see below, Chapter 19), all of which have been sponsored by the ICC. Typically, model codes codify existing trade practice and usage.

International conventions only have the force of law in England if incorporated into our national law by legislation. Even then the convention may be 'voluntary' to the extent that the parties to a commercial transaction can exclude the operation of its provisions. By contrast, model codes only have force when incorporated into a contract either expressly or by previous course of dealing or by custom or usage of the trade.

For further discussion of the harmonisation of international commercial law, see R Goode in 'Reflections on the Harmonization of Commercial Law' and L Del Duca in 'Developing Transnational Harmonization Procedures for the Twenty-first Century', Chs 1 and 2 of R Cranston and R Goode (eds) *Commercial and Consumer Law* (1993). But see also Sir John Hobhouse in (1990) 106 LQR 530, who is severely critical of the recent trend towards harmonisation by international conventions such as the Vienna Sales Convention. He writes (at p 533) that:

> These conventions are inevitably and confessedly drafted as multi-cultural compromises between different schemes of law. Consequently they will normally have less merit than most of the individual legal systems from which they have been derived. They lack coherence and consistency. They create problems about their scope. They introduce uncertainty where no uncertainty existed before. They probably deprive the law of those very features which enable it to be an effective tool for the use of international commerce.

5 The role of equity in commercial law

Principles of contract, tort, restitution, property law, company law, insolvency law, and even criminal law, may be relevant when considering a problem thrown up by a commercial transaction (see, eg, R M Goode *Commercial Law* (1982), p 38). In certain circumstances, equitable principles may also have to be considered.

'Commercial Equity' (1993) 14 *Company Lawyer* 41 (editorial comment)

A significant proportion of litigation in the Chancery Division of the High Court of Justice in London has in recent years been of a commercial nature. Indeed Chancery practitioners of the pre-war era would probably not now recognise the work of the Court.

Commercial frauds and business disputes now seem to be part of the regular diet of this once obscure part of the judicial process. The intrusion of equity into commerce, if intrusion it be, has not always been welcomed. Clearly the City, regulated as much of it is under the Financial Services Act 1986, might prefer the black letter rules of its rule books to oust any possibility of judges applying what to many appear to be maverick or, at least, uncertain principles. Hence the Law Commission's excursus into this area. ['Fiduciary Duties and Regulatory Rules' LCCP No 124 (1992): see below, p 174.] Such fears are not new and are not confined to the City and the business world.

In 1881, Bramwell LJ said in *New Zealand & Australian Land Co v Watson* (1881) 7 QBD 374 at 382:

> Now I do not desire to find fault with the various intricacies and doctrines connected with trusts, but I should be very sorry to see them introduced into commercial transactions, and an agent in a commercial case turned into a trustee with all the troubles that attend that relation.

More modern judicial examples abound, for example Goff LJ, as he then was, in *Scandinavian Trading Tanker Co AB v Flota Petroleum Ecuatoriana* [1983] QB 529 at 541 prayed in aid 'the policy which favours certainty in commercial transactions' to deny equitable relief against forfeiture in a charter case. Indeed he went as far as to say that such a policy was 'antipathetic' to this kind of equitable intervention.

However the fact remains that equitable and common law doctrines can and do co-exist in many factual situations. But when a common law rule is direct and governs the case in all its circumstances, equity cannot override it. As every law student knows, 'equity follows the law' but as that fine New York judge, Cardozo CJ added in *Graf v Hope Building Corpn* 254 NY 1 at 9 (1930) 'but not slavishly nor always'.

Thus contractual and fiduciary relationships may co-exist but their functions will be separate. Indeed where there is purpose in referring to a contractual relationship it is meaningless, as Professor L S Sealy has pointed out, to talk of fiduciary relationships as such because fixed rules and principles do not apply. Hence perhaps the nervousness of those who crave certainty. There has been a worry that equitable principles in the commercial arena will lead to flaccid notions of fairness being applied. This is presumably because the equitable jurisdiction is often discretionary. However, in the case of injunctions, an every day fact of life in commercial law, discretion is at the heart of the jurisdiction. That is not however an excuse for wallowing in any idiosyncratic concept of justice for, as Lord Blackburn said in *Doherty v Allman* (1878) 3 App Cas 709 at 728, discretion was to be exercised judicially and not according 'to the fancy of whoever is to exercise the jurisdiction . . .'.

In recent years, apart from the development of the injunction in commercial contexts it is the area of constructive trusts which shows that equity is not past the age of child bearing and indeed has a vital role in the commercial arena. As Cardozo J observed many years ago in *Beatty v Guggenheim Exploration Co* 225 NY 380 at 389 (1919):

> A court of equity in decreeing a constructive trust is bound by no unyielding formula. The equity of the transaction must shape the measure of relief.

As we observed in a recent editorial on money laundering ((1992) 13 Co Law 162) recent decisions attest to the virility of the Chancery Courts in pursuing and then depriving those who might in practical terms be beyond the reach of the criminal law, of their gains.

Sir John Mummery, speaking at a King's *Company Lawyer* lecture last summer, pointed to four decisions of the Court of Appeal as instances of the circumstances where the courts were developing and applying the concept of constructive trusteeship as a means of achieving a just solution in difficult cases. These four decisions were *Polly Peck International Plc v Nadir (No 2)* [1992] 4 All ER 769; *Finers v Miro* [1991] 1 WLR 35; *Lipkin Gorman v Karpnale Ltd* [1989] 1 WLR 1340 and *Agip (Africa) Ltd v Jackson* [1991] Ch 547.

Essentially these cases concern the basis of and limits to the liability for involvement as constructive trustees. As Sir Peter Millett points out in his article 'Tracing the proceeds of fraud' (1991) 107 LQR 71, the liability of an accessory is limited to the case where the breach of trust was fraudulent and dishonest as in *Belmont Finance Corpn Ltd v Williams Furniture Ltd* [1979] Ch 250. The liability of the recipient is not so limited. The distinction, Sir Peter argues, is fundamental because an accessory is a person who never received the property at all, or who received it in circumstances where his receipt was irrelevant. His liability cannot therefore be receipt based but fault based . . . .

 Now it will doubtless be said that these cases add to the uncertainty which many commercial lawyers fear. The fact is that in intervening equity is merely doing what it has done historically and that is to temper the rigour of purely legal duties where that rigour is inappropriate. If this will prevent bankers and other professionals operating in the commercial world from being used as accessories to fraud, then this is surely to be welcomed.

NOTES

1. Although the principle of certainty in commercial transactions would appear to leave little scope for equitable intervention, this extract illustrates that equity has a role to play in the world of commerce. However, over-reliance on equitable concepts should be avoided. Where businessmen have defined their relationship in the terms of a contract freely negotiated between them, the courts should hesitate before interfering with their bargain. By the terms of their contract each party has accepted certain risks, including the risk of the other party's insolvency before completing performance of the contract, and the law should be slow to confer additional rights upon them through the medium of equitable intervention.

2. In two areas in particular the infiltration of equitable doctrines into English commercial law has been strongly resisted (see W Goodhart and G Jones (1980) 43 MLR 489–490). First, the courts have traditionally opposed the application of the equitable standard of constructive notice to commercial transactions. As Lindley LJ stated forcefully in *Manchester Trust Ltd v Furness* [1895] 2 QB 539 at 545:

> . . . as regards the extension of the equitable doctrines of constructive notice to commercial transactions, the Courts have always set their faces resolutely against it. The equitable doctrines of constructive notice are common enough in dealing with land and estates, with which the Court is familiar; but there have been repeated protests against the introduction into commercial transactions of anything like an extension of those doctrines, and the protest is founded on perfect good sense. In dealing with estates in land title is everything, and it can be leisurely investigated; in commercial transactions possession is everything, and there is no time to investigate title; and if we were to extend the doctrine of constructive notice to commercial transactions we should be doing infinite mischief and paralyzing the trade of the country.

This passage has since been applied by the Court of Appeal in *Greer v Downs Supply Co* [1927] 2 KB 28, by Diplock J in *Port Line Ltd v Ben Line Steamers Ltd* [1958] 2 QB 146 at 167, and by Neill J in *Feuer Leather Corpn v Frank Johnstone & Sons* [1981] Com LR 251. Thus, the appropriate standard of 'notice' for commercial transactions is actual knowledge of a fact or suspicion that something is wrong, coupled with a wilful disregard of the means of knowledge, ie deliberately turning a blind eye (sometimes known as 'inferred knowledge'). Mere failure to make enquiries which ought reasonably to have been made (ie constructive notice) is not enough. The relationship between actual and constructive notice in commercial transactions is considered further below at pp 579–581 and 780–781.

Secondly, unless expressly agreed by the parties, the courts have resisted attempts to introduce the concept of equitable ownership into the sale of goods. An agreement for the sale of goods does not of itself vest equitable ownership in the buyer: he either acquires a legal title or acquires nothing beyond a mere contractual right (see R Goode (1987) 103 LQR 433 at p 438). In *Re Wait* [1927] 1 Ch 606, P bought from S 500 tons of wheat out of 1000 tons on board the ship *Challenger*. P paid S. But S went bankrupt before the 500 tons purchased by P had been appropriated from the bulk. S's trustee claimed the whole 1000 tons as assets in the bankruptcy on the ground that no property in the 500 tons had passed to P (s 16 of the Sale of Goods Act 1979 prevents the passing of property in unascertained goods: see below, p 259). On the other hand, P claimed that there had been an equitable assignment which gave him a *pro rata* equitable interest in the bulk. A majority of the Court of Appeal (Lord Hanworth MR and Atkin LJ) decided against P. In an important obiter dictum, Atkin LJ stated that there could be no place for equitable interests in goods within the confines of an ordinary contract of sale, because the Sale of Goods Act contains a complete code of law in respect of contracts for the sale of goods. He said (at 635–636):

> The total sum of legal relations (meaning by the word 'legal' existing in equity as well as in common law) arising out of the contract for the sale of goods may well be regarded as defined by the Code. It would have been futile in a code intended for commercial men to have created an elaborate structure of rules dealing with rights at law, if at the same time it was intended to leave, subsisting with the legal rights, equitable rights inconsistent with, more extensive, and coming into existence earlier than the rights so carefully set out in the various sections of the Code.
>
> The rules for transfer of property as between seller and buyer, performance of the contract, rights of the unpaid seller against the goods, unpaid sellers' lien, remedies of the seller, remedies of the buyer, appear to be complete and exclusive statements of the legal relations both in law and equity.

Although Atkin LJ's view was not wholly shared by the other majority member of the Court of Appeal, it has, nevertheless, been applied by Oliver J in *Re London Wine Co (Shippers) Ltd* [1986] PCC 121, and has been endorsed by Lord Brandon in *Leigh & Sillavan Ltd v Aliakmon Shipping Co Ltd, The Aliakmon* [1986] AC 785 at 812–813.

3. Despite the rejection of equitable doctrines in those cases referred to above in note 2, you will discover that equity impinges upon our consideration of commercial law at various stages of this book: see, for example, the importance of the fiduciary relationship which usually exists between a principal and agent (below, pp 168–182); the imposition of constructive trusts to combat commercial fraud; the availability of equitable remedies such as the *Mareva* injunction and *Anton Piller* order (above, p 9); the significance of equitable assignment in debt factoring (below, p 753); the use of equitable floating charges as security (below, pp 838–845); the availability of a right to trace in equity (below, pp 541–542). See generally, Kennedy J 'Equity in a Commercial Context' in P D Finn (ed) *Equity and Commercial Relationships* (1987); P D Finn 'Equity and Contract' in P D Finn (ed) *Essays on Contract* (1987).

4. The role of equity is particularly important where money is lent, or payment made for goods in advance of delivery, or goods supplied before payment, and the borrower, seller or purchaser, as the case may be, subsequently becomes insolvent before performing his side of the bargain. Any claim in contract, or for recovery of the price on a total failure of consideration, or in debt, is only a personal claim against the general assets of the insolvent person. As a personal claim it will abate with the claims of other creditors in the insolvency. On the other hand, if the payer or supplier can establish an equitable proprietary interest in the money paid or goods supplied, he will gain priority in the insolvency. Thus, where the payer can show that the money paid is held by the recipient subject to a trust in his favour, the payer will be able to withdraw *his* assets from those available in the insolvency (see *Barclays Bank Ltd v Quistclose Investments Ltd* [1970] AC 567 (money lent for a specified purpose held on trust for the lender when the purpose failed); *Re Kayford Ltd* [1975] 1 WLR 279 (customers' pre-payments for goods held on trust in favour of the customers); *Chase Manhattan Bank NA v Israel–British Bank (London) Ltd* [1981] Ch 105 (money paid under a mistake of fact held on trust for the payer)). It may even be possible for the payer to claim that the money paid is held subject to what is known as a 'remedial constructive trust' in cases where there has been an element of unconscionability on the part of the recipient (*Neste Oy v Lloyds Bank plc* [1983] 2 Lloyd's Rep 658; *Metall und Rohstoff AG v Donaldson Lufkin & Jenrette Inc* [1990] 1 QB 391 at 479, CA; see also SR Scott [1993] LMCLQ 330). Where goods are supplied before payment, the supplier may be able to rely upon a reservation of title clause to make the purchaser a trustee of the goods, their product, or the proceeds of their sale, until he is paid in full – a claim which may involve tracing in equity: see *Aluminium Industrie Vaassen BV v Romalpa Aluminium Ltd* [1976] 1 WLR 676, and those cases considered below at pp 407–425. See generally, W Goodhart and G Jones (1980) 43 MLR 489; R Goode (1987) 103 LQR 433 at pp 434–447.

5. For the relationship between equity and good faith or fair dealing in commercial transactions, see below, pp 28–29.

6 The philosophy and concepts of commercial law

'The Codification of Commercial Law' by R Goode (1988) 14 Mon LR 135, pp 147–155

. . . *are* there concepts of commercial law? Or is commercial law no more than an aggregation of the different rules governing particular forms of commercial contract, with no linking themes of any kind? If this is the case, and if it is what we want, then a commercial code is not for us. I believe that commercial law does exist and that it embodies a philosophy, not always very coherent but nonetheless present, and fundamental concepts, not always very clearly articulated but nonetheless helping to implement that philosophy and to serve the needs of the business community. By the philosophy of commercial law I mean those underlying assumptions of fairness and utility which inform commercial law and run like a thread through its different branches. By concepts of commercial law I mean those principles of law, whether the common law or legislation, which are a particular response to the needs of the commercial community and thus apply with special vigour to commercial transactions, even though they are capable of application to non-commercial dealings.

VI THE PHILOSOPHY AND CONCEPTS OF COMMERCIAL LAW

The primary function of commercial law, in the sense in which I use that term, is to accommodate the legitimate practices and expectations of the business community in relation to their commercial dealings. This sounds much easier than it is. Business law reflects commercial life, and life is not simple. The law and the judges have to balance a range of competing values, the relative weight of which varies not only from one legal system to another but from one age to another within a single jurisdiction. Those who criticise the *Uniform Commercial Code* for appearing to face all ways at once are correct in the accusation but unfair in the criticism, for the Code does no more than reflect the fact that desirable objectives often pull in opposite directions and require conflicting treatments. The problem for the law maker is much the same as that confronting two consultants treating the same patient, one for diabetes which requires insulin and another for hypoglycaemia which reacts adversely to insulin.

1. The philosophy of commercial law

There would seem to me to be eight principles which together make up the philosophy of commercial law. They are: . . .

(a) *Party autonomy*

The general philosophy of the common law is that businessmen should be free to make their own law. A contract is a contract. A party is entitled to the benefit of his bargain and to the strict performance of conditions of the contract, whether they relate to the time of performance or the description or quality of what is to be tendered as performance. Only where contract terms are so restrictive, oppressive or otherwise incompatible with society's goals as to offend against the public interest should the courts intervene to curb the sanctity of contract. One reason for upholding contracts is a philosophical one, that of freedom under the law, including the freedom to fetter one's own freedom. Another is that the enforcement of contractual undertakings helps to promote security and predictability, a matter of some importance to the business world. Hence the *Uniform Commercial Code* makes it clear, in section 1–102(2)(b) and (3), that freedom of contract is a principle of the Code. But freedom of contract cannot be absolute, and the Code itself contains numerous specific restrictions, as well as a general bar on contracting out of the obligations of good faith, diligence, reasonableness and care. The circumstances which are considered to justify legislative or judicial interference in the bargain of the parties to a commercial transaction vary widely according to the *mores* of the particular society, the familiarity of the judges with the problems of business life and the relative importance of a particular State as an international centre of commerce or finance. . . . The view in London, as I see it, may be broadly expressed in these terms: 'business life is rough and tough; if you can't take care of yourself or don't know what you're doing, you shouldn't get into it in the first place!' In other words, in a contest between contract and equity in a commercial dispute, contract wins almost every time; and I suspect that one reason why foreigners so frequently select English law, rather than Continental law, to govern their contacts and English courts to adjudicate their disputes is that they know where they stand on the law and can rely on judges experienced in commercial transactions to give effect to their understanding. Related to the contract/equity conflict is the tension between conflicting goals expressed in the opposing maxims of international law, *pacta sunt servanda* and *rebus sic stantibus*. It takes a great deal to persuade an English court that change of circumstances modifies or discharges even a long-term contract.

(b) *Predictability*

The business world attaches high importance to the predictability of judicial decisions on legal issues. The weight given by a legal system to the need for predictability compared with equity and flexibility will, of course, vary from jurisdiction to jurisdiction and will depend in no small measure on the volume of business and of dispute resolution a particular State has or wishes to attract. A reasonable degree of predictability is needed in the commercial world because so much planning and so many transactions, standardised or high in value, are undertaken on the basis that the courts will continue to follow the rules laid down in preceding cases. But every businessman and his lawyer knows that there are tides in judicial philosophy, that every action ultimately produces a reaction, that a form of liability denied by one generation of judges will be vigorously developed by the next. . . .

(c) *Flexibility*
Needless to say, the man of affairs wishes to have his cake and eat it; to be given predictability on the one hand and flexibility to accommodate new practices and developments on the other. Karl Llewellyn was acutely aware of the need to accommodate these opposing goals in the *Uniform Commercial Code*; and he sought, with a fair measure of success, to achieve that accommodation by building into the Code a range of flexible words and concepts to encourage the organic growth of Code law whilst trusting the courts to observe the general policies and philosophy of the Code as a whole. Thus we find references to 'the continued expansion of commercial practices through custom, usage and agreement of the parties' and to 'obligations of good faith, diligence, reasonableness and care' as well as the preservation of general principles of law and equity. In England the courts are on the whole very responsive to the needs of the business community and reluctant to deny recognition to the legal efficacy of commercial instruments and practices in widespread use: As in the Army, there are two opposing but equally effective techniques to avoid bringing disaster on your head from on high. One is to keep out of the way, proceed in stealth and hope that no one will know you are there, still less what you are doing. The other is the exact opposite, namely to promote your activities with a fanfare of trumpets, persuade the rest of the corps to join you and then defy the authorities to upset such a large number of people and such a huge volume of business by declaring it illegal! In the international markets the latter technique seems to work rather well, always so long as one does not come up against a rural judge whose main interests lie in equity and the avoidance of unconscionable bargains!

(d) *Good faith*
The attitude of the common law to the question of good faith in contracts is curiously ambivalent and is fashioned by English legal history. In civil law jurisdictions the duty of good faith is inherent not only in contractual but in pre-contractual relationships. Particularly vigorous is the general requirement of good faith embodied in section 242 of the German *Civil Code*, which has given rise to a mass of doctrine and jurisprudence and is widely applied. Section 1–203 of the *Uniform Commercial Code* provides that:

> Every contract or duty within this Act imposes an obligation of good faith in its peformance or enforcement.

By contrast, good faith is not a general requirement of English law for the enforcement of *legal* rights or the exercise of *legal* remedies. A party can exercise a right to terminate a contract for breach even though it causes him no loss and his sole motive is to escape the consequences of a bad bargain; and a party able to perform a contract without need of the other party's co-operation can in general proceed with performance against the other party's wishes, and even when that party no longer has an interest in the performance, and then claim payment of the contract sum. Where good faith does surface in commercial transactions is in a priority dispute or where some equitable right or remedy is involved. It is surely high time that English law adopted a general principle of good faith and cast off its historical shackles.

(e) *The encouragement of self-help*
Compared to continental legal systems, the common law is remarkably indulgent towards self-help. Acceleration clauses can be invoked, contracts can be terminated or rescinded, goods repossessed, liens and rights of contractual set-off exercised, receivers and managers appointed and securities realised, all without any need for judicial approval, the only limiting factor (in the absence of special legislation) being that one must not commit a breach of the peace. There seems no pressure to modify this approach in relation to commercial transactions, nor, with the enormous pressure of work on courts all over the world, does a change seem particularly necessary or desirable. Civilised self-help has the advantages of speed, efficiency, flexibility and cheapness upon which the smooth functioning of business life so much depends.

(f) *The facilitation of security aspects*

As an aspect of the common law's attitude towards self-help, but also an independent characteristic, we may note that – again by comparison with continental systems – it is extremely favourable to the creation of security interests. Security can be taken over almost any kind of asset, tangible or intangible, usually with little or no formality; it can cover present and future property without the need for specific description; and it can secure present and future indebtedness. The creditor has the option of security by possession, ownership (mortgage) or mere charge. He has the facility of appointing a receiver over the entirety of a debtor company's assets, with full powers to take over and manage the company's business, without the creditor being in any way responsible for his receiver's acts or omissions so long as the creditor does not intervene in the conduct of the receivership. Moreover, one of the particular features of insolvency law is that it recognizes and protects interests created and perfected under non-insolvency rules, so that in general a security interest will be accepted as having priority over the claims of the general body of unsecured creditors in the debtor's bankruptcy or winding up.

One of the criticisms levelled against Article 9 was that it was *too* favourable to secured creditors and gave inadequate consideration to the claims of the general body of unsecured creditors. But the balance of the interests of secured and unsecured creditors is primarily a function of insolvency law, not of commercial law, for so long as the debtor is solvent the existence of security is of no moment to the unsecured creditor, who can take a judgment and enforce it by execution.

(g) *The protection of vested rights*

(h) *The protection of innocent third parties*

These two well established principles of commercial law do, of course, run in opposite directions. The first reflects a general feeling that an owner should not lose his property without fault; the second, that innocent buyers (including incumbrancers) should be protected against proprietary rights of which they have no notice, in order to ensure the free flow of goods in the stream of trade. Like most legal systems, English law faces both ways. Its starting position is the *nemo dat* principle but its *Sale of Goods Act* moves towards the civilian principle *possession vaut titre*. Third parties may also acquire overriding rights where the holder of a prior security interest has failed to perfect it by registration. No ordering of priorities can do justice in every case, but the position in English law has probably become more incoherent than under most legal systems. Certainly we would expect a commercial code to provide a reasonably rational balance between competing interests and one which, as under the *Uniform Commercial Code*, moves away from distinctions between legal and equitable interests. A rational law should seek to embody two principles: first, that no one should suffer loss or subordination of his rights without fault; secondly, that no one should be affected by a prior interest of which he has neither knowledge nor the means of acquiring knowledge. These two competing principles can be harmonised in some measure by registration requirements, which on the one hand provide the owner of an interest with a means of protecting it and on the other allow third parties to ignore a registrable interest which is unregistered. But we cannot prescribe registration of all real rights, and the problem then is to establish the general, or residuary, rule. For residuary cases I believe the interests of commerce require the civilian principle of *possession vaut titre* rather than the common law principle *nemo dat quod non habet*. A party who puts an article of commerce, tangible or intangible, into the stream of trade must take his chances. This is simply an application in the field of property rights of the policy that dictates that equity should be slow to interfere in commercial transactions.

2. The concepts of commercial law

(a) *The concept of a market*

As one would expect in a body of law concerned with dealings among merchants, the concept of a market is central to commercial law. By this is meant not necessarily a physical market in which traders strike bargains *in praesenti* on the floor of the market but a mechanism for bringing together substantial numbers of participants who deal in commodities, securities or money and who make a market by acting both as buyers and as sellers at prices determined by supply and demand. With the advent of telecommunications physical markets are steadily giving way to markets established by computer networks in which the participants are linked to each other and to a central system operated by the relevant exchange for striking bargains and displaying market prices. Commercial law is influenced by the concept of a market in a variety of ways. Parties dealing in a market are deemed to contract with reference to its established and reasonable customs and usages, which can have the effect of giving a special meaning to ordinary words, of importing rights and obligations not normally implied, of permitting tolerances in performance which would not be accepted in the general law of contract and of expanding or restricting remedies for a shortfall in performance, as where a small deficiency in quantity or quality is compensatable by an allowance against the price, to the exclusion of the remedy of termination of the contract. The market price is taken as the reference point in computing damages against a seller who fails to deliver or a buyer who fails to accept the subject-matter of the contract, and a party who reduces his loss by a subsequent sale at a higher price or a subsequent purchase at a lower price is not normally required to bring this saving into account, contrary to the normal contract rules as to mitigation of damages.

The problem for commercial law is to define the manner in which a usage of the market is to be established, a matter that can be of great difficulty but on which much may turn . . . .

(b) *The importance of customs or usages of a trade or locality*
Even without a market a court will recognize established customs or usages, such as those of a particular trade or locality, where the circumstances indicate that the parties were contracting by reference to the custom or usage. The enforceability of abstract payment undertakings is an important example to which I shall allude in more detail shortly.

(c) *The importance of a course of dealing*
Since traders are often concerned in a continuous and consistent course of dealing with each other, it is taken for granted that the usual terms apply, whether or not spelled out in the contract. Terms implied by a course of dealing are thus a fruitful source of implication into commercial contracts.

(d) *The concept of negotiability*
A key feature of commercial law is its recognition of the need for the ready marketability of commercial assets, in particular goods, money obligations and securities. Hence the development of documents of title and negotiable instruments and securities, the delivery of which (with any necessary indorsement) passes constructive possession (goods) or legal title (instruments and securities) to the underlying rights. Hence also the rule, confined to negotiable instruments, that a holder in due course acquires a title free from equities and defects in the title of his transferor. The concept of negotiability derives from the old law merchant and is a particular characteristic of commercial law. Its importance in facilitating dealings with goods in transit and with negotiable securities may be expected to decline as systems evolve for the paperless transfer of goods and securities, an evolution which the draftsman of a commercial code will have to be ready to accommodate. The same is true of negotiable instruments payable at sight or on demand, since these are payment documents rather than credit instruments and in relative terms are gradually giving way to electronic funds transfers. By contrast, term instruments may be expected to retain their vigour, since there seems no reasonable prospect of devising a commercially viable system for replicating electronically the negotiability of a paper document.

(e) *The enforceability of abstract payment undertakings*
General contract law requires a promise not made under seal to be supported by consideration if it is to be enforceable. But all kinds of legal magic can be worked by mercantile usage. It is generally accepted – though to this day there are no English decisions directly on the point – that certain types of payment undertaking become binding when communicated to the beneficiary, despite the absence of any consideration or any act of reliance on the part of the beneficiary. I refer in particular to the obligations of a bank issuing a documentary credit, a standby credit and a performance bond or guarantee. The contracts

engendered by such undertakings are of a peculiar kind, since they are neither unilateral nor bilateral in the ordinary sense, they involve no acceptance of an offer and no consideration. Exactly what types of payment undertaking will be so enforced remains a matter of conjecture. Is this privileged status confined to undertakings by banks? And if so, which types of undertaking? The answer apparently lies in mercantile custom and usage, a force so powerful that it can sweep aside without argument what is generally considered to be a basic principle of contract law.

I hope I have demonstrated to your satisfaction that there *is* a philosophy of commercial law and there *are* concepts of commercial law which mark out commercial transactions for special treatment. Other concepts may suggest themselves as desirable, such as the irrevocability of firm offers in dealings between merchants. But my purpose is not to produce an exhaustive catalogue, simply to refute the notion still current in some circles that commercial law is merely an aggregation of rules governing particular classes of transaction with no common threads calling for an integrated codification.

NOTES

1. Good faith was a well developed concept in the *lex mercatoria* of the Middle Ages. But it had no counterpart in the common law. With the incorporation of the *lex mercatoria* into the common law in the seventeenth and eighteenth centuries a general principle of good faith in commercial transactions was lost.

Under the common law a party may enforce his *legal* rights and exercise his *legal* remedies without regard to any general requirement of good faith. Professor Goode would like to change this by introducing a general principle of good faith through a commercial code. Others question the need for such wholesale incorporation of the principle of good faith, preferring instead to rely on an incremental approach towards good faith principles. As Bingham LJ stated in *Interfoto Picture Library Ltd v Stiletto Visual Programmes Ltd* [1988] 1 All ER 348 at 352–353:

> In many civil law systems, and perhaps in most legal systems outside the common law world, the law of obligations recognises and enforces an overriding principle that in making and carrying out contracts parties should act in good faith. This does not simply mean that they should not deceive each other, a principle which any legal system must recognise; its effect is most aptly conveyed by such metaphorical colloquialisms as 'playing fair', 'coming clean' or 'putting one's cards face upwards on the table'. It is in essence a principle of fair and open dealing. . . .
>
> English law has, characteristically, committed itself to no such overriding principle but has developed piecemeal solutions in response to demonstrated problems of unfairness. Many examples could be given. Thus equity has intervened to strike down unconscionable bargains. Parliament has stepped in to regulate the imposition of exemption clauses and the form of certain hire-purchase agreements. The common law also has made its contribution, by holding that certain classes of contract require the utmost good faith, by treating as irrecoverable what purport to be agreed estimates of damage but are in truth a disguised penalty for breach, and in many other ways.

As we can see from the extract which appears above, Professor Goode himself recognises that good faith plays an important role in priority disputes (eg the protection given to a good faith purchaser or incumbrancer) and where *equitable* rights or remedies are involved (reflected in the general maxims of equity 'he who seeks equity must do equity' and 'he who comes to equity must come with clean hands'). But it is respectfully submitted that in calling for the incorporation of a general principle of good faith into English law, Professor Goode underplays the alternatives to such a general principle which already regulate the conduct of negotiations and the performance of contracts. Concepts such as election, estoppel, waiver, relief against forfeiture (although the House of Lords has denied its application to commercial contracts: *The Scaptrade* [1983] 2 AC 694), the contra proferentem rule, and the requirement that in exceptional cases an innocent party ought to accept a repudiation and mitigate his loss, can all be added to the list of regulatory mechanisms set out by Bingham LJ in *Interfoto v Stiletto*. In one case, Winn LJ even went so far (probably too far) as to refer to a developing doctrine of 'fair conduct' between parties to commercial contracts (*Panchaud Frères SA v Etablissements General Grain Co* [1970] 1 Lloyd's Rep 53 at 59). See generally, J W Carter (1992) 5 JCL 199 and (1993) 6 JCL 1.

Finally, it is important to acknowledge that the requirement of good faith already features in some of the most important pieces of commercial legislation. Both the Bills of Exchange Act 1882 and the Sale of Goods Act 1979 demand the exercise of good faith before certain rights, particularly those rights protecting third party purchasers, can be acquired (see BEA, ss 12, 29(1), 30(2), 59(1), 60, 79(2), 80; SGA, ss 22–25, 47). Both statutes define good faith in terms of 'honesty in fact' (BEA, s 90; SGA, s 61(3)), although it is clear that wilfully turning a blind eye to one's own suspicions is evidence of dishonesty (*Jones v Gordon* (1877) 2 App Cas 616 at 629 per Lord Blackburn, see below, p 511; *London Joint Stock Bank v Simmons* [1892] AC 201 at 221, per Lord Herschell). See also the Factors Act 1889, ss 2(1), 8 and 9; the Marine Insurance Act 1906, s 17; the Cheques Act 1957, ss 1 and 4; the Hire-Purchase Act 1964, ss 27–29. References in statutes to standards of good faith are likely to increase with the harmonisation of commercial law in the European Community (see, eg, EC Directive 86/653 on Self-Employed Commercial Agents, arts 3(1) and 4(1): below, p 169) and the harmonisation of world trade law (see, eg, the Vienna Convention on Contracts for the International Sale of Goods (1980), art 7(1)). At both levels, the input of jurisprudence from civil law countries ensures that the principle of good faith is recognised by the harmonisation process. But the process also continues, in a piecemeal fashion, on the domestic front. For example, the Law Commission has recently proposed that the Sale of Goods Act 1979 should be reformed to prevent buyers who are not consumers from rejecting goods for minor breaches of certain terms of the sale contract (Law Com No 160, *Sale and Supply of Goods* (1989), paras 4.21 and 6.20). This proposal is an attempt to impose good faith standards in commercial sale transactions.

On the role of good faith in English law, see generally J F O'Connor *Good Faith in English Law* (1990). There is a vast body of literature on the relationship between good faith and contract law, see, eg, R Powell (1956) 9 CLP 16; H Lucke 'Good Faith and Contractual Performance' in P D Finn (ed) *Essays on Contract* (1987), and the literature cited therein. But the concepts of good faith and fair dealing have their critics who see them as too imprecise and reducing the level of legal certainty in transactions: see *White and Carter (Councils) Ltd v McGregor* [1962] AC 413 at 430, per Lord Reid; D Tiplady (1983) 46 MLR 601; M Bridge (1984) 9 Can Bus LJ 385.

2. The concept of the market in commercial law is considered further by Professor Goode in [1991] LMCLQ 177.

7 The codification of commercial law

You will have realised by reading this far that there have been calls for the codification of English commercial law. Those who make that call, such as Professor Goode, do not ask for codification along Victorian lines, where there were virtually no links between the codified statutes. On the contrary, the modern advocates of codification want a comprehensive commercial code along the lines of the American Uniform Commercial Code (UCC) (above, pp 5–6). Such a code would contain statements of principle and would not attempt to deal in detail with every problem that might arise in commerce.

The case for a codification can be summarised as follows: it simplifies the law and makes it easily accessible; the process of codification highlights areas of weakness in the existing law; it enables the law to be modernised and reduces ambiguities and inconsistencies between statutes; it provides an integrated body of commercial law of which the various branches are linked by common concepts, a coherent philosophy and a consistent terminology. It is said that the net effect of commercial codification will be to improve the law and also produce savings in time, effort and money for those who must advise on it and comply with it. See generally, R Goode (1988) 14 Mon LR 135 at pp 137–140, upon which this summary is based.

Yet there has been no call for a commercial code from our commercial judges or practitioners (Lord Goff (1992) 5 JCL 1 at p 3). Furthermore, the opponents of such general codification say that it is unnecessary, inflexible and contrary to our common law tradition of responding to the changing needs of the business community as they arise. Of course, those who see commercial law as an amalgam of distinct subjects, and who deny that there are any general principles of commercial law, see the whole process of general codification as meaningless.

However, as the next extract illustrates, there have been similar calls for wholesale codification of international trade law.

'The Codification of the Law of International Trade' by C M Schmitthoff [1985] JBL 34, pp 41–43

. . . we have to consider whether the creation of a world code on international trade law – a task which, as I have already observed, undoubtedly would fall to UNCITRAL – would be beneficial and feasible. Three questions have here to be examined: what would be the purpose of such codification, what would be the method of it, and what would be the contents of such a code?

As regards the benefits of such codification, they would be, in my view, considerable. Probably the greatest benefit would be that such a code would offer countries in the course of development a compact package deal. If they adopt the code, they would at once have the most modern and comprehensive legal instrument for the conduct of their international business. Secondly, it would be possible to establish in a general part of such code certain principles which should apply to all international trade transactions. I am thinking here, eg, of the obligation of good faith in the performance and enforcement of an international contract, as it is laid down in paragraph 1–203 of the American Uniform Commercial Code. Other equitable rules of the American Code's General Provisions may likewise be suitable for incorporation into a general part of a world code, eg those on severability of an invalid provision, or those on a liberal construction, according to the underlying purposes and policies, in this context, of international Conventions or other international instruments.

Further, a code of international trade law could deal with certain general questions which affect all international trade contracts, such as the effect of telecommunications and the determination of a universal unit of accounts for international conventions, ie the Special

Drawing Rights of the World Bank. Lastly, the creation of a code on international trade law would emphasise the inherent unity of the work of UNCITRAL and other formulating agencies in their efforts to harmonise and unify the legal regulation of international trade on a worldwide basis. This inherent unit is not always clearly discernible in the present state of development as these organisations have often to deal with highly specialised topics of relatively small ambit.

As to the method of codification, little has to be said. It is obvious that the empirical method has to be adopted. The code would thus be nothing more than a technical legal instrument of consolidation.

As to its contents, the code would necessarily have to be built on existing measures of unification. It would have to include, in an integrated manner, the United Nations Conventions so far promulgated and other international measures widely accepted by the practice. It should not be limited to measures sponsored by UNCITRAL but should include suitable texts drafted by other formulating agencies and approved by UNCITRAL. But this may not be enough. A general part would have to be provided, bracketing together the substantive parts. In addition, some further specific subjects may have to be included in order to make the code comprehensive and workable in practice. I have indicated elsewhere what I would consider to be the substance of such a code. I said [C M Schmitthoff *Commercial Law in a Changing Economic Climate* (2nd ed, 1981), p 30]:

> If the Unidroit project on the Code of International Trade Law and the ICC scheme on trade usages are joined together with the United Nations Convention on Contracts for the International Sale of Goods, the ICC Uniform Customs and Practice on Documentary Credits and the Uniform Rules for Collections, the United Nations Hamburg Rules on the Carriage of Goods by Sea, and the UNCITRAL Arbitration Rules, the basis of a world code on international trade is already laid. What has to be done, is to weld together these disjoined pieces of unification into a logical, integrated work and to supplement it by unifications which are still extant, such as the proposed uniform law on international bills of exchange and promissory notes, the regulation of the international contracts of forwarding and warehousing, and other relevant topics.

In the result, the creation of a uniform world code on international trade law would, in my view, serve a useful purpose and, having regard to the existing and planned unificatory measures, is a feasible proposition.

NOTE

Professor Schmitthoff is not referring to the piecemeal harmonisation of trade law that has already taken place via international conventions and codes. He is calling for a worldwide code of international trade. Like Professor Goode, he points to the American UCC as proof that such a code is not a utopian goal. Such a code would create a new *lex mercatoria*.

CHAPTER 2

Basic concepts of personal property

In this chapter, we shall examine some basic concepts of personal property law: the nature of personal property, the characteristics and significance of property rights, ownership, possession and bailment.[1] It is important to understand these concepts as commercial law is primarily concerned with dealings in personal property, eg the sale of goods, the issue and transfer of negotiable instruments and the factoring of debts.

1 The distinction between real and personal property

The common law distinguishes between real property and personal property. In general terms, real property is land and all things built on land. Personal property is all the property that is left after real property has been subtracted from the class of property taken as a whole (see, eg, Bridge, p 1; Bell, p 3). Personal property is, therefore, a residual class of property.

The reason for the division between real and personal property is historical. In the Middle Ages the common law allowed an owner who had been wrongfully dispossessed of his freehold land to bring an action, called a real action, to recover it. On the other hand, an owner of personal property (which, technically, includes leasehold interests in land) could not bring an action to recover it; he was restricted to a personal action for damages against the person who had wrongfully deprived him of his personal property. This procedural distinction still applies today, save that the courts now have a discretion to order delivery of goods back to their owner (Torts (Interference with Goods) Act 1977, s 3).

Leaving aside leasehold interests, which for practical purposes are interests in land, the law treats real and personal property differently. For example, specific performance will rarely be ordered when a buyer fails to deliver goods, whereas it is the usual remedy when a vendor fails to complete a contract for the sale of land; there are different rules for the creation and *inter vivos* transfer of interests in real property (where formalities are required) and personal property (where few

---

1 See generally, R M Goode *Commercial Law* (1982) ('Goode'), Ch 2 (a masterly survey on which much that follows is based); I R Davies *Textbook on Commercial Law* (1992) ('Davies'), Ch 2. For an excellent short commentary on the law of personal property, see M G Bridge *Personal Property Law* (1993) ('Bridge'). See also R G Hammond *Personal Property: Commentary and Materials* (rev ed, 1992) ('Hammond'). For more detailed analysis, see A P Bell *Modern Law of Personal Property in England and Ireland* (1989) ('Bell'); Crossley Vaines *Personal Property* (5th ed, 1973) ('Crossley Vaines').

formalities are required); and, as we have seen, whereas the wrongfully dispossessed owner of real property may recover it as a matter of course, the recovery of personal property is subject to the court's discretion. But why are real and personal property treated so differently? Professor Goode points to the different characteristics of the two types of property: land is generally immovable, relatively permanent, readily split into multiple interests, primarily acquired for use and not intended to circulate in the flow of trade; on the other hand, personal property moves freely in the world of commerce, usually has a relatively short life, has a primary value measured in money and does not readily lend itself to division into multiple interests (Goode, pp 51–52). He concludes:

> . . . land is governed primarily by property law concepts, goods and choses in action by commercial law concepts; land law is concerned essentially with status, commercial law with obligations. But . . . many rules of property law apply equally well to land and chattels.

2 Types of personal property

Personal property may be divided into chattels real and chattels personal. Chattels real consist mainly of leasehold interests in land. Chattels personal are those items of personal property that are not chattels real. Chattels personal may themselves be divided into tangible movables (choses in possession) and intangible movables (choses in action): see *Colonial Bank v Whinney* (1885) 30 Ch D 261 at 285, per Fry LJ.

While tangible movables include goods and money, intangible movables encompass a broader spectrum of personal property ('choses in action' are defined in greater detail below at p 691). Intangible movables can be divided into documentary intangibles and pure intangibles. Documentary intangibles are documents that not only evidence an underlying right to money, goods or securities but also embody that right (considered further, in relation to negotiable instruments, below at pp 469–472). The distinguishing feature of a documentary intangible is that the right the document represents may be pledged or otherwise transferred simply by delivery of the document, together with any necessary indorsement. Examples of documentary intangibles include bills of lading, negotiable instruments, documentary letters of credit and policies of insurance. Pure intangibles are those choses in action that are not documentary intangibles. Examples of pure intangibles include debts, copyright and goodwill.

It should be noted that intellectual property rights such as copyright, patents, trademarks and related rights also fall under the heading of intangible personal property. However, intellectual property forms a subject in its own right and will not be considered further in this book. (Those interested in the subject should consult R Jacob and D Alexander *A Guidebook to Intellectual Property* (4th ed, 1993); J Phillips and A Firth *An Introduction to Intellectual Property Law* (2nd ed, 1990); W R Cornish, *Intellectual Property* (2nd ed, 1989).)

We have already noted that personal property is defined in negative terms, ie all property that is left after real property has been subtracted from the class of property taken as a whole. This means that anything that can be described as property, so long as it is not real property, is personal property. As Andrew Bell has observed: 'the list [of personal property] is an open-ended one: any novel phenomenon that is recognised as property will in practice be classified as personal property' (Bell, p 1). So, what is property?

3 What is property?

Crossley Vaines on Personal Property **(5th ed, 1973) (eds E Tyler and N Palmer), p 3**

'Property' is a word of different meanings. It may mean a thing owned (my watch or my house is 'my property'); it may mean ownership itself as when I speak of my 'property' in my watch which may pass to the person to whom I sell the watch before I actually hand the watch over . . .; or it may even mean an interest in a thing less than ownership but nevertheless conferring certain rights, as when we speak of the 'property' or 'special property' of a bailee in the thing bailed . . . In English law, therefore, 'property' comprehends tangibles and intangibles, movables and immovables; it means a tangible thing (land or chattel) itself, or rights in respect of that thing, or rights, such as a debt, in relation to which no tangible thing exists.

Elements of Land Law **by K Gray (1st ed, 1987), pp 8–14**

THE MEANING OF PROPERTY

It is important at the outset to dispel one common lay notion concerning 'property'. Non-lawyers (and sometimes lawyers) speak loosely of property as the *thing* which is owned. While this usage is harmless enough in day-to-day speech, it has the effect of obscuring certain salient features of property as a legal phenomenon, for semantically 'property' is the condition of being 'proper' to (or belonging to) a particular person.

(1) Property is not a 'thing' but a 'relationship'

It was the philosopher, Jeremy Bentham, who had to remind lawyers that property is not a thing but a relationship. Bentham pointed out that 'in common speech in the phrase *the object of a man's property*, the words *the object of* are commonly left out; and by an ellipsis, which, violent as it is, is now become more familiar than the phrase at length, they have made that part of it which consists of the words *a man's property* perform the office of the whole.' More recently Professor Macpherson has drawn attention to the way in which, in the transition from the pre-capitalist world to the world of the exchange economy, the distinction between a right to a thing (ie the legal relation) and the thing itself, became blurred. 'The thing itself became, in common parlance, the property'.

(a) *Potential multiplicity of competing users*
At one level of analysis, then, 'property' is a relation between the owner and the thing (ie between a 'subject' and an 'object'). However, as has already been suggested, it is unreal to think simply in terms of 'the' owner of any particular thing. It is possible for conflicting claims to be brought by two or more 'subjects' in respect of the same 'object', and therefore the property lawyer is almost always concerned with the relative merits of different claims. In order to establish what belongs to, or is 'proper' to, any particular 'subject', he must first analyse the legal relations between a number of competing subjects vis à vis the same object. A further level of complexity arises because any particular 'object' of property may itself be capable of sustaining a wide variety of different (but not necessarily conflicting) claims. This is demonstrated most clearly in the case of land. Land may, for instance, be the object of a multiplicity of claims made simultaneously by an owner-occupier, a tenant, a building society, a neighbour who enjoys a right of way or restrictive covenant, or even by a spouse who has certain rights not to be evicted from the property.

(b) *A network of 'property' relationships*
In the ultimate analysis the law of property is concerned with entire networks of legal relationship existing between individuals in respect of things. 'Property' is thus the name given to the bundles of mutual rights and obligations which prevail between 'subjects' in respect of certain 'objects', and the study of property law accordingly becomes an inquiry

into a variety of socially defined relationships and morally conditioned obligations. This relational view highlights certain characteristics of property which are essential to any real understanding of land law.

Professor Bruce Ackerman has spoken of the need to disabuse law students of their primitive lay notions regarding ownership. In the words of Ackerman, 'only the ignorant think it meaningful to talk about owning things free and clear of further obligation.' Instead of defining the relationship between a person and 'his' things, property law considers the 'way rights to use things may be parcelled out amongst a host of competing resource users'. Ackerman points out that each resource user is conceived as holding 'a bundle of rights vis à vis other potential users' and that the ways in which user rights may be legally packaged and distributed are 'wondrously diverse.' Ackerman concludes that

> it is probably never true that the law assigns to any single person the right to use any thing in absolutely *any* way he pleases. Hence, it risks serious confusion to identify any single individual as *the* owner of any particular thing. At best, this locution may sometimes serve as identifying the holder of that bundle of rights which contains a range of entitlements more numerous or more valuable than the bundle held by any other person with respect to the thing in question. Yet, like all shorthands, talk about 'the' property owner invites the fallacy of misplaced concreteness, of reification. Once one begins to think sloppily, it is all too easy to start thinking that 'the' property owner, by virtue of being 'the' property owner, must *necessarily* own a particular bundle of rights over a thing. And this is to commit the error that separates layman from lawyer. For the fact (or is it the law?) of the matter is that property is not a thing, but a set of legal relations between persons governing the use of things.

(2) Property is a dynamic relationship

If property is a relationship, it is a dynamic relationship; the content of the relationship is liable to change. The 'subjects' of property may differ from one social era to another. The 'objects' of property are likewise liable to fluctuate with the passage of time and the emergence of new economic conditions. Above all, the ideology of property is profoundly influenced by changing factors of social, political and economic philosophy.

(a) *The changing 'subjects' of property*
An element of social control is exercised over the property relation in every society, in that each social group to a greater or lesser extent determines for itself the categories of person who may be recognised as the potential 'subjects' of property. In some societies of the past various classes of labourer or serf (eg slaves) were excluded from legal competence as potential 'subjects' of property. Even until relatively recently in England, the married woman was deprived of capacity to hold a legal title in her own name. However, the present century has seen the 'emergence of a property-owning, particularly a real-property-mortgaged-to-a-building-society-owning, democracy.' The years of greater affluence following the World Wars brought about, in the words of Lord Wilberforce, 'the extension, beyond the paterfamilias, of rights of ownership, itself following from the diffusion of property and earning capacity.' Less obviously this diffusion of ownership rights has accentuated the demand that other kinds of right should be recognised as 'proprietary' rights on behalf of less advantaged social groups. Those, for instance, who are not owners of the homes in which they live may wish to assert that their occupation rights (eg as tenants) represent a proprietary status equivalent to that of the owner-occupier.

(b) *The changing 'objects' of property*
If the 'objects' of property are those resources to which social or economic value is generally attached, it is inevitable that over time variations of social interest and concern should alter the emphasis of the property relationship. There was, for instance, an age in which both wives and slaves were regarded as appropriate 'objects' of property. In medieval England the husband was viewed as enjoying proprietary rights in relation to his wife, her domestic services and her productive capacity. Much of the concern which generated this assessment of the spousal relationship was itself brought about by the supposed paramountcy of the need

to ensure the devolution of property within a dynastic line of legitimate issue. However, the 'objects' of property are continually redefined by the prevalent social ethic, and today it is no longer acceptable that either wives or certain classes of labourer should be regarded as the 'objects' of a proprietary relation.

(i) *Transformation of material wealth*   The 'objects' of property can, however, change in more subtle degrees. For centuries the most highly prized 'object' of property in the common law world was land. In the 19th century and early 20th century the phenomenon of the company share came close to dislodging land as the pre-eminent 'object' of commercial value, at a time when the bulk of ordinary men and women owned little of value other than perhaps the clothes which they wore. In the modern post-industrial society, however, with the diffusion of ownership amongst classes never before entitled, the traditional concept of a man's wealth has undergone yet another transformation. Nowadays a person's material substance is no longer related particularly to the ownership of tangible assets designed for enjoyment and consumption; it is more readily expressed in terms of intangible, non-assignable, and often non-survivable, claims of a largely personal nature. The things which today are of real value to the man in the street are assets like his job, his pension, and the right to undisturbed possession of his home. On the fringes of these new categories of property lie certain less well defined rights such as the right to education, the right to health and the right to a wholesome environment.

(ii) *The 'new property'*   The changing concept of wealth in the modern world was classically described by Professor Charles Reich in a seminal law review article in 1964. Reich drew attention to the dramatic changes taking place in the nature and forms of wealth in industrial democratic societies. In particular, he pointed to the way in which government has begun to operate today as a major distributor of wealth in the form of welfare payments, salaries for those in public service, pensions for those who have retired from employment, and many other forms of licence, franchise, subsidy and fiscal benefit. As Reich indicated, 'today's distribution of largesse is on a vast, imperial scale.' Reich went on to argue that the principal forms of wealth for most people in our society are comprised in their employment or profession (and in various work-related benefits such as pensions) or in their dependency claims upon government (in the guise of social security payments). These forms of wealth, which for Reich were concerned essentially with income security, have become in fact the 'new property', and Reich's major thesis was that this 'new property' should be accorded the same standard of legal protection as had been accorded in the past to more traditional entitlements of private property. In his view, the goal of future development in this area must be to 'try to build an economic basis for liberty today – a Homestead Act for rootless twentieth century man. We must create a new property.'
    The call for legal recognition of and protection for the 'new property' has intensified during the two decades since the publication of Reich's major article. In 1970, in its fundamentally significant decision in *Goldberg v Kelly*, the Supreme Court of the United States acknowledged the 'new property' to be deserving of constitutional protection. In the years following this decision, the prominence of the 'new property' has been accentuated by developments in other fields of law.

(iii) *The changing balance of family, work and government*   The emergence of the 'new property' can also be placed in the historical context of a more general shift in the relative importance of family, work and government as determinants of social status and as sources of economic security. Today, in an age of liberal divorce and increasingly attenuated family ties, the primary source of economic security for the individual is no longer the family but rather the individual's employment or his dependency relationship with government. . . .

(iv) *Residential security*   The jurisprudence of the 'new property' has emerged largely in the context of the individual's rights in the fields of employment and social security. However, an object which lies more immediately within the ambit of a 'Homestead Act for rootless twentieth century man' is the general provision of security in the enjoyment of residential accommodation. . . .

(c) *The contemporary redefinition of 'property'*

During the present century claims of social welfare have been increasingly recognised through interventionist legislation in the fields of social security, housing and employment protection. By according legal force to various kinds of 'security claim', this legislation has already gone some distance towards ensuring a more equitable distribution of the 'goods of life'. The security claims recognised in these areas broadly cover the kinds of interest which are comprised within the 'new property'. Thus the claim to security in employment is recognised, at least to some extent, by legislation which protects the individual employee from 'unfair dismissal'; the claim to residential security, by the Rent and Housing Acts and other statutory means; the claim to income security, by the vast range of legislation which underpins the social security system. Inherent in all these measures is a significant return to the idea of a 'status'. The individual receives the benefits of protective legislation, not because he has in any sense contracted or bargained to received them, but because he enjoys a defined 'status' which entitles him to some appropriate form of 'security'.

All these developments tend to suggest that, by operating effectively as an agent of distributive justice, the 'new property' has initiated a redefinition of the ideology of property. In the conventional analysis, the concept of property is essentially negative and exclusory: the traditional concept of a property right comprises the right to exclude all others from the use or enjoyment of some thing. The 'new property' comprises by contrast various kinds of claim *not* to be excluded from the use of enjoyment of some thing. Indeed it has been said that the idea of property is gradually being broadened to include a 'right to a kind of society or set of power relations which will enable the individual to live a fully human life.' At least in some incipient form, this perspective may indicate an intellectual shift away from the idea that property is a private right to exclude from personally owned resources, and may point instead towards a reappraisal of property as a public right of access to socially valued resources.

NOTE

Three important points emerge from the extract taken from Professor Gray's textbook on land law. These points are just as relevant to the commercial lawyer as they are to the (real) property lawyer. The points are:

(1) Property is not a thing but rather a set of legal relations existing between persons in respect of things (Ackerman would regard the editors of *Crossley Vaines* as guilty of 'sloppy thinking' because they define property, inter alia, as 'a thing owned').

(2) Property is a relative, not an absolute, concept. Two or more 'subjects' may have concurrent property rights in respect of the same 'object'. These rights may or may not conflict. For example, S sells goods to B1 and then sells the same goods to B2: rights of B1 and B2 conflict; O hires his car to H for a month: O's rights as owner do not conflict with H's rights as bailee. You should keep this point in mind, particularly when you study the basic principle *nemo dat quod non habet* and its exceptions (Chapter 9).

(3) Property is a dynamic relationship. Both the 'subjects' and 'objects' of property may change. Whether a person has property rights in respect of an object may be of great practical significance to the commercial lawyer. For example, is confidential information property? (see below, p 175). Is a debt a personal obligation, or property capable of being the subject of a charge by the creditor in favour of the debtor? (see below, pp 761–765).

4   What are the characteristics of property rights?

National Provincial Bank Ltd v Ainsworth [1965] AC 1175, House of Lords

(The facts are irrelevant.)

Lord Wilberforce: . . . Before a right or an interest can be admitted into the category of property, or of a right affecting property, it must be definable, identifiable by third parties, capable in its nature of assumption by third parties, and have some degree of permanence or stability.

'Property in Thin Air' by K Gray [1991] CLJ 252, pp 292–295

IV. 'PROPERTY' AS CONTROL OVER ACCESS

And so continues our search for the inner mystery of 'property'. Let us look back and see how far we have got since we started. There is no real likelihood that we have arrived at our destination, for the quest for the essential nature of 'property' has beguiled thinkers for many centuries. The essence of 'property' is indeed elusive. That is why, in a sense, we have tried to catch the concept by surprise by asking not 'What is property?' but rather 'What is not property?' We have started from the other end of the earth – both geographically and conceptually – and we have deliberately come by the direction which seemed least probable. But along the way we may have discovered something of value. We may have discovered the irreducible conditions which underlie any claim of 'property'.

The classic common law criteria of 'property' have tended to rest a twin emphasis on the assignability of the benefits inherent in a resource and on the relative permanence of those benefits if unassigned. Before a right can be admitted within the category of 'property' it must, according to Lord Wilberforce in *National Provincial Bank Ltd v Ainsworth*, be 'definable, identifiable by third parties, capable in its nature of assumption by third parties, and have some degree of permanence or stability'. This preoccupation with assignability of benefit and enforceability of burden doubtless owes much to the fact that the formative phases of the common law concept of property coincided with a remarkable culture of bargain and exchange. Non-transferable rights or rights which failed on transfer were simply not 'property'. Within the crucible of transfer lawyers affected to demarcate rights of 'property' from rights founded in contract and tort or, for that matter, from human rights and civil liberties. Only brief reflection is required in order to perceive the horrible circularity of such hallmarks of 'property'. If naively we ask which rights are proprietary, we are told that they are those rights which are assignable to and enforceable against third parties. When we then ask which rights these may be, we are told that they comprise, of course, the rights which are traditionally identified as 'proprietary'. 'Property' is 'property' because it is 'property': property status and proprietary consequence confuse each other in a deadening embrace of cause and effect.

Nor have the philosophers given significantly greater assistance in explaining the phenomenon of 'property'. Perhaps inevitably lawyers have concentrated their attention on locating the *ownership* of 'property', this task of identification assuming vital significance in a legal culture dominated by transfer and conveyance. By contrast philosophers have directed their efforts principally towards rationalising the *institution* of 'property'. While lawyers discuss who owns what, philosophers ask why anyone can legitimately claim to own anything. Justificatory theories of 'property' range diversely from appeals to the investment of labour or the existence of a social contract to arguments based upon first occupancy, utility or personhood. A pervasive influence in all philosophical thinking on 'property' is still the brooding omnipresence of John Locke. But Locke's concentration on original acquisition ill suits legal discourse in a modern world which is based on derivative acquisition and in which original acquisition (except perhaps in the area of intellectual property) is now virtually impossible. Even Locke himself cannot have believed that in late 17th century

England the 'Commons' still contained many unappropriated acorns yet to be 'pickt up under an Oak' or apples to be 'gathered from the Trees in the Wood', even if he did think that 'property' in such things was 'fixed' by the labour invested in their 'first gathering'. As Walton Hamilton noted much later, Locke's natural state is 'a curious affair, peopled with the Indians of North America and run by the scientific principles of his friend Sir Isaac Newton'.

In their respective preoccupations with resource allocation and institutional justification, lawyers and philosophers alike have largely failed to identify the characteristic hallmark of the common law notion of 'property'. If our own travels in search of 'property' have indicated one thing, it is that the criterion of 'excludability' gets us much closer to the core of 'property' than does the conventional legal emphasis on the assignability or enforceability of benefits. For 'property' resides not in consumption of benefits but in control over benefits. 'Property' is not about *enjoyment of access* but about *control over access.* 'Property' is the power-relation constituted by the state's endorsement of private claims to regulate the access of strangers to the benefits of particular resources. If, in respect of a given claimant and a given resource, the exercise of such regulatory control is physically impracticable or legally abortive or morally or socially undesirable, we say that such a claimant can assert no 'property' in that resource and for that matter can lose no 'property' in it either. Herein lies an important key to the 'propertiness' of property.

Here too lies the key to the divergent approaches evident in *Victoria Park Racing and Recreation Grounds Co Ltd v Taylor.* The minority in the High Court of Australia found a misappropriation of 'property' in the sheer fact that the defendants had diminished the plaintiff's *access* to the benefits of certain resources. By contrast the majority found that there has been no taking of 'property', precisely because the defendants' conduct could never in any event have deprived the plaintiff of *control over access* to those resources. For a variety of reasons the resources in dispute had remained at all times inherently non-excludable. The plaintiff might have enjoyed *access* to the benefits of the contested resources, but it never had a *control over access* which could be prejudiced by the actions of the defendants. The resources in issue could never have sustained any claim of 'property' by the plaintiff and could not now therefore support any allegation of loss or misappropriation. Whatever it was the defendants took – and they undeniably took something – they took none of the plaintiff's 'property'.

The concept of excludability thus takes us some way towards discovering a rationally defensible content in the term 'property'. The differentiation of excludable and non-excludable resources points up the irreducible elements which lie at the core of the 'property' notion. But these irreducibles, once isolated and identified, leave little if anything of value to be gathered from the traditional indicia of 'property'. The concept of excludability does not, of course, resolve entirely the issue of justice in holdings; it merely demarcates the categories of resource in which it is possible to claim 'property'. It sets outer limits on claims of 'property', but provides no criteria for justifying such claims on behalf of particular individuals – except to the extent that we accept the initially unpalatable (but historically attested) proposition that the sustained assertion of effective control over access to the benefits of a resource tends ultimately to be constitutive of 'property' in that resource. The precise allocation of 'property' in excludable resources is left to be determined – is indeed constantly formulated and reformulated – by various kinds of social and moral consensus over legitimate modes of acquisition and the relative priority of competing claims. This consensus is reinforced by a machinery of legal recognition and enforcement which thus adds or withholds the legitimacy of state sanction in relation to individual assertions of 'property'.

NOTES

1. In *Victoria Park Racing and Recreation Grounds Co Ltd v Taylor* (1937) 58 CLR 479 the owner of a racecourse applied for an injunction to stop the owner of neighbouring land, and a broadcasting company, from using a platform erected on the neighbouring land to watch horse races which took place at the racecourse and broadcasting a radio commentary of those races. The racecourse owner charged the public for admission to the course and his business had suffered because punters stayed at home, or in the local hostelry, to listen to the defendant's broadcasts. By a majority of 3:2 the High Court of Australia held that the defendants had committed no legal wrong. Although much of the discussion in the case was in terms of the law of nuisance, the central issue was whether the defendants had taken anything that might be regarded as the plaintiff's 'property'. The majority held that they had not because there could be no property in a spectacle such as a horse race. A spectacle, according to Latham CJ, 'cannot be owned in any ordinary sense of the word' (at 496; cf D F Libling (1978) 94 LQR 103 at p 106).

2. According to Professor Gray (op cit, p 268):

> The primordial principle which emerges from the majority judgments in *Victoria Park Racing* is that a resource can be propertised only if it is 'excludable'. A resource is 'excludable' only if it is feasible for a legal person to exercise regulatory control over the access of strangers to the various benefits inherent in the resource.

In *Victoria Park Racing*, it was not reasonably practical to physically exclude the defendants from the benefits of the spectacle provided on the plaintiff's land (Gray, op cit, p 272).

3. A vast literature on the meaning of 'property', and the justification of private property, has been produced by lawyers, philosophers and political scientists. See, for example, Bell, Ch 1; Hammond, Pt 1 (and the literature cited therein); J Waldron (1985) 5 OJLS 313.

QUESTIONS

1. A buys a car from B. Can A exclude others from the car? What if the car had been stolen by B and the true owner wants it back? Does A have 'property' in the car? The sale of goods by a non-owner is considered below in Chapter 9.

2. C owes £100 to D. Can D exclude others from the debt? If C erroneously pays the debt to E, the debt still exists and D continues to look to C for payment. Therefore, does D have 'property' in the debt?

5 Types of property rights

The common law recognises two types of property rights over personal property: (1) ownership, and (2) possession for a limited interest, including liens (below, p 814) and rights arising under pledges (below, p 800). All other rights exist only in equity, eg the rights of a beneficiary under a trust, mere charges (see below, p 836), non-possessory liens (below, p 846) and the mortgagor's right of redemption (below, p 831). But an equitable interest must be distinguished from a 'mere equity', which is no more than a personal right vested in a person who has conferred an interest or right on another to set aside or qualify the document or transaction by which that interest or right is transferred (per Goode, p 72), eg the right to rescind for fraud or the right to rectification for mistake are both mere equities.

As a general rule, these rights display the two traditional characteristics of property rights: they are assignable and they are enforceable against third parties. But this may not always be the case. For example, in certain circumstances common law property rights may be overriden and equitable rights may be defeated by a bona fide purchaser for value without notice. This confirms what we have already noted, property rights are relative, not absolute. For further discussion of this issue, see Bell, pp 6–13.

6 The significance of property rights

'Ownership and Obligation in Commercial Transactions' by R M Goode (1987) 103 LQR 433, pp 433–435, 436–438

I INTRODUCTION

In common with other legal systems, English law sharply distinguishes property rights from mere personal rights to the delivery or transfer of an asset. I *own* property; I am *owed* performance of a transfer obligation. Ownership attracts several advantages, and some disadvantages, in law, and is frequently a condition precedent to the assertion of contractual rights. If I own an asset in the possession of another who becomes bankrupt, I can withdraw it from the reach of his creditors; if I am owed a purely personal obligation to transfer the asset to me I have no right to remove it from the common pool. As owner of a chattel I am entitled to a remedy in tort for negligence if it is carelessly damaged or destroyed by another. Ownership also carries with it a right to possession, where no one else has a better right, and is protected by the law of torts, in particular the tort of conversion. If I own goods, I bear the burden of accidental loss or damage. The transfer of ownership is in general a condition of the seller's right to sue for the price under a contract of sale of goods; and the acquisition of ownership is a prerequisite to certain statutory transfers of contractual rights, such as the transfer of the shipper's rights under a bill of lading to a consignee or indorsee under section 1 of the Bills of Lading Act 1855 [since replaced by section 2 of the Carriage of Goods by Sea Act 1992]. . . .

II OWNERSHIP IN INSOLVENCY

(i) *Practical importance of the question*

In the commercial world the distinction between ownership of an asset and a purely personal right to acquire an asset, eg under a contract, is usually of little significance so long as the debtor is traceable and solvent, for the interest of a commercial creditor in the performance of a transfer undertaking is usually monetary rather than in ownership for its own sake, and if the debtor (using this term in the broad sense of an obligor) fails to deliver then the creditor can simply obtain what is due to him, either in cash or in kind, by suing for it and enforcing any resulting judgment.

It is upon the debtor's insolvency that the distinction between ownership and a personal right to an asset becomes of crucial significance, for it is a basic policy of insolvency law to adopt the non-bankruptcy ordering of rights and thus to respect proprietary rights held by another prior to the debtor's bankruptcy. Hence in principle the estate available for distribution among the general body of creditors is limited to the debtor's own assets. Owners and secured creditors can withdraw from the pool the assets they own or over which they have security, whilst unsecured creditors are left to prove in competition with each other for such crumbs as remain after proprietary rights, the expenses of the insolvency proceedings and the claims of preferential creditors have been satisfied.

It follows that the degree in which the law is willing to recognise rights as proprietary rather than merely personal is of great moment to unsecured creditors, for every extension of the concept of ownership erodes the debtor's estate and thus reduces the significance of the hallowed principle of pari passu distribution. Conversely, every condition precedent attached by the law to the acquisition of ownership represents a pitfall for the would-be investor and the would-be secured creditor who lays out his money in the expectation of receiving in exchange some proprietary interest in the debtor's patrimony. . . .

(iii)   *The growth of equitable property rights*

Property and obligation at law

The common law (in its narrow sense) sharply distinguished transfers of property from mere personal undertakings. A transfer from A to B had to relate to an existing asset in which A had a subsisting interest, and the transfer itself had to be in proper form. Except in the case of a contract for the sale of existing goods, where the agreement was effective by itself to transfer title, an agreement for transfer conferred no proprietary rights on the intended transferee even if he had parted with his money. A purported transfer by A to B of A's after-acquired property was at best a contract and could not of itself operate to vest the property in B even after A had acquired it; a new act of transfer was necessary after the acquisition. Similarly, a transfer by A to C to hold on trust for B conferred no interest on B, for the conveyance was not made to him.

These common law rules still apply in relation to the transfer of a legal title, save for the special case of contracts of sale of goods, in relation to which the Sale of Goods Act prescribes the automatic transfer of title to future goods upon their acquisition by the seller, if the parties so agree.

Property and obligation in equity

Under the influence of equity the distinction between property rights *in* an asset and personal rights *to* an asset became blurred. Acting on the basis that equity treats as done that which ought to be done, courts of equity came to regard an unperfected agreement to assign as an assignment which became perfected by payment of the consideration; they upheld the assignment of future property as effective on acquisition by the debtor without the need for any new act of transfer; they recognised the interest of the beneficiary under a passive trust as a proprietary interest; and they accorded proprietary status to the right of an owner of an asset to trace the products and proceeds of dispositions by the owner's bailee.

Even after all this the ingenuity of the equity lawyers was not exhausted. A person might succeed to a claim by assignment or by subrogation. Equity also came to recognise the existence of proprietary rights not in a specific asset but in a shifting fund of assets, as exemplified by the interest of the beneficiary under an active trust and of a debenture holder under a floating charge, and these interests became included in the category of proprietary rights having priority over the claims of unsecured creditors.

The development of the resulting trust and the constructive trust led to the recognition of proprietary rights in a variety of situations in which one person improperly held assets or benefits to which another had a better right. Among the events that have been held to attract these forms of trust are the payment of money for a purpose which has failed, the payment of money under a mistake of fact and the acquisition of an asset by the defendant from a third party, or the retention of such an asset, in breach of the defendant's fiduciary duty to the plaintiff.

Finally, even a 'mere equity,' such as a right to rescind (eg for fraud or misrepresentation) a contract under which the bankrupt acquired an asset can be asserted against his trustee, thus removing the asset from the general body of creditors even after the commencement of bankruptcy.

The result of this equitable development is that most obligations owed by B to A to transfer an asset to A are proprietary in nature rather than merely personal, though often A has a personal right to the asset running concurrently with his proprietary interest in it. It is unusual to find a situation in which B has a duty to make over to A an asset still in B's hands without A thereby enjoying equitable ownership of the asset. In equity, the obligation to transfer, whatever its source, is itself a transfer provided that the obligation is not merely contingent, the subject-matter is identifiable and the consideration is in due course paid. The one outstanding exception to this rule is the contract of sale of goods, where the buyer either acquires legal title or acquires nothing beyond a mere contract right. This exception reflects not only the universality of the contract of sale of goods, which makes it undesirable to complicate the contract by equitable ownership, but the fact that under a contract of sale title passes by agreement, and except where this is reserved to secure payment a seller who has not reached the stage of passing legal title usually intends to reserve a right to dispose of the goods elsewhere.

NOTES

1. In *Leigh & Sillavan Ltd v Aliakmon Shipping Co Ltd, The Aliakmon* [1986] AC 785, a carrier contracted with sellers to ship steel coils which the sellers had sold to buyers. The goods were damaged during the voyage as a result of negligent stowage by the carrier. The damage occurred at a time when the risk in the goods, but not the property in them, had passed to the buyers. The buyers had no claim against the carrier under the contract of carriage as they were not a party to that contract (the Carriage of Goods by Sea Act 1992, s 2(1) would, however, now give the buyers a contractual right of action against the carrier: see below, pp 444–445). The House of Lords held that the buyers also had no cause of action against the carrier in tort for negligence. Lord Brandon, with whose speech all their Lordships agreed, stated (at 809) that:

> . . . there is a long line of authority for a principle of law that, in order to enable a person to claim in negligence for loss caused to him by reason of loss of or damage to property, he must have had either the legal ownership of or a possessory title to the property concerned at the time the loss or damage occurred, and it is not enough for him to have only had contractual rights in relation to such property which have been adversely affected by the loss of or damage to it.

2. We have already noted that one of the hallmarks of a property right is that it binds third parties. However, in certain circumstances, a personal right relating to personal property may do the same. In *De Mattos v Gibson* (1858) 4 De G & J 276, the owner of a ship entered into a charterparty. The owner subsequently mortgaged the vessel to a mortgagee who at all times was aware of the charterparty and its terms. The mortgagee sought to enforce his security and divert the ship to another port to sell it. The charterer applied for an injunction to prevent the mortgagee from doing anything which would interfere with the performance of the charterparty. Knight Bruce and Turner LJJ granted the charterer's application for an interlocutory injunction. Knight Bruce LJ said (at 282):

> Reason and justice seem to prescribe that, at least as a general rule, where a man, by gift or purchase, acquires property from another, with knowledge of a previous contract, lawfully and for valuable consideration made by him with a third person, to use and employ the property for a particular purpose in a specified manner, the acquirer shall not, to the material damage of the third person, in opposition to the contract and inconsistently with it, use and employ the property in a manner not allowable to the giver or seller. This rule, applicable alike in general as I conceive to moveable and immoveable property, and recognized and adopted, as I apprehend, by the English law, may, like other general rules, be liable to exceptions arising from special circumstances; but I see at present no room for any exception in the instance before us.

At the full hearing Lord Chelmsford refused the injunction for other reasons.

The principle formulated by Knight Bruce LJ in *De Mattos v Gibson* was later applied by the Privy Council in *Lord Strathcona SS Co Ltd v Dominion Coal Co* [1926] AC 108 to restrain the purchaser of a ship from using it inconsistently with a time charter granted by the previous owner. But in *Port Line Ltd v Ben Line Steamers Ltd* [1958] 2 QB 146, Diplock J denied the existence of the principle and thought that the *Strathcona* case had been wrongly decided. However, the principle has since been approved by Browne-Wilkinson J in *Swiss Bank Corpn v Lloyds Bank Ltd* [1979] Ch 548 (revsd CA; affd HL [1982] AC 584 on other grounds); by Scott LJ in *Mac-Jordan Construction Ltd v Brookmount Erostin Ltd* [1992] BCLC 350; and, most recently, by Hoffmann J in *Law Debenture Trust Corpn plc v Ural Caspian Oil Corpn Ltd* [1993] 1 WLR 138 – who emphasised that 'the *De Mattos* principle permits no more than the grant of a negative injunction to restrain the third party from doing acts which would be inconsistent with performance of the contract by the original contracting party' (at 144) – (revsd in part on another ground (1994) Independent, 10 March, CA).

Although the existence of the *De Mattos* principle now appears to be established; it is a principle surrounded by confusion and uncertainty. As Hoffmann J said in the *Ural Caspian* case (at 144):

> I am bound to say that neither *Strathcona* nor *Swiss Bank* make it entirely clear when the principle applies and when it does not. Why, for example, does it apply to a time charter but not to a resale price maintenance agreement?

Furthermore, whilst it appears that liability under the *De Mattos* principle depends on notice, there is considerable uncertainty as to whether notice includes constructive notice or is confined to actual notice. In *Mac-Jordan Construction Ltd v Brookmount Erostin Ltd*, above, Scott LJ recently held that actual notice was essential (cf A Clarke [1992] LMCLQ 448 at pp 455–456, where the arguments in favour of the standard of actual notice are criticised).

For further discussion of the *De Mattos* principle, see generally S Gardner (1982) 98 LQR 279; A Tettenborn [1982] CLJ 58.

7 Ownership

Ownership is conventionally defined as the residue of legal rights in an asset left in a person after lesser rights in the asset have been granted to others (see Goode, p 52; Bell, p 67). Thus, if I lend you my car for a week, I have residual rights, and an absolute interest, in the car; you have special rights of possession as bailee, and a limited interest, in it (in fact, you would have a limited interest in the car if you took it under a pledge, lease, rental, or other form of bailment). Yet such a residual rights analysis of ownership may be misleading where no lesser rights have been granted in the asset. Another way of describing ownership is to identify the incidents attached to it.

'Ownership' by A M Honoré in *Oxford Essays in Jurisprudence* (1961) (ed A G Guest), pp 107–108, 112–123, 126–128

Ownership is one of the characteristic institutions of human society. A people to whom ownership was unknown, or who accorded it a minor place in their arrangements, who meant by *meum* and *tuum* no more than 'what I (or you) presently hold' would live in a world that is not our world. Yet to see why their world would be different, and to assess the plausibility of vaguely conceived schemes to replace 'ownership' by 'public administration', or of vaguely stated claims that the importance of ownership has declined or its character changed in the twentieth century, we need first to have a clear idea of what ownership is.

I propose, therefore, to begin by giving an account of the standard incidents of ownership: i.e. those legal rights, duties and other incidents which apply, in the ordinary case, to the person who has the greatest interest in a thing admitted by a mature legal system. To do so will be to analyse the concept of ownership, by which I mean the 'liberal' concept of 'full' individual ownership, rather than any more restricted notion to which the same label may be attached in certain contexts. . . .

I. THE LIBERAL CONCEPT OF OWNERSHIP

If ownership is provisionally defined as the *greatest possible interest in a thing which a mature system of law recognizes*, then it follows that, since all mature systems admit the existence of 'interests' in 'things', all mature systems have, in a sense, a concept of ownership. Indeed, even primitive systems, like that of the Trobriand islanders, have rules by which certain persons, such as the 'owners' of canoes, have greater interests in certain things than anyone else.

For mature legal systems it is possible to make a larger claim. In them certain important legal incidents are found, which are common to different systems. If it were not so, 'He owns that umbrella', said in a purely English context, would mean something different from 'He owns that umbrella', preferred as a translation of 'Ce parapluie est à lui'. Yet, as we know, they mean the same. There is indeed, a substantial similarity in the position of one who 'owns' an umbrella in England, France, Russia, China, and any other modern country one may care to mention. Everywhere the 'owner' can, in the simple uncomplicated case, in which no other person has an interest in the thing, use it, stop others using it, lend it, sell it or leave it by will. Nowhere may he use it to poke his neighbour in the ribs or to knock over his vase. Ownership, *dominium, propriété, Eigentum* and similar words stand not merely for the greatest interest in things in particular systems but for a type of interest with common features transcending particular systems. It must surely be important to know what these common features are? . . .

The Standard Incidents

I now list what appear to be the standard incidents of ownership. They may be regarded as necessary ingredients in the notion of ownership, in the sense that, if a system did not admit them, and did not provide for them to be united in a single person, we would conclude that it did not know the liberal concept of ownership, though it might still have a modified version of ownership, either of a primitive or sophisticated sort. But the listed incidents are not individually necessary, though they may be together sufficient, conditions for the person of inherence to be designated 'owner' of a particular thing in a given system. As we have seen, the use of 'owner' will extend to cases in which not all the listed incidents are present.

Ownership comprises the right to possess, the right to use, the right to manage, the right to the income of the thing, the right to the capital, the right to security, the rights or incidents of transmissibility and absence of term, the prohibition of harmful use, liability to execution, and the incident of residuarity: this makes eleven leading incidents. Obviously, there are alternative ways of classifying the incidents; moreover, it is fashionable to speak of ownership as if it were just a bundle of rights, in which case at least two items in the list would have to be omitted.

No doubt the concentration in the same person of the right (liberty) of using as one wishes, the right to exclude others, the power of alienating and an immunity from expropriation is a cardinal feature of the institution. Yet it would be a distortion – and one of which the eighteenth century, with its over-emphasis on subjective rights, was patently guilty – to speak as if this concentration of patiently garnered rights was the only legally or socially important characteristic of the owner's position. The present analysis, by emphasizing that the owner is subject to characteristic prohibitions and limitations, and that ownership comprises at least one important incident independent of the owner's choice, is an attempt to redress the balance.

(1) The right to possess
The right to possess, *viz.* to have exclusive physical control of a thing, or to have such control as the nature of the thing admits, is the foundation on which the whole superstructure of ownership rests. It may be divided into two aspects, the right (claim) to be put in exclusive control of a thing and the right to remain in control, *viz.* the claim that others should not, without permission, interfere. Unless a legal system provides some rules and

procedures for attaining these ends it cannot be said to protect ownership.

It is of the essence of the right to possess that it is *in rem* in the sense of availing against persons generally. This does not, of course, mean that an owner is necessarily entitled to exclude everyone from his property. We happily speak of the ownership of land, yet a largish number of officials have the right of entering on private land without the owner's consent, for some limited period and purpose. On the other hand, a general licence so to enter on the 'property' of others would put an end to the institution of landowning as we now know it.

The protection of the right to possess (still using 'possess' in the convenient, although over-simple, sense of 'have exclusive physical control') should be sharply marked off from the protection of mere present possession. To exclude others from what one presently holds is an instinct found in babies and even, as Holmes points out, in animals, of which the seal gives a striking example. To sustain this instinct by legal rules is to protect possession but not, as such, to protect the right to possess and so not to protect ownership. If dispossession without the possessor's consent is, in general, forbidden, the possessor is given a right *in rem*, valid against persons generally, to remain undisturbed, but he has no *right to possess in rem* unless he is entitled to recover from persons generally what he has lost or had taken from him, and to obtain from them what is due to him but not yet handed over. Admittedly there may be borderline cases in which the right to possess is partially recognized, eg where a thief is entitled to recover from those who oust him and all claiming under them, but not from others. . . .

To have worked out the notion of 'having a right to' as distinct from merely 'having', or, if that is too subjective a way of putting it, of rules allocating things to people as opposed to rules merely forbidding forcible taking, was a major intellectual achievement. Without it society would have been impossible. Yet the distinction is apt to be overlooked by English lawyers, who are accustomed to the rule that every adverse possession is a root of title, ie gives rise to a right to possess, or at least that '*de facto* possession is *prima facie* evidence of seisin in fee and right to possession'.

The owner, then, has characteristically a battery of remedies in order to obtain, keep and, if necessary, get back the thing owned. Remedies such as the actions for ejectment and wrongful detention and the *vindicatio* are designed to enable the plaintiff either to obtain or to get back a thing, or at least to put some pressure on the defendant to hand it over. Others, such as the actions for trespass to land and goods, the Roman possessory interdicts and their modern counterparts are primarily directed towards enabling a present possessor to keep possession. Few of the remedies mentioned are confined to the owner; most of them are available also to persons with a right to possess falling short of ownership, and some to mere possessors. Conversely, there will be cases in which they are not available to the owner, for instance because he has voluntarily parted with possession for a temporary purpose, as by hiring the thing out. The availability of such remedies is clearly not a necessary and sufficient condition of owning a thing; what is necessary, in order that there may be ownership of things at all, is that such remedies shall be available to the owner in the usual case in which no other person has a right to exclude him from the thing.

(2) *The right to use*

The present incident and the next two overlap. On a wide interpretation of 'use', management and income fall within use. On a narrow interpretation, 'use' refers to the owner's personal use and enjoyment of the thing owned. On this interpretation it excludes management and income.

The right (liberty) to use at one's discretion has rightly been recognized as a cardinal feature of ownership, and the fact that, as we shall see, certain limitations on use also fall within the standard incidents of ownership does not detract from its imporance, since the standard limitations are, in general, rather precisely defined, while the permissible types of use constitute an open list.

(3) *The right to manage*

The right to manage is the right to decide how and by whom the thing owned shall be used.

This right depends, legally, on a cluster of powers, chiefly powers of licensing acts which would otherwise be unlawful and powers of contracting: the power to admit others to one's land, to permit others to use one's things, to define the limits of such permission, and to contract effectively in regard to the use (in the literal sense) and exploitation of the thing owned. An owner may not merely sit in his own deck chair but may validly license others to sit in it, lend it, impose conditions on the borrower, direct how it is to be painted or cleaned, contract for it to be mended in a particular way. This is the sphere of management in relation to a simple object like a deck chair. When we consider more complex cases, like the ownership of a business, the complex of powers which make up the right to manage seems still more prominent. The power to direct how resources are to be used and exploited is one of the cardinal types of economic and political power; the owner's legal powers of management are one, but only one possible basis for it. Many observers have drawn attention to the growth of managerial power divorced from legal ownership; in such cases it may be that we should speak of split ownership or redefine our notion of the thing owned. This does not affect the fact that the right to manage is an important element in the notion of ownership; indeed, the fact that we feel doubts in these cases whether the 'legal owner' *really* owns is a testimony to its importance. . . .

(4) *The right to the income*
To use or occupy a thing may be regarded as the simplest way of deriving an income from it, of enjoying it. It is, for instance, expressly contemplated by the English income tax legislation that the rent-free use or occupation of a house is a form of income, and only the inconvenience of assessing and collecting the tax presumably prevents the extension of this principle to movables.

Income in the more ordinary sense (fruits, rents, profits) may be thought of as a surrogate of use, a benefit derived from forgoing personal use of a thing and allowing others to use it for reward; as a reward for work done in exploiting the thing; or as the brute product of a thing, made by nature or by other persons. Obviously the line to be drawn between the earned and unearned income from a thing cannot be firmly drawn. . . .

(5) *The right to the capital*
The right to the capital consists in the power to alienate the thing and the liberty to consume, waste or destroy the whole or part of it: clearly it has an important economic aspect. The latter liberty need not be regarded as unrestricted; but a general provision requiring things to be conserved in the public interest, so far as not consumed by use in the ordinary way, would perhaps be inconsistent with the liberal idea of ownership. . . .

An owner normally has both the power of disposition and the power of transferring title. Disposition on death is not permitted in many primitive societies but seems to form an essential element in the mature notion of ownership. The tenacity of the right of testation once it has been recognized is shown by the Soviet experience. The earliest writers were hostile to inheritance, but gradually Soviet law has come to admit that citizens may dispose freely of their 'personal property' on death, subject to limits not unlike those known elsewhere.

(6) *The right to security*
An important aspect of the owner's position is that he should be able to look forward to remaining owner indefinitely if he so chooses and he remains solvent. His right to do so may be called the right to security. Legally, this is in effect an immunity from expropriation, based on rules which provide that, apart from bankrupcty and execution for debt, the transmission of ownership is consensual.

However, a general right to security, availing against others, is consistent with the existence of a power to expropriate or divest in the state or public authorities. From the point of view of security of property, it is important that when expropriation takes place, adequate compensation should be paid; but a general power to expropriate subject to paying compensation would be fatal to the institution of ownership as we know it. Holmes' paradox, that where specific restitution of goods is not a normal remedy, expropriation and wrongful conversion are equivalent, obscures the vital distinction between acts which a legal system permits as rightful and those which it reprobates as wrongful: but if wrongful conversion were general and went unchecked, ownership as we know it would disappear, though damages were regularly paid.

In some systems, as (*semble*) English law, a private individual may destroy another's property without compensation when this is necessary in order to protect his own person or property from a greater danger. Such a rule is consistent with security of property only because of its exceptional character. Again, the state's (or local authority's) power of expropriation is usually limited to certain classes of thing and certain limited purposes. A general power to expropriate any property for any purpose would be inconsistent with the institution of ownership. If, under such a system, compensation were regularly paid, we might say either that ownership was not recognized in that system, or that money alone could be owned, 'money' here meaning a strictly fungible claim on the resources of the community. As we shall see, 'ownership' of such claims is not identical with the ownership of material objects and simple claims.

(7) *The incident of transmissibility*

It is often said that one of the main characteristics of the owner's interest is its 'duration'. In England, at least, the doctrine of estates made lawyers familiar with the notion of the 'duration' of an interest and Maitland, in a luminous metaphor, spoke of estates as 'projected upon the plane of time'.

Yet this notion is by no means as simple as it seems. What is called 'unlimited' duration (*perpétuité*) comprises at least two elements (i) that the interest can be transmitted to the holder's successors and so on *ad infinitum* (The fact that in medieval land law all interests were considered 'temporary' is one reason why the terminology of ownership failed to take root, with consequences which have endured long after the cause has disappeared.); (ii) that it is not certain to determine at a future date. These two elements may be called 'transmissibility' and 'absence of term' respectively. We are here concerned with the former.

No one, as Austin points out, can enjoy a thing after he is dead (except vicariously) so that, in a sense, no interest can outlast death. But an interest which is transmissible to the holder's successors (persons designated by or closely related to the holder who obtain the property after him) is more valuable than one which stops with his death. This is so both because on alienation the alienee or, if transmissibility is generally recognized, the alienee's successors, are thereby enabled to enjoy the thing after the alienor's death so that a better price can be obtained for the thing, and because, even if alienation were not recognized, the present holder would by the very fact of transmissibility be dispensed *pro tanto* from making provision for his intestate heirs. Hence, for example, the moment when the tenant in fee acquired a heritable (though not yet fully alienable) right was a crucial moment in the evolution of the fee simple. Heritability by the state would not, of course, amount to transmissibility in the present sense: it is assumed that the transmission is in some sense *advantageous* to the transmitter.

Transmissibility can, of course, be admitted, yet stop short at the first, second or third generation of transmittees. The owner's interest is characterized by *indefinite* transmissibility, no limit being placed on the possible number of transmissions, though the nature of the thing may well limit the actual number.

In deference to the conventional view that the exercise of a right must depend on the choice of the holder, I have refrained from calling transmissibility a right. It is, however, clearly something in which the holder has an economic interest, and it may be that the notion of a right requires revision in order to take account of incidents not depending on the holder's choice which are nevertheless of value to him.

(8) *The incident of absence of term*

This is the second part of what is vaguely called 'duration'. The rules of a legal system usually seem to provide for determinate, indeterminate and determinable interests. The first are certain to determine at a future date or on the occurrence of a future event which is certain to occur. In this class come leases for however long a term, copyrights, etc. Indeterminate interests are those, such as ownership and easements, to which no term is set. Should the holder live for ever, he would, in the ordinary way, be able to continue in the enjoyment of them for ever. Since human beings are mortal, he will in practice only be able to enjoy them for a limited period, after which the fate of his interest depends on its transmissibility. Again, since human beings are mortal, interests for life, whether of the holder [or] of another, must be regarded as determinate. The notion of an indeterminate interest, in the full sense, therefore requires the notion of transmissibility, but, if the latter were not recognized, there would still be value to the holder in the fact that his interest was not due to determine on a fixed date or on the occurrence of some contingency, like a general election, which is certain to occur sooner or later. . . .

(9) *The prohibition of harmful use*
An owner's liberty to use and manage the thing owned as he chooses is in mature systems of law, as in primitive systems, subject to the condition that uses harmful to other members of society are forbidden. There may, indeed, be much dispute over what is to count as 'harm' and to what extent give and take demands that minor inconvenience between neighbours shall be tolerated. Nevertheless, at least for material objects, one can always point to abuses which a legal system will not allow.

I may use my car freely but not in order to run my neighbour down, or to demolish his gate, or even to go on his land if he protests; nor may I drive uninsured. I may build on my land as I choose, but not in such a way that my building collapses on my neighbour's land. I may let off fireworks on Guy Fawkes night, but not in such a way as to set fire to my neighbour's house. These and similar limitations on the use of things are so familiar and so obviously essential to the existence of an orderly community that they are not often thought of as incidents of ownership; yet, without them 'ownership' would be a destructive force.

(10) *Liability to execution*
Of a somewhat similar character is the liability of the owner's interest to be taken away from him for debt, either by execution of a judgment debt or on insolvency. Without such a general liability the growth of credit would be impeded and ownership would, again, be an instrument by which the owner could defraud his creditors. This incident, therefore, which may be called *executability*, seems to constitute one of the standard ingredients of the liberal idea of ownership. . . .

(11) *Residuary character*
A legal system might recognize interests in things less than ownership and might have a rule that, on the determination of such interests, the rights in question lapsed and could be exercised by no one, or by the first person to exercise them after their lapse. There might be leases and easements; yet, on their extinction, no one would be entitled to exercise rights similar to those of the former lessee or of the holder of the easement. This would be unlike any system known to us and I think we should be driven to say that in such a system the institution of ownership did not extend to any thing in which limited interests existed. In such things there would, paradoxically, be interests less than ownership but no ownership.

This fantasy is intended to bring out the point that it is characteristic of ownership that an owner has a residuary right in the thing owned. In practice, legal systems have rules providing that on the lapse of an interest rights, including liberties, analogous to the rights formerly vested in the holder of the interest, vest in or are exercisable by someone else, who may be said to acquire the 'corresponding rights'. Of course, the 'corresponding rights' are not the same rights as were formerly vested in the holder of the interest. The easement holder had a right to exclude the owner; now the owner has a right to exclude the easement holder. The latter right is not identical with, but corresponds to, the former.

It is true that corresponding rights do not always arise when an interest is determined. Sometimes, when ownership is abandoned, no corresponding right vests in another; the thing is simply *res derelicta*. Sometimes, on the other hand, when ownership is abandoned, a new ownership vests in the state, as is the case in South Africa when land has been abandoned.

It seems, however, a safe generalization that, whenever an interest less than ownership terminates, legal systems always provide for corresponding rights to vest in another. When easements terminate, the 'owner' can exercise the corresponding rights, and when bailments terminate, the same is true. It looks as if we have found a simple explanation of the usage we are investigating, but this turns out to be but another deceptive short cut. For it is not a sufficient condition of *A*'s being the owner of a thing that, on the determination of *B*'s interest in it, corresponding rights vest in or are exercisable by *A*. On the determination of a sub-lease, the rights in question become exercisable by the lessee, not by the 'owner' of the property.

Can we then say that the 'owner' is the ultimate residuary? When the sub-lessee's interest determines the lessee acquires the corresponding rights; but when the lessee's right determines the 'owner' acquires these rights. Hence the 'owner' appears to be identified as the ultimate residuary. The difficulty is that the series may be continued, for on the determination of the 'owner's' interest the state may acquire the corresponding rights; is the state's interest ownership or a mere expectancy?

A warning is here necessary. We are approaching the troubled waters of split ownership. Puzzles about the location of ownership are often generated by the fact that an ultimate residuary right is not coupled with present alienability or with the other standard incidents we have listed. . . .

We are of course here concerned not with the puzzles of split ownership but with simple cases in which the existence of *B*'s lesser interest in a thing is clearly consistent with *A*'s owning it. To explain the usage in such cases it is helpful to point out that it is a necessary but not sufficient condition of *A*'s being owner that, either immediately or ultimately, the extinction of other interests would enure for his benefit. In the end, it turns out that residuarity is merely one of the standard incidents of ownership, important no doubt, but not entitled to any special status.

NOTES

1. *Legal and equitable ownership.* Ownership may be legal or equitable. Legal and equitable ownership of a chattel may be vested in the same person. Alternatively, legal ownership may be vested in one person and equitable ownership vested in another, eg when A (legal owner) holds goods on trust for B (equitable owner). However, it is not possible for legal ownership of a chattel to be split and a smaller legal interest carved out of it: legal ownership must be transferred entire. The only other absolute legal interest that may exist in a chattel at the same time as that of the true owner (the person with the best right to the chattel) is the independent legal interest of a person who holds possession of the chattel with the intention of asserting rights of ownership (who is also treated in law as an owner). In short, it is only possible for two absolute legal interests to exist in a chattel at the same time: the interests of the true owner and the interests of someone holding possession *animo domini*. By contrast, there is no limit to the number of equitable interests which may subsist in a chattel at any one time.

2. *Interest and title.*

> A person's interest in an asset denotes the quantum of rights over it which he enjoys against other persons, though not necessarily against *all* other persons. His title measures the strength of the interest he enjoys in relation to others. . . .
> (Goode, p 53)

Both the true owner of an asset and the person in possession of an asset *animo domini* have an independent legal *interest* in the asset. Each has title to the absolute interest in the asset and each may assert his interest against a third party, so long as the third party does not have a better title. However, as against each other, the true owner has an absolute (or indefeasible) *title* to the asset and the possessor only a relative *title*. The possessor may not assert his title against the true owner, nor anyone deriving title from him or acting with his authority. It is even possible for a third party to defend an action for wrongful interference brought by someone with a possessory title on the ground that the plaintiff is not the true owner, ie he may plead *jus tertii* (Torts (Interference with Goods) Act 1977, s 8(1): see below, p 69).

The concept of relativity of title also applies to equitable interests. But it should be noted that an equitable interest is also liable to be overriden by a transfer of the legal interest to a bona fide purchaser for value without notice.

3. *Co-ownership*. Personal property may be the subject of co-ownership at law and in equity. Although legal ownership is indivisible, two or more persons may be the legal co-owners of a chattel as joint tenants or as tenants in common (eg where A's 75,000 gallons of oil are mixed with B's 25,000 they will share the 100,000 gallons in the ratio 3:1 as tenants in common: *Indian Oil Corpn Ltd v Greenstone Shipping SA* [1988] QB 345, where there was wrongful mixing by one of the parties). It appears that legal co-ownership of a chose in action must be as joint tenants (*Re McKerrell, McKerrell v Gowans* [1912] 2 Ch 648 at 653). If the co-owners are joint tenants and one of them dies the deceased's share passes to the others by survivorship. In the case of tenants in common, the deceased's share forms part of his estate and passes under his will or on his intestacy. Where there is equitable co-ownership, including co-ownership of a chose in action, there is a presumption in favour of a tenancy in common (R M Goode *Proprietary Rights and Insolvency in Sales Transactions* (2nd ed, 1989), p 6).

8 Acquisition and transfer of legal and equitable ownership

(i) *Legal ownership*

Legal ownership may be acquired by any of the following means:

(1) By taking possession of an existing thing which does not have an owner, eg taking possession of a wild animal.
(2) By bringing a new thing into existence. This mode of acquisition of legal ownership is particularly relevant where goods are manufactured. Prima facie, the manufacturer will be the legal owner of the newly manufactured product. However, the position is complicated where the manufacturer has made the new product from material supplied under a contract of sale which reserves ownership of the material in the supplier until payment. Such reservation of title clauses may even purport to claim ownership of the finished product. Further difficulties arise where the finished product is manufactured from material supplied by different suppliers each relying on their own reservation of title clause to claim ownership of the finished product. These issues are fully explored below, at pp 407–425.
(3) By consensual transfer of a thing from the existing owner. Although consensual transfer may be by gift, the typical form of transfer in the commercial world is by sale. At common law there are strict rules controlling the transfer of ownership of personal property: the transferor must have legal title or a power to pass legal title, the transfer must be effected by the delivery of possession or by a grant (by deed in the case of a gift of a chattel, by word of mouth in the case of other transfers of a chattel), and there must be an intention to make a present, not future, transfer of ownership (see Goode, pp 56–57; above, p 42). It is important to note that the common law does not

normally give effect to an agreement to transfer after-acquired property (ie property which the transferor does not yet own or possess). There must be some new act of transfer after the property has been acquired by the transferor for the ownership to vest in the transferee (*Lunn v Thornton* (1845) 1 CB 379). Exceptionally, in the case of contracts for the sale of goods, ownership of future goods will automatically transfer to the buyer when those goods have been acquired by the seller, if the parties have so agreed (Sale of Goods Act 1979, s 2(5), (6). Furthermore, property which does not yet exist, but which will grow out of existing property owned by the transferor, eg the right to receive sums payable in the future under an existing building contract, may be made the subject of a present transfer of legal ownership (see below, pp 696–697).

(4) By transfer which overrides the rights of the existing owner. The general rule is *nemo dat quod non habet*. However, there are exceptions to the *nemo dat* rule which allow A to transfer to B a good title to C's goods without the latter's consent. The rule and its exceptions are considered below in Chapter 9.

(5) By operation of law when goods become fixtures or accessions or through specification, confusion or commingling, Bridge, pp 80–83; Davies, pp 37–43; Bell, pp 71–73; see also P Birks 'Mixtures' in N Palmer and E McKendrick (eds) *Interests in Goods* (1993), Ch 16 (and the literature cited therein).

(6) By operation of law on death or insolvency (see Bell, Chs 17, 18).

(ii) *Equitable ownership*

Equitable ownership may be acquired by any one of the following means:

(1) by an agreement to transfer legal or equitable ownership;
(2) by a defective transfer of legal ownership;
(3) by a purported present transfer of an after-acquired asset;
(4) by declaration of trust: either the transferor of an asset declares himself to hold it on trust for the transferee, or the transferor instructs a third party to hold the asset on trust for the transferee;
(5) by a transfer made by someone who holds merely an equitable title.

Equitable ownership may be transferred by assignment, which must be in writing (Law of Property Act 1925, s 53(1)(c)) or by declaration of trust (Goode, p 59).

It is because equity regards as done that which ought to have been done that the obligation to transfer an asset is treated in equity as a transfer (but an agreement for the sale of goods is an exception to this rule: see above, p 22). The conditions which must exist for such a transfer to operate are that the obligation is not merely contingent, the subject matter is identifiable and the consideration is in due course paid (see above, p 42; see also below, pp 754–757). If the consideration is not paid when the agreement to transfer is made, it seems that the intended transferee merely acquires an inchoate equitable interest at that time. The intended transferee cannot assert an inchoate interest against the intended transferor or third parties until he pays the price and converts that interest into full equitable ownership, which is deemed to relate back to the time the agreement was made (R M Goode (1987) 103 LQR 433 at p 437, fn; *Lysaght v Edwards* (1876) 2 Ch D 499; *Rayner v Preston* (1881) 18 Ch D 1). Similarly, when there has been an agreement to transfer an after-acquired asset, the transferee has an inchoate interest which attaches to the asset when it is acquired by the transferor with effect from the date of the agreement (*Tailby v Official Receiver* (1888) 13 App Cas 523, HL: below, p 755; *Re Lind* [1915] 2 Ch 345, CA).

Finally, it should be noted that legal ownership and equitable ownership may be transferred outright or by way of security. We shall examine the different legal consequences of transfer by way of security, compared to outright transfer, when we consider receivables financing in Chapter 21.

9 Possession

An Essay on Possession in the Common Law by F Pollock and R S Wright (1888), pp 26–28

The Nature of Possession

Throughout our inquiry we have to bear in mind that the following elements are quite distinct in conception, and, though very often found in combination, are also separable and often separated in practice. They are

i. Physical control, detention, or *de facto* possession. This, as an actual relation between a person and a thing, is matter of fact. Nevertheless questions which the Court must decide as matter of law arise as to the proof of the facts.

ii. Legal possession, the state of being a possessor in the eye of the law.

This is a definite legal relation of the possessor to the thing possessed. In its most normal and obvious form, it coexists with the fact of physical control, and with other facts making the exercise of that control rightful. But it may exist either with or without detention, and either with or without a rightful origin.

A tailor sends to JS's house a coat which JS has ordered. JS puts on the coat, and then has both physical control and rightful possession in law.

JS takes off the coat and gives it to a servant to take back to the tailor for some alterations. Now the servant has physical control (in this connexion generally called 'custody' by our authorities) and JS still has the possession in law.

While the servant is going on his errand, Z assaults him and robs him of the coat. Z is not only physically master of the coat, but, so soon as he has complete control of it, he has possession in law, though a wrongful possession. To see what is left to JS we must look to the next head.

iii. Right to possess or to have legal possession. This includes the right to physical possession. It can exist apart from both physical and legal possession; it is, for example, that which remains to a rightful possessor immediately after he has been wrongfully dispossessed. It is a normal incident of ownership or property, and the name of 'property' is often given to it. Unlike possession itself, it is not necessarily exclusive. A may have the right to possess a thing as against B and every one else, while B has at the same time a right to possess it as against every one except A. So joint tenants have both single possession and a single joint right to possess, but tenants in common have a single possession with several rights to possess. When a person having right to possess a thing acquires the physical control of it, he necessarily acquires legal possession also.

Right to possess, when separated from possession, is often called 'constructive possession'. The correct use of the term would seem to be coextensive with and limited to those cases where a person entitled to possess is (or was) allowed the same remedies as if he had really been in possession. But it is also sometimes specially applied to the cases where the legal possession is with one person and the custody with his servant, or some other person for the time being in a like position; and sometimes it is extended to other cases where legal possession is separated from detention.

'Actual possession' as opposed to 'constructive possession' is in the same way an ambiguous term. It is most commonly used to signify physical control, with or without possession in law. 'Bare possession' is sometimes used with the same meaning. 'Lawful possession' means a legal possession which is also rightful or at least excusable; this may be consistent with a superior right to possess in some other person.

The whole terminology of the subject, however, is still very loose and unsettled in the books, and the reader cannot be too strongly warned that careful attention must in every case be paid to the context.

NOTES

1. In *United States of America and Republic of France v Dollfus Mieg et Cie SA and Bank of England* [1952] AC 582 at 605, Earl Jowitt observed that 'English law has never worked out a completely logical and exhaustive definition of "possession" '. As Andrew Bell explains (at p 34):

> The truth is that 'possession' has no single meaning: it is used in different senses in different contexts. This is perfectly reasonable, for the essence of possession is control, but the degree of control required for a particular rule will depend on the purpose of that rule. This flexibility has its price, however, the price of uncertainty.

Despite the fact that many eminent jurists have expended much energy developing various theories to explain the concept of possession (see, eg, D R Harris 'The Concept of Possession in English Law' in *Oxford Essays in Jurisprudence* (ed A G Guest), Ch 4; and see generally, R W M Dias *Jurisprudence* (5th ed, 1985), Ch 13), the subject remains an enigma. It lacks even an agreed terminology to explain the various forms of possession. The warning given by Pollock and Wright at the end of the extract (above) remains as relevant today as it was in 1888.

2. (i) *De facto possession*. Physical control of a chattel may not create possession in law. To constitute possession in law, physical control must be coupled with an intention to exclude others. As Pollock and Wright observe (at p 20): 'Possession in fact, with the manifest intent of sole and exclusive dominion, always imports possession in law.' Control in fact may be acquired by taking physical possession of the chattel itself or possession of an object which gives physical control of the chattel, eg the key to the warehouse in which the chattel is stored (although possession of a key to a container or to a building has been variously described by the courts as giving 'actual', 'constructive' and 'symbolic' possession of the chattels contained therein: see below, pp 802–806). The degree of control necessary to acquire possession will be relative to the nature of the chattel. For example, in *The Tubantia* [1924] P 78, the plaintiffs carried out salvage work on a wreck lying in 100 feet of water in the North Sea. They succeeded in cutting a hole into a hold, had buoyed the wreck and had recovered some of the cargo when the defendants, a rival salvage company, interrupted their work. Sir Henry Drake P held that the plaintiffs had possession of the wreck and were entitled to an injunction and damages against the defendants for trespass. Although the plaintiffs had only been able to work on the wreck for short periods, with long interruptions because of the weather, the President was satisfied that 'There was the use and occupation of which the subject matter was capable'. Finally, it should be noted that the degree of control needed to acquire possession may not have to be maintained for possession to continue (see, eg, Bridge, p 13; Bell, pp 35–36). Once acquired, possession is deemed to continue unless it is acquired by someone else or it is abandoned (Harris, op cit, p 73).

(ii) *Legal possession.* In the examples given by Pollock and Wright, JS has legal possession of the coat when he has both ownership and physical control of it. JS maintains legal possession when he gives up physical control to his employee (servant). The employee does not acquire legal possession of the coat because although he has physical control (or custody) of it, he does not have the necessary intention to control. However, if the employee took possession of the coat for a limited interest of his own, eg holds the coat as bailee under a pledge, he would acquire legal possession of it. As possession is indivisible, JS would have lost legal possession to the employee taking possession for a limited interest. Similarly, Z, the thief, acquires legal possession of the coat, and JS loses such possession, when he steals it from the employee. However, Z holds possession with the intention of asserting ownership rights. Therefore, Z's possession *animo domini* gives him an absolute legal interest in and a relative title to the coat. In this final example, possession gives rise to legal ownership (see above, p 50).

(iii) *Right to possess or to have legal possession.* Where a bailee holds possession of a chattel for his own interest, eg asserting a right of lien or other limited interest, or rights of owner, the bailor maintains a right to possess but he does not have legal possession of the chattel. This is because possession is single and exclusive (per Pollock and Wright, op cit, p 20). Like ownership, possession is indivisible and can only be held and transferred entire. But where the bailee holds possession for the bailor's interest, ie he is a bailee at will holding the chattel to the bailor's order, the bailor and bailee will share legal possession. In such circumstances, the bailor may be said to have constructive possession of the chattel.

Constructive possession may even operate in favour of a person with a mere possessory title. For example, in *Wilson v Lombank Ltd* [1963] 1 All ER 740, W purchased a car from someone who had no title to sell. W took the car to a garage for repairs. The repairs were completed but whilst the car was awaiting collection a representative of L Ltd (who were not the true owners of the car) removed it from the garage in error. Hinchcliffe J held that W was in possession of the car and could sue L Ltd for trespass. W had a possessory title to the car which the garage held as bailees at will. Therefore, W had constructive possession of the car when it was in the actual possession of the garage. See also *United States of America and Republic of France v Dollfus Mieg et Cie SA and Bank of England* [1952] AC 582 at 611, per Lord Porter.

3. In cases of doubt over who has possession of property, eg when the property is on premises which are jointly occupied, the owner is presumed to be the person in possession of it (*Ramsay v Margrett* [1894] 2 QB 18; *French v Gething* [1922] 1 KB 236).

QUESTIONS

1. B steals A's car. C steals the same car from B. Can B assert a possessory title against C and sue him in conversion? Contrast *Solomon v Metropolitan Police Comr* [1982] Crim LR 606 with *Parker v British Airways Board* [1982] QB 1004 at 1010 per Donaldson LJ; cf the Torts (Interference with Goods) Act 1977, s 8: see below, p 69.
2. In *Wilson v Lombank Ltd*, above, Hinchcliffe J held that the garage did not have a lien on the car. Why was this important to the eventual outcome of the case?

10 Attornment

Attornment is an important commercial application of the concept of constructive possession. Attornment is the process by which a person (the attornor) holding actual possession of a chattel for himself or another person (under the terms of a bailment), later undertakes to hold possession of the goods for someone else (the attornee). The attornor must give his undertaking *to the attornee* (*Godts v Rose* (1855) 17 CB 229; Sale of Goods Act 1979, s 29(4)) and, once given, the attornee is deemed to have constructive possession of the chattel. Attornment most frequently arises where goods sold by A to B are held by C, who is a warehouseman or carrier. C will attorn to B when he acknowledges, with A's assent, that he henceforth holds the goods for B. However, for attornment to take place the goods must be identified. Thus, where the goods sold by A to B form an unidentified part of a bulk held by C, the acknowledgment by C that he now holds the goods for B cannot operate as an attornment, but it will estop C from denying that he holds the goods as described on behalf of B (*Re London Wine Co (Shippers) Ltd* [1986] PCC 121; *Maynegrain Pty Ltd v Compafina Bank* [1982] 2 NSWLR 141, Court of Appeal of New South Wales, noted by F M B Reynolds (1984) 4 Ox JLS 434; revsd on another ground (1984) 58 ALJR 389, PC). This process is sometimes known as quasi-attornment (R M Goode *Proprietary Rights in Insolvency and Sales Transactions* (2nd ed, 1989), p 11). The essential difference between attornment and quasi-attornment is that attornment operates to give the attornee property rights in the goods, whereas an estoppel merely gives the 'attornee' a personal right of action in conversion if the 'attornor' fails to release to him, or his order, goods of the requisite description and quantity.

The possession of a document of title to goods held by a third party does not usually carry with it constructive possession of the goods themselves (*Dublin City Distillery Ltd v Doherty* [1914] AC 823: below, p 806). Possession of the goods depends upon further attornment by the third party to the holder of the document of title. An important exception to this rule arises in the case of a bill of lading (see below, p 444), which is the only true document of title recognised at common law (*Official Assignee of Madras v Mercantile Bank of India* [1935] AC 53 at 59, per Lord Wright: below, p 802). The holder of a bill of lading is deemed to have constructive possession of the goods referred to therein, so long as the bill of lading has been properly transferred to him by delivery or by delivery and indorsement as required. No further attornment is required after the transferee has received delivery of the bill of lading: the issue of the bill of lading by the carrier is deemed to be an attornment in advance (Goode, op cit, pp 9–10: considered in *The Future Express* [1993] 2 Lloyd's Rep 542 at 550, CA). On the other hand, a delivery warrant issued by a warehouseman or other bailee is not considered to be an advance attornment and the transferee of such a document must obtain the further attornment of the warehouseman or other bailee before he takes constructive possession of the goods referred to therein (*Farina v Home* (1846) 16 M & W 119). However, certain statutory documents of title are treated in the same way as a negotiable bill of lading, eg statutory dock and warehouse warrants.

11 Transfer of possession

Although the transfer of possession of a chattel may be effected by unilateral assumption of possession (including theft) or by operation of law (on death or personal insolvency), the most common method is voluntary transfer effected by actual or constructive delivery. Actual delivery transfers actual possession of the chattel to the deliveree. Constructive delivery transfers control of the chattel to the deliveree, usually without giving him actual possession. Constructive delivery may take place in any one of the following ways:

(1) where a deliveror, being in actual possession of the chattel, agrees to hold it as bailee for the deliveree;
(2) where a third party, being in actual possession of the chattel as bailee for the deliveror, attorns to the deliveree with the deliveror's consent;
(3) where the deliveror agrees that the deliveree, who is already in actual possession of the chattel as bailee for the deliveror, shall continue to hold the chattel for himself (the deliveree has actual possession after constructive delivery);
(4) where the deliveror agrees that the deliveree, who is already holding custody of the chattel for the deliveror, shall continue to hold the chattel for himself (again, the deliveree has actual possession after constructive delivery);
(5) where the deliveror transfers a document of title to goods to the deliveree (but see above);
(6) where the seller of goods (the deliveror) transfers them to a carrier for the purpose of transmission to the buyer (the deliveree): Sale of Goods Act 1979, s 32(1);
(7) where the deliveror transfers to the deliveree an object giving physical control of the chattel, eg a key to the warehouse where the goods are stored (but see above, p 54).

Delivery is considered further below at pp 378–379. See also *Official Assignee of Madras v Mercantile Bank of India Ltd* [1935] AC 53 at 58–59, per Lord Wright: below, pp 802–803.

12 The importance of possession

Before considering the commercial importance of possession, it is worth making a few preliminary observations. First, possession is a legal concept, it has no counterpart in equity. An agreement to give possession does not create property rights in law or in equity. If a person fails to hand over possession at the contractually agreed time, the best the disappointed party can do is to sue for breach of contract. Second, possession is only relevant to chattels which are capable of physical possession. Goods, money and documentary intangibles are all capable of physical possession, but a pure intangible is not. Third, where a changing fund of assets is given to one person to manage on behalf of another, the person for whom the assets are managed does not have a possessory or proprietary right to any particular component of the fund, unless he has an immediate power to terminate the manager's authority and crystallise the fund (R M Goode (1976) 92 LQR 360 at p 384 and 528 at p 529).

However, even in the light of these limitations, the concept of possession remains important for the following reasons:

(1) Possession is relevant to the acquisition of legal ownership, at least where a possessory title is claimed, and to the acquisition of other legal interests that depend on possession, eg the special property of bailees in general, and pledgees and lienees in particular (Bell, p 33).

(2) Possession is relevant to the transfer of legal ownership, eg as a gift. But the passing of property under a contract for the sale of goods does not depend on the delivery of possession (Sale of Goods Act 1979, s 18, rule 1: below, p 271). However, several exceptions to the *nemo dat* rule do turn on possession (eg, Sale of Goods Act 1979, ss 24, 25: below, pp 327 ff and 332 ff).

(3) Possession is prima facie evidence of ownership (but see *Elliott v Kemp* (1840) 7 M & W 306).

(4) Possession is the basis for certain remedies. The plaintiff in an action for trespass to chattels must have been in possession, or had a right to immediate possession under a bailment at will, at the time of the interference alleged against the defendant (Crossley Vaines, p 23; cf Bridge, p 39). The plaintiff in an action for conversion of chattels must, at the time of conversion, have either been in actual possession of them, or been entitled to the immediate possession of them. Therefore, an owner lacking actual possession or without the right to immediate possession will not be able to sue in conversion: *Gordon v Harper* (1796) 7 Term Rep 9). But such an owner may bring a special action on the case for any damage done to his reversionary interest in the chattel (*Mears v London & South Western Rly Co* (1862) 11 CBNS 850). The plaintiff in an action for negligence causing loss or damage to chattels must have had either legal ownership or a possessory title to the chattels at the time when the loss or damage occurred (*The Aliakmon* [1986] AC 785 at 809, per Lord Brandon). But see ss 7 and 8 of the Torts (Interference with Goods) Act 1977 (and Order 15, r 10A of the Rules of the Supreme Court) which has, to a certain extent, reduced the importance of possessory title in tort: see below, pp 68–69.

(5) Possession may be relevant in cases of insolvency. Where the buyer of goods becomes insolvent, an unpaid seller may still be able to exercise a lien on the goods, despite property in the goods having passed to the buyer, if he retains possession of them, or a right to stop the goods in transit if they have not yet reached the buyer's possession (Sale of Goods Act 1979, ss 39–46).

Furthermore, where the buyer takes possession of goods under an agreement for sale, and the seller later becomes insolvent, the buyer has a right to retain possession of the goods and may complete the transaction by tendering the price (R M Goode *Proprietary Rights and Insolvency in Sales Transactions* (2nd ed, 1989), p 7).

13 Bailment[2]

We have already made a number of references to bailment in this chapter. But what is bailment? In their treatise *An Essay on Possession in the Common Law* (1888), Pollock and Wright wrote (at p 163):

. . . any person is to be considered as a bailee who otherwise than as a servant either receives possession of a thing from another or consents to receive or hold possession of a thing for another upon an undertaking with the other person either to keep and return or deliver to him the specific thing or to (convey and) apply the specific thing according to the directions antecedent or future of the other person.

---

2 What follows deals with certain aspects of the law of bailment. For more detailed coverage, see generally N E Palmer *Bailment* (2nd ed, 1991) ('Palmer'); Bell, Ch 5; Crossley Vaines, Ch 6.

Possession lies at the heart of bailment. In *Ashby v Tolhurst* [1937] 2 KB 242, the owner of a car left it in a private car park. He paid the attendant and received a ticket from him. Whilst the owner went about his business, the attendant allowed a thief to drive off in the car. The thief, who had neither the ticket nor the car key, had misled the attendant into believing that he was taking the car with the owner's permission. The owners of the car park admitted that the attendant had been negligent but, relying on an exclusion clause printed on the ticket, denied liability. The case then turned on whether the owners of the car park had become bailees of the car. Reversing the trial judge, the Court of Appeal held that the relationship between the parties was that of licensor and licensee, and not that of bailor and bailee. The car owner had merely been given permission to park on the car park, the owners of the car park had not received possession of the car.

But possession alone is not enough to create a bailment: two other conditions must also be fulfilled. First, the bailor must retain a superior interest in the chattel to that of the bailee. The bailee acquires a limited possessory interest in the chattel which is subordinate to the bailor's interest. This is reflected in the fact that at the end of the bailment the bailee must redeliver the chattel to the bailor or deal with it according to the bailor's instructions. By contrast, where possession *and ownership* of the chattel are conveyed by the transferor to the transferee there can be no bailment. For example, the buyer of identified goods under a contract of sale would normally acquire ownership of the goods and not hold them as bailee for the seller. However, where goods are sold subject to a reservation of title clause the buyer may hold them as bailee, even though he is given the power to sell the goods to a sub-buyer or use them himself in his own manufacturing process (*Clough Mill Ltd v Martin* [1985] 1 WLR 111 at 116, per Robert Goff LJ).

Second, the bailee must consent to take possession of the chattel for there to be a bailment. This raises the question whether 'involuntary bailments' are really bailments at all. Involuntary bailments arise where a person is in control of a chattel belonging to another without consenting to act as bailee, eg when goods are sent to the 'bailee's' premises by mistake (*AVX Ltd v EGM Solders Ltd* (1982) Times, 7 July). It is probably best to regard these cases as *sui generis*. Another difficult issue is whether the bailor must consent to the bailee having possession of the chattel. Traditionally, bailment has been explained on the basis of mutual consent (see, eg, Pollock and Wright, op cit, p 163: above at p 58). However, in recent years the consensual theory of bailment has been challenged. It has been argued that it is the bailee's, not the bailor's, consent which matters, and that 'any person who voluntarily assumes possession of goods belonging to another will be held to owe at least the principal duties of the bailee at common law' (Palmer, p 37). Although this new theory remains controversial, it has been endorsed by the courts (see, eg, *The Captain Gregos (No 2)* [1990] 2 Lloyd's Rep 395 at 405, per Bingham LJ; *The Pioneer Container* [1994] 2 All ER 250 at 261–262, PC).

14 Types of bailment

Coggs v Bernard (1703) 2 Ld Raym 909, Court of King's Bench

Holt CJ: . . . And there are six sorts of bailments. The first sort of bailment is, a bare naked bailment of goods, delivered by one man to another to keep for the use of the bailor; and this I call a depositum, and it is that sort of bailment which is mentioned in *Southcote's case* ((1601) Cro Eliz 815). The second sort is, when goods or chattels that are useful, are lent to a friend gratis, to be used by him; and this is called commodatum, because the thing is to be restored in specie. The third sort is, when goods are left with the bailee to be used by him for hire; this is called locatio et conductio, and the lender is called locator, and the borrower conductor. The fourth sort is, when goods or chattels are delivered to another as a pawn, to be a security to him for money borrowed of him by the bailor; and this is called in Latin vadium, and in English a pawn or a pledge. The fifth sort is when goods or chattels are delivered to be carried, or something is to be done about them for a reward to be paid by the person who delivers them to the bailee, who is to do the thing about them. The sixth sort is when there is a delivery of goods or chattels to somebody, who is to carry them, or do something about them gratis, without any rewards for such his work or carriage, which is this present case. I mention these things, not so much that they are all of them so necessary in order to maintain the proposition which is to be proved, as to clear the reason of the obligation, which is upon persons in cases of trust.

'Bailment' by N E Palmer (2nd ed, 1991), pp 124–125

Although there seems to have been no particular reason for the order in which these six varieties of bailment were enumerated, it cannot be denied that Holt CJ's descriptive classification corresponded with the major contemporary manifestations of the bailor-bailee relationship and proved markedly influential upon subsequent discussions of the subject. Even today, it is not easy to think of types of bailment that are not accommodated by his categorisation, and the broad sweep of his analysis is one which has been adopted, with certain refinements, in the present treatment of the subject. Nevertheless, Holt CJ's division is governed by a fundamentally consensual concept of bailment and by the most obvious social or commercial examples of that concept. It therefore pays no regard to the more hybrid or peripheral kinds of bailment and, by leaving them out altogether, suggests that they do not belong to the realm of bailment at all. Admittedly, this observation is based in part upon developments which have occurred since *Coggs v Bernard*, and is therefore a statement of Holt CJ's failure to foresee these developments rather than a criticism of his failure to observe them as a contemporary force. The fact remains that a large number of bailments, of a more or less orthodox character, are excluded from his classification. These include bailments by finding, bailments which arise upon a wrongful or mistaken seizure of property, 'mutual loans', bailments which arise when a landlord levies distress upon his tenant's goods or when a finance company calls in its security, bailments existing between an owner of goods and a sub-bailee, and bailments which, although redounding to the mutual benefit of the parties, are not the product of a direct bargain or do not involve a 'reward to be paid' from bailor to bailee or vice-versa. Nor is it clear that certain bailments of a more modern but conventional kind (such as the contract of hire-purchase, the conditional sale arising by virtue of a title retention clause, the issue of a ticket to a railway passenger on condition that he surrender it at the end of his journey, the custody of a will by the testator's solicitor, the delivery of a manuscript to a publisher, or the delivery of a tool to a workman in order that he can perform certain work with it) can find a place within the foregoing classification. Although it would be unfair to criticise Holt CJ's analysis merely for failing to be watertight or comprehensive, it seems that if the value of classification rests in the earmarking of variant obligations within a basic unitary concept, the analysis is not complete. By concentrating exclusively upon the kinds of bailment that arise from some privity or bargain inter parties, the learned Chief Justice's approach neglects the extended or constructive bailment; by concentrating upon the more conventional types of consensual bailment he neglects certain others which fall within the consensual definition; and by stressing only the elements of purpose and reward he discounts certain other criteria which may affect the obligations of the parties.

NOTES

1. There have been numerous attempts to classify the various types of bailment (they are reviewed by Palmer, op cit, pp 125–131). But as Professor Palmer himself acknowledges 'no general pattern is entirely satisfactory' (op cit, p 123). However, it is common practice amongst textbook writers to divide bailments into two categories: gratuitous bailments (eg where you lend this book to a friend to use without charge) and bailments for reward (eg warehousing, carriage, hire, hire-purchase and pledge). In certain circumstances, it may also be important to ascertain whether the bailment is for a fixed term or is determinable at the will of the bailor (see below, p 69).

2. Where there is a contract of bailment, as is usually the case, the contractual incidents will supplement those that arise out of the proprietary relationship of bailor and bailee (Bridge, p 24). But there does not have to be a contract between the parties for one to become the bailee of the other. For example, where the bailor consents, the bailee may bail the chattel to another person, who becomes the sub-bailee of the original bailor even though there is no contract between them (*Morris v C W Martin & Sons Ltd* [1966] 1 QB 716, CA). Where there is a non-contractual bailment, the rights and duties of the bailor and the bailee *inter se* may be defined according to the general law of tort (Bridge, p 24). However, it seems that bailment may also give rise to obligations which are independent of both contract and tort (see Palmer, pp 44–63; cf Bridge, p 24).

15 The bailee's liability

The bailee owes the bailor a duty to take reasonable care of the bailed chattel. This duty of care is central to their relationship. But does the standard of care required of the bailee vary according to whether the bailment is gratuitous or for reward?

Houghland v R R Low (Luxury Coaches) Ltd [1962] 1 QB 694, Court of Appeal

Returning from a trip to Jersey, Mrs H and her husband boarded one of the defendants' coaches at Southampton. Their suitcase was loaded into the boot of the coach, which was locked by the driver. After completing part of the journey the coach stopped at Ternhill, Shropshire, for the passengers to take tea. After tea the driver was unable to restart the coach and so he called for a relief coach which arrived some three hours later. During this period the coach stood unattended in the dark. When the relief coach arrived the driver supervised the loading of the passengers' luggage into it. The unloading of the luggage from the first coach and its transfer to the relief coach was done by the passengers themselves without supervision. The boot of the relief coach was locked. The relief coach continued the journey stopping occasionally to allow passengers to disembark. When the coach arrived at its final destination, Hoylake, Cheshire, Mrs H and her husband could not find their suitcase. Mrs H sued the defendants in detinue and for negligence.

Ormerod LJ: The judge, according to the note that we have of his judgment . . . found in the first place that the driver of the coach was a bailee of the suitcase, and that the bailment was a gratuitous bailment. I am not sure that there is any evidence for the latter finding; and indeed, I might well, I think, have come to a different conclusion. . . .

The judge then found that it was probably at Ternhill that the suitcase was either taken or lost, and in the circumstances he decided that the defendants were liable to pay the plaintiff £82 10s 11d.

The objection made to the judgment, as I understand it, is that, as this was a gratuitous bailment, the high degree of negligence required, otherwise called gross negligence in some of the cases, has not been established; that the judge made no finding of negligence, and that, in the circumstances, the judgment should not stand. I am bound to say that I am not sure what is meant by the term 'gross negligence' which has been in use for a long time in cases of this kind. There is no doubt, of course, that it is a phrase which has been commonly used in cases of this sort since the time of *Coggs v Bernard*, when the distinction was made in a judgment of Lord Holt CJ ((1703) 2 Ld Raym 909, 913) which has been frequently referred to and cited; but as we know from the judgment of Lord Chelmsford in *Giblin v McMullen* ((1868) LR 2 PC 317, 336) that it was said, after referring to the use of the term 'gross negligence' over a long period: 'At last, Lord Cranworth (then Baron Rolfe) in the case of *Wilson v Brett* ((1843) 11 M & W 113, 115) objected to it, saying that he "could see no difference between negligence and gross negligence; that it was the same thing, with the addition of a vituperative epithet." And this critical observation has been since approved of by other eminent judges.'

For my part, I have always found some difficulty in understanding just what was 'gross negligence,' because it appears to me that the standard of care required in a case of bailment, or any other type of case, is the standard demanded by the circumstances of that particular case. It seems to me that to try and put a bailment, for instance, into a watertight compartment – such as gratuitous bailment on the one hand, and bailment for reward on the other – is to overlook the fact that there might well be an infinite variety of cases, which might come into one or the other category. The question that we have to consider in a case of this kind, if it is necessary to consider negligence, is whether in the circumstances of this particular case a sufficient standard of care has been observed by the defendants or their servants.

First, I think, I should deal with the question of detinue. It has been admitted by Mr Somerset Jones on behalf of the defendants that this is a case where a prima facie case has been established by the plaintiff. If that be so, I find it difficult to appreciate that there can be any grounds for appeal. Mr Somerset Jones has endeavoured to establish, and he has done it by reference to authority, that to found a prima facie case is not sufficient – that there must, in addition, be affirmative evidence before the plaintiff can succeed. I am bound to say that is a doctrine which rather surprises me. If a prima facie case is once established, it is something which may be rebutted easily, but it can only be rebutted by evidence, and that is not present in this case; and therefore, the prima facie case having been established, still remains.

Supposing that the claim is one in detinue, then it would appear that once the bailment has been established, and once the failure of the bailee to hand over the articles in question has been proved, there is a prima facie case, and the plaintiff is entitled to recover, unless the defendant can establish to the satisfaction of the court a defence; and that, I think, is very clear from the words used by Bankes LJ in *Coldman v Hill* ([1919] 1 KB 443, 449) in a passage that appears to me to be important in this case: 'I think the law still is that if a bailee is sued in detinue only, it is a good answer for him to say that the goods were stolen without any default on his part, as the general bailment laid in the declaration pledges the plaintiff to the proof of nothing except that the goods were in the defendant's hands and were wrongfully detained.' So far, so good, but it is, of course, in those circumstances for the defendants to establish affirmatively, not only that the goods were stolen, but that they were stolen without default on their part; in other words, that there was no negligence on their part in the care which they took of the goods.

Applying that principle here, Mr Somerset Jones has been at pains to point out that the judge has made no finding that these goods were in fact stolen. The only view that the judge has expressed on the point is: 'It is impossible to say what happened to this suitcase when it was lost on its journey,' and with that I am bound to agree. It was put on the coach at Southampton, and it was not in the boot of the relief coach when it arrived at Hoylake. The judge has come to the conclusion that, on the probabilities, and again I agree with him, something happened to that suitcase when the transfer took place at Ternhill, or when the coach was delayed for some considerable period of time there. There seems to be no doubt that for something like three hours in the darkness that coach remained there unattended.

In these circumstances, I find it difficult to appreciate what substance there is in the complaint made by Mr Somerset Jones that in this case the judge, in treating this as a case of detinue, was in error. But let us suppose for a moment that the issue here is an issue in negligence: then he admits, and I think properly admits, that there is a prima facie case against the defendants derived from the fact that the suitcase was found by the judge to have been put on the coach at Southampton, and was not on the second coach when it arrived at its destination at Hoylake. In those circumstances, it is for the defendants to adduce evidence which will rebut a presumption of negligence.

But the case goes further than that. The evidence is that when the first coach was at Ternhill, and when the relief coach arrived driven by the managing director of the defendants, and whilst he went for his tea, the luggage was transferred from the first coach to the relief coach, and this was done by being supervised at the relief coach end without any supervision of any kind at the first coach end; and anything might have happened to a suitcase being transferred from one coach to the other. The defendants had their managing director there, and it was not unreasonable to expect that he and the driver between them might have supervised the transfer of this luggage from one coach to another. That did not happen; the transfer took place in the manner described. There was no supervision of the baggage being taken from the first coach. The driver of the coach said that he trusted the passengers, and it may be he was justified in doing that. It may well be that the passengers were honest; but in the darkness of the night, who is to know that some suitcase was not stolen by someone who had nothing at all to do with that particular trip?

In the circumstances, I fail to see where the judge went wrong, and I would dismiss this appeal.

Willmer LJ: I agree, and there is not much that I wish to add. In my judgment, this appeal fails on the facts. In saying that I do not think that it makes any difference whether the case is put in detinue, or whether it is treated as an action on the case for negligence. Whichever be the correct approach, it has been admitted in argument that the plaintiff, by proving the delivery of the suitcase at Southampton and its non-return on the arrival of the coach at Hoylake, made out a prima facie case. That prima facie case stands unless and until it is rebutted. The burden was on the defendants to adduce evidence in rebuttal. They could discharge that burden by proving what in fact did happen to the suitcase, and by showing that what did happen happened without any default on their part. They certainly did not succeed in doing that, for the judge was left in the position that he simply did not know what did happen to the suitcase.

Alternatively, the defendants could discharge the burden upon them by showing that, although they could not put their finger on what actually did happen to the suitcase, nevertheless, whatever did occur occurred notwithstanding all reasonable care having been exercised by them throughout the whole of the journey. Clearly the judge was not satisfied that they had proved the exercise of any such degree of care throughout the whole of the journey. On the evidence, particularly having regard to his preference for the plaintiff's evidence as against that called for the defendants, it was plainly open to him to come to that conclusion. All we know is that, in relation to the stop at Ternhill, this coach was apparently standing deserted in the middle of the night for a period of three hours. When the relief coach arrived, and the time came to transfer the luggage, this was done apparently with only the one member of the defendants' staff supervising the reloading on the second coach, and with no supervision at all over the discharge of the luggage from the first coach. In those circumstances, it is only too clear that the defendants entirely failed to show that throughout the period, when they had this suitcase in their custody, they exercised reasonable care.

I, therefore, agree that this appeal must fail.

[Danckwerts LJ concurred.]

NOTES

1. It may be important to ascertain whether a bailment is contractual or non-contractual. First, the Supply of Goods and Services Act 1982 only applies to contractual bailments. The Act contains provisions relating to the bailee's duty of care (when the contract is for the supply of services in the course of business: s 13) and the bailor's obligations to the bailee (when the contract is for the hire of goods: ss 7–10). Secondly, there may be contractual exemption clauses which exclude or limit the bailee's duties, subject to those controls contained in the Unfair Contract Terms Act 1977 (the position is more complicated in the case of sub-bailment: see generally Palmer, Ch 20 and pp 1631–1656; Bell, pp 126–135 – see also A Bell 'Sub-Bailment on Terms' in N Palmer and E McKendrick (eds) *Interests in Goods* (1993), Ch 6). Thirdly, the fact that the bailment may be gratuitous may be relevant when assessing whether the bailee has exercised reasonable care 'in all the circumstances' (for the analogous situation of a gratuitous agent, see *Chaudhry v Prabhakar* [1989] 1 WLR 29: below, p 164).

2. In certain circumstances, the bailee's liability for loss or damage to the bailed chattel may be strict. Strict liability generally arises as follows:

(1) Where the bailee is a common carrier, unless the loss or damage to the goods is caused by an excepted peril, eg Act of God, inherent vice etc. However, strict liability may be avoided by contractual exemption clauses or by the assumption of the status of private carrier, and various statutes permit or prescribe ways by which liability may be excluded or limited: see, eg, the Carriage of Goods by Air Act 1961, the Carriage of Goods by Sea Act 1971.

(2) Where the bailee 'deviates' in the conduct of the bailment, eg by storing the chattel somewhere other than the place agreed (*Lilley v Doubleday* (1881) 7 QBD 510), or by entrusting the chattel without authority to a third person (*Edwards v Newland & Co* [1950] 2 KB 534), or by wrongfully refusing to return the chattel, or negligently failing to return it when called upon to do so by the bailor at the end of the bailment (*Mitchell v Ealing London Borough Council* [1979] QB 1), or by carrying the chattel otherwise than by the agreed route, unless there is no causative link between the deviation and loss or damage to the chattel (*James Morrison & Co Ltd v Shaw, Savill and Albion Co Ltd* [1916] 2 KB 783). Deviation in the conduct of the bailment also has other consequences: it amounts to a repudiatory breach and gives the bailor an immediate right to possess the chattel; where the deviation is so serious as to amount to a blatant disregard of the bailor's interests, it may constitute conversion by the bailee (*Garnham, Harris and Elton Ltd v Alfred W Ellis (Transport) Ltd* [1967] 2 Lloyd's Rep 22); and the bailee will generally lose the protection of any contractual exclusion clauses (*Gibaud v Great Eastern Rly Co* [1921] 2 KB 426; see also Bell, pp 115–118).

3. Detinue was abolished by s 2(1) of the Torts (Interference with Goods) Act 1977. However, s 2(2) of the 1977 Act goes on to provide that: 'An action lies in conversion for loss or destruction of goods which a bailee has allowed to happen in breach of his duty to his bailor (that is to say it lies in a case which is not otherwise conversion, but would have been detinue before detinue was abolished).' This means that if the chattel has been lost or destroyed as a result of the bailee's breach of duty so that the bailee cannot redeliver it back to the bailor, the bailee will be liable to the bailor for breach of duty, breach of bailment (ie breach of the bailee's duty to redeliver) and conversion under s 2(2). By contrast, where the bailee delivers the chattel to the wrong person, the bailee will be held liable to the bailor even if the misdelivery was entirely innocent (*Devereux v Barclay* (1819) 2 B & Ald 702; but an involuntary bailee will only be liable for misdelivery if he acts negligently in making it: *Elvin and Powell Ltd v Plummer Roddis Ltd* (1933) 50

TLR 158, bailee acted reasonably and not held liable; contrast *Hiort v Bott* (1874) LR 9 Exch 86, bailee acted unreasonably and held liable).

4. Finally, it should be noted that an 'involuntary bailee' will not be liable for mere negligence. His sole duty is to refrain from intentional destruction or damage, unless the chattel is of a noxious character (*AVX Ltd v EGM Solders Ltd* (1982) Times, 7 July, per Staughton J: an unsatisfactory case which is best explained as one of 'involuntary bailment', see Palmer, pp 451–455; T Weir *A Casebook on Tort* (7th ed, 1992), pp 495–496). Sometimes, the 'involuntary bailee' will be under no duty whatsoever towards the chattel and may treat it as his own. In certain circumstances, the recipient of unsolicited goods may treat them as an unconditional gift from the sender (Unsolicited Goods and Services Act 1971, s 1).

QUESTIONS

1. Henry took his Rolex watch to Percy to be repaired. Percy agreed to repair the watch for a fee and told Henry to return and collect it the next day. Percy carried out the repair work, then locked the watch away in his safe and properly secured his workshop for the night. That night Toby, a thief, broke into Percy's workshop, forced the safe and stole Henry's watch. Will Percy be liable to Henry for this loss? Would your answer be different if Percy had been tricked into handing over the watch to Toby, who has falsely claimed to be Henry's butler and had produced a cleverly forged letter of authority from Henry to support his claim? Again, would it make any difference to your answer if Toby had executed his fraud some six months after Henry had delivered the watch to Percy and in the interim period Percy had constantly urged Henry to come and collect it?

2. Electron plc, a manufacturer of electrical products, decides to stockpile certain electrical components which it fears will soon be in short supply. It arranges to store a large consignment of these components in Secure Ltd's warehouse in Manchester. Electron pays all storage charges in advance and warns Secure to have the components ready for it to collect in six months' time. After the components are delivered to Secure's warehouse, Secure sells them to Transtech plc, another manufacturer of electrical products, and employs Cargo Ltd, a firm of carriers, to transport the components to Transtech's factory in Leeds. During the transit Cargo's lorry is blown over by freak hurricane-force winds on the Pennines. The lorry and its cargo of electrical components are completely destroyed. What rights, if any, does Electron have against Secure and/or Cargo? See the notes above and also *Hollins v Fowler* (1875) LR 7 HL 757.

16 Bailment and third parties

The Winkfield [1902] P 42, Court of Appeal

(The facts appear from Collins MR's judgment.)

Collins MR: This is an appeal from the order of Sir Francis Jeune dismissing a motion made on behalf of the Postmaster-General in the case of *The Winkfield*.

The question arises out of a collision which occurred on April 5, 1900, between the steamship *Mexican* and the steamship *Winkfield*, and which resulted in the loss of the former with a portion of the mails which she was carrying at the time.

The owners of the *Winkfield* under a decree limiting liability to £32,514 17s 10d paid that amount into court, and the claim in question was one by the Postmaster-General on behalf of himself and the Postmasters-General of Cape Colony and Natal to recover out of that sum the value of letters, parcels, etc, in his custody as bailee and lost on board the *Mexican*.

The case was dealt with by all parties in the Court below as a claim by a bailee who was under no liability to his bailor for the loss in question, as to which it was admitted that the authority of *Claridge v South Staffordshire Tramway Co* ([1892] 1 QB 422) was conclusive, and the President accordingly, without argument and in deference to that authority, dismissed the claim. The Postmaster-General now appeals.

The question for decision, therefore, is whether *Claridge's Case* was well decided. I emphasize this because it disposes of a point which was faintly suggested by the respondents, and which, if good, would distinguish *Claridge's Case*, namely, that the applicant was not himself in actual occupation of the things bailed at the time of the loss. This point was not taken below, and having regard to the course followed by all parties on the hearing of the motion, I think it is not open to the respondents to make it now, and I therefore deal with the case upon the footing upon which it was dealt with on the motion, namely, that it is covered by *Claridge's Case*. I assume, therefore, that the subject-matter of the bailment was in the custody of the Postmaster-General as bailee at the time of the accident. For the reasons which I am about to state I am of opinion that *Claridge's Case* was wrongly decided, and that the law is that in an action against a stranger for loss of goods caused by his negligence, the bailee in possession can recover the value of the goods, although he would have had a good answer to an action by the bailor for damages for the loss of the thing bailed.

It seems to me that the position, that possession is good against a wrongdoer and that the latter cannot set up the jus tertii unless he claims under it, is well established in our law, and really concludes this case against the respondents. As I shall shew presently, a long series of authorities establishes this in actions of trover and trespass at the suit of a possessor. And the principle being the same, it follows that he can equally recover the whole value of the goods in an action on the case for their loss through the tortious conduct of the defendant. I think it involves this also, that the wrongdoer who is not defending under the title of the bailor is quite unconcerned with what the rights are between the bailor and bailee, and must treat the possessor as the owner of the goods for all purposes quite irrespective of the rights and obligations as between him and the bailor.

I think this position is well established in our law, though it may be that reasons for its existence have been given in some of the cases which are not quite satisfactory. I think also that the obligation of the bailee to the bailor to account for what he has received in respect of the destruction or conversion of the thing bailed has been admitted so often in decided cases that it cannot now be questioned; and, further, I think it can be shewn that the right of the bailee to recover cannot be rested on the ground suggested in some of the cases, namely, that he was liable over to the bailor for the loss of the goods converted or destroyed. It cannot be denied that since the case of *Armory v Delamirie* ((1722) 1 Stra 505), not to mention earlier cases from the Year Books onward, a mere finder may recover against a wrongdoer the full value of the thing converted. That decision involves the principle that as between possessor and wrongdoer the presumption of law is, in the words of Lord Campbell in *Jeffries v Great Western Rly Co* ((1856) 5 E & B 802, 806), 'that the person who has possession has the property.' In the same case he says: 'I am of opinion that the law is that a person possessed of goods as his property has a good title as against every stranger, and that one who takes them from him, having no title in himself, is a wrongdoer, and cannot defend himself by shewing that there was title in some third period, for *against a wrongdoer possession is title*. The law is so stated by the very learned annotator in his note to *Wilbraham v Snow* ((1670) 2 Wms Saund 47f).' Therefore it is not open to the defendant, being a wrongdoer, to inquire into the nature or limitation of the possessor's right, and unless it is competent for him to do so the question of his relation to, or liability towards, the true owner cannot come into the discussion at all; and, therefore, as between those two parties full damages have to be paid without any further inquiry. The extent of the liability of the finder to the true owner not being relevant to the discussion between him and the wrongdoer, the facts which would ascertain it would not have been admissible in evidence, and therefore the right of the finder to recover full damages cannot be made to depend upon the extent of his liability over to the true owner. To hold otherwise would, it seems to me, be in effect to permit a wrongdoer to set up a jus tertii under which he cannot claim. But, if this be the fact in the case of a finder, why should it not be equally the fact in the case of a bailee? Why, as against a wrongdoer, should the nature of the plaintiff's interest in the thing converted be any more relevant to the inquiry, and therefore admissible in evidence, than in the case of a finder? It seems to me that neither in one case nor the other ought it to be competent for the defendant to go into evidence on that matter.

[His Lordship then reviewed several cases showing that a bailee had an unqualified right to sue the wrongdoer. He continued:]

The ground of the decision in *Claridge's Case* was that the plaintiff in that case, being under no liability to his bailor, could recover no damages, and though for the reasons I have already given I think this position is untenable, it is necessary to follow it out a little further. There is no doubt that the reason given in *Heydon and Smith's Case* ((1610) 13 Co Rep 67 at 69) – and itself drawn from the Year Books – has been repeated in many subsequent cases. The words are these: 'Clearly, the bailee, or he who hath a special property, shall have a general action of trespass against a stranger, and shall recover all in damages because that he is chargeable over.'

It is now well established that the bailee is accountable, as stated in the passage cited and repeated in many subsequent cases. But whether the obligation to account was a condition of his right to sue, or only an incident arising upon his recovery of damages, is a very different question, though it was easy to confound one view with the other.

Holmes CJ in his admirable lectures on the Common Law, in the chapter devoted to bailments, traces the origin of the bailee's right to sue and recover the whole value of chattels converted, and arrives at the clear conclusion that the bailee's obligation to account arose from the fact that he was originally the only person who could sue, though afterwards by an extension, not perhaps quite logical, the right to sue was conceded to the bailor also. He says at p 167: 'At first the bailee was answerable to the owner because he was the only person who could sue; now it was said he could sue because he was answerable to the owner.' And again at p 170: 'The inverted explanation of Beaumanoir will be remembered, that the bailee could sue because he was answerable over, in place of the original rule that he was answerable over so strictly because only he could sue.' This inversion, as he points out, is traceable through the Year Books, and has survived into modern times, though, as he shews, it has not been acted upon. Pollock and Maitland's History of English Law, vol 2, p 170, puts the position thus:– 'Perhaps we come nearest to historical truth if we say that between the two old rules there was no logical priority. The bailee had the action because he was liable, and was liable because he had the action.' It may be that in early times the obligation of the bailee to the bailor was absolute, that is to say, he was an insurer. But long after the decision of *Coggs v Bernard*, which classified the obligations of bailees, the bailee has, nevertheless, been allowed to recover full damages against a wrongdoer, where the facts would have afforded a complete answer for him against his bailor. The cases above cited are instances of this. In each of them the bailee would have had a good answer to an action by his bailor; for in none of them was it suggested that the act of the wrongdoer was traceable to negligence on the part of the bailee. I think, therefore, that the statement drawn, as I have said, from the Year Books may be explained, as Holmes CJ explains it, but whether that be the true view of it or not, it is clear that it has not been treated as law in our Courts. . . . Therefore, as I said at the outset, and as I think I have now shewn by authority, the root principle of the whole discussion is that, as against a wrongdoer, possession is title. The chattel that has been converted or damaged is deemed to be the chattel of the possessor and of no other, and therefore its loss or deterioration is his loss, and to him, if he demands it, it must be recouped. His obligation to account to the bailor is really not ad rem in the discussion. It only comes in after he has carried his legal position to its logical consequence against a wrongdoer, and serves to soothe a mind disconcerted by the notion that a person who is not himself the complete owner should be entitled to receive back the full value of the chattel converted or destroyed. There is no inconsistency between the two positions; the one is the complement of the other. As between bailee and stranger possession gives title – that is, not a limited interest, but absolute and complete ownership, and he is entitled to receive back a complete equivalent for the whole loss or deterioration of the thing itself. As between bailor and bailee the real interests of each must be inquired into, and, as the bailee has to account for the thing bailed, so he must account for that which has become its equivalent and now represents it. What he has received above his own interest he has received to the use of his bailor. The wrongdoer, having once paid full damages to the bailee, has an answer to any action by the bailor.

[Stirling and Mathew LJJ concurred.]

NOTES

1. A bailee's possession is sufficient to meet the requirement that a plaintiff in an action for trespass, conversion or detinue (now abolished, but see above at p 64) must have been in possession of the chattel at the time of the interference alleged against the wrongdoer (the other prerequisites for a successful action based on these property torts are to be found in the standard tort textbooks, eg *Street on Torts* (9th ed, 1993) (ed M Brazier), Ch 4). The bailee may also rely on his possession to bring an action against the wrongdoer in negligence. Despite having only a limited interest in the chattel, the bailee is entitled, at common law, to recover the full market value of the chattel against the wrongdoer (*The Winkfield*). The same rule applies where the bailee sues the wrongdoer for breach of contract (*Tanenbaum v W J Bell Paper Co Ltd* (1956) 4 DLR (2d) 177). In *The Jag Shakti* [1986] AC 337, the Privy Council even went so far as to apply *The Winkfield* to a bailee who had merely a right to immediate possession of the goods at the time of the wrong (criticised by Palmer, op cit, pp 342–351).

But in three exceptional situations the wrongdoer may raise another person's superior title to the chattel as a defence against an action brought by the bailee. These are as follows:

(1) when the wrongdoer defends the action on behalf of, and with the authority of, the true owner;
(2) when the wrongdoing was committed with the authority of the true owner;
(3) when the wrongdoer has, since the time of the wrongdoing, become the owner of the goods.

2. When the bailee recovers damages in full from the wrongdoer no action may later be maintained by the bailor, even if he would otherwise have a right of action to sue (*Nicolls v Bastard* (1835) 2 Cr M & R 659 at 660, per Parke B). Similarly, the bailee will be prevented from recovering against the wrongdoer if the bailor has already done so. Thus, in *O'Sullivan v Williams* [1992] 3 All ER 385 (noted by N E Palmer & R Merkin All ER Rev 1992 at 22), the owner of a car lent the vehicle to his girlfriend while he was on holiday. The car was damaged while in her possession. His successful claim for damages, based on his right to recover the car from the girlfriend at his will, was held by the Court of Appeal to preclude a second action by the girlfriend, even though she had possession of the car at the time it was damaged. You will be pleased to know that this incident did not stop the owner later marrying his girlfriend!

3. *The Winkfield* must now be read in the light of ss 7 and 8 of the Torts (Interference with Goods) Act 1977 which allow a wrongdoer to join all claimants to an action for wrongful interference with goods (ie an action in tort) so that they may recover according to their actual interests and thus avoid double liability of the wrongdoer. Where all claimants are not joined to the action, s 7(3) imposes on a party with a possessory title the duty to account to another potential claimant 'to such an extent to avoid double liability'. Should the other claimant later bring his own claim, with the result that the wrongdoer pays twice, s 7(4) imposes a duty on that claimant to reimburse the wrongdoer to the extent of his unjust enrichment (which depends on him having also received payment from the first claimant). But this provision offers no additional benefit to a wrongdoer who has already paid the full value of the chattel to the bailee and has a complete defence at common law to any future action brought by the bailor. Section 8 (and Order 15, r 10A of the Rules of the Supreme Court) allows the wrongdoer to set up a third party's superior title as a defence to the plaintiff's claim for wrongful interference (ie to plead *jus tertii*), although he can probably only do this if the person he claims to have a better title than the plaintiff is joined as a party to the action (*De Franco v Metropolitan Police Comr* (1987) Times, 8 May, per Lloyd LJ). It is even possible for the bailee to rely on s 8 and plead *jus tertii* against the bailor, something he cannot generally do at common law (but the common law rule still applies where the bailee is sued by his bailor for breach of contract or breach of bailment).

4. Finally, it should be noted the bailor's right of action in trespass or conversion (including what was detinue) against a wrongdoer depends on the bailor having a right to immediate possession of the bailed chattel at the time of the wrongdoing. Where the bailment is at the will of the bailor he will have such a right (as in *O'Sullivan v Williams*, above). But where the bailment is for a fixed term the bailee has no right to immediate possession, unless the bailee commits a wrongful act amounting to repudiation of the bailment, eg deviation in the conduct of the bailment (see above, p 64), or destroying the subject matter of the bailment (see below, p 811), or the contract of bailment provides that the bailor has the immediate right to terminate the bailment for any breach of its terms (*North Central Wagon & Finance Co Ltd v Graham* [1950] 2 KB 7).

Part II
The law of agency

CHAPTER 3

Introduction

1 The legal concept of agency[1]

(a) Definitions of agency

Agency is the fiduciary relation which results from the manifestation of consent by one person to another that the other shall act on his behalf and subject to his control, and consent by the other so to act.
(American *Restatement of the Law of Agency* (2nd ed, 1958), para 1(1))

Agency is the fiduciary relationship which exists between two persons, one of whom expressly or impliedly consents that the other should act on his behalf, and the other of whom similarly consents so to act or so acts.
(*Bowstead on Agency* (15th ed, 1985), art 1(1))

Agency is the relationship that exists between two persons when one, called the *agent*, is considered in law to represent the other, called the *principal*, in such a way as to be able to affect the principal's legal position in respect of strangers to the relationship by the making of contracts or the disposition of property.
(G H L Fridman *The Law of Agency* (6th ed, 1990), p 9)

NOTES

1. Any concise definition of the concept of agency must be treated with care. Striving for brevity, the definition is likely to be flawed by errors and omissions which may make it misleading (see Markesinis and Munday, p 3). However, the definitions set out above do provide a starting point from which to begin our assessment of the theoretical basis of agency.

2. Various theories have been advanced to explain the concept of agency (they are reviewed by Bowstead, Ch 1; see also Fridman, Ch 1; Markesinis and Munday, Ch 1). The definition provided in Bowstead, which is based on that given in the American *Restatement*, makes consent the basis of the law of agency. In most cases of agency the principal does consent to the agent acting on his behalf and the agent

---

1 In this and the succeeding chapters dealing with the law of agency, the following abbreviations are used in referring to standard textbooks:

Bowstead: F M B Reynolds (ed) *Bowstead on Agency* (15th ed, 1985);
Fridman: G H L Fridman *The Law of Agency* (6th ed, 1990);
Markesinis and Munday: B S Markesinis and R J C Munday *An Outline of the Law of Agency* (3rd ed, 1992).

agrees to do so ('the paradigm case' according to Bowstead, p 4). But the consent theory breaks down when we move away from the paradigm case. The theory fails to account for the fact that agency can also arise out of apparent authority (below, pp 91–100) and by operation of law (below, pp 104–109) irrespective of, and sometimes contrary to, the wishes of the parties (see, for example, *Boardman v Phipps* [1967] 2 AC 46, where the House of Lords held that an agency relationship existed even though there was no consent by the principal). Such cases can only be brought within the consent theory by a strained construction of the term 'consent' (cf Bowstead, p 5). Furthermore, the consent theory turns the existence of an agency relationship into a question of fact (ie if there is consent, there is agency) when it is really a question of law (*Garnac Grain Co Inc v HMF Faure and Fairclough Ltd* [1968] AC 1130n at 1137, per Lord Pearson; see also Fridman, p 12 (also (1968) 84 LQR 224) and Markesinis and Munday, p 5 for contrasting interpretations of Lord Pearson's speech).

3. Fridman's definition of agency is based on a power-liability analysis of the relationship between the principal and agent. The power-liability analysis focuses on the agent's power to alter the principal's *legal* relations with third parties (in particular by making contracts on behalf of the principal and by disposing of the principal's property) and the principal's consequent liability to have his relations so altered. The power-liability relationship of the principal and agent is best explained by Professor Dowrick in the next extract.

'The Relationship of Principal and Agent' by F E Dowrick (1954) 17 MLR 24, pp 36–38

The essential characteristic of an agent is that he is invested with a legal power to alter his principal's legal relations with third persons: the principal is under a correlative liability to have his legal relations altered. It is submitted that this power-liability relation is the essence of the relationship of principal and agent. The rules which normally attach to the parties, the normal incidents of the relation, are ancillary to this power-liability relation. To satisfy principals' claims in a myriad of cases the judges have imposed on agents certain rules constituting safeguards against the abuse of their powers. To satisfy agents' claims for reimbursement the judges have granted certain rights to agents. But the parties, the best judges of their own interests, may exclude these normal incidents of the relation by their agreement.

This power-liability relation, which, it is contended, is the nucleus of the relation of principal and agent, needs to be examined more closely. A power-liability relation is one of the fundamental legal relations. It exists between two persons, A and B, when A has the ability, conferred on him by law, by his own acts to alter B's legal relations. Agency is but one of the numerous kinds of power-liability relations recognised in our legal system. The distinctive feature of the agency power-liability relation is that the power of the one party to alter the legal relations of the other party is a reproduction of the power possessed by the latter to alter his own legal position. In other words, the power conferred by law on the agent is a facsimile of the principal's own power. This is to be inferred from the main principles of the law of agency, notably the following: when an agent acts on behalf of his principal in a legal transaction and uses the principal's name, the result in law is that the principal's legal position is altered but the agent himself drops out of the transaction: persons who are not themselves *sui juris* may nevertheless have the power to act as agents for persons who are: the power of an agent to bind his principal is limited to the power of the principal to bind himself: if the powers of the principal to alter his own legal relations are ended by his death, insanity, or bankruptcy, the agent's powers are terminated automatically. . . .

At this juncture it is tempting to define the relation of principal and agent as that existing between two legal persons, P and A, when A is invested with a legal power to alter P's legal relations which is a facsimile of the legal power possessed by P himself, and further to proceed to distinguish the relation from such other special legal relations as master-servant and trustee-beneficiary on the simple ground that in the latter relations this power-liability nexus is not essential. But in common law special legal relations are not to be confined within the strait-jackets of definitions; *elegantia juris* may be achieved only at the expense of the dynamic element in our law. Moreover the distinctions between agency and these other special legal relations cannot be so sharply drawn. Suffice it to assert that in mid-twentieth-century English law the nucleus of the rules in the doctrine of principal and agent is this power-liability relation.

NOTES

1. The terms 'power' and 'authority' should not be confused. As Professor Dowrick has emphasised (op cit, p 37 fn):

> A power is a legal concept: it connotes the ability of a person to alter legal relations by doing some act: an agent's power is such an ability existing in the eyes of the law. Authority is a matter of fact: it connotes that one person has given instructions or permission to another to act on his behalf. The legal attribute of an agent, his power, may be called into being by the fact that he has his principal's authority to act, but it may be called into being by other facts, such as the necessity of the case.

2. It is clear, therefore, that the principal cannot actually confer power on his agent. As Professor Montrose has explained ((1938) 16 Can Bar Rev 757 at p 761):

> The term power . . . is a legal relation, one which exists by virtue of a legal rule. The power of an agent is not strictly conferred by the principal but by the law: the principal and agent do the acts which bring the rule into operation, as a result of which the agent acquires a power.

The legal rule will be brought into operation if the principal actually authorises the agent to do certain acts. Once the legal rule comes into operation the agent will be vested with power to affect the principal's legal relations with third parties. Even if the principal does not give the agent any authority, or the agent exceeds his authority, the legal rule may still be brought into operation and vest the agent with power. In such circumstances, public policy will determine the existence and extent of the agent's power to affect his principal's relations (see generally, W A Seavey (1920) 29 Yale LJ 859; and J L Montrose, op cit, p 761). For further jurisprudential discussion of the power-liability relation, see W H Hohfeld *Fundamental Legal Conceptions*, pp 50–60; *Salmond on Jurisprudence* (12th ed, 1966), pp 228–231; R W M Dias, *Jurisprudence* (5th ed, 1985), pp 33–39.

3. Explaining agency in terms of a power-liability relationship appears to avoid the criticisms which we have already made of those definitions based on the consent of the parties (see above, p 74). However, the danger with an explanation which focuses on the agent's power to affect the principal's relations with third parties is that it shifts attention away from the *internal* relationship between the principal and agent to the *external* relationship between the principal and third party. It must always be remembered that agency is a triangular relationship between principal, agent and third party. The law of agency is as much concerned with the relationship between the principal and agent (eg the agent's right to remuneration or indemnity from the principal; the agent's fiduciary duties owed to the principal) as it is concerned with the relationship between the principal and third party.

4. It should be noted that not all agency relationships fit into this power-liability analysis. See below, pp 78–79 (estate agents); and below, p 80 (commission agents). Note also Professor Dowrick's caution that: 'In common law special legal relations are not to be confined within the strait jacket of definitions; *elegantia juris* may be achieved only at the expense of the dynamic elements in our law'.

The consequence of an agent having power to affect the legal relations of the principal, in the way just described, is that the agent usually drops out of the transaction. As Wright J said in *Montgomerie v UK Mutual Steamship Association Ltd* [1891] 1 QB 370 at 371:

> There is no doubt whatsoever as to the general rule as regards an agent, that where a person contracts as agent for a principal the contract is the contract of the principal, and not that of the agent; and, prima facie, at common law the only person who may sue is the principal, and the only person who can be sued is the principal.

(b) Agency distinguished from other relationships

We have seen how Professor Dowrick distinguished agency from other power-liability relationships (above, p 75). But what are those other relationships?

Agency and trusts. Agents and trustees are similar in many ways. They can, for example, both affect the legal position of those persons with whose affairs they are dealing and are both accountable to their principals for any profits derived from their position. However, these similarities mask an important conceptual difference between the two institutions. Whereas an agent acts for another, a trustee holds property for another (Bowstead, p 17). This means that the beneficial owner of the property held in trust will usually be able to enforce his rights against the trustee on a proprietary basis, whereas a principal may only be able to enforce his rights against an agent on a personal basis (although the principal may have a proprietary remedy against an agent who has breached his fiduciary duties: see, eg, *A-G for Hong Kong v Reid* [1994] 1 All ER 1, PC). Furthermore, whereas an agent represents his principal to the outside world, the trustee does not represent the beneficiary and so cannot create contractual relations between that beneficiary and third parties. For further differences between agency and trusts, see Fridman, pp 20–23.

Finally, it is important to note that a normal principal and agent relationship does not of itself give rise to a trust relationship (*Kingscroft Insurance Co Ltd v HS Weavers (Underwriting) Agencies Ltd* [1993] 1 Lloyd's Rep 187 at 191, per Harman J). Whether there is a simultaneous trust relationship between the principal and agent will depend on the intentions of the parties (which are often ascertained from the terms of the agency contract: see Bowstead, pp 162–163).

Agency and bailment. Bailment occurs when there is the delivery or transfer of a chattel (or other item of personal property) by one person (the bailor) to another (the bailee) with a specific mandate which requires the identical item to be delivered up to the bailor or to be dealt with in a particular way by the bailee (see above, pp 58 ff). There are two important features which distinguish agency and bailment; namely:

(1) the bailee merely exercises, with leave of the bailor, certain powers over the bailed property but, unlike the agent, the bailee does not represent the bailor; and

(2) the bailee cannot enter into contracts on the bailor's behalf, although he may have power to do things which are reasonably incidental to his use of the goods which he holds (eg to have the property repaired) and thereby make the bailor liable to a third party (see, for example, *Tappenden v Artus* [1964] 2 QB 185, below, p 821).

Agency and sale. Consider the following scenarios:

(1) A asks B to acquire goods for him, and B is held to be A's agent. In these circumstances A will be privy to any contract B makes with his supplier, B will not be liable for failing to acquire the goods if he has used his best endeavours to do so, and B will not be liable if the goods prove defective so long as he exercised due care and skill in his purchase from the third party. On the other hand, if B agrees to obtain the goods and resell them to A there will be no privity between A and B's supplier, B will be absolutely liable to A if he does not obtain the goods, and B will also be liable to A for defects in the goods (under express terms of the contract of sale, or under terms implied by the Sale of Goods Act 1979, ss 13–15).

(2) C agrees to dispose of D's goods, and C is held to be D's agent. In these circumstances D will be privy to any contract of sale made by C with a third party, D (not C) will be liable to the third party on the contract of sale for defects in the goods, and if the third party pays C, who fails to account to D for the money, the third party will only be discharged if C was authorised to receive his payment. On the other hand, if C is held to have purchased the goods from D there will be no privity between D and the third party, C (not D) will be liable to the third party on the contract of sale for defects in the goods, and the third party will be discharged if he pays C.

The importance of distinguishing between agency and sale is clear. But it may not always be easy to make the distinction. In the world of commerce the term 'agent' is often used without regard to its legal meaning (eg a car dealer may describe himself as the 'agent' of a particular manufacturer but it is probably the case that he purchases the vehicles from the manufacturer and resells them to his own customers). However, the distinction can be made according to whether the 'agent' intended to act on his own behalf or on behalf of someone else. If the evidence shows that he intended to act on his own behalf he cannot be an agent, for an agency relationship can only arise when one person intends to act on behalf of another (G H Treitel *The Law of Contract* (8th ed, 1991), pp 609–610; Markesinis and Munday, p 12).

Of particular relevance to this issue is the extent to which the 'agent' is accountable to the 'principal' for moneys received by him and also whether the resale price is fixed by the 'agent' or the 'principal' (see *Michelin Tyre Co Ltd v McFarlane (Glasgow) Ltd* 1917 55 SLR 35, HL). But no single factor need be decisive of the issue and each case must be examined on its facts (see below, p 236).

Agency, distributorship and franchising. When a manufacturer supplies goods to a distributor or a franchisee that person may be described as a 'selling agent' or 'exclusive agent' of the manufacturer. Often the distributor/franchisee will have agreed to promote the sale of the manufacturer's goods and be prohibited from selling goods of rival manufacturers (which may raise restraint of trade and UK and EEC competition law issues: see below, pp 82–83). Yet, whatever the extent of the additional obligations the distributor/franchisee has contractually undertaken, the central relationship between the parties is usually one of sale not agency. This is because the distributor/franchisee will buy the goods from the manufacturer and resell them to his own customers. However, difficult issues of agency law are raised when the contract of sale between the manufacturer and the distributor/franchisee contain reservation of title clauses, which authorise the distributor/franchisee to sell the goods as agent for the manufacturer (see *Aluminium Industrie Vaassen BV v Romalpa Aluminium Ltd* [1976] 1 WLR 676, considered below at pp 408 ff; F M B Reynolds (1978) 94 LQR 224, pp 235–238).

Agency, servants and independent contractors. As some servants and some independent contractors have agency powers, whereas others do not, there may be little practical value in attempting to distinguish these persons from agents (see Bowstead, p 18; *Chitty on Contracts* (26th ed, 1989), Vol 2, para 2504, where the significance of the distinction for the purposes of labour law is noted). But it should be noted that Professor Fridman takes a different view on this issue (Fridman, pp 27–32). According to him, the distinguishing feature is that whereas the main function of an agent is to make contracts and dispose of property on behalf of his principal, the servant and independent contractor cannot normally affect the contractual or proprietary position of the principal.

Finally, it is important to note that the relationships between agency and (1) trusts, (2) bailment, (3) distributors/franchisees, (4) servants/independent contractors, are not mutually exclusive, eg a trustee *may* also have agency powers in appropriate circumstances, an agent *may* hold money or property as trustee or bailee. But the relationship between agency and sale is mutually exclusive. As the editor of Bowstead states (p 20): 'in respect of a particular transaction a person cannot be acting as agent if he is a buyer from or seller to his principal and vice versa'.

(c) Examples of types of agent

There are many different types of agent. They include:

(1) auctioneers, who are agents for the seller but may also be agents for the buyer for certain purposes (*Hinde v Whitehouse* (1806) 7 East 558);
(2) directors, who are agents of the company when they act collectively as a Board of Directors (although the company's Articles of Association usually provide also for delegation of some or all of the Board's functions to individual directors);
(3) partners, who are agents of the firm and their other partners for the purpose of the business of the partnership (Partnership Act 1890, s 5); and
(4) solicitors and counsel, who are agents of their clients when, inter alia, they effect a compromise of matters connected with, but not merely collateral to, the litigation in question (*Waugh v H B Clifford & Sons Ltd* [1982] Ch 374).

There are other types of 'agent' who may have little or no power to change their principal's legal relations with third parties but nevertheless owe fiduciary obligations to their principal. Estate agents are an example of this type of agent, for their powers are extremely limited. Whilst they may have power to make representations about the property (*Sorrell v Finch* [1977] AC 728 at 753), they have no power to make a contract between their client and the prospective purchaser, unless specifically authorised to do so (*Spiro v Lintern* [1973] 1 WLR

1002, where there was such authority). Such agents do not fit into the power-liability analysis of agency outline by Professor Dowrick (above, pp 74–75) and have been described by one commentator as 'anomalous' (Fridman, p 10 fn) and by another as 'incomplete' (Bowstead, p 12). We shall now turn to those agents who play a particular role in commercial transactions.

Factors. The term 'factor' was used to a great extent in the nineteenth century and is now important for the understanding of cases from that era. A factor was an agent who was given possession or control of goods to be sold for his principal. He usually sold the goods in his own name without disclosing the name of his principal (*Baring v Corrie* (1818) 2 B & Ald 137), although he would remain a factor if he sold the goods in his principal's name (*Stevens v Biller* (1883) 25 Ch D 31). Those who purchased goods from the factor could often rely on his apparent authority to sell them, or his apparent ownership of them, to validate any disposition which had not been authorised by the factor's principal. But the term 'factor' is little used in its traditional sense today (although see below, p 753, for the term being used in a different sense). The Factors Act 1889 introduced the term 'mercantile agent' to cover those persons (including factors) who had a statutory power to make unauthorised dispositions which would bind their principal (see below, p 312). It is now more important to identify a person as a mercantile agent than it is to identify him as a factor. For a legal history of the factor, see R J C Munday (1977) 6 Anglo-American LR 221.

Brokers. A broker is a negotiator who makes contracts between buyers and sellers of goods. Unlike a factor, the broker is not given possession or control of the goods he sells and he may not sell those goods in his own name (*Baring v Corrie*, above). But it should be noted that there are other types of broker eg stockbroker, insurance broker and credit-broker (considered by Fridman, p 38; and Chitty, op cit, paras 2512 and 2513).

Del credere agent. A *del credere* agent, in return for an extra commission, undertakes to indemnify the principal should the principal suffer loss as a result of the failure of a customer, introduced by the agent, to pay the purchase price of the goods sold, when the price is ascertained and due (*Morris v Cleasby* (1816) 4 M & S 566). A *del credere* agent can only be made liable to pay the price of the goods on default or insolvency of the buyer; the principal is not entitled to litigate with a *del credere* agent any disputes arising out of the performance of the contract of sale made by the agent (*Thomas Gabriel & Sons v Churchill and Sim* [1914] 3 KB 1272). *Del credere* agents are of particular use to exporters who are uncertain of the financial risks and creditworthiness of overseas buyers introduced by the agent. However, the modern practice is for an exporter to rely on documentary credits (see below, p 640), credit guarantees (see below, p 688) and confirmations (see immediately below) to secure payment from overseas buyers.

Confirming houses. A confirming house usually acts as an agent for an overseas buyer who wishes to import goods. As such the confirming house may do one of the following:

(1) purchase goods in the domestic market as agent for the overseas buyer and not itself become liable to the seller on the contract of sale;
(2) buy from the seller as principal and then resell to the overseas buyer;

(3) act as agent of the overseas buyer with regard to the contract of sale but also enter into a collateral contract with the seller whereby the confirming house agrees to be liable for the solvency of, and performance of the contract of sale by, the overseas buyer: this is known as 'confirmation' (see *Sobell Industries Ltd v Cory Bros & Co* [1955] 2 Lloyd's Rep 82); and

(4) purchase from the seller as principal and yet remain as an agent in relation to the overseas buyer (*Anglo-African Shipping Co of New York Inc v J Mortner Ltd* [1962] 1 Lloyd's Rep 610, may well be an example of this). For further discussion, see D J Hill (1972) J of Maritime Law and Commerce 307.

Commission agents. A commission agent (sometimes called 'commission merchant') contracts with third parties as a principal in his own name, although all contracts will be made by the agent on behalf of his own principal. As a consequence, the commission agent creates privity of contract between himself and the third party (not between his principal and the third party), yet remains in an agency relationship with his own principal. Although this type of agency is well established in civil law countries (where it is called 'indirect representation'), it has not been generally recognised in English law (early recognition by Blackburn J in *Ireland v Livingston* (1872) LR 5 HL 395 and *Robinson v Mollett* (1875) LR 7 HL 802 has found little support in more recent cases: see Bowstead, p 14). One reason why this type of agency has not been assimilated into English law is that it does not sit easily, if at all, with the traditional agency theory that the hallmark of an agent is his power to alter the principal's legal relations with third parties and then drop out of the transaction himself. However, whilst English law has not been prepared to recognise a general category of 'commission agent' there is evidence from commercial practice that certain agents do enter into contracts with third parties as principals and yet remain in an agency relationship with their own principal (see example (4) under 'Confirming houses', above). The doctrine of undisclosed principal is analogous to the civil law contract of commission (where 'commission' refers to the entrusting of a task to the agent and not the method of payment), although, unlike a commission agent, the agent of an undisclosed principal makes his principal liable and entitled on the contract, subject to the rules of election and merger (F M B Reynolds (1978) 94 LQR 224, p 234). For a strong case in support of recognition of the commission agent in English law, see D J Hill (1968) 31 MLR 623; see also [1964] JBL 304; [1967] JBL 122; cf Fridman, pp 25–26, 43–44).

(d) Agency law and the European Community

(i) *Self-employed commercial agents*

On 18 December 1986, the Council of the European Communities adopted Directive 86/653 (OJ 1986, L382/17) on self-employed commercial agents. The main aim of the Directive is to harmonise the domestic laws of the member states as regards the relationship between commercial agents and their principals (art 1(1)). The Directive covers such matters as the rights and obligations of the parties, remuneration of the commercial agent, termination of the agency agreement, the agent's right to compensation or an indemnity on termination of the agency agreement, and restraint of trade clauses.

But what are 'commercial agents'?

Council Directive 86/653 of 18 December 1986 on the Coordination of Laws of the Member States Relating to Self-Employed Commercial Agents states:

Article 1

1. . . .

2. For the purposes of this Directive, 'commercial agent' shall mean a self-employed intermediary who has continuing authority to negotiate the sale or the purchase of goods on behalf of another person, hereinafter called the 'principal', or to negotiate and conclude such transactions on behalf of and in the name of that principal.

3. A commercial agent shall be understood within the meaning of this Directive as not including in particular:

— a person who, in his capacity as an officer, is empowered to enter into commitments binding on a company or association,
— a partner who is lawfully authorised to enter into commitments binding on his partners,
— a receiver and manager, a liquidator or a trustee in bankruptcy.

Article 2

1. This Directive shall not apply to:

— commercial agents whose activities are unpaid,
— commercial agents when they operate on commodity exchanges or in the commodity market, or
— the body known as the Crown Agents for Overseas Governments and Administrations, as set up under the Crown Agents Act 1979 in the United Kingdom, or its subsidiaries.

2. Each of the Member States shall have the right to provide that the Directive shall not apply to those persons whose activities as commercial agents are considered secondary by the law of that Member State.

NOTES

1. Under art 22 of the Directive, the United Kingdom was required to amend its laws to give effect to the Directive by 1 January 1994. The United Kingdom complied with this requirement through secondary legislation under s 2(2) of the European Communities Act 1972. The Commercial Agents (Council Directive) Regulations 1993 (SI 1993/3053) ('the Regulations') came into force on 1 January 1994. The Regulations are retrospective and apply to all commercial agency contracts whether made before or after 1 January 1994 (but the Regulations do not affect the rights and liabilities of a commercial agent or a principal which have accrued before the commencement date): see reg 23.

2. The Regulations adopt the same definition of a commercial agent as appears in the Directive (and note that intermediaries involved in the provision of *services* are excluded from that definition): see reg 2(1), (2). However, the Regulations do not apply to a person whose activities as a commercial agent are considered secondary (see reg 2(3), (4)). Thus, a person who is wholly or mainly engaged in the business of buying or selling goods on his own behalf, or is wholly or mainly engaged in activities other than carrying out of duties as a commercial agent (eg a housewife selling 'Tupperware' as an agent from home), would fall outside the Regulations. The Regulations expressly provide that the activities of mail order catalogue agents for consumer goods and consumer credit agents are presumed to be secondary (Sch, para 5).

Unfortunately, the Regulations are unclear as to whether they are intended to be limited to commercial agents who are individuals or whether they also extend to commercial agents who are partnerships or companies.

3. The provisions of the Directive, and of the Regulations, are reviewed in Schmitthoff's *Agency and Distribution Agreements* (ed S Kenyon-Slade, with M Thornton) (1992). By way of summary, it should be noted that the Directive, and the implementing Regulations, have strengthened the legal position of self-employed commercial agents with regard to their principals: in particular, such agents have been given express rights to demand a written statement of the terms of their agency agreement; to receive customary or reasonable remuneration (unless there has been agreement as to remuneration); and, in certain circumstances, to be indemnified or receive compensation on termination of the agency. Furthermore, the principal must provide the commercial agent with a statement of commission due, together with supporting documentation.

4. Finally, it should be noted that the Regulations mark a shift away from common law regulation to statutory regulation of the relationship between principal and agent, at least where the agent is a commercial agent.

(ii) *Competition law*

Articles 85 and 86 of the Treaty of Rome are the main European Community competition provisions. Article 85 prohibits, as incompatible with the common market, all agreements between undertakings that may affect trade between member states and which have as their object or effect the prevention, restriction or distortion of competition within the common market. Article 86 prohibits, as incompatible with the common market, any abuse by one or more undertakings of a dominant position within the common market or a substantial part of it, in so far as it affects trade between member states. It is beyond the scope of this book to consider these provisions in any detail (see generally, D G Goyder *EC Competition Law* (2nd ed, 1993) for detailed discussion).

There are two ways of obtaining exemption from Article 85. The first is to apply for clearance of the agreement by the EC Commission. The second is by drafting the agreement to comply with the terms of a 'block exemption'. Regulation 1983/83 grants a block exemption to various classes of exclusive distribution agreements (ie agreements under which a supplier agrees with another party to supply exclusively to the latter certain goods for resale within a certain geographical area). Regulation 4087/88 grants a block exemption to various classes of franchise agreements (ie agreements whereby the franchisor grants to the franchisee, for financial consideration, the right to exploit a package of industrial or intellectual property rights relating to trade marks, trade names etc for the purposes of marketing certain goods and/or services). There is no block exemption for agency agreements. But the EC Commission have indicated by a 'Notice' (ie non-binding guidelines) that exclusive agency agreements made with commercial agents have negative clearance from Article 85 so long as the commercial agent undertakes no 'financial risk', other than on a *del credere* basis (EEC Commission Notice on Exclusive Agency Agreements, of 24 December 1962 (OJ 1962, 139/2921), soon to be replaced by a new Notice which applies to both exclusive and non-exclusive agency agreements: see Goyder, op cit, pp 215–216). Exclusive agency agreements are agreements where the agent agrees to represent only the principal, and no other competing principal, within a certain area. If a principal enters into a network of exclusive agency agreements this may amount to an abuse of a dominant position in the common market and breach Article 86 (see *Suiker Unie v Commission* [1976] 1 CMLR 295). There is no exemption procedure for breaches of Article 86.

It should also be noted that under EEC Directive 86/653 on self-employed commercial agents, as implemented by reg 20 of the Commercial Agents (Council Directive) Regulations 1993 (above, pp 80–82), a restraint of trade clause restricting the right of a commercial agent to act as such after termination of an agency contract will only be valid if, and to the extent that, it is in writing; it relates to the geographical area, or to both the group of customers and the geographical area, and to the kind of goods in respect of which the commercial agent has a right to act; it is reasonable from the point of view of the principal and the commercial agent and their common customers; and it does not apply for a period of more than two years after the termination of the agency contract. The restraint of trade clause would also be subject to the common law on restraint of trade agreements (as to which, see Treitel, op cit, pp 401–424): see reg 20(3).

(e) Harmonisation of agency law

To facilitate the unification of international trade law, a diplomatic conference held in Geneva in 1983, and attended by delegations from 58 countries, approved a Convention on Agency in the International Sale of Goods. The Convention, based on a draft prepared by the International Institute for the Unification of Private Law (UNIDROIT), supplements the rules contained in the 1980 Vienna Convention on Contracts for the International Sale of Goods (see below, p 443). Like the Vienna Convention, the Geneva Convention will enter into force when ratified by ten states (art 33(1)). Neither Convention has been ratified by the United Kingdom.

The Geneva Convention only applies where:

(1) the agent has authority or purports to have authority on behalf of the principal to conclude a contract for the sale of goods with a third party (art 1(1));
(2) the principal and the third party have their places of business in different states (art 2(1)); and
(3) the agent has his place of business in a contracting state or the rules of private international law lead to the application of the law of a contracting state (art 2(1)).

If the third party did not know, nor ought to have known, that the agent was acting as an agent, then the Convention will only apply if the agent and the third party had their places of business in different states and if the requirements of art 2(1) are satisfied (art 2(2)). Certain types of agency, eg the agency of a dealer on a stock, commodity or other exchange, fall outside the provisions of the Convention (art 3).

The Geneva Convention is concerned only with relations between the principal or agent on the one hand, and the third party on the other (art 1(3)). The Convention does not regulate the internal relationship between the principal and the agent. This omission, which was necessary to ensure the adoption of the Convention, may reduce the practical importance of the Geneva Convention (M J Bonell (1984) 32 *American Journal of Comparative Law* 717 at p 747). However, within its stated object, the Convention does represent an impressive attempt to assimilate the different common law and civil law rules of agency. For detailed analysis of the Geneva Convention, see M Evans [1984] Uniform Law Review 74; and Bonell, op cit, which contains a copy of the text of the Convention.

CHAPTER 4

Creation of agency and the authority of the agent

1 Creation of the agency relationship

The relationship of principal and agent may be created in any one of the following ways:

(1) by express or implied agreement between principal and agent;
(2) under the doctrine of apparent authority (see below, pp 91–100);
(3) by operation of law (see below, pp 104–109); and
(4) by ratification of the agent's acts by the principal (see below, pp 109–116).

Agency arising out of agreement will always be consensual but it need not be contractual. An agency may be gratuitous. The main differences between a purely consensual and a contractual agency are (1) the presence or absence of consideration, and (2) the fact that with a contractual agency the agent is usually under an *obligation* to carry out his functions and the principal is under a corresponding obligation to remunerate him (Fridman, p 47; Markesinis and Munday, p 17). The agent's contractual right to remuneration must be distinguished from his right to an indemnity for loss and expense incurred in the execution of his duties. The right to an indemnity arises by operation of law irrespective of any agreement between the parties (see below, p 196).

The agreement between the principal and agent may be expressed orally, in writing or by deed (usually called a 'power of attorney'). In general, no formality is required and an agent may be appointed orally even when he is appointed to make a contract which has to be in writing or evidenced in writing, as with a contract for the purchase of land or a contract of guarantee (*Heard v Pilley* (1869) 4 Ch App 548). But there are some statutory exceptions to this rule (eg Law of Property Act 1925, ss 53(1), 54). Furthermore, if an agent is appointed to *execute* a deed, his appointment must be by deed (*Berkeley v Hardy* (1826) 5 B & C 355), unless the agent executes the deed in the presence of the principal (*Ball v Dunsterville* (1791) 4 Term Rep 313). But under s 1(1)(c) of the Law of Property (Miscellaneous Provisions) Act 1989 a deed is no longer required to authorise *delivery* of a deed. Finally, it should be noted that under the EEC Directive on Self-Employed Commercial Agents 86/653, implemented in the UK by the Commercial Agents Regulations 1993 (above, pp 80–82), both the principal and the commercial agent may request from the other a signed written statement of the terms of the agency contract, including any terms agreed after the creation of the agency contract.

Alternatively, the agreement between the principal and agent may be implied from their conduct (see *Garnac Grain Co Inc v HMF Faure and Fairclough Ltd* [1968]

AC 1130n at p 1137, per Lord Pearson). For example, the consent of the principal may be implied from the fact that he appointed a person to a position in which he would usually act as agent for the person who appoints him (see *Pole v Leask* (1863) 33 LJ Ch 155 at 161–162). The principal may simply acquiesce in the acts of another, but consent will not be presumed merely from the principal's silence, unless other factors indicate that he acquiesced in the agency (*Burnside v Dayrell* (1849) 3 Exch 224). The consent of the agent may be inferred from the fact that he purports to act on behalf of the principal (*Roberts v Ogilby* (1821) 9 Price 269). But merely doing what the principal requests does not invariably result in an agency relationship. As Professor Powell has stated (*The Law of Agency* (2nd ed, 1961), p 297):

> Suppose, for example, that A is about to buy for himself a racehorse called Saucy Sally and receives a [telemessage] from P: 'Buy Saucy Sally for me at £900.' Must it be supposed that A's subsequent purchase of the horse, even at £900, makes A P's agent with a liability to deliver the horse to P? Or that P's authorisation imposes on A any obligation to communicate to P his refusal to act as P's agent? If, therefore, the indication of A's consent is to be the performance of an act by A, that act must show unequivocally that A has consented to act as P's agent.

Finally, it should be noted that any person who is capable of consenting can act as an agent, even though he has only limited or no contractual capacity himself (although any contractual liability to his principal or a third party would depend on his contractual capacity). In general, the principal will only be bound by the contracts and acts of his agent if the principal has capacity to contract or to do the act himself (but see s 35 of the Companies Act 1985, as amended by the Companies Act 1989, for an example of an exception to this rule). For further discussion, see Fridman, pp 49–50; G H Treitel *The Law of Contract* (8th ed, 1991), pp 612–613.

QUESTION

Adam writes to Bill asking him to purchase a particular Ming vase for him and promising to reimburse Bill the cost of the purchase. Before Bill receives the letter, he purchases the vase as a birthday present for Adam and gives it to him. The next day Bill receives Adam's letter and now seeks to recover the cost of the vase from him.

Advise Bill. Would it make any difference to your answer if Bill had bought the vase in anticipation of receiving instructions from Adam to do so, rather than as a present for him? See Bowstead, p 44.

2 Authority of the agent

The relationship between the 'power' and 'authority' of an agent was considered in the previous chapter (above, p 75). However, you will see from what appears below that the term 'authority' is not always used in its strict sense.

(a) Actual authority

Whether an agent has authority is a question of fact. If the principal has given prior consent to the agent acting on his behalf then the agent can be said to have 'actual' authority. Actual authority will be conferred on the agent by the principal under the terms of the agreement or contract between them. As Diplock LJ stated in *Freeman and Lockyer v Buckhurst Park Properties (Mangal) Ltd* [1964] 2 QB 480 at 502:

> An 'actual' authority is a legal relationship between principal and agent created by a consensual agreement to which they alone are parties. Its scope is to be ascertained by applying ordinary principles of construction of contracts, including any proper implications from the express words used, the usages of the trade, or the business between the parties.

Ascertaining the scope of the agent's actual authority is important. As a general rule, only if the agent acts within the scope of his actual authority is he entitled to an indemnity from his principal (and the same applies to any remuneration due under a contract of agency). Moreover, if the agent acts outside his actual authority he may be liable to his principal for breach of contract (see below, p 163), or liable to a third party for breach of his implied warranty of authority (see below, pp 140–45). The position would be otherwise if the principal later adopted or ratified the agent's unauthorised actions (see below, pp 109–116 and 144–145).

(i) *Express actual authority*

Ireland v Livingston (1872) LR 5 HL 395, House of Lords

Livingston wrote to Ireland asking him to ship 500 tons of sugar. The letter continued: 'Fifty tons more or less of no moment, if it enables you to get a suitable price.' Ireland shipped 400 tons in one vessel, presumably intending to ship the rest in another vessel. Livingston refused to accept the 400 tons and wrote to Ireland to cancel any further shipment. The House of Lords held that Livingston was bound to accept the sugar.

Lord Chelmsford: My Lords, the difference of opinion which has prevailed amongst the Judges in this case, shews that the order given to the Plaintiffs by the Defendant in his letter of the 25th of July, 1864 (upon which the question principally turns) is of doubtful construction; and this, in my mind, is a sufficient ground in itself for bringing me to the conclusion at which I have arrived. . . .

Now it appears to me that if a principal gives an order to an agent in such uncertain terms as to be susceptible of two different meanings, and the agent *bona fide* adopts one of them and acts upon it, it is not competent to the principal to repudiate the act as unauthorized because he meant the order to be read in the other sense of which it is equally capable. It is a fair answer to such an attempt to disown the agents' authority to tell the principal that the departure from his intention was occasioned by his own fault, and that he should have given his order in clear and unambiguous terms. This view of the case will, in my opinion, dispense with the necessity of determining which is the more correct construction of the contract, that which was adopted unanimously by the Court of Queen's Bench, and by two of the Judges of the Exchequer Chamber, or that which the four other Judges of the Exchequer Chamber considered to be the right interpretation of it. It is sufficient for the justification of the Plaintiffs, that the meaning which they affixed to the order of the Defendant is, that which is sanctioned by so many learned Judges. It would be most unjust, after the Plaintiffs have honestly acted upon what they conceived to be the wishes of the Defendant, as expressed in his order, that he should be allowed to repudiate the whole transaction and throw the loss of it upon the Plaintiffs in order (as his correspondence shews) to escape from a speculation which had become a losing one in consequence of the market prices of sugars having fallen.

The short ground upon which I think the case may be disposed of, renders it unnecessary for me to express my opinion as to the proper interpretation of the letters upon which the Courts below have proceeded. . . .

The Plaintiffs have construed the meaning of the Defendant's language in a manner for which there was a reasonable excuse, if not a complete justification, and with an honest desire to perform their duty to him, and have obeyed his order according to their understanding of its meaning.

[Lords Westbury and Colonsay delivered concurring opinions.]

NOTES

1. In *Woodhouse AC Israel Cocoa Ltd SA v Nigerian Produce Marketing Co Ltd* [1972] AC 741 at 772, Lord Salmon observed that 'in 1872 there were no means by which an agent, at the other end of the world, receiving ambiguous instructions, could communicate with his principal in London to clear up any doubt about their meaning before carrying out his duty to act upon them promptly'. But with the speed of modern communication methods it is unlikely that an agent would be deemed to have a reasonable excuse to adopt one interpretation of ambiguous instructions without first clarifying those instructions with his principal (*European Asian Bank AG v Punjab and Sind Bank (No 2)* [1983] 1 WLR 642 at 656, per Robert Goff LJ).

2. *Ireland v Livingston* was a case where the principal's instruction was conveyed to the agent in a letter. Where the authority of an agent is given by an instruction in a document not under seal, or has been given orally, it is construed liberally, with regard to the purpose of the agency and to the usages of trade or business (*Ashford Shire Council v Dependable Motors Pty Ltd* [1961] AC 336, PC). If the authority is contained in a deed, the usual strict rules of construction apply. In particular, this means that (1) authority will be limited to the purpose for which it was given (*Midland Bank Ltd v Reckett* [1933] AC 1), and (2) general words of appointment will be restricted by other specific words which describe the particular acts the agent is authorised to peform (*Jacobs v Morris* [1902] 1 Ch 816). However, it should be noted that under s 10 of the Powers of Attorney Act 1971, if a general power of attorney is drawn up in the statutory form or in a similar manner and expressed to be made under the Act, it confers on the donee of the power authority to do on behalf of the donor, ie the principal, 'anything which he can lawfully do by an attorney'. Thus, if the words are unqualified, the agent's authority will only be restricted by any incapacity of his principal.

(ii)   *Implied actual authority*

Hely-Hutchinson v Brayhead Ltd [1968] 1 QB 549, Court of Appeal

Richards was the chairman of Brayhead. To the knowledge, and with the acquiescence, of Brayhead's board he also acted as the company's de facto managing director. Brayhead held shares in another company, Perdio Electronics Ltd. To encourage Hely-Hutchinson to inject funds into Period, Richards in his capacity as chairman of Brayhead wrote to him undertaking to indemnify him for any loss he might incur as a result of lending money to Perdio or guaranteeing any loan made to Perdio. In reliance on this undertaking Hely-Hutchinson advanced £45,000 to Perdio. Subsequently, Perdio went into liquidation and Hely-Hutchinson had to pay off a company loan which he had guaranteed. Hely-Hutchinson sought to recover that sum, and the £45,000 lent to Perdio, from Brayhead. He relied on the terms of Brayhead's letter of indemnity and this raised the question of Richard's authority to bind the company. Roskill J upheld the claim on the ground that Richard had ostensible or apparent authority to bind Brayhead. The Court of Appeal dismissed Brayhead's appeal on the ground that Richard had implied actual authority to bind Brayhead.

Lord Denning MR: I need not consider at length the law on the authority of an agent, actual, apparent, or ostensible. That has been done in the judgments of this court in *Freeman & Lockyer v Buckhurst Park Properties (Mangal) Ltd* ([1964] 2 QB 480). It is there shown that actual authority may be express or implied. It is *express* when it is given by express words, such as when a board of directors pass a resolution which authorises two of their number to sign cheques. It is *implied* when it is inferred from the conduct of the parties and the circumstances of the case, such as when the board of directors appoint one of their number to be managing director. They thereby impliedly authorise him to do all such things as fall within the usual scope of that office. Actual authority, express or implied, is binding as between the company and the agent, and also as between the company and others, whether they are within the company or outside it.

Ostensible or apparent authority is the authority of an agent as it *appears* to others. It often coincides with actual authority. Thus, when the board appoint one of their number to be managing director, they invest him not only with implied authority, but also with ostensible authority to do all such things as fall within the usual scope of that office. Other people who see him acting as managing director are entitled to assume that he has the usual authority of a managing director. But sometimes ostensible authority exceeds actual authority. For instance, when the board appoint the managing director, they may expressly limit his authority by saying he is not to order goods worth more than £500 without the sanction of the board. In that case his *actual* authority is subject to the £500 limitation, but his *ostensible* authority includes all the usual authority of a managing director. The company is bound by his ostensible authority in his dealings with those who do not know of the limitation. He may himself do the 'holding-out.' Thus, if he orders goods worth £1,000 and signs himself 'Managing Director for and on behalf of the company,' the company is bound to the other party who does not know of the £500 limitation, see *British Thomson-Houston Co Ltd v Federated European Bank Ltd* ([1932] 2 KB 176), which was quoted for this purpose by Pearson LJ in *Freeman & Lockyer* (at 499). Even if the other party happens himself to be a director of the company, nevertheless the company may be bound by the ostensible authority. Suppose the managing director orders £1,000 worth of goods from a new director who has just joined the company and does not know of the £500 limitation, not having studied the minute book, the company may yet be bound. Lord Simonds in *Morris v Kanssen* ([1946] AC 459 at 475–476), envisaged that sort of case, which was considered by Roskill J in the present case.

Apply these principles here. It is plain that Mr Richards had no express authority to enter into these two contracts on behalf of the company: nor had he any such authority implied from the nature of his office. He had been duly appointed chairman of the company but that office in itself did not carry with it authority to enter into these contracts without the sanction of the board. But I think he had authority implied from the conduct of the parties and the circumstances of the case. The judge did not rest his decision on implied authority, but I think his findings necessarily carry that consequence. The judge finds that Mr Richards acted as de facto managing director of Brayhead. He was the chief executive who made the final decision on any matter concerning finance. He often committed Brayhead to contracts without the knowledge of the board and reported the matter afterwards. The judge said:

> I have no doubt that Mr. Richards was, by virtue of his position as de facto managing director of Brayhead or, as perhaps one might more compendiously put it, as Brayhead's chief executive, the man who had, in Diplock LJ's words, 'actual authority to manage,' and he was acting as such when he signed those two documents.

And later he said:

the board of Brayhead knew of and acquiesced in Mr. Richards acting as de facto managing director of Brayhead.

The judge held that Mr Richards had ostensible or apparent authority to make the contract, but I think his findings carry with it the necessary inference that he had also actual authority, such authority being implied from the circumstances that the board by their conduct over many months had acquiesced in his acting as their chief executive and committing Brayhead Ltd to contracts without the necessity of sanction from the board.

[Lords Wilberforce and Pearson delivered concurring judgments.]

NOTES

1. Implied actual authority may arise in any of the following forms:

(1) Incidental authority, ie an agent has implied actual authority to do everything necessary for, or ordinarily incidental to, the effective execution of his express authority in the usual way. For example, an agent who is instructed to sell a house has incidental authority to sign the agreement of sale (*Rosenbaum v Belson* [1900] 2 Ch 267). But an agent who is instructed to 'find a purchaser', not to 'sell', has no incidental authority to conclude a contract (*Hamer v Sharp* (1874) LR 19 Eq 108). In both cases the scope of the agent's incidental authority turned on construction of his express authority.

(2) Usual authority, ie an agent has implied actual authority to do what is usual in his trade, profession, or business for the purpose of carrying out his authority or anything necessary or incidental thereto (Fridman, p 60). For example, if the board of directors appoint someone to be managing director 'they thereby impliedly authorise him to do all such things as fall within the usual scope of that office' (*Hely-Hutchinson v Brayhead Ltd*, above, p 89, per Lord Denning MR). A solicitor's authority to compromise litigation is a further example of this form of implied actual authority (*Waugh v HB Clifford & Sons Ltd* [1982] Ch 374 , CA; see generally G Fridman (1987) 36 UNB LJ 9 at pp 24–40). For further examples, see Bowstead, pp 109–114; Fridman, pp 69–73; Markesinis and Munday, pp 31–33).

(3) Customary authority, ie an agent has implied actual authority to act in accordance with the usages and customs of the particular place, market or business in which he is employed, so long as those usages or customs are reasonable and lawful. A usage or custom will be unreasonable if it is inconsistent with the instructions given by the principal to the agent, or with the nature of the principal and agent relationship itself. A principal will only be bound by an unreasonable usage or custom if he had actual notice of it at the time he conferred authority on the agent (*Robinson v Mollett* (1875) LR 7 HL 802). Whether an illegal usage or custom can bind a principal, who is aware of the illegality, probably depends on the nature of the illegality (Bowstead, p 116). For the definition of 'usage', see *Cunliffe-Owen v Teather and Greenwood* [1967] 1 WLR 1421 at 1438–1439, per Ungoed-Thomas J; also see above, p 16.

(4) Implied actual authority may be inferred from the conduct of the parties and the circumstances of the case. For example, in *Hely-Hutchinson*, Lord Denning MR held that Richards' authority was to be 'implied from the conduct of the parties and the circumstances of the case' (above, p 89). It should be noted that, unlike the types of implied authority considered under paragraphs (1)–(3) above, the type of implied authority considered in this paragraph corresponds to the creation of an agency relationship by implied agreement (above, pp 85–86).

2. An agent cannot have *actual* authority when he exceeds an express limit on his authority or when he does something which his principal has expressly prohibited. This means that the principal can prevent implied actual authority arising by expressly restricting his agent's authority. However, the principal will continue to be bound by prohibited acts of his agent if (1) those acts fall within the authority which an agent of that type would usually possess (usual authority), and (2) the third party dealing with the agent is not aware of restrictions which the principal has placed on the agent's authority. Here the agent's usual authority will not be a form of implied actual authority (because of the prohibition), rather it goes to invest the agent with apparent authority (see *First Energy (UK) Ltd v Hungarian International Bank Ltd* [1993] 2 Lloyd's Rep 194 at 201, per Steyn LJ; cf Fridman, p 65; also R T H Stone [1993] JBL 325 at pp 336–337). To avoid terminological confusion, it is important to note that the expression 'usual authority' can be used in these two very different senses. Unfortunately, as we shall soon discover, it can also be used in a third sense (below, p 100).

(b) Apparent authority

Rama Corpn Ltd v Proved Tin and General Investments Ltd [1952] 2 QB 147, Queen's Bench Division

(The facts are irrelevant.)

Slade J: Ostensible or apparent authority . . . is merely a form of estoppel, indeed, it has been termed agency by estoppel, and you cannot call in aid an estoppel unless you have three ingredients: (i) a representation, (ii) reliance on the representation, and (iii) an alteration of your position resulting from such reliance.

Freeman & Lockyer v Buckhurst Park Properties (Mangal) Ltd [1964] 2 QB 480, Court of Appeal

K and H formed the defendant company to purchase and resell a large estate. K and H, together with their nominees, were the directors of the company. The articles of association of the company contained a power to appoint a managing director but none was appointed. However, to the knowledge, and with the acquiescence, of the board K acted as de facto managing director and entered into contracts on the company's behalf. On one occasion K employed a firm of architects to apply for planning permission to develop the estate and to do other work in that connection. K had no actual authority to do this and when the architects claimed their fees from the defendant company an issue arose as to whether K had apparent authority to bind it. The trial judge held that K had such apparent authority and the Court of Appeal dismissed the company's appeal.

Diplock LJ: . . . We are concerned in the present case with the authority of an agent to create contractual rights and liabilities between his principal and a third party whom I will call 'the contractor.' This branch of the law has developed pragmatically rather than logically owing to the early history of the action of assumpsit and the consequent absence of a general jus quaesitum tertii in English law. But it is possible (and for the determination of this appeal I think it is desirable) to restate it upon a rational basis.

It is necessary at the outset to distinguish between an 'actual' authority of an agent on the one hand, and an 'apparent' or 'ostensible' authority on the other. Actual authority and apparent authority are quite independent of one another. Generally they co-exist and coincide, but either may exist without the other and their respective scopes may be different. As I shall endeavour to show, it is upon the apparent authority of the agent that the contractor normally relies in the ordinary course of business when entering into contracts.

An 'actual' authority is a legal relationship between principal and agent created by a consensual agreement to which they alone are parties. Its scope is to be ascertained by applying ordinary principles of construction of contracts, including any proper implications from the express words used, the usages of the trade, or the course of business between the parties. To this agreement the contractor is a stranger; he may be totally ignorant of the existence of any authority on the part of the agent. Nevertheless, if the agent does enter into a contract pursuant to the 'actual' authority, it does create contractual rights and liabilities between the principal and the contractor. It may be that this rule relating to 'undisclosed principals,' which is peculiar to English law, can be rationalised as avoiding circuity of action, for the principal could in equity compel the agent to lend his name in an action to enforce the contract against the contractor, and would at common law be liable to indemnify the agent in respect of the performance of the obligations assumed by the agent under the contract.

An 'apparent' or 'ostensible' authority, on the other hand, is a legal relationship between the principal and the contractor created by a representation, made by the principal to the contractor, intended to be and in fact acted upon by the contractor, that the agent has authority to enter on behalf of the principal into a contract of a kind within the scope of the 'apparent' authority, so as to render the principal liable to perform any obligations imposed upon him by such contract. To the relationship so created the agent is a stranger. He need not be (although he generally is) aware of the existence of the representation but he must not purport to make the agreement as principal himself. The representation, when acted upon by the contractor by entering into a contract with the agent, operates as an estoppel, preventing the principal from asserting that he is not bound by the contract. It is irrelevant whether the agent had actual authority to enter into the contract.

In ordinary business dealings the contractor at the time of entering into the contract can in the nature of things hardly ever rely on the 'actual' authority of the agent. His information as to the authority must be derived either from the principal or from the agent or from both, for they alone know what the agent's actual authority is. All that the contractor can know is what they tell him, which may or may not be true. In the ultimate analysis he relies either upon the representation of the principal, that is, apparent authority, or upon the representation of the agent, that is, warranty of authority.

The representation which creates 'apparent' authority may take a variety of forms of which the commonest is representation by conduct, that is, by permitting the agent to act in some way in the conduct of the principal's business with other persons. By so doing the principal represents to anyone who becomes aware that the agent is so acting that the agent has authority to enter on behalf of the principal into contracts with other persons of the kind which an agent so acting in the conduct of his principal's business has usually 'actual' authority to enter into.

In applying the law as I have endeavoured to summarise it to the case where the principal is not a natural person, but a fictitious person, namely, a corporation, two further factors arising from the legal characteristics of a corporation have to be borne in mind. The first is that the capacity of a corporation is limited by its constitution, that is, in the case of a company incorporated under the Companies Act, by its memorandum and articles of association; the second is that a corporation cannot do any act, and that includes making a representation, except through its agent.

Under the doctrine of ultra vires the limitation of the capacity of a corporation by its constitution to do any acts is absolute. This affects the rules as to the 'apparent' authority of an agent of a corporation in two ways. First, no representation can operate to estop the corporation from denying the authority of the agent to do on behalf of the corporation an act which the corporation is not permitted by its constitution to do itself. Secondly, since the conferring of actual authority upon an agent is itself an act of the corporation, the capacity to do which is regulated by its constitution, the corporation cannot be estopped from denying that it has conferred upon a particular agent authority to do acts which by its constitution, it is incapable of delegating to that particular agent.

To recognise that these are direct consequences of the doctrine of ultra vires is, I think, preferable to saying that a contractor who enters into a contract with a corporation has constructive notice of its constitution, for the expression 'constructive notice' tends to disguise that constructive notice is not a positive, but a negative doctrine, like that of estoppel of which it forms a part. It operates to prevent the contractor from saying that he did not know that the constitution of the corporation rendered a particular act or a particular delegation of authority ultra vires the corporation. It does not entitle him to say that he relied upon some unusual provision in the constitution of the corporation if he did not in fact so rely.

The second characteristic of a corporation, namely, that unlike a natural person it can only make a representation through an agent, has the consequence that in order to create an estoppel between the corporation and the contractor, the representation as to the authority of the agent which creates his 'apparent' authority must be made by some person or persons who have 'actual' authority from the corporation to make the representation. Such 'actual' authority may be conferred by the constitution of the corporation itself, as, for example, in the case of a company, upon the board of directors, or it may be conferred by those who under its constitution have the powers of management upon some other person to whom the constitution permits them to delegate authority to make representations of this kind. It follows that where the agent upon whose 'apparent' authority the contractor relies has no 'actual' authority from the corporation to enter into a particular kind of contract with the contractor on behalf of the corporation, the contractor cannot rely upon the agent's own representation as to his actual authority. He can rely only upon a representation by a person or persons who have actual authority to manage or conduct that part of the business of the corporation to which the contract relates.

The commonest form of representation by a principal creating an 'apparent' authority of an agent is by conduct, namely, by permitting the agent to act in the management or conduct of the principal's business. Thus, if in the case of a company the board of directors who have 'actual' authority under the memorandum and articles of association to manage the company's business permit the agent to act in the management or conduct of the company's business, they thereby represent to all persons dealing with such agent that he has authority to enter on behalf of the corporation into contracts of a kind which an agent authorised to do acts of the kind which he is in fact permitted to do usually enters into in the ordinary course of such business. The making of such a representation is itself an act of management of the company's business. Prima facie it falls within the 'actual' authority of the board of directors, and unless the memorandum or articles of the company either make such a contract ultra vires the company or prohibit the delegation of such authority to the agent, the company is estopped from denying to anyone who has entered into a contract with the agent in reliance upon such 'apparent' authority that the agent had authority to contract on behalf of the company.

If the foregoing analysis of the relevant law is correct, it can be summarised by stating four conditions which must be fulfilled to entitle a contractor to enforce against a company a contract entered into on behalf of the company by an agent who had no actual authority to do so. It must be shown:

(1) that a representation that the agent had authority to enter on behalf of the company into a contract of the kind sought to be enforced was made to the contractor;

(2) that such representation was made by a person or persons who had 'actual' authority to manage the business of the company either generally or in respect of those matters to which the contract relates;

(3) that he (the contractor) was induced by such representation to enter into the contract, that is, that he in fact relied upon it; and

(4) that under its memorandum or articles of association the company was not deprived of the capacity either to enter into a contract of the kind sought to be enforced or to delegate authority to enter into a contract of that kind to the agent.

The confusion which, I venture to think, has sometimes crept into the cases is in my view due to a failure to distinguish between these four separate conditions, and in particular to keep steadfastly in mind (a) that the only 'actual' authority which is relevant is that of the persons making the representation relied upon, and (b) that the memorandum and articles of association of the company are always relevant (whether they are in fact known to the contractor or not) to the questions (i) whether condition (2) is fulfilled, and (ii) whether condition (4) is fulfilled, and (but only if they are in fact known to the contractor) may be relevant (iii) as part of the representation on which the contractor relied. . . .

In the present case the findings of fact by the county court judge are sufficient to satisfy the four conditions, and thus to establish that Kapoor had 'apparent' authority to enter into contracts on behalf of the company for their services in connection with the sale of the company's property, including the obtaining of development permission with respect to its use. The judge found that the board knew that Kapoor had throughout been acting as managing director in employing agents and taking other steps to find a purchaser. They permitted him to do so, and by such conduct represented that he had authority to enter into contracts of a kind which a managing director or an executive director responsible for finding a purchaser would in the normal course be authorised to enter into on behalf of the company. Condition (1) was thus fulfilled. The articles of association conferred full powers of management on the board. Condition (2) was thus fulfilled. The plaintiffs, finding Kapoor acting in relation to the company's property as he was authorised by the board to act, were induced to believe that he was authorised by the company to enter into contracts on behalf of the company for their services in connection with the sale of the company's property, including the obtaining of development permission with respect to its use. Condition (3) was thus fulfilled. The articles of association, which contained powers for the board to delegate any of the functions of management to a managing director or to a single director, did not deprive the company of capacity to delegate authority to Kapoor, a director, to enter into contracts of that kind on behalf of the company. Condition (4) was thus fulfilled.

I think the judgment was right, and would dismiss the appeal.

[Willmer and Pearson LJJ delivered concurring judgments.]

NOTES

1. For the inter-relationship between implied actual authority and apparent authority, see *Hely-Hutchinson v Brayhead Ltd*, above, p 88; and *Waugh v HB Clifford & Sons Ltd* [1982] Ch 374, CA.

2. There has been some debate as to whether or not apparent authority is 'real' authority (see Bowstead, pp 290–292 for references to the literature). It has been submitted by some writers that, like actual authority, apparent authority is based on consent and, therefore, is real authority. These writers concentrate on the objective appearance of consent as manifested in the principal's representations and conduct (eg see M Conant (1968) Nebraska LR 678 at pp 681–686; cf Fridman, p 108). However, the objective consent theory has not found favour with the English courts. Since the *Freeman and Lockyer* decision, the English courts have consistently referred to apparent authority as a form of estoppel (eg *Egyptian International Foreign Trade Co v Soplex Wholesale Supplies Ltd and PS Refson & Co Ltd, The Raffaella* [1985] 2 Lloyd's Rep 36 at 41, CA; *Armagas Ltd v Mundogas SA* [1986] AC 717 at 777, HL; *Gurtner v Beaton* [1993] 2 Lloyd's Rep 369 at 379, CA). As such, apparent authority cannot be real authority, rather it creates the appearance of authority which, for policy reasons, the law recognises as giving the agent power to affect the legal relations of the principal (see above, p 75).

3. Although this debate may appear somewhat academic, it does have practical significance. Some of the consequences of the agent having actual authority, as opposed to apparent authority, have already been considered (above, p 87).

Furthermore, as a form of estoppel, apparent authority can only make the principal liable under any contract made by his agent, it cannot give the principal an independent cause of action unless he ratifies his agent's unauthorised act (although Bowstead, at p 292, submits that the principal should be able to make counterclaims and raise defences against any action brought against him by the third party on the unauthorised contract). If apparent authority was true authority the principal could sue and be sued on the contract (Powell, op cit, p 70; Conant, op cit, p 683).

4. In *Freeman and Lockyer*, Diplock LJ considered how limitations in a company's constitution (its memorandum and articles of association) could affect the capacity of the company to do acts and the power of the board to delegate authority to an agent. However, these comments must now be considered in the light of recent changes to the Companies Act 1985, introduced by the Companies Act 1989. In most cases limitations on the company's capacity and on the board's power to delegate are no longer relevant (ss 35, 35A of the Companies Act 1985 Act, as amended). The doctrine of constructive notice has been abolished (s 711A(1) of the Companies Act 1985, as amended), although this does not affect the question whether a person is affected by notice of any matter by reason of a failure to make such enquiries as ought reasonably be made (s 711A(2) of the 1985 Act, as amended). By s 35B of the Companies Act 1985, as amended, 'a party to a transaction with a company is not bound to enquire as to whether it is permitted by the company's memorandum or as to any limitation on the powers of the board of directors to bind the company or authorise others to do so'. For further details of these changes, see J H Farrar, N E Furey, B M Hannigan *Farrar's Company Law* (3rd ed, 1991), Ch 24; L C B Gower *Principles of Modern Company Law* (5th ed, 1992), Ch 8; see also E Ferran (1992) 13 Co Law 124, 177.

The requirements for apparent authority were summarised by Slade J in the *Rama* case (above, p 91) as (i) representation, (ii) reliance, (iii) alteration of position.

(i) *Representation*

Egyptian International Foreign Trade Co v Soplex Wholesale Supplies Ltd and P S Refson & Co Ltd, The Raffaella [1985] 2 Lloyd's Rep 36, Court of Appeal

The plaintiffs sued the defendant bank on a letter of guarantee signed solely by the bank's credit manager, Mr Booth. At the trial it was common ground that, under the bank's internal rules, Mr Booth did not have actual authority to bind the bank to the guarantee on his sole signature (although at the time he signed the guarantee Mr Booth had assured the plaintiff's representative that one signature was sufficient to bind the bank). The trial judge, and the Court of Appeal, held that Mr Booth had apparent authority to bind the bank to the guarantee by virtue of his designation as credit manager and because of what the bank had permitted him to do in the past.

Browne-Wilkinson LJ: I have so far ignored the representation made by Mr Booth that 'in London one signature is sufficient'. Mr Stamler submitted that a principal cannot be held liable as a result of the agent holding himself out as possessing an authority he does not in fact possess: he relied on remarks to that effect in the *Freeman & Lockyer* case at p 505, *A-G for Ceylon v Silva* [1953] 1 Lloyd's Rep 563, [1953] AC 461 at pp 571 and 479, *The British Bank* *of The Middle East* case (sup.) and *Armagas Ltd v Mundogas SA* [1985] 1 Lloyd's Rep 1. As at present advised, I am not satisfied that the principle to be derived from those cases is as wide as Mr Stamler suggests: they were all cases or dicta dealing with the position where the agent had neither authority to enter into the transaction nor authority to make representations on behalf of the principal. It is obviously correct that an agent who has no actual or apparent authority either (a) to enter into a transaction or (b) to make representations as to the transaction cannot hold himself out as having authority to enter into the transaction so as to affect the principal's position. But, suppose a company confers actual or apparent authority on X to make representations and X erroneously represents to a third party that Y has authority to enter into a transaction; why should not such a representation be relied upon as part of the holding out of Y by the company? By parity of reasoning, if a company confers actual or apparent authority on A to make representations on the company's behalf but no actual authority on A to enter into the specific transaction, why should a representation made by A as to his authority not be capable of being relied on as one of the acts of holding out? There is substantial authority that it can be: see *British Thomson-Houston Co Ltd v Federated European Bank Ltd* [1932] 2 KB 176, especially at p 182 (where the only holding out was an erroneous representation by the agent that he was managing director); and the *Freeman & Lockyer* case per Lord Justice Pearson at p 499; *Hely-Hutchinson v Brayhead Ltd* [1968] 1 QB 549 per Lord Denning MR at p 593A–D. If, as I am inclined to think an agent with authority to make representations can make a representation that he has authority to enter into a transaction, then the Judge was entitled to hold, as he did, that Mr Booth, as the representative of Refson in charge of the transaction, had implied or apparent authority to make the representation that only one signature was required and that this representation was a relevant consideration in deciding whether Refson had held out Mr Booth as having authority to sign the undertaking. However, since it is not necessary to decide this point for the purposes of this appeal, I express no concluded view on it.

Kerr LJ: In this summary I have deliberately made no reference to one other matter concerning the letter of July 26, although Mr Sharobeem undoubtedly placed some reliance on it. This was Mr Booth's assurance, in answer to Mr Sharobeem's question, that he was authorized to sign the letter by himself. The recent decision of this Court in *Armagas Ltd v Mundogas SA* shows that, when a third party is aware that an agent has no actual authority to do a particular act, then the agent's untrue subsequent assurance that he has obtained the necessary authority cannot possibly invest him with any apparent authority for this purpose. In the argument before us this situation was aptly referred to as one where the agent is seeking to pull himself up by his own bootstraps. The present case is different, because it is conceded that the plaintiffs had no reason to doubt Mr Booth's authority at any point. Nevertheless, I would not, as at present advised, accept the argument of Mr Johnson QC that the plaintiffs derive some additional support from Mr Booth's assurance to Mr Sharobeem. As I see it, the issue as to Mr Booth's apparent authority must be resolved with the same result even if this question had not been asked and answered as it was, and I therefore prefer to leave this matter there.

[Lawton LJ delivered a concurring judgment.]

NOTES

1. The representation that the agent has authority must be made by the principal and not by the agent himself (*A-G for Ceylon v Silva* [1953] AC 461 at 479, PC). The representation may also be made by another (intermediate) agent with actual authority to make such a representation (Bowstead, p 287). Difficult questions arise as to whether an intermediate agent with no actual authority to make represent- ations can nevertheless have apparent authority to make such representation. Similarly, can an agent have apparent authority to make representations about his own authority?

2. In *Freeman and Lockyer v Buckhurst Park Properties Ltd* (above, p 91), Diplock LJ stated that an intermediate agent could only make a representation about another person's authority if the intermediate agent had actual authority to do the very act that he represented the other person as having authority to do (applied in *Crabtree-Vickers Pty Ltd v Australian Direct Mail Advertising and Addressing Co Pty Ltd* (1975) 133 CLR 72, High Court of Australia). This approach has been criticised as being unduly restrictive (Bowstead, pp 295–296) and there seems no good reason why an intermediate agent, who is held out by the principal as having apparent authority to do an act, should not himself be able to represent that someone else (eg a junior employee) has authority to do the same act. In most cases the intermediate agent will have apparent authority because he has usual authority which has been limited by the principal's secret reservation (*British Bank of the Middle East v Sun Life Assurance Co of Canada (UK) Ltd* [1983] 2 Lloyd's Rep 9, HL, is consistent with this view; the case is noted by J Collier [1984] CLJ 26). If an intermediate agent would not usually have such authority, it is still possible for the principal to represent that he has apparent authority to do the act, and make a representation that someone else has such authority, but in practice this will often be difficult to establish, for in such circumstances the third party would normally have been put on enquiry as to the actual limitation on the intermediate agent's authority (see note 3 below).

3. The same principles apply to the question whether an agent can ever make representations about his own authority. In principle, an agent can have apparent authority to make representations as to his own authority (*The Raffaella*, obiter, above at p 95; *First Energy (UK) Ltd v Hungarian International Bank Ltd* [1993] 2 Lloyd's Rep 194; also *Canadian Laboratory Supplies Ltd v Engelhard Industries Ltd* (1979) 97 DLR (3d) 1 at 10, Supreme Court of Canada). But such cases will be extremely rare (*Suncorp Insurance and Finance v Milano Assicurazioni SpA* [1993] 2 Lloyd's Rep 225 at 232, per Waller J). Unless the agent would usually have authority to do the act in question, it will be very difficult for the third party to rely on a specific representation of the agent's authority to act, as the third party would normally have been put on enquiry as to the actual limitation on the agent's authority (Fridman, p 111). This point is illustrated by *Armagas Ltd v Mundogas SA* [1986] AC 717. In this case, the third party knew that the agent had no general authority to enter into the transaction in question. It was held by both the Court of Appeal and the House of Lords that, with this knowledge, the third party could not rely on the agent's representation of his own authority to enter into this particular transaction, even though the principal had employed the agent to a senior position in its organisation. With regard to any specific representation of authority made by the principal, Lord Keith stated that (at 777):

> It must be a most unusual and peculiar case where an agent who is known to have no general authority to enter into transactions of a certain type can by reason of circumstances created by the principal reasonably be believed to have specific authority to enter into a particular transaction of that type. The facts in the present case fall far short of establishing such a situation.

But in *First Energy (UK) Ltd v Hungarian International Bank Ltd*, above, the Court of Appeal recently held that an agent had apparent authority to communicate his principal's approval for him to enter into a particular transaction on behalf of the principal, even though the third party was aware that the agent did not normally have authority to enter into such transactions. In that case, the agent (J) was the senior manager of the regional office of the defendant bank (HIB). The plaintiffs

(First Energy) approached J to enquire about long term finance facilities and were informed by him that he had no authority to sanction finance facilities. Whilst negotiations continued over the long-term facilities, First Energy approached J over finance for certain specific projects. J wrote to First Energy offering finance facilities for these projects and First Energy accepted that offer. But HIB refused to supply finance for the specific projects, arguing that J had no authority to make an offer of such facilities. Upholding the judgment of the trial judge, the Court of Appeal held that J had no actual or apparent authority to sanction or enter into the transaction himself, but that he did have apparent authority to communicate that the necessary authority had been obtained from HIB for him to make the offer and that J's offer letter contained a representation to that effect. The Court of Appeal held that such apparent authority arose from HIB having placed J into the position of senior manager. As senior manager, J had usual authority to sign and send letters on behalf of HIB and, therefore, he had apparent authority to represent by letter that he had obtained authorisation from HIB to make an offer on their behalf. The Court of Appeal stressed that their judgment was consistent with the reasonable expectations of the parties and that, in the circumstances, it was unrealistic to expect First Energy to have checked with HIB's Head Office in London as to whether an employee as senior as J had obtained necessary approval to make the offer. The Court of Appeal was able to distinguish *Armagas Ltd v Mundogas SA*, for in that case Lord Keith had not said as a matter of law that an apparent authority to communicate approval could never arise where there was no authority in the agent on his own to enter into the transaction.

4. Other points to note about the representation are:

(1) It can be express (oral or in writing); or implied from a course of dealing; or implied from conduct, such as putting the agent in a position that carries with it usual authority (above, p 91); or by entrusting the agent with the indicia of ownership of property (see below, p 301).

(2) It must be made to the particular third party who deals with the agent, or to the public at large when it would be expected that members of the general public would be likely to deal with the agent (*Farquharson Bros & Co v King & Co* [1902] AC 325 at 341, per Lord Lindley).

(3) It must be of fact and not of law (*Chapleo v Brunswick Permanent Building Society* (1881) 6 QBD 696).

(4) It must be that the 'agent' is authorised to act as agent and not as principal (see below, p 101).

(5) It must be made intentionally or, possibly, negligently (Bowstead, p 288; Fridman, p 104; Markesinis and Munday, p 47).

(ii) *Reliance*

There must be a causal connection between the representation and the third party's dealing with the agent. Furthermore, the third party will not be able to say he relied on the representation if he knew, or ought to have known, of the restriction on the agent's authority. In *Overbrooke Estates Ltd v Glencombe Properties Ltd* [1974] 1 WLR 1335, a purchaser of land at an auction failed to establish that the seller was bound by a misrepresentation relating to the property made by his agent (the auctioneer) before the sale. Before any contract was made, and before any representation was made, the purchaser had been in possession of the conditions of sale of the property which contained a clause to the effect that the auctioneer had no authority to give representations or warranties. Brightman J held that the purchaser 'knew, or ought to have known, that [the auctioneer] had no authority to make or give any representation or warranty in relation to this property'. He further held that a clause restricting the agent's authority was not subject to the 'reasonableness' test enshrined in s 3 of the Misrepresentation Act 1967. For further examples of when the third party will be put on notice as to any restrictions on the agent's authority, see Bowstead, pp 305–307; Fridman, pp 112–114, 196–197; Markesinis and Munday, pp 49, 156–158.

(iii) *Alteration of position*

Must the third party alter his position to his detriment? There are cases going either way (eg *Rama Corpn v Proved Tin and General Investments*, above at p 91, and *Freeman and Lockyer v Buckhurst Park (Mangal) Properties Ltd*, above at p 91 call simply for an alteration of position; *Farquharson Bros & Co v King & Co* [1902] AC 325, and *Norfolk County Council v Secretary of State for the Environment* [1973] 3 All ER 673, call for detrimental reliance). The need for detriment is consistent with the strict requirements of an estoppel, but in one of the more recent cases on apparent authority Gatehouse J held that 'The only detriment that has to be shown . . . is the entering into the contract': *The Tatra* [1990] 2 Lloyd's Rep 51 at 59.

Finally, it should be noted that the principal may be bound by a contract, even though the requirements of apparent authority are not satisfied, if he is precluded by his *subsequent* conduct from denying that the contract was made on his behalf. In *Spiro v Lintern* [1973] 1 WLR 1002, a wife contracted to sell her husband's house. The wife had no actual authority to do this and, because she appeared to be the owner of the house (not her husband's agent), she had no apparent authority. However, after the contract was entered into the husband neither stated that his wife was acting without his authority nor indicated that he was not willing for the sale to proceed. On the contrary, the husband allowed the purchaser to incur various expenses with regard to the property. In an action for specific performance of the contract, the Court of Appeal held the husband was estopped from denying that his wife had authority to sell the house on his behalf. As Buckley LJ stated (at 1011):

> If A sees B acting in the mistaken belief that A is under some binding obligation to him and in a manner consistent only with the existence of such an obligation, which would be to B's disadvantage if A were thereafter to deny the obligation, A is under a duty to B to disclose the non-existence of the supposed obligation.

Buckley LJ emphasised that detrimental reliance was necessary for this type of estoppel (contrast this with apparent authority, above) but held that the purchaser had acted to his detriment by incurring expenses. *Spiro v Lintern* has since been followed in *Worboys v Carter* [1987] 2 EGLR 1, CA.

QUESTIONS

1. In *Armagas Ltd v Mundogas SA* (above, p 97) would the third party have any remedy against the 'agent'?

2. Philip, an author, employed Alice as his secretary and instructed Alice that she was to purchase whatever she needed for her work from Trust, the local stationer, charging his account with Trust. Over a period of several months Alice regularly bought from Trust such things as paper, envelopes and typewriter ribbons. These were charged to Philip's account and Philip settled his account without question each month. Alice then ordered from Trust an electric typewriter (£200), a dictating machine (£150) and a photocopying machine (£200). These items were delivered, in accordance with Alice's instructions, to Philip's address in Trust's van, but Alice intercepted the driver before they were unloaded and told him to take them to her own lodgings, which the driver did without demur. Neither Alice nor the valuable items mentioned were ever seen again. Trust now claims £550 from Philip as the price of goods sold and delivered. Is he entitled to be paid?

(c) Usual authority

Watteau v Fenwick [1893] 1 QB 346, Queen's Bench Division

(The facts appear from the judgment of Wills J.)

Lord Coleridge CJ: The judgment which I am about to read has been written by my brother Wills, and I entirely concur in it.

Wills J: The plaintiff sues the defendants for the price of cigars supplied to the Victoria Hotel, Stockton-upon-Tees. The house was kept, not by the defendants, but by a person named Humble, whose name was over the door. The plaintiff gave credit to Humble, and to him alone, and had never heard of the defendants. The business, however, was really the defendants', and they had put Humble into it to manage it for them, and had forbidden him to buy cigars on credit. The cigars, however, were such as would usually be supplied to and dealt in at such an establishment. The learned county court judge held that the defendants were liable. I am of opinion that he was right.

There seems to be less of direct authority on the subject than one would expect. But I think that the Lord Chief Justice during the argument laid down the correct principle, viz, once it is established that the defendant was the real principal, the ordinary doctrine as to principal and agent applies – that the principal is liable for all the acts of the agent which are within the authority usually confided to an agent of that character, notwithstanding limitations, as between the principal and the agent, put upon that authority. It is said that it is only so where there has been a holding out of authority – which cannot be said of a case where the person supplying the goods knew nothing of the existence of a principal. But I do not think so. Otherwise, in every case of undisclosed principal, or at least in every case where the fact of there being a principal was undisclosed, the secret limitation of authority would prevail and defeat the action of the person dealing with the agent and then discovering that he was an agent and had a principal.

But in the case of a dormant partner it is clear law that no limitation of authority as between the dormant and active partner will avail the dormant partner as to things within the ordinary authority of a partner. The law of partnership is, on such a question, nothing but a branch of the general law of principal and agent, and it appears to me to be undisputed and conclusive on the point now under discussion.

The principle laid down by the Lord Chief Justice, and acted upon by the learned county court judge, appears to be identical with that enunciated in the judgments of Cockburn CJ and Mellor J in *Edmunds v Bushell* ((1865) LR 1 QB 97), the circumstances of which case, though not identical with those of the present, come very near to them. There was no holding out, as the plaintiff knew nothing of the defendant. I appreciate the distinction drawn by Mr Finlay in his argument, but the principle laid down in the judgments referred to, if correct, abundantly covers the present case. I cannot find that any doubt has ever been expressed that it is correct, and I think it is right, and that very mischievous consequences would often result if that principle were not upheld.

In my opinion this appeal ought to be dismissed with costs.

Appeal dismissed.

'The Demise of Watteau v Fenwick: Sign-O-Lite Ltd v Metropolitan Life Insurance Co' by G H L Fridman (1991) 70 Can Bar Rev 329, pp 329–333

Introduction

In the law of agency the most difficult and controversial decision is that of Wills J in *Watteau v Fenwick.*[1] It has been criticised by commentators[2] and distinguished or not followed by judges.[3] Several years ago an English judge described the case as puzzling, the argument for the plaintiff as fallacious, and the doctrine of the case as one that courts should be wary about following.[4]

The case concerned the liability of an undisclosed principal for unauthorised contracts entered into by the principal's agent. . . .

The problem with this case is the logical one of saying that someone who is not known to be an agent can be regarded as having been held out by a principal as having an apparent authority, culled from what was usual or customary in the business in which the agent was engaged,[5] to contract in the way he did, although he lacked any actual authority to do so.[6] Since the doctrine of apparent authority is based upon a principal's holding out someone as his agent with authority to act on his, that is, the principal's behalf,[7] it is difficult to conceive of a case of undisclosed agency as involving the application of the doctrine of apparent authority. One who is not apparently an agent cannot logically be said to have been held out as having any authority at all, whether based on custom, what is usual, or otherwise. The only logical way in which such a conclusion can be reached is by starting from the premise that anyone who employs an agent and does not disclose that he is an agent, inferentially accepts liability for any and every transaction into which the undisclosed agent enters as long as such transaction has a connection with the business or other activity which has been entrusted to the undisclosed agent. The difficulty about this, however, from a practical, if not a logical point of view, is that it would expose the undisclosed principal to a potentially very wide, almost limitless liability for what the agent does. This might protect third parties transacting with the agent. It would mean that the principal has accepted a very great risk by employing an agent and allowing him to appear to be the principal.[8]

Not surprisingly other decisions have taken a contrary view of such a situation. They have held that the act of an undisclosed agent would not make an undisclosed principal liable, even where the act or acts in question related to the authority which, unknown to the third party, had been given to the agent.[9] These decisions hold that, if there has been a limitation placed on the agent's authority by the undisclosed principal, this will bind the third party dealing with the agent, even though the third party was unaware that he was dealing with an agent, and, therefore, was necessarily ignorant of any such limitations. What is surprising, however, is that no decision has firmly and decisively held that *Watteau v Fenwick* was wrong and should be discredited. Such a decision can now be found in the judgment of the British Columbia Court of Appeal in *Sign-O-Lite Plastics Ltd v Metropolitan Life Insurance Co.*[10]

Sign-O-Lite Plastics Ltd v Metropolitan Life Insurance Co

The facts in this case were as follows. In 1978 the plaintiff contracted with Calbax Properties Ltd for the renting of an electronic sign to be installed and maintained by the plaintiff at the Market Mall shopping centre in Calgary. This rental agreement was to last for 61 months. It contained a clause providing for automatic renewal for a further term of 60 months in the event that neither party communicated a contrary intention to the other, in writing, more than 30 days before the end of the first term. By virtue of that clause the agreement was renewed in 1984. Prior to that date, however, the defendant, in two stages, acquired ownership of the company which owned and controlled the shopping mall in which the sign was displayed. As part of this transaction the defendants agreed to assume the 1978 rental agreement between Calbax Properties Ltd and the plaintiff. When the defendant acquired ownership of the mall it was agreed with The Baxter Group Ltd that the latter should manage the mall as agent for the defendant. For that purpose the Baxter Group Ltd was given limited authority to enter into contracts on behalf of its principal, the defendants. The plaintiff knew nothing of the change of ownership of the mall. In other words the plaintiff was unaware of the existence of an undiscloped principal of The Baxter Group Ltd. In 1985, after the automatic renewal of the rental agreement in accordance with the original terms of 1978, The Baxter Group Ltd entered into a new rental agreement with the plaintiff intended by both parties to replace the original agreement. At that time the plaintiff believed, as it had every reason to believe, that it was dealing with a different corporate form of the same owner with which the plaintiff had originally contracted in 1978. The new agreement was one which The Baxter Group Ltd had not authority to contract. This was because (a) it did not disclose that The Baxter Group Ltd was acting as agent for the defendant, and (b) it did not provide for cancellation on 60 days' notice. As a result of various later transactions, which are not relevant to the problem in this case, the plaintiff eventually sued the defendant for damages for breach of contract, that is, the contract entered into in 1985 (not the original contract of 1978). At the trial the plaintiff was unsuccessful in establishing liability under the 1985 agreement, and was awarded damages on the 1978 contract. The defendant appealed and the plaintiff cross-appealed.

Two issues were before the court. The first was whether the defendant could be liable, as an undisclosed principal. This raised directly the question whether *Watteau v Fenwick* was good law and was part of the law in British Columbia. After considering the language of Wills J in *Watteau v Fenwick* and the subsequent case-law in which that decision had been rejected in Ontario[11] (as well as in Alberta[12]), Wood JA delivering the judgment of the court, declared that the reports he had researched were 'bereft of any hint that *Watteau v Fenwick* should be considered good law'.[13] In view of the decisions to which reference has been made earlier, it is hardly a matter for surprise that Wood JA should have reached that conclusion.

Wills J had said in 1883 that once it was established that a defendant was a real principal, the ordinary doctrine as to principal and agent applied – that the principal was liable for all the acts of the agent that were within the authority usually confided to an agent of that character, notwithstanding limitations as between the principal and agent upon that authority.[14] In 1919 in *McLaughlin v Gentles*,[15] Hodgins JA of the Ontario Court of Appeal said:

> It seems to me to be straining the doctrine of ostensible agency or holding out to apply it in a case where the fact of agency and the holding out were unknown to the person dealing with the so-called agent at the time, and to permit that person, when he discovered that his purchaser was only an agent, to recover against the principal, on the theory that the latter was estopped from denying that he authorized the purchase. It appears to me that the fact that there was a limitation of authority is at least as important as the fact that the purchaser was an agent.

For reasons previously mentioned, the opinion of Hodgins JA is undoubtedly preferable to that of Wills J. But, as Wood JA said in the *Sign-O-Lite* case:[16]

> It is astonishing that, after all these years, an authority of such doubtful origin, and of such unanimously unfavourable reputation, should still be exhibiting signs of life and disturbing the peace of mind of trial judges.

It was time to end any uncertainty that might linger as to its proper place in the law of agency. He had no difficulty in concluding that the doctrine set out in *Watteau v Fenwick* was not part of the law of British Columbia. On that ground the plaintiff's cross-appeal failed: the defendant was not liable as an undisclosed principal on the 1985 contract.

Although this case dealt only with the law of British Columbia, it does not appear unreasonable to conclude, in light of this decision and the earlier Ontario cases referred to therein, that in common law Canada generally, whatever the state of the law in England, the doctrine of *Watteau v Fenwick* is defunct. It is to be hoped that the same will ultimately prove to be the situation in England. There is every indication that when the time comes for a court to do so, it will give the same short shrift to the decision of Wills J as it has now received at the hands of the British Columbia Court of Appeal.

---

1 [1893] 1 QB 346 (QBD).

2 F M B Reynolds *Bowstead on Agency* (15th ed, 1985), pp 95–97, 317–320; G H L Fridman, *Law of Agency* (6th ed, 1990), pp 61–66; R Powell *Law of Agency* (2d ed, 1961), pp 75–78; S J Stoljar *Law of Agency* (6th ed, 1990), pp 60–66; A L Goodhart and C J Hamson, *Undisclosed Principals in Contract* (1932) 4 Camb LJ 320; J A Hornby *The Usual Authority of An Agent* [1961] Camb LJ 239.

3 *Miles v McIlwraith* (1883) 8 App Cas 120 (PC); *Becherer v Asher* (1896) 23 OAR 202 (Ont CA);

McLaughlin v Gentles (1919) 51 DLR 383, 46 OLR 477 (Ont App Div); *Massey Harris Co Ltd v Bond* [1930] 2 DLR 57, [1930] 1 WWR 72 (Alta SC). See also *Johnston v Reading* (1893) 9 TLR 200 (QBD); *Lloyd's Bank v Suisse Bankverein* (1912) 107 LT 309, aff'd (1913) 108 LT 143 (CA); *Jerome v Bentley* [1952] 2 All ER 114 (QBD); *International Paper Co v Spicer* (1906) 4 CLR 739 (Aust HC).
4 *Rhodian River Shipping Co SA v Halla Maritime Corp* [1984] 1 Lloyds Rep 373, at pp 378–379 (QBD), per Bingham J. Curiously, this case was not referred to in the British Columbia decision that is now under discussion.
5 Bowstead, op cit, footnote 2, pp 93–97, 111–118; Fridman, op cit, footnote 2, pp 60–69, 107–114.
6 On actual authority see Bowstead, ibid, pp 92–93; Fridman, ibid, pp 53–55.
7 See the authorities cited, supra, footnote 5.
8 It also seems to be rejected by the decision of the House of Lords in *Keighley Maxsted & Co v Durant* [1901] AC 240, on which see Bowstead, op cit, footnote 2, pp 57–58; Fridman, op cit, footnote 2, pp 78–79.
9 See, eg, *McLaughlin v Gentles*, supra, footnote 3: cf *Keighley Maxsted & Co v Durant*, supra, footnote 8.
10 (1990) 73 DLR (4th) 541, 49 BCLR (2d) 183 (BCCA).
11 *McLaughlin v Gentles*, supra, footnote 3; *Massey Harris Co Ltd v Bond*, supra, footnote 3.
12 *Massey Harris Co Ltd v Bond*, ibid.
13 Supra, footnote 10, at pp 548 (DLR), 191 (BCLR).
14 *Watteau v Fenwick*, supra, footnote 1, at pp 348–349.
15 Supra, footnote 3, at pp 394–395 (DLR), 490 (OLR).
16 Supra, footnote 10, at pp 548 (DLR), 191 (BCLR).

NOTES

1. A number of theories have been advanced in an attempt to explain *Watteau v Fenwick*: apparent authority (A L Goodhart and C J Hamson (1931) 4 CLJ 320 at 336; but see Fridman's response: above, p 101); 'inherent agency power' (*Restatement of the Law of Agency* (2nd ed, 1958), paras 8A, 140; but see M Conant (1968) 47 Nebraska LR 678, 686); an independent type of usual authority (Bowstead, pp 95–97; Powell, op cit, p 78; but see also Bowstead, p 319); by analogy with the doctrine of vicarious liability in tort (Treitel, op cit, p 620; but see J Collier [1985] CLJ 363 at p 365; and *Chitty on Contracts* (26th ed, 1989) Vol 2, para 2550); and as an extension of the doctrine of apparent ownership (M Conant, op cit, pp 687–688; but see J Hornby [1961] CLJ 239 at p 246). All these theories are open to criticism and none provides a satisfactory explanation of the case.

2. It is submitted that there are good policy reasons against holding an undisclosed principal liable to a third party when the principal's agent exceeds his actual authority (cf Collier, op cit, p 364, who describes *Watteau v Fenwick* as 'eminently just'). It must be remembered that *Watteau v Fenwick* places the undisclosed principal under a personal liability, it does not give him any right to sue the third party (Bowstead, p 320; Markesinis and Munday, p 36). Furthermore, because the agent exceeds his actual authority the principal cannot sue the third party under the doctrine of undisclosed principal (below, p 145); neither can he rely on ratification of the agent's acts, as an undisclosed principal cannot ratify (below, p 110). It seems unjust that the principal should have a liability without a right of action, especially when he never wished to be bound by such a contract in the first place. However, by analogy with the doctrine of apparent authority, if the principal is sued on a contract made by his agent, he can probably make counterclaims as well as adduce defences, as opposed to suing on the contract of his own motion (see above, p 95). The issue remains undecided.

3. Whatever the faults of the decision, *Watteau v Fenwick* has not been overruled in England. However, the limits of the case are clear. It will not apply if (1) the agent acts for himself and not for his principal (this is why *Kinahan & Co Ltd v Parry*

[1910] 2 KB 389, where *Watteau v Fenwick* was followed, was reversed on appeal: [1911] 1 KB 459); or (2) the third party knows, or ought reasonably to know, of the restriction on the agent's authority (*Daun v Simmins* (1879) 41 LT 783, CA).

QUESTION

Pippa appoints Audrey as her general manager for the purchase of houses in Leeds, instructing Audrey, however, not to disclose the existence of the agency, and not to purchase except on a surveyor's report. Audrey discloses her position to Tessa, withholding, however, the requirement of a surveyor's report and purchases houses in Leeds from Tessa as agent for Pippa without a surveyor's report. Is Pippa liable to Tessa for the price of the houses? See Montrose (1939) 17 Can Bar Rev 693 at pp 710–711; Hornby [1961] CLJ 239 at p 240 fn.

(d) Authority by operation of law

(i) *Agency of necessity*

Bowstead on Agency (15th ed, 1985), p 84

Agency of necessity arises by operation of law in certain cases where a person is faced with an emergency in which the property or interests of another are in imminent jeopardy and it becomes necessary, in order to preserve the property or interest, to act for that person without authority.

China-Pacific SA v Food Corpn of India, The Winson [1982] AC 939, House of Lords

The defendant cargo owner chartered a ship to carry wheat from the United States to Bombay. During the voyage the ship stranded on a reef. The ship's managing agents (in effect the ship's master) then entered into a Lloyd's Standard Form of Salvage Agreement No Cure – No Pay (known as the Lloyd's open form) with the plaintiffs, who were professional salvors. To assist the salvage operation, the salvors unloaded several parcels of wheat and shipped them to Manilla. To protect the wheat from deterioration, the salvors contracted with various depositaries to warehouse it at the salvors' expense. The salvors then looked to the cargo owner for reimbursement of these storage charges. Lloyd J held the cargo owner liable to reimburse the salvors but his decision was reversed by the Court of Appeal. The House of Lords upheld the salvors' appeal against the Court of Appeal's ruling and restored the judgment of Lloyd J.

Lord Diplock: Lloyd's open form is expressed by clause 16 to be signed by the master 'as agent for the vessel her cargo and freight and the respective owners thereof and binds each (but not the one for the other or himself personally) to the due performance thereof.' The legal nature of the relationship between the master and the owner of the cargo aboard the vessel in signing the agreement on the latter's behalf is often though not invariably an agency of necessity. It arises only when salvage services by a third party are necessary for the preservation of the cargo. Whether one person is entitled to act as agent of necessity for another person is relevant to the question whether circumstances exist which in law have the effect of conferring on him authority to create contractual rights and obligations between that other person and a third party that are directly enforceable by each against the other. It would, I think, be an aid to clarity of legal thinking if the use of the expression 'agent of necessity' were confined to contexts in which this was the question to be determined and not extended, as it often is, to cases where the only relevant question is whether a person who without obtaining instructions from the owner of goods incurs expense in taking steps that are reasonably necessary for their preservation is in law entitled to recover from the owner of the goods the reasonable expenses incurred by him in taking those steps. Its use in this wider sense may, I think, have led to some confusion in the instant case, since where reimbursement is the only relevant question all of those conditions that must be fulfilled in order to entitle one person to act on behalf of another in creating direct contractual relationships between that other person and a third party may not necessarily apply.

In the instant case it is not disputed that when the Lloyd's open form was signed on January 22, 1975, the circumstances that existed at that time were such as entitled the master to enter into the agreement on the cargo owner's behalf as its agent of necessity. The rendering of salvage services under the Lloyd's open agreement does not usually involve the salvor's taking possession of the vessel or its cargo from the shipowner; the shipowner remains in possession of both ship and cargo while salvage services are being carried out by the salvors on the ship. But salvage services may involve the transfer of possession of cargo from the shipowner to the salvors, and will do so in a case of stranding as respects part of the cargo if it becomes necessary to lighten the vessel in order to refloat her. When, in the course of salvage operations cargo is off-loaded from the vessel by which the contract of carriage was being performed and conveyed separately from that vessel to a place of safety by means (in the instant case, barges) provided by the salvor, the direct relationship of bailor and bailee is created between cargo owner and salvor as soon as the cargo is loaded on vessels provided by the salvor to convey it to a place of safety; and all the mutual rights and duties attaching to that relationship at common law apply, save in so far as any of them are inconsistent with the express terms of the Lloyd's open agreement. . . .

My Lords, in the courts below and in argument before your Lordships there has been some discussion as to whether on their obtaining possession of the cargo from the shipowner the relationship of the salvors to the cargo owner was that of bailee or sub-bailee. A sub-bailee is one to whom actual possession of goods is transferred by someone who is not himself the owner of the goods but has a present right to possession of them as bailee of the owner. In the instant case Lloyd J and the Court of Appeal were of the view that the salvors were bailees of the cargo owner, and this was, in my view also, plainly right. They would only be sub-bailees of the cargo owner if the contract to render salvage services to the cargo under Lloyd's open form had been signed by the master as agent for the shipowner only. This was plainly not the case. The contract was one under which the salvors' remuneration in respect of salvage services to the cargo was a liability of the cargo owner, not of the shipowner, and security for such remuneration could be required by the salvors to be given by the cargo owner alone; so the only consideration for salvage services rendered to the cargo by salvors under Lloyd's open form came from the cargo owner. The only sub-bailments involved in the instant case were those effected by the salvors themselves with the depositaries when they deposited the salved wheat for safe keeping at Manila. . . .

Upon the assumption, whether correct or not, to which I have already referred as being that upon which this case has been argued throughout, that the salvage services which the salvors had contracted to render to the cargo owner came to an end as respects each parcel of salved wheat when it arrived at a place of safety in Manila Harbour, the legal relationship of bailor and bailee between cargo owner and salvors nevertheless continued to subsist until possession of the wheat was accepted by the cargo owner from the depositaries who had been the salvors' sub-bailees. Subject always to the question of the salvors' right to the provision of security before removal of the salved wheat from Manila, with which I shall deal separately later, the bailment which up to the conclusion of the salvage services had been a bailment for valuable consideration became a gratuitous bailment; and so long as that relationship of bailor and bailee continued to subsist the salvors, under the ordinary principles of the law of bailment too well known and too well-established to call for any citation of authority, owed a duty of care to the cargo owner to take such measures to preserve the salved wheat from deterioration by exposure to the elements as a man of ordinary prudence would take for the preservation of his own property. For any breach of such duty the bailee is liable to his bailor in damages for any diminution in value of the goods consequent upon his failure to take such measures; and if he fulfils that duty he has, in my view, a correlative right to charge the owner of the goods with the expenses reasonably incurred in doing so.

My Lords, as I have already said, there is not any direct authority as to the existence of this correlative right to reimbursement of expenses in the specific case of a salvor who retains possession of cargo after the salvage services rendered by him to that cargo have ended; but Lloyd J discerned what he considered to be helpful analogous applications of the principle of the bailee's right to reimbursement in *Cargo ex Argos* (1873) LR 5 PC 134, from which I have taken the expression 'correlative right,' and in *Great Northern Rly Co v Swaffield* (1874) LR 9 Exch 132. Both these were cases of carriage of goods in which the carrier/bailee was left in possession of the goods after the carriage contracted for had terminated. Steps necessary for the preservation of the goods were taken by the bailee in default of any instructions from owner/bailor to do otherwise. To these authorities I would add *Notara v Henderson* (1872) LR 7 QB 225, in which the bailee was held liable in damages for breach of his duty to take steps necessary for the preservation of the goods, and the Scots case of *Garriock v Walker* (1873) 1 R 100 in which the bailee recovered the expenses incurred by him in taking such steps. Although in both these cases, which involved carriage of goods by sea, the steps for the prevention of deterioration of the cargo needed to be taken before the contract voyage was completed, the significance of the Scots case is that the cargo owner was on the spot when the steps were taken by the carrier/bailee and did not acquiesce in them. Nevertheless, he took the benefit of them by taking delivery of the cargo thus preserved at the conclusion of the voyage.

In the instant case the cargo owner was kept informed of the salvors' intentions as to the storage of the salved wheat upon its arrival in Manila; it made no alternative proposals; it made no request to the salvors for delivery of any of the wheat after its arrival at Manila, and a request made by the salvors to the cargo owner through their solicitors on February 25, 1975, after the arrival of the second of the six parcels, to take delivery of the parcels of salved wheat on arrival at Manila remained unanswered and uncomplied with until after notice of abandonment of the charter voyage had been received by the cargo owner from the shipowner.

The failure of the cargo owner as bailor to give any instructions to the salvors as its bailee although it was fully apprised of the need to store the salved wheat under cover on arrival at Manila if it was to be preserved from rapid deterioration was, in the view of Lloyd J, sufficient to attract the application of the principle to which I have referred above and to entitle the salvors to recover from the cargo owner their expenses in taking measures necessary for its preservation. For my part I think that in this he was right and the Court of Appeal, who took the contrary view, were wrong. It is, of course, true that in English law a mere stranger cannot compel an owner of goods to pay for a benefit bestowed upon him against his will; but this latter principle does not apply where there is a pre-existing legal relationship between the owner of the goods and the bestower of the benefit, such as that of bailor and bailee, which imposes upon the bestower of the benefit a legal duty of care in respect of the preservation of the goods that is owed by him to their owner.

In the Court of Appeal Megaw LJ, as I understand his judgment, with which Bridge and Cumming-Bruce LJJ expressed agreement, was of opinion that, in order to entitle the salvors to reimbursement of the expenses incurred by them in storing the salvaged wheat at Manila up to April 24, 1975, they would have to show not only that, looked at objectively, the measures that they took were necessary to preserve it from rapid deterioration, but, in addition, that it was impossible for them to communicate with the cargo owner to obtain from him such instructions (if any) as he might want to give. My Lords, it may be that this would have been so if the question in the instant case had been whether the depositaries could have sued the cargo owner directly for their contractual storage charges on the ground that the cargo owner was party as principal to the contracts of storage made on its behalf by the salvors as its agents of necessity; for English law is economical in recognising situations that give rise to agency of necessity. In my view, inability to communicate with the owner of the goods is not a condition precedent to the bailee's own right to reimbursement of his expenses. The bailor's failure to give any instructions when apprised of the situation is sufficient.

So, on the cargo owner's main propositions of law in this appeal, I think it fails and that on these points the Court of Appeal was wrong in reversing Lloyd J.

Lord Simon of Glaisdale held that the salvors' right of reimbursement arose by implication from the Lloyd's open form agreement and from the common law of bailment. He continued:

Agency of necessity. Lloyd J decided in favour of the salvor on the further ground that he was the cargo owner's agent of necessity and as such entitled to reimbursement of the expenses in issue. The Court of Appeal held that there was no agency of necessity.

One of the ways in which an agency of necessity can arise is where A is in possession of goods the property of B, and an emergency arises which places those goods in imminent jeopardy: If A cannot obtain instructions from B as to how he should act in such circumstances, A is bound to take without authority such action in relation to the goods as B, as a prudent owner, would himself have taken in the circumstances. The relationship between A and B is then known as an 'agency of necessity,' A being the agent and B the principal. This was the situation described by Lloyd J and denied by the Court of Appeal.

Issues as to agency of necessity generally arise forensically when A enters into a contract with C in relation to the goods, the question being whether B is bound by that contract. The purely terminological suggestion that, in order to avoid confusion, 'agent of necessity' should be confined to such contractual situations does not involve that other relevant general incidents of agency are excluded from the relationship between A and B. In particular, if A incurs reasonable expenses in safeguarding B's goods in a situation of emergency, A is entitled to be reimbursed by B: . . .

To confine 'agent of necessity' terminologically to the contractual situations is justified by the fact that the law of bailment will often resolve any issue between alleged principal and agent of necessity, as it has done here. But sometimes the law of agency will be more useful: for example, if available here it would obviate any problem about the correlation of performance of a duty of care with a claim for reimbursement, since an agent is undoubtedly entitled to an indemnity for expenses incurred reasonably to benefit his principal.

However, I respectfully agree with the Court of Appeal [1981] QB 403, 424 that

> The relevant time, for the purpose of considering whether there was a necessity, or an emergency . . . is . . . the time when the existence of the supposed emergency became apparent. The emergency would be the arrival, or expected arrival, of salved cargo at Manila, with no arrangements for its off-loading or for its preservation in proper storage having been made or put in hand. There never was, so far as one can ascertain from the evidential matter here, such an emergency.

In addition to the factual difficulty in treating the case as one of agency of necessity, there are legal difficulties in the way of the salvor. For an agency of necessity to arise, the action taken must be necessary for the protection of the interests of the alleged principal, not of the agent; the alleged agent must have acted bona fide in the interests of the alleged principal: . . . The Court of Appeal [1981] QB 403, 425 held that the salvor's purpose in storing the salved cargo was to maintain his lien on it. This was assuredly at least in part the salvor's purpose. The law does not seem to have determined in this context what ensues where interests are manifold or motives mixed: it may well be that the court will look to the interest mainly served or to the dominant motive. In view of the opinion I have formed on the rights arising by implication from the Lloyd's open form and from the common law bailment, it is unnecessary to come to any conclusion on these issues.

[Lord Keith of Kinkel, Lord Roskill and Lord Brandon of Oakbrook concurred with Lord Diplock.]

NOTES

1. Traditionally, the courts have not distinguished between cases where an agent of necessity creates a contractual relationship between his principal and a third party and those where the agent of necessity simply seeks reimbursement from the principal, or looks to defend an action for wrongful interference with the principal's goods. However, the distinction was made by Lord Diplock in *The Winson* and we shall adopt it here (as does Bowstead, pp 85–90; but you are advised to read Treitel, op cit, p 625 and A Burrows, *The Law of Restitution* (1993), pp 235–236, for a contrary view).

2. (a) *True agents of necessity.* In such cases the agent has power to affect the legal relations of his principal, whether or not there was an existing agency relationship between them (Bowstead, p 85). The agent may contract with third parties on behalf of his principal and he may dispose of his principal's property. The agent will have a defence if sued by his principal and he may be able to claim reimbursement from the principal for expenses incurred. However, agency of necessity will only arise if:

(1) it is impracticable for the agent to communicate with the principal (*Springer v Great Western Rly Co* [1921] 1 KB 257 at 265, per Bankes LJ);
(2) the action is necessary for the benefit of the principal (*Prager v Blatspiel, Stamp and Heacock Ltd* [1924] 1 KB 566 at 571, per McCardie J);
(3) the agent acts bona fide in the interests of the principal (*Prager v Blatspiel*, above, at 572); and
(4) the action taken by the agent is reasonable and prudent (*F v West Berkshire Health Authority* [1989] 2 All ER 545 at 566, per Lord Goff).

The traditional example of an agent of necessity is the master of a ship who acts in an emergency to save the ship or the cargo (*Hawtayne v Bourne* (1841) 7 M & W 595 at 599, per Parke B). Sometimes it is possible to explain the master's agency in terms of implied actual authority, eg when he signs a salvage contract on behalf of the shipowner (*The Unique Mariner* [1978] 1 Lloyd's Rep 438). On other occasions it may only be possible to explain the master's action in terms of necessity, eg in *The Choko Star* [1990] 1 Lloyd's Rep 516 the Court of Appeal stressed that the ship's master had no implied actual authority to sign a salvage agreement on behalf of cargo owners, but he could do so as an agent of necessity (noted by R J C Munday [1991] LMCLQ 1; and I Brown (1992) 55 MLR 414).

There has been considerable debate as to whether agency of necessity is restricted to cases of the carriage of goods by sea. For conflicting dicta, see *Prager v Blatspiel, Stamp and Heacock Ltd* [1924] 1 KB 566 at 569–571, per McCardie J; and *Jebara v Ottoman Bank* [1927] 2 KB 254 at 270–271, per Scrutton LJ. However, it has been established that agency of necessity also extends to the carriage or storage of perishable goods or livestock on land (*Great Northern Rly Co v Swaffield* (1874) LR 9 Exch 132; *Sachs v Miklos* [1948] 2 KB 23) and there seems no reason why non-perishable goods should not be included in this category, although such cases are likely to be rare. The dicta of Lord Simon in *The Winson* appears to support this broader approach (above, p 107; see also Fridman, p 127). See also ss 12, 13 and Sch 1 of the Torts (Interference with Goods) Act 1977.

3. (b) *Agents who act for another in circumstances of necessity and seek reimbursement or look to defend themselves against an action for interference with the principal's property.* The Winson provides an example of this type of agent. Lord Diplock did not think it necessary that such an agent need comply with all the strict rules as apply to true agents of necessity (above, p 105) and this view is tenatively supported by Bowstead (pp 88–89). Whether this type of agency is confined to situations where there it is a pre-existing relationship (contractual or otherwise) between the principal and agent is a difficult question to answer. It is really a question for the law of restitution. In *The Winson* such a relationship existed, ie that of bailor and bailee, and it does seem that in the absence of a pre-existing relationship, there is no general principle (outside the law of maritime salvage) entitling a person who protects or benefits the property of another to seek reimbursement or claim a lien (see Chitty, op cit, para 2525). The long established right of an acceptor of a bill of exchange for honour to seek reimbursement from the drawer would appear to be an exception to this general rule (Bills of Exchange Act 1882, s 68(5)). On the restitutionary rights of the 'necessitous intervener', see generally Goff and Jones *The Law of Restitution* (4th ed, 1993), Ch 15; P Birks *Introduction to the Law of Restitution* (revised paperback edn, 1989), pp 193–202; Burrows, op cit, Ch 8; and also F Rose (1989) 9 OJLS 167.

(ii) *Agency arising from cohabitation*

There is a rebuttable presumption that a wife has authority to pledge her husband's credit for necessaries. The presumption arises from cohabitation and operates even though the couple are not lawfully married. See Fridman, p 135; Markesinis and Munday, pp 63–65; cf Treitel, op cit, pp 631–614.

QUESTION

'Agency by estoppel is really agency by operation of law' (Fridman). Discuss. See Fridman, pp 15, 119–120.

(e) Ratification

If a person (the 'agent') acts without authority, or exceeds his authority, his actions cannot bind the person (the 'principal') on whose behalf he purports to act. Subsequently, however, the principal may ratify the agent's acts. Ratification validates the agent's actions with effect from the time those actions took place. As Lord Sterndale MR stated in *Koenigsblatt v Sweet* [1923] 2 Ch 314 at 325: 'Ratification . . . is equivalent to an antecedent authority'.

Ratification may be express or implied from the principal's unequivocal conduct. If ratification is to be implied from the principal's conduct, he must usually be shown to have had full knowledge of the agent's unauthorised acts and a real choice as to whether or not he wished to adopt them (*The Bonita; The Charlotte* (1861) 1 Lush 252). However, a principal with incomplete knowledge may be held to have ratified the unauthorised acts of his agent if it can be shown that he took a risk as to how the circumstances might turn out (*Marsh v Joseph* [1897] 1 Ch 213; see also Fridman, pp 81–82). Silence or inactivity may also amount to ratification, at least where the principal is aware of all the material facts and appreciated that he was being regarded as having accepted the position of principal, and he takes no steps to disown that character within a reasonable time, or adopts no means of asserting his rights at the earliest possible time (*Suncorp Insurance and Finance v*

Milano Assicurazioni SpA [1993] 2 Lloyd's Rep 225 at 234–235, per Waller J; cf *Crampsey v Deveney* (1969) 2 DLR (3d) 161 at 164, per Judson J). The adoption of part of a transaction operates as a ratification of the whole (*Suncorp v Milano,* above, at 235).

The principal can only ratify acts which the agent purported to do on the principal's behalf. As the next case illustrates, if the agent purports to act on his own behalf the principal cannot ratify.

Keighley, Maxsted & Co v Durant [1901] AC 240, House of Lords

Keighley, Maxstead & Co (KM) instructed Roberts, a corn merchant, to buy wheat at a certain price on the joint account of themselves and Roberts. Roberts could not buy at this price, but he agreed to purchase wheat from Durant at a higher price. Although Roberts intended to buy the wheat on behalf of himself and KM, he bought it in his own name without informing Durant that he was also acting for KM. KM then purported to ratify the agreement. The price was not paid to Durant who claimed to hold KM liable on the contract. Day J dismissed the action, but he was reversed by the Court of Appeal. The House of Lords allowed an appeal from the Court of Appeal's decision.

Lord Macnaghten: As a general rule, only persons who are parties to a contract, acting either by themselves or by an authorized agent, can sue or be sued on the contract. A stranger cannot enforce the contract, nor can it be enforced against a stranger. That is the rule; but there are exceptions. The most remarkable exception, I think, results from the doctrine of ratification as established in English law. That doctrine is thus stated by Tindal CJ in *Wilson v Tumman* ((1843) 6 Man & G 236 at 242): 'That an act done, *for another,* by a person, not assuming to act for himself, but for such other person, though without any precedent authority whatever, becomes the act of the principal, if subsequently ratified by him, is the known and well-established rule of law. In that case the principal is bound by the act, whether it be for his detriment or his advantage, and whether it be founded on a tort or on a contract, to the same effect as by, and with all the consequences which follow from, the same act done by his *previous* authority.' And so by a wholesome and convenient fiction, a person ratifying the act of another, who, without authority, has made a contract openly and avowedly on his behalf, is deemed to be, though in fact he was not, a party to the contract. Does the fiction cover the case of a person who makes no avowal at all, but assumes to act for himself and for no one else? If Tindal CJ's statement of the law is accurate, it would seem to exclude the case of a person who may intend to act for another, but at the same time keeps his intention locked up in his own breast; for it cannot be said that a person who so conducts himself does assume to act for anybody but himself. But ought the doctrine of ratification to be extended to such a case? On principle I should say certainly not. It is, I think, a well-established principle in English law that civil obligations are not to be created by, or founded upon, undisclosed intentions. That is a very old principle. Lord Blackburn, enforcing it in the case of *Brogden v Metropolitan Rly Co* ((1877) 2 App Cas 666 at 692), traces it back to the year-books of Edward IV (17 Edw 4, 2, pl 2) and to a quaint judgment of Brian CJ: 'It is common learning,' said that Chief Justice, who was a great authority in those days, 'that the thought of a man is not triable, for the Devil has not knowledge of man's thoughts.'

Sir E Fry quotes the same observation in his work on Specific Performance, s 295, p 133, 3rd ed. It is, I think, a sound maxim – at least, in its legal aspect: and in my opinion it is not to be put aside or disregarded merely because it may be that, in a case like the present, no injustice might be done to the actual parties to the contract by giving effect to the undisclosed intentions of a would-be agent.

Lord Shand: The question which arises on this state of the facts is whether, where a person who has avowedly made a contract for himself (1) without a suggestion that he is acting to any extent for another (an undisclosed principal), and (2) without any authority to act for another, can effectually bind a third party as principal, or as a joint obligant with himself, to the person with whom he contracted, by the fact that in his own mind merely he made a contract in the hope and expectation that his contract would be ratified or shared by the person as to whom he entertained that hope and expectation. I am clearly of opinion, with all respect to the majority of the Court of Appeal, that he cannot. The only contract actually made is by the person himself and for himself, and it seems to me to be conclusive against the argument for the respondents, that if their reasoning were sound it would be in his power, on an averment of what was passing in his own mind, to make the contract afterwards either one for himself only, as in fact it was, or one affecting or binding on another as a contracting party, even although he had no authority for this. The result would be to give one of two contracting parties in his option, merely from what was passing in his own mind and not disclosed, the power of saying the contract was his alone, or a contract in which others were bound with him. That, I think, he certainly cannot do in any case where he had no authority, when he made the contract, to bind any one but himself.

Lord Davey: The argument seems to be that as the law permits an undisclosed principal, on whose behalf a contract has been made, to sue and be sued on the contract, and as the effect of ratification is equivalent to a previous mandate, a person who ratifies a contract intended but not expressed to be made on his behalf is in the same position as any other undisclosed principal. Further, it is said that whether the intention of the contractor be expressed or not, its existence is mere matter of evidence, and once it is proved the conclusion ought to follow. Romer LJ held that on principle it ought to be held that ratification (in the case before the Court) is possible, and that to hold the contrary would be to establish an anomaly in the law, and moreover a useless one. My Lords, I cannot agree. There is a wide difference between an agency existing at the date of the contract which is susceptible of proof, and a repudiation of which by the agent would be fraudulent, and an intention locked up in the mind of the contractor, which he may either abandon or act on at his own pleasure, and the ascertainment of which involves an inquiry into the state of his mind at the date of the contract. Where the intention to contract on behalf of another is expressed in the contract, it passes from the region of speculation into that of fact, and becomes irrevocable. In what sense, it may be asked, does a man contract for another, when it depends on his own will whether he will give that other the benefit of the contract or not? In the next place, the rule which permits an undisclosed principal to sue and be sued on a contract to which he is not a party, though well settled, is itself an anomaly, and to extend it to the case of a person who accepts the benefit of an undisclosed intention of a party to the contract would, in my opinion, be adding another anomaly to the law, and not correcting an anomaly.

Lord Lindley: That ratification when it exists is equivalent to a previous authority is true enough (subject to some exceptions which need not be referred to). But, before the one expression can be substituted for the other, care must be taken that ratification is established.

It was strongly contended that there was no reason why the doctrine of ratification should not apply to undisclosed principals in general, and that no one could be injured by it if it were so applied. I am not convinced of this. But in this case there is no evidence in existence that, at the time when Roberts made his contract, he was in fact acting, as distinguished from intending to act, for the defendants as possible principals, and the decision appealed from, if affirmed, would introduce a very dangerous doctrine. It would enable one person to make a contract between two others by creating a principal and saying what his own undisclosed intentions were, and these could not be tested.

[The Earl of Halsbury LC, and Lords James of Hereford, Brampton and Robertson delivered concurring opinions.]

NOTES

1. For criticism of the rule precluding ratification by an undisclosed principal, see A Rochvarg (1989) 34 McGill LJ 286; cf Treitel, op cit, p 626. But the rule is well established and unlikely to be altered in the near future, see *Sharp and Roarer Investments Ltd v Sphere Drake Insurance plc, The Moonacre* [1992] 2 Lloyd's Rep 501 at 515, per AD Coleman QC, for a recent application of the rule.

2. In *Keighley, Maxsted & Co v Durant* the undisclosed principal evaded liability. But in *Spiro v Lintern* (discussed above at p 99), where *Keighley, Maxsted & Co v Durant* was followed and applied, the undisclosed principal was held liable to the third party, even though the agent had acted beyond her actual authority. How did this liability arise?

3. As a general rule, an undisclosed principal may sue and be sued on a contract made by an agent acting *within* the scope of his actual authority (see below, p 145).

(i)   *Other requirements for ratification*

(1)   The principal must be in existence at the time of the agent's act. Thus a newly incorporated company cannot ratify a prior contract made by its promoters (*Kelner v Baxter* (1866) LR 2 CP 174), although the contract will normally take effect as one between the third party and the promoter: s 36C of the Companies Act 1985, as inserted by the Companies Act 1989, s 130(4) (but see *Cotronic (UK) Ltd v Dezonie* [1991] BCC 200 for a case where this did not happen; noted by R Hooley [1991] CLJ 413): see generally A Griffiths (1993) 13 LS 241.

(2)   According to Willes J in *Watson v Swann* (1862) 11 CBNS 756 at 771:

> To entitle a person to sue upon a contract, it must clearly be shown that he himself made it, or that it was made on his behalf by an agent authorised to act for him. The law obviously requires that the person for whom the agent professes to act must be a person capable of being ascertained at the time. It is not necessary that he should be named; but there must be such a description of him as shall amount to a reasonable designation of the person intended to be bound by the contract.

> In that case, an agent was instructed to effect a general policy of insurance on goods for a principal. The agent was unable to do this, so he declared the goods on the back of a general policy of insurance which he had previously effected for himself. Later, when the goods had been lost, the principal sued on the policy. It was held that the principal could not recover on the policy because it was not made on his behalf. At the time the policy was effected by the agent the principal was not even known to him. See also *Southern Water Authority v Carey* [1985] 2 All ER 1077 at 1085, per HH Judge Smout QC. But see Bowstead, at p 62, for criticism of the narrow scope of Willes J's dicta (see also Markesinis and Munday, p 72). In fact policies of marine insurance may be taken out 'for and on behalf of any person interested' and such persons can ratify even though not named on the policy (*Hagedorn v Oliverson* (1814) 2 M & S 485).

(3)   The principal must have been competent at the time when the act was done by the agent and at the date of the purported ratification. For example, a principal who was an enemy alien at the time of the agent's act could not ratify: *Boston*

Deep Sea Fishing and Ice Co Ltd v Farnham (Inspector of Taxes) [1957] 1 WLR 1051. A principal could not ratify his agent's acceptance of a contract option when the option period had expired by the time of the ratification: *Dibbins v Dibbins* [1896] 2 Ch 348. Similarly a contract of insurance cannot be ratified by the assured after loss (*Grover & Grover Ltd v Mathews* [1910] 2 KB 401), unless it is a contract of marine insurance (Marine Insurance Act 1906, s 86). But see below at p 115 as to ratification of a contract of insurance by the insurer after loss.

(4) An act which is void ab initio cannot be ratified but a voidable act may be ratified. As Kelly CB said in *Brook v Hook* (1871) LR 6 Exch 89 at 99: 'although a voidable act may be ratified by matter subsequent, it is otherwise when an act is originally and in its inception void'. This case involved forgery of the principal's signature on a promissory note by his agent. It was held that the principal could not ratify the agent's act as the signature was a nullity. It is also possible to explain the case on the grounds that by forging the principal's signature the agent did not purport to act on behalf of the principal; quite the contrary, the agent purported to be the principal himself (Treitel, op cit, p 627). Furthermore, a principal cannot ratify an unauthorised contract which is prohibited by statute (*Bedford Insurance Co Ltd v Instituto de Resseguros do Brasil* [1985] QB 966 at 986), but otherwise a principal can ratify an unlawful act. For discussion of the extent of the ratifying principal's liability for an unlawful act, see Bowstead, pp 54–55; Fridman, pp 81–82; Markesinis and Munday, pp 78–79.

(ii) *Effect of ratification*

Bolton Partners v Lambert (1889) 41 Ch D 295, Court of Appeal

Lambert made an offer to Scratchley, an agent of Bolton Partners, to take the lease of certain properties. The offer was accepted by Scratchley on behalf of Bolton Partners, though he had no authority to do so. Lambert withdrew the offer before Bolton Partners ratified Scratchley's acceptance. Bolton Partners claimed specific performance of the contract. Affirming the decision of Kekewich J, the Court of Appeal held that Bolton Partners were entitled to specific performance of the contract.

Cotton LJ: But then it is said that on the 13th of January, 1887, the Defendant entirely withdrew the offer he had made. Of course the withdrawal could not be effective, if it were made after the contract had become complete. As soon as an offer has been accepted the contract is complete. But it is said that there could be a withdrawal by the Defendant on the 13th of January on this ground, that the offer of the Defendant had been accepted by *Scratchley*, a director of the Plaintiff company, who was not authorized to bind the company by acceptance of the offer, and therefore that until the company ratified *Scratchley*'s act there was no acceptance on behalf of the company binding on the company, and therefore the Defendant could withdraw his offer. Is that so? The rule as to ratification by a principal of acts done by an assumed agent is that the ratification is thrown back to the date of the act done, and that the agent is put in the same position as if he had had authority to do the act at the time the act was done by him. Various cases have been referred to as laying down this principle, but there is no case exactly like the present one. The case of *Hagedorn v Oliverson* ((1814) 2 M & S 485) is a strong case of the application of the principle. It was there pointed out how favourable the rule was to the principal, because till ratification he was not bound, and he had an option to adopt or not to adopt what had been done. In that case the plaintiff had effected an insurance on a ship in which another person was interested, and it was held that long after the ship had been lost the other person might adopt the act of the plaintiff, though done without authority, so as to enable the plaintiff to sue upon the policy. Again, in *Ancona v Marks* ((1862) 7 H & N 686), where a bill was indorsed to and sued on in the name of *Ancona*, who had given no authority for that purpose, yet it was held that *Ancona* could, after the action had been brought, ratify what had been done, and that the subsequent ratification was equivalent to a prior authority so as to entitle *Ancona* to sue upon the bill. It was said by Mr *Brice* that in that case there was a previously existing liability of the defendant towards some person; but the liability of the defendant to *Ancona* was established by *Ancona*'s authorizing and ratifying the act of the agent, and a previously existing liability to others did not affect the principle laid down.

The rule as to ratification is of course subject to some exceptions. An estate once vested cannot be divested, nor can an act lawful at the time of its performance be rendered unlawful, by the application of the doctrine of ratification. The case of *Walter v James* ((1871) LR 6 Exch 124) was relied on by the Appellant, but in that case there was an agreement between the assumed agent of the defendant and the plaintiff to cancel what had been done before any ratification by the defendant; in the present case there was no agreement made between *Scratchley* and the Defendant that what had been done by *Scratchley* should be considered as null and void.

The case of *Bird v Brown* ((1850) 4 Exch 786), which was also relied on by the Appellant, is distinguishable from this case. There it was held that the ratification could not operate to divest the ownership which had previously vested in the purchaser by the delivery of the goods before the ratification of the alleged *stoppage in transitu*. So also in *Lyell v Kennedy* ((1887) 18 QBD 796) the plaintiff, who represented the lawful heir, desired, after the defendant *Kennedy* had acquired a title to the estate by means of the *Statute of Limitations*, and after the title of the heir was gone, to ratify the act of *Kennedy* as to the receipt of rents, so as to make the estate vest in the heir. In my opinion none of these cases support the Appellant's contention.

I think the proper view is that the acceptance by *Scratchley* did constitute a contract, subject to its being shewn that *Scratchley* had authority to bind the company. If that were not shewn there would be no contract on the part of the company, but when and as soon as authority was given to *Scratchley* to bind the company the authority was thrown back to the time when the act was done by *Scratchley*, and prevented the Defendant withdrawing his offer, because it was then no longer an offer, but a binding contract.

Lindley LJ: The question is what is the consequence of the withdrawal of the offer after acceptance by the assumed agent but before the authority of the agent has been ratified? Is the withdrawal in time? It is said on the one hand that the ordinary principle of law applies, viz, that an offer may be withdrawn before acceptance. That proposition is of course true. But the question is – acceptance by whom? It is not a question whether a mere offer can be withdrawn, but the question is whether, when there has been in fact an acceptance which is in form an acceptance by a principal through his agent, though the person assuming to act as agent has not then been so authorized, there can or cannot be a withdrawal of the offer before the ratification of the acceptance? I can find no authority in the books to warrant the contention that an offer made, and in fact accepted by a principal through an agent or otherwise, can be withdrawn. The true view on the contrary appears to be that the doctrine as to the retrospective action of ratification is applicable.

Lopes LJ: An important point is raised with regard to the withdrawal of the offer before ratification in this case.

If there had been no withdrawal of the offer this case would have been simple. The ratification by the Plaintiffs would have related back to the time of the acceptance of the Defendant's offer by *Scratchley*, and the Plaintiffs would have adopted a contract made on their behalf.

It is said that there was no contract which could be ratified, because *Scratchley* at the time he accepted the Defendant's offer had no authority to act for the Plaintiffs. Directly *Scratchley* on behalf and in the name of the Plaintiffs accepted the Defendant's offer I think there was a contract made by *Scratchley* assuming to act for the Plaintiffs, subject to proof by the Plaintiffs that *Scratchley* had that authority.

The Plaintiffs subsequently did adopt the contract, and thereby recognised the authority of their agent *Scratchley*. Directly they did so the doctrine of ratification applied and gave the same effect to the contract made by *Scratchley* as it would have had if *Scratchley* had been clothed with a precedent authority to make it.

If *Scratchley* had acted under a precedent authority the withdrawal of the offer by the Defendant would have been inoperative, and it is equally inoperative where the Plaintiffs have ratified and adopted the contract of the agent. To hold otherwise would be to deprive the doctrine of ratification of its retrospective effect. To use the words of Baron *Martin* in *Brook v Hook* ((1871) LR 6 Exch 89 at 96), the ratification would not be 'dragged back as it were, and made equipollent to a prior command.'

I have nothing to add with regard to the other points raised. I agree with what has been said on those points. The appeal must be dismissed.

NOTES

1. The effect of the rule in *Bolton Partners v Lambert* is limited in a number of ways:

(1) Ratification must take place within a reasonable time after acceptance of the offer by the unauthorised person: *Managers of the Metropolitan Asylums Board v Kingham & Sons* (1890) 6 TLR 217. What is a reasonable time will depend on the facts of the case. The third party offeror may abridge the time within which the ratification must take place by informing the principal of his wish to withdraw from the contract (*Re Portuguese Consolidated Copper Mines Ltd* (1890) 45 Ch D 16).

  Despite the dicta of Fry LJ in the *Metropolitan Asylums Board* case that 'reasonable time can never extend after the time at which the contract is to commence', Parker J (obiter) in *Bedford Insurance Co Ltd v Instituto de Resseguros do Brasil* [1985] QB 966 at 987 doubted whether there was any general rule to that effect (cf Fridman, p 91). In the *Bedford Insurance* case, Parker J held that it was possible for an insurer to ratify a contract of insurance made by an unauthorised agent after claims had been made on the policy, as this would benefit rather than prejudice the third party, ie the insured.

(2) The rule in *Bolton Partners v Lambert* will not apply if the third party's offer was expressly made subject to ratification (*Metropolitan Asylums Board v Kingham*, above, at 218, per Fry LJ), or the third party's acceptance was expressly made subject to ratification (*Watson v Davies* [1931] 1 Ch 455 at 469, per Maugham J), or the '[third] party to the contract has intimation of the limitation of the agent's authority' (*Warehousing and Forwarding Co of East Africa Ltd v Jafferali & Sons Ltd* [1964] AC 1 at 9, per Lord Guest). In all such cases the third party may withdraw his offer at any time before the principal ratifies the agent's unauthorised acceptance.

(3) A third party who commits a breach of contract after the agent's unauthorised acceptance, but before ratification, will not subsequently be held liable to the principal: *Kidderminster Corpn v Hardwick* (1873) LR 9 Exch 13, which was not referred to in, and is not easily reconcilable with, *Bolton Partners v Lambert*. As Fridman observes (pp 90–91):

  > . . . if the third party, between the time of the agent's acceptance and the principal's ratification does something which, in effect, makes the contract between the third party and the principal virtually non-existent (eg commencing to work for another employer, after having agreed to work for the principal) then the third party will be

able to have all the advantages of revocation or withdrawal of his offer, even though he cannot technically revoke or withdraw it.

(4) The agent and the third party may cancel the unauthorised transaction by mutual consent: *Walter v James* (1871) LR 6 Exch 124.

(5) The retroactive effect of ratification will not be allowed to deprive a stranger to the contract of any property rights which had vested in him before ratification: *Bird v Brown* (1850) 4 Exch 786.

(6) In *Presentaciones Musicales SA v Secunda* (1993) Times, 29 November, the Court of Appeal recently affirmed that where a time limit for doing an act is fixed either by statute or by agreement, the doctrine of ratification would not be allowed to apply if it would have the effect of extending that time. However, the Court of Appeal went on to hold that a plaintiff could ratify the unauthorised issue of a writ by his solicitor when the causes of action upon which the writ was based were not time barred at the date of issue of the writ, but had become so, wholly or in part, at the date of ratification.

2. *Bolton Partners v Lambert* has been criticised for putting the third party in a worse position than he would have been in if he had made his offer direct to the principal, for then he could have withdrawn the offer before the principal accepted it (W A Seavey (1920) 29 Yale LJ 859 at p 891). The case was specifically not followed in *Fleming v Bank of New Zealand* [1900] AC 577 (PC), and was disapproved of in the dissenting judgment of Isaacs J in *Davison v Vickery's Motors Ltd* (1925) 37 CLR 1 (High Court of Australia). The case has recently been criticised by the Supreme Court of New South Wales in *NM Superannuation Pty Ltd v Hughes* (1992) 7 ACSR 105 at 115–117, per Cohen J. Furthermore, most jurisdictions in the US allow the third party to withdraw his offer before ratification and the 1983 Geneva Convention on Agency in the International Sale of Goods (above, p 83) allows a third party to withdraw before ratification if, at the time of contracting, he was unaware of the agent's lack of authority (art 15(2)).

Yet *Bolton Partners v Lambert* may not be as prejudicial to the third party as first appears. As we have seen, there are a number of exceptions to the rule. Furthermore, it must be remembered that if the principal ratifies the contract the third party gets what he bargained for, and that if he does not ratify, the third party can sue the agent for breach of warranty of authority. The real prejudice to the third party is the possibility of uncertainty whilst waiting to see whether the principal will ratify the contract or not. However, as we have seen, even this period may be curtailed if the third party serves notice on the principal of his wish to withdraw from the contract (above, p 115).

QUESTIONS

1. Adam contracts with Ted, telling him that he is acting on behalf of Paul. In fact, Adam is acting on his own behalf. Can Paul ratify the contract? See *Re Tiedemann & Ledermann Frères* [1899] 2 QB 66.

2. Thelma approaches Aida, who purports to act for Patricia without in fact having any authority from her, and offers to sell an old and valuable painting. Aida accepts on condition that Thelma keeps it in her strongroom until delivery is made. Thelma agrees, but fails to do so and in consequence the painting is stolen. On hearing this Patricia ratifies Aida's acts and·sues for the price of the painting. Advise Thelma.

CHAPTER 5

Relations with third parties

We have seen how an agent has power to affect the legal relations of his principal with regard to third parties (above, p 74). Typically the agent will do this by contracting on behalf of the principal or by disposing of the principal's proprety. In this chapter we shall concentrate on the effect of contracts made by agents. The unauthorised disposition of property by an agent is considered below at pp 300 ff (see generally Bowstead, pp 353–386; Fridman, Ch 12; Markesinis and Munday, pp 187–199).

When considering the rights and liabilities arising under a contract made by an agent, it is important to ascertain whether the agent was acting for a disclosed or undisclosed principal. A *disclosed* principal is one of whose existence the third party is aware at the time of contracting with the agent. If the name of the principal is known to the third party then the principal is described as 'named'. If the third party does not know the principal's name, but knows of his existence, the principal is described as 'unnamed'. Whether named or unnamed the principal remains disclosed. On the other hand, if the third party is unaware of the existence of the principal at the time he contracts with the agent, ie the third party thinks the agent is contracting on his own behalf and not for someone else, the principal is described as *undisclosed*.

1 Disclosed agency

(a) Relations between principal and third party

The general rule

Montgomerie v United Kingdom Mutual Steamship Association [1891] 1 QB 370, Queen's Bench Division

Montgomerie was the part-owner of a ship which he insured with the defendant mutual insurance association. The policy of insurance was effected by Perry, Raines & Co who acted as Montgomerie's agent. Perry, Raines & Co was a member of the association but Montgomerie was not, and his name did not appear on the policy. When Montgomerie sued the association to recover a loss on the ship, the association claimed that the terms of the policy expressly excluded their liability to anyone other than a member of the association. Wright J gave judgment for the association.

Wright J: There is no doubt whatever as to the general rule as regards an agent, that where a person contracts as agent for a principal the contract is the contract of the principal, and not that of the agent; and, prima facie, at common law the only person who may sue is the principal, and the only person who can be sued is the principal. To that rule there are, of course, many exceptions. First, the agent may be added as the party to the contract if he has so contracted, and is appointed as the party to be sued. Secondly, the principal may be excluded in several other cases. He may be excluded if the contract is made by a deed inter partes, to which the principal is no party. In that case, by ancient rule of common law, it does not matter whether the person made a party is or is not an agent. . . . Another exception is as regards bills and notes. If a person who is an agent makes himself a party in writing to a bill or note, by the law merchant a principal cannot be added. Another exception is that by usage, which is treated as forming part of the contract or of the law merchant, where there is a foreign principal, generally speaking the agent in England is the party to the contract, and not the foreign principal; but this is subject to certain limitations. Then a principal's liability may be limited, though not excluded. If the other party elects to sue the agent, he cannot afterwards sue the principal. Again, where the principal is an undisclosed principal, he must, if he sues, accept the facts as he finds them at the date of his disclosure, so far as those facts are consistent with reasonable and proper conduct on the part of the other party. Again, if the principal is sued, he is entitled to an allowance for payments which he may have made to his agent if the other party gave credit originally to that agent. Also, and this is very important, in all cases the parties can by their express contract provide that the agent shall be the person liable either concurrently with or to the exclusion of the principal, or that the agent shall be the party to sue either concurrently with or to the exclusion of the principal. . . .

. . . The question, then, is, Have the parties so contracted that Montgomerie and his co-plaintiffs cannot sue, the alternative being that the action should have been brought in the name of Perry, Raines & Co? I have come to the conclusion that the parties have so contracted. I think that the rules annexed to the policy and the articles of association which are incorporated with the policy shew plainly that it was the intention of the parties that the association should look to the member only for contribution, and should have to deal with and be entitled to say that they would deal with the member only in respect of the settlements of losses.

NOTES

1. Montgomerie was an undisclosed principal but the statement made by Wright J as to the normal relationship between the principal and the third party applies to disclosed principals generally.

2. Where the principal acts within the scope of his authority on behalf of a disclosed principal, direct contractual relations are established between the principal and the third party. If the agent acts within the scope of his actual authority (express or implied), or the principal subsequently ratifies the agent's unauthorised acts, the principal may sue and be sued on the contract. But, as we have already seen, where the agent has only apparent authority the principal will be liable on the contract made by his agent but he will not be able to sue upon it himself, unless he ratifies his agent's unauthorised act (above, p 95). Professor Markesinis and Dr Munday submit that the same rule applies when an agent of necessity contracts on behalf of a principal (op cit, p 292). But, unlike apparent authority, agency of necessity is not based on estoppel and so it is difficult to see why the principal should be prevented from bringing an action on the contract. Where the agent acts without authority, and there is no ratification, the principal will incur no liability to the third party (eg *Comerford v Britannic Assurance Co Ltd* (1908) 24 TLR 593; *Wiltshire v Sims* (1808) 1 Camp 258).

3. There are two exceptional cases when a disclosed principal will not be privy to a contract made by his agent acting within the scope of his authority.

First, when the agent contracts by deed the principal will not be able to sue and be sued on the contract unless he is described in the deed as a party to it and the deed is executed in his name (*Re International Contract Co, Pickering's Claim* (1871) 6 Ch App 525). However, this general rule is itself subject to a number of exceptions:

(1) if the agent who contracts by deed contracts as trustee for the principal then the principal can sue on the deed (*Harmer v Armstrong* [1934] Ch 65);
(2) under s 7(1) of the Powers of Attorney Act 1971, as amended by the Law of Property (Miscellaneous Provisions) Act 1989, s 1, Sch 1, para 7(1), if the agent was appointed by a power of attorney, and he acts within the scope of his authority, he may execute the deed in his own name and the principal may sue on it (for detailed consideration of this section, see Bowstead, pp 326–327; Fridman, pp 198–199); and
(3) under s 56(1) of the Law of Property Act 1925, a principal may acquire an interest in land or other property, or the benefit of any condition, right of entry, covenant or agreement over or respecting land or other property, even though he is not named as a party to the conveyance or instrument (but note that the ambit of this section has been restrictively construed by the courts: see G H Treitel *The Law of Contract* (8th ed, 1991), pp 571–573).

For recent proposals for reform of the privity of contract rule so as to allow third parties to enforce contractual provisions made in their favour, see The Law Commission Consultation Paper No 121 'Privity of Contract: Contracts for the Benefit of Third Parties' (1991).

Second, a principal cannot be made liable on any negotiable instrument unless his signature appears on it (Bills of Exchange Act 1882, s 23). However, the principal will be liable on the instrument if his signature is written on the document by someone acting by or with his authority (s 91(1) of the 1882 Act). If the agent signs the instrument with the principal's name the principal will be bound. But difficulties can arise when the agent uses a representative signature: see s 26(1) of the 1882 Act; considered below at pp 523–524. A signature by procuration will put the third party on notice that the agent's authority to sign is limited and the principal will only be bound by the signature if the agent was acting within the scope of his actual authority: s 25 of the 1882 Act; considered below at pp 522–523.

4. There is no longer a presumption that an agent contracting for a foreign principal does so personally and cannot establish privity of contract between the principal and the third party. In *Teheran-Europe Co Ltd v ST Belton (Tractors) Ltd* [1968] 2 QB 545, the Court of Appeal held that modern commercial usage does not raise such a presumption. But the foreign character of the principal is not irrelevant, for as Diplock LJ said:

... the fact that the principal is a foreigner is one of the circumstances to be taken into account in determining whether or not the other party to the contract was willing, or led the agent to believe that he was willing, to treat as a party to the contract the agent's principal, and, if he was so willing, whether the mutual intention of the other party and the agent was that the agent should be personally entitled to sue and liable to be sued on the contract as well as his principal. But it is only one of many circumstances, and as respects the creation of privity of contract between the other party and the principal its weight may be minimal, particularly in a case such as the present where the terms of payment are cash before delivery and no credit is extended by the other party to the principal. It may have considerably more weight in determining whether the mutual intention of the other party and the agent was that the agent should be personally liable to be sued as well as the principal, particularly if credit has been extended by the other party.

See also F M B Reynolds [1983] CLP 119 at pp 126–127.

5. *Montgomerie v United Mutual Steamship Assoc* provides an example of a 'commission agent', ie someone who contracts with the third party as principal yet makes the contract on behalf of his own principal (above, p 80).

Professor Markesinis and Dr Munday note that 'in the absence of special circumstances rendering the agent a party to the contract, once contractual relations have been established between the principal and the third party, the agent drops out of the transaction' (op cit, p 204; see also Bowstead, p 424; Fridman, p 200; and Wright J above at p 118). Yet even though the agent is said to 'drop out' of the transaction, the rights and liabilities of the principal and third party may still be affected by the agent in a number of ways.

(i) *Settlement with the agent*

Irvine & Co v Watson & Sons (1880) 5 QBD 414, Court of Appeal

W & Sons employed C, a broker, to purchase oil for them. C purchased the oil from I & Co with payment to be by 'cash on or before delivery'. At the time of purchase C informed I & Co that he was buying for principals, although he did not reveal the name of his principals. I & Co delivered the oil to C without payment, and W & Sons, not knowing that I & Co had not been paid, in good faith paid C. C did not pay I & Co, who then sued W & Sons for the price. Bowen J gave judgment for I & Co. W & Sons appealed.

Bramwell LJ: I am of opinion that the judgment must be affirmed. The facts of the case are shortly these: The plaintiffs sold certain casks of oil, and on the face of the contract of sale Conning appeared as the purchaser. But the plaintiffs knew that he was only an agent buying for principals, for he told them so at the time of the sale, therefore they knew that they had a right against somebody besides Conning. On the other hand, the defendants knew that somebody or other had a remedy against them, for they had authorized Conning, who was an ordinary broker, to pledge their credit, and the invoice specified the goods to have been bought 'per John Conning.' Then, that being so, the defendants paid the broker; and the question is whether such payment discharged them from their liability to the plaintiffs. I think it is impossible to say that it discharged them, unless they were misled by some conduct of the plaintiffs into the belief that the broker had already settled with the plaintiffs, and made such payment in consequence of such belief. But it is contended that the plaintiffs here did mislead the defendants into such belief, by parting with the possession of the oil to Conning without getting the money. The terms of the contract were 'cash on or before delivery,' and it is said that the defendants had a right to suppose that the sellers would not deliver unless they received payment of the price at the time of delivery. I do not think, however, that that is a correct view of the case. The plaintiffs had a perfect right to part with the oil to the broker without insisting strictly upon their right to prepayment, and there is, in my opinion, nothing in the facts of the case to justify the defendants in believing that they would so insist. No doubt if there was an invariable custom in the trade to insist on prepayment where the terms of the contract entitled the seller to it, that might alter the matter; and in such case noninsistence on prepayment might discharge the buyer if he paid the broker on the faith of the seller already having been paid. But that is not the case here; the evidence before Bowen J shews that there is no invariable custom to that effect.

Apart from all authorities, then, I am of opinion that the defendants' contention is wrong, and upon looking at the authorities, I do not think that any of them are in direct conflict with that opinion. It is true that in *Thomson v Davenport* ((1829) 9 B & C 78) both Lord Tenterden and Bayley J suggest in the widest terms that a seller is not entitled to sue the undisclosed principal on discovering him, if in the meantime the state of account between the principal and the agent has been altered to the prejudice of the principal. But it is impossible to construe the dicta of those learned judges in that case literally; it would operate most unjustly to the vendor if we did. I think the judges who uttered them did not intend a strictly literal interpretation to be put on their words. But whether they did or no, the opinion of Parke B in *Heald v Kenworthy* ((1855) 10 Exch 739) seems to me preferable; it is this, that 'If the conduct of the seller would make it unjust for him to call upon the buyer for the money, as for example, where the principal is induced by the conduct of the seller to pay his agent the money on the faith that the agent and seller have come to a settlement on the matter, or if any representation to that effect is made by the seller, either by words or conduct, the seller cannot afterwards throw off the mask and sue the principal.' That is in my judgment a much more accurate statement of the law. But then the defendants rely on the case of *Armstrong v Stokes* ((1872) LR 7 QB 598). Now that is a very remarkable case; it seems to have turned in some measure upon the peculiar character filled by Messrs Ryder as commission merchants. The Court seemed to have thought it would be unreasonable to hold that Messrs Ryder had not authority to receive the money. I think upon the facts of that case that the agents would have been entitled to maintain an action for the money against the defendant, for as commission merchants they were not mere agents of the buyer. Moreover the present case is a case, which Blackburn J there expressly declines to decide. He expressly draws a distinction between a case in which, as in *Armstrong v Stokes*, the seller at the time of the sale supposes the agent to be himself a principal, and gives credit to him alone, and one in which, as here, he knows that the person with whom he is dealing has a principal behind, though he does not know who that principal is.

It is to my mind certainly difficult to understand that distinction, or to see how the mere fact of the vendor knowing or not knowing that the agent has a principal behind can affect the liability of that principal. I should certainly have thought that his liability would depend upon what he himself knew, that is to say whether he knew that the vendor had a claim against him and would look to him for payment in the agent's default. But it is sufficient here that the defendants did know that the sellers had a claim against them, unless the broker had already paid for the goods.

Baggallay LJ: . . . What then was the effect of that payment? If the dicta in *Thomson v Davenport* are to be taken as strictly correct, they certainly go a long way to support the defendants' contention. But it is to be observed that they were mere dicta, and quite unnecessary to the decision. The largeness of those dicta has since been dissented from by Parke B, in the case of *Heald v Kenworthy*, and with his dissent I entirely agree. He sought to limit the qualification of the general rule to cases, in which the seller by some conduct has misled the buyer into believing that a settlement has been made with the agent. And if that limitation is correct, I am of opinion that there is no such payment here as would discharge the defendants.

But reliance is placed upon the case of *Armstrong v Stokes* as establishing the doctrine that the buyer is released from liability, if he pays the agent at a time at which the seller still gives credit to the agent – and it is contended that as that state of facts existed here, the defendants are accordingly discharged. But I think that is not the true view of the decision in *Armstrong v Stokes*. It must be accepted with reference to the particular circumstances of that case. There at the time of the payment by the principal to the brokers, the sellers still gave credit to the brokers and to the brokers alone. But that is not the case here; the plaintiffs it is true gave credit to Conning, but they did not give him exclusive credit. I do not think I am running counter to any of the decided cases in thinking that this judgment must be affirmed.

Brett LJ considered *Thomson v Davenport* and the limitation placed on the dicta in that case by the judgment of Parke B in *Heald v Kenworthy* and continued:

. . . But it is suggested that that limitation was overruled in *Armstrong v Stokes*. I think, however, that the Court there did not intend to overrule it, but to treat the case before them as one to which the limitation did not apply. I think they noticed the peculiar character of Manchester commission merchants. Probably their decision means this, that, when the seller deals with the agent as sole principal, and the nature of the agent's business is such that the buyer ought to believe that the seller has so dealt, in such a case it would be unjust to allow the seller to recover from the principal after he paid the agent. Or it may perhaps be that Blackburn J finding the wider qualification in the very case which lays down the general rule, felt himself bound by the terms of that qualification, and applied them to the case before him.

If the case of *Armstrong v Stokes* arises again, we reserve to ourselves sitting here the right of reconsidering it.

The only other question is whether the present case falls within the qualification as limited by Parke B, whether there was any misleading conduct on the part of the plaintiffs. But the only thing relied on by the defendants on that point was the noninsistence on prepayment by the plaintiffs. And I do not think that that amounted to laches, or was such an act as would justify the defendants in supposing that Conning had already paid the plaintiffs.

NOTES

1. When the principal is disclosed the estoppel theory is generally accepted as explaining those exceptional cases where the right of the third party is affected by the principal having paid or otherwise settled with the agent (see also *Davison v Donaldson* (1882) 9 QBD 623, CA). Cf when the principal is undisclosed, see below, pp 160–161.

2. Mere delay by the third party in enforcing his claim against the principal is not usually sufficient to give rise to an estoppel, unless there are other factors which make the delay misleading to the principal (see *Davison v Donaldson*, above).

A disclosed principal is not bound by the third party making payment to or settling with the agent, unless the agent had actual or apparent authority to receive the payment or settle on behalf of the principal (*Butwick v Grant* [1924] 2 KB 483; cf when the principal is undisclosed, see below, p 161). The third party will only be discharged if payment is made in the manner which the agent is authorised to accept, eg if the agent is authorised to accept payment in cash, payment by bill of exchange will not discharge the third party (*Hine Bros v SS Insurance Syndicate Ltd* (1895) 72 LT 79). If the agent is not authorised to receive payment but he does so and pays over the money to the principal, the principal will be deemed to have ratified the agent's actions and the third party will be discharged. Exceptionally, if the agent has a lien over the principal's goods for a debt owed to him by the principal, and the agent, acting within his authority, sells the goods to a third party who pays the agent (who has no authority to receive payment), the third party can set off the principal's debt to the agent against the price of the goods which remains owing to the principal (*Hudson v Granger* (1821) 5 B & Ald 27).

(ii) *Set-off and other defences available against the agent*

The third party is entitled to set up against the disclosed principal all defences which arise out of the contract itself and all defences which are available against the principal himself (eg set-off, the fact that the principal is an enemy alien): Bowstead, p 334. Defences and set-off which the third party may have against the agent personally and which are unconnected with the contract made by the agent are not available against the disclosed principal (unless set-off is authorised by the principal: *Barker v Greenwood* (1837) 2 Y & C Ex 414).

Particular difficulties arise when the third party seeks to rely on the deceit or other misrepresentation of the agent against the principal. If the principal instigates or ratifies the agent's action, he will be held personally liable to the third party. The principal will also be held liable for the agent's deceit or other misrepresentation if the agent was acting within the scope of his actual or apparent authority at the time he made the representation: *Lloyd v Grace, Smith & Co* [1912] AC 716, HL; *Armagas Ltd v Mundogas SA* [1985] 3 All ER 795, CA; affd [1986] AC 717. In such circumstances, the principal will be liable even if he did not know of the agent's actions (*Refuge Assurance Co Ltd v Kettlewell* [1909] AC 243) and even if the agent was acting for his own benefit and not for the benefit of the principal (*Lloyd v Grace, Smith & Co*, above).

The principal will not be liable in deceit if the agent made an innocent misrepresentation and the principal, who would have known the representation to be false, did not know it had been made (*Armstrong v Strain* [1951] 1 TLR 856; affd [1952] 1 KB 232). However, in such circumstances the principal would be liable to the third party under s 2(1) of the Misrepresentation Act 1967 if the third party had contracted with the principal in reliance upon the agent's misrepresentation (*Gosling v Anderson* (1972) 223 Estates Gazette 1743; although the agent would not be liable to the third party under the statute: *Resolute Maritime Inc v Nippon Kaiji Kyokai* [1983] 2 All ER 1). The principal may also be liable to the third party in negligence on the basis of *Hedley Byrne & Co Ltd v Heller & Partners Ltd* [1964] AC 465, or liable for any negligent misstatement made by the agent when acting within the scope of his authority, if it can be established that the principal and/or the agent owed the third party a duty of care.

A principal, whether disclosed or undisclosed, should be able to raise the agent's defences against the third party as long as those defences arise out of the transaction and are not personal to the agent: Bowstead, p 335. For example, the principal could allege the contract is void for mistake or voidable for misrepresentation but he could not rely on the agent's infancy as that is personal to the agent.

(iii) *Merger and election*

Thomson v Davenport (1829) 9 B & C 78, Court of King's Bench

M'Kune, a 'general Scotch agent' in Liverpool, ordered a quantity of glass and earthenware from Davenport & Co, dealers in Liverpool, for Thomson, who lived in Dumfries. At the time he placed the order M'Kune informed Davenport & Co that he was acting for a principal but he did not reveal the principal's name. The goods were invoiced and debited to M'Kune, but he became bankrupt and Davenport & Co sought to sue Thomson for the price of the goods supplied. The jury of the Borough Court of Liverpool rejected Davenport & Co's claim and delivered a verdict in favour of Thomson. Davenport & Co appealed.

Lord Tenderden CJ: I am of opinion that the direction give by the learned recorder in this case was right, and that the verdict was also right. I take it to be a general rule, that if a person sells goods (supposing at the time of the contract he is dealing with a principal), but afterwards discovers that the person with whom he has been dealing is not the principal in the transaction, but agent for a third person, though he may in the mean time have debited the agent with it, he may afterwards recover the amount from the real principal; subject, however, to this qualification, that the state of the account between the principal and the agent is not altered to the prejudice of the principal. On the other hand, if at the time of the sale the seller knows, not only that the person who is nominally dealing with him is not principal but agent, and also knows who the principal really is, and, notwithstanding all that knowledge, chooses to make the agent his debtor, dealing with him and him alone, then, according to the cases of *Addison v Gandassequi* ((1812) 4 Taunt 574), and *Paterson v Gandasequi* ((1812) 15 East 62), the seller cannot afterwards, on the failure of the agent, turn round and charge the principal, having once made his election at the time when he had the power of choosing between the one and the other. The present is a middle case. At the time of the dealing for the goods, the plaintiffs were informed that M'Kune, who came to them to buy the goods, was dealing for another, that is, that he was an agent, but they were not informed who the principal was. They had not, therefore, at that time the means of making their election. It is true that they might, perhaps, have obtained those means if they had made further enquiry; but they made no further enquiry. Not knowing who the principal really was, they had not the power at that instant of making their election. That being so, it seems to me that this middle case falls in substance and effect within the first proposition which I have mentioned, the case of a person not known to be an agent; and not within the second, where the buyer is not merely known to be agent, but the name of his principal is also known.

[Bayley J delivered a concurring judgment.]

Littledale J: The general principle of law is, that the seller shall have his remedy against the principal, rather than against any other person. Where goods are bought by an agent, who does not at the time disclose that he is acting as agent; the vendor, although he has debited the agent, may upon discovering the principal, resort to him for payment. But if the principal be known to the seller at the time when he makes the contract, and he, with a full knowledge of the principal, chooses to debit the agent, he thereby makes his election, and cannot afterwards charge the principal. Or if in such case he debits the principal, he cannot afterwards charge the agent. There is a third case; the seller may, in his invoice and bill of parcels, mention both principal and agent: he may debit A as a purchaser for goods bought through B, his agent. In that case, he thereby makes his election to charge the principal, and cannot afterwards resort to the agent. The general principle is, that the seller shall have his remedy against the principal, although he may by electing to take the agent as his debtor, abandon his right against the principal. The present case differs from any of those which I have mentioned. Here the agent purchased the goods in his own name. The name of the principal was not then known to the seller, but it afterwards came to his knowledge. It seems to me to be more consistent with the general principle of law, that the seller shall have his remedy against the principal, rather than against any other person, to hold in this case that the seller, who knew that there was a principal, but did not know who that principal was, may resort to him as soon as he is discovered. Here the agent did not communicate to the seller sufficient information to enable him to debit any other individual. The seller was in the same situation, as if at the time of the contract he had not known that there was any principal besides the person with whom he was dealing, and had afterwards discovered that the goods had been purchased on account of another; and, in that case, it is clear that he might have charged the principal. It is said, that he ought to have ascertained by enquiry of the agent who the principal was, but I think that he was not bound to make such enquiry, and that by debiting the agent with the price of the goods, he has not precluded himself from resorting to the principal, whose name was not disclosed to him. . . . For the reasons already given, I think the plaintiff is entitled to recover.

[Parke J, having been concerned as counsel in the case, gave no opinion.]

Debenham's Ltd v Perkins (1925) 133 LT 252, King's Bench Division

In March, April and June 1922 Mrs Perkins purchased various items from Debenham's Ltd (the plaintiffs). In May 1922 Mrs Perkins separated from her husband. The plaintiffs obtained judgment against Mrs Perkins for the items purchased after her separation. They then sued her husband for the price of those items sold to Mrs Perkins before her separation alleging that she acted as his agent. The County Court judge entered judgment for the husband on the ground that the plaintiffs had elected to proceed to judgment against the wife. The plaintiffs appealed and Scrutton and Bankes LJJ, sitting as additional judges of the King's Bench Division, allowed the appeal.

Scrutton LJ: When an agent acts for a disclosed principal, it may be that the agent makes himself or herself personally liable as well as the principal. But in such a case the person with whom the contract is made may not get judgment against both. He may get judgment against the principal or he may get judgment against the agent who is liable as principal, but once he has got judgment against either the principal or the agent who has the liability of the principal, he cannot then proceed against the other party who might be liable on the contract if proceedings had been taken against him or her first. This is sometimes explained by the doctrine of election and sometimes by the doctrine that when one has merged a contract in a judgment, one can have only one judgment, and, having merged the contract in the judgment, one cannot use the contract to get a second judgment. It is unnecessary to consider which is right.

In this case the tradesman first of all sued the married woman for nine dated items, claiming for a lump sum the price of the goods sold and delivered. As far as we can surmise what happened at the trial – and I understand that counsel are agreed as to what did happen at the trial in this case – the judge took the view that as to the first four items in date the wife was the agent of a principal, the husband, and not herself personally liable, and therefore judgment could not be entered against her, but he decided that as to the last five items the wife was then living separately and not with her husband, and she was not acting as his agent, but was personally liable. Then comes a very odd fact, that having held that she was not acting as agent for her husband, so that there was no defence and she was personally liable, in some way, which I do not understand, the learned judge, on a third-party procedure, held that the husband was found to indemnify the wife. The learned judge is so experienced a judge that one cannot help thinking that there is something one does not know which must have led him to take that view. Anyhow, as far as the case against the wife was concerned, the result of that procedure was that the tradesman failed to recover anything under the first four items and succeeded in getting a judgment for the amount of the last five items, though they were not specifically set out in the judgment. Whereupon the tradesman, desiring to get his money from somebody, sued the husband for the first three items. Thereupon objection was taken, which I understand can be put in this way: the plaintiff sued for one cause of action, and although it is quite true he did not get what he wanted, he got a judgment for part of that cause of action. Having taken judgment against the one person for the cause of action, he cannot use the cause of action to try to get a judgment against another party. The cause of action, the contract, is merged in the judgment.

But it appears to me that there are really two causes of action, not one, in this case. There is a cause of action against the wife who is liable personally, there is a cause of action against another person supposed to be acting by the agency of the wife, for different items, at different times, resulting in claims of different amounts. It seems to me, therefore, that this claim for one sum as a debt is really the result of two causes of action. If that is so, the fact that the plaintiff has got judgment against the wife on one cause of action does not merge the cause of action on which he has failed to get judgment, and which still remains available against the person against whom that cause of action should properly be brought.

Another way, perhaps, of putting it, though I think it also involves treating the matter as two causes of action, is that a plaintiff does not elect to sue one of two people alternatively liable, because he brings a proceeding against the other which fails, and in which he does not get judgment. He terminates the liability of the person alternatively liable only if he brings an action against his or her alternate and gets judgment, so that having got judgment against the one, the person who is alternatively liable is discharged. . . .

On the best consideration, therefore, that I can give to the matter, it seems to me that the judgment obtained in the first action was for a cause of action different from the one which is now being sued, and that therefore the tradesman ought not to be estopped from continuing to sue the husband for those items not included in the first account. I quite appreciate that the husband says that he has defences which the County Court judge in the first action ought to have appreciated, and which he is going to raise when he is able to put all the facts before the court. We are not, therefore, deciding for the moment who is going to succeed when this action is tried, but only that the judge was premature in stopping the action on the ground either of an election or of *res judicata*.

[Bankes LJ delivered a concurring judgment.]

NOTES

1. The doctrines of merger and election only become relevant if the agent is personally liable on the main contract he makes with the third party. Remember, in cases of disclosed agency the agent does not normally become personally liable on the contract (above, p 118). But for those exceptional occasions when the agent may contract personally, see below, pp 129–138.

2. In most cases where an agent has been held to contract personally the courts have held the agent's liability to be in the alternative to that of the principal: eg see *Debenham's Ltd v Perkins*, above at p 125, where the assumption of alternative liability underlies Scrutton LJ's judgment; see also Bowstead, p 348. Yet this approach is open to severe criticism. As Professor Markesinis and Dr Munday astutely observe (op cit, p 163):

> . . . if one is endeavouring to discern the intentions of the third party at the time when he concludes his contract with the agent acting for a named or unnamed principal, there is no strong reason to presume that he will always opt for the alternative liability of the agent and the principal rather than for their joint and several liability. After all, joint liability is both more advantageous to the third party and, legally, might appear more conventional. In short, Scrutton LJ's basic assumption in *Debenham's Ltd v Perkins* may be unrealistic and, arguably, contradict the most probable intentions of the parties to the contract.

3. Merger occurs when the third party obtains judgment against the principal, or the agent, when they are both liable in the alternative. Judgment against one releases the other. This is because there is only a single obligation and two judgments cannot arise out of a single obligation. It used to be the case that judgment against one of two joint debtors released the other, but this is no longer the law (Civil Liability (Contribution) Act 1978, s 3). Similarly, if the principal and agent are jointly and severally liable on the contract judgment against one will not release the other. It should be noted that the doctrine of merger can apply even if the third party does not know of the existence of the principal (and, a fortiori, the principal's identity) at the time he obtained judgment against the agent (*Priestly v Fernie* (1865) 3 H & C 977). In this respect merger differs significantly from election.

4. When the principal and agent are liable in the alternative on the contract with the third party, the third party may elect to hold one of them exclusively liable and thereby be barred from suing the other. As with merger, election will not apply if the principal and agent are jointly and severally liable or liable on separate causes of action. Unlike merger, election could be made between joint debtors. The election must be clear and unequivocal. Obtaining judgment against the principal or the agent is clearly the best evidence of election (although strictly speaking this will constitute a merger of actions) but there is no reason why evidence of election cannot come from other sources (eg giving exclusive credit to the agent: see *Thomson v Davenport*). In each case it is a question of fact whether there has been a clear and unequivocal act giving rise to an election. For further discussion as to what may constitute an election, see below, pp 156–157. Furthermore, as illustrated by *Thomson v Davenport*, the third party must have full knowledge of the facts, including the identity of the principal, before he can be said to have elected.

5. The doctrines of merger and election raise a number of difficult issues. Professor Reynolds has written an excellent article on the subject: (1970) 86 LQR 318. Of particular interest is his view that many of the decisions on election in disclosed agency (including *Thomson v Davenport*) are cases involving contract formation rather than concerning election at all (see also Bowstead, pp 350–351; Treitel, op cit, p 639 fn 98).

QUESTION

A bought some goods from T, representing that he was acting on behalf of P Ltd. T charged the price to A's account, but when A became insolvent, T sued P Ltd for the money. Can P Ltd successfully argue that, by debiting A, T made an effective election and can no longer sue P Ltd? Would your answer be different if A, when buying the goods, had made it clear that he was acting for a principal whose identity he refused to disclose?

(b) Relations between agent and third party

(i) *The general rule*

Montgomerie v United Kingdom Mutual Steamship Association [1891] 1 QB 370, Queen's Bench Division

(See above, pp 117–118.)

Lewis v Nicholson and Parker (1852) 18 QB 503, Court of Queen's Bench

Lewis was the mortgagee of a bankrupt's property. Nicholson and Parker were solicitors to assignees of the bankrupt. Purporting to act 'on behalf of the assignees' Nicholson and Parker entered into an agreement with Lewis to sell the bankrupt's property and pay Lewis those sums owed to him out of the proceeds of sale. Although the property was sold Lewis was not paid. In fact it turned out that Nicholson and Parker did not have the authority of the assignees to enter into this particular transaction and so Lewis brought an action against the solicitors personally for breach of the agreement.

Lord Campbell CJ: . . . Looking at the two letters which constitute the contract, I think it appears on the face of them, that the defendants did not intend to make themselves personally liable on the contract, but to make a contract between the plaintiff and the assignees. It is quite clear that the plaintiff's solicitor, to whom the letter of 26th August was addressed, was not himself a contracting party, but was acting as agent, making a contract for the plaintiff: and I think that the true construction of the letters is that the defendants also were not contracting parties, but acting as agents for the assignees, making a contract for them, and, as I think, personally contracting that they had authority to make a contract binding the assignees. The letter expresses that, in consideration of the plaintiff consenting to the sale, 'we hereby, on behalf of the assignees, consent.' My brother Shee in effect asks us to read the contract as if the words on behalf of the assignees were not there; but they are there; and the nature of facts shews that they were meant to express a contract by the assignees; for it was the consent of the assignees to pay over the money that was material to the plaintiff. The answer refers to 'the undertaking given by you herein, and contained in your letter.' That however does not shew that it was understood by the writer to be a personal undertaking by the defendants, but merely refers to the undertaking as made in their letter, and by them. I think therefore that, looking at these two letters which form the contract, it appears to have been the intention of both parties that the consent should be that of the assignees, not that of the defendants. . . .

Then the other point is to be considered. I think the facts raise it, as the trade assignee had no authority to make the official assignee personally liable on such a collateral contract. He might give assent, binding on both, to the disposal of the goods or money; but this goes much beyond such authority. So, the principals not being bound, the question arises whether the defendants are liable in this form of action. In the note to *Thomas v Hewes* ((1834) 2 Cr & M 519, 530, note (*e*), 4 Tyr 335, 338), it is stated to have been said by Bayley B that 'where an agent makes a contract in the name of his principal, and it turns out that the principal is not liable from the want of authority in the agent to make such contract, the agent is personally liable on the contract.' That is a high authority; but I must dissent from it. It is clear that it cannot apply where the contract is peculiarly personal; otherwise this absurdity would follow, that, if A, professing to have but not having authority from B, made a contract that B should marry C, C might sue A for breach of promise of marriage, even though they were of the same sex. . . . I think in no case where it appears that a man did not intend to bind himself, but only to make a contract for a principal, can he be sued as principal, merely because there was no authority. He is liable, if there was any fraud, in an action for deceit, and, in my opinion, as at present advised, on an implied contract that he had authority, whether there was fraud or not. In either way he may be made liable for the damages occasioned by the absence of authority. But I think that to say he is liable as principal is to make a contract, not to construe it. I think therefore that these defendants were liable, but not in this action.

Erle J: The first question is, what is the true construction of this contract. Looking at the terms of the instruments, and the circumstances under which they were written, I think the construction is that the defendants made a contract between the plaintiff and the assignees, and signed it as agents of the assignees. . . .

I also think that the defendants had not the authority of both assignees to make the contract. The question therefore arises, are they liable as principals on the contract, though intending and expressing an intention to act only as agents in making it? I think they are not. I think that, in general, no contract is made by the law contrary to the intention of the parties. The definition of a contract is that it is the mutual intention of the two parties. There is a class of what are called implied contracts, such as the promise to pay money had and received to the plaintiff's use: but, when it is said that such a contract is implied contrary to the intent of the person receiving the money, it is in truth only a technical mode of naming the remedy which the law gives against that wrongdoer. I know of no case in which what is properly called a contract is made by the law contrary to the intent of the parties.

[Wightman and Crompton JJ delivered concurring judgments.]

NOTE

Although the general rule is that the agent 'drops out' of any contract made on behalf of his disclosed principal, the mere fact that a person acts as agent does not prevent him being liable to the third party. As Lord Scarman said in *Yeung Kai Yung v Hong Kong and Shanghai Banking Corpn* [1981] AC 787 at 795 (PC):

> It is not the case that, if a principal is liable, his agent cannot be. The true principle of law is that a person is liable for his engagements (as for his torts) even though he acts for another, unless he can show that by the law of agency he is to be held to have expressly or impliedly negatived his personal liability.

The agent may be liable and entitled on the main contract made with the third party (see below) or on a collateral contract (eg an auctioneer enters into a collateral contract with the buyer whereby he warrants that he has authority to sell and that he knows of no defects in his principal's title, and which allows him to sue the buyer for the price). Even if not liable on the main contract, the agent may be liable for breach of warranty of authority (as recognised by Lord Campbell CJ in *Lewis v Nicholson and Parker*; also see below, p 140). Furthermore, the agent may be personally liable in tort (Fridman, pp 296–302; Bowstead, pp 490–495).

(ii) *When will the agent be liable on the contract made on behalf of his principal?*

Contracts in writing

Universal Steam Navigation Co Ltd v James McKelvie & Co [1923] AC 492, House of Lords

A charterparty was entered into between T H Seed & Co Ltd, as agents for the owners of the vessel, and 'James McKelvie & Co, Newcastle-on-Tyne, Charterers'. The charterparty was signed: 'For and on behalf of James McKelvie & Co (as agents). J A McKelvie'. When sued for breach of the charterparty, McKelvie & Co claimed to have acted as agents for an Italian company, and denied that they were personally liable on the contract. The Court of Appeal entered judgment for McKelvie & Co. The House of Lords dismissed the owners' appeal from that decision.

Viscount Cave LC: My Lords, apart from authority, I should feel no doubt whatever as to the correctness of the judgment of the Court of Appeal. If the respondents had signed the charterparty without qualification, they would of course have been personally liable to the shipowners; but by adding to their signature the words 'as agents' they indicated clearly that they were signing only as agents for others and had no intention of being personally bound as principals. I can imagine no other purpose for which these words could have been added; and unless they had that meaning, they appear to me to have no sense or meaning at all.

When the cases are examined, it appears that the weight of authority is in favour of the above view.

Lord Shaw of Dunfermline: The first question is in what character Messrs McKelvie signed this document? I see no ground whatsoever for denying effect to the express word 'agents': it was undoubtedly in that character that the contract was signed: there is as little ground for cutting out the express character in which it was signed as for cutting out the signature itself.

The second question is, whether, although thus denominating themselves as 'agents,' Messrs McKelvie were yet signing a contract which by its terms made them principals therein. But its terms do not refer to either 'principals' or 'agents'; the body of the document can be applied to either category. As for the names of the parties, I hold that the names of McKelvie followed by 'Charterers' with nothing said of agency, is definitely stamped with agency by the express affirmation of the signature.

A third view is suggested – namely, that they were ex concessu agents, but yet were principals over and above. This answers itself. Such a confused and unusual situation would require the clearest words to make it intelligible and effective. As at present advised, I have doubts as to whether this could be done. . . .

But I desire to say that in my opinion the appending of the word 'agents' to the signature of a party to a mercantile contract is, in all cases, the dominating factor in the solution of the problem of principal or agent. A highly improbable and conjectural case (in which this dominating factor might be overcome by other parts of the contract) may by an effort of the imagination be figured, but, apart from that, the appending of the word 'agent' to the signature is a conclusive assertion of agency, and a conclusive rejection of the responsibility of a principal, and is and must be accepted in that twofold sense by the other contracting party.

Lord Sumner: . . . I agree that for many years past it has, I believe, been generally understood in business, that to add 'as agents' to the signature is all that is necessary to save a party, signing for a principal, from personal liability on the contract, and I agree also that, even as a matter of construction, when a signature so qualified is attached to a general printed form with blanks filled in ad hoc, preponderant importance attaches to the qualification in comparison with printed clauses or even with manuscript insertions in the form. It still, however, remains true, that the qualifying words 'as agents' are a part of the contract and must be construed with the rest of it. They might have been expressed as a separate clause eg, 'it is further agreed that the party signing this charter as charterer does so as agent for an undisclosed principal' – and that clause would obviously have to be construed. They are a form of words and not a mere part of the act of signifying assent and closing a negotiation by duly attaching a name. They purport to limit ar.d explain a liability, and not merely to identify the person signing or to justify the inscription of a name by the hand of another person than the owner of it. They are more than the addition of 'junior' or 'Revd.' to the signature, which serves to identify the signatory by distinguishing him from others. They are more than a mere 'per procuration,' which only alleges authority to write another's name. . . .

. . . It has sometimes been said that when 'agents' is the word added to the signature, it is a mere word of description, and so does not qualify the liability which the act of signing imports. I question this explanation. One's signature is not the place in which to advertise one's calling, nor is 'agent' ordinarily used to describe a trade, as 'tailor' or 'butcher' would be. I have no doubt that, when people add 'agent' to a signature to a contract, they are trying to escape personal liability, but are unaware that the attempt will fail. The result, however, is the same. When words added to a signature in themselves qualify liability, it is because, as words, they can be so construed in conjunction with the contract as a whole.

In construing the words 'as agents,' there is a distinction to be taken. Though it may be somewhat subtle, it has been mentioned in the older cases. Do the words 'as agents' mean 'and as agents,' or 'only as agents'? The positive affirmation, that I sign 'as agent' – that is, for another – is formally consistent with my signing for myself as well. If the act of signing raises a presumption of personal assent and obligation, which has to be sufficiently negatived or qualified by apt words, are the words 'as agent' apt or sufficient to exclude personal liability? For myself, I think that, standing alone, they are. To say 'as agent,' meaning thereby 'also as agent' for some one undisclosed, is substantially useless. If the agent refuses to disclose, the opposite party is no better off. If the statement is true, the rights and liabilities of the principal can be established at any time by proof. The statement only acquires a business efficacy as distinct from a formal content, if it means 'I am not liable but someone else is and he only,' and this is what I think it does mean.

Unless, then, something is to be found to the contrary in the earlier part of this charter, the qualification 'as agents' appears to me to relieve Messrs McKelvie & Co from personal liability on the contract.

Lord Parmoor: . . . The words 'as agents' are, in my opinion, clearly words of qualification and not of description. They denote, in unambiguous language, that the respondents did not sign as principals, and did not intend to incur personal liability. The signature applies to the whole contract, and to every term in the contract. I think it would not be admissible to infer an implied term, or implied terms, in the contract inconsistent with the limitation of liability directly expressed in the qualification of the signature, since the effect of such an implication would be to contradict an express term of the contract. It is not impossible that by plain words in the body of the document, persons signing 'as agents,' may expressly undertake some form of personal liability as principals, but I can find no trace of any intention of the respondents to incur any such liability in the charterparty, which is in question in the present appeal. . . .

Different considerations arise when a person signs a contract without qualification, and the question is raised whether he is to be deemed as contracting personally, or as agent only. In such a case the intention of the parties is to be discovered from the contract itself, and the rule laid down in Smith's Leading Cases has been adopted as the rule to be followed. 'That where a person signs a contract in his own name, without qualification, he is prima facie to be deemed to be a person contracting personally, and in order to prevent this liability from attaching, it must be apparent from the other portions of the document that he did not intend to bind himself as principal.' I agree with Atkin LJ that it would tend to confusion to consider these cases in a case in which the signature itself has been expressly qualified.

Atkin LJ, in giving his decision in the present case, says: 'If the words qualify the signature, they qualify the assent, and nothing more matters.' I do not understand Atkin LJ to exclude the possibility that a person, signing 'as agent,' may nevertheless in the same document expressly undertake some form of personal liability. Such a possibility does not, in my opinion, affect the value of the rule as laid down by Atkin LJ, or its acceptance as an accurate guide in the construction of contracts, not regulated by statute, or considerations of a special character. The rule accords with the dictum of Mellish LJ in *Gadd v Houghton* ((1876) 1 Ex D 357 at 360), 'when the signature comes at the end you apply it to everything which occurs throughout the contract.'

In my opinion the appeal should be dismissed with costs.

Bridges & Salmon Ltd v The Swan (Owner), The Swan [1968] 1 Lloyd's Rep 5, Admiralty Division

The plaintiffs were two firms of boat repairers claiming against the defendant, Mr J D Rodger, for the cost of repairs to the *Swan*. The *Swan* was owned by Mr Rodger but at all material times the vessel had been on hire to J D Rodger Ltd. Mr Rodger was a director of, and shareholder in, J D Rodger Ltd and acted as agent of the company when it ordered repairs to be carried out to the vessel by the plaintiffs. The repairs in question had been ordered partly orally and partly in writing on the company's headed notepaper, signed 'J D Rodger, Director'. At all times the plaintiffs knew that Mr Rodger was the company's agent but they also knew that he was the vessel's owner. The plaintiffs claimed that Mr Rodger was personally liable on the repair contracts, the company having become insolvent.

Brandon J: Where A contracts with B on behalf of a disclosed principal C, the question whether both A and C are liable on the contract or only C depends on the intention of the parties. That intention is to be gathered from (1) the nature of the contract, (2) its terms and (3) the surrounding circumstances: see Bowstead on Agency (12th ed) (1959), at pp 257 and 258, para 113, and the authorities there cited. The intention for which the Court looks is not the subjective intention of A or of B. Their subjective intentions may differ. The intention for which the Court looks is an objective intention of both parties, based on what two reasonable businessmen making a contract of that nature, in those terms and in those surrounding circumstances, must be taken to have intended.

Where a contract is wholly in writing, the intention depends on the true construction, having regard to the nature of the contract and the surrounding circumstances, of the document or documents in which the contract is contained. Where, as in the present case, the contract is partly oral and partly in writing, the intention depends on the true effect, having regard again to the nature of the contract and the surrounding circumstances, of the oral and written terms taken together.

Many of the decided cases on questions of this kind relate to contracts wholly in writing. But it seems to me that, in principle, there can be no difference in the approach to the problem, whether the contract concerned is wholly in writing or partly in writing and partly oral. In either case the terms of the contract must be looked at and their true effect ascertained. I therefore think that, although I am here concerned with contracts which are partly oral and partly written, I can nevertheless properly seek guidance from decided cases on contracts wholly in writing.

. . . a distinction has been drawn between cases in which a person contracts expressly as agent and those in which, although he describes himself as an agent, he does not contract expressly as such.

Where it is stated in the contract that a person makes it 'as agent for', or 'on account of', or 'on behalf of', or simply 'for', a principal, or where words of that kind are added after such person's signature, he is not personally liable: *Gadd v Houghton & Co* (1876) 1 Ex D 357; *Universal Steam Navigation Co Ltd v James McKelvie & Co* [1923] AC 492; *Kimber Coal Co Ltd v Stone and Rolfe Ltd* [1926] AC 414, 24 Ll L Rep 429.

Where such words are not used but the person is merely stated to be an agent, or the word 'agent' is just added after his signature, the result is uncertain, because it is not clear whether the word is used as a qualification or merely as a description: see *Gadd v Houghton & Co, supra*, per Lord Justice James at p 359; and *Universal Steam Navigation Co Ltd v James McKelvie & Co, supra*, per Lord Sumner at p 501. In general it would seem that in such a case the person does not avoid personal liability, although there may be exceptions to this general rule depending on the other terms of the contract or the surrounding circumstances.

Where a person contracts as agent for a company and does nothing more than add the word 'director' or 'secretary' after his signature, it seems that he does not avoid personal liability: *Brebner v Henderson* 1925 SC 643. This was a Scottish Appeal to the Court of Session which turned on the construction of s 26 of the Bills of Exchange Act, 1882, but I think the reasoning is applicable to a similar situation at common law.

Bearing in mind the distinctions drawn in the authorities to which I have referred, I return to an analysis of the facts in the present case. It seems to me that the defendant did not ever contract expressly as agent in the sense of saying either orally or in writing that he was acting 'as agent for', or 'on account of', or 'on behalf of', or 'for' the company. What he did was to describe himself to both plaintiffs at an earlier stage as 'Mr Rodger, of J D Rodger Ltd', and later to write the written orders on the company's notepaper and add the word 'Director' to his signature. On the other hand, the plaintiffs' subsequent conduct shows that they understood clearly that the bills for their work were to be sent to the company. It has been argued with force for the defendant that this shows that the plaintiffs understood the defendant to be contracting 'on account of' the company and it was to the company alone that they were giving credit. I am not sure, however, that this is the only interpretation to be put on the facts, for it is possible for a person to give credit to a principal without at the same time giving exclusive credit to him.

On this analysis, which takes no account of any special factor arising from the surrounding circumstances, the present case appears to be somewhat near the borderline, with strong arguments available either way. But, as indicated earlier, the surrounding circumstances must also be looked at, and when looked at seem to me to assist considerably in the resolution of the problem.

The main surrounding circumstance, in my view, is that the defendant was at all material times the owner of the *Swan* and that both plaintiffs dealt with him either in the knowledge or on the correct assumption that this was so. The consequence of the defendant being the owner of the *Swan* was that he had a personal interest in the repairs in addition to his interest as director of the company in that the effect of the repairs was to preserve or to improve his own property. In particular, the repairs finally ordered and now sued for were of such an extent and character that they must greatly have increased the value of the vessel. All this was, or must be taken to have been, apparent both to Mr Pearce and to Mr Salmon [the managers of the respective plaintiffs].

The difficulty in the present case seems to me to arise mainly from the fact that the defendant had these two roles, one as director of the company which was operating the *Swan*, and the other as her owner. The defendant claims that, in all his dealings with the first and second plaintiffs in connection with repairs to the *Swan*, he was playing solely the first role. But the question is whether he made it clear to the two managers concerned, by his words oral or written, or his conduct, that this was so, or led them to suppose that he was playing the role of owner as well.

It seems to me that, when a person who is known or correctly assumed to be the owner of a boat, has discussions with a repairing company's manager about repairs to her, it is natural for the manager to assume that, if an order for the repairs is placed, that person will accept personal liability for them as such owner unless he makes the contrary clear beyond doubt. In the present case the defendant did make it clear to both Mr Pearce and Mr Salmon that the accounts for the work should be sent to the company. But the question is whether he made it clear to them at the same time that, although he was the owner of the boat and would therefore derive personal benefit from the repairs, he was nevertheless disowning any personal liability to pay for the work. Unless he did so it seems to me that they were entitled to assume that, while he was placing the order for the company to whom the account was to be sent, he remained also personally liable on the contract.

Approaching the matter in that way I have come to the conclusion that nothing said orally at any time to Mr Pearce, whether by the skipper or engineer of the *Swan* or by the defendant, and nothing contained in the written order to the second plaintiffs dated Oct 14, 1966, did make it clear beyond doubt that the defendant, although owner of the vessel, was disowning personal liability for the cost of the repairs which he was ordering.

I have reached a similar conclusion with regard to the first plaintiffs, although in their case the question of anything significant being said to Mr Salmon by anyone other than the defendant does not arise.

In the result, the decision which I have come to, after considering the nature and terms of the two contracts, and the surrounding circumstances, is that both plaintiffs are entitled to succeed on the second of the three points argued on their behalf, namely, that the defendant, though contracting as agent, did not do so solely as agent but in such a way as to be also personally liable.

NOTES

1. Whether an agent is liable on a contract in writing made on behalf of a disclosed principal depends on the objective intention of the parties, ie of the agent and third party. It is axiomatic to say that each case turns on the construction of the document in question. As Hobhouse J has recently emphasised: 'each contract has to be construed in its own context and having regard to the whole of its terms' (*Punjab National Bank v De Boinville* [1992] 1 Lloyd's Rep 7 at 12, see also Staughton LJ in the same case at 31). Furthermore, it is important to note that contracts made by deed, bills of exchange, promissory notes and cheques as governed by their own rules (see below, p 137).

2. Whilst generalisations as to the effect of particular words and phrases must be dangerous (Bowstead, p 445), the following principles offer some general guidance:

(1) If the agent signs the contract in his own name without more, he will be deemed to have contracted personally, unless he can rely on any term of the

contract which *plainly* show he was merely contracting as agent (eg *Gadd v Houghton & Co* (1876) 1 Ex D 357, CA, where brokers signed a contract of sale in their own name without qualification, but were not held personally liable as they were described in the body of the contract as selling 'on account of' someone else; cf *Tudor Marine Ltd v Tradax Export SA, The Virgo* [1976] 2 Lloyd's Rep 135, CA, where one clause of a charterparty referred to the defendants as charterers and another clause stated that the vessel was chartered 'on behalf and for account of' someone else, the defendants were held personally liable when they signed the contract in their own name without qualification; *Jugoslavenska Linijska Plovidba v Hulsman (t/a Brusse & Sippel Import-Export), The Primorje* [1980] 2 Lloyd's Rep 74).

(2) If an agent signs as 'agent', 'broker', 'director' etc, this may amount to no more than a description and not a qualification of his personal liability, unless a contrary intention can be established from the whole of the contract or from the surrounding circumstances (see *Universal Steam Navigation Co v McKelvie*, above at p 130, per Lord Sumner; *The Swan*, above at p 132).

(3) If the agent clearly indicates by a qualification added to his signature that he is contracting solely as agent, he will not be held personally liable (although see Lord Shaw's reference to a 'highly improbable and conjectural case' in *Universal Steam Navigation Co v McKelvie*, above at p 130; see also note 3 below as to the effect of extrinsic evidence of custom or usage).

3. The terms of the written contract indicating that the agent contracted personally cannot be contradicted by parol or other extrinsic evidence (*Higgins v Senior* (1841) 8 M & W 834). However, the agent may have an equitable defence to an action by the third party if he can establish an extrinsic agreement between himself and the third party that he should not be made personally liable (*Wake v Harrop* (1862) 1 H & C 202; Bowstead, p 449; cf Fridman, pp 216–217). But parol evidence of custom or usage may be introduced to show that the agent is personally liable on a contract, when he does not appear otherwise to be so. So long as the parol evidence does not contradict the terms of the written agreement the personal liability of the agent may be established in this way (eg *Hutchinson v Tatham* (1873) LR 8 CP 482, where parol evidence of trade usage was admitted to show the agent was liable if the name of the principal was not disclosed in a reasonable time).

4. When an agent is held personally liable on the contract he makes with the third party, the question arises as to whether he is solely liable or whether he is liable together with his principal. The liability of both principal and agent will often accord with commercial expectations, and there is certainly evidence that the courts have been willing to hold that the agent has undertaken liability as well as the principal (eg see *International Rly Co v Niagara Parks Commission* [1941] AC 328 at 342; *Montgomerie v UK Mutual SS Assn*, above at p 118; *The Swan*, above at p 133; *Teheran-Europe Co Ltd v ST Belton (Tractors) Ltd*, above at pp 119–120; see also F M B Reynolds (1969) 85 LQR 92). But such cases are probably still to be regarded as exceptional (they are often explained as turning on special trade custom) and it is more likely that the agent will either be held solely liable as principal or not liable at all (see *Universal Steam Navigation Co v McKelvie*, above at p 130, per Lord Shaw; Reynolds, op cit, p 94). There is much that remains uncertain and unsatisfactory in this area (see, in particular, the cases on election: discussed above at pp 123–127). Finally, it should be noted that the terms of the agent's liability is an important issue whenever the agent undertakes personal liability to the third party; it is not an issue restricted to contracts in writing.

5. See P N Legh-Jones (1969) 32 MLR 325, who argues that *The Swan* was wrongly decided.

Oral contracts

N & J Vlassopulos Ltd v Ney Shipping Ltd, The Santa Carina [1977] 1 Lloyd's Rep 478, Court of Appeal

The defendants, who were brokers on the Baltic Exchange, telephoned the plaintiffs, who were also brokers there, and asked them to supply bunkers to the vessel *Santa Carina*. Bunkers were supplied but the plaintiffs' invoice remained unpaid. The plaintiffs then brought an action to recover the price from the defendants. The defendants denied liability on the grounds that they were acting merely as agents for their principals, the time charterers of the *Santa Carina*, and that although the plaintiffs did not know the identity of the principals, they did know that the defendants acted as agents. Reversing Mocatta J, the Court of Appeal gave judgment for the defendants.

Lord Denning MR: On the facts I have stated, it is clear that Vlassopulos, the brokers for the suppliers, knew that Ney, the brokers for the time charterers, were ordering the fuel simply as agents. They were agents either for the owners or the time charterers of the vessels. The brokers for the suppliers knew they were agents. They received a telephone message saying: 'Please supply this fuel oil to the vessel'. But they knew it was from the agents as agents.

The Judge held that the brokers who ordered the fuel were personally liable. He was much influenced by the cases where a person gives a written order for goods or signs a written contract when he is known to be acting as an agent. Nevertheless, although he is known to be acting as an agent, he will be liable on that order or liable on that contract if he signs in his own personal name without qualification. That is settled by cases both in this Court and in the House of Lords: see *H O Brandt & Co v H N Morris & Co Ltd* [1917] 2 KB 784 at p 796 per Lord Justice Scrutton, and *Hichens, Harrison, Woolston & Co v Jackson & Sons* [1943] AC 266 at p 273 per Lord Atkin. In order to exclude his liability he has to append to his signature some such words as 'as agent only' or 'for and on behalf of' or such exclusion must be apparent elsewhere in the document. That is clear from *Universal Steam Navigation Co v James McKelvie & Co* [1923] AC 492 at pp 505–6.

The Judge thought that those cases on written orders and written contracts should be applied to the present case of an oral contract. He felt that if there is an oral conversation on the telephone, as in this case ordering bunkers, the broker is liable unless he uses some express words so as to show that he is acting as agent only and is not to be held personally liable. He said ([1976] 2 Lloyd's Rep 223 at p 226):

> Thus some words must be used to indicate that the agent is not himself undertaking any financial obligation or liability.

I have no doubt that those cases on written orders and written contracts arose out of the old rule of evidence whereby it was not permissible to admit oral evidence to alter or contradict a written contract. Those cases still apply today to written orders and written contracts. But they do not apply to oral orders or oral contracts. At any rate not so rigidly. In many cases if a man, who is an agent for another, orders goods or makes a contract by word of mouth, but does not disclose the name or standing of his principal (so that his credit is unknown to the other contracting party) the agent himself is liable to pay for the goods or to fulfil the contract. It may be that the other contracting party knows that the man is only an agent, but, as he does not know who the principal is, it is to be inferred that he does not rely on the credit of the principal but looks to the agent. That, I think, is the thought underlying the dictum of Mr Justice Salter in *Benton v Campbell, Parker & Co Ltd* [1925] 2 KB 410 at p 414, and the American Restatement on Agency in the comment to para 321. But in other cases that may not be the proper inference. There are cases where, although the man who supplied the goods knows that the other is an agent and does not know his principal, nevertheless he is content to look to the credit of that principal whoever he may be. This is something which Lord Justice Diplock contemplated in the case of *Teheran-Europe Co Ltd v S T Belton (Tractors) Ltd* [1968] 2 Lloyd's Rep 37, [1968] 2 QB 545. He said that

> . . . he may be willing to treat as a party to the contract anyone on whose behalf the agent may have been authorised to contract . . .

This applies particularly to the case of a broker. As Mr Justice Blackburn said in *Fleet v Murton* (1871) LR 7 QB 126 at p 131.

> . . . I take it that there is no doubt at all, in principle, that a broker, as such, merely dealing as broker and not as purchaser of the article, makes a contract from the very nature of things between the buyer and the seller and he is not himself either buyer or seller.

It seems to me that the present case falls into that second category. It was known to both sides that the agents, Ney Shipping Ltd, were only brokers. They were brokers ordering bunkers for a vessel. It was obvious that they were only agents, and they were ordering bunkers for the time charterers or the owners of a vessel. They had often done it before. The accounts for the fuel had always been paid by the principals either directly or through the brokers. It cannot be supposed that the brokers were ever intended to be personally liable. The suppliers would look to the time charterers or the owners, whoever they might be, they being the people to be relied upon. Although they were not named or specified or disclosed, they would be the people to whom the suppliers would look for payment of the oil.

It is just the same, it seems to me, as if the brokers had given a written order for the bunkers and added to their signatures 'as agents only'. In that case they would not have been personally liable. Nor should they be liable in this case when it was done by word of mouth and when the inference from the conduct and the whole of the circumstances was that they were ordering the fuel as agents only.

It can be tested by taking the converse case. Suppose the fuel had been of bad quality and the engines of the ship had been damaged, or the ship delayed, could the brokers Ney Shipping have sued for damages? Or the brokers Vlassopulos have been made liable in damages? Clearly not. It would be for the principals on either side to have sued. So here the brokers Vlassopulos could not sue for the price, nor the brokers Ney be liable for it.

I know that in many trades there is a custom by which the broker is liable. Those cases rest on a custom of the trade. There was no such custom alleged or proved in respect of the brokers on the Baltic Exchange. It seems to me that, in the circumstances of this case, the proper inference is that the agents here were, when they gave the telephone message, giving it as agents only. By their conduct it is to be inferred that it was just the same as if they had given a written order excluding their personal liability and the suppliers looked to the owners or time charterers of the vessel who were the people really liable. It is the unfortunate fact that they have proved insolvent or unable to pay, but it seems to me that that is not a sufficient ground for now making the brokers liable. I would therefore allow the appeal and give judgment for the defendant.

[Roskill and Lawton LJJ delivered concurring judgments.]

NOTES

1. With oral contracts it is a question of fact in each particular case whether it was intended that the agent should or should not be entitled to sue, and/or held personally liable, on the contract. The agent's failure to name his principal is merely one factor, albeit a significant one, for the court to take into account when assessing whether the agent intended to contract personally.

2. In *The Santa Carina*, Lord Denning referred to para 321 of the American *Restatement of the Law of Agency* (2nd ed, 1958), which states that:

Unless otherwise agreed, a person purporting to make a contract with another for a partially disclosed principal is a party to the contract.

(A partially disclosed principal is a disclosed but unnamed principal.)

However, the Court of Appeal declined to apply such a general rule to unwritten contracts under English law. This decision has been criticised by Professor Reynolds who argues for a prima facie rule making the agent liable together with the unnamed principal. Professor Reynolds submits that because there is no such prima facie rule the courts have caused confusion by wrongly classifying unnamed principal cases as undisclosed principal cases so as to prevent the agent avoiding personal liability. See F M B Reynolds [1983] CLP 119.

Deeds

If an agent contracts by deed, he will be personally liable so long as he is a party to the deed and has executed it in his own name. In these circumstances, the agent will be liable even if he is described in the deed as acting for and on behalf of a named principal (*Appleton v Binks* (1804) 5 East 148). As to the possible effect of s 7(1) of the Powers of Attorney Act 1971 (as amended) on this rule, see Fridman, p 199 and p 207; Bowstead, pp 326–327 and p 453.

Negotiable instruments

Special rules apply in cases where an agent has signed a bill of exchange, promissory note or cheque. These rules are considered below at pp 522 ff.

Agents for foreign principals

See above, pp 119–120.

Agents for fictitious or non-existent principals

(1) At common law, an agent who purports to act for a non-existent or fictitious principal can be held personally liable on the contract. Whether the agent is liable will turn on the objective construction of the terms of the contract by the court. Even if the parties did not intend the agent to be liable on the contract, he may still be held liable for breach of warranty of authority, in deceit, or, possibly, for negligent misstatement.

(2) By statute, where a contract purports to be made by or on behalf of a company, at a time when the company has not yet been formed, then subject to any agreement to the contrary, the contract has effect as a contract made with the person purporting to act for the company or as agent for it, and he is personally liable on the contract accordingly: s 36C(1) of the Companies Act 1985, as inserted by Companies Act 1989, s 130(4) (above, p 112). If the agent is to avoid liability under the statute there must be 'a clear exclusion of personal liability': signing the contract 'for and on behalf of X Ltd' would not be enough (*Phonogram Ltd v Lane* [1982] QB 938 at 944, per Lord Denning MR). See generally A Griffiths (1993) 13 LS 241.

(3) Where it turns out that the agent is in fact his own principal, there is authority that the apparent agent can be held personally liable on the contract (*Railton v*

Hodgson (1804) 4 Taunt 576n; *Jenkins v Hutchinson* (1849) 13 QB 744; cf Bowstead at pp 474–476, where it is argued that liability on a collateral warranty would be more appropriate).

Statute

A statutory provision may make an agent personally liable on a contract made on behalf of his principal (see Treitel, op cit, pp 638–639). Examples of an agent's liability arising in this way include ss 36C and 349(4) of the Companies Act 1985 (considered above at p 137 and below at pp 524–526 respectively).

(iii) When will the agent be entitled to sue on the contract made on behalf of his principal?

The agent will be entitled to sue on the contract made on behalf of his disclosed principal in any of the following circumstances:

(1) Where it is the intention of the parties that the agent should have rights as well as liabilities on the contract (eg *Short v Spackman* (1831) 2 B & Ad 962).
(2) Where the agent's right of action arises out of a collateral contract with the third party (although, strictly, this does not allow the agent to sue on the main contract).
(3) Where the agent has some special property in the subject matter of the contract, or possesses a lien over it, or has a beneficial interest in completion of the contract, he may sue the third party. For example, the auctioneer's right to sue the highest bidder for the price stems from his special property in, or lien over, the subject matter of the sale he effects (*Benton v Campbell, Parker & Co* [1925] 2 KB 410 at 416, per Salter J); although the right of action actually arises under a collateral contract between the auctioneer and the highest bidder (*Chelmsford Auctions Ltd v Poole* [1973] QB 542 at 548–549, per Lord Denning MR).
(4) Where the agent purports to contract on behalf of a company yet to be formed, the agent may be entitled as well as liable on the contract under s 36C(1) of the Companies Act 1985 (above, p 137; see also Treitel, op cit, p 638).
(5) Where the agent is in fact the principal he may sue the third party (but see the next case).

Rayner v Grote (1846) 15 M & W 359, Court of Exchequer

The plaintiff, purporting to act for a named principal, contracted in writing to sell certain goods to the defendant. After discovering that the plaintiff was in fact the real principal, the defendant accepted delivery and paid for part of the goods. The plaintiff then sued the defendant for non-acceptance of the remainder of the goods. The Court of Exchequer (Pollock CB, Rolfe B and Alderton B) upheld the verdict of the jury in favour of the plaintiff.

Alderton B (delivering the judgment of the Court): . . . At the time when this contract was made, the plaintiff was himself the real principal in the transaction; and although the contract on the face of it appeared to have been made by him as agent for another party, there was evidence given at the trial, tending strongly to shew, that when the first parcel of the goods was delivered to and accepted by the defendants, the name of the plaintiff as the principal was then fully known to the defendants: and we think that it was then properly left to the jury to infer from the evidence, that the defendants, with the full knowledge of the facts, had received that portion of the goods, and that all parties then treated the contract as one made with the plaintiff as the principal in the transaction. The defendants' counsel, in the argument, contended against this view of the case, and cited the case of *Bickerton v Burrell* as an authority that the plaintiff could not sue in such a case in his own name. That case is indeed in one respect stronger than the present, inasmuch as that was an action for money had and received, whereas this is a case of an executory contract. If, indeed, the contract had been wholly unperformed, and one which the plaintiff, by merely proving himself to be the real principal, was seeking to enforce, the question might admit of some doubt. In many such cases, such as, for instance, the case of contracts in which the skill or solvency of the person who is named as the principal may reasonably be considered as a material ingredient in the contract, it is clear that the agent cannot then shew himself to be the real principal, and sue in his own name; and perhaps it may be fairly urged that this, in all executory contracts, if wholly unperformed, or if partly performed without the knowledge of who is the real principal, may be the general rule. But the facts of this case raise a totally different question, as the jury must be taken to have found, under the learned Judge's direction, that this contract has been in part performed, and that part performance accepted by the defendants with full knowledge that the plaintiff was not the agent, but the real principal. If so, we think the plaintiff may, after that, very properly say that they cannot refuse to complete that contract, by receiving the remainder of the goods, and paying the stipulated price for them. And it may be observed that this case is really distinguishable from *Bickerton v Burrell*, on the very ground on which that case was decided; for here, at all events, before action brought and trial had, the defendants knew that the plaintiff was the principal in the transaction. Perhaps it may be doubted whether that case was well decided on such a distinction, as it may fairly be argued that it would have been quite sufficient to prevent any possible inconvenience or injustice, and more in accordance with former authorities, if the Court had held that a party named as agent, under such circumstances as existed in that case, was entitled, on shewing himself to be the real principal, to maintain the action, the defendant being, however, allowed to make any defence to which he could shew himself to be entitled, either as against the plaintiff or as against the person named as principal by the plaintiff in the contract. It is not, however, necessary for us, in the present case, to question the authority of that decision.

NOTES

1. In *Bickerton v Burrell* (1816) 5 M & S 383, it was held that the plaintiff, having signed a contract as agent for a named principal, could not sue as the real principal, at all events unless he had given notice to the defendant of his true status in advance of bringing the action.

2. It would appear from the dictum of Alderton B in *Rayner v Grote* that an agent who purports to act for a named principal may nevertheless sue on the contract as the real principal provided that the identity of the principal was immaterial to the making of the contract by the third party and the agent has informed the third party being suing that he is the real principal, or that the third party, after discovering that the agent is the real principal, has partly performed or otherwise affirmed the contract (see Fridman, p 226; Bowstead, p 473). So long as the identity of the principal is not material to the third party, it is doubtful that there is anything to be gained by preventing the agent from suing on an entirely executory contract once the third party is aware of the true position (see Markesinis and Munday, p 224).

3. Alderton B's dictum was cited with approval by Webster J in *Gewa Chartering BV v Remco Shipping Lines Ltd, The Remco* [1984] 2 Lloyd's Rep 205. In that case an agent, purporting to act on behalf of a named principal, entered into a contract for the charter of a ship. Later the agent revealed himself to be the real principal. Webster J held that the agent could not enforce the contract since the other contracting party, the shipowners, regarded the identity of the charterer as material (because the charterer was responsible for payment of freight). It could be shown that the shipowners would not have agreed to the same terms if they had known that the agent was really the principal.

4. There have been a number of cases where an agent, who purports to act for an unnamed principal, has been allowed to reveal himself as the real principal and sue on the contract, on the ground that the personal characteristics of the supposed principal cannot have influenced the third party (see *Schmaltz v Avery* (1851) 16 QB 655; *Harper & Co v Vigers Bros* [1909] 2 KB 549; cf *Sharman v Brandt* (1871) LR 6 QB 720).

5. For criticism of *Rayner v Grote* and those cases allowing an agent to sue on a contract purportedly made on behalf of an unnamed principal, see Bowstead, pp 477–499; Makesinis and Munday, pp 224–225.

QUESTION

Arnold contracts purportedly on behalf of Percy, a noted dogbreeder, to buy a valuable prize poodle from Thomas. During the negotiations, Thomas says to Arnold: 'I am surprised that a reputable breeder like Percy is acting through a spiv like you'. Arnold is in fact acting for himself. Two weeks after the conclusion of this contract, Arnold telephones Thomas and admits that he is really the purchaser. At first, Thomas accepts the situation philosophically; but after consulting a lawyer, Daisy, he refuses to deliver up the poodle. Advise Arnold.

(iv) *Breach of warranty of authority*

Bowstead on Agency (15th ed, 1985), art 112(1)

Where a person, by words or conduct, represents that he has authority to act on behalf of another, and a third party is induced by such representation to act in a manner in which he would not have acted if such representation had not been made, the first-mentioned person is deemed to warrant that the representation is true, and is liable for any loss caused to such third party by a breach of such implied warranty, even if he acted in good faith, under a mistaken belief that he had such authority.

Yonge v Toynbee [1910] 1 KB 215, Court of Appeal

Solicitors were instructed by Toynbee to defend an action for libel and slander threatened against him by Yonge. Before the action was commenced, and unknown to his solicitors, Toynbee became insane and was certified as being of unsound mind. On commencement of the action the solicitors entered an appearance, delivered a defence and engaged in certain interlocutory proceedings. Subsequently, the solicitors discovered that Toynbee was insane and informed Yonge of that fact. Yonge then applied to have the appearance and all subsequent proceedings struck out and for the solicitors to pay personally his costs of the action, on the ground that they had acted for Toynbee without authority. The Master ordered the appearance and subsequent proceedings to be struck out but refused to make an order that Yonge's costs should be paid by the solicitors personally. The Court of Appeal allowed Yonge's appeal against the Master's refusal to make an order for costs against the solicitors.

Buckley LJ: The interesting and important question in this case is as to the extent to which the principle of *Smout v Ilbery* ((1842) 10 M & W 1) remains good law after the decision in *Collen v Wright* ((1857) 8 E & B 647). In *Smout v Ilbery* Alderson B, in giving the judgment of the Court, dealt with the authorities under three heads: First, the case where the agent made a fraudulent misrepresentation as to his authority with an intention to deceive. In such case the agent is, of course, personally responsible. Secondly, the case where the agent without fraud, but untruly in fact, represented that he had authority when he had none, instancing under this head *Polhill v Walter* ((1832) 3 B & Ad 114). In that case A, having no authority from B to accept a bill on his behalf, did accept it as by his procuration, bona fide believing that B would retrospectively approve that which he was doing. In such case again the agent is personally liable, for he induced the other party to enter into a contract on a misrepresentation of a fact within his own knowledge. The third class is where the agent bona fide believes that he has, but in fact has not, authority. This third class the learned Baron seems to subdivide into two heads – the first where the agent never had authority, but believed that he had (eg, when he acted on a forged warrant of attorney which he thought to be genuine), and the second where the agent had in fact full authority originally, but that authority had come to an end without any knowledge, or means of knowledge, on the part of the agent that such was the fact. The latter was the state of facts in *Smout v Ilbery*. I understand *Smout v Ilbery* not to dispute that in the former of these last two cases (that is, where the agent never had authority) he is liable, but to hold that in the latter (namely, where he originally had authority, but that authority has ceased without his having knowledge, or means of knowledge, that it has ceased) he is not liable. The principle is stated in the following words: 'If, then, the true principle derivable from the cases is, that there must be some wrong or omission of right on the part of the agent, in order to make him personally liable on a contract made in the name of his principal, it will follow that the agent is not responsible in such a case as the present. And to this conclusion we have come.' It seems to me that, if that principle be the true principle, then the former of the last two mentioned cases ought to have been resolved in the same way as the latter. I can see no distinction in principle between the case where the agent never had authority and the case where the agent originally had authority, but that authority has ceased without his knowledge or means of knowledge. In the latter case as much as in the former the proposition, I think, is true that without any mala fides he has at the moment of acting represented that he had an authority which in fact he had not. In my opinion he is then liable on an implied contract that he had authority, whether there was fraud or not. That this is the true principle is, I think, shewn by passages which I will quote from judgments in three which I have selected out of the numerous cases upon this subject. In *Collen v Wright* Willes J in giving the judgment of the Court uses the following language: 'I am of opinion that a person who induces another to contract with him, as the agent of a third party, by an unqualified assertion of his being authorized to act as such agent, is answerable to the person who so contracts for any damages which he may sustain by reason of the assertion of authority being untrue. . . . The fact that the professed agent honestly thinks that he has authority affects the moral character of his act; but his moral innocence, so far as the person whom he has induced to contract is concerned, in no way aids such person or alleviates the inconvenience and damage which he sustains. The obligation arising in such a case is well expressed by saying that a person professing to contract as agent for another, impliedly, if not expressly, undertakes to or promises the person who enters into such contract, upon the faith of the professed agent being duly authorized, that the authority which he professes to have does in point of fact exist.' This language is equally applicable to each of the two classes of cases to which I have referred. The language is not, in my opinion, consistent with maintaining that which *Smout v Ilbery* had laid down as the true principle, that there must be some wrong or omission of right on the part of the agent in order to make him liable. The question is not as to his honesty or bona fides. His liability arises from an implied undertaking or promise made by him that the authority which he professes to have does in point of fact exist. I can see no difference of principle between the case in which the authority never existed at all and the case in which the authority once existed and has ceased to exist. In *Firbank's Executors v Humphreys* ((1886) 18 QBD 54 at 60) the rule is thus stated by Lord Esher: 'The rule to be deduced is that, where a person by asserting that he has the authority of the principal induces another person to enter into any transaction which he would not have entered into but for that assertion, and the assertion turns out to be untrue, to the injury of the person to whom it is made, it must be taken that the person making it undertook that it was true, and he is liable personally for the damage that has occurred.'

Lastly, Lord Davey in *Starkey v Bank of England* ([1903] AC 114 at 119), after stating that the rule extends to every transaction of business into which a third party is induced to enter by a representation that the person with whom he is doing business has the authority of some other person, rejects the argument that the rule in *Collen v Wright* does not extend to cases where the supposed agent did not know that he had no authority, and had not the means of finding out; cites Lord Campbell's language in *Lewis v Nicholson* ((1852) 18 QB 503), that the agent 'is liable, if there was any fraud, in an action for deceit, and, in my opinion, as at present advised, on an implied contract that he had authority, whether there was fraud or not'; and concludes by saying that in his opinion 'it is utterly immaterial for the purpose of the application of this branch of the law whether the supposed agent knew of the defect of his authority or not.'

The result of these judgments, in my opinion, is that the liability of the person who professes to act as agent arises (a) if he has been fraudulent, (b) if he has without fraud untruly represented that he had authority when he had not, and (c) also where he innocently misrepresents that he has authority where the fact is either (1) that he never had authority or (2) that his original authority has ceased by reasons of facts of which he has not knowledge or means of knowledge. Such last-mentioned liability arises from the fact that by professing to act as agent he impliedly contracts that he has authority, and it is immaterial whether he knew of the defect of his authority or not.

This implied contract may, of course, be excluded by the facts of the particular case. If, for instance, the agent proved that at the relevant time he told the party with whom he was contracting that he did not know whether the warrant of attorney under which he was acting was genuine or not, and would not warrant its validity, or that his principal was abroad and he did not know whether he was still living, there will have been no representation upon which the implied contract will arise. This may have been the ratio decidendi in *Smout v Ilbery* as expressed in the passage 'The continuance of the life of the principal was, under these circumstances, a fact equally within the knowledge of both contracting parties'; and this seems to be the ground upon which Story on Agency, s 265a, approves the decision. The husband had left England for China in May, 1839, a time in the history of the world when communication was not what it is now, and the Court seems to have decided upon the ground that the butcher who supplied the goods knew that the facts were such that the wife did not, because she could not, take upon herself to affirm that he was alive. If so, there was no implied contract. The principle, as stated in the words I have quoted, may have been meant to be, but is not in words, rested upon that ground, and, if it is to be understood as it seems to have been understood in *Salton v New Beeston Cycle Co* ([1900] 1 Ch 43), it is not, I think, consistent with *Collen v Wright*. The true principle as deduced from the authorities I have mentioned rests, I think, not upon wrong or omission of right on the part of the agent, but upon implied contract.

The facts here are that the solicitors originally had authority to act for Mr Toynbee; that that authority ceased by reason of his unsoundness of mind; that, subsequently, they on October 30, 1908, undertook to appear, and on November 6 appeared, in the first action, and, after that was discontinued, did on December 21 undertake to appear, and did on December 30 enter an appearance, in the second action; and that they subsequently, on February 22, 1909, delivered a defence pleading privilege, and denying the slander, and did not until April 5 inform the plaintiff that, as the fact was, their client had become of unsound mind. During all this time they were putting the plaintiff to costs, and these costs were incurred upon the faith of their representation that they had authority to act for the defendant. They proved no facts addressed to shew that implied contract was excluded.

It has been pressed upon us that a solicitor is an agent of a special kind with an obligation towards his client to continue to take on his behalf all proper steps in the action. The particular nature of his agency is not, I think, very material. On the other hand it must be borne in mind that after August 21, when the defendant Toynbee wrote to the plaintiff's solicitors, referring them to Messrs Wontner & Sons, the plaintiff could not consistently with professional etiquette communicate personally with the defendant. During the period from August, 1908, to April, 1909, the solicitors had the means of knowing and did not in fact ascertain that the defendant had become of unsound mind. In the interval they did acts which amounted to representations on their part that they were continuing to stand in a position in which they were competent to bind the defendant. This was not the case. They are liable, in my judgment, upon an implied warranty or contract that they had an authority which they had not.

For these reasons I think that the appellent is entitled to succeed and to have an order against the solicitors for damages, and the measure of damage is, no doubt, the amount of the plaintiff's costs thrown away in the action. The appeal, therefore, should be allowed with costs here and below.

Swinfen Eady J: I wish to add that in the conduct of litigation the Court places much reliance upon solicitors, who are its officers; it issues writs at their instance, and accepts appearances for defendants which they enter, as a matter of course, and without questioning their authority; the other parties to the litigation also act upon the same footing, without questioning or investigating the authority of the solicitor on the opposite side; and much confusion and uncertainty would be introduced if a solicitor were not to be under any liability to the opposite party for continuing to act without authority in cases where he originally possessed one. . . . The manner in which business is ordinarily conducted requires that each party should be able to rely upon the solicitor of the other party having obtained a proper authority before assuming to act. It is always open to a solicitor to communicate as best he can with his own client, and obtain from time to time such authority and instructions as may be necessary. But the solicitor on the other side does not communicate with his opponent's client, and, speaking generally, it is not proper for him to do so, as was pointed out by Kekewich J in *Re Margetson & Jones* ([1897] 2 Ch 314). It is in my opinion essential to the proper conduct of legal business that a solicitor should be held to warrant the authority which he claims of representing the client; if it were not so, no one would be safe in assuming that his opponent's solicitor was duly authorized in what he said or did, and it would be impossible to conduct legal business upon the footing now existing; and, whatever the legal liability may be, the Court, in exercising the authority which it possesses over its own officers, ought to proceed upon the footing that a solicitor assuming to act, in an action, for one of the parties to the action warrants his authority.

[Vaughan Williams LJ delivered a concurring judgment.]

NOTES

1. Despite the fact that it was held in *Yonge v Toynbee* that the agent's liability to the third party was contractual, debate has continued as to the nature of an agent's liability to a third party when acting without authority. For example, the agent's liability has been described as 'quasi-contractual' or, alternatively, 'tortious' (see Fridman, pp 221–222) and in *Farley Health Products Ltd v Babylon Trading Co* (1987) Times, 29 July, Sir Neil Lawson even thought that liability for breach of warranty of authority was *sui generis*, not being a claim in contract or tort. However, it is submitted that the better explanation, which reflects the reasoning of Wright J in *Collen v Wright* (1857) 7 E & B 301 and of the Court of Appeal in *Yonge v Toynbee*, is that the agent's liability is based on a collateral contract made with the third party (see Wedderburn [1959] CLJ 58 at p 68; and Cheshire, Fifoot and Furmston *The Law of Contract* (12th ed, 1991) at p 497). Furthermore, the damages awarded for breach of an agent's warranty of authority will be assessed on normal *Hadley v Baxendale* (1854) 9 Exch 341 principles, thus reflecting the contractual nature of the liability (although if the agent has been fraudulent or negligent the third party can ask for damages to be assessed on a different basis).

2. An agent may be liable for breach of warranty of authority whether he is fraudulent, negligent or innocent. Liability is strict and may operates harshly on an agent who is innocently unaware of the initial absence, or subsequent termination, of his authority. However, the harshness of the rule is mitigated in the following respects:

(1) The agent will not be liable where the third party knew, or ought to have known, that the agent was not warranting his authority (eg *Lilly, Wilson & Co v Smales, Eeles & Co* [1892] 1 QB 456, where it was held that trade custom should have put the third party on notice that the agent was not warranting his authority).

(2) The agent's representation of authority must be one of fact and not of law (eg *Rashdall v Ford* (1866) LR 2 Eq 750, where directors of a statutory company, with no borrowing powers on a true construction of the incorporating statute, were held to have made a representation of law, and not of fact, when they purported to borrow from a third party). However, it is often difficult to distinguish representations of fact from representations of law (see Treitel, op cit, pp 641–642).

(3) Under s 5(1) of the Powers of Attorney Act 1971, a donee of a power of attorney who acts in pursuance of the power at a time when it has been revoked does not, by reason of the revocation, incur any liability (either to the donor or to any other person) if at the time he did not know that the power had been revoked.

(4) The agent's warranty is limited. It is that he has authority to make the contract or enter into the transaction, it is not that the contract or transaction will be performed by his principal. This means that if the principal is insolvent, the third party cannot recover more from the agent than he could have recovered from the principal, had the agent had authority.

3. Liability for breach of warranty of authority may extend very widely indeed. Not only may the agent be liable for breach of warranty of his own authority but he may also be liable if he warrants the authority of someone else (*Chapleo v Brunswick Permanent Building Society* (1881) 6 QBD 696). Furthermore, the agent may be held liable to a person unknown to him but who nevertheless relied upon his representation, eg the indorsee of a bill of exchange or a bill of lading (see *Rasnoimport V/O v Guthrie & Co Ltd* [1966] 1 Lloyd's Rep 1, but see F M B Reynolds (1967) 80 LQR 189 for criticism of this decision; see also R Bradgate and N Savage *Commercial Law* (1991), at p 109).

4. Will an agent with no actual authority be in breach of his warranty of authority if he has apparent authority or if the principal subsequently ratifies his actions? Professor Treitel submits that the agent would not be liable for breach of his warranty of authority in either of these circumstances (op cit, p 642, relying, inter alia, on *Rainbow v Howkins* [1904] 2 KB 322). We respectfully disagree with this submission. The agent professes that he has authority and this must be taken to mean that he has actual authority. This is because apparent authority is no authority at all but merely a condition which calls into being the power of an 'agent' to alter the legal relations of his 'principal' (see above, p 94). However, the fact that the agent has apparent authority is significant because it avoids loss to the third party which would otherwise result from the agent's breach of warranty of authority. If the third party can hold the principal to the contract or transaction affected by the agent on grounds of the latter's apparent authority, the third party will have suffered no loss by reason of the agent's breach of warranty of authority (see eg *Drew v Nunn* (1879) 4 QBD 661, below at p 202; but the point was not considered in *Yonge v Toynbee*). A similar conclusion can be reached with regard to the principal's ratification of an agent's unauthorised acts. Ratification is not retrospective for all purposes (above, pp 115–116) and so it is better to regard the agent as technically in breach of his warranty of authority, even though the third party's loss will be limited if the principal ratifies the agent's acts (although the third party could still have incurred loss in pursuing the agent before ratification by the principal).

2 Undisclosed agency

(a) Relations between principal and third party

(i) *The general rule*

Keighley, Maxsted & Co v Durant [1901] AC 240, House of Lords

(The facts appear above at p 110.)

Lord Lindley: The explanation of the doctrine that an undisclosed principal can sue and be sued on a contract made in the name of another person with his authority is, that the contract is in truth, although not in form, that of the undisclosed principal himself. Both the principal and the authority exist when the contract is made; and the person who makes it for him is only the instrument by which the principal acts. In allowing him to sue and be sued upon it, effect is given, so far as he is concerned, to what is true in fact, although that truth may not have been known to the other contracting party.

At the same time, as a contract is constituted by the concurrence of two or more persons and by their agreement to the same terms, there is an anomaly in holding one person bound to another of whom he knows nothing and with whom he did not, in fact, intend to contract. But middlemen, through whom contracts are made, are common and useful in business transactions, and in the great mass of contracts it is a matter of indifference to either party whether there is an undisclosed principal or not. If he exists it is, to say the least, extremely convenient that he should be able to sue and be sued as a principal, and he is only allowed to do so upon terms which exclude injustice.

NOTES

1. An undisclosed principal can sue and be sued on a contract made on his behalf by his agent acting within the scope of his actual authority. This doctrine is generally regarded as anomalous because it gives the undisclosed principal rights, and subjects him to liabilities, that arise under a contract to which he was not originally privy. As Sir Frederick Pollock once commented in (1887) 3 LQR 358 at 359:

The plain truth ought never to be forgotten – that the whole law as to the rights and liabilities of an undisclosed principal is inconsistent with the elementary doctrines of the law of contract. The right of one person to sue another on a contract not really made with the person suing is unknown to every other legal system except that of England and America.

See also Pollock (1896) 12 LQR 204 and (1898) 14 LQR 5. For further criticism of the undisclosed principal doctrine, see Oliver Wendell Holmes 'The History of Agency' in *Selected Essays in Anglo-American Legal History*, Vol 6, p 404, who thought the doctrine was 'opposed to common sense'; and James Barr Ames (1909) 18 Yale LJ 443, who thought the doctrine 'ignores fundamental legal principles' and 'should be recognised as an anomaly'. As to whether the doctrine causes injustice, contrast Ames, op cit, p 453, with W A Seavey (1920) 29 Yale 859 at pp 877–880 and A L Goodhart and C J Hamson (1932) 4 CLJ 320 at p 321.

2. Numerous theories have been advanced to explain the doctrine: they are usefully reviewed by A Rochvarg (1989) 34 McGill LJ 286 at pp 298–314. The theories which have received most attention are those based on trust and assignment. It has been argued that the agent is trustee for the undisclosed principal (see Ames, op cit), but it was held by Ungoed-Thomas J in *Pople v Evans* [1969] 2 Ch 255 at 264, in the context of the *res judicata* doctrine, that 'there is no trust relationship between any of the parties which can be recognised as between the third party on the one hand and the principal and agent, or either of them, on the other hand'. The trust theory has also been criticised by Seavey, op cit, pp 879–880. Probably the best explanation of the doctrine is by analogy with assignment. This explanation accepts (correctly, it is submitted) that the contract is originally made between the agent, not the principal, and the third party (Lord Lindley's dicta to the contrary in *Keighley, Maxsted & Co v Durant*, above at p 145, should be regarded with doubt) and then regards it as automatically transferred to the undisclosed principal by 'a primitive and highly restricted form of assignment' (Goodhart and Hamson, op cit, p 352). However, the analogy is not perfect for, unlike assignment, the undisclosed principal doctrine involves the transfer of liabilities as well as rights and, furthermore, there is no event which can be regarded as an assignment. For further differences between the undisclosed principal doctrine and assignment, see R Powell *The Law of Agency* (2nd ed, 1961), pp 165–166; see also *Siu Yin Kwan v Eastern Insurance Co Ltd* [1994] 1 All ER 213 at 223, PC.

3. The lack of any watertight legal explanation of the undisclosed principal doctrine does not appear to have troubled the courts unduly. The courts have been prepared to justify the doctrine simply on grounds of commercial convenience (see *Keighley, Maxsted & Co v Durant*, above at p 145, per Lord Lindley; *Teheran-Europe Co Ltd v Belton (Tractors) Ltd* [1968] 2 QB 545 at 552, per Lord Denning MR; *Siu Yin Kwan v Eastern Insurance Co Ltd*, above, at 220, per Lord Lloyd; cf *Freeman & Lockyer v Buckhurst Park Properties (Mangal) Ltd* [1964] 2 QB 480 at 503, per Diplock LJ – above at p 92). This pragmatic approach is to be welcomed, but it has meant that certain aspects of the application of the undisclosed principal doctrine remain unclear, eg the effect of a disposition of goods to the agent of an undisclosed principal (considered by the Court of Appeal of New South Wales in *Maynegrain Pty Ltd v Compafina Bank* [1982] 2 NSWLR 141; reversed on the facts by the Privy Council (1984) 58 ALJR 389, noted by F M B Reynolds (1984) 4 Ox JLS 434).

4. For an account of the historical development of the undisclosed principal doctrine, see A L Goodhart and C J Hamson (1932) 4 CLJ 320; also Markesinis and Munday, pp 168–170. For a comparative treatment of the subject, see W Muller-Freienfels (1953) 16 MLR 299 and (1955) 18 MLR 33.

QUESTION

Peter employs Alan to contract with Ted, instructing him to do so in his own name. Ted suspects Alan may be acting for a principal as it is known in the trade that Alan sometimes contracts for himself and sometimes for others. But without making any inquiry as to Alan's status, Ted contracts with him. Peter has now revealed himself to be Alan's principal but Ted wants to hold Alan personally liable on the contract as the agent of an undisclosed principal. Was Peter really an 'undisclosed' principal? See F M B Reynolds [1983] CLP 119 at pp 122–128; Bowstead, pp 316–317.

(ii) *Exclusion of the undisclosed principal*

By the terms of the contract

Fred Drughorn Ltd v Rederiaktiebolaget Trans-Atlantic [1919] AC 203, House of Lords

An undisclosed principal claimed to be entitled to sue on a charterparty signed by its agent as 'charterer'. Affirming the decision of the Court of Appeal, the House of Lords held that evidence was admissible to establish that the agent had contracted on behalf of the principal.

Viscount Haldane: My Lords, by the law of England if B contracts with C prima facie that is a contract between these two only, but if at the time B entered into the contract he was really acting as agent for A, then evidence is generally admissible to show that A was the principal, and A can take advantage of the contract as if it had been actually made between himself and C. . . .

But, my Lords, the principle is limited by [a] consideration, about which . . . there is no doubt, and the applicability of which to the present case is beyond question. In *Humble v Hunter* ((1848) 12 QB 310) it was approved, although it was not necessary to give a decision on the point, and also in *Formby Bros v Formby* ((1910) 102 LT 116) and in other cases. These are authorities for the proposition that evidence of authority of an outside principal is not admissible, if to give such evidence would be to contradict some term in the contract itself. It was held in *Humble v Hunter*, that where a charterer dealt with someone described as the owner, evidence was not admissible to show that some other person was the owner. That is perfectly intelligible. The question is not before us now, but I see no reason to question that where you have the description of a person as the owner of property, and it is a term of the contract that he should contract as owner of that property, you cannot show that another person is the real owner. That is not a question of agency – that is a question of property.

My Lords, in the same way in *Formby Bros v Formby* the term was 'proprietor,' and 'proprietor' was treated in the opinion of the Court of Appeal as on the same footing as the expression 'owner.' But, my Lords, we are not dealing with that case here. The principle remains, but the question is whether the principle applies to a charterparty where the person who says that he signed only as agent describes himself as the charterer.

My Lords, there may be something to be said from the heading of the charterparty in this case, and the reference to the company which claims to have been his principal, for the proposition that, reading the document as a whole, there is evidence that he intended to convey that he was acting as agent for somebody else; but whether that is so or not the term 'charterer' is a very different term from the term 'owner' or the term 'proprietor.' A charterer may be and prima facie is merely entering into a contact. A charterparty is not a lease – it is a chattel that is being dealt with, a chattel that is essentially a mere subject of contract; and although rights of ownership or rights akin to ownership may be given under it prima facie it is a contract for the hiring or use of the vessel. Under these circumstances it is in accordance with ordinary business common-sense and custom that charterers should be able to contract as agents for undisclosed principals who may come in and take the benefit of the charterparty.

But, my Lords, it is said that in this charterparty the terms are such as to exclude that notion. Why is that said to be so? Because the term 'charterer' is used. Well, I have already commented upon that. It is said that the term 'charterer' was meant simply to describe a particular person who is to carry out the nomination of arbitrators and everything else which is contained in the charterparty – to give orders which can only be given by one person, and that for the working out of the charterparty it is essential to treat the person so contracting as designated as a person whose identity cannot be varied or contradicted.

My Lords, the answer is that the principal may take that place, and that the company, in this case acting through its agent, whoever that agent may be, will be in the same position as the charterer contracting originally. There is nothing in that position inconsistent with the stipulations of this charterparty, and therefore it appears to me that the qualifying principle of *Humble v Hunter*, that you shall not contradict the instrument by giving evidence of agency, has no application in this case.

[Lords Shaw of Dunfermline and Wrenbury concurred. Lord Sumner delivered a concurring opinion.]

NOTES

1. In *Humble v Hunter* (1848) 12 QB 310, a son chartered out a vessel owned by his mother but signed the charterparty as 'C J Humble Esq, owner of the good ship or vessel called the *Ann*'. It was held that the mother could not enforce the contract as undisclosed principal on the basis that she was in fact the shipowner, since the description of her son as 'owner' was inconsistent with this. The House of Lords' decision in *Drughorn*'s case clearly limits the effect of *Humble v Hunter* (in *Epps v Rothnie* [1945] KB 562 at 565, Scott LJ went so far as to suggest that *Humble v Hunter* had been overruled by *Drughorn*'s case). As Professor Markesinis and Dr Munday conclude: 'It will now only be in exceptional cases that the undisclosed principal's intervention will be held inconsistent with the terms of the contract, and possibly only in cases where the agent can be construed to have contracted as owner of property' (op cit, p 174; see also Bowstead, p 321; cf Fridman, p 231). But see *Asty Maritime Co Ltd and Panagiotis Stravelakis v Rocco Giuseppe and Figli SNC, The Astyanax* [1985] 2 Lloyd's Rep 109, where the Court of Appeal held that the description of one party to a charterparty as 'disponent owner' of a vessel was neutral, but that the surrounding circumstances and the course of negotiations were inconsistent with that party contracting as mere agent on behalf of the registered owners of the vessel.

2. In cases such as those we have just considered, the test which determines whether the undisclosed principal can intervene is whether the agent has impliedly contracted that there is no principal behind him. If the agent has given such an implied undertaking the undisclosed principal may not intervene (A L Goodhart and C J Hamson (1932) 4 CLJ 320 at p 327 and p 342; Bowstead, pp 320–321; cf Fridman, pp 232–233). However, it is always open to exclude the possibility of intervention by an undisclosed principal through an express term that the agent is the real and only principal (*United Kingdom Mutual SS Assurance Association v Nevill* (1887) 19 QBD 110).

QUESTION

In *Humble v Hunter*, could the mother have intervened if she had been co-owner of the vessel with her son? See Goodhart and Hamson, op cit, p 327.

On grounds of personality

Greer v Downs Supply Co [1927] 2 KB 28, Court of Appeal

Downs Supply Co (the respondent) purchased timber from Godwin for £29, it being agreed that the respondent should have the right to set off against the price the sum of £17 owed by Godwin to the respondent. Godwin was in fact acting for an undisclosed principal (the appellant) who sought to intervene on the contract. The Court of Appeal held that the undisclosed principal had no right of action on the contract.

Scrutton LJ: . . . The appellant issued a plaint for goods sold and delivered, and the original orders given by the respondent to Godwin were furnished as particulars of the contract of sale. When a plaintiff claims as an undisclosed principal the question sometimes arises whether the contract was made with the agent for reasons personal to the agent which induced the other party to contract with the agent to the exclusion of his principal or any one else. When the learned judge at the trial found that the respondent knew nothing about the appellant and honestly believed he was contracting with Godwin and when it was proved that he was contracting with Godwin because Godwin was his debtor, there was an end of the case for the appellant at the trial.

[Bankes and Lawrence LJJ delivered concurring judgments.]

Said v Butt [1920] 3 KB 497, King's Bench Division

Said wished to attend the first night of a new play to be staged at the Palace Theatre. He knew that the theatre owners would not sell a ticket to him because of an existing dispute with them over allegations Said had made concerning the sale of tickets by the theatre. Said therefore asked his friend Pollock to buy a ticket for him. When Said arrived at the theatre for the performance, Butt (the managing director) refused him admittance. Said sued Butt for wrongfully inducing the owners of the theatre to commit a breach of contract.

McCardie J: . . . A first night at the Palace Theatre is, as with other theatres, an event of great importance. The result of a first night may make or mar a play. If the play be good, then word of its success may be spread, not only by the critics, but by members of the audience. The nature and social position and influence of the audience are of obvious importance. First nights have become to a large extent a species of private entertainment given by the theatrical proprietors and management to their friends and acquaintances, and to influential persons, whether critics or otherwise. The boxes, stalls and dress circle are regarded as parts of the theatre which are subject to special allocation by the management. Many tickets for those parts may be given away. The remaining tickets are usually sold by favour only. A first night, therefore, is a special event, with special characteristics. As the plaintiff himself stated in evidence, the management only disposes of first night tickets for the stalls and dress circle to those whom it selects. I may add that it is scarcely likely to choose those who are antagonistic to the management; or who have attacked the character of the theatre officials. . . . The Palace Theatre officials had no idea that they were selling a ticket to an agent of the plaintiff. If they had known it, they would at once have refused to supply a ticket. I find as a fact that the plaintiff used the name of Mr Pollock in order to disguise that he himself was the purchaser; and I also find that the plaintiff well knew that the Palace Theatre would not have sold him personally a ticket for December 23, 1919. I am satisfied that Mr Pollock himself was aware of the above-mentioned circumstances. I may point out that a theatre stands on a wholly different footing from a public inn, or a public service such as a railway. A public inn, for example, is under a common law duty to supply to all who come provided that accommodation exists; and provided also that the guest is of proper character and behaviour. But a theatre stands upon a wholly different footing. It may sell or refuse to sell tickets at its own option. The public cannot compel a theatre to grant admission.

Under these circumstances, the question is whether the plaintiff, as an undisclosed principal of Mr Pollock, can claim that a binding contract existed between the Palace Theatre, Ltd, and himself.

[His Lordship then considered the authorities dealing with the effect of mistake as to the identity of a contracting party and continued:]

In my opinion the defendant can rightly say, upon the special circumstances of this case, that no contract existed on December 23, 1919, upon which the plaintiff could have sued the Palace Theatre. The personal element was here strikingly present. The plaintiff knew that the Palace Theatre would not contract with him for the sale of a seat for December 23. They had expressly refused to do so. He was well aware of their reasons. I hold that by the mere device of utilizing the name and services of Mr Pollock, the plaintiff could not constitute himself a contractor with the Palace Theatre against their knowledge, and contrary to their express refusal. He is disabled from asserting that he was the undisclosed principal of Mr Pollock.

It follows, therefore, that the plaintiff has failed to prove that the defendant caused any breach of a contract between the Palace Theatre, Ltd, and himself.

I realize, however, that the question is one of difficulty. . . .

Dyster v Randall & Sons [1926] Ch 932, Chancery Division

Dyster knowing that Randall and Sons would not sell certain land to him (because they distrusted him), procured his friend Crossley to purchase the land for him without disclosing that he was acting on Dyster's behalf. When Randall and Sons discovered that Crossley had been acting for Dyster, they sought to resist performance of the contract of sale of the land on the grounds that they had been deceived by Dyster.

Lawrence J: . . . it is essential to bear in mind that the agreement which the plaintiff seeks to enforce is not one in which any personal qualifications possessed by Crossley formed a material ingredient, but is a simple agreement for sale of land in consideration of a lump sum to be paid on completion. It is an agreement which the defendants would have entered into with any other person. It is well settled that the benefit of such an agreement is assignable and that the assignee can enforce specific performance of it. If Crossley had entered into the agreement on his own behalf (as the defendants believed he had) he could immediately have assigned it to the plaintiff and the defendants would have been bound to convey the plots to the plaintiff. Moreover, as Crossley had not, before signing the agreement, disclosed the fact that he was acting as agent, he was liable under it as principal and the defendants could have compelled him to complete the purchase.

Further, it is to be noted that in this case there was no direct misrepresentation such as there was in *Archer v Stone* ((1898) 78 LT 34). Crossley was not asked by the defendants whether he was buying for the plaintiff and he made no statement to the defendants on the subject. The real question therefore is whether Crossley's silence, in the circumstances, amounted to a misrepresentation which renders the agreement unenforceable in this Court. In my judgment mere non-disclosure as to the person actually entitled to the benefit of a contract for the sale of real estate does not amount to misrepresentation, even though the contracting party knows that, if the disclosure were made, the other party would not enter into the contract; *secus*, if the contract were one in which some personal consideration formed a material ingredient: see *Nash v Dix* ((1898) 78 LT 445) and *Said v Butt* ([1920] 3 KB 497). In *Nash v Dix* North J held that the ostensible purchaser was acting on his own account and not as agent, but it appears to me that the learned judge would have arrived at the same conclusion if the alleged agency had been established. In *Said v Butt* McCardie J relied entirely on the personal consideration which entered into the contract and would obviously have decided otherwise if the personal element had been absent. I therefore hold that the first ground relied upon by the defendants does not afford a good defence to the plaintiff's claim to specific performance.

NOTES

1. The undisclosed principal will be prohibited from intervening on his agent's contract in the following circumstances:

(1) when there is an express or implied term in the contract between the agent and the third party prohibiting such intervention; and

(2) when the contract is of a personal nature, ie where the third party relied on the skill, solvency or other personal characteristics of the agent (*Greer v Downs Supply Co*); where the benefit of the contract cannot be assigned; or where there cannot be vicarious peformance of the burden of the contract (eg a contract to paint a portrait – but the Privy Council has recently held in *Siu Yin Kwan v Eastern Insurance Co Ltd* [1994] 1 All ER 213, that a contract of indemnity insurance was not a personal contract in that sense, so that an undisclosed principal could intervene and sue on a contact of insurance made by his agent acting within his actual authority).

Whether the undisclosed principal will be prohibited from intervening in cases where the third party would not have dealt with the principal if he had known that the agent was acting for him is a moot point. *Said v Butt* certainly appears to support the exclusion of the undisclosed principal doctrine in these circumstances. In that case there was no term of the contract excluding the principal's intervention and the contract itself could not be described as personal in any of the senses set out above (unless a ticket for a first night performance is regarded as non-assignable). However, unless it is possible to distinguish the case as one involving a non-assignable benefit, it is submitted that it is best to regard *Said v Butt* as wrongly decided. This task is made somewhat easier by reason of the fact that McCardie J's judgment is based on the erroneous premiss that the contract was made between the third party and the undisclosed principal (the correct analysis is that the undisclosed principal intervenes in a contract originally made between the third party and the agent: A L Goodhart and C J Hamson (1932) 4 CLJ 320 at pp 346–352; see also above at p 146). Dicta in *Dyster v Randall and Sons* that personality may prevent the undisclosed principal's intervention if it is a 'material ingredient' or 'strikingly present', to use McCardie J's words in *Said v Butt*, should be rejected in so far as they purport to go beyond the circumstances prohibiting intervention as set out under (1) and (2) above (see Goodhart and Hamson, op cit, pp 349–352). Allowing a further exception to the undisclosed principal doctrine merely heaps a further anomaly upon an anomaly (ie the doctrine itself). Furthermore, whatever the dicta in *Dyster v Randall and Sons* the result was clear:

the mere fact that the third party would not have dealt with the undisclosed principal was not enough to prevent the principal's intervention.

However, for a strong defence of *Said v Butt*, see G H Treitel *The Law of Contract* (8th ed, 1991), pp 632–633; see also Glanville Williams (1945) 23 Can B Rev 380 at pp 406–412, who submits that 'ordinary ideas of fair dealing' lie at the heart of the decision.

2. The problem raised by *Said v Butt* will be avoided if it can be shown that the person the third party dealt with was acting as principal and not agent. In *Nash v Dix* (1898) 78 LT 445, the defendants did not wish to sell a Congregational chapel to a committee of Roman Catholics. Instead they sold the chapel to the plaintiff but later refused to complete the transaction when they discovered the plaintiff was going to on-sell it to the Roman Catholic Committee. North J ordered specific peformance of the contract of sale on the grounds that the plaintiff was not an agent of the committee but was purchasing the chapel for himself with a view to resale at a profit.

3. If the contract between the agent and the third party was induced by the agent's misrepresentation, the principal cannot enforce it against the third party: *Archer v Stone* (1898) 78 LT 34 (third party asked agent if he was acting for S and he untruthfully denied that he was).

QUESTION

Thelma sells her whole crop of strawberries to Agatha. Unknown to Thelma, Agatha is acting as agent for Louise, who Thelma blames for the breakdown of her marriage and has sworn she would never do business with. Before payment, Agatha becomes insolvent and Thelma discovers that Louise is the principal behind her. Thelma now wishes to hold Louise liable for the price. Can Louise successfully resist Thelma's claim on grounds of personality? See Markesinis and Munday, p 180; and Fridman, pp 234–235.

Deeds, bills of exchange and promissory notes

An undisclosed principal cannot sue or be sued on a deed *inter partes* (see above, p 119). An undisclosed principal cannot be made liable on any negotiable instrument (see above, p 119).

(iii) *Particular aspects of the relationship between undisclosed principal and third party*

The rights and liabilities of the undisclosed principal and third party may be affected by the agent in a number of ways.

Merger and election

Clarkson Booker Ltd v Andjel [1964] 2 QB 775, Court of Appeal

Andjel purchased airline tickets on credit from Clarkson Booker Ltd (the plaintiffs), who were travel agents. In fact Andjel was acting for an undisclosed principal, Peters & Milner Ltd (P & M). Subsequently, on being informed that

Andjel was acting for P & M, the plaintiffs wrote to both principal and agent threatening proceedings unless the amount due was paid. Payment was not made and the plaintiffs started proceedings against P & M. However, the plaintiffs were then informed that P & M were insolvent and about to be put into liquidation. The plaintiffs accordingly did not proceed further with their action against the principal, P & M, but started proceedings against the agent, Andjel. Andjel resisted the claim on the ground that the plaintiffs had elected to hold the principal exclusively liable and, therefore, were precluded from proceeding against him, the agent. The County Court judge gave judgment for the plaintiffs. Andjel appealed.

Willmer LJ: . . . the point is taken for the defendant that the plaintiffs, having elected to start proceedings against Peters & Milner Ltd, are now debarred from asserting their claim against the defendant. The contention on behalf of the defendant is that this is a case of true election in that, with full knowledge of the facts, the plaintiffs deliberately and unequivocally chose to pursue their right against the principals, which was a right consistent with their right against the defendant as agent. Reliance is placed on a statement contained in Powell on Agency, 2nd ed (1961), p 270, where the following is put forward as proposition (v): 'T (a third party) starts proceedings against P (the principal) or A (the agent). The initiation of proceedings against P or A is strong evidence of election, though not necessarily conclusive. That is so whether T issues a writ or files proof of his debt in bankruptcy proceedings.' This proposition is not accepted by the plaintiffs as a correct statement of the law. It is submitted on their behalf that a plaintiff is barred only if he has sued one or other (ie, principal or agent) to judgment. It is conceded that he cannot then proceed against the other. But that, it is said, is not a true case of election; the remedy is barred because the cause of action has merged in the judgment. It is contended that nothing short of judgment against the principal is sufficient to bar the plaintiff's remedy against the agent. In the present case it is said that there has been nothing amounting either in law or in fact to an election, so as to preclude the present action against the defendant.

The judge, in dealing with this aspect of the case, quoted at some length from the speech of Lord Blackburn in *Scarf v Jardine* ((1882) 7 App Cas 345 at 354–362). I need not quote again the passage from Lord Blackburn. Suffice it to say that he expressed the view that there could be no more unequivocal act than instituting proceedings against one of two possible debtors; this, he thought, amounted to a final election to treat that debtor as liable so as to preclude the plaintiff thereafter from suing the other debtor. . . .

I cannot, of course, do other than attach the greatest possible weight to the decision of the House of Lords in *Scarf v Jardine*, particularly the reasoning of Lord Blackburn. But I do not understand him to mean that where proceedings have once been commenced against one of two possible debtors a plaintiff is necessarily precluded as a matter of law from subsequently taking proceedings against the other. Indeed, Mr Hamilton freely conceded that there must be some cases at least where the mere issue of a writ could not be held to amount to a binding election – for instance, where it is issued for the purpose of preventing limitation time from running out. Similarly, it has been held that an abortive writ issued against a company not yet incorporated at the time when the order for the plaintiffs' services was given did not amount to a binding election so as to preclude a subsequent action against the agents through whom the order was given: see *Longman v Hill* ((1891) 7 TLR 639). But even allowing for such exceptional cases it is clear that the institution of proceedings against either agent or principal is at least strong evidence of an election such as, if not rebutted, will preclude subsequent proceedings against the other. In other words, it raises a prima facie case of election. . . .

Having regard to those authorities, I think that the judge in the present case was plainly right in regarding the question before him as one of fact. But is has been argued that he came to a wrong conclusion on the facts. Since the relevant evidence is all contained in the correspondence, we have been invited to review his findings and to draw our own inferences from the correspondence. In a case such as the present we are clearly entitled to take this course, for we are in as good a position to draw inferences as was the judge.

In the light of the authorities to which I have referred, I approach the question to be decided on the basis that the institution of proceedings against Peters & Milner Ltd affords at least prima facie evidence of an election on the part of the plaintiffs to look only to them for payment of their debt. The question is whether there is any sufficient evidence to rebut the prima facie inference that arises from the institution of those proceedings.

In order to constitute an election which will bar the present proceedings against the defendant, the decision to sue Peters & Milner Ltd must, in the first place, be shown to have been taken with full knowledge of all the relevant facts. In the circumstances of this case I feel no difficulty on this point, for it cannot be suggested that when the plaintiffs made their decision to sue Peters & Milner Ltd they were in any way ignorant of their rights against the defendant.

But, secondly, it must be shown that the decision to institute proceedings against Peters & Milner Ltd was a truly unequivocal act if it is to preclude the plaintiffs from subsequently suing the defendant. This, I think, involves looking closely at the context in which the decision was taken, for any conclusion must be based on a review of all the relevant circumstances. One highly relevant circumstance is the fact that it was the defendant to whom the plaintiffs gave credit, as they had done over previous transactions. The correspondence shows that down to the letters of July 26 the plaintiffs throughout were looking to the defendant for payment of their debt, ie, to the person to whom they had given credit, although they also adumbrated a possible claim against Peters & Milner Ltd. On July 26, as I have already stated, they caused letters to be written to both the defendant and Peters & Milner Ltd, threatening proceedings against each. Clearly, up to that time there was no election to proceed only against the latter.

The whole case for the defendant rests on the fact that on August 8, having taken instructions, the plaintiffs' solicitors wrote to Peters & Milner Ltd announcing their intention 'to obtain judgment' against them. It is true that they did not at that time write any similar letter to the defendant, but they did not then or at any other time ever withdraw their threat to take proceedings against him. There is not, and could not be, any suggestion that the defendant was in any way prejudiced by the course which the plaintiffs took, or that he was in any sense lulled into a false sense of security.

Had the plaintiffs carried out their threat to obtain judgment against Peters & Milner Ltd they would, of course, have been precluded from subsequently taking proceedings against the defendant, for their cause of action would then have been merged in the judgment obtained against Peters & Milner Ltd. But in fact the plaintiffs took no step against Peters & Milner Ltd beyond the issue and service of the writ. Upon being informed of the proposal to put the company into liquidation they took no further action whatsoever against that company. They did not, for instance (as in *Scarf v Jardine* and other cases cited), seek to prove in the liquidation; instead they proceeded to give effect forthwith to their already announced, and never withdrawn, threat to sue the defendant.

On the whole, though I regard the case as being very near the borderline, I find myself unable to disagree with the conclusion arrived at by the judge. I do not think that the plaintiffs, by the mere institution of proceedings against Peters & Milner Ltd, made such an unequivocal election as to debar them from taking the present proceedings against the defendant.

I would accordingly dismiss the appeal.

[Davies LJ concurred.]

Russell LJ: The defendant having contracted as agent for an undisclosed principal, the plaintiffs were entitled to enforce the contract either against the defendant on the footing that he was contracting and liable as principal, or against the principal on the footing that the defendant was not liable, being merely an agent. The plaintiffs could not enforce the contract against both. Their right against the defendant and their right against the principal were inconsistent rights. At some stage the plaintiffs had to elect to avail themselves of one of those inconsistent rights and abandon the other. The question is whether the correct conclusion from the facts of this case is that, prior to the issue of their writ against the defendant, the plaintiffs had so elected. If they had, the election crystallised their rights, and they could not sue the defendant. The judge concluded that they had not so elected.

What were the facts? . . .

Was the judge on those facts wrong in concluding that the plaintiffs had not elected to treat the principal as liable in exoneration of the defendant?

It was reluctantly (although rightly) accepted by counsel for the defendant that the service of a writ against the principal per se does not show an election. Statements by Lord Blackburn in the *Scarf* case [*Scarf v Jardine* (1882) 7 App Cas 345 at 360] cannot be taken as establishing that position in law. It would be in some respects convenient if it were so, as tending to certainty in the application of the law, but even that would not resolve the problems that would arise in the case of a single writ against the principal and agent claiming in the alternative, or in the case of simultaneous or substantially simultaneous writs. The position is that in every case the external acts of the plaintiff must lead to the conclusion, as a matter of fact, that the plaintiff has settled to a choice involving abandonment of his option to enforce his right against one party. I have no doubt that in a given case this may be shown without his proceeding to the length of obtaining a judgment; indeed, if judgment is obtained against either principal or agent, this is more than election, though frequently referred to as election: the judgment supersedes the contractual right against either, and if obtained against the agent precludes action against the principal even if the plaintiff was ignorant of his existence and therefore unable to elect. Further, I have no doubt that, in assessing the facts of a particular case in pursuit of a conclusion on the question of election, the fact of the service of a writ against one and not against the other points significantly towards a decision to exonerate the other. A letter may assert a claim and demand satisfaction, but it is not capable of bearing fruit, even if wholly ignored by the recipient, whereas service of a writ is the first step in actual enforcement of the claim, to be ignored by the recipient at his peril. On the other hand, it is in terms a statement that the plaintiff makes a claim against the defendant. As I have said, it does not necessarily involve abandonment of a similar alternative claim against another possible defendant. It would not do so if there were a simultaneous writ against the other. Nor would it do so if the plaintiff were simultaneously expressly informing the other that the alternative claim was not abandoned. Nor would it do so if simultaneously the plaintiff was maintaining vis-à-vis the other the attitude that he might be looked to for liability on the contract.

What of the present case? It is said for the defendant that the letters of July 26 maintained the alternative claim against each, and that by contrast the writ against one demonstrated the exoneration of the other as a matter of election. I am not on the whole persuaded by this. I do not think that the letter to the principal's solicitors (as such) of August 3 can really be regarded as any less a determination to enforce the right against the principal than the subsequent issue and service of the writ on the principal, but that letter was contemporaneous with correspondence which demonstrates a retention of the right to claim against the defendant. In those circumstances, I am not able to conclude that the facts demonstrate that the plaintiffs finally elected to rely on the liability of the principal under the contract in exoneration of the agent. Consequently, I agree that this appeal fails.

NOTES

1. In cases of undisclosed agency the third party is able to sue both the agent on the contract made with him and also the principal because of the special rule of law operating in this situation. 'But because the third party has only purported to make one contract with one person, to enter into a single obligation, these two rights of action are commonly said to be alternative': F M B Reynolds (1970) 86 LQR 317 at p 320.

2. There is clear authority that the doctrine of merger applies to cases of undisclosed agency when the third party proceeds to judgment against the principal or the agent (*Priestly v Fernie* (1865) 3 H & C 977; *Kendall v Hamilton* (1879) 4 App Cas 504 at 514–515, per Lord Cairns LC). For further consideration of the doctrine of merger, see above, p 126.

3. It is clear from *Clarkson Booker v Andjel* that in cases of undisclosed agency there can be election by means of an unequivocal act short of obtaining judgment against the principal or the agent. What constitutes an election is a question of fact to be decided in the circumstances of the case. Commencing legal proceedings against one party provides a prima facie case of election, but it is not conclusive (as shown by *Clarkson Booker v Andjel*; applied in *Pyxis Special Shipping Co Ltd v Dritsas & Kaglis Bros Ltd, The Scaplake* [1978] 2 Lloyd's Rep 380; cf *Cyril Lord Carpet Sales Ltd v Browne* (1966) 111 Sol Jo 51, where the Court of Appeal held the commencement of proceedings against the agent was an election barring action against the principal). Debiting one party may also provide evidence of election (*Addison v Gandassequi* (1812) 4 Taunt 574; cf *Thomson v Davenport*, above at p 123).

4. There is no doubt that in most cases where election is invoked the plea fails. In fact Professor Reynolds submits that in cases of undisclosed agency where the plea has succeeded, and was based on an act short of judgment, the doctrine of estoppel, and not election, may provide the real explanation for those decisions (op cit, pp 323–328). He submits that:

> . . . it is open to the courts to make articulate the proposition that, short of a judgment, a plaintiff will only lose his right against one party by a representation of fact that the contract is with the other or has been performed by the other, or by a representation of intention not to enforce his right against that one, in either case acted on by that party in such a way that it would be detrimental to him if the plaintiff changed his mind. The clearest case of such detriment would occur when the representation or conduct induced the principal to settle with the agent, but it may be that other cases could arise.

See also Treitel, op cit, p 639, who supports the estoppel theory. Recently, a New Zealand judge has stated that 'the doctrine of election is frequently misnamed. Rather, it is to be regarded as being an instance of waiver (or estoppel or release)': *L C Fowler & Sons Ltd v St Stephens College Board of Governors* [1991] 3 NZLR 304 at 308, per Thomas J.

Set-off and other defences available against the agent

As a general rule, when an undisclosed principal intervenes on his agent's contract the third party may set up against him any defences, including personal set-off of debts, which would be available to him against the agent as long as those defences accrued before the third party had notice of the principal's existence (*Browning v Provincial Insurance Co of Canada* (1873) LR 5 PC 263 at 272–273; *Rabone v Williams* (1785) 7 Term Rep 360). However, as the next case illustrates, the third party's rights of set-off appear to be subject to an important restriction.

Cooke & Sons v Eshelby (1887) 12 App Cas 271, House of Lords

Livesey & Co, a firm of brokers, who were in fact acting on behalf of an undisclosed principal, sold cotton to Cooke & Sons (the appellants). The price not being paid, Eshelby (the respondent), the trustee in bankruptcy of the undisclosed principal, claimed it from Cooke & Sons. Cooke & Sons attempted to set off against the price a debt owed to them by Livesey & Co. Cooke & Sons knew that Livesey & Co were in the habit of dealing both for principals and on their own account but at the time of the sale in question they had no belief whether Livesey & Co were acting as agents or not. Affirming the decision of the Court of Appeal, the House of Lords held there was no right of set-off.

Lord Halsbury LC: My Lords, in this case a merchant in Liverpool effected two sales through his brokers. The brokers effected the sales in their own names. The appellants, the merchants with whom these contracts were made, knew the brokers to be brokers, and that it was their practice to sell in their own names in transactions in which they were acting only as brokers. They also knew that the brokers were in the habit of buying and selling for themselves. The appellants with commendable candour admit that they are unable to say that they believed the brokers to be principals; they knew they might be either one or the other; they say that they dealt with the brokers as principals, but at the same time they admit that they had no belief one way or the other whether they were dealing with principals or brokers.

It appears to me that the principle upon which this case must be decided has been so long established that in such a state of facts as I have recited the legal result cannot be doubtful. The ground upon which all these cases have been decided is that the agent has been permitted by the principal to hold himself out as the principal, and that the person dealing with the agent has believed that the agent was the principal, and has acted on that belief. With reference to both those propositions, namely, first, the permission of the real principal to the agent to assume his character, and with reference to the fact whether those dealing with the supposed principal have in fact acted upon the belief induced by the real principal's conduct, various difficult questions of fact have from time to time arisen; but I do not believe that any doubt has ever been thrown upon the law as decided by a great variety of judges for something more than a century. The cases are all collected in the notes to *George v Clagett* ((1797) 7 Term Rep 359).

In *Baring v Corrie* ((1818) 2 B & Ald 137), in 1818, Lord Tenterden had before him a very similar case to that which is now before your Lordships, and although in that case the Court had to infer what we have here proved by the candid admission of the party, the principle upon which the case was decided is precisely that which appears to me to govern the case now before your Lordships. Lord Tenterden says of the persons who were in that case insisting that they had a right to treat the brokers as principals: 'They knew that Coles & Co acted both as brokers and merchants, and if they meant to deal with them as merchants, and to derive a benefit from so dealing with them, they ought to have inquired whether in this transaction they acted as brokers or not; but they made no inquiry.' And Bayley J says: 'When Coles & Co stood at least in an equivocal situation, the defendants ought in common honesty, if they bought the goods with a view to cover their own debt, to have asked in what character they sold the goods in question. I therefore cannot think that the defendants believed, when they bought the goods, that Coles & Co sold them on their own account. And if so, they can have no defence to the present action.'

I am therefore of opinion that the judgment of the Court of Appeal was right. The selling in his own name by a broker is only one fact, and by no means a conclusive fact, from which, in the absence of other circumstances, it might be inferred that he was selling his own goods. Upon the facts proved or admitted in this case the fact of selling in the broker's name was neither calculated to induce nor did in fact induce that belief.

Lord Watson: . . . According to the practice of the Liverpool cotton market with which the appellants were familiar, brokers in the position of Livesey Sons & Co buy and sell both for themselves and for principals; and in the latter case they transact, sometimes in their own name without disclosing their agency, and at other times in the name of their principal. In their answer to an interrogation by the plaintiff touching their belief that Livesey Sons & Co were acting on behalf of principals in the two transactions in question, the appellants say: 'We had no belief upon the subject. We dealt with Livesey Sons & Co as principals, not knowing whether they were acting as brokers on behalf of principals or on their own account as the principals.'

That is a very candid statement, but I do not think any other answer could have been honestly made by persons who, at the time of the transactions, were cognisant of the practice followed by members of the Liverpool Cotton Association. A sale by a broker in his own name to persons having that knowledge, does not convey to them an assurance that he is selling on his own account; on the contrary it is equivalent to an express intimation that the cotton is either his own property or the property of a principal who has employed him as an agent to sell. A purchaser who is content to buy on these terms cannot, when the real principal comes forward, allege that the broker sold the cotton as his own. If the intending purchaser desires to deal with the broker as a principal and not as an agent in order to secure a right to set-off, he is put upon his inquiry. Should the broker refuse to state whether he is acting for himself or for a principal, the buyer may decline to enter into the transaction. If he chooses to purchase without inquiry, or notwithstanding the broker's refusal to give information, he does so with notice that there may be a principal for whom the broker is acting as agent; and should that ultimately prove to be the fact, he has, in my opinion, no right to set off his indebtedness to the principal against debts owing to him by the agent.

It was argued for the appellants, that in all cases where a broker, having authority to that effect, sells in his own name for an undisclosed principal, the purchaser, at the time when the principal is disclosed, is entitled to be placed in the same position as if the agent had contracted on his own account. That was said to be the rule established by *George v Clagett* ((1797) 7 Term Rep 359), *Sims v Bond* ((1833) 5 B & Ad 389) and subsequent cases. It is clear that Livesey Sons & Co were not mere brokers or middlemen, but were agents within the meaning of these authorities, and if the argument of the appellants were well founded they would be entitled to prevail in this appeal, because in that case their right of set-off had arisen before the 20th of July 1883, when they first had notice that Maximos was the principal.

I do not think it necessary to enter into a minute examination of the authorities, which were fully discussed in the arguments addressed to us. The case of *George v Clagett* ((1797) 7 Term Rep 359) has been commented upon and its principles explained in many subsequent decisions, and notably in *Baring v Corrie* ((1818) 2 B & Ald 137), *Semenza v Brinsley* ((1865) 18 CBNS 467), and *Borries v Imperial Ottoman Bank* ((1873) LR 9 CP 38). These decisions appear to me to establish conclusively that, in order to sustain the defence pleaded by the appellants, it is not enough to shew that the agent sold in his own name. It must be shewn that he sold the goods as his own, or, in other words, that the circumstances attending the sale were calculated to induce, and did induce, in the mind of the purchaser a reasonable belief that the agent was selling on his own account and not for an undisclosed principal; and it must also be shewn that the agent was enabled to appear as the real contracting party by the conduct, or by the authority, express or implied, of the principal. The rule thus explained is intelligible and just; and I agree with Bowen LJ that it rests upon the doctrine of estoppel. It would be inconsistent with fair dealing that a latent principal should by his own act or omission lead a purchaser to rely upon a right of set-off against the agent as the real seller, and should nevertheless be permitted to intervene and deprive the purchaser of that right at the very time when it had become necessary for his protection.

Lord FitzGerald: I concur with my noble and learned friend [Lord Watson] in adopting at once the decision and the reasons of the Court of Appeal. I have, however, some hesitation in accepting the view that the decisions rest on the doctrine of estoppel. Estoppel in pais involves considerations not necessarily applicable to the case before us. There is some danger in professing to state the principle on which a line of decisions rests, and it seems to me to be sufficient to say in the present case that Maximos did not in any way wilfully or otherwise mislead the defendants (Cooke & Sons) or induce them to believe that Livesey & Co were the owners of the goods or authorized to sell them as their own, or practice any imposition on them. The defendants were not in any way misled.

NOTES

1. Although it has been argued that *Cooke & Sons v Eshelby* might really be a case of an unnamed, as opposed to an undisclosed, principal (because the third party knew there was a risk that the brokers might be acting for a principal), it is generally treated as an undisclosed principal case: see F M B Reynolds (1983) 36 CLP 119 at pp 126 and 133.

2. In *Cooke & Sons v Eshelby* the House of Lords held that an undisclosed principal would not be bound by the third party's rights of set-off against the agent unless the principal had misled the third party by allowing the agent to appear as the principal. This estoppel approach may be criticised on two grounds. First, it is difficult to see how the third party can rely on the representation of a person of whose existence he is unaware. Secondly, it could be said that in all cases of undisclosed agency the agent is held out to be the principal (Bowstead, p 342; Markesinis and Munday, p 185).

3. A preferable approach would be to allow the third party a right of set-off in all cases where he lacks notice of the principal's existence. The undisclosed principal would then intervene on his agent's contract subject to the third party's rights of set-off in much the same way as the assignee of a chose in action takes subject to equities. But what of the case where an undisclosed principal instructs his agent to contract in the principal's name and yet the agent disobeys that instruction and contracts in his own name? On the estoppel theory the principal would not be bound by set-off, whereas under this alternative approach he would be bound. However, it is submitted that this result is not as unjust as it may first appear. It is not the third party's fault that the agent disobeys his instructions, whereas it could be argued that by choosing to deal through an agent the principal takes the risk that the agent may exceed his authority and act as though he is the principal: R Powell *The Law of Agency* (2nd ed, 1961), p 177; S R Derham [1985] CLJ 384 at p 399.

4. A key element of both the estoppel and subject to equities approaches to set-off is that the third party must not have notice of the existence of a principal at the time he contracted with the agent, or at the time that the debt available for setting off accrued if that was later. On the estoppel approach notice would mean that the third party's prejudice would not have been caused by the principal's conduct. On the subject to equities approach notice would mean that there would not be an equity in favour of the third party (see Bowstead, p 343). But what is meant by 'notice'? Is it restricted to actual notice? In *Cooke & Sons v Eshelby* Lord Watson referred to the third party's 'reasonable belief that the agent was selling on his own account and not for an undisclosed principal'. Furthermore, there appears to be common law support for the view that the third party will be put on notice of the principal's existence if the circumstances are such as to put the third party on inquiry as to the status of the agent and he fails to make an inquiry (see Derham, op cit, pp 390–395 and the cases cited therein). This common law duty of inquiry should not be confused with the separate equitable doctrine of constructive notice which has no place in commercial transactions (*Greer v Downs Supply Co* [1927] 2 KB 28; Derham, op cit, p 391). On this basis, even if the House of Lords had applied the subject to equities approach to set-off in *Cooke & Sons v Eshelby*, the third party (Cooke & Sons) would probably still have been denied a right of set-off. Cooke & Sons were aware of the risk that the brokers could have been acting for a principal yet they failed to inquire as to what was the true position.

For defences available to the principal against an action brought by the third party, see above, p 123.

QUESTION

Was it really necessary for the Court of Appeal to consider the personal nature of the contract in *Greer v Downs Supply Co* (above, p 149), or could the court have simply held the third party to have a right of set-off against the undisclosed principal?

Settlement with the agent

Armstrong v Stokes (1872) LR 7 QB 598, Court of Queen's Bench

R & Co were commission merchants who sometimes acted for themselves and sometimes as agents for others. A was a merchant who had dealings with R & Co on a number of occasions but never inquired whether R & Co were acting for themselves or on behalf of others. On one occasion A sold shirts on credit to R & Co when R & Co were acting as agents for S. A delivered the shirts to R & Co who sent them to S. S paid R & Co but R & Co did not pay A. On discovering that R & Co were acting as agents for S, A sued S for the price. The Court of Queen's Bench held that the action failed.

Blackburn J (delivering the judgment of the Court): . . . [In *Heald v Kenworthy* (1855) 10 Exch 739 at 745] Parke B lays down generally that 'if a person orders an agent to make a purchase for him, he is bound to see that the agent pays the debt; and giving the agent money for that purpose does not amount to payment, unless the agent pays it accordingly.' After commenting on several of the cases already referred to, he concludes: 'I think that there is no authority for saying that a payment made to the agent precludes the seller from recovering from the principal, unless it appears that he has induced the principal to believe that a settlement has been made with the agent.' He states this as generally true wherever a principal has allowed himself to be made a party to a contract, and makes no exception as to the case where the other side made the contract with the agent believing him to be principal, and continued in such belief till after the payment was made. He certainly does not in terms say that there is no qualification of the principle he lays down when applicable to such a case; but recollecting how careful Parke B always was to lay down what he thought to be the law fully and with accuracy, we think the counsel for the plaintiff were justified in arguing that Parke B thought the exception did not exist. And this is, in our opinion, a weighty authority in favour of the plaintiff's contention, more especially as Pollock CB assents in his judgment to the remark thrown out by Parke B during the argument, and afterwards more elaborately stated by him in his judgment. And Alderson B, in his judgment, appears entirely to assent to the judgment of Parke B.

We think that we could not, without straining the evidence, hold in this case that the plaintiff had induced the defendants to believe that he (the plaintiff) had settled with J & O Ryder at the time when the defendants paid them.

This makes it necessary to determine whether we agree in what we think was the opinion of Parke B, acquiesced in by Pollock CB and Alderson B.

We think that, if the rigid rule thus laid down were to be applied to those who were only discovered to be principals after they had fairly paid the price to those whom the vendor believed to be the principals, and to whom alone the vendor gave credit, it would produce intolerable hardship. It may be said, perhaps truly, this is the consequence of that which might originally have been a mistake, in allowing the vendor to have recourse at all against one to whom he never gave credit, and that we ought not to establish an illogical exception in order to cure a fault in a rule. But we find an exception (more or less extensively expressed) always mentioned in the very cases that lay down the rule; and without deciding anything as to the case of a broker, who avowedly acts for a principal (though not necessarily named), and confining ourselves to the present case, which is one in which, to borrow Lord Tenterden's phrase in *Thomson v Davenport* ((1829) 9 B & C 78 at 86), the plaintiff sold the goods to Ryder & Co, 'supposing at the time of the contract he was dealing with a principal,' we think such an exception is established.

We wish to be understood as expressing no opinion as to what would have been the effect of the state of the accounts between the parties if J & O Ryder had been indebted to the defendants on a separate account, so as to give rise to a set-off or mutual credit between them. We confine our decision to the case where the defendants, after the contract was made, and in consequence of it, bona fide and without moral blame, paid J & O Ryder at a time when the plaintiff still gave credit to J & O Ryder, and knew of no one else. We think that after that it was too late for the plaintiff to come upon the defendants.

On this ground we make the rule absolute to enter the verdict for the defendants.

NOTES

1. Contrast *Armstrong v Stokes* with *Irvine & Co v Watson & Sons*, above at p 120. In *Irvine & Co v Watson & Sons* the principal was disclosed, whereas in *Armstrong v Stokes* the principal was undisclosed. Unlike the case of a disclosed principal, the general rule for an undisclosed principal appears to be that he can avoid liability to the third party if he settles with his own agent. When the principal is disclosed he can only avoid such liability if the third party induced him to settle with the agent. However, if the existence of the principal is unknown to the third party it is difficult to see how he can have induced the principal to settle with the agent (Bowstead, p 338).

2. *Armstrong v Stokes* has been subjected to considerable criticism, eg see *Irvine & Co v Watson*, above at p 121, per Bramwell LJ. Professor Markesinis and Dr Munday go so far as to state that the decision is 'logically indefensible and almost certainly would not be followed by the courts today' (op cit, p 187; see also Fridman, p 237: '*Armstrong v Stokes* . . . is not a good authority today'). But Professor Reynolds is less critical of the rule that an undisclosed principal will be discharged from liability to the third party if he settles with the agent. In (1983) 36 CLP 119, at p 134, he submits that:

> . . . for a true undisclosed principal situation this might seem again a reasonable rule. The principal has utilised the services of an intermediary who in the transaction into which he has entered has raised no expectation of the accountability of a principal. Surely the principal's duty is performed by keeping the intermediary in funds: if the third party loses, it is because of his misplaced trust in the intermediary. There is no need to make the principal the insurer.

However, we would agree with Professor Treitel who submits that the argument advanced by Professor Reynolds proves to much. For as Professor Treitel notes: 'whenever an undisclosed principal is sued the third party gets a windfall of this kind' (op cit, p 634).

When the third party pays or settles with an agent acting for an undisclosed principal the third party will be discharged from liability to the principal if he was unaware of the principal's existence at the time of payment or settlement (*Coates v Lewes* (1808) 1 Camp 444). However, as in the case of set-off, the third party can only rely on this defence if the principal's conduct induced him to believe that the agent was the principal in the transaction (eg *Ramazotti v Bowring* (1859) 7 CBNS 851). For criticism of this requirement in the context of set-off, see above, p 159.

(b) Relations between the agent and the third party

As the third party contracts in the first instance with the agent and not the undisclosed principal (see above, p 146), it is not surprising to discover that the agent may sue and be sued on that contract (*Sims v Bond* (1833) 5 B & Ad 389 at 393, Denman CJ). If the agent sues the third party on the contract, the third party can set up against him any defence which would have been available against the undisclosed principal, including the fraud of the principal (*Garnac Grain Co Inc v HMF Faure & Fairclough Ltd* [1966] 1 QB 650; revsd on other grounds by the Court of Appeal [1966] 1 QB 650 at 685–668; affd by the House of Lords [1968] AC 1130n; however, set-off may not always be available to the third party: see Fridman, p 242). But should the undisclosed principal intervene on the contract the agent loses his right of action against the third party (*Atkinson v Cotesworth* (1825) 3 B & C 647; aliter if the agent has a lien or other interest over the goods which form the subject matter of the contract).

Even if the principal intervenes on the contract the agent remains liable to the third party until the third party elects whether to hold the principal or the agent liable (above, pp 152–156). In cases of undisclosed agency, the principal and the agent are liable on the contract in the alternative (*Maynegrain Pty Ltd v Compafina Bank* [1982] 2 NSWLR 141 at 150, per Hope JA; revsd on the facts by the Privy Council (1984) 58 ALJR 389).

CHAPTER 6

Relations between principal and agent

In most cases the rights and duties of an agent derive either from a contract made between the principal and agent or from the fiduciary nature of their relationship. But they may also derive from other sources, eg tort, statute or the law of restitution, as in cases of agency of necessity (see above, pp 104–109). See generally, F E Dowrick (1954) 17 MLR 24.

Most agencies are consensual. But some arise because of the apparent or usual authority of the agent (above, pp 91–100 and pp 100–104). Such agencies are non-consensual and it remains uncertain as to whether they give rise to the normal incidents of a principal-agent relationship. They probably do not (see R Powell *The Law of Agency* (2nd ed, 1961), pp 295–296, fn 4; cf Dowrick, op cit, pp 26–27, fn 15).

1 Duties of the agent

(a) Duty to perform his undertaking and obey instructions

If an agent has entered into a bilateral contract with his principal he must do what he has undertaken to do. For example, in *Turpin v Bilton* (1843) 5 Man & G 455 an agent agreed to insure his principal's ship. He failed to do so, which meant that when the ship was lost the principal was uninsured. It was held that the agent was liable for breach of contract.

When performing his undertaking the agent must obey the lawful and reasonable instructions of his principal, even though he genuinely believes that departing from those instructions would be in his principal's best interests (*The Hermione* [1922] P 162; see also the Commercial Agents (Council Directive) Regulations 1993 (SI 1993/3053), reg 3(1), (2)(c)). But a professional agent, such as a solicitor, may be under a duty to warn and advise the principal of any risks inherent in his instructions. For what happens when the instructions are ambiguous, see above, pp 87–88.

In summary, the agent must follow, and not exceed, the terms of his authority, whether they be express or implied (including those terms implied from custom and usage). But an agent is not obliged to do anything that is illegal, or which, at common law or by statute, is null and void (*Cohen v Kittell* (1889) 22 QBD 680; cf *Fraser v BN Furman (Productions) Ltd* [1967] 1 WLR 898).

On the other hand, if the agent acts under a unilateral contract he is under no duty to do anything at all. Similarly, a gratuitous agent is not bound to do anything, unless his failure to act gives rise to liability in tort. Generally, failure to act does not give rise to tortious liability but in certain circumstances it may do so (see generally, J G Logie [1989] CLJ 115). For example, if an agent has agreed to act and then changes his mind, he may be held to have assumed responsibility to the principal to warn him that his intentions have changed (see Powell, op cit, pp 302–303; Bowstead, p 153; R Bradgate and N Savage *Commercial Law* (1991), p 124; contrast Markesinis and Munday, pp 99–100; Fridman, p 140).

(b) Duty of care and skill

A contractually rewarded agent must exercise reasonable care and skill in the performance of his undertaking. This duty arises both in contract and in tort (recently affirmed by the Court of Appeal in *Arbuthnott v Feltrim*; *Deeny v Gooda Walker*; *Henderson v Merrett Syndicates* (1993) The Times, 30 December). Whether the agent complies with the duty is a question of fact. But what is the standard of care which the agent must exercise? Does the same duty and standard of care apply to a gratuitous agent? The next case provides some answers to these questions.

Chaudhry v Prabhakar [1989] 1 WLR 29, Court of Appeal

Chaudhry (C), who had just passed her driving test, asked Prabhakar (P), a close friend, to find a secondhand car, which had not been involved in an accident, for her to buy. P agreed to do so for no payment. C knew nothing about cars but P, though not a qualified mechanic, did know something about them. P found a car offered for sale by someone who was a car sprayer and panel beater. P noticed that the bonnet of the car had been repaired but he made no enquiries as to whether the car had been involved in an accident. P recommended that C should buy the car and, in answer to C's specific enquiry, informed her that the car had not been involved in an accident. C bought the car. When C later discovered that the car had been involved in an accident and was unroadworthy she sued P for breach of a duty of care. The trial judge gave judgment for C. P appealed but his appeal was dismissed by the Court of Appeal.

Stuart-Smith LJ: Mr Hoyle on behalf of the appellant first defendant accepts that he was under a duty of care to the plaintiff, but he submitted that the judge had imposed too high a standard of care, and when the correct standard was applied the first defendant was not in breach. In the forefront of his argument is the proposition that the first defendant was a gratuitous or unpaid agent and that the duty on such a person is to take such care towards his principal as he would in relation to his own affairs and to exhibit such skill as he actually possesses. He further submitted that this standard is an entirely subjective one. This appears to mean in the context of this case that if the first defendant would have bought the car himself, as he said he would, and is an honest man as the judge found him to be, he cannot be held liable because he has acted up to the standard expected of an unpaid agent.

I cannot accept this; the degree of care and skill owed by a gratuitous agent is stated by *Bowstead on Agency*, 15th ed (1985), art 44(3), p 152 to be

> such skill and care as persons ordinarily exercise in their own affairs or, where the agent has expressly or impliedly held himself out to his principal as possessing skill adequate to the performance of a particular undertaking, such skill and care as would normally be shown by one possessing that skill.

But I am quite satisfied that this is an objective standard and is not simply to be measured by the agent's honest statement that he would have similarly acted if he had been transacting the business on his own account, however foolish that may be. For my part, I would prefer to state an agent's duty of care as that which may reasonably be expected of him in all the circumstances. This was the approach of the Court of Appeal in *Houghland v R R Low (Luxury Coaches) Ltd* [1962] 1 QB 694 on the somewhat analogous case of a gratuitous bailee. Ormerod LJ said, at p 698:

> For my part, I have always found some difficulty in understanding just what was 'gross negligence,' because it appears to me that the standard of care required in a case of bailment, or any other type of case, is the standard demanded by the circumstances of that particular case. It seems to me that to try and put a bailment, for instance, into a watertight compartment – such as gratuitous bailment on the one hand, and bailment for reward on the other – is to overlook the fact that there might well be an infinite variety of cases, which might come into one or the other category. The question that we have to consider in a case of this kind, if it is necessary to consider negligence, is whether in the circumstances of this particular case a sufficient standard of care has been observed by the defendants or their servants.

I have no doubt that one of the relevant circumstances is whether or not the agent is paid. If he is, the relationship is a contractual one and there may be express terms upon which the parties can rely. Moreover, if a paid agent exercised any trade, profession or calling, he is required to exercise the degree of skill and diligence reasonably to be expected of a person exercising such trade, profession or calling, irrespective of the degree of skill he may possess. Where the agent is unpaid, any duty of care arises in tort. Relevant circumstances would be the actual skill and experience that the agent had, though, if he has represented such skill and experience to be greater than it in fact is and the principal has relied on such representation, it seems to me to be reasonable to expect him to show that standard of skill and experience which he claims he possesses. Moreover, the fact that principal and agent are friends does not in my judgment affect the existence of the duty of care, though conceivably it may be a relevant circumstance in considering the degree or standard of care.

Mr Scott on behalf of the plaintiff has submitted that the duty of care arises not only because of the relationship of principal and agent, but also under the doctrine enunciated in *Hedley Byrne & Co Ltd v Heller & Partners Ltd* [1964] AC 465. The House of Lords held that a negligent, though honest, misrepresentation, spoken or written, may give rise to an action for damage for financial loss caused thereby, apart from any contract or fiduciary relationship, since the law will imply a duty of care when a party seeking information from a party possessed of special skill trusts him to exercise care, and that party knew, or ought to have known that reliance was being placed on his skill and judgment.

When considering the question of whether a duty of care arises, the relationship between the parties is material. If they are friends, the true view may be that the advice or representation is made upon a purely social occasion and the circumstances show that there has not been a voluntary assumption of responsibility.

Lord Reid in *Hedley Byrne & Co Ltd v Heller & Partners Ltd* said, at pp 482–483:

> The law ought so far as possible to reflect the standards of the reasonable man, and that is what *Donoghue v Stevenson* [1932] AC 562 sets out to do. The most obvious difference between negligent words and negligent acts is this. Quite careful people often express definite options on social or informal occasions even when they see that others are likely to be influenced by them: and they often do that without taking that care which they would take if asked for their opinion professionally or in a business connection. The appellant agrees that there can be no duty of care on such occasions, and we were referred to American and South African authorities where that is recognised, although their law appears to have gone much further than ours has yet done.

But where, as in this case, the relationship of principal and agent exists, such that a contract comes into existence between the principal and the third party, it seems to me that, at the very least, this relationship is powerful evidence that the occasion is not a purely social one, but, to use Lord Reid's expression, is in a business connection. Indeed the relationship between the parties is one that is equivalent to contract, to use the words of Lord Devlin, at p 530, save only for the absence of consideration.

It seems to me that all the necessary ingredients are here present. The plaintiff clearly relied upon the first defendant's skill and judgment, and, although it may not have been great, it was greater than hers and was quite sufficient for the purpose of asking the appropriate questions of the second defendant. The first defendant also knew that the plaintiff was relying on him; indeed he told her that she did not need to have it inspected by a mechanic and she did not do so on the strength of his recommendation. It was clearly in a business connection, because he knew that she was there and then going to commit herself to buying the car for £4,500 through his agency.

If, as I think, the duty of care in this case can equally be said to arise under the *Hedley Byrne* principle, then logically the standard of care, or the nature and extent of the duty, should be the same as that required of an unpaid agent. And this is an additional reason why I prefer to state the duty as I have, namely, to take such care as is reasonably to be expected of him in all the circumstances.

Stocker LJ: This appeal does not raise any question as to whether or not any duty was owed at all, since it was conceded that the defendant was a gratuitous agent and owed the appropriate duty. On the facts of this particular case I agree that the concession was properly made, though the incidence of the duty may be a matter of dispute.

In many cases in which actionable negligence is claimed in respect of the voluntary giving of advice, the first question that arises is whether any duty of care is owed in respect of such advice where the relationship of the parties is such that no voluntary assumption of legal responsibility was intended or can properly be imputed and where the giving of the advice was motivated solely out of friendship. Thus, in my view, in the absence of other factors giving rise to such a duty, the giving of advice sought in the context of family, domestic or social relationships will not in itself give rise to any duty in respect of such advice. The existence of the duty would depend upon all the circumstances in which the advice was sought or tendered. This problem does not arise in this case because of the concession referred to that the duty of care did exist. Whether the duty arises out of a gratuitous agency or by reason of the extension of the *Donoghue v Stevenson* [1932] AC 562 principle to economic loss sustained as a result of negligent advice as enunciated in *Hedley Byrne & Co Ltd v Heller & Partners Ltd* [1964] AC 465, on the facts of this case, even if the existence of the duty had not been conceded, I should, for my part, have felt bound to conclude that it did exist.

The first defendant accepted the task of finding a motor car suitable for the plaintiff in respect of which a specific characteristic was stipulated – viz that it had not been involved in an accident. The first defendant purported to have done so and stated specifically in answer to the plaintiff's question that it had not been involved in any accident and assured that there was no need to have it examined by a mechanic. He gave her information with regard to its provenance which was incorrect since he did not know the vendor before seeing the car. In making these assertions to the plaintiff he went beyond what was required of him in his capacity as a friend, and it seems to me he owed a duty of care to the plaintiff. The issue arising on this appeal, therefore, relates not to the existence of a duty of care but to its extent.

Mr Hoyle submits that the duty was that of a gratuitous agent which is stated in *Bowstead on Agency*, 15th ed, art 44(3) to be: 'Such skill and care as persons ordinarily exercise in their own affairs.' I doubt whether this is an adequate formulation, at least in the circumstances of this case, when applied to advice given to another. However, even if it be the appropriate duty, the words 'ordinarily exercise[d] in their own affairs' seems to me to postulate an objective and not a subjective standard. If a subjective standard be correct, then in my view the duty so expressed becomes virtually meaningless and would cover circumstances in which no care at all had been taken. Objectively regarded, there was sufficient evidence before the judge from which he could properly conclude that the first defendant did not exercise such care, and the fact that he honestly asserted that he would have been happy to purchase the car himself begs the question rather than resolving it. In my view, the fact that he did not ask the vendor specifically whether or not the car had been involved in any accident did not itself establish a breach provided that he had reasonable grounds for belief that it had not and if he had such reasonable grounds it would not necessarily follow that his assertion to this effect to the plaintiff amounted to actionable negligence. This, however, is to consider this aspect of his advice to her in isolation. He did not, in fact, contrary to his assertion, know the vendor. He did not ask for, or examine, any registration documents, nor make any inquiries as to the previous owner of the car or its provenance. He bought it from a person whose trade was that of a panel beater and observed that the car had a crumpled bonnet. In my view, any purchaser of a car in these circumstances, however naïve, would be put on inquiry. Thus, judged even by the standard of care for which Mr Hoyle contends, if objectively considered, the first defendant failed to discharge it.

In my opinion, in the circumstances such as prevailed here, a more appropriate test is that suggested by Ormerod LJ in *Houghland v R R Low (Luxury Coaches) Ltd* [1962] 1 QB 694, 698: 'whether in the circumstances of this particular case a sufficient standard of care has been observed.' On either formulation of the duty, in my view, the first defendant failed to discharge the duty and was accordingly liable for actionable negligence as the judge has found.

I have sympathy for the first defendant. He was, as the judge found, acting honestly and without any apparent motive to mislead the plaintiff. Common prudence would indicate that he should have explained the circumstances in which he obtained the car and not voluntarily have accepted a duty which otherwise might well not have been imposed upon him.

May LJ: The real questions in this case, looked at with common sense and avoiding unnecessary legal jargon, were, first, did the friend seeking the car owe the intending purchaser any duty of care in and about his search; secondly, if he did, what was its nature and extent; thirdly, did he commit any breach of that duty causing the plaintiff any damage?

As Stuart-Smith and Stocker LJJ have recorded in their judgments, counsel for the first defendant conceded that his client owed the intending purchaser at least the duty to take such care in and about her business, namely, the search for a suitable car for her, as he would have about his own affairs had he been looking for a car for himself. In the light of the more cautious approach taken in recent cases by the House of Lords and the Privy Council to the question whether a duty of care exists, as expressed by Lord Wilberforce in the familiar passage from his speech in *Anns v Merton London Borough Council* [1978] AC 728, 751–752 – see, for instance, the opinion of the Privy Council in *Yuen Kun Yeu v A-G of Hong Kong* [1988] AC 175 – I for my part respectfully doubt whether counsel's concession in the instant case was rightly made in law. I do not find the conclusion that one must impose upon a family friend looking out for a first car for a girl of 26 a *Donoghue v Stevenson* duty of care in and about his quest, enforceable with all the formalities of the law of tort, entirely attractive.

Nor do I think, on the facts of this case, that but for the concession one can apply to the young man's answer to the girl's inquiry about the car's history

the principle that a duty of care arises where a party is asked for and gives gratuitous advice upon a matter within his particular skill or knowledge and knows or ought to have known that the person asking for the advice will rely upon it and act accordingly

– see *Yuen Kun Yeu v A-G of Hong Kong* [1988] AC 175, 192, referring to the effect of *Hedley Byrne & Co Ltd v Heller & Partners Ltd* [1964] AC 465. To do so in this and similar cases will make social relations and responsibilities between friends unnecessarily hazardous.

However the concession was made, and I agree with Stuart-Smith and Stocker LJJ that we must accordingly decide this appeal on that basis. In those circumstances I think that one is driven to the conclusion that the findings by the deputy judge that the plaintiff did ask the first defendant if the car had been involved in an accident, that he had answered that it had not without any direct inquiry to the vendor, whereas in truth it had been involved in a serious accident and been extensively but unskilfully repaired, inevitably led to the conclusion that the first defendant did breach his conceded duty of care and that the plaintiff suffered the damage alleged in consequence.

I too would therefore dismiss this appeal.

NOTES

1. This case is noted by K Brinkworth [1990] Bus LR 111. See also Markesinis and Munday, at pp 101–103; and Fridman, at pp 145–147.

2. *Chaudhry v Prabhakar* seems to put pay to the traditional view that there are different standards of care as between gratuitous agents and agents for reward. In that case, the Court of Appeal made it clear that the required standard of any agent is such as is reasonable in all the circumstances. The standard of care will vary with the facts of any particular case and the fact that the agent is acting gratuitously or for reward is simply one of the factors to be taken into account (see Stuart-Smith LJ, above at p 165; cf Powell, op cit, p 304).

3. But *Chaudhry v Prabhakar* leaves one important question without a clear answer: when will a gratuitous agent owe a duty of care to his principal? See Markesinis and Munday, pp 102–103. A further question could be asked: was it really necessary to treat Prabhakar as a gratuitous agent at all? See N E Palmer [1992] SPTL Reporter 35 at p 36, who sees *Chaudhry v Prabhakar* as a straightforward case of liability for negligent advice.

(c) Duties arising from the fiduciary nature of the agency relationship

Most agents are subject to fiduciary duties. This is because the agent has power to affect the legal relations of his principal and the principal normally places trust and confidence in the agent with regard to the exercise of that power. In these circumstances, equity will intervene and subject the agent to fiduciary duties so as to protect the principal from any abuse of power by the agent.[1] These fiduciary duties are sometimes referred to as 'duties of loyalty' (see the American *Restatement of the Law of Agency* (2nd ed, 1958), paras 387–398).

But it is not every agent who is in a fiduciary position vis-à-vis his principal. As Professor Dowrick has noted: 'if P appoints A to be his agent merely to sign a memorandum and places no particular trust in A, the doctrine of fiduciary relations and the incidents of agency which derive from this equitable doctrine would not apply' ((1954) 17 MLR 24 at pp 31–32). Furthermore, the extent of the fiduciary duties of an agent may vary from case to case. As Lord Upjohn said in *Boardman v Phipps* [1967] 2 AC 46 at 123: 'Rules of equity have to be applied to such a great diversity of circumstances that they can be stated only in the most general terms and applied with particular attention to the exact circumstances of each case.' (See also, below at p 172.)

As fiduciary duties of an agent arise in equity, and do not depend upon any contract made between the principal and agent, those duties may apply to both contractual and gratuitous agents alike. However, the principal and agent may incorporate those duties into any contract made between them, or, alternatively, exclude those duties from their relationship by the terms of their contract. But it should be noted that under the Commercial Agents (Council Directive) Regulations

---

1 For detailed discussion of the nature of fiduciary relationships and the topics considered in this section generally, see P D Finn *Fiduciary Obligations* (1977); Goff and Jones *The Law of Restitution* (4th ed, 1993), Ch 33; L S Sealy [1962] CLJ 69 and [1963] CLJ 119; G Jones (1968) 84 LQR 472 and (1970) 86 LQR 463.

1993, implementing EEC Directive 86/653 on self-employed commercial agents, a commercial agent is placed under certain fiduciary duties: when performing his activities he must look after the interests of his principal and act dutifully and in good faith (reg 3(1)). Any term or provision (whether contained in the agency contract or in any other agreement or notice) is void if, and to the extent that, it is inconsistent with these duties (reg 5(1)).[2] For consideration of the problems raised when directors contract out of their fiduciary duties, see *Movitex Ltd v Bulfield* [1988] BCLC 104 (noted by L S Sealy [1987] CLJ 217).

The most important fiduciary duties which may be owed by an agent towards his principal are the following.

(i) *Duty not to put himself in a position where his duties as agent conflict with his own interests, or the interests of another principal*

Armstrong v Jackson [1917] 2 KB 822, King's Bench Division

Armstrong instructed Jackson, a stockbroker, to buy shares in a certain company for him. Although Jackson pretended to purchase the shares on the open market, he actually sold his own shares in the company to Armstrong. On discovering the truth some years later, Armstrong claimed to have the transaction set aside. McCardie J upheld the claim and ordered Jackson to repay all sums paid by Armstrong for the shares.

McCardie J: . . . First as to the claim to avoid the transaction. It is obvious that the defendant gravely failed in his duty to the plaintiff. He was instructed to buy shares. But he never carried out his mandate. A broker who is employed to buy shares cannot sell his own shares unless he makes a full and accurate disclosure of the fact to his principal, and the principal, with a full knowledge, gives his assent to the changed position of the broker. The rule is one not merely of law but of obvious morality. As was said by Lord Cairns in *Parker v McKenna* ((1874) 10 Ch App 96 at 118), 'No man can in this Court, acting as an agent, be allowed to put himself into a position in which his interest and his duty will be in conflict.' Now a broker who secretly sells his own shares is in a wholly false position. As vendor it is to his interest to sell his shares at the highest price. As broker it is his clear duty to the principal to buy at the lowest price and to give unbiassed and independent advice (if such be asked) as to the time when and the price at which shares shall be bought, or whether they shall be bought at all. The law has ever required a high measure of good faith from an agent. He departs from good faith when he secretly sells his own property to the principal. The rule has long been the same, both at law and equity: see Story on Agency, s 210. It matters not that the broker sells at the market price, or that he acts without intent to defraud: see *Bentley v Craven* ((1853) 18 Beav 75). The prohibition of the law is absolute. It will not allow an agent to place himself in a situation which, under ordinary circumstances, would tempt a man to do that which is not the best for his principal: see per Romilly MR in *Bentley v Craven*. The Court will not enter into discussion as to the propriety of the price charged by the broker, nor is it material to inquire whether the principal has or has not suffered a loss. If the breach of duty by the broker be shown, the Court will set aside the transaction: see *Gillett v Peppercorne* ((1840) 3 Beav 78). The rule was strikingly illustrated in the case of *Rothschild v Brookman* ((1831) 5 Bli NS 165 at 197). The facts in that case were not dissimilar to the facts in the present action. The House of Lords (affirming the Court below)

2 Although attempts to impose fiduciary duties on principals have proved largely unsuccessful (see *Jirna Ltd v Mister Donut of Canada Ltd* (1973) 40 DLR (3d) 303, Sup Ct of Canada), the principal of a commercial agent must act dutifully and in good faith towards his agent: Commercial Agents (Council Directive) Regulations 1993, reg 4(1).

set aside transactions in which the agent had secretly acted as principal. In giving his opinion Lord Wynford (formerly Best CJ) used these words: 'If any man who is to be trusted places himself in a condition in which he has an opportunity of taking advantage of his employer, by placing himself in such a situation, whether acting fairly or not, he must suffer the consequence of his situation. Such is the jealousy which the law of England entertains against any such transactions.' . . .

The position of principal and agent gives rise to particular and onerous duties on the part of the agent, and the high standard of conduct required from him springs from the fiduciary relationship between his employer and himself. His position is confidential. It readily lends itself to abuse. A strict and salutary rule is required to meet the special situation. The rules of English law as they now exist spring from the strictness originally required by Courts of Equity in cases where the fiduciary relationship exists. Those requirements are superadded to the common law obligations of diligence and skill: see per Lord Cranworth in *Aberdeen Rly Co v Blaikie Bros* ((1854) 1 Macq 461 at 471 ff) and per Curiam in *Oliver v Court* ((1820) 8 Price 127 at 161).

NOTES

1. In *Aberdeen Rly Co v Blaikie Bros* (1854) 1 Macq 461 at 471, Lord Cranworth LC provided a classic description of the 'no conflict' rule when he said:

> It is a rule of universal application that no one, having [fiduciary] duties to discharge, shall be allowed to enter into engagements in which he has, or can have, a personal interest conflicting, or which may possibly conflict, with the interests of those whom he is bound to protect.

The rule is strictly applied whenever there is an actual conflict of interest and duty or whenever there is 'a real sensible possibility of conflict' (*Boardman v Phipps* [1967] 2 AC 46 at 124, per Lord Upjohn). The fact that the agent has acted in good faith, and produced a benefit for the principal, is irrelevant to the application of the rule (see, eg, *Boardman v Phipps*, below at p 174). The rationale behind the rule is that the agent must be deterred from the temptation to place his own interests above those of his principal. The rule may even apply after the agency relationship has terminated so long as the confidence naturally arising from such a relationship is proved, or may be presumed, to continue and the transaction in question is connected to that continuing relationship (*Allison v Clayhills* (1907) 97 LT 709 at 711–712, per Parker J). Cf *Sears Investment Trust Ltd v Lewis's Group Ltd (in liquidation)* [1992] RA 262, where the agent's duty of loyalty was held to have terminated together with the agency agreement.

2. *Armstrong v Jackson* illustrates one facet of the no conflicts rule, ie an agent instructed to purchase property must not sell his own property to the principal. Another facet of the rule is that an agent instructed to sell his principal's property must not buy it himself (*McPherson v Watt* (1877) 3 App Cas 254, where the House of Lords held that the agent had breached the rule when he purchased the property in his brother's name). Where an agent deals with his principal in breach of duty, the principal may rescind the contract (assuming there are no bars to rescission, eg restitution is impossible, intervention of third party rights, affirmation of the contract evidenced by lapse of time after discovering the truth). Alternatively, the principal may affirm the contract and claim an account of any profit made by the agent (*Bentley v Craven* (1853) 18 Beav 75). But special rules apply when the agent sells property to the principal. If the agent sells property which he acquired after the creation of the agency relationship then he must account to the principal for any profit (*Tyrrell v Bank of London* (1862) 10 HL Cas

26). If the agent already owned the property before the agency was created he will not be accountable for any profit but he will have to pay damages for any loss caused to the principal (*Jacobus Marler Estates Ltd v Marler* (1913) 85 LJPC 167n). See Bowstead, pp 170–171; see also P Watts [1992] LMCLQ 439.

3. There will be no breach of duty if the agent makes full disclosure of all material facts to the principal and obtains the principal's consent before placing himself in a position where his interests and duty conflict (*North and South Trust Co v Berkeley* [1971] 1 WLR 470 at 484–485, per Donaldson J). When an agent sells his own property to the principal, or buys the principal's property from him, the agent must also show that the price was fair and that he did not abuse his position in any way (*Gibson v Jeyes* (1801) 6 Ves 266). Furthermore, as we have already seen, the no conflict rule may be excluded by the terms of any contract made between the principal and agent (above, p 168). Exclusion of the duty may be by express or implied terms of the contract (*Kelly v Cooper* [1993] AC 205, below).

So far we have examined the no conflict rule in terms of the agent's duty not to put himself in a position where his duty to his principal conflicts with his own interests. However, the rule also prevents the agent from placing himself in a position where he owes a duty to another person which is inconsistent with his duty to his principal (see *North and South Trust Co v Berkeley* [1971] 1 WLR 470 at 484–485, per Donaldson J; see also the case next cited).

Kelly v Cooper [1993] AC 205, Privy Council

Kelly instructed Coopers, a firm of estate agents, to sell his house ('Caliban'). Brant, who was the owner of an adjacent house ('Vertigo'), also instructed Coopers to sell his house. Coopers showed Perot, a prospective purchaser, around both houses and Perot made an offer for Vertigo, which was accepted by Brant. Perot then offered to buy Caliban. Coopers did not inform Kelly of the agreement to buy Vertigo. In ignorance of the agreement made between Perot and Brant, Kelly accepted Perot's offer and the sales of both houses were completed. Kelly later brought an action against Coopers claiming that they were in breach of their duties in (1) failing to disclose material information to him and (2) placing themselves in a position where there was a conflict between their duty of disclosure to Kelly and their own interest in ensuring they obtained commission on both houses.

Lord Browne-Wilkinson, delivering the advice of the Privy Council (Lords Keith of Kinkel, Ackner, Browne-Wilkinson, Mustill and Slynn of Hadley), held that Perot's interest in buying both houses was a material factor which could have influenced the negotiations for the price at which Caliban was sold. He continued:

In the view of the Board the resolution of this case depends upon two fundamental propositions: first, agency is a contract made between principal and agent; second, like every other contract, the rights and duties of the principal and agent are dependent upon the terms of the contract between them, whether express or implied. It is not possible to say that all agents owe the same duties to their principals: it is always necessary to have regard to the express or implied terms of the contract. This fact is fully recognised in the introduction to chapter 5 of *Bowstead on Agency*, pp 137–138. . . .

In a case where a principal instructs as selling agent for his property or goods a person who to his knowledge acts and intends to act for other principals selling property or goods of the same description, the terms to be implied into such agency contract must differ from those to be implied where an agent is not carrying on such general agency business. In the case of estate agents, it is their business to act for numerous principals: where properties are of a similar description, there will be a conflict of interest between the principals each of whom will be concerned to attract potential purchasers to their property rather than that of another. Yet, despite this conflict of interest, estate agents must be free to act for several competing principals otherwise they will be unable to perform their function. Yet it is normally said that it is a breach of an agent's duty to act for competing principals. In the course of acting for each of their principals, estate agents will acquire information confidential to that principal. It cannot be sensibly suggested that an estate agency is contractually bound to disclose to any one of his principals information which is confidential to another of his principals. The position as to confidentiality is even clearer in the case of stockbrokers who cannot be contractually bound to disclose to their private clients inside information disclosed to the brokers in confidence by a company for which they also act. Accordingly in such cases there must be an implied term of the contract with such an agent that he is entitled to act for other principals selling competing properties and to keep confidential the information obtained from each of his principals.

Similar considerations apply to the fiduciary duties of agents. The existence and scope of these duties depends upon the terms on which they are acting. In *New Zealand Netherlands Society Oranje Inc v Kuys* [1973] 1 WLR 1126, 1129–1130, Lord Wilberforce, in giving the judgment of this Board, said:

> The obligation not to profit from a position of trust, or, as it is sometimes relevant to put it, not to allow a conflict to arise between duty and interest, is one of strictness. The strength, and indeed the severity, of the rule has recently been emphasised by the House of Lords: *Boardman v Phipps* [1967] 2 AC 46. It retains its vigour in all jurisdictions where the principals of equity are applied. Naturally it has different applications in different contexts. It applies, in principle, whether the case is one of a trust, express or implied, of partnership, of directorship of a limited company, of principal and agent, or master and servant, but the precise scope of it must be moulded according to the nature of the relationship. As Lord Upjohn said in *Boardman v Phipps* at p 123: 'Rules of equity have to be applied to such a great diversity of circumstances that they can be stated only in the most general terms and applied with particular attention to the exact circumstances of each case.'

In *Hospital Products Ltd v United States Surgical Corpn* (1985) 156 CLR 41, 97, Mason J in the High Court of Australia said:

> That contractual and fiduciary relationships may co-exist between the same parties has never been doubted. Indeed, the existence of a basic contractual relationship has in many situations provided a foundation for the erection of a fiduciary relationship. In these situations it is the contractual foundation which is all important because it is the contract that regulates the basic rights and liabilities of the parties. The fiduciary relationship, if it is to exist at all, must accommodate itself to the terms of the contract so that it is consistent with, and conforms to, them. The fiduciary relationship cannot be superimposed upon the contract in such a way as to alter the operation which the contract was intended to have according to its true construction.

Thus, in the present case, the scope of the fiduciary duties owed by the defendants to the plaintiff (and in particular the alleged duty not to put themselves in a position where their duty and their interest conflicted) are to be defined by the terms of the contract of agency.

Applying those considerations to the present case, their Lordships are of the view that since the plaintiff was well aware that the defendants would be acting also for other vendors of comparable properties and in so doing would receive confidential information from those other vendors, the agency contract between the plaintiff and the defendants cannot have included either (a) a term requiring the defendants to disclose such confidential information to the plaintiff or (b) a term precluding the defendants acting for rival vendors or (c) a term precluding the defendants from seeking to earn commission on the sale of the property of a rival vendor.

Their Lordships are therefore of opinion that the defendants committed no breach of duty, whether contractual or fiduciary, by failing to reveal to the plaintiff Mr Perot's interest in buying Vertigo, since such information was confidential to Mr Brant. Nor did the fact that the defendants had a direct financial interest in securing a sale of Vertigo constitute a breach of fiduciary duty since the contract of agency envisaged that they might have such a conflict of interest.

This decision is consistent with *Lothian v Jenolite Ltd* 1969 SC 111 and does not conflict with any of the other authorities to which their Lordships were referred. The failure of estate agents to communicate material information to their principals which was held to exist in *Keppel v Wheeler* [1927] 1 KB 577 and *Dunton Properties Ltd v Coles, Knapp & Kennedy Ltd* (1959) 174 Estates Gazette 723 related to information received by the estate agents in their capacity as agents of the principal who was complaining and was therefore not subject to any duty of confidentiality owed by the agents to other persons.

North and South Trust Co v Berkeley [1971] 1 WLR 470 raised quite a different problem. The plaintiff was insured under a policy which had been effected by brokers. The insured had made a claim against the insurers. The brokers then accepted instructions from the insurers (ie a person having a contrary interest to that of the insured) to obtain a report from assessors. Having obtained such report, the brokers refused to disclose it to their original principals, the assured. Donaldson J rightly held that this was a breach of duty by the brokers to their principals. In that case, there was nothing in the circumstances to justify the implication of any term in the agency between the assured and the brokers that the brokers should be free to act for the opposing party, the insurers. . . .

As to the defendants' claim for commission, even if a breach of fiduciary duty by the defendants had been proved, they would not thereby have lost their right to commission unless they had acted dishonestly. In *Keppel v Wheeler* [1927] 1 KB 577 the agents admitted an honest breach of fiduciary duty by mistake and yet were entitled to their commission. In the present case the plaintiff did not allege, nor did the judge find, any bad faith by the defendants. Even on the view the judge took therefore there was no ground for depriving the defendants of their commission.

NOTES

1. For contrasting reactions to this case, see A Berg [1992] IFLR (December) 26 (approving) and I Brown (1993) 109 LQR 206 (disapproving). Although not applicable in *Kelly v Cooper*, the Estate Agents Act 1979, s 21, imposes a duty of disclosure on estate agents who have a personal interest in land about which they negotiate. Failure to disclose such an interest does not render the agent liable to any criminal or civil sanction but it may lead to disqualification under s 3 of the Act.

2. *Kelly v Cooper* is a case of unrelated agencies, ie Coopers were not acting as agents for competing principals *in the same transaction* (Brown, op cit, pp 207–208). It is most unlikely that a court will imply a term to enable an agent to act for opposing principals in the same transaction. In such circumstances the agent would have to terminate one of the agency relationships or obtain the fully informed consent of *both* principals to his continuing to act for both of them (eg in *Clark Boyce v Mouat* [1993] 4 All ER 268, the Privy Council held that a solicitor was entitled to act for both parties in a transaction even where their interests might conflict provided he obtained the informed consent of both parties to his so acting).

3. The problems facing fiduciaries owing duties to opposing clients are of long standing but they have been highlighted by the recent growth of multi-function fiduciaries, especially in the financial services industry. With the abolition of single-capacity trading in the mid-1980s following 'Big Bang', it became possible for large firms and banking groups to offer a range of financial services to their customers. This has increased the potential for conflicts of interest. For example, the corporate finance department of a bank may be advising with regard to a rumoured bid from an anonymous bidder, whilst the corporate advisory department of the same bank may be advising the bidder. In these circumstances the bank may be in breach of its duties of confidentiality or its duty to give 'undivided loyalty' to each client, even though it has complied with regulatory rules made pursuant to the Financial Services Act 1986. It is by no means certain how far, if at all, such regulatory rules have modified traditional fiduciary duties. The issue is addressed in a recent Law Commission Consultation Paper which proposes that when assessing the scope and content of fiduciary obligations the courts should be allowed to take account of the existence of regulatory provisions and the efforts which the firm has made to observe them (LCCP No 124 *Fiduciary Duties and Regulatory Rules* (1992); noted by L S Sealy [1992] LMCLQ 446). For further consideration of the relationship between the statutory regulation of financial services and general fiduciary obligations, see E McKendrick (ed) *Commercial Aspects of Trusts and Fiduciary Obligations* (1992), Chs 1–3.

The no conflict rule is probably the most important of the agent's fiduciary duties. Many of the other fiduciary duties owed by the agent (see below) can be regarded as particular applications of the no conflict rule.

(ii) *Duty not to make a secret profit*

Unless he makes full disclosure to his principal and obtains his consent, the agent may not use his position as agent, nor his principal's property or confidential information, to make a profit for himself.

The following cases illustrate how the no secret profit rule operates:

(1) *Lamb v Evans* [1893] 1 Ch 218: L, the proprietor of a trades directory, employed canvassers to obtain advertisements from traders to be inserted in the directory. L discovered that some of the canvassers were proposing to assist a rival publication after their agreement with L had come to an end. The Court of Appeal held that the canvassers were 'not entitled to use for the purposes of any other publication the materials which, while in the plaintiff's employment, they had obtained for the purpose of his publication'.

(2) *Hippisley v Knee Bros* [1905] 1 KB 1: H employed KB as agents to sell goods on commission. H also agreed to pay KB's out of pocket expenses. KB sold the goods and charged H with the cost of printing and advertising. KB claimed the full cost even though they had received a discount from those who had provided these services. At all times KB acted honestly and in accordance with trade custom (of which H had no knowledge). The Court of Appeal held that KB were in breach of duty and had to account for the discount as a secret profit. But KB were allowed to keep their commission on the sale because they had acted in good faith and their breach of duty was only incidental to the sale itself.

(3) *Boardman v Phipps* [1967] 2 AC 46: B, a solicitor, and TP, acting together as agents for the trustees of an estate, attended the annual general meeting of a company in which the estate had a minority holding of shares. Later, they obtained information about share prices from the company. They formed the opinion that the company could be made more profitable and, acting honestly and without concealment (but not having first obtained the 'informed consent'

of all the trustees), used their own money to bid for and eventually to acquire a controlling interest in it. Ultimately, they succeeded in making considerable profits for both themselves and the estate from capital distributions on their respective holdings of shares. By a majority of three to two, the House of Lords held that they must account to the trust for the profit that they had made from their own investments: the profit had been made by reason of their fiduciary position as agents and by reason of the opportunity and the knowledge which had come to them while acting in that capacity.

Where the agent breaches his duty not to make a secret profit, he must account to the principal for that profit. A duty to account is a personal liability, but it appears that the agent may also hold his secret profit on constructive trust for the principal (ie the principal has a proprietary remedy). The distinction between a personal and proprietary remedy becomes significant when the agent is bankrupt and the principal wants to rely on a proprietary remedy to claim priority ahead of the general creditors. For a long time it appeared that if the agent had used his principal's property to make a secret profit then such profit was held on constructive trust, but if the profit had been made without the use of the principal's property the agent was only personally accountable to the principal (see *Industrial Development Consultants Ltd v Cooley* [1972] 1 WLR 443; *Lister & Co v Stubbs* (1890) 45 Ch D 1). It was always difficult to explain *Boardman v Phipps* on this reasoning. In that case the House of Lords did not distinguish between accountability and constructive trust (in fact there was no need to do so as B, the solicitor, was solvent) and the agents were held liable to account for their profits *and* hold them on constructive trust even though they did not use their principal's property to acquire those profits. The case has often been explained on the ground that confidential information is a special form of trust property (as some of their Lordships thought it was).

However, in *A-G for Hong Kong v Reid* [1994] 1 All ER 1, the Privy Council has recently held that an agent holds a bribe (which is a secret profit) on constructive trust for his principal (see below, p 180). Although Lord Templeman, delivering the advice of the Privy Council, did not specifically address the question of whether a secret profit would normally be held on constructive trust when it was not a bribe, his reasoning, and the fact that he cited *Boardman v Phipps* with approval, suggests that it too would be held on trust by the agent.

If the agent has used confidential information to acquire a benefit, the principal may seek an injunction to restrain the agent making further use of the information and claim damages for breach of contract (if the agency is contractual), or seek an account of profits from the agent (which profits, as we have just seen, the agent would hold on constructive trust: *Boardman v Phipps*, above). It should be noted that the agent's duty not to use confidential information acquired in the course of the agency may extend beyond the termination of the agency relationship, although the duty will not apply once the information enters the public domain.

The no secret profit rule is designed to deter the agent from abusing his position and is strictly applied. For example, in *Boardman v Phipps* the agents were held liable to account for their profits even though they had acted honestly, the trust benefitted from their actions, and the trust did not want to buy, and could not have bought, the shares. However, the agents were awarded an equitable allowance for their skill and expenditure in making the profit (cf *Guinness plc v Saunders* [1990] 2 AC 663).

(iii) *Duty not to accept bribes*

Boston Deep Sea Fishing and Ice Co v Ansell (1888) 39 Ch D 339, Court of Appeal

Ansell was employed as managing director of the plaintiff company. Acting on behalf of the company, Ansell contracted for the construction of certain fishing-smacks, but, unknown to the company, he took a commission from the shipbuilders on the contract. Ansell also accepted bonuses from two other companies (in which he held shares) with which he had placed orders on behalf of the plaintiff company. Suspecting misconduct, the plaintiff company dismissed Ansell from office and later brought an action against him for an account of the secret commission and bonuses he had received. Reversing Kekewich J, the Court of Appeal held that the receipt of secret commission was a good ground for dismissal. Ansell was also ordered to account for his secret commission and bonuses.

Cotton LJ: . . . If a servant, or a managing director, or any person who is authorized to act, and is acting, for another in the matter of any contract, receives, as regards the contract, any sum, whether by way of percentage or otherwise, from the person with whom he is dealing on behalf of his principal, he is committing a breach of duty. It is not an honest act, and, in my opinion, it is a sufficient act to shew that he cannot be trusted to perform the duties which he has undertaken as servant or agent. He puts himself in such a position that he has a temptation not faithfully to perform his duty to his employer. He has a temptation, especially where he is getting a percentage on expenditure, not to cut down the expenditure, but to let it be increased, so that his percentage may be larger. I do not, however, rely on that, but what I say is this, that where an agent entering into a contract on behalf of his principal, and without the knowledge or assent of that principal, receives money from the person with whom he is dealing, he is doing a wrongful act, he is misconducting himself as regards his agency, and, in my opinion, that gives to his employer, whether a company or an individual, and whether the agent be a servant, or a managing director, power and authority to dismiss him from his employment as a person who by that act is shewn to be incompetent of faithfully discharging his duty to his principal.

Bowen LJ: I will, first of all, deal with what is the cardinal matter of the whole case; whether the Plaintiffs were justified or not in dismissing their managing director as they did. This is an age, I may say, when a large portion of the commercial world makes its livelihood by earning, and by earning honestly, agency commission on sales or other transactions, but it is also a time when a large portion of those who move within the ambit of the commercial world, earn, I am afraid, commission dishonestly by taking commissions not merely from their masters, but from the other parties with whom their master is negotiating, and with whom they are dealing on behalf of their master, and taking such commissions without the knowledge of their master or principal. There never, therefore, was a time in the history of our law when it was more essential that Courts of Justice should draw with precision and firmness the line of demarcation which prevails between commissions which may be honestly received and kept, and commissions taken behind the master's back, and in fraud of the master. . . .

Now, there can be no question that an agent employed by a principal or master to do business with another, who, unknown to that principal or master, takes from that other person a profit arising out of the business which he is employed to transact, is doing a wrongful act inconsistent with his duty towards his master, and the continuance of confidence between them. He does the wrongful act whether such profit be given to him in return for services which he actually performs for the third party, or whether it be given to him for his supposed influence, or whether it be given to him on any other ground at all; if it is a profit which arises out of the transaction, it belongs to his master, and the agent or servant has no right to take it, or keep it, or bargain for it, or to receive it without bargain, unless his master knows it. It is said if the transaction be one of very old date, that in some way deprives the master of his right to treat it as a breach of faith. As the Lord Justice has pointed out, the age of the fraud may be a reason in the master's mind for not acting on his rights; but it is impossible to say that because a fraud has been concealed for six years, therefore the master has not a right when he discovers it to act upon his discovery, and to put an end to the relation of employer and employed with which such fraud was inconsistent. I, therefore, find it impossible to adopt Mr Justice Kekewich's view, or to come to any other conclusion except that the managing director having been guilty of a fraud on his employers was rightly dismissed by them, and dismissed by them rightly even though they did not discover the fraud until after they had actually pronounced the sentence of dismissal. . . .

That really disposes of the most important part of the dispute between the parties. But I also wish to add one word on the subject of the bonuses which he claims to be entitled to retain as received from the *Hull Ice Co* and the *Hull Fishing Co*, otherwise called the *Red Cross Co*. If that was a profit received by him, as it seems to me to have been, while he was agent, and arising out of the duty which he was employed to do for the company, it falls under the same branch of the law as the profits received in respect of the *Shipbuilding Co*. I have some little difficulty in following Mr Justice Kekewich's judgment with regard to that. We may perhaps have an inaccurate note of it, but if Mr Justice Kekewich is of opinion that it is the essence of a title to relief in such a case that the principal would have been able to claim as his own money, as between himself and the other party to the business transaction, the money secretly received by his agent, I do not think that is the law. It is true, as Mr Justice Kekewich says, that the money which is sought to be recovered must be money had and received by the agent for the principal's use; but the use which arises in such a case, and the reception to the use of the principal which arises in such a case, does not depend on any privity between the principal and the opposite party with whom the agent is employed to conduct business – it is not that the money ought to have gone into the principal's hands in the first instance; the use arises from the relation between the principal and the agent himself. It is because it is contrary to equity that the agent or the servant should retain money so received without the knowledge of his master. Then the law implies a use, that is to say, there is an implied contract, if you put it as a legal proposition – there is an equitable right, if you treat it as a matter of equity – as between the principal and agent that the agent should pay it over, which renders the agent liable to be sued for money had and received, and there is an equitable right in the master to receive it, and to take it out of the hands of the agent, which gives the principal a right to relief in equity.

[Fry LJ delivered a concurring judgment.]

Industries & General Mortgage Co Ltd v Lewis [1949] 2 All ER 573, King's Bench Division

Lewis employed an agent to arrange for Industries & General Mortgage Co (IGM) to find someone who could provide him with a short-term loan. IGM arranged the loan and agreed to pay the agent half the fee they would charge Lewis. Lewis was not informed of this payment. Slade J held that although IGM had no dishonest intention to cause the agent to persuade Lewis to accept their rates of commission or to act to his disadvantage, IGM were liable nevertheless to pay Lewis the amount of the bribe as damages or as money had and received.

Slade J: . . . For the purposes of the civil law a bribe means the payment of a secret commission, which only means (i) that the person making the payment makes it to the agent of the other person with whom he is dealing; (ii) that he makes it to that person knowing that that person is acting as the agent of the other person with whom he is dealing; and (iii) that he fails to disclose to the other person with whom he is dealing that he has made that payment to the person whom he knows to be the other person's agent. Those three are the only elements necessary to constitute the payment of a secret commission or bribe for civil purposes. I emphasise 'civil purposes' because the Prevention of Corruption Act 1906, s 1(1), introduces the adverb 'corruptly,' and, except in the cases provided for in s 2 of the amending Act of 1916, the onus is put on the prosecution of showing that the payment has been made corruptly. I hold that proof of corruptness or corrupt motive is unnecessary in a civil action, and my authority is the decision of the Court of Appeal in *Hovenden and Sons v Millhoff* ((1900) 83 LT 41) where the plaintiffs carried on business as hairdressers' sundrymen and the defendant was a member of a firm of wholesale tobacconists. That firm was dissolved and the defendant carried on the business thereafter alone. For the purpose of purchasing cigars and cigarettes the plaintiffs employed buyers on whose judgment they relied and to whom they paid salaries and bonuses in proportion to their profits, and it was the duty of these buyers to order and to obtain for the plaintiffs the necessary supply of cigars and cigarettes for use in their business on the best trade terms. From 1886 to 1889 the defendant had supplied the plaintiffs with large quantities of cigars and cigarettes for which the plaintiffs had paid upwards of £28,000. In 1889 the plaintiffs discovered that regularly, both at Christmas and Midsummer, during the whole period of their connection with the defendants, he or his firm had made gifts of money in the nature of bribes to the buyers employed by the plaintiffs which were calculated as amounting in all to about $2\frac{1}{2}$ per cent on the invoice price of the goods sold and delivered. On making this discovery, the plaintiffs commenced an action alleging conspiracy between the defendant and the plaintiffs' buyers to defraud the plaintiffs and they also claimed the money which the plaintiffs' buyers had received from the defendant as money had and received to the plaintiffs' use. The jury negatived the allegation of conspiracy, and Grantham J gave judgment for the plaintiffs for one farthing damages. The third answer of the jury was that the payments made to the plaintiffs' buyers by the defendant or his firm had an effect on the minds of the buyers in favour of the defendant. Although the learned judge assessed the damages at one farthing, he formed the conclusion that the action had been substantially one of conspiracy, and as that had been disproved be gave judgment for the defendant and the plaintiffs appealed. The appeal proceeded solely on the cause of action for money had and received. I emphasise that because, conspiracy having been negatived by the jury, the arguments and the *ratio decidendi* of the judgments in the Court of Appeal could have proceeded only on the footing that no charge of fraud had been sustained. Romer LJ, in his judgment, said (83 LT 43):

> It may, therefore, be well to point out what is a bribe in the eyes of the law. Without attempting an exhaustive definition I may say that the following is one statement of what constitutes a bribe. If a gift be made to a confidential agent with the view of inducing the agent to act in favour of the donor in relation to transactions between the donor and the agent's principal and that gift is secret as between the donor and the agent – that is to say, without the knowledge and consent of the principal – then the gift is a bribe in the view of the law.

I emphasise the learned judge's words: 'If a gift be made to a confidential agent with the view of inducing the agent' because counsel for the plaintiffs rightly emphasised those words. Romer LJ proceeds (ibid):

> If a bribe be once established to the court's satisfaction, then certain rules apply. Amongst them the following are now established, and, in my opinion, rightly established, in the interests of morality with the view of discouraging the practice of bribery. First, the court will not inquire into the donor's motive in giving the bribe, nor allow evidence to be gone into as to the motive.

In other words, the learned judge is saying that once the bribe is established, there is an irrebuttable presumption that it was given with an intention to induce the agent to act favourably to the payer and, thereafter, unfavourably to the principal. Romer LJ continues:

> Secondly, the court will presume in favour of the principal, and as against the briber and the agent bribed, that the agent was influenced by the bribe; and this presumption is irrebuttable.

That means that the motive of the donor in making the payment to the agent or donee is conclusively presumed against the person who makes the payment, and, secondly, it is conclusively proved against the person making the payment that the donee is affected and influenced by the payment. The lord justice goes on:

> Thirdly, if the agent be a confidential buyer of goods for his principal from the briber, the court will assume as against the briber that the true price of the goods as between him and the purchaser must be taken to be less than the price paid to, or charged by, the vendor by, at any rate, the amount or value of the bribe.

That is to say, it must be presumed that the price is loaded as against the purchaser at least by the amount of the bribe. Counsel for the plaintiffs says: 'Yes, but earlier the learned judge has said that if a gift be made to a confidential agent with a view to inducing him, it is a bribe, and, therefore, in using the later language and referring to bribes the learned judge is in effect saying: "I am using these later presumptions in cases where a bribe has been established and I have already defined a bribe as being only something which has been established as being paid with a certain motive" '. That, of course, would tear up the whole of the learned judge's observations because he says lower down that the courts will not receive evidence as to what is the motive of the person making the payment. The motive will be conclusively inferred against him. The Court of Appeal allowed the appeal and for the verdict of one farthing they substituted the amount of the bribe. . . .

. . . for the purposes of a civil action, where you have two parties to a contract introduced by an agent of one of them, once it is established that one of the parties to a contract makes a secret payment to the person whom he knows to be the agent of the other, the law will presume against him that he has acted corruptly, that the agent has been influenced by the payment to the detriment of his principal, and that the principal, the defendant in this case, has suffered damage to at least the amount of the bribe.

NOTES

1. In *Anangel Atlas Compania Naviera SA v Ishikawajima-Harima Heavy Industries Co Ltd* [1990] 1 Lloyd's Rep 167, Leggatt J proposed the following more succinct definition: 'a bribe consists in a commission or other inducement, which is given by a third party to an agent as such, and which is secret from his principal'. Equally, the bribe may be given by the third party's agent acting in the course of his authority (*Armagas Ltd v Mundogas SA* [1986] AC 717 at 743, per Robert Goff LJ).

2. In the *Anangel* case, Leggatt J accepted as uncontroversial the submission that 'a principal will be unable to recover from his agent or a third party a payment made by the third party to the agent if the principal knows of it, or would have known of it, if he had thought about it' (at 171). However, it is submitted that knowledge alone (which must be of all the facts) does not prevent the payment being a bribe: there must also be express or implied assent by the principal to the payment (Goff and Jones *The Law of Restitution* (4th ed, 1993), p 668).

What remedies are available to the principal if his agent should receive a bribe?

(1) The agent may be dismissed without notice (*Bulfield v Fournier* (1895) 11 TLR 282).
(2) The agent will be liable to forfeit his right to commission or remuneration that he would otherwise have received (*Andrews v Ramsay & Co* [1903] 2 KB 635; cf *Hippisley v Knee Bros* [1905] 1 KB 1, above at p 174).
(3) The principal can recover the amount of the bribe from the agent as money had and received (the briber will also be liable for the bribe on a restitutionary basis: *Arab Monetary Fund v Hashim* [1993] 1 Lloyd's Rep 543 at 564–565, per Evans J). But does the principal also have a proprietary remedy against an

agent who has received a bribe? For many years, applying the decision of a strong Court of Appeal in *Lister & Co v Stubbs* (1890) 45 Ch D 1, the courts held that the principal's claim to recover the amount of the bribe was personal, not proprietary. This meant that the principal could not recover any profit made by the agent through investment of the bribe, nor could the principal gain priority over general creditors on the agent's insolvency. But there was much controversy as to whether *Lister & Co v Stubbs* was right or wrong (the arguments on either side are neatly summarised by P Birks in [1993] LMCLQ 30). This controversy has now been resolved by *A-G for Hong Kong v Reid* [1994] 1 All ER 1. In that case, the Privy Council held that properties purchased in New Zealand by a Crown servant (the Acting Director of Public Prosecutions for Hong Kong), using monies he had received as bribes, was held by him on constructive trust for the Crown. Delivering the advice of the Privy Council, Lord Templeman said:

When a bribe is offered and accepted in money or in kind, the money or property constituting the bribe belongs in law to the recipient. Money paid to the false fiduciary belongs to him. The legal estate in freehold property conveyed to the false fiduciary by way of bribe vests in him. Equity, however, which acts in personam, insists that it is unconscionable for a fiduciary to obtain and retain a benefit in breach of duty. The provider of a bribe cannot recover it because he committed a criminal offence when he paid the bribe. The false fiduciary who received the bribe in breach of duty must pay and account for the bribe to the person to whom that duty was owed. In the present case, as soon as the first respondent received a bribe in breach of the duties he owed to the Government of Hong Kong, he became a debtor in equity to the Crown for the amount of that bribe. So much is admitted. But if the bribe consists of property which increases in value or if a cash bribe is invested advantageously, the false fiduciary will receive a benefit from his breach of duty unless he is accountable not only for the original amount or value of the bribe but also for the increased value of the property representing the bribe. As soon as the bribe was received it should have been paid or transferred instanter to the person who suffered from the breach of duty. Equity considers as done that which ought to have been done. As soon as the bribe was received, whether in cash or in kind, the false fiduciary held the bribe on a constructive trust for the person injured. Two objections have been raised to this analysis. First it is said that if the fiduciary is in equity a debtor to the person injured, he cannot also be a trustee of the bribe. But there is no reason why equity should not provide two remedies, so long as they do not result in double recovery. If the property representing the bribe exceeds the original bribe in value, the fiduciary cannot retain the benefit of the increase in value which he obtained solely as a result of his breach of duty. Secondly, it is said that if the false fiduciary holds property representing the bribe in trust for the person injured, and if the false fiduciary is or becomes insolvent, the unsecured creditors of the false fiduciary will be deprived of their right to share in the proceeds of that property. But the unsecured creditors cannot be in a better position than their debtor. The authorities show that property acquired by a trustee innocently but in breach of trust and the property from time to time representing the same belong in equity to the cestui que trust and not to the trustee personally whether he is solvent or insolvent. Property acquired by a trustee as a result of a criminal breach of trust and the property from time to time representing the same must also belong in equity to his cestui que trust and not to the trustee whether he is solvent or insolvent.

When a bribe is accepted by a fiduciary in breach of his duty then he holds that bribe in trust for the person to whom the duty was owed. If the property representing the bribe decreases in value the fiduciary must pay the difference between that value and the initial amount of the bribe because he should not have accepted the bribe or incurred the risk of loss. If the property increases in value, the fiduciary is not entitled to any surplus in excess of the initial value of the bribe because he is not allowed by any means to make a profit out of a breach of duty.

Lord Templeman concluded that as *Lister & Co v Stubbs* was inconsistent with this analysis it should not be followed in future.

(4) The principal may claim damages for fraud against the agent bribed and the briber (they are jointly and severally liable) for any loss caused as a result of entering into the transaction in respect of which the bribe was given. However, in *Mahesan S/O Thambiah v Malaysia Government Officers' Co-operative Housing Society Ltd* [1979] AC 374, the Privy Council held that as against the agent bribed, and the briber, the principal cannot recover both the bribe *and* damages for fraud for loss caused: he must elect between these two alternative remedies before judgment (per Lord Diplock at 383). Although this decision has been strongly criticised (see A Tettenborn (1979) 95 LQR 68), we believe that the Privy Council were right to put the principal to his election. To allow the principal to recover both the bribe and damages for his loss against a single defendant would allow double recovery and give the principal an undeserved 'windfall' (see C Needham (1979) 95 LQR 536). But there is no reason why the principal cannot recover the bribe from the agent and go on to recover any excess loss in damages from the briber, or vice versa.

(5) The principal may recover the bribe *and* rescind any contract he made with the third party as a consequence of the bribe being paid to his agent (*Logicrose Ltd v Southend United Football Club Ltd* [1988] 1 WLR 1256, noted by G Jones [1989] CLJ 22).

In addition to civil liability, the agent may also be criminally liable. At common law an agent who accepts or agrees to accept a bribe is guilty of conspiracy. Further, under the Prevention of Corruption Act 1906, s 1, the agent and the person who gave the bribe may each be guilty of an offence if they acted corruptly (see the Prevention of Corruption Act 1916, s 2, for when a corrupt motive will be presumed).

(iv) *Duty to account*

An agent is under a duty to keep the money and property of his principal separate from his own. If the agent fails to keep his principal's property separate from his own, the principal will be entitled to the entire mixed fund, unless the agent can establish any part of it as his own property (*Lupton v White* (1808) 15 Ves 432). This duty only arises where money or property is beneficially owned by the principal, so that the agent is treated as if he were a trustee of it. But in many cases this does not happen because the parties intend that the agent should be free to use the money or property received in his business (eg see those reservation of title clause cases considered below at pp 407–425; see also Bowstead, pp 162–163). In such cases, the agent will not hold money or property *qua* trustee, he will simply be liable to account for it *qua* debtor. However, where the agent is instructed to purchase property for his principal, and does so in his own name, the agent will hold that property on trust for his principal (*Lees v Nuttall* (1829) 1 Russ & M 53).

An agent must also keep accurate accounts of all transactions entered into on behalf of his principal. Failure to do so means that everything will be presumed against the agent (*Gray v Haig* (1854) 20 Beav 219 at 226, per Romilly MR). Further, on the termination of the agency, the agent is under a duty to produce for the principal all documents relating to the agency, unless he is entitled to exercise a lien over them (*Dadswell v Jacobs* (1887) 34 Ch D 278).

QUESTION

What are the legal and practical consequences of holding that a principal has a proprietary, as opposed to a personal, remedy against his agent for breach of duty? See Bowstead, pp 160–161.

(d) Duty not to delegate his authority

De Bussche v Alt (1878) 8 Ch D 286, Court of Appeal

A shipowner (De Bussche) employed an agent to sell a ship in India, China or Japan at a certain price. The agent was unable to sell the ship himself but, with the shipowner's consent, he employed a sub-agent (Alt) in Japan to do so. In fact, the sub-agent purchased the ship for himself and then resold it to a third party at a handsome profit. Affirming the judgment of Hall V-C, the Court of Appeal held the sub-agent liable to account for the shipowner for his profit.

Thesiger LJ, delivering the judgment of the Court (James, Baggally and Thesiger LJJ): . . . As a general rule, no doubt, the maxim '*delegatus non potest delegare*' applies so as to prevent an agent from establishing the relationship of principal and agent between his own principal and a third person; but this maxim when analyzed merely imports that an agent cannot, without authority from his principal, devolve upon another obligations to the principal which he has himself undertaken to personally fulfil; and that, inasmuch as confidence in the particular person employed is at the root of the contract of agency, such authority cannot be implied as an ordinary incident in the contract. But the exigencies of business do from time to time render necessary the carrying out of the instructions of a principal by a person other than the agent originally instructed for the purpose, and where that is the case, the reason of the thing requires that the rule should be relaxed, so as, on the one hand, to enable the agent to appoint what has been termed 'a sub-agent' or 'substitute' (the latter of which designations, although it does not exactly denote the legal relationship of the parties, we adopt for want of a better, and for the sake of brevity); and, on the other hand, to constitute, in the interests and for the protection of the principal, a direct privity of contract between him and such substitute. And we are of opinion that an authority to the effect referred to may and should be implied where, from the conduct of the parties to the original contract of agency, the usage of trade, or the nature of the particular business which is the subject of the agency, it may reasonably be presumed that the parties to the contract of agency originally intended that such authority should exist, or where, in the course of the employment, unforeseen emergencies arise which impose upon the agent the necessity of employing a substitute; and that when such authority exists, and is duly exercised, privity of contract arises between the principal and the substitute, and the latter becomes as responsible to the former for the due discharge of the duties which his employment casts upon him, as if he had been appointed agent by the principal himself. The law upon this point is accurately stated in *Story on Agency*. A case like the present, where a shipowner employs an agent for the purpose of effectuating a sale of a ship at any port where the ship may from time to time in the course of its employment under charter happen to be, is pre-eminently one in which the appointment of substitutes at ports other than those where the agent himself carries on business is a necessity, and must reasonably be presumed to be in the contemplation of the parties; and in the present case, we have, over and above that presumption, what cannot but be looked upon as express authority to appoint a substitute, and a complete ratification of the actual appointment of the Defendant in the letters which passed respectively between *Willis & Son* and the Plaintiff on the one side, and *Gilman & Co* on the other. We are, therefore, of opinion that the relationship of principal and agent was, in respect of the sale of the *Columbine*, for a time at least, constituted between the Plaintiff and the Defendant.

NOTES

1. An agent cannot delegate his authority to another person, or appoint a sub-agent to do some of the acts which he himself has to do, unless the agent has the express or implied consent of his principal to do so. The rule applies both where the principal places trust and confidence in the agent, and also where the principal relies on the personal skill of the agent.

2. In *De Bussche v Alt*, Thesiger LJ set out the circumstances when the consent of the principal to delegate will be implied. The performance of purely ministerial acts, which do not involve confidence or discretion, may also be delegated, eg service of a notice to quit by the solicitor of a company which was itself acting as agent (*Allam & Co Ltd v Europa Poster Services Ltd* [1968] 1 WLR 638). For the powers of a trustee to delegate, see the Trustee Act 1925, ss 23, 25 (as amended by the Powers of Attorney Act 1971, s 9).

3. If the agent makes an unauthorised delegation, the acts of, and payment to, the sub-agent will not bind the principal. But a third party dealing with the sub-agent may be able to rely on the apparent authority of the agent to delegate and thereby hold the principal bound by the sub-agent's acts (Bowstead, p 128). Alternatively, the principal will be bound if he ratifies the agent's act of delegation. It should also be noted that where there has been an unauthorised delegation, the principal is not liable to the sub-agent for commission (*Schmaling v Thomlinson* (1815) 6 Taunt 147); the sub-agent has no lien against the principal (*Solly v Rathbone* (1814) 2 M & S 298); the agent will be liable to the principal for wrongful execution of his authority (*Catlin v Bell* (1815) 4 Camp 183) and may be liable for money had and received by the sub-agent (*National Employers' Mutual General Insurance Association Ltd v Elphinstone* [1929] WN 135).

What are the consequences of an authorised delegation of authority by the agent?

Calico Printers' Association Ltd v Barclays Bank Ltd (1931) 145 LT 51, King's Bench Division

The plaintiffs sold cotton to a consignee in Beirut and sent shipping documents to Barclays Bank Ltd with instructions to insure the goods if the documents were not accepted by the consignee. Barclays Bank did not have an office in Beirut and, with the knowledge of the plaintiffs, instructed the Anglo-Palestine Bank in Beirut to act as their agents. Barclays Bank told the Anglo-Palestine Bank to insure the goods if the documents were not accepted. The Anglo-Palestine Bank did not present the shipping documents for payment and failed to insure the cotton, which was destroyed by fire. The plaintiffs then sued Barclays Bank and the Anglo-Palestine Bank for negligence. Wright J dismissed both claims, holding that the Anglo-Palestine Bank was not liable because there was no privity of contract between them and the plaintiffs, and that Barclays Bank were not liable because they could rely on an exclusion clause in their contract with the plaintiffs.

Wright J: . . . to leave the goods uninsured was a gross breach of the most elementary business precautions. . . .

On this ground I should hold these defendants liable to the plaintiffs if there were privity between them and the plaintiffs, and this question must now be considered.

To support the argument that there was privity between the plaintiffs and the Anglo-Palestine Bank, reliance was especially placed on a passage from Story on Agency, s 201, as establishing a general principle that where the employment of a sub-agent was authorised either by express terms or by a known course of business, or some unforeseen exigency necessitating such employment, there was privity established between the principal and the sub-agent, so that the sub-agent and not the agent became directly responsible to the principal for any negligence or misconduct in the performance of the mandate. But I do not think the English law has admitted any such general principle, but has in general applied the rule that even where the sub-agent is properly employed, there is still no privity between him and the principal; the latter is entitled to hold the agent liable for breach of the mandate, which he has accepted, and cannot, in general, claim against the sub-agent for negligence or breach of duty. I know of no English case in which a principal has recovered against a sub-agent for negligence. The agent does not as a rule escape liability to the principal merely because employment of the sub-agent is contemplated. To create privity it must be established not only that the principal contemplated that a sub-agent would perform part of the contract, but also that the principal authorised the agent to create privity of contract between the principal and the sub-agent, which is a very different matter requiring precise proof. In general, where a principal employs an agent to carry out a particular employment, the agent undertakes responsibility for the whole transaction, and is responsible for any negligence in carrying it out, even if the negligence be that of the sub-agent properly or necessarily engaged to perform some part, because there is no privity between the principal and the sub-agent.

I think the rule applies to the present case. The defendants, Barclays, by accepting the employment for $\frac{1}{4}$ per cent commission accepted responsibility for the whole service, including that part of it which necessarily involved the employment of a sub-agent or correspondent at Beyrout. The mere fact that he was nominated by the plaintiffs does not in my judgment affect the position; the defendants, Barclays, accepted the nomination and accepted the defendants, the Anglo-Palestine Bank, as their instrument to fulfil their contract. The case is one of most ordinary banking practice, and to accept the contention that the defendants, Barclays, were not responsible for the acts of the defendants, the Anglo-Palestine Bank, their foreign correspondents, or that there was privity between the latter and the plaintiffs, would be in my judgment to go contrary to the whole commercial understanding of a transaction like this.

The case is quite different from that put by Lord Cave LC in the case of *William H Muller and Co (London) Ltd v Lethem* ([1928] AC 34, 138 LT 241). In that case the question was whether the appellants were agents in London of a Dutch shipping company so as to be assessable to income tax in respect of business done in this country as such agents. The facts were peculiar, and one view was that the agents were directly appointed by the Dutch shipowners. Lord Cave LC said ([1928] AC at p 47, 138 LT at p 250): 'I am disposed to think that in signing both these documents the Dutch firm were acting as directors of the shipping companies, and in that capacity appointed the London firm as direct agents of those companies; but even if that be not so, and if the appointments must be held to have been made by the Dutch firm as shipping-agents for the Dutch companies and not as directors – still it appears to me that they constituted the London firm direct agents of the two companies. In this connection reference may be made to the well-known judgment of Thesiger LJ in *De Bussche v Alt* (38 LT 370, (1878) 8 Ch D 286), where he pointed out that in certain cases, where the exigencies of business require it, an agent must be deemed to have authority to constitute a direct privity of contract between a substitute appointed by him and his principals. In my opinion the present case falls within that category, and the appellants were appointed and became the authorised and regular agents of the two Dutch companies in London.'

For the reasons I have already indicated, I think it should not be held here that the plaintiffs gave any authority to the defendants, Barclays, to constitute a direct privity of contract between them and the Anglo-Palestine Bank; nor is my judgment on this conclusion affected by *De Bussche v Alt* (sup.) where a bill in equity was filed for an account in respect of secret profits made by a sub-agent for the sale of some ships. The plaintiff, the owner, consigned them for sale to a firm in the East, who appointed the defendant agent for sale in

Japan. The plaintiff and the defendant corresponded about the sale; the defendant made large secret profits and was held liable to account. The court there held that the circumstances constituted an express authority to appoint a substitute apart from the complete ratification of the actual appointment, and it was accordingly held that the relationship of principal and agent was constituted as between plaintiff and defendant, at least, *pro hac vice*. But apart from the specific finding of fact that there was authority to create direct privity, the case turned on equitable principles; the sub-agent was *pro tanto* in a fiduciary position as regards the secret profits and could not retain them as against the person whom he knew to be entitled, namely, the actual principal. In a later case of a similar character, *Powell and Thomas v Evan Jones and Co* ([1905] 1 KB 11, 92 LT 430), the Court of Appeal held that there was evidence to justify the jury in finding there was privity of contract on facts which appear to me very different from those in the present case, but held also that in all the circumstances there was such a fiduciary relationship as between the sub-agent and the principal as placed the former under a personal incapacity to receive any secret reward.

I do not think the three last cited authorities require me to depart from the conclusion that I have arrived at on the facts of this case and the other authorities that I have cited. I accordingly hold that the claim against the defendants, the Anglo-Palestine Bank, fails.

[The decision of Wright J was subsequently affirmed by the Court of Appeal: (1931) 145 LT 51 at 58. There was no appeal against that part of Wright J's judgment set out above.]

NOTES

1. The consequences of authorised delegation depend on whether there is privity of contract between the principal and the sub-agent (criticised by Bowstead, pp 134–135). The existence of privity of contract turns on whether the agent was clearly authorised to create it, or whether his act in doing so was ratified by the principal. However, whether there is privity or not, the acts of an authorised sub-agent bind the principal.

2. If there is privity of contract between the principal and the sub-agent the appointing agent need only exercise due care and skill in the appointment of the sub-agent; he is not normally liable for the default of the sub-agent. Further, if there is privity, the sub-agent becomes the agent of the principal and acquires all the usual rights and duties of an agent.

3. If there is no privity of contract between the principal and the sub-agent, the sub-agent generally owes no duty to account to the principal (*Lockwood v Abdy* (1845) 14 Sim 437); he cannot be sued by the principal in contract or for money had and received (*Robbins v Fennell* (1847) 11 QB 248); and he is not liable to the principal for the negligent performance of his work (*Calico Printers' Association v Barclays Bank Ltd*, above). It may be thought that after the landmark decisions of *Donoghue v Stevenson* [1932] AC 562 and *Hedley Byrne & Co Ltd v Heller & Partners Ltd* [1964] AC 465, a sub-agent could now be held liable to the principal for the tort of negligence, irrespective of whether there is privity of contract between them. However, in *Balsamo v Medici* [1984] 1 WLR 951, Walton J held that a sub-agent would only be liable to the principal for the tort of negligence if he had caused loss in respect of money or property belonging to the principal (see S Whittaker (1985) 48 MLR 86). Pure economic loss would not give the principal a tortious claim for negligence against the sub-agent.

4. Even if there is no privity of contract between the principal and the sub-agent, the sub-agent may still be held liable to the principal as a fiduciary (*Powell &*

Thomas v Evan Jones & Co [1905] 1 KB 11); he may also have a lien against the principal (*Fisher v Smith* (1878) 4 App Cas 1; see below, p 197); and he may be able to rely on the appointing agent's apparent authority to claim remuneration from the principal (Bowstead, p 135).

5. It is clear from the *Calico Printers'* case that if there is no privity of contract between the principal and the sub-agent, the appointing agent will be liable to the principal for the defaults of the sub-agent (see also *Mackersy v Ramsays, Bonars & Co* (1843) 9 Cl & Fin 818; cf *Thomas Cheshire & Co v Vaughan Bros & Co* [1920] 3 KB 240 at 259, where Atkin LJ, obiter, suggested that the appointing agent should only be held liable if he did not exercise reasonable care in the selection of the sub-agent). The appointing agent will also be liable to the principal for money had and received by the sub-agent to the use of the principal (*Balsamo v Medici*, above). In these circumstances, the appointing agent must seek redress from the sub-agent.

QUESTION

Pete employs Sell, It & Fast, a firm of estate agents, to sell his flat. Sell, It & Fast advertise the flat in their own shop window and also in the window of Tomkins, another firm of estate agents, with whom they have a reciprocal advertising arrangement. The advertisement states that all enquiries should be made through Sell, It & Fast. Bob sees the advertisement in Tomkins' window and contacts Sell, It & Fast to arrange to view the flat. Subsequently, Pete agrees to sell the flat to Bob and instructs his parents' solicitor, Conway, to act for him in this matter. Conway agrees to do so but, owing to his ill health, asks his old friend Drabble, a partner in another firm of solicitors, to draw up the documents needed to convey the flat to Bob. The sale of the flat is duly completed and Sell, It & Fast and Conway now claim their agreed fees from Pete. However, Pete has just found out about the involvement of Tomkins and Drabble and seeks your advice as to whether he has to pay Sell, It and Fast's and Conway's fees. See *John McCann & Co v Pow* [1974] 1 WLR 1643; and *Re Becket, Purnell v Paine* [1918] 2 Ch 72.

2 Rights of the agent

(a) Remuneration

(i) *A contractual right*

An agent will only be entitled to remuneration from his principal for his services if the agency is contractual and there is an express or implied term of the agency contract to that effect (but see also note 4, below at p 189).

Way v Latilla [1937] 3 All ER 759, House of Lords

An agent, Way, agreed with his principal, Latilla, to send to the principal information concerning gold mines and concessions in West Africa. Although the principal led the agent to believe that he would receive an interest in any concession obtained, no terms as to remuneration were expressly agreed between them. The House of Lords held that the agent was entitled to a reasonable remuneration on an implied contract to pay him a *quantum meruit.*

Lord Atkin: . . . The question now is, what are Mr Way's rights to remuneration? He originally claimed that there was a completed agreement to give him an interest in the concession, which, by custom, or on a reasonable basis, the court was asked to define as one-third. The trial judge accepted this view, holding that he was entitled to assess a reasonable share, and he accordingly awarded him £30,000, as being roughly 3 per cent on the sum of about £1,000,000, which he took to represent Mr Latilla's profits in the transaction. The Court of Appeal rejected this view, and, in my opinion, rightly. There certainly was no concluded contract between the parties as to the amount of the share or interest that Mr Way was to receive, and it appears to me impossible for the court to complete the contract for them. If the parties had proceeded on the terms of a written contract, with a material clause that the remuneration was to be a percentage of the gross returns, but with the figure left blank, the court could not supply the figure. The judge relied upon the decision of this House in *Hillas & Co Ltd v Arcos Ltd* ((1932) 147 LT 503). But in that case this House was able to find, in the contract to give an option for the purchase of timber in a future year, an intention to be bound contractually, and all the elements necessary to form a concluded contract. There is no material in the present case upon which any court would decide what was the share which the parties must be taken to have agreed. But, while there is, therefore, no concluded contract as to the remuneration, it is plain that there existed between the parties a contract of employment under which Mr Way was engaged to do work for Mr Latilla in circumstances which clearly indicated that the work was not to be gratuitous. Mr Way, therefore, is entitled to a reasonable remuneration on the implied contract to pay him *quantum meruit.* . . .

Services of this kind are no doubt usually the subject of an express contract as to remuneration, which may take the form of a fee, but may also take the form of a commission, share of profits, or share of proceeds calculated at a percentage, or on some other basis. In the present case, there was no question of fee between the parties from beginning to end. On the contrary, the parties had discussed remuneration on the footing of what may loosely be called a 'participation,' and nothing else. The reference is analogous to the well known distinction between salary and commission. There are many employments the remuneration of which is, by trade usage, invariably fixed on a commission basis. In such cases, if the amount of the commission has not been finally agreed, the *quantum meruit* would be fixed after taking into account what would be a reasonable commission, in the circumstances, and fixing a sum accordingly. This has been an everyday practice in the courts for years. But, if no trade usage assists the court as to the amount of the commission, it appears to me clear that the court may take into account the bargainings between the parties, not with a view to completing the bargain for them, but as evidence of the value which each of them puts upon the services. If the discussion had ranged between 3 per cent on the one side and 5 per cent on the other, all else being agreed, the court would not be likely to depart from somewhere about those figures, and would be wrong in ignoring them altogether and fixing remuneration on an entirely different basis, upon which, possibly, the services would never have been rendered at all. That, in fixing a salary basis, the court may pay regard to the previous conversation of the parties was decided by the Court of Exchequer in 1869, in *Scarisbrick v Parkinson* ((1869) 20 LT 175), where the terms of an agreement invalid under the Statute of Frauds, were held to be admissible as evidence in a *quantum meruit.* This seems to me to be good law, and to give effect to a principle which has been adopted regularly by the courts not only in fixing remuneration for services but also in fixing prices, sums due for use and occupation, and, indeed, in all cases where the court has to determine what is a reasonable reward for the consideration given by the claimant. As I have said, the rule applied in fixing the amount of the remuneration necessarily applies to the basis on which the amount is to be fixed. I have therefore no hesitation in saying that the basis of remuneration by fee should, in this case, on the evidence of the parties themselves, be rejected, and that Mr Way is entitled to a sum to be calculated on the basis of some reasonable participation.

What this should be is a task primarily to be undertaken by the trial judge. He did make an alternative award, and arrived at the sum of £5,000. I see no reason to differ from this.

Lord Wright: . . . There was, I think, no justification for making for the parties, as Charles J did, a contract which they did not make themselves. It is, however, clear, on the evidence, that the work was done by the appellant and accepted by the respondent on the basis that some remuneration was to be paid to the appellant by the respondent. There was thus an implied promise by the respondent to pay on a *quantum meruit*, that is, to pay what the services were worth. My difference with the Court of Appeal turns on a narrow issue, which is whether the *quantum meruit* should be determined on the footing of a fee as for professional services, or on some other footing. The Court of Appeal took the former view. I cannot, however, with respect, find, on the whole of the evidence in the case, and, in particular, on the discussions between the parties, any sufficient reason for accepting that view. The services of the appellant were, I think, outside the range of his duties as mining engineer, and were those of an agent for purchase, who suggests to his principal a transaction, and negotiates and completes it for him. While it is not unknown that such services should be remunerated by a fee if it is expressly or impliedly so agreed, this is by no means necessarily, and would not generally be, the case. The idea of such a fee being excluded, it follows that the question of the amount to which the appellant is entitled is left at large, and the court must do the best it can to arrive at a figure which seems to it fair and reasonable to both parties, on all the facts of the case. One aspect of the facts to be considered is found in the communings of the parties while the business was going on. Evidence of this nature is admissible to show what the parties had in mind, however indeterminately, with regard to the basis of remuneration. On those facts, the court may be able to infer, or attribute to the parties, an intention that a certain basis of payment should apply. This evidence seems to me to show quite clearly that the appellant was employed on the basis of receiving a remuneration depending on results. If he had been unsuccessful, he would have been entitled to no more than his expenses, but the respondent had led him to believe that, if the concessions he obtained were valuable, his remuneration would be on the basis of some proportion of their value. The realisation of that value was removed from the actual services by the lapse of time (during which large sums of money were expended and adventured), and by many contingencies, and therefore the proper proportion may be comparatively very small, though the fruits of success were very large. The precise figure can be only a rough estimate. If what the court fixes is either too small or too large, the fault must be ascribed to the parties in leaving this important matter in so nebulous a state. But, forming the best judgment I can, I agree with your Lordships that the figure to be awarded to the appellant should be £5,000, which is what Charles J was prepared to adopt if his judgment were reversed.

[Lords Thankerton, Macmillan and Maugham concurred.]

NOTES

1. Whether a term as to remuneration is to be implied into the agency contract will depend on the normal rules as to the implication of terms into contracts (see Cheshire, Fifoot and Furmston's *Law of Contract* (12th ed, 1991), pp 131–146; G H Treitel *The Law of Contract* (8th ed, 1991), pp 185–195). Such a term may be implied by trade custom or usage, on grounds of business efficacy, or to give effect to the intentions of the parties. See also Supply of Goods and Services Act 1982, s 15.

2. When a professional person is employed as an agent, and there is no express agreement as to remuneration, there is a strong presumption that he is to receive reasonable remuneration for his services (*Miller v Beal* (1879) 27 WR 403). What is reasonable may be assessed according to what is customary in the trade, profession or business in which the agent is employed. But the customary rate must produce a reasonable result if it is to bind the principal (*Wilkie v Scottish Aviation Ltd* 1956 SC 198 at 205, per Lord Clyde). On the remuneration of professional agents generally, see J R Murdoch [1981] Conv 424.

3. No term may be implied which would be inconsistent with an express term of the agency contract. In *Kofi Sunkersette Obu v A Strauss & Co Ltd* [1951] AC 243, it was an express term of the agency contract that the agent was to receive £50 for expenses and also commission at the discretion of the principal. No commission was paid so, relying on *Way v Latilla*, the agent claimed that he was nevertheless entitled to a reasonable commission by way of a *quantum meruit* for his services. The Privy Council rejected the claim and distinguished *Way v Latilla* on the ground that in the case before them commission was expressly provided for under the agency contract. The agency contract left the basis and rate of commission at the discretion of the principal and the Privy Council would not substitute their own discretion for that of the principal. For a similar case, see *Re Richmond Gate Property Co Ltd* [1965] 1 WLR 335. Cf *Powell v Braun* [1954] 1 WLR 401, CA.

4. It should also be noted that an agent may be able to claim a reasonable sum on a restitutionary basis if he renders services outside a contract and those services are freely accepted by the principal, with the knowledge that they could not possibly be gratuitous (see, eg, *Michael Elliott & Partners Ltd v UK Land plc* [1991] 1 EGLR 39 at 45; cf *Fairvale Ltd v Sabharwal* [1992] 2 EGLR 27 at 28). Some of the leading writers on the law of restitution submit that this theory of free acceptance offers the best explanation of *Way v Lattila* (P Birks *An Introduction to the Law of Restitution* (revised paperback edn, 1989), p 272; Goff and Jones *The Law of Restitution* (4th ed, 1993), p 485, note 9; cf A Burrows *The Law of Restitution* (1993), p 295).

5. Under reg 6(1) of the Commercial Agents (Council Directive) Regulations 1993, implementing EEC Directive 86/653 on self-employed commercial agents, in the absence of any agreement between the parties as to remuneration, the principal must pay the commercial agent such remuneration as is customary, or, if there is no agreement or custom, he must pay the agent a reasonable remuneration.

(ii) *Effective cause*

Unless otherwise agreed, when an agent is to be paid commission on bringing about a particular event, the agent is not entitled to that commission unless he can show that his services were the effective cause of the event.

Millar, Son & Co v Radford (1903) 19 TLR 575, Court of Appeal

Millar, Son & Co, a firm of estate agents, were instructed by Radford to find a purchaser, or, failing a purchaser, a tenant, for his property. Millars introduced Cook, who took a seven year lease of the property. Millars were paid their commission. Fifteen months later, without Millars' intervention, Cook purchased the freehold from Radford. Millars then claimed commission on the sale. Upholding the decision of trial judge, the Court of Appeal rejected Millars' claim to further commission.

Collins MR: . . . The claim of house agents to be entitled to commission in circumstances like the present is a claim which is often made, and is likely to continue to be made. It is, therefore, important to point out that the right to commission does not arise out of the mere fact that agents have introduced a tenant or a purchaser. It is not sufficient to show that the introduction was a *causa sine qua non*. It is necessary to show that the introduction was an efficient cause in bringing about the letting or the sale. Here the plaintiffs fail to establish what is a condition precedent to their right to commission – viz, that they have brought about the sale. It is open to the defendant in an action like this to say either that, though the plaintiffs effected a sale, they were not his agents, or that, though they were his agents, they had not effected the sale. If the defendant proves either the one or the other, the plaintiffs fail to make out their case.

[Mathew and Cozens-Hardy LJJ delivered concurring judgments.]

NOTES

1. Today, the equivalent word to 'efficient' is 'effective'. In other words, the agent must be the direct or effective cause of the event upon which his commission is to be paid: there must be no break in the chain of causation.

2. For a similar case to *Millar, Son & Co v Radford*, see *Toulmin v Millar* (1887) 3 TLR 836, HL. In that case, Lord Watson stated that 'in order to found a legal claim for commission there must not only be a causal, there must also be a contractual relation between the introduction and the ultimate transaction of sale'. This means, for example, that an agent instructed to find a tenant will not be entitled to commission if the person he introduces to his principal actually buys the property (*Toulmin v Millar*), and an agent instructed to find a purchaser will not be entitled to commission if he introduces a Government Department which goes on to acquire the property compulsorily (*Hodges & Sons v Hackbridge Park Residential Hotel Ltd* [1940] 1 KB 404). Cf *Rimmer v Knowles* (1874) 30 LT 496, where the agent employed to find a purchaser was held entitled to commission when he introduced a tenant who took a 999 year lease of the property.

3. For a useful summary of those cases where the courts have had to consider which of two competing agents was the effective cause of a transaction, see Markesinis and Munday, pp 129–131.

(iii) *Opportunity to earn commission*

Luxor (Eastbourne) Ltd v Cooper [1941] AC 108, House of Lords

Luxor (Eastbourne) Ltd and Regal (Hastings) Ltd (the vendors) employed Cooper, an estate agent, to find a purchaser for four of their cinemas. The vendors agreed to pay Cooper a fee of £10,000 on completion of the sale if he introduced a purchaser who bought the cinemas for not less than £185,000. Cooper introduced Burton who made an offer of £185,000 for the cinemas 'subject to contract'. But the vendors withdrew from the negotiations. Cooper sued the vendors for damages, claiming they had broken an implied term of his agency contract by which they undertook to do nothing to prevent his earning commission. Branson J gave judgment for the vendors and, although reversed by the Court of Appeal, his judgment was upheld by the House of Lords.

Lord Russell of Killowen: A few preliminary observations occur to me. (1) Commission contracts are subject to no peculiar rules or principles of their own; the law which governs them is the law which governs all contracts and all questions of agency. (2) No general rule can be laid down by which the rights of the agent or the liability of the principal under commission contracts are to be determined. In each case these must depend upon the exact terms of the contract in question, and upon the true construction of those terms. And (3) contracts by which owners of property, desiring to dispose of it, put it in the hands of agents on commission terms, are not (in default of specific provisions) contracts of employment in the ordinary meaning of those words. No obligation is imposed on the agent to do anything. The contracts are merely promises binding on the principal to pay a sum of money upon the happening of a specified event, which involves the rendering of some service by the agent. There is no real analogy between such contracts, and contracts of employment by which one party binds himself to do certain work, and the other binds himself to pay remuneration for the doing of it. . . .

As to the claim for damages, this rests upon the implication of some provision in the commission contract, the exact terms of which were variously stated in the course of the argument, the object always being to bind the principal not to refuse to complete the sale to the client whom the agent has introduced.

I can find no safe ground on which to base the introduction of any such implied term. Implied terms, as we all know, can only be justified under the compulsion of some necessity. No such compulsion or necessity exists in the case under consideration. The agent is promised a commission if he introduces a purchaser at a specified or minimum price. The owner is desirous of selling. The chances are largely in favour of the deal going through, if a purchaser is introduced. The agent takes the risk in the hope of a substantial remuneration for comparatively small exertion. In the case of the plaintiff his contract was made on September 23, 1935; his client's offer was made on October 2, 1935. A sum of £10,000 (the equivalent of the remuneration of a year's work by a Lord Chancellor) for work done within a period of eight or nine days is no mean reward, and is one well worth a risk. There is no lack of business efficacy in such a contract, even though the principal is free to refuse to sell to the agent's client.

The position will no doubt be different if the matter has proceeded to the stage of a binding contract having been made between the principal and the agent's client. In that case it can be said with truth that a 'purchaser' has been introduced by the agent; in other words the event has happened upon the occurrence of which a right to the promised commission has become vested in the agent. From that moment no act or omission by the principal can deprive the agent of that vested right. . . .

My Lords, in my opinion there is no necessity in these contracts for any implication: and the legal position can be stated thus: If according to the true construction of the contract the event has happened upon the happening of which the agent has acquired a vested right to the commission (by which I mean that it is debitum in praesenti even though only solvendum in futuro), then no act or omission by the principal or anyone else can deprive the agent of that right; but until that event has happened the agent cannot complain if the principal refuses to proceed with, or carry to completion, the transaction with the agent's client.

I have already expressed my view as to the true meaning of a contract to pay a commission for the introduction of a purchaser at a specified or minimum price. It is possible that an owner may be willing to bind himself to pay a commission for the mere introduction of one who offers to purchase at the specified or minimum price; but such a construction of the contract would in my opinion require clear and unequivocal language.

Lord Wright: . . . what is in question in all these cases is the interpretation of a particular contract. I deprecate in general the attempt to enunciate decisions on the construction of agreements as if they embodied rules of law. To some extent decisions on one contract may help by way of analogy and illustration in the decision of another contract. But however similar the contracts may appear, the decision as to each must depend on the consideration of the language of the particular contract, read in the light of the material circumstances of the parties in view of which the contract is made. I shall therefore in the first instance examine the particular contract in question in the light of the material facts. I shall later touch on certain of the authorities which have been debated before your Lordships. It is important to simplify as far as possible the problem of construing commission agency agreements, especially in regard to the sale of houses and land. These are of common occurrence among all classes of the community and it is most undesirable that subtleties and complications of interpretation calculated to lead to disputes should be allowed to confuse what is ex facie a plain and simple agreement. . . .

There is no indication in the oral evidence that the parties contemplated that the agents should have any right to be paid anything except out of a purchase price paid by the purchasers to the vendors. Still less is there any such indication in the letters of October 2 and 11, 1935. I think indeed the language excludes the suggested implication. The two letters deal with an offer from Colonel Burton which is 'subject to contract.' That phrase is sharply contrasted with the phrase 'completion of the purchase.' These latter words assume at least that the stage of negotiations indicated by 'subject to contract' has been successfully passed. During that stage each negotiating party is free as between himself and the other to change his mind and desist from negotiating. In particular the vendor retains the right which belongs to him as property owner to dispose of his property as he thinks fit. There is no obligation between him and the potential purchaser, assuming, what is not here in question, that he has given no binding option. He may as between himself and the other party discontinue the negotiations for any reason or want of reason however capricious or selfish. But it is said that as between himself and the agent the position is different. There is, it is said, a binding contract with the agent, and at least an inchoate right to commission in the agent who, in a case like the present, may have done everything on his part requisite to earn his commission. But even so his contract is in terms that his right to commission should depend on a particular event, namely, the completion of the sale. His claim to commission when the sale is not completed, involves the contention that the principal in virtue of the contract with the commission agent has surrendered the freedom to dispose of or retain his own property which he unquestionably enjoys vis-à-vis the other negotiating party. The commission agreement is, however, subordinate to the hoped for principal agreement of sale. It would be strange if what was preliminary or accessory should control the freedom of action of the principal in regard to the main transaction which everyone contemplates might never materialize. I cannot think that a property owner can be held, in virtue of a commission contract like this, to have bound himself by mere implication to complete the sale or to pay damages to the agent. Express words are in my opinion necessary to effect this result. Indeed the stipulation 'payment on completion of purchase' is in my opinion contradictory of the implication that there is to be payment, even in the shape of damages, in the event of the sale not being completed.

The case that the suggested term is not properly to be implied becomes, in my opinion, even clearer when account is taken of some of the more general aspects of the course of business in these matters. It is well known that in the ordinary course a property owner intending to sell may put his property on the books of several estate agents with each of whom he makes a contract for payment of commission on a sale. If he effects a sale to the client introduced by one agent, is he to be liable in damages to all the others for preventing them from earning their commission? Common sense and ordinary business understanding clearly give a negative answer. Or suppose that having employed one agent whose client has made an offer, he receives a better offer from a buyer introduced by another agent and concludes the purchase with him. It seems out of the question that he is thereby rendering himself liable in damages to the former agent. Or suppose that owing to changed circumstances he decides that he will not sell at all and breaks off negotiations with the agent's client, is he to be liable for damages to the agent? I can find no justification for such a view. I am assuming a commission contract not containing special terms such as to impose an obligation on the vendor actually to sell through the particular agent to the potential purchaser introduced by that agent. Contracts containing such terms, though not perhaps usual, are possible. But it is said that in the absence of special terms an obligation of that nature can be implied, subject, however, to the qualification that the owner retains his freedom to deal as he likes with his own and to discontinue negotiations, but only so long as in doing so he acts with reasonable excuse or just cause. I find it impossible to define these terms in this connection. If the commission agent has a right to claim commission or damages if the vendor abandons the negotiations and does not complete the sale, his doing so is a breach of contract vis-à-vis the agent and it is immaterial to the agent how sensible or reasonable the vendor's conduct may be from his own point of view. Such a qualified implication seems to me too complicated and artificial. The parties cannot properly be supposed to have intended it, nor can it be taken to be necessary to give business efficacy to the transaction. But I do not discuss this aspect further because, as already explained, I find no basis for the implication, whether general or qualified. And the great difficulty which the Courts have found in defining or applying the idea of 'just cause or reasonable excuse' further goes to show that it is not an implied term necessary to give business efficacy to what the parties must have intended. Nor is the suggested implication made more plausible by expressing it in a negative form as an implied term that the principal will not prevent the agent earning his commission. Such a term must be based upon something which under the contract the principal has agreed to do, of such a nature that failure to do it carries the consequence that the agent cannot earn the commission which would have become due if the principal had done what he had promised. For the purposes of the present problem this promise must be that he would complete the contract. Thus it all comes back to the same issue, namely, that there must be some breach of contract for which damages can be claimed. . . . It may seem hard that an agent who has introduced a potential purchaser, able and willing to complete, should get nothing for what he has done, if, during the negotiations, the principal decides not to complete, according to his own pleasure and without any reason which quoad the agent is a sufficient excuse. But such is the express contract. And people in ordinary life do not seek the services of commission agents without a good prospect and intention of making use of them. The agent in practice takes what is a business risk. I am assuming that the commission contract is of the type exemplified in this case. The agent may, however, secure a form of contract to which what I have said does not apply. But it is necessary to reserve certain eventualities in which an agent may be entitled to damages where there is a failure to complete even under a contract like the contract in this case. For instance, if the negotiations between the vendor and the purchaser have been duly concluded and a binding executory agreement has been achieved, different considerations may arise. The vendor is then no longer free to dispose of his property. Though the sale is not completed the property in equity has passed from him to the purchaser. If he refuses to complete he would be guilty of a breach of agreement vis-à-vis the purchaser. I think, as at present advised, that it ought then to be held that he is also in breach of his contract with the commission agent, that is, of some term which can properly be implied. But that question and possibly some other questions do not arise in this case and may be reserved. Furthermore, I have been dealing with a contract in regard to the sale of real property and there may be differences where the commission agency is in regard to transactions of a different character. On the whole, however, my opinion is that the contract in question means what it says, that the simple construction is the true construction and that there is no justification for the equitable reconstruction which the Court of Appeal, following authorities which bound it, has applied. I would allow the appeal. . . .

It may be said that . . . on the view which I have been propounding, the prospect of the agent getting his reward is speculative and may be defeated by the arbitrary will of the principal. That may perhaps be so in some cases. But it is I think clear that under a contract like the present the agent takes a risk in several respects; thus, for instance, the principal may sell independently of the agent to a purchaser other than the purchaser introduced by him, or where the employment is not as sole agent, he may sell through another agent. Why should not the agent take the chance also of the employer changing his mind and deciding not to sell at all? It is said that according to the term which, it is suggested, should be implied he can change his mind if he has a reasonable excuse or just cause. But then why should his freedom to dispose of his property be fettered even in this way? And what is a reasonable excuse or just cause? Is it to be decided from the point of view of the owner or from the point of view of the commission agent? It is just the difficulty of applying these vague phrases which has already led to so much litigation on this question. In my opinion the implied term is unworkable. Even in this case Branson J has taken one view and the Court of Appeal another. If the suggested implied term is discarded, a contract such as the present will be simple and workable. Commission agents may sometimes fail to get the commission that they expected, but they will be relieved from disputes and litigation. And they can always, if they desire, demand what they consider a more favourable form of contract.

[Viscount Simon LC and Lord Romer delivered concurring opinions.
Lord Thankerton concurred with Lord Russell of Killowen's opinion.]

Company law students will be familiar with another aspect of this case, see *Regal (Hastings) Ltd v Gulliver* [1967] 2 AC 134n, [1942] 1 All ER 378, HL.

NOTES

1. Unless there is an express or implied promise to the contrary in the contract of agency, the principal is free to prevent his agent from earning commission. Such a promise may be implied by trade custom, or to give business efficacy to the agency contract, or otherwise to give effect to the intentions of the parties. But as *Luxor (Eastbourne) Ltd v Cooper* illustrates, the courts are generally reluctant to imply such a promise into an agency contract. This is particularly true where, as in *Luxor's* case itself, the implication of such a promise would restrict the principal's freedom to deal with his own property as he wished. For example, in *L French & Co Ltd v Leeston Shipping Co* [1922] 1 AC 451, a shipbroker's right to commission depended on the continuation of the charterparty he had negotiated for his principal. But the House of Lords refused to imply a term into the shipbroker's agency contract to the effect that his principal, the shipowner, could not sell his ship to the charterer, thereby bringing the charterparty to a premature end. See also *Rhodes v Forwood* (1876) 1 App Cas 256; cf *Turner v Goldsmith* [1891] 1 QB 544 (both cases are considered below at p 201); J F Burrows (1968) 31 MLR 390.

2. In *L French & Co Ltd v Leeston Shipping Co*, the shipbroker (agent) was deprived of commission because the shipowner (principal) and charterer (third party) agreed to terminate the charterparty. No term was to be implied into the agency agreement to prevent this. But a term may well be implied into the agency agreement to the effect that the principal must not break a contract negotiated by the agent with a third party and so deprive the agent of commission due on performance of that contract. In *Alpha Trading Ltd v Dunnshaw-Patten Ltd* [1981] QB 290 such a term was implied. In that case, agents negotiated a contract for the sale of cement by their principal to a third party. The principal breached the sale contract by failing to perform and settled the resulting claim made by the third party. The principal's failure to perform the sale contract prevented the agents earning commission under the terms of their agency contract. The Court of Appeal held that the principal was in breach of an implied term of the agency contract to the effect that he would not breach the sale contract with the third party so as to deprive the agents of their remuneration under the agency contract. Cf *Marcan Shipping (London) Ltd v Polish SS Co, The Manifest Lipkowy* [1989] 2 Lloyd's Rep 138, where the Court of Appeal refused to imply a term into a collateral contract made beween the agent and third party (the seller) to the effect that the third party would not breach a contract for the sale of a ship made between himself and the agent's principal (the buyer), and thereby deprive the agent of commission due under the agency contract made between the principal and agent.

3. In *Alpha Trading Ltd v Dunnshaw-Pattern Ltd*, Brandon and Templeman LJJ accepted that the observations of Lord Wright in *Luxor (Eastbourne) Ltd v Cooper*, although made in the context of estate agency, were capable of being applied to contracts of agency in general. However, most contracts between estate agents and vendors are unilateral, so it is probably more accurate in such cases to speak in terms of an implied collateral contract, rather than an implied term, that the vendor will not deprive the agent of commission (Bowstead, pp 234–235). Aliter, where the vendor and agent enter into a 'sole agency' agreement whereby the vendor agrees not to sell his property through another agent. Sole agency agreements are generally regarded as bilateral contracts (Bowstead, p 235; cf J R Murdoch (1975) 91 LQR 357, pp 374–375). On estate agency agreements generally, see Fridman, pp 381–391; Markesinis and Munday, pp 134–139; see also J R Murdoch (1975) 91 LQR 357; *The Law of Estate Agency and Auctions* (2nd ed, 1984).

(iv) *Loss of right to commission*

The agent will lose his right to commission if he:

(1) acts outside the scope of his actual authority (*Mason v Clifton* (1863) 3 F & F 899);
(2) acts in a manner which he knows, or ought to have known, to be unlawful (*Josephs v Pebrer* (1825) 3 B & C 639); or
(3) commits a serious breach of his duties as agent (*Boston Deep Sea Fishing and Ice Co Ltd v Ansell* (1888) 39 Ch D 339; cf *Hippisley v Knee Brothers* [1905] 1 KB 1; above, p 174).

Unless otherwise agreed, an agent is not entitled to commission on transactions which take place after termination of the agency contract (*Crocker Horlock Ltd v B Lang & Co Ltd* [1949] 1 All ER 526). But the agent's right to commission depends upon the construction of the terms of the agency contract. The agency contract may provide that the agent's right to commission accrues before the time when the commission becomes payable. When the right arises before termination, eg when the agent secures the order, commission must be paid, even if it only becomes payable after termination, eg when the order is executed (*Sellers v London Counties Newspapers* [1951] 1 KB 784). Particular difficulties may arise with the construction of terms providing for the payment of commission on 'repeat orders'.

It should be noted that the Commercial Agents (Council Directive) Regulations 1993, implementing EEC Directive 86/653 on self-employed commercial agents, contain specific provisions dealing with the remuneration of a commercial agent by commission (regs 7–12). See, in particular, reg 8 which, inter alia, gives the agent a right to commission on business transacted after termination of the agency contract, so long as the business is 'mainly attributable' to the efforts of the agent during the period of the agency contract and was transacted within a reasonable period after termination of that contract.

(b) Indemnity

An agent has a right against his principal to be reimbursed all expenses and indemnified against all losses and liabilities incurred by him while acting within the scope of his actual authority.

Rhodes v Fielder, Jones and Harrison (1919) 89 LJKB 15, King's Bench Division

A country solicitor instructed London solicitors to act as his agent in an appeal which was to be heard in the House of Lords. The London solicitors briefed counsel, who went on to win the case. The country solicitors then instructed the London solicitors not to pay counsel's fees, but the London solicitors paid the fees and reimbursed themselves out of monies of the country solicitor in their possession. The country solicitor then brought an action against the London solicitors to recover the monies so retained.

Lush J: . . . I now come to the second point taken by the plaintiffs, which is this: After the case had been heard in the House of Lords, and after consultations with counsel had been asked for and held, the plaintiff revoked the authority to the defendants to pay these fees, and it was argued that when country solicitors instruct London agents to brief counsel and, in the usual way, the agents have consultations with counsel and incur obligations towards counsel in respect of them which are fully recognized, the country solicitors can revoke their authority to their London agents to pay the counsel's fees. I can only say that to my mind such a proposition is absolutely unsustainable. It is, of course, the fact that the London agents could not be sued for these fees by counsel, but that does not dispose of the question. If they did not pay the fees they would be behaving in a way which would unquestionably place them in a serious position. I think it is right to say this, that a solicitor who has undertaken to pay fees to counsel and refuses to pay them is guilty of misconduct, and therefore it is impossible to say that it was open to the country solicitors in this case to revoke their authority. Authority for this was cited before the Master. The defendants did what they did at the request of the plaintiff, and made themselves responsible as honourable members of their profession for the payment of these fees. I think that the Master was perfectly right, and that the appeal must be dismissed.

Sankey J: As to the second point, I so entirely agree with what has fallen from my brother Lush that I think I should be wasting public time if I said anything further. To my mind it is entirely unarguable.

Appeal dismissed.

NOTES

1. Where the agency is contractual, the agent's right to reimbursement and indemnity arises as an express or implied term of the contract. However, the right may be expressly excluded by the parties, or by a term implied through the custom of the trade (eg, unless otherwise agreed, estate agents are not entitled to claim reimbursement for advertising expenses over and above their commission). The agent's contractual right to reimbursement and indemnity is wide. It covers not only payment of debts which are legally binding on the principal, but also payments which the agent is legally bound to make though the principal is not (*Adams v Morgan & Co* [1924] 1 KB 751) and payments which the agent is under a strong moral obligation to meet (*Rhodes v Fielder, Jones and Harrison*, above).

2. Where the agency is gratuitous, the agent has only a restitutionary right to reimbursement of payments which he was compelled to make for the benefit of his principal and which the principal would have been ultimately liable to make himself (see generally Goff and Jones *The Law of Restitution* (4th ed, 1993), Chs 14 and 15). However, if a gratuitous agent can rely on an equitable right to indemnity, eg as a trustee or surety, he may be able to obtain a wider indemnity than that which arises under the restitutionary remedy.

3. The agent has no right to reimbursement for expenses, or to an indemnity for losses and liabilities, incurred in any of the following circumstances:

(1) when he exceeds his actual authority (*Barron v Fitzgerald* (1840) 6 Bing NC 201), unless his unauthorised acts are subsequently ratified by his principal;

(2) as a result of the agent's breach of duty, negligence, default, or insolvency (*Lage v Siemens Bros & Co Ltd* (1932) 42 Ll L Rep 252); or
(3) in the performance of acts which the agent knows, or ought reasonably to know, are unlawful (*Re Parker* (1882) 21 Ch D 408), but the agent may be entitled to a contribution from his principal under the Civil Liability (Contribution) Act 1978.

(c) Lien

To secure his rights of remuneration, reimbursement or indemnity, the agent may be able to exercise a lien over goods belonging to his principal which are in his possession. In general, the lien gives the agent the right to detain his principal's goods until he is paid what he is owed by the principal in respect of those goods, ie it is usually a particular lien (but see below, pp 818–821, as to when a general lien may arise). But the agent can only exercise a lien over his principal's goods if he lawfully acquired possession of them in the course of the agency (*Taylor v Robinson* (1818) 2 Moore CP 730), and he holds them in the same capacity as that in which he claims the lien (*Dixon v Stansfeld* (1850) 10 CB 398). Furthermore, an agent's right to exercise a lien may be excluded by the express or implied terms of the agency contract (*Wolstenholm v Sheffield Union Banking Co* (1886) 54 LT 746).

A sub-agent may also be able to exercise a lien over the principal's goods, even though the sub-agent's claims for remuneration, reimbursement and indemnity are against the appointing agent and not the principal. To exercise such a lien the appointment of the sub-agent must have been authorised by the principal (actual or apparent authority of the appointing agent will do): see *Solly v Rathbone* (1814) 2 M & S 298, where it was held that there was no right of lien because the sub-delegation was unauthorised. So long as the sub-delegation was authorised the sub-agent may exercise his lien, even though the appointing agent may have had no authority to create privity of contract between the principal and the sub-agent. Where the principal authorised sub-delegation by his agent, but the principal remains undisclosed, the sub-agent may exercise a lien over the principal's goods to secure any claim he may have against the appointing agent, so long as the claim arose before the sub-agent discovered the truth (*Mann v Forrester* (1814) 4 Camp 60). For detailed discussion of the nature of a lien, and also the way it may be acquired and lost, see below, pp 814 ff. See also Markesinis and Munday, pp 144–151, for a useful account of the agent's lien.

QUESTIONS

1. If an agent is under a fiduciary duty not to place himself in a position where his own interests conflict with those of his principal (above, p 169), how can an agent ever exercise a lien over his principal's goods without being in breach of fiduciary duty? See *Compania Financiera Soleada SA v Hamoor Tanker Corpn Inc, The Borag* [1980] 1 Lloyd's Rep 111 at 122, per Mustill J, reversed on other grounds [1981] 1 WLR 274.
2. Aldred, an art collector, authorised Bronwen, an antique dealer, to buy Russian art on his behalf. At the same time he wrote to Sergei, an old friend and dealer, saying what he had done. Bronwen in turned asked Natasha, an expert in Russian art, to look for icons and buy any she found on behalf of Aldred.

On 1 March Natasha bought an icon in Aldred's name from Igor, paying cash down. On 1 April Bronwen approached Sergei (who had absent-mindedly thrown away Aldred's letter without reading it) and bought a Russian painting in Aldred's name, agreeing to pay for it in a month's time. She and the painting thereupon disappeared without trace. Meanwhile Aldred died suddenly on 15 March.

Advise (1) Aldred's executors, who want the icon purchased by Natasha; (2) Natasha, who wants to be reimbursed her expenditure; and (3) Sergei, who wants to be paid for his painting.

3 Termination of agency

(a) Termination of the relationship between principal and agent

Campanari v Woodburn (1854) 15 CB 400, Court of Common Pleas

P agreed to pay A £100 if A sold P's picture. P died before the picture was sold. Unaware of P's death, A sold the picture and claimed £100 from A's administratrix. Although the administratrix confirmed the sale she refused to pay A his commission. A then sued the administratrix for his commission.

Jervis CJ: I am of opinion that the defendant in this case is entitled to the judgment of the court. As alleged on the face of the declaration, it does not appear that the original contract between the plaintiff and the intestate conferred upon the former an authority which was irrevocable: it simply states that it was agreed between the plaintiff and the intestate that the plaintiff should endeavour to sell a certain picture of the intestate, and that, if the plaintiff succeeded in selling the same, the intestate should pay him £100. So far, therefore, as appears in the declaration, it was a mere employment of the plaintiff to do the act, not carrying with it any irrevocable authority. It is plain that the intestate might in his life-time have revoked the authority, without rendering himself liable to be called upon to pay the £100, though possibly the plaintiff might have had a remedy for a breach of the contract, if the intestate had wrongfully revoked his authority after he had been put to expense in endeavouring to dispose of the picture. In that way, perhaps, the plaintiff might have recovered damages by reason of the revocation. His death, however, was a revocation by the act of God, and the administratrix is not, in my judgment, responsible for anything. It was no fault of hers, – as in *Smout v Ilbery* ((1842) 10 M & W 1) – that the contract was not carried out. It must be taken to have been part of the original compact between the plaintiff and the intestate, that, whereas, on the one hand, he would receive a large sum if he succeeded in selling the picture, so, on the other hand, he would take the chance of his authority to sell being revoked by death or otherwise. Mr Maude seems to concede, that, but for what took place subsequently to the death of the intestate, the administratrix would have been liable: but he relies upon the allegation in the declaration, that the plaintiff sold the picture, and that the sale was confirmed by the defendant as administratrix; and contends that therefore she is liable. But it seems to me that that consequence by no means follows. If the defendant as administratrix had, after the death of the intestate, ordered the sale of the picture, no doubt that would have been a new retainer, and she would have been liable to the plaintiff on a quantum meruit. If, with full knowledge of the contract under which the plaintiff was to receive £100 as the stipulated reward for his exertions in selling the picture, the defendant had continued the employment, and it had resulted in a sale, the £100 might have been taken by the jury as the measure of damages. But, without shewing that the defendant had any knowledge whatever of the original contract, the confirmation of the sale is relied on as a confirmation of the original contract. It is enough to say that the averment as to the confirmation of the sale by the defendant does not raise the point which Mr Maude desires to raise. That confirmation, however it might make her liable to an action for a reasonable remuneration for the plaintiff's services, clearly is not sufficient to charge the defendant either personally or in her representative character for the breach of the original contract.

Williams J: I am of the same opinion. It may be convenient to consider what the effect would have been if the declaration had omitted the averment of confirmation of the sale by the defendant. It would then have amounted to a mere statement of an agreement between the plaintiff and the intestate that the plaintiff should endeavour to sell the picture, and, if he succeeded in so doing, the intestate should pay him £100. That clearly would have been revoked by the death. In such a state of things, the mere circumstance of something having been done under the contract, does not make it irrevocable. The contract, after the death of the intestate, was not and could not be confirmed according to its terms. It is perfectly clear, that, if the count had stood without the allegation that the administratrix confirmed the sale, it would have been utterly without foundation. What, then, is the effect of that averment? There is no allegation that the contract was confirmed as between the plaintiff and the deceased; but merely an allegation that the sale was confirmed by the defendant as administratrix. That is manifestly different from an averment that the original contract was confirmed by her, with all its incidents and all its consequences. I do not think it necessary, – though I entertain no doubt on the point, – to give any opinion as to what would have been the effect, if the declaration had contained such an allegation. The utmost that can be said is, that the defendant, as administratrix, might have been liable on a quantum meruit for services performed by the plaintiff as her agent in relation to the sale: but she clearly could not be liable in the way in which she is sought to be charged here.

[Crowder J delivered a concurring judgment.]

Frith v Frith [1906] AC 254, Privy Council

The defendant had been appointed by a power of attorney to take possession of and manage an estate owned by the plaintiff. The estate was mortgaged to a third party and the defendant gave a personal guarantee that he would pay the mortgage debt. Neither the mortgage debt nor the guarantee were mentioned in the power of attorney. Later the plaintiff revoked the defendant's authority and demanded possession of the estate from him. The defendant refused to give up possession on the ground that his authority was coupled with an interest, and was, therefore, irrevocable.

Lord Atkinson (delivering the advice of the Privy Council (Earl of Halsbury, Lord Davey, Lord Robertson, Lord Atkinson, and Sir Arthur Wilson)): . . . it cannot be disputed that the general rule of law is that employment of the general character of the appellant's in this case can be terminated at the will of the employer. The proper conduct of the affairs of life necessitates that this should be so. The exception to this rule within which the appellant must bring himself, if he is to succeed, is that where 'an agreement is entered into for sufficient consideration, and either forms part of a security, or is given for the purpose of securing some benefit to the donee of the authority, such authority is irrevocable': Story on Agency, s 476.

It cannot be contended that the ordinary case of an agent or manager employed for pecuniary reward in the shape of a fixed salary comes within this exception, though his employment confers a benefit upon him. And their Lordships are of opinion that the position of the appellant under the instruments appointing him attorney over this estate is in law that of an ordinary agent or manager employed at a salary, and nothing more because the authority which was conferred upon him contains no reference to the special interest in the occupation of his post which his guarantee to Astwood might have given him, was not expressed or intended to be used for the purpose of subserving that interest, and has no connection with it. For these reasons their Lordships think that the authority given to the appellant was revocable. Several cases have been cited by the appellant's counsel in support of his . . . contention. On an examination of them it will be found that the essential distinction between this case and those cited is this, that in each of the latter power and authority were given to a particular individual to do a particular thing, the doing of which conferred a benefit upon him, the authority ceasing when the benefit was reaped, while in this case, as already pointed out, nothing of that kind was ever provided for or contemplated. In *Carmichael's Case* ([1896] 2 Ch 643) the donor of the power, for valuable consideration, conferred upon the donee authority to do a particular thing in which the latter had an interest, namely, to apply for the shares of the company which the donee was promoting for the purpose of purchasing his own property from him, and the donor sought to revoke that authority before the benefit was reaped. In *Spooner v Sandilands* ((1842) 1 Y & C Ch Cas 390) the donor charged his lands with certain debts due and to accrue due to the donees, and put the latter into the possession of those lands and into receipt of the rents and profits of them, for the express purpose of enabling the donees to discharge thereout these same debts; and it was sought to eject the donees before their debts were paid. In *Clerk v Laurie* ((1857) 2 H & N 199) a wife pledged to a bank dividends to which she was entitled to secure advances made to her husband. It was held that while the advances remained unpaid, she could not revoke the bank's authority to receive the dividends. In *Smart v Sandars* ((1848) 5 CB 895) it was decided that the general authority of a factor in whose hands goods were placed for sale, to sell at the best price which could reasonably be obtained, could not be revoked after the factor had made advances on the security of the goods to the owner of them, and while these advances remained unpaid.

NOTES

1. The principal may terminate his agent's authority by revocation (whether or not this constitutes a breach of contract), so long as the agent has not already fulfilled his obligations. The agent's authority can also be terminated by the following means:

(1) execution of the agent's commission (*Blackburn v Scholes* (1810) 2 Camp 341);

(2) if the agent was appointed for a fixed period, expiry of that period (*Dickinson v Lilwall* (1815) 4 Camp 279);

(3) agreement between the principal and agent;

(4) destruction of the subject matter of the agency (*Rhodes v Forwood* (1876) 1 App Cas 256; see below, p 201);

(5) frustration of the agency rendering its performance illegal, impossible or radically different from what the parties originally contemplated (*Marshall v Glanvill* [1917] 2 KB 87);

(6) the death, insanity or bankruptcy of the principal or the agent, or, where the principal or agent is a company, dissolution (but note that the bankruptcy of the agent will only terminate his authority if it renders him unable to perform his duties): see below, pp 202–205;

(7) notice of renunciation of the agency given by the agent and accepted by the principal.

2. Irrevocable agency: an agent's authority cannot be revoked by the principal without the agent's consent, or determined by the death, insanity or bankruptcy of the principal, in any of the following circumstances:

(1) where the authority of the agent is given by deed, or for valuable consideration, for the purpose of securing or protecting any interest of the agent (*Frith v Frith*, above);

(2) where the agent's authority is given under a power of attorney which is expressed to be irrevocable and is given to secure a proprietary interest of, or the performance of an obligation owed to, the agent (so long as the interest or obligation continues): Powers of Attorney Act 1971, s 4 – also note that under the Enduring Powers of Attorney Act 1985, s 1(1)(a), an enduring power of attorney is not revoked by the supervening mental incapacity of the donor: see Fridman, pp 378–380;

(3) where the agent has incurred personal liability in the performance of his authority for which the principal must indemnify him (*Chappell v Bray* (1860) 6 H & N 145; cf Bowstead, pp 511–512).

3. Termination of the agent's authority is prospective and not retrospective. Both principal and agent will be entitled to sue one another on claims which accrued before termination, eg the principal can sue the agent for the negligent performance of his duties; the agent can sue the principal for remuneration already earned. If the agency is contractual, the very act of termination, whilst effective to end the agent's actual authority, may itself give rise to a claim for breach of contract. This can occur, for example, when the principal revokes the agent's authority without notice. In most cases where the agent is engaged under a bilateral contract (which is not for a fixed term, nor specifies a notice period), the agency will only be terminable on reasonable notice (*Martin-Baker Aircraft Co Ltd v Canadian Flight Equipment Ltd* [1955] 2 QB 556), unless the agent has committed a repudiatory breach of contract so that the principal is entitled to terminate the contract summarily (*Boston Deep Sea Fishing and Ice Co v Ansell* (1888) 39 Ch D 339, see above, p 176). But where the principal has made the agent an offer of a unilateral contract (eg as with an estate agent who is not a sole agent: *Luxor (Eastbourne) Ltd v Cooper* [1941] AC 108; above, p 190) the principal can generally withdraw his offer at will.

4. Some agency agreements are for a fixed period. The question then arises whether the principal will be in breach of the agreement if he goes out of business, or disposes of the subject matter of the agency, before the end of that period and thereby prevents the agent from earning further commission. As the following cases illustrate, the answer depends on the court's construction of the terms of the particular agency agreement in issue.

(1) *Rhodes v Forwood* (1876) 1 App Cas 256: Rhodes, a colliery owner, employed Forwood as sole agent to sell the colliery's coal in Liverpool for seven years. Rhodes sold the colliery and went out of business after four years. Forwood sued Rhodes for breach of the agency contract. The House of Lords rejected Forwood's claim holding that there was no express or implied term of the agency contract that the agreement must continue to seven years. The agency contract had been made subject to the risk that Rhodes might sell the colliery.

(2) *Turner v Goldsmith* [1891] 1 QB 544: Goldsmith, a shirt manufacturer, employed Turner for a period of five years to sell 'the various goods manufactured or sold' by Goldsmith. After two years Goldsmith's shirt factory burnt down and he closed down his business. Turner sued Goldsmith for breach of the agency contract. Reversing the judgment of the trial judge in favour of Goldsmith, the Court of Appeal refused to imply a term making the agency contract subject to the continued existence of the factory. On a true construction of the agency contract, Goldsmith could supply Turner with shirts manufactured by someone else or with other goods altogether.

For further consideration of this issue, see above, pp 194–195.

5. It should be noted that the Commercial Agents (Council Directive) Regulations 1993, implementing EEC Directive 86/653 on self-employed commercial agents, regulate the termination of agency contracts of commercial agents (regs 14–19). In particular, reg 17 provides that the principal must indemnify the agent where he has brought in new customers or has significantly increased the principal's business, or pay compensation to the agent for loss of future commission, and unrecovered costs and expenses, resulting from termination of the agency relationship (including termination as a result of the death of the commercial agent). The compensation provisions will apply unless an indemnity has been specifically agreed upon. However, the indemnity or compensation will not be payable to the commercial agent where

(1) the principal terminates the agency contract because of the agent's repudiatory breach; or
(2) the commercial agent himself terminates the agency contract (unless such termination is 'justified by circumstances attributable to the principal', or on grounds of the age, infirmity or illness of the agent); or
(3) the commercial agent, with the agreement of the principal, assigns his rights and duties under the agency contract to another person (see reg 18).

The agent must claim his indemnity or compensation within one year following the termination of the agency contract (reg 17(9)). The parties cannot contract out of these provisions (reg 19).

(b) Termination and third parties

Drew v Nunn (1879) 4 QBD 661, Court of Appeal

Nunn appointed his wife as his agent to purchase goods from Drew. Nunn was present when some of the goods were ordered by his wife and he paid for some of them. Nunn then became insane and was confined to an asylum. But his wife continued to purchase goods on his behalf from Drew, who was unaware of Nunn's insanity. When Nunn regained his sanity he refused to pay for those goods ordered by his wife when he was in the asylum. Mellor J directed the jury that Drew was entitled to recover the price of the goods from Nunn. Nunn appealed.

Brett LJ: This appeal has stood over for a long time, principally on my account, in order to ascertain whether it can be determined upon some clear principle. I have found, however, that the law upon this subject stands upon a very unsatisfactory footing.

[His Lordship then set out the facts of the case. He continued:]

Upon this state of facts two questions arise. Does insanity put an end to the authority of the agent? One would expect to find that this question has been long decided on clear principles; but on looking into Story on Agency, Scotch authorities, Pothier, and other French authorities, I find that no satisfactory conclusion has been arrived at. If such insanity as existed here did not put an end to the agent's authority, it would be clear that the plaintiff is entitled to succeed; but in my opinion insanity of this kind does put an end to the agent's authority. It cannot be disputed that some cases of change of status in the principal put an end to the authority of the agent; thus, the bankruptcy and death of the principal, the marriage of a female principal, all put an end to the authority of the agent. It may be argued that this result follows from the circumstance that a different principle is created. Upon bankruptcy the trustee becomes the principal; upon death the heir or devisee as to realty, the executor or administrator as to personalty; and upon the marriage of a female principal her husband takes her place. And it has been argued that by analogy the lunatic continues liable until a fresh principal, namely, his committee, is appointed. But I cannot think that this is the true ground, for executors are, at least in some instances, bound to carry out the contracts entered into by their testators. I think that the satisfactory principle to be adopted is that, where such a change occurs as to the principal that he can no longer act for himself, the agent whom he has appointed can no longer act for him. In the present case a great change had occurred in the condition of the principal: he was so far afflicted with insanity as to be disabled from acting for himself; therefore his wife, who was his agent, could no longer act for him. Upon the ground which I have pointed out, I think that her authority was terminated. It seems to me that an agent is liable to be sued by a third person, if he assumes to act on his principal's behalf after he had knowledge of his principal's incompetency to act. In a case of that kind he is acting wrongfully. The defendant's wife must be taken to have been aware of her husband's lunacy; and if she had assumed to act on his behalf with any one to whom he himself had not held her out as his agent, she would have been acting wrongfully, and, but for the circumstance that she is married, would have been liable in an action to compensate the person with whom she assumed to act on her husband's behalf. In my opinion, if a person who has not been held out as agent assumes to act on behalf of a lunatic, the contract is void against the supposed principal, and the pretended agent is liable to an action for misleading an innocent person.

The second question then arises, what is the consequence where a principal, who has held out another as his agent, subsequently becomes insane, and a third person deals with the agent without notice that the principal is a lunatic? Authority may be given to an agent in two ways. First, it may be given by some instrument, which of itself asserts that the authority is thereby created, such as a power of attorney; it is of itself an assertion by the principal that the agent may act for him. Secondly, an authority may also be created from the principal holding out the agent as entitled to act generally for him. The agency in the present case was created in the manner last-mentioned. As between the defendant and his wife, the agency expired upon his becoming to her knowledge insane; but it seems to me that the person dealing with the agent without knowledge of the principal's insanity has a right to enter into a contract with him, and the principal, although a lunatic, is bound so that he cannot repudiate the contract assumed to be made upon his behalf. It is difficult to assign the ground upon which this doctrine, which however seems to me to be the true principle, exists. It is said that the right to hold the insane principal liable depends upon contract. I have a difficulty in assenting to this. It has been said also that the right depends upon estoppel. I cannot see that an estoppel is created. But it has been said also that the right depends upon representations made by the principal and entitling third persons to act upon them, until they hear that those representations are withdrawn. The authorities collected in Story on Agency, ch xviii § 481, p 610 (7th ed), seem to base the right upon the ground of public policy: it is there said in effect that the existence of the right goes in aid of public business. It is however a better way of stating the rule to say that the holding out of another person as agent is a representation upon which, at the time when it was made, third parties had a right to act, and if no insanity had supervened would still have had a right to act. In this case the wife was held out as agent, and the plaintiff acted upon the defendant's representation as to her authority without notice that it had been withdrawn. The defendant cannot escape from the consequences of the representation which he has made; he cannot withdraw the agent's authority as to third persons without giving them notice of the withdrawal. The principal is bound, although he retracts the agent's authority, if he has not given notice and the latter wrongfully enters into a contract upon his behalf. The defendant became insane and was unable to withdraw the authority which he had conferred upon his wife: he may be an innocent sufferer by her conduct, but the plaintiff, who dealt with her bona fide, is also innocent, and where one of two persons both innocent must suffer by the wrongful act of a third person, that person making the representation which, as between the two, was the original cause of the mischief, must be the sufferer and must bear the loss. Here it does not lie in the defendant's mouth to say that the plaintiff shall be the sufferer.

A difficulty may arise in the application of a general principle such as this is. Suppose that a person makes a representation which after his death is acted upon by another in ignorance that his death has happened: in my view the estate of the deceased will be bound to make good any loss, which may have occurred through acting upon that representation. It is, however, unnecessary to decide this point to-day.

Upon the grounds above stated I am of opinion that, although the authority of the defendant's wife was put an end to by his insanity, and although she had no authority to deal with the plaintiff, nevertheless the latter is entitled to recover, because the defendant whilst he was sane made representations to the plaintiff, upon which he was entitled to act until he had notice of the defendant's insanity, and he had no notice of the insanity until after he had supplied the goods for the price of which he now sues. The direction of Mellor J was right.

Bramwell LJ: I agree with the judgment just delivered by Brett LJ. It must be taken that the defendant told the plaintiff that his wife had authority to bind him; when that authority had been given, it continued to exist, so far as the plaintiff was concerned, until it was revoked and until he received notice of that revocation. It may be urged that this doctrine does not extend to insanity, which is not an intentional revocation; but I think that insanity forms no exception to the general law as to principal and agent. It may be hard upon an insane principal, if his agent abuses his authority; but, on the other hand, it must be recollected that insanity is not a privilege, it is a misfortune, which must not be allowed to injure innocent persons: it would be productive of mischievous consequences, if insanity annulled every representation made by the person afflicted with it without any notice being given of his malady. If the argument for the defendant were correct, every act done by him or on his behalf after he became insane must be treated as a nullity. . . .

It has been assumed by Brett LJ that the insanity of the defendant was such as to amount to a revocation of his wife's authority. I doubt whether partial mental derangement would have that effect. I think that in order to annul the authority of an agent, insanity must amount to dementia. If a man becomes so far insane as to have no mind, perhaps he ought to be deemed dead for the purpose of contracting. I think that the direction of Mellor J was right.

Brett LJ: I am requested by Cotton LJ to state that he agrees with the conclusion at which we have arrived; but that he does not wish to decide whether the authority of the defendant's wife was terminated, or whether the liability of a contractor lasts until a committee has been appointed. He bases his decision simply upon the ground that the defendant, by holding out his wife as agent, entered into a contract with the plaintiff that she had authority to act upon his behalf, and that until the plaintiff had notice that this authority was revoked he was entitled to act upon the defendant's representations.

I wish to add that if there had been any real question as to the extent of the defendant's insanity, it ought to have been left to the jury; and that as no question was asked of the jury, I must assume that the defendant was insane to the extent which I have mentioned. I may remark that from the mere fact of mental derangement it ought not to be assumed that a person is incompetent to contract; mere weakness of mind or partial derangement is insufficient to exempt a person from responsibility upon the engagements into which he has entered.

NOTES

1. Compare *Drew v Nunn* and *Yonge v Toynbee* [1910] 1 KB 215 (above, p 140, and see notes at pp 144–145). See R Powell *The Law of Agency* (2nd ed, 1961), pp 405–406; Bowstead, p 524; and Treitel, op cit, p 651, fn 26, for ways of distinguishing these cases. It should be noted that both the agent and third party may be protected from the normal consequences of the principal's supervening mental incapacity by the Powers of Attorney Act 1971, s 5 (above, p 144) and the Enduring Powers of Attorney Act 1985, ss 1(1)(c); 1(3); 9 (see *Re K* [1988] Ch 310; but see also R J C Munday [1989] 13 NZULR 253).

2. Despite occasional dicta to the contrary (eg Brett LJ in *Drew v Nunn*), it is probably the case that where the principal dies there can be no apparent authority. For as Lord Ellenborough said in *Watson v King* (1815) 4 Camp 272 at 274: 'How can a valid act be done in the name of a dead man?' Following this reasoning, it is submitted that the personal representatives of a dead principal cannot ratify any contract made on behalf of the deceased after his death (cf *Foster v Bates* (1843) 12 M & W 226; *Campanari v Woodburn*, above, p 198; but neither case is authority against this submission: Bowstead, p 515; Powell, op cit, p 388, fn 7).

3. There can be no apparent authority when the principal is adjudged bankrupt. This is because when the principal is adjudged bankrupt his estate vests in the trustee in bankruptcy leaving the principal with no capacity to perform the acts which are the subject of the apparent agency. But those dealing with the agent of a bankrupt may have statutory protection under the Insolvency Act 1986, s 284(4),(5). Furthermore, as in cases of death or insanity of the donor of a power of attorney, a third party who deals with the donee of a power of attorney may be able to rely on the Powers of Attorney Act 1971, s 5, to avoid the normal consequences of the donor's supervening bankruptcy.

4. Revocation of the agent's actual authority by the principal does not prevent the principal being bound by the agent's apparent authority, so long as the third party has no notice that the agency has terminated (see *Scarf v Jardine* (1882) 7 App Cas 345 at 356–357, per Lord Blackburn; see also *Curlewis v Birkbeck* (1863) 3 F & F 894).

QUESTION

An insane principal is bound by the apparent authority of his agent, whereas the estate of a dead principal is not. What policy reasons, if any, justify this distinction?

Part III

Domestic sales law

CHAPTER 7

Introduction and definitions[1]

1 Introduction

Prior to 1893, the law governing the sale of goods was almost entirely based on cases decided by the courts at common law. There were a few statutory provisions, but only a few: the two most important were the Factors Acts, discussed below at p 311, and the Statute of Frauds 1677, s 17 (now repealed) which required written evidence for the enforcement of a contract of sale of goods to the value of over £10.

Towards the end of the nineteenth century the subject was much influenced by two leading textbooks, *Blackburn on Sale* and *Benjamin on Sale*. In 1888 the celebrated statutory draftsman, Sir Mackenzie Chalmers, who had already drafted the Bills of Exchange Act 1882 (below, Chapter 16) was commissioned to prepare a Bill for the codification of the law; and this was enacted, with some modifications, as the Sale of Goods Act 1893. Although in more recent times this Act has come in for criticism from some quarters, primarily because it did not, as originally drafted, provide wholly satisfactory remedies for the buyer in consumer contracts, Chalmers' codification has to be seen as a *tour de force*, particularly as a merchant's code – and, since this is a book on commercial law, it is this aspect of the subject with which we shall primarily be concerned. It was not until 1973 (in the Supply of Goods (Implied Terms) Act 1973 – an Act mainly concerned with consumer transactions) that significant changes were made to any part of Chalmers' text, and it is a tribute to his skill that it is still in use, virtually unchanged, a century later, as the basis of all commercial sales of goods within the United Kingdom and a very large share of the world's international sales as well.

Following the 1973 amendments and some further changes made by the Unfair Contract Terms Act 1977, the Act of 1893 was consolidated and re-enacted as the Sale of Goods Act 1979, which is now the principal source of the law. All statutory references in this section of the book will be to this Act of 1979 unless otherwise stated: it will usually be referred to simply as 'the Act'. In the consolidation, some minor changes of language were made from the 1893 text, and there was some re-numbering of the sections – which calls for a degree of caution when reading

---

1 In this and the succeeding chapters dealing with the law of sale of goods, the following abbreviations are used in referring to standard textbooks:

Atiyah: P S Atiyah *The Sale of Goods* (8th ed, 1990)
Benjamin: A G Guest and others (eds) *Benjamin's Sale of Goods* (4th ed, 1992)
Goode: R M Goode *Commercial Law* (1982)

judgments based on the former Act. (However, since *most* sections of the 1893 Act have retained their old numbers in the new Act, cross-references will be given only where this is not the case.)

A codifying Act, such as the Sale of Goods Act 1893, is intended to *replace* the previous case law by a fresh statement of what the law is to be; and it is not normally proper to look to the earlier cases for guidance as to the interpretation of such an Act (see the remarks of Lord Herschell in *Bank of England v Vagliano Bros* [1891] AC 107, quoted below, p 484 – a case on the Bills of Exchange Act 1882). But in fact this principle has not always been respected, and there are many cases where judges have had regard to the former law. In some circumstances this practice is, perhaps, justified by s 62(2) of the Act, which declares that 'the rules of the common law, . . . except in so far as they are inconsistent with the provisions of the Act, . . . apply to contracts for the sale of goods'.

However, there is room for debate as to which 'rules of the common law' are 'inconsistent with the provisions of the Act'. In the leading case of *Re Wait* (below), Atkin LJ not only endorsed the *Vagliano* approach referred to above, saying ([1927] 1 Ch 606, 631): 'Inasmuch as we are now bound by the plain language of the Code I do not think that decisions in cases before 1893 are of much value', but went on to suggest that some provisions of the Act (which Atkin LJ refers to as 'the Code') were intended to displace general provisions of the common law and equity which might otherwise be thought applicable.

Re Wait [1927] 1 Ch 606, Court of Appeal

Wait contracted to buy from Balfour, Williamson & Co 1000 tons of wheat which was to arrive at Avonmouth from the US on the MV *Challenger*. The following day, he agreed to sell 500 tons of this wheat to Humphries & Bobbett, who paid him the price in advance. A few days before the *Challenger* arrived, Wait went bankrupt. By the time that this action was brought, some of the wheat had been disposed of to other buyers, but 530 tons remained which was still in law the property of Wait (or his trustee in bankruptcy) and in his possession. Nothing had been done to identify the 500 tons which was to be used to fulfil Humphries & Bobbett's contract. The Court of Appeal (by a majority, the Chancery judge, Sargant LJ, dissenting) held that Humphries & Bobbett had no claim to any of the wheat, but could only prove in Wait's bankruptcy for the return of the price. In this passage, Atkin LJ rejected an argument that the buyers might be able to assert a claim of a proprietary nature to their share of the wheat based on principles of equity independently of the Act.

Atkin LJ: . . . I am of opinion that the claimants fail, and that to grant the relief claimed would violate well established principles of common law and equity. It would also appear to embarrass to a most serious degree the ordinary operations of buying and selling goods, and the banking operations which attend them. . . .

I do not think that at any time here there was an equitable assignment which ever gave the claimants a beneficial interest in these goods. It has been difficult to elicit the moment of time at which the beneficial interest came into existence. At various times in the argument it has been the moment when the 1000 tons were shipped; when they were declared to the debtor by Balfour Williamson & Co; when the bills of lading came into the possession of the bank; when the claimants paid the £5933 5s to the debtor; when the goods were taken up by the trustee [in bankruptcy]; and when the 530 tons came into the possession of the trustee. The difficulty illustrates the danger of seeking to conduct well established principles into territory where they are trespassers. Without deciding the point, I think that much may be said for the proposition that an agreement for the sale of goods does not import any agreement to transfer property other than in accordance with the terms of the Code, that is, the intention of the parties to be derived from the terms of the contract, the conduct of the parties and the circumstances of the case, and, unless a different intention appears, from the rules set out in s 18. The Code was passed at a time when the principles of equity and equitable remedies were recognized and given effect to in all our Courts, and the particular equitable remedy of specific performance is specially referred to in s 52. The total sum of legal relations (meaning by the word 'legal' existing in equity as well as in common law) arising out of the contract for the sale of goods may well be regarded as defined by the Code. It would have been futile in a code intended for commercial men to have created an elaborate structure of rules dealing with rights at law, if at the same time it was intended to leave, subsisting with the legal rights, equitable rights inconsistent with, more extensive, and coming into existence earlier than the rights so carefully set out in the various sections of the Code.

The rules for transfer of property as between seller and buyer, performance of the contract, rights of the unpaid seller against the goods, unpaid sellers' lien, remedies of the seller, remedies of the buyer, appear to be complete and exclusive statements of the legal relations both in law and equity. They have, of course, no relevance when one is considering rights, legal or equitable, which may come into existence dehors the contract for sale. A seller or a purchaser may, of course, create any equity he pleases by way of charge, equitable assignment or any other dealing with or disposition of goods, the subject-matter of sale; and he may, of course, create such an equity as one of the terms expressed in the contract of sale. But the mere sale or agreement to sell or the acts in pursuance of such a contract mentioned in the Code will only produce the legal effects which the Code states.

[Lord Hanworth MR delivered a concurring judgment.
Sargant LJ dissented.]

The Act applies to contracts for the sale of all types of goods (though in regard to some, eg ships and aircraft, other statutes may be applicable in addition). In general, its provisions govern commercial sales, sales to consumers and transactions between private parties, but in some sections (particularly ss 12–15) a distinction is made between these categories.

2 Definitions

It is impossible to follow the Act properly without a clear understanding of a few key definitions, which form the basis of its whole structure. The draftsman has used these words and phrases with great precision, and it is clearly important for us also to learn to do so.

(a) 'Contract for the sale of goods'

The Act applies only to 'contracts for the sale of goods'. Such a contract is defined in s 2(1) as 'a contract by which the seller transfers or agrees to transfer the property in goods to the buyer for a money consideration, called the price'. There are a number of transactions closely analogous to sales of goods, as we shall see shortly – some of them governed by rules and principles which are similar, if not identical, to those contained in the Act; but plainly it is legitimate to refer to the Act only when we are concerned with contracts for the sale of goods within the statutory definition. These other transactions are distinguished from contracts for the sale of goods below, at pp 223–237.

(b) 'Sale' and 'agreement to sell'

Where under a contract of sale the 'property' in the goods (a term which we may take as broadly equivalent to 'ownership') is transferred from the seller to the buyer, the contract is called in the Act a 'sale' (s 2(4)). Where the transfer of the property is to take place at a future time or is subject to some condition to be fulfilled later, it is called an 'agreement to sell' (s 2(5)). The term 'contract for the sale of goods' is thus a comprehensive expression, embracing both 'sale' and 'agreement to sell'.

A *sale* may be seen as both a contract and a conveyance: by virtue of the contract itself, the buyer becomes the owner of the goods. An *agreement to sell*, in contrast, is purely a contract: ownership does not pass to the buyer until some later time.

(c) 'Goods'

Sown crops

The term 'goods' is defined in s 61(1) as including 'all personal chattels other than things in action and money, and in Scotland all corporeal moveables except money'; and in particular as including 'emblements, industrial growing crops and things attached to or forming part of the land which are agreed to be severed before sale or under the contract of sale'.

'Personal chattels' (or 'chattels personal') are to be contrasted with 'chattels real', such as leasehold interests in land. The term may be subdivided into 'things in possession' (sometimes referred to as tangibles) and things in action (intangibles, or 'choses in action'). The Act is concerned only with the former.

Apart from chattels real and things in action, it is probably right to assume that the following are not 'goods' for the purposes of the Act (though they may be 'goods', 'things' or 'articles' under other statutory definitions): animals in the wild state; electricity and other forms of energy; human remains, tissue and organs and bodily products (eg blood); the various forms of intellectual property; computer software (as distinct from the disk or other object on which it is stored); information (and, *a fortiori*, even more nebulous concepts, such as an opportunity). It is perhaps wrong to be too categorical about some of these items: human hair, for instance, is regularly bought by wig-makers, and skeletons by medical students. Money is expressly excluded from the statutory definition, but a coin may be sold as a collector's item and is then regarded as 'goods' (*Moss v Hancock* [1899] 2 QB 111).

On the other hand, the following are all 'goods' capable of being the subject matter of a contract of sale within the Act: ships, aircraft and vehicles; domestic animals, and wild animals which have been reduced into captivity or are dead; water, oil and gases (even air, in the form of compressed air).

The dividing line between goods and land (or rather between goods and an interest in land) is very difficult to draw. In fact, there *is* no dividing line. The Act itself declares that 'goods', for the purposes of its provisions, includes crops of every description and things attached to *or forming part of* the land which are agreed to be severed before sale or under the contract of sale. But if this is compared with the definition of 'land' under the Law of Property Act 1925, s 205, we find that 'land' is there defined as including 'land of any tenure, and mines and minerals, . . . buildings or parts of buildings . . . and an easement, right, privilege or benefit in, over, or derived from land'. The only possible conclusion is that some types of transaction may be *both* a contract of sale of goods under the Sale of Goods Act *and* a contract for the sale or transfer of an interest in land under the

Law of Property Act. Examples include a contract by a landowner giving another person the right to enter upon his land and fell trees and remove the timber; the right to pick fruit or cut hay; the right to extract minerals or take water; the right to shoot and take away game; and the right to dismantle and remove a building. In land law, these can be seen as easements or *profits à prendre*. In relation to such contracts it may be necessary to look at both statutes and to comply with any mandatory provisions imposed by either (eg the need for writing under the Law of Property (Miscellaneous Provisions) Act 1989, s 2). When it comes to a clash, it is the rules of land law which will ordinarily prevail: so, for instance, if A owns land on which a building is erected and he sells the building to B for removal, any right of B to the building (as 'goods') would be overridden by the claims of a bona fide purchaser of a legal estate in the land who was unaware of the contract with B.

The reference in s 61(1) to 'industrial growing crops' is at first sight puzzling. It reflects the traditional distinction made at common law between *fructus industriales* (produce which was regarded as primarily the end-product of labour, particularly annual or seasonal labour, such as corn, potatoes, etc) and *fructus naturales* (things which were considered part of the natural growth of the soil, for which tilling and cultivating were regarded as unnecessary, or at least not so vital, and which tended to be the product of perennial growth: grass, timber, the fruit from trees). Under the old law, crops in the former category were regarded as goods which could be bought and sold independently of any question of severance: a half-grown crop of potatoes could be sold to a buyer *as goods*. But *fructus naturales* were regarded as part of the land until severance. It is plain that this distinction has not survived the enactment of the Sale of Goods Act. However, even under the Act, severance is essential. In *Saunders v Pilcher* [1949] 2 All ER 1097 a cherry orchard was sold together with its crop of cherries which were ripe and ready to be picked. For tax purposes, the parties purported to make separate sales of the land and the cherries. But the court held that there was only one transaction – a conveyance of the land. The parties did not contemplate that the cherries would be severed *under the contract of sale*, as s 61(1) requires.

The following cases throw light on this issue.

Morgan v Russell & Sons [1909] 1 KB 357, King's Bench Divisional Court

Morgan was the lessee of land in South Wales on which slag and cinders had been tipped, and adjoining this property was land occupied by other persons on which were two disused cinder-tips, fifty years old. He obtained a licence from these persons to remove this material, and then agreed to sell to Russell & Sons the cinders and slag from all three tips. After a considerable amount of cinders and slag had been removed and paid for, Morgan's lessor and the occupiers of the adjoining properties forbade the removal of any more. Under the law at that time the damages recoverable from Morgan for breach of contract varied, depending upon whether the contract was one for the sale of goods or of an interest in land. (The distinction no longer exists, following the abolition of the rule in *Bain v Fothergill* (1874) LR 7 HL 158 by the Law of Property (Miscellaneous Provisions) Act 1989, s 3.) The court ruled that it was a sale of an interest in land.

Lord Alverstone CJ: The learned judge has found, and we have no power to interfere with that finding, that the cinders and slag had become part of the ground or soil itself, and were not definite or detached heaps resting, so to speak, upon the ground. The learned judge considered that under these circumstances the default, if any, in the carrying out of the agreement arose from a defect in the respondent's title, and that therefore, upon the principle of *Bain v Fothergill*, the appellants were not entitled to recover damages for the loss of their bargain. The case for the appellants was rested upon two grounds: it was first said that this was a contract for the sale of goods within s 62 of the Sale of Goods Act 1893, and therefore the ordinary rule of damages applies; and secondly that, even assuming that the cinders and slag were not goods, the principle of *Bain v Fothergill* would not apply, and the appellants were entitled to general damages. I am clearly of opinion that this was not a contract for the sale of goods. The respondent Morgan did not contract to sell any definite quantity of mineral, nor was it a contract for the sale of a heap of earth which could be said to be a separate thing. In my view the contract was a contract to give free access to certain tips for the purpose of removing cinders and slag which formed part of the soil at the price of 2*s* 3*d* per ton, to include the value of the slag so taken, for so long as the appellants chose to exercise their option to take. The contract appears to me to be exactly analogous to a contract which gives a man a right to enter upon land with liberty to dig from the earth in situ so much gravel or brick earth or coal on payment of a price per ton. The first ground therefore in my opinion is not one upon which the appeal can succeed. . . .

[Walton J delivered a concurring judgment.]

Underwood Ltd v Burgh Castle Brick & Cement Syndicate [1922] 1 KB 343, King's Bench Division

Underwoods agreed to sell to the Syndicate a large horizontal tandem condensing engine which was a trade fixture on their leasehold premises. As part of the contract, the sellers were to detach the engine from the land and load it on to a railway truck. It was damaged during the loading process and the buyers refused to accept it. They were held entitled to do so, since (for reasons explained below, p 276) the engine was still the seller's property at the time when it was damaged. In his judgment, Rowlatt J assumed throughout that the transaction was governed by the Sale of Goods Act, but his remarks are of interest on the general question of the sale of fixtures.

Rowlatt J: This case raises an important point under the Sale of Goods Act, 1893. This turns on the question whether the property in the engine had passed to the defendants at the time when the accident happened when the engine was being loaded. This engine weighed some thirty tons and was at the time when it was inspected by the defendants affixed to a bed of concrete by means of Lewis bolts and screwed down. By reason of its weight it had sunk into the concrete and become closely united with it, so that the operation of removing it not only involved unfastening it but taking it to pieces. . . .

I think the important point is that the parties were dealing with an article which was a fixture to the premises, and that is different from the case of a loose chattel. The buyers' intention was to buy an article which would be a loose chattel when the processes of detaching and dismantling it were completed, and to convert it into a loose chattel these processes had first to be performed. The case of a tenant's fixtures seems an analogous case. It seems a safe rule to adopt that if a fixture has to be detached so as to make it a chattel again, the act of detaching has to be done before the chattel can be deliverable. The same result is arrived at if the matter be looked at a little more technically. This fixture was not personal property any more than are tenant's fixtures, but was part of the freehold, and what was sold was not personal property but a part of the realty which the sellers had a right to detach and convert into personal property. . . . In the present case the plaintiffs did not sell their right to sever, but were to sever the fixtures themselves, and when they had done so, and so produced the chattel, they were to deliver it. That was the contract if the matter is analysed. The plaintiffs contended that as between the parties the intention was that the property should pass at the time of the contract and that s 17 of the Sale of Goods Act, 1893, applied. The fallacy of that argument seems to be that it assumes that the sellers had the property in the engine at the time when the contract was made. They had not, although it is true that they had rights which reduced the rights of property of the freeholder in whom the property was to a vanishing quantity. If the property had been mortgaged it would have been no answer to the mortgagees' claim to say that in the Sale of Goods Act, 1893, there is a provision that as between buyer and seller fixtures are goods and chattels. That could not affect the property of the freeholder.

For these reasons I think that the property in this engine did not pass to the defendants at the time when the contract was made, and there must be judgment for them.

NOTE

In *Marshall v Green* (1875) 1 CPD 35, a case decided before the passing of the first Sale of Goods Act in 1893, the court was concerned to decide whether a contract to sell timber which was still standing on the seller's land was a contract to sell the timber as goods, or an interest in land: the court plainly thought that such a contract must be one thing or the other. Grove J said, at 44:

> It seems to me that, in determining the question whether there was a contract for an interest in land, we must look to what the parties intended to contract for. . . . Here the trees were to be cut as soon as possible, but even assuming that they were not to be cut for a month, I think that the test would be whether the parties really looked to their deriving benefit from the land, or merely intended that the land should be in the nature of a warehouse for the trees during that period. Here the parties clearly never contemplated that the purchaser should have anything in the nature of an interest in the land; he was only to have so much timber, which happened to be affixed to the land at the time, but was to be removed as soon as possible, and was to derive no benefit from the soil. If the contract had been for the sale of a young plantation of some rapidly-growing timber, which was not to be cut down until it had become substantially changed and had derived benefit from the land, there might have been an interest in land, but this is not such a case.

This approach may be contrasted with that of the Court of Appeal in *Kursell v Timber Operators & Contractors Ltd* (below, p 218), which was decided many years after the Act of 1893 was passed. The judgments in this later case all treat the issue as a question of sale of goods law, to be decided by reference to the Act.

Part-interests in goods (eg a half or one-third share in a horse, or in a specific heap of grain) pose special problems. It is plain from various sections of the Act (eg s 2(2)) that a contract to transfer a part-interest in goods may at least in some circumstances be classed as a contract of sale of goods. But there are cases which suggest that this may not always be so: in *Re Sugar Properties (Derisley Wood) Ltd* [1988] BCLC 146, 151 Mervyn Davies J treated shares in a racehorse as choses in action. And there are other decisions which have held that the transfer between part-owners of an undivided share in goods is not a 'sale' at all, even though made for a money consideration. *Graff v Evans*, for instance, is typical of a number of older cases concerned with the supply of liquor in members' clubs.

Graff v Evans (1882) 8 QBD 373, Queen's Bench Divisional Court

Graff, as manager of the Grosvenor Club, had been convicted of selling liquor by retail without a licence when Foster, a member of the club, had purchased a bottle of whisky and a bottle of pale ale for 3s 11d (20p) at the club bar. The Divisional Court quashed the conviction, on the ground that supplying a member was not 'selling' the drink.

Field J: The question here is, Did Graff, the manager, who supplied the liquors to Foster, effect a 'sale' by retail? I think not. I think Foster was an owner of the property together with all the other members of the club. Any member was entitled to obtain the goods on payment of the price. A sale involves the element of a bargain. There was no bargain here, nor any contract with Graff with respect to the goods. Foster was acting upon his rights as a member of the club, not by reason of any new contract, but under his old contract of association by which he subscribed a sum to the funds of the club, and became entitled to have ale and whisky supplied to him as a member at a certain price. I cannot conceive it possible that Graff could have sued him for the price as the price of goods sold and delivered. There was no contract between two persons, because Foster was vendor as well as buyer. Taking the transaction to be a purchase by Foster of all the other members' shares in the goods, Foster was as much a co-owner as the vendor. I think it was a transfer of a special property in the goods to Foster, which was not a sale within the meaning of the section.

[Huddleston B delivered a concurring judgment.]

NOTES

1. It is not clear what inference we should draw from the line of cases of which *Graff v Evans* is an example. It may be suggested alternatively that:

(1) a part-interest in goods is not itself 'goods';
(2) it is essential to a sale that there are only two parties, a buyer and a seller (or persons jointly acting as one or the other): a multipartite transaction is something else; or _between themselves_
(3) the reallocation between co-owners <u>inter se</u> of their part-interests in goods is not a transfer of 'the property' in the goods, but of something different – a 'special property'.

2. The supply of liquor in clubs is now specially dealt with in the Licensing Acts.

QUESTIONS

1. If A and B jointly own a bottle of whisky and A agrees to transfer his share to B for £5, is this a contract for the sale of goods?
2. If A, B and C jointly own a bottle of whisky and B and C (1) separately agree to transfer their respective shares to A for £5 each; (2) together agree to transfer both their shares to A for £10; is this in either case a contract for the sale of goods?
3. If A owns two-thirds and B owns one-third of a bottle of whisky, and A agrees to transfer half of his interest (ie a one-third share) to B for £5, is this a contract for the sale of goods?

It is obviously not easy, and in some cases not possible, to apply many provisions of the Act literally to a contract for the sale of a part-interest in goods (eg those relating to delivery). The Law Commission has recommended that the Act be amended by adding to the definition of 'goods' a statement that the term includes an undivided share in goods (and also that an undivided share, specified as a fraction or percentage, in specific goods shall itself be regarded as 'specific goods'): *Sale of Goods forming Part of a Bulk* (Law Com No 215, 1993), Part V.

(d) 'Existing goods' and 'future goods'

Section 5 divides 'goods' into two categories: (1) 'existing goods', ie goods owned or possessed by the seller, and (2) 'future goods' – goods to be manufactured or acquired by the seller after the making of the contract of sale. It goes on to make it plain that there cannot be a 'sale' (in the statutory sense, involving an immediate conveyance) of future goods, by declaring that where a seller purports to effect a present sale of future goods, the contract operates as an agreement to sell the goods (s 5(3)).

'Existing' does not mean 'in existence' in an everyday sense. Goods which are in existence, but are not yet owned or possessed by the seller, are 'future goods' for the purposes of the Act. So if S and B are in a supermarket together, and they agree that S will buy a dozen bottles of wine which are at a special discount if bought by the dozen, and will then resell six bottles to B, their contract is for 'future goods', even though the bottles are in existence and even if the particular six which B is to take have been identified.

It may be helpful at times to classify 'future goods' into various sub-categories. These will include:

(1) goods to be manufactured by the seller;
(2) goods to be acquired by the seller (by purchase, gift, succession, or otherwise – eg fish which he expects or hopes to catch); goods not yet in existence (eg lambs to be born next spring, fruit or potatoes to be harvested next autumn); and
(3) (possibly) things which do exist, but are not yet 'goods' (eg minerals not yet extracted but still forming part of the land).

The reference in s 5(2) to possession of the goods ('owned or *possessed* by the seller') is, at first sight, puzzling. But some sections of the Act (eg ss 12(3), 22, 24, 25(1) and 48(2)) contemplate a sale being made by a person who has no title or a defective title, and it is probably provisions such as these which the draftsman had in mind when formulating the wording of s 5(2).

The time taken as a reference point for the purpose of s 5(1) is that when the contract of sale is made. This is also the case in relation to the other major classification of goods, into 'specific' and 'unascertained' goods, which is examined next.

(e) 'Specific goods' and 'unascertained goods'

By s 61(1), 'specific goods' means goods identified and agreed on at the time a contract of sale is made. The counterpart expression used in the Act, 'unascertained goods', is curiously not defined anywhere, but must by inference mean goods *not* identified and agreed on at the time the contract of sale is made. For goods to be specific, they must be designated as the unique article or articles that the contract is concerned with, and must be capable of being so designated (and actually so designated) at the time of the contract. It is not necessary that the goods in question should be physically present before the parties at that time, although that would be the most obvious example of 'specific goods': goods can also be specific even though they are identified only by words of description (eg 'the grey horse now in my stable' – there being only one grey horse there). Typically (though not, as we shall see, exclusively), unascertained goods are goods sold 'by description', that is, the goods are commodities of a generic kind such as grain, coal, oil, etc, and the seller undertakes to procure for the buyer the agreed quantity of such goods, with such further characteristics as to quality, etc as may be specified – eg a 'new white 2.0 litre VW Golf GTI car, 5 door', or '100 tons of King Edward potatoes, East Anglia grown'.

Unascertained goods fall into three main categories:

(1) generic goods sold by description, as described above;
(2) goods not yet in existence, to be grown or manufactured, such as a suit to be made by a tailor;
(3) a part as yet unidentified out of a specific or identified bulk, eg 10 tons out of the 100 tons (or out of the unmeasured heap) of potatoes now in my store.

The most important reason for distinguishing between specific goods and unascertained goods is to be found in the rule contained in s 16: it is not possible to transfer the property in unascertained goods to the buyer – not, at least, until the contract goods are 'ascertained'. Nothing that the parties can agree to or do or say can breach this fundamental principle. The leading cases on this point include *Re Wait*, which has already been referred to, and *Kursell v Timber Operators & Contractors Ltd*.

Re Wait [1927] 1 Ch 606, Court of Appeal

(For the facts and other parts of judgments in this case, see above, p 210, and below, p 256.)

Lord Hanworth MR: The problem to be solved comes back to the question: were the 500 tons specific goods? They were never appropriated, and it is admitted that the legal property has not passed, for these were future goods within s 5 of the Code in respect of which no property passed to the purchaser: see ss 16, 17 and 18, sub-s 5. There was no ascertainment or identification of the 500 tons out of the cargo in bulk of the motor vessel *Challenger*.

The bankruptcy of the vendor does not in my judgment affect the question, though it may emphasize the hardship to the purchasers, for the question must be determined upon the rights of the parties under the contract upon the arrival of the wheat.

Kursell v Timber Operators & Contractors Ltd [1927] 1 KB 298, Court of Appeal

The contract between the parties was for the sale of all the merchantable timber growing on a certain date in a forest in Latvia, 'merchantable timber' being defined in the contract as 'all trunks and branches of trees but not seedlings and young trees of less than six inches in diameter at a height of four feet from the ground'. The buyers were to have 15 years to cut the timber. Shortly afterwards, the Latvian government passed a law nationalising the forest. The sellers argued that the property in the timber had passed to the buyers and that accordingly the consequences of the nationalisation decree fell on them. The Court held, however, that the timber which was the subject of the contract of sale was not 'specific goods', since the trees answering to the contract measurements had not been identified (and could not, in fact, be identified until the time came to cut them, which could be at any time within the fifteen-year period); it followed that the timber was still the property of the sellers and the contract was frustrated.

Scrutton LJ: What is the legal result of these facts? In the first place has the property passed? It was said that this was a contract for the sale of specific goods in a deliverable state under s 18, r 1, of the Sale of Goods Act. Specific goods are defined as goods identified and agreed upon at the time a contract of sale is made. It appears to me these goods were neither identified nor agreed upon. Not every tree in the forest passed, but only those complying with a certain measurement not then made. How much of each tree passed depended on where it was cut, how far from the ground. Nor does the timber seem to be in a deliverable state until the buyer has severed it. He cannot under the definition be bound to take delivery of an undetermined part of a tree not yet identified. . . .

For these reasons in my opinion the property had not passed under s 18, r 1, and, therefore, the timber was not at the risk of the purchasers.

Sargant LJ: . . . It is . . . necessary in the first place to consider whether the contract effected an immediate transfer of the property in the timber to the respondents; and this, in my judgment, depends upon whether, under r 1 in s 18 of the Sale of Goods Act 1893, the contract was one for the sale of specific goods in a deliverable state. This question again divides itself into two heads – namely, first, was the timber agreed to be sold specific goods; and, secondly, was it in a deliverable state?

As to the first head, there is a curious ambiguity in the wording of the contract. The merchantable timber sold is obviously limited to trees planted at the date of the contract, and does not include any trees subsequently planted. But is it limited to such of these existing trees as were merchantable (that is of the required size) at the date of the contract; or does it include trees which being unmerchantable at the date of the contract become merchantable at that period of the subsequent fifteen years when the purchasers come to exercise their right of felling? The former construction is one that is more in accordance with a very strict view of the language of the contract, but it would necessarily involve such extreme and obvious difficulty in the working out of the contract, that I am for myself inclined to adopt the second of these two constructions.

If then this view is correct it seems hopeless to contend that the timber sold was specific, for the items of timber sold depend upon the rate of growth of the trees, and the time at which the purchasers come to fell the various sections of the forest. Accordingly the appellants contended strenuously that the date for ascertaining the size of the trees was the date of the contract. And I will consider the question whether the goods sold were specific on this view of the construction, which is the more favourable to the appellants.

Even on this view, however, I cannot think that the timber sold was at the date of the contract identified, or more than merely identifiable; and in order that goods may be specific they must in my view be identified and not merely identifiable. The appellants relied on the maxim 'Id certum est quod certum reddi potest'; but I do not think that this maxim applies in the present connection. . . . For the purpose of the passing of the actual property in goods as distinguished from a right to ultimately claim a title to the goods as against the vendor or volunteers under him, a present identification of the goods as specific goods appears to be required by the statute. There must be a transfer of the right in re not merely of the right ad rem.

Further I am of opinion that under the contract in question the timber sold did not form goods in a deliverable state. . . .

[Lord Hanworth MR delivered a concurring judgment.]

Section 16, and also some other sections (ss 17, 52) use the further expression, 'ascertained goods'. Like 'unascertained goods', this phrase has no statutory definition. But Atkin LJ in *Re Wait* (above) explained it as meaning goods which at the time of the making of the contract as unascertained but which become identified as the contract goods at some later time. For instance, in *Aldridge v Johnson* (below, p 224), the buyer, who had agreed to buy a quantity of barley, left his own sacks with the seller to be filled with barley from his bulk store. It was held that the barley became 'ascertained' (ie identified as the buyer's) as it was shovelled into his sacks, sackful by sackful, even before the total contract quantity had been measured out.

QUESTIONS

1. *Atiyah*, at p 53 says: 'It is probably safe to say that future goods can never be specific goods within the meaning of the Act.' Do you agree? (Consider the example of the six bottles of wine, above, p 217.)

2. Can goods not yet in existence ever be specific goods in the statutory sense?

(f) 'The property'

The definition of a contract of sale in s 2(1) requires that the seller should transfer or agree to transfer 'the property' in goods to the buyer. In s 61(1) we are told that 'property' means 'the general property in goods, and not merely a special property'. This expression, 'special property', is sometimes used to describe the interest of a pledgee, in order to emphasise the fact that he has something more than mere possession of the goods which have been pledged. (On pledge, see below, p 800.) A pledgee has title to an interest in the goods which he can deal with, eg by sub-pledge or assignment, and in certain circumstances he has a power of sale. But he does not have *the general property* in the goods, in the statutory sense, and so a transfer of his interest as pledgee cannot be a sale. (The expression 'special property' was also used by Field J in *Graff v Evans* (above, p 215) when describing the transfer of an interest between co-owners, but it is unlikely that 'special property' in this sense was contemplated by the draftsman of the Act.)

In loose terms, we may think of 'the property' as meaning simply 'ownership'. To be more precise, however, 'the property' which a seller transfers or agrees to transfer is his title to *the absolute legal interest* in the goods: see the article by Battersby and Preston of which an extract is cited below. A pledgee has title only to a more limited interest, which is therefore excluded from the statutory definition. For this reason, the Act will not apply to a transfer by an owner of goods to someone else of an interest less than full ownership – eg a contract of hire or some other form of bailment, or which creates a charge over goods. Nor will it apply to the transfer of such an interest by the hirer or bailee or chargee to a third party. And since we are concerned only with the *legal* interest in goods, the Act is not concerned with transfers of beneficial ownership, such as may arise on the creation of a trust.

It does not follow, however, that a seller has to have, or to purport to transfer, a complete or perfect legal title to the goods in order to bring a transaction within the statutory definition of a 'sale of goods'. Sections 21–25 and 48(2) all deal with cases where the seller has no title, or a defective title. And s 12(3) (a provision first inserted by the Supply of Goods (Implied Terms) Act 1973) expressly contemplates that a seller who has only a limited title to goods may contract to sell that title. So, a person who has found an article and has failed to trace its owner may sell his title to it as a finder. The subsection also states that a seller may contract to sell whatever title a third person may have to the goods. This might happen, for instance, when a pawnbroker sells goods as unredeemed pledges: he does not contract to confer on the buyers any better title than the various pledgors may have. This analysis is entirely consistent with the views of Battersby and Preston referred to above: the seller here is contracting to sell such title as he (or the third person) has to an absolute legal interest in the goods, not a title to some more limited interest.

G Battersby and A D Preston 'The Concepts of "Property", "Title" and "Owner" used in the Sale of Goods Act 1893' (1972) 35 MLR 268, pp 268–272, 288

(Footnotes in the original article are omitted.)

A. THE THREE ELEMENTS INVOLVED IN A TRANSFER OF TANGIBLE PROPERTY

In the transfer of any tangible property, whether land or chattels, three elements are distinguishable, namely, the estate or interest which is transferred, the title to that estate or interest, and the evidence of that title.

(1) *Estate or interest transferred*

What rights are being transferred and what is their duration? In the context of land, the rights must be, for example, the fee simple, the residue of a 999-year lease, a life estate, or some lesser interest such as a perpetual easement. Similarly, in relation to chattels, although the range of interests recognised by the law is restricted, one needs to distinguish life interests, entailed interests and absolute interests, as well as various kinds of incumbrance. Whether the transfer involves land or chattels, therefore, its nature can be understood only when the estate or interest to be transferred is defined.

(2) *Title to that estate or interest*

Is there anyone who can show that the transferor's title to the estate or interest is defective? The fundamental rule of the English law of property affecting title is *nemo dat quod non habet*. Its effect is that, although a transfer may comply with the legal formalities required for the transfer of the interest in question, it may yet fail to take effect because the transferor has no title to transfer. It is equally possible, however, that the transferor may have a title, but one which is less than perfect. This follows from the elementary proposition of our law that title to tangible property, whether land or chattels, is relative. The title to such property is protected by the possessory actions, which require only that the plaintiff must have possession or the immediate right to possession. This principle, and the converse rule that, subject to very narrow exceptions, the defendant cannot plead *jus tertii*, mean that mere adverse possession of property confers a title which is good against all the world except a person who can prove a better title, that is to say, a person with a continuing prior title. This notion of relative title permeates our law, and is one of the key concepts in the law of property, though in sale of goods, unlike conveyancing of land, it is frequently forgotten. Given such a concept, the phrase 'owner of property' assumes significance only in relation to a particular issue with a particular person. . . . The concept of absolute ownership, by which is meant an indefeasible title to the absolute interest in the particular property, is as elusive in the realm of chattels as in that of land. True, there are exceptional cases of absolute ownership: a sale of goods in market overt to a purchaser in good faith is an exception relating to chattels, and in the case of land one may instance the statutory procedure by which all existing interests may be compulsorily purchased. These exceptional cases, however, in no way derogate from the general principle. In a legal system which guaranteed that all transfers would vest an indefeasible title in the transferee the distinction between title and interest would be unnecessary, but English law, adopting the *nemo dat* rule, does not provide such a guarantee. In any given situation, therefore, the phrase 'transfer of property' needs expanding to 'the transfer of such-and-such a title to such-and-such an interest.'

(3) *Evidence of title*

By what facts does the transferor of property prove his title? This question assumes great importance in transactions concerning land; in the case of transactions concerning chattels, however, there is normally no investigation of title, the transferor's possession of the chattels apparently as owner affording the only evidence. The reasons for this are not hard to find: it is extremely rare for any documentary title to exist; the transient value of most chattels means that the chain of title will usually be short; there are exceptions to the rule *nemo dat quod non habet* which reduce the risk of bad titles; in any event, the value of chattels must often render investigation of title something of an excess. The question of evidence of title to chattels can accordingly be forgotten.

Our basic submission, therefore, is that the two objects of currency in the English system of property and conveyancing are interests and title, and that what is dealt with in a particular transfer is a particular title to a particular interest in the property in question.

B. THE DEFINITION OF A SALE OF GOODS

With these basic points in mind, we turn to examine in more detail the nature of a sale of goods. The transaction is defined in section 1 of the Sale of Goods Act. Section 1(1) reads:

> A contract of sale of goods is a contract whereby the seller transfers or agrees to transfer the property in goods to the buyer for a money consideration, called the price. There may be a contract of sale between one part owner and another.

This definition is amplified in section 1(8) as follows:

> Where under a contract of sale the property in the goods is transferred from the seller to the buyer the contract is called a sale; but where the transfer of the property in the goods is to take place at a future time or subject to some condition thereafter to be fulfilled the contract is called an agreement to sell.

It will be observed first that the person selling the goods is called 'the seller,' not 'the owner.' The latter term is used at the end of subsection (1) (a 'sale between one part owner and another'), but it is clear from the context that the word 'owner' is not intended to have any flavour different from the word 'seller'; just as 'the seller' is a person who sells or agrees to sell a particular title, so 'the owner' is a person who owns a particular title, and as part owner owns that title concurrently with another. These words and phrases do not, therefore, indicate the use of any concept of absolute ownership.

Secondly, it will be observed that both subsections refer to the transfer of 'property in goods.' What is the concept of 'property' here employed? It is self-evident from the context that the word 'property' is not used in the sense of the physical chattels themselves, for the word 'goods' is used for that purpose. 'Property' therefore refers in some way to the proprietary right which is transferred by the sale. In our submission, 'property' comprises the two elements distinguished earlier as being involved in any transfer of property, namely, interest and title. So far as the interest is concerned, the purpose is to define a sale as involving the transfer of the absolute legal interest in the goods (analogous to the legal fee simple estate in land), as opposed to any lesser interest. This is made clear by the definition of 'property' in section 62 as 'the general property in the goods and not merely a special property.' Clearly, therefore, the creation for value of a bailment, which involves the transfer merely of possession and not of the absolute interest (analogous in many ways to the grant of a lease of land), is not a sale. Equally, in our submission, the transfer for value of a life interest in goods would not be a sale as defined, but would be regarded as an assignment of that life interest. But the concept of 'property' involves also the notion of title, for a sale must involve the transfer of a *particular title* to the absolute interest. In this general definition of sale, however, nothing is said about the *quality* of that title, which may be good, bad or indifferent on the scale of relativity. Nor would one expect anything to be said about the quality of title in the definition of the transaction: it would be logically and linguistically inapposite. What section 1 of the Act really achieves, therefore, is a definition of the nature of the contract of sale of goods, and this definition is expanded into two forms: (i) 'a contract whereby the seller transfers . . . the property in goods to the buyer' (ii) 'a contract whereby the seller . . . agrees to transfer the property in goods to the buyer.' These formulations of the definition differ in that the latter separates the stages of contracting to convey and conveyance, while the former telescopes the two stages so that both contract to convey and conveyance occur simultaneously; this telescoping, however, in no way detracts from the point that contract and conveyance are independent notions. More importantly these formulations share the feature that the contract of sale of goods concerns the transfer of a title to the absolute legal interest in the goods. In exactly the same way, one could define a contract for the sale of land as 'a contract for the transfer for value of a title to the fee simple estate' (ie separating the two elements of 'property'); that is merely an explanation of the nature of the transaction, corresponding to the second of the above formulations of the definition of a contract for the sale of goods, and containing within itself no promise as to quality of title, for which the parties are left to provide, if they wish, by appropriate contractual terms. Again, one could define a gift of goods as 'a voluntary transfer of the property in goods,' this merely serving to explain the nature of the transaction, for it is in the last degree unlikely that any undertakings as to the quality of the title will be given. Our point is that in all these cases it is the nature of the transaction that is being defined, and that nature is the transfer of a title to the absolute legal interest. The title which is in fact transferred, unless the case falls within an exception to the *nemo dat* rule, will always be the title vested in the seller at the time of the transfer: if it is poorer than that contracted for, the seller will be liable to the buyer for breach of contract, whilst if it is better than that contracted for, the risk assumed by the buyer will be proportionately less burdensome. . . .

SUMMARY

The above arguments have led to the following principal conclusions:

(1) The notion of relative title is fundamental in English law, and is the main key to understanding the proprietary concepts used in the law of sale of goods.

(2) A distinction must be drawn between title and interest, the law of sale of goods being concerned with the transfer of a title to the absolute legal interest in the goods sold.

(3) The concept of 'property' in the Sale of Goods Act, despite the limited meaning assigned to it by section 62(1), must be expanded to mean 'a title to the absolute legal interest in the goods sold,' which meaning is used consistently throughout the Act.

(4) The concept of 'title,' as used in sections 21–26 of the Act, must be expanded to take in the notion that the transfer relates to the absolute legal interest in the goods sold, with the result that 'title' bears a similar meaning to 'property' in the above sense.

(5) A contract of sale is a contract which involves the transfer of a title to the absolute legal interest, and not necessarily a good title; a transfer which excludes the implied undertakings as to good title is still a sale, and there is no bar to such exclusion as the law now stands.

(6) Care is needed in applying the exceptions to the *nemo dat* rule, because of the ambiguity of expressions such as 'owner' and 'good title.' A few of the exceptions have the effect of generating a new perfect title, but the majority have the much more limited effect of transferring a particular title, which may itself be defeasible, by overriding some prior transaction or interest.

(The whole of this important article is particularly worthy of study.)

3 Sale of goods distinguished from other transactions

There are various types of transaction which in some ways resemble contracts for the sale of goods, but do not fall within the statutory definition. This means that the Act cannot be directly applied to such contracts. However, it may be of indirect relevance, since the Act of 1893 may have codified a rule of the common law which, prior to that date, had an application wider than the sale of goods. The common law rules, in their uncodified form, may be assumed to continue to apply to these other contracts. So it may be that many sale of goods rules are equally applicable to contracts of barter: it is only the dearth of litigated cases on barter that prevents us from knowing how far the similarity extends. Again, in formulating legislation to govern some of these other types of transaction (eg the Supply of Goods and Services Act 1982), the statutory draftsman has often modelled his new law on the Sale of Goods Act and sometimes copied its language verbatim. It would be surprising if a court were to rule that cases decided on the construction of this language in the Sale of Goods Act were not relevant guides to its meaning in the context of the later Act.

(a) Sale distinguished from gift

A gift differs from a sale because there is no consideration for the transfer of the property in the goods. This is usually an obvious matter, but in borderline cases the court may be faced with a very difficult question. Eg, in the well-known case *Esso Petroleum Ltd v Customs & Excise Comrs* [1976] 1 All ER 117, motorists were offered a 'free' medallion with each purchase of four gallons of petrol. There was a difference of judicial opinion whether the medallions were the subject of a gift or a sale, or of a contract collateral to the purchase of the petrol which fell into neither of these categories.

(b) Sale distinguished from barter or exchange

The Act stipulates that the consideration in a contract of sale should be in money. If it takes some other form (eg where goods are exchanged for other goods, for services, or for any other thing of value), it is a contract of barter or exchange and not one of sale and the Act will not apply to it. This may not always be important, for it is likely that many of the rules which applied to sales at common law also applied (and continue to apply) to barter. But in the absence of clear precedents we cannot be sure that this is invariably so.

Where goods are exchanged for other goods (and particularly where some money is paid by one of the parties as well), it is not always necessary or appropriate to construe the transaction as one of barter. In *Aldridge v Johnson* (below), the evidence seems to have pointed to an arrangement under which there were reciprocal *sales* of the bullocks and the barley; the prices of each were calculated and then set off against each other, and the balance of £23 was agreed to be paid in cash. In other words, there were two separate contracts of sale, and it is consistent with this analysis that sale of goods principles were applied. In *Dawson v Dutfield*, however (a typical 'trading-in' case), the court preferred to take the view that there was only *one* contract of sale, namely that by Dawson to Dutfield of the newer lorries for £475; there was then a subsidiary arrangement that *if* Dutfield chose to deliver the two older lorries in part exchange, he would be allowed £225 off the price.

Aldridge v Johnson (1857) 7 E & B 885, Court of Queen's Bench

Aldridge made a deal with Knights to exchange 32 bullocks for 100 quarters of barley, to be measured out of a larger amount lying in Knights' granary which Aldridge had inspected the day before. They valued the bullocks at £6 each (ie £192 in all) and the barley at £215, and agreed that the difference of £23 would be paid in cash. Knights took delivery of the bullocks, and Aldridge sent 200 of his own sacks, each holding half a quarter, to Knights to be filled with barley from the heap in the granary and put on the railway by Knights' men. 155 of the 200 sacks had been filled when, on Knights' instructions, they were emptied out into the heap again. Aldridge then learned that Knights was about to be declared bankrupt. In this action brought against Johnson, Knights' trustee in bankruptcy, Aldridge claimed the right to 100 quarters out of the barley in the heap; but the court held that only the barley in the 155 sacks had become Aldridge's property. It also held that he had not been divested of it when the sacks were emptied back into the heap. But Aldridge had no claim to the rest of the 100 quarters which had never been put into his sacks.

Lord Campbell CJ: I think that no portion of what remained in bulk ever vested in the plaintiff. We cannot tell what part of that is to vest. No rule of the law of vendor and purchaser is more clear than this: that, until the appropriation and separation of a particular quantity, or signification of assent to the particular quantity, the property is not transferred. Therefore, except as to what was put into the 155 sacks, there must be judgment for the defendant. It is equally clear that, as to what was put into those sacks, there must be judgment for the plaintiff. Looking to all that was done, when the bankrupt put the barley into the sacks eo instanti the property in each sack-full vested in the plaintiff. I consider that here was a priori an assent by the plaintiff. He had inspected and approved of the barley in bulk. He sent his sacks to be filled out of that bulk. There can be no doubt of his assent to the appropriation of such bulk as should have been put into the sacks. There was also evidence of his subsequent appropriation, by his order that it should be sent on. There remained nothing to be done by the vendor, who had appropriated a part by the direction of the vendee. It is the same as if boxes had been filled and sent on by the bankrupt, in which case it cannot be disputed that the property would pass: and it can make no difference that the plaintiff ordered the sacks to be forwarded by the vendor. As to the question of conversion, the property being in the plaintiff, he has done nothing to divest himself of it. It is not like the case of confusion of goods, where the owner of such articles as oil or wine mixes them with similar articles belonging to another. That is a wrongful act by the owner, for which he is punished by losing his property. Here the plaintiff has done nothing wrong. It was wrong of the bankrupt to mix what had been put into the sacks with the rest of the barley; but no wrong has been done by the plaintiff. That being so, the plaintiff's property comes into the hands of the defendant as the bankrupt's assignee. . . . He claims all the barley, and claims all of it as being the property of the bankrupt. He therefore has converted the plaintiff's property.

[Coleridge, Erle and Crompton JJ delivered concurring judgments.]

G J Dawson (Clapham) Ltd v H & G Dutfield [1936] 2 All ER 232, King's Bench Division

Dawson, a dealer in secondhand vehicles, agreed to sell Dutfields two lorries, a Leyland and a Saurer, for a combined price of £475 of which £250 was paid or credited at the time. He also agreed to allow Dutfields £225 as the trade-in price of two Leyland vehicles, which Dutfields were allowed to use while their new purchases were being overhauled, provided that they were delivered to him within a month. The Saurer turned out to be in a much worse condition than the parties expected and, after arrangements to provide another vehicle in its place had proved abortive, Dawson sued for the balance of the price of the two lorries. It was held that he could sue for this sum and was not bound to take the other vehicles as trade-ins.

Hilbery J: The first agreement was a complete one and completely executed by the plaintiffs; all that remained to be done was to be done by the defendants. The plaintiffs had discharged their duty. Further the agreement was not a severable one. . . . There is no evidence of any agreement to put aside the old agreement and treat it as non-existent. There is no more than an expression by the plaintiffs of intention to placate the defendants, an expression of willingness to take back the Saurer and try and find a suitable lorry in order to ease the situation for the defendants. It was the expression of a pious – or I should say business – hope.

Someone must bear the burden of a bad bargain and the loss arising from the fact that the condition of the lorry was so much worse than expected. The thing was sold as it stood, and bought after examination by people who understood that there was much to be done to it. Neither party understood how bad it was. My decision is that the plaintiffs are entitled to the balance of the purchase money in the terms of the claim, owing to the non-delivery of the two Leylands. These had to be delivered within one month and if they had so delivered them, the defendants would have been entitled so to satisfy the purchase price to the extent of £225. They did not do so and there remains £225 as part of the purchase price due to the plaintiffs. The action in such circumstances is not one in detinue, and therefore no demand is necessary. Nor are the plaintiffs bound to claim the lorries. The defendants were merely given the right to satisfy £225 of the purchase price by the delivery of the lorries within one month or thereabouts. Such an arrangement does not deprive the plaintiffs of their right to the purchase price in cash. The defendants have not delivered and there must be judgment for the plaintiffs for the balance of the purchase price.

NOTES

1. In the United States, the price in a contract of sale may be paid in money or otherwise; if it is payable in whole or part in goods, each party is a seller of the goods which he wishes to transfer (Uniform Commercial Code, para 2–304(1)).

2. Some aspects of the contract of barter are now governed by the Supply of Goods and Services Act 1982. This Act provides for statutory terms as to title, quality, etc to be implied into contracts of barter, using much the same language as ss 12–15 of the Sale of Goods Act; but it does not deal with the question – when does the property pass? – which was vital in *Aldridge v Johnson* and might have been answered differently if the transaction had been viewed as one of pure barter.

QUESTIONS

1. If Dutfield *had* traded in the two older lorries, what would have been the nature of that second transaction – a sale, a barter, or something else? What was the consideration given by Dawson?

2. In the Irish case *Flynn v Mackin* [1974] IR 101 a motor dealer agreed to supply Father Mackin with a new car in exchange for his old car plus a cash payment of £250. No valuation or price was put by the parties on either vehicle. Was there a sale of (1) the new car, (2) the old car, (3) neither?

(c) Sale of goods distinguished from transfer of an interest in land

There is an overlap between these categories of contract, as has been noted above (p 212). A contract under which a person is to come on to another's land and remove gravel, for instance, may be so drawn as to appear to be a grant of mineral rights, on the one hand, or a sale of the gravel, as goods, on the other. Although it is possible to frame such a contract so as to give it an emphasis either way, it should be borne in mind that more than one statutory regime may be applicable (see above, pp 212–213), and that even though the parties may intend to make a sale of goods, the transaction may be overriden before severance by the claim of a third party with a superior title to the land.

(d) Sale distinguished from bailment   *goods to be returned or passed on*

A bailment involves the delivery of goods by one person to another for a limited purpose, on terms that the identical goods will be returned to the bailor or delivered to a third party in accordance with his instructions at the conclusion of the bailment. There is normally no likelihood that a contract of bailment will be confused with one of sale, but the question did arise in *South Australian Insurance Co v Randell* (1869) LR 3 PC 101. In that case, a farmer had delivered corn to a miller and tipped it into a common store, on terms which allowed him to claim at any time *either* the redelivery of an equivalent quantity of corn *or* the market price of such corn ruling on the day in which he made his demand. Since the identity of the corn was lost when it was delivered, and there was no obligation on the miller, if redelivery was demanded, to make the redelivery from the same store – or, indeed, from any particular source – it was held that the transaction could not be a bailment but was more in the nature of a sale.

The distinction between sale and bailment may be blurred in some cases involving a manufacturer. For instance, components or part-finished goods may be delivered to a manufacturer, on terms that they will be combined with other goods belonging to the latter and used to make an end-product which is then either redelivered to the original supplier for a charge, or sold on to a third party for a price for which, or out of which, the seller will account to the supplier. The question whether the transaction is a bailment by the supplier of his goods to the manufacturer or one involving a transfer (perhaps a sale) of the property in his goods and a resale back to him (or a sale on to the third party) can be very complex: the answer turns essentially on the terms of the contract, but may also be influenced by such factors as whether one party has supplied the 'principal' goods, and by whether the goods supplied remain identifiable throughout the manufacturing process. Some aspects of this question are discussed below when we examine the *Romalpa* line of cases: see below, p 408.

QUESTIONS

1. Would the Sale of Goods Act apply to a transaction such as that in *South Australian Insurance Co v Randell*?

2. Twenty farmers agree to rent a store owned by Bloggs, where they tip their grain into a common bulk when it is harvested in August. It is agreed that Bloggs will sell one-tenth of the total quantity on the first of each month, beginning on 1 October and ending on 1 July, and share out the proceeds (less the rent and a commission) among the farmers on a pro rata basis, proportionate to the total quantity which each has contributed. What is the nature of this arrangement?

3. A day-old chick costs £1 and the food, etc required to rear it until it is ready to lay costs £2. It can then be sold for £3.50. Consider what arrangements might be made between A, who hatches chicks, and B, who grows foodstuffs for poultry and has the facilities for rearing them.

A contract of sale should also be distinguished from other forms of bailment, such as a contract to lease or hire goods, and a pledge.

In the commercial world, specialised forms of lease have developed, notably the 'finance lease', under which the position of the lessee is in many respects similar to that of a buyer. The finance lease can be used in relation to plant and vehicles of all sorts, ranging all the way from a photocopier to a jet airliner. In the normal case the term of the lease approximates to that of the expected working life of the goods in question, and the total of the hire charges paid by the lessee over this period is roughly equal to its capital cost plus the lessor's profit from the transaction. The lessee undertakes responsibility for the maintenance and repair of the goods, and to pay the hire charges whether the goods are in working order or not. Thus his position, though different in law, is in practical terms little different from that of a buyer who has agreed to pay the purchase price of the goods by instalments over a similar period, at the end of which they will have come to the end of their useful life. The finance lease may have tax advantages and, as a form of 'off balance-sheet accounting' may be used to enhance the appearance of a firm's financial statements.

A contract of hire-purchase is a form of bailment, but is sufficiently important to be discussed separately.

(e) Sale distinguished from hire-purchase

In a contract of hire-purchase, goods are hired by their owner to a person for a period, at the end of which he may exercise an option, conferred upon him by the contract, to buy the goods, usually by making a further nominal payment. In practical terms (though not in legal form), the position of the hirer under such a contract is very similar to that of a person who has agreed to buy the goods on the understanding that he is to take immediate delivery, but pay the price by instalments over a period. Such a contract of sale may take two forms. If the property passes to the buyer at once, it is commonly called a 'credit sale'. If the seller retains the property in the goods until the whole of the price is paid, it is termed a 'conditional sale'. Each of these forms of contract of sale differs from a contract of hire-purchase because the buyer is contractually bound to complete the transaction: he has 'agreed to buy'. The hirer under a contract of hire-purchase, in contrast, has only an *option* to buy, which he is free to exercise or not as he chooses; and he also commonly has the right to terminate the hiring before the expiry of the contemplated period. The effectiveness of hire-purchase – as a transaction which gives possession and use of the goods to the hirer whilst at the same time ensuring that the seller's retention of title gives him maximum protection as regards payment – was established in the leading case of *Helby v Matthews* (below). This followed the decision in *Lee v Butler* (below, p 332), where the transaction took the form of a conditional sale agreement, and it was held that the rights of the seller (though protected in the event of the buyer's insolvency) could be defeated by an unauthorised resale of the goods by the buyer to a bona fide third party.

The distinction between hire-purchase and sale can be important. In particular, it should be noted that the two popular forms of 'instalment credit' transaction referred to above – the credit sale and the conditional sale – are in law contracts of sale to which (subject to the consumer credit legislation referred to below) the Sale of Goods Act is applicable, whereas a contract of hire-purchase is wholly outside the scope of the Act, at least until the option to purchase is exercised.

Helby v Matthews [1895] AC 471, House of Lords

Helby contracted to hire a piano to Brewster for three years at a rental of 10s 6d (52p) a month. The contract included the following provisions:

The owner agrees:

A. That the hirer may terminate the hiring by delivering up to the owner the said instrument.

B. If the hirer shall punctually pay the full sum of £18 18s by 10s 6d at date of signing, and by 36 monthly instalments of 10s 6d in advance as aforesaid, the said instrument shall become the sole and absolute property of the hirer.

C. Unless and until the full sum of £18 18s be paid, the said instrument shall be and continue to be the sole property of the owner.

Brewster, without any authority from Helby, pledged the piano with Matthews, a pawnbroker, as security for a loan. Although Brewster was not the owner of the piano, the pledge would have been effective under the Factors Act 1889, s 9, if the contract had been one of conditional sale (see *Lee v Butler*, below, p 332). The House of Lords, reversing the Court of Appeal, held that it was not a conditional sale, and that therefore Helby was entitled to claim the piano from the pawnbroker.

Lord Herschell LC: My Lords, I cannot, with all respect, concur in the view of the Court of Appeal, that upon the true construction of the agreement Brewster had 'agreed to buy' the piano. An agreement to buy imports a legal obligation to buy. If there was no such legal obligation, there cannot, in my opinion, properly be said to have been an agreement to buy. Where is any such legal obligation to be found? Brewster might buy or not just as he pleased. He did not agree to make thirty-six or any number of monthly payments. All that he undertook was to make the monthly payment of 10s 6d as long as he kept the piano. He had an option no doubt to buy it by continuing the stipulated payments for a sufficient length of time. If he had exercised that option he would have become the purchaser. I cannot see under these circumstances how he can be said either to have bought or agreed to buy the piano. The terms of the contract did not upon its execution bind him to buy, but left him free to do so or not as he pleased, and nothing happened after the contract was made to impose that obligation.

The Master of the Rolls said: 'It is a contract by the seller to sell, and a contract by the purchaser, if he does not change his mind, to buy; and if this agreement goes on to its end, it ends in a purchase. Therefore, it seems to me that the true and proper construction of this instrument, after all, is this: it is an agreement by the one to sell, and an agreement by the other to buy, but with an option on the part of the buyer if he changes his mind to put an end to the contract.' I cannot think that an agreement to buy, 'if he does not change his mind,' is any agreement to buy at all in the eye of the law. If it rests with me to do or not to do a certain thing at a future time, according to the then state of my mind, I cannot be said to have contracted to do it. It appears to me that the contract in question was in reality a contract of hiring, and not in name or pretence only. But for the provision that if the hirer punctually paid the 10s 6d a month for thirty-six months, the piano should be his property, it could not be doubted that it was a mere agreement for its hire, and I cannot see how the fact that this provision was added made it any the less a contract of hiring until that condition had been fulfilled.

I think it very likely that both parties thought it would probably end in a purchase, but this is far from shewing that it was an agreement to buy. The monthly payments were no doubt somewhat higher than they would have been if the agreement had contained no such provision. One can well conceive cases, however, in which a person who had not made up his mind to continue the payments for three years would nevertheless enter into such an agreement. It might be worth his while to make somewhat larger monthly payments for the use of the piano in order that he might enjoy that option if he chose to exercise it. In such a case how could it be said that he had agreed to buy when he had not only come under no obligation to buy, but had not even made up his mind to do so? The agreement is, in its terms, just as applicable to such a case as to one where the hirer had resolved to continue the payments for the three years, and it must be construed upon a consideration of the obligations which its terms create, and not upon a mere speculation as to what was contemplated, or what would probably be done under it.

It was said in the Court of Appeal that there was an agreement by the appellant to sell, and that an agreement to sell connotes an agreement to buy. This is undoubtedly true if the words 'agreement to sell' be used in their strict legal sense; but when a person has, for valuable consideration, bound himself to sell to another on certain terms, if the other chooses to avail himself of the binding offer, he may, in popular language, be said to have agreed to sell, though an agreement to sell in this sense, which is in truth merely an offer which cannot be withdrawn, certainly does not connote an agreement to buy, and it is only in this sense that there can be said to have been an agreement to sell in the present case.

[Lords Watson, Macnaghten and Shand delivered concurring opinions. Lord Morris concurred.]

NOTES

1. This case established that the owner of the goods which are let out under a hire-purchase agreement cannot lose his title under s 9 of the Factors Act 1889 (or its equivalent, s 25(1) of the Sale of Goods Act 1979). A second ruling of the House of Lords in *McEntire v Crossley Bros Ltd* [1895] AC 457 held that a contract in similar form was not a disguised transaction by way of security and accordingly liable to be held void if not registered as a bill of sale under the Bills of Sale Act (1878) Amendment Act of 1882. The two principal difficulties which had arguably stood in the way of the hire-purchase form being fully effective were thus surmounted by these near-contemporaneous decisions; and the way was cleared for it to become the principal instrument for instalment purchases for a century to come.

2. Since 1938, there has been legislation designed to protect consumers who fall into difficulties under hire-purchase transactions – whether because the terms of the hiring are onerous or because they encounter difficulties in keeping up the agreed hire payments and run the risk that the owner will repossess the goods, leaving them little or no redress. The statutory controls have applied for the most part only to transactions coming within prescribed financial and other limits. The legislation currently in force is the Consumer Credit Act 1974, which regulates transactions where credit is given to *individuals* (a term which excludes companies and other corporate bodies) to an amount not exceeding £15,000. This legislation applies not only to loans and similar arrangements which involve 'credit' in an everyday sense, but includes hire-purchase contracts where the 'balance financed' (ie the total charge, less any deposit paid) is under £15,000, and also conditional sales (within similar limits) and some forms of credit-sale. For many purposes, this Act treats hire-purchase and conditional sale contracts as equivalent, thus eroding the distinction between *Lee v Butler* and *Helby v Matthews* which proved so important a hundred years ago. The distinction remains an important one, of course, where the transaction falls outside the statutory limits.

3. The Supply of Goods (Implied Terms) Act 1973 (which applies to all hire-purchase agreements and not just to 'consumer' transactions) imports into contracts of hire-purchase implied terms as to title, description, quality, etc which closely parallel those implied into contracts of sale by ss 12–15 of the Sale of Goods Act 1979 (see below, Chapter 10). Moreover, the Unfair Contract Terms Act 1977 treats exemption clauses in the two categories of contract in precisely similar terms.

4. Notwithstanding the clear fact that in law the supplier of goods under a hire-purchase agreement is and remains their owner and is not merely the holder of a security interest in goods which he has 'sold' to the hirer, there is a strong argument for saying that in economic reality this *is* the case, and that it would be better if the law recognised it. The legal position is even further divorced from reality if the credit is given, not by the dealer who supplies the goods to his customer, but by a finance company which takes no part in the actual negotiations. If we take the common situation where a customer inspects a car in a dealer's showroom and agrees to take it on hire-purchase, a layman might reasonably think that the dealer was selling the car, the customer buying it, and the finance company lending the buyer the money to pay the price, and taking security over the car until this borrowed money was repaid by instalments over time. But in law, what the parties in England do is quite different: the dealer, who has persuaded his customer to take the car, sells it to the finance company, and the latter then lets it to the customer on hire-purchase. So the 'buyer' is in law a hirer (and a hirer from a faceless institution that he has never met); the dealer is not a seller vis-à-vis his customer – indeed, he is in no direct contractual relationship towards him at all; and the supposed lender on security is a buyer who becomes the owner of the car for so long as any part of the price is outstanding! In other jurisdictions, such as the United States and Canada, general personal property security laws have been introduced (eg the US Uniform Commercial Code, art 9) which assimilate into one regime all transactions that *in effect* involve the giving of security over personal chattels, regardless of their legal form. This makes unnecessary the elaborate type of legal charade described above which the technicalities of English law impose on similar transactions here. Successive reports (the report of the Crowther Committee on Consumer Credit (Cmnd 1781, 1962) and the report of Professor Diamond on Security Interests in Property (HMSO, 1989)) have recommended that there should be wholesale reform of this area of English law, along the lines of the transatlantic codes. But governments have shown no interest in putting these recommendations into effect: see below, p 854.

(f) Sale distinguished from transaction by way of security

Among the forms of security considered later in this book are the pledge, the lien, the mortgage, and the charge: see Chapters 23 and 24. Since neither pledge nor lien involve the transfer of the property in the goods concerned, they are plainly distinguishable from a contract of sale. The same may be said of a charge: the chargor grants an interest in or over his goods in favour of the chargee, which is of a proprietary nature, but he retains the property in his own hands, and the chargee's interest is a defeasible one, which is automatically terminated on payment of the debt which it secures. A mortgage resembles a sale rather more closely, in that the legal title to the goods is transferred to the creditor in order to secure the debt: the general property in the goods (to use the wording of the Act) passes to him. But whereas in a sale it passes absolutely, so that the seller has no further interest in the goods, in a mortgage it passes subject to the condition that the mortgagor is entitled to redeem – that is, to have the goods transferred back to him when the debt is paid. The parties remain in a continuing relationship of debtor and creditor, and both retain an interest in the goods during the currency of the mortgage.

Section 62(4) states that the provisions of the Act do not apply to a transaction in the form of a sale which is intended to operate by way of mortgage, pledge, charge or other security. This draws our attention to the possibility that a transaction which is to all appearances a contract of sale may in fact be intended by the parties to do no more than create a security interest in favour of the purported 'buyer': there may be a secret understanding, or an agreement recorded in another document, that the transfer of property in the goods is only conditional and that it will be retransferred when the seller's indebtedness to the buyer has been discharged. Or the sale may be part of a composite transaction (eg a sale followed by a lease-back of the goods to the seller) which, viewed overall, is really meant to be a way of raising money on the security of the goods. In situations falling into these categories, it is not s 62(4) which is likely to pose legal problems, but rather the Bills of Sale Act of 1882 (see below, p 847); for under this latter Act (which traditionally looks to the substance rather than the form) the transaction, if it *is* held to be a security transaction, risks being declared void for non-compliance with the statute or for want of registration.

This means that the courts may be faced with the difficult task of determining the 'true intention' of the parties in many borderline cases. In older cases, many of which involved consumers dealing with finance companies, transactions were frequently struck down as disguised loans on security (eg *Polsky v S & A Services* [1951] 1 All ER 1062n, CA). The sale and lease-back is, however, a well-established form of transaction, especially in commercial circles, which ought nowadays to be recognised as valid in its own right (see, for example, *Eastern Distributors Ltd v Goldring* (below, p 301) and *Mercantile Credit Ltd v Hamblin* (below, p 308)). Even so, surprisingly, we do find an occasional decision (eg *Re Curtain Dream plc* [1990] BCLC 925) ruling that the parties had created a concealed charge which was unenforceable for want of registration.

(g) Sale of goods distinguished from contract for work and materials

There has always been a difficult – indeed an impossible – line to draw here. I take my car to a garage to have a new set of tyres fitted. Does the garage *sell* me the tyres and fit them as something incidental to the sale? Or is it performing a *service*, doing work on the car, and providing the materials ancillary to that service? Is the position different where the work required is a more substantial component in the overall job – fitting new brake linings or replacing a head gasket, say? Does a customer who eats a meal in a hotel or restaurant *buy* the food, or have it supplied incidentally to the provision of services?

The courts have wavered in their approach to this question. In some early cases, such as *Clay v Yates* (below), what seems to have mattered was the relative importance of the two elements – the labour and the materials. Later, in cases like *Lee v Griffin* (below), they made the issue turn on whether or not there was an end-product in the form of a chattel in which the property was transferred; and most recently, in *Robinson v Graves* (below) the question was said to be determined by the 'substance' of the transaction. However, this is not always a meaningful test – a point which the court may have failed to appreciate – and the decisions which have been reached are far from consistent.

The following have been held to be contracts for work and materials:

–   a contract to print a book: *Clay v Yates* (1856) 1 H & N 73;
–   a contract to paint a portrait: *Robinson v Graves* [1935] 1 KB 579, CA (below);
–   the supply of drugs by a veterinary surgeon when inoculating cattle: *Dodd v Wilson* [1946] 2 All ER 691.

In contrast, the following have been held (or assumed) to be sales of goods:

–   a contract to make a set of dentures: *Lee v Griffin* (1861) 1 B & S 272;
–   the supply of a meal in a restaurant: *Lockett v Charles Ltd* [1938] 4 All ER 170;

- the supply of a fur jacket made to the customer's order: *J Marcel (Furriers) Ltd v Tapper* [1953] 1 WLR 49;
- the supply and laying of a fitted carpet: *Philip Head & Sons Ltd v Showfronts Ltd* [1970] 1 Lloyd's Rep 140;
- the supply and installation of an animal feed hopper: *H Parsons (Livestock) Ltd v Uttley Ingham & Co Ltd* [1978] QB 791, CA.

It is difficult to resist the conclusion that these decisions have been made on an impressionistic, rather than a logical, basis. Fortunately, the question is less important nowadays than formerly, for two reasons. First, prior to the repeal in 1954 of s 4 of the Sale of Goods Act 1893 (itself traceable back to the Statute of Frauds 1677), a contract for the sale of goods was not normally enforceable without written evidence, but writing was not required in the case of a contract for services. This distinction has now disappeared (and with it the temptation for judges to make somewhat arbitrary rulings leading to an outcome to meet the justice of the case!). Secondly, in many respects the legal rules applicable are the same whatever classification is given to the transaction: for instance, in relation to the obligation to supply goods or materials of merchantable quality and suitable for their purpose. In a sale of goods, the relevant rules are to be found in ss 12–15 of the Act; in a contract for work and services, equivalent rules were applied at common law until 1982, and are now set out in statutory form in the Supply of Goods and Services Act 1982, ss 2–5.

However, there are other areas of the law where the two types of transaction may be governed by different legal rules – eg, perhaps, in regard to the passing of property and risk; and here the distinction will remain important. Ironically, in the most recent case in which this issue might have been crucial, *Hyundai Heavy Industries Co Ltd v Papadopoulos* (below), the House of Lords did not give a clear ruling. This case concerned a contract to build and deliver a ship, and it was held that the contract was of a hybrid nature which, although essentially one of sale, had some characteristics of a contract to do building work: for so long as the ship was unfinished, it was appropriate to apply rules analogous to those of building law, even though the contract would be treated as being one of sale when the work was finished and the ship was ready to deliver.

Robinson v Graves [1935] 1 KB 579, Court of Appeal

(The facts appear from the judgment.)

Greer LJ: This appeal raises a very interesting question, which has been well argued and is not free from difficulty, having regard to the fact that there has not yet been any actual decision on the point involved in this case, though there have been in some of the cases dicta tending in one direction and in others dicta tending in the other direction. The question to be decided is this: Whether when a person goes to an artist to have a portrait painted, it may be his own portrait or the portrait of some friend (as for instance his wife), and the commission is accepted by the artist, they are making a bargain for the manufacture of future goods to be delivered when those goods come into existence in circumstances which make it a sale of goods within the meaning of s 4 of the Sale of Goods Act 1893, which has now taken the place of s 17 of the Statute of Frauds relating to the sale of goods.

I propose to look at the question first without dealing with the authorities, because after all we are dealing with the meaning of the English language in the statute and its application to particular facts. I can imagine that nothing would be more surprising to a client going to a portrait painter to have his portrait painted and to the artist who was accepting the commission than to be told that they were making a bargain about the sale of goods. It is, of course, possible that a picture may be ordered in such circumstances as will make it an order for goods to be supplied in the future, but it does not follow that this is the inference to be drawn in every case as between the client and the artist. Looking at the propositions involved from the point of view of interpreting the words in the English language it seems to me that the painting of a portrait in these circumstances would not, in the ordinary use of the English language, be deemed to be the purchase and sale of that which is produced by the artist. It would, on the contrary, be held to be an undertaking by the artist to exercise such skill as he was possessed of in order to produce for reward a thing which would ultimately have to be accepted by the client. If that is so, the contract in this case was not a contract for the sale of goods within the meaning of s 4 of the Sale of Goods Act 1893.

There are only two cases to which I think it is necessary to refer. The first case is *Clay v Yates* ((1856) 1 H & N 73). That case was concerned with the question whether a contract with a printer to print and deliver a book to a customer who desired to have it printed was or was not a sale of goods. In the course of the argument Martin B said this: 'Suppose an artist paints a portrait for 300 guineas, and supplies the canvas for it, which is worth 10*s*, surely he might recover under a count for work and labour.' I regard that as an expression of opinion by a high authority on all questions of the common law that in those circumstances there would not be any sale of goods, but there would be a contract for work and labour; and in the judgments which follow the learned judges seem to me to agree with that view. . . .

Now it is said that that case is inconsistent with the subsequent case of *Lee v Griffin* ((1861) 1 B & S 272). So far as the facts of that case are concerned it affords no help to the decision of the present case, because it was concerned with the question whether, when a dentist undertakes to make a plate of false teeth – more frequently called a denture – that is or is not a sale of goods. In that case the principal part of that which the parties are dealing with is the chattel which will come into existence when such skill as may be necessary to produce it has been applied by the dentist and those who work for him; but in the course of delivering the judgments in that case Crompton J and Hill J said nothing whatever which would throw any doubt upon the views expressed in the earlier case of *Clay v Yates*. Crompton J says: 'However, on the point which was made at the trial, whether the plaintiff could not succeed on the count for work, labour, and materials, I am also clearly of opinion against the plaintiff. Whether the cause of action be work and labour, or goods sold and delivered, depends on the particular nature of each individual contract'; and then he refers to the case of *Clay v Yates* as turning upon the peculiar circumstances of the case, and concludes with these words: 'I do not agree with the proposition, that whenever skill is to be exercised in carrying out the contract, that fact makes it a contract for work and labour, and not for the sale of a chattel; it may be the cause of action is for work and labour, when the materials supplied are merely ancillary, as in the case put of an attorney or printer. But in the present case the goods to be furnished, viz, the teeth, are the principal subject-matter; and the case is nearer that of a tailor, who measures for a garment and afterwards supplies the article fitted.'. . .

If you find, as they did in *Lee v Griffin*, that the substance of the contract was the production of something to be sold by the dentist to the dentist's customer, then that is a sale of goods. But if the substance of the contract, on the other hand, is that skill and labour have to be exercised for the production of the article and that it is only ancillary to that that there will pass from the artist to his client or customer some materials in addition to the skill involved in the production of the portrait, that does not make any difference to the result, because the substance of the contract is the skill and experience of the artist in producing the picture.

For these reasons I am of opinion that in this case the substance of the matter was an agreement for the exercise of skill and it was only incidental that some materials would have to pass from the artist to the gentleman who commissioned the portrait. For these reasons I think that this was not a contract for the sale of goods within the meaning of s 4 of the Sale of Goods Act 1893, but it was a contract for work and labour and materials. . . .

[Slesser and Roche LJJ delivered concurring judgments. Greer LJ added:]

I intended to say and would like to add, that in deciding as we have done we are not deciding anything which is necessarily contrary to the decision of Mathew J in the shortly reported case of *Isaacs v Hardy* ((1884) Cab & El 287), which dealt with a contract of a very different kind – namely, where a picture dealer, whose sole object was to acquire something which he might sell in his business, engaged an artist to paint and deliver to him a picture of a given subject at an agreed price. It must not be taken that we are in any way overruling that case or deciding whether it was right or wrong.

Hyundai Heavy Industries Co Ltd v Papadopoulos [1980] 1 WLR 1129, House of Lords

Hyundai contracted to 'build, launch, equip and complete' a 24,000 ton cargo ship and 'deliver and sell' her to a Liberian company for $14.3m. (Perhaps significantly, the parties were described in the contract respectively as 'the builder' and 'the buyer'.) Payment of the price, which was guaranteed by Papadopoulos, was to be made by five instalments at stated stages of the work. The second instalment fell due on 15 July, but it was still unpaid on 6 September and Hyundai then exercised a contractual right to cancel the contract on the basis of this default. The question for the court to decide was whether the July instalment remained payable notwithstanding the termination of the contract. The House of Lords assumed (although not without some doubt) the correctness of the decision in *Dies v British & International Mining & Finance Corpn Ltd* [1939] 1 KB 724 that, if the contract was one for the sale of goods, the seller had no right to retain or to enforce such a payment. In contrast, if it was a contract for work and materials, there was no doubt that it could be claimed. Their ruling was that, while the ship was in the course of construction, the contract had sufficient of the characteristics of a contract for work and materials for the latter rule to apply.

Viscount Dilhorne: Counsel for the guarantors in the instant case argued that if the buyer in the *Dies* case was entitled to recover an advance which had already been paid, then a fortiori the buyer in the instant case could not be liable to make an advance that was due but unpaid: if he did make it, said counsel, he would be entitled to immediate repayment of it.

I do not accept that argument. In my opinion the *Dies* case [1939] 1 KB 724 and *Palmer v Temple* (1839) 9 Ad & El 508 are both distinguishable from the present case because in both these cases the contracts were simply contracts of sale which did not require the vendor to perform any work or incur any expense on the subjects of sale. But the contract in the instant case is not of that comparatively simple character. The obligations of the buyer were not confined to selling the vessel but they included designing and building it and there were special provisions (article 2) that the contract price 'shall include payment for services in the inspection, tests, survey and classification of the vessel' and also 'all costs and expenses for designing and supplying all necessary drawings for the vessel in accordance with the specifications.' Accordingly the builder was obliged to carry out work and to incur expense, starting from the moment that the contract had been signed, including the wages of designers and workmen, fees for inspection and for cost of purchasing materials. It seems very likely that the increasing proportions of the contract price represented by the five instalments bore some relation to the anticipated rate of expenditure, but we have no information on which to make any nice comparison between the amount of expenses that the builder would have to bear from time to time, and the amounts of the instalments payable by the buyer. I do not think that such comparisons are necessary. It is enough that the builder was bound to incur considerable expense in carrying out his part of the contract long before the actual sale could take place. That no doubt is the explanation for the provision in article 10(b) of the shipbuilding contract that:

> . . . all payments under the provisions of this article shall not be delayed or withheld by the buyer due to any dispute of whatever nature arising between the builder and the buyer hereto, unless the buyer shall have claimed to cancel the contract under the terms thereof. . . .

The importance evidently attached by the parties to maintaining the cash flow seems to support my view of the contract.

There was no evidence either way as to whether the builders had in fact carried out their obligations to start designing and building the vessel, but in my opinion we must assume, in the absence of evidence or even averment to the contrary, that they had carried out their part of the bargain up till the date of cancellation.

Much of the plausibility of the argument on behalf of the guarantors seemed to me to be derived from the assumption that the *contract* price was simply a *purchase* price. That is not so, and once that misconception has been removed I think it is clear that the shipbuilding contract has little similarity with a contract of sale and much more similarity, so far as the present issues are concerned, with contracts in which the party entitled to be paid had either performed work or provided services for which payment is due by the date of cancellation. In contracts of the latter class, which of course includes building and construction contracts, accrued rights to payment are not (in the absence of express provisions) destroyed by cancellation of the contract. . . .

[Lords Edmund-Davies and Fraser of Tullybelton delivered concurring opinions. Lords Russell of Killowen and Keith of Kinkel concurred.]

(h) Contract of sale distinguished from agency

As we saw in Chapter 3, there is again sometimes a difficult line to draw between a contract for the sale of goods and one of agency; and the question can arise both between a seller and an agent, on the one hand, and a buyer and an agent, on the other.

Suppose, first, that X is an antiques dealer who travels the country attending auction sales, etc, and Y asks him to look out for a particular kind of sideboard and, if he finds one, to buy it for him. This could be done either on the basis that X would buy as Y's agent, taking remuneration by way of a commission, or by X himself buying the sideboard from its owner and reselling it to Y at a profit. In the former case there is only one contract of sale, with two principal parties; in the latter, two sales and three principal parties. If X and Y have not clearly spelt out the details of their arrangement, the court may be left with a difficult decision.

On the other hand, we may find the converse case. Z may have a showroom in which he displays Ford cars, above which is exhibited the sign 'Sole agent for the sale of Ford cars in the County of Whimshire'. If Z really is an agent, then a customer who agrees to buy a car will actually be buying it from the Ford motor company, and Z is simply a go-between. But it is far more likely that Z is not an agent in the legal sense at all, but a retailer who has bought his stock of cars from Ford and resells each car to the particular customer. Again, there is only one contract of sale in the former case, with one buyer and one seller; in the latter, two contracts of sale, and three principal parties. It is clear that the description which the parties give to their relationship will not be decisive of its true nature in law. The use of the word 'agent' or 'agency' may be a loose, popular usage, obscuring the fact that the person in question is a buyer or a seller.

The courts can have regard to several pointers, none of them in itself conclusive, in reaching a decision in a borderline case. What degree of independence does the 'middle' man have? Is he free to fix his own prices? Is he remunerated by a commission or similar payment, or by taking a profit? Does he have to account to his supplier for the payments he receives, or is he simply invoiced by the supplier for the goods he orders?

The position may be even more complicated. A person may be constituted by the same transaction both someone who has agreed to buy goods and, in addition, the seller's agent (eg in some 'retention of title' or *Romalpa* cases (see below, p 408), the seller's agent to resell the goods). In the world of exporting and importing, it is common for a buyer who is based abroad to be represented in the seller's country by an agent who gives a guarantee to the seller that his principal, the buyer, will pay the price. This, as we saw above, p 79, is called a *del credere* agency; and such an agent has some of the rights given to a seller by the Sale of Goods Act – eg the right to hold the goods under a lien until his principal, the buyer, has reimbursed him for the price (s 38(2)). Again, there is a counterpart: a *confirming agent*, an agent acting for a seller (usually based overseas) who guarantees to the buyer that his principal, the seller, will deliver the goods: see above, p 79.

4 Formation of the contract of sale

A contract of sale, like any other contract, depends upon establishing an agreement between the parties, which usually follows from the acceptance by one party of an offer made by the other. No special rules apply to sales of goods, except perhaps in regard to the price. As has been noted, the consideration in a contract of sale must consist of money. It may happen that the parties have reached agreement on all aspects of their contract except for fixing the price. In most other types of contract, a failure to agree on the consideration would result in the bargain being incomplete, and void for uncertainty. However, in regard to contracts for the sale of goods, the Act goes some way to fill possible gaps by providing as follows, in s 8:

8. (1) The price in a contract of sale may be fixed by the contract, or may be left to be fixed in a manner agreed by the contract, or may be determined by the course of dealing between the parties.

(2) Where the price is not determined as mentioned in subsection (1) above the buyer must pay a reasonable price.

(3) What is a reasonable price is a question of fact dependent on the circumstances of each particular case.

It is clear from these provisions that the court has power to fix a reasonable price where there has been agreement on all the terms of a contract of sale other than the price. However, if the parties have purposefully left the price open, as something to be negotiated between them in the future, the court may have no option but to declare that there is as yet no binding contract. In *May & Butcher Ltd v R* [1934] 2 KB 17n, HL, an agreement to buy war surplus tentage from the Crown at prices to be agreed upon from time to time between the parties was held not to be a concluded contract. This case may be contrasted with *Hillas & Co Ltd v Arcos Ltd* (1932) 147 LT 503, HL, where the parties had already been in a contractual relationship for the supply of timber in the year 1930, and the buyers sought to exercise an option under that contract to purchase further timber in 1931. The sellers argued that this second contract was not binding because various of its terms were not fully spelt out, but the House of Lords, distinguishing *May & Butcher*, held that the uncertainty could be resolved by reference to the previous course of dealing between the parties.

It may be noted in passing that the Supply of Goods and Services Act 1982, s 15 similarly provides for a reasonable price to be paid in a contract for the supply of a service, where no price has been otherwise fixed.

Section 9 of the Sale of Goods Act deals with the special case where the price is left to be fixed by a valuation made by a third party. Here the contract will not be binding if the third party cannot or does not make the valuation (unless he is prevented from doing so by the fault of one of the parties: s 9(2)); but if the goods have been delivered to the buyer and 'appropriated' by him, he must pay a reasonable price for them (s 9(1)). ('Appropriated' here may be taken as meaning 'dealt with in some way as if he were their owner': elsewhere in the Act, it is used in a rather more technical sense: see below, p 284.)

CHAPTER 8

Passing of the property in the goods as between seller and buyer

1 Significance of the passing of property

The concept of 'the property' in the goods dominates much of the thinking in English sale of goods law – so much so that Professor Goode calls our preoccupation with the concept 'excessive, not to say obsessional' (*Commercial Law*, p 154). We saw when discussing s 2(4)–(5) that the Act makes a distinction between a *sale*, where the property is transferred to the buyer under the contract of sale itself, and an *agreement to sell*, when the property is to be transferred some time after the making of the contract. In this chapter, we examine this concept of the passing of the property – the event upon which the seller ceases to be, and the buyer becomes, the owner of the goods. This event has significance for many purposes in law, the most important of which are listed below. It should be noted, however, that not all of these are fixed rules of law: some of them may be varied by agreement between the parties, and others state only a provisional or presumptive rule which may in particular situations have to give way to another which in the circumstances has an overriding effect. Subject to these qualifications, which are discussed in more detail below, we may list the following points of distinction:

Where the contract is an *agreement to sell*, and the property remains with the seller:

(1) The contract is still executory.
(2) The buyer has only rights *in personam* against the seller: the seller can exercise proprietary rights in relation to the goods (eg sue a third party in tort if the goods are wrongly detained, stolen or damaged), but the buyer cannot: see *The Aliakmon*, below.
(3) The buyer's remedy against the seller, if he is in breach of contract, is for damages for non-delivery (s 51) (except in the rare case where specific peformance is available (s 52: see below, p 439)).
(4) The seller's remedy against the buyer, if he is in breach, is for damages for non-acceptance (s 50); the seller continues to be responsible for the goods (storage charges, disposing of them if perishable, etc).
(5) A seller who has retained the property can in principle sell the goods to a different buyer and give this second buyer a good title, whereas a buyer who has not got title cannot do more than *agree to sell* them to a third party.

(6) The risk of loss is on the seller (s 20).

(7) The contract may be frustrated if the goods perish (s 7).

(8) If the goods are requisitioned, taken as prize, etc, the loss is borne by the seller, and any compensation is payable to the seller.

(9) In the event of the seller's insolvency, the buyer has no right to the goods, but only the right to prove in the insolvency for the return of any part of the price which he has paid, and for damages in respect of any loss that he has suffered: *Re Wait* (above, p 210).

(10) In the event of the buyer's insolvency, the seller can claim back the goods even though they have been delivered to the buyer: the *Romalpa* case (below, p 408).

(11) Any profits or increase (eg young born to livestock) belong to the seller.

Where the contract is a *sale*, and the property has passed to the buyer:

(1) The contract is executed, ie there is a conveyance as well as a contract.

(2) The buyer has rights *in rem* (proprietary rights) in relation to the goods (eg the right to sue a third party in tort if the goods are wrongly detained, stolen or damaged).

(3) The buyer's remedies against the seller, if he is in breach, are not only for damages for non-delivery (s 51), but also lie in tort.

(4) The seller's remedies against the buyer, if he is in breach, are not only for damages for non-acceptance (s 50), but also for the contract price (s 49(1)); the buyer is left with all responsibility for the goods.

(5) A seller who has parted with title cannot in principle sell the goods to a second buyer, while a buyer to whom the property in goods has passed can sell them on to a third party and give that person a good title.

(6) The risk of loss is on the buyer (s 20).

(7) The contract is not frustrated if the goods perish.

(8) If the goods are requisitioned, taken as prize, etc, the loss is borne by the buyer, and any compensation is payable to the buyer.

(9) In the event of the seller's insolvency, the buyer may claim the goods: *Aldridge v Johnson* (above, p 224).

(10) In the event of the buyer's insolvency, the seller cannot claim back any goods which have been delivered to the buyer, but can only prove in the insolvency for so much of the price as is outstanding, and also for any loss that he has suffered.

(11) Any profits or increase (eg young born to livestock) belong to the buyer.

The distinction between a sale and an agreement to sell may also affect criminal liability – eg if the property has already passed to the buyer he cannot be guilty of theft of the goods (*Edwards v Ddin* [1976] 1 WLR 942).

Leigh v Sillavan Ltd v Aliakmon Shipping Co Ltd, *The Aliakmon* [1986] AC 785, House of Lords

Leigh & Sillavan Ltd agreed to buy a quantity of steel coils from Kinsho-Mataishi Corpn, to be shipped from Korea to Immingham, Humberside. The contract was on C & F terms (see below, p 461), which meant that at the relevant time the goods were at the buyers' risk; but the property had not passed to them because this was not to take place until payment of the price. The steel was damaged whilst being stowed on the defendants' vessel, the *Aliakmon*, allegedly due to negligence for which the defendants were responsible. The House of Lords held that since the goods were not the buyers' property at the time when the damage was caused, their only claim was for economic loss, in respect of which the defendants owed them no duty of care.

Lord Brandon of Oakbrook: My Lords, this appeal arises in an action in the Commercial Court in which the appellants, who were the c and f buyers of goods carried in the respondents' ship, the *Aliakmon*, claim damages against the latter for damage done to such goods at a time when the risk, but not yet the legal property in them, had passed to the appellants. The main question to be determined is whether, in the circumstances just stated, the respondents owed a duty of care in tort to the appellants in respect of the carriage of such goods. . . .

My Lords, there is a long line of authority for a principle of law that, in order to enable a person to claim in negligence for loss caused to him by reason of loss of or damage to property, he must have had either the legal ownership of or a possessory title to the property concerned at the time when the loss or damage occurred, and it is not enough for him to have only had contractual rights in relation to such property which have been adversely affected by the loss of or damage to it.

[His Lordship examined the authorities, and continued:]

None of these cases concerns a claim by cif or c and f buyers of goods to recover from the owners of the ship in which the goods are carried loss suffered by reason of want of care in the carriage of the goods resulting in their being lost or damaged at a time when the risk in the goods, but not yet the legal property in them, has passed to such buyers. The question whether such a claim would lie, however, came up for decision in *Margarine Union GmbH v Cambay Prince SS Co Ltd (The Wear Breeze)* [1969] 1 QB 219. In that case cif buyers had accepted four delivery orders in respect of as yet undivided portions of a cargo of copra in bulk shipped under two bills of lading. It was common ground that, by doing so, they did not acquire either the legal property in, nor a possessory title to, the portions of copra concerned: they only acquired the legal property later when four portions each of 500 tons were separated from the bulk on or shortly after discharge in Hamburg. The copra having been damaged by want of care by the shipowners' servants or agents in not properly fumigating the holds of the carrying ship before loading, the question arose whether the buyers were entitled to recover from the shipowners in tort for negligence the loss which they had suffered by reason of the copra having been so damaged. Roskill J held that they were not, founding his decision largely on the principle of law established by the line of authority to which I have referred.

[His Lordship then considered and rejected a number of grounds on which it was contended that *The Wear Breeze* had been wrongly decided. He concluded that the plaintiffs had no cause of action in tort.]

[Lords Keith of Kinkel, Brightman, Griffiths and Ackner concurred.]

As has already been emphasised, some of the differences between a sale and an agreement to sell which have been listed above depend upon rules that are only of *prima facie* application. For instance, s 20, which declares that risk passes with the property in the goods, applies only 'unless otherwise agreed'. Many of the other propositions are qualified by further provisions of the Act – for example, although s 49(2) gives the seller a right to sue for the price once the property has passed, s 28 adds the further condition that, unless otherwise agreed, the seller must also be ready and willing to deliver the goods in exchange for the price: this means that normally no action for the price will lie unless *both* property and possession have passed to the buyer. And it is true that both a seller who has retained possession of the goods can in some circumstances confer a good title on a second buyer even though the property may have passed to the first buyer (s 24), and a buyer who has been given possession has a corresponding power to give a good title to a sub-buyer and so defeat the original seller's title (s 25(1)). For reasons such as this, Professor Lawson (1949) 65 LQR 362 and Professor Atiyah (*Sale of Goods*, Ch 17, but more particularly in earlier editions of his book) have argued that the significance of the concept of property is less than has traditionally been thought: the exceptions and qualifications to the 'rules' listed above are so great as virtually to eat up the rules themselves, so that 'property' should be seen as playing only a marginal, rather than a central, role on our law of sale. In the United States, the law of sale (as contained in the Uniform Commercial Code) has been drafted without using the concept of 'property' at all. This is, of course, perfectly possible, just as it would be possible to draw up the rules for the game of football without using the word 'offside'; but it does have two consequences: first, each of the 'rules' set out above (as to risk, liability to pay the price, etc) has to be separately stated, and stated in more individual and detailed terms because it is not possible to use the word 'property' as a conceptual short-cut; and secondly, there is no convenient 'peg' on which to hang any new rule to cover a situation that the draftsman may not have thought of. (By way of example, the Act contains no rule about goods taken as prize in wartime; but the court was able to use the established concept of 'property' to resolve the issues which arose when the question did come up: see *The Odessa* [1916] 1 AC 145, PC. An American court would have had to resort to more elaborate reasoning.)

The importance of the concept of 'the property' is highlighted when we look at a further question. As a matter of rock-bottom theory, it is the property in the goods which the buyer bargains for when he enters into a contract for the sale of goods – not their possession or use or any of the other aspects of ownership. This is so not simply because that is what the definition in s 2(1) says, but because it is well established by the cases that if the buyer does *not* get the ownership that he has bargained for, he can recover the whole of the price that he has paid, as money paid on a total failure of consideration, despite the fact that he may have had the possession and use of the goods for a considerable time before this fact is discovered: see *Rowland v Divall* (below, p 344). If the buyer in such a case chose instead to frame his claim in damages, he would of course receive a smaller sum, reflecting what he had lost in practical, rather than conceptual, terms.

2 Relationship of property to risk

The Act in various sections speaks of 'the risk' passing to the buyer, but the term 'risk' is nowhere defined. We may ask: Risk of what? The parties to a contract of sale face many risks: the risk that the market value of the goods in question may go up or down, the risk that perishable goods may deteriorate, and so on. However, we may glean from the decided cases that 'the risk' that the Act is concerned with is the risk that the goods will be wholly or partly destroyed or damaged, for instance by fire or flood or the sinking of the ship on which they are being carried, or lost by theft. It is also clear that we are concerned only with events that are not attributable to the act or fault of either of the parties, or which are dealt with expressly by the terms of the contract (eg by a 'force majeure' clause).

' "Risk" in the Law of Sale' by L S Sealy [1972B] CLJ 225, pp 226–227

. . . The truth is that risk is a derivative, and essentially negative, concept – an elliptical way of saying that either or both of the primary obligations of one party shall be enforceable, and that those of the other party shall be deemed to have been discharged, even though the normally prerequisite conditions have not been satisfied. That is to say, the legal consequences attaching to 'the risk' fall to be defined purely in terms of the parties' other duties and the corresponding rights and remedies: the seller's right to claim the price, and the buyer's right to resist payment or to demand its return; and the right to claim damages (eg, for non-delivery or non-acceptance) or to resist such a claim.

Head v Tattersall may be seen as an illustration of the doctrine of risk, although the word 'risk' does not appear in any of the judgments.

Head v Tattersall (1871) LR 7 Exch 7, Court of Exchequer

Head bought from Tattersall, an auctioneer, a horse described in the catalogue as having been hunted with the Bicester and Duke of Grafton's hounds. This information was incorrect. The sale contract contained a condition that 'horses not answering the description must be returned before 5 o'clock on the Wednesday evening next; otherwise the purchaser shall be obliged to keep the lot with all faults'. Head took the horse away and during the time that it was in his custody it was accidentally injured when it took fright and ran against the splinter-bar of a carriage. He returned the horse in its damaged state before the 5 o'clock deadline, on the ground that it did not correspond with its description. It was held that he was entitled to do so, and to have the whole of his money back.

Cleasby B: The effect of the contract is to give the buyer an option of returning the horse in a particular event and within a specified time; and although it is clear that he might by his conduct have disentitled himself to exercise his option, he has not, in my judgment, done anything so to disentitle himself in the present case. By taking the horse away he did no more than, under his contract, he had a right to do. . . . This being so, the second question remains, whether the right given by the contract was limited, so as only to confer a right to return the horse, provided it remained in the same condition as it was in when sold. It is a sufficient answer to say, that as a time for returning the horse was expressly fixed by the contract, an accident occurring within the time from a cause beyond the plaintiff's control ought not to deprive him of his right, provided he can return the horse in some shape or other. . . . Moreover, the matter may be put thus: – As a general rule, damage from the depreciation of a chattel ought to fall on the person who is the owner of it. Now here the effect of the contract was to vest the property in the buyer subject to a right of rescission in a particular event when it would revest in the seller. I think in such a case that the person who is eventually entitled to the property in the chattel ought to bear any loss arising from any depreciation in its value caused by an accident for which nobody is in fault. Here the defendant is the person in whom the property is revested, and he must therefore bear the loss. The cases cited seem to me to be beside the present question, for here there was an express condition in the contract itself giving to the purchaser an absolute right, under certain circumstances, to return the horse. I think, therefore, the plaintiff is entitled to recover.

[Kelly CB and Bramwell B delivered concurring judgments.]

The prima facie rule relating to risk is contained in s 20(1): unless otherwise agreed, the goods remain at the seller's risk until the property is transferred to the buyer, but from and after the transfer of the property they are at the buyer's risk, whether delivery has been made to him or not. This is, however, only the prima facie rule; and in fact *Head v Tattersall* is a case where such an agreement must, by inference, have been found to exist, for the injury occurred at a time when the property had passed to the buyer and was (at least provisionally) vested in him. *The Aliakmon* (above, p 240) is another example of the parties 'agreeing otherwise'.

There, the sale was on 'C & F' terms, which meant under the conventions of international sales law that the goods were at the buyers' risk 'as from shipment' (see below, p 461). However, it was also a term of the contract that the property was not to pass until the price had been paid. So the risk of damage was carried by the buyers even during the time when the goods remained the sellers' property.

Subsections (2) and (3) of s 20 list two further exceptions to the prima facie rule laid down by s 20(1): fault of either party, and liability as a bailee. *Demby Hamilton & Co Ltd v Barden* and *Wiehe v Dennis Bros* respectively provide illustrations of these two exceptions.

Demby Hamilton & Co Ltd v Barden [1949] 1 All ER 435, King's Bench Division

In November 1945 Barden, a wine merchant, agreed to buy from Demby Hamilton 30 tons of apple juice, to be collected at the rate of one truckload per week by third parties to whom the juice had been sub-sold. The sellers crushed apples sufficient to fulfil this contract (the last apples they had for that season) and put the juice into barrels. If the juice had been collected punctually in accordance with the contract, deliveries would have finished in February 1946, but only two truckloads were collected after 11 December 1945, and eventually, on 7 November 1946, the sellers informed the buyer that the remaining juice had become putrid and had been thrown away. It was held that the loss lay on the buyer, because the delay in taking delivery was due to his fault.

Sellers J: I am not going so far in this case as to say that I place the onus on the buyer to show that the loss did not occur or might not have occurred. I think that all the facts and circumstances have to be looked at in very much the same way as a jury would look at them in order to see whether the loss can properly be attributed to the failure of the buyer to take delivery of the goods at the proper time. That, I think, is essentially a matter for the jury – a question of fact – having regard to all the circumstances. The first requirement of the proviso in question is that delivery has been delayed through the fault of the buyer. I am satisfied on the facts in the present case that a good delivery, which would have avoided all loss, was delayed through the fault of the buyer, and that of the third parties. The next requirement of the proviso is that, where delivery has been delayed through the fault of the buyer, the goods are at the risk of the party in fault 'as regards any loss which might not have occurred but for such fault.' The goods referred to there must be the contractual goods which have been assembled by the seller for the purpose of fulfilling his contract and making delivery. The goods may have been defined goods, goods manufactured for the purpose of delivery, or goods which had been acquired by the seller from somebody else for the purpose of fulfilling his contract. It does not seem to me that the Act requires to be construed in any narrow sense. The real question is whether the loss which has accrued was brought about by the delay in delivery, and that must have regard to the goods which were there to be delivered. Different circumstances may arise in different cases. It may be that the seller was in a position to sell the goods elsewhere and acquire other goods for the postponed time of delivery, and if he does not do that and there is some loss in the meantime the responsibility for the loss would be held to fall upon him. Again, there may be cases (and I think this is one of them) where the seller has his goods ready for delivery and has to keep them ready for delivery as and when the buyer proposes to take them. In the present case the position is clear. The casks of apple juice which were not accepted were manufactured at the time of the contract, and the contract required that delivery should be in accordance with sample. It would have been very difficult to have obtained goods which complied with the sample unless the apples had all been crushed at the same time. They would have had to be apples from the same district and the juice from them, when obtained, would have had to be of the same maturity. The condition of apples changes. They may be unripe at one time and too ripe at another. The 30 tons of juice were goods which the sellers rightly and reasonably kept for the fulfilment of their contract. These were the last apples which the sellers had that season for crushing, and, therefore, the goods in question were goods which the sellers had awaiting delivery in fulfilment of their contract with the buyer.

I have to ask myself whether this loss might not have occurred but for the fault of the buyer. I am satisfied that it would not have occurred but for his fault. There is, of course, an obligation on a seller to act reasonably, and, if possible, to avoid any loss. As to that, one or two questions arise for consideration. Was there anything the sellers could reasonably do to dispose of these goods when they still had an outstanding obligation to keep them at the disposal of the buyer and when they had to be ready and willing to deliver them when requested? If delivery had been asked for at a later date and they had let these goods go elsewhere they could not have fulfilled their contract. I do not hesitate to find (although to construe this proviso is not easy) that in a practical and business sense this loss has fallen on the sellers by reason of the fact that the buyer refused to take delivery at the proper time and postponed the date of delivery until the goods had deteriorated, and I come to the conclusion that the liability for that loss falls on the buyer. . . .

Wiehe v Dennis Bros (1913) 29 TLR 250, King's Bench Division

Wiehe in London contracted to buy a Shetland pony called 'Tiny' from Dennis Bros, intended to be presented along with a car and harness to Princess Juliana, daughter of the Queen of the Netherlands. The pony and car were to be delivered in Rotterdam in a month's time. While the pony was in the sellers' custody, a charitable ball was held at Olympia, in the course of which an unauthorised person took the pony out of its stall and led it among the dancers; but it was mishandled and suffered injuries. The sellers were held liable on the basis that they had failed to show that they had taken proper care of it as bailees pending delivery.

Scrutton J: In his Lordship's view one cause of action against the defendants was that they were the bailees of the pony and that the pony was injured without their being able to give any explanation how such injuries were caused. The case therefore fell within *Bullen v Swan Electric Engraving Co* ((1906) 22 TLR 275), where Mr Justice Walton said that there was in the case of a gratuitous bailee an obligation to use such care as a reasonably prudent owner would take of his own property, and also that in an action such as the present it was not sufficient for the defendants, in order to escape liability, merely to prove that the goods were not in their possession because they had been lost, but that they must prove much more than that in order to escape liability.

In this case the defendants did not satisfy the jury as to how the injuries were caused, and they had not satisfied his Lordship that they had used reasonable care. Therefore in his Lordship's opinion the defendants were liable to pay damages for the injuries to the pony which occurred while it was in their custody and as to which no satisfactory explanation had been given as to how they happened. That relieved him from deciding a difficult question of law; namely, whether the property in the pony had passed at the time of the accident, so that it was at the risk of the plaintiff. His Lordship said that he was inclined to think that it had; that the contract was for the sale of a specific object as to which nothing had to be done in order to put it into a deliverable state except to deliver it. . . .

One further point should be made about 'risk'. It is a cardinal rule in English law that property can never pass in unascertained goods (s 16: see above, p 218 and below, p 259). But the law does not put a similar obstacle in the way when it comes to the passing of risk. The parties may, by agreement, place the risk of loss on the buyer even before the contract goods have been identified as such. Plainly, this cannot be done in the case of goods sold purely by description, so long as no steps have been taken to appropriate goods to the contract or to identify the source from which they will be appropriated. But in other circumstances it is well established that the risk of loss of goods which are unascertained in the statutory sense may be placed on the buyer. This is illustrated by *Sterns Ltd v Vickers Ltd*, a case concerning a contract to sell an unascertained part out of an identified bulk.

Sterns Ltd v Vickers Ltd [1923] 1 KB 78, Court of Appeal

The Admiralty sold to Vickers 200,000 gallons of white spirit which was being stored by the London and Thames Haven Oil Wharves Co in 'tank No 78'. Two weeks later, Vickers contracted to sell 120,000 gallons of this spirit to Sterns. Sterns resold the spirit which they had bought to Lazarus. Vickers obtained from the storage company a warrant acknowledging that 120,000 gallons of spirit were being held on Sterns' behalf, and this warrant was indorsed by Sterns to Lazarus. As Lazarus did not want to take immediate delivery of the spirit, he made his own arrangements with the company for further storage and paid them storage rent. Several months later, when Lazarus came to take the spirit, it was found to have been adulterated by being mixed with a spirit of heavier specific gravity. The Court of Appeal held that even though property in the spirit had not passed to the buyers, they had assumed the risk of loss or damage in respect of their share of the bulk spirit from the time when they accepted the storage company's warrant.

Scrutton LJ: I think Mr Thorn Drury is right in saying that as at the material time there had been no severance of the quantity purchased from the larger bulk there were no specific 120,000 gallons in which the property passed. The question as to the effect of such a sale of an undivided portion of a larger bulk has frequently arisen in the Courts, and was much discussed in the well-known case of *Inglis v Stock* ((1885) 10 App Cas 263), where a similar argument to that which was addressed to us here was addressed to the Court for the purpose of showing that a person who had bought a certain number of tons of sugar, part of a larger stock, had no insurable interest in the quantity bought, because no specific bags had been appropriated to the contract and consequently the property in them had not passed. But as Lord Blackburn there pointed out, although the purchaser did not acquire the property in any particular number of tons of sugar he did acquire an undivided interest in the larger bulk and that undivided interest the House of Lords held to be insurable. The acquisition of an undivided interest in a larger bulk clearly will not suffice to pass the property when the appropriation to the contract has to be made by the vendor himself. As Bayley B said in *Gillett v Hill* ((1834) 2 Cr & M 530): 'Where there is a bargain for a certain quantity' of goods 'ex a greater quantity, and there is a power of selection in the vendor to deliver which he thinks fit, then the right to them does not pass to the vendee until the vendor has made his selection, and trover is not maintainable before that is done.' Nor probably will the acquisition of such an undivided interest pass the property, so as to entitle the purchaser to sue for a conversion, in a case where the power of appropriation is, as here, in a third party. But in that latter case, whether the property passes or not, the transfer of the undivided interest carries with it the risk of loss from something happening to the goods, such as a deterioration in their quality, at all events after the vendor has given the purchaser a delivery order upon the party in possession of them, and that party has assented to it. The vendor of a specified quantity out of a bulk in the possession of a third party discharges his obligation to the purchaser as soon as the third party undertakes to the purchaser to deliver him that quantity out of the bulk. In the present case, what happened was that at the date of the contract there was a bulk larger than the quantity sold, and it was of the contract quality according to sample. A delivery warrant was issued by the Thames Haven Company undertaking to deliver that quantity from the bulk which at that time corresponded with the sample. That warrant was accepted by the purchaser and by their sub-purchaser, Lazarus, who proceeded to pay rent for the storage from the date of the warrant. In those circumstances I come clearly to the conclusion that as between the plaintiffs and the defendants the risk was on the plaintiffs the purchasers. The vendors had done all that they undertook to do. The purchasers had the right to go to the storage company and demand delivery, and if they had done so at the time they would have got all that the defendants had undertaken to sell them. What the purchasers here are trying to do is to put the risk after acceptance of the warrant upon persons who had then no control over the goods, for it seems plain that after the acceptance of that warrant the vendors would have had no right to go to the storage company and request them to refuse delivery to the purchaser. For these reasons, treating the matter as a question rather of the transfer of risk than of the passing of property – for strictly I do not think the property passed, but only a right to an undivided share in the bulk to be selected by a third person – I think the view taken by the judge below was erroneous. He seems to have considered the question of transferring the risk, and thought there was no evidence of it. With that view I cannot agree. I think the only conclusion to be drawn from the evidence is that the risk did pass. . . .

[Bankes LJ delivered a concurring judgment. Eve J concurred.]

QUESTIONS

1. Who carried the risk in respect of the other 80,000 gallons?
2. Suppose that when Lazarus came to collect the spirit which he had purchased, there had been no adulteration but 80,000 gallons had been stolen. How much would he be (1) entitled, (2) bound, to take?
3. If other spirit had been mixed with the 200,000 gallons so that the bulk was *improved* in quality, could he have claimed 120,000 gallons of it?

What is the effect, as between the parties, of the passing of the risk? We may summarise the position as follows:

(1) If the risk has passed, the buyer will have to pay the price even though he does not (and will not ever) get the goods, if they have been lost or destroyed; and similarly he must pay the full price even though the goods have been partly lost, or damaged. The buyer, for his part, cannot sue the seller in damages for failing to make delivery, or for delivering less than the contract quantity or damaged goods.
(2) If the risk has not passed at the time when the loss or damage happens, the seller cannot compel the buyer to pay the price, or to take delivery of any remaining goods, or of the goods in their damaged state, or sue him for damages for refusing to do so.

3 Statutory provisions relating to perishing of specific goods

Sections 6 and 7 of the Act contain provisions relating to the 'perishing' of the goods which bear some relationship to the question of risk. They may be seen respectively as particular instances of the contractual doctrines of common mistake and frustration. Each section applies only to contracts for the sale of *specific* goods.

(a) Section 6: specific goods which have perished

Where there is a contract for the sale of specific goods, and the goods without the knowledge of the seller have perished at the time when the contract is made, s 6 of the Act declares that the contract is void.

Section 6 is said by Chalmers himself (*The Sale of Goods* (1st ed, 1890), p 10) to have been based on the well-known House of Lords' decision in *Couturier v Hastie*.

Couturier v Hastie (1856) 5 HL Cas 673, House of Lords

A cargo of corn was shipped by Couturier in February 1848 for delivery in London. In May Hastie, acting for Couturier on a *del credere* commission (ie, as an agent who assumed personal liability for the buyer's obligations: see above, p 79), contracted to sell this cargo to Callander. Unknown to either Hastie or Callander, the cargo had been sold in April by the ship's captain in Tunis, en route to London, because it was overheating. Callander refused to pay for the corn, and so Couturier sued Hastie for the price. Mr Wilde, counsel for Couturier, argued:

> The purchase here was not of the cargo absolutely as a thing assumed to be in existence, but merely of the benefit of the expectation of its arrival, and of the securities against the contingency of its loss. The purchaser bought in fact the shipping documents, the rights and interests of the vendor.

In effect, his contention was that the buyer had not bought the cargo of corn, as specific goods, but had contracted to take over the benefit of the voyage, as a venture. (Compare the position of the buyer under a contract made on CIF terms, below, p 452.) However, the court held, as a matter of construction, that the subject matter of the contract was the cargo. As it had not been delivered, the seller could not sue for the price.

Lord Cranworth LC: Looking to the contract itself alone, it appears to me clearly that what the parties contemplated, those who bought and those who sold, was that there was an existing something to be sold and bought, and if sold and bought, then the benefit of insurance should go with it. I do not feel pressed by the latter argument, which has been brought forward very ably by Mr Wilde, derived from the subject of insurance. I think the full benefit of the insurance was meant to go as well to losses and damage that occurred previously to the 15th of May, as to losses and damage that occurred subsequently, always assuming that something passed by the contract of the 15th of May. If the contract of the 15th of May had been an operating contract, and there had been a valid sale of a cargo at that time existing, I think the purchaser would have had the benefit of insurance in respect of all damage previously occurring. The contract plainly imports that there was something which was to be sold at the time of the contract, and something to be purchased. No such thing existing, I think the Court of Exchequer Chamber has come to the only reasonable conclusion upon it, and consequently that there must be judgment given by your Lordships for the Defendants. . . .

QUESTION

Is *Couturier v Hastie* authority for the proposition stated in s 6?

Some commentators have found the following decision of the Australian High Court difficult to reconcile with the statutory rule laid down by s 6.

McRae v Commonwealth Disposals Commission (1950) 84 CLR 377, High Court of Australia

The Commission, an agency of the Australian government, advertised for sale 'an oil tanker lying on the Jourmand Reef, which is approximately 100 miles north of

Samarai. The vessel is said to contain oil'. McRae agreed to buy the tanker and its contents for £285. He fitted out a salvage expedition at considerable expense and went to the advertised locality, but there was no tanker there – and in fact no reef. No such tanker had ever existed. The High Court held the Commission liable for breach of a contractual promise that there was an oil tanker at the position specified.

Dixon and Fullagar JJ (in a joint judgment): . . . It was not decided in *Couturier v Hastie* ((1856) 5 HL Cas 673) that the contract in that case was void. The question whether it was void or not did not arise. If it had arisen, as in an action by the purchaser for damages, it would have turned on the ulterior question whether the contract was subject to an implied condition precedent. Whatever might then have been held on the facts of *Couturier v Hastie*, it is impossible in this case to imply any such term. The terms of the contract and the surrounding circumstances clearly exclude any such implication. The buyers relied upon, and acted upon, the assertion of the seller that there was a tanker in existence. It is not a case in which the parties can be seen to have proceeded on the basis of a common assumption of fact so as to justify the conclusion that the correctness of the assumption was intended by both parties to be a condition precedent to the creation of contractual obligations. The officers of the Commission made an assumption, but the plaintiffs did not make an assumption in the same sense. They knew nothing except what the Commission had told them. If they had been asked, they would certainly not have said: 'Of course, if there is no tanker, there is no contract.' They would have said: 'We shall have to go and take posession of the tanker. We simply accept the Commission's assurance that there is a tanker and the Commission's promise to give us that tanker.' The only proper construction of the contract is that it included a promise by the Commission that there was a tanker in the position specified. The Commission contracted that there was a tanker there. 'The sale in this case of a ship implies a contract that the subject of the transfer did exist in the character of a ship' (*Barr v Gibson* ((1838) 3 M & W 390)). If, on the other hand, the case of *Couturier v Hastie* and this case ought to be treated as cases raising a question of 'mistake', then the Commission cannot in this case rely on any mistake as avoiding the contract, because any mistake was induced by the serious fault of their own servants, who asserted the existence of a tanker recklessly and without any reasonable ground. There *was* a contract, and the Commission contracted that a tanker existed in the position specified. Since there was no such tanker, there has been a breach of contract, and the plaintiffs are entitled to damages for that breach.

Before proceeding to consider the measure of damages, one other matter should be briefly mentioned. The contract was made in Melbourne, and it would seem that its proper law is Victorian law. Section 11 of the Victorian *Goods Act* 1928 corresponds to s 6 of the English *Sale of Goods Act* [1979], and provides that 'where there is a contract for the sale of specific goods, and the goods without the knowledge of the seller have perished at the time when the contract is made the contract is void'. This has been generally supposed to represent the legislature's view of the effect of *Couturier v Hastie*. Whether it correctly represents the effect of the decision in that case or not, it seems clear that the section has no application to the facts of the present case. Here the goods never existed, and the seller ought to have known that they did not exist. . . .

[McTiernan J concurred.]

NOTE

It is possible to explain why s 6 (or rather the Australian equivalent) was not applied in *McRae's* case by reference to the literal wording of the section: the tanker had not 'perished', because no tanker had ever existed. But this is not the *ratio decidendi* of the judgment. The court found that the Commission had contracted to sell a ship and, as a term of that contract, *warranted that they had a ship to sell*. They were held liable to pay damages for breach of this term.

As pointed out by Professor Atiyah (Atiyah, p 74), the parties to a contract on facts similar to *Couturier v Hastie* or *McRae's* case are free to make any one of three bargains:

(1) Their contract might be subject to an implied condition precedent that the goods are in existence; if they are not, neither party incurs any liability.
(2) The seller might contract (warrant) that the goods do exist; if they are not, he will be liable in damages to the buyer.
(3) The buyer may agree to take the risk that the goods may have perished prior to the contract – ie, he agrees to pay for the *chance* of getting the goods.

In (1), neither party takes the risk that the goods may not exist; in (2), the seller does; in (3), the buyer does. Where this question of risk is not spelt out clearly, all are possible interpretations of the bargain which the parties have made.

QUESTIONS

1. The decision in *Hedley Byrne & Co Ltd v Heller & Partners Ltd* [1964] AC 465, HL was not even a glimmer on the horizon in 1950, when *McRae* was decided (apart from the long-sighted eyes of Lord Denning!: see *Candler v Crane, Christmas & Co Ltd* [1951] 2 KB 164, CA). If the same facts were to occur in England today, would you advise McRae to rely on *Hedley Byrne* or the Misrepresentation Act 1967, rather than on the *ratio* in that case, and would the outcome be any different?
2. In earlier editions of Cheshire and Fifoot's *Law of Contract* (though not with the same confidence in the current (12th) edition co-authored by Professor Furmston: see p 235), it was suggested that the decision in *McRae* could be better supported on the basis that, although the contract of sale itself was void under s 6, the Commission had also entered into a *collateral* contract with McRae in which they promised that the ship existed. Consider this suggestion.
3. McRae, who paid the Commission £285 for the salvage rights to a vessel and its contents worth possibly many thousands of pounds, is reported as having said: 'One often had a couple of hundred pounds on a horse on a Saturday and I might as well have a gamble on this.' Was this not a case, then, of *emptio spei*, the third of Professor Atiyah's possible contracts?

(b) Section 7: specific goods which subsequently perish

In a provision which closely parallels s 6 (above), s 7 states:

> Where there is an *agreement to sell* specific goods and subsequently the goods, without any fault on the part of the seller or buyer, perish before the risk passes to the buyer, the agreement is avoided.

Just as a contract lawyer might see s 6 as an instance of common mistake as to the existence of the subject matter (or *res extincta*), so s 7 may be seen as a specific case of the operation of the doctrine of frustration through the destruction of the subject matter of the contract.

The wording of ss 6 and 7 is similar in several places, and it is generally assumed that decisions on the meaning of any common terms are relevant for both. Among these is 'perish'.

Barrow, Lane & Ballard Ltd v Phillip Phillips & Co [1929] 1 KB 574, King's Bench Division

On 11 October 1927, Phillips contracted to sell to Ballards a specific parcel consisting of 700 bags of Chinese ground nuts in shell, held in the stores of a wharf company. Unknown to the parties, 109 of the bags had been stolen before the contract was made; and, after delivery had been made of 150 bags, all the rest were also stolen. Phillips sued Ballards for the price of all 700 bags. It was held that s 6 applied, since the *parcel* of 700 bags had perished when the 109 were stolen.

Wright J: . . . I regard this parcel as an indivisible parcel of goods within the description given by Bailhache J in the case of *Behrend & Co v Produce Brokers' Co* ([1920] 3 KB 530). In that case the parcel was a parcel of 200 tons of Egyptian cotton-seed and the learned judge there held, and I think rightly, that in commerce that was an indivisible parcel of goods. The same is certainly true, in my judgment, a fortiori of this specific parcel of 700 bags, the location of which was expressly defined in the contract. . . . It has now been ascertained and agreed that at the date of the contract on October 11, 1927, there were not 700 bags in the parcel but only 591 bags, 109 having by that time been fraudulently abstracted or irregularly delivered. In the interval between October 11 and December 6 or 7 other bags had been taken, so that on December 12, after the 150 bags had been delivered to the defendants, none were left at all.

If the whole 700 bags had remained in the wharf on October 11, 1927, the fraudulent abstraction being subsequent to that date, and the parcel intact on that date, there could be no question, I think, that the property must have passed on October 12 from the plaintiffs to the defendants. But that in fact was not so. When the contract of October 11 was made, there was not in existence any parcel such as is described in the contract. There was a parcel of 591 bags, but there was not a parcel of 700 bags.

If, on the other hand, the whole 700 bags had been stolen on October 11, 1927, without the knowledge of either party, or if it had been destroyed by fire – if for any such reason it did not exist as a parcel at all on October 11, there can be no doubt that s 6 of the Sale of Goods Act 1893, would have applied. [His Lordship read that section.] The section says that as the contract has reference to specific goods and as those goods, without the knowledge of the seller, are not in existence at the date of the contract, there is nothing on which the contract can operate and it is void. In other words, because the parties are contracting about something which, unknown to them, has no existence in fact, the intention of both of them is completely frustrated and there is no contract between them. The rule has been established for many years that, where a contract relates to specific goods which do not then exist, the case is not to be treated as one in which the seller warrants the existence of those specific goods, but as one in which there has been a failure of consideration and mistake.

This case raises a further problem, which, so far as I know, and so far as learned counsel have been able to ascertain, has never hitherto come before the Court. The problem is this: Where there is a contract for the sale of specific goods, such as the parcel of goods in this case, and some, but not all, of the goods have then ceased to exist for all purposes relevant to the contract because they have been stolen and taken away and cannot be followed or discovered anywhere, what then is the position? Does the case come within s 6 of the Sale of Goods Act, so that it would be the same as if the whole parcel had ceased to exist? In my judgment it does. The contract here was for a parcel of 700 bags, and at the time when it was made there were only 591 bags. A contract for a parcel of 700 bags is something different from a contract for 591 bags, and the position appears to me to be in no way different from what it would have been if the whole 700 bags had ceased to exist. The result is that the parties were contracting about something which, at the date of the contract, without the knowledge or fault of either party, did not exist. To compel the buyer in those circumstances to take 591 bags would be to compel him to take something which he had not contracted to take, and would in my judgment be unjust. . . .

A question of some difficulty arises when the goods are not lost or destroyed, but simply deteriorate in quality. Normally, this question will be determined by considering one or other of the following questions (or perhaps both: see s 33): (1) whether the seller has given any warranty as to the condition which the goods will be in at the material time (see, eg *Mash & Murrell Ltd v J I Emanuel Ltd* (below, p 363)), and (2) which party has the risk. But if the goods have deteriorated beyond the point where they cease to conform to their contract description, or are no longer of any commercial use, there is a case for saying that they have 'perished'. Although this is not borne out by one of the few cases on the point, *Horn v Minister of Food* [1948] 2 All ER 1036 (where potatoes which had rotted to a degree which made them useless even to be fed to cattle were held, *obiter*, not to have perished), most writers agree that the ruling was wrong. In other contexts, where the question in issue has been essentially the same, there are authoritative decisions the other way. For instance, in *Asfar & Co v Blundell* [1896] 1 QB 123, CA a consignment of dates aboard a ship sank in the Thames and was contaminated by sea water and sewage. When salvaged, they were unfit for human consumption (but, surprisingly, still worth a considerable sum for distillation into spirit!). For insurance purposes, however, the cargo was held to be a 'constructive total loss' – surely equivalent to a finding that they had 'perished' had s 6 or s 7 been in issue.

(c) 'Perishing' of unascertained goods

Both s 6 and s 7, as has been noted, apply only to specific goods. This raises the question whether unascertained goods can ever be said to have perished, and if so what the consequences are in law. It is best to consider the various categories of unascertained goods in sequence.

Generic goods. Goods of this kind which are sold purely by description (the typical 'commodity sale', such as '100 tons of King Edward potatoes') are subject to a firm rule, which in principle admits of no exceptions. Such contracts are made on the understanding that the seller undertakes the entire responsibility of ensuring that potatoes answering the contract description will be available for delivery to the buyer on the agreed date, and that he accepts all risks incidental to seeing that they are supplied. The whole point of contracts to buy goods for forward delivery is to hedge the buyer's position against adverse movements in the market, including the risk that supplies may run out. As the extract from the *Intertradex* case (below) shows, this is part of the 'warp and woof' of commerce. The leading case is *Blackburn Bobbin Co Ltd v T W Allen & Sons Ltd*.

Blackburn Bobbin Co Ltd v T W Allen & Sons Ltd [1918] 2 KB 467, Court of Appeal

Allens contracted to sell the Blackburn company 70 standards of Finland birch timber [a standard is 165 cubic feet], to be delivered on rail at Hull (where Allens were based) over the period from June to November 1914. Because there had been no sailings from Finnish ports, no deliveries at all had been made when war broke out in August of that year, and thereafter it became impossible to obtain Finnish timber either directly from Finland or from any other source. It was normal practice for merchants to import all Finnish timber direct from Finland to meet their customers' orders, and stockpiles were not held in England. The Court of Appeal, affirming McCardie J, held that Allens were not excused from their contractual obligations.

Pickford LJ: The defendants contend that the contract was at an end because it was in the contemplation of both parties that the defendants should be able to supply the timber according to the ordinary method of supplying it in the trade, and that when that became impossible both parties were discharged from their obligations. . . .

[His Lordship discussed a number of cases dealing with the doctrine of frustration, and continued:]

In my opinion McCardie J was right in saying that the principle of these cases did not apply to discharge the defendants in this case. He has found that the plaintiffs were unaware at the time of the contract of the circumstance that the timber from Finland was shipped direct from a Finnish port to Hull, and that they did not know whether the transport was or was not partly by rail across Scandinavia, nor did they know that timber merchants in this country did not hold stocks of Finnish birch. I accept the finding that in fact the method of dispatching this timber was not known to the plaintiffs. But there remains the question, Must they be deemed to have contracted on the basis of the continuance of that method although they did not in fact know of it? I see no reason for saying so. Why should a purchaser of goods, not specific goods, be deemed to concern himself with the way in which the seller is going to fulfil his contract by providing the goods he has agreed to sell? The sellers in this case agreed to deliver the timber free on rail at Hull, and it was no concern of the buyers as to how the sellers intended to get the timber there. I can see no reason for saying – and to free the defendants from liability this would have to be said – that the continuance of the normal mode of shipping the timber from Finland was a matter which both parties contemplated as necessary for the fulfilment of the contract. To dissolve the contract the matter relied on must be something which both parties had in their minds when they entered into the contract, such for instance as the existence of the music-hall in *Taylor v Caldwell* ((1863) 3 B & S 826), or the continuance of the vessel in readiness to perform the contract, as in *Jackson v Union Marine Insurance Co* ((1874) LR 10 CP 125). Here there is nothing to show that the plaintiffs contemplated, and there is no reason why they should be deemed to have contemplated, that the sellers should continue to have the ordinary facilities for dispatching the timber from Finland. As I have said, that was a matter which to the plaintiffs was wholly immaterial. It was not a matter forming the basis of the contract they entered into. . . .

For the reasons I have given the defendants have failed on the facts to make out their case that the contract was dissolved. The appeal will be dismissed.

[Bankes and Warrington LJJ delivered concurring judgments.]

Intertradex SA v Lesieur-Tourteaux SARL [1977] 2 Lloyd's Rep 146, [1978] 2 Lloyd's Rep 509, Queen's Bench Division and Court of Appeal

Intertradex contracted to sell to Lesieur-Tourteaux 800 tonnes of Mali groundnut expellers, CIF Rouen. (On CIF contracts, see below, p 452.) The sellers intended to fulfil their obligations from a consignment of 1000 tonnes which they in turn had contracted to buy from suppliers, 'SEPOM', who (as they, but not the buyers, knew) were the sole crushers and producers of Mali groundnut expellers. The suppliers' factory at Koulikoro was ten days by rail from Abidjan, and four days from Dakar, the only export ports. The suppliers were unable to meet their commitments due to a mechanical breakdown at their factory (for which a replacement part had to be obtained from Germany) and interruptions in the supply by rail of raw materials to their factory. The sellers claimed that they were excused from performance – a view which was upheld by a board of arbitration to which the dispute was referred. Donaldson J, in a judgment affirmed by the Court of Appeal, held that they were not excused.

Donaldson J: That this situation was aggravating or frustrating both for SEPOM and the sellers is not in doubt, but the legal doctrine of frustration is not based upon psychology or emotion. . . .

The sellers' basic obligation was to deliver the goods (or documents covering the goods) in accordance with their contract. The basic risks which they assumed were those of shortage of supply and a rise in price. It was for the assumption of these risks that they would have agreed a price which, hopefully, would have produced a profit. They have qualified this obligation by reference in cll 21 and 22 to a very wide variety of events which might place obstacles in their way. Ingenuity may suggest some concatination of events to which these clauses do not apply, but which are of so outlandish a nature that the obligation to deliver cannot have been intended to survive in the changed circumstances. But a mere reduction in the supplies available, even from a sole supplier, due to such commonplace events as a breakdown of machinery or the inadequacies of a railway are far removed from this category. They are the warp and woof of industrial and commercial aggravation. Giving the fullest effect to the board's findings of fact and paying the fullest respect to their view of the commercial realities, in my judgment there are no possible grounds for holding the contract between the buyers and sellers to have been frustrated.

Of course, the parties are free to make a contract for the sale of commodities of this kind on other terms; and indeed it is customary in most international sales contracts to incorporate 'force majeure' clauses designed to protect the seller against liability in such events as a failure of supply or a breakdown of transport. In fact, in *Intertradex* itself, there was such a clause, but it was held on the facts that the sellers were not able to rely on it.

In *Re Badische Co Ltd* [1921] 2 Ch 331 Russell J *implied* into a contract, made in England between two English companies, for the supply of dyestuffs (which it was known would come from a German source) a term to the effect that supplies from Germany should not be interrupted by the outbreak of war; and he held the sellers excused when this condition could no longer be met. This reasoning, it is submitted, cannot be supported in the light of the strong line of authority to the contrary exemplified by the cases above – a principle summed up in the Latin maxim *genus nunquam perit* ('generic goods can never perish').

It is also possible for the parties to make their contract on altogether different terms, so that it is not a contract of sale at all, but one in which the 'seller' does not commit himself to procure the goods. This was the construction put upon the contract in *Monkland v Jack Barclay Ltd* [1951] 2 KB 252. At that time, new Bentley cars were in short supply and there was a waiting list of over a year. Monkland ordered a Bentley Mark VI from Barclays, but when the expected time for delivery came they refused to let him have one because he was unwilling to comply with a stipulation demanded by the manufacturers that he would not resell the car in the first six months after purchase. The court held that Barclays were under no liability to Monkland because by the terms of their contract they had agreed only to *use their best endeavours* to procure a car for him (an obligation which they had performed), rather than to *sell* him one.

Goods to be manufactured or acquired by the seller. On principle, the same approach should normally govern contracts for the sale of goods which are to be manufactured or otherwise acquired (eg fish to be caught) by the seller. If a tailor agrees to make a suit for a customer or a shipbuilder to build a boat, and the suit or boat is destroyed in a fire when it is 90 per cent finished, the seller has no choice but to obtain a new supply of materials and begin work all over again. And the same would be true if the seller's boatload of fish was swept overboard in a storm on its way back to port. However, the parties may again agree to the contrary, and of course this will be the only possible construction where there is something about the contract which makes the seller's obligation conditional upon the continued availability of the materials which have been lost – for instance, where it has been agreed that a suit shall be made from a specific piece of cloth which is later destroyed.

Goods which are to be appropriated from a specific bulk or source. A different rule applies to this class of unascertained goods, since the contract of sale will necessarily be impossible to perform if the source from which the goods are to be appropriated fails. Where, for instance, the parties' contract is not simply one for 100 tons of King Edward potatoes, but for 100 tons of King Edward potatoes *out of the 200 tons now in the seller's store*, the contract will be frustrated if the entire 200 tons are destroyed. Similarly, if the 100 tons contracted for are to come from the crop to be harvested from a particular field, and bad weather causes the whole crop to fail. The case of *Howell v Coupland* was concerned with a slight variant of these facts.

Howell v Coupland (1876) 1 QBD 258, Court of Appeal

Coupland, a Lincolnshire farmer, in March 1872 contracted to sell to Howell 200 tons of Regent potatoes to be grown on specified land belonging to Coupland, to be delivered in the following September and October. Coupland planted potatoes on 68 acres of the land – an area sufficient in a normal season to yield over 450 tons; but the crop was struck by an unpreventable disease in August and only 80 tons were produced. Howell took delivery of the 80 tons and paid for them at the contract rate, and sued in this action for damages for Coupland's failure to deliver the balance. It was held that the failure should be excused.

Lord Coleridge CJ: I am of opinion that the judgment ought to be affirmed. . . . The true ground, as it seems to me, on which the contract should be interpreted, and which is the ground on which, I believe, the Court of Queen's Bench proceeded, is that by the simple and obvious construction of the agreement both parties understood and agreed, that there should be a condition implied that before the time for the performance of the contract the potatoes should be, or should have been, in existence, and should still be existing when the time came for the performance. They had been in existence, and had been destroyed by causes over which the defendant, the contractor, had no control, and it became impossible for him to perform his contract; and, according to the condition which the parties had understood should be in the contract, he was excused from the performance. It was not an absolute contract of delivery under all circumstances, but a contract to deliver so many potatoes, of a particular kind, grown on a specific place, if deliverable from that place. On the facts the condition did arise and the performance was excused. I am, therefore, of opinion that the judgment of the Queen's Bench should be affirmed.

[James and Mellish LJJ, Baggallay JA and Cleasby B delivered concurring judgments.]

QUESTIONS

1. Why would a potato merchant make a contract in March to buy potatoes as yet unplanted which would not be grown until September?

2. If a natural calamity such as frost or disease has struck one farmer's crop, it is likely to have affected others also. What would happen to the market price in such circumstances?

3. If Howell had not wanted the 80 tons, was he bound to take them? (See s 30(1).)

NOTE

There has never been any doubt that *Howell v Coupland* is a correct decision, but there has been some debate as to the principle on which it should be regarded as having been based in modern law. Underlying the uncertainty is the note appended by Chalmers to s 7 of the Act, from which it is plain that he considered that that section is illustrated by *Howell v Coupland* (see his *Sale of Goods* (1st ed, 1890), p 11). However, s 7 by its terms applies only to contracts for the sale of *specific* goods, and the potatoes in that case were not 'specific' within the statutory definition (as set out in s 61(1)), since no particular 200 tons were identified by the parties at the time when they made their contract – indeed, the crop had not even been planted then. Mellish LJ in his judgment did, in fact, describe the contract as an agreement to sell 'specific things'; but of course he was speaking many years before the Act was drafted and so this statement is not relevant. The suggestion sometimes made that the words 'specific goods' should be given a meaning outside the statutory definition solely for the purposes of ss 6 and 7 is hard to defend. Nor is it wholly appropriate to explain *Howell v Coupland* as a simple case of common-law frustration, for the consequence of frustration is that the entire contract is avoided, whereas the court in that case ruled that the seller should be excused only in regard to the part of the crop which had failed; and as we shall see shortly from the ruling in *H R & S Sainsbury Ltd v Street* (below), the seller is not excused from his obligation to deliver so much as he has been able to produce.

In *Re Wait* (above, p 210), Atkin LJ made the following comments ([1927] 1 Ch 606 at 631):

> An attempt was made to show that the goods were specific goods by citing the decision of *Howell v Coupland*, and arguing that as the goods were called specific there, the term in the Sale of Goods Act, despite the statutory definition, must be used in the same sense. And it was said that in any case s 7 of the Code reproduces the decision in *Howell v Coupland*, and as it uses the word 'specific,' the meaning must differ from the statutory definition. These contentions appear to me to ignore the true use of the Code, and to misinterpret *Howell v Coupland*.

> [His Lordship stated the facts of *Howell v Coupland*, and continued:]

> It was held that on the principle of *Taylor v Caldwell* ((1863) 3 B & S 826) he was relieved from further performance of the contract. Blackburn J says it is a contract for the delivery at a future time of a specific thing so far as this, that it is for the delivery of a portion of a specific thing, in other words the Court implied a condition that a particular thing, the crop, should come into existence or remain in existence. This case had no reference to 'specific or ascertained' for the purpose of passing the property or of specific performance, and I conceive that it would have startled Lord Blackburn if the whole crop had come into existence, to have it contended that 200 tons under the contract had been ascertained before they were both separated and riddled. The case of *Howell v Coupland* would now be covered either by s 5, sub-s 2, of the Code or, as is suggested by the learned authors of the last two editions of Benjamin on Sale, by common law principles retained by s 61, sub-s 2, of the Code.

Section 5(2) of the Act states that there may be a contract for the sale of goods, the acquisition of which depends upon a contingency which may or may not happen. In *Howell v Coupland*, the contingency was a condition implied by the court that the specified land would yield the amount of potatoes necessary to fulfil the contract. The use of an implied term in this way gives the court more flexibility than the doctrine of frustration would allow, for it makes it possible also to imply an understanding that if there is a shortfall the seller is bound to let the buyer have the smaller amount which has been produced. This was in fact the ruling in *H R & S Sainsbury Ltd v Street*.

H R & S Sainsbury Ltd v Street [1972] 1 WLR 834, Queen's Bench Division

(The facts appear from the judgment.)

MacKenna J: The plaintiff buyers claim damages against the defendant seller under an alleged contract for the sale of 'about 275 tons' of feed barley for delivery in August or September 1970. The defendant denies the contract. He alleges in the alternative that if he agreed to sell it was a condition precedent of his obligation to deliver that he should in 1970 harvest a crop of at least that tonnage on his farm at East Knoyle, Wiltshire, that he did not harvest such a crop but one of only 140 tons, and that his failure to harvest the larger crop excused him from the obligation to delivery any barley, even the smaller tonnage. He admittedly delivered none. The plaintiffs concede that he harvested only the smaller tonnage and further concede that they are not entitled to damages for his failure to deliver barley which he did not harvest, but assert that they are entitled to recover damages for his failure to deliver the 140 tons harvested. It is agreed that if they are entitled to recover any damages these should be computed at £7.50 per ton.

There are two questions which I must decide. (1) Did the defendant agree to sell 'about 275 tons' of feed barley to the plaintiffs? If he did, (2) was he under any obligation to deliver the 140 tons which he actually harvested? . . .

[His Lordship reviewed the evidence and concluded:]

As to the first question I find that there was a contract between the plaintiffs and the defendant for the purchase of 275 tons of feed barley (5 per cent more or less) to be grown by the defendant on his farm. . . .

As to the second, I am prepared to assume, consistently with the plaintiffs' abandonment of their claim for damages for the tonnage not in fact produced, that it was an implied condition of the contract that if the defendant, through no fault of his, failed to produce the stipulated tonnage of his growing crop, he should not be required to pay damages. It seems a very reasonable condition, considering the risks of agriculture and the fact that the crop was at the contract date still growing. But a condition that he need not deliver any if, through some misfortune, he could not deliver the whole is a very different one, and in my opinion so unreasonable that I would not imply it unless compelled to do so by authority. The way in which the parties chose the more or less conventional figure of one and a half hundredweights as the estimated yield of the crop is, I think, an additional reason in this case against the implication. If they had intended that a failure to achieve this optimistic tonnage would mean the end of the contract for both of them, they would have gone about the business of estimating yield in a much more cautious manner.

Mr Rawlins argued that it was reasonable that the defendant should be freed of all his obligations under the contract if without his fault he failed to produce the whole tonnage. 275 tons (5 per cent more or less) set an upper limit to the quantity which the plaintiffs could be compelled to take. It was reasonable, he said, that there should be a lower limit to the amount which the defendant could be compelled to deliver. In a year when the latter's yield was high, market prices would probably be low, and it would be a benefit to the plaintiffs not to be required to take more than an agreed tonnage at the contract price fixed in advance. In a year when the yield was low, as in the present case, it would be a benefit to the defendant if he were free to disregard his contract and to sell his crop to some other buyer at the higher market price. The contract should, if possible, be construed as giving him this freedom. I am not persuaded by the argument. The upper limit of 275 tons might in the circumstances of a particular case be beneficial to both parties. But even if it could be beneficial only to the buyer that is no reason for implying a term that the same figure shall serve as a lower limit to the seller's obligation to deliver, so that his failure to reach that figure, if blameless, would release him from the contract.

[The buyers were accordingly held to be entitled to damages. His Lordship said, in relation to *Howell v Coupland*:]

It is clear from the statement of the facts in the headnote that the case raised no question about the seller's obligation to deliver the potatoes which he had in fact produced, and clear from the last sentence quoted from the judgment of Blackburn J that it gives no support to the view that the bargain was off both as to the 120 tons and the 80. There is nothing in the judgments of the Court of Appeal which touches this question.

After the decision of *Howell v Coupland* the Sale of Goods Act 1893 was passed.

[His Lordship quoted ss 5(2), 6, 7 and 61(2) of the Act, and continued:]

The rule of *Howell v Coupland* is, I think, preserved by s 5(2). If I am wrong in that view, because the growing of a crop cannot be considered the 'acquisition' of goods within the meaning of that section, then it is preserved by s 61(2). I do not think that it is preserved by ss 6 or 7. These sections are, in my opinion, dealing with goods existing, and a crop not yet grown does not answer either description.

NOTE

There is one further problem, for which English law does not offer a wholly satisfactory solution. What if Coupland had made a second contract to sell 200 tons of potatoes to another merchant? What would be the rights of the respective parties? Or, to identify the issues more clearly, suppose that S has 20 boxes of champagne in his cellar and in separate contracts he agrees to sell '10 boxes of the champagne in my cellar' to B1 and the same to B2. Before any boxes have been appropriated to either contract, a thief steals 10 boxes, leaving S in the position where he can perform one or other of his contracts, but not both. Cases in other contexts suggest that in the absence of some provision in the contracts indicating that one of them should be performed first, or that each buyer should take a proportionate share of what goods are available, the seller is not excused for his failure to honour the contract that he chooses not to perform. In the language of the doctrine of frustration, this failure is 'self-induced', resulting from his own election to perform the other: see *Maritime National Fish Ltd v Ocean Trawlers Ltd* [1935] AC 524, PC and *The Super Servant Two* [1990] 1 Lloyd's Rep 1, CA (two cases on the hiring of ships). In the United States, the Uniform Commercial Code, s 2-615 offers a much fairer solution: the seller is allowed to 'prorate' his performance, ie distribute those goods which he does have available *pro rata* amongst the various buyers. (On prorating, see A H Hudson (1968) 31 MLR 535; (1978) 123 Sol Jo 137.) In England this solution is possible only if there is a clause in the contract which permits the seller to take such a way out: as is, in fact, commonly the case in international sales contracts.

4 Frustration of sale of goods contracts

In the discussion above, we have been concerned with the destruction of the subject matter of the contract – which is, of course, one of the grounds upon which a contract can be held to be frustrated at common law. Nothing in the Act prevents the doctrine of frustration from being applied to contracts for the sale of goods where any of the other recognised grounds is relied on, eg supervening illegality, or impossibility caused by such an event as the closing of the port designated by the contract for the shipping of the goods or the sinking of the named ship in which they are to be carried. Many leading 'frustration' cases were concerned with sales of goods: the *Fibrosa* case [1943] AC 32, HL, and the 'Suez' cases such as *Tsakiroglou & Co Ltd v Noblee Thorl GmbH* [1962] AC 93, HL. But we should remember that, as the latter case and the *Intertradex* judgment cited above show, impossibility of performance is not readily inferred in the case of ordinary commodity sales.

Returning to those situations where there has been destruction of the goods which are the subject matter of the contract, we may ask: what is the relation between the concept of 'risk', which we have been examining, and the doctrine of frustration? First, by definition, frustration deals with an *unforeseen* event – something not contemplated by the parties and not provided for by a term of the contract. The rules as to risk *are* terms of the contract, express or implied; and if the parties have agreed that one or the other of them shall carry the risk of accidental loss or damage to the goods, or if the seller has undertaken an *absolute* obligation to see that goods of the contract description will be delivered to the buyer (as in the typical contract to sell generic goods, eg *Blackburn Bobbin Co Ltd v T W Allen & Sons Ltd*, above), there is no scope for the doctrine of frustration to apply in regard to such an event. Second, we should note that there is a difference in the respective *effects* of risk and frustration: the former exposes one party to liability, whereas frustration lets both parties off their obligations. Third, it should be remembered that the Law Reform (Frustrated Contracts) Act 1943, which gives the court some discretionary powers to adjust the losses between the respective parties following a frustrating event, is expressly not made applicable to contracts for the sale of specific goods which, under s 7 or otherwise, are frustrated by reason of the fact that the goods have perished (s 2(5)(c) of the 1943 Act). This is in itself a statutory acknowledgment that there is no room for other solutions to a problem where the concept of risk applies.

5 Rules for determining when the property passes

So many issues in our sale of goods law are made to turn on the question whether the property in the goods is still vested in the seller or has passed to the buyer that it is plainly a matter of the greatest importance to identify the point in time when the property passes. The Act deals with this in ss 16–19 by a few basic rules, supplemented by a number of presumptions.

(a) The basic rules

(i) *No property can pass in unascertained goods*

Section 16 has already been referred to more than once. Where the contract is for unascertained goods, no property in the goods can be transferred to the buyer unless and until the goods have been ascertained. In *Re Wait* (above, p 210), the Court of Appeal (and in particular, Atkin LJ) with considerable emphasis made it plain that there was no room in sale of goods law even for the notion that an *equitable* title might pass or an equitable interest be created, however well established and appropriate such a doctrine might be in relation to the transfer of other types of property such as land or book-debts (*Tailby v Official Receiver* (1888) 13 App Cas 523: see below, p 755). Perhaps this is to put the point too strongly, for of course the parties to a contract of sale can create an equitable interest in goods *by express agreement* (and may even do so as a term of their sale contract, as in some of the *Romalpa* cases: see below, p 408); but *Re Wait* has eliminated any possibility that such an interest will be held to have arisen by inference or by operation of law.) *Re London Wine Co (Shippers) Ltd* [1986] PCC 121 offers a further illustration.

Re London Wine Co (Shippers) Ltd [1986] PCC 121, Chancery Division

The company had executed a debenture giving a floating charge to its bank secured over all its assets; and the bank, acting under a power conferred by the charge instrument, had appointed a receiver. Certain customers of the company claimed that they had bought wine which was in the possession of the company and that it was their property, either at law or in equity. The bank contended that, since no wine had been appropriated to answer any of the contracts in question, all the wine remained the property of the company and was therefore subject to the charge.

The company had acquired stocks of wine which were held in various warehouses, some of it in bond, some duty paid. These customers had each contracted to buy wine of a particular description from the company (eg '40 cases [of 12 bottles] Volnay Santenots 1969 Domaine Jacques Prieur') and, having paid the price in full, had received from the company a document called a 'Certificate of Title' which described the buyer as the 'sole and beneficial owner' of the wine in question. The company charged the buyer for storage and insurance until he chose to take delivery of the wine, or sold it on to someone else. But there was no procedure for identifying or segregating the wine sold to any particular customer. The court considered separately three typical cases:

(1)   those (eg that of Mr Strong) where a customer had bought the company's total stock of a particular wine at the date of the purchase;

(2)   those (eg that of Mr Button) where two or more customers had bought quantities of a particular wine which, taken together, exhausted the whole of the company's stock of that wine;

(3)   those (eg that of Mr Bailey) where the purchase did not exhaust the particular stock, but there had been an acknowledgment that the appropriate quantity of the particular wine was being held to the customer's order. In some of these cases, the customer had pledged his right to the wine as security for a loan – eg a customer called Vinum Ltd had pledged its wine to a finance company called Compass, and a similar acknowledgment had been given to the pledgee.

Oliver J held that in none of these instances had the property, or any other legal or equitable interest of a proprietary nature, passed to the buyer. The bank's security interest therefore prevailed, and the buyers were simply unsecured creditors for the return of the money which they had paid. (Where, however, in case (3), there had been an acknowledgment by the *warehousekeeper* that wine of a particular description was held to the customer's order, it was said that an action for damages based on an estoppel might lie against him, independently of the issue before the court.)

Oliver J: . . .There, then, are the three categories with which I have to deal and the question which has arisen in each case is whether the wines which have been sold belong to the purchasers and those claiming through or under them or whether on the relevant date they remained the company's property and so became subject to the charge in the debenture which then crystallised. I should perhaps say that there is no question of stocks being insufficient to fulfil all the purchase orders so that there is no competition between purchasers *inter se.*

The question is easier to pose than to answer and I am indebted to counsel for all the respondents for sustained and instructive arguments. It will, I think, be convenient to deal with these in a different order from that in which they were advanced, because there are certain arguments common to all three cases which, if accepted, would render it unnecessary to consider the special features applicable to any particular case.

As regards the case of Mr Strong and Mr Button, Mr Wright's primary submission on their behalf is that the legal title to the goods passed and that, accordingly, the matter ends there. If, however, that is wrong, he submits first that the goods became subject to a valid and effective trust before the relevant date, and, as an alternative to this, that each purchaser had, before the relevant date, a right to specific performance of his contract and that, when the floating charge crystallised, the bank took subject to that right. These two submissions apply equally to the third category and have been adopted and expanded by Mr Stamler on behalf of the respondents Vinum and Compass and since they are, therefore, common to all cases, and, if correct, are conclusive of the whole case, they can conveniently be dealt with first.

As regards the creation of a trust, this is put in this way. On the assumption that no property passed in the goods at law – and it is not argued that this could possibly be the case in the third category represented by Mr Bailey and by Mr Stamler's clients – there was, it is submitted, clearly an intention that the property should pass so far as the company had it in its power to make it do so. One has only to look at the terms of its circulars with their references to '*your* wines,' to the purchaser being 'the beneficial owner' and to the company having a lien. This is reinforced when one looks at the terms of the letters of confirmation which list the quantities and types of wine and confirm that the purchaser is 'the sole beneficial owner of these wines,' and is indeed further reinforced in the case of Compass and Vinum when reference is made to the master agreements with Compass and the company where the company joins in to warrant title to the wine. By issuing these documents, the acknowledged purpose of which was to enable the purchasers to deal with their wines by sale or charge, the company, it is said, evinced the clearest possible intention to declare itself a trustee and once you find such an intention, it matters not that the instrument expressing it fails to do so in unequivocal terms or, indeed, that there is no instrument at all. Reliance is placed upon the recent case of *Re Kayford Ltd* ([1975] 1 WLR 279 at 282) where Megarry J said: '. . . [i]t is well settled that a trust can be created without using the words "trust" or "confidence" or the like: the question is whether in substance a sufficient intention to create a trust has been manifested.'

That, of course, is a proposition with which it is impossible to quarrel but I do not find that case, where the evidence of intention to create a trust was exceptionally clear and where the trust property was from the outset specifically set aside and identified, one which assists me very much in ascertaining whether, in the very different circumstances of the instant case, a trust has been effectively declared. Mr Wright, in his reply, put it rather differently. A trust, he said, may be constituted not merely by direct and express declaration but also by the consequences flowing from the acts of the persons themselves to which consequences the law attaches the label 'trust.' A trust, to put it another way, is the technical description of a legal situation; and where you find (i) an intention to create a beneficial interest in someone else, (ii) an acknowledgment of that intention and (iii) property in the ownership of the person making the acknowledgment which answers the description in the acknowledgment, then there is, at the date of the acknowledgment, an effective and completed trust of all the property of the acknowledger answering to that description. This is, I think, in essence the same submission as that made by Mr Stamler – he submits that where one is dealing with a homogeneous mass there is no problem about certainty. So long as the mass can be identified and there is no uncertainty about the quantitative interest of the beneficiary, the court will find no difficulty in administering the trust if it once finds the necessary intention to create an equitable interest in property of the type comprised in the mass. I think, indeed, that if the case is to be made out at all, it must be put in this way, for the submission itself is based on the premise that there are no specific or ascertained goods in which the beneficiary is interested. Were it otherwise there would be no need to invoke the concept of trust for the title would have passed under the Sale of Goods Act (as, indeed, Mr Wright submits in categories 1 and 2, it did). If trust there be, then it must be a trust of the homogeneous *whole* and the terms of the trust must be that the trustee is to hold that whole upon trust to give effect thereout to the proportionate interest of the beneficiary. Thus if we postulate the case of the company having in warehouse 1,000 cases of a particular wine and selling 100 cases to X the circumstances of this case indicate, it is submitted, that the company created an equitable tenancy in common between itself and X in the whole 1,000 cases in the proportions of 9/10ths and 1/10th.

It is with regret that I feel compelled to reject these submissions, for I feel great sympathy with those who paid for their wine and received an assurance that they had title to it. But I find it impossible to spell either out of the acknowledgments signed by the company or out of the circumstances any such trust as is now sought to be set up. Granted that the references to 'beneficial interest' are appropriate words for the creation of a trust; granted, even (although this I think is very difficult to spell out) that that was the company's intention, it seems to me that any such trust must fail on the ground of uncertainty of subject-matter. I appreciate the point taken that the subject-matter is part of a homogeneous mass so that specific identity is of as little importance as it is, for instance, in the case of money. Nevertheless, as it seems to me, to create a trust it must be possible to ascertain with certainty not only what the interest of the beneficiary is to be but to what property it is to attach.

I cannot see how, for instance, a farmer who declares himself to be a trustee of two sheep (without identifying them) can be said to have created a perfect and complete trust whatever rights he may confer by such declaration as a matter of contract. And it would seem to me to be immaterial that at the time he has a flock of sheep out of which he could satisfy the interest. Of course, he could by appropriate words, declare himself to be a trustee of a specified proportion of his whole flock and thus create an equitable tenancy in common between himself and the named beneficiary, so that a proprietary interest would arise in the beneficiary in an undivided share of all the flock and its produce. But the *mere* declaration that a given number of animals would be held upon trust could not, I should have thought, without very clear words pointing to such an intention, result in the creation of an interest in common in the proportion which that number bears to the number of the whole at the time of the declaration. And where the mass from which the numerical interest is to take effect is not itself ascertainable at the date of the declaration such a conclusion becomes impossible.

In the instant case, even if I were satisfied on the evidence that the mass was itself identifiable at the date of the various letters of confirmation I should find the very greatest difficulty in construing the assertion that 'you are the *sole* and beneficial owner of' 10 cases of such and such a wine as meaning or being intended to mean 'you are the owner of such proportion of the total stock of such and such a wine now held by me as 10 bears to the total number of cases comprised in such stock.' All other things apart, such construction would be a total negation of the assertion 'you are the *sole* owner.' But in fact, (leaving aside the first category for the moment) it is far from clear what, at the date of any individual letter of confirmation, was the composition of the mass from which the interest was to take effect. It was suggested in argument that the words 'lying in bond' on the invoice was a reference to the stocks held by the company in bond at that date and that therefore it was possible to predicate of any individual letter of confirmation that it referred to cases forming part of a then existing mass. I do not think that these words signify that, but in any event if does not seem necessarily to have been the case at all that there was an ascertainable existing mass at the time of the individual letter. For example, in the case of Mr Bailey, the exhibited correspondence shows that a quantity of wines of various descriptions was invoiced on August 16th, 1972 and described as 'lying in bond.' At the same time the company wrote to Mr Bailey's bankers undertaking that the wines on the invoice 'will not be removed from the bond without your written authority.' On September 29th, 1972 the bankers wrote to the company asking for the warehouse warrants, and on October 6th Mr Baring replied saying that the wines had 'now just arrived in the country.' The warehouse receipts were actually sent on November 10th, 1972. So that it appears that, at least in this case, the wines described as 'lying in bond' in August were not in fact in the warehouse at all at that date. . . .

I turn now, therefore, to the submissions peculiar to the individual cases. Now in the case of Mr Strong, although the goods were sold by generic description, it happened that at the material time the quantity described was in the company's possession and was the only wine of that description in its possession, although it is not claimed that it could not, without undue difficulty, obtain additional quantities from elsewhere if it required to do so. Mr Wright argues that the result of this was to ascertain the goods and that the property passed; and to make this good he has to rely either upon s 17 or upon an appropriation under s 18, r 5(1) of the Sale of Goods Act. Section 16 states quite clearly that the property is not transferred to the buyer unless and until the goods are ascertained but it is not a necessary corollary of this that the property *does* pass to the buyer when they *are* ascertained. To produce that result one either has had to find an appropriation (from which an intention to pass the property will be inferred) or one has to find an intention manifested in some other way. Mr Wright relies upon what has been referred to as an 'ascertainment by exhaustion' and has drawn my attention to the decision of Roche J in *Wait & James v Midland Bank* ((1926) 31 Com Cas 172).

[His Lordship referred to the facts of that case (below, p 266), and continued:]

The decision in that case was one of obvious common sense because in fact from November 16th onwards there were no goods from which the seller could have fulfilled the contracts except the 850 quarters. They could, no doubt, have delivered 850 quarters of Australian wheat but not 850 quarters 'ex store Avonmouth ex *Thistleros* [sic].' The instant case seems to me quite different. It is not and cannot be alleged that the sale to Mr Strong was a sale of specific goods. What the company undertook to do was to deliver so many cases and bottles of the specified type of wine 'lying in bond.' This does not in my judgment link the wine sold with any given consignment or warehouse. The fact that the company had at the date of the invoice that amount of wine and that amount only is really irrelevant to the contract. No doubt it could have fulfilled the order from this wine but it could equally have fulfilled it from any other source. It is not contended that there was any act of appropriation and Mr Wright's case is that the property passed under s 17 when the usual title letter mentioning the wine described in the invoice was sent some three months later, by which date, he says, the wine was ascertained. I cannot draw that conclusion from the material before me, for it seems to me clear that the company was, under the contract, at liberty to deliver to the purchaser any bottles of wine which tallied with the description. It never has been, therefore, to use Roche J's words, ascertained what the goods are which are covered by the contract.

The argument in relation to the second category of case is very similar. It will be remembered that in the *Wait & James* case Roche J restricts his remarks to the case of one buyer under several contracts. It is, however, submitted that where you have several buyers under several contracts, then, when you reach a stage where the totality of those contracted quantities exhausts the whole of the mass from which the individual contracts are to be fulfilled, there is no longer any property in the seller but the buyers own the mass as tenants in common. . . .

I think, with Ridley J that there are insuperable difficulties in the way of Mr Wright's argument, but even if I am wrong about that, I think that the same objection applies here as in the case of Mr Strong. Even if Mr Wright's argument is correct as a matter of law, its underlying basis must be that there is an identifiable whole which has been appropriated in some way to answer for the quantities which it is said exhaust the entire parcel. That simply does not appear to me to be the case here. I cannot construe the words 'lying in bond' as providing an identifying label for the mass from which the goods were to be selected. In my view, the company remained free to fulfil the contracts to its various purchasers from any source, as, for instance, by importing further wine of the same description. That being so, the mere fact that the company sold quantities of wine which in fact exhausted all the stocks which it held cannot, in my judgment, have had the effect of passing a proprietary interest in those stocks to the various purchasers so that they can now claim the goods collectively and ignore the bank's charge.

In the case of the third category of purchaser, represented by Mr Bailey and by Vinum Ltd and their respective pledgees, the case is put rather differently. It is not contended that any proprietary interest passed at law, but what is said is that an interest by estoppel was vested in the purchasers. . . .

In the case of Mr Bailey, the correspondence exhibited shows how, in very many cases, the company, at the instance of the pledgee from the purchaser, invited the warehouseman to issue warehouse receipts acknowledging that he held wine to the account of the pledgee. The case of Compass is even clearer, for here there was a master agreement to which the company was a party and under which it warranted the validity of the warehouse receipts and that the wine was held by it as a custodian for the pledgor.

There is no doubt that the pledgees were intended to and did alter their position on the faith of these representations by advancing money to Mr Bailey and Vinum Ltd respectively.

In these circumstances Mr Wright on behalf of Mr Bailey and Mr Stamler on behalf of Vinum Ltd and its pledgees submit that both the company and the warehouseman are estopped and that there were created in the purchasers and their pledgees proprietary interests by estoppel created before the bank's charge crystallised and so binding upon it.

None of the warehousemen is a party to these proceedings so that nothing that I say would be binding upon them in any event but in fact I cannot see how an estoppel affecting the warehousemen could affect the bank except in so far as such an estoppel created a proprietary interest in the goods in the warehouse subject to which the bank's charge takes effect. But the authorities to which I have referred above make one thing quite clear and that is that no property *actually* passes, although the estoppel operates to enable the plaintiff to prosecute an action in trover in which he can obtain damages from the warehouseman.

I can find here no estoppel which, in my judgment, can affect the bank or preclude it from asserting its real title to the assets of the company at the relevant date. . . .

Accordingly, I have felt compelled, perhaps rather reluctantly, to the conclusion that I must direct: (1) that all three categories of goods described in the schedule to the summons should be dealt with by the receiver as being the property of the company on the relevant date and so subject to the floating charge and (2) that no such goods are subject to any lien or other interest having priority to the floating charge in favour of the respondent purchasers or their respective assigns or mortgagees.

NOTE

Just as property cannot be transferred in unascertained goods, so also we may note that there cannot be a valid trust of unidentified property (*Re Wait* (above, p 210); *Re London Wine Co (Shippers) Ltd* (above)); nor can possession be effectively transferred or an attornment made in respect of unascertained goods (*Re London Wine Co*). However, we have seen that the same limitation does not apply to the passing of risk (above, p 245).

The Law Commissions have made recommendations for the reform of the law so as to meet a number of the criticisms which these inflexible rules have attracted (*Sale of Goods forming Part of a Bulk*, L Com No 215, 1993). They were prompted to do so partly because of the decision of the Commercial Court in Rotterdam in *The Gosforth*, S en S 1985 Nr 91 (noted in [1986] LMCLQ 4). Here purchasers of goods forming part of a bulk cargo, who had paid for the goods and received delivery orders, found that the goods still belonged to the seller and could be arrested by an unpaid creditor who was suing the seller. The Dutch court in giving judgment referred to s 16 of the UK Sale of Goods Act 1979, under which the ruling that the property had not passed would have been the same. After extensive consultation, the Law Commissions have made the following recommendations. It will be seen that the effect of these reforms, if enacted, would be to reverse the effect of cases such as *Re Wait*, but only where the price has been paid in advance.

Sale of Goods forming Part of a Bulk (L Com No 215, 1993)

SUMMARY OF RECOMMENDATIONS

6.1 There should be a new rule on sales of goods out of bulk which would enable property in an undivided share in the bulk to pass before ascertainment of goods relating to specific sale contracts.

6.2 The new rule should apply only to contracts for the sale of a specified quantity of unascertained goods.

6.3 (a) The new rule should apply only where the goods or some of them form part of an identified bulk.
(b) 'Identified' for this purpose should mean identified in the contract or by subsequent agreement between the parties as containing goods covered by the contract.
(c) 'Bulk' for this purpose should mean a mass or collection of goods of the same kind contained or stored in a defined space or area and such that any goods in the bulk are interchangeable with any other goods therein of the same number or quantity.

6.4 (a) The new rule should apply only where the buyer has paid for some or all of the goods covered by the contract and forming part of the bulk.
(b) Where the buyer has paid for some only of those goods, any deliveries to the buyer out of the bulk should be ascribed in the first place to the pre-paid goods.

6.5 (a) Property in an undivided share in the bulk should pass to the buyer at such time as the parties may agree, provided that the bulk has been identified and the price for at least some of the goods in the bulk has been paid.
(b) In the absence of such agreement property in an undivided share in the bulk should pass to the buyer as soon as the bulk has been identified and the price for at least some of the goods in the bulk has been paid.
(c) The parties should be free to agree that property in an undivided share is not to pass at all and that the existing rule in s 16 of the Sale of Goods Act 1979 is to apply.

6.6 The buyer's undivided share in the bulk at any time should be such a share as the quantity of goods paid for and due to the buyer out of the bulk at that time bears to the quantity of goods in the bulk at that time. This would be subject to the rule on ascertainment by exhaustion (whereby a single buyer would own the whole of the bulk if it were reduced to or below the quantity purchased) and to a rule that the aggregate of the shares of two or more buyers can never exceed the whole of the bulk. The rule on ascertainment by exhaustion should be included in the Sale of Goods Act 1979 by adding a paragraph to rule 5.

6.7 In order to facilitate normal trading where co-ownership arises under the new rules, each co-owner should be deemed to have consented to –

(a) any removal, dealing with, delivery or disposal of goods in the bulk by any other co-owner in so far as the goods fall within that co-owner's share, and
(b) delivery out of the bulk to any other co-owner of goods which are contractually due to that co-owner even if the delivery would bring about or increase a shortfall.

It should be made clear that the deemed consent protects those acting in reliance on it, including office-holders in insolvency, from legal action based on those actions.

6.8 A co-owning buyer who takes delivery of goods out of the bulk should not be liable under the new provisions to compensate any other buyer who receives short delivery.

6.9 The new provisions on passing of property in an undivided share in a bulk should not affect a buyer's contractual rights, including in particular the right to delivery of actual goods conforming to the contract in quantity and quality.

6.10 For the removal of any doubt, it should be made clear –

  (a) that 'goods' in the Sale of Goods Act 1979 includes an undivided share in goods, and
  (b) that an undivided share of specific goods is itself regarded as specific goods.

QUESTIONS

1. If the Law Commissions' recommendations had been enacted, would buyers in any of the three categories considered in *Re London Wine Co* (above) have been successful in their claims?

2. Consider the case of the two contracts to sell champagne (above, p 258), and suppose that both buyers have paid the price. What difference would the enactment of the Law Commissions' recommendations make to the position of (1) the buyers; (2) the seller?

'Ascertainment'

Goods which are unascertained – ie not 'identified and agreed on' at the time when the contract of sale is made (s 61(1)) – will become 'ascertained' by being 'identified in accordance with the agreement after the time a contract of sale is made' (per Atkin LJ in *Re Wait* [1927] 1 Ch 606 at 630). Normally this will follow from the act of one or both of the parties or someone designated by them, eg a warehouseman. Sometimes, where the contract goods are capable of prospective identification (eg 'the next calf to be born to my cow "Buttercup" '), ascertainment may happen automatically, when the goods come into existence. Also, occasionally, ascertainment may take place without the act of either party, 'by exhaustion'.

Wait & James v Midland Bank (1926) 31 Com Cas 172, King's Bench Division

Wait & James (yes, the same Mr Wait as in *Re Wait*!) owned a consignment of wheat which had arrived on the SS *Thistleross* and was placed in a warehouse of the Bristol Dock Authority at Avonmouth. They had entered into contracts to sell various quantities of this wheat to a number of buyers, including contracts respectively for 250, 750 and 250 quarters to a firm called Redlers. Redlers had taken away 400 quarters out of the total of 1250 quarters due to them, and had pledged the remaining 850 quarters (equal to 6800 bushels) to the Midland Bank. All the other buyers then took delivery of their wheat, so that exactly 850 quarters remained in the warehouse. Both Wait & James, who had not been paid, and the Bank, claimed to be entitled to this wheat. Roche J held that wheat to satisfy Redlers' contract had been 'ascertained by exhaustion', and that the bank's claim prevailed.

Roche J: It is said, on the other hand, that no property passed to the respondents, because when there purported to be a transfer to them on September 25 in the first case, or at a later date, there was no property in any ascertained goods in Messrs Redlers, the transferors, which was transferred to the bank. The answer to that, I think, is this, that Messrs Wait and

James agreed to sell the goods to Messrs Redlers Limited, and that Messrs Redlers Limited, agreed to transfer those goods to the bank. Those goods were in fact transferred to Messrs Redlers Limited, and through Messrs Redlers Limited, to the bank, as soon as they became ascertained on November 16, and then the property passed. That was some 10 or 11 days before Messrs Wait and James sought to exercise their right as unpaid vendors.

The next point which is interposed against the claim of the bank is an objection that this method of ascertainment by exhaustion, as it was usefully expressed by Mr Rayner Goddard, is not a method of ascertainment which does ascertain, but that the only effective way of ascertaining the goods which are in bulk, such as these, and which are sold by weight, is by weighing; and I agree that the most usual and most natural way is to weigh. But I am not prepared to hold that that is the only way of ascertaining the goods dealt with, and that without such weighing there could be no ascertainment. It is not a case such as may arise under s 18 of the Sale of Goods Act, where weighing is required for the purpose of ascertaining the price; there is no such requirement in this case. . . . In my judgment, the matter has been dealt with automatically by the facts, and the facts have provided the method of ascertainment in the manner I have already described through the delivery of the rest of the goods to other purchasers. I therefore hold that what remains in the warehouse has been ascertained to be the quantity of goods agreed to be sold by Messrs Wait and James to Messrs Redlers Limited, and to be the goods transferred by Messrs Redlers Limited to the Midland Bank.

It remains to consider one other argument based upon the construction of s 16 of the Sale of Goods Act. There are here three contracts, and the section provides as follows: 'Where there is a contract for the sale of unascertained goods, no property in the goods is transferred to the buyer unless and until the goods are ascertained.' The claimants contend that there has been no differentiation or ascertainment of distinct goods as being either the goods dealt with under the contract of September 25, or of the goods dealt with and comprised under the contract of October 1, or those dealt with under the contract of October 13. This objection is well founded in fact; but I think that it is altogether too narrow a construction of the section. These contracts were always in one hand. That is to say, they were all sales to Messrs Redlers, Limited, and they were all transferred to the bank, and I cannot imagine unless there were sub-divisions, that there would be any weighing taking place under any circumstances which would stop with breaks of 250, 750, or 250, and I cannot conceive that if there were not such breaks in weighing if it took place that it would be said: 'Well, you have ascertained that there are 6,800 quarters here, but you have never ascertained what is left under each particular one of these contracts.' In my judgment it is sufficient if, where there are contracts for the sale of unascertained goods to one buyer, it is ascertained what the goods are which are covered by those contracts; and I hold that that is the permissible and proper construction of s 16. In this case my judgment falls within that construction, and accordingly I think that that objection fails.

Karlshamns Oljefabriker v Eastport Navigation Corpn, The Elafi [1982] 1 All ER 208, Queen's Bench Division

Karlshamns, a Swedish firm, had agreed to buy 6000 metric tons of copra, part of a cargo (believed to be of 22,000 tons) which had been loaded on the *Elafi* in the Philippines. It was then discovered that more than 22,000 tons had been shipped, and Fehr, having agreed to buy this excess, resold it to Karlshamns. The 16,000 tons which had been sold to other buyers was offloaded at Hamburg and Rotterdam and the rest of the cargo taken to Sweden for delivery to Karlshamns. During discharge of the copra, water was let into a hold as a result of the shipowners' negligence and 825 tons were damaged. Karlshamns claimed to be entitled, as owners of the whole of what was left of the cargo, to sue the shipowners in tort. Mustill J held that the separate quantities which Karlshamns had agreed to buy could be aggregated and that, the total amount having been ascertained by exhaustion, the property had passed to them.

Mustill J: There is no doubt as to the general principles to be applied when deciding an issue of this nature. Whatever the intentions of the parties, where the contract is for the sale of unascertained goods, no property can pass until the goods are ascertained: see s 16 of the Sale of Goods Act 1893. Once ascertainment has taken place, the passing of the property depends on the intention of the parties which is to be collected from the terms of the contract, the conduct of the parties, and the circumstances of the case: see s 17. As part, but only part, of the process of drawing the necessary inference, the court must have regard to the prima facie presumption, created by s 18, r 5(1) that the parties intended the property in unascertained goods to pass when goods of the contract description in a deliverable state were unconditionally appropriated to the contract, either by the seller with the assent of the buyer or by the buyer with the assent of the seller.

It is convenient to approach the present case in stages, in the light of these general principles. First, what would have been the position if the entire cargo had been sold to the claimants under a single contract? Here, since the contract was on cif terms, it is very probable that the property would have passed to the claimants when the shipping documents were negotiated, for the cargo was ascertained and appropriated from the outset, and the general rule is that under a cif contract the property passes with the documents. The only cause for uncertainty is the fact that the claimants had a right to reject goods in excess of the stipulated quantity, so that it would not be possible to know during the voyage whether any individual portion of cargo might not ultimately revert to the vendors. I believe, however, that in such a situation the property in the entire cargo would pass conditionally to the claimants, subject to a retransfer of any excess if the claimants so elected, and that this would be sufficient to found a claim in tort in respect of all such cargo as the claimants chose to accept.

Next, there is the situation which would exist if (say) half of the cargo was sold to each of two buyers. Here, it would be clear that no property would pass until the goods had been discharged and a physical separation effected between the goods delivered under each contract, notwithstanding that the contract was on cif terms: see, for example, *Comptoir d'Achat et de Vente du Boerenbond Belge SA v Luis de Ridder Ltda, The Julia* [1949] 1 All ER 269, [1949] AC 293. The absence of any ascertainment during the voyage would mean that s 16 prevented the property from passing, whatever the parties may have intended; hence there could be no claim in tort: see *Margarine Union GmbH v Cambay Prince SS Co Ltd* [1969] 1 QB 219, [1967] 3 All ER 775.

The next step is to see what the position would have been if the whole of the cargo had been sold to the claimants under four rather than one contract of sale. There was no physical separation of the goods in the holds of the vessel, as between the various contracts. Did this prevent the property from passing before delivery? Here, there is an authority very close to the point, in the shape of *Wait & James v Midland Bank* [above].

[His Lordship discussed that case and continued:]

In the present case, counsel for the respondents did not question that there might be ascertainment of goods by exhaustion, rather than by an explicit separation of each consignment from the bulk; and I am sure that he was right to make this concession. He does, however, make two criticisms of the judgments of Roche J.

First, counsel contends that Roche J was mistaken in giving a broad interpretation of s 16. If the section is looked at in isolation, there is force in this argument. The section refers to 'a contract for the sale of unascertained goods' and says that the property shall not pass 'unless and until the goods are ascertained'. In their most natural sense the words 'the goods' would be read as referring to the goods which are the subject of the contract in question, so that one can say of them that '*these* are the goods which refer to *that* contract'. But when one comes to deal with an unusual situation, such as exists here, it is in my view legitimate to look at the reasoning which underlies the legislation. This is quite plain. The passing of property is concerned with the creation of rights in rem, which the purchaser can assert not only against the vendor but against the world at large, and which he can alienate in such a way as to create similar rights in a transferee. Where there are multiple contracts of sale in the hands of different buyers, in relation to an undivided bulk, there are only two possible solutions. First, to hold that the buyers take as joint owners in undivided shares. English law has rejected this solution. The only alternative is to hold that the property does not pass until the goods are not only physically separated but separated in a way which enables an individual buyer to say that a particular portion has become his property under his contract of sale, for until then, to adopt the words of Bayley B in *Gillett v Hill* (1834) 2 Cr & M 530 at 535, 149 ER 871 at 873, no one can say which part of the whole quantity the seller has agreed to deliver. There is, however, no need to impose this solution on a case where there are parallel contracts between the parties together comprising the whole of the bulk. Here it is known which part of the whole the seller has agreed to deliver, namely all of the parts. I am unable to envisage a situation in which it would make the least practical difference whether or not the purchaser of an entire cargo from the same seller under a series of contracts for homogeneous goods is able to identify which ton or bag of the whole relates to which contract. So far as the creation of rights in rem it does not matter; nor does it for the purposes of a claim arising from non-delivery or short delivery. If the seller delivers nothing at all, the buyer sues in respect of the whole quantity. If he delivers only part, then he can appropriate the delivery to whichever of the contracts he prefers, paying the price fixed by that contract and claiming damages in accordance with the prices under the other contracts.

In the present case, there is nothing in the award to suggest that the contracts differed even as regards price. This being so, it seems to me quite unnecessary to read s 16 so as to produce a different result in the case of four contracts comprising the entire bulk from the one which would have been reached if there had been a single contract for the whole. . . .

There is, however, another criticism which counsel for the respondents directs at the judgment of Roche J, namely that it omits any mention of s 18, r 5. Whatever may be the position, he says, as regards *ascertainment*, there was here no *appropriation* of the goods to the individual contracts before the moment of loss.

In my judgment, this objection adds nothing to the argument in relation to ascertainment. It is true that in some cases the ascertainment of goods may not be the same as the unconditional appropriation of them, although the distinction will usually be difficult if not impossible to draw. But here I cannot see any difference. On the hypothesis that all the goods were the subject of parallel contracts between the same parties, the facts which constituted the ascertainment of the goods so as to release the inhibition created by s 16 on the passing of the property must have been the same as those which constituted appropriation for the purpose of ascertaining the parties' intention as to the passing of the property for the purposes of s 18, r 5. Counsel for the respondents did not suggest how, in a case like this, it would be possible to have ascertainment without appropriation, or vice versa. This being so, it appears legitimate to place appropriation on the same broad basis as ascertainment, and hold that it is sufficient if the whole of the bulk can be identified with the contracts taken as a group.

[His Lordship held, finally, that it was immaterial that title to the two lots had passed to the buyers through different chains of sellers, and gave judgment in their favour.]

Future goods. Sections 16 and 17 make no mention of future goods; but it is made plain elsewhere in the Act that there cannot be a present sale of future goods – in other words, the parties cannot merely by the terms of their contract cause the property in such goods to pass then and there to the buyer. But such a contract is not without effect. Section 5(3) states that where the seller purports to effect a present sale of future goods, the contract operates as an agreement to sell the goods.

(ii) *Section 17: intention of the parties paramount*

Subject always to s 16 (above), the primary rule governing the passing of property is contained in s 17: the property in the goods is transferred at such time as the parties intend it to be transferred. Section 17(2) adds, not very helpfully, that for the purpose of ascertaining the intention of the parties, regard is to be had to the terms of the contract, the conduct of the parties and the circumstances of the case.

It follows that the parties are free to express an intention which is the opposite of that which would normally be inferred, and that the court will give effect to such an intention. So, for instance, in *Re Blyth Shipbuilding & Dry Docks Co Ltd* [1926] Ch 494, CA, the parties to a contract to build and deliver a ship, which was to be paid for by instalments, had agreed that on payment of the first instalment of the price the property in the vessel should pass to the buyers. The buyers thus became the owners of the uncompleted vessel, even though in an ordinary case it would plainly have been expected that no property would pass until the ship was finished. Conversely, in the well-known line of *Romalpa* cases (below, p 408), where goods are sold to a manufacturing company in the knowledge that they are to be used in a manufacturing process, the obvious assumption would be that property in the goods should pass to the buyer before they were dealt with in this way, but the courts have on a number of occasions given effect to an express provision in the contract that the seller should retain title until the price has been paid.

However, the parties' expressed intention sometimes has to be overriden by considerations of practicality or by weightier rules of law. Thus, in *Re Blyth Shipbuilding*, the court declined to give effect to a further provision in the contract that 'all materials appropriated' for building the vessel should also become the property of the buyers: this would have made them owners of all the unworked material and the surplus and scrap material that did not end up incorporated into the ship – a result which the parties could not have intended. And in some of the *Romalpa* cases (eg *Borden (UK) Ltd v Scottish Timber Products Ltd* (below, p 418), retention of title clauses have been held ineffective once the goods have lost their identity – eg, in that case, resin, once it had been used in the process of manufacturing chipboard.

Section 17 allows the court to give effect to the implied, as well as the express, intention of the parties. In *Re Anchor Line (Henderson Bros) Ltd* [1937] Ch 1, where there was a contract to sell a crane for a deferred purchase price, the court inferred an intention that the property in the crane should remain with the seller from the fact that there was an express clause placing the *risk* on the buyer. It reasoned that since this clause would have been unnecessary if the property had passed when the contract was made, the parties must have intended the opposite.

One important category of contracts where the normal rules may be held to be overridden by the implied intention of the parties is in the area of retail sales, and in particular consumer sales. We shall see shortly that the property in goods is frequently presumed to pass in law at some time earlier than that of delivery and payment – eg at the time when the contract is made (s 18, rule 1) or when goods of the contract description are 'appropriated' to the contract (rule 5). But in *RV Ward Ltd v Bignall* [1967] 1 QB 534 at 545, CA Diplock LJ said that 'in modern times, very little is needed to give rise to the inference that the property in specific goods is to pass only on delivery or payment' – an observation which, though made in a different context, is clearly appropriate to most retail and consumer sales, including both contracts for the sale of unascertained goods and contracts for specific goods.

(b) Statutory presumptions – s 18

Sections 16 and 17 are the only two *rules of law* relating to the passing of property.

But there are many cases in which s 17 will give no guidance, because the parties to a contract of sale do not normally give any thought to such abstract questions as the transfer of title (and, if they do, they are as like as not to get it wrong! – see *Dennant v Skinner and Collom* (below, p 272)); and there may well be nothing in the express terms of their contract or the surrounding circumstances to throw light on the issue. So the Act, in s 18, sets up a series of *presumptive rules* for ascertaining the intention of the parties which the court can apply. However, we must always bear in mind the opening words of s 18 itself, echoing those of s 17, 'Unless a different intention appears . . .': the 'rules' in s 18 are no more than prima facie *presumptions as to the intention of the parties* which may be rebutted by evidence to the contrary; they are not to be regarded as rules of law.

(i) *Rule 1: unconditional contracts for the sale of specific goods*

Where there is an *unconditional* contract for the sale of *specific goods* which are in *a deliverable state*, rule 1 states the the property in the goods passes to the buyer when the contract is made; and that it is immaterial whether the time of payment or the time of delivery, or both, are postponed.

This is a rule which is virtually unique to the common law systems, in contrast to the laws of other jurisdictions which usually link the passing of property with the delivery of possession.

Tarling v Baxter (1827) 6 B & C 360, Court of King's Bench

On 4 January, the parties agreed on the sale and purchase of a stack of hay, standing on land belonging to the seller's brother. Payment was to be made in a month's time, and no hay was to be cut or taken away until the price had been paid. Before the price was due, the hay was destroyed in a fire. The buyer was held bound to pay the price.

Bayley J: It is quite clear that the loss must fall upon him in whom the property was vested at the time when it was destroyed by fire. And the question is, in whom the property in this hay was vested at that time? By the note of the contract delivered to the plaintiff, the defendant agreed to sell the plaintiff a stack of hay standing in Canonbury Field at the sum of £145, the same to be paid for on the 4th day of February next, and to be allowed to stand on the premises until the first day of May next. Now this was a contract for an immediate, not a prospective sale. Then the question is, in whom did the property vest by virtue of this contract? The right of property and the right of possession are distinct from each other; the right of possession may be in one person, the right of property in another. A vendor may have a qualified right to retain the goods unless payment is duly made, and yet the property in these goods may be in the vendee. The fact in this case, that the hay was not to be paid for until a future period, and that it was not to be cut until it was paid for, makes no difference, provided it was the intention of the parties that the vendee should, by the contract, immediately acquire a right of property in the goods, and the vendor a right of property in the price. The rule of law is, that where there is an immediate sale, and nothing remains to be done by the vendor as between him and the vendee, the property in the thing sold vests in the vendee, and then all the consequences resulting from the vesting of the property follow, one of which is, that if it be destroyed, the loss falls upon the vendee. The note of the buyer imports also an immediate, perfect, absolute agreement of sale. It seems to me that the true construction of the contract is, that the parties intended an immediate sale, and if that be so, the property vested in the vendee, and the loss must fall upon him.

[Holroyd and Littledale JJ delivered concurring judgments.]

Dennant v Skinner and Collom [1948] 2 KB 164, King's Bench Division

At an auction of cars held by Dennant, a Standard car was knocked down for £345 to a man calling himself King, who also bought five other vehicles. King falsely said that he was the son of a reputable motor dealer and, in reliance on this statement, Dennant allowed him to pay with an uncleared cheque and take the Standard car away, after signing a document acknowledging that the ownership of the vehicles would not pass to him until payment had been received under the cheque. The cheque was dishonoured on presentation. The car was later sold to Collom who resold to Skinner. Dennant claimed the return of the car, as his property; but Hallett J held that property had passed to King on the fall of the hammer, and that the subsequent purported reservation of ownership by Dennant was ineffective.

Hallett J (after dealing with a point based on larceny): I come now to consider the second point on which the plaintiff relies, which I understand is this; that the property in the circumstances of this case did not pass until the price was paid by the cheque being in order or cash substituted for it. The circumstances in regard to that I have already stated, and it remains only to consider the law. In the first place, as I have said, I think that a contract of sale is concluded at an auction sale on the fall of the hammer. The Sale of Goods Act 1893, s 18, r 1, provides: 'Where there is an unconditional contract for the sale of specific goods, in a deliverable state, the property in the goods passes to the buyer when the contract is made, and it is immaterial whether the time of payment or the time of delivery, or both, be postponed.' Accordingly, upon the fall of the hammer the property of this car passed to King unless that prima facie rule is excluded from applying because of a different intention appearing or because there was some condition in the contract which prevented the rule from applying. In my view, this was clearly an unconditional contract of sale, and I can see nothing whatever to make a different intention appear. The only evidence upon which it was ever suggested to exist was the printed conditions, but I can see nothing in those conditions to negative an intention that the property should pass on the fall of the hammer. I think the conditions are entirely consistent with such an intention. By the Sale of Goods Act, s 28: 'Unless otherwise agreed, delivery of the goods and payment of the price are concurrent conditions,' and finally, by yet another section of the Act, namely, s 39(1)(a), an unpaid seller of goods has a lien on the goods or right to retain them for the price while he is in possession of them, and he also has a right of re-sale as limited by the Act. Passing of the property and right to possession are two different things: here the property had passed upon the fall of the hammer, but still Mr Dennant had a right to retain possession of the goods until payment was made. If, when he was ready to deliver the goods, payment was not made, he could have sued for the price, or he could have exercised powers of re-sale, and he could have secured himself by way of lien on the goods for the price, but once he chose, for reasons good, bad, or indifferent as a result of statements fraudulent or honest, to part with the possession of the vehicle by giving delivery of it, he then lost his seller's lien and no longer had a right to possession of the vehicle. . . .

In my view, therefore, the second contention for the plaintiff also fails. However, there was a third aspect of the matter and that arises out of the document which I have already read. Now the document in its terms contemplates that the ownership of the vehicle has not passed to the bidder, but, as I have already said, in my judgment it had passed upon the fall of the hammer, and if subsequently the bidder executed the document acknowledging that ownership of the vehicle would not pass to him, that could not have any effect on what had already taken place. Can it be said that this document and the transaction it records as regards payment had the effect of divesting the property from King and re-vesting it in Mr Dennant, the seller? That is the only way in which Mr Brundrit has been able to suggest it that the document assists the plaintiff. I have considered that aspect of the matter, but I do not think that such a view of the document is sound. In my view the property had passed on the fall of the hammer; the right to possession had passed when Mr Dennant, persuaded and misled by King's lies, parted with his seller's lien, and there was nothing left upon which Mr

Dennant could found a claim in detinue against some third person, in this case Mr Skinner, who was thus in possession of the vehicle.

The result seems to me to be that here the sufferer from the lies of King and from the reliance which Mr Dennant unfortunately placed on him must be Mr Dennant himself and not the innocent parties who are represented by the defendant and the third party in this action. Accordingly there must be judgment for the defendant and the third party.

In order for rule 1 to apply, all three of the conditions indicated by the phrases italicised on p 271 above must be met. 'Specific goods' is a term which has already been discussed (above, p 217); we proceed now to consider the concepts of 'unconditional' contract and 'deliverable state'.

Unconditional. 'Unconditional' obviously means 'not subject to any conditions', but this is not very helpful, since the term 'condition' is itself notorious for the many different meanings or shades of meaning which it may have in the law of contract. (Professor Stoljar once identified twelve! – see (1953) 69 LQR 485.) In two early cases, *Varley v Whipp* [1900] 1 QB 513 and *Ollett v Jordan* [1918] 2 KB 41, contracts were held to be 'conditional' in the present context because the conditions implied by the Act as to conformity with description (s 13) and merchantable quality (s 14(2)) remained unfulfilled. This construction would lead to absurd conclusions: if 'unconditional' in rule 1 means 'containing no conditions (in the sense of a major or vital term) unfulfilled by the seller', then it would not be possible to ascertain whether the property had passed until the goods had been delivered and inspected and found to be in order. However, these cases are considered not to represent the true position in modern law (see, eg *Benjamin*, para 5–019); instead, the preferred view is that 'unconditional' means 'not subject to any condition upon the fulfilment of which the passing of the property depends'. Although this leaves us with a rather cyclic or question-begging piece of reasoning – the property passes if the contract is unconditional; the contract is unconditional if there is nothing to prevent the property from passing – it will not be the only legal definition that is subject to this criticism.

We can see the concept well illustrated by the *Romalpa* line of cases (below, p 408), where the passing of the property in the goods is made conditional on payment of the price. In contracts for the sale of things attached to or forming part of the soil, there will usually (and in some cases necessarily) be an implied condition that property in the goods will not pass until they have been severed from the freehold. However, as the cases of *Kursell v Timber Operators & Contractors Ltd* and *Underwood v Burgh Castle Cement* (see below) show, there may be other grounds in such circumstances for holding that the property has not passed.

NOTE

It is probably not appreciated by most of today's lawyers that the use of the word 'condition' to mean 'vital term', in contrast with 'warranty', is not a practice of long standing and might well not have been used or understood in this sense by Chalmers himself. In the first edition of his *Sale of Goods* (1890) he included a substantial appendix on the construction of 'terms and conditions' in which the word 'condition' is used only to refer to a contingency, or in the neutral sense of 'term'. Moreover, in his original draft of the Bill, only the implied terms that goods sold by description should correspond with their description (s 13) and that where goods are sold by sample the buyer should have an opportunity of comparing the bulk with the sample (s 15(2)(b)) were characterised as conditions: all the other statutorily implied terms were called warranties.

Consider also his draft for what is now s 11 (his clause 14):

14. (1) Where a contract of sale is subject to any condition for the benefit of the buyer, the buyer may elect to treat the non-performance of such condition as a breach of warranty, and not as a ground for rescinding the contract.

(2) Whether a stipulation in a contract of sale is a condition or a warranty depends in each case on the construction of the contract.

(3) Where a contract of sale is not severable, and the buyer has accepted part performance of the contract, a breach of any condition on the part of the seller can only be treated by the buyer as a breach of warranty.

Note that there is here no reference to a right to treat the contract as repudiated or to reject the goods, and note also the use of 'rescind' in sub-clause (1). These and other slight variations in the wording of what is now s 11 make it possible to read the whole of Chalmers' Bill in a way which allows 'condition' to be given the meaning of 'pure condition' rather than 'vital term', and more particularly a (pure) condition upon the fulfilment of which the passing of the property and/or the obligation of the buyer to accept the goods is made to depend. He did plainly appreciate that such a condition may be promissory (ie, something which the seller undertakes will be fulfilled) or non-promissory, for he makes a distinction between the 'non-performance' of a condition (sub-clause (1)) and the 'breach of any condition on the part of the seller' (sub-clause (3)). But there can be little doubt that it is we in later generations (and the unknown parliamentary hand which drew up the amendments to Chalmers' draft) who have created the kind of problem which we have just been discussing, by uncritically allowing the word 'condition' to be used in a way which fudges its many possible meanings and so distorts the scheme which Chalmers envisaged and set out in his rather more subtle language.

Deliverable state. There is a statutory definition of 'deliverable state'. Section 61(5) provides that goods are in a deliverable state when they are in such a state that the buyer would under the contract be bound to take delivery of them. And in turn, we are told that 'delivery' means 'the voluntary transfer of possession from one person to another' (s 61(1)). (This does not necessarily mean physical delivery – see above, p 56, and below, p 378). Again, there are problems with this definition. If the goods do not answer their description or are not of merchantable quality, the buyer has the right to reject them for breach of condition (see ss 11(3), 13, 14(2) and below, p 426). So it might be inferred that the property could never pass in goods which were defective in any respect such as this. But to accept this reasoning is in effect to revive the discredited arguments in *Varley v Whipp* and *Ollett v Jordan* referred to above. Although the question has not been the subject of any direct judicial ruling, writers are generally in agreement that 'deliverable state' in s 18 must be given a more restrictive interpretation so as to avoid this consequence. Professor Goode, for instance, suggests that rule 1 should be read as applying 'where, *on the assumption that the goods are what they purport to be*, the seller has not, by the terms of the contract, undertaken to do anything to them as a prerequisite of the buyer's acceptance of delivery' (*Commercial Law*, p 182). This may, in its turn, be too narrow, for it is not obvious that the rule should apply only where the acts in question are to be performed by the seller: the acts could be those of a third party, for instance. (As regards acts to be performed by the buyer, see below, p 278.) Such cases as have been reported on the meaning of 'deliverable state' have been concerned with more straightforward issues.

Kursell v Timber Operators & Contractors Ltd [1927] 1 KB 298, Court of Appeal   *Merchantable timber growing in Latvian forest not deliverable state*

(See the extracts from the judgments of Scrutton and Sargant LJJ quoted above, pp 218–219.)

Underwood Ltd v Burgh Castle Brick & Cement Syndicate Ltd [1922] 1 KB 123, King's Bench Division

(For the facts, see above, p 214.)

Rowlatt J: The sale was that of a specific chattel to be delivered by the plaintiffs, but the fact that it was to be delivered by them is not the test whether the property passed. The test is whether anything remained to be done to the engine by the sellers to put it into a deliverable state; and by that I understand a state in which the thing will be the article contracted for by the buyer; I do not mean deliverable in the sense that it is properly packed or anything of that kind. It must have everything done to it that the sellers had to do to it as an article. I do not think therefore that the fact by itself that the sellers had to take the engine to pieces would postpone the time when the property passed. Many chattels have to be taken to pieces before they can be delivered – eg a sideboard or a billiard table; nevertheless the property in these passes on the sale and is not postponed until the article is actually taken to pieces and delivered. I do not, therefore, lay any stress on the fact of the engine having to be taken to pieces. I think the important point is that the parties were dealing with an article which was a fixture to the premises, and that is different from the case of a loose chattel. The buyers' intention was to buy an article which would be a loose chattel when the processes of detaching and dismantling it were completed, and to convert it into a loose chattel these processes had first to be performed. The case of a tenant's fixtures seems an analogous case. It seems a safe rule to adopt that if a fixture has to be detached so as to make it a chattel again, the act of detaching has to be done before the chattel can be deliverable.

Philip Head & Sons Ltd v Showfronts Ltd [1970] 1 Lloyd's Rep 140, Queen's Bench Division

Showfront contracted with Heads to supply and lay fitted carpeting for a number of rooms in an office block which they were refurbishing. The carpet for the largest room, a showroom measuring about 40 ft × 20 ft, had to be made from several lengths stitched together: it was very unwieldy and took up to six men to lift it. After being assembled, it was left on the premises on a Friday afternoon and was stolen in the course of the weekend. The court held that it was not in a 'deliverable state' until it had been satisfactorily laid, and so it was the sellers' property and at their risk when it was stolen.

Mocatta J: The problem here is, I think, however, whether it can be said that carpeting in a deliverable state was unconditionally appropriated to the contract. That phrase is defined in s 62(4) of the statute as follows:

> Goods are in a 'deliverable state' within the meaning of this Act when they are in such a state that the buyer would under the contract be bound to take delivery of them.

There is not much assistance in the authorities as to the meaning of this phrase. It is, however, both interesting and, I think, helpful to read a passage from an opinion of Lord Blackburn in *Seath & Co v Moore* (1886) 11 App Cas 350, in which many of the points subsequently codified in the Sale of Goods Act 1893, including some of the problems which I have to deal with here, are discussed. It is true that that case was one dealing with problems arising out of a shipbuilding contract, but in this particular passage Lord Blackburn is purporting to state the relevant principles of English law in general terms. He stated in relation to the passing of property (ibid, at p 370):

> It is essential that the article should be specific and ascertained in a manner binding on both parties, for unless that be so it cannot be construed as a contract to pass the property in that article. And in general, if there are things remaining to be done by the seller to the article before it is in the state in which it is to be finally delivered to the purchaser, the contract will not be construed to be one to pass the property till those things are done. . . .

I find that passage to give valuable guidance here.

I have described as best I can the state of the carpeting subsequently stolen at the time that it came back to these premises after having been stitched up; it was plainly a heavy bundle, very difficult to move. Although I have determined that this was a contract to which the Sale of Goods Act, 1893, applied, nevertheless an important feature of it was undoubtedly the laying of the carpeting following on the planning. It seems to me that one has to consider – in each case it is a case of fact – where there is work to be done in relation to the article sold before the contractual obligations of the sellers are completed, what is the relevant importance of that work in relation to the contract when deciding whether the property has passed and in particular whether the article or goods in question is or are at a particular moment of time in a deliverable state under s 18, rule 5(1). I think one is entitled to apply everyday common sense to the matter; a householder, for example, purchasing carpeting under a contract providing that it should be delivered and laid in his house would be very surprised to be told that carpeting, which was in bales which he could hardly move deposited by his contractor in his garage, was then in a deliverable state and his property.

I take the view because of the condition of this carpeting at the time it was stolen and the importance of the last stage in the obligations to be performed by the plaintiffs under this contract, that at the moment when this carpeting was stolen it had not been unconditionally appropriated to the contract in a deliverable state, and accordingly, in my judgment, the property had not passed at the moment that the carpeting was stolen. In those circumstances the plaintiffs' case must fail. . . .

(ii) *Rule 2: specific goods to be put into a deliverable state by the seller*

Where there is a contract for the sale of *specific goods* and the seller is bound to do something to the goods for the purpose of putting them into a *deliverable state*, rule 2 states as a presumption that the property will not pass until the seller has done that thing and the buyer has notice that it has been done. The operation of the rule may be illustrated by two cases which have already been mentioned:

Underwood Ltd v Burgh Castle Brick & Cement Syndicate

(See above, p 214.)

Philip Head & Sons Ltd v Showfronts Ltd

(See above, p 275.)

In most respects, rule 2 seems straightforward enough. The terms 'specific goods' and 'deliverable state' have been discussed above, at pp 217, 274. It should be observed that it is necessary not only that the goods should be put into a deliverable state, but that the buyer must also have notice of this before the property will pass. The one point which may cause some surprise is that the wording of the rule is restricted to acts to be performed *by the seller*. This leaves the position unresolved where the act of putting the goods into a deliverable state is to be performed by the buyer, or by some third party. The only inference which we can draw from the fact that the Act is silent on this point is that there is no presumption either way in such a case. Of course, in many situations it will be possible – and perhaps even necessary – for the court to imply a condition into the contract of sale to the effect that the property is not to pass until the goods have been put into a deliverable state. For instance, if there is a contract to sell a second-hand car if it passes the test for an MOT certificate, the car will not be in a 'deliverable state' (within the definition contained in s 61(5)) until it has passed the test, and it will be immaterial whether it is for the seller or the buyer to arrange the test under the contract. Again, if we suppose that in *Underwood Ltd v Burgh Castle Brick & Cement Syndicate* (above) it was the buyer who had to detach the engine from the land, it is hardly conceivable that a court would consider the goods to have been in a 'deliverable state' until this had been done. The same would be true of a sale of standing timber: in the famous words used in *Liford's Case* (1614) 11 Co Rep 46b, 50a: 'Timber trees cannot be felled with a goose quill'. But it will not always be necessary to draw such an inference, particularly if we bear in mind that under s 61(5), 'deliverable' is not restricted in its meaning to 'physically deliverable'. Fruit ready for picking (and, *a fortiori*, crops in the category *fructus industriales*, such as potatoes, ready to be harvested) can surely be 'in such a state that the buyer would under the contract be bound to take delivery of them' even though they are still attached to the land. And the analogy with cases decided under rule 3 (such as *Nanka-Bruce v Commonwealth Trust Ltd* (below)) suggests that the courts may be less ready than might at first be supposed to treat contracts not falling strictly within rule 2 as conditional.

(iii) *Rule 3: specific goods to be weighed or measured, etc by the seller for the purpose of ascertaining the price*

Where there is a contract for the sale of *specific goods* in a *deliverable state*, but the seller is bound to weigh, measure, test or do some other act or thing to the goods for the purpose of ascertaining the price, rule 3 lays down a presumption that the property in the goods will not pass until the act or thing has been done and the buyer has notice that it has been done.

Turley v Bates (1863) 2 H & C 200, Court of Exchequer

Turley contracted to sell Bates a heap of fireclay lying on Turley's land at the price of 2s (10p) per ton, to be carted away by Bates and weighed at his own expense. Bates had taken away about 270 tons of clay and paid for it. This action was brought for the price of the remaining clay, estimated to have a value of £110 10s 6d. Bates argued that the property in the heap had not passed to him, so that he was liable only for damages which, in the absence of evidence that the clay had fallen in value, should be nominal damages only. The court held that the property had passed and that he was liable for the price.

The judgment of the court (Channell and Bramwell BB) was delivered by **Channell B:** . . . For the plaintiff it was contended, that where full authority was given to the buyer to remove the clay sold, and all that the seller had to do according to the contract was complete, and where everything that remained to be done was to be done by the buyer at his own expense, viz, as in this case, to cart away and have the clay weighed at his own expense, it must be taken as if there had been such a bargain and sale as to pass the property though the clay had not been removed and weighed, and that the contract price might be recoverable on the count for goods bargained and sold.

For the defendant it was contended, that taking the case on the plaintiff's evidence, and as found by the jury, that there had been a removal and weighing of part of the clay, yet no property passed in any clay until the clay had been weighed at Johnson's machine and the quantity and price thus ascertained, so as to entitle the plaintiff to recover on the count for goods bargained and sold.

In the course of the argument for the defendant we were referred to several cases decided in our Courts which were said to govern the question, and to a passage from my brother Blackburn's Treatise on Contract of Sale, part 2, chap 2, p 152. It was argued that the rule reducible from these authorities was, that so long as a price had been agreed upon according to quantity, to be ascertained by weighing, that until the goods had been weighed and the price so ascertained the contract was incomplete. . . .

It is very doubtful whether in stating the rule to be that where anything remains to be done to the goods for ascertaining the price as weighing, etc, the performance was a condition precedent to the transfer of the property, it was meant by the learned author to include a case where all that remained to be done was to be done by the buyer with full authority from the seller to do the act.

[Channell B referred to a number of cases, and continued:]

From a consideration of these cases, it appears that the principle involved in the rule above quoted is, that something remains to be done by the seller. It is, therefore, very doubtful, as before stated, whether the present case comes within the principle of the rule. But, however that may be, it is clear that this rule does not apply if the parties have made it sufficiently clear whether or not they intend that the property shall pass at once, and that their intention must be looked at in every case. . . .

In the present case the jury have, in effect, adopted the plaintiff's version of the bargain, by their finding that it was for the whole heap. And taking that view of the case, it seems to us clear that the intention of the parties was that the property in the whole heap should pass, notwithstanding the clay was to be weighed at Johnson's machine; and we, therefore, think that the rule to reduce the damages must be discharged.

Most of the comments made in relation to rule 2 apply also to rule 3. The following case underlines the fact that the presumption laid down by rule 3 applies only in the case where the act in question is to be performed *by the seller*.

Nanka-Bruce v Commonwealth Trust [1926] AC 77, Privy Council

(The facts appear from the judgment.)

The opinion of the Privy Council was delivered by **Lord Shaw:** This is an appeal from the judgment of the Full Court of the Gold Coast Colony affirming a judgment of Beatty J without a jury.

The appellant is a planter and shipper of cocoa, carrying on business at Accra. The respondents carry on business at Accra as general exporters and importers.

One, Laing (the co-defendant with the respondents in the action), was an editor of a newspaper in Accra and a buyer and seller of cocoa. He had previously made purchases of cocoa from the appellant.

The claim of the appellant against the respondents is for damages for conversion of 160 bags of cocoa. The history of this cocoa, so far as is material to the present case, and stated neutrally, is as follows: The appellant entered into a general arrangement with Laing, under which Laing was to receive cocoa from the appellant at the price of 59*s* per load of 60 lbs. It was recognized that Laing would resell the cocoa to other merchants, and that when these other merchants took delivery by a transfer of the consignment notes the goods would be weighed up at their premises and the weights tested there. That operation being completed, the amount payable by Laing on the contract made with the appellant was, of course, ascertained.

On April 24, 1920, the 160 bags of cocoa were despatched by rail by the appellant to Accra under a consignment note made out in favour of Laing. Laing then acted with the goods thus: He sold them to the respondents, and handed to the respondents' representatives the railway consignment note. The respondents took delivery and, against a large debt due to them from Laing, credited him with the price at which they had purchased the goods. Laing's conduct seems unquestionably to have been dishonest conduct. Both Courts have, however, found that the conduct of the respondents was quite honest, and that they purchased the goods for value and without any notice of any objection to, or defect in, the title of Laing, or the contract under which he had acquired the goods. Both Courts have concurrently found that Laing purchased the cocoa from the appellant. The appellant attacked this finding as erroneous in law, alleging that the weighing up of the goods must be treated as having been a condition precedent to an operative sale.

Their Lordships agree that the provision as to the weight of the goods being tested was not a condition precedent to a sale. The goods were transferred, their price was fixed, and the testing was merely to see whether the goods fitted the weights as represented, but this testing was not suspensive of the contract of sale or a condition precedent to it. To effect such suspension or impose such a condition would require a clear contract between vendor and vendee to that effect. In this case there was no contract whatsoever to carry into effect the weighing, which was simply a means to satisfy the purchaser that he had what he had bargained for and that the full price claimed per the contract was therefore due.

[His Lordship referred to *Cundy v Lindsay* (below, p 297), and continued:]

Applying that law their Lordships find no difficulty in affirming that these goods were de facto sold to Laing by the appellant, and that so far as the respondents were concerned they were honestly and for value bought by them from Laing. Suppose it to be the case that the appellent, defrauded by Laing, to whom he had sold the goods, could have treated the transaction as voidable on that account and sued Laing for remission accordingly, that cannot in law form a ground of impeachment as against buyers in good faith and for value from the person, like Laing, thus vested in the goods by a de facto contract.

This is an end of the case. . . .

QUESTION

Once the property has passed to the buyer, the seller may in principle sue the buyer for the price (see s 49(1)). In *Nanka-Bruce* it would not have been difficult to quantify the amount which the seller could claim, because the cocoa had already been provisionally weighed. But if the buyer is to do the weighing and the goods are destroyed before the weighing has been done, how is the price to be reckoned? The following case (which turned on the fact that *risk*, as distinct from property, had passed to the buyer), gives a clue.

Castle v Playford (1872) LR 7 Exch 98, Court of Exchequer Chamber

Castle agreed to sell to Playford a cargo of ice, to be shipped to a port in the United Kingdom and paid for on arrival at the rate of £1 per ton 'weighed on board during delivery'. Under the contract, the risk lay with the buyer. The ship and cargo were lost at sea. The court ruled that the buyer was liable to pay the price which, in the circumstances, had to be an estimated price.

Blackburn J: My impression is, if it were necessary to decide it now, that the effect of this contract is that the property passed; but I think it is unnecessary to decide the matter. The parties in this case have agreed, whether the property passed or not, that the purchaser should, from the time he received the bills of lading, take upon himself all risks and dangers of the seas; and, according to Mr Littler's construction, I do not see what risk he took upon himself at all, unless it was this – that he said, 'If the property perishes by the dangers of the seas, I shall take the risk of having lost the property, whether it be mine or not.'

The difficulty in the court below arose in reference to the alteration of the time of payment. No doubt it was afterwards provided that payment should be made on the ship's arrival and according to what was delivered. Now here, the ship and cargo have gone to the bottom of the sea; but in the cases of *Alexander v Gardner* ((1835) 1 Bing NC 671), and *Fragano v Long* ((1825) 4 B & C 219), it was held, that if the property did perish before the time for payment came, the time being dependent upon delivery, and if the delivery was prevented by the destruction of the property, the purchaser was to pay an equivalent sum. In the present case, when the ship went down there would be so much ice on board, and, in all probability, upon an ordinary voyage so much would have melted; and what the defendant has taken upon himself to pay is the amount which, in all probability, would have been payable for the ice. It would be the same amount as on an open insurance; and, doubtless, the merchants, in inserting this clause, were considering who were to pay the premiums of insurance for insuring the cargo, and the defendant seems to have said, 'As soon as the bills of lading come to me, I will pay the premiums, or stand my own insurer.' I am, therefore, of opinion that the judgment below should be reversed.

[Cockburn CJ delivered a concurring judgment.
Mellor, Brett and Grove JJ concurred.]

NOTE

In *National Coal Board v Gamble* [1959] 1 QB 11 (a case concerned with a sale of *unascertained* goods), coal was loaded on to a lorry pursuant to a bulk contract and taken to a weighbridge on the seller's premises, where the lorry was found to be nearly 4 tons overladen. The driver said that he would take his chance on the overloading, took the weighbridge ticket and left the premises. He was later stopped by the police and his firm convicted of permitting the lorry to be overweight. The Divisional Court held that the Coal Board, as seller, had rightly been convicted of aiding and abetting the driver in the commission of the offence, since until the goods had been weighed (so that the price could be ascertained) and the weighbridge ticket handed to the driver, the property in the coal remained with the seller, whose employee (the weighbridgeman) could have insisted that the excess be unloaded.

(iv) *Rule 4: goods delivered on approval or on sale or return*

When goods have been delivered to a buyer 'on approval' or on 'sale or return', or other similar terms, rule 4 prescribes that the property passes to the buyer:

(1) when he signifies his approval or acceptance to the seller or does any other act adopting or approving the transaction; or

(2) if he does not signify his approval or acceptance but retains the goods without giving notice of rejection, then, if a time has been fixed for the return of the goods, on the expiration of that time and, if no time has been fixed, on the expiration of a reasonable time.

This is the only time that a contract for the sale of goods 'on approval' or 'on sale or return' is mentioned in the Act. These two expressions may be taken to have the same meaning in English law – namely, that the person to whom the goods have been delivered has the option of buying the goods or not as he chooses, and until he has bought them (or is deemed by rule 4 to have done so), the property in the goods remains with the seller. Strictly speaking, therefore, there is no 'sale' at all (and not even an agreement to sell or to buy, but only an offer to sell), until the buyer has exercised his option; and the use in the Act of the terms 'seller' and 'buyer' is anomalous. We may note, in contrast, that in the United States the two expressions 'on approval' and 'on sale or return' are given different meanings: there, the former term is used in the same sense as in England, but 'on sale or return' means that there *is* a sale, and the buyer becomes the owner, subject however to a condition that he may return the goods within an agreed or a reasonable time and rescind the transaction. This analysis is similar to that in *Head v Tattersall* (above, p 243), but with the difference that the buyer is free to return the goods for any reason – even because he simply decides that he does not want them.

An example of an act 'adopting the transaction' is where the 'buyer' sells or pledges the goods, as illustrated by the following case.

Kirkham v Attenborough [1897] 1 QB 201, Court of Appeal

Kirkham, a manufacturing jeweller, delivered to Winter a quantity of jewellery on sale or return. Winter pledged some of the jewellery to Attenborough. In this action, Kirkham claimed that the goods pledged were still his property, but was unsuccessful.

Lopes LJ: The position of a person who has received goods on sale or return is that he has the option of becoming the purchaser of them, and may become so in three different ways. He may pay the price, or he may retain the goods beyond a reasonable time for their return, or he may do an act inconsistent with his being other than a purchaser. The words of the Act are difficult to construe; but it seems to me that if the recipient of the goods retains them for an unreasonable time he does something inconsistent with the exercise of his option to return them, and thereby adopts the transaction. So if he does any other act inconsistent with their return, as if he sells them or pledges them, because if he pledges them he no longer has the free control over them so as to be in a position to return them. In all these cases he brings himself within the words of the section by adopting the transaction, and the property in the goods passes to him. If that is the state of the law, applying it to this case, it is clear that the plaintiff is not entitled to recover from the defendant either the goods or their price, and the judgment in favour of the plaintiff cannot be supported.

[Lord Esher MR delivered a concurring judgment.
Rigby LJ concurred.]

For the buyer to 'adopt' a transaction under rule 4(a), there must be some act of election on his part (by words or conduct). It is not sufficient simply to show that he is unable to return the goods. In *Elphick v Barnes* (1880) 5 CPD 321 a horse which was delivered on eight days' trial died from an illness on the third day. Lord Denman CJ, treating the contract as one of a sale on approval, said (at 326): 'Here, I think, there was no sale at the time of the horse's death, which happened without the fault of either party, and therefore that the action for goods sold and delivered must fail.'

Rule 4, like the other rules in s 18, only lays down a presumption. It is open to the parties to make any other arrangement as regards the passing of the property –

for instance, that it shall not pass to the buyer until the price has been paid. *Kirkham v Attenborough* (above) may be contrasted with *Weiner v Gill.*

Weiner v Gill [1906] 2 KB 574, Court of Appeal

Weiner, a jeweller, delivered a diamond brooch and other articles to another jeweller, Huhn, on the terms: 'On approbation. On sale only for cash or return. . . . Goods had on approbation or on sale or return remain the property of Samuel Weiner until such goods are settled for or charged.' Huhn delivered the articles to Longman who said that he had a customer for them, but in fact he pawned them with Gill.

Sir Gorell Barnes P: The only question which we have to consider is whether the property in these goods had passed from the plaintiff to Huhn. As a general rule a person in the possession of goods cannot convey a better title to them than he himself has. There are exceptions to that rule, examples of which are to be found in the Factors Act 1889, and in s 25 of the Sale of Goods Act 1893. It has been argued that in the present case the defendants are protected by s 25 of the latter Act, but, having regard to the facts of the case, I do not think that that argument can be successfully maintained. In considering the question whether the property passed from the plaintiff to Huhn regard must be had to the terms of s 17 and s 18 of the Sale of Goods Act.

[The President read the sections and continued:]

If the present case were one falling within the terms 'on sale or return' in r 4, then the case of *Kirkham v Attenborough* [above] would no doubt be in point, because, as was said by Wightman J in *Moss v Sweet* ((1851) 16 QB 493), the meaning of a contract of sale or return is 'that the goods were to be taken as sold, unless returned within a reasonable time.' In the present case, however, we are dealing with a contract of an entirely different character, for on the face of the contract there appears a different intention as to when the property shall pass from that laid down in r 4 of s 18. The terms of the contract shew a clear intention that no property in the goods shall vest in Huhn until he has paid for them or been charged by the plaintiff for them. So that no means existed by which the buyer could exercise such an option as was indicated in r 4. The only thing he could do was to pay cash for them or to get the plaintiff to debit him with the price. That was not done, and therefore, in my opinion, the property in the goods never passed to Huhn, and consequently the defendants have no answer to the plaintiff's claim.

[Lord Alverstone CJ and Farwell LJ delivered concurring judgments.]

QUESTION

Gill was in the position of a bona fide purchaser without notice of the special terms of Weiner's contract, and with no possibility of finding out about them. Should the law do more to protect such a person?

Paragraph (b) of rule 4, in contrast with paragraph (a), contemplates that the buyer under a contract on sale or return terms may sometimes become the owner of the goods by inaction. This is illustrated by the case which follows.

Poole v Smith's Car Sales (Balham) Ltd [1962] 1 WLR 744, Court of Appeal

Both parties were car dealers. In August 1960 Poole, who was about to go on holiday, delivered a Vauxhall car to Smiths with authority to sell it, provided that he received £325, Smiths being allowed to retain any sum received in excess of that figure. In October Poole telephoned several times and asked for the return of the car, and eventually wrote a letter on 7 November stating that if it was not returned by 10 November it would be deemed to have been sold to Smiths. The car was not returned until the end of November, when Poole refused to take it back. It had been driven for some 1600 miles and had been badly damaged as a result of an accident sustained when two of Smiths' employees had, without authority, taken it out on a joyride. In this action Poole sued for the price, alleging that the property had passed, and was successful.

Ormerod LJ: The whole question now is whether, in the circumstances, the plaintiff is entitled to recover from the defendants either the sum of £325 as the price of goods sold and delivered, or such sum as may be proper as damages for detinue.

The plaintiff, in the first place, says that the car was sent to the defendants on sale or return, and the question which first arises to be determined is whether this was a transaction for sale or return. The judge held, that this was not a transaction having the sharply defined qualities of a contract for sale or return as envisaged by the Sale of Goods Act 1893. Mr Chedlow has raised the point that a contract for sale or return in the ordinary way is a contract where the person to whom the chattel is delivered is intending either to purchase the chattel or to send it back, whereas this was a contract where the defendants might expect to sell the car to one of their customers and if they could not sell it, then to return it, and, in those circumstances, it was not a contract for sale or return. So far as I am concerned, I am afraid I do not understand that distinction. I know of no authority for it, and in the absence of authority which is binding on this court, for my part, I would not make it. . . .

If that was the contract then the questions which arise are when and how did the property pass? It appears that we must be governed either by the express or implied intentions of the parties, or, failing those intentions, by the provisions of s 18 of the Act of 1893, and the rules there laid down. It has been contended on behalf of the plaintiff that the rule which applies here is r 4, which reads as follows: 'When goods are delivered to the buyer on approval or "on sale or return" or other similar terms the property therein passes to the buyer: – (a) When he signifies his approval or acceptance to the seller or does any other act adopting the transaction.' The question is whether he has in this case. Or: '(b) If he does not signify his approval or acceptance to the seller but retains the goods without giving notice of rejection, then, if a time has been fixed for the return of the goods, on the expiration of such time, and, if no time has been fixed, on the expiration of a reasonable time. What is a reasonable time is a question of fact.'

The question next arises whether that particular rule which I have read applies; that is to say, whether the property has passed. Mr Chedlow has argued that that rule cannot apply, and the reason why it cannot apply is because of the first words of s 18 of the Sale of Goods Act 1893, which reads: 'Unless a different intention appears.' It was argued that on the evidence in this case it was clear that a different intention appeared, and that it was not the intention that the property should pass in the manner indicated by r 4. I think I need only say here, in dealing with Mr Chedlow's argument, that I can see nothing which warrants the conclusion that any different intention is to be discovered from the circumstances of the case.

So we are thrown back on r 4. By that rule if the parties have fixed a time for the property to pass, then the property will pass at that time. In this case there is no suggestion that any time had been fixed. Failing that, and it is a question of fact, the time for the property to pass is at the expiry of a reasonable time, and the question which arises is what is a reasonable time. . . .

It is a well-known fact that people go on holidays in the months of July, August and September. It has become obvious, I think, in recent years that when people go on holidays, they like to take their cars with them. It may be that many people, when the holidays are over, like to sell those cars and, therefore, it may be a well-recognised fact, and I think it is, that the sellers' market for secondhand motor-cars in October and November is not so good as it is before the holiday season begins or is still in its early stages. In any event, I see no reason why in these days a court should not take judicial notice of the way the market in secondhand cars is carried on and come to a conclusion as to what is a reasonable time.

For my part I am fully satisfied, both on the knowledge which has come to me in the ordinary course of life and through sitting in these courts, and from the evidence before the court in this case, that a reasonable time had expired, certainly in November, for the return of this car; and if that reasonable time had expired, it is clear by reason of the operation of s 18 of the Act of 1893 that the property in the car had passed from the plaintiff to the defendants. . . .

The position remains, therefore, that here was a car delivered on sale or return, that a reasonable time expired without the car being returned and, therefore, there must have been or must be deemed to have been a sale of the car. That being so, the defendants become liable for the purchase price.

[Willmer LJ delivered a concurring judgment.
Danckwerts LJ concurred.]

QUESTION

Suppose that the car had been damaged as a result of Smiths' negligence before the expiry of a reasonable time: what would the legal position be?

(v) *Rule 5: unascertained goods*

Rules 1–4 of s 18 are all concerned with specific goods. The only rule dealing with *unascertained* goods is r 5. It states:

(1) Where there is a contract for the sale of unascertained or future goods by description, and goods of that description and in a deliverable state are unconditionally appropriated to the contract, either by the seller with the assent of the buyer or by the buyer with the assent of the seller, the property in the goods then passes to the buyer; and the assent may be given either before or after the appropriation is made.

(2) Where, in pursuance of the contract, the seller delivers the goods to the buyer or to a carrier or other bailee . . . (whether named by the buyer or not) for the purpose of transmission to the buyer, and does not reserve the right of disposal, he is to be taken to have unconditionally appropriated the goods to the contract.

We have already met some of the terms used in this rule. As well as *unascertained goods* (see above, p 217) and *future goods* (above, p 216), which were dealt with in Chapter 7, the expression *deliverable state* (p 274) occurs in rules 1 and 2 and has been discussed above. *Unconditionally* in this context is probably analogous with 'unconditional contract', as used in r 1 (see above, p 273), but in the present context, where it refers to 'appropriation', it has been the subject of special judicial consideration on a number of occasions, as will be seen in the cases which follow. Of the new expressions, it is best to start with the term 'appropriation'.

'Appropriation' literally means 'taking or dealing with as one's property' – in which sense it is used in s 9(1); but in r 5 it has the rather different connotation of a selecting or setting aside. But even within the broad idea of a setting aside, the word can have a range of meanings. Suppose that a wine merchant who has an order for one dozen bottles of a particular wine for a customer selects a box containing twelve bottles of the wine from a larger quantity in his cellar with the intention of using it to fulfil that order: we may say that he has 'appropriated' the box in question to the contract. But, of course, there is nothing at this stage to stop him changing his mind: if a second customer wants wine of the same description, he could sell him that box without infringing any commitment to the first buyer, and then select (or even procure from elsewhere) another dozen bottles to meet the original order. Nothing that the merchant has done by this 'appropriation' affects his ownership of the wine in question, or his ability to sell it to anyone he may choose. No subjective decision on his part, or unilateral or private act of setting aside, gives the first customer any claim to that box. Nor would an act by the merchant such as putting the goods in his delivery van to be taken to the customer's address, or even writing the customer's name and address on the box: these acts are all reversible or revocable, and the second customer, especially if he is in a hurry, might not mind at all being given a box with writing on it. 'Appropriation', for the purpose of r 5, must mean something more than this.

A second use of the word goes somewhat further, but still does not bring r 5 into play. It may be a term of the contract that at some stage the seller will earmark goods of the particular description for the purpose of meeting his obligations, so that from then onwards he is bound under the contract to deliver those goods and those goods only, but *without* any understanding that the property in the goods is to pass at that stage. So, for example, in a typical CIF contract (see below, p 452), an importer may agree to buy goods of a particular description to be delivered at a specified port in his own country – eg, a Dutch merchant may contract to buy 2000 tonnes of soya bean meal of US origin to be delivered to him at Rotterdam. The seller may very likely have no identified goods in mind at the time of the contract. But it will normally be a term of the contract that, once he has located a suitable consignment, he will give the buyer a 'notice of appropriation' of the goods which he has chosen. This is a contractually binding act, obliging him to use those goods, and those goods only, in fulfilment of the contract. But it will not necessarily follow that such an act of appropriation, even when notified to the buyer, has the added consequence of passing the property in the goods to the buyer – indeed, this would be most unusual for, as we shall see, the normal understanding in a contract on CIF terms is that property will only pass when the shipping documents relating to the goods are handed over in exchange for the purchase price. 'Appropriation', for the purposes of r 5, has to be more than an act of selection, and more than a purely contractual earmarking of goods to answer the contract: it must be an act which is intended and agreed, in terms of the contract, to transfer ownership to the buyer.

Wait v Baker (1848) 2 Exch 1, Court of Exchequer Chamber

(The facts are immaterial.)

Parke B: . . . It is admitted by the learned counsel for the defendant, that the property does not pass, unless there is a subsequent appropriation of the goods. The word appropriation may be understood in different senses. It may mean a selection on the part of the vendor, where he has the right to choose the article which he has to supply in performance of his contract; and the contract will shew when the word is used in that sense. Or the word may mean, that both parties have agreed that a certain article shall be delivered in pursuance of the contract, and yet the property may not pass in either case. For the purpose of illustrating this position, suppose a carriage is ordered to be built at a coachmaker's, he may make any one he pleases, and, if it agree with the order, the party is bound to accept it. Now suppose that, at some period subsequent to the order, a further bargain is entered into between this party and the coachbuilder, by which it is agreed that a particular carriage shall be delivered.

It would depend upon circumstances whether the property passes, or whether merely the original contract is altered from one which would have been satisfied by the delivery of any carriage answering the terms of the contract, into another contract to supply the particular carriage – which, in the Roman law, was called obligatio certi corporis, where a person is bound to deliver a particular chattel, but where the property does not pass, as it never did by the Roman law, until actual delivery; although the property, after the contract, remained at the risk of the vendee, and if lost without any fault in the vendor, the vendee, and not the vendor, was the sufferer. The law of England is different: here, property does not pass until there is a bargain with respect to a specific article, and everything is done which, according to the intention of the parties to the bargain, was necessary to transfer the property in it. 'Appropriation' may also be used in another sense, and is the one in which Mr Butt uses it on the present occasion; viz where both parties agree upon the specific article in which the property is to pass, and nothing remains to be done in order to pass it. . . .

The application of the presumption contained in r 5 is illustrated by the following cases (some of which have already been discussed):

Aldridge v Johnson

(See above, p 224.)

Philip Head & Sons Ltd v Showfronts Ltd

(See above, p 275.)

Rohde v Thwaites (1827) 6 B & C 388, Court of King's Bench

Thwaites had contracted to buy twenty hogsheads of sugar out of the bulk held by Rohde in his warehouse. Rohde filled twenty hogsheads, of which four were delivered to Thwaites and accepted by him; but he refused to collect the remaining sixteen. In this action it was held that Rohde could sue for the price of all twenty hogsheads.

Holroyd J: The sugars agreed to be sold being part of a larger parcel, the vendors were to select twenty hogsheads for the vendee. That selection was made by the plaintiffs, and they notified it to the defendant, and the latter then promised to take them away. That is equivalent to an actual acceptance of the sixteen hogsheads by the defendant. That acceptance made the goods his own, subject to the vendor's lien as to the price. If the sugars had afterwards been destroyed by fire, the loss must have fallen on the defendant. I am of opinion that the selection of the sixteen hogsheads by the plaintiffs, and the adoption of that act by the defendants, converted that which before was a mere agreement to sell into an actual sale, and that the property in the sugars thereby passed to the defendant; and, consequently, that [the vendors were] entitled to recover to the value of the whole under the count for goods bargained and sold.

[Bayley J delivered a concurring judgment.
Littledale J concurred.]

Langton v Higgins (1859) 4 H & N 402, Court of Exchequer

Carter, a Cambridgeshire farmer, who owed money to Mrs Langton, agreed to sell her all the oil of peppermint to be distilled from the crop to be grown on his farm in

1858. Mrs Langton sent him the necessary bottles and his wife filled them with the oil; but Carter then sold them to Higgins and shortly afterwards disappeared. It was held that Mrs Langton could sue Higgins in detinue, since the property in the oil had passed to her when the bottles were filled.

Bramwell B: . . . The contract is to sell the whole of the vendor's crop of oil of peppermint grown in a certain year. I do not think that when the oil was made the property passed, – possibly there may have been an obligatio certi corporis; but it appears to me that when the oil was put into the plaintiff's bottles the property in it vested in her. . . . It may be that the vendor would be bound to shew some act of delivery before he could sue for the price; but however that may be, I am of opinion that the property vested in the plaintiff when the oil was put into her bottles. Looking at the principle, there ought to be no doubt. A person agrees to buy a certain article, and sends his bottles to the seller to put the article into. The seller puts the article into the buyer's bottles, then is there any rule to say that the property does not pass? The buyer in effect says, 'I will trust you to deliver into my bottles, and by that means to appropriate to me, the article which I have bought of you.' On the other hand the seller must be taken to say, 'You have sent your bottles and I will put the article in them for you.' In all reason, when a vendee sends his ship, or cart, or cask, or bottle to the vendor, and he puts the article sold into it, that is a delivery to the vendee. If we could suppose the case of a metal vessel filled with a commodity which rendered the vessel useless for subsequent purposes, it would be monstrous if the vendor could say 'I have destroyed your vessel by putting into it the article you purchased, but still the property in the article never passed to you.' Or suppose a vendor was to deliver a ton of coals into the vendee's cellar, could he say 'I have put the coals in your cellar, but I have a right to take them away again?' But, independently of reason, there is an authority on the subject.

[His Lordship referred to *Blackburn on Sale*, and continued:]

Can there be more complete evidence of intention to pass the property than when the vendee sends her bottles to be filled with the article purchased, and the vendor puts it into the bottles? Therefore, both upon principle and authority, I think that the property in the oil passed to the plaintiff when it was put into the bottles.

[Pollock CB and Martin B delivered concurring judgments.]

Mucklow v Mangles (1808) 1 Taunt 318, Court of Common Pleas

Royland contracted to build a barge for Pocock. The whole of the agreed price was paid as the work progressed. When it was nearly finished, Pocock's name was painted on the stern. Two days after it had been completed, it was seized by Mangles, a sheriff's officer, who was executing a judgment against Royland. Royland was later adjudicated bankrupt. The question before the court was whether the sheriff had rightly seized the barge, or whether it had become Pocock's property. It was held that the property had not passed to Pocock.

Mansfield CJ: The only effect of the payment, is, that the bankrupt was under a contract to finish the barge: that is quite a different thing from a contract of sale, and until the barge was finished we cannot say that it was so far Pocock's property, that he could have taken it away. It was not finished at the time when Royland committed the act of bankruptcy: it was finished only two days before the execution. . . .

Heath J: . . . A tradesman often finishes goods, which he is making in pursuance of an order given by one person, and sells them to another. If the first customer has other goods made for him within the stipulated time, he has no right to complain; he could not bring trover against the purchaser for the goods so sold. The painting of the name on the stern in this case makes no difference. If the thing be in existence at the time of the order, the property of it passes by the contract, but not so, where the subject is to be made.

[Lawrence J concurred.]

NOTE

We really need to know more facts than are stated in the report of this case. Under the law then in force, the 'commencement' of Royland's bankruptcy would have been back-dated to some 'act of bankruptcy' (which is referred to by Mansfield CJ), which plainly took place between the painting of the name and the completion of the work. The title of the trustee in bankruptcy would be deemed to have vested on the date of that act.

Noblett v Hopkinson [1905] 2 KB 214, King's Bench Divisional Court

The licensee of a public house was charged with unlawfully opening his premises for the sale of intoxicating liquor on a Sunday, in the circumstances described by Lord Alverstone CJ. The justices had dismissed the charge on the ground that there had been an 'appropriation' of the liquor on the Saturday evening, and consequently no 'sale' on the Sunday. The decision of the justices was reversed on appeal and a conviction entered.

Lord Alverstone CJ: It appears that two men went to the respondent's public-house on Saturday and asked for half a gallon of beer, and asked if it could be sent down to them on Sunday morning; the inference that I think may properly be drawn from this is that they would not have ordered the beer if they could not have had it sent to them on the Sunday. They then paid for the beer, which was drawn and put into a bottle; then, as the case states, the bottle was corked and put on the bar counter, whence it was taken to the brewhouse stable (which was within the curtilage) and remained there till the Sunday morning, when it was given to the barman behind the counter to hand to the two men when they called for it; as a matter of fact the barman seems to have taken it off the premises himself and gone with it to the place where the two men were, where he was stopped by the constable. There was in my opinion no evidence that what was done with the beer on the Saturday evening was done under the licence or by the authority of the purchaser; the evidence seems to shew that it was done by the vendor on his own responsibility, and, if the bottle of beer had been broken during the Saturday night, other beer would have had to be supplied to the men on the Sunday morning. I think therefore that there was not sufficient evidence on which it could properly be found that there was an appropriation of the beer on the Saturday night – I mean of an appropriation made by the respondent as the agent of the purchasers. The statement in the case does not of necessity mean that the beer was put aside in the way described with the consent of the purchasers, and in my opinion, when the justices speak of appropriation, they mean simply an appropriation by the publican.

That is enough for the decision of this case. . . .

[Kennedy and Ridley JJ delivered concurring judgments.]

It should be noted that r 5 requires an appropriation by or under the authority of one party with the *assent* of the other. This assent may be given before or after the appropriation, and will sometimes be inferred (eg from the fact that the seller's appropriation is made by filling containers supplied by the buyer). Rules 2 and 3, in contrast, require only that the buyer should have *notice* that the seller has performed the outstanding act. It is clear that mere notice to the other party will not necessarily give rise to an inference of assent. But the following case shows that such an inference may sometimes be drawn.

Pignataro v Gilroy [1919] 1 KB 459, King's Bench Divisional Court

The defendants contracted to sell by sample to the plaintiff 140 bags of rice, then unascertained, and in due course notified the buyer that 125 bags were available for collection at one address and 15 at another. Despite two reminders by letter, the plaintiff did not send to collect the 15 bags for nearly a month, by which time they had been stolen. It was held that the property had passed to the plaintiff and that the risk of loss therefore lay on him.

The judgment of the court (Lawrence and Rowlatt JJ) was delivered by **Rowlatt J:** Under the above contract it would be the duty of the sellers to appropriate the goods to the contract; and if such appropriation were assented to, expressly or impliedly, by the buyer the property would have passed. When they received the cheque for the goods and were asked for a delivery order it was right and proper for them to appropriate and place at the disposal of the buyer the goods for which he thus paid in order to effectuate a delivery or its equivalent concurrently with the receipt of the money. They did send a delivery order for the goods at Chambers' Wharf, and as to the 15 bags, told the plaintiff that they were ready, and asked that they should be taken away. It might well be contended that not only as regards the goods covered by the delivery order, but also as regards the goods at the defendants' own premises which they thus told the plaintiff were ready to be taken away in response to the plaintiff's request for a delivery order, there was an appropriation to which by asking for the delivery order the plaintiff had assented in advance. We do not think it necessary to decide this, because we think there was what amounted to an assent subsequent. If the plaintiff had replied saying that he would remove the goods the case would be precisely the same as *Rohde v Thwaites* ((1827) 6 B & C 388). The plaintiff, however, did nothing for a month, and the question is what is the effect of that? If the goods were of the required quality it is difficult to see how the plaintiff could have dissented from the appropriation. He could not object to the place from which he was required to fetch them, because he had inspected rice lying at those premises at the time and for the purposes of this very contract. For the same reason it is not easy to see how he could have objected to their quality unless there happened to be some bags inferior to those which he had inspected. At any rate, he made no objection at all. Now it is obvious that if he made any objection he ought to do so promptly, because he could not place upon the vendors the risk involved in the continued possession of these goods, nor prolong the encumbrance of the vendors' premises. As he chose merely to say nothing for a whole month in response to an appropriation made in consequence of his own letter, we think that comes to precisely the same thing as if he had written saying he would remove them and did not. The learned judge said that there was no evidence of an appropriation with the assent of the buyer. He could only say this if he was looking for an express assent. As the assent may be implied we think that there was not only evidence of it but that it is the only inference possible upon the facts. For these reasons the appeal must be allowed, and judgment entered for the defendants. . . .

Carlos Federspiel & Co SA v Charles Twigg & Co Ltd [1957] 1 Lloyd's Rep 240, Queen's Bench Division

Federspiels in Costa Rica agreed to buy a number of cycles from Twiggs in England and paid them the price. Under the contract, the goods were to be loaded aboard the SS *Brittanic* at Liverpool. Cycles were manufactured to answer the contract and packed in crates marked with the buyers' name, and steps were taken to send the crates to Liverpool for shipment. But the sellers went into receivership before shipment took place. The buyers argued unsuccessfully that the property in the cycles had passed to them.

Pearson J: It is admitted that if the goods were the property of the buyers, that is to say, the plaintiff company, there was conversion by the defendants.

The issue in the case appears from para 5 of the defence. I should perhaps read also part, at any rate, of para 4:

> This defendant . . . denies that any bicycles or tricycles were made available to the plaintiffs or appropriated to the said agreement.

In para 5 it is said:

> This defendant denies that the property in any bicycles or tricycles manufactured by the defendant company passed to the plaintiffs, either as alleged or at all. This defendant admits that no bicycles or tricycles have been delivered to the plaintiffs pursuant to the said agreement but he denies that he or the defendant company detain wrongfully or in breach of the said agreement any goods belonging to the plaintiffs.

That, therefore, is the main issue: whether or not the goods were appropriated to the contract by the sellers with the consent of the buyers so as to pass the ownership to the buyers. . . .

[His Lordship quoted several sections from the Sale of Goods Act, and continued:]

This is a case in which the contract is for the sale of unascertained goods by description, for the sale of future goods probably still to be manufactured. Afterwards certain goods were manufactured, and the sellers at one time apparently expected to use them in fulfilment of the contract. The question is whether there was an appropriation of those goods to the contract by the sellers with the assent of the buyers within the meaning of Rule 5 of s 18.

I think it is convenient just, in effect, to lay a foundation for the understanding of the exact meaning and effect of s 18 by reading a short passage from an old case, *Mirabita v Imperial Ottoman Bank* (1878) 3 Ex D 164. The relevant passage is from the judgment of Lord Justice Cotton, at p 172, where he says:

> Under a contract for sale of chattels not specific the property does not pass to the purchaser unless there is afterwards an appropriation of the specific chattels to pass under the contract, that is, unless both parties agree as to the specific chattels in which the property is to pass, and nothing remains to be done in order to pass it. In the case of such a contract the delivery by the vendor to a common carrier, or (unless the effect of the shipment is restricted by the terms of the bill of lading) shipment on board a ship of, or chartered for, the purchaser, is an appropriation sufficient to pass the property.

[His Lordship referred to a number of other cases, including *Wait v Baker* (above, p 285) and *Pignataro v Gilroy* (above, p 289), and continued:]

On those authorities, what are the principles emerging? I think one can distinguish these principles. First, r 5 of s 18 of the Act is one of the rules for ascertaining the intention of the parties as to the time at which the property in the goods is to pass to the buyer unless a different intention appears. Therefore the element of common intention has always to be borne in mind. A mere setting apart or selection of the seller of the goods which he expects to use in performance of the contract is not enough. If that is all, he can change his mind and use those goods in performance of some other contract and use some other goods in performance of this contract. To constitute an appropriation of the goods to the contract, the parties must have had, or be reasonably supposed to have had, an intention to attach the contract irrevocably to those goods, so that those goods and no others are the subject of the sale and become the property of the buyer.

Secondly, it is by agreement of the parties that the appropriation, involving a change of ownership, is made, although in some cases the buyer's assent to an appropriation by the seller is conferred in advance by the contract itself or otherwise.

Thirdly, an appropriation by the seller, with the assent of the buyer, may be said always to involve an actual or constructive delivery. If the seller retains possession, he does so as bailee for the buyer. There is a passage in Chalmers' Sale of Goods Act, 12th ed, at p 75, where it is said:

> In the second place, if the decisions be carefully examined, it will be found that in every case where the property has been held to pass, there has been an actual or constructive delivery of the goods to the buyer.

I think that is right, subject only to this possible qualification, that there may be after such constructive delivery an actual delivery still to be made by the seller under the contract. Of course, that is quite possible, because delivery is the transfer of possession, whereas appropriation transfers ownership. So there may be first an appropriation, constructive delivery, whereby the seller becomes bailee for the buyer, and then a subsequent actual delivery involving actual possession, and when I say that I have in mind in particular the two cases cited, namely, *Aldridge v Johnson*, (above, p 224), and *Langton v Higgins*, (above, p 286).

Fourthly, one has to remember s 20 of the Sale of Goods Act, whereby the ownership and the risk are normally associated. Therefore as it appears that there is reason for thinking, on the construction of the relevant documents, that the goods were, at all material times, still at the seller's risk, that is *prima facie* an indication that the property had not passed to the buyer.

Fifthly, usually but not necessarily, the appropriating act is the last act to be performed by the seller. For instance, if delivery is to be taken by the buyer at the seller's premises and the seller has completed his part of the contract and has appropriated the goods when he has made the goods ready and has identified them and placed them in position to be taken by the buyer and has so informed the buyer, and if the buyer agrees to come and take them, that is the assent to the appropriation. But if there is a further act, an important and decisive act to be done by the seller, then there is *prima facie* evidence that probably the property does not pass until the final act is done.

Applying those principles to the present case I would say this. Firstly, the intention was that the ownership should pass on shipment (or possibly at some later date) because the emphasis is throughout on shipment as the decisive act to be done by the seller in performance of the contract. Secondly, it is impossible to find in this correspondence an agreement to a change of ownership before the time of shipment. The letters, especially those of Aug 27 and Sept 14, which are particularly relied on by the plaintiff, do not contain any provision or implication of any earlier change of ownership. Thirdly, there is no actual or constructive delivery; no suggestion of the seller becoming a bailee for the buyer. Fourthly, there is no suggestion of the goods being at the buyer's risk at any time before shipment; no suggestion that the buyer should insist on the seller arranging insurance for them. Fifthly, the last two acts to be performed by the seller, namely, sending the goods to Liverpool and having the goods shipped on board, were not performed.

Therefore, my decision that the *prima facie* inference which one would have drawn from the contract is that the property was not to pass at any time before shipment, is in my view not displaced by the subsequent correspondence between the parties. It follows, therefore, that there was no appropriation of these goods and therefore the action fails.

An act of appropriation sufficient to pass the property in goods may be performed by a third party, eg a warehouseman. In such a case, the third party may be regarded as the agent of one (or possibly both) of the parties for the purpose.

Wardar's (Import & Export) Co Ltd v W Norwood & Sons Ltd [1968] 2 QB 663, Court of Appeal

Wardar's agreed to buy from Norwood 600 cartons of frozen ox kidneys out of a consignment of 1500 cartons which had been imported from Argentina and were lying in a cold store in Smithfield. A driver, McBeath, employed by a firm of carriers, arrived at 8 am on an October morning to pick up the goods on behalf of Wardar's and take them to Scotland. He had a refrigerated lorry but had forgotten to turn on the refrigerating machinery. When he arrived, 600 cartons had been taken out of the store by the storage firm and placed on the pavement. McBeath handed over a delivery order and the Smithfield porters began to loan the van. Loading took until noon (in part because the porters took a one-hour tea-break), by which time the day was warm and some of the cartons were leaking, and the refrigeration in the van was still not fully effective. The kidneys were unfit for consumption when they arrived in Scotland. The Court of Appeal held that the loss fell on the buyers, since property and risk had passed at 8 am and the deterioration had occurred after that time.

Salmon LJ: When McBeath arrived at the cold store at 8 am on October 14, the frozen kidneys which he was to take to Scotland were there on the pavement waiting for him. There is no doubt that they had been in the cold store the day before and, indeed, had then been examined by the buyers soon after they made their oral contract of purchase. As far as the evidence goes, there was absolutely nothing the matter with the kidneys on October 13. There is no evidence as to when these 600 cartons were taken out of the cold store. It seems unlikely that they would have been left on the pavement overnight. Had they been left on the pavement overnight, it is perhaps even more unlikely that they would all have been there in the morning. The natural inference, I think, is that they must have been taken out of the cold store at some time on the morning of October 14 prior to 8 am.

These 600 cartons were part of a consignment of 1500 cartons of frozen kidneys that had been stored in the cold store. The evidence called at the trial showed that the rest of the cartons – that is, 900 of the cartons – had also been sold, and no complaint was made in respect of them. At the time of the sale it was a sale of unascertained goods: 600 cartons were bought out of a total of 1500 cartons. This case really turns upon the question as to when the property passed to the buyers. It is plain that as a rule the goods remain at the sellers' risk until the property does pass to the buyers. After the property passes, the goods are at the buyers' risk: s 20 of the Act of 1893. There are special circumstances (of which *Sterns Ltd v Vickers Ltd* ([1923] 1 KB 78, CA) is an example) when the risk may pass to the buyers even before the property has passed to them; but there are no such special circumstances here. The case depends entirely upon when the property passed.

Under r 5 of s 18, the property passes to the buyers in the case of unascertained goods, such as these, when the goods are unconditionally appropriated to the contract. At 8 am the carrier arrived; and the carrier was the buyers' agent. There were the goods, which had been left on the pavement by the sellers' agent for the purpose of fulfilling the contract. The carrier handed over the delivery note, with the clear intention that those goods should be accepted for loading; and the loading commenced.

It is unnecessary to decide the point whether there was an unconditional appropriation to the contract at the moment when the goods were put onto the pavement, which is perhaps fortunate, because we do not know precisely when that was; but, in my view, there can be no doubt that there was a clear, unconditional appropriation when the delivery order was handed over in respect of the goods which had been deposited on the pavement for loading. There is certainly no evidence that they were not then of merchantable quality. It would seem from the evidence of Mr McBeath, the driver of the lorry, that at some stage the porters wished to take a tea-break. The driver was apparently concerned at the goods being left standing on the pavement, but he was told, according to his evidence, that the tea-break would take only five minutes. It appears that it took about an hour; and it was after the tea-break, according to Mr McBeath, that he first noticed that some of the cartons were dripping, which would be a strong indication that the goods had by then started to deteriorate. Meantime, however, a good many of the cartons had already been loaded into the lorry. Since, however, the goods were appropriated to the contract when the delivery order was handed over and accepted in respect of the goods standing on the pavement, any deterioration that occurred thereafter was at the risk of the buyers. We know that when the goods arrived at their destination the vast bulk of them were not of merchantable quality. We also know from the driver of the lorry that he did not turn on the refrigeration, so he said, until the tea-break was taken. At any rate, the refrigeration did not become effective until 1 pm. It may not be very material, but it does not seem to me to be at all unlikely, if the goods were left in a stuffy lorry, as they were, for some hours, that the deterioration may have occurred during that time. The driver said that this was a hot day. Unless it was a very exceptional day for October 14 in this country, I cannot think that the sun had much strength in it by 8 am. In any event, none of this, I think, matters, because at 8 am these goods were appropriated to the contract and the risk of deterioration then fell on the buyers; and there is no evidence that there was any deterioration before that time. . . .

[Harman LJ delivered a concurring judgment.
Phillimore J concurred.]

Paragraph (2) of r 5 deems goods to have been unconditionally appropriated to the contract when the seller has delivered them to a carrier or other bailee for the purpose of transmission to the buyer. It was unsuccessfully argued in *Wardar's* case that there had been no 'delivery' under this provision until the cartons had actually been put on the lorry; but it is plain that the court considered that delivery had taken place at the time when the delivery order was handed over by McBeath to the cold store firm and accepted. Paragraph (2) also refers to a *reservation of the right of disposal* by the buyer – an expression which is also used, and its meaning elaborated, in s 19(1) and (2). These are perhaps rather superfluous provisions, because it is plain from the whole tenor of ss 17 and 18 that no property can pass under the contract so long as some condition remains to be fulfilled, and that an appropriation to be effective must also be unconditional; and obviously if the seller makes a stipulation that he is reserving a right of disposal even after delivery to the buyer or the carrier, the appropriation will not be unconditional. However, it does no harm for the details in question to be spelt out in the Act, and it is helpful to have it clearly stated as a prima facie rule that where goods are loaded on to a ship for the purposes of transmission to the buyer, and the seller takes the bill of lading in his own name, intending to transfer it to the buyer at some later stage (normally against payment of the price), the property is not to be taken to have passed (s 19(2)). On this question, see further below, p 448.

(c) Acceptance and rejection

Before we leave the topic of the passing of property, it may be appropriate to ask: what is the *latest* time at which property can pass under a contract of sale? The answer would appear to be found in s 35: that is, when the buyer has *accepted* the goods, as explained in that section. (On acceptance, see below, p 380.) This is the point at which the buyer loses, or abandons, any right which he may have to reject the goods (eg because they are not of the contract description or quality), after which his remedy, if any, is confined to a damages claim.

It is sometimes possible for a buyer to reject goods even *after* the property has passed to him. In such a case, the effect of rejection is that the buyer divests himself of his ownership and causes it to revest in the seller. *Head v Tattersall* (above, p 243) is perhaps an early example of this: the risk, as well as the property, being deemed to have revested in the seller with retrospective effect. Two more modern cases illustrate the same principle.

Kwei Tek Chao v British Traders & Shippers Ltd [1954] 2 QB 459, Queen's Bench Division

Buyers in Hong Kong contracted to buy from sellers in London a chemical of Swedish origin known as 'Rongalite C'. Under the contract, property passed to the buyers when the price was paid in exchange for the shipping documents: this happened on 12 November. By the time that the goods arrived in Hong Kong on 17 December, the buyers had ascertained that the goods had been shipped outside the contractual period for shipment and that the shipping documents had been forged (by a third party) to conceal this fact. Devlin J held that the buyers could reject the goods for this reason, and that they could do so even though the property had already passed to them: it must be regarded as having passed defeasibly, ie subject to a condition subsequent that in an event such as that which had happened, it could be revested in the sellers by the buyers properly exercising a right of rejection. It followed that the buyers, who had pledged the documents to their bank, had not dealt with the goods in a manner inconsistent with the sellers' ownership so as to lose their right of rejection under s 35 of the Act.

Devlin J: In *Hardy & Co v Hillerns and Fowler* ([1923] 2 KB 490) the question which arose for decision was whether the buyers had accepted the goods under s 35. The goods had arrived, and the case showed that the time during which he had the right to examine them was still running. During that time the buyer delivered some of the goods to a sub-buyer. That was an act which was inconsistent with the ownership of the seller. . . . The court held that, notwithstanding that his time for examination was still open, the buyer could, if he chose to commit an act under s 35 such as intimating that he accepted the goods, accept them.

Mr Roskill has argued that when the goods are delivered to the buyer and he does any act in relation to them which is inconsistent with the ownership of the seller the word 'delivered' there means physical delivery of the goods from the ship. If that is so, no dealing with the documents would be within the meaning of the clause, because it would all have been done before the goods had been delivered. I cannot take that view of it. 'Delivery' as defined by the Act means a voluntary transfer of possession, and I think that it means, therefore, transfer of possession under the contract of sale. In a cif contract the goods are delivered, so far as they are physically delivered, when they are put on board a ship at the port of shipment. The documents are delivered when they are tendered. A buyer who takes delivery from the ship at the port of destination is not taking delivery of the goods under the contract of sale, but merely taking delivery out of his own warehouse, as it were, by the presentation of the document of title to the goods, the master of the ship having been his bailee ever since he became entitled to the bill of lading.

I think that the true answer may be found rather differently. Atkin LJ, in the course of his judgment in *Hardy & Co v Hillerns and Fowler*, dealt with the situation which is always a little puzzling under the cif contract: if the property passes when the documents are handed over, by what legal machinery does the buyer retain a right, as he undoubtedly does, to examine the goods when they arrive, and to reject them if they are not in conformity with the contract? Atkin LJ put forward two views for consideration. One was that the property in the goods, notwithstanding the tendering of the documents, did not pass until the goods had been examined or until an opportunity for examination had been given. The other was that it passed at the time of the tendering of the documents, but only conditionally and could be revested if the buyer properly rejected the goods. Mr Roskill argues (and I think rightly) that for the first possible view indicated by Atkin LJ no other authority can be found, and it would clearly create considerable complications. If there is no property in the goods, how can the buyer pledge them? It would provide a simple answer to the point had it arisen in this case, since there could not be a pledge. I think that the true view is that what the buyer obtains, when the title under the documents is given to him, is the property in the goods, subject to the condition that they revest if upon examination he finds them to be not in accordance with the contract. That means that he gets only conditional property in the goods, the condition being a condition subsequent. All his dealings with the documents are dealings only with that conditional property in the goods. It follows, therefore, that there can be no dealing which is inconsistent with the seller's ownership unless he deals with something more than the conditional property. If the property passes altogether, not being subject to any condition, there is no ownership left in the seller with which any inconsistent act under s 35 could be committed. If the property passes conditionally the only ownership left in the seller is the reversionary interest in the property in the event of the condition subsequent operating to restore it to him. It is that reversionary interest with which the buyer must not, save with the penalty of accepting the goods, commit an inconsistent act. So long as he is merely dealing with the documents he is not purporting to do anything more than pledge the conditional property which he has. Similarly, if he sells the documents of title he sells the conditional property. But if, as was done in *Hardy & Co v Hillerns and Fowler*, when the goods have been landed, he physically deals with the goods and delivers them to his sub-buyer, he is doing an act which is inconsistent with the seller's reversionary interest. The seller's reversionary interest entitles him, immediately upon the operation of the condition subsequent, that is, as soon as opportunity for examination has been given, to have the goods physically returned to him in the place where the examination has taken place without their being dispatched to third parties. The dispatch to a third party is an act, therefore, which interferes with the reversionary interest. A pledge or a transfer of documents such as that which takes place on the ordinary string contract does not. . . .

McDougall v Aeromarine of Emsworth Ltd [1958] 1 WLR 1126, Queen's Bench Division

Aeromarine contracted to build for McDougall a four-ton cruiser/racer yacht for use in the 1957 yachting season. Payment of the price was to be made by five intalments. The contract contained a term (clause 8) similar to that in *Re Blyth Shipbuilding Co Ltd* (see above, p 270) by virtue of which the property in the uncompleted vessel passed to the buyer on payment of the first instalment. The yacht had defects rendering it unseaworthy when it was launched in June 1957, and these defects had not been remedied several months later when Aeromarine offered to finish the work on varied terms which McDougall was not prepared to accept. Diplock J held that the buyer was justified in rejecting the yacht and that, although the property may have passed pursuant to clause 8, it had passed only defeasibly, and had been revested in Aeromarine when McDougall rightly exercised his right to reject.

Diplock J: The defendants' failure to tender the yacht for delivery in accordance with the contract by September 5 was itself, I think, a breach of condition which the plaintiff was entitled to treat as rescinding the contract. Their intimation, for that was what their offer amounted to, that they could not complete it before the end of the 1957 yachting season was a fortiori, in my opinion, a wrongful repudiation of the contract by the defendants, as was their intimation that they would only complete the contract upon terms different from those of the original contract. The plaintiff by his letter of September 19 elected to treat the defendants' wrongful repudiation of the contract as rescinding it.

I hold that, in all the circumstances of the case, he was entitled to do so; but even if he were not, the defendants cannot rely on the plaintiff's purported rescission of the contract of September 19 as a wrongful repudiation on his part of the contract, thus relieving them from any further obligation to perform it, because they did not accept his repudiation but continued to hold him to the contract; and on October 30 they informed the plaintiff that they would insist either on completing the vessel on terms inconsistent with and less favourable to the plaintiff than those in the original contract, or those that they had offered in their letter of September 5, or upon delivering the vessel in its defective state with an allowance of 50 guineas off the contract price. This was, I think, yet another wrongful repudiation by the defendants of the contract, which the plaintiff was entitled to and did accept. Such part of the property, if any, in the vessel or any portion thereof as had previously vested in him under clause 8 of the contract accordingly revested then in the defendants.

CHAPTER 9

Transfer of title

1 The rule *nemo dat quod non habet*

In most contexts, it would be reasonable to regard the expressions 'Transfer of property as between seller and buyer' and 'Transfer of title' as meaning much the same thing. It therefore comes as something of a surprise to find that the Sale of Goods Act 1979 uses these terms to refer to quite different topics. The 'Transfer of property as between seller and buyer', dealt with in ss 16–19, does indeed have the fairly obvious meaning, ie the process by which ownership passes from the one party to the other. In contrast, under 'Transfer of title', the concern is with a number of situations in which a seller who is a *non-owner*, or a person with a *defective title*, can nevertheless confer a good title on his buyer, and in doing so defeat the claims of the true owner or of a person with a superior title. Of course, these are exceptional situations – as s 21, which sets out the basic rule, makes clear. This rule (summed up in the ancient maxim *nemo dat quod non habet* – or, for short, *nemo dat*), states that, subject to the Act,

> where goods are sold by a person who is not their owner, and who does not sell them under the authority or with the consent of the owner, the buyer acquires no better title to the goods than the seller had. . . .

The same, or a similar, basic rule applies (unless there are statutory or common law exceptions) to sales of land and other forms of property, to gifts, to bailments such as hire and pledge, and to the assignment of choses in action; and its importance cannot be over-emphasised – especially since the rule itself can be stated in a few lines, and the bulk of the discussion which is to follow will go into the exceptions at length and in some detail! Two well-known cases illustrate the *nemo dat* rule.

Cundy v Lindsay (1878) 3 App Cas 459, House of Lords

A rogue called Blenkarn, impersonating a well-known firm named Blenkiron which carried on business in the same street, ordered a quantity of linen by post from Lindsay & Co in Belfast. When the linen arrived, Blenkarn sold part of it to Messrs Cundy, who bought in good faith and without knowledge of Blenkarn's fraud. The first contract was held to be void (in modern terms, on the ground of mistake of identity), so that no title in the linen passed to Blenkarn. It followed that he could not confer any title on Cundy, who were consequently liable to Lindsay & Co in conversion.

Lord Cairns LC: My Lords, you have in this case to discharge a duty which is always a disagreeable one for any Court, namely, to determine as between two parties, both of whom are perfectly innocent, upon which of the two the consequences of a fraud practised upon both of them must fall. My Lords, in discharging that duty your Lordships can do no more than apply, rigorously, the settled and well known rules of law. Now, with regard to the title to personal property, the settled and well known rules of the law may, I take it, be thus expressed: by the law of our country the purchaser of a chattel takes the chattel as a general rule subject to what may turn out to be certain infirmities in the title. If he purchases the chattel in market overt, he obtains a title which is good against all the world; but if he does not purchase the chattel in market overt, and if it turns out that the chattel has been found by the person who professed to sell it, the purchaser will not obtain a title good as against the real owner. If it turns out that the chattel has been stolen by the person who has professed to sell it, the purchaser will not obtain a title. If it turns out that the chattel has come into the hands of the person who professed to sell it, by a *de facto* contract, that is to say, a contract which has purported to pass the property to him from the owner of the property, there the purchaser will obtain a good title, even although afterwards it should appear that there were circumstances connected with that contract, which would enable the original owner of the goods to reduce it, and to set it aside, because these circumstances so enabling the original owner of the goods, or of the chattel, to reduce the contract and to set it aside, will not be allowed to interfere with a title for valuable consideration obtained by some third party during the interval while the contract remained unreduced.

My Lords, the question, therefore, in the present case, as your Lordships will observe, really becomes the very short and simple one which I am about to state. Was there any contract which, with regard to the goods in question in this case, had pased the property in the goods from the Messrs Lindsay to Alfred Blenkarn? If there was any contract passing that property, even although, as I have said, that contract might afterwards be open to a process of reduction, upon the ground of fraud, still, in the meantime, Blenkarn might have conveyed a good title for valuable consideration to the present Appellants.

Now, my Lords, there are two observations bearing upon the solution of that question which I desire to make. In the first place, if the property in the goods in question passed, it could only pass by way of contract; there is nothing else which could have passed the property. The second observation is this, your Lordships are not here embarrassed by any conflict of evidence, or any evidence whatever as to conversations or as to acts done, the whole history of the whole transaction lies upon paper. . . .

Now, my Lords, . . . what the jurors have found is in substance this: it is not necessary to spell out the words, because the substance of it is beyond all doubt. They have found that by the form of the signatures to the letters which were written by Blenkarn, by the mode in which his letters and his applications to the Respondents were made out, and by the way in which he left uncorrected the mode and form in which, in turn, he was addressed by the Respondents; that by all those means he led, and intended to lead, the Respondents to believe, and they did believe, that the person with whom they were communicating was not Blenkarn, the dishonest and irresponsible man, but was a well known and solvent house of Blenkiron & Co, doing business in the same street. My Lords, those things are found as matters of fact, and they are placed beyond the range of dispute and controversy in the case.

If that is so, what is the consequence? It is that Blenkarn – the dishonest man, as I call him – was acting here just in the same way as if he had forged the signature of Blenkiron & Co, the respectable firm, to the applications for goods, and as if, when, in return, the goods were forwarded and letters were sent, accompanying them, he had intercepted the goods and intercepted the letters, and had taken possession of the goods, and of the letters which were addressed to, and intended for, not himself but, the firm of Blenkiron & Co. Now, my Lords, stating the matter shortly in that way, I ask the question, how is it possible to imagine that in that state of things any contract could have arisen between the Respondents and Blenkarn, the dishonest man? Of him they knew nothing, and of him they never thought. With him they never intended to deal. Their minds never, even for an instant of time rested upon him, and as between him and them there was no *consensus* of mind which could lead to any agreement or any contract whatever. As between him and them there was merely the one side to a contract, where, in order to produce a contract, two sides would be required. With the firm of Blenkiron & Co of course there was no contract, for as to them the matter was entirely unknown, and therefore the pretence of a contract was a failure.

The result, therefore, my Lords, is this, that your Lordships have not here to deal with one of those cases in which there is *de facto* a contract made which may afterwards be impeached and set aside, on the ground of fraud; but you have to deal with a case which ranges itself under a completely different chapter of law, the case namely in which a contract never comes into existence. My Lords, that being so, it is idle to talk of the property passing. The property remained, as it originally had been, the property of the Respondents, and the title which was attempted to be given to the Appellants was a title which could not be given to them.

My Lords, I therefore move your Lordships that this appeal be dismissed with costs, and the judgment of the Court of Appeal affirmed.

[Lords Hatherley and Penzance delivered concurring opinions.]

Jerome v Bentley & Co [1952] 2 All ER 114, Queen's Bench Division

Jerome entrusted a stranger, Major Tatham, with a diamond ring on terms that if he could sell it for more than £550 he could keep any surplus for himself, and that if he had not sold it within seven days he was to return it. Twelve days later, Tatham sold the ring for £175 to Bentleys, who bought in good faith thinking that he was the owner. After Bentleys had resold the ring, Jerome sued them in conversion and succeeded, on the ground that Tatham had had no authority to sell the ring to them.

Donovan J: Major Tatham belonged to no . . . well-known class of agent. He was simply a private individual, carrying on, so far as I know, no calling at all, to whom a ring had been entrusted for sale. . . . When Major Tatham sold the ring he was not the plaintiff's agent at all except, perhaps, for the purpose of safe custody of the ring. Major Tatham did more than exceed an authority to sell – he usurped it. . . .

It is said here that the plaintiff gave Major Tatham the ring to sell, and if he put limitations on the authority, such as a period of seven days, he should have communicated that fact to any interested third party. I cannot help wondering how the plaintiff was to do this, for he did not know to whom out of the whole population Major Tatham would offer the ring.

[His Lordship referred to a number of cases, and continued:]

That brings me to the circumstances in which Major Tatham sold the ring, the subject of the present dispute. On Jan 11, 1947, his sole duty was to hand the ring back to the plaintiff, and he had no authority to deal with it in any way except for the purpose of its safe custody. He has admitted that he stole the ring as a bailee. In other words, when he entered the shop he intended fraudulently to convert the ring to his own use, and he accomplished that purpose. He then became a thief of the ring. . . . No one represented Major Tatham to the defendants as the plaintiff's agent with authority to sell the ring. The defendants knew nothing of the plaintiff. In fact, they made Major Tatham show his identity card and sign a declaration that the ring was his. So they dealt with him on the footing of a principal selling his own property.

It is said that, even on the footing that Major Tatham was a thief, the defendants are entitled to succeed on the dictum of Ashhurst J, in *Lickbarrow v Mason* (below, p 300). Everything, however, depends on the construction to be put on the word 'enabled' in this passage. If I carelessly leave my front door unlocked so that a thief walks in and steals my silver, I have, in a sense, enabled him to steal it by not locking my door, but that does not prevent my recovering it from some innocent purchaser from the thief otherwise than in market overt. 'Enabled' in this context means the doing of something by one of the innocent parties which in fact misled the other. This is clearly to be deduced from Lord Lindley's speech in *Farquharson Bros & Co v King & Co* ([1902] AC 325). The plaintiff here did nothing which misled the defendants. In the circumstances I hold that no property in this ring passed to the defendants, and there is nothing to prevent the plaintiff from setting up his title as against them. Therefore, I decide in his favour.

Many of the exceptions to the *nemo dat* rule reflect a concern for the bona fide purchaser in a commercial transaction which is well put by Lord Denning in the following passage.

Bishopsgate Motor Finance Corpn Ltd v Transport Brakes Ltd [1949] 1 KB 322, Court of Appeal

(The facts are immaterial.)

Denning LJ: In the development of our law, two principles have striven for mastery. The first is for the protection of property: no one can give a better title than he himself possesses. The second is for the protection of commercial transactions: the person who takes in good faith and for value without notice should get a good title. The first principle has held sway for a long time, but it has been modified by the common law itself and by statute so as to meet the needs of our own times.

2 First exception: estoppel

At the beginning of this discussion, only part of s 21(1) was quoted. In full, the subsection reads as follows:

> Subject to this Act, where goods are sold by a person who is not their owner, and who does not sell them under the authority or with the consent of the owner, the buyer acquires no better title to the goods than the seller had, unless the owner of the goods is by his conduct precluded from denying the seller's authority to sell.

The word 'precluded' is more or less equivalent to 'estopped', which is perhaps a more familiar term for English lawyers. (Laymen and Scottish lawyers, however, will no doubt feel more at home with the word which the statute actually uses.) There are various ways in which the owner of goods might find himself 'precluded' from denying that he has given another person authority to sell them, but in essence this will be based either on (1) a representation to the buyer (or to the world at large) that that person (the person whom the Act calls 'the seller') is the owner's *agent* to sell the goods, or (2) a similar representation that the 'seller' is the *owner* of the goods. Most of the reported cases turn on the representation of an agency; and so there will necessarily be some overlap between the discussion in the present section and that in Chapter 5. There is also, at least in theory, the possibility that the owner may be in some way 'precluded' by his own negligence from denying the seller's authority to sell, but (as we shall see) this is largely an illusory concept.

At the outset, it is perhaps prudent to refer to the ancient dictum of Ashhurst J in *Lickbarrow v Mason* (1787) 2 Term Rep 63 at 70, which it is customary to cite in the present context. Ashhurst J said:

> We may lay it down as a broad general principle that, wherever one of two innocent persons must suffer by the acts of a third, he who has enabled such third person to occasion the loss must sustain it.

This statement is notorious as having been frequently cited (not least in examination questions!), and rarely, if ever, applied: indeed, on the one occasion when it was followed without proper analysis (*Commonwealth Trust v Akotey*, below), the court almost certainly came to the wrong answer. The word 'enabled', if broadly construed, would allow a third party to defeat the claims of the true owner of goods in far too wide a range of circumstances. For instance, if A lent a book to B and B then dishonestly sold it to C, it would be hard to deny that A had 'enabled' B to deceive C into buying the book; but it is unthinkable that the law would allow the proprietary rights of A to be defeated in such circumstances. Similar considerations would apply in the case where A forgot to lock the door of his house and so made it easier for B to steal the book and then sell it to C. So the dictum of Ashhurst J (which was in fact quite appropriate in the special context in which it was used) is nowadays cited largely for the purpose of discrediting it.

Commonwealth Trust v Akotey [1926] AC 72, Privy Council

Akotey sent 1050 bags of cocoa by rail to Laing, and sent him the consignment notes. He had previously sold cocoa to Laing, but on this occasion no agreement to sell had been concluded, Laing's offer of £2.50 a ton having been rejected as too low. Laing sold the cocoa to Commonwealth Trust, who bought in good faith. He handed over the consignment notes and was paid the price. Akotey claimed that the cocoa was still his, and sued Commonwealth Trust in conversion. The Privy Council, applying the dictum of Ashhurst J cited above, held that Akotey was estopped by his conduct from setting up his title.

The advice of the Privy Council was delivered by **Lord Shaw:** . . . It was further argued before their Lordships that although the property in the cocoa had not passed from the respondent, yet that the respondent had so acted as to estop him from setting up his title in answer to the claim of the appellants. Reliance was placed on the well-known statement of Ashhurst J in *Lickbarrow v Mason* [above], 'that wherever one of two innocent persons must suffer by the acts of a third, he who has enabled such third person to occasion the loss must sustain it.' Their Lordships are clearly of opinion that the present is a plain case for the application of that principle. There is no kind of specialty in this case such as occurred in *Farquharson Bros & Co v King & Co* ([1902] AC 325), the parallel to which would be that the goods were delivered to Laing by the fraudulent act of respondent's agent: the goods were in fact delivered over to Laing by the direct act of the respondent himself.

To permit goods to go into the possession of another, with all the insignia of possession thereof and of apparent title, and to leave it open to go behind that possession so given and accompanied, and upset a purchase of the goods made for full value and in good faith, would bring confusion into mercantile transactions, and would be inconsistent with law and with the principles so frequently affirmed, following *Lickbarrow v Mason*.

The owner of goods will lose his title to a third party (called in s 21(1) the 'buyer') if he has in some way *represented* (or 'held out') the truth of a fact or state of affairs which has led the buyer to believe that the seller is the owner of the goods or is authorised to deal with them on the owner's behalf, and the buyer has relied on this representation. Such a representation may be made by words or by conduct. A well-known case on estoppel by representation is *Eastern Distributors Ltd v Goldring*.

Eastern Distributors Ltd v Goldring [1957] 2 QB 600, Court of Appeal

(The facts appear from the judgment.)

The judgment of the court (Lord Goddard CJ, Romer LJ and Devlin J) was read by **Devlin J:**
... In 1955 the third party, Murphy, was in business, which he describes as that of a mobile greengrocer, and he owned a Bedford utility van which he used in the business and which is the subject-matter of this action. He wanted to buy a Chrysler car from a motor dealer called Coker, but he had no money to pay for it – not even enough for a deposit under a hire-purchase contract, so Coker suggested that he should raise the deposit on the security of the Bedford van by means of a hire-purchase contract on it. If the money was simply borrowed on the security of the van, the necessary instrument would be a bill of sale and would have to be registered as such. But there is nothing to prevent the owner of a vehicle from selling it to a hire-purchase company, pocketing the price and paying it back by instalments; and provided the sale is a genuine one and not a sham, effect will be given to it as a hire-purchase contract. Murphy would then be in a position to buy the Chrysler on hire-purchase terms, using the price of the Bedford to cover the deposit.

Coker was in touch with the plaintiffs, who are a hire-purchase company. The simplest way of carrying out the scheme, so far as it affected the Bedford, would have been for Murphy to have dealt direct with the plaintiffs, but Coker – perhaps because he wanted the deposit for the Chrysler to go straight to him or possibly for some other reason – suggested a different arrangement, and Murphy acquiesced in it. This was, that Coker should pretend to the plaintiffs that he was selling to Murphy the Bedford as well as the Chrysler. This involved also the pretence that Murphy had paid the deposit on both vehicles. Coker would then collect from the plaintiffs the balance of the price of both cars, which would in effect be the money for which he was selling the Chrysler to Murphy; and by paying off the instalments on both cars Murphy would pay the price of the Chrysler. In order to accomplish this plan, Murphy on May 5, 1955, signed in blank four hire-purchase documents – namely, the proposal forms and the memoranda of agreement for the Chrystler and the Bedford respectively. He left these for Coker to fill in. He signed also on the same day a delivery note stating that he had taken delivery of the Bedford.

What happened afterwards is uncertain. Coker, whom the judge has found not to be fraudulent, was not available to give evidence. The records of the plaintiffs were in confusion owing to a change of ownership. The judge has found that the proposal for the Chrysler did not go through. Nevertheless, Coker proceeded with the proposal for the Bedford. He did this without Murphy's authority, for the essence of the scheme was that the Bedford transaction was only ancillary to the purchase of the Chrysler. The judge has found that the plaintiffs accepted the Bedford proposal as a genuine hire-purchase transaction and dealt with it accordingly. On May 10, 1955, the plaintiffs bought the Bedford from Coker, as recorded in a sales note, for £180 less an initial payment of £60. The memorandum of hire-purchase agreement was completed on May 19, and the counterpart signed by the plaintiffs was sent to Murphy the same day. Coker let Murphy have the Chrysler for a bit, but then it was taken away and Coker appears to have told Murphy that the whole transaction was cancelled. Murphy says that he regarded himself as the lawful owner of the Bedford. He advertised his greengrocery business for sale and on June 24, 1955, he sold it, including the Bedford, to the defendant for £200. It is not disputed that the defendant bought in good faith and without any knowledge of Murphy's dealings with the Bedford.

Murphy paid no instalments under the hire-purchase contract. On August 22, 1955, the plaintiffs notified him that they would take possession of the Bedford. Later they ascertained that the defendant had it, and in January, 1956, they claimed it from him. He refused to give it up and they issued proceedings against him in the St Albans County Court claiming the vehicle or £180 as its value. The defendant joined Murphy as third party. On January 31, 1957, judgment was given for the plaintiffs against the defendant and for the defendant against the third party. The defendant says that his judgment against the third party is worthless, and the plaintiffs have not even bothered to sue him. So the case raises the familiar question of which of two innocent parties, the plaintiffs or the defendant, shall suffer for the misconduct of a third; and it is necessary to determine which of the two is in law entitled to the Bedford van.

The plaintiffs depend for their title upon the transaction with Coker. If Coker had sold the van on behalf of Murphy and with his authority, that would dispose of the matter. So it would if Murphy had actually transferred the property to Coker so as to give him something which he could sell in his own name. But in fact Murphy never transferred the van to Coker; and although he gave a general authorization to Coker to act in the way in which he did, he put, as the judge has found, a specific limitation upon Coker's authority and one which indeed followed from the nature of the transaction contemplated: this was that the two proposals should go forward together. Coker, the judge has found, had no authority to deal with the Bedford separately from the Chrysler. So the plaintiffs cannot claim that they bought the van from the owner or from one who had his actual authority to sell.

But equally it is clear that as against Murphy the plaintiffs acquired a good title to the Bedford. Coker represented that the car was his, and Murphy was privy to that representation being made; so neither can be heard to say that Coker had not a good title to transfer to the plaintiffs. Or, if the matter be looked at as one of principal and agent, the plaintiffs, being ignorant of the limitation placed on Coker's authority, are not affected by it. . . .

[On the relationship between s 21 and the doctrine of estoppel, his Lordship said:]

Of course, there are many cases of sale of goods where an agent has been held out or represented to have an authority to sell which he has not in fact got, and the solution of the difficulty so created might no doubt have been found by the application of the doctrine of estoppel, but in fact the courts of common law approached the problem of the unauthorized sale from a different angle.

They began with the principle that no one could pass a better title than that which he had: nemo dat quod non habet. To this general principle they admitted a number of exceptions, simply on the ground of mercantile convenience. The best known relate to transfers of currency and negotiable instruments. Sales in market overt afford another example. In these cases, as is well known, a transferee may acquire a better title than that of his transferor. In the same way, and for the same reason of mercantile convenience, the courts of common law allowed a good title to a buyer who bought in good faith from a man who apparently had been given by the true owner the right to dispose of the goods. Such a buyer did not merely acquire a title by estoppel, based on the implied representation by the owner that there was a right of disposition and vulnerable at the suit of anyone who was not bound by that representation. He acquired in the same way as the transferee of a negotiable instrument or the buyer in market overt a good title against all the world. . . .

[His Lordship quoted s 21(1), and continued:]

This section expresses the old principle that apparent authority to sell is an exception to the maxim nemo dat quod non habet; and it is plain from the wording that if the owner of the goods is precluded from denying authority, the buyer will in fact acquire a better title than the seller.

We doubt whether this principle, which is sometimes referred to – for example, by Wright J in *Lowther v Harris* [above] – as common law estoppel, ought really to be regarded as part of the law of estoppel. At any rate it differs from what is sometimes called 'equitable estoppel' in this vital respect, that the effect of its application is to transfer a real title and not merely a metaphorical title by estoppel. It is unnecessary to determine in this case whether it covers the exercise of every sort of apparent authority in relation to the sale of goods or whether it is confined to apparent authority to sell. . . .

It is sufficient to say that, whatever the limits of the doctrine, it clearly applies to the facts of this case. Coker was armed by Murphy with documents which enabled him to represent to the plaintiffs that he was the owner of the Bedford car and had the right to sell it. The result is that Murphy is, in the words of s 21, precluded from denying Coker's authority to sell, and consequently the plaintiffs acquired the title to the goods which Murphy himself had and Murphy had no title left to pass to the defendant. . . .

Very often, the estoppel which brings the exception to the *nemo dat* rule into play will be based on a representation (express or implied) that the 'seller' has the owner's *authority* to sell the goods as his *agent*.

Henderson & Co v Williams [1895] 1 QB 521, Court of Appeal

(The facts appear from the judgment.)

Lindley LJ: In this case a Liverpool sugar merchant, named Grey had 150 bags of sugar belonging to him warehoused in his name in the defendant's warehouse at Goole. On June 6, 1894, Grey was induced by the fraud of one Fletcher to authorize the defendant to hold these bags of sugar according to Fletcher's order. On the same day Fletcher agreed to sell them to the plaintiffs; but before the plaintiffs paid him for them they insisted on having them transferred into their own name. This was done on June 7, and the defendant informed the plaintiffs that he held the sugar at the plaintiffs' order and disposal. Thereupon the plaintiffs paid Fletcher for the goods. Grey afterwards discovered that he had been defrauded, and he gave notice to the defendant not to part with the bags of sugar. The defendant, being indemnified by Grey, has refused to deliver them to the plaintiffs, whereupon they bring this action to recover their value. The defendant defends this action for and on behalf of Grey. . . .

He contends – (1) that he is not estopped from setting up Grey's title; and (2) that his title is better than that of the plaintiffs. I am of opinion that the defendant is wrong upon the first point, even if he is right on the second. The distinct attornment by the defendant to the plaintiffs on June 7, 1894, clearly, in my opinion, estopped the defendant from denying the plaintiffs' title. . . .

[Lord Halsbury LC and A L Smith LJ delivered concurring judgments.]

Henderson v Williams may be contrasted with *Farquharson Bros v King.*

Farquharson Bros & Co v C King & Co [1902] AC 325, House of Lords

Farquharsons were timber merchants who warehoused in the Surrey Commercial Docks timber which they imported from abroad. They employed a confidential clerk, Capon, who was authorised to sign delivery orders addressed to the dock company, on the strength of which timber would be released to Farquharsons' customers. In 1896, Capon began a series of frauds. Using the name Brown, and working from an address in Battersea, he entered into contracts to sell timber to the respondents, King & Co, representing that 'Brown' was acting as the agent of someone called Bayley. He then issued delivery orders to the dock company directing it to transfer the appropriate quantity of Farquharsons' timber to 'Brown' or deliver it to Brown's order. As 'Brown', he sent further orders to the dock company authorising it to deliver this timber to King & Co. After the frauds had been discovered, Farquharsons sued King & Co in conversion. The House of Lords held that nothing which Farquharsons had done precluded them from denying that Capon had had authority to sell their timber.

Lord Lindley: Capon sold the plaintiffs' timber without their authority, and sold it to the defendants. The defendants honestly bought the timber, and they had no notice that Capon had no right to sell it; but there was no sale in market overt, and the Factors Acts do not apply. The mere fact, therefore, that the defendants acted honestly does not confer upon them a good title as against the plaintiffs, the real owners of the timber. The plaintiffs are entitled to recover the timber or its value, unless they are precluded by their conduct from denying Capon's authority to sell. (Sale of Goods Act 1893, s 21, and see s 61.) Capon sold under the name of Brown, representing himself to be an agent of some persons named Bayley, who were well known in the timber trade. The defendants bought on the faith of his being what he pretended to be. What have the plaintiffs done which precludes them from denying, as against the defendants, Capon's right to do what he pretended he was entitled to do? Putting the question in another form: What have the plaintiffs done to preclude them from denying, as against the defendants, Capon's right to sell to them? To answer those questions it is necessary to consider what the plaintiffs did.

Capon was the plaintiffs' confidential clerk; they gave him a limited power of sale to certain customers, and a general written authority to sign delivery orders on their behalf; and the plaintiffs sent that written authority to the dock company which stored the plaintiffs' timber. This authority would, of course, protect the dock company in delivering timber as ordered by Capon, however fraudulently he might be acting, if the dock company had no notice of anything wrong. By abusing his authority Capon made timber belonging to the plaintiffs deliverable by the dock company to himself under the name of Brown. In that name he sold it, and procured it to be delivered to the defendants. What is there here which precludes the plaintiffs from denying Capon's right to sell to the defendants?

What have the plaintiffs done to mislead the defendants and to induce them to trust Capon? Absolutely nothing. The question for decision ought to be narrowed in this way, for it is in my opinion clear that, when s 21 of the Sale of Goods Act has to be applied to a particular case, the inquiry which has to be made is not a general inquiry as to the authority to sell, apart from all reference to the particular case, but an inquiry into the real or apparent authority of the seller to do that which the defendants say induced them to buy.

It was pointed out by Parke J, afterwards Lord Wensleydale, in *Dickinson v Valpy* ((1829) 10 B & C 128, 140), that 'holding out to the world' is a loose expression; the 'holding out' must be to the particular individual who says he relied on it, or under such circumstances of publicity as to justify the inference that he knew of it and acted upon it. The same principle must be borne in mind in dealing with cases like the present. I do not myself see upon what ground a person can be precluded from denying as against another an authority which has never been given in fact, and which the other has never supposed to exist.

It was argued that the dock company were led by the plaintiffs to obey Capon's orders and to deliver to Brown, and that the defendants were induced by the dock company to deal with Brown, or at all events to pay him on the faith of his being entitled to the timber; so that in fact the plaintiffs, through the dock company, misled the defendants. This is ingenious but unsound. Except that delivery orders were sent in the name of Brown to the defendants, and were acted on by the dock company, there is no evidence connecting the dock company with the defendants in these transactions; and the answer to the contention is that the defendants were misled, not by what the plaintiffs did nor by what the plaintiffs authorized the dock company to do, but by Capon's frauds.

It is, of course, true that by employing Capon and trusting him as they did the plaintiffs enabled him to transfer the timber to any one; in other words, the plaintiffs in one sense enabled him to cheat both themselves and others. In that sense, every one who has a servant enables him to steal whatever is within his reach. But if the word 'enable' is used in this wide sense, it is clearly untrue to say, as Ashhurst J said in *Lickbarrow v Mason* (above, p 300), 'that wherever one of two innocent persons must suffer by the acts of a third, he who has enabled such third person to occasion the loss must sustain it.' Such a doctrine is far too wide; and the cases referred to in the argument . . . shew that it cannot be relied upon without considerable qualification. . . .

In the present case, in my view of it, Capon simply stole the plaintiff's goods and sold them to the defendants, and the defendants' title is not improved by the circumstance that the theft was the result of an ingenious fraud on the plaintiffs and on the defendants alike. The defendants were not in any way misled by any act of the plaintiffs on which they placed reliance; and the plaintiffs are not, therefore, precluded from denying Capon's authority to sell. . . .

[The Earl of Halsbury LC and Lords Macnaghten, Shand and Robertson delivered concurring opinions.]

In all of the cases discussed so far, there has been a representation, express or implied, on the part of the owner on which the alleged estoppel was based. It is usual to make a distinction between an *estoppel by representation* and an *estoppel by conduct*, although nothing in law appears to turn on this. Although s 21(1) itself uses the word 'conduct', it tells us nothing about the kinds of conduct (other than a representation) which might 'preclude' an owner from denying the 'seller's' authority to sell his goods. However, one point is well established. This is that for an owner merely to allow another person to have *possession* of his goods carries with it no implication that that person has any authority to sell them, even if the possession is given with a view to the person trying to find a buyer. This point is clearly illustrated by the case of *Jerome v Bentley* (above, p 299). In *Central Newbury Car Auctions Ltd v Unity Finance Ltd* (below), the same principle was applied in a case where the owner of a car had allowed a person to have possession not only of the car, but also of its registration certificate. It was held that the fact that the owner was allowed to arm himself with this document, as well as the car, made no difference, and that even though the owner might have acted negligently in not checking the identity and credentials of this person (see below, p 307), the position would be the same. Another case, *Mercantile Bank of India Ltd v Central Bank of India Ltd* [1938] AC 287, PC, confirms that to entrust another with possession of the *documents of title* to goods (in that case, railway receipts, which in Indian practice were treated as documents of title) can no more be relied on for the purposes of an estoppel than entrusting him with the goods themselves.

Central Newbury Car Auctions Ltd v Unity Finance Ltd [1957] 1 QB 371, Court of Appeal

Central Newbury bought a Morris car at auction and put it on display in their showroom. Its registration book (now called a registration certificate) was in the name of a previous owner, Ashley. A distinguished-looking person calling himself Cullis agreed to take the car on hire-purchase and was allowed to take it away, together with the registration book. Three days later, a man calling himself Ashley (no doubt the same swindler who had previously called himself Cullis) sold the car to Mercury Motors, signing the transfer of ownership form on the registration book with the name of Ashley. Mercury Motors later sold the car to Unity Finance, who resisted a claim by Central Newbury to have it back. It was held that Mercury Motors were not precluded from denying the swindler's authority to sell.

Morris LJ: . . . Now it is clear that the person who purported to sell the Morris car to Mercury Motors was not the owner of the car and he did not sell it under the authority or with the consent of the owner. The suggestion is therefore that if possession of a car and of its registration book is given to someone who has no authority to sell, but who wrongly purports to sell, the true owner may lose his ownership. Perhaps, however, the suggestion is more limited and should be stated as being that if an owner negligently gives possession of a car and of its registration book to someone who has no authority to sell but who wrongly purports to sell, the true owner may lose his ownership. But the element of negligence so introduced involves and implies a duty to take care and to be circumspect in regard to one's own property. That in turn raises the question as to whom the duty is owed. So as to cover every potential purchaser it must therefore be asserted that the owner owes a duty to the whole world.

What is said in the present case is that the plaintiffs gave Cullis possession both of the car and of the registration book and were negligent in so doing: it is said, therefore, that because of their conduct in being negligent they are precluded from denying that Cullis had any authority to sell. In other words, it is said that they cannot be heard to say to the defendants that Cullis had no right to sell. Why? Not because they were deceived by Cullis into letting him have the car – but because they also let him have the registration book. This must involve that if A gives to B possession of A's car with its registration book, A cannot be heard to say that he has not given to B an 'authority to sell.' This proposition seems to me to be far-reaching and to involve giving to a registration book a significance which it does not possess.

When Cullis presented himself at Birkenhead he was a complete stranger to Mercury Motors. They accepted what he said to them. They believed that he was Mr Ashley, who was selling his own car. They, of course, did not know that the car belonged to the plaintiffs and had no sort of thought of the plaintiffs in their mind. There was no question of any kind of representation from the plaintiffs. Mercury Motors proceeded to buy because they were duped by Cullis. Cullis would not have had the registration book but for the decision of the plaintiffs to allow him to have it, but, so far as Mercury Motors were concerned, they merely had what Cullis said to them, coupled with the fact of his physical possession of the car and the registration book. If the plaintiffs are to be precluded from denying Cullis's authority to sell, it seems to me that it must be because of the mere circumstance that they gave possession of the book as well as the car to Cullis. If they had given the car and book to Cullis in circumstances which involved no criticism upon them and without any carelessness, the situation would have been exactly the same so far as Mercury Motors are concerned. Therefore, it seems to me that the plaintiffs should only lose their ownership or be precluded from asserting it if it can be said that by parting with their car and its registration book they endowed the possessor of these with an apparent authority to sell. The proposition must be that though no apparent authority to sell can be assumed from mere possession of a car, nor from mere possession of a car registration book, the possession of a car with its book carries an apparent authority to sell. If Mercury Motors can assume that Cullis had a right to sell because Cullis had the car and its book, then it seems immaterial whether the plaintiffs put Cullis into possession because they were deceived without any carelessness on their part or because they were deceived and were in some ways careless. It cannot be that ownership is lost on the basis of enduring punishment for carelessness. The improvident householder who has left a window open at night which gives easy access for a thief is not in a worse position in asserting ownership of stolen articles than is the cautious householder who has checked the secure closing of his house.

It is doubtless true that criticism, particularly when available in the light of after events and after acquired knowledge, can be levelled against the plaintiffs. But it hardly seems entirely appropriate that the criticism should come from the Birkenhead purchasers. Are the plaintiffs to be estopped by negligence while the purchasers may be negligent with impunity? Nor does it seem fitting to weigh in the balance the respective criticisms of the actions of the parties and to see in which direction the scales are tipped. . . .

[Denning and Hodson LJJ delivered concurring judgments.]

There are suggestions in a number of cases that, in addition to estoppel by representation and estoppel by conduct, it may be possible for an owner of goods to be precluded by his *negligence* from asserting his title against a third party. The concept of estoppel by negligence is not unknown in other parts of the law. For instance, in relation to negotiable instruments: a person who carelessly draws a cheque leaving spaces which allow the amount to be altered by a rogue from 'two pounds' to 'two hundred pounds' may be liable to a holder of the cheque for the latter amount. But – despite the many dicta – it is difficult to find any case which gives support to the view that this concept of estoppel by negligence has any really significant role to play in the law of sale of goods. In *Central Newbury Car Auctions Ltd v Unity Finance Ltd* (above), we saw that Morris LJ said: 'It cannot be that ownership is lost on the basis of enduring punishment for carelessness.'

It is clear from this and other cases (eg *Jerome v Bentley* (above, p 299)) that the courts are not prepared to find that an owner of goods owes a duty of care to the world in general which would be broken merely by entrusting possession of his goods to another, even if the circumstances are somewhat dubious. Recent trends in the law of tort in relation to liability for negligently caused economic loss give no encouragement to the view that we are likely to see much relaxation in this attitude.

And even where it is possible to argue that the owner owed a duty of care to a specific plaintiff, rather than to all the world, it seems that the courts show the same reluctance to hold that the owner's negligence should cause him to lose the title to his goods. There are still two further hurdles for the plaintiff to overcome: he must persuade the court (1) that the duty of care was broken, on the facts of the case, and (2) that this breach of duty was the effective cause of the plaintiff's action in entering into the transaction by which he claims to have acquired the goods. In the cases which are next cited, one or more of these arguments failed.

Mercantile Credit Co Ltd v Hamblin [1965] 2 QB 242, Court of Appeal

The facts are somewhat similar to *Eastern Distributors Ltd v Goldring* (above, p 301). Mrs Hamblin wished to raise money on the security of her Jaguar car, and a car dealer called Phelan said that he could arrange for her to do this by selling the car to a finance company, Mercantile Credit, and taking it back from the company on hire purchase. He persuaded her to sign blank forms of a hire-purchase agreement with Mercantile Credit and other documents on the understanding that he would find out how much money could be raised and would report back to her before proceeding. In breach of the arrangement and without any authority from her he completed the blank forms and put the deal through and was paid £800 by the finance company. The Court of Appeal held that she was not estopped by negligence from claiming that the car still belonged to her.

Pearson LJ: In order to establish an estoppel by negligence, the finance company has to show (i) that the defendant owed it a duty to be careful, (ii) that in breach of that duty she was negligent, (iii) that her negligence was the proximate or real cause of it being induced to part with the £800 to the dealer. A great many cases were cited in the argument, but to my mind the principal task is to find what situations or relationships may give rise to the duty to be careful. . . .

In the present case, at the time when the defendant signed the documents in blank she was not then making a contract, but she was contemplating and contingently intending that she would eventually enter into a contract with some persons who would provide her with money on the security of the car. In fact the documents identified those persons as the finance company, but she had not read the documents: consequently, she did not have the finance company in contemplation, but she did contemplate that there would or might be some such persons with whom she would contract. She intended to make such a contract if and when the conditions were fulfilled, ie, if and when the amount and terms obtainable were reported to and agreed by her. She signed in blank the documents which would, if the conditions were fulfilled, constitute her offer to be accepted by the providers of the money, whoever they might be. She entrusted the documents to a dealer, who would be able, if so minded, to fill them in and present them to the providers of the money and secure their acceptance. She was arming the dealer with the means to make a contract ostensibly on her behalf. In my judgment, there was a sufficient relationship of proximity between the defendant and any persons who might contract to provide her with the money that she was seeking, to impose upon her a duty of care with regard to the preparation and custody of the contractual documents. The duty was owing to those persons, whoever they might eventually be found to be. They were in fact the finance company.

The next question is whether she committed any breach of duty, that is to say, whether she was negligent. On the peculiar facts of this case I think that there should not be a finding of negligence against her. She was well acquainted with the dealer, who was apparently respectable, solvent and prosperous, and the blank cheque which he gave her would naturally give her confidence that she could rely on his due performance of the arrangement which they had made.

Suppose, however, that she was negligent. There is then the question whether her negligence was the proximate or real cause of the finance company being induced to part with the money. In my judgment, the proximate or real cause was the fraud of the dealer. She gave him the means to commit his fraud, but his fraud was not, in the situation as it reasonably appeared to her, a natural or foreseeable consequence of what she did, and she should not be held responsible for it. I agree with the judge's finding on this point.

It follows that there is no estoppel by negligence, and no ostensible authority or holding out; the alleged hire-purchase agreement was invalid and not binding on the defendant; she has retained her ownership of the car; the finance company's claim fails, and the appeal should be dismissed. . . .

Salmon LJ: No doubt as a general rule the doctrine of estoppel by negligence applies only to negotiable instruments. I am not, however, by any means persuaded that there are no exceptions to this rule.

If the defendant had known that the dealer was a rogue likely to obtain money by fraud on the strength of the documents, then, in my judgment, she would have owed a duty to the world, of whom the finance company was a part, not to leave the signed documents in the dealer's possession. Her negligence in doing so would have precluded her from denying the truth of any representations the documents contained and on which the finance company had acted to its detriment. . . .

In the special circumstances of this case I do not consider that the defendant was careless in entrusting the dealer with the documents which she had signed in blank. After all, he was one of the most reputable car dealers in Nottingham and in a very large way of business. She could not reasonably foresee that he might use the documents for an improper purpose. She had every reason to trust him and none to doubt him. She left the forms which she had signed in blank with him, so that if she approved on the telephone of the terms and the amount of the loan he could obtain for her, he could immediately close the transaction for her without waiting for her to make the journey to his business premises in order to sign the documents. No doubt it is usually highly imprudent to sign documents in blank but it is not always so, and in the special circumstances of this case the defendant ought not to be blamed. This seems to me to dispose of the case against her. . . .

[Sellers LJ delivered a concurring judgment.]

Moorgate Mercantile Co Ltd v Twitchings [1977] AC 890, House of Lords

HP Information Ltd (HPI) maintained a register on which car dealers and finance companies recorded all motor-vehicle hire-purchase agreements that were notified to it by its members. At the time of the case, 98 per cent of all such hire-purchase agreements were on this record. The appellants and the respondents were both members of HPI. Moorgate had let a car on hire purchase to a man named McLorg, who then dishonestly sold it to Twitchings. By some error or oversight, Moorgate had failed to notify HPI that the car was on hire-purchase, and so when Twitchings made an inquiry HPI informed him that no hire-purchase agreement was recorded in respect of the car. Moorgate sued Twitchings claiming damages for conversion. Twitchings pleaded in reply that Moorgate were estopped by their negligence in having failed to notify the existence of the hire-purchase agreement; and alternatively they claimed to be entitled to set off the value of the car by way of damages in negligence. The House of Lords, by a majority, held that there was no estoppel, and no liability based on negligence.

Lord Fraser of Tullybelton: The conduct of Moorgate, by which it is said to be estopped from denying McLorg's authority to sell, is its omission to register with HPI its hire purchase agreement with him. That omission is said to have been negligent and is also the basis for the counterclaim of damages for negligence. So there is no practical difference as regards this case between the defence of estoppel by conduct and the counterclaim for damages; both depend upon establishing that Moorgate's omission to register the agreement was negligent. Negative conduct or omission will of course only be negligent, in the sense of wrongful, if there was a duty to act. If Twitchings are to succeed under either head they must therefore show (a) that Moorgate owed a duty to them to take reasonable care to register the agreement, (b) that Moorgate negligently failed to perform that duty, and (c) that their negligence was the proximate or real cause of Twitchings's loss. . . .

The first question then is whether Moorgate was under such a duty to Twitchings. The mere fact that registering hire purchase agreements was a usual practice in the business of finance houses such as Moorgate will not by itself give rise to a duty on the part of Moorgate towards Twitchings to register its agreements: see *Mercantile Bank of India Ltd v Central Bank of India Ltd* [1938] AC 287, 304. The reason why it is said that the duty was owed is that both parties were members of, or subscribers to, the registration scheme operated through HPI. Moorgate, as a finance house, was a full member of HPI and Twitchings, as dealers, was an affiliated member. At an earlier stage of the case it was contended on behalf of Twitchings that there had been a multi-lateral contract to which Moorgate and themselves had been parties, but that contention was not maintained in this House. The proposition here was that their common membership of the scheme created a relationship or propinquity between them which made them 'neighbours' in the sense of *Donoghue v Stevenson* [1932] AC 562, as extended by *Hedley Byrne & Co Ltd v Heller & Partners Ltd* [1964] AC 465, and so gave rise to the duty. If that proposition is right, it means that a finance house, by joining the registration scheme operated by HPI, subjected itself to a duty to other members including affiliated members, and perhaps to all users of the scheme, to take reasonable care to register all its hire purchase agreements with HPI.

[His Lordship examined the 'aims and objects' of HPI, and concluded:]

The primary purpose of the HPI scheme is, in my opinion, to provide protection to finance houses. But finance houses which are members of the scheme are under no obligation to anyone else to protect their own property by using the facilities of HPI. The owner of property is entitled to be careless with it if he likes, and even extreme carelessness with his own property will not preclude him from recovering it from a person who has bought it from someone who dishonestly purported to sell it: see *Farquharson Bros & Co v King & Co* [1902] AC 325 *per* Lord Macnaghten at pp 335–336, and *Swan v North British Australasian Co Ltd* (1863) 2 H & C 175. In my opinion Moorgate's conduct in not registering the hire purchase agreement with McLorg was, at worst, careless in respect of Moorgate's own property, and it was not in breach of any duty to other parties. It was quite different from the kind of conduct considered in *Eastern Distributors Ltd v Goldring* [1957] 2 QB 600, where the owner of a motor vehicle who had in effect armed a dishonest person with documents enabling him to represent himself as owner was held to be estopped from denying his authority to sell, and see also *Mercantile Credit Co Ltd v Hamblin* [1965] 2 QB 242, 275c. When Moorgate gave possession of its vehicle to McLorg on hire purchase terms, it was not doing anything of that sort. It is notorious that the person in possession of a motor vehicle is often not the owner of it, and the vehicle log book contains a warning that it is not proof of ownership of the vehicle. The very fact that dealers like Twitchings check with HPI before buying a vehicle from a stranger shows that they are well aware that possession and ownership may be separate. Accordingly, I am of opinion that when Moorgate, having given possession of their vehicle to McLorg under a hire purchase agreement, did not register the agreement with HPI, they were not in breach of any duty owed by them to Twitchings. Twitchings therefore fail to show the first of the three things that they have to establish if their defence is to be upheld. . . .

[Lords Edmund-Davies and Russell of Killowen delivered concurring opinions.]

Lord Wilberforce (dissenting): . . . [The contention] is that the appellants are estopped from asserting their ownership of the car by their conduct, ie, by their negligent omission to register their agreement.

In a consideration of this argument it is first necessary to be clear as to what elements are necessary in order to validate a claim of estoppel, a question which requires to be answered in the light of the fact that what, on this argument, is relied upon as founding the estoppel is inaction or silence rather than positive conduct. English law has generally taken the robust line that a man who owns property is not under any general duty to safeguard it and that he may sue for its recovery any person into whose hands it has come: see *Farquharson Bros & Co v King & Co* [1902] AC 325 *per* Earl of Halsbury, p 332 and piu andante Lord Macnaghten, p 336. He is not estopped from asserting his title by mere inaction or silence, because inaction or silence, by contrast with positive conduct or statement, is colourless: it cannot influence a person to act to his detriment unless it acquires a positive content such that that person is entitled to rely on it. In order that silence or inaction may acquire a positive content it is usually said that there must be a duty to speak or to act in a particular way, owed to the peson prejudiced, or to the public or to a class of the public of which he in the event turns out to be one. . . .

[Lord Wilberforce held that a duty lay, as between the parties as members of HPI, in the instant case. Lord Salmon, also dissenting, agreed.]

NOTES

1. As appears from the remarks of Devlin J in *Eastern Distributors Ltd v Goldring*, quoted above, it is perhaps a misnomer to speak of the title conferred upon the buyer under the exception to s 21(1) as being based on an estoppel. Normally, the effect of an estoppel is limited to the two parties in question, and it is binding only on the person making the representation. But the title which the buyer acquires under this exception is a title good against third parties and not just against the representor – for example, he may sue a third party in tort for wrongful interference with the goods.

2. A curious point of construction was raised in *Shaw v Metropolitan Police Comr* [1987] 1 WLR 1332. It will be noted that s 21(1) uses the phrase 'where goods are *sold* . . .', and not some wider expression such as 'where there has been a contract to sell . . .'. The Court of Appeal held that the word 'sold' had to be read literally and that the 'estoppel' exception did not apply where there had been only an agreement to sell. Here an overseas student who was about to leave Britain for his home country had entrusted a rogue (calling himself 'Mr London') with possession of his Porsche car, and had signed papers which were certainly sufficient to preclude him from denying London's authority to sell. London delivered the car to the plaintiff, Shaw, pursuant to an agreement to sell it to him, and disappeared. Shaw claimed to be entitled to keep the car under the exception to s 21(1), but the Court of Appeal held that this was not the case because there had been no *sale* to him – only an agreement to sell.

3 Second exception: sale under the Factors Act 1889, s 2

The second exception to the *nemo dat* rule is alluded to in s 21(2)(a) of the Sale of Goods Act 1979, which declares that 'nothing in this Act affects the provisions of the Factors Acts or any enactment enabling the apparent owner of goods to dispose of them as if he were their true owner'.

There have been Factors Acts going as far back as 1823; the latest is the Factors Act 1889. One of the oddest things about these Acts is the word 'factor' itself, which has survived in the statutory title even though the term is not used in the Act itself and (in this sense) has dropped out of commercial usage. In modern business, the expression 'factoring' is used in a wholly unrelated technical sense (the assignment or discounting of book-debts) which is described in Chapter 21. There is also a fairly common practice of describing dealers in certain components or spare parts as 'factors' – eg 'motor factors', or 'electrical factors'. The Factors Acts, however, refer to the type of commercial agent described in Chapter 3, who typically handles the goods of his client (or at the very least the documents of title relating to such goods) in the course of finding a buyer or seller for them: one everyday example is an auctioneer selling furniture or similar goods which are displayed prior to the sale in his showroom. (In this sense, the expression 'factor' is to be contrasted with 'broker', who is an agent who buys or sells without, as a rule, physically handling the property or documents: see above, p 79.) The statute uses the term 'mercantile agent' instead of the obsolete 'factor', and defines it as follows (Factors Act 1889, s 1(1)):

> For the purposes of this Act the expression 'mercantile agent' shall mean a mercantile agent having in the customary course of his business as such agent authority either to sell goods or to consign goods for the purpose of sale, or to buy goods, or to raise money on the security of goods.

We can infer from this not very helpful definition that a mercantile agent must be someone who has a business, and who in the course of that business buys or sells goods for other people.

A more complete picture may be gained if we look also at s 2(1), which is the section of the Factors Act that contains the second of our exceptions to the *nemo dat* rule:

> Where a mercantile agent is, with the consent of the owner, in possession of goods or of the documents of title to goods, any sale, pledge, or other disposition of the goods, made by him when acting in the ordinary course of business of a mercantile agent, shall, subject to the provisions of this Act, be as valid as if he were expressly authorised by the owner of the goods to make the same; provided that the person taking under the disposition acts in good faith, and has not at the time of the disposition notice that the person making the disposition has not authority to make the same.

It will thus be seen that the exception applies, broadly, where the mercantile agent has in the course of his business possession of the owner's goods for the purposes of sale, consistently with the traditional but now obsolete meaning of the word 'factor'.

The effect of the exception set out in s 2 is that in the special case where goods are in the possession of a mercantile agent, the ruling laid down in such cases as *Jerome v Bentley* (above, p 299) is reversed. Normally, as we have seen, the mere fact that S has possession of O's goods gives rise to no inference that S has O's authority to sell them to B, and if S has purported to make such a sale, O is not estopped from denying that S has such authority. The same rule applies where S has documents of title relating to the goods (*Mercantile Bank of India v Central Bank of India*, above, p 306). But if S is a *mercantile agent* and the other conditions of s 2(1) are satisfied, B is entitled to infer that S is acting with O's authority, and B will get a good title as against O. An example is *Weiner v Harris*.

Weiner v Harris [1910] 1 KB 285, Court of Appeal

Weiner, a manufacturing jeweller, entrusted goods to Fisher as his agent for the purposes of sale. Fisher had a shop in Harrogate from which he sold jewellery, and he also travelled the country selling jewellery for other people. The case concerned certain items which Fisher had without Weiner's authority pledged with Harris, a Cardiff pawnbroker.

Cozens-Hardy MR: . . . Then it is said that . . . this case is not within the Factors Act. It is necessary for that purpose to refer only to ss 1 and 2. Section 1, sub-s 1, says 'For the purposes of this Act the expression "mercantile agent" shall mean a mercantile agent having in the customary course of his business as such agent authority either to sell goods' – that is the only part which is material. Then s 2, sub-s 1, says this: 'Where a mercantile agent is, with the consent of the owner, in possession of goods or of documents of title to goods, any sale, pledge, or other disposition of the goods, made by him when acting in the ordinary course of business of a mercantile agent, shall . . . be valid.' Apply that first section. Many thousand pounds' worth of goods were handed over by Weiner to be dealt with on the footing of this letter. I am bound to say I cannot imagine a mercantile agent within the meaning of this section if Fisher was not. He was sent all over the country by Weiner for the very purpose of disposing of the goods upon the footing of the letter, and to say that his business was that of a shopkeeper is altogether irrelevant to any question we have to decide here. . . . In my opinion . . . the defendant, having regard to the provisions of the Factors Act, has a perfectly good title to this pledge.

[Fletcher Moulton and Farwell LJJ delivered concurring judgments.]

A mercantile agent must, as we have seen, have a business. What sort of business? How much of a business? Is it possible to be a mercantile agent on a single occasion? After all, everyone intending to set up in business as a mercantile agent has to begin with his first transaction! The next two cases give an indication of the courts' approach to this question.

Lowther v Harris [1927] 1 KB 393, King's Bench Division

Colonel Lowther kept furniture and antiques (including two valuable tapestries) stored in a house in Chelsea. Prior had a shop nearby from which he sold mainly glass and china. Lowther engaged Prior to seek buyers for the stored articles, but Prior was not authorised to sell anything without obtaining Lowther's approval. Customers were brought to the house to see the tapestries, and after one such visit Prior obtained Lowther's consent to remove one of the tapestries by falsely telling Lowther that he had sold it to Woodhall for £525. In fact, he had not sold the tapestry to anyone; but he later sold it to Harris for £250. Wright J held that Prior had been entrusted with possession of this tapestry as a mercantile agent, with the consequence that Harris obtained a good title under the Factors Act. (A claim in respect of a second tapestry which Prior had simply stolen and then sold to Harris failed, because it was held that Prior had never had possession of it with Lowther's consent.)

Wright J: . . . Unless the defendant has a defence under the Factors Act 1889, or on the ground of common law estoppel, it is clear that he is liable in damages for conversion, which damages, if recoverable by the plaintiff, I fix at £350 in the case of the Aubusson tapestry, and at £270 in the case of the Leopard tapestry. The circumstances relating to the two pieces of tapestry are different and require separate consideration. I shall first deal with the Aubusson tapestry, and shall first consider the defence based on the Factors Act 1889, in order to ascertain if the conditions of the Act are fulfilled. The first question is whether Prior was a mercantile agent – that is, an agent doing a business in buying or selling, or both, having in the customary course of his business such authority to sell goods. I hold that he was. Various objections have been raised. It was contended that Prior was a mere servant or shopman, and had no independent status such as is essential to constitute a mercantile agent. It was held under the earlier Acts that the agent must not be a mere servant or shopman: *Cole v North Western Bank* ((1875) LR 10 CP 354, 372); *Lamb v Attenborough* ((1862) 1 B & S 831); *Hyman v Flewker* ((1863) 13 CBNS 519). I think this is still law under the present Act. In my opinion Prior, who had his own shops, and who gave receipts and took cheques in his own registered business name and earned commissions, was not a mere servant but an agent, even though his discretionary authority was limited. It is also contended that even if he were an agent he was acting as such for one principal only, the plaintiff, and that the Factors Act 1889, requires a general occupation as agent. This, I think, is erroneous. The contrary was decided under the old Acts in *Hyman v Flewker*, and I think the same is the law under the present Act. . . .

The next question is whether Prior was in possession of the Aubusson tapestry, and, if so, with the consent of the plaintiff, and, if he had such possession, whether it was in his capacity as mercantile agent. I add the last consideration because I think that, just as such a condition was imported in the old Factors Acts (see *Cole v North Western Bank* and cases there cited), the same condition must be satisfied under the Factors Act of 1889. For the defendant it was contended that the tapestry, while lying at 10 Palace Street, was in the possession of Prior, relying on the facts that Prior had the use for residence of the top floor and the sitting room below, and further that he had disposing control over the goods in the house. As to Prior's residence in the house, I hold that the furniture in it, including the tapestry, was in the possession of the plaintiff, because Mr Urwin, who was the lessee and occupier of the house, and who was in attendance during business hours, was merely a servant of the plaintiff, so that his possession was the plaintiff's possession. I adopt the language of Pollock and Wright on Possession, p 38: 'It will hardly be denied that a man is in possession in fact, as well as possessor in law, of his own goods in the house which he occupies, whether he be in the room at a given moment, or even in the house, or not.' The plaintiff did all in his power to exclude any unauthorized dealing with the goods by Prior while they were in the house. As to Prior's use of the top floor and sitting room, I think Prior was merely in the position of a licensee, and perhaps caretaker, but never in possession of the plaintiff's goods in 10 Palace Street. . . . But I do hold that Prior became in possession of the Aubusson tapestry when he was allowed to take it away in the van after the plaintiff had sanctioned a sale to Woodhall. It is true that no such sale had in fact been made or was intended to be made, and that the possession was obtained by the fraud of Prior. Possession, however, was in fact obtained by Prior, and obtained by him in his capacity as mercantile agent. For the plaintiff it was contended that Prior obtained the tapestry under colour of an actually completed sale, and merely for purpose of delivery and as a sort of carrier between vendor and vendee. I think that is erroneous. Prior's functions as a mercantile agent were not completed even if a bargain had been concluded, but extended to the delivery of the goods, the collecting of the price, and the giving of a receipt and a subsequent accounting to the plaintiff. Delivery of possession to Prior was a necessary step to enable him to complete his office.

I accordingly hold that Prior obtained possession of the Aubusson tapestry in his capacity as a mercantile agent and with the consent of the plaintiff; having such possession, he made (as I have found above), in the ordinary course of business of a mercantile agent, a sale to the defendant, who, it is not contested, acted in good faith and with no notice of Prior's want of authority. I hold that the defendant establishes his defence as regards the Aubusson tapestry under the Factors Act 1889. This conclusion renders it unnecessary to discuss the plea based on estoppel at common law. I merely observe that on the facts established the defendant had no notice of the actual relations between the plaintiff and Prior, or how as between them business was conducted, and knew nothing except that the tapestry belonged to the plaintiff, and that Prior, whom the defendant regarded as a commission dealer, stated he was selling it on behalf of the plaintiff.

[His Lordship then dealt with the sale of the Leopard tapestry, and held that as to this the defence under the Factors Act 1889, failed, because Prior never had possession of it with the consent of the plaintiff, and therefore the conditions of the Act were not fulfilled. He held that as to this tapestry the plaintiff was entitled to recover.]

Budberg v Jerwood (1934) 51 TLR 99, King's Bench Division

The Baroness Marie de Budberg had escaped from Russia in 1921, bringing with her a pearl necklace worth £600 which she had smuggled out of the country by concealing it in her mouth. In London she decided to sell it, and entrusted it to Dr Thadee de Wittchinsky, an eminent Russian lawyer who since the revolution had acted as a legal adviser to Russian refugees in England. Dr de Wittchinsky pawned the necklace for £50 without telling the Baroness, and kept the money. Later, he redeemed the pledge and sold the necklace to Jerwood, who bought in good faith. After the death of Dr de Wittchinsky, the true facts were discovered and the Baroness sued to recover her necklace. A plea that Dr de Wittchinsky had acted as a mercantile agent failed.

Macnaghten J in his judgment stated that: . . . a mercantile agent was a person who in the ordinary course of his business as such agent had authority to sell goods. Now, Dr de Wittchinsky was a doctor of laws, who, towards the end of his life, had a permanent residence in London and there carried on business as a lawyer advising Russians living in this country. None of the witnesses had treated him as having any other business than that of a lawyer. But it was suggested that he acted as a mercantile agent in this transaction. It was said that it was possible that a man could be a mercantile agent although he had only one customer. In support of that proposition the defendants cited *Lowther v Harris* ([1927] 1 KB 393). He accepted that proposition, but it was qualified to this extent, that the alleged agent must be acting in the particular transaction in a business capacity. Here it was clear that the relationship between the plaintiff and Dr de Wittchinsky was not a business relationship. There was no suggestion of remuneration, and he was acting merely as a friend. In those circumstances the Factors Act did not apply. . . .

For s 2(1) to apply, all the conditions specified in the section must, of course, be satisfied. It is best to take the key phrases one by one, since many of them have been the subject of judicial consideration.

(a) 'Where a mercantile agent is, *with the consent of the owner*, in possession of goods . . .'

This requirement of consent is amplified by subss (2) and (3) of s 2. These provisions state respectively that (1) where the owner has once given consent to the mercantile agent having possession, that consent is deemed to continue even although it has been determined, unless the person dealing with the agent has notice of the determination; and (2) a consent to possession of goods carries with it a deemed consent to the possession of any documents of title relating to the goods which the agent has obtained by reason of his having or having had possession of the goods.

The cases establish that it is not sufficient that the owner should have consented to the agent having possession: he must consent to his having possession *in his capacity as mercantile agent*. The older Factors Acts used the word 'intrusted'; and the essential idea is that this 'intrusting' should be with a view to a sale, or a possible sale, by the agent – that is, for a purpose connected with his business as a selling agent. However, the courts have taken a fairly broad approach to this question, as Denning LJ explained in the following extract:

Pearson v Rose & Young Ltd [1951] 1 KB 275, Court of Appeal

(The facts are irrelevant.)

Denning LJ: In the early days of the common law the governing principle of our law of property was that no person could give a better title than he himself had. But the needs of commerce have led to a progressive modification of this principle so as to protect innocent purchasers. We have had cases in this court quite recently about sales in market overt and sales by a sheriff; and now we have the present case about sales by a mercantile agent. The cases show how difficult it is to strike the right balance between the claims of true owners and the claims of innocent purchasers. The way that Parliament has done it in the case of mercantile agents is this: Parliament has protected the true owner by making it clear that he does not lose his right to goods when they are taken from him without his consent, as for instance when they have been stolen from his house by a burglar who has handed them over to a mercantile agent. The true owner can in that case claim them back from any person into whose hands they came, even from an innocent purchaser who has bought from a mercantile agent. But Parliament has not protected the true owner, if he has himself consented to a mercantile agent having possession of them: because, by leaving them in the agent's possession, he has clothed the agent with apparent authority to sell them; and he should not therefore be allowed to claim them back from an innocent purchaser.

The critical question, therefore, in every case is whether the true owner consented to the mercantile agent having possession of the goods. This is often a very difficult question to decide. . . .

If the true owner consents to the mercantile agent having the goods for repair but not for sale, is that a consent which enables the Factors Act to operate? The answer would seem at first sight to be 'Yes', because it is undoubtedly a consent to the agent having possession. But this needs testing. Suppose, for instance, that the owner of furniture leaves it with a repairer for repair, and that the repairer happens to be a dealer as well, does that mean that the repairer can deprive the true owner of his goods by selling them to a buyer? Clearly not, if the owner did not know the repairer to be a dealer; and even if he did, why should that incidental knowledge deprive the true owner of his goods? Such considerations have led the courts to the conclusion that the consent, which is to enable the Factors Act 1889, to operate, must be a consent to the possession of the goods by a mercantile agent as mercantile agent. . . . That means that the owner must consent to the agent having them for a purpose which is in some way or other connected with his business as a mercantile agent. It may not actually be for sale. It may be for display or to get offers, or merely to put in his showroom; but there must be a consent to something of that kind before the owner can be deprived of his goods.

[Somervell LJ and Vaisey J delivered concurring judgments.]

This point, which was also emphasised in *Lowther v Harris* (above), is confirmed by the following cases.

Staffs Motor Guarantee Ltd v British Wagon Co Ltd [1934] 2 KB 305, King's Bench Division

Heap was a mercantile agent who dealt in secondhand lorries. He had in his possession a six-ton Commer lorry which he had once owned, but had sold to British Wagon and then taken back on hire-purchase. Without authority from British Wagon, he later sold it to Staffs Motor. When Heap failed to keep up his hire-purchase payments, British Wagon repossessed the lorry. Staffs Motor in this action claimed that this action was a violation of their rights as owners, arguing that their purchase from Heap had given them a good title under s 2 of the Factors Act 1889. The Court of Appeal rejected this claim, on the ground that Heap's possession had been qua hirer under the hire-purchase agreement, and not qua mercantile agent.

MacKinnon J: . . . The plaintiffs say that the defendants entrusted the possession of the lorry to Heap, who was a mercantile agent for the sale of second-hand lorries, and that they, the plaintiffs, in good faith and without any notice of his want of authority, entered into a contract with him for the purchase of the lorry, and, therefore, they claim that they have a good title to the lorry as against the defendants pursuant to the provisions of that section. There was no doubt some evidence that Heap did deal in second-hand motor vehicles as an ordinary seller of them. I will suppose that, if an ordinary owner of a motor-car had brought his car to Heap and asked him to sell it for him and Heap had sold it to some one at a lower price than that authorized by the true owner or otherwise not in accordance with his instructions, the purchaser from Heap would be entitled under the section which I have quoted to claim as against the true owner. I think, however, that it has rightly been pointed out on behalf of the defendants that there would be this difficulty in the way of the plaintiffs' assertion of that claim, that if the transaction between the defendants and Heap was a genuine transaction – and the plaintiffs' claim in this respect arises on that basis – then the lorry had been sold by Heap to the defendants and had been entrusted by the defendants to Heap not as a mercantile agent dealing in or selling motor vehicles, but to Heap as a hirer of the car and therefore as its bailee. In these circumstances I do not think that it is open to the plaintiffs to say that the defendants entrusted the car to Heap as a mercantile agent. . . .

Because one happens to entrust his goods to a man who is in other respects a mercantile agent, but with whom he is dealing not as a mercantile agent but in a different capacity, I do not think that it is open to a third party who buys the goods from that man to say that they were in his possession as a mercantile agent and that therefore he had power to sell them to a purchaser and so give him a good title to them. The claimant must be able to assert not only that the goods were in the man's possession as a mercantile agent, but also that they were entrusted by the owner to him as a mercantile agent. . . .

[MacKinnon J also thought that similar reasoning applied to a claim based on s 25(1) of the *NB* Sale of Goods Act 1893 [SGA 1979, s 24], but on this point his judgment has since been overruled: see below, p 328.]

Astley Industrial Trust Ltd v Miller [1968] 2 All ER 36, Queen's Bench Division

This decision is primarily of importance because it confirmed the authority of the above line of cases even although another ground of decision in the *Staffs Motor* case had since been overruled, as mentioned above. A firm called Droylesden had two businesses: hiring out cars, and dealing in cars. It did not own its hire cars, but took them on hire-purchase from Astley through a dealer called Lomas. Droylesden acquired a new Vauxhall car on hire-purchase from Astley to put into its rental fleet, and the following day, without authority from Astley, sold it to Miller, who bought in good faith. It was held that since Droylesden had possession of the car qua hire-purchaser and not qua motor dealer, s 2 of the Factors Act 1889 did not apply to the transaction, and in consequence Miller was bound to return the car to Astley or pay its value.

Chapman J: . . . It is plain on the facts as I have found them: (a) that at the material time the car in question was in the possession of Droylesden, who were not then the true owners; (b) that this possession by Droylesden was with the consent of the true owner, Lomas; (c) that Droylesden were persons who were, albeit as a sideline and as a subsidiary to their main business of hire car operators, trading as motor dealers in the sense that they bought and sold cars, at any rate on the second-hand market.

Counsel for the defendant has contended that, if these three conditions are satisfied, the situation is that a person who is in fact a mercantile agent, and who has in fact possession of someone else's property with the consent of that someone else, is clothed with ostensible or apparent authority to make any sale, pledge or other disposition of it which may appeal to his lust for pecuniary gain or his urge to perpetrate a fraud. Counsel for the plaintiffs, on the other hand, has contended that there is inherent in the statutory language a fourth condition, namely, that the goods must have been entrusted by the true owner or with his permission to the mercantile agent in his capacity as a mercantile agent; unless this is so, there is, he contends, no basis for saying that the true owner has clothed the mercantile agent with authority to act in that capacity. Counsel for the defendant has disputed this interpretation of the statute on the basis that it involves reading into the statute words which are not there.

Of course, one must always construe the words of an Act of Parliament strictly; that is, with precision. This is particularly true when questions of title are concerned and especially when the title is that of a completely honest, respectable and blameless person. The meaning of words, however, does not always end at the minimal dictionary content of each word taken as a separate entity, and this is as true of words in a section of an Act of Parliament as of words in a passage of verse or poetry. Counsel for the defendant's construction would, for example, lead to this result: if I take my car into the local garage to have a puncture repaired, or to be greased, or to have a general check-up before going on holiday, I would be at the risk of the garage not only purporting to sell it, but actually passing good title if, besides carrying out repairs and servicing for customers, they professed the business of buying and selling motor cars (whether second-hand or new). This would seem a startling conclusion. Or to go further to extremes: if my next-door neighbour (being in fact a motor dealer) came to me and said, 'My car has to go into dock for a fortnight. You are going on a cruise for your holidays. Would you, as a friend, lend me your car while you are away?' If, as one neighbour to another, I yielded to his importunity, I would, according to counsel's argument, be at risk of losing my car, merely because he happened to be a motor dealer, if he decided to flog it to some fly-by-night. At such a conclusion one's commonsense revolts.

The authorities seem to be all one way on this point, namely, in favour of counsel for the plaintiff's argument and against counsel for the defendant.

[His Lordship referred to a number of cases, and continued:]

Counsel for the defendant has contended that this formidable body of authority has all been swept away by *Pacific Motor Auctions Pty Ltd v Motor Credits (Hire Finance) Ltd* (below, p 328). That case dealt with s 28(1) of the Sale of Goods Act 1923–1953, of New South Wales, which covers cases where a person, having sold goods, continues in possession of the goods. That is the equivalent of s 25(1) of our Sale of Goods Act 1893 [now s 24 of the Act of 1979]. The Privy Council, in a judgment delivered by Lord Pearce, held that the continuity of possession required by the section was continuity of a physical possession, and that it did not matter if, by a private transaction, there was a change in the legal nature of the possession, eg, from possession of a seller, paid or unpaid, to possession of a bailee under a hire-purchase agreement. In so holding, the Privy Council expressly dissented from the view expressed by MacKinnon J, in *Staffs Motor Guarantee Ltd v British Wagon Co Ltd* [above]. . . . But this view of MacKinnon J, as to the effect of s 25(1) of the Sale of Goods Act 1893, is entirely separate and distinct from the view expressed by the same judge in the same case on the effect of s 2(1) of the Factors Act 1889. On the Sale of Goods Act point, the learned judge has been overruled, but I find nothing in the *Pacific Motor Auctions* case to suggest that the learned judge's point of view on the Factors Act point has been in any way eroded. . . .

Accordingly, I take it to be well settled and unchallenged law that the statutory power to pass title which is vested in a mercantile agent depends on his having possession in his capacity as a mercantile agent and on the true owner having consented to his having possession in that capacity. In the present case, on the facts as I have found them, Droylesden did not have possession of the Vauxhall in their capacity as mercantile agents, nor did Lomas consent to their having possession in that capacity. Droylesden, therefore, had no power to pass title to anybody.

The consent of the owner for the purposes of applying s 2 is regarded as having been given even though it has been obtained by deception.

Folkes v King [1923] 1 KB 282, Court of Appeal

Folkes entrusted his Austin touring car to Hudson, a mercantile agent, with a view to sale, but on the express understanding that the car would not be sold for less than

£575 without Folkes's permission. Hudson dishonestly sold the car at once to Alvarez, who bought in good faith, for £340 and, after several further sales, it was eventually bought by King. Folkes sued King for the return of the car, but his claim was held barred by s 2 of the Factors Act 1889. The main issue in the case turned on the now-obsolete distinction in the criminal law between 'obtaining by false pretences' and 'larceny by a trick'. Older cases had held that there was 'consent' for the purposes of s 2 in the former case, but no 'consent' in the latter. In this case, the Court of Appeal ruled that the distinction was immaterial, and that there was 'consent' in both situations.

Scrutton LJ: . . . First on the question whether to prove larceny by a trick is a defence to the Factors Act as excluding consent of the true owner. I can understand that where by a trick there is error in the person there is no true consent and the Factors Act is excluded. But where there is agreement on the person and the true owner intends to give him possession, it does not seem to me that the fact that the person apparently agreeing to accept an agency really means to disregard the agency, and act for his own benefit, destroys the consent of the true owner under the Factors Act. That Act intended to protect a purchaser in good faith carrying out an ordinary mercantile transaction with a person in the position of a mercantile agent. It does not do so completely, for it requires the purchaser to prove that the goods were in possession of the mercantile agent 'with the consent of the owner.' But it does not require the purchaser in addition to prove that the mercantile agent agreed both openly and secretly, ostensibly and really, to the terms on which the owner transferred possession to the mercantile agent. It appears to me to be enough to show that the true owner did intentionally deposit in the hands of the mercantile agent the goods in question. It is admitted that if he was induced to deposit the goods by a fraudulent misrepresentation as to external facts, he has yet consented to give possession, and the Factors Act applies, but it is argued that if he deposits the goods in the possession of an agent who secretly intends to break his contract of agency the Factors Act does not apply. I do not think Parliament had any intention of applying the artificial distinctions of the criminal law to a commercial transaction, defeating it if there were larceny by a trick, but not if there were only larceny by a bailee, or possession obtained by false pretences.

[Bankes LJ and Eve J delivered concurring judgments.]

NOTES

1. Compare *Du Jardin v Beadman Bros Ltd* [1952] 2 QB 712, where a similar interpretation was given to the expression 'consent of the seller' in s 25(1) of the Sale of Goods Act 1979 (see below, p 332).

2. It is still conceivable that a court would hold that a consent obtained by fraud might amount to no consent at all, if the circumstances were such as to make the owner the victim of a material mistake of identity, as in such contract cases as *Cundy v Lindsay* (above, p 297) and *Ingram v Little* [1961] 1 QB 31, CA. In *Folkes v King* (above), Scrutton LJ said ([1923] 1 KB 282 at 305): 'I can understand that where by a trick there is error in the person there is no true consent and the Factors Act is excluded.'

3. In *Beverley Acceptances Ltd v Oakley* [1982] RTR 417, CA it was held that the 'possession' and the 'disposition' referred to in s 2(1) had to be simultaneous: it was not sufficient that the person in question had once had possession qua mercantile agent but had lost it prior to the purported disposition.

4. In two cases, the court seems to have put a rather strained interpretation on the wording of s 2 out of indulgence for a car-owner who had been defrauded by a dishonest dealer. In each case the car had been delivered to a dealer with instructions to obtain offers, but with no authority to sell. The dealer had, however, sold the car to a purchaser in circumstances which would have been covered by s 2 but for the fact that the dealer had got possession of the car's registration certificate without the owner's consent. In the first, *Pearson v Rose & Young Ltd* [1951] 1 KB 275, CA the registration certificate had been unintentionally left with the dealer when the owner was called away on an errand of mercy; in the second, *Stadium Finance Ltd v Robbins* [1962] 2 QB 664, CA the owner had retained the ignition key, but the dealer had used a duplicate key and opened the glove-box where the registration certificate had been locked away. The court in each case seized on the fact that there was no consent to the dealer having possession of the registration certificate and found for the owner, in *Pearson* on the ground that 'the goods' in s 2 meant the car *with* its registration certificate, and the owner had not consented to the dealer having possession of the latter; in *Stadium Finance* on the rather narrower ground that the sale of the car having been made (to a finance company with a view to letting it to a customer on hire-purchase) without either the ignition key or the registration certificate, was not a sale 'in the ordinary course of business'.

QUESTION

Mary entrusts her car to Jock, a back-street car dealer, with instructions not to sell it for less than £4000. Jock has induced Mary to do so by telling her that he is Jake, a well-known and reputable dealer with showrooms in the High Street. Jock at once sells the car for £3000 to Lucy, who buys in good faith. Advise Mary.

(b) 'When acting in the ordinary course of business as a mercantile agent'

This phrase was explained by Buckley LJ in *Oppenheimer v Attenborough & Son* [1908] 1 KB 221 at 230–231 as follows:

> I think it means, 'acting in such a way as a mercantile agent acting in the ordinary course of business of a mercantile agent would act'; that is to say, within business hours, at a proper place of business, and in other respects in the ordinary way in which a mercantile agent would act, so that there is nothing to lead the [buyer] to suppose that anything wrong is being done, or to give him notice that the disposition is one which the mercantile agent had no authority to make.

In *Stadium Finance Ltd v Robbins* (above), we saw that the sale of a vehicle without an ignition key or registration certificate might be regarded as not being within the ordinary course of business. This would, of couse, depend upon the circumstances: a car might quite properly be sold at a time when the registration certificate had been sent to the authorities (eg to have a change of address recorded).

NOTE

Oppenheimer v Attenborough & Son (above) was, in fact, a case where the mercantile agent had *pledged* the goods, and in the extract which has been quoted the word 'pledgee' occurs where we have substituted the word 'buyer'. This case serves as a timely reminder that s 2 of the Factors Act 1889 does, in fact, apply to pledges and other dispositions of goods by a mercantile agent, as well as to sales; and we may note also that it is sufficient that the mercantile agent has possession of the *documents of title* to the goods, and not necessarily of the goods themselves.

QUESTIONS

1. In *Pearson v Rose & Young Ltd* (above), Vaisey J expressed the view that the sale by a mercantile agent of a car with only three wheels would not be a sale in the ordinary course of business. Do you agree?
2. Consider the facts of *Pacific Motor Auctions Pty Ltd v Motor Credits (Hire Finance) Ltd* (below, p 328). Could the buyers in that case have relied on s 2 of the Factors Act (or its Australian equivalent)?

(c) 'Provided that the person taking under the disposition acts in good faith, and has not at the time of the disposition notice that the person making the disposition has not authority to make the same'

The onus of proof on these issues lies upon the buyer: *Heap v Motorist's Advisory Agency Ltd* (below). The requirement that the buyer should act in good faith and without notice of any irregularity is closely tied up with the 'ordinary course of business' point which we have just discussed, for any departure from the ordinary course of business may well put the buyer on notice that the circumstances are suspicious.

Heap v Motorists' Advisory Agency Ltd [1923] 1 KB 577, King's Bench Division

A rogue called North (who was assumed for the purpose of the present question to have been a mercantile agent) obtained possession of Heap's Citroen car, which was worth about £210, and sold it without Heap's authority to the defendants for the very low price of £110. North did not effect the sale himself, but ('apparently for reasons of prudence') used a friend, Cory, to do so. Lush J held that the onus was on the defendants to prove that they had acted in good faith and without notice of the want of authority, and that they had failed to do so, so that s 2 did not protect the defendants.

Lush J: Under s 2 of the Factors Act 1889, however, the buyer gets no title apart from the section. He is allowed to get what I may call a statutory title provided he complies with the terms of the section. In order to acquire a title which he would not otherwise have, the buyer has to prove all these things that I have mentioned: that the owner consented to the mercantile agent having possession, that the agent acted in the ordinary course of business, and also, I think, that the buyer acted in good faith and had no notice.

If the onus is on the defendants, they have certainly failed to satisfy me that they had no notice that the person selling the car, that is North, had no authority to sell. Indeed, I think that, for this purpose, wherever the onus rests, the defendants must be taken to have had notice. To begin with, the car appears to have been bought considerably under value, though I do not say that the undervalue was so great as to show actual dishonesty. The defendants have endeavoured to prove that it would have cost them £50 or £60 to put it right, and that must no doubt be taken into account; but to my mind it would not have cost them more than £10 or £12, an outlay which would have left the car a remarkably cheap one for the defendants. Another peculiar circumstance was that North did not himself come to the defendants about the car, but got Cory to sell it to them. The defendants admit that they were a little suspicious, and made a point of not buying the car from North but from Cory, whom they knew. Neither North nor Cory produced the registration book, and the defendant never asked for it, though the whole object of registration is to facilitate transfers of cars and enable people to know who owns the car. Another circumstance which I cannot overlook is that after the defendants had given a crossed cheque to Cory he came back and asked for an open cheque because, according to him, North had no banking account near at hand and he wanted the money at once, and the defendants then allowed their cashier to cancel the crossed cheque and give an open cheque. All these circumstances were, in my opinion, enough to put the defendants on their guard and to fix them with notice. I do not say that they wickedly shut their eyes to an obvious fraud, but I do say that they did not do what any reasonable man would have done in this case – namely, decline to buy this car without knowing more about it. They thought it was a good bargain and made up their minds too easily to buy the car. I think they must be taken to have had notice of some want of authority in those who purported to sell it to them. Their manager told me in evidence that he felt rather uncomfortable and suspicious about the sale. In my view the defendants ought not in the circumstances to have bought the car.

The result is that all the defences fail, and I therefore give judgment for the plaintiff for the return of the car or its value with costs.

4 Third exception: sale under power of sale or court order

Section 21(2)(b) of the Sale of Goods Act states that the provisions of the Act do not affect the validity of any contract of sale under any special common law or statutory power of sale or under the order of a court of competent jurisdiction.

It is not necessary to list at length the various situations where a sale of goods may be effected without the authority of the owner under the powers referred to in this provision. It is sufficient to cite a few examples.

Goods may be sold under common law powers by a pledgee: *Burdick v Sewell* (1884) 13 QBD 159 (see below, p 812) and by an agent of necessity (see above, p 104).

There are many statutory provisions which confer a power of sale, eg upon an unpaid seller of goods (below, p 402), a bailee of uncollected goods (below, p 825), a landlord who has distrained upon his tenant's goods, and a sheriff who has seized goods under a writ of execution.

In addition, the court may order a sale of goods, either under its inherent powers (eg to enforce a charge) or pursuant to the rules of court (eg to dispose of goods which are perishable or likely to deteriorate); and it may do this even against the wishes of the owner: *Larner v Fawcett* [1950] 2 All ER 727.

5 Fourth exception: sale in market overt

Section 22 provides that where goods are sold in market overt, according to the usage of the market, the buyer acquires a good title to the goods, provided that he buys them in good faith and without notice of any defect or want of title on the part of the seller.

This is a very quaint and archaic exception to the *nemo dat* rule, as is indicated by the fact that the leading case was decided in 1596! It has no real place in a modern code of commercial law. Indeed, it has recently attracted growing criticism on the ground that it facilitates – and, indeed, may possibly even encourage – trafficking in stolen goods. The Law Reform Committee in its 12th Report (Cmnd 2958, 1967), paras 31–33, perhaps surprisingly did not recommend the outright abolition of the market overt rule, but instead suggested that it should be replaced by a provision that gave protection to anyone who bought goods by retail at trade premises or at a public auction, in good faith and without notice of any defect or want of title on the part of the seller. However, this recommendation has not been implemented.

The following points relating to the market overt rule may be noted:

(1) It applies only in England, and not in Scotland or Wales or any other common-law country.
(2) It is the only exception to the *nemo dat* rule which applies to goods which have been stolen, so that the true owner loses all claim to them. The buyer in market overt gets an absolute title – even, perhaps, a better title than the previous 'owner' had.
(3) It applies only to sales, and not to pledges or other dispositions of goods.
(4) The market in question must be an open, established public market constituted by law or custom. Many well-known markets are not so recognised. Exceptionally, the whole of the City of London is treated as such a market.

Case of Market Overt (1596) 5 Co Rep 83b, Newgate Sessions

Coke's report reads as follows (footnotes omitted):

At the sessions of Newgate, now last past, it was resolved by Popham, Chief Justice of England, Anderson, Ch Justice of the Common Pleas, Sir Thomas Egerton, Master of the Rolls, the Attorney-General, and the Court, that if plate be stolen and sold openly in a scrivener's shop on the market-day (as every day is a market-day in London except Sunday) that this sale should not change the property, but the party should have restitution; for a scrivener's shop is not a market-overt for plate; for none would search there for such a thing; & *sic de similibus*, etc. But if the sale had been openly in a goldsmith's shop in London, so that any one who stood or passed by the shop might see it, there it would change the property. But if the sale be in the shop of a goldsmith, either behind a hanging, or behind a cupboard upon which his plate stands, so that one that stood or passed by the shop could not see it, it would not change the property: so if the sale be not in the shop, but in the warehouse, or other place of the house, it would not change the property, for that is not in market-overt, and none would search there for his goods. So every shop in London is a market-overt for such things only which by the trade of the owner are put there to sale; and when I was Recorder of London, I certified the custom of London accordingly. Note, reader, the reason of this case extends to all markets-overt in England.

Reid v Metropolitan Police Comr [1973] QB 551, Court of Appeal

(The facts appear from the judgment.)

Scarman LJ: . . . The appeal raises a question as to the extent of the rule protecting the title of one who buys in market overt. The rule is retained in our law by s 22(1) of the Sale of Goods Act 1893.

On the night of December 13, 1969, thieves broke into the house of Mr Reid and stole a quantity of his property including a pair of Adam candelabra worth today about £800. In March 1970, he found the candelabra in an antique dealer's shop in Motcombe Street, which is in the City of Westminster. The police took charge of them, and Mr Reid commenced proceedings in the county court to recover them.

Not surprisingly, the career of the candelabra from Mr Reid's house to the West End shop where he found them remains something of a mystery. But we do know that Mr Cocks, himself an antique dealer, acquired them in the New Caledonian Market, Bermondsey, and placed them in the Motcombe Street shop, with the consent of the shopowner, for the purpose of sale.

The New Caledonian Market is a market established by the Bermondsey Borough Council under powers conferred by the London County Council (General Powers) Act 1903. . . .

Mr Cocks has, therefore, intervened in the action, claiming that he bought in market overt and so has a good title to the candelabra. The deputy county court judge upheld his contention, and Mr Reid, who is admittedly their owner if Mr Cocks' claim should fail, now appeals to this court.

The transaction, which Mr Cocks claims was a sale in market overt, has a strangely secretive air about it. Our predecessors in the law merchant, from which the doctrines of market overt derives, would, I suspect, have been surprised at such a claim, had the transaction occurred in their time. Mr Cocks, whom the judge found to have acted honestly and to have bought in good faith, went, as was his wont, to the market early in the morning of Friday, February 13, 1970, where he saw a man setting up a stall. This man had with him the two candelabra, dismantled and in a box. After a short haggle, Mr Cocks paid him £200 in cash and took the candelabra. He did not ask for a receipt. He did not then, and does not now, know who the vendor was. The transaction took place early in the 'semi-light' (as one witness described conditions after the sale). The judge found that the transaction took place after 7 am, the hour at which the market opened, but before sunrise which that day was at 8.19 am. The vendor was not a regular stall-holder. He displayed neither name nor licence, and has not been seen or heard of since.

Because the transaction occurred within the permitted hours of trading in the market the judge held that it was a sale in market overt. But Mr Reid contends that a market sale confers upon the purchaser a good title only if it occurs in business hours between sunrise and sunset.

The reason why the law permitted a sale in market overt to confer a good title upon the bona fide purchaser was the openness of the transaction: see the judgment of Scrutton J in *Clayton v Le Roy* [1911] 2 KB 1031, 1040–1045. When shops were scarce, the market was the place, and market day the occasion, for the public to buy and sell. The market was regulated by the franchise-holder. The place, the day, and the hours of business were established under the authority of the franchise and were well known. Thus any person whose goods had been stolen would know where and when the thief was likely to seek to dispose of them, and would have an opportunity of finding and recovering them before they were sold in the open market. *Blackstone's Commentaries*, vol II, p 449, describes the ancient safeguards for the true owner (including in Saxon times 'the presence of credible witnesses') and at p 450 of his *Commentaries*, vol II, says:

> By which wise regulations the common law has secured the right of the proprietor in personal chattels from being divested, so far as was consistent with that other necessary policy, that purchasers, bona fide, in a fair, open, and regular manner, should not afterwards put to difficulties by reason of the previous knavery of the seller.

Safeguards, such as Blackstone describes, were notably absent in this case. Instead of the 'credible witnesses' of ancient time, there was no witness, no clue as to the identity of the seller, very little exposure of the goods for sale, but a transaction effected in the 'semi-light' before dawn, and before the vendor's stall was erected. The only attributes of openness were the place and the fact that the transaction was effected within permitted hours of trading. Any chance of the true owner intervening before the candelabra were sold was minimal.

[His Lordship examined a number of authorities, some of which were conflicting, and concluded:]

The basic safeguard offered by the law to the owner is the opportunity to recover his property before it is sold. If stolen goods are sold outside either the City of London or any franchise or statutory market, the owner can recover them. If they are sold in the City of

London or any regularly established market, he may be defeated by a sale in market overt. His safeguard must be the openness of the transaction. If the protection of title given to the market purchaser arises only if the sale be effected during the hours of daylight, the owner knows at the very least that he cannot be defeated save by a transaction done in daytime.

Accordingly, in my opinion, the protection of title afforded by the law to a purchaser in market overt is available only if the sale takes place between sunrise and sunset. I would, therefore, allow the appeal.

[Lord Denning MR and Phillimore LJ delivered concurring judgments.]

Reform of the law. On 8 December 1993, Lord Renton introduced into the House of Lords a Sale of Goods (Amendment) Bill to abolish the market overt exception to the *nemo dat* rule. The Bill was later withdrawn, but the Department of Trade and Industry has since published a consultation document in which abolition is again proposed.

6 Fifth exception: sale under a voidable title

Section 23 of the Act confirms the well-known common law rule that where the seller of goods has a voidable title to them, and the title has not been avoided at the time of the sale, the buyer acquires a good title provided that he buys in good faith and without notice of the seller's defect of title. A similar rule applies to pledges of goods.

The commonest case in which a seller will have a voidable title is where he has obtained the goods under a contract induced by misrepresentation (whether fraudulent or innocent). But a contract may also be voidable on other grounds, such as undue influence, duress, and drunkenness.

A voidable transaction must be distinguished from one which is wholly void, eg on the ground of mistake of identity: contrast *Cundy v Lindsay* (above, p 297) with *Lewis v Averay*, below.

Lewis v Averay [1972] 1 QB 198, Court of Appeal

Lewis, in Bristol, advertised his Austin Cooper car for sale in a newspaper and agreed to sell it for £450 to a man calling himself Greene, who claimed to be a well-known actor, Richard Greene, and showed a Pinewood Studio pass as evidence of this identity. The rogue 'Greene' was allowed to take the car away in exchange for a cheque which later proved to be worthless. Three days later the rogue sold the car for £200 to Averay, a music student living in London, who bought in good faith. The Court of Appeal held that the first sale was voidable for fraud, but not void for mistake of identity, with the result that Averay got a good title.

Phillimore LJ: . . . I think the law was conveniently stated by Pearce LJ in the course of his judgment in *Ingram v Little* [1961] 1 QB 31 to which reference has already been made. He said, at p 61:

> Each case must be decided on its own facts. The question in such cases is this. Has it been sufficiently shown in the particular circumstances that, contrary to the prima facie presumption' – and I would emphasise those words – 'a party was not contracting with the physical person to whom he uttered the offer, but with another individual whom (as

the other party ought to have understood) he believed to be the physical person present. The answer to that question is a finding of fact.

Now, in that particular case the Court of Appeal, by a majority and in the very special and unusual facts of the case, decided that it had been sufficiently shown in the particular circumstances that, contrary to the prima facie presumption, the lady who was selling the motor car was not dealing with the person actually present. But in the present case I am bound to say that I do not think there was anything which could displace the prima facie presumption that Mr Lewis was dealing with the gentleman present there in the flat – the rogue. It seems to me that when, at the conclusion of the transaction, the car was handed over, the logbook was handed over, the cheque was accepted, and the receipts were given, it is really impossible to say that a contract had not been made. I think this case really is on all fours with *Phillips v Brooks* ([1919] 2 KB 243), which has been good law for over 50 years. True, the contract was induced by fraud, and Mr Lewis, when he discovered that he had been defrauded, was entitled to avoid it; but in the meanwhile the rogue had parted with the property in this motor car which he had obtained to Mr Averay, who bought it bona fide without any notice of the fraud, and accordingly he thereby, as I think, acquired a good title.

[Lord Denning MR and Megaw LJ delivered concurring judgments.]

The claim of a buyer who relies on s 23 will be defeated if, before he makes his purchase, the original owner has validly exercised his right to avoid the first transaction. This is normally done by giving notice to the other party, or by retaking possession of the goods. However, in *Car & Universal Finance Co Ltd v Caldwell* it was held that, at least in exceptional circumstances such as occurred in that case, some other action on the owner's part might be sufficient to evince an intention to rescind.

Car & Universal Finance Co Ltd v Caldwell [1965] 1 QB 525, Court of Appeal

Caldwell was induced to sell his Jaguar car to Norris by fraud. Norris took the car away and sold it to a company called Motobella. After passing through several hands, it was eventually sold several months later to the plaintiffs, who bought in good faith. When Caldwell discovered the fraud, he had at once notified the police and the Automobile Association, but he was unable to communicate with Norris, who had disappeared. The Court of Appeal held that the first contract of sale had been effectively avoided before the car was sold to Motobella, so that Caldwell had the right to claim the car.

Upjohn LJ: On the footing that on January 13 the defendant did everything he reasonably could to avoid the contract of sale, short of communicating his intention so to do to Norris, the whole question is whether such acts of avoidance were effective in law to avoid the contract on that day, or whether communication to Norris of intention to avoid the contract was necessary in law.

Where one party to a contract has an option unilaterally to rescind or disaffirm it by reason of the fraud or misrepresentation of the other party, he must elect to do so within a reasonable time, and cannot do so after he has done anything to affirm the contract with knowledge of the facts giving rise to the option to rescind. In principle and on authority, however, he must, in my judgment, in the ordinary course communicate his intention to rescind to the other party. This must be so because the other party is entitled to treat the contractual nexus as continuing until he is made aware of the intention of the other to exercise his option to rescind. So the intention must be communicated and an uncommunicated intention, for example, by speaking to a third party or making a private note, will be ineffective. The textbooks to which we were referred are unanimous on the subject. 'If a party elects to rescind he must within a reasonable time manifest that election by communicating to the other party his intention to rescind the transaction and claim no interest under it. The communication need not be formal provided it is a distinct and positive repudiation of the transaction': Kerr on Fraud and Mistake, 7th ed (1952), p 530. . . .

Such in my view must be the general principle. Does it admit of any exception? Mr Caplan concedes that there is one: where the subject-matter of the contract is a transfer of property, then the party entitled to do so may disaffirm the contract by retaking possession of the property. Mr Caplan, however, submits this is really a method of communication, though for my part I do not see how that can be true of every case that could be suggested. Is there any other exception? Mr Caplan submits not and that, apart from recaption, there should be a universal rule of law that communication is essential to break the nexus. On the facts of this case, it is clear that Norris intended quite deliberately to disappear and render it impossible for the defendant to communicate with him or to recover the car. While I appreciate Mr Caplan's argument that this point can only arise in cases between the vendor and a third party, I agree with Sellers LJ that this problem must be solved by consideration of the rights between the two contracting parties. Admittedly one of two innocent parties must suffer for the fraud of a third, but that cannot be helped and does not assist to solve the problem. . . . It is indeed strange that there is no authority in point.

If one party, by absconding, deliberately puts it out of the power of the other to communicate his intention to rescind which he knows the other will almost certainly want to do, I do not think he can any longer insist on his right to be made aware of the election to determine the contract. In these circumstances communication is a useless formality. I think that the law must allow the innocent party to exercise his right of recession otherwise than by communication or repossession. To hold otherwise would be to allow a fraudulent contracting party by his very fraud to prevent the innocent party from exercising his undoubted right. I would hold that in circumstances such as these the innocent party may evince his intention to disaffirm the contract by overt means falling short of communication or repossession.

We heard much interesting argument on the position where one party makes an innocent misrepresentation which entitles the other to elect to rescind and then innocently so acts that the other cannot find him to communicate his election to him. I say nothing about that case and would leave it to be decided if and when it arises. I am solely concerned with the fraudulent rogue who deliberately makes it impossible for the other to communicate with him or to retake the property.

[Sellers and Davies LJJ delivered concurring judgments.]

For another case where the same issue arose, see *Newtons of Wembley Ltd v Williams* (below, p 333).

7 Sixth exception: sale by seller continuing in possession

The exception which we are about to discuss is, anomalously, governed by two overlapping statutory provisions – the Sale of Goods Act 1979, s 24 and s 8 of the Factors Act 1889. There is a similar overlap between s 25(1) and s 9 (respectively) of these two Acts, which contain the seventh of our exceptions to the *nemo dat* rule. The explanation usually put forward is that when the Sale of Goods Bill 1893 was drafted, it was intended to repeal ss 8 and 9 of the Factors Act, but that this was overlooked when that Act was passed. (Just to add further to the confusion, in the Act of 1893, the present ss 24 and 25(1) were numbered respectively ss 25(1) and 25(2)!) The wording of the two sets of provisions is very nearly the same, and it will be sufficient for most purposes to refer simply to ss 24 and 25(1). There will, however, be one occasion where it will be necessary to draw attention to the differences (see below, p 340).

Section 24 reads as follows:

Where a person having sold goods continues or is in possession of the goods, or of the goods or documents of title to the goods, the delivery or transfer by that person, or by a mercantile agent acting for him, of the goods or documents of title under any sale, pledge, or other disposition thereof, to any person receiving the same in good faith and without notice of the previous sale, has the same effect as if the person making the delivery or transfer were expressly authorised by the owner of the goods to make the same.

Section 8 of the Factors Act 1889 differs from s 24 only in that the words 'or under any agreement for the sale, pledge or other disposition thereof' are inserted before 'to any person'.

A number of detailed points call for discussion.

First, it will be recalled that in the case of *Staffs Motor Guarantee Ltd v British Wagon Co Ltd* (above, p 316), MacKinnon J held that the possession of a mercantile agent, for the purposes of s 2 of the Factors Act 1889, had to be possession *in his capacity as mercantile agent*, and that because Heap, the seller, had possession of the lorry in that case qua hirer or bailee and not qua mercantile agent, the section did not apply. As it happened, Heap was not only a mercantile agent, but also a person who had previously sold the lorry to another buyer and had continued in possession of it, and so a second argument was advanced that title to the lorry had passed to the second buyer, Staffs Motor, by virtue of the provision which is now s 24. However, once again, the point was taken that Heap's continuing possession was qua hirer and not qua seller (under the former sale), and MacKinnon J held that this was also fatal to Staff Motors' claim.

But the law has now changed, and on this second point the *Staffs Motor* case has been overruled. The 'qua seller' gloss is not to be put on the phrase 'continues or is in possession' in s 24, at least where the seller has remained in unbroken possession throughout. The new construction was first put forward in the *Pacific Motor Auctions* case (below) which, being a Privy Council decision, did not technically overrule *Staffs Motor*; but the Court of Appeal in *Worcester Works Finance Ltd v Cooden Engineering Co Ltd* [1972] 1 QB 210, CA has since adopted the same approach and so *Staffs Motor* can now be regarded as having been formally overruled, so far as concerns the construction of s 24.

Pacific Motor Auctions Pty Ltd v Motor Credits (Hire Finance) Ltd [1965] AC 867, Privy Council

A car retailing firm in Sydney called Motordom held its stock of used cars under an arrangement which is sometimes called a 'display' or 'stocking' agreement and sometimes a 'floor plan'. When it bought a car, it would pay the seller in cash (or credit him with the price, if the car was taken as a trade-in) and then immediately resell it to Motor Credits at a discounted price equal to 90 per cent of the price which they had paid. In that way, it kept itself in funds to finance its future trading. The car would not leave Motordom's premises, but remained there on display for the purposes of sale. Motordom thus was in possession of the car as bailee for Motor Credits as owners; it was also a seller who had 'continued in possession' of the car after selling it. Sales of the cars, when effected, were made by Motordom as agents for Motor Credits. When Motordom got into financial difficulties, Motor Credits revoked its authority to sell any further cars. Pacific Auctions, a creditor of Motordom, was owed a substantial amount of money, and its manager called in the evening on that same day to demand payment. When payment was not forthcoming he bought a total of 29 cars at prices which added up to approximately the amount owed, and took them away. Motor Credits demanded the return of these cars from Pacific Auctions.

The advice of the Privy Council was delivered by **Lord Pearce:** . . . The point under s 28(1) [of the Sale of Goods Act 1923 (NSW), equivalent to s 24 (UK)] turns on the construction of the words 'where a person having sold goods continues or is in possession of the goods.' Are those words to be construed in their full sense so that wherever a person is found to be in possession of goods which he has previously sold he can, whatever be the capacity in which he has possession, pass a good title? Or is some, and if so what, limitation to be placed on them by considering the quality and title of the seller's possession at the time when he sells them again to an innocent purchaser? . . .

The first reported question that arose about the construction of those same words is to be found in *Mitchell v Jones* ((1905) 24 NZLR 932), a case under the New Zealand Sale of Goods Act 1895. There the owner of a horse sold it to a buyer and some days later obtained it back from him on lease. Then, having possession of the horse in the capacity of lessee, he sold it a second time to an innocent purchaser. The full court held that the innocent purchaser was not protected. Stout CJ said: 'The point turns on how the words "or is in possession of the goods" in the subsection are to be construed. . . . The meaning is – first, that if a person sells goods and continues in possession, even though he has made a valid contract of sale, provided that he has not delivered them, he may to a bona fide buyer make a good title; and, secondly, the putting-in of the words "or is in possession of the goods" was meant to apply to a case of this character: if a vendor had not the goods when he sold them, but they came into his possession afterwards, then he would have possession of the goods, and if he sold them to a bona fide purchaser he could make a good title to them. He would be in the same position as if he had continued in possession of the goods when he made his first sale. In such a case as that he could make a good title to a bona fide purchaser.

That is not this case. In this case the person who sold the goods gave up possession of them, and gave delivery of them to the buyer. The relationship, therefore, of buyer and seller between them was at an end. It is true that the seller got possession of the goods again, but not as a seller. He got the goods the second time as the bailee of the buyer, and as the bailee he had no warrant, in my opinion, to sell the goods again, nor could he make a good title to them to even a bona fide purchaser.'

And Williams J said that the section 'does not . . . apply where a sale has been absolutely final by delivery, and possession has been obtained by the vendee.' It has not been doubted in argument nor do their Lordships doubt that that case was rightly decided.

In 1934, however, Mackinnon J, founding on that case, put a further gloss on the statutory provision in *Staffs Motor Guarantee Ltd v British Wagon Co* [above]. In April one Heap agreed with a finance company to sell his lorry to it and then to hire it from the company on hire-purchase terms. He filled up a proposal form which was accepted, and a hire-purchase agreement dated May 2 was signed. During the term of the hiring he sold it to an innocent purchaser. It seems that there was an interval between the agreement to sell and the hire-purchase agreement, but it does not appear from the report that there was any physical delivery or interruption of Heap's physical possession. Mackinnon J held that 'Heap's possession of the lorry' (at the time of the second sale) 'was not the possession of a seller who had not yet delivered the article sold to the buyer, but was the possession of a bailee under the hire-purchase agreement. . . .' Although the sale had not been completed by physical delivery nor had there been interruption of the seller's physical possession, he held that the case was covered by the principle in *Mitchell v Jones*.

[His Lordship discussed certain other cases, including *Eastern Distributors Ltd v Goldring* (above, p 301), and continued:]

It is plainly right to read the section as inapplicable to cases where there has been a break in the continuity of the physical possession. On this point their Lordships accept the observations of the judges in *Mitchell v Jones* as to the words 'or is' which are the sole grounds for any doubt on this point. But what is the justification for saying that a person does not continue in possession where his physical possession does continue although the title under or by virtue of which he is in possession has changed? The fact that a person having sold goods is described as *continuing* in possession would seem to indicate that the section is not contemplating as relevant a change in the legal title under which he possesses. For the legal title by which he is in possession *cannot* continue. Before the sale he is in possession as an owner, whereas after the sale he is in possession as a bailee holding goods for the new owner. The possession continues unchanged but the title under which he possesses has changed. One may, perhaps, say in loose terms that a person having sold goods continues in possession as long as he is holding because of and only because of the sale; but what justification is there for imposing such an elaborate and artificial construction on the natural meaning of the words? The object of the section is to protect an innocent purchaser who is deceived by the vendor's physical possession of goods or documents and who is inevitably unaware of legal rights which fetter the apparent power to dispose. Where a vendor retains uninterrupted physical possession of the goods why should an unknown arrangement, which substitutes a bailment for ownership, disentitle the innocent purchaser to protection from a danger which is just as great as that from which the section is admittedly intended to protect him?

[His Lordship discussed the history of s 24 and its relation to various provisions in the earlier Factors Acts. He concluded:]

There is therefore the strongest reason for supposing that the words 'continues in possession' were intended to refer to the continuity of physical possession regardless of any private transactions between the seller and purchaser which might alter the legal title under which the possession was held.

Their Lordships do not think that such a view of the law which they believe Parliament to have intended could in practice create any adverse effect. It would mean that when a person sells a car to a finance house in order to take it back on hire-purchase the finance house must take physical delivery if it is to avoid the risk of an innocent purchaser acquiring title to it. But in any event such arrangements where there is no delivery are not without some jeopardy owing to the Bills of Sale Acts.

It seems to their Lordships that *Staffs Motor Guarantee Ltd v British Wagon Co* (and *Eastern Distributors Ltd v Goldring* in so far as it followed it), was wrongly decided. Even if it were rightly decided, it would not cover the facts of this case. For even assuming that a separate agreement of bailment, following a sale, without any break in the seller's physical possession, were sufficient to break its continuity for the purposes of the section, here there was no separate bailment. Motordom's continued physical possession was solely attributable to the arrangement which constituted the sale. It was a term of the sale by Motordom to the respondent that Motordom should be entitled to retain possession of the cars for the purpose of selling them to customers. Motordom only received 90 per cent of the price on the sale to the respondent, and it cannot be argued that the sale ended at that stage. It would be absurd to suppose that either party intended Motordom to sell its stock for 90 per cent of its value without getting a right to any further benefit. The transaction by which Motordom sold the cars to the respondent was inextricably mixed with Motordom's right to keep the cars for display at its premises. In their Lordship's opinion Motordom having sold the goods whose ownership is disputed, continued in possession of them. . . .

Documents of title. Section 24 refers not only to the case where the seller is in possession of the *goods*, but also where he is in possession of the *documents of title* to the goods. This expression also occurred in s 2 of the Factors Act 1889 (above, p 311). It is time to examine this concept of a 'document of title' more closely.

The first comment to make is that the term 'document of title' is misleading, because in most cases the documents concerned have nothing to do with the title to the goods. (The bill of lading is an exception.) What the documents do have in common is that they give or evidence a person's right to the *possession* of goods, so that whoever has the document can demand that they be delivered to him or to his order. The statutory definition (Factors Act 1889, s 1(4), adopted by the Sale of Goods Act 1979, s 61(1)), is as follows:

> The expression 'document of title' shall include any bill of lading, dock warrant, warehouse-keeper's certificate, and warrant or order for the delivery of goods, and any other document used in the ordinary course of business as proof of the possession or control of goods, or authorising or purporting to authorise, either by indorsement or delivery, the possessor of the document to transfer or receive goods thereby represented.

In practical terms, documents of title fall into two classes.

The first category is an *acknowledgment*, signed by a person who has physical possession of the goods (usually a bailee, such as a warehouseman or a carrier) that he is holding them on a particular person's behalf, and available for delivery to that person. (This latter person may or may not be the owner of the goods: what matters is that he has the right to demand possession from the former.) A seller of goods who holds them as bailee for his buyer may issue such a 'document of title' in favour of the latter. Typically, an acknowledgment of this kind is called a *warrant* (eg a dock warrant, warehouseman's warrant, railway warrant). The category also includes a bill of lading, ie a document issued by a sea carrier which acknowledges that the goods in question have been received on board, and which also contains the terms of the contract of carriage: see below, p 444.

The second type of document of title is an *order*, signed by the owner of goods or other person entitled to possession of them, addressed to the warehouseman, carrier or other bailee in whose custody they are, instructing him to deliver the goods to a named person or to his order. Such a document is usually called a *delivery order*.

Although (with the exception of the bill of lading) these documents do not confer rights of ownership on their holders or serve to evidence such rights, they do operate to *protect* an owner's title, because they give the holder the power to control the right of disposal of the goods which they represent. So, for instance, the owner of goods stored in a warehouse can give security over the goods (eg to a bank) by pledging the warehouseman's warrant with the bank. And the use of documents of title is facilitated by the commercial practice of treating the rights evidenced by such documents as being transferable by the physical delivery of the document, usually accompanied by an endorsement written on the document itself.

When we turn to look at the provisions of s 24 relating to documents of title, we see that in this context they do have a bearing on questions of ownership. For this purpose, it is not the document itself or the issuing of such a document which confers rights of ownership; it is the *transfer* to a second buyer of a document of title *which is already in the possession of the seller*, and which he has not parted with under the first contract of sale, that defeats the claims of the first buyer. So, a person who has sold goods to buyer A, but has kept possession of either the goods themselves or a document of title relating to the goods, has the power to defeat A's title and confer a good title on buyer B, by delivering the goods or the document of title to B. But under s 24 (and also, as we shall see, under s 25(1)), actual delivery of one or the other is essential: the mere fact that he has purportedly sold the goods to B will give B no proprietary rights. In contrast, delivery is not necessary to bring a transaction within the exception created by s 2 of the Factors Act 1889 (sale by a mercantile agent).

Of course, in many circumstances any such action by a seller in reselling the goods will be a breach of his contract with the first buyer, and also constitute the tort of conversion or wrongful interference with the goods. The question whether the seller will be liable under these heads is discussed later (see below, p 401).

8 Seventh exception: sale by buyer in possession

Section 25(1) of the Sale of Goods Act 1979 (which is similar to the Factors Act 1889, s 9) is the counterpart of s 24. It reads:

> Where a person having bought or agreed to buy goods obtains, with the consent of the seller, possession of the goods or the documents of title to the goods, the delivery or transfer by that person, or by a mercantile agent acting for him, of the goods or documents of title, under any sale, pledge or other disposition thereof, to any person receiving the same in good faith and without notice of any lien or other right of the seller in respect of the goods, has the same effect as if the person making the delivery or transfer were a mercantile agent in possession of the goods or documents of title with the consent of the owner.

Once again, the Factors Act 1889, s 9 differs from this wording only by the inclusion of the phrase 'or under any agreement for the sale, pledge or other disposition thereof' before the words 'to any person'.

Care is needed in reading cases decided before 1979, since in the Act of 1893 the present s 25(1) was numbered 25(2).

Here we can see another situation where the principle of *Jerome v Bentley* (above, p 299) does not apply: although the fact that an owner has let another person have possession of his goods carries no implication or representation that that person has authority to sell them, this latter person may, exceptionally, be deemed to have the power to do so when he is someone who has contracted to buy the goods.

A leading case on this section (or rather on s 9 of the Factors Act 1889, since the Sale of Goods Act 1893 had not then been enacted) is *Lee v Butler*, which marked an important step in the evolution of the hire-purchase agreement.

Lee v Butler [1893] 2 QB 318, Court of Appeal

Mrs Lloyd agreed to take on 'hire' certain furniture from Hardy under the terms of an agreement, called a 'hire and purchase agreement', paying over a period of three months sums described as 'rent' which totalled £97 4s. It was declared that the furniture should remain the property of Hardy throughout, but that when the full £97 4s had been paid, the furniture would become the sole and absolute property of Mrs Lloyd. Mrs Lloyd, before all the instalments had been paid under the agreement, sold the furniture to Butler. Lee, who had taken an assignment of Hardy's rights under the agreement, claimed to be entitled to the goods, but the court found for Butler under s 9 of the Factors Act 1889 (SGA, s 25(1)).

Lord Esher MR: This is a very plain case, and the construction of the statute is very clear. It deals with 'Dispositions by mercantile agents' in one set of sections, and with 'Dispositions by sellers and buyers of goods' in another set of sections, in which s 9 is included. The case is clearly within that section. [His Lordship read s 9.] Mrs Lloyd had agreed by this hire and purchase agreement to buy the goods, and they were put into her possession with the consent of the owner. Mrs Lloyd sold the goods to the defendant without notice that they were not hers, and he, acting in good faith and with no notice of the plaintiff's rights, received them. Section 9 was passed to meet this very kind of case. I am of opinion that the judgment of Wright J was right, and this appeal should be dismissed.

[Kay LJ delivered a concurring judgment.
Bowen LJ concurred.]

NOTE

The key point in *Lee v Butler* is that Mrs Lloyd, though described as a 'hirer', was *bound* to complete the purchase of the goods. In other words, this was a *conditional sale* agreement, under which the seller retained the property in the goods until the whole of the agreed price had been paid. In a true hire-purchase agreement, the hirer has only an *option* to buy the goods, which he exercises by paying all the hire instalments (and sometimes also a nominal 'option fee'); and he is free at any time to discontinue the hiring. In the test case of *Helby v Matthews* (above, p 228), the House of Lords held that a purported sale of the goods by the hirer under such a contract to a third person did not come within s 25(1), and so an owner in the position of Hardy is protected against unauthorised sales by the hirer. This ruling has been the basis of the hire-purchase agreement ever since.

Paradoxically, the Consumer Credit Act 1974 now declares that conditional sale agreements coming within certain financial and other limits are to be treated for many purposes as hire-purchase agreements, so as to give consumers who buy under conditional sale agreements the statutory protection conferred by that Act; and s 25(2) of the Sale of Goods Act 1979 expressly reverses *Lee v Butler* in relation to agreements falling within the statutory limits: see above, p 230.

The wording of s 25(1) has some curious features.

First, for a long time the words '*bought* or agreed to buy' were regarded as puzzling, because it was thought that if a person had *bought* goods he would have a good title anyway, which would enable him to sell to a sub-buyer without any need to invoke s 25(1). But in *Newtons of Wembley Ltd v Williams* it was demonstrated that the draftsman of the section had truly remarkable foresight, and that there is indeed a role for the word 'bought'.

Newtons of Wembley Ltd v Williams [1965] 1 QB 560, Court of Appeal

On 16 June 1962 Newtons sold a Sunbeam Rapier car to Andrew and allowed him to take it away. Andrew's purchase was fraudulent, because he paid for the car with a worthless cheque. Newtons were unable to trace Andrew, but they informed the police and Hire Purchase Information Ltd (see above, p 309), and sent out two men to try and trace and seize the car. About a month later Andrew sold the car to Biss at a streetside market in Warren Street, London, paying Andrew the whole price in £5 notes. Biss resold the car to Williams, who refused to give it up to Newtons after it had been traced.

Sellers LJ followed *Car & Universal Finance Co Ltd v Caldwell* (above, p 326) in holding that Newtons had effectively avoided the sale to Andrew by informing the police etc, and continued: The title the defendant seeks to advance is the title of Biss, when Biss was the buyer, or the purported buyer, of the car from Andrew in the Warren Street market on or about July 6, 1962.

Quite clearly, at common law, Andrew at that date had no title to give, and at common law Biss obtained no title. It was submitted before us that at that stage Andrew was a complete stranger in this matter, that the case is clear, and that possession should be given to the plaintiffs, or damages in lieu thereof. But in fact Andrew was not a complete stranger. Andrew had in fact the possession of the car, which had been given to him or which he had obtained when he acquired the car on the handing over of the cheque on June 15.

In those circumstances, notwithstanding the position at common law – or because of it – the defendant has relied on the Factors Act, 1889; and the question which arises in this case is whether the transaction between Andrew and Biss can be brought within the provisions of that Act.

I turn first to s 9. It is one of two sections, ss 8 and 9, dealing with dispositions by sellers and buyers of goods, s 8 dealing with the disposition by a seller remaining in possession, s 9 with disposition by a buyer obtaining possession.

[His Lordship read s 9 and continued:]

Andrew had bought the goods and obtained them with the consent of the plaintiffs. He had subsequently delivered them on a sale to Biss and, if Biss was a person receiving the same in good faith and without notice of any lien or other right of the original seller, then this section provides that the transaction shall have the same effect as if the person making the delivery, ie, Andrew, were a mercantile agent in possession of the goods or documents of title with the consent of the owner. So the first part of s 9 is complied with on the facts of this case, and the question arises whether the second part, the receiving of the goods in good faith (and it is not suggested that Biss had notice of any lien or other right of the original seller), has been complied with, and whether, treating Andrew as a mercantile agent, the requirements of s 9 in that respect have been complied with.

That requires a consideration in the first place of the question: What is a mercantile agent? In s 1(1), 'The expression "mercantile agent" shall mean a mercantile agent having in the customary course of his business as such agent authority either to sell goods, or to consign goods for the purpose of sale, or to buy goods, or to raise money on the security of goods.' That description is to be applied to Andrew on the facts of this case.

Section 2(1) concerns the powers of a mercantile agent with respect to the disposition of goods thus.

[His Lordship read s 2(1) and continued:]

One of the points taken by the plaintiffs was that although at the outset Andrew was a person who had obtained, with the consent of the seller, possession of the goods, at the time when this transaction took place that consent no longer operated: it had been withdrawn by the rescission of the contract. But Andrew was in possession of the goods of the plaintiffs, a possession which he had obtained at the outset with their consent. Section 2(2) provides that 'Where a mercantile agent has, with the consent of the owner, been in possession of goods . . . any sale . . . which would have been valid if the consent had continued, shall be valid notwithstanding the determination of the consent. . . .' That is an express provision which altered the law as it had been laid down in an earlier case (*Fuentes v Montis* (1868) LR 3 CP 268; affd LR 4 CP 93) some time in 1868. Notwithstanding that which the plaintiffs had done to terminate their contract and withdraw their consent, they had in fact – true, through inability to do otherwise – left the possession of their car with Andrew.

[Other parts of the judgment of Sellers LJ are set out below.]

[Pearson LJ delivered a concurring judgment.
Diplock LJ concurred.]

The second puzzle arising from the wording of s 25(1) is concerned with the concluding words:

> has the same effect as if the person making the delivery or transfer were a mercantile agent in possession of the goods or documents of title with the consent of the owner.

It will be noticed that this wording differs markedly from the concluding words of s 24:

> has the same effect as if the person making the delivery or transfer were expressly authorised by the owner of the goods to make the same.

No case prior to *Newtons of Wembley*, at least in England, had ever considered the meaning of these words, which cannot be given full effect without invoking s 2 of the Factors Act 1889 and all the accumulated learning relating to that section. Taken literally, it would appear that s 25(1) could not be successfully invoked unless the first buyer had access to a place of business and conducted the second sale 'in the ordinary course of business of a mercantile agent'. This would seem to rule out most private buyers, and would suggest that the seminal case of *Lee v Butler* (above, p 332) was decided *per incuriam*. In *Newtons of Wembley* itself, the court was able to reach a fairly easy answer on the rather fortuitous facts of the case, but the basic question remains unresolved.

Newtons of Wembley Ltd v Williams [1965] 1 QB 560, Court of Appeal

(The facts are given above.)

Sellers LJ: The only other question which arises is how far s 9, on its true construction, takes the ultimate sub-buyer (the defendant in the present case), relying, as he does, on what happened between Andrew and Biss. The judge treated s 9 as placing Andrew in the position of a mercantile agent, but with the obligation on the defendant of establishing not only that Biss took in good faith (I leave out the other requirement of no notice of the plaintiff's rights; nothing arose on that), but also that in the transaction between Andrew and Biss (Andrew being treated as a mercantile agent in accordance with s 9), Andrew was 'acting in the ordinary course of business of a mercantile agent.' There is a possible construction, which was urged upon us by the defendant, that Andrew must be deemed to be acting under s 9 as a mercantile agent, that it must be assumed or deemed that he was acting in the ordinary course of business of a mercantile agent; and investigations were made in other parts of the Act of 1889, in particular s 8, to see whether any support could be had for that view.

Section 8 makes a different provision. It states that where a person, having sold goods, continues, or is, in possession of the goods and then sells them, then, providing the person who receives them does so in good faith and without notice of the previous sale, the transaction will have 'the same effect as if the person making the delivery or transfer were expressly authorised by the owner of the goods to make the same.' The words are different in s 9, and for myself I do not find much help, in constructing s 9, from looking at s 8, except for the fact that since they are different they are intended to have a different effect.

Before one takes too favourable a view for the sub-buyer and too harsh a view against the true owner of the goods as to the cases where s 9 can be invoked, one must remember that it is taking away the right which would have existed at common law, and for myself I should not be prepared to enlarge it more than the words clearly permitted and required. It seems to me that all that s 9 can be said clearly to do is to place the buyer in possession in the position of a mercantile agent when he has in fact in his possession the goods of somebody else, and it does no more than clothe him with that fictitious or notional position on any disposition of those goods. Section 2(1) makes it clear that the sub-buyer from a mercantile agent, to whom that section applies, has in order to obtain the full advantage of the subsection, to establish that the mercantile agent was acting in the ordinary course of business. It is said that that is a somewhat vague phrase, and we have been referred to some authorities with regard to that. It may be that in some cases precisely what is in 'the ordinary course of business' of a mercantile agent may call for some special investigation, but on the face of it it seems to me that it envisages a transaction by a mercantile agent and is to be derived from such evidence as is either known to the court or established by evidence as to what would be the ordinary course of business. . . .

The question arises here on the evidence whether this transaction is to be said to have been in the ordinary course of business of a mercantile agent. Counsel for the plaintiffs sought to establish that a transaction taking place in this somewhat unusual market, the street kerb in

Warren Street, was, on the face of it, something which was not an ordinary business transaction in any way, by a mercantile agent or anybody else, but was to some extent suspect. But the judge had evidence about this and he said, and I think it is within the knowledge of the court, that there had been an established market in secondhand cars in this area on this very site for a long time. Although he said that he had some doubt at one time about the sale to Biss being in the ordinary course of business, for, as he pointed out, there were no business premises, the sale was in the street, and it was for cash, yet he came to the conclusion, which I think cannot be challenged, that there was in Warren Street and its neighbourhood an established street market for cash dealing in cars. When one looks at what took place in that area and finds the prospective buyer coming up and getting into contact with the prospective seller in regard to a car, with an offer and an acceptance, trial of the car and a looking over it and some questions asked and a delivery – I do not find anything to indicate that it was not in the ordinary course of business of a mercantile agent. It seems to me that the defendant has established that essential fact.

NOTE

L A Rutherford and I A Todd [1979] CLJ 346 draw attention to the fact that s 25(1) deems the *delivery or transfer* of the goods or documents to have been expressly authorised, and not the 'sale, pledge or other disposition'. In the light of this, they argue that the scope of the subsection may be more limited than has generally been assumed.

The final conundrum concerning s 25(1) focuses on its very last word: 'with the consent of the *owner*'. In the earlier parts of the subsection, all the relevant references are to the 'seller'. At least at first sight, this would suggest that the 'owner' mentioned at the end is a different person from the seller; and it could very readily be taken to mean 'the true owner'. From this it would follow that if S agreed to sell goods to B1 and gave him possession, and B1 then sold them to B2, B2 would get a good title even against a true owner, O, from whom the goods had been stolen before they were acquired by S. Although not an impossible construction, this would be surprising, for none of the other exceptions to the *nemo dat* rule (market overt apart) has ever been understood to allow title to be conferred through a thief. Some commentators therefore concluded that the word 'owner' in the section had to be read as a slip for 'seller'. The question has now been resolved more happily by the House of Lords, which favoured a still different approach.

National Employers' Mutual General Insurance Association Ltd v Jones [1990] 1 AC 24, House of Lords

Miss Hopkin owned a Ford Fiesta car which was stolen in 1983 and, after passing through several hands, was bought by a firm called Autochoice, which sold it to Mid-Glamorgan Motors, who resold it to Jones. When Miss Hopkin's insurers (who had been subrogated to her rights: see below, p 893) claimed the car from Jones, he sought the protection of s 25(1). All the courts found for the insurers. The trial judge and a majority of the Court of Appeal took the view that the word 'owner' in s 25(1) had to be read as 'seller'. The House of Lords upheld the finding on a different construction: the section was to be taken as referring to a *notional* sale by a *notional* mercantile agent in possession of the goods with the consent of their *notional* owner.

Lord Goff of Chieveley outlined the history of the Factors Acts prior to 1889, and continued: Such are the statutory precursors of the Factors Act 1889. This Act is, as I have already recorded, entitled simply 'An Act to amend and consolidate the Factors Acts.' There is no hint of any change of fundamental policy in the title; nor is there any preamble to the Act, in which any such change of policy would surely have been set out, had it been intended by Parliament to make such a change. As I have previously said, the relevant sections are s 2, 8 and 9. Section 2 is concerned to provide for the validity of sales, pledges and other dispositions of goods by mercantile agents who are, 'with the consent of the owner,' in possession of the goods or of documents of title to the goods; such transactions, it is provided, shall be as valid as if the mercantile agents were expressly authorised 'by the owner of the goods to make the same.' Plainly, the owner of the goods here referred to is the owner with whose consent the agent is in possession of them. The section cannot be read as having the effect of adversely affecting the title of any person, other than the person who had entrusted the goods or documents of title to the mercantile agents; it cannot adversely affect the title of one from whom the goods had been stolen, whose goods have come into possession of the mercantile agent from the thief, or from a person deriving the title from the thief. The policy underlying this section is, therefore, wholly consistent with the policy underlying the earlier Factors Acts.

I come therefore to ss 8 and 9. I will, for the sake of clarity set out the two sections again, in order to identify with initials the relevant actors in the drama. In s 8, I have identified the vendor as A; the first purchaser, who has allowed A to remain in possession of the goods or documents of title, I shall hereafter refer to as B1; and the second purchaser, to whom A has sold, pledged or otherwise disposed of the goods or documents of title, I have identified as B2. In s 9, I have identified the seller referred to in line 2 of the section as A; the person who bought or agreed to buy the goods from A, and who obtained possession of the goods or documents of title with A's consent, I have identified as B; and the person to whom B delivers or transfers the goods or documents of title under a sale, pledge or other disposal, or an agreement for the same, I have identified as C. Interpolating these initials, the sections read:

8. Where a person (A), having sold goods, continues, or is, in possession of the goods or of the documents of title to the goods, the delivery or transfer by that person (A), or by a mercantile agent acting for him, of the goods or documents of title under any sale, pledge, or other disposition thereof, or under any agreement for sale, pledge, or other disposition thereof, to any person (B2) receiving the same in good faith and without notice of the previous sale, shall have the same effect as if the person making the delivery or transfer were expressly authorised by the owner of the goods to make the same.

9. Where a person (B), having bought or agreed to buy goods, obtains with the consent of the seller (A) possession of the goods or the documents of title to the goods, the delivery or transfer, by that person (B) or by a mercantile agent acting for him, of the goods or documents of title, under any sale, pledge, or other disposition thereof, or under any agreement for sale, pledge, or other disposition thereof, to any person (C) receiving the same in good faith and without notice of any lien or other right of the original seller (A) in respect of the goods, shall have the same effect as if the person (B) making the delivery or transfer were a mercantile agent in possession of the goods or documents of title with the consent of the owner.

These two sections, of course, go slightly further than ss 3 and 4 of the Factors Act 1877, in that they take effect not only when the relevant person ((A) in s 8, and (B) in s 9) is allowed to be in possession of the documents of title to the goods, but also when he is allowed to be in possession of the goods themselves. It is relevant to observe also that, whereas the statutory hypothesis at the end of ss 3 and 4 of the Factors Act 1877 refers to the transaction taking effect as if the person making the delivery or transfer was a person entrusted by the *vendee* with the goods or documents, or entrusted by the *vendor* with the documents, as the case may be, we now see, in ss 8 and 9 of the Factors Act 1889, a different phraseology, referring not to the vendee (B1) or the vendor (A), but just to the 'owner of the goods' or 'the owner.' It is upon the slender foundation of this change of phraseology that the appellant, in the present case, has sought to build his argument that s 9 has the effect of adversely affecting the title, not only of a person (A) who has allowed another person (B) to be in possession of the relevant goods or documents, but also of anybody from whom the goods have been stolen, and whose goods have come into the possession of another who sells them.

For s 9 to have any such effect would constitute a change in policy of a fundamental kind, of which there is no evidence whatsoever in the remainder of the Act of 1889. I add for good measure that when, in 1893, s 9 was effectively incorporated (with changes which are immaterial for present purposes) as s 25(2) of the Sale of Goods Act of that year, it was incorporated into an Act of Parliament which expressly maintained the fundamental principle nemo dat quod non habet, in s 21(1) of the Act (now s 21(1) of the Act of 1979, quoted above). The succeeding sections enact what appear to be minor exceptions to that fundamental principle: yet, if the appellant's contention were to be correct, s 25(2) would have made not so much an exception to the principle, but would have substantially amounted to a reversal of it.

For the reasons I have set out, the statutory context provides overwhelming evidence that the legislature never intended, either in s 9 of the Factors Act 1889, or in s 25(2) of the Sale of Goods Act 1893 (or its successor, s 25(1) of the Sale of Goods Act 1979) to achieve the result contended for by the appellant. But there is further internal evidence, in the Act of 1889, that such a result can never have been intended.

Let me concentrate for a moment, not on s 9, but on s 8, of the Factors Act 1889. The submission for the appellant has to be that, when A has sold goods to B1, and B1 allows A to remain in possession of the goods after the sale, a subsequent sale by A to B2 will be effective to divest the title of a person from whom the goods have previously been stolen before they came into the hands of A. It is obvious that this can never have been the intention of the legislature. If it was, what was the relevance of the sale to B1, and the fact that B1 has allowed A to remain in possession? Assuming B1 to have acted in good faith, why should not A, whom I will assume to be the thief, give as good a title to B1 as to B2? Each is relying equally upon the possession of A of the goods. In truth, the whole section proceeds upon the assumption that the relevant owner of the goods, who is deemed to have authorised their delivery and transfer, is B1 – the person to whom the goods have been sold by A, and who has allowed A to remain in possession of them. And exactly the same point can be made in relation to s 9 itself. What is the relevance of the fact that B is in possession of the goods or documents of title with the permission of A? Again, there seems to be no good reason why C should get a good title, but that B (whom I assume to be acting in good faith) should not; each is simply relying, in good faith, upon the possession of his vendor.

Furthermore, if the construction of s 9 (and, by implication, s 8) urged by the appellant is correct, then we find a startling contrast between the policy underlying those two sections, and that underlying s 2. For s 2 goes no further than to divest the title of a person who has entrusted the mercantile agent with the possession of the relevant goods or documents of title; if ss 8 and 9 were to have the effect of divesting the title of a person from whom the goods have been stolen, and who has not entrusted them to the person who has purported to sell them to the purchaser, it is difficult to see why s 2 should have been so limited in its effect.

As a matter of construction of the relevant statutory provisions, therefore, I have reached the conclusion that the submission advanced by the appellant cannot be sustained. In my opinion, s 9 of the Factors Act 1889 must be read as providing that the delivery or transfer given by the intermediate transferor (B) shall have the same effect as if he was a mercantile agent in possession of the goods or documents of title with the consent of the owner who entrusted them to him (A). Such a construction is, in my opinion, to be derived from the terms of s 2(1) of the Act, to which s 9 evidently refers, and also from the legislative context which I have already discussed. The same construction must, of course, be placed upon s 25(1) of the Sale of Goods Act 1979.

[Lords Bridge of Harwich, Lowry, Brandon of Oakbrook and Griffiths concurred.]

The following case is also of relevance, and raised some interesting incidental points.

D F Mount Ltd v Jay & Jay (Provisions) Co Ltd [1960] 1 QB 159, Queen's Bench Division

Jays agreed to sell to Merrick 250 cartons of Australian canned peaches, part of a larger consignment owed by them and lying in the warehouse of Delta Storage Ltd, Greenwich. Merrick made it plain that he would pay the price from the moneys which he would receive from his own customers when the goods had been resold. Jays made out two delivery orders addressed to Delta in favour of Merrick, one for 150 cartons and another for 100. Merrick sent the delivery orders to Delta endorsed with the words 'Please transfer to our sub-order'. Merrick then agreed to resell the 250 cartons to Mount, and received the price from Mount in exchange for a delivery order addressed to Delta and signed by Merrick. Jays were never paid by Merrick. Both Jays and Mount claimed to be entitled to the peaches, which were still in the hands of Delta. Judgment was given in favour of Mount on the ground that Jays had 'assented' to the resale under s 47(1) (see below, p 397); but the case also contains a discussion of two points relevant to the present *nemo dat* exception: (1) does it matter that the contract goods are not identified, but unascertained? and (2) is it necessary under s 25(1) for the sub-buyer to receive the *same* delivery order that the buyer received from the original seller?

Salmon J held that Jays had 'assented' to the subsale by Mount under s 47(1), and continued: The sale of the 250 cartons was a sale of unascertained goods. In my judgment, however, there is no reason why s 47 should not apply to unascertained goods, although I respectfully agree with Pickford J that an inference can in some circumstances more readily be drawn against the seller in the case of a sale of specific goods than in the case of a sale of unascertained goods. I hold that the defendants assented to the sale of the cartons by Merrick within the meaning of s 47.

This is enough to dispose of the case, but I will deal briefly with some of the other points which have been canvassed. Mr Silkin argues that even had there been no sufficient assent by the defendants, he would be entitled to succeed under the proviso to s 47 [now s 47(2)].

[His Lordship read the proviso and continued:]

It is conceded that the plaintiffs took that delivery order in good faith and for valuable consideration. Mr Noakes argues, however, that there has been no transfer by Merrick within the meaning of the proviso. The material words to consider are: '. . . where a document of title to goods has been lawfully transferred to any person as buyer, . . . and that person transfers the document to a person. . . .'

It seems to me that these words confine the proviso to cases where a document is transferred to the buyer and the same document is then transferred by him to the person who takes in good faith and for valuable consideration. If Merrick had indorsed the delivery orders he received from the defendants and transferred them to the plaintiffs, the proviso would, in my judgment, have applied; but he did not do so. He sent those delivery orders to the wharf, and made out a fresh delivery order in favour of the plaintiffs.

It is strange that there appears to be no authority on this point. It is clear that the person who transfers the document of title to the buyer may originate it himself and need not have received it from some third party in order to 'transfer' it within the meaning of the proviso: see *Ant Jurgens Margarinefabrieken v Louis Dreyfus & Co* ([1914] 3 KB 40). In my judgment, however, on the plain language of the section, it must be that very document which is transferred by the buyer for the proviso to operate. I am conscious that this construction leads to a very artificial result, but I cannot avoid it without doing violence to the plain language of the section.

Mr Silkin, however, also relies on s 25(2) of the Sale of Goods Act 1893 [now s 25(1)].

[His Lordship read the subsection and continued:]

It seems to me that the language of this subsection is less rigorous than that of the proviso to s 47 and does not compel me to hold that the subsection applies only in those cases where the buyer transfers the same document as that of which he is in possession with the consent of the seller. I would observe that there seems to be no authority on this point.

The object of the subsection is to protect an innocent person in his dealings with a buyer who appears to have the right to deal with the goods in that he has been allowed by the seller to be in possession of the goods or documents of title relating to them. In such a case the subsection provides that any transfer of the goods or documents of title by the buyer to a person acting in good faith and without notice of any want of authority on the part of the buyer shall be as valid as if expressly authorised by the seller.

In the present case the defendants sent the documents of title to Merrick with the intention that they should enable him to obtain money from his customers. With the help of these documents, which he sent to the wharf so that the wharfingers would give a reassuring reply to any inquiry that the plaintiffs might make, or at least not query any delivery order they received from the plaintiffs, Merrick managed to obtain a substantial sum of money from the plaintiffs.

In my view, the transfer by Merrick of the delivery order . . . was, by virtue of s 25(2), as valid as if expressly authorised by the defendants.

NOTES

1. While the judgment of Salmon J does refer to the fact that the goods were unascertained, the discussion is perfunctory and refers only to s 47, and not also to s 25(1). Section 25(1) in fact uses the phrase 'sale, pledge or other disposition thereof', which would appear to exclude a mere agreement to sell. However, if this point had been taken, it could have been resolved by invoking s 9 of the Factors Act 1889 instead of s 25(1). The wording of these two sections is almost the same, but s 9 crucially adds the words 'or under any *agreement for sale*, pledge or other disposition thereof'. This appears to be the only case in the reports where the difference in wording between s 25(1) and s 9 might have been significant. There is a similar variation, as we have seen, between s 24 and s 8 of the 1989 Act.

2. This draws our attention to the significance of the slight differences in wording between s 25(2), s 47 and s 9 of the Factors Act 1889. It surely cannot have been the intention of the legislature to say nearly the same thing in three different ways. It is a matter for regret that the opportunity was not taken to clarify the position (and also that involving s 24 and s 8) when the legislation was consolidated in 1979.

3. As is the case with s 24, it is essential for s 25(1) to apply that the person claiming the benefit of this exception should have taken delivery of the goods from the original buyer, or had a document of title transferred to him. The mere fact of a sale without such delivery or transfer is not sufficient. (But note also (as Salmon J confirms) that the *issue* of a delivery order by the seller or buyer is treated as equivalent to the 'transfer' of a similar document which has emanated from a third party.)

4. It should be noted that the section uses the phrase 'under any sale, pledge, *or other disposition thereof*' (as also does s 24). These two exceptions to the *nemo dat* rule are therefore not confined to the case of a second sale or pledge. Where, for instance, a builder who has agreed to buy materials on terms that title remains in the seller uses these materials in constructing a house for a customer, there is a 'disposition' within s 25(1): the customer gets a good title and cannot be sued in conversion by the original seller: *W Hanson (Harrow) Ltd v Rapid Civil Engineering Ltd* (1987) 38 BLR 106. However, a 'disposition' probably requires some voluntary act on the part of the first buyer: see *The Saetta* (below, p 424), where the owners of the chartered ship simply took over the fuel oil on board when they resumed possession of her: the court, without ruling whether there had been a 'disposition' by the charterers, held that in the absence of any voluntary act there had been no 'delivery' by them of the oil, and that s 25(1) did not apply.

5. In *Four Point Garage Ltd v Carter* [1985] 3 All ER 12, the goods in question were delivered by the seller directly to the sub-purchaser. Simon Brown J held that s 25(1) applied, because the buyer was deemed to have taken constructive delivery of the goods and the seller to have acted as the buyer's agent in making delivery to the sub-purchaser.

9 Eighth exception: sale by *unpaid* seller under SGA 1979, s 48

This exception to the *nemo dat* rule overlaps to some extent with the sixth (sale by seller in possession), but there are important points of difference. It is discussed with the other seller's remedies below, at p 402.

10 Ninth exception: private purchase of motor vehicle held on hire purchase

Most of the Hire-Purchase Act 1964 has long since been repealed, but Part III remains in force (in the form of a revised text which incorporates some amendments made by the Consumer Credit Act 1974). This part of the Act is concerned to protect *private purchasers* acting in good faith who buy *motor vehicles* which have been let out on hire purchase without notice of the existence of the hire-purchase agreement. It will be recalled that *Helby v Matthews* (above, p 228) confirmed that a person who has taken goods on hire purchase is merely a hirer and not someone who has 'bought or agreed to buy' the goods, and so he cannot give a good title to under s 25(1) to someone who buys the goods from him. When the Hire-Purchase Act 1964 was enacted, this special exception to the *nemo dat* rule was introduced as a result of a concession made by the motor trade. (The alternative proposed by the government was to set up a registration system for the ownership of vehicles which would have been very costly to administer.)

The details of Part III are quite complex. The most important points are as follows:

(1) It applies only to 'motor vehicles' – mechanically propelled vehicles intended or adapted for use on public roads (s 29(1)) – a definition which would include cars, motor-cycles, motorised caravans and lorries, but not caravans, trailers and boats. Agricultural machines such as combine harvesters could pose a problem of construction.

(2) 'Private purchaser' has a special meaning: someone who is not a 'trade or finance purchaser' (s 29(2)). This excludes all motor dealers and finance companies, but not other forms of business purchaser.

(3) The Act applies to vehicles which have been acquired under conditional sale contracts (such as the contract in *Lee v Butler*, above, p 332) as well as under hire-purchase agreements (s 27(1)). There is no financial or other statutory limitation on the scope of the Act (in contrast with most other hire-purchase legislation, which is confined to *consumer* transactions).

(4) Only the *first* private purchaser from the hirer (or 'debtor', as he is termed in the Act) is protected. Thus, if the debtor sells the vehicle to X, who has notice of the hire-purchase agreement, X will not get a good title, and neither will Y, if X sells on to Y, even if Y is a bona fide purchaser without notice. (This is surely an oversight on the part of the draftsman.) However, if a vehicle which is on hire purchase is disposed of to a trade or finance purchaser, the first private purchaser from that trade or finance purchaser is protected (s 27(2)–(5)).

Reform of the law. On 20 January 1994 the Department of Trade and Industry published a Consultation Document containing proposals for the reform of some of the exceptions to the *nemo dat* rule, including abolition of the market overt exception, and extending Part III of the Hire-Purchase Act 1964 to cover all goods on hire-purchase and similar contracts. More controversially, it is also proposed that anyone who is in possession of goods with the owner's consent should have power to confer a good title on an innocent purchaser. It is a reasonably safe prediction that this last suggestion, with its potentially far-reaching consequences, will not gain support: see the criticism of B J Davenport (1994) 110 LQR 165.

CHAPTER 10

Statutory implied terms

1 Introduction

Sections 12–15 contain the statutory rules governing the seller's obligations to give a good title, ensure that the buyer enjoys quiet possession, etc and to deliver goods of the description and quality that the contract specifies. These are set out in the form of *implied terms*. In principle (and certainly in the Act as originally enacted), the parties are free to exclude or vary these implied terms, since s 55(1) states that 'where a right, duty or liability would arise under a contract of sale of goods by implication of law, it may . . . be negatived or varied by express agreement, or by the course of dealing between the parties, or by such usage as binds both parties to the contract'. But the parties' freedom to do this has, since 1977, been considerably limited by the Unfair Contract Terms Act 1977, which expressly makes s 55(1) subject to its provisions. These statutory restrictions on freedom of contract are more severe in the case of consumer sales than other contracts of sale; and in regard to international sales (called in the 1977 Act 'international supply contracts') they do not apply at all. We shall note the effect of these restrictions later in this chapter.

All the statutory implied terms are classified by the Sale of Goods Act as *conditions* or *warranties*. The Act does not contemplate the possibility that there may also be 'innominate' terms of the kind recognised in *Hong Kong Fir Shipping Co Ltd v Kawasaki Kisen Kaisha Ltd* [1962] 2 QB 26, CA – that is, terms where the remedy for breach is made to depend on the seriousness of the breach. However, there is clearly nothing to prevent a court from categorising an *express* term in a contract of sale of goods as innominate; and, in fact, the Court of Appeal did so in *Cehave NV v Bremer Handelsgesellschaft mbH, The Hansa Nord* [1976] QB 44, CA, in relation to the term 'shipment to be made in good condition'. Where this construction is put upon an obligation to be fulfilled by the seller, the buyer will have a right to reject the goods only if the breach is such as to go to the root of the contract; failing this, he will be confined to a remedy in damages.

Section 11 sets out in statutory form the definition of a condition (and, by implication, of a warranty), and the conventional rules of the general law of contract relating to the breach of such terms.

2 The implied condition as to title (s 12(1))

Subject to one statutory exception (s 12(3), discussed below), in every contract of sale there is an implied condition on the part of the seller that in the case of a sale he has a right to sell the goods, and in the case of an agreement to sell he will have such a right at the time when the property is to pass (s 12(1)). So, if goods are sold which turn out to have been stolen, the buyer is entitled to the return of the whole of the purchase price.

Rowland v Divall [1923] 2 KB 500, Court of Appeal

(The facts appear from the judgment.)

Scrutton LJ: The plaintiff purchased a car from the defendant for £334. He drove it from Brighton, where he bought it, to the place where he had a garage, painted it and kept it there for about two months. He then sold it to a third person who had it in his possession for another two months. Then came the police, who claimed it as the stolen car for which they had been looking. It appears that it had been stolen before the defendant became possessed of it, and consequently he had no title that he could convey to the plaintiff. In these circumstances the plaintiff sued the defendant for the price he paid for the car as on a total failure of consideration. Now before the passing of the Sale of Goods Act there was a good deal of confusion in the authorities as to the exact nature of the vendor's contract with respect to his title to sell. It was originally said that a vendor did not warrant his title. But gradually a number of exceptions crept in, till at last the exceptions became the rule, the rule being that the vendor warranted that he had title to what he purported to sell, except in certain special cases, such as that of a sale by a sheriff, who does not so warrant. Then came the Sale of Goods Act, which re-enacted that rule, but did so with this alteration: it re-enacted it as a condition, not as a warranty. Section 12 says in express terms that there shall be 'An implied condition on the part of the seller that . . . he has a right to sell the goods.' It being now a condition, wherever that condition is broken the contract can be rescinded, and with the rescission the buyer can demand a return of the purchase money, unless he has, with knowledge of the facts, held on to the bargain so as to waive the condition. But Mr Doughty argues that there can never be a rescission where a restitutio in integrum is impossible, and that here the plaintiff cannot rescind because he cannot return the car. To that the buyer's answer is that the reason of his inability to return it – namely, the fact that the defendant had no title to it – is the very thing of which he is complaining, and that it does not lie in the defendant's mouth to set up as a defence to the action his own breach of the implied condition that he had a right to sell. In my opinion that answer is well founded, and it would, I think, be absurd to apply the rule as to restitutio in integrum to such a state of facts. No doubt the general rule is that a buyer cannot rescind a contract of sale and get back the purchase money unless he can restore the subject matter. There are a large number of cases on the subject, some of which are not very easy to reconcile with others. Some of them make it highly probable that a certain degree of deterioration of the goods is not sufficient to take away the right to recover the purchase money. However I do not think it necessary to refer to them. It certainly seems to me that, in a case of rescission for the breach of the condition that the seller had a right to sell the goods, it cannot be that the buyer is deprived of his right to get back the purchase money because he cannot restore the goods which, from the nature of the transaction, are not the goods of the seller at all, and which the seller therefore has no right to under any circumstances. For these reasons I think that the plaintiff is entitled to recover the whole of the purchase money as for a total failure of consideration, and that the appeal must be allowed.

Atkin LJ: I agree. It seems to me that in this case there has been a total failure of consideration, that is to say that the buyer has not got any part of that for which he paid the purchase money. He paid the money in order that he might get the property, and he has not got it. It is true that the seller delivered to him the de facto possession, but the seller had not got the right to possession and consequently could not give it to the buyer. Therefore the buyer, during the time that he had the car in his actual possession had no right to it, and was at all times liable to the true owner for its conversion. Now there is no doubt that what the buyer had a right to get was the property in the car, for the Sale of Goods Act expressly provides that in every contract of sale there is an implied condition that the seller has a right to sell. . . . The whole object of a sale is to transfer property from one person to another. . . .

It seems to me that in this case there must be a right to reject, and also a right to sue for the price paid as money had and received on failure of the consideration, and further that there is no obligation on the part of the buyer to return the car, for ex hypothesi the seller had no right to receive it. Under these circumstances can it make any difference that the buyer has used the car before he found out that there was a breach of the condition? To my mind it makes no difference at all. The buyer accepted the car on the representation of the seller that he had a right to sell it, and inasmuch as the seller had no such right he is not entitled to say that the buyer has enjoyed a benefit under the contract. In fact the buyer has not received any part of that which he contracted to receive – namely, the property and right to possession – and, that being so, there has been a total failure of consideration. The plaintiff is entitled to recover the £334 which he paid.

[Bankes LJ delivered a concurring judgment.]

NOTE

This rule can work considerable injustice, as is shown by the later case of *Butterworth v Kingsway Motors* [1954] 1 WLR 1286, where a car which was owned by a finance company and let on hire purchase was wrongfully sold by the hirer and passed through several hands before being bought by the plaintiff, who used it for nearly a whole year before it was reclaimed by the finance company. (The Hire-Purchase Act 1964, Part III (above, p 341) was not yet in force.) It was held, following *Rowland v Divall*, that the plaintiff could recover all of his purchase price (£1725) from his immediate seller because of the breach of the *condition* implied by s 12(1), even though he had had the use of the car for almost a year, and the far smaller sum of £175 would have been sufficient to pay off the finance company's interest in the car. Had the plaintiff been restricted to a remedy in damages, he would of course have been entitled to be paid much less.

The Law Reform Committee, in its Twelfth Report (*Transfer of Title to Chattels*, Cmnd 2958, 1967), para 36, recommended that a buyer in these circumstances should be entitled to recover no more than his actual loss, giving credit for any benefit he may have had from the goods while they were in his possession.

The following case shows that s 12(1) (which uses the phrase 'a right to sell the goods') is wider in its scope than might be inferred from the label 'implied condition as to title' which is commonly applied to it.

Niblett Ltd v Confectioners' Materials Co Ltd [1921] 3 KB 387, Court of Appeal

(The facts appear from the judgment.)

Bankes LJ: In August 1919, the parties entered into a contract for the sale of 3000 cases of condensed milk. The contract was originally made at an interview, but it was subsequently confirmed by writing in the form of a sold note dated August 18 sent by the respondents to the appellants with a request that they would sign a counterpart, that is to say, a bought note, in the same terms, which the appellants did. The contract appears to be wholly embodied in the writing. Notwithstanding this both parties seem to have treated the contract as partly oral and partly in writing, and to have adduced parol evidence as to its terms, and counsel for the respondents have contended that it was agreed that one or more of three brands of condensed milk, including the 'Nissly' brand, might be delivered in fulfilment of the contract, and Bailhache J appears to have dealt with the case on that footing. Two thousand cases were delivered, and give rise to no question. One thousand arrived bearing labels with the word 'Nissly' upon them. It came to the knowledge of the Nestlé and Anglo-Swiss Co that parcels of condensed milk were being imported with this label upon them, and they took up the position that these 1000 cases infringed their registered trade mark. They objected to these goods being dealt with in any way. The justice of their objection was admitted by the respondents, who gave an undertaking not to sell, offer for sale, or dispose of any condensed milk under the title of 'Nissly.' The appellants did their best to sell, exchange, or export the goods, but found that the only possible way of dealing with them was to strip them of their labels and sell them without marks or labels.

Bailhache J came to the clear conclusion that if s 12 of the Sale of Goods Act 1893 is to be construed literally the respondents had no right to sell the goods as they were, and that the appellants were not enjoying and never had enjoyed quiet possession of the goods; that they could never get them from the Commissioners of Customs, and that if they had got them they were never in a position to deal with them, because of the Nestlé Co's threat. But he felt himself bound by the judgment of Lord Russell CJ in *Monforts v Marsden* ((1895) 12 RPC 266) to give to s 12 a meaning and effect which he would not have attributed to it but for that case. With the greatest respect to Lord Russell CJ I think the doubts cast by Bailhache J upon that decision are justified. The case was heard and decided by Lord Russell CJ on circuit. He took the view that s 12 was to be read with qualifications like those which limit the implied covenant for quiet enjoyment in a conveyance of real property by a grantor who conveys as beneficial owner under s 7 of the Conveyancing Act 1881, and he imposed upon the implied obligations in s 12 of the Sale of Goods Act 1893, a restriction limiting their operation to acts and omissions of the vendor and those acting by his authority. I cannot agree with the view thus expressed by Lord Russell. I think s 12 has a much wider effect, and that the language does not warrant the limitation imposed by Lord Russell. I express no opinion as to what 'circumstances' of a contract are 'such as to show a different intention,' to use the earlier words of s 12. Mr Spence contended that these circumstances are not confined to matters relating to the making of the contract, but would include the fact that at the time of making a written contract for the sale of goods it was understood that the goods would be of one or another brand. He argued that this was a circumstance which would show an intention to exclude the warranties otherwise implied. But assuming that goods of one or more of three brands might be delivered under the contract, that circumstance does not show any intention that if two of those brands are free from objection, and the third is an infringement of trade mark rights, the vendor may tender goods of the third brand in fulfilment of his contract. The goods tendered must still be goods which the vendor has a right to sell. Therefore in my opinion the appellants have established a right of action under s 12, sub-s 1, of the Act.

It is not necessary to consider whether there is also a good cause of action under s 12, sub-s 2, and I say nothing upon that point. I think there is also a cause of action under s 14, sub-s 2, because these goods were not 'of merchantable quality.' Quality includes the state or condition of the goods. The state of this condensed milk was that it was packed in tins bearing labels. The labels were as much part of the state or condition of the goods as the tins were. The state of the packing affected the merchantable quality of the goods. . . .

[Scrutton and Atkin LJJ delivered concurring judgments.]

3 Sale of a limited title

Prior to 1973, there was considerable academic debate over the question whether the implied condition as to title could be excluded by an express stipulation in the contract (and, if so, whether the resulting transaction was a contract of sale of goods at all). However, the issue is now resolved by s 12(3), an amendment which was first introduced by the Supply of Goods (Implied Terms) Act 1973. This provision allows a person to contract to sell such title to goods as he (or another person) may have – so that a person who has found a watch and cannot trace the owner can sell his 'finder's title', and a landlord distraining on his tenant's goods or a sheriff who has seized goods in execution to satisfy a judgment debt can sell them on the understanding that the buyer shall get whatever title to them the tenant or debtor may have had. But, apart from this special provision, the condition implied by s 12(1) cannot be excluded or modified in any way by the operation of an exemption clause (Unfair Contract Terms Act 1977, s 6(1)(a)) – unless the contract is of a kind to which that Act does not apply at all, such as an international sale contract.

4 The implied warranties as to freedom from encumbrances and quiet possession (s 12(2)(a), (b))

Section 12 goes on to supplement the implied condition as to title by providing for two implied *warranties*: first, that the goods are, and will remain, free from any undisclosed encumbrances (s 12(2)(a)) and, secondly, that the buyer will enjoy quiet and undisturbed possession (s 12(2)(b)). These are the only statutory implied terms that are characterised as warranties and not conditions. It follows that if either of these implied terms is broken, the buyer will have only a remedy in damages and will not be able to reject the goods.

Where there has been a breach of s 12(1) (title), there will normally be a breach of s 12(2)(b) (quiet possession) also. In *Niblett v Confectioners' Materials Ltd* (above), the Court of Appeal held that there had also been a breach of s 12(2)(b). In *Mason v Burningham* [1949] 2 KB 545, CA, where the plaintiff bought a secondhand typewriter which turned out to have been stolen and had to be returned to its rightful owner, she could plainly have sued under s 12(1) (as in *Rowland v Divall* (above)), but chose instead to rely only on s 12(2)(b). She was awarded by way of damages not only a refund of the purchase price, but also a sum which she had reasonably (in the view of the court) paid to have the typewriter overhauled and put into first-class condition following the purchase.

Microbeads AC v Vinhurst Road Markings Ltd [1975] 1 WLR 218, CA, is a case which closely parallels *Niblett v Confectioners' Materials Ltd* (above): here the road-marking machines which were the subject of the contract turned out two years later to infringe the patent of a third party, who threatened to institute proceedings against the buyer. Since the patent was not granted to the third party until after the date of the contract of sale, there had been no breach of the condition as to title at the time when the property in the goods passed to the buyer, and so it was not possible to invoke s 12(1). But the court held that a remedy lay under s 12(2)(b).

The scope of s 12(2)(b) has never been fully explored. From the above cases, it is plain that there will be a breach of the statutory warranty if the buyer's possession is disturbed by the lawful act of a third person who asserts a superior title or a right which impairs the buyer's title or his freedom to possess and use the goods. On the other hand, it is plain that the seller will not be in breach of his undertaking if a stranger who has no connection with the seller (eg a trespasser or a vandal) simply commits a tort which interferes with the buyer's rights. However, a tort committed by the seller himself or his agent will cause him to incur liability under s 12(2)(b).

In *Empresa Exportadora de Azucar v Industria Azucarera Nacional SA, The Playa Larga* [1983] 2 Lloyd's Rep 171 the seller, the Cuban state sugar trading agency, had sold sugar to a buyer in Chile and had sent a cargo of sugar aboard the *Playa Larga* to Valparaiso in part fulfilment of its obligations. When the Allende regime in Chile was overthrown and replaced by a right-wing military dictatorship, the Cuban government ordered the seller to break off all trading relations with its Chilean buyer, and the seller ordered the ship not to unload the sugar. This action was held to amount to a breach of s 12(2)(b), and the seller was obliged to pay damages.

Subsections (4) and (5) of s 12 apply to the case where a contract of sale is made under s 12(3) – that is, where the seller contracts to transfer a limited title. Under these subsections, modified forms of the warranties as to freedom from encumbrances and quiet possession are implied in such a contract.

QUESTION

Why do you think that the draftsman of the Act chose to characterise the implied terms in s 12(2) and 12(3) as warranties rather than conditions?

5 The implied condition that the goods will correspond with their description (s 13)

Where there is a contract for the sale of goods by description, there is an implied condition that the goods will correspond with the description (s 13(1)). Section 13(2) goes on to say that if the sale is by sample as well as by description, the goods must comply with both the sample and their description.

This provision has been regarded as curious by some commentators, who have expressed surprise that the Act should bother to include such a rule at all, and thought it even more odd that the obligation should be described as an *implied* condition when there is surely an *express* obligation to deliver goods of the description by which they were sold.

The explanation has to be sought in the earlier history of the law of sale, some time before the codifying Act. In many of the older cases, a distinction was made between a sale of specific goods, on the one hand, and a sale of goods 'by description' on the other. An identified horse or vehicle may be regarded as typical of the former: the buyer could inspect it, have his own experts look at it, and was expected to rely on his own judgment in order to satisfy himself that he was getting what he wanted: *caveat emptor*. Alternatively, he could ask the seller for an express warranty (eg as to a horse's soundness) if he wanted to have the seller accept responsibility in some particular respect. Where, however, the sale was for generic goods which had no identity (eg '100 tons of King Edward potatoes'), the qualities of the goods which the buyer was bargaining to have could be ascertained only by reference to the contractual description by which they were sold (and, in commercial contracts, a further term, implied by law, that they should be of 'merchantable' quality under that description (now SGA 1979, s 14(2); but in the modern version of this subsection references to the contractual description have been eliminated). It was thus vital that, in the case of goods sold by description, the seller should be required to deliver goods conforming exactly to the description that the contract specified, and that the law should allow the buyer to reject the goods if they did not. Hence, in Chalmers' original draft, the implied term as to conformity with description was one of only two implied terms which he made *conditions* (the other, for similar reasons, being what is now s 15(2)(b), relating to sales by sample). All the other statutory implied terms – even the implied term as to title – were characterised merely as warranties, it being left to the buyer to stipulate expressly that compliance with any particular term should be a 'condition' for his benefit if he thought it sufficiently important.

In the event, the law took a quite different turn soon after the Act of 1893 was passed. Chalmers did not clearly incorporate into this part of his Bill the distinction between sales of specific goods and sales by description that is explained above, and his Bill was altered during its passage through Parliament so as to make most of the statutory implied terms conditions, and not merely warranties. (At much the same time, lawyers allowed the meaning of the word 'condition' to slip from that of 'pure' condition to its barely defensible modern connotation, 'term of vital importance'.) In *Varley v Whipp* [1900] 1 QB 513 the term 'sale by description' was interpreted as including a secondhand reaping machine (ie specific goods) which the buyer had not seen, and since then it has been extended to goods which the buyer has seen and inspected (*Grant v Australian Knitting Mills Ltd* [1936] AC 85, PC (woollen underpants bought in a retail shop); *Beale v Taylor* [1967] 1 WLR 1193, CA (a secondhand car advertised for sale in a newspaper)). These cases have led to the term 'sale by description' being given a meaning so attenuated as to give rise to speculation whether any contract of sale will be regarded as *not* being made 'by description': in *Grant* Lord Wright said ([1936] AC 85 at 100):

> . . . there is a sale by description even though the buyer is buying something displayed before him on the counter: a thing is sold by description, though it is specific, so long as it is sold not merely as the specific thing but as a thing corresponding to a description, eg, woollen under-garments.

Section 13(3), a new provision inserted by an amendment made in 1973, puts this matter even further beyond doubt by providing:

> A sale of goods is not prevented from being a sale by description by reason only that, being exposed for sale or hire, they are selected by the buyer.

The main explanation for this extraordinary widening of the meaning of the term 'sale by description' is to be found in relation not to s 13, but to s 14(2), where the phrase was, prior to 1973, used as a precondition for the statutory implication of a duty to supply goods of 'merchantable quality'. The reason for implying such a term in a mercantile context has been explained above; but in more recent times s 14(2) has had to be pressed more and more into service for the purpose of giving the buyer in a *consumer* sale a remedy where he has been sold defective goods. The customer who bought the underpants in *Grant v Australian Knitting Mills Ltd* suffered severe dermatitis because there were excess sulphites, a chemical irritant, in the pants which had not been washed out in the process of   he could not, in 1936, have been given a remedy under s 14(2) withou that the goods had been sold to him 'by description' – a Council simply took in cavalier fashion without any great c

When we move out of the consumer sphere and back int with which this book is primarily concerned, we see that th correspondence with description has an important role 'commodity' sales – contracts for the sale of generic go only the contract description to rely on in order to ensure the goods that he wants. This is illustrated by the two ca

Re Moore & Co Ltd and Landauer & Co's Arbitration [1921] 2 KB 519, Court of Appeal

Moore & Co contracted to sell to Landauer & Co 3100 cases of Australian canned fruits, described as being packed in cases containing 30 cans each. When the ship containing the goods arrived in London, it was found that only about half of the consignment was packed in cases of 30, the rest being in cases of 24. The buyers rejected the goods without giving any reason; and were held by the Court of Appeal to have been entitled to do so under s 13.

Atkin LJ: It appears to me to be clear that the stipulation in the contract that there shall be 2½ dozen tins in a case is part of the description of the goods. There is, therefore, an implied condition that the goods when tendered shall correspond with the description. That condition was broken, and there was a right to reject. It appears to me also to be plain that by reason of s 30, sub-s 3, of the Sale of Goods Act 1893, the sellers were not entitled to insist upon the buyers accepting so much of the goods tendered as happened to correspond with the description. I think the buyers were entitled to reject the whole.

[Bankes and Scrutton LJJ delivered concurring judgments.]

Arcos Ltd v E A Ronaasen & Son [1933] AC 470, House of Lords

This was a contract for the sale of Russian timber cut into staves for the purpose of making cement barrels. The contract specified that the staves should be ½ inch in thickness. The buyers claimed to be entitled to reject the timber because most of the staves were thicker than half an inch, although a large proportion were not more than $9/16$ of an inch. It was found that the staves were fit for making cement barrels and merchantable under the contract specification. The House of Lords upheld the buyers' right to reject.

Lord Atkin: The decisions of the learned judge and of the Court of Appeal appear to me to have been unquestionably right. On the facts as stated by the umpire as of the time of inspection only about 5 per cent of the goods corresponded with the description: and the umpire finds it impossible to say what proportion conformed at the time of shipment.

It was contended that in all commercial contracts the question was whether there was a 'substantial' compliance with the contract: there always must be some margin: and it is for the tribunal of fact to determine whether the margin is exceeded or not. I cannot agree. If the written contract specifies conditions of weight, measurement and the like, those conditions must be complied with. A ton does not mean about a ton, or a yard about a yard. Still less when you descend to minute measurements does ½ inch mean about ½ inch. If the seller wants a margin he must and in my experience does stipulate for it. Of course by recognized trade usage particular figures may be given a different meaning, as in a baker's dozen; or there may be even incorporated a definite margin more or less: but there is no evidence or finding of such a usage in the present case.

No doubt there may be microscopic deviations which business men and therefore lawyers will ignore. And in this respect it is necessary to remember that description and quantity are not necessarily the same: and that the legal rights in respect of them are regulated by different sections of the code, description by s 13, quantity, by s 30. It will be found that most of the cases that admit any deviation from the contract are cases where there has been an excess or deficiency in quantity which the Court has considered negligible. But apart from this consideration the right view is that the conditions of the contract must be strictly performed. If a condition is not performed the buyer has a right to reject.

[Buckmaster and Warrington of Clyffe delivered concurring opinions. ... urgh and Macmillan concurred.]

NOTE

These two decisions have been heavily criticised by some commentators, who have drawn attention to the fact that the goods delivered were apparently in each case perfectly suitable for the buyers' purpose, and that the buyers' undenied reason for wanting to reject them was that the market price for such goods had fallen and they wanted to get out of an unprofitable bargain. But there are important arguments which fully justify the court's strict approach to the requirement of conformity with description, *in the commercial context in which these cases were decided*. First, merchants put a high premium on certainty: a firm rule means that they know where they stand, whereas much delay would be caused if every case had to go to court in order to ascertain whether the deviation from the contract was significant, or what the real motives of the parties were. Secondly, more often than not, the buyers of commodities are not merchants who intend to use the goods themselves, but dealers who have bought to sell on, and who may well already have resold the goods to sub-buyers; and in such a case they will usually have resold the goods by the same description.

There could well be a long chain of further sub-contracts. If there is a dispute over conformity with description under the first sale, the court is not to know what use for the goods the ultimate buyer may have in mind, or whether it is such as would entitle him to reject them. Thirdly, as we shall see (below, p 465) the completion of these contracts of sale is very often carried out not by the parties themselves, but by others on their behalf (such as their respective banks) by payment of the price in exchange for the shipping documents relating to the goods – possibly in a foreign country. These representatives will not be in a position to know whether goods which do not fully comply with the contract description will nevertheless be suitable for their clients' purpose (still less, their clients' sub-purchasers' purpose), and so the only workable rule has to be one calling for strict conformity.

Against the background of this discussion, we are in a better position to look a little more closely at the concept of 'sale by description', and in particular to ask which out of the many words used in reference to the goods being sold are part of their contract 'description'.

The approach of the courts will depend upon the context. In the commercial context of commodity sales, we have seen from *Re Moore and Landauer* and *Arcos v Ronaasen* (above) that words regarding the packing of the goods and their dimensions may be part of their description. The same may be true of references to the origin of the goods, their analysis, etc: the parties can make any element or item part of the description and, if the court concludes that that was their intention, the buyer is entitled to stipulate that that, and that alone, is what he shall get. In contrast, particularly when the case is concerned with specific or identifiable goods, it is open to the court to hold that, although descriptive words were used, the goods were not 'sold by' that description. This is clear from *Reardon Smith Line Ltd v Yngvar Hansen-Tangen* (where a contract to charter a ship raised analogous questions) and even more so, in the somewhat specialist world of the art market, from *Harlingdon & Leinster Enterprises Ltd v Christopher Hull Fine Art Ltd*. The issue for the court is then to decide whether the parties attached sufficient weight to the particular words as to warrant their being treated as part of the contractual description.

Reardon Smith Line Ltd v Yngvar Hansen-Tangen [1976] 1 WLR 989, House of Lords

In 1972 Sanko, a Japanese shipbuilding company, contracted to charter to Hansen-Tangen a new 80,000-ton tanker, to be delivered when construction was completed in 1974. Since at the time when the contract was entered into construction had not begun, it was provided that Sanko would declare the yard where the vessel was to be built and its hull number at a later date. In fulfilment of this requirement, Sanko notified Hansen-Tangen that the vessel was to be built by the Osaka company and 'known as Hull No 354 until named'. Osaka's own yard was not large enough to build an 80,000-ton ship, and so it arranged for the work to be done by a subsidiary company, Oshima, 300 miles away, and Oshima gave the proposed vessel its own hull number, 004, though it continued to be shown in Osaka's own books as No 354. Hansan-Tangen later contracted to sub-charter the tanker to Reardon Smith, describing it as 'newbuilding motor tank vessel called Yard No 354 at Osaka'. When the ship was ready for delivery the market had collapsed owing to the oil crisis of 1974, and the charterers sought to reject it on the ground that it did not correspond with the contractual description.

Lord Wilberforce stated the facts and continued: These being the background facts, the whole case . . . turns, in my opinion, upon the long italicised passage in the sub-charter set out above which, for convenience of reference I repeat:

> '(the good) Japanese flag (subject to Clause 41) Newbuilding motor tank vessel called Yard No 354 at Osaka Zosen'.

I shall refer to this as the 'box' since it appears enclosed in a typed box on the document. . . .

I ask what was the commercial purpose of these charterparties and what was the factual background against which they were made? The purpose is clear: it was to make available to (1) Hansen-Tangen and (2) to Reardon Smith a medium-sized tanker suitable for use as such, this tanker not being in existence, or even under construction at the date of either charter, and, at the date of the intermediate charter not even the subject of contracts made by the supplying company. The vessel was to be constructed in a Japanese yard and made available on charter to Sanko as part of a programme. At the date of the sub-charter the vessel was identified in contracts for its construction in Japan and had a serial number. In order to ensure that the tanker was suitable for its purpose a detailed specification was drawn up – by way of a warranted description with which of course the vessel must strictly comply.

In addition, since at the time of either charterparty the vessel was not in existence or under construction, some means had to be agreed upon for identifying the particular vessel – one out of a programme – which would form the subject matter of the charters. This was indispensable so as to enable those committing themselves to hire the vessel, to sub-hire it, if they wished, and if necessary to arrange finance. This necessary identification was to be effected by nomination, by Sanko in the first place and then by Hansen-Tangen.

The text of the charterparties confirms beyond doubt that this was what was intended and done. The preamble, in the Shelltime 3 form, provides for the insertion of a name – 'being owners of the good . . . tank vessel called. . . .' The box insertion in the subcharter was made in this place – 'called Yard No 354 at Osaka Zosen.' The intermediate charter, entered into before Sanko had nominated any vessel, provided in its preamble – instead of 'called . . .' for declaration by the owners together with the Hull number, and the addendum, entered into after Sanko had nominated, provided 'to be built by Osaka Shipbuilding Co Ltd and known as Hull No 354 until named.' What is vital about each of these insertions is that they were simple substitutes for a name, serving no purpose but to provide a means whereby the charterers could identify the ship. At the dates when these insertions were made no importance could have been attached to the matters now said to be so significant – they were not a matter of negotiation, but of unilateral declaration. What is now sought is to elevate them into strict contractual terms in the nature of 'conditions.'

The appellants sought, necessarily, to give to the box and the corresponding provision in the intermediate charter contractual effect. They argued that these words formed part of the 'description' of the future goods contracted to be provided that, by analogy with contracts for the sale of goods, any departure from the description entitled the other party to reject, that there were departures in that the vessel was not built by Osaka Shipbuilding Co Ltd and was not Hull No 354. I shall attempt to deal with each of these contentions.

In the first place, I am not prepared to accept that authorities as to 'description' in sale of goods cases are to be extended, or applied, to such a contract as we have here. Some of these cases either in themselves (*Re Moore and Co and Landauer and Co* [1921] 2 KB 519) or as they have been interpreted (eg *Behn v Burness* (1863) 3 B & S 751) I find to be excessively technical and due for fresh examination in this House. Even if a strict and technical view must be taken as regards the description of unascertained future goods (eg, commodities) as to which each detail of the description must be assumed to be vital, it may be, and in my opinion is, right to treat other contracts of sale of goods in a similar manner to other contracts generally so as to ask whether a particular item in a description constitutes a substantial ingredient of the 'identity' of the thing sold, and only if it does to treat it as a condition (see *Couchman v Hill* [1947] KB 554, 559, per Scott LJ). I would respectfully endorse what was recently said by Roskill LJ in *Cehave NV v Bremer Handelsgesellschaft mbH* [1976] QB 44, 71:

> In principle it is not easy to see why the law relating to contracts for the sale of goods should be different from the law relating to the performance of other contractual obligations, whether charterparties or other types of contract. Sale of goods law is but one branch of the general law of contract. It is desirable that the same legal principles should apply to the law of contract as a whole and that different legal principles should not apply to different branches of that law. . . .

The general law of contract has developed, along much more rational lines (eg, *Hong Kong Fir Shipping Co Ltd v Kawasaki Kisen Kaisha Ltd* [1962] 2 QB 26), in attending to the nature and gravity of a breach or departure rather than in accepting rigid categories which do or do not automatically give a right to rescind, and if the choice were between extending cases under the Sale of Goods Act 1893 into other fields, or allowing more modern doctrine to infect those cases, my preference would be clear. The importance of this line of argument is that Mocatta J and Lord Denning MR used it in the present case so as to reject the appellants' argument on 'description' and I agree with them. But in case it does not appeal to this House, I am also satisfied that the appellants fail to bring the present case within the strictest rules as to 'description.'

In my opinion the fatal defect in their argument consists in their use of the words 'identity' or 'identification' to bridge two meanings. It is one thing to say of given words that their purpose is to state (identify) an essential part of the description of the goods. It is another to say that they provide one party with a specific indication (identification) of the goods so that he can find them and if he wishes sub-dispose of them. The appellants wish to say of words which 'identify' the goods in the second sense, that they describe them in the first. I have already given reasons why I can only read the words in the second sense.

The difference is vital. If the words are read in the first sense, then, unless I am right in the legal argument above, each element in them has to be given contractual force. The vessel must, as a matter of contract, and as an essential term, be built by Osaka and must bear their Yard No 354 – if not the description is not complied with and the vessel tendered is not that contracted for.

If in the second sense, the only question is whether the words provide a means of identifying the vessel. If they fairly do this, they have fulfilled their function. It follows that if the second sense is correct, the words used can be construed much more liberally than they would have to be construed if they were providing essential elements of the description. . . .

So the question becomes simply whether, as a matter of fact, it can fairly be said that – as a means of identification – the vessel was Yard No 354 at Osaka Zosen or 'built by Osaka Shipping Co Ltd and known as Hull No 354 until named.' To answer this, regard may be had to the actual arrangements for building the vessel and numbering it before named.

My Lords, I have no doubt, for the reasons given by the Court of Appeal, that an affirmative answer must be given. I shall not set out the evidence which clearly makes this good. The fact is that the vessel always was Osaka Hull No 354 – though also Oshima No 4 – and equally it can fairly be said to have been 'built' by Osaka Shipbuilding Co Ltd as the company which planned, organised and directed the building and contractually engaged with Sculptor to build it, though also it could be said to have been built by Oshima Shipbuilding Co Ltd. For the purpose of the identificatory clause, the words used are quite sufficient to cover the facts. No other vessel could be referred to: the reference fits the vessel in question.

[Viscount Dilhorne and Lord Russell of Killowen delivered concurring opinions. Lords Simon of Glaisdale and Kilbrandon concurred.]

Harlingdon & Leinster Enterprises Ltd v Christopher Hull Fine Art Ltd [1991] 1 QB 564, Court of Appeal

This contract concerned the sale for £6000 of a painting described as being the work of Gabriele Münter, a painter of the German expressionist school. The parties were both art dealers, the buyers (but not the sellers) being specialists in this area of the art market. The painting was a forgery worth £50 to £100. The Court of Appeal held that although the seller had used the words 'by Münter' in describing the painting, it had not been *sold by* that description – the buyer having relied on his own judgment in regard to this question of attribution. Accordingly, he was not liable to the buyer for breach of s 13.

Nourse LJ: The judge [Judge Oddie] found that both at the time when the agreement was made and subsequently when the invoice was made out both Mr Hull and Mr Runkel [the representatives respectively of the sellers and the buyers] believed that the painting was by Münter and that, if either had not believed that, the deal would not have been made. He made the following further findings:

> In my judgment Runkel must have known and accepted that Hull was disclaiming any judgment, knowledge or private information which would or could have grounded the latter's earlier statement to Braasch that he had two paintings by Gabriele Münter for sale . . . I think the only conclusion which can be drawn from the unusual facts of this case is that it was Runkel's exercise of his own judgment as to the quality of the pictures, including the factor of the identity of their painter, which induced him to enter into the agreement he made with Hull. However, I am not satisfied that without the attribution, given what followed in the circumstances in which it was made, Runkel would not have purchased the painting. If it had never been made, Runkel would never have gone to see the paintings. But when he did go and examine the painting, he considered whether it was a Münter or not; he did agree to buy it, regardless of the attribution, because he relied on his own judgment. . . . It was reliance on his own assessment and not upon anything said by a man who had gone out of his way to stress his ignorance of the paintings which led Runkel astray.

Thus did the judge find as fact that the plaintiffs did not rely on the description of the painting as one by Gabriele Münter. They relied only on their own assessment. . . .

Section 13(1) of the Sale of Goods Act 1979 is in these terms:

> Where there is a contract for the sale of goods by description, there is an implied condition that the goods will correspond with the description.

The sales to which the subsection is expressed to apply are sales 'by description.' Authority apart, those words would suggest that the description must be influential in the sale, not necessarily alone, but so as to become an essential term, ie a condition, of the contract. Without such influence a description cannot be said to be one *by* which the contract for the sale of the goods is made.

I think that the authorities to which we were referred are consistent with this view of s 13(1).

[His Lordship referred to a number of earlier cases, and continued:]

In *Gill & Duffus SA v Berger & Co Inc (No 2)* [1984] AC 382, the facts of which need not be stated, Lord Diplock, with whose speech the other members of the House of Lords agreed, said this of s 13, at p 394:

> while 'description' itself is an ordinary English word, the Act contains no definition of what it means when it speaks in that section of a contract for the sale of goods being a sale '*by* description'. One must look to the contract as a whole to identify the kind of goods that the seller was agreeing to sell and the buyer to buy. . . . where, as in the instant case, the sale (to use the words of s 13) is '*by* sample as well as *by* description,' characteristics of the goods which would be apparent on reasonable examination of the sample are unlikely to have been intended by the parties to form part of the 'description' *by* which the goods were sold, even though such characteristics are mentioned in references in the contract to the goods that are its subject matter.

Those observations, in emphasising the significance to be attached to the word 'by,' show that one must look to the contract as a whole in order to identify what stated characteristics of the goods are intended to form part of the description *by* which they are sold. . . .

In theory it is no doubt possible for a description of goods which is not relied on by the buyer to become an essential term of a contract for their sale. But in practice it is very difficult, and perhaps impossible, to think of facts where that would be so. The description must have a sufficient influence in the sale to become an essential term of the contract and the correlative of influence is reliance. Indeed, reliance by the buyer is the natural index of a sale by description. . . . For all practical purposes, I would say that there cannot be a contract for the sale of goods by description where it is not within the reasonable contemplation of the parties that the buyer is relying on the description. For those purposes, I think that the law is correctly summarised in these words of *Benjamin on Sale*, which should be understood to lay down an objective test: 'Specific goods may be sold as such . . . where, though the goods are described, the description is not relied upon, as where the buyer buys the goods such as they are.' . . .

In giving his decision on this question, Judge Oddie said:

> There can clearly be a sale by description where the buyer has inspected the goods if the description relates to something not apparent on inspection.

Later, having said that he had not been referred to any similar case where a sale in reliance on a statement that a painting was by a particular artist had been held to be a sale by description, the judge continued:

> In my judgment such a statement could amount to a description and a sale in reliance on it to a sale by description within the meaning of the Act. However, on the facts of this case, I am satisfied that the description by Hull before the agreement was not relied on by Runkel in making his offer to purchase which was accepted by Hull. I conclude that he bought the painting as it was. In these circumstances there was not in my judgment a sale by description.

I agree. On a view of their words and deeds as a whole, the parties could not reasonably have contemplated that the plaintiffs were relying on the defendants' statement that the painting was by Gabriele Münter. On the facts which he found the judge could not, by a correct application of the law, have come to any other decision.

[Slade LJ delivered a concurring judgment.
Stuart-Smith LJ dissented.]

We may contrast the cases above with *Beale v Taylor* [1967] 1 WLR 1193, CA, where a car was advertised for sale in a newspaper as a 'Herald convertible, white, 1961, twin carbs', and was bought after the buyer had inspected it. It was in fact a hybrid made up of the back half of a 1961 Triumph Herald convertible welded to the front half of an older model. The Court of Appeal held that the date, 1961, was part of the contract description and that the buyer could reject under s 13. It is plain that the court has considerable discretion in the scope which it may give to the concept of a sale 'by description' where the sale is of a specific article.

NOTE

Where goods have deteriorated or been adulterated, there will come a point where it is arguable that they are not simply different in *quality* from what might have been expected, but are not goods answering to the contract 'description' at all – for instance, cement which has been allowed to become wet so as to be commercially useless. The question must be resolved as a matter of degree. In *Pinnock Bros v Lewis & Peat Ltd* [1923] 1 KB 690 copra cake intended to be fed to livestock which had been adulterated with castor beans and rendered poisonous was described by Roche J as something 'which could not properly be described as copra cake at all'. In contrast, in *Ashington Piggeries Ltd v Christopher Hill Ltd* [1972] AC 441, HL, herring meal mixed into a feeding compound for mink which had become toxic through reaction to a preservative was held still to answer the description 'herring meal': it was not shown to be toxic to other animals, and remained suitable for other commercial purposes, such as a fertiliser.

6 Implied terms as to quality and fitness

(a) No general rule

The Sale of Goods Act 1979, s 14, contains provisions by which undertakings on the part of the seller as to the quality of the goods and their fitness for a particular purpose are implied into certain contracts of sale. However, it is most important to note that these provisions constitute *exceptions* to the general rule, and that the basic rule denies that a seller is deemed to give any such undertakings. In other words, the traditional broad principle of *caveat emptor* governs this aspect of the law of sale, as so many others. Section 14(1) confirms this:

> Except as provided by this section and s 15 below and subject to any other enactment, there is no implied condition or warranty about the quality or fitness for any particular purpose of goods supplied under a contract of sale.

However, apart from statute, a condition or warranty about quality or fitness may be implied by usage (s 14(4)).

(b) Statutory exceptions: 'where the seller sells goods in the course of a business'

The two exceptions contained in s 14(2) and 14(3) apply only 'where the seller sells goods in the course of a business'. These subsections have established an important code for the protection of people who buy as consumers from a retailer or manufacturer; but their scope is much wider than consumer protection measures; and, indeed, they were not originally conceived as primarily intended for this purpose. The exceptions apply also to transactions between one merchant and another, whether they are manufacturers, wholesalers, importers, retailers or any other kind of dealer. The provisions also apply where a sale is made by a person who in the course of a business is acting as agent for another, except where the fact that the seller (the agent's principal) is not selling in the course of a business is known to the buyer or reasonable steps have been taken to bring this fact to the buyer's notice (s 14(5)). But where a private person sells to a business buyer or to another private person, it will be a case of *caveat emptor*.

It has not yet been authoritatively established whether a person whose business does not normally include that of selling goods, or of selling goods of the type in question, is included within the statutory phrase 'sells goods in the course of a business' – for example, a solicitor who sells off a surplus desk.

(c) Implied condition that the goods are of merchantable quality

Where a seller sells goods in the course of a business, there is a condition implied by statute that the goods supplied under the contract are of merchantable quality. There is, however, no such condition (1) as regards defects specifically drawn to the buyer's attention before the contract is made, or (2) if the buyer examines the goods before the contract is made, as regards defects which that examination ought to reveal (s 14(2)).

The concept of 'merchantable quality' was not given any statutory definition in the original Act of 1893. This was, no doubt, understandable in an Act which at the time was thought of primarily as a merchants' code: whether a consignment of goods was of 'merchantable' quality under its contract description was a question which could be resolved by bringing in as evidence the opinion of other merchants who dealt in such goods, or by referring the question to an arbitrator or umpire who was expert in the particular trade. But problems have since arisen where s 14(2) has been invoked in a consumer context – eg in relation to such questions as whether a car which has a mechanical fault or damaged bodywork or upholstery is 'merchantable', and whether it makes a difference that the car is sold as new or secondhand. In 1973, a statutory definition of 'merchantable quality' was introduced in an endeavour to give the courts guidance on this question. This is to be found in s 14(6), which reads as follows:

> Goods of any kind are of merchantable quality within the meaning of [s 14(2)] if they are as fit for the purpose or purposes for which goods of that kind are commonly bought as it is reasonable to expect having regard to any description applied to them, the price (if relevant) and all the other relevant circumstances.

This definition is something of an amalgam of various 'tests' for merchantability which had been put forward at different times in the case law (and, indeed, in *M/S Aswan Engineering Establishment Co v Lupdine Ltd* (below, p 359), Lloyd J expressed the opinion that the statutory definition had not changed the meaning of the term as it had previously been understood at common law). Whether this is accepted or not, the position is still regarded by many as unsatisfactory; and the Law Commission has recommended that the concept of merchantability be removed altogether from the Act and replaced by a new implied term which more closely matches the expectations of consumer buyers. This proposal is discussed further below, at p 364.

Before looking at the cases, we may note two preliminary points. First, 'quality', in relation to goods, includes their state or condition (s 61(1)). So, in *Niblett v Confectioners' Materials Ltd* (above, p 345), the tinned milk with labels which infringed the Nestlé trade mark were held not to be of merchantable quality, with the result that there was a breach of s 14(2) as well as of s 12(1). Second, s 14(2) states that the implied term is that the goods *supplied under the contract of sale* are of merchantable quality, and not just 'the goods sold'. This more general phrase has been construed as including the container in which the goods were supplied. In *Geddling v Marsh* [1920] 1 KB 668 mineral water was sold to the plaintiff in a 'returnable' bottle which was bailed and not sold to her: the bottle burst and injured her. The court ruled that the bottle was 'supplied under a contract of sale' and that she could recover damages under s 14(2).

In the earliest cases in which the term 'merchantable quality' were examined, it seems to have been construed as equivalent to 'saleability' or 'resaleability'. For instance, *Jackson v Rotax Motor & Cycle Co* [1910] 2 KB 937, CA, concerned a consignment of motor horns (evidently the type consisting of a rubber bulb connected to a large polished brass bell which adorned the exterior of cars of Edwardian vintage) which were sold for a total price of £450. Some of the horns arrived dented and scratched. The consignment of horns was held not to be of merchantable quality 'in the sense that they could without more have been disposed of reasonably and properly by the buyers as dealers in horns to any customer who wanted then and there a horn for a motor car', even though the cost of repairing and repolishing the defective horns would have been only £35.

A second set of judicial definitions have turned on the notion of what a reasonable buyer would accept in performance of a contract of sale of goods under that description. For example, in *Bristol Tramways etc Carriage Co Ltd v Fiat Motors Ltd* [1910] 2 KB 831 at 841, CA, Farwell LJ said:

> The phrase in s 14(2) is, in my opinion, used as meaning that the article is of such quality and in such condition that a reasonable man acting reasonably would after a full examination accept it under the circumstances of the case in performance of his offer to buy that article whether he buys for his own use or to sell again.

However – as was pointed out by Dixon J of the Australian High Court in *Grant v Australian Knitting Mills Ltd* (1933) 50 CLR 387 at 418 (reversed on appeal, but without reference to this point, [1936] AC 85, PC) – such a test becomes workable only if there is some reference to the contract *price* as well as to the description: without taking the price into account, it is difficult to fix the level of quality which ought to be regarded as acceptable. This point was endorsed by the House of Lords in *B S Brown & Sons Ltd v Craiks Ltd* [1970] 1 WLR 752, HL, where cloth suitable for industrial use but not suitable for dressmaking (as intended by the buyer) was sold at 36 pence per yard: it was held to be 'merchantable' at this price, which was within a range appropriate to industrial cloth.

Another way of looking at the issue raised by *Brown & Sons Ltd v Craiks Ltd* is to have regard to the question of the *purpose* for which the goods are required; not the buyer's specific purpose (which is a distinct question dealt with by s 14(3)), but the usual or normal purpose for which such goods are bought. The problem here is that (as in that case), some kinds of goods may have more than one purpose; and the definition must on the one hand avoid saying that to be merchantable goods must be suitable for *every* conceivable purpose, and on the other that it is sufficient that they should be fit for *any one* purpose, for which they might be used. In *Henry Kendall & Sons v William Lillico & Sons Ltd* [1969] 2 AC 31, HL (a case sometimes referred to as *Hardwick Game Farm Ltd v SAPPA*), a Brazilian groundnut extraction was sold by importers to a firm of feedstuff merchants and used to make a compound poultry meal for feeding by farmers to pheasants. The extraction contained a substance which made it poisonous to poultry, but it was perfectly suitable to feed to other kinds of livestock, such as cattle and pigs. A majority of the House of Lords held that it was merchantable.

The statutory definition of 'merchantable quality' in s 14(6) (quoted above, p 358) appears to draw together all these elements. It was discussed in the following case.

Aswan Engineering Establishment Co v Lupdine Ltd [1987] 1 WLR 1, Court of Appeal

Aswan bought a consignment of liquid waterproofing compound in plastic pails for shipment to Kuwait, where they carried on an engineering business. The pails were stacked five or six high in shipping containers which, on arrival in Kuwait, were left standing in the sun on the quayside. The temperature inside the containers reached 70°C, with the result that the pails collapsed. The buyers sued the sellers, alleging (inter alia) that the goods were not of merchantable quality, and the sellers in turn sued the manufacturers of the pails, Thurgar Bolle, on the same ground. There was evidence that the pails would have stood a temperature of 70° if the rows of pails had been separated by wooden battens (a packing technique known as the 'eggbox' method). The court held that the pails were merchantable as 'heavy duty pails suitable for export' (the contract description), and both claims failed.

Lloyd LJ: I take first the judge's finding that the pails were merchantable. As to the cause of failure, experts were instructed on both sides. Shortly before the trial, the experts were able to reach agreement on all important issues of primary fact. They incorporated their agreement into a joint memorandum which was put before the court. In particular they agreed that the pails were bound to fail at 60° centigrade (140° Fahrenheit) or above when stacked five or six high with a load of 25 kilogrammes per pail, so that the lid of the lowest pail was bearing a weight of 100 or 125 kilogrammes. However the pails would not have failed if the temperature had been 52° centigrade (122° Fahrenheit) or below. Nor would they have failed, even at 70° centigrade if the rows had been separated horizontally with wooden battens (a method of stuffing containers which became known as the 'eggbox' method), so that the weight of each row of pails was taken, not by the row below, but directly by the floor of the container through vertical supports. There was no agreement as to whether the pails would have survived 70° centigrade and, if so, for how long, if stacked two, three or four rows high *without* horizontal separation and vertical supports. But one of the experts gave evidence, on which Mr Aikens relied, that a stack of three would have been in trouble, and even a stack of two if left long enough. There was evidence that pails had been used for export to other parts of the world without mishap.

On those primary facts, the judge stated his conclusion:

> It was nevertheless necessary for the V.20 pails to be merchantable as heavy duty pails suitable for export. Having heard and read the expert evidence, however, I am satisfied that these pails were merchantable within the meaning ascribed to that term by s 14(6) of the Act of 1979. They were very strong pails and they were nearly able to withstand the high temperature of the Gulf.

That conclusion would have been unassailable on the law as it stood before the Supply of Goods (Implied Terms) Act 1973. As I shall hope to show in a moment, the law had developed to a point where the dividing line, and overlap such as it was, between ss 14(1) [s 14(3) of the 1979 Act] and 14(2) of the Sale of Goods Act 1893, and the meaning to be attached to the words 'merchantable quality' in the latter subsection, then undefined, had become tolerably clear. But Mr Aikens submits that that state of affairs has been changed by the definition of 'merchantable quality' introduced by the Act of 1973, and now contained in s 14(6) of the Act of 1979. That subsection provides:

Goods of any kind are of merchantable quality within the meaning of subs (2) above if they are as fit for the purpose or purposes for which goods of that kind are commonly bought as it is reasonable to expect having regard to any description applied to them, the price (if relevant) and all the other relevant circumstances.

It is not possible to appreciate the change which that definition is said to have brought about without first looking at the law as it stood before the Act of 1973. But if I may anticipate Mr Aikens's argument, he submits that the reference in the subsection to 'the purpose or purposes' (in the plural) as distinct from *a* purpose (in the singular) has brought about a fundamental shift in the relationship between the old s 14(1) and s 14(2), by very largely extending the scope of s 14(2) at the expense of s 14(1). Mr Aikens concedes that unless he is right on his construction of s 14(6), then his argument on s 14(2) must fail.

[His Lordship discussed a very large number of cases decided prior to 1973, in the course of which he referred to Lord Reid's judgment in the *Hardwick Game Farm* case (above, p 358) as follows:]

It is in Lord Reid's speech that the clearest guidance is to be found as to the state of the law before the Act of 1973 was passed. 'Merchantable,' he said . . . 'can only mean commercially saleable.' He continued:

If the description is a familiar one it may be that in practice only one quality of goods answers that description – then that quality and only that quality is merchantable quality. Or it may be that various qualities of goods are commonly sold under that description – then it is not disputed that the lowest quality commonly so sold is what is meant by merchantable quality: it is commercially saleable under that description.

[He continued:]

I will now attempt to summarise the position as it was in my own words. To bring s 14(2) into operation, a buyer had to show that the goods had been bought by description from a seller dealing in goods of that description. If they were, then subject to a proviso which is immaterial for present purposes, the goods were required to be of merchantable quality. In order to comply with that requirement, the goods did not have to be suitable for every purpose within a range of purposes for which goods were normally bought under that description. It was sufficient that they were suitable for one or more such purposes without abatement of price since, if they were, they were commercially saleable under that description.

Mr Aikens submits that the direction in which the law has developed over the last century and a half, and which I have attempted to describe, has been radically changed by s 14(6) of the Act of 1979. There is, of course, no reason why Parliament should not have intended to bring about such a change. But it prompts careful consideration. . . .

Mr Aikens's argument is that the definition in s 14(6) refers to the purpose or *purposes* for which goods of any kind are commonly bought. Therefore the goods are not merchantable unless they are as fit as it is reasonable to expect for all the purposes for which those goods are commonly bought. It is no longer sufficient that they should be fit for *one* such purpose. Mr Stevenson, on the other hand, submits that the definition has changed little if anything. It enacts the common law definition proposed by Lord Reid in the *Hardwick Game Farm* case [1969] 2 AC 31.

Mr Aikens's argument is undoubtedly attractive at first sight. If Parliament had intended to enact Lord Reid's formulation, it might have been expected that the definition would have referred to *one* of the purposes for which goods are commonly bought. But there is an equally strong, and perhaps even stronger, argument the other way. If Parliament had intended to enact what Mr Aikens submits is the meaning of s 14(6), then the definition would surely have referred specifically to *all* purposes, not just the purpose or purposes. The reason why Parliament did not adopt either of those courses is, I think, to be found in the speech of Lord Reid in the *Hardwick Game Farm* case. . . . Lord Reid points out that goods of any one kind may be sold under more than one description, corresponding to different qualities.

To take the facts of the present case, heavy duty pails are no doubt of higher quality than ordinary pails, and for that reason no doubt command a higher price. Pails which are suitable for the lower quality purpose may not be suitable for the higher quality purpose. It would obviously be wrong that pails sold under a description appropriate to the higher quality should be held to be merchantable because they are fit for a purpose for which pails are sold under the description appropriate to the lower quality. Since the definition presupposes that goods of any one kind may be sold under more than one description, it follows that the definition had, of necessity, to refer to more than one purpose. In my opinion, this is the true and sufficient explanation for the reference to 'purposes' in the plural. The reference to *the* purpose in the singular was required in order to cover one-purpose goods, such as the pants in *Grant v Australian Knitting Mills Ltd* (1933) 50 CLR 387. It would be wrong to infer from the use of the phrase 'purpose or purposes' that Parliament intended any such far-reaching change in the law as that for which Mr Aikens contends. On the contrary, I agree with Mr Stevenson that the definition is as accurate a reproduction of Lord Reid's speech in the *Hardwick Game Farm* case [1969] 2 AC 31 as it is possible to compress into a single sentence.

We were told that there is no reported case in which it has fallen to a court to construe and apply the definition in s 14(6). But the definition was considered by Lord Denning MR in *Cehave NV v Bremer Handelsgesellschaft mbH* [1976] QB 44. That was a case which fell to be decided under the old law. But Lord Denning MR clearly regarded the statutory definition as encapsulating the existing common law. He said, at p 62:

> For myself, I think the definition in the latest statute is the best that has yet been devised. . . . The statute itself only applies to contracts made after 18 May 1973. But the definition seems to me appropriate for contracts made before it.

Mr Aikens had a further argument in relation to s 14(2) based on the language of s 14(3). . . . On s 14(2) he submits that the inclusion in s 14(3) of the phrase 'whether or not that is a purpose for which such goods are commonly supplied' shows that Parliament did indeed intend to bring about a fundamental shift of emphasis between s 14(2) and s 14(3). Hitherto, as Lord Reid pointed out in the *Hardwick Game Farm* case [1969] 2 AC 31, there has been a tendency to confine the scope of s 14(2) and extend the scope of s 14(3). The inclusion in s 14(3) of the words to which I have referred shows, says Mr Aikens, that in future s 14(2) is intended to cover use for all normal purposes, thus very greatly extending the scope of that subsection; whereas s 14(3) is to be confined to use for special or abnormal purposes.

I cannot accept that argument for three reasons. In the first place it is not what the words say. Section 14(3) is clearly intended to cover normal as well as abnormal purposes. In those circumstances, if s 14(2) is also to cover use for all normal purposes, in the sense that goods are to be regarded as unmerchantable unless they are fit for all normal purposes, then the distinction between the two subsections would be largely obliterated. Secondly, it would mean that Parliament had enacted a consequence which Lord Morris, in . . . his speech in the *Hardwick Game Farm* case [1969] 2 AC 31, described as being unreasonable. Thirdly, it would mean that the law had gone even further in the direction of caveat venditor than it did in the *Hardwick Game Farm* case, past a point which Lord Diplock, in his dissenting speech in the *Ashington Piggeries* case [1972] AC 441, regarded as already too far. Of course, all these things are possible, but I would require clearer words in s 14(3) and (6) to persuade me that this is what Parliament has done.

So I would reject Mr Aikens's argument on the construction of s 14(6). The definition has not revolutionised the law. As mentioned earlier, Mr Aikens conceded that if he were wrong on s 14(6), he could not successfully attack the judge's finding that these pails were merchantable. But it is as well to mention why, in my view, that concession was properly made.

I can well understand an argument that goods should be regarded as unmerchantable if they contain a hidden defect which, while leaving the goods suitable for some purposes, renders them unsuitable for others. If the buyer does not know, and cannot find out, for what purposes the goods are unsuitable, they are no more than a trap. That was the argument which appealed to Lord Pearce in the *Hardwick Game Farm* case {1969] 2 AC 31, and was one of the two reasons why he dissented on the point. But the majority took the opposite view. One must assume that the hypothetical buyer knows not only that the goods on offer are defective, but also what the nature of the particular defect is; so that in the present case one must assume that the hypothetical buyer knows that the pails are incapable of withstanding temperatures in excess of 60° centigrade when stacked five or six high, or perhaps two or three high, without separation. Does that make them unmerchantable within the meaning of s 14(6)? Clearly not. I will assume, as was conceded by Mr Stevenson, that the 'description applied' to the pails was that they were to be heavy duty pails for export shipment. There was no evidence that a hypothetical buyer who wanted the pails for export, say, to Europe, and who knew of the particular defect, would insist on an abatement in the price. I would be astonished if he had. The pails were perfectly suitable for that purpose, and therefore of merchantable quality within the definition. Indeed, they were suitable for export to the Middle East as well as Europe. For if the eggbox method of stuffing had been used, the pails would have survived despite the temperature. . . .

[Nicholls LJ delivered a concurring judgment.
Fox LJ concurred.]

In *Harlingdon & Leinster Enterprises Ltd v Christopher Hull Fine Art Ltd* (above, p 354), where a painting sold as by Münter turned out to be a relatively worthless forgery, the majority of the Court of Appeal held that there had been no breach of s 14(2), but the definition in s 14(6) was not discussed at length. Nourse LJ said ([1991] 1 QB 564 at 576):

> The first question which arises out of the words of s 14(6) is for what purpose or purposes are paintings of this kind commonly bought. The second question is whether this painting was as fit for that purpose or those purposes as it was reasonable to expect having regard to any description applied to it, the price (if relevant) and all the other relevant circumstances. Those were both questions of fact to be decided by the judge, who answered them thus:

>> In my view the purpose or purposes for which goods of this kind are commonly bought are the aesthetic appreciation of the owner or anyone else he permits to enjoy the experience when the picture is displayed for view. Having regard to . . . the description before the agreement was entered, the price and all other relevant circumstances disclosed by the material facts of this transaction, I am not satisfied that this painting was not of merchantable quality.

> The first of these findings was attacked by Mr Crystal on the ground that the purpose for which a painting is commonly bought by one dealer from another is resale. I see some force in that attack, but all that it means is that the purpose or purposes contemplated by s 14(6) are either resale alone or resale and aesthetic appreciation together. In either case, I do not think that Judge Oddie's second finding is invalidated. It is true that the painting was defective in that it was not the work of the artist by whom it appeared to have been painted. I agree with Denning LJ in *Leaf v International Galleries* [1950] 2 KB 86, 89 that that was a defect in the quality of the painting. But it was not one which made it unsaleable. The evidence was that it could have been resold for £50 to £100. Admittedly that would have been a very long way below the £6,000 which the plaintiffs paid for it. But the question whether goods are reasonably fit for resale cannot depend on whether they can or cannot be resold without making a loss. Nor did the defect make the painting unfit for aesthetic appreciation. It could still have been hung on a wall somewhere and been enjoyed for what it was, albeit not for what it might have been.

> I do not think that the views which I have so far expressed are affected by the regard which s 14(6) requires there to be had to the description applied to the painting, its price and any other relevant circumstances. I will take those matters in turn. I will assume that a description which is not relied on by the buyer can nevertheless be one which is 'applied to' the painting. But having held that the sale was not made *by* that description, I cannot think that it would be right, in having regard to it, to give it the significance which it

would have had if s 13(1) had applied. I arrive at a similar view in regard to the price. Having been prepared to pay £6,000 in reliance only on their own assessment, the plaintiffs cannot use their own error of judgment as a basis for saying that a painting which would otherwise be reasonably fit for resale or for aesthetic appreciation is thereby rendered unfit for those purposes. As for any other relevant circumstances, I do not think that Mr Crystal suggested that there were any in the present case. In the result, I would also reject the plaintiffs' claim under s 14(2).

Slade LJ said (at 586):

As to the claim based on s 14, I hope that my opinion is not too simplistic, but it is very clear. The complaint, and only complaint as to the quality of the picture, relates to the identity of the artist. There is no other complaint of any kind as to its condition or quality. If the verdict of the experts had been that the artist was in truth Gabriele Münter, the claim would not have arisen. Having concluded that this was not a contract for the sale of goods by description because it was not a term of the contract that she was the artist, I see no room for the application of s 14. If the plaintiffs fail to establish a breach of contract through the front door of s 13(1), they cannot succeed through the back door of s 14.

QUESTIONS

Industrial cloth

1. If the price was relevant in *Brown & Sons v Craiks*, was it not equally relevant in *Harlingdon v Christopher Hull*?
2. Do you think that the herring meal sold in *Ashingdon Piggeries Ltd v Christopher Hill Ltd* (above, p 356) was of merchantable quality?

The time factor. Suppose that goods are sold and delivered by S to B which, to the knowledge of S, B intends to transport to a distant place. Must the goods be of merchantable quality *both* at the time when they are delivered *and* at the time when they arrive at that place, or is it sufficient that they are merchantable at the former time? Or is there some other test? The courts have settled this issue with something of a compromise formulation. It is settled that the relevant time is the time of delivery (*Cordova Land Co Ltd v Victor Bros Inc* [1966] 1 WLR 793, where skins sold to be shipped from the United States to Hull were found to be damaged on arrival at Hull: held, there could be no breach of any implied term in the absence of evidence that the goods were defective at the time when they were shipped). But, where it is contemplated that the goods are to undergo a journey, they will not be regarded as of merchantable quality unless, at the time they are delivered, they are in a fit state to endure a normal journey of that kind and to be in a merchantable condition when they arrive.

Mash & Murrell Ltd v Joseph I Emanuel Ltd [1961] 1 WLR 862, Queen's Bench Division (reversed by the Court of Appeal on other grounds, [1962] 1 WLR 16n)

The contract was for the sale of Cyprus spring crop potatoes, C & F Liverpool, to be shipped on the SS *Ionian* from a port in Cyprus (Limassol). (On C & F contracts, see below, p 461.) When the potatoes arrived in Liverpool they were rotten and unfit for human consumption.

Diplock J found on the evidence that the potatoes when loaded at Limassol were not fit to travel to Liverpool, and said: . . . These goods being bought c & f Liverpool, the warranty as to merchantability was a warranty that they should remain merchantable for a reasonable time, the time reasonable in all the circumstances, which means a time for the normal transit to the destination, Liverpool, and for disposal after. That warranty was, in my view, broken.

[The Court of Appeal ([1962] 1 WLR 16n) reversed this decision on the facts, finding that the potatoes had suffered from excess heat and lack of ventilation on the voyage. For the purpose of this finding, it assumed that the view of Diplock J correctly expressed the law.]

Proposals for reform of the law. The concept of 'merchantable quality' has in recent times come in for a considerable amount of criticism, both because its meaning has eluded clear definition and because the condition implied by s 14(2) has not proved capable of dealing with many of the problems which arise where sub-standard goods are sold in consumer transactions. The Law Commissions have twice been asked to make recommendations for reform of the law. Their first recommendation, made in their report, 'Exemption Clauses in Contracts First Report: Amendments to the Sale of Goods Act 1893' (L Com No 24, Scot L Com No 12, 1969), led to two amendments which were introduced by the Supply of Goods (Implied Terms) Act 1973 and have since been incorporated into the Sale of Goods Act 1979: the removal of the requirement that the term should be implied only when goods are sold 'by description'; and the introduction of a statutory definition of 'merchantable quality', which now appears in the Act as s 14(6). Their second set of recommendations which is contained in the report, 'Sale and Supply of Goods' (L Com No 160, Scot L Com No 104, Cd 137 (1987)) have not yet become law, although they were in part included in the Consumer Guarantees Bill 1989, which failed to reach the statute-book. A similar Bill received a first reading in Parliament in June 1993, but was not proceeded with.

The Law Commissions in their 1987 report recommend that the concept of merchantable quality be abolished and replaced by new concept of 'acceptable' quality. The new provision (s 14(2)–(2B)) would read:

(2) Where the seller sells goods in the course of a business, there is an implied term that the goods supplied under the contract are of acceptable quality.
(2A) For the purposes of this Act, goods are of acceptable quality if they meet the standard that a reasonable person would regard as acceptable, taking account of any description of the goods, the price (if relevant) and all the other relevant circumstances.
(2B) For the purposes of this Act, the quality of goods includes their state and condition and the following (among others) are in appropriate cases aspects of the quality of goods—

(a) fitness for all the purposes for which goods of the kind in question are commonly supplied,
(b) appearance and finish,
(c) freedom from minor defects,
(d) safety, and
(e) durability.

Corresponding changes are proposed in regard to the use of the concept of 'merchantability' in s 15 (sale by sample).

QUESTION

What difference, if any, would the Law Commissions' proposals make to the law governing (1) a contract of sale between merchants; (2) a consumer sale?

Before leaving s 14(2), mention should be made of the two statutory exceptions:

Defects specifically drawn to the buyer's attention*. In *Bartlett v Sidney Marcus Ltd* [1965] 1 WLR 1013 the buyer could not be heard to complain of a defective clutch in a secondhand car which he had been told about before entering into the contract.

Defects which an examination made by the buyer ought to have revealed*. This proviso was altered in 1973: previously, it appeared from the decided cases that a buyer who had only been able to make a cursory examination might be debarred from a remedy if a more thorough examination would have revealed the defect in question. This was based on the former wording of the proviso ('as regards defects which *such* examination ought to have revealed'). The revised wording ('as regards defects which *that* examination ought to have revealed') makes it fairly clear that the exception will apply only if the buyer has examined the goods and the defect ought to have been revealed by such an examination as he actually did make.

NOTE

Many textbooks on the law of sale of goods contain detailed discussions of cases such as *Bartlett v Sidney Marcus Ltd* (above) which were concerned with consumers who complained that the cars which they had been sold were not as good as they had expected. The statutory implied term as to merchantable quality, in its present form, has not always provided a satisfactory remedy in such cases. For instance, in *Business Application Specialists Ltd v Nationwide Credit Corpn Ltd* [1988] RTR 332 a secondhand Mercedes sold for nearly £15,000 was found to need repairs costing £635: it was nevertheless held to be merchantable. And in *Rogers v Parish (Scarborough) Ltd* [1987] QB 933, CA, there was a difference of opinion between the trial judge and the Court of Appeal whether a car with leaking oil seals which was driven 5000 miles before being repaired (and was in fact repaired by the seller at no cost to the buyer) was merchantable. In contrast, *Bartlett v Sydney Marcus Ltd* [1965] 1 WLR 1013 a secondhand car, known when sold to have a defective clutch, cost rather more to repair than the buyer expected: it was held to be merchantable. It is not thought necessary to discuss these 'consumer' cases in detail in a book on commercial law. For a full account, see Atiyah, pp 165ff, 174ff.

(d) Implied condition as to fitness for purpose (s 14(3))

We have seen that the definition of 'merchantable quality' under s 14(2) carries within it the notion that the goods sold should be fit for the purposes (or some of the purposes) for which goods of that description are commonly used. If the buyer wants the goods for a *particular* purpose, his case will be stronger if he can bring it within the wording of s 14(3) – which, confusingly, was numbered as s 14(1) in the Act of 1893. This reads as follows:

> Where the seller sells goods in the course of a business and the buyer, expressly or by implication, makes known ... to the seller ... any particular purpose for which the goods are being bought, there is an implied condition that the goods supplied under the contract are reasonably fit for that purpose, whether or not that is a purpose for which such goods are commonly supplied, except where the circumstances show that the buyer does not rely, or that it is unreasonable for him to rely, on the skill or judgment of the seller. ...

It will be noted that s 14(3) contains a number of phrases which are used also in s 14(2) and have been discussed above in relation to that provision. These include 'where the seller sells goods in the course of a business' and 'the goods supplied under the contract'.

Again, we should bear in mind that the condition implied by s 14(3) is the *exception*, and not the rule: the basic rule is *caveat emptor*, as set out in s 14(1).

The words 'particular purpose' have always been given a very broad interpretation. It would be natural to assume that they were intended to be construed in a restrictive sense, and confined to the situation where the goods in question have a potentially wide range of purposes and the buyer wants them for just one such purpose – eg, perhaps, where he buys paint and makes it known to the seller that he wishes to use it to paint metal that is exposed outdoors. (Compare the *Cammell Laird* case (below), where a propeller was ordered for the special purpose of being fitted to a particular ship.) But this is not the approach which the courts have adopted. Where goods have only one purpose, or one obvious purpose, this has been regarded as the 'particular' purpose – and, indeed, if it is the obvious purpose the courts will take it for granted that this purpose was made known to the seller, so that the case will be very readily deemed to fall within the section. So, for instance, food will be taken to have been bought for the 'particular' purpose of being eaten (*Wallis v Russell* [1902] 2 IR 585), milk to be drunk (*Frost v Aylesbury Dairy Co* [1905] 1 KB 608, CA) and a hot-water bottle for filling with hot water to warm a bed (*Preist v Last* [1903] 2 KB 148, CA). This construction is given added support by the inclusion in the section of the words 'whether or not that is a purpose for which such goods are commonly supplied'. The main reason why the courts adopted this generous interpretation of the statutory language was, once again, to broaden the scope of the remedies available to a buyer in a consumer sale: if, for some reason, s 14(2) could not be invoked, he had a second-string argument under s 14(3). In a very large number of cases, both s 14(2) and s 14(3) will be held to have been broken on the same facts.

The key issue in regard to s 14(3) is that of *reliance*: there must have been something said or done to bring home to the seller the fact that he was being relied upon to supply goods fit for the buyer's particular purpose. This onus will be an easy one to discharge where the purpose is a natural or likely one (eg that food is fit to eat). The section in its current form (the wording was revised in 1973) helps the court in determining this question of reliance by laying down a presumption that once a particular purpose has been made known to the seller, it is assumed that the buyer will have relied on the seller to provide goods fit for that purpose; but, even so, it must be found that such reliance was reasonable on the facts. The cases cited below illustrate the courts' approach to the questions of 'particular purpose' and reliance.

Bristol Tramways etc Carriage Co Ltd v Fiat Motors Ltd [1910] 2 KB 831, Court of Appeal

The plaintiffs successfully claimed damages in respect of seven omnibuses sold to them by the defendants (as the trial judge found) for the purpose 'of conveying passengers in and near Bristol, a heavy traffic in a hilly district'. The omnibuses were not sufficiently robust for this work, and had to be reconstructed. The sellers were held to be in breach of the condition implied under s 14(1) of the 1893 Act (now s 14(3)) that they would be fit for this purpose.

Cozens-Hardy MR: This is an action in which the plaintiffs claim damages in respect of seven Fiat motor omnibuses sold by the defendants to the plaintiffs. The learned judge,

Lawrance J, who tried this case without a jury, has held that the omnibuses as delivered were not fit to perform the duty required of them, and that the plaintiffs made fully known to the defendants the particular purpose for which the omnibuses were required, and that they relied upon the defendants' skill and judgment in the matter.

The case really turns upon s 14 of the Sale of Goods Act, 1893. . . .

Turning to s 14, it is plain that the defendants were told that the omnibuses were required for heavy passenger traffic at Bristol. I am disposed to think that such a statement of purpose suffices to shew that the buyer relied upon the seller's skill or judgment without any further evidence on the point, but, however that may be, I think there was in the present case ample evidence that the plaintiffs did rely upon the defendants' skill or judgment. This being so, there was an implied condition that the omnibuses should be reasonably fit for the declared purpose. . . .

[Farwell and Kennedy LJJ delivered concurring judgments.]

Cammell Laird & Co Ltd v Manganese Bronze & Brass Co Ltd [1934] AC 402, House of Lords

Cammell Laird had agreed to build two ships for the United Molasses Company, and had contracted with Manganese Bronze to have propellers made for these ships to designs which specified the general dimensions of the propellers but not the thickness and shaping of the blades, which it was left to Manganese Bronze, as specialist suppliers, to determine. Four propellers had to be made before two were produced which performed satisfactorily. Cammell Laird claimed damages for the delay in finishing their work caused by the fact that the first propellers supplied were defective, alleging a breach of s 14(3) [s 14(1) of the 1893 Act]. The House of Lords held that the defects in the propellers lay in those areas of the design where Cammell Laird had relied on Manganese Bronze's specialist skill and judgment, and upheld the claim.

Lord Macmillan: The appellants also contended that they were entitled to succeed under s 14, sub-s 1, of the Sale of Goods Act 1893 [1979 Act, s 14(3)]. That section contains what is left of the rule of caveat emptor, but the exceptions have made large inroads upon it. The rule does not apply 'where the buyer, expressly or by implication, makes known to the seller the particular purpose for which the goods are required, so as to show that the buyer relies on the seller's skill or judgment, and the goods are of a description which it is in the course of the seller's business to supply'; in such a case 'there is an implied condition that the goods shall be reasonably fit for such purpose.'

Now there is no question that it is in the course of the respondents' business to supply ships' propellers. But there is room for argument as to whether the appellants made known to the respondents 'the particular purpose' for which the propeller was wanted. On the one hand it was contended that no particular purpose was expressed or implied which the propeller was to serve, and that if any purpose was implied it was merely the ordinary and general purpose which all ships' propellers serve – namely, as the word itself connotes, the purpose of propulsion. On the other hand it was contended that the contract disclosed that the propeller was wanted for a particular purpose – the purpose, namely, of being fitted to and working in association with the ship and engines No 972 which the appellants were building. Having regard to the decision and the reasoning in the case of *Manchester Liners Ltd v Rea Ltd* ([1922] 2 AC 74), I am of opinion that there was in the present instance sufficient disclosure of a particular purpose within the statutory meaning.

But that is not enough. To get the benefit of s 14, sub-s 1, the particular purpose must be so made known as to show that the buyer relies on the seller's skill or judgment. The respondents' argument was that the appellants by their detailed specification so tied the respondents' hands as to negative the idea that anything was left or intended to be left to their skill or judgment, except mere matters of material and workmanship, as to which there was no suggestion of failure on their part. That there was an important margin within which the respondents' skill and judgment had scope for exercise is best demonstrated by the fact already mentioned that while all the three propellers which they made for this ship were in conformity with the specification, it was only at the third attempt that the respondents succeeded in supplying a propeller that would work.

The defect, whatever it was, which existed in the first two propellers as well as the remedying of that defect achieved in the third propeller, thus lay in the region within which the respondents were free, so far as the specification went, to exercise their skill and judgment. I therefore reach the conclusion that there was room here for the exercise of the respondents' skill and judgment and I hold that the particular purpose for which the propeller was wanted was so made known to the respondents as to show that the appellants relied on their skill and judgment.

The appellants are thus entitled, in my opinion, to succeed. . . .

[Lords Tomlin, Warrington of Clyffe, Russell of Killowen and Wright delivered concurring opinions.]

Teheran-Europe Co Ltd v S T Belton (Tractors) Ltd [1968] 2 QB 545, Court of Appeal

Belton, an English company, contracted to sell mobile air compressors which they had acquired as government surplus to Teheran-Europe Ltd, a company incorporated in Iran (then known as Persia) and carrying on business in Teheran. The buyers made known to the sellers that the compressors were required for resale as 'new and unused' machines in Iran. An action under s 14(3) [then s 14(1)] failed because, although this 'particular purpose' had been made known to the sellers, the circumstances were not such as to show that the buyers had relied on their skill and judgment.

Lord Denning MR: Now, as I read this contract, it was a contract for the sale of goods by description. These were air compressors, described as new and unused – described in the catalogue and in the correspondence. There was clearly an implied term that they should comply with the description as set out in s 13(1) of the Sale of Goods Act.

So far as s 14(1) is concerned, it is quite clear that the buyers made known to the sellers that they were required for resale in Persia. In the letter of August 10, 1967, Richards Marketing Ltd wrote to S T Belton (Tractors) Ltd: 'We have now received provisional estimates for packing these units singly suitable for shipment to Khorranshahr, and cross-country transit.' Khorranshahr, as far as I understand it, is in Persia. And then in the letter of August 19, 1957, they said: 'Our clients are asking for a liberal supply of descriptive literature for advertising purposes in Iran.' So that it is quite clear that the buyers made known to the sellers that they required them for resale in Persia.

But the section of the statute contains a further requirement before a condition is implied. The particular purpose must be made known to the seller so as to show that the buyer relies on the seller's skill and judgment. The judge held that, once the purpose was made known, there was an inference that the buyer relied on the seller's skill and judgment. He quoted some of the speeches in *Manchester Liners Ltd v Rea Ltd* ([1922] 2 AC 74). But that case has, in the last few days, been considered by the House of Lords in the *Hardwick Game Farm v Suffolk Agricultural Poultry Producers' Association* ([1969] 2 AC 31) case. Lord Reid said:

I do not think that this case [*Manchester Liners Ltd v Rea Ltd*] is any authority for the view which has sometimes been expressed that if the seller knows the purpose for which the buyer wants the goods it will be presumed that the buyer relied on his skill and judgment.

So the observations in *Manchester Liners Ltd v Rea Ltd* have received a knock-out blow. We can revert once more to the statute. The particular purpose must be made known 'so as to show that the buyer relies on the seller's skill or judgment.' That means that the buyer makes the particular purpose known to the seller in such a way that the seller knows that he is being relied upon. That cannot be said here. The sellers here did not know they were being relied on for resale in Persia. They knew nothing of conditions in Persia. The buyers knew all about those conditions. The buyers saw the machine here. They read its description. They relied upon their own skill and judgment to see that it was suitable for resale in Persia, and not on the seller's. At all events, they did not make the purpose known to the seller in such circumstances as to show him that they relied on the seller's skill and judgment. So I do not think there was an implied term that they should be fit for the purpose of being resold in Persia.

[Diplock and Sachs LJJ delivered concurring judgments.]

NOTE

Manchester Liners Ltd v Rea Ltd [1922] 2 AC 74, which was referred to by both Lord Macmillan and Lord Denning, concerned a contract between a shipping company and a firm of coal merchants to supply coal to fuel a named ship. The House of Lords held that it should be assumed that the sellers knew the nature of the particular ship's furnaces and the character of the coal she used. It would appear that stronger evidence of reliance would now be needed to bring a seller within the section.

Henry Kendall & Sons v William Lillico & Sons Ltd [1969] 2 AC 31 (also sometimes known as Hardwick Garm Farm v SAPPA), House of Lords

(This case also raised questions under s 14(2): see above, p 358.)

Lord Pearce: . . . My Lords, young pheasants on the Hardwick Game Farm were killed or stunted through eating food which was compounded and supplied by Suffolk Agricultural and Poultry Producers Association Ltd ('SAPPA'). Nobody has doubted that the Hardwick Garm Farm had a good cause of action or that SAPPA were right in admitting it. The question is, how far that loss can be handed on to the various merchants up the line of supply. The claims are based on breaches of condition or warranty under the Sale of Goods Act 1893. . . .

The damage came from a latent toxin in Brazilian groundnut meal which SAPPA used as an ingredient in their compound food. They had bought the meal from Grimsdale (and from Lillico who have not appealed from the judgment against them and have therefore passed out of the picture). Grimsdale have been held liable under s 14(1) of the Sale of Goods Act 1893 [1979 Act, s 14(3)], in that the meal was not reasonably fit for the purpose, but not liable under s 14(2) since the meal was held to be merchantable. Grimsdale bought the meal from Kendall who have likewise been held liable under s 14[(3)] but not under s 14(2). Kendall appeal against this liability. Grimsdale are content to accept their own liability so long as they can hand it on to Kendall. But if Kendall succeed in disclaiming liability, then Grimsdale in turn seek to disclaim their own liability to SAPPA.

When Grimsdale orally sold to SAPPA, it was in the course of Grimsdale's business to sell cattle and poultry feeding stuffs to the manufacturers of compound feeding stuffs. Grimsdale knew that the meal was 'liable to be used in the manufacture of compound feeding stuffs for cattle or poultry.' They were further aware that SAPPA 'only compounded feeding stuffs for poultry, pheasants and pigs' and 'did not compound feeding stuffs for cattle.' It was held that the particular purpose was made known so as to show that SAPPA relied on Grimsdale's skill and judgment. It has been held unanimously by the trial judge and the Court of Appeal that the condition of fitness implied by s 14[(3)] has been proved and that the meal was not fit for the purpose for which it was supplied. In my opinion, that view is right. And it is clear that the injury to the pheasants was well within the range of damages recoverable. Therefore, whether or not Grimsdale can hand on their liability to Kendall, they cannot avoid liability themselves. . . .

The more difficult question is whether Grimsdale's purchase from Kendall contained under s 14[(3)] or 14(2) conditions which were broken. . . .

When Kendall sold to Grimsdale they were aware that the purpose of Grimsdale was 'to resell in smaller quantities to be compounded into food for cattle and poultry'. . . . If, therefore, a condition resulted under s 14[(3)] from that knowledge, the food must be fit for cattle and poultry. Fitness for one coupled with unfitness for the other would not suffice.

The judge and the Court of Appeal held that the purpose of Grimsdale was 'a particular purpose' within s 14[(3)]. It was argued that such a purpose was too wide and had not enough particularity to constitute a particular purpose. I do not accept this contention. Almost every purpose is capable of some sub-division, some further and better particulars. But a particular purpose means a given purpose, known or communicated. It is not necessarily a narrow or closely particularised purpose (see *Benjamin on Sale* (1950), 8th ed, p 630: 'A particular purpose is not some purpose necessarily distinct from a general purpose'). A purpose may be put in wide terms or it may be circumscribed or narrowed. An example of the former is to be found in *Bartlett v Sydney Marcus Ltd* [1965] 1 WLR 1013, where the purpose was that of a car to drive on the road. See also *Baldry v Marshall* [1925] 1 KB 260 ['a comfortable car suitable for touring purposes']. A somewhat narrower purpose was to be found in *Bristol Tramways, etc, Carriage Co Ltd v Fiat Motors Ltd* [1910] 2 KB 831 ['an omnibus for heavy traffic in a hilly district']. The less circumscribed the purpose, the less circumscribed will be, as a rule, the range of goods which are reasonably fit for such purpose. The purpose of a car to drive on the road will be satisfied by almost any car so long as it will function reasonably; but the narrower purpose of an omnibus suitable to the crowded streets of a city can only be achieved by a narrower range of vehicles. This, however, is a question of fact and degree. Lord Herschell said in *Drummond v Van Ingen* (1887) 12 App Cas 284, 293:

> Where the article may be used as one of the elements in a variety of other manufactures, I think it may be too much to impute to the maker of this common article a knowledge of the details of every manufacture into which it may enter in combination with other materials.

In general it would be wrong to say, as was suggested in argument, that a wide purpose is unfair to the seller because it purports to require fitness for every conceivable subdivision of purpose within the main purpose.

I would expect a tribunal of fact to decide that a car sold in this country was reasonably fit for touring even though it was not well adapted for conditions in a heat wave; but not, if it could not cope adequately with rain. If, however, it developed some lethal or dangerous trick in very hot weather, I would expect it to be found unfit. In deciding the question of fact the rarity of the unsuitability would be weighed against the gravity of its consequences. Again, if food was merely unpalatable or useless on rare occasions, it might well be reasonably suitable for food. But I should certainly not expect it to be held reasonably suitable if even on very rare occasions it killed the consumer. The question for the tribunal of fact is simply 'were these goods reasonably fit for the specified purpose?'

'To resell in smaller quantities to be compounded into food for cattle and poultry' was, therefore, a particular purpose within s 14[(3)]. If a particular purpose is made known, that is sufficient to raise the inference that the buyer relies on the seller's skill and judgment unless there is something to displace the inference. There is no need for a buyer formally to 'make known' that which is already known. . . . The reliance need not be exclusive. Partial reliance will suffice.

The judge considered that the inference that the buyer relied on the seller's skill and judgment was displaced by the fact that Grimsdale and Kendall were members of the same Association, the London Cattle Food Traders Association. I do not, with respect, accept this view. The whole trend of authority has inclined towards an assumption of reliance wherever the seller knows the particular purpose. And where there are several subsales and the purpose is obvious, the liability is frequently passed up the line. To cut the chain of liability at one particular point is not fair unless there is some cogent reason for doing so. In the present case I see no grounds for holding that Kendall were in any relevantly different position from Grimsdale. The fellow-membership of the CTFA was irrelevant. One member may rely on another member just as much as he relies on an outside trader. The fellow-membership may even increase his reliance.

Reliance is not excluded by the fact that the seller may not himself have seen the goods he sells. In *Bigge v Parkinson* (1862) 7 H & N 955, 959 where it was implied that stores for troops in India must be fit for their purpose, Cockburn CJ said:

> Where a person undertakes to supply provisions, and they are supplied in cases hermetically sealed, but turn out to be putrid, it is no answer to say that he has been deceived by the person from whom he got them.

The seller, not the buyer, is aware of the provenance of the goods and has chosen to acquire them for disposal. It would, therefore, be not unreasonable that the buyer should rely on the seller's 'knowledge and trade wisdom' to use a phrase quoted in *Grant v Australian Knitting Mills Ltd* (1933) 50 CLR 387, 446 by Evatt J from *Ward v Great Atlantic & Pacific Tea Co* 231 Mass 90, 93, 94 (1918). And Walton J in *Preist v Last* (1903) 89 LT 33, 35, refers to the buyer's reliance that the seller will not sell him 'mere rubbish.' This expression is echoed in the evidence in the present case where Mr Brown of Lillico said that they relied on Kendall 'not to sell what they knew was rubbish'.

It is argued that the width of the purpose should prevent one from inferring that there was reliance. I do not think so. The compounders of food for cattle and poultry need healthy ingredients, as the sellers knew. The parties were not considering what admixture of healthy groundnut meal would be good for particular animals or birds, but whether assuming a certain quantity of groundnut meal would be a fit ingredient, the goods delivered would be healthy or harmful groundnut meal. It was reasonable that the buyer should rely on the seller to deliver groundnut meal which would, as groundnut meal, be a healthy and not a harmful ingredient in a compound.

In my opinion, there was on the circumstances of this case sufficient to establish reliance by Grimsdale on Kendall and a resulting condition.

The condition did not mean that the food was fit, however strange or unsuitable the proportions of the compound might prove to be. It meant that the food was fit if compounded reasonably and competently according to current standards. Goods are not fit if they have hidden limitations requiring special precautions unknown to the buyer or seller. The groundnut meal delivered was plainly not fit for the purpose of reselling in small lots to compounders of food for cattle and poultry. It was highly toxic. It is beside the point that Kendalls were unaware of the proportions in which it was to be compounded. It was unfit for use in the normal range of proportions. The evidence shows that 10 per cent was included in the feeding stuff for pheasants. This was not abnormal. When the toxicity had been discovered and investigated the recommendation of a reputable working party was that not more than 5 per cent of meal with a high toxicity should be included even in cattle rations and none should be included in rations for birds. Moreover, while its toxicity was unknown, the meal was thereby far more harmful and dangerous. Even had the buyer known of its toxic qualities, it was not fit for compounding for poultry. For a compounder's business is to mix healthy foods in suitable compounds. It is quite unsuitable that he should get toxic meal which can only be used by inserting it in quantities so abnormally small that the dilution of other compounds removes its lethal effect. All the courts below have held rightly, without any dissent, that this meal was not reasonably fit for the purpose for which it was supplied by Kendall to Grimsdale.

Kendall are therefore liable in breach of the condition under s 14[(3)]. . . .

[Lords Reid, Morris of Borth-y-Gest, Guest and Wilberforce delivered opinions concurring on this issue. Lord Guest dissented on another point.]

In *Ashington Piggeries Ltd v Christopher Hill Ltd* [1972] AC 441, HL (see above, p 356), similar questions arose in relation to a feeding compound, mixed by the sellers to the buyers' formula, which contained herring meal that was contaminated by a toxic preservative and proved fatal when fed to the buyers' mink. The herring meal had in turn been bought by the sellers from Norwegian suppliers who had no knowledge of the precise use to which it was to be put, but knew that the herring meal was to be used in compounding animal foodstuffs, and it was held that they ought reasonably to have foreseen that it might be fed to mink. The toxin affected different species of animals in varying degrees, but it was especially harmful to mink. Although only the buyers had any expertise relating to mink, it was held that both the sellers and their Norwegian suppliers were in breach of s 14(3), because they had been relied on to supply goods which were reasonably fit for feeding to animals generally (not limited specifically to mink).

Aswan Engineering Establishment Co v Lupdine Ltd [1987] 1 WLR 1, Court of Appeal

(For the facts, see above, p 359. This part of the judgment is concerned with the case against the manufacturers, Thurgar Bolle.)

Lloyd LJ: . . . It was said that Lupdine made known to Thurgar Bolle that the pails were wanted for export; that this was a stated purpose distinct from, for example, use for domestic purposes; and that the purpose was sufficiently defined to be a 'particular purpose' within s 14(3). A particular purpose need not be a narrow purpose.

Mr Aikens relied on the two decisions in the House of Lords to which I have already referred, namely, the *Hardwick Game Farm* case [1969] 2 AC 31 and the *Ashington Piggeries* case [1972] AC 441. In the former case the purchase of groundnut extractions for compounding into food for cattle and poultry, and in the latter case the purchase of herring meal for inclusion in animal feeding stuffs, though wide purposes, were nevertheless held to be particular purposes within the meaning of what is now s 14(3). In the *Ashington Piggeries* case the narrow purpose for which the herring meal was required was compounding into mink food. That purpose was never made known to the sellers. But the sellers were held liable under what is now s 14(3), since feeding to mink was found to be a normal use within the wider stated purpose of compounding into food for cattle and poultry. In the same way, submitted Mr Aikens, exporting to the Middle East is a normal use within the wider stated purpose of exporting generally. There is no finding that the conditions on the voyage, or after arrival, were abnormal in any way. Since the pails were not suitable for exporting to the Middle East, Thurgar Bolle are in breach of s 14(3). So ran the argument. I see the force of that argument, but it fails, for a reason which I have not so far mentioned.

Section 14(3), like the old s 14(1), depends on reliance. Unless the buyer relies on the seller's skill or judgment in selecting the appropriate goods for the stated purpose, there is no implied condition. In many cases reliance can be inferred. But in the present case the circumstances show quite clearly that Lupdine never relied on Thurgar Bolle's skill or judgment in any relevant sense at all.

In September 1979 Mr Hamilton, of Lupdine, saw a description of the pail in a catalogue. He made inquiries of Thurgar Bolle, and was sent a sample. The following June Lupdine wrote:

> We are currently involved in considerable export of our waterproofing compound and feel that this V.20 container will be more suitable and robust than the ones we are currently using.

A week later they placed a trial order. Neill J concluded that this was not a case where any special characteristics had been made known to the sellers in circumstances which showed the buyers relied on their skill and judgment. It would require a strong case for us to go behind that finding of fact. I would, however, go further than the judge. In my judgment the circumstances showed positively that the buyers did *not* rely on the sellers' skill or judgment in any relevant sense. In those circumstances there can be no question of an implied condition under s 14(3).

Moreover, even if there had been an implied condition, I should have declined to hold that Thurgar Bolle were in breach. In the *Hardwick Game Farm* case [1969] 2 AC 31, 114–115, Lord Pearce said:

> It was argued that such a purpose was too wide and had not enough particularity to constitute a particular purpose. I do not accept this contention. Almost every purpose is capable of some sub-division, some further and better particulars. . . . A purpose may be put in wide terms or it may be circumscribed or narrowed. . . . The less circumscribed the purpose, the less circumscribed will be, as a rule, the range of goods which are reasonably fit for such purpose.

To the same effect is an observation of Lord Wilberforce in the *Ashington Piggeries* case [1972] AC 441, 497, that width of purpose is compensated, from the seller's point of view, by the dilution of his responsibility. If making known that the pails were wanted for export is a particular purpose within s 14(3), as Mr Aikens contends, then the purpose could hardly be wider. A very wide range of goods must be regarded as reasonably fit for that purpose. On the facts, these pails fell within that range. Indeed, so wide is the purpose that it could be said that the pails needed to be little, if anything, more than merchantable.

NOTES

1. In *Wormell v RHM Agriculture (East) Ltd* [1987] 1 WLR 1091, CA it was held that instructions, supplied with the goods (in that case, a herbicide) have to be taken into account in considering whether goods are fit for their purpose.
2. The passages which, in the interests of simplification, were omitted when quoting s 14(3) (above, p 365) contain references to a mysterious figure called a 'credit-broker'. This more elaborate wording is intended to bring within the scope of s 14(3) the 'triangular' transaction where (for example) a vehicle is bought on conditional-sale or credit-sale terms from a finance company after the customer has chosen it from the stock of a motor dealer. The finance company will be bound to supply a vehicle fit for the buyer's particular purpose if the buyer has made that purpose known to the dealer (the 'credit-broker'). A similar provision (s 10(3) of the Supply of Goods (Implied Terms) Act 1973) governs transactions where the customer takes the goods on hire purchase.

7 Terms implied in sales of goods by sample (s 15)

Section 15 deals with goods which are sold by sample. There are three implied conditions, set out in s 15(2):

(1) that the bulk will correspond with the sample in quality;
(2) that the buyer will have a reasonable opportunity of comparing the bulk with the sample;
(3) that the goods will be free from any defect, rendering them unmerchantable, which would not be apparent on reasonable examination of the sample.

These provisions are in themselves more or less self-explanatory. The only likely surprise lies in the concept of a 'sale by sample' itself, and its legal function. The term is defined, not very helpfully, in s 15(1):

> A contract of sale is a contract for sale by sample where there is an express or implied term to that effect in the contract.

This makes it plain that it is not sufficient that the buyer should merely have seen a specimen of the goods in question; the parties must have agreed that the sale shall be a sale *by reference to* that sample.

The cases show that the function of a sample is very similar to that of a contractual description, or perhaps to supplement the contractual description. In *Drummond v Van Ingen* (1887) 12 App Cas 284 at 297, HL, Lord Macnaghten explained this function as follows:

> The office of a sample is to present to the eye the real meaning and intention of the parties with regard to the subject matter of the contract which, owing to the imperfection of language, it may be difficult or impossible to express in words. The sample speaks for itself. But it cannot be treated as saying more than such a sample would tell a merchant of the class to which the buyer belongs, using due care and diligence, and appealing to it in the ordinary way and with the knowledge possessed by merchants of that class at the time. No doubt the sample might be made to say a great deal more. Pulled to pieces and examined by unusual tests which curiosity or suspicion might suggest, it would doubtless reveal every secret of its construction. But that is not the way in which business is done in this country.

From this statement we can infer that a seller in a sale by sample does not guarantee that the bulk will comply with the sample in every possible respect: but only that it will be as like the sample as an ordinary comparison or inspection would reveal. Over and above this, the buyer must rely on the implied terms contained in s 14(2) and (3), or stipulate for an express warranty. However, there is limited further protection conferred by s 15(2)(c), which implies a condition that the goods will be free from any latent defect which renders them unmerchantable. The case next cited confirms the restricted scope both of the function of a 'sale by sample' and of this latter condition.

Steels & Busks Ltd v Bleecker Bik & Co Ltd [1956] 1 Lloyd's Rep 228, Queen's Bench Division

Steels & Busks contracted to buy from Bleecker Bik five tons of pale crepe rubber, 'quality as previously delivered'. The court construed this as a sale by sample, the 'sample' being the rubber delivered under previous contracts. Steels & Busks used the rubber to manufacture corsets, but it turned out (unlike the earlier deliveries) to contain an invisible preservative, PNP, which stained the fabric of the corsets. Sellers J held that there had been no breach of the condition implied by s 15(2)(a): the rubber was in accordance with the sample on any visual test. Nor had there been a breach of the condition as to merchantability implied by s 15(2)(c): this rubber was perfectly useful for commercial purposes once the staining chemical had been washed out or neutralised.

Sellers J: In assessing the quality of the goods and their state and condition on delivery, the Appeal Committee have applied the normal market standard and applied the normal tests. Para 8 of the award deals with the arbitrators' views:

> As understood in the market, quality is determined by visual inspection of samples drawn in the wharves after rubber has been landed; such inspection extends to colour, texture, and the possibility of impurities such as specks of bark, sand, bits of cotton, and deterioration. The kind of chemical used in the preparation of rubber has never been regarded as entering into the quality of rubber. If the quality of pale crepe were to depend on the chemical preservative used, there might be as many qualities as there are preservatives; no such idea is known to the trade. 'PNP' is not a defect in rubber nor is it an adulterant or impurity. It is a preservative used, though less frequently in pale crepe than in other types of rubber, and its presence does not affect quality. We have not

overlooked the statutory definition of 'quality of goods' in s 62(1) of the Sale of Goods Act, but we do not regard the presence of 'PNP' as a matter affecting state or condition. . . .

If the buyers are to succeed in their claim, it must, I think, only be on the ground that the 21 bales did not comply with the sample, that is, the first delivery. In one respect the bales complained of did not so comply. They contained 'PNP,' whereas the sample did not, and it was submitted that s 15(2)(a) of the Sale of Goods Act had not been complied with as the bulk did not correspond with the sample in quality.

[His Lordship quoted the section, and continued:]

Section 15(2) is not inconsistent with the view that where there is (as here) a defect not apparent on reasonable examination of the sample, the buyers' rights arise, if at all, under sub-s (2)(c) and not under sub-s (2)(a), but it is not, I think, conclusive as a matter of construction. . . .

Drummond v Van Ingen (1887) 12 App Cas 284, is the case upon which s 15 is largely based. . . .

In that case, the contract expressly provided that quality and weight should be equal to certain numbered samples; and the Earl of Selborne LC, at p 288, said this about its construction:

I think that the word 'quality' as used in the contracts, ought to be restricted to those qualities which were patent, or discoverable from such examination and inspection of the samples as, under the circumstances, the respondents might reasonably be expected to make.

In *Drummond v Van Ingen* the House of Lords was able, by giving the sample clause a restricted meaning, to hold that its terms did not exclude an implied warranty covering latent defects. It is of the essence of this reasoning that a clause of this sort does not cover latent qualities or defects at all. In that case it was the seller's argument that was defeated by this construction. But, by the same token, it is not open to a buyer to submit a sample to an analysis unusual in the trade so as to reveal in it certain attributes or qualities hitherto unsuspected, and then to require, by virtue of the sample clause alone, that the bulk should contain the same qualities. If, for example, a buyer, to use the words of Lord Macnaghten, pulls a sample of cloth to pieces and discovers by means of analysis that the dye contains a certain proportion of a certain chemical, he cannot by virtue of the same clause require that the dye in the bulk shall contain the same proportion of the same chemical. He may, of course, complain that if it does not contain that proportion, it would be unmerchantable or would fail to satisfy some other express or implied condition as to quality; but he cannot say that it breaks the condition that the bulk shall correspond with the sample in quality, for that condition is dealing only with apparent quality. . . .

I am in complete agreement with that construction of s 15(2)(a), and I am grateful for that passage, which I adopt and apply here. *Drummond v Van Ingen, sup,* as Mr Justice Devlin indicates, is the forerunner very largely of s 15. Although it is before the Act and therefore perhaps not technically an authority, I should not feel emboldened to disregard it even if I wished to do so.

The extent to which a sample may be held to 'speak' must depend on the contract and what is contemplated by the parties in regard to it. A sample may be analysed, X-rayed – tested to destruction. In the present case the parties were content, in accordance with the normal practice of the trade, to rely on a visual examination. Neither 'PNP' nor, I think, any other chemical in general use for coagulation and preservation or either is detectable by visual examination, and therefore the presence or absence of the chemical cannot in itself be a breach of the sample clause. . . .

The buyers had in fact used the first delivery and found it satisfactory and that no doubt resulted in the repeat orders. The crude rubber had received treatment and processing by them and revealed no defect. Such circumstances would not enlarge the liability of the sellers, as the contract remained, as far as the compliance with a sample was concerned, a contract which called for compliance in those matters revealed by visual examination and those matters only.

In my judgment, the Appeal Committee (and also, indeed, the original arbitrators) were entitled to come to the decision that the goods delivered under the last contract were in accordance with the contractual terms, and I answer the question raised accordingly.

8 Exclusion of seller's liability

The Unfair Contract Terms Act 1977 ('UCTA'), s 6, restricts the ability of a seller to negative or vary the terms implied by ss 12–15 of the Sale of Goods Act 1979.

Two preliminary points must be made. First, the Act of 1977 does not apply at all to 'international supply contracts' – a term which includes contracts for the sale of goods where the seller and buyer are based in different jurisdictions *and* one of three additional conditions applies:

(1) the goods are to be carried from one state to another;
(2) the acts constituting the offer and acceptance have been done in different territories; or
(3) the goods are to be delivered to a territory other than that in which the offer and acceptance took place (UCTA, s 26).

Second, s 6 (unlike the rest of UCTA) is not restricted in its application to 'business liability' (as defined in s 1(3)). So, for instance, liability for breach of s 12 of the Sale of Goods Act (the condition as to title, etc) cannot be excluded even in a contract of sale made between two private persons.

Section 12 of UCTA makes a distinction between contracts in which a person (in the present context, the buyer) 'deals as consumer', and other contracts of sale. A buyer will deal as consumer if:

(1) he neither makes the contract in the course of a business nor holds himself out as doing so; and
(2) the other party (ie, the seller) does make the contract in the course of a business; and
(3) the goods are of a type ordinarily supplied for private use or consumption.

However, if the contract is one for sale by auction or by competitive tender the buyer will not in any circumstances be regarded as dealing as consumer (UCTA, s 12(2)).

The onus is on the seller to prove that the buyer is not dealing as consumer (UCTA, s 12(3)).

Section 6 of UCTA makes the following rules regarding clauses purporting to exempt a seller from liability under ss 12–15 of the Sale of Goods Act:

–   Liability under s 12 (undertakings as to title, etc) cannot be excluded or restricted at all. (Note, however, that s 12 itself makes provision for the case where a seller purports to sell only a limited title: see s 12(3) (above, p 346).)
–   Liability under ss 13 (conformity with description), 14(2) (merchantability), 14(3) (fitness for purpose) and 15 (conformity with sample) *cannot* be excluded or restricted *as against a person dealing as consumer*; and, as against any other buyer, can be excluded or restricted only in so far as the term satisfies the 'requirement of reasonableness'.

The 'requirement of reasonableness' is defined for the purposes of the Act generally as 'that the term shall have been a fair and reasonable one to be included having regard to the circumstances which were, or ought reasonably to have been, known to or in the contemplation of the parties when the contract was made' (UCTA, s 11(1)). More particularly, in regard to contracts for the sale of goods, the court is directed to have regard to a number of guidelines which are set out in Sch 2 of UCTA (s 11(2)). These include such matters as the relative bargaining strength of the parties, the amount of choice available to the buyer, and whether the goods were specially made or adapted to his order.

Of course, the exemption clauses in a contract for the sale of goods will not necessarily be confined to those which purport to exclude or restrict liability under ss 12–15 of the Sale of Goods Act. In the case of other exemption clauses (eg terms seeking to restrict the buyer's remedies in the case of a late delivery or short delivery) it will be necessary to have regard to other provisions of UCTA to see whether they apply – eg s 2 (terms excluding liability for negligence), s 3 (liability arising in contract, where one of the parties deals as consumer or on the other's written standard terms of business).

Some reported cases dealing with exemption clauses in contracts for the sale of goods were decided under earlier legislation – eg *George Mitchell (Chesterhall) Ltd v Finney Lock Seeds Ltd* [1983] 2 AC 803, HL, and *R W Green Ltd v Cade Bros Farms* [1978] 1 Lloyd's Rep 602. These rulings should be treated with caution, because the wording of the previous legislation was different: in particular, in applying the test of 'reasonableness', the court was formerly empowered to have regard to events occurring *after* the formation of the contract – something which UCTA does not allow (see s 11(1)).

9 Product liability

In 1985, after much debate, the EC Council adopted a Directive (85/374/EEC) which required member states to introduce legislation making manufacturers and other 'producers' strictly liable for damage caused by their products. The Directive was implemented in this country by Part I of the Consumer Protection Act 1987. The liability established by this statute will not, of course, apply primarily as between a seller and a buyer of goods, since the buyer will already have remedies under the contract of sale which are likely to be rather more extensive; but it may provide a direct remedy for a buyer against the original 'producer' of the goods, or (if the seller is himself their 'producer') give a cause of action to consumers of the goods and other parties who are not themselves buyers.

Under the Act of 1987, where damage is caused by a defect in a product, the producer is liable to the victim without the need for proof of fault. 'Damage' is defined as meaning death or personal injury or damage to property – but only property which is of a type ordinarily intended for private use or consumption. Accordingly, economic loss is excluded, as is damage to commercial and public property. It should be noted also that no claim lies in respect of the defective product itself. Other points to note are:

(1) primary agricultural products are excluded, if unprocessed;
(2) 'producer' includes an importer, and also a supplier where the original producer cannot be identified; and
(3) the law allows a 'state of the art' defence – ie a plea that the product met technical or scientific standards which were regarded as acceptable at the relevant time.

CHAPTER 11

Performance of the contract

The Act sets out in ss 27–37 a number of rules about the parties' respective obligations in regard to the payment of the price and the delivery of the goods. The selection of only these rules and their grouping into a separate Part is somewhat arbitrary. The terms implied into contracts of sale by ss 12–15, for instance, could very well have been expressed by the draftsman as 'duties of the seller' – a duty to pass a good title to the buyer, a duty to deliver goods of the contract description, etc. We shall, however, follow the lead given by the Act.

1 Duties of the seller

(a) To deliver the goods

Sections 27ff of the Sale of Goods Act 1979 spell out the duties of the seller in regard to delivery, in terms which are more or less self-explanatory. It is the duty of the seller to deliver the goods in accordance with the terms of the contract of sale (s 27). Unless otherwise agreed, he must be ready and willing to give possession of the goods to the buyer in exchange for the price (s 28).

The meaning of 'delivery'. The term 'delivery' may be the source of some confusion, as we saw in relation to the term 'deliverable state' (above, p 274). 'Delivery', in the statutory sense, means 'voluntary transfer of possession from one person to another'. Thus, it does not necessarily mean *physical* delivery, still less 'delivery' in the popular sense of sending the goods in a vehicle to the buyer's premises. In fact, the Act says that, in the absence of some express or implied provision in the contract, the place of delivery is the seller's place of business, if he has one, and if not, his residence; except that, if the contract is for specific goods, which are known when the contract is made to be in some other place, then that place is the place of delivery (s 29(2)).

Under the statutory definition, the term 'delivery' is dependent upon the common law concept of possession, whose meaning (as we saw in Chapter 2) is rather elusive. Three forms of delivery are particularly relevant for present purposes:

(1) actual, or physical delivery: this means the handing over of the goods themselves, whether to a buyer, a carrier or other person;
(2) symbolic delivery: handing over something which symbolises the goods; in particular, a bill of lading relating to goods which are at sea, and possibly the ignition key of a vehicle or the key of a locked building in which the goods are stored;

(3) constructive delivery: this refers to a transfer of the *right* to possession of goods which are in the physical custody of a third party, and is effected by a procedure known as *attornment*, which has been described above, p 56.

Attornment, it will be recalled, involves all three parties: (1) the seller (S) must instruct the third party (T) to hold the goods to the order of the buyer (B); and (2) T must acknowledge to B that he is now holding the goods on B's behalf. Most commonly, this will be done by the issue of a *delivery order* by S addressed to T, and handed to B or sent directly to T; T will then either make acknowledgment of the new state of affairs by some form of endorsement on the delivery order, or by issuing a *warrant* made out in favour of B (see above, p 331). Either way, the attornment will then be complete, and the right to possession which was formerly vested in S will have been transferred to B, and T becomes a bailee of the goods for B. There will, however, be no effective transfer of possession in this sense without step (2) above: neither an agreement solely between S and B, nor any arrangement between S and T alone, is sufficient. This is confirmed by s 29(4) of the Act.

Delivery and payment. Section 28 makes delivery and payment 'concurrent conditions', in the absence of any agreement to the contrary: that is to say (in the words of the Act) the seller must be ready and willing to give possession of the goods to the buyer in exchange for the price, and the buyer must be ready and willing to pay the price in exchange for possession of the goods. This provision raises some conceptual difficulties, since in theory (as we have seen: above, p 242) it is the *property* in the goods which the buyer bargains for in exchange for the price, and not possession. But s 28 says, in effect, that (unless otherwise agreed) a buyer can withhold payment if he does not get possession, and a seller can withhold delivery unless he gets payment; and so as a *practical* matter, it is often more realistic to think of delivery and payment as given in exchange for each other, rather than in abstract terms of property.

Time of delivery. Stipulations as to the time of performance of a contractual obligation may be made 'of the essence' of the contract or not (ie may made be conditions or warranties), as determined by their agreement. Section 10(2) confirms this in relation to contracts for the sale of goods, adding a presumptive rule (s 10(1)) that stipulations as to the time of payment are *not* of the essence. It is therefore up to the parties to settle whether a term relating to the time of delivery is to be regarded as a condition. However, in many mercantile transactions, it is well established by case law that stipulations as to the time of delivery will be so construed – particularly where the goods are to travel by sea transport. Thus, in *Bowes v Shand* (1877) 2 App Cas 455, HL, rice which was to be shipped 'during the months of March and/or April' was in fact loaded in February; the buyer was held entitled to reject. (Compare *Kwei Tek Chao v British Traders & Shippers NV* (above, p 294).)

Section 29(3) states that where, under the contract of sale, the seller is to send the goods to the buyer, but no time for doing so is fixed, he is bound to send them within a reasonable time. What is a reasonable time is a question of fact (s 59). It is also provided that a demand or tender of delivery may be treated as ineffectual unless made at a reasonable hour – again, a question of fact (s 29(5)).

Other rules about delivery. As we have seen, there is no rule of law which obliges the seller to 'deliver' the goods to the buyer, in the sense of taking or sending them to the buyer: whether it is for him to do this or for the buyer to take possession of the goods is a question that depends on the terms of the contract, express or implied (s 29(1)). But since, apart from any such contractual provision, the place of delivery will, prima facie, be the seller's place of business or his residence – or, in the case of specific goods, the place where they are known to be (s 29(2)) – it will normally be for the buyer to make arrangements to take delivery at that place. Unless otherwise agreed, the expenses of and incidental to putting the goods into a deliverable state must be borne by the seller (s 29(6)).

The seller must deliver the exact contract quantity – neither more nor less (s 30); and he cannot require the buyer to accept delivery by instalments (s 31). Nor, in fact, can the buyer require the seller to make delivery by instalments – although the Act does not mention this. These rules are examined in more detail below, at pp 381 and 426, when we discuss the buyer's remedies.

If the contract provides that the seller may, or must, send the goods to the buyer, delivery of the goods to a carrier (whether named by the buyer or not) for the purpose of transmission to the buyer is prima facie deemed to be a delivery of goods to the buyer (s 32(1)). 'Carrier', for this purpose, of course includes a ship. Section 32 goes on to provide that the seller must make a contract with the carrier on reasonable terms and, if it involves sea transit, give adequate notice to the buyer to enable him to insure them during their sea transit (s 32(3)). Any risk of deterioration in the goods necessarily incidental to the course of transit is to be borne by the buyer (s 33).

2 Duties of the buyer

The statutory duties of the buyer are: to take delivery (ss 27, 28, 37(1)); to accept the goods (s 27); and to pay the price (ss 27, 28).

(a) To take delivery

The basic rules regarding the place, time, etc of delivery have already been discussed (above, p 378). If the seller is ready and willing to deliver the goods and requests the buyer to take delivery, and the buyer does not within a reasonable time after such a request take delivery of the goods, the buyer will be liable in damages to the seller (s 37(1)). Where the seller makes a defective tender, the buyer is not bound to take delivery of the goods tendered but has the choice of remedies set out in s 30, discussed below at p 426.

(b) To accept the goods

The meaning of the term 'acceptance' in this context is explained in s 35. The buyer is deemed to have accepted the goods (a) by intimating that fact to the seller, (b) by dealing with the goods as owner (but see below, p 428) and (c) by retaining the goods beyond a reasonable time.

(c) To pay the price

The buyer is bound to pay the price in accordance with the terms of the contract of sale (s 27). But unless otherwise agreed, he is not required to make payment unless the seller is ready and willing to give him possession of the goods in exchange for the price (s 28).

A payment by cheque or any other form of negotiable instrument is normally regarded as only a conditional payment; and if it is not met or is dishonoured the seller's right to sue for the price, and his statutory rights as an unpaid seller, are revived (s 38(1)(b)). Exceptionally, the seller may agree to accept payment in this form in satisfaction of the buyer's obligation to pay the price. In this case, if the cheque is not met, his only remedy is on the instrument itself.

The contract may provide for payment in a foreign currency, and in this case the court has power to give its judgment in that currency: *Miliangos v George Frank (Textiles) Ltd* [1976] AC 443, HL.

3 Instalment contracts

(a) Introduction

A contract of sale may be provided for delivery of the goods, or payment of the price, or both, to be made by instalments. In general, such contracts will be governed by the ordinary rules of the law of contract. It may be crucial, for instance, to determine whether the contract (or, more accurately, the seller's obligation) is 'entire' or 'divisible'. An example of the former might be the sale by a mail-order company of an encyclopedia set, to be delivered to the buyer by posting one volume every month; and of the latter, the sale of 100 tons of coal to be delivered at the rate of 10 tons on the Monday of each week. The failure by the seller to deliver one volume of the encyclopedia would justify a claim by the buyer to be entitled to reject all the volumes so far received and have his money back. But a similar failure to deliver one instalment of the coal would, at the most, entitle the buyer to terminate the contract as regards *future* deliveries: there would be no question of a right to *restitutio in integrum* with retrospective effect. It is important to appreciate that the Act deals with only some points relating to instalment contracts, and leaves others (such as the distinction just made between entire and divisible obligations) to be decided by reference to the general law.

(b) Buyer not bound to accept delivery by instalments (s 31(1))

Section 31(1) declares that, unless otherwise agreed, the buyer of goods is not bound to accept delivery by instalments. It is also a rule (although not stated in the Act) that the buyer is not entitled to *require* delivery to be made by instalments (*Honck v Muller* (1881) 7 QBD 92, CA, especially at 99).

Behrend & Co v Produce Brokers' Co [1920] 3 KB 530, King's Bench Division

(The facts appear from the judgment.)

Bailhache J: In this case the sellers, by two contracts of sale . . . bound themselves to the buyers to deliver in London, ex the steamship *Port Inglis*, to the buyers' craft alongside, two separate parcels of cotton seed, one of 176 tons and the other of 400 tons. The buyers on their part had to pay for these parcels against shipping documents and to send craft to receive the goods. The buyers fulfilled both these obligations and received from the *Port Inglis* some fifteen tons of one parcel and twenty-two tons of the other. When these had been delivered it was discovered that the rest of the seed was lying under cargo for Hull, and the *Port Inglis* stopped delivery and left for that port, promising to return and deliver the rest of the seed. She returned in about a fortnight's time and the seed was tendered to the buyers, but the buyers had meantime informed the sellers that they regarded the departure of the *Port Inglis* with the remainder of the seed on board as a failure to deliver and a breach of contract. They kept so much of the seed as had been delivered to them and demanded repayment of so much of the contract price as represented the seed undelivered.

The umpire has decided in the buyers' favour and I am asked to say whether he was right. Everything depends upon whether the departure of the *Port Inglis* for Hull with the greater part of both parcels of seed on board was a failure to deliver, notwithstanding the promise to return and complete delivery. Both contracts between the parties are in the same terms and neither has any express provision on the subject. In my opinion, the buyer under such a contract, and where each parcel of goods is indivisible, as here, has the right to have delivery on the arrival of the steamship, not necessarily immediately or continuously; he must take his turn or the goods may be so stowed that other goods have to be discharged before the whole of the buyers' parcel can be got out. To such delays and others which may occur in the course of unloading the buyer must submit, but in the absence of any stipulation to the contrary the buyer, being ready with his craft, is entitled to delivery of the whole of an indivisible parcel of goods sold to him for delivery from a vessel which has begun delivery to him before she leaves the port to deliver goods elsewhere. If this is so the rest of the case is covered by s 30 of the Sale of Goods Act, and the buyer can either reject the whole of the goods, including those actually delivered, in which case he can recover the whole of his money; or he may keep the goods actually delivered and reject the rest, in which case he must pay for the goods kept at the contract price, and he can recover the price paid for the undelivered portion. . . . I think that the award is right.

(c) Breach in respect of one or more instalments (s 31(2))

Section 31(2) makes provision for one particular type of instalment contract. It states:

> Where there is a contract for the sale of goods to be delivered by stated instalments, which are to be separately paid for, and the seller makes defective deliveries in respect of one or more instalments, or the buyer neglects or refuses to take delivery of or pay for one or more instalments, it is a question in each case depending on the terms of the contract and the circumstances of the case whether the breach of the contract is a repudiation of the whole contract or whether it is a severable breach giving rise to a claim for compensation but not to a right to treat the whole contract as repudiated.

It is likely that the rules stated in this subsection reflect propositions of the common law which have a wider application: for instance, similar rules would surely govern a contract for the sale of goods to be delivered by instalments which are not to be separately paid for but, perhaps, paid for in some other way. The operation of s 31(2) in practice is illustrated by the following cases.

Maple Flock Co Ltd v Universal Furniture Products (Wembley) Ltd [1934] 1 KB 148, Court of Appeal

Maple contracted to sell to Universal 100 tons of rag flock 'to be delivered three loads per week as required'. The weekly deliveries were to be separately paid for. After 18 loads, each of one and a half tons, had been delivered, the buyers wrote purporting to cancel the remainder of the contract on the ground that an analysis of the sixteenth load had shown that its chlorine content was over eight times the government standard. The court held that this single breach did not justify termination of the contract as a whole.

Lord Hewart CJ delivered the judgment of the court (Lord Hewart CJ, Lord Wright and Slesser LJ): The decision of this case depends on the true construction and application of s 31, sub-s 2, of the Sale of Goods Act 1893, which is in the following terms: 'Where there is a contract for the sale of goods to be delivered by stated instalments, which are to be separately paid for, and the seller makes defective deliveries in respect of one or more instalments, or the buyer neglects or refuses to take delivery of or pay for one or more instalments, it is a question in each case depending on the terms of the contract and the circumstances of the case, whether the breach of contract is a repudiation of the whole contract or whether it is a severable breach giving rise to a claim for compensation but not to a right to treat the whole contract as repudiated.' That sub-section was based on decisions before the Act, and has been the subject of decisions since the Act. A contract for the sale of goods by instalments is a single contract, not a complex of as many contracts as there are instalments under it. The law might have been determined in the sense that any breach of condition in respect of any one or more instalments would entitle the party aggrieved to claim that the contract has been repudiated as a whole; or on the other hand the law as established might have been that any breach, however serious, in respect of one or more instalments should not have consequences extending beyond the particular instalment or instalments or affecting the contract as a whole. The sub-section, however, which deals equally with breaches either by the buyer or the seller, requires the Court to decide on the merits of the particular case what effect, if any, the breach or breaches should have on the contract as a whole.

[His Lordship referred to a number of decided cases, and continued:]

With the help of these authorities we deduce that the main tests to be considered in applying the sub-section to the present case are, first, the ratio quantitatively which the breach bears to the contract as a whole, and secondly the degree of probability or improbability that such a breach will be repeated. On the first point, the delivery complained of amounts to no more than $1\frac{1}{2}$ tons out of a contract for 100 tons. On the second point, our conclusion is that the chance of the breach being repeated is practically negligible. We assume that the sample found defective fairly represents the bulk; but bearing in mind the judge's finding that the breach was extraordinary and that the appellant's business was carefully conducted, bearing in mind also that the appellants were warned, and bearing in mind that the delivery complained of was an isolated instance out of 20 satisfactory deliveries actually made both before and after the instalment objected to, we hold that it cannot reasonably be inferred that similar breaches would occur in regard to subsequent deliveries. Indeed, we do not understand that the learned Judge came to any different conclusion. He seems, however, to have decided against the appellants on a third and separate ground, that is, that a delivery not satisfying the Government requirements would or might lead to the respondents being prosecuted. . . . Though we think he exaggerates the likelihood of the respondents in such a case being held responsible, we do not wish to underrate the gravity to the respondents of their being even prosecuted. But we cannot follow the Judge's reasoning that the bare possibility, however remote, of this happening would justify the respondents in rescinding in this case. There may indeed be such cases, as also cases where the consequences of a single breach of contract may be so serious as to involve a frustration of the contract and justify rescission, or furthermore, the contract might contain an express condition that a breach would justify rescission, in which case effect would be given to such a condition by the Court. But none of these circumstances can be predicated of this case. We think the deciding factor here is the extreme improbability of the breach being repeated, and on that ground, and on the isolated and limited character of the breach complained of, there was, in our judgment, no sufficient justification to entitle the respondents to refuse further deliveries as they did.

The appeal must accordingly be allowed and judgment entered for the appellants, with costs here and below, for damages for their breach of contract in refusing further deliveries.

Withers v Reynolds (1831) 2 B & Ad 882, Court of King's Bench

Withers, a stable-keeper, contracted to buy wheat straw from Reynolds, to be delivered at the rate of three loads per fortnight, and paid for on delivery. After about ten weeks, Withers insisted on paying for the straw one delivery in arrear. The court ruled that this was a repudiation which justified Reynolds in refusing all further performance.

Parke J: The substance of the agreement was, that the straw should be paid for on delivery. The defendant clearly did not contemplate giving credit. When, therefore, the plaintiff said that he would not pay on delivery, (as he did, in substance, when he insisted on keeping one load on hand,) the defendant was not obliged to go on supplying him.

Patteson J: If the plaintiff had merely failed to pay for any particular load, that, of itself, might not have been an excuse to the defendant for delivering no more straw: but the plaintiff here expressly refuses to pay for the loads as delivered; the defendant, therefore, is not liable for ceasing to perform his part of the contract.

[Lord Tenterden CJ and Taunton J delivered concurring judgments.]

Warinco AG v Samor SpA [1977] 2 Lloyd's Rep 582, [1979] 1 Lloyd's Rep 450, Queen's Bench Division and Court of Appeal

(The facts are immaterial.)

Donaldson J: It is a popular myth, which lawyers do little to dispel, that the law is a highly technical matter with mysterious rules leading to results which are contrary to commonsense. Nothing could be further from the truth, both in general and in the particular instance of the law relating to the repudiation of contracts.

If a buyer under a contract calling for delivery by instalments commits a breach of that contract before all the deliveries have been made and that breach is so serious as to go to the root of the contract – in other words, to destroy the basis of the contract – commonsense suggests that the seller should not be expected to go to the trouble and expense of tendering later instalments if he does not want to. The law so provides.

Again, if it becomes clear that the buyer will be unable to accept or to pay for later instalments, commonsense suggests that the seller should, if he wishes, be discharged from any obligation further to perform his part of the contract. The law so provides.

Finally, if a buyer acts or speaks in a manner which declares in clear terms that he will not in future perform his part of the contract, the seller should, in common sense and fairness, have the option of being discharged from further obligation under the contract. And that is the law.

But common sense also suggests that there can be borderline cases in which it is not quite so clear what should happen. The law is at a disadvantage here in that it must draw a line. The line which it draws is indicated by the question: 'Has the buyer evinced an intention to abandon or to refuse to perform the contract?'. In answering this question, the law has regard to such factors as the degree to which the delivery of one instalment is linked with another, the proportion of the contract which has been affected by the allegedly repudiatory breach and the probability that the breach will be repeated. However, these are merely part of the raw material for answering the question. They cannot be conclusive in themselves.

Two other cases may be mentioned:

(1) *Robert A Munro & Co Ltd v Meyer* [1930] 2 KB 312, where there was a contract to supply 1500 tons of meat-and-bone meal by instalments of 125 tons

per month. After 631 tons had been delivered, it was discovered that all the meal delivered so far had been deliberately adulterated with cocoa husk, so that it failed to conform to its description. Wright J granted a declaration that the buyers were not bound to take delivery of any further instalments.

(2) *Regent OHG Aisenstadt und Barig v Francesco of Jermyn Street Ltd* [1981] 3 All ER 327: Regent, a firm of German clothing manufacturers, agreed to sell 62 suits to Francesco, retailers of menswear. Delivery was to be by instalments, the number and size to be at Regent's discretion. Francesco told Regent that they wished to cancel the order, but Regent insisted on continuing to make deliveries because the suits were already in production. Francesco then purported to cancel the contract on the ground that one delivery had been one suit short, relying on s 30(1) of the Act (see below, p 426), which entitles a buyer who is tendered short delivery to reject all the contract goods. Mustill J ruled that where the contract provided for delivery to be made by instalments, s 31(2) applied to the exclusion of s 30(1), and the repudiation was wrongful in the circumstances.

NOTE

The statement of the law in the *Maple Flock* case may be regarded as an instance of the 'innominate term' approach to the question of breach of contract favoured by the Court of Appeal in *Hong Kong Fir Shipping Co Ltd v Kawasaki Kisen Kaisha Ltd* [1962] 2 QB 26.

CHAPTER 12

Remedies of the seller

1 Action for the price

The seller's right to bring an action for the price is described in s 49 of the Act in rather surprisingly restrictive terms. Section 49 states that he is entitled to do so only in two specified situations:

(1) where, under the contract of sale, the property in the goods has passed to the buyer, and he wrongfully neglects or refuses to pay for the goods according to the terms of the contract (s 49(1));

(2) where, under the contract, the price is payable on a day certain irrespective of delivery, and the buyer wrongfully neglects or refuses to pay the price (s 49(2)).

However, there are some other situations where the seller may sue for the price (see paragraph (c) below); so s 49 cannot be regarded as a complete statement of the law.

(a) Where the property has passed to the buyer (s 49(1))

For the seller to be able to sue for the price under this section, it is not sufficient that the property has passed to the buyer. The buyer must also have wrongfully neglected or refused to pay the price; and this neglect or refusal will not be 'wrongful' if the price is not yet due under the terms of the contract (eg, where the seller has agreed to give credit), or if the seller is in breach of certain obligations on his part (eg, where s 28 applies, to be ready and willing to give possession of the goods to the buyer in exchange for the price).

(b) Where the price is payable on a day certain irrespective of delivery (s 49(2))

If the contract stipulates a fixed date for payment, or a date that can be calculated by reference to some objective fact (eg 'seven days after arrival of ship'), irrespective of delivery, the seller can sue for the price even though the property has not passed, and even though no goods have yet been appropriated to the contract. Again, however, the buyer must have wrongfully neglected or refused to pay for the goods. The meaning of the phrase 'a day certain irrespective of delivery' was discussed in *Workman Clark & Co Ltd v Lloyd Brazileno* (below, p 390).

(c) Where the risk has passed

The draftsman appears to have overlooked the fact that there are some other situations, not covered by s 49, where the seller may sue for the price. The most obvious is where the risk has passed to the buyer before the property has passed and the goods are destroyed or lost in an event covered by the concept of 'risk': see *Castle v Playford* (above, p 279) and *Manbre Saccharine Co Ltd v Corn Products Co Ltd* (below, p 455).

(d) Other situations

However, in other situations where it might with justice have been held that the price was payable even though neither of the s 49 requirements had been complied with, the courts have held that the seller has only an action for damages for non-acceptance of the goods under s 50. The unsatisfactory consequence may then be, not only that the seller is kept out of his money for a long time, but that he is left with the goods on his hands and the burden of seeing to their disposal. These are cases where the buyer by his own wrongful act has prevented the price from becoming due and payable, such as the two following.

Stein, Forbes & Co v County Tailoring Co (1916) 86 LJKB 448, King's Bench Division

Stein Forbes contracted to sell sheepskins on CIF terms (see below, p 452) to County Tailoring, 'Payment: Net cash against documents on arrival of the steamer'. The steamer arrived, but County Tailoring wrongfully refused to take up the documents or to pay the price. Atkin J held them liable in damages but not bound to pay the price.

Atkin J held that the defendants had been guilty of breach of contract, and continued: The material question that remains is as to the plaintiffs' remedy. The plaintiffs have sued only for the price of the goods. Their counsel contended that they were entitled to the price, even though the property in the goods had not passed to the defendants, on the ground that here was a sum certain payable at a fixed time, and that, as the defendants had prevented delivery, they could not rely upon non-delivery. I do not think, however, that the plaintiffs can establish their claim on that footing. This is not the case of a day being appointed for payment of money, and the day happening before the thing which is the consideration for the payment. In such a case, which falls within one of the well known rules in the notes to *Pordage v Cole* [1669] 1 Wms Saund (1871 ed), 548 at 551, the money can be claimed before performance. Such a case is provided for by the Sale of Goods Act 1893, s 49, sub-s 2. But this is not a case where the price is payable on a day certain irrespective of delivery. On the contrary, it is payable expressly against delivery.

Counsel for the plaintiffs further said that the property had in fact passed to the defendants, and that, upon the plaintiffs being willing to transfer possession, they were entitled to the price. I think that there are many objections to this view. At what time property passes under a contract of sale depends upon the intention of the parties.

[His Lordship read ss 16 and 17, sub-s 1 of the Sale of Goods Act 1893, and continued:]

The Act provides certain rules for ascertaining the intention of the parties unless a different intention appears. Counsel for the plaintiffs contends that, as soon as the goods are unconditionally appropriated to the contract and the seller holds the documents at the disposal of the buyer, the property passes. The value of that proposition depends on the meaning of 'unconditionally.' I doubt whether goods are appropriated unconditionally if the seller does not mean the buyer to have them unless he pays for them. But it seems to me impossible to lay down a general rule applicable to all cif contracts. The overruling question is, 'Does the intention of the parties appear in the course of the making and the fulfilment of the contract?'

[His Lordship read s 19 of the Sale of Goods Act 1893, and continued:]

In the present case the goods were shipped at New York on behalf of the plaintiffs, and the bill of lading was taken to the order of the banking firm which financed the transaction for the plaintiffs. On arrival of the ship the plaintiffs had to take up the bill of lading from the bankers, and, as the defendants would not take up the documents, the plaintiffs had to take delivery of the goods from the ship. It seems quite plain that the seller or his banker reserved the *jus disponendi*. It was said that the property passed to the buyer on shipment, and the seller only received his unpaid vendor's lien. That view seems to me inconsistent with s 19 of the Sale of Goods Act 1893, and with every business probability.

   Then it is said that, whatever the original intention may be, at any rate the property passes when there is an appropriation of specific goods, as by the invoice in this case and a tender or willingness to tender. It would be a remarkable intention in a commercial man to keep the property on shipment in order to secure payment, but yet in taking the necessary steps to procure payment by appropriation and tender to part with the property before payment is in fact made. I think that in such cases the ordinary inference to be drawn is that the seller does not intend to part with the property except against payment. It seems to me that this view is confirmed by the provision of s 19, sub-s 3 of the Act.

   Unless the property has passed, I do not think that in this case the plaintiffs can sue for the price, and in my opinion it has not passed. The plaintiffs' claim is, therefore, for damages.

Colley v Overseas Exporters Ltd [1921] 3 KB 302, King's Bench Division

Colley agreed to sell leather belting to the defendant company on FOB terms (see below, p 447). The contract obliged the buyers to nominate a ship on to which the seller was to make arrangements to load the goods, and provided that the price was to be paid when delivery was made to the ship. The buyers failed to nominate a ship, despite five abortive attempts, and the goods lay on the docks. It was held that the seller could not sue for the price, even though it was due to the buyer's own default that the event which would have made the price payable under the contract had not occurred.

McCardie J: This action is brought upon a writ specially indorsed within Order xiv to recover the sum of £985 17s 4d alleged to be due from the defendants to the plaintiff as the price of goods. The only question is whether that liquidated sum is due. No question arises as yet as to damages against the defendants. The case raises a point of legal interest and practical utility as to the circumstances under which the purchase price of goods can be sued for. . . .

   The defendants committed no deliberate breach of contract; they suffered a series of misfortunes. They failed however to name an effective ship. The plaintiff on his part did all he could to carry out his obligations. Under these circumstances the plaintiff seeks to recover the price of the goods in question. The able argument of Mr Willes for the plaintiff rested on two well-known passages in the judgment of Lord Blackburn in *Mackay v Dick* ((1881) 6

App Cas 251). The first passage is this: 'I think I may safely say, as a general rule, that where in a written contract it appears that both parties have agreed that something shall be done, which cannot effectually be done unless both concur in doing it, the construction of the contract is that each agrees to do all that is necessary to be done on his part for the carrying out of that thing, though there may be no express words to that effect.' The second passage is this: 'It would follow in point of law that the defender having had the machine delivered to him, was by his contract to keep it, unless on a fair test according to the contract it failed to do the stipulated quantity of work, in which case he would be entitled to call on the pursuers to remove it. And *by his own default* he can now never be in a position to call upon the pursuers to take back the machine, on the ground that the test had not been satisfied, he must, as far as regards that, keep, and consequently pay for it.' I will consider later on the facts in *Mackay v Dick*. The contention of Mr Willes before me was that inasmuch as the defendants' own fault had here prevented the goods from being put on board they were disabled from saying that the price, which would have been payable if and when the goods had actually been put on board, was not now due to the plaintiff. This is a novel and interesting submission. An action for the price of goods is, of course, essentially an action for a liquidated sum. It involves special and technical elements. . . .

The circumstances . . . under which a claim to the price may be made (as distinguished from a claim of damages for breach of contract) are indicated in s 49 of [the Sale of Goods] Act.

[His Lordship read the section, and continued:]

Here sub-s 2 of s 49 does not apply, as it apparently did in *Workman, Clark & Co v Lloyd Brazileño* ([1908] 1 KB 968), where the price was payable by stated instalments on stated dates. The parties before me here made no special agreement as to the payment of the price. Nor can it be said that sub-s 1 of s 49 applies here, for the property in the goods has not in fact and law passed to the buyer. Several rules for the passing of property in sale of goods contracts are indicated in ss 16, 17, 18, and also in s 32. The Act does not deal specifically with fob or cif contracts. Judicially settled rules exist however with respect to them. I need only deal with fob contracts. The presumed intention (see s 18 of the Act) of the parties has been settled. It seems clear that in the absence of special agreement the property and risk in goods does not in the case of an fob contract pass from the seller to the buyer till the goods are actually put on board: see *Browne v Hare* ((1859) 4 H & N 822); *Inglis v Stock* ((1885) 10 App Cas 263); *Wimble v Rosenberg* ([1913] 3 KB 743) Benjamin on Sale, 6th ed, p 785, where several useful cases are collected. Unless therefore the principle involved in the words of Lord Blackburn in the second passage cited from *Mackay v Dick* applies here the plaintiff will fail. Does the principle go to the extent submitted by Mr Willes? It is well to consider *Mackay v Dick*. The headnote says: 'If, in the case of a contract of sale and delivery, which makes acceptance of the thing sold and payment of the price conditional on a certain thing being done by the seller, the buyer prevents the possibility of the seller fulfilling the condition, the contract is to be taken as satisfied.' If this headnote be given its full apparent effect then the principle it suggests would be most far reaching and the results extraordinary. The facts in *Mackay v Dick* must be remembered. Concisely put they were these. By a contract in two letters the seller agreed to sell and deliver at the buyer's works a digging machine. The price of £1125 was payable after the machine had satisfactorily performed certain tests. If it failed to perform them the buyer was to remove the machine. The machine was actually delivered into the buyer's possession. Owing however to the buyer's own default it did not perform the tests. He refused to pay the price, and the seller thereupon brought his action for the £1125. The plaintiff succeeded on the principle stated by Lord Blackburn. It is to be clearly noted that a specific machine was fully deliverable by the seller to the buyer. Apparently the property in the machine actually passed to the buyer. . . . Hence I think that the sale and delivery of the machine must in *Mackay v Dick* be deemed to have been complete, and payment of the price was therefore subject only to the 'resolutive condition' imposed by the clause as to the test: see Chalmers' Sale of Goods, 8th ed, pp 6, 7, and the cases there cited as to resolutive conditions. Default by the buyer as to the test was proved, and thus the seller got his judgment for the price. The actual decision in *Mackay v*

Dick does not therefore aid the plaintiff here. The real question is as to the extent to which the principle indicated by Lord Blackburn in the second passage I have quoted operates to make a price payable which, apart from that principle, would not be payable. Although, as I have said, *Mackay v Dick* turned on Scotch law yet I think that that principle is equally well settled in English law. . . .

Now in deciding whether the argument of Mr Willes in this case be sound, and in determining the extent to which the principle stated in the second cited passage from Lord Blackburn may be applied, it is necessary to remember the law which existed before the Act of 1893 was passed. In former days an action for the price of goods would only lie upon one or other of two counts. First, upon the indebitatus count for goods sold and delivered, which was pleaded as follows: 'Money payable by the defendant to the plaintiff for goods sold and delivered by the plaintiff to the defendant': Bullen and Leake, Precedents of Pleading, 3rd ed, p 38. This count would not lie before delivery: *Boulter v Arnott* ((1833) 1 Cr & M 333). The count was applicable where upon a sale of goods the property had passed and the goods had been delivered to the purchaser and the price was payable at the time of action brought. Secondly, upon the indebitatus count for goods bargained and sold, which was pleaded as follows: 'Money payable by the defendant to the plaintiff for goods bargained and sold by the plaintiff to the defendant': Bullen and Leake, p 39. This count was applicable where upon a sale of goods the property had passed to the purchaser and the contract had been completed in all respects except delivery, and the delivery was not a part of the consideration for the price or a condition precedent to its payment. If the property had not passed the count would not lie: *Atkinson v Bell* ((1828) 8 B & C 277). In my view the law as to the circumstances under which an action will lie for the price of goods has not been changed by the Sale of Goods Act 1893. That enactment appears to crystallise and confirm the old law. . . .

In my opinion . . . no action will lie for the price of goods until the property has passed, save only in the special cases provided for by s 49, sub-s 2. This seems plain both on the code and on common law principle. I have searched in vain for authority to the contrary. A clear distinction exists between cases where the default of the buyer has occurred after the property has passed and cases where that default has been before the property has passed. To the former cases *Mackay v Dick* may be applied on appropriate facts. To the latter cases *Mackay v Dick* does not apply so as to enable the buyer to recover the price as distinguished from damages for breach of contract. To hold that *Mackay v Dick* applies where the property has not passed would lead to extraordinary results. Here the substantial allegation against the defendants is that their default prevented the plaintiff from passing the property and so entitling him to the price. Just the same default however would, in substance, have been committed if the defendants had repudiated the contract before the goods had been sent from Sheffield. So too every buyer who refuses to take delivery of unascertained goods and thereby prevents the transference of property in them from the seller commits a similar default. If the ingenious contention of Mr Willes were correct it would be difficult to imagine a case of sale of goods, even though unascertained, to which *Mackay v Dick* would not apply. . . .

It follows therefore for the reasons given that the plaintiff is not entitled to recover the price of the goods in question. If he desires to claim damages he must amend his writ. On the record at present before me he cannot ask for judgment.

Where by the terms of a contract of sale the price is to be paid by instalments, each payable 'on a day certain', each instalment of the price may be sued for as it becomes due: *Workman, Clark & Co Ltd v Lloyd Brazileno* [1908] 1 KB 968, CA – a case like *Re Blyth Shipbuilding & Dry Docks Co Ltd* (above, p 270), where the price of a ship to be built for the buyer was to be paid for by five instalments as the work progressed. In a case like this, we can see again the advantage of an action for the price, in comparison with a mere claim for damages: if the seller cannot sue for instalments of the price, when due, his position will be particularly onerous, as he will be left with an uncompleted ship and no source to look to to maintain his cash-flow.

(e) The right to interest on the price

Section 54 preserves any right that the seller may have, apart from the Act, to claim interest on the price. At common law, interest is payable only if the contract so provides; but the courts now have a wide statutory discretion to award interest in many cases, eg under the Supreme Court Act 1981, s 35A. In practice, interest is regularly awarded in commercial claims for debt.

2 Action for damages for non-acceptance

The seller may bring an action against the buyer for damages for non-acceptance when the buyer has wrongfully neglected to accept and pay for the goods (s 50(1)). The buyer has a counterpart claim against the seller for damages for non-delivery (s 51(1)). Both sections then go on to state in similar terms the rule as to remoteness of damage which contract lawyers will recognise as the 'first rule' in *Hadley v Baxendale* (1854) 9 Exch 341: that the measure of damages is the estimated loss directly and naturally resulting, in the ordinary course of events, from the defendant party's breach of contract (ss 50(2), 51(2)); and they then continue with a statement of another well-known formula for the assessment of damages, the 'market price' rule (ss 50(3), 51(3)). For the action for damages for non-acceptance, this reads as follows:

> Where there is an available market for the goods in question the measure of damages is prima facie to be ascertained by the difference between the contract price and the market or current price at the time or times when the goods ought to have been accepted or (if no time was fixed for acceptance) at the time of the refusal to accept (s 50(3)).

Thus, the statutory rules restate principles which are part of the normal damages rules in the law of contract. But they go only so far: they do not, for instance, mention the 'second rule' in *Hadley v Baxendale*, which deals with claims for 'unusual' losses for which the buyer is deemed to have assumed liability by reason of special facts known to the parties at the time when the contract was entered into. In such cases, we must fall back on the common law.

The 'market price' rule is closely connected with the general principle that a party seeking damages is under an obligation to take steps to mitigate his loss. If, when the buyer refuses to accept the goods, there is a market where other buyers are ready to take them off the seller's hands and to pay the going price for them, he will have discharged his duty to mitigate if he disposes of the goods promptly to such a buyer. Looking at it the other way, if the seller does not do this and he is later able to obtain only a smaller price for the goods – perhaps because they have deteriorated, or because demand has fallen off – the buyer will rightly be able to argue that he should not be liable for the whole of the seller's loss because the opportunity to mitigate was not taken.

Section 50(3) will apply only if there is an 'available market' for the goods in question. There have been various judicial definitions of this term. It is sufficient to quote one, from the judgment of Jenkins LJ in *Charter v Sullivan* [1957] 2 QB 117 at 128, CA:

> I . . . will content myself with the negative proposition that I doubt if there can be an available market for particular goods in any sense relevant to s 50(3) of the Sale of Goods Act [1979] unless those goods are available for sale in the market at the market or current price in the sense of the price, whatever it may be, fixed by reference to supply and

demand as the price at which a purchaser for the goods in question can be found, be it greater or less than or equal to the contract price.

In that case, the contract was for the sale of a new Hillman car, at a time when the retail price of all such cars was fixed by the manufacturers. Jenkins LJ held that in these circumstances s 50(3) should not be applied, since the price of Hillman cars was not free to fluctuate in response to supply and demand. Since demand for such cars then exceeded the supply available, and the seller had been able to resell the car for the same price within a few days, he had suffered no loss and was held entitled only to nominal damages. This case may be contrasted with *W L Thompson Ltd v Robinson (Gunmakers) Ltd* [1955] Ch 177, where once again the retail price of the car (a 'Vanguard') was fixed by the manufacturers, but at that time the supply of Vanguard cars exceeded the demand. This meant that when the buyer refused to accept the car the seller lost the profit on a sale, and he was awarded this sum as damages for loss of bargain. In *Lazenby Garages Ltd v Wright* [1976] 1 WLR 459, CA, it was held that there is no 'available market' for secondhand cars: the court took the rather surprising view that every secondhand car is a unique article, so that the measure of the seller's loss if the buyer refuses to accept is not reckoned by reference to a market price, but by the actual loss (if any) which the seller has sustained.

Section 50(3) states that the relevant market price is that available at the *time* of the failure or refusal to accept. It is also established by the cases that a similar test applies in regard to the *place* of the relevant market: the court asks whether a market existed for goods of the contract description at the place where the buyer ought to have taken delivery, and uses as a yardstick the price prevailing on that market.

More complicated questions may arise where there is an *anticipatory* repudiation by the buyer which is accepted by the seller: although, once again, damages are prima facie to be assessed by reference to the market price at the time when the goods ought to have been accepted – ie the time fixed for delivery by the contract (s 50(3)), the seller's duty to mitigate his loss may well place him under an obligation to resell the goods as soon as possible after he has accepted the buyer's repudiation, if this takes place against the background of a falling market. (If the seller does not accept the repudiation, of course, he is under no duty to mitigate until an actual breach occurs: *Tredegar Iron & Coal Co Ltd v Hawthorn Bros & Co* (1902) 18 TLR 716.)

Further difficult issues may be encountered in the case of an international sale, where the buyer's breach takes place after the goods have been shipped. If there is an available market for such goods 'afloat', to which the seller can have recourse, the price on this market will be appropriate; but if there is not, the first possible place where he will be able to dispose of them will be the port of arrival. (Section 50(3) is, after all, only a prima facie rule.) Thus, in *Muller, MacLean & Co v Leslie & Anderson* (1921) 8 Ll L Rep 328, the contract was for a consignment of padlocks FOB New York, to be shipped to India. The buyers wrongly refused to accept the shipping documents after the goods had been shipped. Damages were awarded to the sellers based on the market price in India at the time of the ship's arrival.

Where, because there is no available market, s 50(3) does not apply, the court must fall back on the ordinary rules of the law of contract as to the assessment of damages, estimating the seller's loss as best it can. If he has lost a profit on a retail sale, as in *Thompson v Robinson* (above), he can claim the amount of that profit. If he has resold to a substitute buyer at a lower price, the resale price will be at least prima facie evidence of his loss.

The seller will also be able to claim as damages the reasonable costs of reselling the goods and any incidental expenses, eg for storage, transport, etc. This is confirmed by s 37(1).

3 Seller's right to terminate contract upon breach or repudiation by buyer

If the buyer wrongfully fails or refuses to perform one or more of his obligations under the contract, this may be a breach or repudiation of the contract which will allow the seller to terminate the contract and treat himself as discharged from further performance. Whether he can do so or not falls to be determined by normal contract principles. Thus, in *Bunge Corpn v Tradax SA* [1981] 1 WLR 711, HL, the buyers were required by a term of the contract to provide a vessel and to give the sellers at least 15 days' notice of the readiness of the vessel to load. They were four days late in doing so. It was held that this provision as to time was a condition, breach of which entitled the sellers to treat the contract as repudiated. A similar consequence would follow where the buyer is held to have been in breach of an intermediate or innominate term, and the breach is regarded as serious.

4 Remedies of an unpaid seller

(a) Introduction

In addition to the remedies described above, which are simply applications to the law of sale of ordinary principles of the law of contract, the Act confers additional remedies upon a seller who is *unpaid*. These are set out in s 39(2) as follows:

(1) a *lien* on the goods or right to retain them for the price while he is in possession of them;

(2) in the case of the insolvency of the buyer, a right of *stopping the goods in transit* after he has parted with the possession of them; and

(3) a *right of resale*, as limited by the Act.

Section 39(2) states that an unpaid seller who is still the owner of the goods (ie where the property has not passed to the buyer) has rights analogous to the right of lien and stoppage in transit set out in s 39(1). This confirms that the rights of the seller in such a case are no less than they would be if the property had passed. It is arguable that he would in many circumstances be able to assert such rights anyway, by virtue of the fact that he is the owner of the goods; but the Act removes any doubts which there might be on the point.

The rights described in s 39(1) and elaborated in the rest of Part V of the Act are described as 'rights against the goods'. In contrast with the seller's rights to sue for the price and for damages, which are rights to proceed *in personam* against the buyer by way of a money claim in the courts, these rights give the seller powers, in the nature of self-help remedies, which he can exercise directly against the goods. For this reason, they are sometimes referred to as the seller's 'real' remedies.

A seller is an 'unpaid seller' for the purposes of s 39 in the circumstances set out in s 38(1). This will be the case

(1)   when the whole of the price has not been paid or tendered; or
(2)   when a bill of exchange or other negotiable instrument has been received by the seller as conditional payment, and the condition on which it was received has not been fulfilled by reason of the dishonour of the instrument or otherwise.

By s 38(2), certain other persons are given the same rights as the seller – an agent of the seller to whom a bill of lading respecting the goods has been indorsed, and a consignor or agent who has himself paid or is directly responsible to the buyer for the price.

The question whether a seller is 'unpaid' turns simply upon the *fact* whether payment has been made (or tendered) or not: it is not concerned with the rights and wrongs of the situation, such as whether payment is actually due. A seller who has agreed to allow his buyer credit is thus an unpaid seller, even during the time when the period for credit is still running. Note also (1) that a seller is 'unpaid' so long as *any part* of the price is outstanding, and (2) that if payment has been *tendered*, this is treated as equivalent to payment, so that a seller who has refused to accept payment when tendered will lose his unpaid seller's remedies.

Where the seller has accepted a cheque or other negotiable instrument in payment of the price, the normal understanding is that he receives it as a conditional payment, rather than in satisfaction of the buyer's obligations. In this case, his remedies as an unpaid seller are suspended while the instrument is current, but revive if the instrument is dishonoured, or if the buyer becomes insolvent.

(b) Unpaid seller's lien

The unpaid seller's right of *lien* is his right, if he is in possession of the goods, to retain possession of them until the price is paid or tendered (s 41(1)). A lien is thus a form of possessory security. As discussed more fully in Chapter 23, it is a right to *retain* goods which are already in the party's possession (in contrast with the pledge, which is based on a *delivery* of possession). Not every unpaid seller may claim a lien. The right arises in the following cases (s 41(1)):

(1)   where the goods have been sold without any stipulation as to credit;
(2)   where the goods have been sold on credit but the term of credit has expired;
(3)   where the buyer becomes insolvent.

The seller may assert his lien even though he is in possession as the buyer's bailee or agent (s 41(2)).

A seller has a right of lien even though part only of the price is unpaid (s 38(1)(a)); and he may exercise his lien (for the whole price, if appropriate) against part only of the goods, if he has already delivered the rest to the buyer, unless he is held to have waived his lien (s 42).

An unpaid seller loses his lien in three circumstances (s 43(1)):

(1)   when he delivers the goods to a carrier or other bailee for the purpose of transmission to the buyer without reserving the right of disposal of the goods;
(2)   when the buyer or his agent lawfully obtains possession of the goods;
(3)   by waiver.

In addition, of course, he will lose his lien if the price is paid or tendered to him; but not by reason only that he obtains a judgment for the price (s 43(2)).

Section 43(1) underlines the essential nature of the lien as a right to *retain* possession: if the unpaid seller parts with the goods, he cannot reassert his lien even if he gets back possession: *Valpy v Gibson*, below. He may also lose his lien by delivering the goods to a carrier for the purpose of transmission to the buyer, unless he 'reserves the right of disposal' – a phrase which, as we saw in relation to s 19 (above, p 293), most often refers to a seller who ships goods and takes the bill of lading in his own name.

Valpy v Gibson (1847) 4 CB 837, Court of Common Pleas

Brown, a merchant in Birmingham, bought cloth from Gibson. Gibson sent the cloth to Leech, Harrison & Co, shipping agents, at Liverpool, in four cases marked for shipment to Valparaiso, requesting Leech & Co to put them on board as directed by Brown. After the goods had been loaded on to a ship, Brown's agent, Alison, ordered them to be returned to Gibson to be repacked in eight cases instead of four. Gibson was still in possession of the goods, and unpaid, when Brown was declared bankrupt. It was held that it was too late for Gibson to claim an unpaid seller's lien.

The judgment of the court (Wilde CJ, Coltman, Maule and Cresswell JJ) was delivered by **Wilde CJ:** With regard to the right of stoppage in transitu, it appears to us, that, though the defendants knew the goods were to be sent to Valparaiso, and so informed Leech, Harrison & Co, when they forwarded them to Liverpool, yet that Leech, Harrison & Co, could not, simply on that information, forward the goods to Valparaiso, but that they held them subject to such orders as Brown might give as to forwarding them to Valparaiso, or elsewhere; and the transitus was consequently at an end as soon as the goods came to the hands of Leech, Harrison & Co. But, when Leech, Harrison & Co, by the order of Brown, re-landed the goods; and, by order of Alison (who must be taken to have acted under the authority of Brown), sent them to the defendants to be re-packed, the possession of the goods, as well as the property, vested in Brown, who, in causing them to be re-landed and sent to the defendants, dealt with the good as owner; and this would certainly put an end to the transitus, even if it had not been determined, as we think it was, by the original delivery to Leech, Harrison & Co.

The right which it was contended the defendants had, as vendors in the actual and lawful possession of the goods, on the insolvency of the vendee, cannot, we think, be sustained. The goods being sold on credit, and the complete property and possession having vested in Brown, they became his absolutely, without any lien or right of the vendors attaching to them, any more than on any other property of Brown; and their delivery to the defendants to be re-packed, could not have the effect of creating a lien for the price, without an agreement to that effect. We therefore think there must be judgment for the plaintiffs.

Section 43(1) has to be read in conjunction with s 47, which describes other situations in which an unpaid seller will lose his right of lien. (Section 47 also applies to the unpaid seller's right of stoppage in transit (below, p 398).) There is a further overlap: s 47 links in also with s 25(1) and the almost identical Factors Act 1889, s 9 (concerning sales by a buyer in possession), which we discussed as an exception to the *nemo dat* rule (see above, p 332). Section 47 is concerned with the effect on the unpaid seller's real remedies of a sub-sale or other disposition of the goods made by the buyer. It reads:

(1) Subject to this Act, the unpaid seller's right of lien or retention or stoppage in transit is not affected by any sale or other disposition of the goods which the buyer may have made, unless the seller has assented to it.
(2) Where a document of title to goods has been lawfully transferred to any person as buyer or owner of the goods, and that person transfers the document to a person who takes it in good faith and for valuable consideration, then

(a) if the last-mentioned transfer was by way of sale, the unpaid seller's right of lien or retention or stoppage in transit is defeated; and

(b) if the last-mentioned transfer was made by way of pledge or other disposition for value, the unpaid seller's right of lien or retention or stoppage in transit can only be exercised subject to the rights of the transferee.

Note that in the Act of 1893, s 47 was not divided into subsections; instead, what is now s 47(2) appeared as a proviso to the general rule now stated in s 47(1).

Section 47(2) deals with the position when the seller has delivered or transferred a 'document of title' to the buyer. (For the definition of this term, see above, p 330.) It is important to note that the mere fact that the seller has handed a document of title to the buyer will not of itself affect the seller's rights of lien and stoppage: there must be *two* 'transfers' of the document before s 47(2) can apply.

Mordaunt Bros v British Oil and Cake Mills Ltd illustrates the general proposition stated in s 47(1), while *Mount v Jay* throws light on the two exceptions referred to in s 47: assent of the seller (s 47(1)), and the transfer of a document of title (s 47(2)(a)); however, on the special facts of the case, the wording of s 25(1) proved to be more appropriate than that of s 47(2)(a).

Mordaunt Bros v British Oil and Cake Mills Ltd [1910] 2 KB 502, King's Bench Division

BOCM contracted to sell various lots of boiled linseed oil to Crichton Bros, who resold it to Mordaunts. Mordaunts had paid Crichtons all or most of the price of their purchases. Possession remained with BOCM, who had not been paid by Crichtons. Delivery orders had been sent by Crichtons to BOCM, directing BOCM to deliver to Mordaunts an amount of oil appropriate to each contract, which BOCM usually acknowledged and recorded in its books. It was held that these acts did not constitute an 'assent' by BOCM to the resale for the purposes of s 47(1).

Pickford J: It was next argued that the plaintiffs were entitled to succeed by virtue of s 47 of the Sale of Goods Act 1893, on the ground that the defendants had assented to the sales by Crichton Brothers to the plaintiffs. Several cases were cited in which it was held that unpaid vendors had assented to sub-sales so as to preclude themselves from asserting their right of lien. As a matter of fact all those cases related to sub-sales of specific goods. I am not, however, going to decide that s 47 has no application to unascertained goods; but I wish to point out that such acts as presenting to an unpaid vendor delivery orders in favour of sub-purchasers and the entry accordingly of the names of the sub-purchasers in the books of the unpaid vendor may have a very different effect according as the goods are specific or unascertained. In the former case it may be more readily inferred that the unpaid vendor has assumed the position of an agent or bailee holding the goods for and on behalf of the sub-purchaser or holder of the delivery order, and the acceptance of the delivery order and entry of the holder's name in the books by the unpaid vendor might in the case of specific goods justify the inference that the unpaid vendor had accepted that position. No such inference could be drawn if the goods were not in existence, and it does not follow that because the inference may be drawn in the case of specific goods it will also be drawn in the case of goods in existence but unascertained. In my opinion the assent which affects the unpaid seller's right of lien must be such an assent as in the circumstances shews that the seller intends to renounce his rights against the goods. It is not enough to shew that the fact of a sub-contract has been brought to his notice and that he has assented to it merely in the sense of acknowledging the receipt of the information. His assent to the sub-contract in that sense would simply mean that he acknowledged the right of the purchaser under the sub-contract to have the goods subject to his own paramount right under the contract with his original purchaser to hold the goods until he is paid the purchase-money. Such an assent would imply no intention of making delivery to a sub-purchaser until payment was made under the original contract. The assent contemplated by s 47 of the Sale of Good Act 1893, means something more than that; it means an assent given in such circumstances as shew that the unpaid seller intends that the sub-contract shall be carried out irrespective of the terms of the original contract.

Now in the circumstances of this case what was the effect of the inquiry by the plaintiffs whether the delivery orders of Crichton Brothers were 'in order' and the defendants' reply that they were? I think some light is thrown on the nature and purpose of this inquiry by the fact that the plaintiffs parted with their money before making the inquiry. Neither party regarded those inquiries as directed to the questions whether the defendants were to hold the oil as agents for the plaintiffs, renouncing any rights they might have to hold the goods till they were paid for by Crichton Brothers, and whether they were prepared to deliver to the plaintiffs and look elsewhere than to the goods themselves for any rights they might have in respect of them. Whatever might have been the effect of such an inquiry and answer in a case where specific goods were in question, I think in the present case where the goods were unascertained the inquiry and answer amounted to no more than this – that the defendants were ready to carry out the contract between themselves and Crichton Brothers with this modification, that delivery should be made to the plaintiffs instead of to Crichton Brothers, but that the delivery should be subject to all the other terms and incidents of the contract with Crichton Brothers.

In two or three instances a certain portion of the goods specified in delivery orders was delivered before the defendants refused to make any further deliveries. In my opinion that makes no difference; it simply means that they were carrying out their contract with Crichton Brothers so long as that firm were punctual in their payments. In my opinion the plaintiffs' case fails and there must be judgment for the defendants.

D F Mount Ltd v Jay & Jay (Provisions) Co Ltd [1960] 1 QB 159, Queen's Bench Division

(For the facts and another part of the decision, see above, p 339. This part of Salmon J's judgment is concerned with the question of 'assent'.)

Salmon J: The case raises the familiar problem – which of two innocent persons, the plaintiffs or the defendants, shall suffer for the trickery of a rogue.

The plaintiffs rely first on s 47 of the Sale of Goods Act 1893.

[His Lordship read s 47, and continued:]

There is a proviso to the section, with which I shall deal in a moment. The plaintiffs contend that the defendants assented to the sale or disposition of the 250 cartons by Merrick to the plaintiffs, and thereby lost their right as unpaid sellers to the lien which they would otherwise have had upon the cartons. The defendants contend that if they assented to the sub-sale by Merrick, their assent was not an assent within the meaning of s 47, and rely upon *Mordaunt Bros v British Oil and Cake Mills Ltd* [above]. It is clear from Pickford J's judgment in that case that the assent contemplated by s 47 means 'an assent given in such circumstances as show that the unpaid seller intends that the sub-contract shall be carried out irrespective of the terms of the original contract' and must be 'such an assent as in the circumstances shows that the seller intends to renounce his rights against the goods.' Pickford J held that there had been no such assent on the part of the sellers.

The facts of that case are, however, very different from those of the present case. There the sellers had at no time any reason to doubt the buyer's ability to pay, and were not informed of the sub-sale until after the sale was effected. Pickford J held that the sellers had assented to the sub-sale merely in the sense that they acknowledged its existence and the right of the sub-buyer to have the goods subject to their own paramount rights under the contract with the original buyer to hold the goods until paid the purchase price.

In the present case the defendants were anxious to get rid of the goods on a falling market. They knew that Merrick could only pay for them out of the money he obtained from his customers, and that he could only obtain the money from his customers against delivery orders in favour of those customers. In my view, the true inference is that the defendants assented to Merrick reselling the goods, in the sense that they intended to renounce their rights against the goods and to take the risk of Merrick's honesty. The defendants are reputable merchants and I am sure that it was not their intention to get rid of their goods on a falling market through Merrick on the basis that, if he defaulted, they could hold the goods against the customers from whom he obtained the money out of which they were to be paid. . . .

[His Lordship then expressed the view that it was immaterial that the goods were unascertained: see above, p 339.]

[Salmon J also upheld a second argument that Mount was entitled to succeed under s 25(1) (see above, p 339), since Merrick, the first buyer, had received a document of title from Jays and had delivered a second document of title to Mount. It would not have been possible for Mount to rely on the similar provision in s 47(2), however, because the language of s 47(2) is clearly restricted to the case where the *same* document of title is transferred to the sub-buyer.]

QUESTIONS

1. Is it reasonable to suppose that the draftsman of the Act intended s 25(1) to be construed differently from s 47(2)?
2. Both the cases cited above accept that s 47(2) can apply to a sale of unascertained goods, which have at no stage been appropriated to the contract. Section 39(2) may give some support to this view. But could not Jays have responded to Mount's demand simply by saying that whatever peaches were still in their hands were their own property, to do what they liked with? Is the decision in *Mount v Jay* consistent with s 16? (On this point, see the contrasting arguments of A G L Nicol (1979) 42 MLR 129 and R M Goode *Proprietary Rights and Insolvency in Sales Transactions* (2nd ed, 1989), pp 64–68.)
3. What would have been the position if Jays had become insolvent after Merrick had sub-sold to Mount and the goods had remained unascertained?

(c) Seller's right to stop the goods in transit

Sections 44–46 set out the second of the unpaid seller's 'real' remedies: to stop the goods if they are still in transit to the buyer, before they have actually reached him. For this remedy to be available, it is not sufficient that the seller should be 'unpaid'; the buyer must also have become insolvent. (For the definition of 'insolvent', see s 61(4), which makes it plain that it is 'commercial' or 'cash-flow' insolvency that matters, and not the buyer's asset position. On insolvency generally, see below, Chapter 27.)

In the Act of 1893, the Latin phrase 'in transitu' was used. The anglicised version was introduced in 1979.

When a seller delivers possession of the goods to a carrier for transmission to the buyer and does not reserve the right of disposal, he loses his lien (s 43(1)(a)). The right of stoppage enables him to resume possession of the goods, at any time during the period that they are in transit, thus allowing him to exercise rights similar to those that he would have under a lien. Once again, s 39(2) confirms that it is immaterial whether the property in the goods has passed to the buyer or not.

The function of the 'carrier' may involve any form of transport: ship, rail, road, air, or a combination of methods.

Section 45 sets out the rules which define the duration of the transit and defines the events in which it will terminate and put an end to the seller's right of stoppage. These events are:

(1) delivery of the goods by the carrier to the buyer or his agent, whether after they have arrived or before they have reached the appointed destination (s 45(1), (2));
(2) attornment by the carrier to the buyer or his agent after they have reached the appointed destination (s 45(3));
(3) a wrongful refusal by the carrier to deliver the goods to the buyer or his agent (s 45(6)).

A delivery of part of the goods does not prevent the seller from exercising his right of stoppage against the remainder, unless the part delivery indicates an agreement to give up possession of the whole of the goods (s 45(7)).

If the buyer rejects the goods and they remain in the possession of the carrier, the transit is deemed to continue, even though the seller has refused to take them back (s 45(4)).

Section 46 describes how the right of stoppage is effected, and defines the obligations of the carrier and the seller in the circumstances. The seller must either take actual possession of the goods, or give notice of his claim to the carrier or other person who has possession of the goods, either directly to that person or to his principal (s 46(1)–(3)). The carrier must then redeliver the goods to the seller at the latter's expense (s 46(4)).

The seller's right of stoppage is not affected by any subsale which the buyer may have made, unless a document of title has been transferred to the buyer and from him to the subpurchaser, in circumstances which bring into play the provisions of s 47(2) (which has been discussed above at p 395 in the context of the unpaid seller's lien). The following cases illustrate the exercise of the seller's right of stoppage.

The *Tigress* (1863) 32 LJPM & A 97, Court of Admiralty

Lucy & Son had sold Bushe wheat which was at sea aboard the *Tigress*, and had endorsed one copy of the bill of lading to Bushe, although they had not been paid. Bushe had become bankrupt while the wheat was still on board. Lucy & Son, purportedly exercising their right of stoppage, directed the master to deliver the wheat to themselves, and tendered payment of the freight. The ship's master refused to deliver the wheat to Lucy & Co without proof that the wheat belonged to them. It was held that he was wrong to do so: he had to assume that the seller was acting within his rights.

Dr Lushington: . . . All that is necessary is for the vendor to assert his claim as vendor and owner. Were it otherwise, were the vendor obliged formally to prove his title to exercise the right of stoppage *in transitu*, that right would be worthless; for the validity of a stoppage *in transitu* depends upon several conditions. First, the vendor must be unpaid; secondly, the vendee must be insolvent; thirdly, the vendee must not have indorsed over for value. But the proof that these conditions have been fulfilled would always be difficult for the vendor – often impossible; for instance, whether the vendor is or is not unpaid may depend upon the balance of a current account; whether the vendee is insolvent may not transpire till afterwards, when the bill of exchange for the goods becomes due. . . . And, lastly, whether the vendee has or has not indorsed the bill of lading over, is a matter not within the cognizance of the vendor. He exercises his right of stoppage *in transitu* at his own peril, and it is incumbent upon the master to give effect to a claim as soon as he is satisfied it is made by the vendor, unless he is aware of a legal defeasance of the vendor's claim. Such, according to my opinion, is the law as laid down by Lord Campbell, in *Gurney v Behrend* ((1854) 3 E & B 622). Lord Campbell uses these words: '*Prima facie* the defendants had a right to stop the wheat, for it was still *in transitu*, and they were unpaid vendors. The onus is on the plaintiffs to prove that they had become the owners, and that the right to stop *in transitu* was gone.' Moreover, I find that the indemnity set out as an exhibit to the petition, and stated in the petition to have been presented to the master, recites that Bushe is the holder of the bill of lading, and claims the wheat under it. So that, in fact, the master had full knowledge of all the circumstances at the time. The defendant then further objects thus: assuming the plaintiffs had a right to stop *in transitu*, and duly asserted that right, yet the master was guilty of no breach of duty in refusing to deliver; he simply is retaining the custody of the wheat for the right owner, as soon as the claim shall be established. Now to this argument I cannot accede; for I think there are cases without number to shew that the right to stop means the right not only to countermand delivery to the vendee, but to order delivery to the vendor. Were it otherwise, the right to stop would be useless, and trade would be impeded. The refusal of the master to deliver upon demand is, in cases like the present, sufficient evidence of conversion – *Wilson v Anderton* ((1830) 1 B & Ad 450). The master may indeed sometimes suffer for an innocent mistake; but he can always protect himself from liability by filing a bill of interpleader in Chancery. For these reasons, I am satisfied that this petition sufficiently shews a *prima facie* case of such breach of duty as renders the vessel liable in this Court, and therefore the objections must be overruled.

Taylor v Great Eastern Rly Co (1901) 17 TLR 394, King's Bench Division

Barnard Bros sold a quantity of barley to Sanders and consigned it to Elsenham station, where the railway company acknowledged that it was holding the grain to Sanders' order. Later, when Sanders became insolvent, Barnard Bros purported to exercise a right of stoppage. But it was held that they could not do so, because the transit had determined when the acknowledgment was issued.

Bigham J: The first question is whether Barnard Brothers were on November 30 entitled to stop the goods as being still *in transitu*. I am of opinion that they were not. The *transitus* was over as soon as a reasonable time had elapsed for Sanders to elect whether he would take the goods away or leave them in the defendants' depôt on rent. Such a reasonable time had elapsed, and, having regard to the fact that it was the practice of the defendants to hold goods for Sanders as warehousekeepers at rent when they were not removed after arrival at the stations, I find that, by agreement between Sanders and the defendants, the goods were at the time when Barnards took them away in the possession of the defendants as warehousekeepers for Sanders. I should have been of the same opinion even if there had been no course of business, for I do not think that after service of a notice such as that used in this case it is competent for a consignee by silence indefinitely to fix upon a railway company the onerous responsibilities of common carriers. I am satisfied that, if the defendants had sued Sanders for rent, Sanders could not have successfully resisted the claim. It was argued that the words in the advice note 'the grain is now held at owner's sole risk and subject to the usual warehouse charges' meant that the goods were held by the defendants on account of whom it might concern, and that 'owners' did not necessarily mean Sanders, but might mean Barnards or any one else who should turn out to be the owners. I do not think there is anything in this point. The advice note is addressed to Sanders for the purpose of affecting him, not for the purpose of affecting any one else, and, moreover, Sanders was the owner of the goods; a right in the vendor to stop *in transitu* does not prevent the buyer from being the owner of the goods; in fact, it necessarily supposes him to be the owner.

Reddall v Union Castle Mail SS Co Ltd (1914) 84 LJKB 360, King's Bench Division

Rutherfords sold a bale of goods to Snow, knowing that he was buying for someone in South Africa. Snow instructed Rutherfords to send the goods to the Union Co's ship *Armadale Castle* at Southampton, to be marked for shipment to Algoa Bay in South Africa. Rutherfords consigned the bale by rail to Southampton as instructed, where Snow, 'in anticipation of insolvency' told the Union Co to 'stop all shipments'. In consequence, the bale did not leave with the ship, but was kept in storage at Snow's expense until it was handed to Rutherfords in response to a claim to stop in transit. Reddall, Snow's trustee in bankruptcy, sued the Union Co in conversion, and was successful: the court ruled that the transit had ceased when the buyers intercepted the goods before they had been loaded.

Bailhache J: I think, upon these facts, the original transit was to Algoa Bay. The cases upon stoppage *in transitu* are very numerous, and, where the transit is made in stages, difficult to reconcile. I think, however, that it is true to say that, where goods are delivered by the seller or his agent to a carrier, and pass at each successive stage of the transit from the hands of one carrier to another, without the intervention of a forwarding agent, to the destination indicated by the buyer to the seller, the transit continues until that destination is reached. It makes no difference in such a case whether an intermediate carrier receives his instructions direct from the buyer or from the seller, provided that those instructions are given to facilitate the transit of the goods upon the journey originally intended and communicated to the buyer. . . .

This does not dispose of the case, because the goods were intercepted at Southampton and the journey to Algoa Bay was stopped. The buyers, not having contracted with the sellers that the goods should go to Algoa Bay, were within their rights in doing this. . . . The defendants thereafter held the goods at rent at the buyers' disposal, and would not and could not have sent them forward to Algoa Bay, or to any other destination, without fresh instructions from the buyers. I think, therefore, that, although the original transit was to Algoa Bay, that transit had been ended at Southampton, and that under the circumstances the pretended stoppage *in transitu* was too late, and the defendants were wrong in delivering the goods to the sellers. Where the original *transitus* is interrupted by the buyers, I think the test is whether the goods will be set in motion again without further orders from the buyers; if not, the transit is ended and the right to stop lost.

There will be judgment, therefore, for the plaintiff in this case.

If, when he receives notice of stoppage, the carrier has a lien on the goods for unpaid freight, the seller is liable to pay the freight, and also the costs of redelivery: *Booth SS Co Ltd v Cargo Fleet Iron Co Ltd* [1916] 2 KB 570, CA.

(d) Rescission and resale by the seller

No automatic rescission. Section 48(1) states that, except as provided later in s 48, a contract of sale is not rescinded by the mere fact that an unpaid seller has exercised his right of lien or stoppage. The contract continues on foot, so that if the buyer (or his trustee in bankruptcy) tenders the price and any other moneys owing, he can require that the goods be delivered to him. If the property in the goods has passed to the buyer, it will remain with him notwithstanding the fact that the seller has exercised his right of lien or stoppage. The seller must take some further step in order to terminate the contract and revest the property in himself or vest it in a new buyer.

Section 48 confusingly runs together various issues which are not necessarily related. Subsections (1), (2) and (3) refer to an *unpaid* seller, but subs (4) applies to all sellers; subss (1) and (4) and (it has been held, by implication, also) subs (3), are concerned with the question of 'rescission' of the contract of sale – but not subs (2); while subss (3) and (4) deal with a seller's *right* of resale (as explained below), whereas in contrast subs (2) is concerned with the *effect* of a resale, whether rightful or not! We shall do our best to disentangle these questions in the discussion that follows.

When the seller has a right of resale. Section 48(3)–(4) sets out the circumstances in which a seller has a right of resale, and the consequences of such a resale. The use of the word 'right' is important. We saw earlier that a seller who continues or is in possession of the goods has the power in certain circumstances to confer a good title upon a second buyer if he resells the goods (s 24; Factors Act 1889, s 8: above, p 327). But those provisions give the seller nothing more than the *power* to pass a good title: a seller who relies on s 24 or s 8 without more will, at least prima facie, be acting in breach of his contract with the first buyer and liable to him in damages accordingly. If the property has passed to the buyer, he may also be liable to him in tort. However, if the seller resells in exercise of a *right* to do so, he will not be so liable. In fact, it is only s 48(4) which expressly states that the contract of sale is rescinded when the seller exercises his right of resale, but this was held to be also implicit in s 48(3) in *R V Ward Ltd v Bignall* (below). The three situations in which s 48 confers such a right are:

(1) where the *unpaid* seller gives *notice* to the buyer of his intention to resell, and the buyer does not within a reasonable time pay or tender the price (s 48(3));
(2) where the seller is *unpaid* and the goods are *perishable* (s 48(3));
(3) where the seller *expressly reserves* the right of resale in case the buyer should make default (s 48(4)).

R V Ward Ltd v Bignall [1967] 1 QB 534, Court of Appeal

On 6 May Bignall contracted to buy from Wards two cars, a Vanguard estate and a Ford Zodiac, for a total price of £850, paying a deposit of £25. Later in the same day, he refused to pay the balance or take delivery of either car. Wards the next day gave notice to him through their solicitors that if he did not complete the purchase by 11 May they would dispose of the cars. The Vanguard was later sold for £350, but the Zodiac remained unsold. In this action Wards sued Bignall, claiming the balance of the contract price less the amount received for the Vanguard, together with certain expenses. The Court of Appeal held that by reselling the Vanguard, Wards had rescinded the whole contract, so that their only claim was for damages for non-acceptance, obliging them to bring into account the market value of the unsold Zodiac, which remained their property.

Sellers LJ: I would hold that the property had not passed to the buyer; all that has happened since May 6, 1965, fits in with that view, and is not in harmony with the two vehicles having been transferred to the buyer when the bargain was made. The plaintiffs' remedy was rightly pursued below as damages for non-acceptance.

I need not develop that further, as, in my view, the result of this case would be the same whether the property had passed at the time of the sale or not.

As soon as the appeal was opened on behalf of the defendant against the judgment for £497 10s, counsel for the plaintiffs, the respondents here, asked leave to amend the grounds of his cross-appeal. His contention was that the claim throughout had been for the balance of the price of the two cars bargained and sold, and that the Zodiac car had been the defendant's vehicle and not the plaintiffs' since the moment of the contract of sale. He relied on s 48 of the Sale of Goods Act 1893. . . .

The question on this part of the appeal is whether, [on the assumption that] the property passed on the sale, the Zodiac car which has not been [resold] remains the buyer's property so that the action of the plaintiffs is for the price, or whether by the sale of the Vanguard the plaintiffs have rescinded the whole contract on the buyer's breach of it so that the ownership of the Zodiac reverted back to the plaintiffs and their remedy is in damages under the statute, or, in effect, damages for non-acceptance, giving credit for what they have received from the sale of the goods or part thereof.

Subsections (1) and (2) of s 48 speak clearly. Subsection (4) expressly provides: 'the original contract of sale is thereby rescinded.' That was necessary because, where the seller 'expressly reserves a right of re-sale in case the buyer should make default,' a seller who re-sold under such a contract would be applying and affirming the contract, and his action would be consistent with it. Under subs (3) no such provision of rescission is necessary, for, if an unpaid seller re-sells, he puts it out of his power to perform his contract and his action is inconsistent with a subsisting sale to the original buyer. Once there is a re-sale in accordance with s 48 by an unpaid seller in possession of the contractual goods the contract of sale is rescinded, whether the re-sale be of the whole of the goods or of part of them, and in this respect subss (3) and (4) fall into line.

As the property in the goods reverts on such a re-sale, the seller retains the proceeds of sale whether they be greater or less than the contractual price. The probability in normal trade is that the price would be less, giving rise to a claim for damages, as for non-acceptance of the goods. . . .

Subsection (4) makes the resale operate as a rescission and leaves the remedy, if any loss ensues, in damages. That brings it into harmony with subs (3), which also gives a claim for damages for any loss occasioned by the original buyer's breach of contract. If the unpaid seller resells the goods, he puts it out of his power to perform his obligation under the original contract, that is, to deliver the contractual goods to the buyer. By the notice to the buyer, the seller makes payment of the price 'of the essence of the contract,' as it is sometimes put. It requires the buyer to pay the price or tender it within a reasonable time.

If he fails to do so, the seller in possession of the goods may treat the bargain as rescinded and resell the goods. The suit for damages becomes comparable to a claim for damages for non-acceptance of the goods where the property never has passed. The property has reverted on the resale, and the second buyer gets a good title. The seller resells as owner. Subsection (2) expressly gives the buyer a good title thereto as against the original buyer.

On this view of the law the plaintiffs cannot recover the price of the Zodiac, which is in the circumstances their property. They can, however, recover any loss which they have sustained by the buyer's default. The parties have sensibly agreed that the value of the Zodiac in May, 1965, was £450. The total contract price was £850, against which the plaintiffs have received £25 in cash and £350 in respect of the Vanguard, and have to give credit for £450 for the Zodiac. To the loss of £25 must be added the sum for advertising, which was admittedly reasonably incurred – £22 10s. The plaintiffs' loss was, therefore, £47 10s.

I would allow the appeal and enter judgment for £47 10s in favour of the plaintiffs in substitution for the award of the deputy judge.

Diplock LJ: Whether or not the property had passed on May 6, 1965, the seller was only liable to deliver upon payment or tender of the balance of the purchase price (see the Sale of Goods Act, s 28) and was entitled until then to retain possession, either by virtue of his lien as an unpaid seller if the property had passed (Sale of Goods Act, s 39(1)), or by virtue of his right to withhold delivery if the property had not passed (subs (2) of the same section). In either case, the unpaid seller has a right to resell the goods if he gives notice of his intention to do so and the buyer does not within a reasonable time pay or tender the price (Sale of Goods Act, s 48(3)). The note in the current edition of Chalmers that the right of resale only arises where the seller exercises his right of lien or stoppage in transitu, that is, where the property has passed to the buyer, is in my view wrong. This subsection enables a seller in possession of the goods to make time of payment of the purchase price of the essence of the contract whether the property has passed or not. The seller cannot have greater rights of resale if the property has already passed to the buyer than those which he would have if the property had remained in him.

In this court it has been contended on behalf of the seller that, when an unpaid seller who retains possession of goods the property in which has passed to the buyer exercises his statutory right of resale under s 48(3) of the Sale of Goods Act, he does not thereby elect to treat the contract as rescinded, but remains entitled to recover the purchase price from the buyer although he must give credit for the net proceeds of sale of any of the goods which he has sold. Authority for this proposition is to be found in the judgment of Finnemore J in *Gallagher v Shilcock* ([1949] 2 KB 765), and the question in this appeal is whether that judgment is right or not.

Finnemore J based his conclusion on his view as to the construction of s 48 of the Sale of Goods Act, and in particular upon the contrast between the express reference in subs (4) of s 48 to the contract being rescinded when goods are resold under an express right of resale and the absence of any reference to rescission in subs (3) of s 48. With great respect, however, I think that that disregards basic principles of the law of contract, and that there is another explanation for the contrast between the two subsections.

Rescission of a contract discharges both parties from any further liability to perform their respective primary obligations under the contract, that is to say, to do thereafter those things which by their contract they had stipulated they would do. Where rescission occurs as a result of one party exercising his right to treat a breach by the other party of a stipulation in the contract as a repudiation of the contract, this gives rise to a secondary obligation of the party in breach to compensate the other party for the loss occasioned to him as a consequence of the rescission, and this secondary obligation is enforceable in an action for damages. Until, however, there is rescission by acceptance of the repudiation, the liability of both parties to perform their primary obligations under the contract continues. Thus, under a contract for the sale of goods which has not been rescinded, the seller remains liable to transfer the property in the goods to the buyer and to deliver possession of them to him until he has discharged those obligations by performing them, and the buyer remains correspondingly liable to pay for the goods and to accept possession of them.

The election by a party not in default to exercise his right of rescission by treating the contract as repudiated may be evinced by words or by conduct. Any act which puts it out of his power to perform thereafter his primary obligations under the contract, if it is an act which he is entitled to do without notice to the party in default, must amount to an election to rescind the contract. If it is an act which he is not entitled to do, it will amount to a wrongful repudiation of the contract on his part which the other party can in turn elect to treat as rescinding the contract.

Part IV of the Sale of Goods Act, ss 38 to 48, deals with the rights of an unpaid seller both before the property in the goods has passed to the buyer and after it has passed. The mere fact that a seller is unpaid does not necessarily mean that the buyer is in breach of the contract, or, if he is, that his breach is one which entitles the seller to exercise his right to treat the contract as repudiated.

[His Lordship referred to ss 39 and 48, and continued:]

If the contract provided for delivery upon a specified date, the seller's conduct in failing to deliver on that date would put it out of his power to perform one of his primary obligations under the contract if time were of the essence of the contract. It was, therefore, necessary, or at least prudent, to provide expressly that if his failure to deliver were in the mere exercise of a lien or right of stoppage in transitu it did not discharge his liability to deliver the goods upon tender of the contract price, or the buyer's liability to accept the goods and to pay for them.

Subsection (2) deals with a different topic, videlicet, the title of a new buyer to whom the goods are resold by the seller. If the property in the goods at the time of the resale remained in the seller, the new buyer would obtain a good title at common law and would require no statutory protection. The subsection is, therefore, limited to cases where the property in the goods at the time of resale had already passed to the original buyer, and provides that, where the seller is in possession of the goods in the exercise of his unpaid seller's lien or right of stoppage in transitu, the new buyer shall acquire a good title, and this is so whether or not the seller had a right of resale as against the original buyer.

Subsection (3) reads as follows:

> Where the goods are of a perishable nature, or where the unpaid seller gives notice to the buyer of his intention to resell, and the buyer does not within a reasonable time pay or tender the price, the unpaid seller may resell the goods and recover from the original buyer damages for any loss occasioned by his breach of contract.

This is the provision of the Act which confers 'a right of resale as limited by this Act,' referred to in s 39(1)(c). The right dealt with in this subsection is a right as against the original buyer. As a stipulation as to time of payment is not deemed to be of the essence of a contract of sale unless a different intention appears from the terms of the contract (Sale of Goods Act, s 10(1)), failure by the buyer to pay on the stipulated date is not conduct by him which entitles the unpaid seller to treat the contract as repudiated. He remains liable to deliver the goods to the buyer upon tender of the contract price (Sale of Goods Act, s 28). Apart from this subsection, if the unpaid seller resold the goods before or after the property had passed to the original buyer, he would remain liable to the original buyer for damages for non-delivery if the original buyer tendered the purchase price after the resale, and if the property had already passed to the original buyer at the time of the resale he would be liable to an alternative action by the original buyer for damages for conversion. The purpose of the subsection is to make time of payment of the essence of the contract whenever the goods are of a perishable nature, and to enable an unpaid seller, whatever the nature of the goods, to make payment within a reasonable time after notice of the essence of the contract. As already pointed out, an unpaid seller who resells the goods before the property has passed puts it out of his power to perform his primary obligation to the buyer to transfer the property in the goods to the buyer and, whether or not the property has already passed, to deliver up possession of the goods to the buyer. By making the act of resale one which the unpaid seller is entitled to perform, the subsection empowers the seller by his conduct in doing that act to exercise his right to treat the contract as repudiated by the buyer, that is, as rescinded, with the consequence that the buyer is discharged from any further liability to perform his primary obligation to pay the purchase price, and becomes subject to the secondary obligation to pay damages for non-acceptance of the goods. If the contract were not rescinded by the resale the seller would still be entitled to bring an action against the buyer for the price of the goods although, no doubt, he would have to credit the buyer with the proceeds of the resale. If that were the intention of the subsection one would have expected it to provide this in express terms. That it was not the intention is, however, apparent from the words used to define the remedy of the unpaid seller who has exercised his right of resale, videlicet, to 'recover from the original buyer damages for any loss occasioned by his breach of contract.' It is, of course, well-established that where a contract for the sale of goods is rescinded after the property in the goods has passed to the buyer the rescission divests the buyer of his property in the goods.

Subsection (4) deals with the consequences of a resale by a seller, not necessarily an 'unpaid seller' as defined in s 38, made in the exercise of an express right of resale reserved in the contract on the buyer making default. If such an express right were exercisable after the property in the goods had passed to the buyer, its exercise might, on one view, be regarded as an alternative mode of performance of the seller's primary obligations under the contract, and the resale as being made by the seller as agent for the buyer. It was, therefore, necessary to provide expressly that the exercise of an express power of resale should rescind the original contract of sale. That is, in my view, the explanation of the express reference to rescission in subs (4). The absence of a similar express reference to rescission in subs (3) is no sufficient ground for ascribing to subs (3) a meaning which the actual words of the subsection would appear to contradict and which would, in my view, conflict with the general principles of the law of contract.

In the present case the unpaid seller only resold part of the goods which he had contracted to sell to the original buyer. This makes no difference, however. His primary duty under the contract was to deliver both cars to the buyer. If he delivered only one, the buyer would be entitled to reject it (Sale of Goods Act, s 30(1)). By his conduct in selling the Vanguard on May 24, 1965, the unpaid seller put it out of his power to perform his primary obligation under the contract. He thereby elected to treat the contract as rescinded. The property in the Zodiac thereupon reverted to him, and his only remedy against the buyer after May 24, 1965, was for damages for non-acceptance of the two cars, of which the prima facie measure is the difference between the contract price and their market value on May 24, 1965.

I, too, would allow this appeal, and enter judgment for the plaintiffs for £47 10s instead of £497 10s.

[Russell LJ concurred.]

NOTES

1. The word 'rescind' is used in varying senses in different textbooks on the law of contract. In many contexts, it is helpful to distinguish between (1) 'terminating' a contract for breach, which discharges the parties from further performance of such primary obligations as are outstanding, but leaves open to the party not in breach his remedy in damages, and (2) 'rescinding' a contract (eg for misrepresentation), which has the effect of restoring the parties to their original positions (rescission *'ab initio'*). In s 48 and the judgments in *Ward v Bignall* the word 'rescind' is used as equivalent to 'terminate for breach', so far as the *contractual* position is concerned, but is preferred to 'terminate' because the focus is on the destination of the *property* in the goods. It is made clear that, when a seller validly exercises a right of resale, there is a 'rescission' in the sense that the property is revested in him before passing to the new buyer. It follows that if the resale is made for a higher price, the seller may keep it all (*Commission Car Sales (Hastings) Ltd v Saul* [1957] NZLR 144).

2. We may infer from the judgments in this case the following additional points:

(1) A resale of *part* of the goods operates to rescind the whole contract.
(2) An unpaid seller's right of resale is said to be 'as limited by this Act' (s 39(1)(c)). But this does not mean that the right of resale is limited to those cases where he has exercised his right of lien or stoppage in transit. There could, for instance, be a right of resale reserved by the terms of the contract of sale in specified events, as in some of the *Romalpa* cases (see below, p 408). Alternatively, the buyer could be in breach of his obligation to pay the price on the agreed date, in a case where time has been made of the essence of the contract. Section 48 does not have the effect of excluding or restricting any power of resale which the seller may have at common law.
(3) Section 48(4) applies whether the seller is an unpaid seller or not.

(e) Effect of resale by an unpaid seller

Section 48(2) states that where an unpaid seller *who has exercised his right of lien or retention or stoppage in transit* resells the goods, the second buyer acquires a good title to them as against the original buyer. There is a degree of overlap between this provision and s 24 (sale by seller in possession, broadly equivalent to s 8 of the Factors Act 1889: above, p 327), but there are also important differences, which we may list as follows:

(1) Section 24 applies whether the seller is an unpaid seller or not; for s 48(2) to apply, he must be unpaid.

(2) Section 24 applies where the seller 'continues or is in possession of the goods, or of the documents of title to the goods'; s 48(2) applies where an unpaid seller 'has exercised his right of lien or retention or stoppage in transit'. There are plainly circumstances when one only of these requirements will have been met.

(3) Section 24 applies only where the goods or document of title are *delivered* to the second buyer; there is no such requirement in s 48(2).

(4) Section 24 operates only in favour of a bona fide purchaser who takes without notice; again, there is no such requirement in s 48(2).

(5) Section 24 is expressed to operate for the benefit not only of a sub-buyer, but also someone who takes under a pledge or other disposition of the goods (and, under s 8 of the Factors Act, also someone who has *agreed* to buy or take under a pledge or other disposition); s 48 applies only to a resale.

NOTE

In the opinion of Lord Diplock in *Ward v Bignall*, s 48(2) applies – and is needed – only where the property in the goods has passed to the buyer. Where a seller who has *retained* the property resells the goods, he can confer a good title on the second buyer by virtue of his ownership, and there is no need to invoke s 48(2). The seller may, however, still be liable to the first buyer for breach of contract. Since s 24 also speaks only of a person who has *sold* goods, we may infer that a person who has retained title to the goods (ie, only agreed to sell them) can confer a good title on a second purchaser by virtue of his ownership and does not need to invoke the provisions of that section.

QUESTION

S agrees to sell to B1 goods which are stored in W's warehouse. S retains the property in the goods but gives B1 a delivery order addressed to W. Not having been paid by B1, S resells the goods to B2, telling him that he has been let down by a previous buyer, B1. S gives B2 a delivery order. The following day, B1 contracts to sell the goods to X, and endorses his delivery order over to X. Who is entitled to the goods (1) before any delivery order is presented to W; (2) if B2 presents his delivery order to W before X; (3) if X presents his delivery order to W before B2?

(f) Retention of title clauses

It is of course axiomatic that a clause in a contract of sale may stipulate that the seller shall retain the title to the goods until a stated event has happened, and in particular until he has been paid the price; and this may be done even though possession of the goods is given to the buyer: see s 2(5). The case of *Lee v Butler* (above, p 332) is an example. The term 'retention of title clause' has, however, come to have a special connotation in a commercial context as a result of the landmark decision in the *Romalpa* case (below). In a typical 'retention of title' contract, the buyer is likely to be either a company engaged in the manufacturing or construction industry which buys raw materials or components for the purposes of its business, or a company which acquires the goods with a view to reselling them or letting them on hire or lease to its own customers. (An individual may also buy goods subject to a retention of title – as, indeed, was the case in *Lee v Butler* – but we shall assume that the buyer is a company, since it is in relation to company buyers that the most interesting (and most complex!) issues arise.) Another point of distinction, in practice, is that cases like *Lee v Butler* (and similarly in the hire-purchase cases) the goods are normally durables of some type which are to be paid for by instalments; and one of the main risks which the seller wishes to guard against is that the buyer will resell the goods before he has paid the whole of the price: in contrast, the *Romalpa* cases are concerned with goods – often of a consumable kind – which both parties contemplate will be used up or disposed of in some way before the price is paid, and the main risk for the seller is the buyer's insolvency.

Aluminium Industrie Vaassen BV v Romalpa Aluminium Ltd [1976] 1 WLR 676, Queen's Bench Division and Court of Appeal

The plaintiffs (AIV), a Dutch company, supplied aluminium foil to Romalpa in England on AIV's standard terms of trading, parts of which are quoted in the judgment of Mocatta J. Romalpa went into receivership owing AIV £122,000. The receiver had in his possession unprocessed aluminium foil worth £50,000 and £35,000 representing the proceeds of subsales of foil which had been made by Romalpa. It was held (1) that AIV's claim to the unprocessed foil prevailed over that of the receiver, because AIV had effectively retained title to it; and (2) that AIV was entitled to the money representing the proceeds of subsales on the basis of the doctrine of tracing established in *Re Hallett's Estate* (1880) 13 Ch D 696, CA.

Mocatta J: The first major issue in this case turns on whether clause 13, in what the plaintiffs say are their general selling terms and conditions for aluminium foil, applied to the transactions done between the plaintiffs and the defendants, in respect of which £122,239 is owing. That clause began with this important reservation of title. The first sentence of the clause reads as follows:

> 'The ownership of the material to be delivered by AIV' (that is the plaintiffs) 'will only be transferred to purchaser when he has met all that is owing to AIV, no matter on what grounds.'

I read the remainder of the clause in view of its somewhat elaborate nature and of subsequent issues arising:

> Until the date of payment, purchaser, if AIV so desires, is required to store this material in such a way that it is clearly the property of AIV. AIV and purchaser agree that, if purchaser should make (a) new object(s) from the material, mix this material with (an)other object(s) or if this material in any way whatsoever becomes a constituent of (an)other object(s) AIV will be given the ownership of this (these) new object(s) as surety of the full payment of what purchaser owes AIV. To this end AIV and purchaser now agree that the ownership of the article(s) in question, whether finished or not, are to be transferred to AIV and that this transfer of ownership will be considered to have taken place through and at the moment of the single operation or event by which the material is converted into (a) new object(s), or is mixed with or becomes a constituent or (an)other object(s). Until the moment of full payment of what purchaser owes AIV purchaser shall keep the object(s) in question for AIV in his capacity of fiduciary owner and, if required, shall store this (these) object(s) in such a way that it (they) can be recognized as such. Nevertheless, purchaser will be entitled to sell these objects to a third party within the framework of the normal carrying on of his business and to deliver them on condition that – if AIV so requires – purchaser, as long as he has not fully discharged his debt to AIV shall hand over to AIV the claims he has against the buyer emanating from this transaction.

If the plaintiffs can establish that clause 13 does apply, as between themselves and the defendants, they are admittedly entitled to succeed on their second claim, the goods in question in the possession of the defendants still being their property. But their first claim, namely, the right to trace, is disputed. I must therefore deal first with the hotly contested point whether clause 13 did apply between the plaintiffs and the defendants.

[His Lordship referred to the course of dealing between the parties, and answered this question in the affirmative. He continued:]

Having decided that clause 13 did apply to the many transactions between the plaintiffs and defendants after September 1, 1973, when the defendants took over the aluminium foil business that the partnership had previously conducted with the plaintiffs, I now have to deal with the consequences of that decision as applying to the claims in the action.

In the first place, it is admitted that the plaintiffs are the owners of the remaining unsold aluminium foil held by the receiver, and that they are entitled to an order for its delivery up to them. The real contest arose in relation to the plaintiffs' right to a charge on the receiver's account with the [bank] to the extent of £35,152.66 representing, as certified by the receiver, the sum recovered by him from customers of the defendants as a result of AIV materials supplied to the defendants by the plaintiffs. This right the plaintiffs claim on the basis of the principle established in *Re Hallett's Estate* (1880) 13 Ch D 696 entitling them to trace the proceeds of the sale of their property sold by the plaintiffs into the receiver's bank account. It is common ground that the effect of clause 13 is that, while money was owing by the defendants to the plaintiffs, any aluminium foil delivered by the plaintiffs to the defendants, while still in their possession, was held by them as bailees.

It is further common ground that the clause must be read subject to the necessary implication that the defendants were entitled to sell the foil to sub-purchasers. It is curious that this is not said about sales of unmixed foil whilst it is said in the last sentence of the clause about foil mixed with other material. In respect of this, it is to be noted that the defendants were, if required, to assign to the plaintiffs their rights against sub-purchasers in respect of the mixed materials sold to them. Notwithstanding the generally far-reaching and somewhat elaborate provisions in clause 13, reserving the plaintiff's right of ownership in the goods until nothing was owing from the purchasers, and the admission that the clause had the effect of making the defendants bailees of the goods while in their possession until all money owing had been paid, the argument for the defendants was that once foil had been sold to bona fide purchasers, the relationship between the plaintiffs and the defendants was purely one of debtor and creditor. As against this, the plaintiffs argued that a fiduciary relationship stemming from the bailment continued after sales to third parties, and that in consequence equitable remedies applied, including the right to trace proceeds of the sub-sales. It was not necessary, said the plaintiffs, to find as a prerequisite to the right to trace an express or constructive trust. The equitable proprietary remedy followed as a consequence of the finding that the defendants were bailees.

Having indicated the general nature of the competing arguments, I can go straight to the judgment of Sir George Jessel MR in *Re Hallett's Estate* (1880) 13 Ch D 696. Although in that case there had been breaches of express trust, it is clear from the passages I am about to read that the reasoning was not founded on this, and that the principle stated applied to much wider circumstances. It is necessary to make certain fairly extensive quotations. Sir George Jessel MR said, at p 708:

> The modern doctrine of equity as regards property disposed of by persons in a fiduciary position is a very clear and well-established doctrine. You can, if the sale was rightful, take the proceeds of the sale, if you can identify them. If the sale was wrongful, you can still take the proceeds of the sale, in a sense adopting the sale for the purpose of taking the proceeds, if you can identify them. There is no distinction, therefore, between a rightful and a wrongful disposition of the property, so far as regards the right of the beneficial owner to follow the proceeds. . . .

Pausing there for a moment, it is not, of course, suggested here that there was a wrongful disposition of the plaintiff's property when the defendants sold the foil to bona fide sub-purchasers. . . .

There then follows this passage showing the width of the application of the principle:

Has it ever been suggested, until very recently, that there is any distinction between an express trustee, or an agent, or a bailee, or a collector of rents, or anybody else in a fiduciary position? I have never heard, until quite recently, such a distinction suggested. . . . It can have no foundation in principle, because the beneficial ownership is the same, wherever the legal ownership may be.

There is the following short passage, at p 710:

Now that being the established doctrine of equity on this point, I will take the case of the pure bailee. If the bailee sells the goods bailed, the bailor can in equity follow the proceeds, and can follow the proceeds wherever they can be distinguished, either being actually kept separate, or being mixed up with other moneys.

These passages are clearly most apposite, since they refer to the position of a mere bailee, and were strongly relied upon by Mr Lincoln. Mr Pickering sought to avoid them by saying that they were obiter or had in some way been modified in *Re Diplock* [1948] Ch 465 and that it was necessary that there should be some express or constructive trust before the equitable doctrine could apply. My attention was not drawn to any passage in *Re Diplock* criticising or modifying, in any way, the statements of principle which I have quoted. Although I fully recognise that in considering this problem I find myself in a most unfamiliar field, I feel it my duty to follow and apply those statements. Mr Pickering drew my attention to two authorities as illustrating the simple debtor/creditor relationship, namely, *King v Hutton* [1900] 2 QB 504 and *Henry v Hammond* [1913] 2 KB 515. It is unnecessary to refer to these in detail, save to say that the former makes it clear that the special facts of each case are crucial in determining whether there is a simple debtor/creditor relationship, although the intention of the parties as ascertained from the terms of their contract shows that some kind of fiduciary relationship exists. The preservation of ownership clause contains unusual and fairly elaborate provisions departing substantially from the debtor/creditor relationship and shows, in my view, the intention to create a fiduciary relationship to which the principle stated in *Re Hallett's Estate* applies. A further point made by Mr Pickering was that if the plaintiffs were to succeed in their tracing claim this would, in effect, be a method available against a liquidator to a creditor of avoiding the provisions establishing the need to register charges on book debts: see s 95(1)(2)(e) of the Companies Act 1948. He used this only as an argument against the effect of clause 13 contended for by Mr Lincoln. As to this, I think Mr Lincoln's answer was well founded, namely, that if property in the foil never passed to the defendants with the result that the proceeds of sub-sales belonged in equity to the plaintiffs, s 95(1) had no application.

The plaintiffs accordingly succeed. . . .

[The defendants appealed.]

Roskill LJ: . . . Are the plaintiffs entitled to the proceeds of sales to sub-purchasers now held by the receiver? We were told both by Mr Price and by Mr Lincoln that the receiver received these moneys after he had entered into his receivership from sales made by the defendants to sub-purchasers before that date. The receiver, properly if I may say so, kept those moneys separate; as we were told that there is no complication arising of those moneys having become mixed with other moneys, because they were always kept separate. There was no suggestion that the sub-sales in question were other than authorised by the plaintiffs or that the sub-purchasers concerned did not acquire a valid title to the several quantities of foil which each of them bought. The sole question is whether, on the facts and on the true construction of the bargain, including the general conditions, between the plaintiffs and the defendants, the plaintiffs are entitled to trace and recover those proceeds of the sub-sales, upon the well-known principles laid down in the judgment of Sir George Jessel MR in *Re Hallett's Estate*. . . .

The critical question is whether there was a fiduciary relationship between the plaintiffs and the defendants which entitles the plaintiffs successfully to claim these moneys in the way and upon the footing which I have just described. Mr Price strenuously argued that the bargain between the parties was a perfectly ordinary bargain, creating the ordinary contractual relationship of seller and buyer, with the consequence that if the buyers – that is to say the defendants – became insolvent before payment for the goods was made by them to the sellers, – that is, the plaintiffs – the sellers were left with their ordinary contractual or, as he put it, personal remedy as unsecured creditors of the buyers, and that there was no additional proprietary remedy (again to borrow his language) available to them justifying their seeking to trace and recover the proceeds of the sub-sales which had come from the sub-purchasers into the hands of the receiver.

It seems to me clear that, but for the provisions of clause 13 – which have to be read in conjunction with the other relevant clauses I have mentioned – this would be the position. The individual contracts were for delivery ex the plaintiffs' works in Holland, and, apart from special provisions, in English law at least – as already stated, there is no evidence of Dutch law and therefore we must apply English law to these contracts – both property and risk would have passed to the defendants upon such delivery.

But clause 13 plainly provides otherwise. The defendants as sellers were to retain the property in the goods until all – and I underline '*all*' – that was owing to them had been paid. . . . It is obvious, to my mind, that the business purpose of the whole of this clause, read in its context in the general conditions, was to secure the plaintiffs, so far as possible, against the risks of non-payment after they had parted with possession of the goods delivered, whether or not those goods retained their identity after delivery. I unhesitatingly accept that part of Mr Lincoln's submission. In the case of unmanufactured goods this was to be achieved by the plaintiffs retaining the property until all payments due had been made, to which were added the special rights given by clause 25. In the case of mixed or manufactured goods, more elaborate provisions were made and indeed were obviously required if the avowed object of clause 13 were to be achieved in the case of the latter class of goods. The plaintiffs were to be given the ownership of these mixed or manufactured goods as 'surety' for 'full payment.' 'Surety' I think in this context must mean, as Mr Lincoln contended yesterday, 'security.' This is as between the defendants and the plaintiffs, and it is not necessary to consider how far this provision would protect the plaintiffs against adverse claims, at any rate in this country, by third parties. Further, the clause later provides that until 'full payment' is made the defendants shall keep the mixed goods for the plaintiffs as 'fiduciary owners' – not perhaps the happiest of phrases but one which suggests, at least to an English lawyer, that in relation to mixed or manufactured goods there was produced what in English law would be called a fiduciary relationship in this respect. The clause goes on to give to the defendants an express power of sale of such goods, and the right to deliver them; and adds an obligation upon the defendants, if required by the plaintiffs so to do, to assign (to use English legal language) to the plaintiffs the benefit of any claim against a sub-purchaser so long as the defendants have not fully discharged all their indebtedness to the plaintiffs. . . .

The burden of Mr Lincoln's argument was, first, that all goods dealt with in pursuance of clause 13 were, until *all* debts were discharged, the plaintiffs' goods which the defendants were authorised to sell on the plaintiffs' behalf and for the plaintiffs' account but only within the framework of clause 13. Since the goods were the plaintiffs', the defendants remained accountable to the plaintiffs for them or for their proceeds of sale, so long as any indebtedness whatever remained outstanding from the defendants to the plaintiffs. Hence the creation of the fiduciary relationship upon which Mr Lincoln sought to rely. The burden of Mr Price's argument was, as already stated, that the clause created in the first part no more than the ordinary debtor/creditor, buyer/seller, relationship, and that nothing in the second part justified placing additional fiduciary obligations upon the defendants in respect of unmanufactured goods, referred to in the first part of the clause.

[His Lordship held that clause 13 impliedly authorised Romalpa to sell the unmanufactured, as well as the manufactured, goods, on terms that they were accountable to AIV for the proceeds of sale. He continued:]

I see no difficulty in the contractual concept that, as between the defendants and their sub-purchasers, the defendants sold as principals, but that, as between themselves and the plaintiffs, those goods which they were selling as principals within their implied authority from the plaintiffs were the plaintiffs' goods which they were selling as agents for the plaintiffs to whom they remained fully accountable. If an agent lawfully sells his principal's goods, he stands in a fiduciary relationship to his principal and remains accountable to his principal for those goods and their proceeds. A bailee is in like position in relation to his bailor's goods. What, then, is there here to relieve the defendants from their obligation to account to the plaintiffs for those goods of the plaintiffs which they lawfully sell to sub-purchasers? The fact that they so sold them as principals does not, as I think, affect their relationship with the plaintiffs; nor (as at present advised) do I think – contrary to Mr Price's argument – that the sub-purchasers could on this analysis have sued the plaintiffs upon the sub-contracts as undisclosed principals for, say, breach of warranty of quality.

It seems to me clear . . . that to give effect to what I regard as the obvious purpose of clause 13 one must imply into the first part of the clause not only the power to sell but also the obligation to account in accordance with the normal fiduciary relationship of principal and agent, bailor and bailee. Accordingly, like the judge I find no difficulty in holding that the principles in *Hallett's* case are of immediate application, and I think that the plaintiffs are entitled to trace these proceeds of sale and to recover them, as Mocatta J has held by his judgment.

It is ironic that the starting point for this major modern commercial development was not a high-powered collaboration between the best brains in the City and the Temple, but a rather poor translation into English of a document drafted by a Dutch lawyer! It is perhaps also significant, with hindsight, that this seminal case came before a commercial court in which some key issues of an equitable nature were not argued. The same cannot be said of the second leading case in the series, *Re Bond Worth Ltd* (below), where the hearing lasted for 15 full days and over 90 authorities were cited in argument. But before looking at *Re Bond Worth*, it is necessary to understand something of the way in which companies normally finance their operations. Most companies depend upon some degree of borrowing in order to maintain their cash-flow. When a company borrows money, and more particularly when it borrows it on overdraft from a bank, it is usually required to give security in the form of a general *floating charge* to the bank. Such a charge (as is explained more fully below, p 838) allows the company to carry on its business without interference from the bank, unless and until it defaults on the terms of its loan. If that does happen (for instance, if the company's overdraft is run up beyond the agreed limit), the bank can move in immediately and take possession of all of the company's assets, most commonly by the appointment of a receiver – an insolvency practitioner whose role it is to enforce the bank's security, if necessary by selling up these assets. If we take the case of B, a company manufacturing furniture, which has given a floating charge to its bank, and suppose that S is a timber firm which is asked to supply timber to B on credit, it is easy to see that if S simply sells the wood to B and is not paid, and then the bank intervenes by appointing a receiver (or some other insolvency procedure, such as liquidation, ensues), the bank is in a position to claim the timber as part of B's assets while S, who has supplied the timber which has gone to swell the assets, is a mere unsecured creditor whose debt will rank after that of the bank. The obvious answer to S's predicament is for him to supply the timber to B on terms that it will remain S's property until it has been paid for – ie, to insert a 'retention of title' clause into the contract of sale. The *Romalpa* case, and several other cases since, have upheld the validity of such a clause – at least where the goods in question remain identifiable as the contract goods, or part of them: *Clough Mill Ltd v Martin* (below), or where they have been used in a manufacturing process which is reversible (eg motors fitted to air compressors but which can be detached simply by unbolting them: *Hendy Lennox (Industrial Engines) Ltd v Grahame Puttick Ltd* [1984] 1 WLR 485).

But the position becomes more complicated in a number of situations:

(1) where the goods have been used in an irreversible manufacturing process (eg resin, in the manufacture of chipboard), so that the original goods have lost their identity: *Borden (UK) Ltd v Scottish Timber Products Ltd* (below);

(2) where the goods have been mixed with other goods, so that, again, it is impossible to determine which are the goods that were sold under the contract in question: *Re Andrabell Ltd* (below);

(3) where the goods have ceased to be the property of either seller or buyer, eg by being resold to a customer of B, or being built into a house belonging to a third party, or used to repair a third party's chattel (*Specialist Plant Services Ltd v Braithwaite Ltd* [1987] BCLC 1, CA).

In an attempt to meet some of these problems, the draftsmen have endeavoured to make their retention of title clauses more elaborate. A variety of ancillary clauses have been developed. These include:

(1) a provision which requires the buyer (B) to keep the goods separate from other goods, perhaps also stipulating that he shall hold the goods as bailee for the seller (S);

(2) a provision which seeks to confer upon S proprietary rights in relation to the proceeds of any sale of the goods made by B to a third party; such a provision may be reinforced by other terms which require B to keep such proceeds separate from other moneys, to hold them on a fiduciary basis, to pay them into a special account, etc;

(3) a provision which seeks to extend S's proprietary rights into any goods which may be manufactured by B and which incorporate the goods which S has sold;

(4) (a combination of (2) and (3)): a provision which declares that S shall have a proprietary interest in the proceeds of any sale made by B of goods which are the product of such a manufacturing process;

(5) (an 'all moneys' clause): a stipulation that S shall retain the property in the goods sold (and possibly have some or all of the other rights listed in (2), (3) and (4) above) until S has been paid not only the price of those goods, but all other debts which are outstanding between S and B.

The ingenuity of the draftsman will not necessarily stop there. He will, for instance, almost certainly include a power for S or his agents to enter B's premises and seize the sale goods, and any other goods in which by virtue of the contract S has acquired a proprietary interest.

Unhappily for many sellers, the precedent set in the *Romalpa* case ran into difficulties in the very next reported case, *Re Bond Worth Ltd* (below). Many of the devices suggested above have since encountered similar problems in subsequent test cases. These difficulties stem from the fact that there is a very fine line between a true 'retention of title' clause and a provision which creates a *charge*.

A *charge* is a proprietary right created by a debtor in favour of another person empowering the latter to look to specified property of the debtor for satisfaction of the debt. (For a full discussion of this concept, see below, p 836.) Where, under a contract of sale of goods, the seller reserves to himself the entire property in the goods until the price is paid, there is no charge, since the buyer has never owned the property over which the supposed charge could have been created. Where, however, the property first passes to the buyer and he in turn purports to *revest* it in the seller, or to confer some interest in it on the seller, until the price is paid, all the elements of a charge are likely to be present. It was held in *Re Bond Worth Ltd* (below) that if the seller purports to reserve to himself an *equitable* interest in the goods until the price is paid, and meantime to transfer only a bare legal title to the buyer, this may also constitute a charge. And it is almost inevitable, in the nature of things, that where the contract seeks to confer upon the seller a right to look for satisfaction of the price to property which is worth more than that amount (or to a sum of money which exceeds the price which he is owed), the courts will construe the transaction as one involving a charge. So it is likely that this construction will be placed on any contract which attempts to vest in the seller the property in the *product* resulting from work done by the buyer on the goods, or from some manufacturing process to which they have been subjected, until the price is paid, for it is hardly credible that the parties would have intended that the buyer should abandon to the seller the value which he has added to the original sale goods. In the same way, any claim asserted by the seller against the *proceeds of sale* of the goods or their product to a subpurchaser will be regarded as a charge. Had an argument along these lines been fully explored in the *Romalpa* case itself, the outcome (at least as regards the proceeds of sale of the foil) might well have been different.

In principle, there can be no objection to the creation of a charge, as such, in any of these circumstances. But there is a clear practical reason why the parties will not wish to do so. Where the buyer is a company which has already given a floating charge over all of its assets, present and future, to its bank, that charge will almost always include a term which prohibits the company from creating any other charge ranking ahead of that of the bank. If the seller has actual or constructive notice of this term (which under the rules of company law he will almost certainly be deemed to have), of course any attempt on his part to create a prior charge in his own favour is doomed to fail. And so he will avoid at all costs making any concession that the contract of sale involves a charge. And in so doing, he falls into a second trap; for if the court does hold that there is a charge, it will be void because it has not been registered under the Companies Act. The cases which follow show many examples where a purported reservation of title has been construed as falling on the wrong side of this critical line, and struck down as an unregistered charge.

Re Bond Worth Ltd [1980] Ch 228, Chancery Division

'Acrilan' fibre was supplied by Monsanto to Bond Worth for use in the manufacture of carpets. The contract of sale provided that 'equitable and beneficial ownership' of the Acrilan should remain in the sellers until the price had been paid, or until prior resale, in which case Monsanto's beneficial ownership was to attach to the proceeds of the resale. It was also stipulated that Monsanto should have the equitable and beneficial ownership in any products made out of the fibre. Slade J held that these provisions were consistent only with the creation of a floating charge, and that the transaction was void for non-registration as a charge under the Companies Act.

Slade J: I turn to consider the relevant contracts. In my judgment at least the following points are fairly clear:

(1) They were absolute contracts for the sale of goods within the meaning of s 1(2) of the Sale of Goods Act 1893, though this is not to say that they did not comprise other features in addition.

(2) The legal title or property in the Acrilan fibre comprised in any one of the contracts passed to Bond Worth when the fibre was delivered to Bond Worth: see s 18, rule 1 of the Sale of Goods Act 1893. In using the term 'property' in this context I refer to the general property in the goods (which is the definition given to the word in s 62(1) of that Act) and

not merely a special property, such as that possessed by a bailee.

(3) The risk in the goods likewise passed to Bond Worth on delivery. This followed not only from s 20 of the Sale of Goods Act 1893, but also from the opening words of sub-clause (a) of the retention of title clause. Thus if, after delivery, the goods had been stolen or destroyed before Bond Worth had had the opportunity to use them in any way, Bond Worth would nevertheless have had to pay the full purchase price for them.

(4) Though sub-clause (a) of the retention of title clause provided that 'equitable and beneficial ownership' in the goods would remain with Monsanto until full payment for the whole amount of the relevant order had been received or until prior resale, it was manifestly not the intention to confer on or reserve to Monsanto all the rights which would normally be enjoyed by a sui juris person, having the sole beneficial title to property, as against the trustee holding the legal title. Mr Sears, on behalf of Monsanto, expressly conceded and affirmed that Monsanto would not, by virtue of its so called 'equitable and beneficial ownership,' have had the right to call for re-delivery of the goods, at any rate so long as Bond Worth was not in default under its payments. Bond Worth, on the other hand, was to have far-reaching rights even before payment to deal with the goods, which would not normally be possessed by a trustee holding the legal title therein on behalf of one sole, sui juris beneficiary.

(5) Even during the period before full payment had been received by Monsanto and notwithstanding the provisions relating to 'equitable and beneficial ownership,' Bond Worth were to be at liberty to sell all or any part of the goods and to transfer the property therein to a purchaser. The words 'until prior resale,' in sub-clause (a) of the retention of title clause, render the implication of such authority to resell inevitable. They go far beyond the provisions of s 25(1) of the Sale of Goods Act 1893 which empower a buyer of goods in possession after sale in some circumstances, even without the authority of his vendor, to resell and pass a good title to a purchaser on a resale, but confer no authority on him to effect such resale, as between him and his vendor.

(6) The parties nevertheless intended that if Bond Worth were to resell all or any part of the goods at a time when Monsanto had not yet been paid the full price due under the order, Monsanto's 'equitable and beneficial ownership,' whatever that meant, would attach to the proceeds of sale or to the claim for such proceeds.

(7) Even during the period before full payment had been received by Monsanto and notwithstanding the provisions relating to 'equitable and beneficial ownership,' Bond Worth were to be at liberty to use the goods for the purposes of manufacture. . . .

(8) The parties nevertheless intended that if, by virtue of such last-mentioned use, the goods should become constituents of or be converted into other products, the retention of title clause should attach to such other products as if they had been the original subject matter of the sale. . . .

Thus far, the position would seem to me reasonably clear. The real difficulty arises concerning the meaning and legal effect, if any, of the provisions in the retention of title clause concerning 'equitable and beneficial ownership.' If the contracts embody something more than a mere sale, what is this additional feature? What is the nature of the relationship beyond a mere vendor-purchaser relationship between Monsanto and Bond Worth that comes into existence by virtue of the provisions relating to 'equitable and beneficial ownership?'

In *Aluminium Industrie Vaassen BV v Romalpa Aluminium Ltd* [1976] 1 WLR 676, to which I shall have to refer in greater detail later, it was expressly admitted that the retention of title clause had the effect of making the defendants *bailees* of the relevant goods while in their possession until all money owing had been paid. . . . On the different facts of the present case, however, there can be no question of a bailor-bailee relationship, since it is common ground that the property in the Acrilan fibre passed to Bond Worth at latest when it was delivered, while it is of the essence of a bailment that the general property in the goods concerned remains in the bailor, while only a special property passes to the bailee, which entitles him to exercise certain possessory remedies. Nor can the relationship be one of agency, since the documents contain no suggestion that Bond Worth is to be regarded as an agent and the rights which by necessary implication are given to it deal with the goods on its own behalf are quite inconsistent with a principal-agent relationship.

In these circumstances, I think it plain that, if the retention of title clause operated to create any effective rights at all for the benefit of Monsanto, such rights can only have been rights either (i) by way of a trust under which Monsanto was the sole beneficiary or (ii) by way of a trust under which Monsanto had a charge in equity over the relevant assets to secure payment of the unpaid purchase price. No possible third alternative has occurred to me.

[His Lordship examined the authorities, and continued:]

The implicit authority and freedom of Bond Worth to employ the relevant raw materials, products and other moneys as it pleased and for its own purposes during the subsistence of the operation of the retention of title clause were in my judgment quite incompatible with the existence of a relationship of Bond Worth as trustee and Monsanto as beneficiary solely and absolutely entitled to such assets, which is the relationship asserted.

I have, however, already indicated that this is not my own view of the effect, if any, of the retention of title clause when properly construed, but that such effect, if any, is a declaration of trust by Bond Worth in respect of the relevant assets by way of equitable charge to secure repayment of the moneys from time to time owing in respect of the relevant order. Does the authority and freedom of Bond Worth, to which I have last referred, by itself negative the existence of a valid trust by way of equitable charge? In my judgment, in so far as it might be suggested that the clause operated to create in this manner an immediate *specific* charge, the answer to this question must be 'yes.' It is in my judgment quite incompatible with the existence of an effective trust by way of specific charge in equity over specific assets that the alleged trustee should be free to use them as he pleases for his own benefit in the course of his own business.

There is, however, one type of charge (and I think one type only) which, by its very nature, leaves a company at liberty to deal with the assets charged in the ordinary course of its business, without regard to the charge, until stopped by a winding up or by the appointment of a receiver or the happening of some other agreed event. I refer to what is commonly known as a 'floating charge'. . . . Such a charge remains unattached to any particular property and leaves the company with a licence to deal with, and even sell, the assets falling within its ambit in the ordinary course of business, as if the charge had not been given, until it is stopped by one or other of the events to which I have referred, when it is said to 'crystallise"; it then becomes effectively fixed to the assets within its scope.

Romer LJ in *Re Yorkshire Woolcombers' Association Ltd* [1903] 2 Ch 284, 295 gave the following description of a floating charge:

> I certainly do not intend to attempt to give an exact definition of the term 'floating charge' nor am I prepared to say that there will not be a floating charge within the meaning of the Act, which does not contain all of the three characteristics that I am about to mention, but I certainly think that if a charge has the three characteristics that I am about to mention, it is a floating charge. (1) If it is a charge on a class of assets of a company present and future; (2) if that class is one which, in the ordinary course of the business of the company, would be changing from time to time; and (3) if you find that by the charge it is contemplated that, until some future step is taken by or on behalf of those interested in the charge, the company may carry on its business in the ordinary way as far as concerns the particular class of assets I am dealing with.

This description of a floating charge shows that it need not extend to all the assets of the company. It may cover assets merely of a specified category or categories. The third characteristic mentioned by Romer LJ is clearly present in relation to each of the four categories of charged assets in the present case; it was clearly contemplated that until some future step was taken by or on behalf of Monsanto, Bond Worth might carry on its business in the ordinary way in relation to each of these four categories. The second characteristic mentioned by him is likewise clearly present at least in relation to each of the second, third and fourth categories of charged assets; these are ex hypothesi classes of assets which in the ordinary course of business will be changing from time to time.

This much could be said against the existence of floating charges in the present case. As regards the first characteristic mentioned by Romer LJ, the charge on the first category of charged assets is exclusively a charge on present assets of the company, while the charges on the other three categories of charged assets are exclusively charges on future assets of the company. If the charges are looked at separately, they do not comprise classes of mixed present and future assets. Furthermore, the second characteristic mentioned by him is present in relation to the first category of charged assets (the raw fibre) only in the sense that the assets comprised in this category may diminish by being used for the purposes of manufacture or sale; they cannot be increased. I do not, however, think that these points of possible distinction prevent all or any of the four relevant charges from being floating charges within the ordinary meaning of legal terminology. Romer LJ himself disclaimed any intention of saying that there could not be a floating charge within the meaning of the Companies Acts which did not contain all the three characteristics that he mentioned.

The critical distinction in my judgment is that between a specific charge on the one hand and a floating charge on the other. Vaughan Williams LJ pointed out in the *Woolcombers* case [1903] 2 Ch 284 that it is quite inconsistent with the nature of a specific charge, though not of a floating charge, that the mortgagor is at liberty to deal with the relevant property as he pleases. He said, at p 294:

I do not think that for a 'specific security' you need have a security of a subject matter which is then in existence. I mean by 'then' at the time of the execution of the security; but what you do require to make a specific security is that the security whenever it has once come into existence, and been identified or appropriated as a security, shall never thereafter at the will of the mortgagor cease to be a security. If at the will of the mortgagor he can dispose of it and prevent its being any longer a security, although something else may be substituted more or less for it, that is not a 'specific security'.

When that case went on appeal to the House of Lords, under the name *Illingworth v Houldsworth* [1904] AC 355, Lord Macnaghten drew the distinction between a specific charge and a floating charge in the following terms, at p 358:

A specific charge, I think, is one that without more fastens on ascertained and definite property or property capable of being ascertained and defined; a floating charge, on the other hand, is ambulatory and shifting in its nature, hovering over and so to speak floating with the property which it is intended to affect until some event occurs or some act is done which causes it to settle and fasten on the subject of the charge within its reach and grasp.

In the present case, in my judgment, the respective charges on each of the four categories of charged assets were ambulatory and shifting in their nature, and were intended to hover over them until the happening of an event which caused them to crystallise. The assets comprised in each of the four categories were of a fluctuating class, albeit in the case of the first category liable to fluctuate only by diminution. Until a crystallising event occurred, it was clearly not intended that any restriction should be placed on Bond Worth to deal with them in the ordinary course of its business.

Accordingly in the end I answer [the] question by saying that in my judgment the effect of the retention of title clause was to create floating equitable charges over the four categories of charged assets, for the purpose of securing payment of the purchase prices due under the relevant orders, and to constitute Bond Worth a trustee of such assets for the purpose of such security, but for no other purpose. . . .

[Since no particulars of this charge had been registered, it was held void under what is now Part XII of the Companies Act 1985.]

NOTES

1. In the course of his judgment, Slade J said ([1980] Ch 228 at 248):

In my judgment, any contract which, by way of security for the payment of a debt, confers an interest in property defeasible or destructible upon payment of such debt, or appropriates such property for the discharge of the debt, must necessarily be regarded as creating a mortgage or charge, as the case may be. The existence of the equity of redemption is quite inconsistent with the existence of a bare trustee-beneficiary relationship.

This passage has been frequently quoted in later cases.

2. Although Monsanto, by the terms of the contract, purported to *retain* equitable and beneficial ownership in the goods, Slade J held that the contract had to be construed as taking effect in two steps: there was first a *sale* of the entire property in the fibre to Bond Worth, which was then 'followed by a security, *eo instanti*, given back by Bond Worth to the vendor, Monsanto'. Bond Worth had therefore *created* a charge, which brought the transaction within the registration requirements of the Companies Act. Commentators (eg R Gregory (1990) 106 LQR 551) have since queried whether this vital link in Slade J's reasoning has survived the rejection by the House of Lords of the '*scintilla temporis*' fiction in the conveyancing case of *Abbey National Building Society v Cann* [1991] 1 AC 56, HL; but *Bond Worth* was followed on this point in the recent case of *Stroud Architectural Systems Ltd v John Laing Construction Ltd* [1994] BCC 18.

Borden (UK) Ltd v Scottish Timber Products Ltd [1981] Ch 25, Court of Appeal

Bordens sold resin to Scottish Timber, on terms that the property in the resin was not to pass to the buyers until payment had been made for all goods supplied to them by Bordens. The resin was bought to be mixed with hardeners and wood chippings and made into chipboard (an irreversible process), and was normally used within two days. Bordens were owed over £300,000 when the buyers went into receivership. They claimed to be entitled to trace their proprietary interest in the resin into the finished chipboard and the proceeds of sale of the chipboard. The Court of Appeal held, however, that the resin ceased to exist as such once it was used in making the chipboard, and that the sellers lost their title to it in consequence.

Buckley LJ: It is common ground that it was the common intention of the parties that the defendants should be at liberty to use the resin in the manufacture of chipboard. After they had so used the resin there could, in my opinion, be no property in the resin distinct from the property in the chipboard produced by the process. The manufacture had amalgamated the resin and the other ingredients into a new product by an irreversible process and the resin, as resin, could not be recovered for any purpose; for all practical purposes it had ceased to exist and the ownership in that resin must also have ceased to exist.

The [retention of title] condition does not expressly deal with any property in the chipboard, or create any equitable charge upon the chipboard, produced by the manufacture. If any term is to be implied, that must be a term which is necessary to give the contract business efficacy, but it must also be a term which the court can see unambiguously to be a term which the parties would have inserted into their contract had they thought it appropriate to express it. If no such term can be identified, then the court may have to conclude that the contract was inept to achieve any valuable, practical result in that respect.

Is it possible here to imply any term giving the plaintiffs a proprietary interest in the chipboard manufactured by the defendants, or giving the plaintiffs an equitable charge upon that chipboard?

Common ownership of the chipboard at law is not asserted by the defendants; so the plaintiffs must either have the entire ownership of the chipboard, which is not suggested, or they must have some equitable interest in the chipboard or an equitable charge of some kind upon the chipboard. For my part, I find it quite impossible to spell out of this condition any provision properly to be implied to that effect.

It was impossible for the plaintiffs to reserve any property in the manufactured chipboard, because they never had any property in it; the property in that product originates in the defendants when the chipboard is manufactured. Any interest which the plaintiffs might have had in the chipboard must have arisen either by transfer of ownership or by some constructive trust or equitable charge, and, as I say, I find it impossible to spell out of this condition anything of that nature.

Mr Mowbray, in a very valiant argument, has contended that he can achieve his end by relying upon the doctrine of tracing. But in my judgment it is a fundamental feature of the doctrine of tracing that the property to be traced can be identified at every stage of its journey through life, and that it can be identified as property to which a fiduciary obligation still attaches in favour of the person who traces it.

In the present case, in the circumstances that I have described of the resin losing its identity in the chipboard, I find it impossible to hold that the resin can be traced into the chipboard, or to any other form of property into which the chipboard might at any time be converted. Accordingly, it seems to me that the doctrine of tracing is inapplicable to a case such as this. . . .

[Bridge and Templeman LJJ delivered concurring judgments.]

Re Peachdart Ltd [1984] Ch 131, Chancery Division

Leather was supplied by Freudenbergs to Peachdart to be made into handbags, on terms that until payment of the price the sellers retained ownership in the leather and the right to trace their interest into any proceeds of sale of the leather or of goods made out of it, by virtue of a fiduciary relationship created between the buyer and sellers. Vinelott J held, however, that the sellers' interest was lost once the leather had been appropriated in the handbag-making process.

Vinelott J: Turning to the partly or wholly manufactured handbags and the proceeds of sale of those sold before the receiver was appointed, Mr Littman's submission was shortly as follows. It was said that under the terms of the bailment of each parcel of leather supplied by Freudenbergs pending payment in full of the price for that parcel the company as bailee was entitled to use the leather in the manufacture of handbags, a process which involved cutting and shaping and sewing a piece of leather and attaching to it hinges, handles, clasps and the like, in the course of which the piece of leather would remain identifiable throughout. The thread and attachments which were, it was said (and I do not think it is disputed) of comparatively minor value, then became the property of Freudenbergs as accessories to the leather. Thus the company remained a bailee of the handbags throughout the process of manufacture, and when the company sold the handbag it sold it (as in *Romalpa*) as agent for Freudenbergs, and was accordingly accountable to Freudenbergs as owner for the entire proceeds of sale. Freudenbergs was not entitled to a mere charge. Mr Littman instanced as an analogy a sportsman who having shot a rare animal takes the skin to a leather worker and instructs him to make it into a game bag. There the property in the skin would remain with the sportsman notwithstanding that the skin would undergo many operations and would have thread and other material added to it. He distinguished the *Borden* case on the ground that in that case the resin was inevitably consumed and destroyed as a separate substance when used in the manufacture of chipboard. The title retention clause accordingly did not purport to vest the property in the chipboard in the vendor, and if it had done so the vesting could only have been by way of equitable transfer of something not in existence when the resin was sold.

To my mind it is impossible to suppose that in the instant case, even assuming in Freudenbergs' favour that the company became a bailee of the leather when it was first delivered to it, the parties intended that until a parcel of leather had been fully paid for the company would remain a bailee of each piece of leather comprised in the parcel throughout the whole process of manufacture, that Freudenbergs should have the right until the parcel had been fully paid for, to enter the company's premises and identify and take away any partly or completely manufactured handbag derived from it, and that on the sale of a completed handbag the company would be under an obligation to pay the proceeds of sale into a separate interest bearing account and to keep them apart from their other moneys and not employ them in the trade.

It may be that, as Mr Littman asserts, an expert in the leather trade could identify each handbag whether partly or completely manufactured as made from a skin comprised in a particular parcel of leather. But after a handbag had been sold it would be impossible to do so. There is nothing in the conditions of sale which requires the company to keep a record of handbags sold so as to identify those of which it was a bailee and agent of Freudenbergs. No such records were in fact kept and there is nothing in the evidence which suggests that the parties contemplated that they would be. Indeed on the facts of this case it would be impossible for Freudenbergs now to prove that the handbags sold by the company but not paid for when the receiver was appointed were in fact made out of leather comprised in any of the parcels to which the unpaid invoices relied on by Freudenbergs relate. It seems to me that the parties must have intended that at least after a piece of leather had been appropriated to be manufactured into a handbag and work had started on it (when the leather would cease to have any significant value as raw material) the leather would cease to be the exclusive property of Freudenbergs (whether as bailor or as unpaid vendor) and that Freudenbergs would thereafter have a charge on handbags in the course of manufacture and on the distinctive products which would come into existence at the end of the process of manufacture (the value of which would be derived for the most part from Mr Launer's reputation and skill in design and the skill in his workforce). The charge would in due course shift to the proceeds of sale. That I accept does some violence to the language of clause 11(b) in so far as that clause provides that, 'The property in the whole or such other goods shall be *and remain* with the seller' (my emphasis). I do not think that those words compel the conclusion that the company was to be a mere bailee throughout the whole process of manufacture until the whole purchase price of the relevant parcel had been paid, and that on a sale before that time it would be no more than an agent for Freudenbergs. The language is, I think, consistent with the view that once the process of manufacture had started so that in the course of manufacture work and materials provided by the company would result in the leather being converted into (that is incorporated in or used as material for) other goods of a distinctive character the property in those other goods would vest in Freudenbergs only as security for any outstanding balance of the price of the relevant parcel of leather. What the draftsman has done is to elide and I think confuse two quite different relationships, that of bailor and bailee, with a superimposed contract of sale (or of vendor and purchaser) on the one hand and that of chargor and chargee on the other hand.

Mr Littman conceded, and I think he must concede, that if Freudenbergs had no more than a charge on the partly completed and completed handbags the charge was void for non-registration. It was also void as regards the book debts against the bank, which under the debenture had a prior fixed charge. . . .

NOTE

N E Palmer *Bailment* (2nd ed, 1991), at pp 166–168 suggests that Vinelott J perhaps too readily (given the clear wording of the contract) rejected the argument that the leather would remain the sellers' property after it had been made into handbags. Unlike the resin in the *Borden* case (above, p 418), which ceased to exist, the leather here was still the dominant constituent in the end-product. However, in the more recent case of *Modelboard Ltd v Outer Box Ltd* [1993] BCLC 623, it was held that cardboard which had been made into cardboard boxes had ceased to be 'the goods' (ie the cardboard) which had been the subject of the original sale, and so it is not likely that this argument would have prevailed. (The *result* in *Peachdart* can, however, be justified on other grounds, for there was no provision in the contract requiring that either the handbags made from Freudenberg's leather should be kept separate from other handbags or that the proceeds of sale of such handbags should similarly be kept separate.)

QUESTIONS

1. X, who raises day-old chicks, sells them for £1 to Y, a farmer, who will rear them on foodstuffs costing £3 per bird before selling them on. Can X effectively reserve title to the chicks until the price is paid? (Ignore the possibility that the transaction may be construed as creating a charge.)
2. Y, a supplier of poultry foodstuffs, sells chicken feed to X, who breeds and rears chickens. The birds are worth £1 each when day-old but will eat £3 worth of food before reaching maturity, when X will sell them on. Can Y effectively reserve title to the chicken feed until the price is paid? (Ignore the possibility that the transaction may be construed as creating a charge.)

Hendy Lennox (Industrial Engines) Ltd v Grahame Puttick Ltd [1984] 1 WLR 485, Queen's Bench Division

Lennox had supplied Puttick with diesel engines under contracts which reserved their title as sellers until full payment of the price. The engines were incorporated into generating sets which would then be sold to Puttick's customers; but each engine remained identifiable by its serial number and could easily be unbolted from the generating set. Puttick went into receivership at a time when three generating sets were in its possession. Two sets were in a deliverable state and Staughton J held that the property in them had passed to Puttick's customers, so that Lennox's claim to the two engines concerned was lost; but since the third set was not in a deliverable state (although its engine had been affixed) he held that Lennox could assert a proprietary claim to retake that engine.

Staughton J: I am aware that until very recently the radio and radar apparatus on a ship was commonly hired by the shipowner rather than bought by him. No doubt it was attached to the ship; but I do not suppose that it thereby became the property of the shipowner or his mortgagee. Nor in my judgment would an engine which was the property of A become the property of B merely because B incorporated it in a generator set otherwise composed of his own materials.

Those reflections and the facts of this case persuade me that the proprietary rights of the sellers in the engines were not affected when the engines were wholly or partially incorporated into generator sets. They were not like the Acrilan which became yarn and then carpet (the *Bond Worth* case), or the resin which became chipboard (*Borden's* case), or the leather which became handbags (the *Peachdart* case). . . . They just remained engines, albeit connected to other things.

Clough Mill Ltd v Martin [1985] 1 WLR 111, Court of Appeal

Clough Mill, spinners of yarn, sold yarn to Heatherdale, a manufacturer of fabrics, on terms which included the following (as the first and fourth sentences respectively of condition 12):

> However, the ownership of the material shall remain with the seller, which reserves the

right to dispose of the material until payment in full for all the material has been received by it in accordance with the terms of this contract or until such time as the buyer sells the material to its customers by way of bona fide sale at full market value. . . .

If any of the material is incorporated in or used as material for other goods before such payment the property in the whole of such goods shall be and remain with the seller until such payment has been made, or the other goods have been sold as aforesaid, and all the seller's rights hereunder in the material shall extend to those other goods.

The Court of Appeal held that Clough Mill could claim to be the owner of unused yarn which was in Heatherdale's possession when it went into receivership.

Sir John Donaldson MR: . . . Section 95 of the Companies Act 1948 provides:

(1) . . . every charge created . . . by a company . . . shall, so far as any security on the company's property . . . is conferred thereby, be void against the liquidator and any creditor of the company . . .

Accordingly s 95 can only apply if (a) the company creates a charge, and (b) that charge *confers* a security on *the company's property.*

The plaintiff's demands upon the defendant related solely to unused and unsold yarn and it is quite clear that if the first sentence of condition 12 had stood alone, s 95 would have had no application. The agreement between the plaintiff and the buyer involved the plaintiff *retaining* property in the goods. It did not involve the buyer *conferring* a charge on any property, but still less on its own property.

The argument that the object of the exercise was to give the plaintiff security for the price of the yarn does not of itself advance the matter. Just as it is possible to increase the amount of cash available to a business by borrowing, buying on hire-purchase or credit sale terms, factoring book debts or raising additional share capital, all with different legal incidents, so it is possible to achieve security for an unpaid purchase price in different ways, with different legal consequences. The parties have chosen not to use the charging method in relation to unused yarn.

Fortunately we do not have to decide whether the fourth sentence of condition 12 creates a charge to which s 95 of the Act of 1948 would apply. I say 'fortunately,' because this seems to me to be a difficult question. If the incorporation of the yarn in, or its use as material for, other goods leaves the yarn in a separate and identifiable state, I see no reason why the plaintiff should not retain property in it and thereby avoid the application of s 95. However, in that situation I should have thought that the buyer was clearly purporting to create a charge on the 'other goods' which would never have been the plaintiff's goods. I say 'purporting,' because those goods might themselves remain the property of another supplier in consequence of the inclusion of the equivalent of the first sentence of condition 12 in the relevant sale contract. If, on the other hand, the incorporation of the yarn created a situation in which it ceased to be identifiable and a new product was created consisting of the yarn and the other material, it would be necessary to determine who owned that product. If, and to the extent that, the answer was the buyer, it seems to me that the fourth sentence would create a charge.

For present purposes I am content to assume that in some circumstances the fourth sentence of condition 12 would indeed give rise to a charge to which s 95 of the Act of 1948 would apply, but they are not the circumstances which exist in the instant appeal and I see no reason to distort the plain language of the first sentence on the false assumption that the parties must be deemed to have intended that the same legal framework should apply both before and after the yarn was made up into other goods.

There remains one other aspect which creates problems, but again is not, I think, determinative of this appeal. The first sentence of condition 12 retains property in all the material to which the contract relates until the price of that material has been paid in full. Thus if three-quarters of the yarn had been paid for, the plaintiffs would retain ownership of, and have a right to resell, all the material. Such a resale would be likely to realise more than was owed by the buyer. What happens then? I am inclined to think that the word 'until' in the phrase 'reserves the right to dispose of the material until payment in full for all the material has been received' connotes not only a temporal, but also a quantitative limitation.

In other words, the plaintiff can go on selling hank by hank until they have been paid in full, but if thereafter they continue to sell, they are accountable to the buyer for having sold goods which, upon full payment having been achieved, became the buyer's goods.

Other cases concerned with retention of title clauses include the following:

(1) *Re Andrabell Ltd* [1984] 3 All ER 407: In a number of contracts of sale Airborne Accessories Ltd supplied travel bags to Andrabell, a retailer, on terms that ownership should not pass to Andrabell until it had paid Airborne the 'total purchase price'. When Andrabell went into liquidation, Airborne claimed to be entitled to certain bags which were in its possession and to moneys, allegedly representing the proceeds of sale of bags, which Airborne had paid into its general bank account. In view of the following facts, Peter Gibson J held that no fiduciary relationship had been created:
   (a) the passing of the property in the bags was postponed only until full payment was made for the particular consignment, rather than Andrabell's total indebtedness;
   (b) there was no provision requiring the bags to be stored separately;
   (c) there was no express acknowledgment of a fiduciary relationship, and no provision that Airborne should have the benefit of the subsales;
   (d) Andrabell was not constituted Airborne's agent to resell;
   (e) there was no obligation to keep the proceeds of sale separate from other moneys;
   (f) the contracts provided for a 45-day period of credit, during which time Andrabell was free to use the proceeds of any subsales in any way that it liked.

In the absence of a fiduciary relationship, he said, the parties had to be treated simply as creditor and debtor, and there was no duty to account. Nor could Airborne claim any of the bags.

QUESTION

Assuming that all the bags in Andrabell's possession were identifiable as having been supplied by Airborne, why did the claim for return of the bags fail? Could Airborne have succeeded if the contract had been differently worded?

(2) *Specialist Plant Services Ltd v Braithwaite Ltd* [1987] BCLC 1, CA: The plaintiff company supplied parts and materials for the purposes of repairing a machine owned by Braithwaite. The contract contained a provision that the supplier should be given ownership of the machine 'as surety for the full payment' of what the customer owed. This was held to create a charge.

(3) *E Pfeiffer Weinkellerei-Weineinkauf GmbH & Co v Arbuthnot Factors Ltd* [1988] 1 WLR 150 and *Compaq Computer Ltd v Abercorn Group Ltd* [1991] BCC 484: In each of these cases goods (respectively wines and computing equipment) were supplied on retention of title terms to a retailer who sold or leased them to customers. The supplier purported to reserve title to the goods, and also a proprietary interest in the moneys representing the proceeds of the subsales and leases, until the price of the goods was paid; and its claim in each case was against these moneys. Since the suppliers' claim was only in respect of so much of the proceeds as was necessary to satisfy the outstanding price, the court held that the contracts amounted to an equitable assignment of the proceeds by way of charge, which was inconsistent with the fiduciary

relationship on which a proprietary claim would be based; and because no charge had been registered, the suppliers could not succeed. (The suppliers also failed on a second ground, namely that the proceeds had been assigned to a factoring house which was held to have priority: see below, p 739.)

(4) *Tatung (UK) Ltd v Galex Telesure Ltd* (1988) 5 BCC 325: This case concerned television and video equipment which was sold to a retailer on terms which authorised the goods to be resold or let on hire to customers, but which purported to reserve title in the goods to the suppliers and to confer on them rights to the proceeds of sale or hire of the goods until the purchase price and any other sums owing to the suppliers had been paid. Since the suppliers' interest in the proceeds was defeasible upon payment of whatever the retailers owed to the suppliers, it was held that the contract created rights by way of security rather than an absolute interest.

(5) *Armour v Thyssen Edelstahlwerke AG* [1991] 2 AC 339, HL: Here German sellers successfully claimed to have retained title to steel sold and delivered to a Scottish company. It was held that a retention of title clause in standard form was effective (in regard to the original goods, which were identifiable) in Scots law.

(6) *Forsythe International (UK) Ltd v Silver Shipping Co Ltd, The Saetta* [1993] 2 Lloyd's Rep 268: The *Saetta* was owned by Silver and chartered to Petroglobe. Forsythe sold fuel oil to Petroglobe which was delivered into the ship's bunkers. The sale contract reserved title in the oil to the sellers. When Petroglobe failed to pay the hire charges on time Silver repossessed the ship under a power conferred by a clause in the charterparty which provided that any fuel oil on board thereupon became the property of Silver. Clarke J held that the oil still belonged to Forsythe and that in consequence Silver's act amounted to the tort of conversion as against Forsythe. (He also held that the taking of possession by Silver was not a 'delivery' by Petroglobe which would give Silver a good title under s 25(1) (see above, p 341): 'delivery' required a conscious, voluntary act on the part of the party making delivery.)

Reform of the law. It is clear from the cases that the theoretical basis of many of the customary *Romalpa* terms – at least the more elaborate ones – is unclear, and that much uncertainty would be avoided if this topic were made the subject of clarifying legislation. But views differ as to the best course to be taken.

There are some who argue that the law should be changed so that, regardless of contractual form, all retention of title clauses should be deemed to create a charge and require registration. This would, of course, suit the banks, who would almost always be able to enforce their own charges in priority.

There is a counter-argument which stresses the commercial importance and utility of *Romalpa* terms, and expresses concern that already much of the protection which sellers have sought to secure for themselves has been whittled away by successive judgments: a simple business need, it is contended, is being thwarted by over-elaborate legal niceties.

It is probably true to say that there is this commercial need, and that it would be wrong to ignore it. Moreover, there is a working 'retention of title' regime in many other EC countries (as evidenced by the fact that German and Dutch plaintiffs feature prominently in the list of English cases cited above), and with the progressive removal of barriers to trade within the Community, it makes little sense for the United Kingdom to be the odd one out.

The topic has received attention in three official reports.

The Crowther Committee (Cmnd 4596, 1971, para 5.2.19) recommended that the whole subject be taken out of the law of sale of goods and made part of a general Lending and Security Act, in which all transactions which give any kind of de facto security would be registrable as such.

The Cork Committee (Cmnd 8558, 1982, para 1639) suggested that a *separate* registration system should be set up for retention of title contracts; but it resisted arguments that there should be legislation aimed at providing certainty in this area (eg by defining what is and is not a charge), preferring to leave it to market forces and the evolutionary processes of case law to reduce the subject to a more settled state over time.

Professor Diamond, in his report (*A Review of Security Interests in Property* (HMSO, 1989), Ch 17) suggests a compromise: that (at least until a more comprehensive lending and security law is introduced) a seller should be protected by being allowed to assert a proprietary claim against the sale goods themselves and the proceeds of any subsale, without any requirement of registration under the Companies Act – but only in regard to a claim for the actual price of the goods: if he wants wider protection (eg with an 'all moneys' clause or a claim to processed goods), the transaction will be regarded as creating a charge and will have to be registered.

QUESTION

In *Borden (UK) Ltd v Scottish Timber Products Ltd* (above, p 418), Templeman LJ said ([1981] Ch 25 at 42):

> Unsecured creditors rank after preferential creditors, mortgagees and the holders of floating charges and they receive a raw deal: see *Business Computers Ltd v Anglo-African Leasing Ltd* [1977] 1 WLR 578, 580. It is not therefore surprising that this court looked with sympathy on an invention designed to provide some protection for one class of unsecured creditors, namely unpaid sellers of goods: see *Aluminium Industrie Vaassen BV v Romalpa Aluminium Ltd* [1976] 1 WLR 676, although there is no logical reason why this class of creditor should be favoured as against other creditors such as the suppliers of consumables and services.

Do you agree that there is 'no logical reason' for this distinction? If so, what attitude should the law take?

CHAPTER 13

Remedies of the buyer

1 Introduction

This topic, which is of course the counterpart of 'Duties of the seller' (above, p 378), is relatively straightforward, and largely restates principles of the general law of contract.

2 To reject the goods

If the seller delivers or tenders goods which are not of the contract description, whether as regards quantity or quality, the first and most obvious remedy of the buyer will be to reject them. As we saw earlier, the right to reject may be exercised even after the property has passed to the buyer, provided that he has not 'accepted' the goods within the meaning of s 35 (*Kwei Tek Chao v British Traders & Shippers Ltd*; *McDougall v Aeromarine of Emsworth Ltd* (above, p 294).

Where the seller has delivered the wrong *quantity* of goods, the buyer has the choice of remedies set out in s 30:

(1) in the case of a short delivery, to reject the goods or to accept them and pay at the contract rate;

(2) in the case of an excessive delivery, to reject the goods, to accept the contract quantity and reject the rest, or to accept all the goods and pay for the excess at the contract rate;

(3) in the case where the contract goods are delivered mixed with other goods not contracted for, to accept the contract goods and reject the remainder, or to reject the whole consignment.

The one qualification to these provisions is that the law is prepared to overlook a disparity in measurement which is commercially insignificant (the *de minimis* exception). In *Shipton, Anderson & Co v Weil Bros & Co* [1912] 1 KB 574, this principle was applied: there, a cargo of 4950 tons of wheat was overweight by 55 lbs (a difference in price of 20p in £40,000, which the sellers did not claim). But such cases will be rare, for (as we saw in relation to the seller's obligation to deliver goods conforming with their description (above, p 348)), the approach of the courts is a strict one.

The right to reject will also lie if the seller has broken a condition of the contract, or has committed a serious breach of an innominate term. The most common breaches of terms as to *quality* will be breaches of the statutory conditions implied by ss 12–15 of the Act, although of course there may be express conditions as well. An example of a breach of an innominate term is *Cehave NV v Bremer Handelsgesellschaft mbH, The Hansa Nord* [1976] QB 44, CA, where the seller of a cargo of citrus pulp pellets was in breach of an express term, 'shipment to be made in good condition', but not in the view of the Court of Appeal to a degree which went to the root of the contract. Accordingly, the buyer was entitled to damages only, and not to reject the goods. The same approach is also appropriate where there has been a breach of a contract to be performed by instalments (where s 31(2) applies, to the exclusion of s 30: see above, p 385).

A seller normally has the right to cure a defective tender of goods, if this can be done within the time allowed by the contract and is not otherwise inconsistent with the contract.

Borrowman, Phillips & Co v Free & Hollis (1878) 4 QBD 500, Court of Appeal

This case concerned a contract to buy a cargo of American maize, to be shipped between 15 May and 30 June. The sellers offered the buyers a cargo on the *Charles Platt*, but the buyers rejected this offer (it was held, by an arbitrator, rightly) because the sellers had no shipping documents. The sellers then offered a second cargo on the *Maria D*, which the buyers also rejected. The sellers had to resell the cargo of the *Maria D* at a loss, and sued the buyers for damages for non-acceptance. The trial judge (Denman J) ruled that the buyers were not bound to accept the second tender once the sellers had appropriated the first cargo to the contract; but the Court of Appeal reversed this decision.

Brett LJ: I now pass to the point, upon which the judgment of Denman J was given. It has been argued by the defendants' counsel that the plaintiffs could not lawfully tender the cargo of the *Maria D*, because they had already tendered that of the *Charles Platt*, and had insisted upon that tender. The doctrine of election was relied upon, and it was urged that, even if the offer of the *Charles Platt* was not of itself a sufficient election, the plaintiffs were ousted of their right to sue in this action by referring the matter to arbitration. It may be that that if the plaintiffs had recovered damages in an action for not accepting the cargo of the *Charles Platt* they could not maintain this suit; but in the present case there were no trial and judgment, it was only a reference to arbitration, whether the plaintiffs could according to mercantile usage tender the cargo of the *Charles Platt*. The question comes down to the narrow point, whether the plaintiffs are barred by the doctrine of election. For the defendants reliance has been placed upon a passage in Blackburn on Contract of Sale, pp 128, 129, to the effect that when in pursuance of a contract to sell unspecified goods the vendor has appropriated certain goods, he has made an election which is irrevocable; but I think that passage has nothing to do with the principle to be applied in the present case. It may be that, where goods which fulfil the terms of a contract are appropriated for sale in performance thereof, there is an election by the vendor which is irrevocable; but here the contention for the defendants is that the cargo of the *Charles Platt* was not in accordance with the contract. . . .

I have only to add that a different rule might have been applied, if the defendants had accepted the cargo of the *Charles Platt*; it is possible that the tender of the plaintiffs could not in that case have been withdrawn. I wish it however to be understood, that this is a point upon which I express no opinion.

[Bramwell and Cotton LJJ delivered concurring judgments.]

The buyer loses the right to reject the goods when he 'accepts' the goods (or is deemed to have accepted them) in the circumstances set out in s 35. (On acceptance, see above, p 380.) The loss of the right to reject does not affect his right to claim damages in respect of any shortfall or defect in the delivery (s 11(4)). However, s 35 is declared to be subject to s 34: the words 'except where s 34 above otherwise provides' having been inserted into s 35 by an amendment made in 1967. Section 34 sets out rules regarding the buyer's right to examine the goods in the following terms:

(1) Where goods are delivered to the buyer, and he has not previously examined them, he is not deemed to have accepted them until he has had a reasonable opportunity of examining them for the purpose of ascertaining whether they are in conformity with the contract.

(2) Unless otherwise agreed, when the seller tenders delivery of goods to the buyer, he is bound on request to afford the buyer a reasonable opportunity of examining the goods for the purpose of ascertaining whether they are in conformity with the contract.

Before the amending words were inserted into s 35, there were circumstances in which a buyer had been held to have accepted the goods (and thus lost any right of rejection) even though he had had no opportunity to examine them. This was held to be the case where the buyer had resold the goods before they were delivered to him, and delivery had been made either to the sub-buyer directly or the goods were in containers which had been sent on to the sub-buyer unopened. The courts took the view (eg in *Hardy & Co v Hillerns & Fowler* (below) and *E & S Ruben Ltd v Faire Bros & Co Ltd* [1949] 1 KB 254) that because the buyer in reselling the goods had 'done an act in relation to the goods which was inconsistent with the ownership of the seller' (see s 35), his right to reject was lost. This ruling had the unhappy consequence that the sub-buyer could throw the goods back into the hands of the first buyer, but the latter could not in turn reject the goods and leave them with the original seller, who was the person responsible for the defective delivery. In *Perkins v Bell* (below) this question did not arise, because the court took the view that the buyer had had an opportunity to examine the goods before sending them on; but it did in *Hardy & Co v Hillerns & Fowler*.

Perkins v Bell [1893] 1 QB 193, Court of Appeal

Perkins, a Leicestershire farmer, contracted to sell barley to Bell, a corn merchant, to be delivered in sacks at his local railway station. Bell resold the barley to brewers in another county. The barley, which was below the contract quality, was delivered to the station, where Bell had a sample taken and 'considered it a fair delivery' (though he seems to have assumed that this was only a provisional examination), and ordered the stationmaster to send the consignment on to the brewers. They rejected it as 'quite unfit for the brewing of ale'. The court held that Bell must be deemed to have accepted the goods.

A L Smith LJ delivered the judgment of the court (Lindley, Bowen and A L Smith LJJ): It will be noticed that by the contract the plaintiff was to deliver the barley at Theddingworth Station. No other destination was known to him, and we cannot doubt that if this had been a sale of specific ascertained barley, the property therein would have passed to the defendant upon its delivery to the railway company at the station by the plaintiff. The railway company would thereupon have become the agents of the defendant to receive it and to carry it to any place or places the defendant might direct. But it was said by Mr Loyd for the defendant that inasmuch as this was a sale by sample, the defendant was entitled to a fair opportunity of comparing the bulk with the sale sample after delivery, before the property in the barley passed to him, and that the place for inspection need not necessarily be the place at which delivery is to be made; and in this we agree. The question, however, is if there can be read into this contract an implied term that the inspection was to be had at any place fixed by the vendee without the knowledge of the vendor. This is not a case in which before a sale by sample it is agreed that the destination of the goods shall be the vendee's premises or some other named locality, and that the transit thereto shall be performed partly by the vendor and partly by the vendee. In such a case it would be right to imply that the place of destination agreed upon was the place for inspection, and that the joint transit was only an agreed mode of getting the goods there: see *Grimoldby v Wells* ((1875) LR 10 CP 391). This is a case in which at the time of sale the only known destination was Theddingworth Station, at which the vendor undertook to deliver the barley at his own risk and expense. Of all that should take place afterwards as regards the barley, the vendor knew nothing. It was entirely at the disposal of the vendee, who might send it where and to whom he pleased, and when he pleased, and over which disposition the seller could exercise no control. We find no evidence in this case to dislodge the presumption which prima facie arises, that the place of delivery is the place for inspection. To hold otherwise would be to expose the vendor to unknown risks, impossible of calculation, when the contract was entered into. The vendee might consign the barley not only to one, but to different sub-vendees, living in different places and at different distances from Theddingworth Station, and until arrival at these places the barley would be at the risk of the vendor. If the barley was rejected by these sub-vendees upon arrival, the vendor would have at his own risk and cost to take the barley back from whatever places it might happen to be in, no matter how far they might be from Theddingworth Station, or to arrange for its sale at the places where it then was. As to these risks the contract is wholly silent, and in our judgment it is impossible to read into it that the vendor undertook these risks, as we were invited by Mr Loyd to do.

Hardy & Co v Hillerns & Fowler [1923] 2 KB 490, Court of Appeal

(The facts appear from the judgment of Bankes LJ. This case would, of course, now be decided differently, in view of the amendment to s 35.)

Bankes LJ: Messrs Hillerns & Fowler bought a large quantity of Rosario or Santa Fé wheat to be shipped from a port in Uruguay to Hull at a certain price including freight and insurance, payment to be by cash in London against shipping documents. The ship sailed and arrived in Hull on March 18. On March 20 the buyers' bankers in London took up the shipping documents. On the 21st the ship commenced to discharge the wheat, and on the same day the buyers sold to sub-purchasers portions of the wheat so discharged, 200 qrs to a purchaser at Barnsley, 100 qrs to a purchaser at Nottingham, and 500 qrs to a purchaser at Southwell. In order to fulfil those sub-contracts they on the same day, March 21, despatched the quantities so sold by rail to Barnsley and Nottingham respectively, and to Southwell by barge. They had taken samples of wheat on the 21st, which samples had raised a suspicion that the cargo was not according to the contract description. But they allowed the discharge to continue, and on the 22nd took further samples, which satisfied them that their suspicions were well founded, and on the 23rd they gave the sellers notice that they rejected the wheat. Upon those facts the sellers contended that under the terms of s 35 the buyers must be deemed to have accepted the goods and lost their right of rejection. The arbitration tribunal found that the wheat was not in accordance with the contract, but that owing to the difficulty of getting a fairly representative sample until a considerable portion of the cargo had been discharged it was reasonable for the buyers to delay making up their mind to reject until the 23rd.

The question now arises whether the buyers by so reselling and forwarding to the sub-purchasers portions of the wheat had lost the right to reject and were confined to their remedy in damages. The construction which Greer J has placed upon ss 34 and 35 of the Sale of Goods Act is one with which I entirely agree. Section 34 gives a buyer to whom goods have been delivered, which he has not previously examined, a reasonable opportunity of examining them before he shall be deemed to have accepted them. Then s 35 provides as follows:

[The Lord Justice read the section.]

I understand that to mean that if during the currency of the reasonable time within which the examination is to be made the buyer does certain things, one of which is an 'act in relation to (the goods) which is inconsistent with the ownership of the seller,' he shall be deemed to have accepted them. Section 35 is, in my opinion, independent of s 34, and it is quite immaterial for the purposes of that section that the reasonable time for examining the goods had not expired when the act was done. The finding therefore of the arbitration tribunal that in the present case that time had not expired may be disregarded.

It remains to be considered whether the act of reselling to the sub-purchasers was an act which was inconsistent with the ownership of the sellers. Mr Le Quesne has argued that s 35 has no application to this case, because the contract under which the wheat was sold to the buyers was a cif contract, and that upon the bank taking up the shipping documents upon March 20 the property passed to the buyers, and that consequently when they resold on the 21st there was no ownership left in the sellers with which that act of resale could be inconsistent. It seems to me that that is attempting to put a meaning on the language of the section which it cannot reasonably bear. I understand the section to refer to an act which is inconsistent with the seller being the owner at the material date; and the material date for the purposes of this case is not the date of the resale, but the date of the notice of rejection, upon receipt of which the ownership revested in the sellers. It is with that revested ownership that in my opinion the act of resale was inconsistent. And it was inconsistent with it for this reason: Where under a contract of sale goods are delivered to the buyer which are not in accordance with the contract, so that the buyer has a right to reject them, the seller upon receipt of notice of rejection is entitled to have the goods placed at his disposal so as to allow of his resuming possession forthwith, and if the buyer has done any act which prevents him from so resuming possession that act is necessarily inconsistent with his right. It is not enough that the buyer should, as in the present case, be in a position to give the seller possession at some later date, he must be able to do so at the time of the rejection. For these reasons I have come to the conclusion that the decision of Greer J was right and that the appeal should be dismissed.

[Atkin LJ delivered a concurring judgment. Young LJ concurred.]

NOTE

In a New Zealand case, *Hammer & Barrow v Coca Cola* [1962] NZLR 723 the goods (200,000 yo-yos) had to the knowledge of the sellers been resold to sub-buyers before they were due to be delivered and, indeed, the contract provided that delivery was to be made by the sellers directly to the sub-buyers' premises. It was held (even on the unamended wording of s 35) that (1) the place for examination contemplated by the contract was the premises of the sub-buyer, and (2) that since there had been no act inconsistent with the ownership of the sellers *after* delivery of the goods, there had been no acceptance.

If a buyer has rightly rejected the goods, he is not bound to return them to the seller. It is sufficient if he informs the seller that he refuses to accept them (s 36). It is then up to the seller to make arrangements for them to be collected or disposed of.

If a buyer who has rejected goods has paid all or part of the price and the seller does not make an effective substituted delivery, he may of course claim restitution of the money that he has paid. He may also claim damages for any incidental or consequential losses, provided that they are not too remote.

3 Buyer's action for damages for non-delivery

The buyer's right to sue the seller for damages for non-delivery closely parallels the seller's action for damages for non-acceptance (s 50: see above, p 391). Section 51 provides:

(1) Where the seller wrongfully neglects or refuses to deliver the goods to the buyer, the buyer may maintain an action against the seller for damages for non-delivery.

(2) The measure of damages is the estimated loss directly or naturally resulting, in the ordinary course of events, from the seller's breach of contract.

(3) Where there is an available market for the goods in question the measure of damages is prima facie to be ascertained by the difference between the contract price and the market or current price of the goods at the time or times when they ought to have been delivered or (if no time was fixed) at the time of the refusal to deliver.

The concept of 'an available market' and the rule that, where there is such a market, the price prevailing there is prima facie to be used to ascertain the measure of damages, have already been discussed in relation to the seller's action for damages for non-acceptance (see above, p 391). The place and time when the delivery ought to have been made will once again, prima facie, be the relevant time and place for the reckoning of the market price; and this will be true whether there is an actual or an anticipatory breach. However, in the case of an anticipatory breach, once the seller's repudiation has been accepted, the buyer's duty to mitigate his loss may oblige him to accept lower damages if he fails to buy against a rising market. These points are illustrated by the following cases.

Melachrino v Nickoll & Knight [1920] 1 KB 693, King's Bench Division

Melachrino agreed in two separate contracts to sell Egyptian cotton seed to Nickoll & Knight, to be shipped to London on the SS *Asaos*, expected to arrive between 10 January and 10 February 1917. The sellers repudiated the contracts on 14 December 1916, and the buyers accepted their repudiation on the same day. On 14 December the market price of cotton seed was above the contract price; for the whole of the period between 10 January and 10 February it was below it. The court held that the buyer was entitled to only nominal damages.

Bailhache J: Upon these facts the question arises: Are the buyers' damages to be fixed with reference to the market prices on December 14, 1916, or with reference to the prices ruling at the time when the goods might be expected to be delivered? If the former the damages are substantial, if the latter nominal. The arbitrators have assessed the damages as at the date of the anticipatory breach.

There was a market for the goods and in that case the prima facie rules for the measurement of damages as laid down in s 51 of the Sale of Goods Act 1893, vary according to whether there is a fixed time for delivery or not. If there is no fixed time the measure is the difference between the contract price and the market price at the time of refusal to deliver. The first point to determine therefore is whether this was a contract of that kind. In my opinion it was not. The time was not certain but it was fixed by reference to the happening of an event – namely, the arrival of the *Asaos* in the United Kingdom. I take it that when s 51 speaks of no time being fixed for delivery it refers to those contracts in which no mention of time is made and which therefore are to be performed within the indefinite period known as a reasonable time under the circumstances.

In regard to other cases of which this is one the prima facie measure of damages is said to be the difference between the contract price and the market price at the time the goods ought to have been delivered – in this case the period between January 10 and February 10, 1917. In a constantly fluctuating market and if the prices during that period had ruled higher than the contract prices there might have been some difficulty in determining the proper price to be taken, but in this case that point does not arise, as at all times between those dates the market prices were below the contract prices.

Section 51 does not in terms deal with an anticipatory breach, and in the case of a breach by effluxion of time it is clear that it makes no difference to the measure of damages whether a buyer goes into the market or is content to take the difference in price without troubling to buy against the defaulting seller. The question to be decided is whether the same rule applies in the case of an anticipatory breach.

An anticipatory breach occurs when the seller refuses to deliver before the contractual time for delivery has arrived and the buyer accepts his refusal as a breach of contract.

In that case the following rules are well established, subject of course to any express provisions to the contrary in any particular contract.

Immediately upon the anticipatory breach the buyer may bring his action whether he buys against the seller or not.

It is the duty of the buyer to go into the market and buy against the defaulting seller if a reasonable opportunity offers. This is expressed by the phrase 'It is the buyer's duty to mitigate damages.' In that event the damages are assessed with reference to the market price on the date of the repurchase. If the buyer does not perform his duty in this respect the seller is none the less entitled to have damages assessed as at the date when a fresh contract might and ought to have been made.

As a corollary to this rule the buyer may if he pleases go into the market and buy against the seller: as he is bound to do so to mitigate damages, so he is entitled to do so to cover himself against his commitments or to secure the goods. In that case again the damages are assessed with reference to the market price at the date of the repurchase.

It is also settled law that when default is made by the seller by refusal to deliver within the contract time the buyer is under no duty to accept the repudiation and buy against him but may claim the difference between the contract price and the market price at the date when under the contract the goods should have been delivered.

Further, in the case of an anticipatory breach the contract is at an end and the defaulting seller cannot take advantage of any subsequent circumstances which would have afforded him a justification for non-performance of his contract had his repudiation not been accepted.

In logical strictness it would appear to follow that equally the defaulting seller cannot take advantage of a fall in the market before the due date for delivery to escape liability for damages.

It looks therefore at first sight as though the date at which the difference between the contract price and the market price ought to be taken for the assessment of damages when the buyer does not buy against the seller should follow by analogy the rule adopted where the buyer goes into the market and buys, or where the breach is failure to deliver at the due date and should be at or about the date when the buyer intimates his acceptance of the repudiation though he does not actually go into the market against the seller. If so, in this case, the date would be about December 14, when the buyer claimed arbitration and so the arbitrators have found.

As against this line of reasoning it must be remembered that the object of damages is to place a person whose contract is broken in as nearly as possible the same position as if it had been performed. This result is secured by measuring damages either at the date of the repurchase, in the case of repurchase on an ancitipatory breach, or at the date when the goods ought to have been delivered when there is no anticipatory breach whether there is a repurchase or not. In these cases the buyer gets a new contract as nearly as may be like the broken contract and the defaulting seller pays the extra expense incurred by the buyer in restoring his position.

Where however there is an anticipatory breach but no buying against the defaulting seller, and the price falls below the contract price between the date of the anticipatory breach and the date when the goods ought to have been delivered, the adoption of the date of the anticipatory breach as the date at which the market price ought to be taken would put the buyer in a better position than if his contract had been duly performed. He would if that date were adopted be given a profit and retain his money wherewith to buy the goods if so minded on the fall of the market. It would be in effect, to use a homely phrase, to allow him to eat his cake and have it. Perhaps it is better to avoid figures of speech however picturesque and to say, to make a profit from the anticipatory breach while the contract if duly performed would have shown a loss – a position which is I think irreconcilable with the principles upon which damages are awarded as between buyer and seller.

In my opinion the true rule is that where there is an ancitipatory breach by a seller to deliver goods for which there is a market at a fixed date the buyer without buying against the seller may bring his action at once, but that if he does so his damages must be assessed with reference to the market price of the goods at the time when they ought to have been delivered under the contract. If the action comes to trial before the contractual date for delivery has arrived the Court must arrive at that price as best it can.

To this rule there is one exception for the benefit of the defaulting seller – namely, that if he can show that the buyer acted unreasonably in not buying against him the date to be taken is the date at which the buyer ought to have gone into the market to mitigate damages. . . .

The result in this case is that the damages are nominal.

Tai Hing Cotton Mill Ltd v Kamsing Knitting Factory [1979] AC 91, Privy Council

Tai Hing contracted to sell 1500 bales of cotton yarn to Kamsing at HK$1335 per bale, delivery to be made as required by the buyers on giving one month's notice. In July 1973, when 424 bales remained undelivered, the sellers wrote to the buyers repudiating the contract. The buyers for some months pressed the sellers to continue to deliver supplies, but eventually on 28 November 1973 they issued a writ claiming damages for breach. The market price of cotton was $3300 per bale in August 1973 but fell steadily from September 1973 onwards. The Privy Council held that this was a case of an anticipatory breach which was not accepted until 28 November; that this was the latest date on which the buyers could have given the sellers notice requiring delivery of all the outstanding bales; and that accordingly damages should be assessed by reference to the market price one month after that, ie on 28 December 1973.

The advice of the Privy Council was delivered by **Lord Keith of Kinkel:** The principal question in the appeal is whether the majority of the Full Court were right in holding that damages for the sellers' admitted breach of contract fell to be ascertained as at July 31, 1973, the date of the sellers' repudiation of the contract, notwithstanding that the buyers did not accept the repudiation, and rescind the contract, until they issued and served their writ in the present action on November 28, 1973.

The answer to that question turns on the proper construction of s 53 of the Hong Kong Sale of Goods Ordinance, which provides:

(1) Where the seller wrongfully neglects or refuses to deliver the goods to the buyer, the buyer may maintain an action against the seller for damages for non-delivery. (2) The measure of damages is the estimated loss directly and naturally resulting, in the ordinary course of events, from the seller's breach of contract. (3) Where there is an available market for the goods in question, the measure of damages is prima facie to be ascertained by the difference between the contract price and the market or current price of the goods at the time or times when they ought to have been delivered, or, if no time was fixed for delivery, then at the time of the neglect or refusal to deliver.

These provisions are identical with those of s 51 of the (United Kingdom) Sale of Goods Act 1893, except that in the latter the words 'for delivery' and 'neglect or' in the latter part of subs (3) do not appear. Their Lordships do not consider that this difference can properly lead to any distinction of construction between the two enactments.

In the Full Court both Huggins J and McMullin J took the view that the present contract was one which did not fix any time for delivery, that the sellers on July 31, 1973, intimated their refusal to deliver the balance of the contractual goods, and that the second limb of s 53(3) consequently required that damages be ascertained by reference to market price at July 31, 1973. Cons J dissented on this matter, and he therefore was in favour of dismissing the cross-appeal and allowing the learned Chief Justice's assessment of damages to stand.

Before this Board it was contended for the sellers that the second limb of subs (3) did not apply to cases of anticipatory breach of contract, that damages fell to be assessed by reference to market price at the time when the goods ought to have been delivered, and that such time was a reasonable period (say, one month) after the last date upon which the buyers might have called for delivery of the balance of the contractual goods. That date was November 28, 1973, being the date upon which the buyers, by issuing and serving their writ, had accepted the sellers' repudiation and rescinded the contract. Thus the damages fell to be ascertained by reference to the market price of comparable goods at December 28, 1973, and since the buyers had led no evidence about market price on that date they had failed to prove any loss and the damages should be nominal.

In support of their proposition that the second limb of s 53(3) does not apply in cases of anticipatory breach of contract the sellers relied strongly on *Millett v Van Heek & Co* [1920] 3 KB 535, [1921] 2 KB 369.

[His Lordship set out the facts of that case, and continued:]

Bray J, delivering the judgment of the court, went on to express the opinion that a contract providing for delivery within a reasonable time was not, within the meaning of s 51(3) of the Act of 1893, a contract for delivery at a fixed time, even if the contract was for delivery within a reasonable time after some future date. He then said, at p 542:

> The next point was whether this case fell within the rule mentioned in the last two lines of s 51(3). We hold that this rule cannot apply to this case. It does not apply to a case where the breach is an anticipatory breach. We hold that there is no specific rule in s 51 within which the present case falls, except the rule in subs (2), and that this case must be decided according to that rule, but with the light thrown upon it by subs (3).

This judgment was affirmed by the Court of Appeal (Bankes, Warrington and Atkin LJJ) upon the ground that the second limb of s 51(3) had no application to the case of an anticipatory breach by repudiation of the contract before the time for performance arrived, the question whether a contract for delivery within a reasonable time is not a contract for delivery at a fixed time being reserved. . . .

As Atkin LJ rightly said [in that case], there was in 1921 ample authority for the proposition that in cases of rescission of a contract providing a fixed time for performance by acceptance of a repudiation, damages are to be assessed as at the time fixed for performance (subject to considerations of mitigation of loss), and not as at the date of repudiation. . . .

Mr Gatehouse for the buyers, while accepting that the second limb of s 51(3) of the Sale of Goods Act 1893 and of s 53(3) of the Hong Kong Ordinance did not apply to cases of anticipatory breach where the contract stipulated a fixed time for delivery, argued that it did apply to such cases where no fixed time was stipulated, and that *Millett v Van Heek & Co* was wrongly decided.

[His Lordship referred to a number of cases, and continued:]

In their Lordships' opinion the cases referred to by Mr Gatehouse are not authoritative upon the point at issue and have in themselves no persuasive effect. The force of Mr Gatehouse's argument resides essentially in the plain terms of the second limb of s 51(3). Their Lordships are attracted by the consideration that this may have been enacted in order to provide a universal rule of simple application for cases where the contract fixes no time for delivery, as where delivery is to be within a reasonable time or on demand by the purchaser. In such cases there may be great difficulty in determining when the contract ought to have been performed, and there could be much convenience in assessing damages as at the date of repudiation by the seller, assuming the buyer accepts it. Further, if the enactment is not intended to apply to a repudiation in such cases, it is difficult to see what content it can have. It could not apply, in cases where delivery is to be made on demand by the buyer, to a refusal to deliver following on a demand duly made, because the demand, having been made in accordance with the contract, would fix the time for delivery. It might be intended to apply, where delivery is to be made within a reasonable time, to a refusal to deliver intimated at the expiry of the period of reasonable time, but if so nothing significant would have been added to the first limb. It may well be, however, that the enactment was introduced into the subsection without consideration in depth of the juristic position, and that on analysis it proves, exceptionally, to have no content whatever. It would be surprising if the first limb of one and the same subsection were intended to be a specific application of the general principle in the preceding subsection, and the second limb to be a radical departure from it. If Parliament had intended to introduce a new rule of the nature contended for, their Lordships would have expected this to be done by clearer and more specific language than appears in the second limb of subs (3).

Atkin LJ, in the course of that part of his judgment in *Millett v Van Heek & Co* which dealt with the question whether the second limb of s 51(3) applied to cases of anticipatory breach, expressed the view that it was anomalous that a plaintiff should not only have the option, but be compelled, to fix his damages in reference to the time when the repudiation takes place. It appears to their Lordships that a plaintiff in such a case is not necessarily so compelled. He is not required to accept the repudiation, and if he does not do so the repudiation has no effect. He may wait until there has been an actual failure by the defendant to perform the contract, either on account of an unmet demand or on account of a reasonable time having elapsed without delivery. In this event the damages would be assessed, not at the date of the unaccepted repudiation, but at the date of the actual failure to perform. A more important consideration, in their Lordships' view, is that if the plaintiff did accept the repudiation, and if the market were to fall substantially up to the time when in the event the contract ought to have been performed, the plaintiff would be placed in a better position than if there had been due performance. This would represent an important inroad on a fundamental principle of assessment of damages, namely, that they should be no more than compensatory. In the result, their Lordships have not been satisfied that *Millett v Van Heek & Co* was wrongly decided. . . .

Their Lordships therefore affirm the principle that the second limb of s 51(3) of the Act of 1893 and of s 53(3) of the Hong Kong Ordinance, does not apply in any case of anticipatory breach of contract.

It follows that the majority of the Full Court in the present case were wrong to assess damages on the basis of the market price of cotton yarn on July 31, 1973. The applicable rule for ascertaining the measure of damages is that contined in s 53(2) of the Hong Kong Ordinance, namely that it is 'the estimated loss directly and naturally resulting, in the ordinary course of events, from the seller's breach of contract.' As their Lordships have noticed, the contract here was for delivery of the cotton yarn in such instalments as might be demanded by the buyers upon reasonable notice. It was common ground between the parties that the period of reasonable notice for delivery of the balance of 424.20 bales of yarn was one month. . . . The buyers did not accept the sellers' repudiation of July 31, and at any time thereafter could have demanded delivery of the balance of yarn on one month's notice. That situation continued until November 28, 1973, when the buyers issued and served their writ, thereby accepting the repudiation and rescinding the contract. November 28 was thus the last day upon which the buyers could have given reasonable notice requiring delivery of the yarn, and in their Lordships' opinion the appropriate date upon which to consider the market price of yarn for the purpose of assessing damages was one month thereafter, namely December 28, 1973.

The 'market price' rule makes it unnecessary to award the buyer additional damages for any loss of profit which he expected to make from reselling the goods – even if the seller knew, or ought to have foreseen, at the time of making the contract that this was the buyer's intention. For, if there *is* a market available for the purchase of equivalent goods, the buyer can have recourse to it (and ordinarily must do so, to fulfil his duty to mitigate) in order to meet his obligations under the sub-sale. This is so whether the market price is higher or lower than the original sale price, as is shown by the two cases below.

Williams v Reynolds (1865) 6 B & S 495, Court of Queen's Bench

(The facts appear from the judgment.)

Blackburn J: The plaintiff and the defendants entered into a contract on the 1st April, by which the defendants agreed to sell 500 piculs of China cotton at $16^{3}/_{4}$d per lb, guaranteed fair, to be delivered in August, so that the defendants had all that month to supply a certain quantity of cotton, answering the description given, at a certain price. At the end of August they had failed to fulfil their contract. And if the case stood there, the measure of damages would have been the difference between the contact price of $16^{3}/_{4}$d and the market price at the end of August, the latest time for delivery, which was $18^{1}/_{4}$d.

The question is, whether the plaintiff is entitled to recover a further sum, this being a contract, not for the delivery of specific cotton, but of cotton of a particular description. . . . The additional facts here are that, on the 25th May, nearly two months after the original contract and three months before its completion, the plaintiff made a contract to supply Mayall & Anderson, at Liverpool, with the same quantity and quality of cotton at $19^{3}/_{4}$d, to be delivered in August. If the defendants had fulfilled their contract the plaintiff would have handed over the cotton to his purchasers, and would have gained a considerable profit by the transaction. It was argued that because this purchase was made on the Liverpool Cotton Exchange, where all persons know that cotton is bought on speculation to sell again, the defendants would be aware that the plaintiff would enter into a fresh contract, relying on the performance by them of their contract, and that the nonfulfilment of it would occasion the breach of the second contract, and so the loss of profit by the resale would be a natural consequence of the defendants' breach of contract. . . . I cannot see that loss of profit from a contract subsequently made by the purchaser . . . follows as a natural consequence from the original seller's breach of contract. Though the purchaser might naturally rely on the seller's contract to enable him to fulfil his own, it is not necessary that he should do so; and if the seller was a slippery customer it would be imprudent to do it: in that case the purchaser would, as a prudent man, go into the market and supply himself from thence. Here the plaintiff had reason to rely on the defendants, but that does not entitle him to throw upon them the loss of the profit he would have made.

[Crompton and Shee JJ delivered concurring judgments.]

Williams Bros v E T Agius Ltd [1914] AC 510, House of Lords

Agius contracted to sell 4500 tons of coal to Williams at 16s 3d (81p) per ton, and Williams then contracted to sell coal of the same description to Ghiron at 19s (95p) per ton. Agius failed to deliver. The market price at the time of Agius's breach was 23s 6d (£1.18) per ton. The court awarded Williams damages based on the market price, and held that the subsale was irrelevant.

Lord Moulton: My Lords, the question for the decision of your Lordships in this appeal is set out very plainly in the award, in the form of a special case, which forms the basis of this litigation. It is whether the appellants are right in their contention that the measure of damages put forward by them in respect of the admitted breach by the respondents of the contract to deliver a cargo of coals in November, 1910, is correct. That contention is that the proper measure of damages is the difference between the contract price of 16s 3d per ton and the market price on the date of the breach of contract, which the arbitrator finds to be 23s 6d per ton.

Inasmuch as this is a plain case of a failure to deliver a specified quantity of an article obtainable in the market, the measure of damages is well established. The case comes under the rule laid down in the case of *Rodocanachi v Milburn* ((1886) 18 QBD 67), and regularly and repeatedly followed ever since, and ultimately embodied in the Sale of Goods Act 1893, s 51, sub-s 3. The contention of the appellants is in accordance with that rule, and the question put to the Court in the special case must accordingly be answered in their favour.

This consideration is, in my opinion, sufficient to decide this appeal, but, in deference to the opinions expressed by the majority of the Court of Appeal, I propose to examine the matters which it is suggested make the measure of damages in the present case other than that given by the recognized rule to which I have already referred.

From the facts of the case as found in the award, and the documents therein referred to, we learn that the appellants made a contract to sell a cargo of coal to the Italian firm of P Ghiron, and that they intended to fulfil that contract by the cargo to be delivered by the respondents in November. The price to be paid by the said P Ghiron was 19s per ton, and the respondents contend that it is the difference between 19s per ton and the contract price of 16s 3d per ton which is the true measure of damages.

If these were the only facts of the case the contention of the respondents would be precisely that view of the damages in the case of an article purchasable in the market which was negatived by the decision in *Rodocanachi v Milburn*. That case rests on the sound ground that it is immaterial what the buyer is intending to do with the purchased goods. He is entitled to recover the expense of putting himself into the position of having those goods, and this he can do by going into the market and purchasing them at the market price. To do so he must pay a sum which is larger than that which he would have had to pay under the contract by the difference between the two prices. This difference is, therefore, the true measure of his loss from the breach, for it is that which it will cost him to put himself in the same position as if the contract had been fulfilled.

[His Lordship then considered and rejected an argument that there had not been a subsale to Ghiron, but an assignment to him of the benefit of the first contract. Damages based on the market price were accordingly awarded.]

[Viscount Haldane LC and Lords Dunedin and Atkinson delivered concurring opinions. Lord Parker of Waddington concurred.]

Where there is no available market for goods of the contract description, the court must make its own assessment of the amount of the buyer's loss. It may, for instance, have regard to price movements in other, comparable markets (eg *The Arpad* [1934] P 189, where there was no available market for 'Roumanian wheat', but the price of wheat generally had fallen), or, if a subsale by the buyer was within the reasonable contemplation of the parties, the buyer's lost profit on the resale (*Patrick v Russo-British Grain Export Co Ltd* [1927] 2 KB 535).

4 Action for damages for late delivery

The Act contains no provision relating to the assessment of damages when the seller fails to deliver on the due date but the buyer accepts them when they are tendered late. The issue therefore falls to be determined on ordinary contractual principles. If there is an available market for the goods, prima facie the measure of the buyer's loss is the difference in the market price on the two dates: thus, if the market is rising, he will get substantial damages, while if it is falling, he will have suffered no loss. (Compare the well-known case of *Koufos v C Czarnikow Ltd, The Heron II* [1969] 1 AC 350, HL, where late delivery was made by a carrier.) If there is no available market, ordinary contract principles will still apply: indeed, the equally well-known case of *Victoria Laundry (Windsor) Ltd v Newman Industries Ltd* [1949] 2 KB 528, CA, where the plaintiffs recovered the profits which they had foreseeably lost during the period of the delay, was itself a case of late delivery in a sale of goods contract.

5 Action for damages for breach of warranty

Section 53 sets out a series of propositions about the buyer's remedies where there has been a breach of warranty by the seller, or where the buyer has elected (or is compelled) to treat a breach of condition as a breach of warranty. His remedy is for damages only: he cannot reject the goods. Alternatively, he may 'set up against the seller the breach of warranty in diminution or extinction of the price' (s 53(1)).

The measure of damages (again, echoing the rule in *Hadley v Baxendale* (1854) 9 Exch 341) is the estimated loss directly and naturally resulting, in the ordinary course of events, from the breach of warranty (s 53(2)). Where there is an available market, the measure of damages for breach of a warranty of quality is prima facie the difference between the value of the goods at the time they were delivered to the buyer and the value they would have had if they had fulfilled the warranty (s 53(3)). In such a case, the fact that there has been a subsale of the goods is irrelevant (*Slater v Hoyle & Smith Ltd* [1920] 2 KB 11, CA). Exceptionally, in *Van Den Hurk v Martens & Co Ltd* [1920] 1 KB 850, where it was known that the goods had been resold to a sub-buyer abroad and that they were to be despatched to him unopened and without any examination, the court substituted the market price at the time and place of the second delivery abroad as being more appropriate for the assessment of damages than the time and place of delivery under the principal contract.

Consequential losses for breach of warranty are assessed on ordinary contractual principles: *H Parsons (Livestock) Ltd v Uttley Ingham & Co Ltd* [1978] QB 791, CA – again, a sale of goods case which has a leading place in the contract syllabus.

6 Buyer's remedies at common law

Like the seller (see above, p ?), the buyer may have remedies at common law for breaches of the contract of sale by the seller which are not specifically dealt with by the Act. So, if the seller under a contract on CIF terms fails to give a notice of appropriation as required by the contract, the buyer may treat this as justification for terminating the contract (*Société Italo-Belge v Palm & Vegetable Oils (Malaysia) Sdn Bhd, The Post Chaser* [1981] 2 Lloyd's Rep 695). Where the breach does not entitle the buyer to terminate, he has of course a remedy in damages for any loss that he has suffered (*Cehave NV v Bremer Handelsgesellschaft mbH, The Hansa Nord* (above, p ?).

7 Specific performance

Section 52(1) empowers the court, in an action by a buyer for breach of contract for failure to deliver *specific or ascertained goods*, to order (if it thinks fit) that the contract be performed specifically, without giving the seller the option of retaining the goods on payment of damages.

We saw earlier in *Re Wait* [1927] 1 Ch 606, CA (above, p ?), that a person who has contracted to buy *unascertained* goods cannot invoke this provision, at least for so long as the goods remain unascertained, and that the court will not grant corresponding relief on general equitable principles in such a case. The court has a discretion under s 52, which it will not exercise if the contract is concerned with goods of an ordinary description which the buyer intends to resell (*Cohen v Roche* [1927] 1 KB 169: the 'ordinary' goods were in fact 'eight genuine Hepplewhite chairs'!). An order under s 52 has been made in respect of a ship, of a design especially suited to the buyer's needs (*Behnke v Bede Shipping Co Ltd* [1927] 1 KB 649) and (though not specifically under s 52) of an ornamental door designed by Adam (*Phillips v Lamdin* [1949] 2 KB 33).

Part IV

International sales

CHAPTER 14

International sales

1 Introduction

There is more than one way in which a sale of goods contract may have an international element – for example, the seller and buyer may be domiciled in different jurisdictions, or the contract may contemplate that the goods are to be carried from one country to another. The Unfair Contract Terms Act 1977 has its own special definition (see above, p 376). We are concerned in this section with contracts that involve the transport of the goods from one country to another. These will not necessarily be the countries in which the seller and buyer are respectively based – indeed, they may be based anywhere, even in the same country. A contract of this kind exposes the parties to greater risks than a purely domestic sale: physical risks associated with sea or air travel and the associated extra handling; financial risks, such as movements in exchange rates; political risks (extending even to the possibility of war, blockades, etc); and legal risks if a foreign system of law is involved, or a judgment or award has to be enforced in a foreign country. Some of these risks can be covered by insurance. Others may be avoided by careful drafting of the sales contract – a choice of law clause, for instance, will normally ensure that the contract is governed by a known set of legal rules. Much uncertainty can be resolved if the parties use one of the standard contract forms of the relevant trade association, which have been tried and tested over the years, eg the GAFTA forms of the Grain and Feed Trade Association, or those of the London Metal Exchange. There are also standard international terms of trade, such as INCOTERMS (the International Rules for the Interpretation of Trade Terms promulgated by the International Chamber of Commerce). These may have customary or even statutory force in some jurisdictions, but will be applied in English law only if chosen by the parties.

Two attempts have been made to establish standard terms of trade on a supra-national basis by international treaty. The first, the Uniform Law on International Sales, based on a convention signed at The Hague in 1964, failed to gain wide support and has not been a success. The United Kingdom has, in fact, ratified this convention, but on the basis that it will apply only where the parties have agreed that this will be the case – ie 'opted in' (Uniform Laws on International Sales Act 1967). Since in practice parties have rarely, if ever, done this, the Uniform Law is in effect a dead letter in this country. The second treaty, the United Nations Convention on Contracts for the International Sale of Goods (commonly known as the Vienna Convention), is clearly destined to supersede the Uniform Law, since it has gained wide support. The Convention was adopted at a UN conference held in Vienna in 1980 and became operative at the beginning of 1988. However, since the United Kingdom has not ratified this Convention and has no present plans to do so, we shall not discuss it further in this work. (For further reading, see J O Honnold *Uniform Law for International Sales under the 1980 United Nations Convention* (1982); P Slechtreim *Uniform Sales Law – the UN Convention on Contracts for the International Sale of Goods* (1986); C M Schmitthoff *The Export Trade* (9th ed, 1990), Ch 14; B A K Nicholas (1989) 105 LQR 201.)

For many reasons, it makes best sense to take as our example of an international sale a contract where the goods are to be carried by sea – this being the traditional export-import transaction and so the one for which well-established legal rules have evolved. Because of the time which it takes for goods to travel by sea, it is also particularly necessary in this type of transaction for the parties to be able to make arrangements to finance the deal and for this purpose to give security over the goods to their respective banks. To meet these problems, the *documents* relating to the sale and carriage of the goods have been elevated to a position of special symbolic importance, to the point where for many purposes they are treated in law as representing the goods themselves: for instance, 'delivery' of the goods can be effected by handing over these documents.

The principal documents for this purpose are:

(1) the bill of lading;
(2) the commercial invoice;
(3) the policy of marine insurance.

The bill of lading. The bill of lading is a document with a threefold purpose. (For an illustration, see Form 2 in the Appendix.) It is issued by the carrier (ie the owner or charterer of the ship) to the consignor of the goods, or to someone nominated by him, shortly after the goods have been loaded. First, it acknowledges the fact that the goods have been received, describing them in an itemised list, and evidences the fact that they have been loaded in apparent good order and condition. (If not, the defect is noted – eg that some barrels were leaking – and the bill is then called a 'claused', as distinct from a 'clean', bill.) Second, it normally contains the terms of the contract of carriage, identifying the route and destination. Third, it is regarded in law as evidencing the rights of possession and ownership in respect of the goods, so that these rights are deemed (at least prima facie) to be vested in the holder of the bill of lading – the person who is in possession. Delivery of the goods at their destination is normally made by the carrier to the holder against the surrender of the bill.

The commercial invoice. This is an invoice itemising the goods sold and describing them in a way which makes it possible to identify them as the contract goods, or as answering to the description of the contract goods.

The policy of marine insurance. This must be expressed in such a way as to make it clear that it covers the goods specified in the other two documents for the whole of the voyage covered by the bill of lading. When the bill of lading is transferred from one person to another, the policy of insurance will be assigned at the same time.

Other documents which may be required under particular contracts may include: a certificate of origin; a certificate of quality; export and/or import licences.

The Carriage of Goods by Sea Act 1992 (replacing the Bills of Lading Act 1855) overcomes problems which would arise at common law under the doctrine of privity of contract when a bill of lading is transferred from one holder to another. The original parties to a bill are the carrier and (normally) the consignor. Where the goods are the subject of a contract of sale, the consignor may already be the seller of the goods, or he may sell them after shipment. His buyer may, in turn, resell the goods, and this may be repeated so that there is a chain of sub-buyers. Any of these parties who is entitled to the goods at a particular time may have pledged his interest in the goods as security to his bank, and deposited the bill with the bank. Alternatively, the consignor may have had the bill made out in the name of the consignee, who is already the owner of the goods. If the doctrine of privity of contract were applied strictly, the contractual rights and duties evidenced by the bill would be enforceable only as between the consignor and the carrier; and the buyer, the sub-buyer or the consignee in the circumstances described above would be in no contractual relationship with the carrier. The Act of 1992 modifies this position by providing that whoever is the lawful holder of a bill is entitled to sue the carrier on the contract of carriage, and that anyone who is thus entitled to assert contractual rights against the carrier assumes the corresponding contractual duties. (In fact, the Act applies also to certain other documents commonly used in sea transport, such as sea waybills and ship's delivery orders. These documents are not bills of lading in the full sense: they do not contain the terms of the contract of carriage, and they are not regarded as symbolising the goods for the purpose of transferring title. The Act of 1855 did not apply to them, or give rights to the holder as the 1992 Act now does.)

A buyer of goods to whom this package of shipping documents has been effectively transferred can therefore assert:

(1) contractual rights against his immediate seller under the contract of sale;
(2) contractual rights against the carrier under the contract of carriage, by virtue of the Act of 1992: in turn, he will be liable to the carrier for the freight;
(3) his rights, as assignee of the benefit of the insurance policy, against the insurer, if the goods are lost or damaged by an event which the policy covers.

In addition, if the property in the goods has passed to him, he will have rights in tort against anyone who has wrongfully interfered with the goods or refused to deliver them up, or negligently damaged them. However, this will not be so if he does not own the goods, even though they may be at his risk (*The Aliakmon* [1986] AC 785, HL: above, p 240). This gap in the law which was not remedied by the Act of 1992: *The Aliakmon* is still an authority as a tort case – although, ironically, the buyers would now have rights in contract against the carrier under the new Act, since they had become holders of the bill of lading.

2 Typical export transactions

The parties to an international contract of sale are free to make any arrangement they choose as regards delivery, risk and the other incidents of the transaction. In practice, the contract is likely to fall under one or another of a series of recognised heads, which we can set out in a list that covers a whole spectrum of possible arrangements, beginning with the 'ex works' contract (where all the responsibilities connected with transport, etc are assumed by the buyer) and ranging all the way to the contract 'delivered, duty paid' (where the entire burden in these respects is carried by the seller). The main heads are:

Ex works (and variants: ex factory, warehouse, store);
Free carrier;
Free alongside (FAS);
Free on board (FOB);
Cost and freight (C & F);
Cost, insurance, freight (CIF, or CF & I) (variants: CIF & C (commission), CIF &
    E (exchange), CIF & C & I (commission and interest));
Carriage paid;
Carriage and insurance paid;
Delivered at frontier;
Delivered ex ship (also called 'arrival');
Delivered ex quay;
Delivered duty unpaid;
Delivered duty paid.

Examples of such contracts can be found going back for well over a century, and in some cases for many centuries. More modern methods of transport have led to the introduction of variants, such as FOB airport, where the goods are to be carried by air. The *container trade* (where the goods are stowed in a container before being carried by road, rail or sea or a combination of modes) has spawned a further variety of trade terms:

Full container load (FCL);
Less than full container load (LCL);
Free carrier (broadly equivalent to FOB);
Freight carriage paid (equivalent to C & F);
Freight carriage and insurance paid (equivalent to CIF).

The contracts at the two extremes of the first list above differ very little from domestic sales. Where a seller sells on 'ex works' or similar terms, he has only to make delivery at or near his own place of business, as he might do to a local buyer, and everything else is up to the buyer. The fact that the goods are destined for export, if the seller knows this, may have some bearing on the question of merchantability (*Mash & Murrell Ltd v Emmanuel*, above, p ?), and he may be expected under the terms of the contract to provide a certificate of origin or other documentation (or, alternatively, to co-operate with the buyer in procuring it); but property, possession and risk will normally pass at the point of delivery, and all the problems thereafter are the buyer's. Where a seller undertakes to 'deliver, duty paid', in contrast, it is his business to get the goods all the way to the point of delivery in the buyer's country, and the buyer's position will be little different from that of a buyer under a domestic purchase in that country.

In this book, we shall look in more detail at four of the more common of the traditional standard-form contracts: FAS, FOB, CIF and 'arrival'. For further information, reference may be made to Schmitthoff *The Export Trade* (9th ed, 1990).

3 FAS contracts

'FAS' stands for 'free alongside ship'. Here the first, inland, journey to the port of shipment is the seller's responsibility, but he assumes no obligation beyond that (except, perhaps, obligations in regard to procuring certificates of origin, etc). The contract is really no different in essence from a domestic sale on FOR ('free on rail') terms, or even from one where the seller agrees to deliver the goods at any other place within the seller's own country. Typically, the seller's duties might include the following:

- to supply the goods, with evidence of conformity with the contract;
- to deliver the goods alongside the ship, at the place and at or within the time stipulated by the contract or nominated by the buyer;
- to give the buyer notice of the above;
- to provide a certificate of origin;
- to co-operate with the buyer in obtaining other necessary documentation, eg an export licence.

The buyer, for his part, will have the following duties:

- to procure a ship, or shipping space, and give the seller due notice of the name of the ship and the place and time of loading;
- to pay the price;
- to bear all the costs of loading from alongside ship;
- to bear the costs of procuring all documentation, including the export licence, bill of lading, etc.

Property, possession and risk will normally pass to the buyer on delivery – ie when the goods have been placed alongside the ship so that they can be taken on board by crane, ship's tackle or the equivalent. 'Alongside' may mean (depending upon the custom of the particular port) on the docks, in a lighter, etc.

4 FOB contracts

The contract on FOB ('free on board') terms is the first of the two 'mainstream' export transactions for which detailed rules have been very fully worked out over the years. There can, of course, be a wide variety of FOB arrangements, but we shall look first at a contract on 'classic' or 'strict' FOB terms. Here, the seller undertakes not just to get the goods *to* the ship, but to see them loaded *on to* the ship, and to bear the cost of loading them; but it is the buyer's business to make all the arrangements regarding the shipping and insurance of the goods. The contract will state, typically: 'FOB, Felixstowe, shipment in August', or, perhaps, 'FOB, East Anglian port'. The understanding then is that the seller must hold himself ready to put the goods on any ship nominated by the buyer at the nominated port at any time during the month of August. The first step in performance will be taken by the buyer, who has the right (and the duty) to find a suitable ship calling at the port of loading within the contract period: he may, for instance, nominate the 'MV *Neptune*, expected ready to load at Felixstowe, 7 August'. This may mean chartering a ship, if the goods are enough to constitute a whole cargo, or booking space on a general cargo ship if what he is buying is less than a shipload. Then the respective duties of the parties unfold in sequence. The seller must have the goods ready to ship at that time and place; then he has to have them loaded on to the ship at his own expense; the buyer must be ready to pay the price on completion of the loading; and so on. At the conclusion of the loading of the goods, the consignor is issued with a document called a 'mate's receipt', which acknowledges receipt of the goods, itemised as to quantity and description, and confirmed to be in apparent good order and condition. In an FOB contract, this will be given to the seller, who receives it on behalf of the buyer; and the price may be payable under the contract in exchange for this document. In that case, the buyer will shortly afterwards surrender the mate's receipt to the carrier and receive in its place the bill of lading, which will of course be made out in the buyer's name. Alternatively, the contract may provide for the seller to procure the bill of lading, in which case he will retain the mate's receipt and have the bill of lading issued in either his own name or that of the buyer (depending upon the provisions of the contract) and receive payment in exchange for the bill itself. If the bill is made out to the seller, he will be a party to the contract of carriage; and he will also have 'reserved the right of disposal' in regard to the goods, which will normally prevent the property from passing to the buyer until the bill is transferred to him (s 18, rule 5(2); s 19(1),(2)).

The critical moment in an FOB contract occurs when the goods 'cross the ship's rail', normally by being swung by a crane or derrick, but sometimes less dramatically (eg in the case of oil or grain) in the course of being pumped or sucked through a pipe from shore to ship. At this point risk normally passes, and possession and property may pass also. But the property will not pass if the seller has 'reserved the right of disposal' (eg by retaining the bill of lading), or the contract goods are unascertained, or the contract provides otherwise. For a recent example of a case where the seller reserved the right of disposal, see *The Ciudad de Pasto* [1989] 1 All ER 951, where the seller of a consignment of prawns destined for Japan had retained the shipping documents until the outstanding balance (20 per cent) of the price was paid.

Under an FOB contract of this traditional type, the seller's and buyer's duties may be listed as follows.

The seller's duties will typically include:

- to supply the goods, with evidence of conformity with contract;
- to deliver the goods on board the ship, at the place and time stipulated by the contract or nominated by the buyer;
- to obtain the export licence;
- to bear all costs up to and including loading (across the ship's rail);
- to provide documents evidencing delivery to the ship, certificate of origin, etc;
- to co-operate with the buyer in procuring the bill of lading and other documentation;
- to give notice to the buyer to enable him to insure the goods during their sea transit (see s 32(3)).

The buyer's duties are as follows:

- to procure a suitable ship or shipping space and give the seller due notice of the ship and place and time of loading;
- to pay the price;
- to bear all costs subsequent to the goods passing the ship's rail;
- to bear the costs of procuring all documentation, including the bill of lading and certificate of origin.

Variations on the 'classic' FOB contract are very common. In the 'extended' FOB contract, the seller takes on the additional responsibilities of making the shipping and insurance arrangements. It may be more convenient for the seller to do this, especially where the goods sold do not amount to a complete cargo. The seller is often better placed to deal with exporting agencies in his own country – or he may be in the exporting business himself. Of course, every additional duty which the seller undertakes is likely to be reflected in the price which he charges the buyer.

Some of the cases which have been cited in earlier chapters were concerned with contracts made on FOB terms – eg *Colley v Overseas Exporters Ltd* (above, p 388) and *Carlos Federspiel & Co SA v Charles Twigg & Co Ltd* (above, p 289). The case which follows contains a description of this type of contract, and shows the importance in law of the moment when the goods pass the ship's rail.

Pyrene Co Ltd v Scindia Navigation Co Ltd [1954] 2 QB 402, Queen's Bench Division

An airport fire tender, which had been sold on FOB terms by Pyrene to the government of India, was dropped and damaged while being loaded for export on to a ship belonging to Scindia. It had not crossed the ship's rail. Contracts for the carriage of goods by sea were at the material time regulated by an international convention known as the Hague Rules (now superseded by the Hague-Visby Rules), which limited the liability of the carrier for negligent damage to the goods to £200. But the contract of carriage here had been made between Scindia and the buyers. This action was brought in tort by the sellers (as consignors of the goods in question), claiming £966 damages against Scindia for negligently damaging the tender. The question was whether the limitation of liability under the Hague Rules could be pleaded in defence. It was argued that the doctrine of privity prevented Scindia from relying directly on the contract of carriage. Devlin J held, however, that on the facts the sellers had 'participated' in the contract of carriage sufficiently for them to be bound by the Hague Rules, or that (alternatively) there was a *collateral* contract between the parties, into which the Hague Rules could be incorporated on the basis of usage or custom. In the course of his judgment, he explained some details regarding the nature of FOB contracts and the incidents of their performance.

Devlin J: I have now arrived at the conclusion that the rules apply to the contract between the defendants and ISD [the relevant department of the Indian government] so as to entitle the defendants, if they were sued by ISD, to limit their liability. The plaintiffs' last contention is that they were not a party to the contract between the defendants and ISD or to any similar contract; and that, even if they were, the limitation would not apply to them.

[His Lordship held that the Hague Rules did not support this last point, and continued:]

I come next to the question whether the plaintiffs are privy to the contract of carriage. A similar question has arisen before in relation to stevedores and other agents of the carrier. If the carrier employs a third party, such as stevedores, to perform part of his duties under the contract of carriage, can the third party claim the protection of the contract; or can the shipper, if his goods are damaged, sue the third party in tort? The point arose in *Elder, Dempster & Co Ltd v Paterson, Zochonis & Co Ltd* ([1924] AC 522). The bill of lading was issued on behalf of time charterers; but the goods were handled and damaged by the crew who were servants of the shipowner. The charterers were protected by exceptions in the bill of lading; but the shipper claimed to sue the shipowner in tort for the action of his servants. The claim failed. Scrutton LJ in the Court of Appeal, and Viscount Cave, put it on the ground of agency: the charterer in entering into the contract of carriage acted on behalf and for the benefit of those others who might be given duties to perform under it. There is in the case another ratio decidendi which I shall note later; but recently Denning LJ in *White v John Warwick & Co Ltd* ([1953] 1 WLR 1285), preferred the view I have just stated. *Elder, Dempster & Co Ltd v Paterson, Zochonis & Co Ltd* was not concerned with exceptions or immunities in the Hague Rules, but the principle is the same. Two New South Wales cases, *Gilbert, Stokes and Kerr Pty Ltd v Dalgety & Co Ltd* ((1948) 48 SRNSW 435), and *Waters*

Trading Co Ltd v Dalgety & Co Ltd ((1951) 52 SRNSW 4), and one United States case, *Collins & Co v Panama Rly Co* (197 F2d, 893 (1952)), have been concerned with the Hague Rules and have allowed stevedores to claim the benefit of them. In the last of the three the majority judgment in the United States Court of Appeals applied the law as set out in the Restatement of the Law, tit. Agency, s 347: 'An agent who is acting in pursuance of his authority has such immunities of the principal as are not personal to the principal.'. . .

In the case I have to consider the third party is on the shipper's side; if he was privy to the contract it was the act of the shipper that made him so. If he was privy to it he cannot, of course, take the benefits without the burdens, or enforce liability without limitation if the contract gives limitation.

There is nothing novel about the idea of a third party coming in to enforce a contract either as an undisclosed principal or as a beneficiary. Denning LJ, in *Smith and Snipes Hall Farm Ltd v River Douglas Catchment Board* ([1949] 2 KB 500), reviews the main categories into which such third parties commonly fall. The principle is very familiar in mercantile contracts: *Affréteurs Réunis SA v Leopold Walford (London) Ltd* ([1919] AC 801) is an example given by Denning LJ arising out of a charterparty. It is a principle which has constantly to be invoked where the property in the subject-matter of the contract is likely to be transferred during the currency of the contract. In marine insurance the policy is always expressly taken out for the benefit of those to whom the property 'doth, may or shall appertain.'. . . In bills of lading the indorsement of the bill passes the title to the goods by virtue of the custom of merchants, as found in *Lickbarrow v Mason* ((1794) 5 Term Rep 683), but did not at common law transfer the benefit of the contract of carriage. The Bills of Lading Act 1855, s 1, gives the indorsee or named consignee a statutory right to sue; the Judicature Act 1873, s 25(6), later performed the same function for the assignee under the ordinary contract. But just as before 1873 the assignee could always sue in the name of the assignor, so before 1855 the consignee could sue in the name of the consignor. . . .

In this type of case the seller as shipper makes the contract for the benefit of the buyer. The converse may be equally true. There is no difficulty in principle about the concept of an fob buyer making a contract of affreightment for the benefit of the seller as well as for himself. But it is necessary that I should examine in greater detail than I have hitherto done the circumstances in which the contract was made in order to determine whether the inference of agency can properly be drawn from them.

The contract of sale provided for delivery fob London, the price including dock and harbour dues and port rates to be paid by the seller; and further expressly provided that freight was to be engaged by the buyer, who was to give due notice to the seller when and on board what vessel the goods were to be delivered. Payment was to be made twenty-one days after delivery and after receipt of certain documents for which the contract called, such as invoice, inspection certificate, etc, and of the dock company's or mate's receipt. In the special circumstances of this case and because of delay in shipment, payment was in fact made in advance, but on the terms that that should not affect the seller's obligations as to delivery. As I have said, it was agreed that the property did not pass till delivery over the ship's rail.

It is worth noting that the problem which I have to consider does not arise as a matter of course in every fob contract. The fob contract has become a flexible instrument. In what counsel called the classic type as described, for example, in *Wimble, Sons & Co v Rosenberg & Sons* ([1913] 3 KB 743), the buyer's duty is to nominate the ship, and the seller's to put the goods on board for account of the buyer and procure a bill of lading in terms usual in the trade. In such a case the seller is directly a party to the contract of carriage at least until he takes out the bill of lading in the buyer's name. Probably the classic type is based on the assumption that the ship nominated will be willing to load any goods brought down to the berth or at least those of which she is notified. Under present conditions, when space often has to be booked well in advance, the contract of carriage comes into existence at an earlier point of time. Sometimes the seller is asked to make the necessary arrangements; and the contract may then provide for his taking the bill of lading in his own name and obtaining payment against the transfer, as in a cif contract. Sometimes the buyer engages his own forwarding agent at the port of loading to book space and to procure the bill of lading; if freight has to be paid in advance this method may be the most convenient. In such a case the seller discharges his duty by putting the goods on board, getting the mate's receipt and handing it to the forwarding agent to enable him to obtain the bill of lading. The present case belongs to this third type; and it is only in this type, I think, that any doubt can arise about the seller being a party to the contract.

The contract of carriage in this case was made in the office of Bahr Behrend & Co, for they are both agents for ISD and freight brokers for the defendants. An instruction came to Bahr Behrend from ISD to arrange for the shipment of these goods among other cargo, and a note by Bahr Behrend dated March 29, 1951, records that the shipment was booked per the *Jalazed*. The ordinary practice is for ISD to prepare a bill of lading (the defendants have a special form for Government of India shipments) and to send it to Bahr Behrend. Bahr Behrend check the items on it from a return made out by the cargo superintendent after shipment and then sign and issue the bill of lading on behalf of the defendants generally some days after the ship has sailed, dependent on the volume of the cargo to be dealt with.

It is the practice in the Port of London for all loading to be done by the port authority at the ship's expense. The whole charge, therefore, for loading from alongside is paid by the ship and covered by the freight; in this case, it included the cost of lighterage from the dock to the ship's side. On April 7 Bahr Behrend, on behalf of ISD, notified the plaintiffs that space had been engaged, and instructed them to dispatch the goods to arrive alongside the vessel.

The question at once arises: if, as the plaintiffs contend, there is no contractual relationship between them and the defendants, how do they get these goods on board? If the ship sails off without loading the goods the plaintiffs are in breach of their contract of sale. Have they no redress against the ship? Mr Megaw argues that they would have none, and that vis-à-vis the sellers the ship in loading acts as a volunteer. This seems to me to be a position which none of the three parties would have accepted for a moment.

Let me look at the situation first from the standpoint of the shipper, ISD. In the ordinary case, such as I have been considering above, where the shipper takes out a bill of lading or an insurance policy, he has at the time of the contract himself got the property in the goods; the question whether he contracts for the benefit of subsequent owners depends on proof of his intention at the time of contracting. But where, as in this case, he has not got the property at the time of the contract, and does not intend to acquire it before the contract begins to operate, he must act as agent. He cannot intend otherwise; the intention is inherent in the act; he must either profess agency or confess himself a wrongdoer. For if the shipowner lifts the seller's goods from the dock without the seller's authority he is guilty of conversion to which the shipper, by requiring him to do it, makes himself a party.

Let me look at it now from the standpoint of the ship. If the shipowners were sued for conversion they would surely have redress against the shipper. A person who requests a carrier to handle goods must have the right to deal with them or it would not be safe to contract with him. A shipowner cannot be supposed to inquire whether the goods he handles do or do not belong to the shipper who entrusts them to his care; if the goods are not the shipper's there must be implied a warranty of authority by him that he has the right to contract with regard to them.

Then from the standpoint of the seller, if his goods are left behind, and it is said to him: 'You made no contract with the ship; what else did you expect?' he would answer, I think, that he naturally supposed that all the necessary arrangements had been made by the shippers.

In brief, I think the inference irresistible that it was the intention of all three parties that the seller should participate in the contract of affreightment so far as it affected him. If it were intended that he should be a party to the whole of the contract his position would be that of an undisclosed principal and the ordinary law of agency would apply. But that is obviously not intended; he could not, for example, be sued for the freight. This is the sort of situation that is covered by the wider principle; the third party takes those benefits of the contract which appertain to his interest therein, but takes them, of course, subject to whatever qualifications with regard to them the contract imposes. It is argued that it is not reasonable to suppose that the seller would submit to the terms of a contract whose detail he does not know and which might not give him the sort of protection of which he would approve. I do not think that as a matter of business this is so. Most people board a bus or train without considering what protection they will get in the event of an accident. I see nothing unreasonably imprudent in a seller assuming that the buyer, whose stake in the contract is greater than his, would have obtained whatever terms are usual in the trade; if he were legally minded enough to inquire what they were, the answer would be that by statutory requirement the contract was governed by the Hague Rules.

If this conclusion is wrong, there is an alternative way by which, on the facts of this case, the same result would be achieved. By delivering the goods alongside the seller impliedly invited the shipowner to load them, and the shipowner by lifting the goods impliedly accepted that invitation. The implied contract so created must incorporate the shipowner's usual terms; none other could have been contemplated; the shipowner would not contract for the loading of the goods on terms different from those which he offered for the voyage as a whole. This simple solution was the one which Lord Sumner preferred in *Elder, Dempster & Co Ltd v Paterson, Zochonis & Co Ltd*, and which was adopted in respect of the stevedores' liability in the cases I have mentioned. But, as I have said, the problem in those cases was a rather different one, and I do not think that the solution fits so well the circumstances of this case. First, it means that if the goods were not lifted there would be no contract; and while that does not arise in this case, a solution that leaves it in the air is not so acceptable as one that covers it. Secondly, I find it difficult to infer that the shipowner by lifting the goods intended to make any new contract; he would not know where the property in the goods lay; I think he must have supposed that he was acting under a contract already made through Bahr Behrend, and on the assumption that Bahr Behrend had authority to make it. Thirdly, I doubt whether the seller intended to make any separate contract when he sent down the goods; I think that he, too, would have supposed that they would be dealt with under the contract of affreightment. . . .

In my judgment the plaintiffs are bound by the Hague Rules as embodied in the contract of carriage and, accordingly, can recover no more than £200. There will be judgment for them for that sum.

NOTE

Devlin J's view that the sellers 'participated' in the contract of carriage is difficult to understand, since it is clear that he did not consider that they were bound by all of its terms – their participation was at best partial, and whatever consideration moved from them was not the promise to pay the freight, but something else, which was unexpressed. It seems that the content of this part-contract, if spelt out, would have been little different from that of the collateral contract which the judge put forward as an alternative; and this alternative reasoning is easier to accept.

5 CIF contracts

This is the second of the 'classic' export-sale forms. The letters 'CIF' stand for 'cost, insurance, freight'. In this type of contract the point of delivery is moved further down the sequence, to a time *after* the goods have been shipped; but in reality we are looking at a contract of a wholly different character. In a CIF contract, the buyer looks to the seller to make the whole of the shipping arrangements, including those relating to insurance, and the buyer takes delivery of the goods symbolically, commonly while they are somewhere at sea, by taking over the shipping documents relating to the consignment – including, at least, the bill of lading, commercial invoice and insurance policy. As will become apparent, what the buyer bargains for is not so much to acquire the goods in a physical sense, as to take over the whole commercial *venture*. It has even been suggested on occasion that in a CIF contract the subject matter of the contract is not the goods, but the documents; but this view has no judicial support and there is no doubt that the Sale of Goods Act applies to such contracts.

In contrast with the FOB contract, which specifies the port of loading, a CIF contract specifies the port of arrival: thus, if goods are sold on terms 'CIF Felixstowe', the seller undertakes to provide goods which are destined to arrive at that port. Most contracts for the sale of goods on CIF terms are for commodities of some sort, such as crude oil or sugar or grain – in legal terms, unascertained goods which are sold by description; and it will be no concern of the buyer how the seller finds the goods to meet his contract. In other words, if we suppose a contract for the sale of 2000 tonnes of Missouri wheat sold CIF Rotterdam, the likelihood is not that the seller will be the American farmer who grew the wheat, or even the American merchant who shipped it, but a commodity dealer who has sold wheat of this description 'forward' (perhaps several months previously) and seeks to honour his commitment by finding wheat *already afloat* which answers the contract description. (The buyer may well also be another middleman – a dealer or importer, and not the European farmer who will eventually feed the wheat to his livestock or the miller who will turn it into flour.) So, when we read through the lists of the respective duties of the seller and buyer, we should bear in mind that our notional seller and buyer are pictured as the parties at the very beginning of what may be quite a long chain of successive sales, all made on similar CIF terms, and that not all of these duties will be applicable to parties further down the chain.

The seller's duties will include:

- to ship at the agreed port of shipment goods of the contract description (or procure goods afloat which have been so shipped);
- to procure a contract of sea carriage by which the goods will be delivered to the contract destination;
- to insure the goods under an insurance contract which will be available for the benefit of the buyer;
- to procure a commercial invoice in conformity with the contract;
- to tender these documents to the buyer (or his agent or bank).

The buyer's duties will be:

- to accept the documents, if they are in conformity with the contract, and pay the price;
- to take delivery of the goods at the agreed destination, and pay all unloading costs;
- to pay customs and other duties at the port of arrival;
- to procure any necessary import licence.

In practice, the freight is often deducted from the overall price and left to be paid by the buyer when the ship has reached its destination.

(a) The importance of the shipping documents

The key feature of the CIF contract is the role played by the documents in the performance of the contract. Once the buyer has had these documents delivered to him in a way which effectively transfers or assigns to him the rights which they embody, he is in a position to assert his title to the goods (since property normally passes on delivery of the bill of lading), and with it, the right to possession; he can demand delivery of the goods at the port of arrival, and sue a wrongdoer in tort if the goods are wrongfully damaged or lost or detained; he has contractual rights against the carrier, if the goods are missing or damaged or delayed in delivery; and he has the right to claim on the policy of insurance in the event of accidental loss or damage – say, in a storm at sea. The buyer takes over from the seller the whole *package* of rights and liabilities which make up the commercial venture. This means that he is bound to go through with the deal – to pay the price and take up the documents, when tendered – even though the goods may have been lost (see the *Manbre Saccharine* case, below). However, since he has only the documents to go on, the law rightly says that he is bound to complete by taking up the documents only if the documents tendered are strictly in conformity with the contract. It must be apparent from the documents themselves that everything is in order. The commercial invoice, the bill of lading and the insurance policy must describe the goods in exactly the same terms as the contract description; the quantities must tally; the contract of carriage must also be consistent with the contract, as regards date of shipment, route, etc; and the policy of insurance must accurately reflect the details of the voyage contemplated by the contract and the risks which the contract stipulates that it must guard against. Moreover, the buyer is entitled to insist on 'continuous documentary cover': the contract of carriage must cover the whole of the period during which the goods are in transit, the insurance policy must likewise cover all the normal risks to all the goods continuously for the whole period from shipment to arrival. The buyer may insist on this even though at the time of performance the discrepancy appears to have become irrelevant (eg, even if the voyage has been safely completed), for the documentation may turn out to be necessary later if an unforeseen claim should arise.

The buyer under a CIF contract has two rights of rejection (*Kwei Tek Chao v British Traders*, above, p 294): if the documents are not in order, he may refuse to take them up, and treat this as a repudiatory breach by the seller; and even after he has accepted the documents, he has a right to reject the goods if, on arrival, they prove not to be in conformity with the contract. Conversely, if the buyer rejects the documents when they are apparently in order, the seller may elect to treat this as a repudiation on the part of the buyer, and is relieved from the duty of delivering the goods themselves (*Gill & Duffus*, below).

In a CIF contract the property in the goods and the right to possession normally pass to the buyer when the documents are handed over. But the risk is deemed to have passed retrospectively 'as from' shipment – in other words, the buyer takes over the risk with retrospective effect back to the time of shipment. This may mean that he has to pay the price and take up the documents even though the goods have been lost; *Manbre Saccharine Co Ltd v Corn Products Co Ltd* (below). He will, however, succeed to the such rights as the seller may have against the carrier and insurer in such a case.

Ross T Smyth & Co Ltd v T D Bailey, Sons & Co [1940] 3 All ER 60, House of Lords

(The facts are immaterial.)

Lord Wright: The contract in question here is of a type familiar in commerce, and is described as a cif contract. The initials indicate that the price is to include cost, insurance and freight. It is a type of contract which is more widely and more frequently in use than any other contract used for purposes of sea-borne commerce. An enormous number of transactions, in value amounting to untold sums, are carried out every year under cif contracts. The essential characteristics of this contract have often been described. The seller has to ship or acquire after that shipment the contract goods, as to which, is unascertained, he is generally required to give a notice of appropriation. On or after shipment, he has to obtain proper bills of lading and proper policies of insurance. He fulfils his contract by transferring the bills of lading and the policies to the buyer. As a general rule, he does so only against payment of the price, less the freight, which the buyer has to pay. In the invoice which accompanies the tender of the documents on the 'prompt' – that is, the date fixed for payment – the freight is deducted, for this reason. In this course of business, the general property in the goods remains in the seller until he transfers the bills of lading. These rules, which are simple enough to state in general terms, are of the utmost importance in commercial transactions. I have dwelt upon them perhaps unnecessarily, because the judgment of the Court of Appeal might seem to throw doubt on one of their most essential aspects. The property which the seller retains while he or his agent, or the banker to whom he has pledged the documents, retains the bills of lading is the general property, and not a special property by way of security. In general, however, the importance of the retention of the property is not only to secure payment from the buyer but for purposes of finance. The general course of international commerce involves the practice of raising money on the documents so as to bridge the period between shipment and the time of obtaining payment against documents. These credit facilities, which are of the first importance, would be completely unsettled if the incidence of the property were made a matter of doubt. By mercantile law, the bills of lading are the symbols of the goods. The general property in the goods must be in the seller if he is to be able to pledge them. The whole system of commercial credits depends on the seller's ability to give a charge on the goods and the policies of insurance. A mere unpaid seller's lien would, for obvious reasons, be inadequate and unsatisfactory. . . .

Manbre Saccharine Co Ltd v Corn Products Co Ltd [1919] 1 KB 198, King's Bench Division

Under two separate contracts, Corn Products sold starch and corn syrup to Manbre Saccharine on terms CIF London. Goods answering the contract description were shipped aboard the SS *Algonquin*, which was sunk by a torpedo or mine on 12 March 1917. The sellers tendered the documents relating to the goods on 14 March, but the buyers refused to take them up or pay the price. It was held that they were bound to do so, and that this was a breach of contract.

McCardie J: The first question arising can be briefly stated as follows: Can a vendor under an ordinary cif contract effectively tender appropriate documents to the buyer in respect of goods shipped on a vessel which at the time of tender the vendor knows to have been totally lost? . . .

I conceive that the essential feature of an ordinary cif contract as compared with an ordinary contract for the sale of goods rests in the fact that performance of the bargain is to be fulfilled by delivery of documents and not by the actual physical delivery of goods by the vendor. All that the buyer can call for is delivery of the customary documents. This represents the measure of the buyer's right and the extent of the vendor's duty. The buyer cannot refuse the documents and ask for the actual goods, nor can the vendor withhold the documents and tender the goods they represent. The position is stated with weight and clearness in the treatise on charterparties by Scrutton LJ, 8th ed, p 167, in the notes to article 59 as follows: 'The best way of approaching the consideration of all questions on cif sales is to realise that this form of the sale of goods is one to be performed by the delivery of documents representing the goods – ie, of documents giving the right to have the goods delivered or the possible right, if they are lost or damaged, of recovering their value from the shipowner or from underwriters. It results from this that various rules in the Sale of Goods Act 1893, which is primarily drafted in relation to the sale and delivery of goods on land, can only be applied to cif sales mutatis mutandis. And there may be cases in which the buyer must pay the full price for delivery of the documents, though he can get nothing out of them, and though in any intelligible sense no property in the goods can ever pass to him – ie, if the goods have been lost by a peril excepted by the bill of lading, and by a peril not insured by the policy, the bill of lading and the policy yet being in the proper commercial form called for by the contract.'

In *Arnhold Karberg & Co v Blythe, Green, Jourdain & Co* ([1915] 2 KB 379, 388), Scrutton LJ, when a judge of first instance, described a cif contract as being a sale of documents relating to goods and not a sale of goods. But when the Court of Appeal considered that case ([1916] 1 KB 495, 510, 514) Bankes LJ and Warrington LJ commented on the language of Scrutton J and indicated their view that a cif contract is a contract for the sale of goods to be performed by the delivery of documents. But I respectfully venture to think that the difference is one of phrase only. For in reality, as I have said, the obligation of the vendor is to deliver documents rather than goods – to transfer symbols rather than the physical property represented thereby. If the vendor fulfils his contract by shipping the appropriate goods in the appropriate manner under a proper contract of carriage, and if he also obtains the proper documents for tender to the purchaser, I am unable to see how the rights or duties of either party are affected by the loss of ship or goods, or by knowledge of such loss by the vendor, prior to actual tender of the documents. If the ship be lost prior to tender but without the knowledge of the seller it was, I assume, always clear that he could make an effective proffer of the documents to the buyer. In my opinion it is also clear that he can make an effective tender even though he possess at the time of tender actual knowledge of the loss of the ship or goods. For the purchaser in case of loss will get the documents he bargained for; and if the policy be that required by the contract, and if the loss be covered thereby, he will secure the insurance moneys. The contingency of loss is within and not outside the contemplation of the parties to a cif contract. I therefore hold that the plaintiffs were not entitled to reject the tender of documents in the present case upon the ground that the *Algonquin* had, to the knowledge of the defendants, sunk prior to the tender of documents. This view will simplify the performance of cif contracts and prevent delay either through doubts as to the loss of ship or goods or through difficult questions with regard to the knowledge or suspicion of a vendor as to the actual occurrence of a loss.

Arnhold Karberg & Co v Blythe, Green, Jourdain & Co [1916] 1 KB 495, Court of Appeal

In this case it was held that the documents tendered under a CIF contract must be valid and effective at the time of tender: it is not sufficient that they were valid when issued. Blythe & Co had contracted to buy Chinese horse beans CIF Naples. Beans were duly shipped in July 1914 aboard a German ship, the *Gernis*; but before the documents were due to be tendered war was declared against Germany, with the consequence that the contract of carriage contained in the bill of lading became void for illegality. The Court of Appeal, affirming Scrutton J, held that the buyers were entitled to reject this bill.

Bankes LJ: We have had in this case a very full and interesting discussion on the question of the effect of the outbreak of war upon certain cif contracts entered into before the outbreak of war. . . . In my opinion the answer to the question which the Court has to decide is to be found on the face of the contracts, and upon consideration of what the terms of those contracts provide. The contract on the part of the sellers is a contract for the sale of goods whereby the sellers also undertake, inter alia, to enter into a contract of affreightment to the appointed destination, which contract will be evidenced by the bill of lading, and secondly to take out a policy or policies of insurance upon the terms current in the trade, but which policy or policies were not in this case to include war risks. On the buyers' part they undertook to pay net cash in London in exchange for the bill or bills of lading and policies of insurance, either on arrival of the goods at the port of discharge, or at the expiration of three months from the date of the bills of lading should the goods not sooner arrive, or on the posting of the vessel at Lloyd's as a total loss. In any case, however, the payment is to be in exchange for the bill or bills of lading and policy or policies of insurance. What is the meaning of the buyer's contract thus expressed, that he is to pay in exchange for a bill of lading? In my opinion it means what it says, that in exchange for the price he is to receive a bill of lading which is still a subsisting contract of affreightment of the goods to the port of destination, and a policy or policies of insurance which is, or are still, a subsisting contract, or subsisting contracts, of insurance. It is said that this construction, which seems to me so obviously the natural construction, ignores the fact that in a contract of this kind certain risks fall upon the buyer. I quite accept the contention that certain risks do fall upon the buyer. For instance, in the present cases all war risks fell on the buyer, as the parties have agreed that the seller shall be under no obligation to obtain policies covering war risks. I agree also that the condition of the goods at the time of the tender of the shipping documents is not material, nor is the value of the documents at the time of tender material. In all such matters the risk is on the buyer. He may be obliged to pay for goods although they may be at the bottom of the sea, or although through some unforeseen circumstance they may never arrive, or although they may have been lost owing to some cause not covered by the agreed form of policy. All these risks, however, are risks affecting the goods. In effect the contention of the appellants appears to me to be a contention that one of the risks undertaken by the buyer is a risk affecting his contract, and not the goods the subject-matter of the contract. I cannot agree with this view. It appears to me that the question of the construction of the contract must depend upon the language used, and not upon any such considerations as these. In the present case it is not disputed that the outbreak of war dissolved the contract of affreightment, and that so far as any further prosecution of the voyage was concerned the bill of lading was no longer an effective document. Under those circumstances, in my opinion that bill of lading was not a bill of lading within the meaning of the contract in respect of which the seller was under an obligation to pay cash in exchange.

Scrutton J in his judgment has used one expression with which I do not agree. The expression is the one in which he says that 'the key to many of the difficulties arising in cif contracts is to keep firmly in mind the cardinal distinction that a cif sale is not a sale of goods, but a sale of documents relating to goods.' I am not able to agree with that view of the contract, that it is a sale of documents relating to goods. I prefer to look upon it as a contract for the sale of goods to be performed by the delivery of documents, and what those documents are must depend upon the terms of the contract itself. The conclusion at which Scrutton J arrives he expresses in this way. He says: 'It is clearly not essential that if the goods do not arrive, the buyer should have a good claim on one of the contracts,' – I have already dealt with that, and with that I fully agree – 'but I think it is essential that each contract should be one into which he can legally enter as a contracting party, and when the legal relations of the seller under the contract of affreightment tendered have become void, and it is illegal for the buyer to enter into any similar relations with shipowner or insurer, I cannot hold that such documents are good tender.' He puts there two grounds upon which he bases his decision, and in so far as the first ground depends upon the construction of the contract I entirely agree with him; but the second ground he bases upon the contention apparently that it was illegal for the buyer to enter into any similar legal relation with the shipowner or the insurer, and upon that point we have had an extremely interesting discussion. Mr Wright has contended that the taking of the bill of lading by the buyer in this particular case would not have involved him in any illegal contract upon the ground that the bill of lading had ceased to be an operative contract of affreightment, and that the taking of it would not involve the buyer in any legal relations with the shipowner, and that the bill of lading has become merely a document of title in respect of the goods, which may or may not at some future time be capable of enforcement. This contention seems to me to be a very strong ground for arriving at the conclusion that the tender of such a document is not a good tender under the contract. Mr Wright further contended that it is not true to say that a bill of lading is a piece of wastepaper, because in so far as it covered the period from the time of shipment until the time this vessel took refuge it was an effective document, and some rights may still exist in respect of that period which may be evidenced by this bill of lading. How that may be I am not prepared to say. The contract has come to an end. It has not come to an end in the sense that Mr Wright refers to where the goods are lost; it has not come to an end in the sense that although it is a perfectly good and enforceable contract it is valueless; but it has come to an end in the sense indicated by Willes J in *Esposito v Bowden* ((1857) 7 E & B

763) [ie, on the ground of frustration]. He says the contract is dissolved, which seems to me to be an entirely different thing and to involve entirely different consequences.

In my opinion this appeal fails, and the judgment of Scrutton J, subject to the point which I have indicated, was correct.

[Swinfen Eady and Warrington LJJ delivered concurring judgments.]

Hansson v Hamel & Horley Ltd [1922] 2 AC 36, House of Lords

Hansson agreed to sell 350 tons of Norwegian cod guano to Hamel & Horley CIF Kobe or Yokohama. Since there were no ships running directly from Norway to these Japanese ports, the guano was sent on a local ship, the *Kiev*, from Braatvag in Norway to Hamburg and there transshipped to the *Atlas Maru* for the ocean voyage to Japan. After the *Atlas Maru* had sailed, the seller tendered to the buyers in purported performance of his contract a bill of lading which related only to the 'ocean' leg of the transport. The buyers were held entitled to insist on 'continuous documentary cover', ie documentary evidence of a contract or contracts of carriage covering both legs of the journey and the period of transshipment, and to reject this tender.

Lord Sumner: A cf and i [CIF] seller, as has often been pointed out, has to cover the buyer by procuring and tendering documents which will be available for his protection from shipment to destination, and I think that this ocean bill of lading afforded the buyer no protection in regard to the interval of thirteen days which elapsed between the dates of the two bills of lading and presumably between the departure from Braatvag and the arrival at Hamburg. . . .

When documents are to be taken up the buyer is entitled to documents which substantially confer protective rights throughout. He is not buying a litigation, as Lord Trevethin (then A T Lawrence J) says in the *General Trading Co's Case* ((1911) 16 Com Cas 95, 101). These documents have to be handled by banks, they have to be taken up or rejected promptly and without any opportunity for prolonged inquiry, they have to be such as can be re-tendered to sub-purchasers, and it is essential that they should so conform to the accustomed shipping documents as to be reasonably and readily fit to pass current in commerce. I am quite sure that, under the circumstances of this case, this ocean bill of lading does not satisfy these conditions. It bears notice of its insufficiency and ambiguity on its face: for, though called a through bill of lading, it is not really so. It is the contract of the subsequent carrier only, without any complementary promises to bind the prior carriers in the through transit. . . . As things stood, the buyer was plainly left with a considerable lacuna in the documentary cover to which the contract entitled him. . . .

[Lords Buckmaster, Atkinson, Wrenbury and Carson concurred.]

Kwei Tek Chao v British Traders & Shippers Ltd [1954] 2 QB 459, Queen's Bench Division

(See the extract cited above, p 294. This case confirms that the buyer has two rights to reject: he may refuse to take up the documents if they are not in conformity with the contract, and he may reject the goods even after having accepted the documents, if he later discovers a breach on the seller's part.)

Berger & Co Inc v Gill & Duffus SA [1984] AC 382, House of Lords

Bergers contracted to sell to Gill & Duffus 500 tonnes of Argentine bolita beans CIF Le Havre. The contract provided for payment to be made against shipping documents, and also that a certificate given by independent assessors (GSC) as to the quality of the beans at the port of discharge should be final. The sellers first delivered only 445 tonnes at Le Havre, and overcarried the remaining 55 tonnes to Rotterdam. Before the 55 tonnes had reached Le Havre and been inspected there by GSC, the buyers twice rejected the documents, on grounds relating to the certificate of quality as regards the 445 tonnes which the House of Lords held to be irrelevant. The buyers were accordingly guilty of a repudiatory breach which, it was held, discharged the sellers from their obligation to deliver the 55 tonnes and debarred the buyers from any right that they might have had to reject the goods. In consequence, the buyers were held liable in damages for non-acceptance in respect of the entire 500 tonnes.

Lord Diplock: In the instant case it has never been contended that the actual shipping documents tendered by the sellers to the buyers on 22 March 1977 and re-tendered on 30 March did not relate to the whole quantity of 500 tonnes or did not upon the face of them conform to the terms of the cif contract of 22 December 1976. That being so it is, in my view, a legal characteristic of a cif contract so well established in English law as to be beyond the realm of controversy that the refusal by the buyer under such a contract to pay to the seller, or to a banker nominated in the contract if the contract so provides, the purchase price upon presentation at the place stipulated in the contract, of shipping documents which on their face conform to those called for by the contract, constitutes a fundamental breach of contract, which the seller is entitled to elect to treat as rescinding the contract and relieving him of any obligation to continue to perform any of his own primary obligations under it; or, to use the terminology of the Sale of Goods Act 1893, 'to treat the contract as repudiated.' So far as concerns the instant case the relevant primary obligation of the sellers of which they were relieved, was any further obligation to deliver to the buyers any of the goods that were the subject matter of the contract.

That a refusal by the buyer to accept the tender of shipping documents which on the face of them conform to the requirements of a cif contract and upon such acceptance to pay the contract price amounts to a breach of condition (in the meaning given to that expression in the Sale of Goods Act 1893) has been taken for granted so universally by English courts as not to have attracted any subsequent positive exposition worthy of citation, ever since Lord Cairns put it thus in *Shepherd v Harrison* (1871) LR 5 HL 116, 132, a case where payment was to be by acceptance of a documentary bill of exchange:

> I hold it to be perfectly clear that when a cargo comes in this way, protected by a bill of lading and a bill of exchange, it is the duty of those to whom the bill of lading and the bill of exchange are transmitted in a letter, *either 'to approbate or to reprobate' entirely and completely, then and there.*

Recognition of the principle so stated (to which I have myself supplied the emphasis) is implicit in all judgments dealing with bankers' confirmed credits as a mode of payment including the most recent judgments of this House. . . .

In the instant case the sellers did elect to treat the contract as repudiated on 1 April 1977. They then ceased to be under any contractual obligation to deliver to the buyers any 'Argentine bolita beans – 1974 crop.' The buyers on the other hand became liable to the sellers in damages for breach of contract. Prima facie the measure of such damages would be the difference between the contract price of the 500 tonnes of beans that were the subject matter of the contract and the price obtainable on the market for the documents representing the goods at date of the acceptance of the repudiation. Such prima facie measure might, however, fall to be reduced by any sum which the buyers could establish they would have been entitled to set up in diminution of the contract price by reason of a breach of warranty as to description or quality of the goods represented by the shipping documents that had been actually shipped by the sellers if those goods had in fact been delivered to them. . . .

I turn now to analyse what it was that went wrong with the case in the Court of Appeal. Here it was recognised that the cif contract was a single contract for a consignment of 500 tonnes. What appears to have been wholly overlooked is that the sellers, on 1 April 1977, had in fact elected, as they were entitled to do, to treat the buyers' rejection of the shipping documents as a repudiatory breach that had brought to an end their primary obligation under the contract to deliver any goods at all to the buyers. No mention of this election on the sellers' part is to be found in any of the judgments. Robert Goff LJ, in his dissenting judgment, does say that on rejection of the documents by the buyers 'the sellers became entitled to bring the contract [sc. for the 500 tonnes] to an end,' but there is nothing to indicate that his attention was directed to the fact that the sellers had acted on that entitlement and *had* brought the contract to an end.

My Lords, it is trite law for which I do not find it necessary to refer to any other authority than the judgment of Devlin J in *Kwei Tek Chao v British Traders and Shippers Ltd* [1954] 2 QB 459, 487–488, that when a buyer under a cif contract accepts shipping documents which transfer the property in the goods to him, the property in the goods that he obtains is subject to the condition subsequent that it will revest in the seller if upon examination of the goods themselves upon arrival the buyer finds them to be not in accordance with the contract in some respect which would entitle him to reject them, and he does in fact reject them. But this is because the cif contract remains on foot; and being a contract for the sale of goods, the buyer has the right under s 34 of the Sale of Goods Act 1893 to reject the goods themselves for non-conformity with the contract and retains this right until he has had a reasonable opportunity of examining the goods after they have been delivered.

My Lords, it is not necessary in the instant case to consider whether a similar right to reject the goods upon delivery is retained by a buyer who, in breach of contract, has refused to accept the shipping documents when duly presented in accordance with the provisions of the contract, and the seller has *not* elected to treat such refusal as a repudiatory breach bringing all further primary obligations on his part under the contract to an end. . . .

Whatever legal problems might be presented by a situation resulting from a seller's failure to treat the buyer's rejection of conforming shipping documents as bringing the contract to an end, it would, in my view, be contrary to the basic concepts of the law of contract that deal with the different remedies for different categories of breach, if a seller of goods who had elected to treat the buyer's breach of a condition of the contract, or a fundamental breach of an innominate term, as bringing to an end his own further primary obligations under the contract (or in the terminology of the Sale of Goods Act 1893 'to treat the contract as repudiated') continued to be under any legal obligation to deliver to the buyer any goods, if the election so to treat the buyer's breach were made before the actual goods had been delivered to him. As already mentioned, if the seller sued the buyer for damages for his failure to pay the price of the goods against tender of conforming shipping documents, the buyer, if he could prove that the seller would not have been able to deliver goods under those shipping documents that conformed with the contract of sale, would be able to displace the prima facie measure of damages by an amount by which the value of the goods was reduced below the contract price by that disconformity; but this goes to a quantum of damages alone. . . .

Given the absence of any suggestion of difference in quality between the 55 tonnes and the 445 [tonnes] that GSC had certified as equal to the sealed sample by reference to which the cif contract was made, the buyers lacked the finding of fact essential to their defence in part to the sellers' claim in damages, that on balance of probabilities GSC would not have issued a similar certificate in respect of the 55 tonnes. . . .

[His Lordship accordingly held that the buyers were liable in damages for non-acceptance of the whole 500 tonnes, reckoned by reference to the market price at the relevant date.]

[Lords Keith of Kinkel, Roskill, Brandon of Oakbrook and Templeman concurred.]

(b) Variants of the CIF contract

The basic principles applicable to a CIF contract apply with the necessary modifications to contracts where the buyer agrees to pay, in addition to cost, insurance and freight, for some extra items such as commission, exchange and interest (CIF & C, etc, referred to in the list on p 446). The same is true of the C & F contract, where it is the buyer rather than the seller who has the responsibility of arranging the insurance cover. (One reason for this may be that the laws of the buyer's country require him to take out insurance with a local insurer, or possibly with a state-owned insurance agency, in order to save foreign exchange.) It is more likely that a C & F contract will be one which contemplates that the seller is an exporter who will procure and despatch the goods, rather than one which can be fulfilled by buying goods already afloat, since in the latter case there will be insurance cover in place which it is assumed the buyer will take over.

6 Ex ship or 'arrival' contracts

Under a contract of this description, the buyer is bound to pay the price only if actual delivery of the goods is made to him at the port of delivery, the seller bearing all costs up to but not including unloading costs and import duties. Property and risk will pass with delivery of possession. It is not sufficient that the seller tenders a valid set of shipping documents: the buyer is entitled to the goods, not just the documents; and if the seller cannot procure the delivery of the goods from the ship, he has not fulfilled his obligations.

Comptoir d'Achat et de Vente du Boerenbond Belge S/A v Luis de Ridder Ltda, *The Julia* [1949] AC 293, House of Lords

Rye was sold to a Belgian company under a contract expressed to be on terms 'CIF Antwerp', but which was held to be an 'arrival' contract. While the goods were at sea, the buyer paid the price in exchange for documents which included a delivery order, but the ship was prevented from unloading at Antwerp when the Germans invaded Belgium. The goods were unloaded at Lisbon instead. The buyers claimed their money back, alleging a total failure of consideration; the sellers argued in reply that the delivery of the documents was at least part performance, which was enough to defeat the buyer's claim. It was held that since the contract, as an 'arrival' contract, required actual delivery to be made at Antwerp, the consideration had totally failed.

Lord Porter: My Lords, this is an appeal for a judgment of the Court of Appeal affirming by a majority the judgment of Morris J who upheld an award of an umpire stated in the form of a special case under the Arbitration Acts 1889 to 1934. The arbitration arose out of a contract for the sale of rye by the respondents (the sellers) to the appellants (the buyers). The buyers, who were the claimants in the arbitration, asked for the refund of the purchase price paid by them under the contract on the ground that the consideration had wholly failed. The question for your Lordships' consideration is whether there was such total failure of consideration.

The learned judge in agreement with the umpire, as I understand him, regarded the contract as a cif contract modified to some extent, but not altered in its essential characteristics. The buyers had, in his view, entered into a contract for the purchase of documents or, more accurately, for the purchase of a parcel of rye, the fulfilment of which was to be implemented by the handing over of documents. The documents, he considered, might be varied at the option of the sellers, who would fulfil their contract if they chose to tender a delivery order instead of a bill of lading, and a certificate instead of a policy of insurance. Even the stringency of these obligations he regarded as reduced by the practice of the parties with the result that delivery order meant an instruction to their own agents (countersigned, it is true, by those agents) and a certificate of insurance which was never tendered to or held on behalf or at the disposal of the buyers. The delivery order, Morris J considered, 'doubtless possessed commercial value.' In other words, the buyers were purchasers of documents and had received that for which they stipulated, ie, the usual delivery order and a certificate of insurance which would compel or incite the sellers to recover any loss from underwriters and pay it over to the buyers.

My Lords, the obligations imposed upon a seller under a cif contract are well known, and in the ordinary case include the tender of a bill of lading covering the goods contracted to be sold and no others, coupled with an insurance policy in the normal form and accompanied by an invoice which shows the price and, as in this case, usually contains a deduction of the freight which the buyer pays before delivery at the port of discharge. Against tender of these documents the purchaser must pay the price. In such a case the property may pass either on shipment or on tender, the risk generally passes on shipment or as from shipment, but possession does not pass until the documents which represent the goods are handed over in exchange for the price. In the result the buyer after receipt of the documents can claim against the ship for breach of the contract of carriage and against the underwriter for any loss covered by the policy. The strict form of cif contract may, however, be modified: a provision that a delivery order may be substituted for a bill of lading or a certificate of insurance for a policy would not, I think, make the contract concluded upon something other than cif terms, but in deciding whether it comes within that category or not all the permutations and combinations of provision and circumstance must be taken into consideration. Not every contract which is expressed to be a cif contract is such. . . . In the present case therefore it is not as if a usual form of delivery order had been given and accepted or an insurance certificate covering the parcel was in the hands of Van Bree as agents for the buyers, nor can a solution be found in the mere designation of the contract as cif. . . . The true effect of all its terms must be taken into account, though, of course, the description cif must not be neglected. It is true, no doubt, to say that some steps had been taken towards the performance of this contract, eg, the goods had been shipped, an invoice sent, the customary so-called delivery order had been transmitted and that delivery order amongst its provisions contained a declaration by the sellers' agents, Belgian Grain and Produce Co Ltd that they gave a share of the present delivery order of $4,973 in a certificate of insurance. But the taking of steps towards performance is not necessarily a part performance of a contract. The question is whether the purchaser has got what he is entitled to in return for the price. Of course, if the buyers paid the sum claimed in order to obtain the delivery order and the share purported to be given by it in the certificate of insurance, the contract would have been performed in part at least, but I do not so construe the contract, even when illuminated by the practice adopted by the parties. That practice seems to me rather to show that the payment was not made for the documents but as an advance payment for a contract afterwards to be performed. With all due respect to the learned judge and the Master of the Rolls, I can see no sufficient reason for supposing . . . that the delivery order had some commercial value. . . . There was no evidence of commercial value and the document itself was merely an instruction by one agent of the sellers to another. . . . The document appears to me to be no more than an indication that a promise already made by the sellers would be carried out in due course, but in no way increases their obligations or adds to the security of the buyers.

My Lords, the object and the result of a cif contract is to enable sellers and buyers to deal with cargoes or parcels afloat and to transfer them freely from hand to hand by giving constructive possession of the goods which are being dealt with. Undoubtedly the practice of shipping and insuring produce in bulk is to make the process more difficult, but a ship's delivery order and a certificate of insurance transferred to or held for a buyer still leaves it possible for some, though less satisfactory, dealing with the goods whilst at sea to take place. The practice adopted between buyers and sellers in the present case renders such dealing well nigh impossible. The buyer gets neither property nor possession until the goods are delivered to him at Antwerp, and the certificate of insurance, if it enures to his benefit at all, except on the journey from ship to warehouse, has never been held for or delivered to him. . . .

The vital question in the present case, as I see it, is whether the buyers paid for the documents as representing the goods or for the delivery of the goods themselves. The time and place of payment are elements to be considered but by no means conclusive of the question: such considerations may, on the one hand, indicate a payment in advance or, on the other, they may show a payment postponed until the arrival of the ship, though the property in the goods or the risk have passed to the buyer whilst the goods are still at sea, as in *Castle v Playford* ((1872) LR 7 Exch 98). But the whole circumstances have to be looked at and where, as, in my opinion, is the case here, no further security beyond that contained in the original contract passed to the buyers as a result of payment, where the property and possession both remained in the sellers until delivery in Antwerp, where the sellers were to pay for deficiency in bill of lading weight, guaranteed condition on arrival and made themselves responsible for all averages, the true view, I think, is that it is not a cif contract even in a modified form but a contract to deliver at Antwerp. Nor do I think it matters that payment is said to be not only on presentation but 'in exchange for' documents. There are many ways of carrying out the contract to which that expression would apply, but in truth whether the payment is described as made on presentation of or in exchange for a document, the document was not a fulfilment or even a partial fulfilment of the contract: it was but a step on the way. What the buyers wanted was delivery of the goods in Antwerp. What the sellers wanted was payment of the price before that date, and the delivery of the documents furnished the date for payment, but had no effect on the property or possession of the goods or the buyers' rights against the sellers. If this be the true view there was plainly a frustration of the adventure – indeed the sellers admit so much in their pleading – and no part performance and the consideration had wholly failed. The buyers are accordingly entitled to recover the money which they have paid. . . .

[Lords Simonds, du Parcq, Normand and MacDermott delivered concurring opinions.]

7 Contracts for the international sale of goods shipped in bulk

It is, of course, a basic proposition under the Sale of Goods Act 1979, s 16 that no *property* in goods can pass until the goods have been ascertained (normally, in an export-sale context, by some act of appropriation). At common law, *possession* also cannot exist in an unascertained part of a larger bulk. So problems arise in the case of bulk shipments – eg where a seller ships 10,000 tons as a complete cargo and then contracts to resell 1000 tons to each of ten separate subpurchasers. Even if the carrier (as is common) issues multiple bills of lading in respect of the goods (eg ten bills each relating to 1000 tons), the delivery of such a bill to a buyer is not effective to pass rights of ownership or possession to him. He would have to claim at common law or in equity to the goods in the event of the seller's insolvency (*Re Wait*, above, p 210), no right to sue a third party in tort (*The Aliakmon*, above, p 240), and he had no rights against the carrier either at common law or under the Bills of Lading Act 1855. (However, the Carriage of Goods by Sea Act 1992 now does give him *contractual* rights against the carrier in such a case.) The position is certainly no more favourable if the buyer receives a document of even lower standing than a bill of lading, such as a ship's waybill or a delivery order – although, once again, the Act of 1992 has given the buyer rights against the carrier which can be exercised by the holder of such a document). In all of these situations, the usual assumptions as to the passing of property and the right to possession cannot apply, whether the contract is made on FOB, CIF or any other terms. Instead, the very earliest time at which property can pass will be when goods are appropriated to answer the particular contract. It is unlikely that this will take place before actual delivery.

But *risk* can pass in respect of an unascertained part of a specific bulk (*Sterns v Vickers,* above, p 246), and so a buyer does have an insurable interest in such goods.

The Law Commissions have recommended that s 16 of the Act should be modified so as to allow for the passing of property in part of a bulk, if the buyer has paid some or all of the price ('Sale of Goods forming Part of a Bulk' (L Com No 215, Scot L Com No 145, 1993: see the extract cited above, p 265). This recommendation is not confined to *international* contracts of sale.

8 Contracts of sale involving road, rail, and/or air transport

There is no equivalent to the bill of lading in a contract for the sale of goods involving air transport. The whole procedure happens too quickly for there to be any need to deal with the goods while they are in transit, or for either party's bank to wish to have security of a documentary kind over the goods during this period. Instead, an 'air waybill' is issued, which is usually made out in the name of the buyer as consignee. The usual terms on which the goods are carried are 'FOB airport'. Under such a contract, the seller's responsibilities will cease when the goods are delivered to the air carrier or his agent at the exporting airport.

The CIM (*Convention internationale concernant le transport de merchandises par chemin de fer*) and CMR (*Convention relative au contrat de transport international de merchandises par route*) are international conventions which deal respectively with the rail and road transport of goods across frontiers. (On the CIM and CMR, see M A Clarke *International Carriage of Goods by Road: CMR* (1991); D A Glass and C Cashmore *Introduction to the Law of Carriage of Goods* (1989) Chs 3, 4.) The United Kingdom is a party to both conventions. These conventions apply even where the goods are handled by successive carriers. The position is more complicated when multimodal transport is involved, as is common in the container transport business. Here, it is normal for the principal contract of carriage to be made with a single firm called a 'combined transport operator', which assumes overall responsibility and subcontracts to others for all or some of the separate parts of the journey. The contract is evidenced by a 'combined transport document', which necessarily lacks many of the advantages that are accorded to a bill of lading. The International Chamber of Commerce has worked out a number of standard forms of contract which are appropriate in a variety of circumstances. As a result, although the practical difficulties associated with multimodal transport have largely been overcome, at least as between the immediate parties, the legal problems arising from questions of privity of contract and the conflict of laws are potentially very complex. The position, especially as regards risk, is likely to be all the worse when a container carries a mixed load (LFL, ie less than a full load), and so cannot be sealed up by the seller before he parts with possession.

9 Payment in international sales transactions

In earlier times, payment in international contracts of sale was commonly effected by bill of exchange: the seller would draw a bill on the buyer for the price and transmit it and the bill of lading to him together (a 'documentary bill': see below, p 639); and the understanding was that the buyer would take up the bill of lading only if he accepted the bill of exchange or honoured it by payment (see Sale of Goods Act 1979, s 19(3)). This method has been superseded by modern practices and is now little used. Instead, it will usually be a term of the contract that the buyer will procure the opening of a confirmed letter of credit in the seller's favour before the goods are shipped (a requirement which has been construed as a condition of the contract: *Trans Trust SPRL v Danubian Trading Co Ltd* [1952] 2 QB 297).

Payment by banker's commercial letter of credit is considered in detail below, in Chapter 19. In practice, the working of the system depends upon two fundamental rules. The first is the doctrine of strict compliance: the bank is entitled to reject the shipping documents if not in strict conformity with the contract: *Equitable Trust Co of New York v Dawson Partners Ltd* (below, p 650); *J H Rayner & Co Ltd v Hambro's Bank Ltd* (below, p 651). The second is the autonomy of the credit: the bank must pay against the documents if they are in order, regardless of any later instructions from the buyer, his bankruptcy, suspicions regarding the validity of the underlying sale transaction, etc (*Urquhart Lindsay & Co Ltd v Eastern Bank Ltd* (below, p 647); *Hamzeh Malas & Sons v British Imex Industries Ltd* (below, p 648).

Part V

Bills of exchange and banking

CHAPTER 15

Negotiable instruments

In this chapter we seek to: (1) define the term 'negotiable instrument'; (2) establish how documents come to be recognised as negotiable; (3) list those documents regarded as negotiable instruments; and (4) examine the advantages of using negotiable instruments.[1]

1 Definition

There is no statutory definition of the term 'negotiable instrument'. Any definition must be drawn from the common law. To define the term the concepts of 'instrument' and 'negotiability' require separate consideration.

(a) Instrument

If A owes money to B, B has an intangible right to payment of that money. An instrument is a document which physically embodies that payment obligation. It has been described by Professor Goode as 'a document of title to money' (R M Goode *Commercial Law* (1982), p 428) and must be distinguished from a document of title to goods, such as a bill of lading. To be a document of title to money an instrument must contain an undertaking to pay a sum of money (eg as in a promissory note) or an order to another to pay a sum of money to the person giving the order or a third person (eg as in a bill of exchange). Alternatively, the undertaking or order may relate to the delivery of a security for money (*Goodwin v Robarts* (1876) 1 App Cas 476). A document which is primarily a receipt for money, even if coupled with a promise to pay it, is not an instrument: *Akbar Khan v Attar Singh* [1936] 2 All ER 545, PC; applied in *Claydon v Bradley* [1987] 1 All ER 522, CA.

If an instrument is made payable to bearer, or if it is made payable to a specified person or his order and it has been indorsed by or with the authority of that person, it is described as being 'in a deliverable state'. The possessor, otherwise known as the 'holder', of an instrument in a deliverable state is presumed to be entitled to payment of the money due under it. This is because the instrument embodies the

---

1 See generally, J James *Richardson's Guide to Negotiable Instruments* (8th ed, 1991); R Bradgate & N Savage *Commercial Law* (1991), Chs 25–27; R M Goode *Commercial Law* (1982), Part 3. For detailed analysis, see A G Guest *Chalmers and Guest on Bills of Exchange, Cheques and Promissory Notes* (14th ed, 1991); F R Ryder and others *Byles on Bills of Exchange* (26th ed, 1988).

contractual right to payment and that right is transferable by mere delivery. However, the holder may not be the true owner of the instrument, as it may, for example, have been lost or stolen, and so it is more accurate to say that he has the *power* (but not necessarily the entitlement) to enforce the payment obligation contained in the instrument and give a valid discharge. In such a case, the true owner of the instrument will have the *entitlement* (but not necessarily the power) to enforce the underlying right to payment of the money and also have a superior title to the instrument itself. The true owner maintains his right to payment because it exists independently of the instrument. Whether the holder has an indefeasible title to the instrument will depend on whether it is negotiable and whether he took it for value and in good faith.

'The Nature of the Negotiable Instrument' by A Barak (1983) 18 Israel LR 49, pp 53–55, 57–58, 60–63, 65

III. THE NEGOTIABLE INSTRUMENT AS A CHATTEL

(a) *Rights on and to the negotiable instrument*

In discussing the negotiable instrument one refers not only to rights on it, but also to rights in, or to it. While this is not accurate terminology from a strictly juridical point of view, it does reflect the proprietary character of the negotiable instrument. The negotiable instrument is a physically tangible thing, and just as one speaks of ownership of, or title to, a chair or a car, so one can speak of ownership of a negotiable instrument. . . .

(b) *Consequences of the proprietary nature of the negotiable instrument*

The negotiable instrument is, then, seen to be a chattel. Its owner has the same powers as the owner of any other property. He can retain possession of it, sell it, transfer it, give it away as a gift, destroy it, or alter it. These actions may, of course, affect the very ownership of the instrument or its value. When the owner of the instrument has possession of it, there is a unity of ownership and possession. This, however, is not essential and the two can equally well be in separate hands. For example, an instrument to the order of A is stolen from him. A remains the owner, but the thief has possession. When possession is unlawfully separated from ownership, the law of conversion comes into operation and gives the owner – who is entitled to immediate possession – the right to demand restitution of the instrument or its value. But, of course, possession can also be separated from ownership lawfully when, for example, the owner delivers it into the custody of another person for safekeeping or as a deposit. . . .

(c) *The negotiable instrument as a special kind of chattel*

It cannot be denied that the negotiable instrument is unlike other chattels. One does not refer to it as a chattel naturally and as a matter of course. Its proprietary nature is not its most important side, for its inherent value as a chattel is negligible. The real value of the negotiable instrument lies in the obligations it embodies. A legal system in which the proprietary nature of the negotiable instrument is hardly stressed at all is conceivable. It is not absolutely essential to dwell on the instrument's proprietary qualities. Reference to it as a chattel in the common law countries is for the purpose of attaining certain results. Just as a chattel can be transferred from hand to hand, so too can a negotiable instrument be transferred, since it is itself a chattel. However, it embodies an obligation and, by transferring the chattel, one transfers the obligation as well. Thus, it was possible to transfer the obligation embodied in a negotiable instrument at a time when ordinary obligations could not, as a rule, be transferred.

The common law did not recognize the transferability of a debt, but accepted that the owner of a chattel could sell, pledge or deliver it to someone else at will. If the debt be given the outward appearance of a chattel, why should it not be transferable just as a chattel is? Why should such a debt not be subject to the law of property which allows a chattel to be transferred from hand to hand without difficulty? While the law remained steadfast in its refusal to allow the transfer of debts, men of commerce came to grasp that, by giving a debt the qualities of a chattel, the problem of freely transferring it would be solved. [Sussman, *The Law of Bills of Exchange* (6th ed, 1983), p 4.]

Today, reference to the negotiable instrument as a chattel has further consequences – for example, the possibility of resorting to the law of conversion when the instrument is taken from its owner unlawfully. . . .

IV. THE NEGOTIABLE INSTRUMENT AS AN OBLIGATION

(a) *The negotiable instrument as a new and independent obligation*

In most cases bills are drawn in the course of commercial transactions between the parties. When A draws a bill to the order of B the reason generally is that A owes B money, either on account of a loan which B has given him, or of goods supplied to him by B. In cases of this kind, the instrument is evidence of the existence of A's liability to B. The obligation does not derive from the instrument itself, but from the initial transaction between the two. However, the instrument is not merely a piece of evidence. A's signature on it creates a new and independent obligation, whereby A is liable to B and to any person to whom B transfers the instrument. This obligation is in addition to – and often even in place of – that deriving from the initial transaction. Accordingly, if a bill, given by A to B as a conditional discharge of the initial transaction, is dishonoured, B has two causes of action: one on the initial transaction between him and A; the other on the obligation created by the instrument itself. Insofar as the former is concerned, the instrument is no more than written evidence. As for the latter, the initial transaction constitutes the consideration. Thus, by virtue of the signatures on it, the negotiable instrument creates a new and independent obligation, completely different from the obligation deriving from the initial transaction. Moreover, the instrument does not only give rise to one single obligation; there are as many obligations as there are signatures on it – some of them primary obligations, some secondary.

(b) *The negotiable instrument as a contract*

The wording of the Bills of Exchange Ordinance clearly indicates that the obligation on a bill is a contract. This contract, however, is – it will be noted – unilateral, not bilateral. There is no mutual exchange of undertakings and only one party is liable on such a contract; the rules of offer and acceptance do not apply to it. True, the contract on a negotiable instrument is not complete until the instrument is delivered 'in order to give effect thereto'; but delivery is not the same as acceptance of an offer in the law of contract.

Frequently, a negotiable instrument is made within the framework of a bilateral contract. For example, A undertakes to sell goods to B and in consideration B gives A a bill. That is a bilateral contract; but the bill has an existence of its own. Once it has been made, an additional contract arises – that on the bill itself. If B fails to pay the bill, A will generally have two contractual remedies – one based on the bilateral contract, the other on the bill. There is, of course, a close connection between the two contracts: payment of the bill discharges the bilateral contract; failure on the part of A to perform his undertaking under the bilateral contract may provide B with a defence to an action brought on the bill. But this connection must not be allowed to blur the material difference between the two or hide the fact that the bill has a separate existence of its own as a unilateral contract.

(c) *Consequences of the contractual nature of the negotiable instrument*

Subject to the special rules which follow from the negotiability of the instrument, the obligation on it is just like any other contractual obligation to pay a certain sum of money. Thus, capacity to incur liability, as a party to a bill is coextensive with capacity to contract. Events which invalidate contracts generally, also invalidate liability on a bill. Defences available under the general law of contract, such as duress, fraud, failure of consideration and so on, are equally a part of the law of negotiable instruments. It is a well-known fact that the plea of *non est factum*, so common in the law of contract, was first raised in a case concerning a negotiable instrument. The contractual nature of the negotiable instrument is similarly reflected in the application of the doctrine of consideration. A number of legal systems, in which consideration is essential for the creation of contractual liability, make consideration a prerequisite of liability on a negotiable instrument too – since that liability is itself a form of contractual liability. On the other hand, systems in which consideration is not one of the elements of the contract, and which require no more than *causa* for example, are found to forgo the need for consideration and make do with *causa* in the case of liability on a negotiable instrument too.

Since the obligations on a negotiable instrument are contractual obligations, there is nothing to prevent the guarantor known to the general law of contract being used in this connection. And, indeed, the ordinary rules applicable to the relations between guarantor and the person to whom he gives the guarantee do apply in the case of negotiable instruments as well. These obligations are, moreover, themselves divisible into principal and secondary obligations, the latter being by way of guarantee for the performance of the former. Accordingly, the relations between the two are governed by the general rules of guarantee.

Again, the fact that the obligations we are considering are contractual obligations, which – by their very nature – are transferable, means that, in principle, there is no reason why they cannot be transferred from one person to another in accordance with the rules of assignment applicable to ordinary contractual obligations. And, in fact, this is the position in English Law. . . .

(d) *The negotiable instrument as a special kind of contract*

While the obligation on a negotiable instrument is of a contractual nature, what characterizes it is the fact that it is 'negotiable'. Accordingly, apart from being transferable under the general law of contract, it can be transferred in the special manner established by the law merchant – namely, by negotiation. . . .

(b) Negotiable

Crouch v Crédit Foncier of England (1873) LR 8 QB 374, Court of Queen's Bench

Blackburn J: In the present case the plaintiff has taken upon himself the burden of establishing both that the property in the debenture passed to him by delivery, and that the right to sue in his own name was transferred to him.

The two propositions are very much connected, but not identical. The holder of an overdue bill or note may confer the right on the transferee to sue in his own name, but he conveys no better title than he had himself. So the assignee of a Scotch bond, which is assignable by the law of Scotland, may sue in his own name in the courts of this country: see *Innes v Dunlop* ((1800) 8 Term Rep 595); but he has not a better title than those from whom he took the bond, unless, perhaps, if the contract is by the law of Scotland not merely assignable but also negotiable. As to this, in *Dixon v Bovill* ((1856) 3 Macq 1 at 16), Lord Cranworth, then Lord Chancellor, in delivering the judgment of the House of Lords in a Scotch case as to iron scrip notes, says, 'I have no hesitation in saying, that independently of the law merchant and of positive statute, within neither of which classes do these scrip notes range themselves, the law does not, either in Scotland or in England, enable any man by a written engagement to give a floating right of action at the suit of any one into whose hands the writing may come, and who may thus acquire a right of action better than the right of him under whom he derives title'.

But the two questions go very much together; and, indeed, in the notes to *Miller v Race* ((1758) 1 Burr 452 1 Smith LC (13th ed, 1929) pp 452, 533), where all the authorities are collected, the very learned author says: 'It may therefore be laid down as a safe rule that where an instrument is by the custom of trade transferable, like cash, by delivery, and is also capable of being sued upon by the person holding it pro tempore, then it is entitled to the name of a *negotiable instrument*, and the property in it passes to a bona fide transferee for value, though the transfer may not have taken place in market overt. But that if either of the above requisites be wanting, ie, if it be either not accustomably transferable, or, though it be accustomably transferable, yet, if its nature be such as to render it incapable of being put in suit by the party holding it pro tempore, it is not a *negotiable instrument*, nor will delivery of it pass the property of it to a vendee, however bona fide, if the transferor himself have not a good title to it, and the transfer be made out of market overt.'

Bills of exchange and promissory notes, whether payable to order or to bearer, are by the law merchant negotiable in both senses of the word. The person who, by a genuine indorsement, or, where it is payable to bearer, by a delivery, becomes holder, may sue in his own name on the contract, and if he is a bona fide holder for value, he has a good title notwithstanding any defect of title in the party (whether indorser or deliverer) from whom he took it. . . .

NOTES

1. According to Blackburn J a negotiable instrument has two characteristics, namely: (1) it is 'transferable, like cash, by delivery' (which assumes it is in a deliverable state) so that the transferee can enforce the rights embodied in it in his own name; and (2) the transferee, being a bona fide holder for value, can acquire a better title to it than that of his transferor.

2. It is its capacity to be acquired free from equities of prior parties (ie free from any defects of title of prior parties and from personal defences available to prior parties) which characterises an instrument as 'negotiable' in the strict sense of the word. By contrast, a bill of lading in a deliverable state is transferable by delivery and so can be described as 'negotiable' in one sense of the word. But it is not 'negotiable' in the strict sense as it cannot pass a title free from equities of prior parties: *Kum v Wah Tat Bank Ltd* [1971] 1 Lloyd's Rep 439 at 446, per Lord Diplock, PC. Cf C Debattista *Sale of Goods Carried by Sea* (1990), pp 22–23 who argues that a bill of lading can be described as 'negotiable' in the strict sense of the word because, under the Factors Act 1889 and ss 24 and 25 of the Sale of Goods Act 1979, its transferee may be able to take a better title to the goods it represents than his transferor had. For a comprehensive rebuttal of Debattista's theory see A Tettenborn [1991] LMCLQ 538 at pp 541–542. However, note that under s 47(2) of the Sale of Goods Act 1979 a bona fide transferee for value of a bill of lading may defeat an unpaid seller's right of stoppage in transit even though the right of stoppage may have been valid against his transferor.

3. The distinction between using the term 'negotiable' to mean 'transferable' and using it in its strict sense was made clear by Bowen LJ in *Simmons v London Joint Stock Bank* [1891] 1 Ch 270 at 294 when he said that:

A negotiable instrument payable to bearer is one which, by the custom of trade, passes from hand to hand by delivery, and the holder of which for the time being, if he is a *bona fide* holder for value without notice, has a good title, notwithstanding any defect of title in the person from whom he took it. A contractual document in other words may be such that, by virtue of its delivery, all the rights of the transferor are transferred to and can be enforced by the transferee against the original contracting party, but it may yet fall short of being a completely negotiable instrument, because the transferee acquires by mere delivery no better title than his transferor.

See s 8(1) of the Bills of Exchange Act 1882 and s 6(2) of the Cheques Act 1957 for examples of when the term 'negotiable' is used only in the sense of 'transferable'.

4. In its Report on Banking Services Law and Practice (1989 Cm 622), a Review Committee chaired by Professor Jacks recommended a statutory definition of the term 'negotiable', which would apply to all negotiable instruments (Rec. 8(3)). This recommendation was rejected by the Government in its subsequent White Paper on banking services (1990 Cm 1026, Annex 6).

QUESTIONS

1. Negotiable instruments are one of the most important exceptions to the nemo dat rule. Why should they be given such a privileged status? See Chafee (1918) 31 Harvard LR 1104 at p 1146.
2. Although the bona fide transferee for value of a non-negotiable instrument does not automatically take free from equities, can such a transferee ever take the instrument free from defects in the title of his transferor? See *Goodwin v Robarts* (1876) 1 App Cas 476 at 489, HL; *Easton v London Joint Stock Bank* (1886) 34 Ch D 95 at 113–114, CA; *Colonial Bank v Cady and Williams* (1890) 15 App Cas 267 at 285, HL.

A suggested definition of a negotiable instrument:

Cowen *The Law of Negotiable Instruments in South Africa* (5th ed, 1985), Vol 1, p 52

A negotiable instrument is a document of title embodying rights to the payment of money or a security for money, which, by custom or legislation, is (a) transferable by delivery (or by indorsement and delivery) in such a way that the holder *pro tempore* may sue on it in his own name and in his own right, and (b) a *bona fide* transferee *ex causa onerosa* may acquire a good and complete title to the document and the rights embodied therein, notwithstanding that his predecessor had a defective title or no title at all.

2 How instruments come to be negotiable

There are two ways in which documents may come to be recognised as negotiable instruments: (1) statute; and (2) mercantile usage.

(a) Statute

In most, perhaps all, cases statutory recognition of negotiability merely confirms previous judicial acceptance of a mercantile usage which recognised an instrument as negotiable. For example, bills of exchange and cheques were accepted as negotiable by the courts before they were recognised as such by the Bills of Exchange Act 1882.

There has been some debate as to whether the Promissory Notes Act 1704 made promissory notes negotiable when that had not previously been the case, or whether it was merely declaratory of the law as it stood before Lord Holt's landmark decision in *Clerke v Martin* (1702) 2 Ld Raym 757. In that case Lord Holt held that a promissory note payable to order was not a bill of exchange, and was, therefore, not negotiable. He said:

> . . . that this note could not be a bill of exchange. That the maintaining of these actions upon such notes, were innovations upon the rules of the common law; and that it amounted to the setting up a new sort of specialty, unknown to the common law, and invented in Lombard Street, which attempted in these matters of bills of exchange to give laws to Westminster Hall. That the continuing to declare upon these notes upon the custom of merchants proceeded from obstinacy and opinionativeness, since he had always expressed his opinion against them, and since there was so easy a method, as to declare upon a general indebitatus assumpsit for money lent, etc. . . .

Most commentators have interpreted this decision as wrong and have held the 1704 Act to be declaratory of the case law as it existed prior to *Clerke v Martin* (for a judicial statement to this effect see *Goodwin v Robarts* (1875) LR 10 Exch 337 at 350, per Cockburn CJ delivering the judgment of the Exchequer Chamber). But Professor Holden has argued that Lord Holt's decision was correct and that promissory notes had not been recognised as negotiable prior to his decision (J Milnes Holden *The History of Negotiable Instruments in English Law* (1955), pp 79–84). If Holden is right than the 1704 Act was constitutive of negotiability.

As to whether the East India Company Bonds Act 1811 actually made bonds of the East India Company negotiable or merely transferable by delivery, see *Holden*, op cit, p 245 and Chorley (1932) 48 LQR 51 at p 53.

(b) Mercantile usage

Goodwin v Robarts (1875) LR 10 Exch 337, Exchequer Chamber

Through his stockbroker Goodwin purchased certain Russian and Hungarian Government scrip. The scrip promised to give the bearer, after all instalments had been paid, a bond for the amount paid, with interest. Goodwin allowed his stockbroker to retain possession of the scrip and the stockbroker fraudulently pledged it with the defendant bankers as security for a loan. The stockbroker went bankrupt and the bankers sold the scrip. Goodwin brought an action against the bankers to recover the amount realised on the sale. The bankers argued that through mercantile usage such scrip had been treated as negotiable by delivery so that Goodwin had lost his title to it. The judgment of the Exchequer Chamber was delivered by Cockburn CJ.

Cockburn CJ: . . . The substance of [the defendants'] argument is, that, because the scrip does not correspond with any of the forms of the securities for money which have been hitherto held to be negotiable by the law merchant, and does not contain a direct promise to pay money, but only a promise to give security for money, it is not a security to which, by the law merchant, the character of negotiability can attach.

Having given the fullest consideration to this argument, we are of opinion that it cannot prevail. It is founded on the view that the law merchant thus referred to is fixed and stereotyped, and incapable of being expanded and enlarged so as to meet the wants and requirements of trade in the varying circumstances of commerce. It is true that the law merchant is sometimes spoken of as a fixed body of law, forming part of the common law, and as it were coeval with it. But as a matter of legal history, this view is altogether incorrect. The law merchant thus spoken of with reference to bills of exchange and other negotiable securities, though forming part of the general body of the lex mercatoria, is of comparatively recent origin. It is neither more nor less than the usages of merchants and traders in the different departments of trade, ratified by the decisions of Courts of law, which, upon such usages being proved before them, have adopted them as settled law with a view to the interests of trade and the public convenience, the Court proceeding herein on the well-known principle of law that, with reference to transactions in the different departments of trade, Courts of law, in giving effect to the contracts and dealings of the parties, will assume that the latter have dealt with one another on the footing of any custom or usage prevailing generally in the particular department. By this process, what before was usage only, unsanctioned by legal decision, has become engrafted upon, or incorporated into, the common law, and may thus be said to form part of it. 'When a general usage has been judicially ascertained and established,' says Lord Campbell, in *Brandao v Barnett* ((1846) 12 Cl & Fin 787 at 805), 'it becomes a part of the law merchant, which Courts of justice are bound to know and recognise.'

[Cockburn CJ then traced the history of how bills of exchange, promissory notes, bankers' notes, exchequer bills and cheques came to be regarded as negotiable and continued:]

It thus appears that all these instruments which are said to have derived their negotiability from the law merchant had their origin, and that at no very remote period, in mercantile usage, and were adopted into the law by our Courts as being in conformity with the usages of trade; of which, if it were needed, a further confirmation might be found in the fact that, according to the old form of declaring on bills of exchange, the declaration always was founded on the custom of merchants.

Usage, adopted by the Courts, having been thus the origin of the whole of the so-called law merchant as to negotiable securities, what is there to prevent our acting upon the principle acted upon by our predecessors, and followed in the precedents they have left to us? Why is it to be said that a new usage which has sprung up under altered circumstances, is to be less admissible than the usages of past times? Why is the door to be now shut to the admission and adoption of usage in a matter altogether of cognate character, as though the law had been finally stereotyped and settled by some positive and peremptory enactment?

[Cockburn CJ then distinguished several cases relied on by Goodwin and continued:]

We must by no means be understood as saying that mercantile usage, however extensive, should be allowed to prevail if contrary to positive law, including in the latter such usages as, having been made the subject of legal decision, and having been sanctioned and adopted by the Courts, have become, by such adoption, part of the common law. To give effect to a usage which involves a defiance or disregard of the law would be obviously contrary to a fundamental principle. And we quite agree that this would apply quite as strongly to an attempt to set up a new usage against one which has become settled and adopted by the common law as to one in conflict with the more ancient rules of the common law itself. . . .

If we could see our way to the conclusion that, in holding the scrip in question to pass by delivery, and to be available to bearer, we were giving effect to a usage incompatible either with the common law or with the law merchant as incorporated into and embodied in it, our decision would be a very different one from that which we are about to pronounce. But so far from this being the case, we are, on the contrary, in our opinion, only acting on an established principle of that law in giving legal effect to a usage, now become universal, to treat this form of security, being on the face of it expressly made transferable to bearer, as the representative of money, and as such, being made to bearer, as assignable by delivery. This being the conclusion at which we have arrived, the judgment of the Court of Exchequer will be affirmed.

[The House of Lords upheld the judgment of the Court of Exchequer Chamber and approved the ratio decidendi of that decision: (1876) 1 App Cas 476.]

NOTES

1. Compare the willingness of Cockburn CJ to ratify mercantile usage with the unwillingness of Lord Holt to do the same in *Clerke v Martin* (above, at p 475). W S Holdsworth remarked that one of the effects of *Clerke v Martin*, and its statutory reversal in the Promissory Notes Act 1704, was to teach the courts that 'they could not wholly ignore approved mercantile custom; that they must adapt their rules to such customs; that in fact there were cases in which "Lombard Street must be allowed to give laws to Westminster Hall" ' (W S Holdsworth *A History of English Law*, Vol VIII, p 176). Chorley went so far as to say that Cockburn CJ's statements on the judicial recognition of mercantile usage 'should be inscribed in letters of gold in every Court handling commercial litigation': (1932) 48 LQR 51 at p 55.

2. Even if the usage is of recent origin the courts will still recognise it (*Bechuanaland Exploration Co v London Trading Bank Ltd* [1898] 2 QB 658). As Bigham J stated in *Edelstein v Schuler & Co* [1902] 2 KB 144 at 154:

> . . . but it is to be remembered that in these days usage is established much more quickly than it was in days gone by; more depends on the number of the transactions which help to create it than on the time over which the transactions are spread. . . .

3. Before a court will recognise an instrument as negotiable through mercantile usage the following conditions must be satisfied:

(1) the usage must be 'reasonable, certain and notorious': *Devonald v Rosser & Sons* [1906] 2 KB 728 at 743, per Farwell LJ, CA;
(2) the usage must be general and not 'a custom or habit which prevails only in a particular market or particular section of the commercial world': *Easton v London Joint Stock Bank* (1886) 34 Ch D 95 at 113, per Bowen LJ, CA; reversed on a different point sub nom *Sheffield (Earl of) v London Joint Stock Bank* (1888) 13 App Cas 333;
(3) the instrument's terms must not be incompatible with negotiability (eg not marked 'non-negotiable') nor stated to be transferable by some method other than delivery: *London and County Banking Co Ltd v London and River Plate Bank Ltd* (1887) 20 QBD 232 at 239, per Manisty J.

QUESTION

Unless recognised as negotiable by statute or mercantile usage, an instrument cannot be made negotiable simply by an express specification to that effect in its terms (*Crouch v Crédit Foncier of England* (1873) LR 8 QB 374 at 386, per Blackburn J). Why? What advantage would there be in recognising such an instrument as negotiable?

3 Types of negotiable instrument

Negotiable instruments include the following documents:

(1) bills of exchange;
(2) cheques;
(3) promissory notes;
(4) bank notes;

(5) treasury bills;
(6) banker's drafts;
(7) dividend warrants;
(8) share warrants;
(9) bearer scrip;
(10) bearer debentures;
(11) bearer bonds;
(12) floating rate notes;
(13) certificates of deposit.

The following documents are not negotiable instruments:

(1) bills of lading;
(2) dock warrants;
(3) delivery orders;
(4) postal or money orders;
(5) registered share certificates;
(6) registered debentures;
(7) insurance policies;
(8) IOUs.

4 Advantages of a negotiable instrument

Before 1874 the assignment of a promise to pay money was not permitted (apart from limited exceptions) at common law. It was the refusal of the common law to allow the transfer of promises to pay money which contributed to the use of negotiable instruments to achieve that end. Only with the enactment of s 25(6) of the Supreme Court of Judicature Act 1873 have promises to pay money been generally assignable at law (since repealed and substantially re-enacted by s 136 of the Law of Property Act 1925: see below, pp 699 ff). However, there remain a number of distinct advantages in embodying a payment obligation in a negotiable instrument and transferring it by delivery (or delivery and indorsement) rather than merely assigning the obligation under the 1925 Act. These advantages can be summarised as follows:

(1) the transferee of a negotiable instrument can sue in his own name, even though there has been no assignment in writing, or notice to the obligor or even if the transfer is not absolute, as required for assignments under the statute; and
(2) the transferee of a negotiable instrument who takes it for value and in good faith acquires a good title free from equities, whereas an assignee under the statute may take subject to equities.

The ease with which a negotiable instrument can be transferred, and the security of title which it can provide, means it can be readily sold to raise cash before the payment obligation on the instrument becomes due.

Even if the payee does not intend to transfer the payment obligation there are advantages in receiving payment by means of a negotiable instrument. As the instrument embodies its own payment obligation divorced from the underlying transaction from which it originates, payment under the instrument, at least in theory, becomes certain, regardless of any breach of that underlying transaction. This has led bills of exchange to be treated as cash ensuring that in most cases the courts will give summary judgment on the instrument and refuse to stay execution of that judgment pending trial of any counter-claim.

Cebora SNC v SIP (Industrial Products) Ltd [1976] 1 Lloyd's Rep 271, Court of Appeal

The plaintiffs entered into a distribution agreement with the defendants whereby the defendants were given the exclusive right to sell the plaintiffs' products in the United Kingdom. In payment of the price of products supplied by the plaintiffs under this agreement the defendants drew five bills of exchange. Following disputes between the parties, the defendants gave instructions that the bills should be dishonoured. The plaintiffs applied for summary judgment on the bills and the defendants counterclaimed for non-delivery of goods, delivery of defective goods and loss of profit. The District Registrar entered judgment for the plaintiffs and refused the defendants' application for a stay of execution pending trial of their counterclaim. May J dismissed the defendants' appeal, as did the Court of Appeal (Buckley and Stephenson LJJ, and Sir Eric Sachs).

Sir Eric Sachs: Any erosion of the certainties of the application by our Courts of the law merchant relating to bills of exchange is likely to work to the detriment of this country, which depends on international trade to a degree that needs no emphasis. For some generations one of those certainties has been that the bona fide holder for value of a bill of exchange is entitled, save in truly exceptional circumstances, on its maturity to have it treated as cash, so that in an action upon it the Court will refuse to regard either as a defence or as grounds for a stay of execution any set off, legal or equitable, or any counterclaim, whether arising on the particular transaction upon which the bill of exchange came into existence, or, a fortiori, arising in any other way. This rule of practice is thus, in effect, pay up on the bill of exchange first and pursue claims later. . . .

In my judgment, the Courts should be really careful not to whittle away the rule of practice by introducing unnecessary exceptions to it under the influence of sympathy-evoking stories, and should have due regard to the maxim that hard cases can make bad law. Indeed, in these days of increasing international interdependence and increasing need to foster liquidity of resources, the rule may be said to be of special import to the business community. Pleas to leave in Court large sums to deteriorate in value while official referee scale proceedings are fought out may well to that community seem rather divorced from business realities, and should perhaps be examined with considerable caution.

Nova (Jersey) Knit Ltd v Kammgarn Spinnerei GmbH [1977] 2 All ER 463, House of Lords

An English company and a German company set up a partnership in Germany. The English company sold machines to the German company to be used for the partnership and the German company issued bills of exchange for the price. The English company brought an action on the bills. The German company sought to bring a defence and counterclaim for unliquidated damages for mismanagement of the partnership and defects in the machines. The House of Lords (Lord Wilberforce, Viscount Dilhorne, Lords Salmon, Fraser and Russell) held the German company liable to pay the bills in full without set-off or counterclaim. By a majority (Lord Salmon dissenting), their Lordships refused a stay of execution of the judgment based on an arbitration agreement contained in the underlying contract.

Lord Wilberforce: . . . When one person buys goods from another, it is often, one would think generally, important for the seller to be sure of his price: he may (as indeed the appellants here) have bought the goods from someone else whom he has to pay. He may demand payment in cash; but if the buyer cannot provide this at once, he may agree to take bills of exchange payable at future dates. These are taken as equivalent to deferred instalments of cash. Unless they are to be treated as unconditionally payable instruments (as in the Act, s 3, says 'an unconditional order in writing'), which the seller can negotiate for cash, the seller might just as well give credit. And it is for this reason that English law (and German law appears to be no different) does not allow cross-claims, or defences, except such limited defences as those based on fraud, invalidity, or failure of consideration, to be made. . . .

Lord Russell of Killowen: . . . It is in my opinion well established that a claim for unliquidated damages under a contract for sale is no defence to a claim under a bill of exchange accepted by the purchaser: nor is it available as set-off or counterclaim. This is a deep rooted concept of English commercial law. A vendor and purchaser who agree upon payment by acceptance of bills of exchange do so not simply upon the basis that credit is given to the purchaser so that the vendor must in due course sue for the price under the contract of sale. The bill is itself a contract separate from the contract of sale. Its purpose is not merely to serve as a negotiable instrument, it is also to avoid postponement of the purchaser's liability to the vendor himself, a postponement grounded upon some allegation of failure in some respect by the vendor under the underlying contract, unless it be total or quantified partial failure of consideration. . . .

NOTES

1. Also see *James Lamont & Co Ltd v Hyland Ltd* [1950] 1 KB 585; *Brown Shipley & Co Ltd v Alicia Hosiery Ltd* [1966] 1 Lloyd's Rep 668; and *Montecchi v Shimco (UK) Ltd* [1979] 1 WLR 1180.

2. Although treated as the equivalent of cash, a bill of exchange is not legal tender and, subject to any agreement or usage to the contrary, a creditor is only obliged to accept legal tender, ie cash, in payment of a debt (*Gordon v Strange* (1847) 1 Exch 477). If a bill of exchange, promissory note or cheque is accepted in payment of a debt it depends on the intention of the parties as to whether it is taken in absolute or conditional payment of the debt. In *Re Charge Card Services Ltd* [1989] Ch 497 at 511, CA, Browne-Wilkinson V-C stated that:

> . . . It is common ground that where a debt is 'paid' by cheque or bill of exchange, there is a presumption that such payment is conditional on the cheque or bill being honoured. If it is not honoured, the condition is not satisfied and the liability of the purchaser to pay the price remains. Such presumption can be rebutted by showing an express or implied intention that the cheque or bill is taken in total satisfaction of the liability. . . .

Browne-Wilkinson V-C left open the question whether the presumption of conditional payment would be rebutted merely by the fact that the cheque had been accompanied by a bank card (at 517). At first instance, in the same case, Millett J stated (obiter) that the presumption would not be rebutted in those circumstances: [1987] Ch 150 at 166. For recent emphasis on the conditional nature of payment by cheque, see *Crockfords Club Ltd v Mehta* [1992] 1 WLR 355, Henry J and the Court of Appeal.

QUESTIONS

1. Is there any advantage to a creditor in accepting payment by negotiable instrument as opposed to cash? If so, would this enable a debtor to argue that payment by negotiable instrument provided its own consideration to support the creditor's agreement to accept a lesser sum in settlement of an undisputed debt?

See *D & C Builders v Rees* [1966] 2 QB 617, CA. Also see McLauchlan (1987) 12 NZULR 259 and *James Cook Hotel Ltd v Caux Corporate Services Ltd* [1989] LRC (Comm) 518 (New Zealand).

2. If a negotiable instrument is used to pay a debt and, when in the creditor's hands, the instrument is accidentally destroyed before its maturity, can the creditor return to the debtor demanding payment of the debt?

CHAPTER 16

Bills of exchange

1 The use of bills of exchange

E P Ellinger 'Electronic Funds Transfer as a Deferred Settlement System' in
Electronic Banking, the Legal Implications **(Goode, ed), pp 40–41**

Bills of exchange are used predominantly in the context of two facilities associated with international trade: the documentary credit (which is used exclusively in this context) and the acceptance credit (which is used in domestic projects as well). In the case of documentary credits, the seller usually draws a bill of exchange on the issuing or confirming bank for the amount of the credit. The bill, which may be payable at 90 or 180 days after sight, will be 'discounted' by the seller's own bank, who thereupon becomes the negotiating bank. This bank arranges for the presentment of the bill for acceptance and for payment, usually by engaging a correspondent.

The arrangement differs in an acceptance credit. Here an industrialist or manufacturer, who requires extra liquidity, may be unable to obtain a loan from his bank. But the bank may be prepared to lend him its credit. To do so, it authorises him to draw on itself bills of exchange for an amount not exceeding a stated ceiling. The bills are, thus, signed by the industrialist as drawer and by the bank as acceptor. The industrialist obtains his required finance by discounting the bill. He is able to arrange for this on the strength of the combined effect of the signatures of the bank and of himself. The instrument may be discounted several times on the bills market. At maturity, it is met by the bank (the acceptor), which seeks reimbursement from the drawer. If the drawer is not in a position to settle, another set of bills is 'rolled over'.

There are, of course, other transactions in which bills of exchange are being used. Thus, a bill accompanies cif documents transmitted by the seller of the goods to the purchaser. But in all the cases involved, the bill serves the same two objects. First, it purports to charge the person on whom it is drawn (the 'drawee'), whose consent to the demand ('acceptance') constitutes a deferred payment undertaking. Secondly, the bill is meant to be discounted. It therefore has to be negotiable. . . .

A bill of exchange payable on demand appears as Figure 1 and a bill of exchange payable at a usance of 90 days after sight appears as Figure 2.

FIGURE 1   **BILL OF EXCHANGE PAYABLE ON DEMAND**

Fitzwilliam College
Cambridge

1 January 1994

£100

On demand pay to Leonard Sealy[3] or order the sum of one hundred pounds.

For and on behalf of Hooley Holdings Ltd,[1]

To   Corporate Capital Ltd[2]
St Catherine's Street
London

R Hooley

Director

Notes
1 The 'drawer'.
2 The 'drawee'.
3 The 'payee' (when the bill is delivered to him he becomes the first 'holder').

FIGURE 2   **BILL OF EXCHANGE PAYABLE AT A USANCE OF 90 DAYS
AFTER SIGHT**

Accepted payable at ABC Bank Ltd,
Lombard St, London. For and on behalf of
Corporate Capital Ltd,[4] *P. Ropeson* Director.

Fitzwilliam College
Cambridge

1 January 1994

£100

At 90 days sight pay to Hooley Holdings Ltd[3] or order the sum of
one hundred pounds for value received.

For and on behalf of Hooley Holdings Ltd,[1]

To   Corporate Capital Ltd[2]
St Catherine's Street
London

R Hooley

Director

Notes
1 The 'drawer'.
2 The 'drawee'.
3 The 'payee' (when the bill is delivered to him he becomes the first 'holder').
4 The 'acceptor' (when the 'drawee' has accepted the bill he is then called the 'acceptor').

484 Bills of exchange

2 The Bills of Exchange Act 1882

The primary source of the law of bills of exchange is the Bills of Exchange Act 1882. The Act was drafted by Sir Mackenzie Chalmers who also drafted the Sale of Goods Act 1893 and the Marine Insurance Act 1906. (Unless expressly stated to be otherwise, all statutory provisions referred to in this chapter are to sections of the Bills of Exchange Act 1882.)

Bank of England v Vagliano Bros [1891] AC 107, House of Lords

(The facts appear below on p 492. The case turned on the meaning of s 7(3). The Court of Appeal had qualified the wording of the subsection by introducing a limitation to be found in the common law.)

Lord Herschell: My Lords, with sincere respect for the learned Judges who have taken this view, I cannot bring myself to think that this is the proper way to deal with such a statute as the Bills of Exchange Act, which was intended to be a code of the law relating to negotiable instruments. I think the proper course is in the first instance to examine the language of the statute and to ask what is its natural meaning, uninfluenced by any considerations derived from the previous state of the law and not to start with inquiring how the law previously stood, and then, assuming that it was probably intended to leave it unaltered, to see if the words of the enactment will bear an interpretation in conformity with this view.

If a statute, intended to embody in a code a particular branch of the law, is to be treated in this fashion, it appears to me that its utility will be almost entirely destroyed, and the very object with which it was enacted will be frustrated. The purpose of such a statute surely was that on any point specifically dealt with by it, the law should be ascertained by interpreting the language used instead of, as before, by roaming over a vast number of authorities in order to discover what the law was, extracting it by a minute critical examination of the prior decisions, dependent upon a knowledge of the exact effect even of an obsolete proceeding such as a demurrer to evidence. I am of course far from asserting that resort may never be had to the previous state of the law for the purpose of aiding in the construction of the provisions of the code. If, for example, a provision be of doubtful import, such resort would be perfectly legitimate. Or, again, if in a code of the law of negotiable instruments words be found which have previously acquired a technical meaning, or been used in a sense other than their ordinary one, in relation to such instruments, the same interpretation might well be put upon them in the code. I give these as examples merely; they, of course, do not exhaust the category. What, however, I am venturing to insist upon is, that the first step taken should be to interpret the language of the statute, and that an appeal to earlier decisions can only be justified on some special ground.

One further remark I have to make before I proceed to consider the language of the statute. The Bills of Exchange Act was certainly not intended to be merely a code of the existing law. It is not open to question that it was intended to alter, and did alter it in certain respects. And I do not think that it is to be presumed that any particular provision was intended to be a statement of the existing law, rather than a substituted enactment.

NOTES

1. Although the Preamble to the 1882 Act states that it was intended 'to codify the law relating to Bills of Exchange, Cheques, and Promissory Notes', it did, in fact, alter the common law in a number of respects (see, inter alia, s 4(2), s 7(2) and (3), s 12).

2. The Act does not, in general, extend to negotiable instruments other than bills of exchange, cheques and promissory notes (although see s 95 of the 1882 Act and s 5 of the Cheques Act 1957).

3. Lord Herschell gave examples of when it would be legitimate to examine the common law as an aid to construction of the provisions of the 1882 Act. The common law remains relevant in many other ways. This is emphasised by A Barak in the following extract.

'The Nature of the Negotiable Instrument' by A Barak (1983) 18 Israel LR 49, pp 69–70

. . . that several different sets of rules apply to the negotiable instrument: since it is a chattel – the general law applicable to chattels (such as sales and torts); since it is an obligation – the general law of obligations (for example the rules as to capacity); and since it is a negotiable paper – the special rules applicable to such instruments. In most countries, the law of negotiable instruments is normally confined to that latter body of rules. Israel's Bills of Exchange Ordinance deals almost entirely with the bill as a negotiable instrument; it makes virtually no reference at all to the bill as a chattel or an obligation. Those aspects of the bill are covered by the general law. Hence, one can draw a distinction between the law of negotiable instruments in the strict sense and the law of negotiable instruments in the broad sense. The former deals with the bill as a negotiable paper and, as said, is usually to be found in special legislation. The latter deals with the bill as a chattel and an obligation and is usually to be found in the general law. The parallel existence of the two has been possible because legislation on negotiable instruments was never intended to provide an exhaustive list of the rules of law dealing with such instruments. From the time of the very earliest legislation in this field it has been clear that, alongside the special rules governing the bill as a negotiable instrument, the ordinary rules relating to it as a chattel and an obligation continue to apply. . . .

NOTES

1. Israel's Bills of Exchange Ordinance is based on the English Bills of Exchange Act 1882 and so Barak's comments are equally relevant to the 1882 Act.

2. Section 97(2) provides that: 'The rules of common law including the law merchant, save in so far as they are inconsistent with the express provisions of this Act, shall continue to apply to bills of exchange, promissory notes, and cheques.'

3. An example of the general law applicable to chattels relevant to bills is the tort of conversion. This is the remedy usually, but not always, available to the true owner of a stolen bill. An example of the general law of obligations applicable to bills is the doctrine of consideration. In this case the Act expressly imports the common law rules as s 27(1)(a) states that valuable consideration for a bill may be constituted by any consideration sufficient to support a simple contract.

QUESTION

Lord Herschell's restrictive method of interpreting a codifying statute has not always been followed by the courts (eg *Ashington Piggeries Ltd v Christopher Hill Ltd* [1972] AC 441). What are its disadvantages?

3 Definition of a bill of exchange

Bills of Exchange Act 1882, s 3

(1) A bill of exchange is an unconditional order in writing, addressed by one person to another, signed by the person giving it, requiring the person to whom it is addressed to pay on demand or at a fixed or determinable future time a sum certain in money to or to the order of a specified person, or to bearer.

(2) An instrument which does not comply with these conditions, or which orders any act to be done in addition to the payment of money, is not a bill of exchange.

Korea Exchange Bank v Debenhams (Central Buying) Ltd [1979] 1 Lloyd's Rep 548, Court of Appeal

Korea Exchange Bank's claim was for the balance of moneys due under an instrument which was on a bill of exchange form drawn payable 'at 90 days D/A of this First Bill of Exchange'. The word 'sight', which was part of the original printed form of the instrument coming between the typed letters 'D/A' and the printed word 'of', had been deleted by overtyping. As a preliminary issue the Court of Appeal was asked to decide whether the instrument was expressed to be payable at a fixed or determinable future time and whether it was, therefore, a bill of exchange within the meaning of s 3(1).

Megaw LJ: . . . The common ground between the parties as to the meaning of the symbol 'D/A' in commercial usage is that it means 'documents against acceptance'. Write those words in, and the result is:

At 90 days documents against acceptance . . . pay.

That is gibberish, in the absence of some exposition which conforms with common sense or commercial usage or both.

The defendants say the symbol 'D/A' or the words 'documents against acceptance' commonly appear in the margins of bills of exchange or at some place in the bill outside the actual words of the order to pay. They say that their purpose is simply to call to the attention of holders or potential holders of the bill the fact that the drawee will not accept unless the proper documents are produced, relating to the sale transaction which underlies the bill. The symbol, or the phrase which it represents, is in no respect directed to the drawee. If it were, it would, or might, make the purported bill a conditional order to pay, and hence prevent it from being a bill of exchange under the Act. The inclusion of 'D/A' in the place where it occurs in the present bill is, the defendants say, most unusual, if not unique. . . .

The defendants' submission is that 'D/A', where it is placed in this instrument, has no more and no less effect than if it were in the margin of the instrument. It is not any part of the order to the drawee. The result, necessarily, is that, since 'sight' has been crossed out, and 'D/A' is no part of the order to the drawee, the order to the drawee means as 'At 90 days . . . pay'. It thus gives no starting point for the 90 days. Hence the instrument is not a bill, since it fails to require payment 'at a fixed or determinable future time'. The words 'At 90 days' are left hanging in the air. But it does leave the symbol 'D/A', and the words which, as a matter of common ground, they represent (documents against acceptance), introduced parenthetically in an unusual and inappropriate place, but at least having their generally understood meaning and effect merely as a notification to potential holders.

The plaintiffs' submission, as accepted by the Judge, involves, first, the transmutation and alteration of the words which it is common ground that 'D/A' represents. That is, the words 'documents against acceptance' are transmuted into 'acceptance in exchange for documents'. The plaintiffs' submission, again as accepted by the learned Judge, involves, secondly, that the word which is represented by the second part of the symbol 'D/A' (the 'A' for 'acceptance') has to be treated as having become a part – and a vital part – of the order from the drawer to the drawee: so that 'At 90 days . . . /A . . . pay' becomes 'At 90 days after acceptance pay'. But the first part of the symbol 'D/A' (the 'D' for 'documents against') is not a part of the order from the drawer to the drawee, but, having been transmuted into 'in exchange for documents', becomes merely an informative description of the other half of the symbol. All this is done so as to achieve precisely the result which, the plaintiffs concede, could have been achieved by leaving in the word 'sight', which in fact was deleted, presumably before the instrument was signed by the drawer.

There are objections to either of the rival submissions. In the end, with great respect to the contrary view taken by the learned Judge, I have come to the conclusion that the plaintiffs have not established that those who have to handle bills of exchange from day to day in the market should be expected to understand with reasonable assurance that this unusual wording is to be interpreted as including the 'acceptance' part of the symbol 'D/A' as being part of the order to the drawee to pay. 'D/A' in commercial usage is ordinarily, at least, not any part of the order to pay directed to the drawee. If a part of the symbol is to become an essential part of the drawer's order to the drawee, this has to be made clear on the face of the instrument. In this instrument, in my judgment, it, at the best, falls short of the necessary clarity.

If I were wrong on this first question, I should have arrived at the same answer on another ground. . . .

If the plaintiffs were right on the first question discussed above, so that 'At 90 days D/A pay . . .' means 'At 90 days after acceptance . . . pay', the plaintiffs would have surmounted their first hurdle under s 3 of the Act. But they would still have to surmount a barrier placed in the way by s 11.

Section 11 sets out the conditions in which a bill is payable at a determinable future time within the meaning of the Act. We can dispense at once with the conditions in para (2) of s 11. It is not suggested that they would avail the plaintiffs, for a bill payable 90 days after acceptance is not payable at a fixed period after the occurrence of a specified event which is certain to happen. The bill may never be accepted. So the plaintiffs have to come within para (1), or else they fail.

The plaintiffs, then, have to establish that the bill is –

. . . expressed to be payable – (1) At a fixed period after date or sight.

No one suggests that this bill was payable 'after date'. So the question is: was this bill *expressed to be* payable at a fixed period after sight? . . .

. . . The answer I should have thought was necessarily 'No'. 90 days is a fixed period. But 'after acceptance' is a different expression from 'after sight'. It is, to my mind, a bold submission that in a document in which the word 'sight' has been struck out and 'acceptance' put in, the document is nevertheless 'expressed to be' payable at a fixed period after sight.

It is not a proposition which I feel able to accept. Even if the position were, as Mr Staughton submitted, that for the purpose of s 11 'sight' and 'acceptance' mean the same thing, I should not be prepared to accept that the statutory phrase 'expressed to be payable . . . after sight' could be interpreted as though it permitted the bill to be expressed otherwise than by the use of the word 'sight'. But, in any event, while it may be right to say that for the purpose of s 11 sight *includes* acceptance, there can be sight without acceptance. For a bill can be seen but not accepted. Therefore, while '90 days after acceptance' provides a fixed period in respect of an accepted bill which would coincide with the fixed period after sight, it provides no fixed period if the bill, as may well happen, is not accepted. A provision for payment at a fixed period after sight, therefore, ensures certainty as to the date of maturity by reference to either contingency: acceptance or refusal. The certainty as to the date of maturity in the event of refusal to accept is important. For example, by s 57(1) of the Act, the holder could recover interest on the amount of the bill from the drawer or prior indorser, in the event of a refusal of acceptance, only from the date of maturity of the bill. The bill, to achieve the required certainty, must therefore contain provisions as to the date of maturity in the event of non-acceptance as well as in the event of acceptance. That is properly covered by a bill providing for payment so many days after sight. It is not covered by a bill providing for payment so many days after acceptance.

[Waller and Eveleigh LJJ concurred.]

NOTES

1. In *Carlos v Fancourt* (1794) 5 Term Rep 482 at 486 Ashhurst J emphasised that '[c]ertainty is a great object in commercial instruments; and unless they carry their own validity on the face of them, they are not negotiable . . .'. This requirement ensures that negotiable instruments are freely negotiable and saleable and it lies at the heart of the definition of a bill of exchange contained in s 3(1). The instrument in the *Korea Exchange Bank* case was held not to be a bill of exchange because it lacked that essential element of certainty. At first instance, Donaldson J had found in favour of the bank because he regarded the drawer's intention that the instrument should be a bill of exchange as decisive. The Court of Appeal's emphasis was on certainty in the market place amongst those who would deal in such instruments. Whilst the Court of Appeal's approach is consistent with the comments of Ashhurst J, it should be noted that the courts are prepared to overcome faulty expressions in an instrument where the true meaning is obvious despite the defect: see A H Hudson [1981] JBL 101 at pp 102–103. In the *Korea Exchange Bank* case the true meaning was not obvious. For an example of a case where the true meaning was obvious see *Chamberlain v Young and Tower* [1893] 2 QB 206 (below, p 491).

2. In the *Korea Exchange Bank* case the preliminary issue had been narrowly drawn. In his judgment, Megaw LJ touched on two further questions but he was not prepared to answer them as they fell ouside the ambit of the preliminary issue. The first question was whether the instrument contained a conditional order to the drawee so as to fall ouside the definition of a bill of exchange in s 3(1). The defendants had accepted that the symbol 'D/A' was not directed to the drawee and so the court did not have to decide the issue. A clear order to the drawee to pay, or accept the bill, only against the tender of certain documents would be conditional. Whether a bill marked 'documents against acceptance' contains such a conditional order remains undecided: see *Rosenhain v Commonwealth Bank of Australia* (1922) 31 CLR 46 at 52, High Court of Australia.

3. The second question left unanswered by Megaw LJ was whether the bill in question was a bill payable on demand by virtue of s 10(1)(b). Under s 10(1)(b) a bill is payable on demand 'in which no time for payment is expressed'. As the Court of Appeal held that the symbol 'D/A' lacked the necessary clarity to be part of the drawer's order to the drawee, then it is arguable that the effect of this finding was that no time for payment was stipulated in the bill with the result that s 10(1)(b) applied. Such an argument is unlikely to meet with much success. It is generally accepted that if a time for payment *is* expressed but that time is not a fixed or determinable future time within ss 3(1) and 11 then s 10(1)(b) does not apply. It is submitted that this will also be the case if the wording intended to express a time for payment is defective or unintelligible. In a case like the *Korea Exchange Bank* case, to hold otherwise would benefit the party responsible for the defect (*Byles on Bills of Exchange* (26th ed, 1988) (hereafter referred to as 'Byles'), p 17).

4. *Williamson v Rider* [1963] 1 QB 89, CA, is also an important case on certainty of time of payment. In this case a promissory note was drawn payable 'on or before December 31st 1956'. Under s 83(1) a promissory note, like a bill of exchange, must be payable 'on demand or at a fixed or determinable future time'. The Court of Appeal held, by a majority, that the instrument was not a promissory note since it was not payable at a fixed future time. Willmer and Danckwerts LJJ held that as the maker of the instrument had an option to pay at an earlier date than the specified date this created an uncertainty and contingency in the time for payment. Ormerod LJ, dissenting, stated that there was no uncertainty as to the time of payment as the maker's obligation to pay only arose on the specified date, even though he is given a right to pay earlier. In *Claydon v Bradley* [1987] 1 All ER 522, CA, where an instrument was payable 'by July 1, 1983', the Court of Appeal felt bound to follow *Williamson v Rider*. However, the decision of the majority in *Williamson v Rider* has been the subject of widespread criticism (see, in particular, A H Hudson (1962) 25 MLR 593 at pp 595–596) and the dissenting judgment of Ormerod LJ has been followed in Canada and Ireland (*John Burrows Ltd v Subsurface Surveys Ltd* (1968) 68 DLR (2d) 354; *Creative Press Ltd v Harman* [1973] IR 313; cf *Salot v Naidoo* 1981 (3) SA 959). It would take a decision of the House of Lords to overrule *Williamson v Rider*.

QUESTION

If I draw and sign an instrument promising to pay X £100 on the death of the oak tree I have just planted in my garden, is the instrument a promissory note?

Orbit Mining and Trading Co Ltd v Westminster Bank Ltd [1963] 1 QB 794, Court of Appeal

Orbit Mining had two directors, Wolff and Epstein. Wolff often went abroad and when he did so he left signed cheque forms with Epstein, drawn on Midland Bank. Epstein added his signature to three such forms drawn to 'cash or order', indorsed them and paid them in for the credit of his account with Westminster Bank. Westminster Bank did not know that Epstein was employed by Orbit Mining. It was conceded at the trial that Westminster Bank had converted these instruments but it contested liability on the ground of the statutory protection given to it as a collecting bank acting in good faith and without negligence within, what is now, s 4 of the Cheques Act 1957. Mackenna J held that the three instruments were not cheques within s 73 of the 1882 Act, but that they were documents intended to enable a person to obtain payment from a banker within s 4(2)(b) of the Cheques Act 1957 and so fell within the protection of s 4 of the 1957 Act. However, the judge went on to hold that the bank had lost its statutory protection because it had been negligent. The Court of Appeal allowed the bank's appeal on the issue of negligence but upheld Mackenna J's finding as to the nature of the documents.

Sellers LJ: In the light of these provisions [ss 3(1), 8(3) and 73 of the 1882 Act], in my judgment, the three instruments in this case where the order is 'Pay cash or order' cannot be held to be cheques because they are not bills of exchange. They are not to or to the order of a specified person and they are not 'to bearer'. A subtle argument was addressed to us submitting that the effect of the instruction 'Pay cash or order' was to make payment to bearer and that is the meaning to be derived from the words and therefore the cheques were 'expressed to be so payable.' It is so easy, and indeed has for so long been customary, to make a clear payment to 'bearer' that I think the Act requires 'bearer' to be stated and that it does not apply to a possible implied or derived interpretation of the words used. 'Or order' in itself is in contrast to 'bearer,' although as 'cash' can give no order the effect is no doubt that it is equivalent to a payment to bearer.

Section 7(3) expressly provides that 'Where the payee is a fictitious or non-existing person the bill may be treated as payable to bearer.' 'Cash' cannot be said to be a fictitious or non-existing person and it would be enlarging the provisions of the Act to read the bill as expressed to be payable to bearer where the payee is 'cash.'

Harman LJ: . . . In order to be a cheque within s 73 the document must be a bill of exchange. This is defined by s 3(1) of the Act of 1882, under which there must be a sum payable 'to the order of a specified person or to bearer.' Clearly 'cash' is not a specified person, and I do not think that unless made expressly in favour of the bearer it is enough to argue that 'cash or order' in the end as a matter of construction means 'bearer,' and I agree with the judge below that the mandate to pay bearer must be expressed and not implied.

As to s 4(2)(b), this is clearly a document intended to enable a person to obtain payment of the sum mentioned in the document. 'Person' here means any person and does not require a named person: therefore, 'cash' is good enough. The question is whether the document was 'issued by a customer of a banker.' In my opinion this clearly was so issued. It was a good cheque so far as the plaintiff company was concerned, on which its own bank did pay and was admittedly liable so to do. A written document is intended to bring about that which its written terms indicate. It is not legitimate to inquire into the mind of the creator of the document. . . .

[Davies LJ delivered a concurring judgment.]

NOTES

1. Prior to this case there had been some debate as to whether instruments drawn 'pay cash or order' or 'pay wages or order' could be treated as bearer cheques. The decision in the *Orbit Mining* case confirmed the view that such instruments are not to be regarded as payable 'to bearer' although, as Sellers LJ noted, they can act as a mandate which directs payment to the bearer of the instrument. As a mandate the instrument cannot be transferred by delivery or by indorsement and delivery. See also *Gader v Flower* (1979) 129 NLJ 1266, CA, where *Orbit Mining* appears to have been followed. But a bill drawn payable to 'cash or bearer' would appear to be a valid bill payable to bearer (*Grant v Vaughan* (1764) 3 Burr 1516) as is a bill payable to 'X or bearer' (*M K International Development Co Ltd v The Housing Bank* [1991] 1 Bank LR 74, CA). *Sed quaere* an instrument drawn payable to 'bearer or order'?

2. It is important for a bill of exchange to specify to whom it is payable. This notifies the drawee, who has accepted the bill, of the identity of the person to whom he should make payment so that he can discharge himself from all further liability on the bill. This requirement is reflected in the wording of ss 3(1) and 7(1). However, it will not be fatal to the status of an instrument as a bill of exchange if the payee is described on the bill in an ambiguous way (*Bird & Co (London) Ltd v Thomas Cook & Son Ltd* [1937] 2 All ER 227 at 230–231 which was a case concerning an ambiguous indorsement). So long as the ambiguity is latent (ie the payee is misnamed or designated by description only) then extrinsic evidence will be admissible to establish who the drawer intended to be the payee. Where the ambiguity is patent on the instrument then extrinsic evidence is not available and the instrument will not be a bill of exchange, unless it may be treated as payable to a fictitious or non-existent person within s 7(3) (see below, p 492).

3. Under s 32(4) the payee or indorsee, if he is wrongly designated or his name is misspelt, may indorse the bill as he is described in it (eg if a bill is drawn payable to 'J Browne or order', whereas the true name of the payee is 'J Brown', he can validly negotiate the bill by signing it as 'J Browne').

4. In *Chamberlain v Young and Tower* [1893] 2 QB 206 an instrument drawn 'pay to .... order' was construed as being a valid bill payable 'to my order' so as to give effect to the drawer's clear intention to create a negotiable instrument. It is a moot point whether an instrument drawn 'pay .... or order' is a valid bill. The words 'or order' negative any inference that it is payable to bearer (cf *Wookey v Pole* (1820) 4 B & Ald 1). Despite a number of early nineteenth century cases holding that such an instrument was not a bill of exchange (*R v Richards* (1811) Russ & Ry 193; *R v Randall* (1811) Russ & Ry 195), it is generally accepted (see *Chalmers and Guest on Bills of Exchange* (14th ed, 1991) (hereafter referred to as 'Chalmers and Guest'), p 46; *Chitty on Contracts* (26th ed, 1989) (hereafter referred to as 'Chitty'), Vol 2, para 2763; cf Byles, p 32) that an instrument drawn 'pay .... or order' would now be construed as payable 'to myself or order'. In the Scottish case of *Henderson, Sons & Co Ltd v Wallace and Pennell* (1902) 40 SLR 70 Lord Traynor treated an instrument drawn 'pay .... or order' as a promissory note. However, the issue was left undecided in *Chamberlain v Tower and Young* and in *North and South Insurance Corpn v National Provincial Bank* [1936] 1 KB 328.

5. If the name of the payee is left blank the instrument is described as 'inchoate' and the person in possession of it may insert the name of the payee under s 20(1), so long as he does do 'within a reasonable time, and strictly in accordance with the authority given' (s 20(2)). There must be some doubt as to whether completion of a bill by a person acting beyond his actual authority, but within his apparent or ostensible authority, will be 'strictly' in accordance with the authority given (see Chalmers and Guest, p 100). If these prerequisites are not complied with the bill will not be enforceable against any person who became a party to it prior to its completion, unless the instrument is negotiated to a holder in due course after completion (s 20(2)). Even if the holder of the bill cannot rely on s 20, he may be able to argue that the person who signs a negotiable instrument in blank or while it is otherwise incomplete is estopped from denying the validity of the completed instrument against him, if he has acted to his detriment in reliance upon it (*Lloyds Bank Ltd v Cooke* [1907] 1 KB 794, CA). In *Wilson & Meeson v Pickering* [1946] KB 422, the Court of Appeal emphasised that this type of estoppel was confined to the case of negotiable instruments so that a cheque which had lost its negotiability because it had been crossed 'not negotiable' (see s 81) fell outside its ambit (cf *Mercantile Credit Co Ltd v Hamblin* [1965] 2 QB 242 at 274–275, 278–279).

4 Transfer of a bill of exchange

By s 31(1) a bill is 'negotiated' when it is transferred from one person to another in such a manner as to constitute the transferee the holder of the bill. In this section the word 'negotiated' is used to mean 'transferred', whether or not such transfer is free from equities of prior parties. The actual mode of transfer depends on whether the bill is a bearer bill or payable to order.

(a) Bearer bills

By s 31(2) a bearer bill is transferred by delivery. According to s 2, 'delivery' means the transfer of possession, whether actual or constructive, from one person to another. Section 8(3) describes a bill as payable to bearer when it is expressed to be so payable, or on which the only or last indorsement is an indorsement in blank. An indorsement in blank occurs when the indorser simply signs the bill without specifying an indorsee (s 34(1)) and is to be contrasted with a special indorsement which occurs when the indorser specifies the person to whom, or to whose order, the bill is to be payable (s 34(2)). The back of the bill reproduced as Figure 1 appears as Figure 3. This shows a special indorsement by the payee and an indorsement in blank by the indorsee.

FIGURE 3   **BACK OF BILL OF EXCHANGE REPRODUCED AS FIGURE 1**

Notes
4 Special indorsement.
5 Indorsement in blank.

By s 7(3), where the payee is a fictitious or non-existing person the bill may be treated as payable to bearer. By virtue of s 34(3) this provision is extended to the case where an indorsee under a special indorsement is a fictitious or non-existent person so that the bill can then be treated as having been indorsed in blank.

Bank of England v Vagliano Bros [1891] AC 107, House of Lords

Vagliano Brothers regularly accepted bills drawn on them by their foreign correspondent, Vucina. Glyka, a clerk employed by Vagliano Brothers, forged Vucina's signature as drawer on a number of such bills. The bills were drawn payable to the order of C Petridi & Co, who carried on business in Constantinople, and had been the payee of some genuine bills previously drawn by Vucina upon Vagliano Brothers. In ignorance of the forgery, Vagliano Brothers accepted these bills payable at the Bank of England. Glyka then forged the indorsement of C Petridi & Co and obtained payment from the Bank of England in the name of a fictitious indorsee. The issue was whether the Bank of England was entitled to treat the bills as payable to bearer and debit Vagliano Brothers' account with the amount of their acceptances. The House of Lords by a majority (Lords Bramwell and Field dissenting) held that the Bank of England had been entitled to do so.

Lord Herschell: . . . If I am right in thinking that in the case of a payee who is a fictitious person (whatever be the meaning of that expression) a bill may, as against the acceptor, be treated by a lawful holder as payable to bearer whether the acceptor knew of the fiction or not, why should this right and liability differ according as the name inserted as payee be a creature of the imagination or correspond to that of a real person, the drawer in neither case intending a person so designated to receive payment, and in each case himself indorsing the bill in the name of the nominal payee before putting it into circulation? I am at a loss for any reason why this distinction should exist. It is true that there is this difference between the two cases – that in the one an indorsement by the named payee is physically impossible, whilst in the other it is not. But I do not think this difference affords a sound basis for a distinction between the respective rights and liabilities of the drawer, acceptor, and holder. It seems to me that it would in each case be reasonable, and on the same grounds, that the acceptor should be liable to the holder of the bill, indemnifying himself out of the funds of the drawer or obtaining reimbursement from him. . . .

Do the words, 'where the payee is a fictitious person,' apply only where the payee named never had a real existence? I take it to be clear that by the word 'payee' must be understood the payee named on the face of the bill; for of course by the hypothesis there is no intention that payment should be made to any such person. Where, then, the payee named is so named by way of pretence only, without the intention that he shall be the person to receive payment, is it doing violence to language to say that the payee is a fictitious person? I think not. I do not think that the word 'fictitious' is exclusively used to qualify that which has no real existence. When we speak of a fictitious entry in a book of accounts, we do not mean that the entry has no real existence, but only that it purports to be that which it is not – that it is an entry made for the purpose of pretending that the transaction took place which is represented by it. . . .

I have arrived at the conclusion that, whenever the name inserted as that of the payee is so inserted by way of pretence merely, without any intention that payment shall only be made in conformity therewith, the payee is a fictitious person within the meaning of the statute, whether the name be that of an existing person, or of one who has no existence, and that the bill may, in each case, be treated by a lawful holder as payable to bearer.

I have hitherto been considering the case of a bill drawn by the person whose name is attached to it as drawer, whilst the bills which have given rise to this litigation were not drawn by Vucina, who purported to be the drawer, his name being forged by Glyka. I think it was hardly contended on behalf of the respondents that this made any difference. The bills must, under the circumstances, as against the acceptor, be taken to have been drawn by Vucina, and if they have been made payable to a fictitious person within the meaning of the statute, I do not think it is open to question that they may, as against the acceptor, be treated as payable to bearer, in every case in which they could have been so treated if Vucina had drawn them. If, in the present case, Vucina had himself drawn the bills and inserted the name of C Petridi & Co as payees, as a mere pretence without intending any such persons to receive payment, it follows from what I have said that in my opinion they would have been bills whose payee was a fictitious person, and I do not think they can be regarded as any the less so, in view of the circumstances under which the name of C Petridi & Co was inserted.

Lord Macnaghten: On behalf of the bank, it was pointed out that these pretended bills, being duly accepted and regular and complete on the face of them, were presented for payment apparently in due course; and it was said that although no doubt at the time they were taken to be payable to order, and to be duly indorsed by the payee, yet when it turns out that the payee was a fictitious person, they may be treated as payable to bearer, and so the payment is justified though all the indorsements are inoperative.

On behalf of Vagliano Bros, it was contended that a bill payable to a fictitious person is not payable to bearer unless the acceptor is proved to have been aware of the fiction; and further, it was contended that nothing but a creature of the imagination can properly be described as a fictitious person. I do not think that either of these contentions on behalf of the respondents can be maintained.

Before the Act of 1882, the law seems to have been, as laid down by Lord Ellenborough in *Bennett v Farnell* ((1807) 1 Camp 130 at 180), that 'a bill of exchange made payable to a fictitious person or his order, is neither in effect payable to the order of the drawer nor to bearer, unless it can be shewn that the circumstances of the payee being a fictitious person was known to the acceptor.' The Act of 1882, s 7, sub-s 3, enacts that, 'Where the payee is a fictitious or non-existing person, the bill may be treated as payable to bearer.' As a statement of law before the Act that would have been incomplete and inaccurate. The omission of the qualification required to make it complete and accurate as the law then stood seems to shew that the object of the enactment was to do away with that qualification altogether. The section appears to me to have effected a change in the law in the direction of the more complete negotiability of bills of exchange – a change in accordance, I think, with the tendency of modern views and one in favour of holders in due course, and not, so far as I can see, likely to lead to any hardships or injustice.

Then it was said that the proper meaning of 'fictitious' is 'imaginary.' I do not think so. I think the proper meaning of the word is 'feigned' or 'counterfeit.' It seems to me that the 'C Petridi & Co' named as payees on these pretended bills were, strictly speaking, fictitious persons. When the bills came before Vagliano for acceptance they were fictitious from beginning to end. The drawer was fictitious; the payee was fictitious; the person indicated as agent for presentation was fictitious. One and all they were feigned or counterfeit persons put forward as real persons, each in a several and distinct capacity; whereas, in truth, they were mere make-believes for the persons whose names appeared on the instrument. They were not, I think, the less fictitious because there were in existence real persons for whom these names were intended to pass muster.

[Lord Halsbury LC and Lords Selbourne, Watson and Macnaghten based their opinions mainly on the ground that Vagliano Brothers had misled the Bank of England into making the payments and so the bank was not to be held responsible for them. However, as an additional ground for their opinions Lord Halsbury LC and Lord Watson, together with Lord Morris, held that s 7(3) was to be interpreted as interpreted by Lords Herschell and Macnaghten.]

NOTES

1. The only genuine signature on these 'bills' was that of Vagliano Brothers as acceptor. The drawer's and payee's signatures were forgeries. As s 3(1) requires the drawer's signature to appear on the bill, and Vucina had not signed these bills, they could not fall within the statutory definition of a bill of exchange. This was recognised by Lord Halsbury LC (at 116) and by Lords Watson (at 134), Macnaghten (at 160) and Morris (at 162). As s 7(3) states that '. . . *the bill* may be treated as payable to bearer', the subsection would appear to have little relevance to the 'bills' in the *Vagliano* case. Lords Watson (at 134) and Macnaghten (at 160) stated that as the instruments were not genuine bills of exchange, s 7(3) was not intended to apply to them (also, see J R Adams (1891) 7 LQR 295–296). Lord Halsbury LC (at 116 and 120) overcame this difficulty by holding that Vagliano Brothers, as acceptor, were estopped from denying that the instrument was a valid bill. Lords Herschell (at 154) and Morris (at 162–163) appear to concur with that view. The estoppel operates at common law and prevents the acceptor from asserting against a bona fide holder for value without notice that the drawer's signature was forged (it is not a statutory estoppel under s 54(2)(a) – can you see why?). The estoppel will operate against the acceptor so that the instrument, upon which the drawer's signature has been forged, is deemed to be a bill of exchange. Section 7(3) will then treat the bill as payable to bearer if the forger did not intend the named payee to receive payment.

2. The drawer's intention is, therefore, of utmost importance when deciding whether a payee is fictitious. That this should be so seems anomalous in a case like *Bank of*

England v Vagliano Bros. In his book *Modern Banking Law* (1987) Professor Ellinger has remarked that whilst such emphasis on the intention of the drawer:

> . . . is supportable in the case of cheques in which the drawer determines the tenor of the bill and is, in effect, the main party to be charged in the event of its dishonour, it is difficult to see that the principle of the *Vagliano* case is appropriate in the case of bills of exchange. In such an instrument, the main obligor is the acceptor and not the drawer. If the acceptor – eg the plaintiffs in the *Vagliano* case – intends the instrument to be payable to a designated payee, such as P & Co, why should the court be guided by the intention of a person whose name does not even appear on the bill, such as the forger G? This argument is reinforced in the case of a bill of exchange because the order to pay the bill is given to the designated bank, the defendants in the *Vagliano* case, by the acceptor!

3. Focusing on the drawer's intention means that if the drawer does intend the named payee to receive payment that payee is not fictitious, even though the drawer may have been fraudulently induced into drawing the bill in that way. Such a bill falls outside s 7(1) and remains payable to order. This was held to have occurred in the following cases.

In *Vinden v Hughes* [1905] 1 KB 795 a fraudulent clerk made out cheques to certain well known customers and persuaded Vinden, his employer, to sign the cheques even though no money was in fact owing to those customers. The employee then forged the customers' signatures and sold the cheques to Hughes for cash. Hughes passed the cheques through his own bank account, and had the proceeds placed to his credit. Warrington J held that Vinden believed he owed money to his customers when he signed the cheques as drawer and intended those customers to receive their proceeds. So far as Vinden was concerned at that time, the names of the customers/payees had not been inserted as a mere pretence and, therefore, they were not fictitious persons. Vinden could, therefore, recover the proceeds of the cheques from Hughes because the clerk's forged indorsements were wholly ineffective and did not entitle Hughes to receive payment of those proceeds.

In *North and South Wales Bank v Macbeth* [1908] AC 137 White fraudulently induced Macbeth to draw a cheque in favour of Kerr or order. Kerr was an existing person, and Macbeth, who had been misled by the fraud, intended him to receive the proceeds of the cheque. White then forged Kerr's indorsement and paid the cheque into his account with the appellant bank who received payment of it. Macbeth sued the bank for conversion of the cheque. The House of Lords held that s 7(3) did not apply as, although misled, Macbeth intended Kerr or his transferee to receive the proceeds of the cheque. This meant the cheque was payable to order and without Kerr's genuine indorsement the bank was not entitled to receive payment of it.

4. The intention of the drawer is irrelevant if the payee is non-existing. For example, the drawer may intended the named payee to receive payment but, unknown to the drawer, that payee may have died before the bill is issued. The problem arose in *Clutton v Attenborough & Son* [1897] AC 90 where a clerk, employed by Clutton, induced his employer to draw cheques payable to one George Brett by falsely representing that a person of that name was entitled to payment for certain work done for Clutton. The clerk obtained possession of the cheques, indorsed them in the name of George Brett and negotiated them to Attenborough & Son who gave value for them in good faith. The House of Lords held that as the cheques fell within s 7(3) they were to be treated as payable to bearer and so Attenborough & Son were entitled to receive their proceeds. Lord Halsbury LC noted rather abruptly that 'it has in this case never been suggested that on the face of these instruments the name of George Brett is anything other than the name of a non-existing person'. Despite the possibility that there was at least one person in the world called George Brett when Clutton signed the cheques, the 'George Brett' named as payee did not exist because there was no person of that name who had done work for Clutton. Clutton did not know that George Brett did not exist. However, if the drawer knows that the payee does not exist then he cannot intend payment to be made to him. In these circumstances (eg a cheque drawn payable to 'Ivanhoe'), the payee will be both a fictitious and non-existent person.

5. There is no practical difference whether the payee is fictitious or non-existent, as s 7(3) treats them both in exactly the same way. The subsection is important because it circumvents the effects of s 24. By s 24 a forged or unauthorised signature is treated as wholly inoperative. This means that if the payee's or indorsee's signature is forged any subsequent possessor of the instrument will not be an 'indorsee' and, therefore, not a 'holder' within the definition contained in s 2. However, if the bill is treated as payable to bearer, any forged indorsement is irrelevant because the possessor of a bearer bill will be, in any event, a 'holder' within the statutory definition. A 'holder' who has given value can enforce the bill and an acceptor who pays such a holder gets a good discharge under s 59. Where a bill is payable to order, payment to a person who has acquired it through or under a forged indorsement will not constitute a discharge because payment has not been made to a holder and so has not been made in due course as required by s 59. If the acceptor's bank pays someone who is not capable of giving the acceptor a good discharge then it acts in breach of mandate and may not debit its customer's account. If the acceptor's bank pays a 'holder' then it acts within its mandate (because the acceptor is discharged) and may debit its customer's account. This explains why it was so important in *Bank of England v Vagliano Bros* for the bank to establish that the bills in question were payable to bearer. Given that the payee's signature had been forged, only if the bill was payable to bearer could the acceptor be discharged from his liability and the bank act within its mandate. But see J R Adams (1891) 7 LQR 295 who questions whether the discharge of Vagliano Brothers was a relevant issue given that the drawer's signature was a forgery.

6. Finally, note that s 7(3) is permissive and not preremptory in its wording ie '. . . the bill *may* be treated as payable to bearer'. It may be possible, therefore, to draw a bill using words prohibiting its transfer, or indicating an intention that it should not be transferred, which prevent the bill being treated as payable to bearer under s 7(3) (see *Rhostar (Pvt) Ltd v Netherlands Bank of Rhodesia Ltd* 1972 (2) SA 703 at 709–711).

QUESTIONS

1. If a bill of exchange is drawn 'pay cash or order', is it treated as payable to bearer under s 7(3)?

2. In *Vinden v Hughes* the clerk used the names of existing customers as payees and s 7(3) was held not to apply. The loss occasioned by the clerk's fraud, therefore, fell on the third party, Hughes. If the clerk had simply invented names of non-existing customers then s 7(3) would have applied and the loss would have fallen on the employer, Vinden. Is it reasonable that the third party's rights should depend upon the nature of the misrepresentation made by the person who has induced the drawer to issue the instrument? If not, how should the third party's rights be determined? (see *Royal Bank of Canada v Concrete Column Clamps (1961) Ltd* (1976) 74 DLR (3d) 26 (Can SC) at 31–32, per Laskin CJC (dissenting); although Laskin CJC's view has not subsequently been adopted: see *Fok Cheong Shing Investments Co Ltd v Bank of Nova Scotia* (1981) 32 OR (2d) 705 (Can)). See also P E Salvatori (1979) 3 Can Bus LJ 296.

(b) Order bills

By s 31(3) a bill payable to the order of a specified payee is negotiated (meaning 'transferred') by the indorsement of the payee, or the holder to whom the bill has been specially indorsed, and delivery of it. Section 8(4) states that a bill is payable to order which is expressed to be so payable, or which is expressed to be payable to a particular person, and does not contain words prohibiting transfer or indicating an intention that it should not be transferable. Furthermore, a bill whose only or last indorsement is in blank (and, therefore, payable to bearer), will become payable to order if a holder inserts above the indorsement in blank a direction to pay the bill to or to the order of himself or some other person ie he converts the indorsement in blank into a special indorsement (s 34(4)).

Professor Ellinger asserts that s 34(4) reflects the policy of the Act and, to be consistent with that policy, submits that a bill originally drawn payable to bearer may also be converted into a order bill by the execution of a special indorsement (*Modern Banking Law* (1989), p 243). However, in *Miller Associates (Australia) Pty Ltd v Bennington Pty Ltd* (1975) 7 ALR 144 at 149, Sup Ct of New South Wales, Sheppard J held that such a bill remains payable to bearer regardless of the 'indorsement'. Sheppard J appeared to be of the opinion that as a bill drawn payable to bearer can be transferred by mere delivery, the signature of a holder of such a bill is irrelevant to its transfer and is not, therefore, an indorsement within the meaning of the Act (cf W J Chappenden (1981) 55 ALJ 135 at 137). However, the holder's signature will expose him to the same liabilities imposed on an indorser under s 55(2) (see Goode *Commercial Law* (1982) (hereafter referred to as 'Goode'), p 459). The Report of the Review Committee on Banking Law and Services (1989) Cm 622 recommended that within a new Negotiable Instruments Act there should be confirmation of the view that a bill drawn payable to bearer remains unaffected by any indorsement (Rec 8(10); Appendix A, para 20.8 and Appendix N, para 25). As the Government's subsequent White Paper (1990) Cm 1026 does not envisage a new Act, it did not adopt this recommendation (Annex 6, para 6.11). The issue remains open.

By s 31(4) where a holder of a bill payable to his order transfers it for value without indorsing it, the transfer gives the transferee such title as the transferor had in the bill, and the transferee in addition acquires the right to have the indorsement of the transferor. In these circumstances the transferee is placed in the position of an assignee of an ordinary chose in action and takes subject to equities of prior parties. If the transferor does indorse the bill he will be liable on it as an indorser but, as the indorsement only takes effect from that time, the transferee will take the instrument subject to any defect of title of which he has become aware between the date of the transfer and the date of the indorsement (see *Whistler v Forster* (1863) 14 CBNS 248).

(c) Destruction of transferability

Hibernian Bank Ltd v Gysin and Hanson [1939] 1 KB 483, Court of Appeal

The Irish Casing Co Ltd drew a bill of exchange payable three months after date 'to the order of the Irish Casing Co Ltd only the sum of £500 effective value received'. The bill was also crossed 'not negotiable'. After acceptance by the defendants the bill was indorsed by the drawers and transferred to the plaintiffs for value. On presentation for payment by the plaintiffs, as indorsees and holders for value, the bill was dishonoured. The defendants claimed that by its wording the bill was not transferable. Lewis J held that the words 'not negotiable' meant that the bill was not transferable or negotiable and gave judgment for the defendants. The Court of Appeal affirmed his decision.

Slesser LJ: . . . I am unable to see, construing the document as indicating the intention of the parties, that there was any acceptance of the bill except upon the basis that it was 'not negotiable.' If that be so, then it is difficult to see how the plaintiffs in this case can show any title to sue at all, because it is by reason, and by reason only, of the bill being capable of being transferred in such a manner as to constitute them the holders of the bill that they have any title to sue. If the matter ended there, and the only words for consideration were the words 'not negotiable,' then I think the case would clearly fall within s 8, sub-s 1, of the Act, which provides that 'when a bill contains words prohibiting transfer, or indicating an intention that it should not be transferable, it is valid as between the parties thereto, but is not negotiable.' Section 81 of the Act, defining the words 'not negotiable,' is in terms limited to cheques, and cannot be extended to bills not cheques to alter the natural meaning. But it is said that those words 'not negotiable' must be read subject to the other words, that the bill is payable 'to the order of the Irish Casing Co Ltd, only,' and Mr Murphy [counsel for the plaintiffs] seeks, as I understand him, to reconcile those words by saying that the bill is not negotiable after the order has been given by the Irish Casing Company, and that the absence of negotiability does not exclude the giving of the first order by the Irish Casing Company. I am unable to accept that construction. I think that the words 'not negotiable' are affirmative and govern the whole tenor of the instrument. The matter then comes to this, that either the words 'Not negotiable – Pay to the order of the Irish Casing Company only' make the whole instrument really no bill at all, or some other and more limited meaning must be given to the words 'To the order of the Irish Casing Company only.'

The surrounding circumstances of the case support a view which my brother Clauson has suggested and which has been adopted by Mr Willink [counsel for the defendants], that those words 'To the order of the Irish Casing Co Ltd, only,' are, so to speak, words of convenience, requiring payment to an agent of the Irish Casing Company, but do not, when they are read subject to the words 'not negotiable' amount to constituting the bill a bill payable to order within the meaning of s 8 at all. Fry LJ in *National Bank v Silke* ([1891] 1 QB 435 at 439) says that he is 'inclined to think that s 8 divides bills into three classes – bills not negotiable, bills payable to order, and bills payable to bearer.' In my view, adopting that classification, this is a bill 'not negotiable,' and when Fry LJ goes on to say 'so that a bill payable to order must always be negotiable,' he supports, I think, my conclusion that, in so far as this bill is not negotiable, it is not a bill payable to order within the meaning of the Bills of Exchange Act, and must have some lesser and more conditional effect. I think that that effect may be carried out by limiting it to cases where the order is merely for money to be paid to some one as agent for or for the purposes of the Irish Casing Company, and no more. In that view the instrument does not become irreconcilable or impossible of interpretation. It remains a non-negotiable instrument drawn by the Irish Casing Company Ltd, and accepted by the defendants, but limited as to its effect as between those two parties. It is not transferable; it produces no rights of action in the Hibernian Bank at all . . . .

[Clauson and Du Parcq LJJ concurred.]

NOTES

1. Under s 8(1) a bill is 'negotiable' (meaning 'transferable' in this section) when drawn, unless it contains words prohibiting transfer, or indicating an intention that it should not be transferable. If the bill is drawn so that it is not transferable then only the original payee can enforce it although the bill remains a valid bill of exchange within the definition contained in s 3(1). It is obvious that if the bill is not transferable then it is not 'negotiable' in the technical sense of the word (ie it cannot be acquired free from equities of prior parties). The reverse is not necessarily true. A bill which is not 'negotiable', in the technical sense of the word, can still be transferable.

2. In *Hibernian Bank v Gysin and Young* the Court of Appeal held that where a bill (not a cheque) is drawn: 'Pay to the order of X only' and is crossed 'not negotiable', it is not transferable. But what if the words 'not negotiable' had been omitted from the bill? Neither the Court of Appeal, nor Lewis J, gave much thought as to whether the word 'only' was effective in itself to override the statement that the bill was to be payable to order. The editors of Byles (p 86) believe it did and submit that the case could have been decided on the basis of the fact that the bill was drawn in favour of the payee 'only', without involving the question of the effect of the words 'not negotiable'.

3. What if a bill (not a cheque) is drawn: 'Pay X or order' and crossed 'not negotiable'. Can it be transferred? Professor Guest submits that such words would probably be construed as indicating an intention that the bill should not be transferable within s 8(1), although he accepts the possibility that the words 'not negotiable' might be regarded as an error and have no legal effect (Chalmers and Guest, p 654). The reasoning of the Court of Appeal, and Lewis J, in the *Hibernian Bank* case strongly supports Professor Guest's submission that the words 'not negotiable' are decisive of the issue. But the issue turns on which words ('Pay X or order' or 'not negotiable') are the best evidence of the drawer's intention.

4. The words 'not negotiable' have a special statutory meaning when written on a crossed cheque: see s 81 (below, p 600).

5. What if, on a bill written on a standard form, the drawer makes it payable to a particular person and deletes the words 'or order'. Is the bill transferable? Professor Ellinger has come to 'an inescapable conclusion from a strict construction of s 8' that it remains transferable (Chitty, Vol 2, para 2765). This is because under s 8(4) a bill payable to a particular person is payable to that person's order in any event. The deletion of the words 'or order' would have no practical effect. If the bill was to be made non-transferable the word 'only' should be inserted after the name of the payee.

6. If a bill is 'negotiable' (meaning 'transferable') when drawn it will remain so until it is restrictively indorsed or discharged by payment or otherwise: see ss 35, 36(1) and 59.

QUESTIONS

1. A standard printed form of an uncrossed cheque states 'Pay . . . or order'. The drawer inserts X's name between the words 'Pay' and 'or order' and adds the words 'not negotiable' to the cheque. Is the cheque transferable? Would your answer be different if the cheque had been drawn in these terms on a blank piece of paper?

2. If a standard printed form of order cheque is drawn 'Pay X only or order', is it transferable?

5 Persons entitled to the benefit of the obligation on the bill

(a) Holder

A 'holder' is defined by s 2 as the payee or indorsee of a bill or note who is in possession of it, or the bearer thereof. By s 38(1), any holder of a bill may sue in his own name and payment to the holder, within the terms of s 59(1), will discharge the bill. However, the 'holder' may not be the 'true owner' of the bill. According to Byles (p 329), 'the true owner is the person entitled to the property in and possession of the bill as against all other claimants'. For example, the finder or a thief of a bearer bill is the holder, but the person who lost it or from whom it was stolen remains the true owner and may recover it, unless or until it is negotiated to a holder in due course, who thereupon becomes the true owner. Subject to certain statutory defences available to banks (see Chapter 18), the true owner (and anyone with an immediate right to possession of the bill) retains the right to sue for conversion of the bill or claim the proceeds of the bill as money had and received.

The rights of a holder depend upon whether he is a 'mere holder', a 'holder for value' or a 'holder in due course'. A 'mere holder' is a holder otherwise than for value who does not claim title through a holder in due course (see below, p 507). He takes the bill subject to any defect in the title of prior parties and most personal defences available against such parties (see below, p 513). Furthermore, he can be met by the defence of absence or failure of consideration, whether his claim is against an immediate or remote party (see below, p 503).

(b) Holder for value

The liabilities of the drawer, acceptor and indorser of a bill are contractual in nature. Section 21(1) specifically refers to the 'contract on the bill' of the drawer, acceptor or indorser. This means not only that those persons must have the capacity to contract on the bill (s 22) but also that consideration has been provided for their contractual 'engagement' on the bill (ss 55(1)(a), 54(1), 55(2)(a)). The same pre-conditions apply to the maker's contractual engagement on a promissory note (s 88(1)). However, note that under s 30(1) every party whose signature appears on a bill is prima facie deemed to have become a party thereto for value.

Oliver v Davis [1949] 2 KB 727, Court of Appeal

Davis borrowed £350 from Oliver and gave him a post-dated cheque for £400. Later, he told his fiancee's sister, Miss Woodcock, that he was in difficulty about repaying Oliver, and as a result Miss Woodcock drew a cheque for £400 in favour of Oliver. Before the cheque was presented Miss Woodcock learnt that Davis was already married and stopped her cheque. When sued by Oliver on the cheque, Miss Woodcock contended that there had been no consideration for it. Oliver succeeded before Finnemore J, but Miss Woodcock succeeded on appeal.

Evershed MR: Section 27, sub-s 1 of the Bills of Exchange Act 1882, on which the whole argument turns, is in these terms: 'Valuable consideration for a bill may be constituted by (a) Any consideration sufficient to support a simple contract; (b) An antecedent debt or liability. Such a debt or liability is deemed valuable consideration whether the bill is payable on demand or at a future time.' It is pointed out by Mr Lawson that para (b), referring to an antecedent debt or liability, is on the face of it something distinct in subject-matter from para (a), which refers to considerations sufficient to support a simple contract. I think for myself that the proper construction of the words in (b) 'An antecedent debt or liability' is that they refer to an antecedent debt or liability of the promisor or drawer of the bill and are intended to get over what would otherwise have been prima facie the result that at common law the giving of a cheque for an amount for which you are already indebted imports no consideration, since the obligation is past and has been already incurred. On the facts of this case it may not be strictly necessary to express a concluded view on that matter. But the case in this court of *Crears v Hunter* ((1887) 19 QBD 341) (which, though decided after the date of the Act of 1882, related to the law in regard to bills of exchange which the Act generally codified) including the argument addressed to the court on behalf of the defendant, in my judgment strongly supports the view that 'an antecedent debt or liability' ought so to be construed. This at any rate is plain – that if the antecedent debt or liability of a third party is to be relied upon as supplying 'valuable consideration for a bill,' there must at least be some relationship between the receipt of the bill and the antecedent debt or liability. And for practical purposes it is difficult to see how there can be any distinction between a case in which there is a sufficient relationship for this purpose between the bill and the antecedent debt or liability and a case in which, as a result of that relationship, there is in the ordinary sense a consideration passing from the payee to the drawer of the bill. Otherwise the creditor might recover both on the debt from the third party and on the cheque from the drawer. . . .

Somervell LJ: . . . the antecedent debt or liability in s 27, sub-s 1 (b) is a debt or liability due from the maker or negotiator of the instrument and not from a third party. That being so, in this case the plaintiff cannot rely on (b). He cannot say: 'Because there was an antecedent debt or liability from the third party, therefore I am entitled to succeed.' *Crears v Hunter*, in my opinion, makes it clear that when dealing with a negotiable instrument given in respect of a debt of a third party, consideration has to be found such as is now referred to in s 27, sub-s 1 (a), namely, consideration sufficient to support a simple contract. If that is right, the plaintiff has here to show a consideration sufficient to support a simple contract. . . .

Denning LJ: . . . Section 27, sub-s 1(b) of the Act . . . does not apply to a promise to pay an antecedent debt or liability of a third party. In such a case in order that the promise may be enforced there must be shown a consideration which is sufficient to support a simple contract.

NOTES

1. What 'consideration sufficient to support a simple contract' could have been provided by Oliver? If he had promised to forbear from suing Davis, or had actually forborne from suing him at the express or implied request of Miss Woodcock, then he would have provided consideration for the cheque (see

AEG (UK) Ltd v Lewis [1993] 2 Bank LR 119, CA). This would have provided *present* consideration under s 27(1)(a), not consideration arising out of the antecedent debt or liability of Davis under s 27(1)(b). On the facts of the case, the Court of Appeal found no evidence of such forbearance.

2. Certain dicta of Evershed MR may have gone somewhat further than the opinion expressed by Somervell and Denning LJJ. He stated that the antecedent debt or liability of a third party could be relied on as providing consideration if there was 'some relationship between the receipt of the bill and the antecedent debt or liability'. What did he mean by 'some relationship'? Could it mean something other than actual forbearance, or a promise to forbear, to sue? In *Bonior v Siery Ltd* [1968] NZLR 254 the payee took a cheque drawn by a company in payment of an antecedent debt owed to him by a director of that company. As a result, the company was entitled to reduce its own indebtedness to the director. Applying the wider dicta of Evershed MR in *Oliver v Davis*, Speight J held that 'there was such a close relationship between payment on behalf of the third party and the affairs of [the company] as constitutes consideration' (at 261). However, Speight J also found a degree of forbearance by the payee and it is submitted by Chalmers and Guest (p 245) that this orthodox approach is to be preferred as it is consistent with the established principle that, as between immediate parties (see below, p 503), consideration must move from the promisee.

3. Professor Goode argues that, save in relation to a bill taken as security for an existing debt, it is a misconception to regard s 27(1)(b) as an exception to the common law rule as to past consideration (Goode, p 444). This is because it was established by Lush J in *Currie v Misa* (1875) LR 10 Exch 153 at 163–164 that a negotiable instrument is given for value when it is offered, and accepted, as conditional payment of an existing debt. This leaves open the question: why should the conditional payment rule not equally apply where the debt is that of a third party?

Diamond v Graham [1968] 1 WLR 1061, Court of Appeal

To induce Diamond to lend £1,650 to Herman, Graham drew a cheque for £1,665 in favour of Diamond. In return, Herman drew a cheque for £1,665 in favour of Graham and Diamond made the loan to Herman. Later, Graham's cheque in favour of Diamond was dishonoured when presented for payment. When sued on the cheque, Graham argued that Diamond was not a holder for value because no value had passed directly between Diamond and himself, as drawer.

Danckwerts LJ: Prima facie, of course, a bill of exchange is presumed to be for value, and the onus is upon the drawer of the cheque to show that it was not for value, and the discussion which has taken place before us has really revolved round the provisions of s 27(2) of the Bills of Exchange Act, which says:

> Where value has at any time been given for a bill the holder is deemed to be a holder for value as regards the acceptor and all parties to the bill who become parties prior to such time.

The contention of Mr Tibber on behalf of the defendant is that Mr Diamond was not a holder for value because no value had passed directly between him and Mr Graham, the drawer; I think that was the effect of his argument.

There is one thing that I have not mentioned, I think, and that is that when Mr Graham drew the cheque in favour of Mr Diamond, Mr Herman drew his own cheque for the amount and gave it to Mr Graham, but unfortunately Mr Herman's cheque was dishonoured, and I gather that he has since become bankrupt.

It seems to me that in presenting the argument which he did, Mr Tibber was giving a meaning which the words of s 27(2) do not bear, and is not in accordance with the words of that subsection. There is nothing in the subsection which appears to require value to have been given by the holder as long as value has been given for the cheque, and in the present case it seems to me that double value was given for the cheque first of all by Mr Herman, who gave his own cheque to Mr Graham in return for Mr Graham drawing a cheque in favour of Mr Diamond, and as it appears to me further value was given by Mr Diamond when he thereupon released his cheque to Mr Herman, and consequently there was clearly value for the cheque given, and therefore Mr Diamond was a holder for value. It seems to me, therefore, the defence fails, the plaintiff succeeds, and the appeal must be dismissed. . . .

Diplock LJ: . . . Here there clearly passed between Mr Diamond and Mr Herman 'consideration to support a simple contract.' Was that consideration given for a bill? A bill is defined by s 3(1) in these terms: . . .

Plainly this was a bill, an unconditional order in writing, and it was for the bill that consideration was given to Mr Herman. 'Holder' is defined in s 2: ' "Holder" means the payee or indorsee of a bill or note who is in possession of it.' Mr Diamond was plainly the payee of the bill who acquired possession of it as the result of the consideration which he gave to Mr Herman. It seems to me that clearly he falls within all the requirements of the section.

I should add that Mr Graham became a party to the bill 'prior to such time.' Section 21, which deals with delivery, in sub-s (3) says:

Where a bill is no longer in the possession of a party who has signed it as drawer . . . a valid and unconditional delivery by him is presumed until the contrary is proved.

Mr Tibber has argued, as my Lord has said, that one must not read the words in their literal meaning, but subject to a qualification that it applies only where the consideration has passed directly between one party to the bill and another party to the bill. I can see nothing in the authorities which requires that qualification, and I can see nothing in common sense or justice which requires that qualification in circumstances (though they must be rare) such as existed in this case.

I too would dismiss the appeal.

Sachs LJ: I agree. Not only has the defendant got nowhere near establishing that he did not become a party for value to this cheque, but upon the evidence it is abundantly clear to my mind that there was valuable consideration given for it within the meaning of s 27(1)(a), and in addition that the value was given for it within the meaning of s 27(2).

Accordingly the appeal must be dismissed.

NOTES

1. In Chitty, Vol 2, para 2790, Professor Ellinger states that:

. . . Immediate parties are those who, in addition to the privity created by the bill, have a direct legal relationship with each other. The drawer and the acceptor, the drawer and the payee and an indorser and his indorsee are usually parties who have entered into a contract with one another, such as an agreement to extend credit, a sale of goods or an arrangement for the discount of negotiable instruments; they are therefore predominantly immediate parties. But in certain circumstances even these parties may be remote parties, eg where the drawer makes the bill payable to the payee's order, or where the drawee executes his acceptance, at the request of a stranger to the bill. It is maintained by some writers that, generally, the defences which can be pleaded against a remote party are more restricted than those available against an immediate party. It will be shown, however, that the distinction between remote and immediate parties is relevant mainly in respect of actions brought on a bill by a holder for value. The superior rights of a holder in due course are defined in s 38(2) of the Act, which does not draw a distinction between remote and immediate parties. At the other end of the scale, a mere holder, who has not furnished value, appears to hold the bill subject to virtually all equities available against prior parties, including immediate parties.

2. In *Churchill and Sim v Goddard* [1937] 1 KB 92 at 110 Scott LJ held that '. . . as between immediate parties, the defendant is entitled to prove absence of consideration moving from the plaintiff as a defence to an action on the bill . . .'. The accuracy of this statement of law was thrown into doubt by Danckwerts LJ's obiter dictum in *Diamond v Graham* that there was nothing in s 27(2) 'which appears to require value to have been given by the holder as long as value has been given for the cheque'. However, Danckwerts LJ's interpretation of s 27(2) was subsequently doubted by Roskill LJ in *Pollway Ltd v Abdullah* [1974] 1 WLR 493 at 497 and in *Hasan v Willson* [1977] 1 Lloyd's Rep 431 at 442 Robert Goff J observed that:

> . . . If Lord Justice Danckwerts is to be understood as having stated that, as between immediate parties to a bill, valid consideration may move otherwise than from the promisee, then I have to say, with the greatest respect, that I find it impossible to reconcile this statement with the analysis of the law by the Court of Appeal in *Oliver v Davis*.

Also, see J Thornley [1968] CLJ 196 and S Scott (1969) 15 McGill LJ 487.

3. A holder can rely on s 27(2) to make him a holder for value as against a remote party, even though he has not himself provided consideration for the bill. But if the consideration relied upon is provided by someone who his not himself a party to the bill, can the holder who wishes to be a holder for value under s 27(2) still rely upon it? In *Diamond v Graham*, Herman was not a party to the cheque yet this did not stop Danckwerts LJ holding that Diamond was a holder for value under s 27(2). The question arose in *MK International Development Co Ltd v The Housing Bank* [1991] 1 Bank LR 74, CA, where, following instructions from one of their customers, the Housing Bank drew a bill of exchange payable to 'MK International or bearer' and debited their customer's account accordingly. The bill was first handed to their customer, who then delivered it to MK International. The Court of Appeal held that as the customer gave value for this bearer bill and held it as bearer, MK International could rely on s 27(2) as holders for value. However, Mustill LJ also considered whether MK International could have relied on s 27(2) if the customer had not been a party to the bill. Mustill LJ expressed a tentative opinion that s 27(2) was:

> . . . not to be read as envisaging value being provided by strangers to the instrument, but rather as a special provision, directed to the position of a holder who wishes to establish that he is a holder for value in good faith without notice and must as a first step show that he is a holder for value; and it relieves him of the necessity to show that he himself gave value. But it does not alter the requirement created by s 27(1) that some party to the instrument must have done so.

This case involved an interlocutory judgment on the question of whether leave should be granted to serve a writ out of the jurisdiction under RSC Ord 11. Mustill LJ acknowledged his remarks on s 27(2) to be obiter dicta and emphasised that he should not wish any court seized of the action to regard his decision as foreclosing its decision on this 'new' point. See R Hooley [1991] LMCLQ 463 for further discussion of the case.

4. Section 27(2) states that a holder is deemed to be a holder for value as regards the acceptor 'and all parties to the bill who became parties prior to [the time when value had been given for the bill]'. In *Diamond v Graham* it appears from Danckwerts LJ's judgment that when Graham drew his cheque in favour of Diamond, Herman simultaneously drew his cheque in favour of Graham. The precise sequence of events is not clear from the report. As Graham's liability as drawer would only be complete and irrevocable when the bill was delivered to Diamond (s 21(1)), it seems likely that he received Herman's cheque, and hence value, before that time. However, in *MK International Development Co Ltd v The Housing Bank*, above, when the issue arose of the simultaneous provision of value for a cheque at the time it was drawn, Staughton LJ held that '. . . It cannot be right that s 27(2) does not cover the case where a person becomes a party to the bill and receives value simultaneously'.

5. It has generally been accepted that absence, or failure, of consideration from the defendant's promisee is not a defect of title or equity attaching to a bill, but a mere personal defence which operates against an immediate party, or a remote party who is not a holder for value (see Chalmers and Guest, p 249; Byles, p 213). On this understanding, if a remote party is a holder for value because of value given by a previous party to the bill, the defence of absence, or failure, of consideration cannot be raised against him (see below, p 506 for an exceptional case when total failure of consideration can prove a defence against such a holder for value). However, this orthodox view has not gone unchallenged. Professor Goode sees no sound basis for the distinction that a holder for value who is an immediate party takes subject to equities (ie personal defences), but that a holder for value who is a remote party does not do so (Goode, p 467). The orthodox analysis has also been challenged by Professor Geva ((1980) 5 Can Bus LJ 53 and [1980] CLJ 360). In [1980] CLJ 360 Professor Geva submits that the cases thought to establish that 'absence of consideration is not a defect of title or equity attaching to the instrument', can be distinguished as concerning the special case of an 'accommodation party' (p 363). After emphasising that a negotiable instrument is both a chattel and a chose in action (p 361), he goes on to submit (pp 367–368) that:

> . . . in its true sense the 'holder for value' provision means that absence of consideration is not an equity as to ownership. The provision does not deal with absence of consideration as an equity as to liability. Its effect is indeed that only inasmuch as a holder seeks to establish his property in the instrument rather than to charge a party with liability, absence of consideration is not a defect of title. Thus, as 'the outgrowth of the fundamental idea in the law of negotiable paper . . . that a bill or note is a species of property,' the provision means that once 'value has . . . been given for the instrument, it becomes the subject of gift.' Accordingly, '[i]f a party gives to another a negotiable instrument, *on which other parties are liable*, the man who makes the gift cannot recover the bill back, and the man to whom the bill is given may recover against the other parties on the bill.' As such the 'holder for value' provision is merely a 'sheltering' provision which is complementary to the section conferring on the transferee for value 'such title as the transferor had,' as well as to another section giving to '[a] holder . . . who derives his title to a bill through a holder in due course' the same 'rights of that holder in due course.' Its effect is thus to confer the endorser's title on a holder who took the instrument without giving value thereto, thereby giving him a cause of action against *prior parties already liable on the instrument*. This indeed means that absence of consideration is not an equity as to ownership of the instrument. But it falls short from providing that absence of consideration is also not an equity as to liability on the instrument. In fact, it is submitted, the section does not even deal with the latter.
> This analysis dispells the myth of the 'holder for value' as an intermediate concept who

though not a holder in due course overcomes the defence of absence of consideration. As consideration given by his promisee is required to charge a promisor with liability on an instrument, the 'holder for value' is in fact the only holder entitled to recover thereon. Where no promisor is a party to consideration there is neither liability nor a 'holder for value.' Consideration thus gives rise to liability as well as to the emergence of a 'holder for value.' Yet unless the latter is a holder in due course, his right is subject to all equities affecting the instrument. As the nature of the liability on a bill or note is not 'different from that on any other written contract for payment of money,' absence of consideration to a promise thereon is an equity as to liability. It is available as a defence to an immediate as well as remote party against every holder not in due course.

6. If a holder is deemed to be a holder for value under s 27(2), can he establish 'that he took the bill . . . for value' under s 29(1)(b) and so become a holder in due course? In *Mackenzie Mills (a firm) v Buono* [1986] BTLC 399, Buono drew a cheque in favour of his Italian suppliers as payment for certain furniture to be supplied to him. Mackenzie Mills were solicitors to the Italians and were owed legal fees by them. In payment for the legal fees, the Italians indorsed Buono's cheque in blank and delivered it to Mackenzie Mills. However, the cheque was subsequently dishonoured for non-payment and Mackenzie Mills sued Buono claiming as holders in due course. Buono argued that Mackenzie Mills were mere holders and pleaded total failure of consideration for the cheque as the furniture had not been supplied to them. The issue was whether Mackenzie Mills had given value for the cheque within s 29(1)(b). May LJ accepted a concession made by Buono's counsel that if the Italians had given value for the cheque to Buono, then the case fell within s 27(2) and the solicitors were holders in due course by virtue of the combined effect of s 27(2) and s 29. May LJ went on to hold that consideration had been given for the cheque at the time the Italians promised to deliver the furniture and their subsequent failure to deliver did not affect this (although note that even a remote party could not sue if he knew at the time he took the bill that the consideration had totally failed, as this would be in the nature of a fraud: *Lloyd v Davis* (1824) 3 LJ OS KB 38; cf *Fairclough v Pavia* (1854) 9 Exch 690). May LJ went on to hold that, if he was wrong on the s 27(2) point, Mackenzie Mills had provided consideration for the cheque by taking it against the legal fees owed to them by the Italians.

Support for the concession made in the *Mackenzie Mills* case can be found in *Barclays Bank Ltd v Astley Industrial Trust Ltd* [1970] 2 QB 527 at 539 where Milmo J held that the holder of a cheque who had a lien on it was, by virtue of s 27(3), deemed to have taken it for value within the meaning of s 29(1)(b) to the extent of the sum for which he had a lien. Milmo J appeared to accept the view of a number of textbooks that no distinction was to be drawn between the expressions 'holder for value', 'holder who has taken for value' and 'holder who has given value'. See also, *Re Keever* [1967] Ch 182 at 193, per Ungoed-Thomas J.

In *MK International Development Co Ltd v The Housing Bank*, above, Mustill LJ clearly thought, albeit obiter only, that a holder in due course did not have to provide value himself but that he could rely on s 27(2). Furthermore, in *Clifford Chance v Silver* [1992] 2 Bank LR 11, the Court of Appeal recently held that a cheque received by the plaintiff solicitors as stakeholders (ie without themselves giving value for it) was nevertheless held by them as holders in due course because they were deemed to be 'holders for value' pursuant to s 27(2). But in neither case does it appear that the Court of Appeal considered the views of the majority of commentators who believe that it is necessary for a person claiming to be a holder in due course under s 29(1) to have given value personally (see, eg, J James

Richardson's Guide to Negotiable Instruments (8th ed, 1991), p 77; R Bradgate and N Savage *Commercial Law* (1991), p 412; B Geva [1980] CLJ 360 at p 364; A G Guest *Chalmers and Guest on Bills of Exchange, Cheques and Promissory Notes* (14th ed, 1991), p 274). There is certainly a case for saying that the phrase 'he took the bill in good faith and for value' in s 29(1)(b) implies that a holder in due course must give value personally (R M Goode *Commercial Law* (1982), p 448, fn 102). The issue is considered further by L P Hitchens in [1993] JBL 571.

QUESTION

The Report of the Review Committee on Banking Services Law and Practice (paras 8.14–8.16; rec 8(4)) recommended that the need for consideration as a test of the negotiability of negotiable instruments should be abolished. The Review Committee felt that the requirement produced unnecessary complications when used to distinguish between the various types of holders and was unnecessary evidence of an intention to create legal relations. What 'unnecessary complications' could the Review Committee have been referring to? Other than the need for consideration, what evidence is there to show that a party to a bill intends to enter into legal relations? The Government's subsequent White Paper on banking services did not take up this recommendation on consideration ((1990) Cm 1026).

(c) Holder in due course

Bills of Exchange Act 1882, s 29

(1) A holder in due course is a holder who has taken a bill, complete and regular on the face of it, under the following conditions; namely,
  (a) That he became the holder of it before it was overdue, and without notice that it had been previously dishonoured, if such was the fact:
  (b) That he took the bill in good faith and for value, and that at the time the bill was negotiated to him he had no notice of any defect in the title of the person who negotiated it.
(2) In particular the title of a person who negotiates a bill is defective within the meaning of this Act when he obtained the bill, or the acceptance thereof, by fraud, duress, or force and fear, or other unlawful means, or for an illegal consideration, or when he negotiates it in breach of faith, or under such circumstances as amount to a fraud.

By s 30(2) every holder of a bill is prima facie deemed to be a holder in due course. This presumption will apply if the plaintiff can establish that the instrument in question is a valid bill and that it has been validly negotiated to him to make him a holder of it. To rebut the statutory presumption, the defendant must prove that the requirements for holder in due course status, set out in s 29(1), have not been satisfied (see Chalmers and Guest, pp 289–290).

Section 30(2) goes on to provide that if in an action on a bill it is admitted or proved that the acceptance, issue, or subsequent negotiation of the bill is affected with fraud, duress, or force or fear, or illegality, the burden of proof is shifted, unless and until the holder proves that, subsequent to the alleged fraud or illegality, value has in good faith been given for the bill. If the holder can discharge the burden of proof the statutory presumption of holder in due course status will apply, once again, in his favour. It would then be up to the defendant to rebut the presumption by proving that the requirements set out in s 29(1) had not been satisfied.

R E Jones Ltd v Waring and Gillow Ltd [1926] AC 670, House of Lords

A rogue, by fraud, induced the appellants to draw two cheques, one for £2000 and another for £3000, payable to the order of the respondents (who were totally innocent of the fraud). The rogue tendered the cheques to the respondents in payment of his existing indebtedness to them. Subsequently, the respondents raised an objection to the signature on the cheques and returned the cheques to the appellants. The appellants then issued the respondents with a new cheque for £5000. On discovering the fraud the appellants claimed repayment of the proceeds of the cheque from the respondents. By a majority (Viscount Cave LC and Lord Atkinson dissenting), the House of Lords gave judgment for the appellants.

Viscount Cave LC: My Lords, it was contended on behalf of the respondents that they were 'holders in due course' of the cheque for £5000 within the meaning of s 21, sub-s 2, of the Bills of Exchange Act 1882, and entitled on that ground to retain the proceeds of the cheque. I do not think that the expression 'holder in due course' includes the original payee of a cheque. It is true that under the definition clause in the Act (s 2) the word 'holder' includes the payee of a bill unless the context otherwise requires; but it appears from s 29, sub-s 1, that a 'holder in due course' is a person to whom a bill has been 'negotiated,' and from s 31 that a bill is negotiated by being transferred from one person to another and (if payable to order) by indorsement and delivery. In view of these definitions it is difficult to see how the original payee of a cheque can be a 'holder in due course' within the meaning of the Act. Section 21, sub-s 2, which distinguishes immediate from remote parties and includes a holder in due course among the latter, points to the same conclusion. The decision of Lord Russell in *Lewis v Clay* ((1897) 67 LJQB 224) was to the effect that the expression does not include a payee; and the opinion to the contrary expressed by Fletcher Moulton LJ in *Lloyds Bank v Cooke* ([1907] 1 KB 794) does not appear to have been accepted by the other members of the Court of Appeal. This contention therefore fails.

[On the issue of whether the respondents were holders in due course, the majority (Lords Shaw of Dunfermline, Sumner and Carson) delivered opinions concurring with that of the Lord Chancellor. Lord Atkinson concurred.]

NOTES

1. As a payee cannot be a holder in due course, he cannot be deemed to be one under s 30(2). However, Byles states that *R E Jones Ltd v Waring and Gillow* 'did not, specifically, at any rate, reduce the rights of a payee-holder for value below those of a holder in due course. And it is submitted that the decision did not affect the rights of the payee-holder for value whatever they may be' (p 232). It appears that if the issue or acceptance of a bill is affected by the fraud or duress of a third party, that can only be raised as a defence against the original payee who has taken the bill in good faith and for value, if the party sued on the bill can prove that when the payee took it he had notice of the defect (*Talbot v Von Boris* [1911] 1 KB 854, CA; followed by Robert Goff J in *Hasan v Willson* [1977] 1 Lloyd's Rep 431 at 444). Note how the burden of proof rests on the party sued and not the payee, as would be the case if s 30(2) applied (see Chalmers and Guest, p 293 and p 341).

2. A payee can be given the rights of a holder in due course under s 29(3). See below, p 514.

Arab Bank Ltd v Ross [1952] 2 QB 216, Court of Appeal

Ross was the maker of two promissory notes naming a Palestine firm, 'Fathi and Faysal Nabulsy Company', as payees. One of the partners in that firm indorsed the notes 'Fathi and Faysal Nabulsy' (the word 'Company' being omitted) and discounted them to the Arab Bank. The issue arose whether the notes were 'complete and regular on [their] face' so that the Arab Bank could succeed with a claim against Ross as holders in due course under s 29. The Court of Appeal held that the indorsements were irregular and that the Arab Bank were not holders in due course. Nevertheless, the bank were held entitled to succeed with their claim on the notes as a holders for value.

Denning LJ: The first question in this case is whether the Arab Bank Ltd were holders in due course of the promissory note, and that depends on whether, at the time they took it, it was 'complete and regular on the face of it' within s 29 of the Bills of Exchange Act 1882. Strangely enough, no one doubts that the 'face' of a bill includes the back of it. I say strangely enough, because people so often insist on the literal interpretation of Acts of Parliament, whereas here everyone agrees that the literal interpretation must be ignored because the meaning is obvious. The meaning is that, looking at the bill, front and back, without the aid of outside evidence, it must be complete and regular in itself.

Regularity is a different thing from validity. The Act itself makes a careful distinction between them. On the one hand an indorsement which is quite invalid may be regular on the face of it. Thus the indorsement may be forged or unauthorized and, therefore, invalid under s 24 of the Act, but nevertheless there may be nothing about it to give rise to any suspicion. The bill is then quite regular on the face of it. Conversely, an indorsement which is quite irregular may nevertheless be valid. Thus, by a misnomer, a payee may be described on the face of the bill by the wrong name, nevertheless, if it is quite plain that the drawer intended him as payee, then an indorsement on the back by the payee in his own true name is valid and sufficient to pass the property in the bill (*Leonard v Wilson* ((1834) 2 Cr & M 589); *Bird & Co v Thomas Cook & Son Ltd* ([1937] 2 All ER 227); *Hadley v Henry* ((1896) 22 VLR 230), but the difference between front and back makes the indorsement irregular unless the payee adds also the misnomer by which he was described on the front of the bill. This is what he eventually did in *Leonard v Wilson*.

Regularity is also different from liability. The Act makes a distinction between these two also. On the one hand a person who makes an irregular indorsement is liable thereon despite the irregularity. Thus, if a payee, who is wrongly described on the front of the bill, indorses it in his own true name, the indorsement is irregular, but he is liable to any subsequent holder and cannot set up the irregularity as a defence; or, if he is rightly described on the front of the bill, but indorses it in an assumed name, the indorsement is irregular but he is liable thereon as if he had indorsed it in his own name: see s 28(1) and s 55(2) of the Act. Conversely, a regular indorsement will not impose liability if it is forged or unauthorized. Thus, where a firm is the payee, but is described in an unauthorized name which is substantially different from its real name, an indorsement by one partner in that name does not impose liability on the other partners: *Kirk v Blurton* ((1841) 9 M & W 284). It would be otherwise if the name was substantially the same: *Forbes v Marshall* ((1855) 11 Exch 166).

Once regularity is seen to differ both from validity and from liability, the question is when is an indorsement irregular? The answer is, I think, that it is irregular whenever it is such as to give rise to doubt whether it is the indorsement of the named payee. A bill of exchange is like currency. It should be above suspicion. But if it is asked: When does an indorsement give rise to doubt? I would say that that is a practical question which is, as a rule, better answered by a banker than a lawyer. Bankers have to consider the regularity of indorsements every week, and every day of every week, and every hour of every day; whereas the judges sitting in this court have not had to consider it for these last 20 years. So far as I know the last occasion was in *Slingsby's* case ([1932] 1 KB 544).

The Law Merchant is founded on the custom of merchants, and we shall not go far wrong if we follow the custom of bankers of the City of London on this point. They have given evidence that they would not accept the indorsements in this case as a regular indorsement. They said that if a bill is made payable to 'Fathi and Faysal Nabulsy Company' they would not accept an indorsement 'Fathi and Faysal Nabulsy.' I think there is good sense in their view. For aught they know, in Palestine the word 'company' may be of vital significance. It may there signify a different legal entity, just as the word 'limited' does here (*Bank of Montreal v Exhibit and Trading Co* ((1906) 11 Com Cas 250), or it may signify a firm of many partners and not merely two of them. I agree with the bankers that this indorsement does give rise to doubt whether it is the indorsement of the named payee. It was, therefore, irregular. . . .

The truth is, I think, that the bankers adopted this strict attitude both in their own interests and also in the interests of their customers. It would be quite impossible for them to make inquiries to see that all the indorsements on a bill are in fact genuine; but they can at least see that they are regular on the face of them: see *Bank of England v Vagliano* ([1891] AC 107 at 157), per Lord Macnaghten. That is some safeguard against dishonesty. It is a safeguard which the bankers have taken for the past 120 years at least, and I do not think we should throw any doubt today on the correctness of their practice.

I do not stay to discuss the regularity of indorsements by married women or titled folk, except to say that titles and descriptions can often be omitted without impairing the regularity of the indorsement. The word 'company' in this case is not, however, mere description. It is part of the name itself. It was suggested that an indorsement in Arabic letters would be regular. I cannot accept this view. The indorsement should be in the same lettering as the name of the payee; for otherwise it could not be seen on the face of it to be regular. My conclusion is, therefore, that this promissory note, when it was taken by the Arab Bank Ltd, was not complete and regular on the face of it. They were not, therefore, holders in due course.

[Somervell and Romer LJJ delivered concurring judgments.]

NOTES

1. A bill is considered 'incomplete' if any material detail is missing, eg, the name of the payee, the amount payable, any necessary indorsement and the date (although see Goode, p 447 as to whether omission of the date renders a bill incomplete).

2. However, under s 20 a holder taking an incomplete bill may fill it up within a reasonable time and strictly in accordance with the authority given and so convert himself retrospectively into a holder in due course (*Glenie v Smith* [1908] 1 KB 263 at 268–269). Furthermore, by s 2 of the Cheques Act 1957 if a collecting bank takes for value a cheque payable to order without the cheque having been indorsed to it, the cheque will be treated as indorsed in blank and, therefore, payable to bearer. Notwithstanding the omission of the indorsement the cheque is transferable by mere delivery and the bank can take it as a holder in due course (*Midland Bank Ltd v R V Harris Ltd* [1963] 1 WLR 1021 at 1024–1025; *Westminster Bank Ltd v Zang* [1966] AC 182 at 190).

Jones v Gordon (1877) 2 App Cas 616, House of Lords

G and S, both being insolvent and contemplating bankruptcy, drew bills on each other and accepted them. After declining to discount four bills drawn by S and accepted by G, amounting in total to £1,727, J purchased them for £200. At the time he purchased the bills, J knew G was in financial difficulties but believed he had assets. He also knew that certain people could give information as to G's financial affairs, but he did not contact them. G became bankrupt and J tried to prove against his estate for the full amount of the bills. The House of Lords held that J was not a bona fide purchaser who could take the bills free of defects in title, as he was deemed to have known of the fraud. His proof in bankruptcy was limited to £200.

Lord Blackburn: . . . my Lords, I think it is right to say that I consider it to be fully and thoroughly established that if value be given for a bill of exchange, it is not enough to shew that there was carelessness, negligence, or foolishness in not suspecting that the bill was wrong, when there were circumstances which might have led a man to suspect that. All these are matters which tend to shew that there was dishonesty in not doing it, but they do not in themselves make a defence to an action upon a bill of exchange. I take it that in order to make such a defence, whether in the case of a party who is solvent and *sui juris*, or when it is sought to be proved against the estate of a bankrupt, it is necessary to shew that the person who gave value for the bill, whether the value given be great or small, was affected with notice that there was something wrong about it when he took it. I do not think it is necessary that he should have notice of what the particular wrong was. If a man, knowing that a bill was in the hands of a person who had no right to it, should happen to think that perhaps the man had stolen it, when if he had known the real truth he would have found, not that the man had stolen it, but that he had obtained it by false pretences, I think that would not make any difference if he knew that there was something wrong about it and took it. If he takes it in that way he takes it at his peril.

But then I think that such evidence of carelessness or blindness as I have referred to may with other evidence be good evidence upon the question which, I take it, is the real one, whether he did know that there was something wrong in it. If he was (if I may use the phrase) honestly blundering and careless, and so took a bill of exchange or a bank-note when he ought not to have taken it, still he would be entitled to recover. But if the facts and circumstances are such that the jury, or whoever has to try the question, came to the conclusion that he was not honestly blundering and careless, but that he must have had a suspicion that there was something wrong, and that he refrained from asking questions, not because he was an honest blunderer or a stupid man, but because he thought in his own secret mind – I suspect there is something wrong, and if I ask questions and make farther inquiry, it will no longer be my suspecting it, but my knowing it, and then I shall not be able to recover – I think that is dishonesty. I think, my Lords, that that is established, not only by good sense and reason, but by the authority of the cases themselves.

[Lords O'Hagan and Gordon delivered concurring judgments.]

NOTES

1. In this case, the separate issues of J's knowledge of the fraud and his lack of good faith were merged together. However, under s 29 there are separate requirements that:

(1) when he becomes holder of the bill he does not have notice of previous dishonour;

(2) at the time the bill was negotiated to him the holder does not have notice of any defect in the title of the person who negotiated it; and

(3) the holder takes the bill in good faith.

By s 90, the expression 'good faith' is defined in terms of the holder's honesty (not negligence) and there is no doubt that notice of defects in title will reflect on the holder's honesty.

2. The expression 'notice' in s 29 means either actual knowledge of a fact or suspicion that something is wrong, coupled with a wilful disregard of the means of knowledge. It does not mean 'constructive knowledge' (see above, p 21). A holder may have notice imputed to him if his agent has such notice. Notice will be imputed to the principal even if the agent is acting contrary to the principal's interests (*Bank of Credit and Commerce International SA v Dawson* [1987] FLR 342), although not if the agent is a party to the commission of a fraud on his principal (*Re European Bank, ex p Oriental Commercial Bank* (1870) 5 Ch App 358).

3. J paid £200 for bills with a total value of £1,727. This caused Lord Blackburn to note at 631–632 that:

> . . . since the repeal of the Usury Laws we can never inquire into the question as to how much was given for a bill, and if [J's vendor] was in such a position that he could have proved against the estate it would have been no objection at all that he conveyed these bills to another for a nominal amount, that he sold bills nominally amounting to £1,727 for £200. Although I think that could not have been inquired into, yet the amount given in comparison with the apparent value is an important piece of evidence guiding us to a conclusion as to whether or not it was a bona fide transaction.

In *MK International Development Co Ltd v The Housing Bank*, above, p 504, Mustill LJ noted Lord Blackburn's remarks in *Jones v Gordon* and continued:

> . . . It may also be the law that where the bill is given as the price of an indivisible obligation the maker cannot complain even as against an immediate party that the obligation was not worth the amount of the bill, ie that he made a bad bargain: unless perhaps the consideration is so trifling as not to be consideration at all: see *Young v Gordon* (1896) 23 R 419.

In the *MK International* case a cheque was drawn for £50,965 to settle claims for payment of various debts allegedly owed to a group of companies (including the plaintiff company) and their controller. The cheque named the plaintiff company as payee although that company claimed payment of only one of the debts that the cheque was intended to settle. As the cheque had been given for full consideration (ie in settlement of all the debts) and yet only part of the consideration was furnished by the payee (by forbearing to sue for its own debt), the issue arose whether there had been a partial absence of consideration giving the drawer a good defence pro tanto against the plaintiff company. Mustill LJ could see no logical reason why, if subsequent failure of an ascertained part of the consideration is a defence as between immediate parties the same should not be so where, as to part, the consideration was never there in the first place. He held that the plaintiff's cause of action on the cheque was limited to the amount of the particular debt owed to it. However, it must be noted that Mustill LJ stressed that he reached this conclusion 'without any of the confidence which one ought to be able to feel on a point so apparently simple' and the other members of the court, Staughton and McCowen LJJ, did not address this issue.

What are the benefits of holder in due course status?

Cebora SNC v SIP (Industrial Products) Ltd [1976] 1 Lloyd's Rep 271, Court of Appeal

(See above, p 479.)

NOTES

1. Under s 38(2), a holder in due course holds the bill free from any defects of title of prior parties, as well as from mere personal defences available to prior parties amongst themselves, and may enforce payment against all parties liable on the bill. A list of 'defects of title' can be found in s 29(2), although this list is probably not exhaustive (Geva [1980] CLJ 360 at 363 and above, p 507; Byles, p 228). For an example of a defect of title not included in s 29(2), see s 125(2) of the Consumer Credit Act 1974. The expression 'mere personal defences' is not defined in the 1882 Act and covers defences not founded on the bill itself but arising out of the relationship between the parties themselves. It appears to include matters of set-off or counterclaim and general contractual defences, such as any misrepresentation inducing the contract on the bill. We have already noted that there has been some debate as to whether absence or failure of consideration is a mere personal defence or a defect of title (see above, p 505).

2. If the holder in due course is not subject to defects of title or mere personal defences of prior parties, what are the 'exceptional circumstances', referred to by Sir Erich Sachs in the *Ceborra* case, when a bill will not be treated as cash in the hands of such a holder. They are as follows:

(1) when there are 'real' or 'absolute' defences arising from the invalidity of the bill itself, or the invalidity of the defendant's apparent contract on the bill (eg contractual incapacity, forged or unauthorised signature, non est factum): Chalmers and Guest, p 336–337; cf Byles at p 229;

(2) when the holder in due course sues as agent or trustee for another person, or when he sues wholly or in part for another person, as any defence or set-off available against that person is available pro tanto against the holder: see *Barclays Bank Ltd v Aschaffenburger Zellstoffwerke AG* [1967] 1 Lloyd's Rep 387, CA;

(3) when the holder in due course does not comply with his duties as to presentment for acceptance and/or payment, or when he fails to comply with the proper procedure on dishonour (see below, p 516).

3. In the context of 'regulated' consumer credit and consumer hire agreements (unless they are non-commercial agreements), s 123(1) of the Consumer Credit Act 1974 prohibits the taking of negotiable instruments other than cheques in discharge of amounts payable by the debtor or hirer or by a surety. Section 123(3) prohibits the taking of any negotiable instrument (including cheques) as a security for an amount payable under such an agreement. Under s 125(1) a person who takes a negotiable instrument in contravention of s 123(1) or (3) is not a holder in due course, and is not entitled to enforce the instrument. However, the transferee of a negotiable instrument from such an owner or creditor can be a holder in due course and is entitled to enforce the instrument (s 125(4)). Even a transferee who is not a holder in due course can enforce such an instrument as the contravention of s 123(1) or (3) is probably not a defect of title within s 29(2) of the 1882 Act (Chalmers and Guest, p 282; Chitty, pp 220–221). In these circumstances the person forced to pay on the instrument is entitled to be indemnified by the owner or creditor (s 125(3)).

QUESTION

Why did Parliament seek to restrict the use of negotiable instruments in the manner set out in ss 123–125 of the Consumer Credit Act 1974? Note that the Consumer Credit (Negotiable Instruments) Order 1984, SI 1984/435, exempts from these restrictions credit transactions financing international trade where credit is provided to the debtor in the course of his business.

(d) Holder in due course by derivation

Bills of Exchange Act 1882, s 29

. . .

(3) A holder (whether for value or not), who derives his title to a bill through a holder in due course, and who is not himself a party to any fraud or illegality affecting it, has all the rights of that holder in due course as regards the acceptor and all parties to the bill prior to that holder.

Jade International Steel Stahl und Eisen GmbH & Co KG v Robert Nicholas (Steels) Ltd [1978] QB 917, Court of Appeal

Jade drew a bill of exchange, payable to themselves or order, on Nicholas for the price of steel supplied by them to Nicholas. Jade indorsed the bill and discounted it to a German bank (Sparkasse), who discounted it to another German bank, and they, in turn, discounted it to Midland Bank. Each bank took the bill as a holder in due course. The Midland Bank presented the bill to Nicholas for acceptance. Nicholas accepted the bill but later dishonoured it when presented for payment owing to a dispute about the quality of the steel supplied by Jade. Midland Bank then indorsed the bill in blank and, as each bank exercised its rights of recourse, the bill was passed back down the line until it reached Jade, whose account Sparkasse had debited with its amount. Jade then brought an action on the bill against Nicholas, who raised the defective quality of the steel as a defence. The issue was whether, under s 29(3), Jade could claim the benefits of holder in due course status enjoyed by the banks. Donaldson J held Jade were entitled to summary judgment on the bill. His decision was upheld on appeal.

Cumming-Bruce LJ: So the short point which is raised as the first point on this appeal is whether in those circumstances the drawer/payee to whom the bill was delivered pursuant to the Midland Bank or Sparkasse's right of recourse is properly to be regarded as a holder who derives his title to the bill through a holder in due course, within the meaning of s 29(3) of the Act.

The submission of Mr Bowsher is that when the plaintiffs recovered the bill pursuant to the Sparkasse Bank's right of recourse they did not thereby derive their title to the bill through the Sparkasse Bank, or through any of the other indorsers, but that it came back to them in their initial capacity as drawer pursuant to their liability as drawer under s 47(2) of the Act. Thus, he submits, that whether or not it is right within the meaning of the subsection to regard the plaintiffs at that stage as holders they were not holders who derived their title through a holder in due course. Initially as drawers they derive title from nobody. When they negotiated the bill in the first instance they then lost their title. All that was left was their liability under s 47(2), the liability to a right of recourse against them in their capacity as drawers. And so the submission is that the words of s 29(3) ought to be read strictly so as to limit the meaning of the words 'derive title to the bill' to those situations in which the bill is negotiated, what I would call on its way upwards, from the original drawer to indorser and subsequent indorsers. . . .

I see the force as a matter of mercantile practice of the submission of Mr Bowsher that there is not any good commercial reason to deprive the defendants of the contractual rights that they initially had before they discounted the bill merely because in the last stages of the story when the bill was being dishonoured it comes back into the drawer's hands pursuant to the right of recourse of a party to whom the bill has been negotiated. The question which in the absence of authority I do not find perfectly straightforward is whether it can be right to place a restricted meaning on the apparently clear words of the subsection so as to exclude these plaintiffs from a capacity which at first sight they have, namely, a holder deriving title to the bill from a holder in due course; and faced with the words of the statute I am persuaded that there is not sufficient reason shown for placing upon those words the restricted meaning for which he contends.

I remain, which may be only a reflection of my inexperience, surprised that in the year 1977, one hundred years almost since this section was placed on the Statute Book, that the point does not appear ever to have come up for decision and is without authority.

For the reasons that I have stated on the first point, which is the only point that has been argued, I would agree that the appeal should be dismissed.

Geoffrey Lane LJ: It seems to me that once the drawers/payees (the plaintiffs in this case) have discounted the bill to the Sparkasse (Sparkasse then becoming the holders in due course), they lose the capacity which they had as immediate parties to the bill as drawers. Then when in the effluxion of time they once again become holders of the bill in the way that I have described, it is in that new fresh capacity of holders via the Sparkasse and the other bank that their situation must be judged. It is unreal as I see it to regard them as having a dual capacity. Indeed, it is something of a logical difficulty to see how they could. I repeat, when they discounted the bill they lost the benefit of their original capacity, and the guise under which they held it on the second occasion becomes the dominating guise for the purpose of deciding whether or not the judge was in a position to consider the question of discretion. . . .

On the first ground I would dismiss this appeal.

[Stephenson LJ delivered a concurring judgment.]

NOTES

1. This decision has been criticised. In [1978] CLJ 236 at pp 237–238, John Thornley noted that:

> If unqualified, this decision would radically affect cases involving want or failure of consideration. It hardly fits with the provisions that an accommodation bill is discharged when paid in due course by the party accommodated (usually the payee) (s 59(3)) and that an accommodation party is liable on the bill to a holder *for value* (s 28(2)). Suppose A, wishing to make B a gift but lacking ready cash, gratuitously accepts a bill drawn on him by, and payable to, B, who negotiates it to C, a holder in due course. If A dishonours and C has recourse to B, returning the bill, A's formerly effective defence of want of consideration moving from B could no longer prevail against B as a holder in due course by derivation. Logic drives one further. If C were a holder for value, but not in due course (eg, because he took the bill when overdue), B would on recourse become a holder for value against A, since 'Where value has at any time been given for a bill the holder is deemed to be a holder for value as regards the acceptor and all parties to the bill who became parties prior to such time' (s 27(2)). Relationships other than drawer and acceptor would be similarly affected; eg, the original payee of a gratuitous cheque could, on recourse, recover from the drawer.

2. It was submitted by Jade's counsel that Jade gave value for the bill when Sparkasse debited their account. However, Crawford and Falconbridge argue that in these circumstances the bill was in effect paid by the drawer-indorser and s 59(2)(b) provides in such a case that such a party 'is remitted to his former rights against the acceptor' (*Crawford and Falconbridge on Banking and Bills of Exchange* (8th ed), p 1467).

3. Also, note that s 29(3) only gives the holder the same rights as the holder in due course through whom he derived his title to the bill. As certain 'real' defences are available against a holder in due course (eg contractual incapacity, forged or unauthorised signature, non est factum), they will also be available against a holder in due course by derivation.

6 Duties of the holder

To enforce the bill and claim payment from the drawer and indorsers, the holder must comply with a number of duties. These can be summarised as:

(1) a duty to present the bill for acceptance (ss 39–44: although these provisions do not apply to cheques or promissory notes which do not contemplate acceptance) and payment (ss 45–47);
(2) a duty to give notice of dishonour by non-acceptance or non-payment to the drawer and prior indorsers (ss 48–51); and
(3) a duty to protest a foreign bill if dishonoured for non-acceptance or non-payment (ss 4, 51 and 94).

In most cases failure to comply with these duties will release the drawer and indorsers from their liability on the bill. Special rules modify the holder's duties to the drawee or acceptor (s 52).

Yeoman Credit Ltd v Gregory [1963] 1 WLR 343, Queen's Bench Division

The plaintiffs drew two bills of exchange on a company called Express Coachcraft Ltd which accepted them, payable at National Provincial Bank Ltd. The defendant was a director of Express Coachcraft Ltd and indorsed the bills as surety. One bill was a 'fixed date' bill payable on 9 December, the other was an 'on demand' bill. Before the plaintiffs presented the bills they were informed by Mr Thornton, a director of Express Coachcraft Ltd, that the bills should be presented at a branch of Midland Bank where there were funds to meet them. The plaintiffs noted this instruction in pencil on the bills. The bills were presented for payment at Midland Bank on 9 December but the bank refused to meet them. They were then presented to National Provincial Bank on 11 December but that bank also dishonoured them.

Megaw J: The two bills which were presented in December were a 'fixed date' bill for £2,000 and an 'on demand' bill for £900. The date for payment of the 'fixed date' bill was December 9, 1959. Section 45, r (1), of the Bills of Exchange Act 1882, provides: 'Where the bill is not payable on demand, presentment must be made on the day it falls due.' Now presentment was made on December 9, the date when this bill fell due, to Midland Bank Ltd, because of the pencil notation on it. In my view, that cannot be treated as being a proper presentment of a bill which was drawn as payable at a different bank at a different place, and I am quite unable to say that that is in any way altered by the fact that, as the result of a telephone conversation, the pencil notation had been made on it and the plaintiffs had been told that it was to be presented at a different place and there, and there only, to be met. Certainly it cannot be a circumstance which could in any way affect the rights or liabilities of the defendant unless it was established that he knew and had consented to those instructions being given to the plaintiffs. What Mr Collins [credit controller of the plaintiffs] quite clearly ought to have done, and what I am sure in retrospect he realises that he ought to have done, was, after that telephone conversation, to have gone to the defendant and to have gone to all indorsers and said: 'I have had this information. Will you please, with our consent, alter the bill so as to put a different place of payment on it, and each of you indicate on the bill your consent to that alteration?' If that had been so, the matter would have been in order. But, whatever may be said about an estoppel in relation to Coachcraft or in relation to Mr Thornton, that cannot apply to the defendant. So far as the defendant is concerned, he was entitled to have the bill presented on December 9 to the named bank, National Provincial Ltd. That was not done. It was presented at the named bank on the following day. That was a bad presentment, and the result of that, under s 45, r (1), of the Act of 1882, is that, without any proof that the defendant was in any way prejudiced by that late presentation, he is excused from liability on the bill. No question arises here – I do not think that any question was sought to be raised by the plaintiffs – under s 46(1) of the Act of 1882 with regard to the excuse of delay in making presentment for payment. If it had been raised, there would, in my view, have been no facts which would have justified any bringing in of that subsection against the defendant. Accordingly, the claim for the bill for £2,000 fails.

With regard to the other bill, for £900, it being a bill payable on demand, that question of time of presentment does not arise. Counsel for the defendant has contended that it was a bad presentment for payment none the less, because of the pencil writing of a different bank on it. In my judgment, that is not a valid contention, and I say no more about it.

NOTES

1. By s 52(1), where a bill is accepted generally, presentment for payment is not necessary to render an acceptor liable on the bill. This is because an acceptor, like any other debtor, is under a duty to seek out his creditors. Professor Goode (Goode, p 461) has criticised this reasoning as 'arrant nonsense' for the bill may have been negotiated since its original acceptance and until presented for payment the acceptor will not know the identity of his creditor.

2. There are some nineteenth century cases which have been interpreted as authority for the proposition that failure to present a bill for payment not only discharges the drawer and indorsers on the bill but also deprives the holder of his right to sue on the underlying contract for which the bill was given (see, for example, *Soward v Palmer* (1818) 8 Taunt 277; *Peacock v Pursell* (1863) 14 CBNS 728 and Byles, p 122). Professor Goode maintains that this line of authority does not support this supposed rule (Goode, p 462). In any event it is questionable whether such a draconian rule represents the law today (Goode, p 462; Chalmers and Guest, p 362). Professor Goode submits that the appropriate solution is to treat the drawer as discharged from liability on the underlying contract to the extent that he has suffered prejudice by the non-presentment.

3. By s 74, where a cheque is not presented for payment within a reasonable time of its issue, the drawer is only discharged to the extent of the actual damage suffered by him through the delay. However, an indorser would be discharged if the cheque was not presented for payment within a reasonable time of its issue, even if he was not prejudiced by the delay (s 73; cf *King & Boyd v Porter* [1925] NI 107). As to the liability of the maker and indorsers of a promissory note, if it is not duly presented for payment, see ss 86, 87 and 89.

Eaglehill Ltd v J Needham Builders Ltd [1973] AC 992, House of Lords

The defendants drew a bill of exchange on F Ltd, payable on 31 December 1970. F Ltd accepted the bill payable at Lloyd's Bank, High Wycombe. The bill was then discounted to the plaintiffs. Shortly afterwards, F Ltd went into liquidation and both plaintiffs and defendants knew that the bill would be dishonoured when presented for payment. The plaintiffs prepared a notice of dishonour dated 1

January 1971 but posted it in error on 30 December so that it was received by the defendants in the first post on the morning on 31 December. On 31 December the bill was received by Lloyd's Bank in the first post and dishonoured at some point that day. The plaintiffs brought an action against the defendants on the bill. A majority of the Court of Appeal (Lord Denning dissenting) accepted the defendants' argument that they were discharged from liability because the notice of dishonour was ineffective under s 49 as it had been given before the bill had actually been dishonoured. The House of Lords unanimously allowed the plaintiffs' appeal.

Lord Cross of Chelsea:

Was the notice in itself a good notice?
Counsel for the respondents conceded what is, indeed, obvious, that the holder of a bill who knows or fears that it will be dishonoured on the due date can write out and sign before the due date a notice stating that the bill has been dishonoured on the due date and keep it in his desk for use if and when the bill is dishonoured. He also conceded that if the holder hands such a notice to a servant or agent the day before the due date with instructions to deliver it to the drawer next day after the bill has been dishonoured the notice so delivered will be a good notice taking effect when it is received. He submitted, however, that if the holder posts the notice the night before the due date the notice will be bad since it will have been 'given' before the bill is dishonoured even though it does not reach the drawer until after the dishonour. I can see nothing in s 49 of the Bills of Exchange Act 1882 to warrant such an illogical distinction. Rule (15) provides that where a notice of dishonour is duly addressed and posted the sender is deemed to have given due notice of dishonour notwithstanding any miscarriage by the Post Office; but that rule affords no ground for the view that if there is no miscarriage and the notice is received in the ordinary course of post it is given when it is posted and not when it is received. Indeed, the word 'deemed' suggests the contrary. The same conclusion is suggested by r (12)(a) which provides that where the person giving and the person to receive notice reside in the same place a notice is to be deemed to have been given within a reasonable time if it is either given (ie delivered) to the recipient on the day after dishonour or sent off (eg by post) in time to reach the recipient on the day after dishonour. These rules indicate that a notice is only truly given when it is received but that in certain circumstances the 'sending off' of a notice may be treated notionally as the 'giving' of it. Of couse, the wording of a notice written out before the bill is dishonoured may show that it refers to the state of affairs existing when it was written. If, for example, the notice in this case had been dated December 30, it might have been argued that, notwithstanding that it mentioned that the due date was December 31, it was saying either that the bill had been dishonoured on or before the 30th or that it would be dishonoured on the 31st and was on that account bad. But the notice in this case was dated January 1. The recipient – if he noticed the date at all – would realise that the notice had been posted two days earlier than had been intended; but nothing in the wording of the notice would lead him to think that it was referring to anything other than a dishonour which had already occurred on the 31st. In my view therefore this notice was a good notice unless it was received before the bill was dishonoured.

The time of dishonour and the time of the receipt of the notice of dishonour
Lord Denning MR says in his judgment that it is a general rule that the law pays no regard to parts of a day. That is, of course, true if what one is concerned with is the calculation of a period of time. But, with respect, it is not true if what one is concerned with is a sequence of events happening on the same day. In that context the law does, in general, pay regard to parts of a day (see eg *Clarke v Bradlaugh* (1881) 8 QBD 63 and *Re North* [1895] 2 QB 264) and I can see nothing in the Bills of Exchange Act 1882 to suggest that a notice of dishonour given on the due date but before the dishonour of the bill is a good notice. Section 49, r (12), says that a notice of dishonour may be given 'as soon as' the bill is dishonoured, not that it may be given 'on the day' on which the bill is dishonoured. On this point I agree with Sachs LJ.

It is, therefore, necessary to inquire at what time on December 31 the bill was dishonoured and at what time on that day the notice of dishonour was received. The wording of the Bills of Exchange Act 1882, which codified the law as laid down in hundreds of cases decided over the previous century and a half, appears in places to presuppose a manner of doing business which must have been unusual even in 1882 and is a thing of the past today. For example, s 52(4) which provides that 'Where the holder of a bill presents it for payment, he shall exhibit the bill to the person from whom he demands payment,' conjures up the picture of the holder going into the counting house of the acceptor with the bill in his hand and of the acceptor either opening his till and handing over the appropriate number of sovereigns in exchange for the bill or there and then refusing to honour it. In fact nowadays both holder and acceptor normally employ their banks to carry out the transaction. If it is believed that the bill will be met, the collecting bank will credit the holder in advance with the amount of the bill which it sends by post to the paying bank. If the bill is met the paying bank will debit its customer, the acceptor, and credit the collecting bank with the appropriate amount in its daily settlement with it. If the bill is not met it will be returned to the collecting bank which will cancel the credit which it has given the holder. This case was, however, exceptional as the acceptor was, to the knowledge of both drawer and holder, in liquidation and there was no possibility of the bill being met though it was necessary for it to be presented and dishonoured and for notice of dishonour to be given to the drawer if the drawer was to be made liable on it. It was suggested in argument that when, as happened here, the bill is sent by post to the paying bank on the due date the paying bank becomes the agent of the holder or the collecting bank to present the bill to itself. I see no need for such a fiction. Section 41(1)(a) provides that presentment must be made to the drawer by or on behalf of the holder, but (e) provides that where authorised by agreement or usage a presentment through the Post Office is authorised. So when this bill arrived by post at Lloyds Bank, High Wycombe, on December 31, and was laid before some clerk with authority to deal with it, it can be said to have been presented and exhibited to the acceptor's agent by the holder or his agent, the collecting bank, through the medium of the Post Office. If the acceptor is not bankrupt or in liquidation but has not a credit with the paying bank sufficient to cover the bill and that bank is not prepared to advance him the necessary money to cover it, it may well be that the bill is not dishonoured until it is returned through the post to the holder or the collecting bank. If, for instance, the paying bank were to ring up its customer saying that the bill would be dishonoured unless he put them in funds to meet it and he provided the necessary money that day I am not satisfied that the bill would have been dishonoured simply because the paying bank did not debit their customer's account with the necessary sum as soon as they saw it. But in this case where there could be no question of the acceptor meeting the bill I think that it was dishonoured as soon as the bank clerk who had authority to deal with the matter saw it and recognised that it was a bill which could not be met and would have to be returned to the holder or the collecting bank. One must next consider at what time on December 31 the notice of dishonour was received by the respondents. I do not think that such a notice is 'received' as soon as it is put into the drawer's letter box either by the postman or a private messenger. On the other hand, it is the duty of the drawer if he be absent from his place of business or residence to see that there is someone there to receive notice on his behalf: see *Chalmers on Bills of Exchange*, 13th ed (1964), p 159. So I think that such a notice is received when it is opened in the ordinary course of business or would be so opened if the ordinary course of business was followed.

Not surprisingly there was no evidence to show at what precise moments of time on the morning of December 31 these two pieces of paper were first seen in the offices of the bank and the respondents respectively by persons competent to deal with them. I cannot agree with Sachs LJ that it is more probable that the notice of dishonour was received before than after the bill was dishonoured. It is impossible to say which event happened first. All that one can say is that it is probable that there was only a short interval of time between them. That being so, the respondents say that the appellants have failed to prove that due notice of dishonour was given, while the appellants say that it should be presumed in their favour, in the absence of evidence to the contrary, that the dishonour preceded the notice of dishonour.

The presumption for which the appellants contend may be expressed as follows:

If two acts have been done one of which ought to have been done after the other if it was to be valid and the evidence which could reasonably be expected to be available does not show which was done first they will be presumed to have been done in the proper order.

Such a presumption would not be – as was suggested in argument – an application of the maxim omnia praesumuntur rite esse acta for it is abundantly clear that the posting of the notice on December 30 was wholly irregular. It would be an extension into another field of the maxim that a document which is reasonably capable of two constructions should be construed ut res magis valeat quam pereat. Such an extension appears to me to be justified – at all events in the case of commercial documents such as those with which we are here concerned. As it would be rebuttable its existence would not encourage those in whose favour it might operate to be careless whether or not the due time had arrived for the doing of the act in question. In practice it would only operate when as here there had been a mistake and it would have the merit of discouraging those against whom it would operate from seeking to take advantage of a slip by the other side in cases where they could not prove that the slip had led to the acts in question being done in the wrong order.

Viscount Dilhorne: It was contended that where two events occur on the same day the principle ut res magis valeat quam pereat should be applied or the presumption omnia praesumuntur pro rite esse acta applied. No such presumption or principle was relied on in *Castrique v Bernabo* but Alderson B in *Aikman v Conway* (1837) 3 M & W 71, 72 said: 'It is a good rule, that when two things are done on the same day, that shall be presumed to have been done first which ought to be so.' In that case it was contended that judgment should be set aside on the ground that a rule to plead had been deposited before a declaration had been filed, when the rule to plead should not have been deposited until after the notice had been filed.

Lord Denning MR in this case founded on Alderson B's observations and agreed with the opinion expressed obiter by Megaw J in *Yeoman Credit Ltd v Gregory* [1963] 1 All ER 245, 255 that if notice of dishonour is sent on the day on which the bill is dishonoured it is sufficient and that 'one simply does not look at hours and minutes in relation to this matter.'

I feel considerable doubt about whether that is correct for under the Bills of Exchange Act 1882 the notice to be valid cannot be given before the dishonour. If it was established that the notice was given at 9 a.m. and the bill had been dishonoured at 5 p.m. the same day the actual decision in *Aikman v Conway* would seem to imply that one could disregard the facts and hold the notice valid. Despite the evidence in *Aikman v Conway*, Alderson B was apparently prepared to presume that the events had occurred in the right order when in fact the evidence clearly showed that they had not.

I doubt, too, whether it is right to extend the application of the principles ut res magis valeat and omnia pro rite esse acta to the facts of this case. I see no authority for doing so, but I do not consider that this case really requires a decision on that question.

On the facts the evidence shows that the bill was delivered to the bank and the notice to the respondent by the first post on the same day at premises only a short distance apart. They must have been delivered within a period of a few minutes. The bill was received by the bank at the commencement of business, which I take to mean when the post was dealt with. I think one is entitled to infer that the notice was received by the respondents when their post was opened at the commencement of the day's work and also to infer that work commenced in the absence of evidence to the contrary at about the same time.

On this basis, though the facts do not show that the notice was received after the dishonour of the bill, on the balance of probabilities it appears to me that the dishonour and receipt of the notice must have occurred at practically the same time and that the balance of probabilities is against the notice having been received first. I agree with Megaw J that one need not have regard to minutes or indeed to seconds and on the balance of probabilities, in my view, the notice was received to all intents and purposes as soon as and not before the bill was dishonoured. That suffices to make the notice a good notice within the Bills of Exchange Act 1882 and for these reasons in my opinion this appeal should be allowed.

[Lords Reid, Diplock and Simon of Glaisdale concurred with Lord Cross of Chelsea.]

NOTES

1. Byles notes (pp 177–178) that:

> The law presumes that, if the drawer has not had due notice, he is injured because otherwise he might have immediately withdrawn his effects from the hands of the drawee and that, if the indorser has not had timely notice, the remedy against the parties liable to him is rendered more precarious. The consequence, therefore, of neglect of notice is, that the party to whom it should have been given is discharged from all liability, whether on the bill or on the consideration for which the bill was paid.

2. Discharge from liability on the bill does not depend, therefore, upon the drawer or indorser having suffered any prejudice by the failure to give notice of dishonour. Contrast this approach to that found in the Geneva Uniform Laws on Bills of Exchange and Promissory Notes (Art 45) and the United Nations Convention on International Bills of Exchange and International Promissory Notes (Art 68) which provide only for an action for damages for loss caused by failure to give notice of dishonour.

3. Byles' conclusion that the holder who fails to give notice of dishonour loses his right on the original consideration for which the bill was given, is open to the same criticism as made against the supposed rule to similar effect with regard to non-presentment for payment (see above, p 517 and Goode, p 463; Chalmers and Guest, p 389).

4. For the limited protection given to a holder in due course when there is a failure to give notice of dishonour by non-acceptance, see s 48(1).

7 Liability on the bill of exchange: general principles

It has already been noted that the liability created by a bill of exchange is contractual (see above, at p 500). However, the drawer, acceptor or indorser will only be liable on the bill if:

(1) he has capacity to contract;
(2) his contract on the bill is complete and irrevocable; and
(3) he has signed the instrument as such.

(a) Capacity to contract

By s 22(1), capacity to incur liability as a party to a bill is determined by the general law relating to capacity to contract. If a drawer, acceptor or indorser has no capacity to contract, he is not liable on the bill. With the recent abolition of the *ultra vires* rule in so far as it affects third parties, a company will rarely be able to plead against a holder of a bill that it does not have capacity to contract (see ss 35(1) and (4) of the Companies Act 1985, as substituted by s 108 of the Companies Act 1989). However, the fact that one party does not have the capacity to contract does not, in itself, release other parties from liability on the bill. Section 5(2) deals with the situation where the drawee has no capacity to contract.

(b) Complete and irrevocable contract

By s 21(1), every contract on the bill is incomplete and revocable until delivery of the bill. Section 2 defines 'delivery' as the transfer of possession, actual or constructive, from one person to another. However, the acceptor's contract can also become complete and irrevocable if the drawee gives notice to, or according to, the directions of the person entitled to the bill that he has accepted it. If the bill is in the hands of a holder in due course a valid delivery of the bill by all parties prior to him, so as to make them liable to him, is conclusively presumed (s 21(2) and see *Clifford Chance v Silver* [1992] 2 Bank LR 11, CA). If the bill is in the hands of a holder, who is not a holder in due course, there is a rebuttable presumption that there was a valid and unconditional delivery by the drawer, acceptor or indorser (s 21(3)). See *Citibank NA v Brown Shipley & Co Ltd* [1991] 2 All ER 690 for a case where there was an unsuccessful attempt to rebut this presumption (noted by A H Hudson [1991] LMCLQ 291 and A Phang [1992] JCL 69).

(c) Signature essential to liability

Under s 23, a person is liable as drawer, acceptor or indorser of a bill only if he has signed it as such. This does not mean that the bill has to be signed personally by such a person, for under s 91(1) it is enough that *his* signature is written on the bill by some other person 'by or under his authority'. Bills and promissory notes are exceptions to the undisclosed principal rule, so if the agent signs in his own name no extrinsic evidence may be adduced to show that the principal is the party liable on the bill. Unless the fact he is acting as agent appears from the wording of his signature, the agent will be personally liable if he signs in his own name (*Leadbitter v Farrow* (1816) 5 M & S 345, 349). If the agent signs in his principal's name, or signs in his own name with an express indication that he acts as agent for another, then, whether he acts with or without authority, he will incur no personal liability on the bill. However, if the agent acts without authority he may be liable for misrepresentation or breach of warranty of authority (*Starkey v Bank of England* [1903] AC 114). If the 'agent' signs in the name of a fictitious or non-existing principal he may be personally liable (see *Bowstead on Agency* (15th ed), p 469).

The principal's signature will be written on the bill 'by or under his authority', if the agent has actual (express or implied) or apparent (or ostensible) authority to sign. However, if the agent acts outside the bounds of his actual authority and signs by procuration (eg 'per procurationem', 'per pro' or 'pp'), the principal is not bound by the signature. This is the effect of s 25, which provides that a signature by procuration operates as notice to third parties that the agent's authority is limited so that the principal will only be liable on signatures within the actual limits of the agent's authority. Even a holder in due course will be put on notice by such a signature and will not be able to enforce the bill against the principal if the agent has exceeded his authority (*Morison v London County & Westminster Bank Ltd* [1914] 3 KB 356 at 367, per Lord Reading CJ). Unfortunately, the effect of s 25 means that a principal who has misled a third party, by holding his agent out as having authority, will avoid liability simply because of the form of the agent's signature. This will occur even if the third party has no reasonable opportunity to check the agent's authority.

It is not clear whether s 25 extends to all forms of representative signature (eg signatures 'for' or 'on behalf of' the principal). For strong arguments that s 25 should be given a narrow interpretation, see Chalmers and Guest at p 210 and Byles at p 68. For further criticism of the section and a recommendation that it should be repealed see the Report of the Review Committee on Banking Law and Practice ((1989) Cm 622, Rec 8(10), Appendix A, pp 228–229, Appendix N, para 6). The recommendation was not adopted by the Government in its subsequent White Paper ((1990) Cm 1026, Annex 6, para 6.11).

(i) *Company bills, cheques and promissory notes*

Companies Act 1985, s 37

> A bill of exchange or promissory note is deemed to have been made, accepted or endorsed on behalf of a company if made, accepted or endorsed in the name of, or by or on behalf or on account of, the company by a person acting under its authority.

Section 91(2) confirms that a bill or note of a company does not have to be executed under seal. If the bill or note is not executed under seal (or under the procedure set out in s 36A of the Companies Act 1985, as inserted by s 130(2) of the Companies Act 1989), then a person acting within his actual authority can bind the company, and not himself, if he (1) signs the company's name (although, in practice, banks regard this as irregular: *Paget's Law of Banking* (10th ed, 1989), p 140); or (2) signs the company's name and accompanies it with his signature, and either a 'per pro' or other representative indication. However, the agent will be personally liable on the bill or note in the following circumstances:

(1) under s 26(1), if he does not indicate that he signs for or on behalf of the company, or in a representative capacity, but merely describes himself as agent or some other representative of the company.

Bondina Ltd v Rollaway Shower Blinds Ltd [1986] 1 All ER 564, Court of Appeal

Mr Ward, a company director, signed a cheque by placing his signature (without additional words) below the pre-printed name of the company as drawer. At the bottom of the cheque there was a pre-printed line of figures designating the number of the cheque, the branch of the bank and the number of the account which was the company's account. The director denied he was personally liable on the cheque.

Dillon LJ: Counsel for the plaintiffs founds himself on s 26 of the Bills of Exchange Act 1882, which provides by sub-s (1):

> Where a person signs a bill as drawer, indorser, or acceptor, and adds words to his signature, indicating that he signs for or on behalf of a principal, or in a representative character, he is not personally liable thereon; but the mere addition to his signature of words describing him as an agent, or as filling a representative character, does not exempt him from personal liability.

Counsel for the plaintiffs says that Mr Ward has merely signed a printed form of cheque and has not added any relevant words to his signature. As it seems to me, however, when Mr Ward signed the cheque he adopted all the printing and writing on it; not merely the writing designating the payee and the amount for which the cheque was drawn, if that had been written out for him and not by himself, but also the printing of the company's name and the printing of the numbers which designate the company's account. The effect of this is to show that the cheque is drawn on the company's account and not on any other account. It is not a case of a joint liability of several people. It shows plainly, as I construe it, looking no further than the form of the cheque itself, that the drawer of the cheque was the company and not Mr Ward. . . .

[Sir George Waller delivered a concurring judgment.]

If there is doubt as to whether a signature on the bill or note is that of the principal or of the agent, then the construction most favourable to the validity of the instrument is adopted (s 26(2)).

Rolfe Lubell & Co (a firm) v Keith [1979] 1 All ER 860, Queen's Bench Division

The plaintiffs would only supply goods to G F Ltd if bills of exchange drawn in payment were personally indorsed by two officers of the company. The bills were accepted by the company and indorsed by the managing director and company secretary who placed their signatures within a rubber-stamped box on the back of the bill, so that it read 'For and on behalf of G F Ltd, X (*signature*) director, Y (*signature*) secretary'. The plaintiffs brought an action against the director claiming he was personally liable on the bills.

Kilner-Brown J: . . . In the instant case the form of signature as acceptors on the face of the bill and as indorser on the back of the bill is precisely the same. The two defendants signed for and on behalf of the company and made the company liable on the bill as acceptor. By signing in similar form on the back of the bill they produced what counsel for the plaintiffs described as a mercantile nonsense. An indorsement on the back of a bill amounts to a warrant that the bill will be honoured and imposes in certain circumstances a transfer of liability to the indorser. No one can transfer liability from himself to himself. The only way in which validity can be given to this indorsement is by construing it to bind someone other than the acceptor. As soon therefore as it becomes obvious that the indorsement as worded is meaningless and of no value there is a patent ambiguity which allows evidence to be admitted to give effect to the intentions of the parties. . . .

On the evidence I find as a fact that the first defendant agreed personally to indorse the bills; that his signature is evidence of that agreement and consequently a valid indorsement in a personal capacity and that he is personally liable on the two bills which were dishonoured on presentation. It follows that in my judgment the words 'for and on behalf of the company' are of no significance in so far as the relationship between the plaintiffs and the first defendant are concerned; they do not vary or amend a clear agreement personally to indorse and thereby to warrant and assume liability for the default of the company. The signature is the relevant and significant act.

(2) under s 349(4) of the Companies Act 1985, if a director or other officer of a company signs or authorises to be signed on behalf of the company any bill of exchange, promissory note, cheque or order for money or goods in which its name is not mentioned in legible characters, he is liable to a fine; and he is further personally liable to the holder of the bill etc for the amount of it (unless it is fully paid by the company).

Durham Fancy Goods Ltd v Michael Jackson (Fancy Goods) Ltd [1968] 2 QB 839, Queen's Bench Division

The drawer of a bill of exchange drawn on a company whose correct name was 'Michael Jackson (Fancy Goods) Ltd' typed on it a form of acceptance describing the company as 'M Jackson (Fancy Goods) Ltd'. The defendant, a director of the company, accepted the bill by adding his signature beneath the typed words of the acceptance. The company went into liquidation and the bill remained unpaid. The drawer brought an action against the director claiming he was personally liable for the amount of the bill under s 108 of the Companies Act 1948 (a similar provision to s 349 in the 1985 Act).

Donaldson J: Mr Rokison for Mr Jackson submits that there was sufficient compliance with the section in the present case because (a) the bill made it clear that the acceptors were a limited company and (b) there was no confusion as to their identity. In support of the first of these submissions he relied upon *Penrose v Martyr* ((1858) EB & E 499) in which Crompton J stated (at 503) that the purpose of the corresponding statutory provision

> was to prevent persons from being deceived into the belief that they had a security with the unlimited liability of common law, when they had but the security of a company limited

and upon the judgment of Scrutton J in *F Stacey & Co Ltd v Wallis* ((1912) 28 TLR 209 at 211) affirming this view and deciding that 'Ltd' was an acceptable abbreviation for 'Limited.' Unfortunately for Mr Jackson, the second submission is unsupported by authority. Indeed it is contrary to the tenor of the decision of Denman J and of the Court of Appeal in *Atkins v Wardle* ((1889) 5 TLR 734). There the drawer of the bill was a shareholder in the 'South Shields Salt Water Baths Company (Limited)' but he drew on 'Salt Water Baths Company (Limited), South Shields' and the directors accepted on behalf of 'South Shields Salt Water Bath Company' which was equally incorrect. No question of confusion as to identity or as to the status of the drawers as a limited liability company could have arisen. Nevertheless the directors were held to be personally liable, Lord Esher MR pointing out that the statute did not require the misdescription to be material.

Mr Rokison also submitted that just as 'Ltd' was an acceptable abbreviation for 'Limited,' so 'M' was an acceptable abbreviation for 'Michael.' This I do not accept. The word 'Limited' is included in a company's name by way of description and not identification. Accordingly a generally accepted abbreviation will serve this purpose as well as the word in full. The rest of the name, by contrast, serves as a means of identification and may be compounded of or include initials or abbreviations. The use of any abbreviation of the registered name is calculated to create problems of identification which are not created by an abbreviation of 'Limited.' I should therefore be prepared to hold that no abbreviation was permissible of any part of a company's name other than 'Ltd' for 'Limited' and, possibly, the ampersand for 'and.' However it is not necessary to go as far as this. Any abbreviation must convey the full word unambiguously and the initial 'M' neither shows that it is an abbreviation nor does it convey 'Michael.'

I have therefore no doubt that Mr Jackson committed an offence under s 108 of the Act of 1948, although a court might well decide to impose no penalty. I have also no doubt that he is liable to the plaintiffs who are admitted to be the holders of the bill of exchange since this is what the statute says. But can the plaintiffs enforce that liability? That is a different question.

This case is distinguished from all previous cases under the earlier statutory versions of the section in that here it was the holders of the bill of exchange who inscribed the words of acceptance, who chose the wrong words and who now seek to rely upon their own error, coupled it is true with the defendant's failure to detect and remedy it, as entitling them to relief. Common sense and justice seem to me to dictate that they shall fail. If I am right thus far, I should be surprised if the law compelled me to find in the plaintiffs' favour because, contrary to popular belief, the law, justice and common sense are not unrelated concepts.

In my judgment the principle of equity upon which the promissory estoppel cases are based is applicable to and bars the plaintiffs' claim.

NOTES

1. The abbreviation 'Co' for 'Company' is permitted: *Banque de L'Indochine et de Suez SA v Euroseas Group Finance Co Ltd* [1981] 3 All ER 198 at 202, per Robert Goff J. But using a company's business name is not permitted: *Maxform SpA v Mariani & Goodville Ltd* [1979] 2 Lloyd's Rep 385; affd [1981] 2 Lloyd's Rep 54 (criticised by C M Schmitthoff [1980] JBL 79 at p 80).

2. In the *Durham Fancy Goods* case, counsel for the plaintiffs (Mr J S Hobhouse, now Lord Justice Hobhouse) submitted that in the light of the penal provisions of s 108 (now s 349) and the clear and unqualified legal statutory duty and liability which it imposed on the defendant, a plea of estoppel could not operate. Donaldson J did not deal with this submission in any detail and in the recent cases of *Blum v OCP Repartition SA* [1988] BCLC 170, CA, and *Rafsanjan Pistachio Producers Co-operative v Reiss* [1990] BCLC 352 (Potter J) it was submitted by counsel that the *Durham Fancy Goods* case was wrongly decided because it turned on an estoppel. However, in neither case did the court find evidence of any inequitable conduct and, therefore, did not have to decide this issue. In the *Blum* case, May LJ (at 175) expressly reserved his position as to whether the *Durham Fancy Goods* case was wrongly decided.

3. The cases since the *Durham Fancy Goods* case have shown that it is particularly difficult to establish the estoppel necessary to avoid liability under s 349, although they generally assume that the *Durham Fancy Goods* case was correctly decided. For example, in *Maxform SpA v Mariani & Goodville Ltd*, above, the plaintiffs drew bills of exchange addressed to 'Italdesign' which was the registered business name of a company called Mariani and Goodville Limited. The defendant accepted the bills in his own name. It was held by Mocatta J, and affirmed by the Court of Appeal, that the defendant was personally liable under s 108(4) of the Companies Act 1948. A plea of estoppel failed, for although the plaintiffs had addressed the bills to 'Italdesign' this did not determine how the bills should have been accepted. The defendant could have accepted them by signing 'Mariani and Goodville trading as Italdesign'.

4. In (1982) 3 Company Lawyer 156 at 157, Keith Wright describes what is now s 349 as 'a special form of statutory liability which . . . is harsh and rigid and not constrained by any particular bounds of fairness, common sense or presumed legislative policy'. It is clear from Donaldson J's judgment in the *Durham Fancy Goods* case that liability will accrue under s 349 even though no one was misled by any misdescription of the company's name (but mere mis-spelling of the company's name, when it does not cause confusion, falls outside s 349: *Jenice Ltd v Dan* [1993] BCLC 1349, where Primekeen Ltd was spelt Primkeen Ltd on the relevant cheque). In this respect s 349 does not purport to be remedial and the civil liability arising under the section can more accurately be described as a 'quasi-penalty' (per Potter J in the *Rafsanjan Pistachio* case at 363). For further criticism of the section and a recommendation for its reform, see C M Schmitthoff [1969] JBL 45, [1979] JBL 214 and [1980] JBL 79.

(3) under s 36C of the Companies Act 1985 (inserted by s 130(4) of the Companies Act 1989), where a contract purports to be made by a company, or

by a person as agent for a company, at a time when the company has not been formed, then subject to any agreement to the contrary the contract had effect as a contract entered into by the person purporting to act for the company or as agent for it, and he is personally liable on the contract accordingly. See *Phonogram Ltd v Lane* [1982] QB 938, CA; cf *Cotronic (UK) Ltd v Dezonie (t/a Wendaland Builders Ltd)* [1991] BCC 200, CA. See generally, A Griffiths (1993) 13 LS 241.

QUESTIONS

XYZ Ltd was incorporated on 1 October 1992 and A was appointed its sole director. Advise A as to his personal liability in the following circumstances:

(1) On 1 September 1992 A draws a cheque and signs it 'For and on behalf of XYZ Ltd, A (*signature*), director'.
(2) On 1 November 1992 XYZ Ltd opens a current account with B Bank and is issued with a cheque book which, due to the bank's error, names XYY Ltd as drawer on all the cheques. To pay for goods supplied to XYZ Ltd, A draws one of the cheques from the cheque book and signs it as in (1) above. The cheque is not paid when presented.
(3) A uses one of the cheques from the cheque book referred to in (2) above and draws it 'Pay cash or order'. A signs the cheque 'A (signature), director'. The cheque is not paid when presented. See *Gader v Flower* (1979) 129 NLJ 1266.
(4) To pay for services supplied by C to XYZ Ltd, A uses one of the cheques from the cheque book referred to in (2) above and draws it 'pay C or order'. A signs it 'A (signature), director'. The cheque is not paid when presented. Does A have any claim against B Bank? See *Hendon v Adelman* (1973) 117 Sol Jo 631.

(ii) *Forged or unauthorised signatures*

Section 24 provides that where a signature on a bill is forged or placed on it without the authority of the person whose signature it purports to be, the forged or unauthorised signature is wholly inoperative, and no right to retain the bill, discharge it or enforce it can be acquired through or under that signature, unless the party against whom it is sought to retain it or enforce payment of the bill is precluded from setting up the forgery or want of authority. The section also provides that it does not affect the ratification of an unauthorised signature not amounting to a forgery. But what is a forgery?

Forgery and Counterfeiting Act 1981

1. A person is guilty of forgery if he makes a false instrument, with the intention that he or another shall use it to induce somebody to accept it as genuine, and by reason of so accepting it to do or not to do some act to his own or any other person's prejudice.

9. (1) An instrument is false for the purposes of this Part of the Act—
. . .
    (d) if it purports to have been made in the terms in which it is made on the authority of a person who did not in fact authorise its making in those terms; . . .
(2) A person is to be treated for the purposes of this Part of this Act as making a false

instrument if he alters an instrument so as to make it false in any respect (whether or not it is false in some other respect apart from that alteration).

NOTES

1. Section 9(1)(d) of the Forgery and Counterfeiting Act 1981 superseded s 1 of the Forgery Act 1913, which was drafted in similar terms. In *Kreditbank Cassel GmbH v Schenkers Ltd* [1927] 1 KB 826 a branch manager of the defendant company, without authority and fraudulently, drew and indorsed bills on behalf of the company for his own benefit. The Court of Appeal held that the company was not liable on the bills as they were forgeries within the Forgery Act 1913 and the plaintiffs could not rely on the rule in *Turquand's* case ((1856) 6 E & B 327) because that rule does not apply where the bills are forgeries. It would appear, therefore, that a fraudulent unauthorised signature amounts to a forgery and cannot be ratified (*Brook v Hook* (1871) LR 6 Exch 89). Yet this cannot be what was intended by s 24 which distinguishes between unauthorised signatures (which are ratifiable) and forged signatures (which are not ratifiable). The explanation appears to be that when the Bills of Exchange Act 1882 was passed the Forgery Act 1861 was in force and that Act did not treat an unauthorised signature as a forgery (see *Morison v London County and Westminster Bank Ltd* [1914] 3 KB 356 at 366, CA). Consistent with what appears to have been Parliament's intention when the Bills of Exchange Act 1882 was passed, it is submitted by Chalmers and Guest (pp 167–168) that the definition of forgery now contained in the Forgery and Counterfeiting Act 1981 should not be applied to s 24 (cf Goode, pp 468–469, who, nevertheless, sees no reason why a signature on behalf of another without his authority should not be ratified even though it is a forgery as defined by the 1981 Act). Yet even if the 1981 Act's definition of forgery is applied to the 1882 Act, it is submitted that, so far as ratification is concerned, the distinction between forged and unauthorised signatures, emphasised by s 24, should be maintained (see Chitty, Vol 2, p 206). This is because a true forger does not act, or purport to act, under the authority of the person whose signature he forges and so his signature cannot be ratified; whereas an unauthorised signature can be ratified when the agent purports to act on behalf of a principal.

2. A fraudulent alteration in the body of the bill may amount to a forgery under ss 9(1) and (2) of the Forgery and Counterfeiting Act 1981 but it does not come within the ambit of s 24. Section 64 deals with the situation where a bill is materially altered.

3. It has already been noted that any person in possession of an order bill bearing a forged or unauthorised indorsement cannot be a holder in due course (nor any other form of 'holder') of that bill and has no right to enforce it against any person who became a party to the bill prior to the forgery (see above, p 496 and *Lacave & Co v Crédit Lyonnais* [1897] 1 QB 148 at 152, per Collins J; cf *Embiricos v Anglo-Austrian Bank* [1905] 1 KB 677, CA). However, if after the forged or unauthorised indorsement, the bill is subsequently indorsed, then, under s 55(2)(b) the subsequent indorsers will be precluded from denying to a holder in due course the genuineness and regularity in all respects of the previous indorsements. In this context, the term 'holder in due course' must be taken to include a person who would, but for the forged or unauthorised indorsement, have been a holder of the bill (Chalmers and Guest, p 184).

Greenwood v Martins Bank Ltd [1933] AC 51, House of Lords

A husband opened an account in his sole name with the respondent bank. His wife forged his signature on various cheques and drew money out of this account. The husband found out about the forgeries but was persuaded by his wife to say nothing. The husband remained silent for eight months and when he finally decided to tell the bank of his wife's action she shot herself. The husband brought an action against the bank to recover the sums paid out of his account on the cheques to which his signature had been forged.

Lord Tomlin: . . . Now it may be said at once that there can be no question of ratification or of adoption in this case. The necessary elements for ratification were not present, and adoption as understood in English law requires valuable consideration, which is not even suggested here.

The sole question is whether in the circumstances of this case the respondents are entitled to set up an estoppel.

The essential factors giving rise to an estoppel are I think:

(1) A representation or conduct amounting to a representation intended to induce a course of conduct on the part of the person to whom the representation is made.

(2) An act or omission resulting from the representation, whether actual or by conduct, by the person to whom the representation is made.

(3) Detriment to such person as a consequence of the act or omission.

Mere silence cannot amount to a representation, but when there is a duty to disclose deliberate silence may become significant and amount to a representation.

The existence of a duty on the part of the customer of a bank to disclose to the bank his knowledge of such a forgery as the one in question in this case was rightly admitted.

The respondents' case is that the duty ought to have been discharged by the appellant immediately upon his discovery in October, 1929, and that if it had been then discharged they could have sued the appellant's wife in tort and the appellant himself would have been responsible for his wife's tort. They claim that his silence until after his wife's death amounted in these circumstances to a representation that the cheques were not forgeries and deprived the respondents of their remedy.

[Lord Tomlin emphasised that the husband had known of his wife's actions for some months and continued:]

The appellant's silence, therefore, was deliberate and intended to produce the effect which it in fact produced – namely, the leaving of the respondents in ignorance of the true facts so that no action might be taken by them against the appellant's wife. The deliberate abstention from speaking in those circumstances seems to me to amount to a representation to the respondents that the forged cheques were in fact in order, and assuming that detriment to the respondents followed there were, it seems to me, present all the elements essential to estoppel. Further, I do not think that it is any answer to say that if the respondents had not been negligent initially the detriment would not have occurred. The course of conduct relied upon as founding the estoppel was adopted in order to leave the respondents in the condition of ignorance in which the appellant knew they were. It was the duty of the appellant to remove that condition however caused. It is the existence of this duty, coupled with the appellant's deliberate intention to maintain the respondents in their condition of ignorance, that gives its significance to the appellant's silence. What difference can it make that the condition of ignorance was primarily induced by the respondents' own negligence? In my judgment it can make none. For the purposes of the estoppel, which is a procedural matter, the cause of the ignorance is an irrelevant consideration.

[Lords Atkin, Warrington, Thankerton and Macmillan concurred in Lord Tomlin's opinion and the husband's appeal was dismissed.]

NOTES

1. This was a case of estoppel by representation. Estoppel may also arise by negligence as where a customer of a bank draws a cheque in such a way as to facilitate the fraud or forgery: see *London Joint Stock Bank v Macmillan* [1918] AC 777, HL. *Greenwood v Martins Bank Ltd* was a case where the estoppel prevented the person charged with liability on the bill from relying on the forgery of his own signature. Such a common law estoppel may also prevent a party to the bill from asserting that the signature of another party to the bill is forged or unauthorised: see *Bank of England v Vagliano Bros*, above at p 492.

2. Although a forged signature cannot be ratified, it may be adopted. This would occur, for example, if a customer's signature on a cheque is forged but he subsequently agrees that his bank may debit his account with the cheque. Whether adoption is an example of estoppel by representation or derives from a separate contractual promise, which must be supported by its own consideration, is undecided. In *Greenwood v Martins Bank Ltd*, Lord Tomlin clearly saw it falling into the category of contractual promise. Whether the adoption of a person's forged indorsement on a bill would give that person rights against prior parties, as opposed to simply making him liable to subsequent parties, has not been addressed by the courts.

3. Various statutory estoppels also operate to prevent a party to the bill from denying the genuineness, and in some cases genuineness and regularity, of another party's signature: see ss 54(2)(a) and 55(2)(b). These estoppels are specifically preserved by s 24 which is stated to be 'Subject to the provisions of this Act'. For other statutory provisions covered by this proviso see ss 7(3), 60, 64, 80.

8 Liability on the bill: specific parties

Section 53(1) provides that a bill of exchange, of itself, does not operate as an assignment of funds which the drawer has in the hands of the drawee and that, unless he accepts the bill, the drawee is not liable on the instrument. This does not prevent the drawee being bound by some extrinsic contractual obligation to accept the bill or pay the sum due on it, eg where a bank issues a cheque guarantee card it gives an undertaking to any supplier of goods or services to the cardholder that it will honour its customer's cheques (see generally *First Sport Ltd v Barclays Bank plc* [1993] 1 WLR 1229, CA).

A drawee who accepts a bill (called the 'acceptor') becomes the person primarily liable on it (s 54(1)). However, if the bill is accepted by an accommodation party (as defined by s 28) it is an 'accommodation bill' and the person primarily liable on the bill is the person accommodated and not the acceptor who is deemed merely a surety for that liability. This is important because with an accommodation bill payment in due course by the person accommodated will discharge the bill (s 59(3)), whereas the usual rule is that only payment in due course by the drawee or acceptor will discharge the bill (s 59(1) and (2)).

For the various statutory estoppels which operate against the acceptor in favour of a holder in due course, see s 54(2). We have already noted that certain common law estoppels may also operate against the acceptor in favour of a holder (see above, p 494).

The liability of the drawer and any indorser on the bill is conditional on dishonour by the drawee/acceptor. They each warrant that the bill will be accepted and paid according to its tenor and that if it is dishonoured each will compensate the holder and any indorser (who must be a subsequent indorser in the case of the indorser's warranty) who is compelled to pay the bill (s 55(1)(a) and s 55(2)(a)). When a bill has been accepted for value, the relationship between the drawer and indorsers on the one hand and the acceptor on the other is analogous, therefore, to that of suretyship. This explains why the drawer and any indorser are discharged from liability if the requisite proceedings on dishonour are not followed. It also ensures that they are entitled to the equities of a surety, although in the case of an indorser this will only accrue when the bill has been dishonoured (*Duncan, Fox & Co v North and South Wales Bank* (1880) 6 App Cas 1 at 18–19, HL, per Lord Blackburn).

For the various statutory estoppels binding the drawer see s 55(1)(b) and for those binding the indorser see s 55(2)(b) and (c). Other common law estoppels may arise on the facts of any particular case.

For the measure of damages recoverable against a drawer, indorser and acceptor, see s 57. Note that under s 16(1) the drawer, and any indorser (even an anomalous indorser under s 56), may negative or limit his liability to the holder by an express stipulation on the bill to that effect. The most an acceptor can do to limit his liability is to give a qualified acceptance to the order of the drawer contained in the bill (s 19). If the acceptor purports to exclude his liability completely he would not be deemed to have accepted the bill at all (Chalmers and Guest, pp 79 and 91; cf *Decroix Verley et Cie v Meyer & Co* (1890) 25 QBD 343 at 347, per Bowen LJ; affd [1891] AC 520). As to the liability of the drawer and any indorser where a qualified acceptance is taken by the holder, see s 44.

Can a 'stranger' be liable on the bill?

G & H Montage GmbH v Irvani [1990] 2 All ER 225, Court of Appeal

The plaintiffs drew bills of exchange in Germany which were accepted in Iran. The defendant 'backed' the bills in Iran by signing the back of each bill. The bills were returned to the plaintiffs in Germany who, with the defendant's authority, added an 'aval' or guarantee in favour of the drawer by inserting the words 'bon pour aval pour les tires' (good as guarantee for the drawees) above the defendant's signature on the back of the bills. The bills were expressed to be payable to the plaintiff's order in London but when presented for payment they were dishonoured. The plaintiffs sued the defendant on his 'aval'. The Court of Appeal, upholding the decision of Saville J, found for the plaintiffs. The case turned on issues of conflict of laws. In particular, the Court of Appeal held that the legal effect of the 'aval' was determined by s 72(2), or by analogy thereto, by German law as the law of the place were the contract of 'aval' was made. Under German law, the 'aval' was treated as a guarantee by the defendant to the plaintiffs of payment by the drawees.

Mustill LJ:

Signature by way of 'aval'
The placing of a signature on a bill of exchange by someone who is neither drawer nor acceptor coupled with delivery of the bill thus signed is a potential source of liability in two directions. First, towards those who subsequently become holders of the bill. Second, towards prior parties, including in particular the drawer.

English law distinguishes between the liabilities of a signatory who is a holder of the bill and of one who is not. Where the person signing is a holder, then his signature will be that of an indorser, and his liability is defined by s 55(2)(a) of the 1882 Act as follows:

> The indorser of a bill by indorsing it – (a) Engages that on due presentment it shall be accepted and paid according to its tenor, and that if it be dishonoured he will compensate the holder or a subsequent indorser who is compelled to pay it, provided that the requisite proceedings on dishonour be duly taken . . .

As stated in *Byles on Bills of Exchange* (26th ed, 1988) p 198, 'Every indorser of a bill is in the nature of a new drawer . . .' Evidently the indorser will not be liable to the drawer as such, whatever his liability to that person as named payee and holder may be (*Byles* p 200).

Where the party is not the holder of the bill, but a stranger to it, he may incur liabilities in more than one way. (I omit from consideration the liabilities of persons who sign as agents, or as accommodation parties, or for honour only, since these are not material to the present case.) Where the stranger simply 'backs' the bill by appending his signature without qualification or explanation, his position is prima facie governed by s 56 of the 1882 Act as follows:

> Where a person signs a bill otherwise than as drawer or acceptor, he thereby incurs the liabilities of an indorser to a holder in due course.

Thus, the quasi-indorser, or anomalous indorser, as he had been described, will be liable to subsequent parties in the event of dishonour, even if at the time of indorsement the drawer has not yet signed: see s 20. But he will not by his signature alone incur liability to the drawer/payee. Additional facts may, however, serve to create such a liability in two ways.

First, there may be an explicit indication that the signature is intended to bind the stranger as a guarantor of a liability on the bill. If so, and if sufficient particulars of the guarantee are given to constitute a memorandum or note in writing for the purpose of s 4 of the Statute of Frauds (1677), the guarantee may be enforced as such, independently of any liability of the signatory as a party to the bill.

Second, the courts have found it possible, by an ingenious use of the Act, to make the signatory liable to the drawer/payee as guarantor for the acceptor, on proof that this is what the parties intended, even in the absence of a writing sufficient to satisfy the Statute of Frauds. *Gerald McDonald & Co v Nash & Co* [1924] AC 625, [1924] All ER Rep 601 arose from a sale by McDonalds to Archer & Co of goods for which it transpired the latter were unable to pay. Nash agreed to provide finance to enable the transaction to be completed. To give effect to this agreement, McDonalds drew bills on Archer, payable to McDonalds' order. Archer accepted the bills and Nash indorsed them and handed them to McDonalds. When it became clear that some of the bills would go unpaid by Archer, McDonalds indorsed their own name (whether in blank or to their own order does not appear) on each bill over the signature of Nash. When the bills were presented for payment to Archer, they were dishonoured, and McDonalds then claimed payment from Nash as indorsers.

It is unnecessary to go into great detail as to the reasoning of the House of Lords in upholding McDonalds' claim. Suffice it to say that it proceeded by the following stages. (1) At the time when Nash indorsed the bills McDonalds had not themselves signed their own names, so as to make the bills payable to anyone other than themselves. (2) Nash could not therefore have been holders in due course. (3) But it was the intention of the parties that Nash by signing the bills should become liable to McDonalds or to other payees of the bills. (4) The bills were therefore incomplete. (5) Under s 20 of the 1882 Act McDonalds as possessors of the incomplete bill had authority to fill it up in any way they thought fit. (6) They exercised this authority by signing their own names as indorsers, thus completing the chain of parties. (7) Although this act took place after the indorsement by Nash, its effect was to make the bill complete ab initio, so that retrospectively Nash could be treated as holders at the moment when they added their indorsement. (8) Nash were therefore liable to McDonalds as payees. (9) Nash could be treated as having waived the right of recourse against McDonalds (as drawers) which would otherwise have defeated McDonalds' claim by circuity of action.

Thus, although in *Steele v M'Kinlay* (1880) 5 App Cas 754 a somewhat similar claim had failed, the proof (absent in *Steele*) that Nash had been intended to sign as surety for the acceptors took the case out of s 56, and enabled a prior party to sue as indorser, proof which, it may be noted, did not depend on any written memorandum sufficient to satisfy the statute.

Other systems of law have no need for this device, since their laws recognise the concept of an 'aval'. This is most conveniently illustrated by some extracts from the English text and Annex I to the Convention providing a Uniform Law for Bills of Exchange and Promissory Notes (Geneva, 7 June 1930, 143 LoNTS 257):

Article   30

Payment of a bill of exchange may be guaranteed by an 'aval' as to the whole or part of its amount.

This guarantee may be given by a third person or even by a person who has signed as a party to the bill.

Article 31

The 'aval' is given either on the bill itself or on an 'allonge'.

It is expressed by the words 'good as aval' ('*bon pour aval*') or by any other equivalent formula. It is signed by the giver of the 'aval'.

It is deemed to be constituted by the mere signature of the giver of the 'aval' placed on the face of the bill, except in the case of the signature of the drawee or of the drawer.

An 'aval' must specify for whose account it is given. In default of this, it is deemed to be given for the drawer.

Article 32

The giver of an 'aval' is bound in the same manner as the person for whom he has become guarantor.

His undertaking is valid even when the liability which he has guaranteed is inoperative for any reason other than defect of form.

He has, when he pays a bill of exchange, the rights arising out of the bill of exchange against the person guaranteed and against those who are liable to the latter on the bill of exchange.

Thus, the party who has given an aval for the acceptor (the party for whom the aval will usually be given) is liable to the drawer, without the need to establish a guarantee in writing or to create retrospectively, through the notion of the bill being 'incomplete', an unbroken chain of indorsements.

Turning to the two foreign laws in contention here, Germany has enacted legislation in close conformity with the 1930 convention. It has been found convenient throughout to work from the text of the convention, rather than an ad hoc translation of the German statute, and I will take the same course. In particular, I prefer to use the term 'aval' rather than 'bill of exchange guarantee' (a rendering of 'Wechselbürgschaft'), because the latter may tend to beg some questions relevant to the appeal.

The gist of the expert evidence of German law, if I correctly understand it, is that if placed on the front of the bill a bare signature by a stranger will operate as an aval, but will not do so if placed on the reverse, unless qualified by words showing that an aval is what it is intended to be: art 31, third paragraph. If not so qualified, it will have a similar effect to an 'anomalous' indorsement under English law, making the signatory liable to subsequent, but not prior, parties to the bill.

[Woolf and Purchas LJJ delivered concurring judgments.]

NOTES

1. Mustill LJ went on to hold (Woolf and Purchas LJJ agreeing) that as the liability sued on was deemed by German law to be a liability on the bill, the requirement of s 4 of the Statute of Frauds was irrelevant (following *McCall Bros Ltd v Hargreaves* [1932] 2 KB 423 at 429–430, [1932] All ER Rep 854 at 857, per Goddard J). In any event, even if the Statute of Frauds did apply, Mustill LJ held that the bills themselves were sufficient writings to satisfy the requirement of s 4 (at 238–239).

2. Mustill LJ noted that under s 56 the quasi-indorser will only be liable to subsequent parties and that he will not by his signature alone be liable to the drawer/payee. Why should it be so restrictively interpreted? For a wider interpretation of the wording of the section, see Goode, p 457 and Byles, p 199.

3. This restrictive interpretation of s 56 has forced the courts to develop the device used in *Gerald McDonald & Co v Nash & Co* [1924] AC 625, when there is extrinsic evidence to establish an intention to make the signatory liable to prior parties. The desire to remedy a perceived injustice has meant that the courts have been prepared to overlook the strict requirement of s 31(3) that an indorsement is completed by delivery. As Professor Goode points out, the payee would not have parted with the bill to the quasi-indorser after completing the bill by indorsing it with his own signature above that of the quasi-indorser (Goode, p 458).

4. For the Government's proposal to recognise a guarantee given by way of an aval, see below, p 543.

A 'transferor by delivery' is also a stranger to the bill. He is the transferor of a bearer bill who transfers it by mere delivery (s 58(1)), although a holder who presents the bill for payment to the drawer is not a transferor by delivery (*Guaranty Trust Co of New York v Hannay & Co* [1918] 2 KB 623 at 631–632). As the transferor by delivery does not sign the bill he is not liable on it (s 58(2)), although in the case of a cheque delivered to a bank for collection he may be liable on the bill because of the effect of s 2 of the Cheques Act 1957. The transferor may incur liability outside the bill for on transfer he warrants to his immediate transferee (provided the transferee is a holder for value), that the bill is what it purports to be, that he has a right to transfer it and that he is not aware of any fact which renders it valueless (s 58(3)). The fact that a claim against a transferor by delivery is for breach of warranty arising outside the bill means that:

(1) the claim is not for the amount of the bill but for damages or restitution of money paid on a total failure of consideration; and
(2) the transferor by delivery may be able to meet the claim with a counterclaim on the underlying contract.

QUESTION

In his article 'The Nature of the Negotiable Instrument' (1983) 18 Israel LR 49 at p 70, Aharon Barak notes that s 58 (or rather its Israeli equivalent) 'is no more than a repetition of the general law of sale and its place is there, not in the law of negotiable instruments.' Is s 58, therefore, a redundant provision?

9 Discharge of the bill

A bill can be discharged by any of the following methods:

(1) payment in due course by or on behalf of the drawee or acceptor (s 59);
(2) the acceptor becoming the holder of the bill in his own right at or after maturity (s 61);
(3) express waiver by the holder of his rights against the acceptor at or after maturity (s 62);
(4) intentional cancellation of the bill by the holder when this is apparent from the bill itself (s 63); and
(5) in certain circumstances, the material alteration of the bill without the assent of the parties liable on it (s 64).

Can the acceptor of a discharged bill, or the maker of a discharged note, incur any further liability on the instrument if it is transferred to a bona fide purchaser for value without notice of the discharge?

Glasscock v Balls (1889) 24 QBD 13, Court of Appeal

As security for a debt, the defendant gave to W a promissory note payable on demand to W's order. On becoming further indebted to W, the defendant executed a mortgage in favour of W to secure all his indebtedness, including the debt already secured by the promissory note. W then transferred the mortgage to H and received from him a sum equal to the amount of the defendant's total indebtedness to W. As security for a debt owed by W to the plaintiff, W indorsed and delivered the promissory note to the plaintiff who took it without knowledge of the previous transactions. The plaintiff's claim on the note against the defendant was upheld by Lord Coleridge CJ. The defendant appealed.

Lord Esher MR: In this case the plaintiff sues the maker of a promissory note payable on demand as indorsee. It was admitted that the plaintiff was indorsee of the note for value without notice of anything that had occurred. The plaintiff cannot be said to have taken the note when overdue, because it was not shewn that payment was ever applied for, and the cases shew that such a note is not to be treated as overdue merely because it is payable on demand and bears date some time back. Under such circumstances prima facie the indorsee for value without notice is entitled to recover on the note. It lies on the defendant to bring the case within some recognised rule which would prevent such an indorsee from recovering upon the note. . . . If a negotiable instrument remains current, even though it has been paid, there is nothing to prevent a person to whom it has been indorsed for value without knowledge that it has been paid from suing . . . the note here has not been paid. Nothing has happened which would prove a plea of payment. Something has happened which would entitle the maker to certain rights as against the payee, but which is not payment of the note. The maker might be entitled to an injunction to prevent the payee from suing on the note, but there has not been a payment of the note. It was said by the defendant's counsel that the note was extinguished. I cannot say I understand the meaning of the term 'extinguished' as used in the argument. I never heard of a plea of extinguishment of a bill or note. . . . No other principle could be suggested by the defendant under which the case could be brought, and therefore it must come under the general principle that the maker of the note, having issued it and allowed it to be in circulation as a negotiable instrument, is liable upon it to an indorsee for value without notice of anything wrong. For these reasons I think the appeal must be dismissed.

[Lindley LJ delivered a concurring judgment.
Lopes LJ concurred.]

NOTES

1. Even though W applied the money received from H in satisfaction of the defendant's indebtedness, the note was not discharged by payment in due course. Payment had not been made by the maker of the note, nor had it been made to the holder as required by s 59(1).

2. Lord Esher's remarks as to the rights of a holder in due course who takes a negotiable instrument after it has been paid are clearly obiter dicta. In any event, if a bill, or note, is payable at a fixed date and the holder transfers it after maturity, the transferee could not be a holder in due course as he would take the instrument after it had become overdue (s 29(1)(a)). The issue seems, therefore, to arise only with regard to a bill, or note, payable on demand which will not be overdue unless it has been in circulation for an unreasonable period of time (s 36(3)). Even then, the holder of a discharged bill, or note, will probably not be a holder in due course. Under s 36(1), which applies to promissory notes by virtue of s 89(1), where a bill is negotiable in its origin it continues to be negotiable 'until it has been . . . (b) discharged by payment or otherwise'. Chalmers and Guest (pp 482–483) state that the section infers that a bill, or note, which has been discharged by payment in due course ceases thereafter to be negotiable and that the bill could not then be 'negotiated' to a holder in due course as required by s 29(1)(b). Cf L Kadirgamar in (1959) 22 MLR 146 at pp 149–153 who, alternatively, goes on to argue that if a promissory note has been discharged by payment and the maker fails to obtain the instrument, or fails to note on it that it has been paid, then he may be estopped (by negligence or by representation) from setting up the payment as a defence to a claim on the note by a holder who takes it for value and without notice (pp 153–163).

3. If an order bill is indorsed and transferred after discharge, the indorser will be precluded by s 55(2)(c) from denying to his immediate or subsequent indorsee that the bill was at the time of his indorsement a valid and subsisting bill. If a bearer bill is transferred after discharge, the transferor will be liable to his transferee for value for breach of warranty under s 58(3).

   What happens if the drawee or acceptor of an order bill pays someone who has taken the bill under a forged or unauthorised indorsement? As the payee will not be a 'holder' (due to s 24), the bill is not discharged by payment (subject to the special protection given to bankers, see Chapter 18). The true owner can turn to the drawee/acceptor for payment forcing the latter to attempt to recover their original payment from the erroneous payee as money paid under a mistake of fact. Similar problems arise if a drawee banker pays a cheque after the drawer has countermanded his original order to pay. If the recipient knew of the mistake as to the facts at the time he received the payment he will be ordered to make restoration (*Kendal v Wood* (1871) LR 6 Exch 243). But what if the payment was received in good faith and in ignorance of the mistake?

Barclays Bank Ltd v W J Simms, Son & Cooke (Southern) Ltd [1980] QB 677, Queen's Bench Division

The first defendants contracted to do certain building works for a housing association. On the issue of an interim certificate of completion of some of the work, the association sent the first defendants a cheque for £24,000 drawn on the plaintiffs. At all times there were sufficient funds in the first defendants' account held with the plaintiffs to meet the cheque. The following day the National Westminster Bank, exercising its powers under a debenture, appointed the second defendant as receiver over the property and assets of the first defendants. On hearing of the receiver's appointment, the association instructed the plaintiffs not to pay the cheque. Due to a clerical error, the plaintiffs overlooked the stop order and paid the cheque when presented by the receiver. The plaintiffs demanded repayment of the £24,000 from the defendants.

Robert Goff J: . . . This case raises for decision the question whether a bank, which overlooks its customer's instructions to stop payment of a cheque and in consequence pays the cheque on presentation, can recover the money from the payee as having been paid under a mistake of fact. The point is one on which there is no decision in this country; and it is a point, I was told, of considerable importance to bankers, not only because it is an everyday hazard that customers' instructions may be overlooked, but because modern technology, rather than eliminating the risk, has if anything increased it.

[After setting out the facts and reviewing, inter alia, the decisions of the House of Lords in *Kleinwort Sons & Co v Dunlop Rubber Co* (1907) 97 LT 263; *Kerrison v Glyn, Mills, Currie & Co* (1911) 81 LJKB 465 and *R E Jones Ltd v Waring and Gillow Ltd* [1926] AC 670, his Lordship continued:]

From this formidable line of authority certain simple principles can, in my judgment, be deduced: (1) If a person pays money to another under a mistake of fact which causes him to make the payment, he is prima facie entitled to recover it as money paid under a mistake of fact. (2) His claim may however fail if (a) the payer intends that the payee shall have the money at all events, whether the fact be true or false, or is deemed in law so to intend; or (b) the payment is made for good consideration, in particular if the money is paid to discharge, and does discharge, a debt owed to the payee (or a principal on whose behalf he is authorised to receive the payment) by the payer or by a third party by whom he is authorised to discharge the debt; or (c) the payee has changed his position in good faith, or is deemed in law to have done so. . . .

I have ignored, in stating the principle of recovery, defences of general application in the law of restitution, for example where public policy precludes restitution. . . .

Where a bank pays a cheque drawn upon it by a customer of the bank, in what circumstances may the bank recover the payment from the payee on the ground that it was paid under a mistake of fact?

It is a basic obligation owed by a bank to its customer that it will honour on presentation cheques drawn by the customer on the bank, provided that there are sufficient funds in the customer's account to meet the cheque, or the bank has agreed to provide the customer with overdraft facilities sufficient to meet the cheque. Where the bank honours such a cheque, it acts within its mandate, with the result that the bank is entitled to debit the customer's account with the amount of the cheque, and further that the bank's payment is effective to discharge the obligation of the customer to the payee on the cheque, because the bank has paid the cheque with the authority of the customer.

In other circumstances, the bank is under no obligation to honour its customer's cheques. If however a customer draws a cheque on the bank without funds in his account or agreed overdraft facilities sufficient to meet it, the cheque on presentation constitutes a request to the bank to provide overdraft facilities sufficient to meet the cheque. The bank has an option whether or not to comply with that request. If it declines to do so, it acts entirely within its rights and no legal consequences follow as between the bank and its customer. If however the bank pays the cheque, it accepts the request and the payment has the same legal consequences as if the payment had been made pursuant to previously agreed overdraft facilities; the payment is made within the bank's mandate, and in particular the bank is entitled to debit the customer's account, and the bank's payment discharges the customer's obligation to the payee on the cheque.

In other cases, however, a bank which pays a cheque drawn or purported to be drawn by its customer pays without mandate. A bank does so if, for example, it overlooks or ignores notice of its customer's death, or if it pays a cheque bearing the forged signature of its customer as drawer, but, more important for present purposes, a bank will pay without mandate if it overlooks or ignores notice of countermand of the customer who has drawn the cheque. In such cases the bank, if it pays the cheque, pays without mandate from its customer; and unless the customer is able to and does ratify the payment, the bank cannot debit the customer's account, nor will its payment be effective to discharge the obligation (if any) of the customer on the cheque, because the bank had no authority to discharge such obligation.

It is against the background of these principles, which were not in dispute before me, that I have to consider the position of a bank which pays a cheque under a mistake of fact. In such a case, the crucial question is, in my judgment, whether the payment was with or without mandate. The two typical situations, which exemplify payment with or without mandate, arise first where the bank pays in the mistaken belief that there are sufficient funds or overdraft facilities to meet the cheque, and second where the bank overlooks notice of countermand given by the customer. In each case, there is a mistake by the bank which causes the bank to make the payment. But in the first case, the effect of the bank's payment is to accept the customer's request for overdraft facilities; the payment is therefore within the bank's mandate, with the result that not only is the bank entitled to have recourse to its customer, but the customer's obligation to the payee is discharged. It follows that the payee has given consideration for the payment; with the consequence that, although the payment has been caused by the bank's mistake, the money is irrecoverable from the payee unless the transaction of payment is itself set aside. Although the bank is unable to recover the money, it has a right of recourse to its customer. In the second case, however, the bank's payment is without mandate. The bank has no recourse to its customer; and the debt of the customer to the payee on the cheque is not discharged. Prima facie, the bank is entitled to recover the money from the payee, unless the payee has changed his position in good faith, or is deemed in law to have done so. . . .

If a bank pays a cheque under a mistake of fact, in what circumstances has the payee a good defence to the bank's claim to recover the money, on the principle in Cocks v Masterman (1829) 9 B & C 902?

The authorities on this topic have recently been analysed by Kerr J in *National Westminster Bank Ltd v Barclays Bank International Ltd* [1975] QB 654, an analysis which I gratefully adopt and which makes it unnecessary for me to burden this judgment with a full analysis of the authorities. The case before Kerr J was concerned with a claim by the plaintiff bank to recover from the defendant bank a sum paid by it on a forged cheque presented by the defendant bank on behalf of a customer for special collection, which the plaintiff bank had paid to the defendant bank in ignorance of the forgery, and the defendant bank had then credited to its customer's account. A principal question in the case was whether the plaintiff bank was estopped from claiming repayment by a representation, in honouring the cheque, that the cheque was genuine. Kerr J, in holding that the bank made no such representation and was not so estopped, considered the line of cases, commencing with the decision of Lord Mansfield in *Price v Neal* (1762) 3 Burr 1354, in which payments of bills of exchange which contained forged signatures had been held irrecoverable on a number of grounds. The early cases on the topic culminated in the leading case of *Cocks v Masterman* (1829) 9 B & C 902. In that case the plaintiff bankers paid a bill which purported to have been accepted by their customer, in ignorance of the fact that the acceptance was forged – a fact they did not discover until the day after payment. It was held by the Court of King's Bench that they could not recover the money from the defendants, the holders' bankers. Bayley J, who delivered the judgment of the court, said, at pp 908–909:

. . . we are all of opinion that the holder of a bill is entitled to know, on the day when it becomes due, whether it is an honoured or dishonoured bill, and that, if he receive the money and is suffered to retain it during the whole of that day, the parties who paid it cannot recover it back. The holder, indeed, is not bound by law (if the bill be dishonoured by the acceptor) to take any steps against the other parties to the bill till the day after it is dishonoured. But he is entitled so to do, if he thinks fit, and the parties who pay the bill ought not by their negligence to deprive the holder of any right or privilege. If we were to hold that the plaintiffs were entitled to recover, it would be in effect saying that the plaintiffs might deprive the holder of a bill of his right to take steps against the parties to the bill on the day when it becomes due.

The principle to be derived from this case is probably that, if the plaintiff fails to give notice on the day of payment that the bill contained a forged signature and that the money, having been paid in ignorance of that fact, is being claimed back, the defendant is deprived of the opportunity of giving notice of dishonour on the day when the bill falls due, and so is deemed to have changed his position and has a good defence to the claim on that ground. But, whatever the precise basis of the defence, it is clearly founded on the need for the defendant to give notice of dishonour; and it can therefore have no application where notice of dishonour is not required. Thus in *Imperial Bank of Canada v Bank of Hamilton* [1903] AC 49, it was held by the Privy Council that the defence had no application to an unendorsed cheque in which the amount of the cheque had been fraudulently increased by the drawer after it had been certified. The cheque was regarded as a total forgery, and not as a negotiable instrument at all. Lord Lindley, who delivered the advice of the Board, said, at p 58:

> The cheque for the larger amount was a simple forgery; and Bauer, the drawer and forger, was not entitled to any notice of its dishonour by non-payment. There were no indorsers to whom notice of dishonour had to be given. The law as to the necessity of giving notice of dishonour has therefore no application. The rule laid down in *Cocks v Masterman* (1829) 9 B & C 902, and recently reasserted in even wider language by Mathew J in *London and River Plate Bank Ltd v Bank of Liverpool Ltd* [1896] 1 QB 7, has reference to negotiable instruments, on the dishonour of which notice has to be given to some one, namely, to some drawer or indorser, who would be discharged from liability unless such notice were given in proper time. Their Lordships are not aware of any authority for applying so stringent a rule to any other cases. Assuming it to be as stringent as is alleged in such cases as those above described, their Lordships are not prepared to extend it to other cases where notice of the mistake is given in reasonable time, and no loss has been occasioned by the delay in giving it.

Likewise, in *National Westminster Bank Ltd v Barclays Bank International Ltd* [1975] QB 654, Kerr J held that the defence had no application in the case which he had to consider of a wholly forged cheque, which was also not a negotiable instrument at all. . . .

It is therefore a prerequisite of the application of the defence that the defendant should be under a duty to give notice of dishonour. The provisions regarding notice of dishonour in the Bills of Exchange Act 1882 are contained in ss 48 to 50 of the Act. In s 50(2) are set out the circumstances in which notice of dishonour is dispensed with. For present purposes, the relevant provision is contained in s 50(2)(c), which provides (inter alia) that notice of dishonour is dispensed with, as regards the drawer, where the drawer has countermanded payment. It follows that in the case of a simple unendorsed cheque, payment of which is countermanded by the drawer, notice of dishonour is not required; and in such a case the payee cannot invoke the defence established in *Cocks v Masterman* (1829) 9 B & C 902.

It is to be observed that, in *Imperial Bank of Canada v Bank of Hamilton* [1903] AC 49, Lord Lindley described the rule laid down in *Cocks v Masterman* as a stringent rule. It is not merely stringent, but very technical. It is possible that if, in due course, full recognition is accorded to the defence of change of position, there will be no further need for any such stringent rule and the law can be reformulated on a more rational and less technical basis. Whether the law will hereafter develop in this way remains to be seen.

IV. *Application of the foregoing principles to the present case*
In the light of the above principles, it is plain that in the present case the plaintiff bank is entitled to succeed in its claim. First, it is clear that the mistake of the bank, in overlooking the drawer's instruction to stop payment of the cheque, caused the bank to pay the cheque. Second, since the drawer had in fact countermanded payment, the bank was acting without mandate and so the payment was not effective to discharge the drawer's obligation on the cheque; from this it follows that the payee gave no consideration for the payment, and the

claim cannot be defeated on that ground. Third, there is no evidence of any actual change of position on the part of either of the defendants or on the part of the National Westminster Bank; and, since notice of dishonour is not required in a case such as this, the payee is not deemed to have changed his position by reason of lapse of time in notifying them of the plaintiff's error and claiming repayment.

I must confess that I am happy to be able to reach the conclusion that the money is recoverable by the plaintiff bank. If the bank had not failed to overlook its customer's instructions, the cheque would have been returned by it marked 'Orders not to pay,' and there would have followed a perfectly bona fide dispute between the association and the receiver on the question, arising on the terms of the building contract, whether the association was entitled to stop the cheque – which ought to be the real dispute in the case. If the plaintiff bank had been unable to recover the money, not only would that dispute not have been ventilated and resolved on its merits but, in the absence of ratification by the association, the plaintiff bank would have had no recourse to the association. Indeed, if under the terms of the building contract the money had not been due to the defendant company, non-recovery by the plaintiff bank would have meant quite simply a windfall for the preferred creditors of the defendant company at the plaintiff bank's expense. As however I have held that the money is recoverable, the situation is as it should have been; nobody is harmed, and the true dispute between the association and the receiver can be resolved on its merits.

NOTES

1. As a specific technical defence turning on the holder's prejudice in not being able to give notice of dishonour to prior parties, the rule in *Cocks v Masterman* is flawed. Section 50(1) provides that delay in giving notice of dishonour is excused where the delay is caused by circumstances beyond the control of the party giving notice, and is not imputable to his default, misconduct, or negligence. If the holder gives notice of dishonour when informed that the payment was made in mistake of the facts then, under s 50(1), he should not be prejudiced by the delay in giving such notice.

2. For as long as English law did not recognise any general defence of change of position, the rule in *Cocks v Masterman* had to be based on the technical ground of failure to give notice of dishonour. In *Barclays Bank v Simms*, Goff J recognised that this could all change if full recognition was accorded to the general defence. This came with *Lipkin Gorman v Karpnale Ltd* [1991] 2 AC 548 where the House of Lords finally recognised that a general defence of change of position in good faith is available against restitution claims based on unjust enrichment of the defendant. Although their Lordships were at pains to point out that they did not wish to define the scope of the defence in abstract terms, but to let it develop on a case by case basis, Lord Goff (as he now is) did emphasise (at 580) 'that the defence is available to a person whose position has so changed that it would be inequitable in all the circumstances to require him to make restitution, or alternatively to make restitution in full'. This would mean that if the holder, who had been wrongly paid, had actually suffered prejudice because, for example, he had lost an immediate right of recourse against a prior party who had since become insolvent, the defence of change of position would apply. In so far as the rule in *Cocks v Masterman* can be justified on this wider ground it should now be regarded as a specific application of the general defence. For further discussion of the *Lipkin Gorman* case, see W Cornish [1991] CLJ 407, P Watts (1991) 107 LQR 521, P Birks [1991] LMCLQ 473 and E McKendrick (1992) 55 MLR 377.

3. Professor Goode has been particularly critical of the decision in *Barclays Bank v Simms*. In (1981) 97 LQR 254 at pp 255–256 he argued that:

> . . . the defendants ought to have succeeded on two grounds, neither of which appears to have been argued. The first is that whilst the countermand of payment terminated the bank's *actual* authority to pay the cheque, the payee was entitled to rely on the bank's continued *apparent* authority to make payment, so that this was effective to discharge the drawer's liability to the payee on the cheque. The second is that a payee who gives up a cheque on which he has a valid claim in exchange for payment inevitably suffers a change of position, for he no longer has the instrument in his hands, and any claim he wishes to pursue against the drawer will have to be on the original consideration, not on the cheque, so that he loses valuable rights. It will further be argued that if the claim had been dismissed the rights of the parties could then have been adjusted by reference to the principle of subrogation, without unjust enrichment of the drawer or unjust detriment to the bank.

Although Professor Goode's submissions may have the merits of encouraging certainty and finality in transactions involving apparently valid commercial paper, they have themselves been subjected to criticism by Lord Goff and Professor Jones in *The Law of Restitution* (4th ed, 1993) (hereafter referred to as 'Goff & Jones'), pp 139–140. For further comments on this case, see A Tettenborn (1980) 130 NLJ 273 and P Matthews (1980) 130 NLJ 587.

4. Other grounds for denying a restitutionary claim for money paid under a mistake of fact include:

(1) if the payee presented the instrument as agent and has since remitted the proceeds to his principal – the payor can only look to the principal, and not the agent, for repayment (*Buller v Harrison* (1777) 2 Cowp 565 at 568); and

(2) if the payee is estopped from alleging that he made the payment under a mistake (although mere payment of money cannot in itself constitute a representation which will estop the payer from recovering payment: Goff & Jones, p 747).

Whether these specific defences will now be subsumed under the general defence of change of position remains to be seen.

5. It is a general rule of English law that payments made under a mistake of law, as opposed to fact, are not recoverable (*Bilbie v Lumley* (1802) 2 East 469). The rule does not apply in most other common law jurisdictions, see, eg, *Air Canada v British Columbia* (1989) 59 DLR (4d) 161, Supreme Court of Canada; *David Securities Pty Ltd v Commonwealth Bank of Australia* (1992) 109 ALR 57, High Court of Australia, noted by G Jones [1993] CLJ 225; P Birks (1993) 108 LQR 164; and A Burrows (1993) 13 OJLS 584. Furthermore, the Law Commission have provisionally recommended that the approach for mistake of law should be equated to that for mistake of fact (Law Com CP No 120 (1991)). See generally, *Woolwich Equitable Building Society v IRC* [1993] AC 70, noted by J Beatson (1993) 109 LQR 1, P Birks [1992] PL 580, E McKendrick [1993] LMCLQ 88 and G Virgo [1993] CLJ 31.

6. Money paid by a bank under a mistake of fact may be traced and recovered in equity. For such an equitable tracing remedy to get off the ground the bank must establish the existence of a fiduciary relationship (or equitable right of property). This should not be difficult where a bank has made a payment under a mistake of fact. In *Chase Manhattan Bank NA v Israel-British Bank (London) Ltd* [1981] Ch

105, the plaintiff bank made two payments of US $2 million to the defendant bank. The second payment was as a result of a clerical error. The defendant later become insolvent but Goulding J held that the plaintiff could trace its payment into the defendant's assets in priority to the general creditors. Goulding J held that the plaintiff retained an equitable proprietary interest in the money and that the defendant was subject to a fiduciary duty to the plaintiff (criticised by A Tettenborn in [1982] CLJ 272, but recently approved by Hobhouse J in *Westdeutsche Landesbank Girozentrale v Islington Borough Council* and *Kleinwort Benson Ltd v Sandwell Borough Council* (1993) Times, 23 February, noted by A Burrows (1993) 143 NLJ 480 and D Cowan [1993] LMCLQ 300; affd (1993) Times, 30 December). It may also be possible for a bank to trace a mistaken payment at common law. But common law tracing is only available where the bank's money has not been mixed with other money (*Agip (Africa) Ltd v Jackson* [1990] Ch 265; affd [1991] Ch 547 (noted by C Harpum [1990] CLJ 217 and [1991] CLJ 409)). Mixing does not prevent tracing in equity (*El Ajou v Dollar Land Holdings plc* [1993] 3 All ER 717; revsd on other grounds (1994) Times, 3 January). However, equitable tracing is only available where it is possible for the bank to 'identify' an asset in the recipient's hands which represents, in mixed or unmixed form, the money paid by mistake (*Re Diplock* [1948] Ch 465; cf *Space Investments Ltd v Canadian Imperial Bank of Commerce* [1986] 1 WLR 1072 at 1074, per Lord Templeman (criticised by R M Goode (1987) 103 LQR 433 at pp 446–447; D Hayton (1990) 106 LQR 87 at p 101), recently applied in *Liggett v Kensington* [1993] 1 NZLR 257 (NZ CA) (noted by P Zohrab [1993] NZ Law Journal 294). On tracing generally, see Hanbury and Martin *Modern Equity* (14th ed, 1993), pp 640–671; A Burrows *The Law of Restitution* (1993), pp 57–76; R M Goode (1976) 92 LQR 360 and 528.

QUESTION

What are the rights and obligations of a drawee or acceptor who pays a bearer bill to a holder who is not its true owner?

10 Reform

In 1987 the Government, together with the Bank of England, commissioned a Review of Banking Services Law and Practice. The Review Committee's report was published in 1989: (1989) Cm 622. Amongst its recommendations, the Review Committee proposed a new Negotiable Instruments Act (based on the language and style of the 1882 Act) covering not only bills of exchange and promissory notes but also, insofar as their negotiability is concerned, all other negotiable instruments.

In 1990 the Government presented a White Paper which set out its response to the Report of the Review Committee: (1990) Cm 1026. The Government rejected the Review Committee's recommendation to extend the 1882 Act to embrace other negotiable instruments but, following the Review Committee's recommendations, it stated its intention, when the Parliamentary timetable permits, to make the following changes to the law relating to negotiable instruments:

(1) To amend the 1882 Act so that the expression 'a sum certain in money' (see ss 3(1) and 83(1)) is defined to include 'a monetary unit of account established by an inter-governmental institution' or by agreement with two or more states.

The amendment is intended to facilitate the use of instruments denominated in units of account like European Currency Units (ECUs) which probably fall outside the existing definition of a bill of exchange or promissory note. Cf A Berg [1991] JIBFL (November) 538.

(2) To amend the 1882 Act so that the mandatory requirement for noting and protesting a dishonoured foreign bill is abolished and replaced by a simplified voluntary procedure.

(3) To amend the 1882 Act to recognise a guarantee given by way of an aval.

(4) To amend the 1882 Act to allow notice of dishonour to be given by electronic communication or by telecommunication.

(5) To legislate to give transactions in 'dematerialised' instruments (ie issued and traded in purely electronic form) the same status as transactions in negotiable instruments generally. The Government considered that it was already possible, within the framework of existing legislation, to engage in screen-based transfers of negotiable instruments held in a paper form in a central depositary. However, it concluded that existing legislation would not necessarily apply to the trading of an obligation not contained in a written instrument.

These proposals for reform have yet to be implemented. However, on 1 October 1990 the Bank of England's Central Moneymarkets Office Service came into operation. The Service provides its members with a central depository for money market instruments (in paper form) and an electronic book-entry transfer system. By eliminating the handling of paper between its members the Service provides a speedier, more efficient and more secure way of transferring money market instruments and producing the associated payment instructions.

CHAPTER 17

Banks and their customers

In this chapter we will concentrate on the relationship of banker and customer. To place this relationship in its proper context, we will begin with an outline of the way banking activities are controlled in the United Kingdom.

1 Banking regulation

Prior to 1979 supervision of the UK banking system was operated primarily on a non-statutory basis. The Bank of England (the Bank) operated a self-regulatory system based on personal knowledge, mutual trust and co-operation. The system worked reasonably well when the UK banking community was relatively small and homogeneous but was unsuited to the rapid expansion of the banking sector in the 1960s and 1970s.

The Banking Act 1979 placed the Bank's system of informal regulation on a statutory footing, at least in so far as deposit-taking was concerned. The Act was born out of the secondary banking crisis of the mid-1970s when unsupervised deposit-taking institutions, which had 'borrowed short and lent long', faced a liquidity crisis and also out of the first EEC Banking Directive 77/780 which demanded harmony in controls of credit institutions throughout the member states of the EEC. The Act prohibited the taking of a deposit in the course of a deposit-taking business unless it was taken by an exempt institution or was an exempt transaction. Under s 2(1) of the Act, exempt institutions were the Bank, recognised banks, licensed institutions (generally known as 'licensed deposit-takers') and certain bodies listed in Sch 1 of the Act, such as the central banks of the EEC countries and building societies. The Bank was given power to 'recognise' banks and 'license' deposit-takers according to criteria laid down in Sch 2 of the Act. The Bank was also given power to supervise an institution's continuing ability to satisfy the conditions for authorisation. However, it was clear from the collapse of Johnson Matthey Bankers Ltd (a recognised bank) in 1984 that recognised banks were not subject to as rigorous supervision as licensed deposit-takers.

The collapse of Johnson Matthey Bankers Ltd led to the Banking Act 1987 which abolished the two-tier division between recognised banks and licensed deposit-takers replacing it with a sole category of 'authorised institutions'. Save for certain institutions exempted by s 4 of the Act (including building societies which are regulated by the Building Societies Act 1986), only an institution authorised by the Bank may accept a deposit in the UK in the course of carrying on a deposit-taking business (s 3(1)). An institution will be authorised provided the Bank is satisfied that the criteria laid down in Sch 3 of the Act (as amended) have been met (s 9(2)). These criteria are primarily concerned with the fitness of the applicant's directors, controllers or managers to conduct the type of business involved and they aim to ensure that the business itself will be conducted with prudence, integrity and skill. Additionally, an applicant must have initial capital of not less than ECU 5 million.

The Banking Act 1987 contains many of the features of the 1979 Act. As with the 1979 Act, its main objective is depositor protection. The term 'deposit' and 'deposit-taking business' are defined in the Act (ss 5 and 6). The Act does not seek to regulate deposits paid by way of security or as an advance or part payment under a contract of sale, or hire, or 'other provision of property or services' (see *SCF Finance Co Ltd v Masri (No 2)* [1987] QB 1002, CA). The Banking Act 1987 continues the depositor protection scheme, established by the 1979 Act, whereby depositors are compensated in the event of a bank failing. The scheme guarantees that in such circumstances a depositor will receive back 75 per cent of any deposit up to £20,000 (ss 50–66). The House of Lords has recently held in *Deposit Protection Board v Dalia* (1994) Times, 20 May, that, for these purposes, a 'depositor' is the person who originally made the deposit, including his personal representatives and trustee in bankruptcy, but that an assignee of the whole or part of the debt represented by the deposit falls outside the scheme.

Further changes in UK bank regulation have resulted from the implementation of the EC Single Market in Banking. The EC Second Banking Coordination Directive 89/646 (which member states were required to implement by 1 January 1993) introduced the concept of a single banking licence enabling a bank (or 'credit institution') incorporated in a member state to enjoy mutual recognition throughout the Community by virtue of recognition in its home country. Once the appropriate licence or authorisation is granted by the home supervisor, the bank can establish and offer certain 'listed' banking services (including acceptance of deposits and other repayable funds from the public and most ordinary types of banking business) in any Community country without first having to obtain host country authorisation. The main burden of the continued supervision of the bank's activities is then placed on the home supervisor and not the host state.

The Banking Coordination (Second Council Directive) Regulations 1992 (SI 1992/3218), which came into force on 1 January 1993, implement the Directive in the UK by making the necessary amendments to the Banking Act 1987. Under the Regulations, a *European institution* (defined as a 'credit institution' whose principal place of business is in the member state in which it is formed or incorporated, which holds an authorisation issued by the supervisory authority of that state, and which has given to this authority notice of its intention to carry on listed banking activities in the UK) is effectively excluded from the general provisions of the Banking Act 1987. Subject to certain procedural requirements, the prohibition imposed under s 3(1) of the 1987 Act on the acceptance of deposits from the public in the course of a deposit taking business does not apply to European institutions (reg 5(1)). The changes introduced by the new Regulations are considered further by E P Ellinger in [1993] JBL 271.

To ensure the necessary harmonisation of prudential controls across member states, the Second Banking Coordination Directive is supplemented by the 'Own Funds' Directive 89/299, the 'Solvency Ratio' Directive 89/647, and the new Directive on Deposit Guarantee Schemes. For further details, see *The Single Market and the Law of Banking* (1991), edited by R Cranston.

Banking Act 1987

1. (1) The Bank of England (in this Act referred to as 'the Bank') shall have the powers conferred on it by this Act and the duty generally to supervise the institutions authorised by it in the exercise of those powers.

(2) It shall also be the duty of the Bank to keep under review the operation of this Act and developments in the field of banking which appear to it to be relevant to the exercise of its powers and the discharge of its duties.

. . .

(4) Neither the Bank nor any person who is a member of its Court of Directors or who is, or is acting as, an officer or servant of the Bank shall be liable in damages for anything done or omitted in the discharge or purported discharge of the functions of the Bank under this Act unless it is shown that the act or omission was in bad faith.

. . .

2. . . . (7) Section 1(4) above shall apply to an act or omission by a member of the Board [of Banking Supervision] in the discharge or purported discharge of his functions under this section as it applies to an act or omission of a person there mentioned in the discharge or purported discharge of the functions of the Bank.

NOTES

1. After an institution has been authorised the Bank can ensure that it observes proper standards of practice by exercising a range of powers given to it under the Act. These include: power to demand that an institution produce an accountant's report on any matter on which the Bank requires information (s 39), power to appoint competent persons to investigate the affairs of an authorised institution (ss 41–44), power to control the publication of any deposit advertisement issued or proposed to be issued by an authorised institution (s 33(2)) and power to present a petition for the winding up of an authorised institution (s 92). To assist the Bank in the discharge of its duties a Board of Banking Supervision has been established whose members include the Governor, Deputy Governor and Executive Director of the Bank, as well as six independent members.

2. Does a supervisory authority owe a depositor a duty of care? Section 1(4) has made the question somewhat less important than it used to be, although it should be noted that the immunity only extends to suit for liability in damages and 'does not prevent an application for judicial review, nor does it exclude claims in respect of acts or omissions shown to be in bad faith' (Graham Penn *Banking Supervision: Regulation of the UK Banking Sector under the Banking Act 1987* (1989), p 22). In any event the difficulties of establishing that the supervisory authority owes a duty of care to depositors were made clear in *Yuen Kun Yeu v A-G of Hong Kong* [1988] AC 175, PC. In that case the Privy Council held that the Hong Kong Commissioner of Deposit-taking Companies owed no duty of care to persons who might make deposits in companies subject to the licensing and regulation provisions of the Deposit-taking Companies Ordinance. The depositors alleged that the Commissioner had been negligent in registering the company concerned or in failing to revoke that registration in circumstances where it was alleged the Commissioner should have appreciated that the company was not fit to carry on a deposit-taking business. The Privy Council rejected these allegations holding that '. . . the Ordinance placed a duty on the commissioner to supervise deposit-taking companies in the general public interest, but no special responsibility towards individual members of the public' (at 787). In *Minories Finance Ltd v Arthur*

Young (a firm) [1989] 2 All ER 105 it was submitted before Saville J that the *Yuen Kun Yeu* case was conclusive authority against the proposition that the Bank owed a duty of care to depositors in the UK. Whilst it did not prove necessary for Saville J to decide the issue, he noted that '. . . [a]lthough this submission is formidable, I am not persuaded that it is so strong that the contrary argument can simply be dismissed as unsustainable. The Privy Council were concerned with a Hong Kong ordinance; the present case concerns a different supervisiory banking authority in a different country . . .' (at 111). However, the Privy Council followed the *Yuen Kun Yeu* case in *Davis v Radcliffe* [1990] 1 WLR 821 in holding that the Isle of Man Finance Board and the Treasurer owed no duty to plaintiffs who had deposited money in an Isle of Man bank licensed under the Isle of Man Banking Act 1975.

3. Following the collapse of the Bank of Credit and Commerce International in 1991 amid widespread allegations of fraud, the Chancellor of the Exchequer and the Governor of the Bank of England asked Lord Justice Bingham to report on the supervision of BCCI under the Banking Acts. In his report, *Inquiry into the Supervision of the Bank of Credit and Commerce International* (October 1992), Lord Justice Bingham made a number of serious criticisms of the way the Bank of England had supervised BCCI. As a result of these criticisms, the liquidators of BCCI, suing on behalf of the bank's depositors, commenced legal proceedings against the Bank of England alleging negligent supervision of BCCI (the action has yet to come to trial). To avoid the defence of statutory immunity under s 1(4) of the Banking Act 1987, the liquidators have alleged that the Bank of England acted in bad faith. It is part of the Bank's defence that it was unaware, and should not have been aware, of the problems at BCCI until it received a report from BCCI's auditors immediately before the bank collapsed. This has raised the question of whether an auditor should be placed under a legal duty to report to the Bank of England upon matters which may affect the continued authorisation of a bank under the Banking Act. Section 47 of the Banking Act 1987 gives the auditors of an authorised institution statutory immunity from any action for breach of duty for communicating to the Bank of England in good faith any information or opinion on a matter of which they become aware in their capacity as auditors and which relates to their client's business or affairs. But until recently an auditor was under no legal duty to report on such matters to the Bank of England. However, since 1 May 1994, following a recommendation made by Lord Justice Bingham, accountants who are auditors of authorised institutions are now under a statutory duty to report to the Bank of England matters of which they have become aware in their capacity as auditors where they have reasonable cause to believe that the institution concerned may not be meeting one or more of the minimum criteria for authorisation in Sch 3 to the Banking Act 1987 (as amended) and that the matters are likely to be of a material significance for the exercise of the Bank's regulatory functions. (For comparative purposes see *Deloitte Haskins & Sells v National Mutual Life Nominees Ltd* [1993] AC 774, where the Privy Council had to determine the extent of an auditor's statutory duty to report to regulators under New Zealand law.)

4. For a detailed commentary on the Banking Act 1987, see Graham Penn *Banking Supervision: Regulation of the UK Banking Sector under the Banking Act 1987* (1989). See also, J J Norton (ed) *Bank Regulation and Supervision in the 1990s* (1991); K McGuire 'Emergent Trends in Bank Supervision in the United Kingdom' (1993) 56 MLR 669.

2 What is a 'bank'?

United Dominions Trust Ltd v Kirkwood [1966] 2 QB 431, Court of Appeal

UDT was a well established finance house with high standing. UDT lent £5,000 to Lonsdale Motors Ltd to enable them to buy cars to put in their showroom to sell. In return Lonsdale Motors Ltd accepted five bills of exchange, each for £1,000, drawn on them by UDT. The defendant was the managing director of Lonsdale Motors Ltd and he indorsed the bills. The bills were not met on presentation and, Lonsdale Motors Ltd having gone into liquidation, UDT sued the defendant as indorsee. The defendant's only defence was that UDT was an unregistered moneylender and that the loan was illegal as it contravened the provisions of the Moneylenders Act 1900. The case turned on whether UDT was 'bona fide carrying on the business of banking' within the meaning of s 6(d) of the Moneylenders Act 1900 so as to exempt it from the provisions of the Act. Mocatta J found for UDT and the defendant appealed.

Lord Denning MR: . . . Parliament has conferred many privileges on 'banks' and 'bankers' but it has never defined what is a 'bank' and who is a 'banker'. It has said many times that a banker is a person who carries on 'the business of banking,' but it has never told us what is the business of banking. It has imposed penalties on persons who describe themselves as a 'bank' or 'bankers' when they are not, but it has never told us how to decide whether or not they are bankers.

The characteristics of banking
Seeing that there is no statutory definition of banking, we must do the best we can to find out the usual characteristics which go to make up the business of banking. In the eighteenth century, before cheques came into common use, the principal characteristics were that the banker accepted the money of others on the terms that the persons who deposited it could have it back again from the banker when they asked for it, sometimes on demand, at other times on notice, according to the stipulation made at the time of deposit; and meanwhile the banker was at liberty to make use of the money by lending it out at interest or investing it on mortgage or otherwise. Thus, Dr Johnson in 1755 in his dictionary defined a 'bank' as a 'place where money is laid up to be called for occasionally' and a 'banker' as 'one that traffics in money, one that keeps or manages a bank.' Those characteristics continued for a long time to dominate thought on the subject. Thus, in 1914, Isaacs J in the High Court of Australia said that

> The essential characteristics of the business of banking . . . may be described as the collection of money by receiving deposits on loan, repayable when and as expressly or impliedly agreed upon, and the utilisation of the money so collected by lending it again in such sums as are required': see *State Savings Bank of Victoria Comrs v Permewan Wright & Co Ltd* ((1915) 19 CLR 457 at 470–471).

You will notice that those characteristics do not mention the use of cheques, or the keeping of current accounts. Accordingly, we find in the courts cases in which a company was held to carry on the business of banking even though it issued no cheques and kept no current accounts but only issued deposit receipts, repayable on notice (see *Re Shields' Estate, Bank of Ireland (Governor & Co) Petitioners*) ([1901] 1 IR 172), or only kept deposit accounts from which the depositors could withdraw their money on demand or on notice, this being on production of a passbook, not by cheque: see *Re Bottomgate Industrial Co-operative Society* ((1891) 65 LT 712); *State Savings Bank of Victoria Comrs v Permewan Wright & Co Ltd* ((1915) 19 CLR 457). If that were still the law, it would mean that the building societies were all bankers.

The march of time has taken us far beyond those cases of 50 years ago. Money is now paid and received by cheque to such an extent that no person can be considered a banker unless he handles cheques as freely as cash. A customer nowadays who wishes to pay money into his bank takes with him his cash and the cheques, crossed and uncrossed, payable to him. Whereas in the old days it was a characteristic of a banker that he should receive *money* for deposit, it is nowadays a characteristic that he should receive *cheques for collection* on behalf of his customer. How otherwise is the customer to pay his money into the bank? It is the only practicable means, particularly in the case of crossed cheques. Next, when a customer wishes to withdraw the money which he has deposited or to pay his creditors with it, he does it in most cases by drawing a cheque on the bank. Occasionally he does it by a draft on the bank or a written order. Whereas in the old days he might withdraw it on production of a passbook and no cheque, it is nowadays a characteristic of a bank that the customer should be able to withdraw it by cheque, draft or order. This view has gradually gained acceptance: see *Re District Savings Bank Ltd, ex p Coe* ((1861) 3 De GF & J 335, at 338), per Turner LJ; *Re Shields' Estate* ([1901] 1 IR 172 at 195), per Lord Ashbourne.

In 1924 Aitkin LJ gave a modern picture of a characteristic banking account in *Joachimson v Swiss Bank Corpn* ([1921] 3 KB 110 at 127):

> The bank undertakes to receive money and collect bills for its customer's account. The proceeds so received are not to be held in trust for the customer, but the bank borrows the proceeds and undertakes to repay them. The promise to repay is to repay at the branch of the bank where the account is kept, and during banking hours. It includes a promise to repay any part of the amount due against the written order of the customer addressed to the bank at the branch . . . bankers never do make a payment to a customer in respect of a current account except on demand.

This was followed in 1948 by the *Bank of Chettinad Ltd of Colombo v IT Comrs, Colombo* ([1948] AC 378 at 383), where the Privy Council accepted the Ceylon description of a 'banking company' as

> a company which carries on as its principal business the accepting of deposits of money on current account or otherwise, subject to withdrawal by cheque, draft or order.

And now the Shorter Oxford Dictionary gives the meaning of a 'bank' in modern use as:

> An establishment for the custody of money received from, or on behalf of, its customers. Its essential duty is to pay their drafts on it: its profits arise from the use of money left unemployed by them.

There are, therefore, two characteristics usually found in bankers today: (i) They accept money from, and collect cheques for, their customers and place them to their credit; (ii) They honour cheques or orders drawn on them by their customers when presented for payment and debit their customers accordingly. These two characteristics carry with them also a third, namely: (iii) They keep current accounts, or something of that nature, in their books in which the credits and debits are entered.

Those three characteristics are much the same as those stated in *Paget's Law of Banking*, 6th ed (1961), p 8:

> No-one and nobody, corporate or otherwise, can be a 'banker' who does not (i) take current accounts; (ii) pay cheques drawn on himself; (iii) collect cheques for his customers.

[Lord Denning then reviewed the evidence holding that: (1) whilst UDT did receive money on deposit, these were short-term investments repayable on agreed dates after maturity and were not repayable on notice; and (2) there was no evidence that UDT collected cheques on behalf of customers. He continued:]

Long acceptance as bankers
Thus far the evidence adduced by UDT would not suffice to show that it has the usual characteristics of a banker. But it must be remembered that a recital of *usual* characteristics is not equivalent to a definition. The *usual* characteristics are not the *sole* characteristics. There are other characteristics which go to make a banker. In particular stability, soundness and probity. Parliament would not dream of granting the special privileges of a banker to a

ramshackle concern which had no reserves or whose methods were dubious. Like many other beings, a banker is easier to recognise than to define. In case of doubt, it is, I think, permissible to look at the reputation of the firm amongst ordinary intelligent commercial men. If they recognise it as carrying on the business of banking, that should turn the scale. Here it is that UDT comes out well. It has for many years been accepted in the most responsible quarters as being a bank. There was impressive evidence from four of the Big Five Banks that they regarded UDT as a bank; and that UDT was generally regarded in the City of London as a bank. These bankers accorded to UDT all the privileges of being a banker. They paid crossed cheques presented by UDT. They gave it clearance house facilities. They answered references regarding customers, and such like. . . .

Reputation may exclude a person from being a banker: so also it may make him one. Our commercial law has been founded on the opinion of merchants. Lord Mansfield himself used to have his own special jurymen of the City of London who sat regularly with him. He took their opinion as to what was the practice: and laid down the law accordingly – see, for instance, *Lewis v Rucker*, and Campbell, Lives of the Chief Justices, ii, p 407. I would follow his example. In such a matter as this, when Parliament has given no guidance, we cannot do better than look at the reputation of the concern amongst intelligent men of commerce.

This reputation has, moreover, formed the basis of practice which we should not disturb. When merchants have established a course of business which is running smoothly and well with no inconvenience or injustice, it is not for the judges to put a spoke in the wheel and bring it to a halt. Even if someone is able to point to a flaw, the courts should not seize on it so as to invalidate past transactions or produce confusion. So you will find it said from the time of Lord Coke that the law so favours the public good that it will in some cases permit a common error to pass for right: see the 4th Institute, p 240. Communis error facit jus. That is to say, when business has been regulated on the faith of it and the position of parties altered in consequence (Lord Blackburn on several occasions so said): see *R v Sussex Justices* ((1862) 2 B & S 664 at 680); *Davidson v Sinclair* ((1878) 3 App Cas 765 at 788); *Dalton v Angus* ((1881) 6 App Cas 740 at 812). This applies with especial force to commercial practice. When it has grown up and become established, the courts will overlook suggested defects and support it rather than throw it down. Thus it will enforce commercial credits rather than hold them bad for want of consideration. It is a maxim of English law to give effect to everything which appears to have been established for a considerable course of time and to presume that what has been done was done of right, and not in wrong: see *Gibson v Doeg* ((1857) 2 H & N 615 at 623). This maxim is of particular force here where innumerable transactions have been effected on the faith of UDT being a banker. UDT has itself made loans of millions of pounds which are recoverable if its claim to be a banker is correct; but irrecoverable if it is not. Are we to throw all these over? It has described itself on all its documents and cheques as 'bankers' and continues so to do. But if it is not a banker, it is guilty of a criminal offence for each document it so issues. Are we to suggest that it should be prosecuted now? Thousands of its customers have claimed repayment of tax on form R.62 on the basis that it was a banker and the revenue have paid. Has all this been unlawful? Are all its transactions to be thrown into confusion by the suggestion now made for the first time that it is an unregistered moneylender? Rather than come to any such conclusion, we should presume that it has done whatever is necessary to constitute it a banker.

Harman LJ (dissenting): . . . It is notoriously difficult to define the business of banking and no statute has attempted it. Perhaps the best is that stated in the Privy Council case of *Bank of Chettinad Ltd of Colombo v IT Comrs, Colombo* ([1948] AC 378 at 383). The definition there stated as applying in Ceylon is said in the judgment of the board to conflict in no way with the meaning attached to the word 'banking' in England in 1932, which I think has not changed today. The definition is

a company which carries on as its principal business the accepting of deposits of money on current account or otherwise, subject to withdrawal by cheque, draft or order.

All the witnesses called on UDT's behalf agreed that the keeping of what they called 'current accounts' was an essential part of a banker's business. This involved, according to all the banking witnesses, the collection of customers' cheques.

[Harman LJ then reviewed the evidence and held that UDT did not satisfy this definition of the business of banking. He continued:]

UDT relied also on its reputation and called impressive evidence to show that it was regarded by the Big Five Banks, by the Board of Trade and by the Inland Revenue Commissioners as being a banker. It had a clearing house number and various banker's privileges, for instance, that of compounding for the stamp duty on its cheques. I confess to having been impressed by this evidence: it was said in a dissenting judgment in *Davies v Kennedy* ((1868) 17 WR 305) that a banker is one who is considered in commercial circles to be one, but on the whole I have come to the conclusion that reputation alone is not enough. There must be some performance behind it. The other bankers, seeing UDT's cheques in circulation through the clearing office, did not have any call to inquire into the nature of the business being done as we have had to do and I reluctantly conclude that, on the evidence at present before us, this defence succeeds and that the appeal ought to be allowed accordingly. I regret to find myself unable to subscribe to the views expressed by the Master of the Rolls on this topic. His judgment seems to me to prove that UDT is not a banker.

There remains, however, the fact that UDT is apparently reputed in commercial and financial circles as being a banker. It has for many years enjoyed that reputation and its accompanying privileges and has styled itself bankers. If it is not so, it has been committing a criminal offence and the very large amounts owing to it are all irrecoverable in law. I cannot conceal from myself the serious consequences of my decision on a concern of the highest repute and undoubted probity.

Diplock LJ: . . . [UDT] asserts that it is bona fide carrying on the business of banking and is therefore not a 'moneylender' within the meaning of the Act. It has been lending money in the course of its business for many years. It has been treated as if it were a banker by government departments and by commercial men, including those who indisputably are themselves bankers. To hold that all these have been mistaken throughout the years it not a decision which a court should reach lightly.

But this, in my view, is not an issue on which communis error jus facere potest. Evidence that a company is generally regarded by commercial men and bankers as being itself a banker is some evidence that it is carrying on the business of banking. If supported by even slight evidence of some banking transactions which it carries out, it may be sufficient proof that in law it is a banker. But if there is actual evidence of the business which it does carry on and relies upon as constituting the business of banking and the court is driven to the conclusion that this, at any rate, is not banking business, the court cannot abdicate its duty so to decide because commercial men and bankers, however numerous or influential, have thought it to be a banker upon whatever information may have been available to them. . . .

What makes a person a banker is not what he does with the money of which he obtains the use, as, for instance, by lending it at interest (as mentioned by Holmes LJ [*Re Shields' Estate, Bank of Ireland (Governor & Co), Petitioners* [1901] 1 IR 172 at 207] and Isaacs J [*State Savings Bank of Victoria Comrs v Permewan, Wright & Co Ltd* (1915) 19 CLR 457 at 471]), by investing it, by discounting bills, etc, but the terms upon which he obtains from other persons, his banking customers, loans of money which he can use as he thinks fit. What I think is common to all modern definitions and essential to the carrying on of the business of banking is that the banker should accept from his customers loans of money on 'deposit,' that is to say, loans for an indefinite period upon running account, repayable as to the whole or any part thereof upon demand by the customer either without notice or upon an agreed period of notice.

Some verbal confusion and perhaps some misunderstanding of the less recent judgments may arise from the fact that an account kept by a banker of his customer's loans made without interest and repayable on demand is nowadays generally called a 'current account,' while the account kept of his customer's loans made at interest and repayable only upon notice is generally known as a 'deposit account.' But accounts of both these types possess the essential characteristics of running accounts of 'deposits' of money by the customer.

Accordingly it is, in my view, essential to the business of banking that a banker should accept money from his customers upon a running account into which sums of money are from time to time paid by the customer and from time to time withdrawn by him by cheque, draft or order. I am inclined to agree with the Master of the Rolls and the author of the current edition of *Paget on Banking*, 6th ed (1961), p 8, that to constitute the business of banking today the banker must also undertake to pay cheques drawn upon himself (the banker) by his customers in favour of third parties up to the amount standing to their credit in their 'current accounts' and to collect cheques for his customers and credit the proceeds to their current accounts. This view of the essential characteristics of the business of banking today is supported by the evidence of the witnesses who were unquestionably bankers who gave expert evidence in the present case. . . .

The . . . question is whether the evidence in this case is sufficient to satisfy the onus which lies upon UDT of proving that it was at the material time in 1961 a 'person bona fide carrying on the business of banking.' . . . But the requirement that his carrying on of the business of banking must be bona fide does, I think, involve two requirements. The first is that the banking transactions which he carries out in the course of his business must not be negligible in size and number when compared with the rest of his business. The second is that the transactions relied upon as constituting the accepting of deposits of money from customers on running account must be genuinely of this legal nature and not a mere disguise for transactions of a different legal nature. The court must look to the true nature of the transactions, not merely to their form.

[Diplock LJ then reviewed the evidence and held that UDT carried out a limited banking business in that some customers used 'current accounts' for the payment of cheques drawn in favour of third parties or collection of cheques drawn by third parties. He continued:]

Once one eliminates the kinds of transactions recorded in the 'current accounts' of Lonsdale Motors Ltd as not being in the legal nature of banking transactions at all, the evidence of Mr Garrett in my judgment leaves a complete lacuna as to whether or not the banking transactions which UDT carries out constitute more than a negligible part of their business.

Is that lacuna capable of being filled by evidence of the reputation which UDT enjoys in banking and commercial circles of being 'bankers'? After anxious reflection I think it is, but for reasons which differ from those which have commended themselves to the Master of the Rolls, for which, with great respect, I cannot find sufficient authority in the cases which he cites. Most transactions of the relevant kind would come to the knowledge of bankers, for the cheques would pass through the clearing or would be specially presented and would involve ancillary transactions between such bankers and UDT. Evidence given by bankers that they have regarded UDT as carrying on the business of banking would thus be based upon transactions undertaken by UDT which would be within the general knowledge of the persons giving evidence. Unless the grounds of the witnesses' belief were probed in cross-examination and shown to be mistaken, such evidence in an ordinary case might be sufficient in itself to establish a prima facie case that UDT was bona fide carrying on the business of banking. . . .

[As there had been no cross-examination of the 'banker' witnesses at the trial as to whether the basis of their evidence was mistaken, Diplock LJ was prepared to assume that the grounds of the witnesses' belief were based on the genuine banking transactions undertaken by UDT and were not based on transactions which were later proved not to have been genuine banking transactions, although thought to be so at the time. He concluded:]

For these reasons I agree with the Master of the Rolls that this appeal should be dismissed. My decision is based entirely upon the state in which the evidence was left at the conclusion of this trial. As between UDT and the defendant, the status of UDT as bankers becomes res judicata – but between these two parties only. It does not follow that if, in some other case, the evidence were more complete or more closely probed, the result would be the same; but it would at least be more satisfactory.

NOTES

1. In his *Modern Banking Law* (1987) Professor Ellinger commented on *UDT v Kirkwood* as follows (p 55):

> It is clear that the three judgments in the *Kirkwood* case take divergent views regarding the importance of reputation for determining whether or not a given institution is a bank. As a rigorous analysis of law, Harman LJ's view is to be preferred. According to the common law definition, a bank is an institution that actually carries on banking business; not an institution which has the reputation of doing so or of being a bank. This definition postulates an objective test. Lord Denning, and to a lesser extent Diplock LJ, propounded a test based on subjective criteria. However, their view derives support from other cases. [See *Stafford v Henry* (1850) Ir 12 Eq 400, *Ex p Coe* (1861) 3 De GF & J 335.]

There must be some doubt as to how much the majority's decision was based on the law and how much it was based on policy. All the merits were with UDT (Kirkwood had no other defence) and the majority were appalled by what would happen if UDT were not recognised as carrying on a banking business. In *UDT v Kirkwood* certainty appears to have been the victim of expediency. For further criticism of this case see M Megrah (1967) 30 MLR 86 and R R Pennington, A H Hudson and J E Mann *Commercial Banking Law* (1978), p 15.

2. *UDT v Kirkwood* involved an assessment of what was meant by the statutory phrase 'bona fide carrying on the business of banking'. *Paget's Law of Banking* (10th ed, 1989) ('Paget') makes the point that the words 'bona fide' are perhaps implicit in every statutory reference to carrying on a banking business (p 125). In the *Kirkwood* case Diplock LJ went some way to explaining what they meant (see above, p 552). Diplock LJ's dictum has since been explained by Lawton LJ in *Re Roe's Legal Charge* [1982] 2 Lloyd's Rep 370. Although Lawton LJ emphasised that he had no intention of defining a bona fide banking business, he did state that an institution could still be regarded as a bank even if:

(1) its banking business was negligible in size compared with that of a clearing bank; and
(2) it carried on business in other fields so long as its banking business was not negligible in size when compared to those other areas of business activity.

3. The Moneylenders Act 1900 was repealed by the Consumer Credit Act 1974, s 192(4) and Sch 5, Part I, as was s 123 of the Companies Act 1967, which enabled financial institutions like UDT to be listed as bankers for the purpose of exemption under the Moneylenders Acts. But *UDT v Kirkwood* remains an important case as some statutes simply refer to a 'bank' or 'banker' or use similar expressions without further definition. See, for example, the Post Office Act 1969, the Insurance Companies Act 1982, the Building Societies Act 1986 and the Income and Corporation Taxes Act 1988. Section 2 of the Bills of Exchange Act 1882 defines a 'banker' to include a body of persons whether incorporated or not who carry on the 'business of banking'. This definition is also important for the Cheques Act 1957 which, by virtue of s 6(1), is to be construed as one with the Bills of Exchange Act 1882. Furthermore, under the general law certain rights are only conferred on a 'bank' or 'banker'. These rights are the banker's lien and banker's right of set-off. Also, if the relationship is one of banker-customer certain incidents may be presumed to attach to it, eg a banker's duty of confidentiality.

4. Some statutes contain their own definition of a 'bank'. With the enactment of the Banking Act 1987 most such statutes simply define a bank as 'an institution authorised under the Banking Act 1987' (see s 108 and Sch 6 of the 1987 Act). See, for example, s 9(1)(a) of the Bankers' Books Evidence Act 1879, s 5(7) of the Agricultural Credits Act 1928 and s 87(1) of the Solicitors Act 1974 (as amended by the Banking Act 1987).

5. By s 67 of the Banking Act 1987, and subject to the exceptions contained in s 68 (eg the National Savings Bank, any penny savings banks, a school bank), only an authorised institution which is a corporation, whose paid-up share capital or undistributable reserves amount to not less than £5 million, may use a name which indicates it is a 'bank'. Similar capital requirements apply to partnerships using 'bank' in their name. It should be noted that under s 67 an institution can be called a 'bank' even though it does not provide all the traditional facilities of a banking business set out in *UDT v Kirkwood*. Under s 69(1) of the 1987 Act, there are restrictions on persons describing themselves as carrying on banking business when they are not authorised institutions (as restricted by s 69(2)) or specifically exempt under the section. However, by s 69(4) of the 1987 Act, s 69(1) 'does not prohibit a person from using the expression "bank" or "banker" (or similar expression) where it is necessary for him to do so in order to be able to assert that he is complying with, or entitled to take advantage of, any enactment, any instrument made under any enactment, any international agreement, any rule of law or any commercial usage or practice which applies to a person by virtue of his being a bank or banker'.

QUESTIONS

1. How does Lord Denning's judgment differ from that of Lord Justice Diplock in the *Kirkwood* case?
2. How relevant are the criteria of a banking business set out in the *Kirkwood* case as the use of cheques declines and funds are transferred increasingly by electronic means (eg by ATMs and EFTPOS; see below, pp 631 ff)?
3. Should there be a uniform functional definition of a 'bank'? See E P Ellinger *Modern Banking Law* (1987), p 75.

3 Who is a 'customer'?

Taxation Comrs v English, Scottish and Australian Bank Ltd [1920] AC 683, Privy Council

A thief stole a cheque payable to bearer from the Commissioner of Taxation. The thief then opened an account at the respondent bank in the name of 'Stuart Thallon'. The next day 'Thallon' paid the stolen cheque into the account and, after it had been cleared, he drew cheques on the proceeds. 'Thallon' then disappeared. The Commissioner brought an action against the bank for conversion of the cheque. In its defence the bank pleaded s 88 of the Bills of Exchange Act 1909 (Commonwealth of Australia), which was similar to s 82 of the Bills of Exchange Act 1882 (now s 4 of the Cheques Act 1957). The Commissioner alleged, inter alia, that 'Thallon' was not a customer within the meaning of the section. Upholding the decision of the Supreme Court of New South Wales, the Privy Council (Viscount Haldane, Lords Buckmaster, Dunedin and Atkinson) held that 'Thallon' was a customer and that the bank came within the protection of the Act.

Lord Dunedin (delivering the advice of the Privy Council): . . . Their Lordships are of opinion that the word 'customer' signifies a relationship in which duration is not of the essence. A person whose money has been accepted by a bank on the footing that they undertake to honour cheques up to the amount standing to his credit is, in the view of their Lordships, a customer of the bank in the sense of the statute, irrespective of whether his connection is of short or long standing. The contrast is not between an habitué and a newcomer, but between a person for whom the bank performs a casual service, such as, for instance, cashing a cheque for a person introduced by one of their customers, and a person who has an account of his own at the bank.

NOTES

1. In *Woods v Martins Bank Ltd* [1959] 1 QB 55, the plaintiff wrote to the defendant bank asking it to collect monies he had ordered a building society to pay to the bank, to pay part of the sum received to a particular company and 'retain to my order the balance of the proceeds'. The bank agreed to comply with the instructions, even though the plaintiff did not have an account with them at the time. Salmon J held that (at 63):

> . . . In my view the defendant bank accepted the instructions contained in this letter as the plaintiff's bankers, and at any rate from that date the relationship of banker and customer existed between them.

And in *Warren Metals Ltd v Colonial Catering Co Ltd* [1975] 1 NZLR 273 (Supreme Court of New Zealand) McMullin J held that (at 276):

> . . . A customer is someone who has an account with a bank or who is in such a relationship with the bank that the relationship of banker and customer exists, even though at that stage he has no account. . . .

2. It would appear from *Woods v Martins Bank Ltd* that a person can become a customer as soon as the bank agrees to open an account for him. But can he ever be a customer if he deals with a bank without intending to open a current or deposit account? For example, would the holder of a credit card issued and operated by a bank be a customer even though he held no account with that bank?

3. The Code of Banking Practice (2nd ed, 1994) (see below, p 562) sets out the standards of good banking practice to be observed by banks, building societies and card issuers when dealing with 'personal customers' in the UK. Although the Code does not purport to give a precise legal or technical definition of the term 'personal customers', it is interesting to note that it intends that term to cover:

> A private individual who maintains an account (including a joint account with another private individual or an account held as an executor or trustee, but excluding the accounts of sole traders, clubs and societies) *or who takes other services from a bank or building society.* [Emphasis added.]

4. The term 'customer' appears in s 75 of the Bills of Exchange Act 1882 and ss 1 and 4 of the Cheques Act 1957. Neither statute defines the term and so the common law definition is of prime importance.

Stoney Stanton Supplies (Coventry) Ltd v Midland Bank Ltd [1966] 2 Lloyd's Rep 373, Court of Appeal

As part of a scheme to defraud a third party, F forged the signature of the directors of the plaintiff company on documents requesting the defendant bank to open an account in the plaintiff company's name. The account was opened. The plaintiff company was unaware of this and at no time was F authorised to act on the company's behalf. Money which should have been paid to the third party was paid into the account and, by forging the signature of one of the plaintiff company's directors on various cheques, F drew out £9,000 for his own use. The plaintiff company subsequently went into liquidation and the liquidator sought to recover the £9,000 from the bank alleging, inter alia, that the bank were the bankers of the plaintiff company and were under a duty to the company to use reasonable care and they failed in that duty. McNair J found for the bank and the liquidator appealed.

Lord Denning MR: . . . As to the claim against the Bank for breach of duty, that too fails, for the simple reason that there was never any relationship of banker and customer. As far as the opening of the account was concerned, it was not taken out by the company but by Fox, who forged all the documents. The company did not authorize it at all. It is quite impossible to hold that there was any relationship of banker and customer between this company and the Bank. The company never authorized anything at all. It is rather like the case of Mr A in *Robinson v Midland Bank Ltd* (1925) 41 TLR 402. Where a person opens an account in the name of another person without any authority so to do, it is quite plain there is no relationship of banker and customer and so no question of breach of duty arises.

[Danckwerts LJ delivered a concurring judgment.
Winn LJ concurred.]

NOTE

In *Thavorn v Bank of Credit and Commerce International SA* [1985] 1 Lloyd's Rep 259 the plaintiff, an elderly woman, opened an account in her nephew's name but stipulated that during her lifetime she was to be the only person authorised to draw on it. Lloyd J held that the aunt was the customer of the bank and that the nephew was merely her nominee (at 263). Contrast this case with *Rowlandson v National Westminster Bank Ltd* [1978] 1 WLR 798 where a woman drew a cheque payable at a bank where she was known, but with which she did not have an account, and explained that the proceeds were a gift for her grandchildren. The bank credited the cheque to an account opened in the grandchildren's names and gave their guardians the power to draw on the account. The guardians were not specifically informed of this arrangement and did not expressly approve of it. However, when the guardians eventually learned of the account one of them did draw a cheque on it. It was held by John Mills QC, sitting as a Deputy High Court Judge, that the bank was in breach of its duty to the grandchildren by allowing that guardian to draw on the account for his own use. As Professor Ellinger has noted '[i]t would appear to follow that a contract of banker and customer came into existence between the defendant bank and the grandchildren, presumably as a result of the tacit approval of the opening of the account by the guardians. The case may, undoubtedly, rest on its exceptional facts' (*Modern Banking Law* (1987), p 80).

QUESTION

In *Stoney Stanton Supplies (Coventry) Ltd v Midland Bank Ltd* (above), who, if anyone, was the bank's customer? See above, pp 138–140.

4 The nature of the banker–customer relationship

Libyan Arab Foreign Bank v Bankers Trust Co [1989] QB 728, Queen's Bench Division

Staughton J: . . . It is elementary, or hornbook law to use an American expression, that the customer does not own any money in a bank. He has a personal and not a real right. Students are taught at an early stage of their studies in the law that it is incorrect to speak of 'all my money in the bank.' See *Foley v Hill* (1848) 2 HL Cas 28, 36, where Lord Cottenham said:

> Money, when paid into a bank, ceases altogether to be the money of the principal . . . it is then the money of the banker, who is bound to return an equivalent by paying a similar sum to that deposited with him when he is asked for it. . . . The money placed in the custody of a banker is, to all intents and purposes, the money of the banker, to do with as he pleases. . . .

Naturally the bank does not retain all the money it receives as cash in its vaults; if it did, there would be no point or profit in being a banker. What the bank does is to have available a sufficient sum in cash to meet all demands that are expected to be made on any particular day.

Joachimson v Swiss Bank Corpn [1921] 3 KB 110, Court of Appeal

On 1 August 1914, one of the partners in the firm of N Joachimson died. As a result, the partnership was dissolved. At the date of dissolution the sum of £2,321 was standing to the credit of the partnership on current account at the defendant bank. At the end of the First World War one of the former partners brought an action in the firm's name to recover that sum. The bank's defence was that, as no demand had been made, no cause of action had accrued to the firm on 1 August 1914 and that, therefore, the action was not maintainable. Roche J found for the firm holding that the debt owing by a banker to his customer could be sued for without any previous demand. The bank appealed.

Bankes LJ: . . . The question whether there was an accrued cause of action on August 1, 1914, depends upon whether a demand upon a banker is necessary before he comes under an obligation to pay his customer the amount standing to the customer's credit on his current account. This sounds as though it was an important question. In a sense no doubt it is, but it is very rarely that the question will in practice arise. In most of the cases in which the question is likely to arise, even if a demand is necessary to complete the cause of action, a writ is a sufficient demand. It is only therefore in the unlikely case of a banker pleading the Statute of Limitations, or in a case like the present where the facts are very special, that the question becomes important. . . .

In the ordinary case of banker and customer their relations depend either entirely or mainly upon an implied contract. . . .

In [*Foley v Hill* (1848) 2 HL Cas 28] the Law Lords expressed their opinions as to the ordinary relation existing between banker and customer, and those opinions are correctly summarized in the headnote as follows: 'The relation between a banker and customer, who pays money into the bank, is the ordinary relation of debtor and creditor, with a superadded obligation arising out of the custom of bankers to honour the customer's drafts; and that relation is not altered by an agreement by the banker to allow the interest on the balances in the bank.' The point which is raised in the present appeal was not mentioned or discussed, either in the Court below or in the House of Lords, and in my opinion the decision cannot be treated as an exhaustive definition of all the obligations arising out of the relation between banker and customer, or as ruling out the possibility of an implied term of that relation, requiring an express demand of repayment as a condition precedent to the right to sue the banker for the amount standing to the credit of the customer's current account. The recent decision of the House of Lords in *London Joint Stock Bank v Macmillan* ([1918] AC 777), approving *Young v Grote* ((1827) 4 Bing 253), affords one striking instance of an obligation implied in the relation of banker and customer to which no reference was made in *Foley v Hill*. . . .

Having regard to the peculiarity of that relation there must be, I consider, quite a number of implied superadded obligations beyond the one specifically mentioned in *Foley v Hill* and *Pott v Clegg* ((1847) 16 M & W 321). Unless this were so, the banker, like any ordinary debtor, must seek out his creditor and repay him his loan immediately it becomes due – that is to say, directly after the customer has paid the money into his account – and the customer, like any ordinary creditor, can demand repayment of the loan by his debtor at any time and any place. It is only necessary in the present case to consider the one question whether there is, arising out of the relation of banker and customer, the implied obligation on the part of the customer to make an actual demand for the amount standing to his credit on current account as a condition precedent to a right to sue for that amount.

[Bankes LJ then reviewed a number of cases, including *Foley v Hill*, which contain dicta to the effect that a customer's cause of action against a bank for repayment of money only accrues when demand has been made. He continued:]

These dicta all favour the contention of the present appellants, and they are supported by the very strong body of expert opinion which was given in evidence in the Court below as to the practice of bankers. Applying Lord Esher's test, as laid down in *Hamlyn v Wood* ([1891] 2 QB 488 at 491), to the question whether the term contended for by the appellants must be implied in the contract between banker and customer, I have no hesitation in saying that it must. It seems to me impossible to imagine the relation between banker and customer, as it exists to-day, without the stipulation that, if the customer seeks to withdraw his loan, he must make application to the banker for it. . . . As no demand for payment in the present case was made on or before August 1, 1914, it follows, in my opinion, that the plaintiffs had no accrued cause of action on that date, and the claim fails on that ground.

Atkin LJ: This case raises the question whether the customer of a bank may sue the banker for the balance standing to the credit of his current account without making a previous demand upon the banker for payment. . . .

The question seems to turn upon the terms of the contract made between banker and customer in ordinary course of business when a current account is opened by the bank. It is said on the one hand that it is a simple contract of loan; it is admitted that there is added, or superadded, an obligation of the bank to honour the customer's drafts to any amount not exceeding the credit balance at any material time; but it is contended that this added obligation does not affect the main contract. The bank has borrowed the money and is under the ordinary obligation of a borrower to repay. The lender can sue for his debt whenever he pleases. I am unable to accept this contention. I think that there is only one contract made between the bank and its customer. The terms of that contract involve obligations on both sides and require careful statement. They appear upon consideration to include the following provisions. The bank undertakes to receive money and to collect bills for its customer's account. The proceeds so received are not to be held in trust for the customer, but the bank borrows the proceeds and undertakes to repay them. The promise to repay is to repay at the branch of the bank where the account is kept, and during banking hours. It includes a promise to repay any part of the amount due against the written order of the customer addressed to the bank at the branch, and as such written orders may be outstanding in the ordinary course of business for two or three days, it is a term of the contract that the bank will not cease to do business with the customer except upon reasonable notice. The customer on his part undertakes to exercise reasonable care in executing his written orders so as not to mislead the bank or to facilitate forgery. I think it is necessarily a term of such contract that the bank is not liable to pay the customer the full amount of his balance until he demands payment from the bank at the branch at which the current account is kept. Whether he must demand it in writing it is not necessary now to determine. The result I have mentioned seems to follow from the ordinary relations of banker and customer, but if it were necessary to fall back upon the course of business and the custom of bankers, I think that it was clearly established by undisputed evidence in this case that bankers never do make a payment to a customer in respect of a current account except upon demand. The contention of the plaintiffs appears to me to ignore the fact that the contract between banker and customer contains special terms, and cannot in its entirety by expressed in the phrasing of an ordinary indebitatus count. . . .

The question appears to me to be in every case, did the parties in fact intend to make the demand a term of the contract? If they did, effect will be given to their contract, whether it be a direct promise to pay or a collateral promise, though in seeking to ascertain their intention the nature of the contract may be material. In the case of such a contract as this, if I have correctly stated the manifold terms of it, it appears to me that the parties must have intended that the money handed to the banker is only payable after a demand. The nature of the contract negatives the duty of the debtor to find out his creditor and pay him his debt. If such a duty existed and were performed, the creditor might be ruined by reason of outstanding cheques being dishonoured. Moreover, payment can only be due, as it appears to me, at the branch where the account is kept, and where the precise liabilities are known. And if this is so, I apprehend that demand at the place where alone the money is payable must be necessary. A decision to the contrary would subvert banking business. . . .

Finally it is perhaps unnecessary to say that the necessity for a demand may be got rid of by special contract or by waiver. A repudiation by a bank of the customer's right to be paid any particular sum would no doubt be a waiver of any demand in respect of such sum.

For these reasons, I am of opinion that the appeal should be allowed, and that judgment should be entered for the defendants on the claim with costs.

[Warrington LJ delivered a concurring judgment.]

NOTES

1. Atkin LJ saw the banker–customer relationship giving rise to 'one contract'. Bankes LJ differed on this point. He felt the relationship of banker and customer was that of debtor and creditor supplemented with a 'number of implied superadded obligations'. Paget notes that 'Atkin LJ's concept of a single contract is the more convincing, and it is this concept which has prevailed' (p 162). Furthermore, in *Tai Hing Cotton Mill Ltd v Liu Chong Hing Bank Ltd* [1985] 2 All ER 947 at 956, PC, Lord Scarman described Atkin LJ's judgment in *Joachimson v Swiss Bank Corpn* as '[t]he classic, though not necessarily exhaustive, analysis of the incidents of the contract [between banker and customer]'. As to other incidents of the contract, not referred to by Atkin LJ, see below generally.

2. Although the banker–customer relationship gives rise to a single contract, that contract may be governed by more than one proper law. The point arose in *Libyan Arab Foreign Bank v Bankers Trust Co* (above, p 557) where a customer had one account in London and another one in New York. Staughton J held that although there was one contract between the bank and its customer it was 'governed in part by the law of England and in part by the law of New York' (at 747). The general rule is that the contract between a bank and its customer is governed by the law of the place where the account is kept, unless there is an agreement to the contrary: *Libyan Arab Foreign Bank v Manufacturers Hanover Trust Co* [1988] 2 Lloyd's Rep 494; *Attock Cement Co Ltd v Romanian Bank for Foreign Trade* [1989] 1 WLR 1147, CA and *Libyan Arab Foreign Bank v Manufacturers Hanover Trust Co (No 2)* [1989] 1 Lloyd's Rep 608. The Contracts (Applicable Law) Act 1990, implementing the Rome Convention on the Law Applicable to Contractual Obligations 1980, does not alter this general rule.

3. *Joachimson v Swiss Bank Corpn* was a case concerned with the contract between a bank and its customer arising out of the central account relationship. Once that relationship is established the bank is bound to provide its customer with certain services. But banks also provide their customers with many other services which fall outside the terms of the contract of debtor and creditor. These additional services are provided under specific or 'special contracts' and although banks generally provide them to their customers, they are not bound to do so. Which services are banks bound to provide to their customers (arising under the central debtor–creditor contract) and which are optional (arising out of a specific agreement)? In *Libyan Arab Foreign Bank v Bankers Trust Co* (above, p 557), Staughton J asked a similar question (at 749):

> What is the customer entitled to demand? In answering that question one must, I think, distinguish between services which a bank is obliged to provide if asked, and services which many bankers habitually do, but are not bound to, provide. For a private customer with a current account I would include in the first category the delivery of cash in legal tender over the bank's counter and the honouring of cheques drawn by the customer. Other services, such as standing orders, direct debits, banker's drafts, letters of credit, automatic cash tills and foreign currency for travel abroad, may be in the second category of services which the bank is not bound to but usually will supply on demand. I need not decide that point. The answer may depend on the circumstances of a particular case.

4. It is clear, therefore, that the relationship of debtor and creditor is not the only relationship which may exist between a bank and its customer. Other relationships which may exist between them include, inter alia, those of:

(1) *principal and agent* (which coexists with that of debtor and creditor) for purposes of a customer's instructions to his banker to carry out particular transactions on his account, eg when drawing a cheque or bill of exchange, the customer, as principal, authorises his bank, as agent, to make payment;

(2) *bailor and bailee* if valuables are left with the bank for safe keeping, eg when a bank provides a safe deposit service; and

(3) *beneficiary and trustee* if a bank receives money as a trustee (but not if the bank is appointed a trustee and, exercising an express power in the trust deed, deposits trust money with itself *qua banker*: see *Space Investments Ltd v Canadian Imperial Bank of Commerce Trust Co (Bahamas) Ltd* [1986] 3 All ER 75 where the Privy Council held that in such circumstances the bank held the money absolutely (being a mere debtor) and that the beneficiaries had no proprietary interest in the money so deposited which gave them priority over other unsecured creditors to the assets of the bank on its insolvency; also see *Ross v Lord Advocate* [1986] 1 WLR 1077 at 1094. For a critical analysis of other aspects of Lord Templeman's speech in *Space Investments*, see R M Goode (1987) 103 LQR 433 at pp 445–447. Also see Penn, Shea and Arora *The Law Relating to Domestic Banking* (1987), Vol 1, para 3.08 which examines the impact of the *Space Investments* case on money deposited with a

bank for the specific purpose of being paid to other persons, ie as in *Barclays Bank Ltd v Quistclose Investments Ltd* [1970] AC 567, see below, p 557).

For further discussion of those exceptional situations when a bank may become a fiduciary in relation to its customer, see below, pp 557 ff.

QUESTIONS

1. Is it necessary for a customer to make a demand in the case of a fixed deposit maturing at a predetermined time?
2. What is the nature of the relationship between a bank and its customer when the customer's account is overdrawn? See E P Ellinger *Modern Banking Law* (1987), pp 83–84.

5 Terms of the banker–customer contract

Banking Services: Law and Practice Report by the Review Committee (Chairman: Professor R B Jack CBE) 1989, Cm 622

2.07 Statute law relating to banking services is limited, and mostly of venerable age; what exists is largely of a technical character, concerned with the usage of cheques and bills of exchange. Thus, the banker–customer relationship has been largely left to implied contract, whose terms have been elucidated by a patchwork of judicial decisions. Much of this case law is again somewhat ancient, and has changed remarkably little over time. Until fairly recently, there had been scant use of express contractual terms agreed between the parties concerned.

2.08 We shall begin by examining the statutory component of banking services law, move onto common law, and finally look at express contract. . . .

2.13 *Express contract*, the third leg of the legal framework, symbolises the modern trend towards a more arms-length relationship between banker and customer, the reasons for which we shall be examining. For the central account relationship, express contract is so far the exception in this country, although we give at Appendix G [terms and conditions of Midland Bank plc] one instance where the principal terms and conditions of that relationship have been reduced to writing for the bank's personal customers. In this area implied contract still, for the most part, holds sway, and the future is far from clear.

2.14 The situation is different when we turn to more sophisticated banking services, and it is here that express contract has been making inroads, in the last two decades, into the traditional implied basis of the relationship. The use of credit cards, introduced in this country in the late 1960's, has normally been governed by express contract. The same is true of cheque guarantee cards, first introduced about the same time, and of automated teller machines (ATM's, which evolved from cash dispensers in the mid-1970's). The national EFT-POS scheme (Electronic Funds Transfer at Point of Sale) will be underpinned by a network of written contracts between the various parties involved, including a contract between the bank as card issuer and its customer as a user of the EFT-POS system. Express contract has also characterised the various bank-to-bank relationships in the clearing system since the setting up of the Association for Payment Clearing Services (APACS) in 1985.

In 1987 the Review Committee chaired by Professor Jack (the Jack Committee) was appointed by the Government and the Bank of England to examine the need for reform of the law and practice relating to the provision of banking services within the UK. It produced its Report in 1989.

When considering proposals for reform, the Jack Committee felt constrained by an overriding need to 'preserve flexibility, so as not to discourage competition and innovation by excessive regulation' (para 4.02). However, within the bounds of this overriding constraint the Jack Committee recognised, inter alia, the need to 'achieve fairness and transparency in the banker–customer relationship' (para 4.04). The Jack Committee recommended a self-regulating code of practice governing banker–customer relations (paras 16.10–16.12). On the issue of communication of a bank's terms and conditions to its customer the Jack Committee concluded as follows:

6.23 It was earlier made clear that there is at present no general legal requirement as to the form in which the banker–customer contract should be expressed. We have ourselves rejected the option of model contract, on the argument that flexibility is needed to maintain competition: banks should, in other words, be allowed room for manoeuvre in how they conduct their customer relations. Such considerations would argue equally against any other kind of uniform procedure imposed from above, such as the standard industry-wide booklet canvassed by the National Consumer Council in their 1983 report 'Banking Services and the Consumer'.

6.24 On two points however we are persuaded of the need for regulation, in order to ensure fairness and transparency in the relationship. First it can be seen that, in areas where banks do choose to set out their terms and conditions in express contract, they will sometimes frame these in a way which, while not perhaps unreasonable in the terms of the Unfair Contract Terms Act 1977 (whose Section 4 sets a 'requirement of reasonableness' for all contracts with consumers), will still slant them somewhat to the banks' advantage: such terms and conditions may, for example, over-stress the rights of the banker on the one hand, and the obligations of the customer on the other. . . . We would therefore look for a standard of best practice that requires a bank, in any communication to its customer of the terms of the contract, to ensure he is given a fair and balanced view of those terms, and of the rights and obligations that exist on each side.

6.25 The second point concerns contract variation. Banks' present terms and conditions will often allow them to change those terms and conditions unilaterally overnight, and present their customers with a *fait accompli* which may be to their disadvantage. We see no case for requiring banks to negotiate changes in contract terms with individual customers, which would clearly be unmanageable, as would a similar requirement applying to the original contract. But we do think it fair to expect that customers are given reasonable notice of any proposals for contract variation, to allow them to make any necessary adjustment. The US EFT Act 1978 requires 21 days, and the Australian code of good practice on EFT 30 days, for this purpose. We would not stipulate a precise period ourselves, but would look for a standard of best practice to be established on the matter.

In its White Paper 'Banking Services Law and Practice' (1990, Cm 1026), the Government accepted the need for a voluntary code of banking practice and welcomed the Jack Committee's recommendations relating to the terms and conditions of the banker–customer contract (Annex 1, paras 1.7–1.9). The result has been that the British Bankers' Association, the Building Societies Association and the Association for Payment Clearing Services have drawn up a Code to promote good banking practice when dealing with *personal* customers (defined above, p 555) in the United Kingdom. The Code is called *Good Banking* and it first came into operation on 16 March 1992 (noted by P Morris [1992] LMCLQ 474). Following a review conducted by an independent Review Committee, the second edition of the Code came into operation on 28 March 1994 (save for para 5.3: see below, p 564).

All further references to the Code in this chapter will be to the second edition.

Although voluntary, by February 1994 the first edition of the Code had been adopted by 289 banks (including all the major UK clearing banks) and building societies. The Review Committee monitors compliance with the Code. A defaulting institution can be reported to its regulator, the Bank of England or the Building Societies Commission. In the case of banks, the Bank of England's *Statement of Principles* (1993) makes it plain that banking authorisation is dependent upon observing 'high ethical standards' which would be called into doubt:

> if the institution fails to comply with the recognised ethical standards of conduct such as those embodied in the various codes of conduct. (Examples of such codes would be the London Code of Conduct for the wholesale markets, . . . the Code of Banking Practice, and the Takeover Code.)

The stated objectives (referred to as 'governing principles') of the Code are:

(1) to set out the standards of good banking practice when dealing with customers;
(2) to require banks, building societies and card issuers to act fairly and reasonably in dealing with their customers;
(3) to require banks, building societies and card issuers to help customers to understand how their accounts operate and promote their understanding of banking services generally; and
(4) to maintain confidence in the security and integrity of banking and card payment systems (para 2.1).

These objectives provide valuable guidelines to the interpretation and application of the substantive provisions of the Code.

Good Banking: Code of Banking Practice (2nd ed, 1994)

4.0 TERMS AND CONDITIONS

4.1 Written terms and conditions of a banking service will be expressed in plain language and will provide a fair and balanced description of the relationship between the customer and bank or building society.

4.2 Banks and building societies will tell customers how any variation of the terms and conditions will be notified. Banks and building societies will give customers reasonable notice before any variation takes effect.

4.3 Banks and building societies should issue to their customers, if there are sufficient changes in a 12 month period to warrant it, a single document to provide a consolidation of the variations made to their terms and conditions over that period.

4.4 Banks and building societies will provide new customers with a written summary or explanation of the key features of the more common services that they provide. This will include an explanation, when accounts are held in the names of more than one customer, of the rights and responsibilities of each customer.

4.5 Banks and building societies will not close customers' accounts without first giving reasonable notice.

4.6 To help customers manage their accounts and check entries, banks and building societies will provide them with regular statements of account. Except where this would be inappropriate to the nature of the account (eg where passbooks are issued) this should be at no less than 12 monthly intervals but customers will be encouraged to request statements at shorter intervals.

[The Code goes on to demand that banks and building societies provide their customers with details of the basis of charges, if any, payable in connection with the operation of their accounts (paras 5.1–5.2). The Code also provides for the publication of interest rates applicable to a customer's account (paras 5.4–5.5). A new paragraph 5.3 provides that banks and building societies must introduce systems to come into effect by 31 December 1996 to ensure that they will give no less than 14 days' notice of the amount to be deducted from their customers' current and savings accounts in respect of interest and charges for account activity that have accumulated during the charging period.]

NOTES

1. Broadly similar provisions to those found in paras 4.0–4.6 apply to banks, building societies and others who provide financial services by means of plastic cards, eg credit cards, charge cards, debit cards (paras 16.1–16.5).

2. Under the Consumer Credit Act 1974, there already exists a limited statutory control on a creditor's power to vary a 'regulated agreement' (essentially one offering credit not exceeding £15,000). Section 82 of the 1974 Act provides that where a regulated agreement contains a power of variation, then no variation can take effect before notice of it is given in the manner prescribed in the Consumer Credit (Notice of Variation of Agreements) Regulations 1977 (SI 1977/328) as amended by SI 1979/661, SI 1979/667. These notice provisions cover overdrafts and credit cards.

3. The next revision of the Code will be completed by March 1997.

Where the customer is a 'consumer', or deals on the bank's written standard terms of business, any term in the banker–customer contract which seeks to exclude or limit the liability of the bank for breach of contract, or allows the bank to render a contractual performance substantially different from that which was reasonably expected, or allows the bank to render no performance at all, will be ineffective except in so far as it satisfies the requirement of reasonableness (Unfair Contract Terms Act 1977, ss 3, 11). However, students should also be aware that under the new EC Directive on Unfair Contract Terms (93/13 EEC, OJ 95, 21/4/93, p 29), which must be implemented in the UK by 1 January 1995, these *and other terms* in the banker–customer contract may be declared not to bind the bank's customer. The Directive applies to unfair terms in consumer contracts which have not been individually negotiated. Article 3(1) provides that for the purposes of the Directive: 'A contract term which has not been individually negotiated shall be regarded as unfair if, contrary to the requirement of good faith, it causes a significant imbalance in the parties' rights and obligations under the contract, to the detriment of the consumer'. An 'indicative and non-exhaustive' list of terms which may be regarded as unfair is set out in the Annex to the Directive (it includes any term allowing the seller or supplier to alter the terms of the contract unilaterally without a valid reason specified in the contract or to alter without a valid reason any characteristics of the product or service to be provided). The important point to note is that the Directive applies to a much broader spectrum of terms than simply 'exclusion' and 'limitation' clauses. The Directive will be particularly relevant to banks using standard form contracts with their personal customers.

6 Bank's duty to honour the customer's mandate

Libyan Arab Foreign Bank v Bankers Trust Co

(See above, p 557.)

Joachimson v Swiss Bank Corpn

(See above, p 557.)

NOTES

1. In *Joachimson v Swiss Bank Corpn*, Atkin LJ left open the question whether the customer's mandate (ie his demand for repayment) need be in writing. Paget submits that the bank should be able to insist upon a written demand (p 200). Today banks usually allow their customers to demand payment in writing (eg by cheque, standing order or direct debit) or by electronic means (eg ATM or EFTPOS). If a cheque is cashed at a branch where the account is not kept, this branch is probably to be considered as discounting or collecting the cheque (*Woodland v Fear* (1857) 7 E & B 519).

2. The bank is only obliged to honour its customer's mandate if the account is actually in credit, or, where it is in debit, if the customer has been granted an overdraft (*Bank of New South Wales v Laing* [1954] AC 135 at 154, PC).

3. A bank may combine a customer's accounts by setting one account off against another to determine the total state of indebtedness between the customer and the bank. This is purely 'an accounting situation' and is not to be confused with the exercise of a banker's lien (*Halesowen Presswork and Assemblies Ltd v National Westminster Bank Ltd* [1971] 1 QB 1 at 46, per Buckley LJ, approved in the House of Lords [1972] AC 785 at 802 and 810). The right is lost if the bank and customer have agreed to keep accounts separate (*Barclays Bank Ltd v Okenarhe* [1966] 2 Lloyd's Rep 87 at 95; contrast the statutory right of set-off under s 323 of the Insolvency Act 1986, which cannot be overridden by contract: House of Lords in *Halesowen*, above, at 805, 809, 824). Such an agreement may be implied, as is usually the case when a customer opens a loan account (*Bradford Old Bank Ltd v Sutcliffe* [1918] 2 KB 833). Combination is also inapplicable where a fund is deposited with the bank for a special purpose of which it has knowledge (*Barclays Bank Ltd v Quistclose Investments Ltd* [1970] AC 567, HL; but compare this case with *Neste Oy v Lloyds Bank plc* [1983] 2 Lloyd's Rep 658 where the bank was entitled to set off the balance in the account). Further, an account opened by a customer as trustee, agent or nominee of another person, may not be combined with the customer's private account (*Union Bank of Australia v Murray-Aynsley* [1898] AC 693). However, the bank may be able to exercise an equitable right of set-off between a personal account and a 'nominee' account, if there is clear and undisputed evidence that the customer entitled to the funds in both accounts was one and the same person (*Uttamchandami v Central Bank of India* (1989) 133 Sol Jo 262, CA; *Bhogal v Punjab National Bank* [1988] 2 All ER 296, CA).

4. A bank is not obliged to combine a customer's accounts held at different branches of the same bank in order to meet a cheque where there are insufficient funds in the account at the branch on which it is drawn (*Garnett v McKewan* (1872) LR 8 Exch 10 at 14). Whether the bank is obliged to combine accounts kept at the same branch remains an open question (compare Penn, Shea and Arora *The Law Relating to Domestic Banking* (1987), Vol 1, p 146 (bank is obliged) with E P Ellinger *Modern Banking Law* (1987), pp 159–160 (bank not obliged)).

5. If the bank dishonours the customer's cheque without good cause the bank will be liable in damages for breach of contract. If the customer is a trader he will recover substantial damages for injury to his reputation without having to prove that he suffered special damage (*Marzetti v Williams* (1830) 1 B & Ad 415). If the customer is not a trader he will only recover nominal damages unless he can prove actual loss (*Gibbons v Westminster Bank* [1939] 2 KB 882; *Rae v Yorkshire Bank plc* [1988] FLR 1, CA). However, this distinction between traders and others is now difficult to justify as certain non-trader members of the public (eg solicitors, accountants, doctors and dentists) may suffer at least as serious damage to their reputation as a trader if their cheques are dishonoured (E P Ellinger *Modern Banking Law* (1987), p 312). A customer may also have an action for libel if a cheque is returned dishonoured due to supposed lack of funds in the customer's account (*Davidson v Barclays Bank Ltd* [1940] 1 All ER 316).

6. When does the bank have 'good cause' to refuse to honour the customer's mandate? The main ground is lack of funds (above) but other grounds include:

(1) The mandate must be unambiguous in form, otherwise the bank may refuse payment (*London Joint Stock Bank Ltd v Macmillan* [1918] AC 777 at 815, per Lord Haldane). Where the mandate is a cheque, the bank may refuse to pay if the cheque is not properly drawn (*Cunliffe Brooks & Co v Blackburn and District Benefit Building Society* (1884) 9 App Cas 857 at 864, per Lord Blackburn).

(2) In the absence of special instructions to the contrary from their customers, it is the practice of banks not to pay cheques which are stale. Usually a cheque is treated as stale if presented for payment six months or more after the date written on it. The practice is so widespread that there is probably a term implied into the banker–customer contract that the bank may refuse to honour a cheque if not presented until an unreasonable time after its date (Penn, Shea, Arora *The Law Relating to Domestic Banking* (1987), Vol 1, p 70).

(3) A bank is entitled to refuse to pay a cheque drawn on it if to do so would involve a breach of duty of care to its customer in carrying out the mandate (see below, p 572). Furthermore, a bank is bound to refuse to pay a demand where to do so would render the bank liable as a constructive trustee (see below, p 579).

(4) Restraint orders under the Drug Trafficking Offences Act 1986 (s 8) and the Prevention of Terrorism (Temporary Provisions) Act 1989 (s 13(8) and Sch 4) will effect the bank's duty to pay on its customer's mandate. In *Re K (Restraint Order)* [1990] 2 QB 298, Otton J held that an order under the Drug Trafficking Offences Act 1986 did not prevent the bank from exercising its right to combine accounts.

(5) A bank may be prevented from honouring its customer's mandate by a garnishee order or a *Mareva* injunction. A garnishee order is an order of the court granted to a judgment creditor, which attaches to funds held by a third

party (eg a bank) who owes money to the judgment debtor (eg the bank's customer). The bank's obligation to honour its customer's cheques ceases if it is served with a garnishee order nisi (the order is first made provisionally) even if the credit balance of the customer exceeds the amount of the judgment (*Rogers v Whiteley* [1892] AC 118), unless the order is stated to be for a limited sum. The order applies to a trust account as well as the customer's private account (*Plunkett v Barclays Bank Ltd* [1936] 2 KB 107). A Mareva injunction freezes the customer's assets when there is a danger that the customer will spend, or otherwise dissipate, those assets to avoid execution of a judgment which may be made against him. If the bank has notice of a *Mareva* injunction directed to the customer then this may suspend the bank's duty to pay its customer's cheques (*Z Ltd v A-Z and AA-LL* [1982] QB 558). However, cheques supported by cheque guarantee cards, and drawn prior to the date the order is served on the bank, fall outside the ambit of the injunction. As the bank is entitled and bound to honour its own collateral obligation to the third party (made via the cheque guarantee card) to pay the cheque, it may debit its customer's account accordingly (*Z Ltd v A-Z and AA-LL*, above, at 592–593, per Kerr LJ). Similarly, Mareva injunctions have been held not to affect a bank's duty to make payment under letters of credit, negotiable instruments and documentary collections, save in very exceptional circumstances (*Z Ltd v A-Z and AA-LL*, above; *Lewis & Peat (Produce) Ltd v Almatu Properties Ltd* [1993] 2 Bank LR 45, CA). It should be noted that the courts are most reluctant to grant a Mareva injunction against a bank itself as this would affect the bank's ability to pay its creditors their due debts (*Polly Peck International plc v Nadir (No 2)* [1992] 4 All ER 769, CA).

(6) The bankruptcy of an individual commences with the day on which the bankruptcy order is made (s 278(a) of the Insolvency Act 1986). From that day the bank no longer has authority to pay the bankrupt customer's cheques, whether or not the bank knows that the order has been made. By s 284(1) of the 1986 Act any payment made by the bankrupt between the presentation of the bankruptcy petition and the vesting of the bankrupt's estate in his trustee (ie the day he is appointed) is void, except to the extent that it is made with the consent of, or is ratified by, the court. If the bank makes a payment which is caught by s 284(1) without knowledge of presentation of the petition, then the court may well ratify it. By s 284(4), the amount paid is irrecoverable if received by the payee before the commencement of the bankruptcy in good faith, for value and without knowledge of the presentation of the petition. The bank may be protected by sub-s (4) if it receives payment into the account after presentation of the petition. The bank is given further protection by s 284(5) which allows it to maintain a debit if the bank pays a bankrupt's cheque after the making of the order, unless the bank did so with notice of the bankruptcy or it is not reasonably practical to recover the amount from the payee (see Paget, p 310).

(7) By s 127 of the Insolvency Act 1986, in a winding-up of a company by the court, any disposition of the company's property made after the commencement of the winding-up is, unless the court otherwise orders, void. The winding-up is deemed to commence on the presentation of the petition, unless it is a voluntary winding-up, which is deemed to commence when the resolution is passed (s 129). If a disposition is made in good faith in the ordinary course of business when the parties are unaware of the presentation of the petition, and it is completed before the winding-up order is made, the court is likely to validate it (unless it can be challenged as a preference). But if the

bank knows of the presentation of the petition and yet pays the company's cheques to third parties in respect of pre-liquidation debts, the payments are unlikely to be validated and the bank will be required to account to the liquidator for those sums (*Re Gray's Inn Construction Co Ltd* [1980] 1 WLR 711, CA: see below, p 917). In these circumstances the bank would be entitled to refuse to honour its customer's cheques without a validation order. A winding-up order terminates the bank's authority to pay its customer's cheques (*National Westminster Bank Ltd v Halesowen Presswork and Assemblies Ltd* [1972] AC 785).

7 Bank's duty to obey the customer's countermand

The converse of the bank's duty to obey the customer's mandate is the bank's obligation to obey his countermand – with regard to cheques, this obligation is defined by statute.

Bills of Exchange Act 1882

75. The duty and authority of a banker to pay a cheque drawn on him by his customer are determined by—
(1) Countermand of payment:
(2) Notice of the customer's death.

Curtice v London City and Midland Bank Ltd [1908] 1 KB 293, Court of Appeal

The plaintiff was a customer of the Willesden Green branch of the defendant bank. He drew a cheque on that branch payable to Jones. After business hours on the same day, the plaintiff telegraphed the branch to stop payment of the cheque. The Post Office's telegram messenger, finding the bank closed, placed the telegram in the bank's letter-box at 6.15 pm. By an oversight, the telegram was not taken out of the letter-box and shown to the branch manager until two days later, by which time the cheque had been paid. The plaintiff then drew a cheque for the whole of the balance of his account, including the amount of the cheque which he had drawn in favour of Jones. The defendant bank dishonoured the cheque and the plaintiff then sued for the whole balance as money had and received. The county court judge found for the plaintiff holding that there had been a good countermand of payment and that decision was upheld on appeal to the Divisional Court. The bank further appealed to the Court of Appeal.

Cozens-Hardy MR: . . . Countermand is really a matter of fact. It means much more than a change of purpose on the part of the customer. It means, in addition, the notification of that change of purpose to the bank. There is no such thing as a constructive countermand in a commercial transaction of this kind.

In my opinion, on the admitted facts of this case, the cheque was not countermanded, although it may well be that it was due to the negligence of the bank that they did not receive notice of the customer's desire to stop the cheque. For such negligence the bank might be liable, but the measure of damage would be by no means the same as in an action for money had and received. I agree with the judgment of A T Lawrence J on this point, and that is sufficient to dispose of the appeal. But as we have had an argument addressed to us as to the effect upon the duty of a bank of the mere receipt of a telegram, I wish to add a few words on that. A telegram may, reasonably and in the ordinary course of business, be acted upon by the bank, at least to the extent of postponing the honouring of the cheque until further inquiry can be made. But I am not satisfied that the bank is bound as a matter of law to accept an unauthenticated telegram as sufficient authority for the serious step of refusing to pay a cheque.

The result is that the appeal is allowed, with costs here and below.

Fletcher Moulton LJ: . . . A banker (although so far as his financial relations to his customer are concerned he stands in the position of debtor and creditor) is for such a purpose as this only a particular type of agent; he is in the possession of money of the customer, and his duty is to obey the directions of the customer as to paying that money out. If an order is given to him he has the ordinary rights of any agent with regard to the mode in which that order shall be given to him. I use the word 'mode' in its widest sense. It has long been held that an order must be unambiguous. If a master chooses to give an order to his servant that bears two meanings, he cannot find fault with his servant for having taken the meaning which it was not in fact intended to bear; and that applies to a banker when receiving orders as much as to agents generally.

Now that principle which applies to the duty of conveying the mandate in a form in which the meaning is unambiguous applies, in my opinion, mutatis mutandis to the question of its authenticity. If the mandate is sent in a form in which a servant, acting reasonably, has no security that the mandate comes from his employer, the employer cannot grumble that he did not act upon it. Authenticity and meaning appear to me, in the general law of agency, to stand on the same footing, subject, of course, to the broad difference of circumstances which are due to the difference of nature of the two. In my opinion a telegram which is only an official but unauthenticated copy of a document, in itself unauthenticated, cannot be said to be necessarily and as a matter of law a mandate communicated in such a way that its provenance is unambiguous. . . .

With regard to the second point, as to the doctrine that there may be in law constructive notice of the meaning of a countermand which has not reached the mind of the servant, I agree entirely with what the Master of the Rolls has said.

Farwell LJ: . . . There is no contract that the banker will do more than honour the cheque. On that is superadded the statute, which shews that the duty and authority of a banker to pay a cheque drawn on him by his customer may be countermanded on notice being given to him. In my opinion that must be actual notice brought to his attention. On the evidence here it is clear that the banker is simply put on inquiry by the receipt of a telegram, and his duty is not to pay at once, but to make inquiries; and, if the mere receipt of a letter or telegram were sufficient countermand, the position of a banker in large business would be most difficult. Supposing a midday post comes in with so many letters that it takes a quarter of an hour (not an unreasonable time) to open them – it is during bank hours, and just as the post comes in or within five minutes afterwards a number of cheques are presented, is it to be said that the banker must thereupon refuse to cash any of those cheques until he has opened all his letters? On the general question of stopping by telegram I am disposed to think that it would depend a great deal on the custom of the bankers, and the agreement, if any, between the customers and their bankers, that business should be conducted by telegram, and this would depend on the evidence in each case. I therefore agree with the result which has been arrived at.

NOTES

1. An example of an ambiguous countermand arose in *Westminster Bank Ltd v Hilton* (1926) 43 TLR 124. In that case the customer telegraphed his bank to stop payment of a post-dated cheque, giving the wrong cheque number but otherwise correctly stating the details of the cheque. In fact, a cheque with the number specified by the customer (which the customer had not intended to stop) had already been paid. As the post-dated cheque (which the customer had intended to stop) had a later serial number than the cheque which had already been paid and was dated one day later than the stop order, the bank concluded that the stop order did not apply to the post-dated cheque and duly paid it, believing it to be a replacement for the other cheque. The House of Lords held the bank had not been negligent in paying the post-dated cheque. Lord Shaw emphasised that as this was a post-dated cheque the onus was on the customer to inform the bank of this fact, which he had not done (at 129–130). If a principal's instructions are ambiguous and can be interpreted in different ways, the agent will be excused if he acted bona fide in one way even if it is not the way intended by his principal (*Ireland v Livingston* (1872) LR 5 HL 395; see above, p 87). However, if the agent has the opportunity to seek clarification from his principal he will not be absolved from liability if he fails to do so (see *Giordano v Royal Bank of Canada* (1973) 38 DLR (3d) 191; *Remfor Industries Ltd v Bank of Montreal* (1978) 90 DLR (3d) 316; cf *Westminster Bank Ltd v Hilton*, above, at 126; *Shapera v Toronto-Dominion Bank* (1970) 17 DLR (3d) 122).

2. A countermand must be given to the branch upon which the cheque is drawn and will be ineffective if given to a different branch (*London, Provincial and South-Western Bank Ltd v Buszard* (1918) 35 TLR 142; *Burnett v Westminster Bank Ltd* [1966] 1 QB 742).

3. Up to what stage of the payment process does the customer have the right to countermand his payment instruction? Clearly the bank must receive the countermand in time to refuse payment. A countermand made after the bank has paid a cheque across the counter would be too late. Where the drawer and payee maintain accounts at different banks, or at different branches of the same bank, the cheque will pass through the clearing process. Notwithstanding that settlement takes place between banks at the end of each trading day, as the Clearing House Rules make provision for later dishonour by the branch on which the cheque is drawn, a notice of countermand should be effective if received before the time limited by the Rules has run out (*Chalmers and Guest on Bills of Exchange, Cheques and Promissory Notes* (14th ed, 1991) ('Chalmers and Guest'), p 619). If the drawer and payee maintain accounts at the same branch of the same bank, payment is 'made' as soon as the bank has set in motion the bank's internal process for crediting the payee's account (*Momm v Barclays Bank International Ltd* [1977] QB 790; Chalmers and Guest, p 619). Particular problems arise in ascertaining when payment is made with regard to Electronic Funds Transfer (see below, p 633) (see Report of the Jack Committee, Ch 12; Goode 'Electronic Funds Transfer as an Immediate Payment System' in *Electronic Banking, the Legal Implications* (Goode, ed), at p 15 and, generally, R M Goode *Payment Obligations in Commercial and Financial Transactions* (1983), Parts I and IV).

4. When a cheque is supported by a cheque guarantee card the bank gives a contractual undertaking to the payee, through the agency of the customer, that the bank will not dishonour the cheque on presentation for want of funds in the account, so that it is obliged if necessary to advance moneys to the customer to meet it (*Re Charge Card Services Ltd* [1987] Ch 150, 166; affd [1989] Ch 497, CA; see also *First Sport Ltd v Barclays Bank plc* [1993] 1 WLR 1229, CA). Can a cheque be countermanded when supported by a cheque guarantee card? Usually the terms and conditions on which the card is supplied to the customer include an undertaking by the customer not to countermand payment of any cheque backed by the card. Whether this means that any countermand is ineffective, or alternatively that the countermand is effective but the customer is in breach of contract to the bank, has yet to be judicially determined. Academic opinion supports the view that the countermand would be ineffective as the customer has authorised its agent, the bank, to incur a personal liability to the payee, for which the customer has a contractual duty to indemnify the bank (Penn, Shea and Arora *The Law Relating To Domestic Banking* (1987), Vol 1, p 75; E P Ellinger *Modern Banking Law* (1987), p 397; Chalmers and Guest, p 622).

5. Section 75(2) of the Bills of Exchange Act 1882 overcomes the normal rule that the authority of the agent is automatically determined by the principal's death (*Campanari v Woodburn* (1854) 15 CB 400; see above, p 198). The effect of s 75(2) on *donatio mortis causa* and *inter vivos* gifts is summarised by Chalmers and Guest, op cit, p 623, as follows:

> ... if a customer draws a cheque and hands it to another in contemplation of death, there will be no valid donatio mortis causa if the cheque is not presented to and paid by the banker before he has notice of the death [*Re Beaumont* [1902] 1 Ch 889], unless the gift has in the lifetime of the donor been completed by a dealing with the cheque [*Rolls v Pearce* (1877) 5 Ch D 730]. Nor is there an effective gift inter vivos of the amount of the cheque at law or in equity, for equity will not intervene to perfect an imperfect gift [*Re Swinburne* [1926] Ch 38; but the gift of a cheque drawn by a third party, which the donor holds, would appear to be good: *Clement v Cheesman* (1884) 27 Ch D 631].

6. The Bills of Exchange Act 1882 does not deal with the effect of the insanity of the customer on the bank's duty to honour his mandate. Under general agency principles, an agent's authority automatically terminates on his principal's insanity (notice of insanity being irrelevant): *Yonge v Toynbee* [1910] 1 KB 215 (see above, p 140). But as the relationship between customer and bank is not solely that of principal and agent, the better view is that only notice of the customer's insanity terminates the bank's authority to pay cheques (F H Ryder (1934) 55 JIB 14). However, where an order is made in relation to a customer under Part VII of the Mental Health Act 1983, it is probable that this automatically determines the customer's mandate (Chalmers and Guest, op cit, p 623; cf Paget, p 227).

7. The remedies available to the bank when it pays money in error by overlooking a countermand or notice of the customer's death or insanity are:

(1) an action for recovery of money paid under a mistake of fact (*Barclays Bank Ltd v W J Simms, Son & Cooke (Southern) Ltd* [1980] QB 677; see above, p 536);

(2) a right to trace the money, or its substitute, into the hands of the recipient (*Chase Manhattan Bank NA v Israel–British Bank (London) Ltd* [1981] Ch 105; see above, p 541);

(3) raising a defence in equity to the customer's claim that his account was wrongly debited, by pleading that the payment was made for the benefit of the customer in payment of his debts (*Scarth v National Provincial Bank Ltd* (1930) 4 Legal Decisions Affecting Bankers 241, following *Liggett (B) Liverpool Ltd v Barclays Bank Ltd* [1928] 1 KB 48).

8 Bank's duty of care

Lipkin Gorman v Karpnale Ltd [1989] 1 WLR 1340, Court of Appeal

Cass was a partner in the plaintiff firm of solicitors and had authority to draw on the solicitors' client account with the defendant bank by his signature alone. Cass was a compulsive gambler and to fund his addiction he wrongfully drew cheques on the client account. The bank honoured the cheques even though its branch manager knew Cass was a gambler and was aware that the method used for drawing and paying the relevant cheques was unusual. The bank did not inform the solicitors that Cass was a gambler or that large sums were being withdrawn from the client account under his authority and made no enquiries as to the propriety of those withdrawals. When the frauds were discovered, the solicitors brought an action against the bank and against the casino where Cass had gambled away the money. The claim against the bank was that it had been in breach of duty to the solicitors and was liable as a constructive trustee of the moneys stolen. The solicitors' claim succeeded before Alliott J and the bank appealed.

May LJ:. . . I turn to the solicitors' claim against the bank based on contract or negligence. We are here concerned with the general relationship between a banker and his customer in the common case where the latter has a current account with the former which is in credit. The underlying basis of this relationship is that it is one of debtor and creditor. The money deposited with a bank becomes its own. It is prima facie bound to meet its debt when called on to do so. . . . Indeed any failure by a bank to honour its customer's instructions may well redound to the serious discredit of the customer himself. On the authorities it is clear that at least in the last century the terms of a customer's mandate to his banker in respect of his current account were sacrosanct.

[His Lordship then cited the judgment of Kindersley V-C in *Bodeham v Hoskins* (1852) 21 LJ Ch 864 at 869 and of Lord Cairns LC and Lord Westbury in *Gray v Johnston* (1868) LR 3 HL 1 at 11, 14. He continued:]

Finally, in *Bank of New South Wales v Goulburn Valley Butter Co Pty Ltd* [1902] AC 543, 550, Lord Davey, in giving the opinion of the Privy Council, said: 'The law is well settled that in the absence of notice of fraud or irregularity a banker is bound to honour his customer's cheque.'

However, in two relatively recent decisions, strongly relied on by counsel for the solicitors, it seems to me that at first instance two judges went appreciably further. These two decisions were *Selangor United Rubber Estates Ltd v Cradock (No 3)* [1968] 1 WLR 1555 and *Karak Rubber Co Ltd v Burden (No 2)* [1972] 1 WLR 602. The facts of each case were complicated and it is unnecessary to set them out in detail. The disputes were concerned with the use of a limited company's moneys to finance the purchase of its own shares. In addition to claims against personal defendants the several banks involved in the relevant transaction were also sued, first, as constructive trustees with the directors of the company's funds in respect of breach of trust, secondly, in negligence in relation to the way the banks paid cheques drawn on them. . . .

When Ungoed-Thomas J turned to consider the claim against the banks in *Selangor United Rubber Estates Ltd v Cradock (No 3)* [1968] 1 WLR 1555 based on negligence, he said, at p 1591:

A further and alternative claim is made against the defendant banks for negligence. This is a claim for damages at common law, as contrasted with a claim for equitable relief against the banks, as well as against other defendants, to replace moneys misapplied as trustees or constructive trustees. Both these equitable and common law claims, as against both defendant banks, involve the allegations that they ought to have made inquiry. Such allegations, though differing in the case of each bank, are identical under both the equitable and common law claim, and it is common ground that any standard of care which puts on inquiry or notice is the same under both claims.

In my opinion, whether it was by concession or not, it was wrong to equate the duty to inquire where there has been fraud and the bank is proved to have known of it with that where all that is being alleged is that the bank had been negligent. Nor was it necessary to rely on any such equivalence in order to decide the issues in the *Selangor* case. It was because of this error I think that both Ungoed-Thomas J in the *Selangor* case, at p 1608, and Brightman J in *Karak Rubber Co Ltd v Burden (No 2)* [1972] 1 WLR 602, 628–629 stated the common law of duty of care on a paying banker in the normal case of a current account in credit too highly. The relationship between the parties is contractual. The principal obligation is on the bank to honour its customers' cheques in accordance with its mandate on instructions. There is nothing in such a contract, express or implied, which could require a banker to consider the commercial wisdom or otherwise of the particular transaction. Nor is there normally any express term in the contract requiring the banker to exercise any degree of care in deciding whether to honour a customer's cheque which his instructions require him to pay. In my opinion any implied term requiring the banker to exercise care must be limited. To a substantial extent the banker's obligation under such a contract is largely automatic or mechanical. Presented with a cheque drawn in accordance with the terms of that contract, the banker must honour it save in what I would expect to be exceptional circumstances. . . .

For my part I would hesitate to try to lay down any detailed rules in this context. In the simple case of a current account in credit the basic obligation on the banker is to pay his customer's cheques in accordance with his mandate. Having in mind the vast numbers of cheques which are presented for payment every day in this country, whether over a bank counter or through the clearing bank, it is, in my opinion, only when the circumstances are such that any reasonable cashier would hesitate to pay a cheque at once and refer it to his or her superior, and when any reasonable superior would hesitate to authorise payment without inquiry, that a cheque should not be paid immediately on presentation and such inquiry made. Further, it would, I think, be only in rare circumstances, and only when any reasonable bank manager would do the same, that a manager should instruct his staff to refer all or some of his customers' cheques to him before they are paid. In this analysis I have respectfully derived substantial assistance from the material parts of the judgment of Steyn J in *Barclays Bank Plc v Quincecare Ltd*, (1988) Times, 2 March, in which judgment was given on 24 February 1988 [now reported at [1992] 4 All ER 363].

Parker LJ: . . . All the cheques were within the bank's mandate and, there being funds to meet them, the bank's primary obligation was to honour them. Such obligation is however not absolute. It is common ground that in some circumstances a bank would, notwithstanding that it honoured a cheque duly signed by a person whose signature it was authorised and required to honour, nevertheless be acting in breach of contract. An extreme example would be where the bank in fact knows a cheque is being drawn in fraud of the customer or, what amounts to the same, they turn a blind eye to the obvious.

The solicitors' claim against the bank in the present case is based on the alternative grounds that in honouring the cheques the bank acted in breach of contract or rendered itself liable as a constructive trustee. . . .

It is in my view clear that the bank could not have rendered itself liable as constructive trustee unless it was also liable for breach of contract and that if it was not liable for breach of contract it could not be liable as constructive trustee. This is because, stated in broad terms, the bank's duty to pay cheques signed in accordance with its mandate is subject to the qualification that it must be performed without negligence and that (i) negligence may exist where there is no question of the circumstances giving rise to a finding of constructive trusteeship; (ii) if there is no negligence I cannot envisage, at least in this case, any facts which would found liability on the ground of constructive trusteeship. . . .

That a bank has a duty of care to its customer when carrying out its mandate is beyond doubt, but so to state advances matters but little, for in each case the question for decision is whether a bank has failed in that duty and there are very many cases on the subject, a considerable number of which were cited in argument. In my view such cases must be approached with caution, for essentially they are no more than decisions of fact, ie of the application of the law to an endless variety of circumstances. Expressions in them, such as that a paying bank must pay under its mandate save in extreme cases, or that a bank is not obliged to act as an amateur detective, or that suspicion is not enough to justify failing to pay according to the mandate, or other like observations which are to be found in the cases, are no more than comments on particular facts or situations and embody in my view no principles of law. Furthermore what would or might have been held to be a breach of duty at one time may not be a breach of duty at another. As Diplock LJ said in *Marfani & Co Ltd v Midland Bank Ltd* [1968] 1 WLR 956, 972:

> What facts ought to be known to the banker, ie, what inquiries he should make, and what facts are sufficient to cause him reasonably to suspect that the customer is not the true owner, must depend upon current banking practice, and change as that practice changes. Cases decided 30 years ago, when the use by the general public of banking facilities was much less widespread, may not be a reliable guide to what the duty of a careful banker in relation to inquiries, and as to facts which should give rise to suspicion, is today.

In addition, cases relating to a collecting banker being sued in conversion and those relating to a paying banker sued for breach of contract raise different considerations. In the former class of case it is for the banker to establish that he collected without negligence, in the latter the burden is on the customer to prove negligence. The statutory protection is also different in the two types of case, as can be seen from the observation of Greer LJ in *Carpenters' Co v British Mutual Banking Co Ltd* [1938] 1 KB 511, 529:

> In my judgment s 60 of the Bills of Exchange Act 1882 only protects a bank when that bank is merely a paying bank, and is not a bank which receives the cheque for collection.

Finally, it is to be noted that the distinction between liability as a constructive trustee and liability for breach of contract is frequently blurred or unconsidered. . . .

So far as breach of contract is concerned. . . . If a reasonable banker would have had reasonable grounds for believing that Cass was operating the client account in fraud, then, in continuing to pay the cash cheques without inquiry the bank would, in my view, be negligent and thus liable for breach of contract, albeit neither Mr Fox nor anyone else appreciated that the facts did afford reasonable grounds and was thus innocent of any sort of dishonesty. . . .

The question must be whether, if a reasonable and honest banker knew of the relevant facts, he would have considered that there was a serious or real possibility, albeit not amounting to a probability, that its customer might be being defrauded, or, in this case, that there was a serious or real possibility that Cass was drawing on the client account and using the funds so obtained for his own and not the solicitors' or beneficiaries' purposes. That, at least, the customer must establish. If it is established, then in my view a reasonable banker would be in breach of duty if he continued to pay cheques without inquiry. He could not simply sit back and ignore the situation. In order so to establish the customer cannot, of course, rely on matters which a meticulous ex post facto examination would have brought to light. Such an examination may well show that it was indeed obvious what Cass was doing, but in the present case the inquiry is simply whether Mr Fox, and therefore the bank, had, on the basis of the facts and banking practices established at the time, reason to believe that there was a serious possibility that Cass was misusing his authority to sign under the mandate in order to obtain and misapply the cash . . . in fraud of the solicitors.

[His Lordship then reviewed the volume of cheque transactions carried out at the branch where the solicitors' client account was held and concluded:]

The overall situation which has therefore to be considered is one in which there were a maximum of 63 fraudulent cash cheques drawn by an authorised signatory on one of some 2,800 current accounts over a period during which there were many thousands of cash transactions and during which the total debit entries on the fraudulently operated account were about seven times the number of fraudulent entries. In order for Mr Fox to have had any reason to believe that there even might be something wrong with the operation of the client account, he would have had to examine the paid cheques and conclude that on the basis of their signatures, amounts and frequency, this was a serious possibility.

On the evidence I can see no basis on which it could be said that a reasonable banker would either have done so or, had he done so, would have had reason to believe any such thing. . . .

I do not consider that a case of negligence has been made out, still less a case that the bank was liable as constructive trustee. I would therefore allow the appeal of the bank and dismiss the cross-appeal of the solicitors under this head.

Nicholls LJ: For the reasons given by Parker LJ I would allow the bank's cross-appeal. . . .

Appeal allowed with costs.

NOTES

1. For commentary on the Court of Appeal's decision in *Lipkin Gorman*, see E P Ellinger [1989] JBL 255; G Jones [1990] CLJ 17. The case was appealed to the House of Lords but not on the question of the duties of the paying bank: [1991] 2 AC 548.

2. *Lipkin Gorman* concerned the duties of the paying bank. Although the relationship between a banker and customer is that of debtor and creditor, the drawing and payment of the customer's cheques as against the customer's money in the banker's hands creates the relationship of principal and agent: *Westminster Bank Ltd v Hilton* (1926) 43 TLR 124 at 126, per Lord Atkinson. As agent the bank owes fiduciary duties to its customer (*Bowstead on Agency* (15th ed), pp 156–160) and every agent for reward is also bound to exercise reasonable care and skill in carrying out the instructions of his principal (Bowstead, op cit, p 144). It is an implied term of the contract between the bank and the customer that the bank will observe reasonable skill and care in and about executing the customer's orders: *Barclays Bank plc v Quincecare Ltd* [1992] 4 All ER 363 at 376, per Steyn J. However, this can create a conflict between the bank's duty to honour the customer's mandate and its duty to exercise reasonable care and skill in and about the execution of the mandate. It is to the resolution of this conflict of duties that the Court of Appeal's decision in *Lipkin Gorman* is directed.

3. The bank's general duty of reasonable care and skill extends over the whole range of banking business within the ambit of the bank's contract with its customer (*Selangor United Rubber Estates Ltd v Cradock (No 3)* [1968] 1 WLR 1555; cf *Weir v National Westminster Bank* (1992) Times, 7 November: Lord Abernethy, sitting in the Outer House of the Court of Session, held that a bank did not owe a duty of care to its customer's agent in his personal capacity where the customer was a disclosed principal). The duty may be implied into the contract by the common law or by s 13 of the Supply of Goods and Services Act 1982. When the bank provides services under the terms of a contract with its customer, the courts will not impose on the bank a wider duty of care in tort than that arising under its contractual duty (*Tai Hing Cotton Mill Ltd v Liu Chong Hing Bank Ltd* [1986] AC 80 at 107, per Lord Scarman (see below, p 592), applied in *National Bank of Greece SA v Pinios Shipping Co No 1, The Maira* [1990] 1 AC 637, CA (reversed on other grounds [1990] 1 AC 637 at 666), although Lloyd LJ (at 651) pointed out that the position would be different if the contract and the tort lay in different fields). Yet the bank's duty to exercise reasonable care and skill may also arise when services are provided outside a contractual relationship. Thus a bank may be held liable in tort for negligent advice and negligent statements made to customers (*Box v Midland Bank Ltd* [1979] 2 Lloyd's Rep 391) and to non-customers (*Hedley Byrne & Co Ltd v Heller & Partners Ltd* [1964] AC 465, HL). However, a bank will not be liable if information or advice supplied by it to a customer is passed on (without the bank's knowledge) to third parties who rely on it (*Caparo Industries plc v Dickman* [1990] 2 AC 605, HL; *Al Saudi Banque v Clark Pixley (a firm)* [1990] Ch 313; *James McNaughton Paper Group Ltd v Hicks Anderson and Co* [1991] 2 QB 113, CA; cf *Morgan Crucible Co plc v Hill Samuel & Co Ltd* [1991] Ch 295, CA). Finally, it should be noted that by s 6 of the Statute of Frauds Amendment Act 1828 no action can be brought against a bank (or any other person) which makes a false representation regarding another person's credit unless such representation is in writing and signed. This provision is particularly relevant where a bank gives a credit reference for one of its customers. In *Banbury v Bank of Montreal* [1918] AC 626 the House of Lords held that the section applies only to claims of fraudulent misrepresentation, although in *UBAF Ltd v European American Banking Corpn* [1984] QB 713 the Court of Appeal extended its application to claims under s 2(1) of the Misrepresentation Act 1967 because under that subsection the person making the representation is liable only if he 'would be liable to damages in respect thereof had the misrepresentation been made fraudulently'.

4. There are limits to the extent of a bank's duty of care.

(1) A bank is not required to warn a customer of the risks involved in paying into his account a generally indorsed cheque of which he is not named as payee and which is crossed 'not negotiable – account payee only' (*Redmond v Allied Irish Banks plc* [1987] FLR 307).

(2) A bank is under no duty to consider the prudence of lending from the customer's point of view or to advise the customer with reference to it (*Williams & Glyn's Bank Ltd v Barnes* [1981] Com LR 205).

(3) In the normal course of events, a bank is under no duty to advise on the nature and effect of a security document (eg guarantee, mortgage or charge) to be executed by a customer or non-customer in favour of the bank for the benefit of a third party, or to advise that person to take independent legal advice: see *Chetwynd-Talbot v Midland Bank Ltd* (1982) 132 NLJ 901; *Westpac Banking Corpn v McCreanor* [1990] 1 NZLR 580; *Barclays Bank plc v Khaira* [1992] 1 WLR 623, defendants' notice of appeal struck out by the Court of Appeal (without commenting on this issue) 30 April 1992 (unreported); but contrast *Cornish v Midland Bank plc* [1985] 3 All ER 513 at 522–523, per Kerr LJ – see also *O'Hara v Allied Irish Banks Ltd* [1985] BCLC 52, a case concerning a *non-customer* giving security for a third party, where Harman J said (at 53) 'short of course of fraud or some deliberate misrepresentation, or some existing fiduciary relationship, there is no ordinary duty of care'. See further R Cranston [1990] JBL 163; D Faber (1991) 12 Co Law 213.

But in special circumstances (eg where a wife guarantees her husband's indebtedness) the bank may have to advise a customer or non-customer executing third party security as to the nature of their potential liability, the risks they are running and to take independent legal advice, if it is to ensure that the security will not be set aside for undue influence, misrepresentation or some other legal wrong: see *Barclays Bank plc v O'Brien* [1994] 1 AC 180, HL; *CIBC Mortgages plc v Pitt* [1994] 1 AC 200, HL; and the Code of Banking Practice (2nd ed, 1994), paras 14.1–14.2.

(4) A bank is under no duty to ensure that a chattel (a ship), mortgaged to the bank

by a customer, is adequately insured (*National Bank of Greece SA v Pinios Shipping Co No 1, The Maira* [1990] 1 AC 637, CA; reversed on other grounds: [1990] 1 AC 637 at 666);

(5) A bank need not consider 'all relevant matters' before exercising a power to appoint a receiver (*Shamji v Johnson Matthey Bankers Ltd* [1986] BCLC 278; affd [1991] BCLC 36: see below, p 904).

9 Bank's fiduciary duties

The bank acts as the customer's agent when making and collecting payments and, when doing so, owes the usual fiduciary duties of an agent to its principal (see above, p 575). However, the existence of a banker–customer relationship does not, of itself, make the bank a fiduciary. The normal banker–customer relationship does not give rise to a presumption of undue influence (*National Westminster Bank plc v Morgan* [1985] AC 686, HL), nor is the bank under a duty of disclosure (see generally *Banque Keyser Ullman SA v Skandia (UK) Insurance Co Ltd* [1990] 1 QB 665 at 798, CA; affd [1991] 2 AC 251, HL; *Bank of Nova Scotia v Hellenic Mutual War Risks Association (Bermuda) Ltd* [1990] 1 QB 818, CA; revsd on other grounds [1992] 1 AC 233).

Exceptionally, the bank may be treated as a fiduciary in the following circumstances:

(1) When the bank is expressly appointed as a trustee. However, the level of care and skill demanded of a bank when acting as trustee has recently been described by Leggatt LJ in *Nestlé v National Westminster Bank plc* [1993] 1 WLR 1260 at 1285 (noted by J Martin (1992) 142 NLJ 1279; A Kenny [1993] Conv 63), as an 'undemanding standard of prudence'. In that case the bank had misunderstood an investment clause in the trust deed and failed to conduct a regular and periodic review of investments. The beneficiary under the trust alleged that by this failure the trust fund, although preserved, had not increased in size as much as it should have done if properly managed. The Court of Appeal found for the bank on the ground that the beneficiary could not prove loss but went on to hold that the bank was not in breach of trust in any event as the importance of preserving a trust fund would always outweigh success in its advancement. If the trustee is a bank trust corporation with a specialist staff of trained trust officers and managers, a higher standard of care may be demanded of it (*Bartlett v Barclays Bank Trust Co Ltd* [1980] Ch 515 at 534, per Brightman J). The point that more should be expected from a corporate trustee was not analysed by the Court of Appeal in the *Nestlé* case (Kenny, op cit, pp 65–66). As to what happens when the bank *qua* trustee deposits trust money with itself *qua* banker, see above, p 560.

(2) Where the customer pays money to the bank for a specific purpose which has been made known to the bank, the bank holds the money on a primary purpose trust which the customer may enforce. The primary purpose trust must be clearly intended and expressed. If the primary purpose trust fails because the expressed purpose becomes impossible to perform, or if the primary purpose trust ends through performance leaving a surplus of money in the bank's hands, then the bank holds the money on an automatic resulting trust for the customer (*Barclays Bank Ltd v Quistclose Investments Ltd* [1970] AC 567 at 580–581, per Lord Wilberforce: see below, p 915; *Re Northern Developments*

(Holdings) Ltd (6 October 1978, unreported); *Carreras Rothmans Ltd v Freeman Mathews Treasure Ltd* [1985] Ch 207; *Re EVTR Ltd* [1987] BCLC 646: see also P Millett (1985) 101 LQR 269; C Rickett [1991] 107 LQR 608; N Clayton [1992] 5 JIBL 183; and M Bridge (1992) 12 OJLS 331 at pp 345–361). If an automatic resulting trust arises and the bank refuses to repay the customer, the bank will be liable to pay compound interest on the money wrongfully retained (*Guardian Ocean Cargoes Ltd v Banco do Brasil SA (No 3), The Golden Med* [1992] 2 Lloyd's Rep 193, Hirst J).

(3) When the bank offers advice on a transaction from which it derives a benefit. In *Woods v Martins Bank Ltd* [1959] 1 QB 55 the bank advised the plaintiff to invest in a company which was in debt to the bank. The bank did not disclose this fact to the plaintiff. The plaintiff, who was inexperienced in financial matters, lost the full amount invested in the shares. Salmon J held that even if the plaintiff was not the bank's customer, the bank owed him a fiduciary duty of care when it gave him financial advice. There has been some scepticism over this case (R Cranston [1990] JBL 163 at p 164). As it pre-dates *Hedley Byrne & Co Ltd v Heller & Partners Ltd* [1964] AC 465, Salmon J was forced to establish a fiduciary relationship for liability to be imposed on the bank for pre-contractual advice. However, the decision has been followed in the leading Canadian case of *Standard Investments Ltd v Canadian Imperial Bank of Commerce* (1985) 22 DLR (4th) 410.

(4) When there is a 'special relationship' between the bank and its customer so that the former owes the latter a fiduciary duty of care. In *Lloyd's Bank Ltd v Bundy* [1975] QB 326, an elderly father gave his bank a guarantee of his son's business debts. The father also agreed to charge his home to the bank. Sir Eric Sachs held that the bank owed the father a fiduciary duty of care which it had breached by failing to give him proper advice or suggesting that he should obtain independent legal advice. Accordingly, he held that the guarantee and charge should be set aside (Lord Denning and Cairns LJ agreed but based their decisions on other grounds). Sir Eric Sachs emphasised that such a duty would not normally arise between a bank and a customer who had guaranteed the debts of a third party. However, in this case the duty arose because the father was a long-standing customer of the bank who relied on it for advice. In other words, there was a 'special relationship' between the bank and its customer. As Sir Eric Sachs stated (at 341):

> Such cases tend to arise where someone relies on the guidance or advice of another, where the other is aware of that reliance and where the person upon whom reliance is placed obtains or may well obtain, a benefit from the transaction or has some other interest in it being concluded. In addition, there must, of course, be shown to exist a vital element which in this judgment will for convenience by referred to as confidentiality.

It is by no means certain that a fiduciary duty of care arises between a bank and its customer in the way described by Sir Eric Sachs. The decision of the Court of Appeal in *Lloyd's Bank Ltd v Bundy* can be upheld on grounds of undue influence alone, without reliance upon the existence of a fiduciary duty of care. This is how the House of Lords viewed the *Bundy* case in *National Westminster Bank plc v Morgan* [1985] AC 686. See further, N Clayton [1992] 8 JIBL 315 at pp 319–321.

(5) Where money is paid by one bank to another as a result of a mistake of fact, the payment gives rise to a fiduciary relationship between the two banks enabling the paying bank to exercise an equitable tracing remedy to recover the

money mistakenly transferred (*Chase Manhattan Bank NA v Israel–British Bank (London) Ltd* [1981] Ch 105; criticised by A Tettenborn [1980] CLJ 272).

10 Anomalous situations: undue influence and liability as a constructive trustee

(a) Undue influence

Where a bank, or its agent, acquires a dominating influence over a person (customer or non-customer) who contracts with the bank, usually by giving the bank a guarantee for the indebtedness of a third party, the contract may be set aside on grounds of undue influence. This principle also applies where the bank has actual or constructive knowledge of influence exercised over the other contracting party by a third party (*Bank of Credit and Commerce International SA v Aboody* [1990] 1 QB 923, CA). To protect its position the bank should explain (in private) to the person influenced the nature of the liability, the risks of the transaction and insist that person takes independent legal advice before entering into the transaction (*Barclays Bank plc v O'Brien* [1994] 1 AC 180, HL).

The main cases on undue influence are *Lloyds Bank Ltd v Bundy* [1975] QB 326, CA; *National Westminster Bank plc v Morgan* [1985] AC 686, HL; *Avon Finance Co Ltd v Bridger* [1985] 2 All ER 281, CA; *Kingsnorth Trust Ltd v Bell* [1986] 1 WLR 119, CA; *Coldunell Ltd v Gallon* [1986] QB 1184, CA; *Goldsworthy v Brickell* [1987] Ch 378, CA; *Midland Bank plc v Shephard* [1988] 3 All ER 17, CA; *Midland Bank plc v Perry* [1988] 1 FLR 161, CA; *Bank of Baroda v Shah* [1988] 3 All ER 24, CA; *Barclays Bank plc v Kennedy* [1989] 1 FLR 356, CA; *Bank of Credit and Commerce International SA v Aboody* [1990] 1 QB 923, CA; *Lloyds Bank plc v Egremont* [1990] 2 FLR 351, CA (a misrepresentation case); *Barclays Bank plc v O'Brien* [1994] 1 AC 180, HL; *CIBC Mortgages plc v Pitt* [1994] 1 AC 200, HL.

Undue influence is an equitable concept but it does not create a fiduciary relationship (*National Westminster Bank plc v Morgan* [1985] AC 686).

(b) Liability as a constructive trustee

A bank may be held liable *as a constructive trustee* if it knowingly receives and becomes chargeable with trust property or assists with knowledge in a dishonest and fraudulent design on the part of the trustees (*Barnes v Addy* (1874) 9 Ch App 244 at 251, per Lord Selborne LC). Agents who receive trust money in a ministerial capacity, ie for the benefit of their principal and not for their own use and benefit, are not to be made liable under the first category of 'knowing receipt' (P Birks (1989) 105 LQR 352, (1989) 105 LQR 528, [1989] LMCLQ 296, Y L Tan [1991] LMCLQ 357). In *Agip (Africa) Ltd v Jackson* [1990] Ch 265 at 292, Millett J expressed the clear view (obiter) that paying and collecting banks could not normally be brought within the 'knowing receipt' category since they do not generally receive money for their own benefit. However, if the bank does receive or deal with the money for its own benefit, eg the collecting bank uses the money to reduce or discharge the customer's overdraft, it may be held liable as a constructive trustee. However, even if the bank receives trust property in a ministerial capacity knowing that it has been paid in breach of trust, the bank will not be held liable under the 'knowing receipt' category of constructive trust. It may, however, be liable under the 'knowing assistance' category.

Liability under the 'knowing receipt' category of constructive trust depends on the bank's knowledge that the transfer to the bank was in breach of trust or knowledge that the property was subject to a trust before the bank dealt with the property in a manner inconsistent with the trust. Liability under the 'knowing assistance' category of constructive trust depends on the bank's knowledge of the trust, the dishonest and fraudulent design and the bank's own assistance in the design (*Baden Delvaux and Lecuit v Société Général pour Favoriser le Développement du Commerce et de l'Industrie en France SA* [1983] BCLC 325 at 403, 407). But the authorities have been unclear as to what level of knowledge is required for liability under each category.

So far as the 'knowing assistance' category is concerned it now appears to be settled that liability only arises if the bank has been dishonest rather than negligent, ie liability arises in cases of 'actual' as opposed to 'constructive' knowledge (see *Lipkin Gorman v Karpnale Ltd* [1989[1 WLR 1340, CA; *Agip (Africa) Ltd v Jackson* [1990] Ch 265 and, on appeal [1991] Ch 547; *Eagle Trust plc v SBC Securities Ltd* [1992] 4 All ER 488; *Cowan de Groot Properties Ltd v Eagle Trust plc* [1992] 4 All ER 700 (where the point was conceded); *Polly Peck International plc v Nadir (No 2)* [1992] 4 All ER 769). For these purposes, 'actual' knowledge includes wilfully shutting one's eyes to the obvious and wilfully and recklessly failing to make such inquiries as an honest and reasonable man would make.

The standard of liability under the 'knowing receipt' category is less certain. Some cases support the view that liability only arises if the bank has been dishonest (see *Carl-Zeiss-Stiftung v Herbert Smith & Co (No 2)* [1969] 2 Ch 276; *Competitive Insurance Co Ltd v Davies Investments Ltd* [1975] 1 WLR 1240; *Re Montagu's Settlement Trusts* [1987] Ch 264; *Eagle Trust plc v SBC Securities Ltd*, above, where Vinelott J accepted the dishonesty standard for commercial transactions, although he clouded the issue by relying on the concept of 'inferred knowledge'; *Cowan de Groot Properties Ltd v Eagle Trust plc*, above, where Knox J also emphasised the commercial nature of the transaction; *Polly Peck International plc v Nadir (No 2)*, above, where Scott LJ, without deciding the issue, appeared to favour the standard of dishonesty rather than negligence). On the other hand, there are a substantial number of cases which favour the negligence standard for 'knowing receipt', ie liability arises in cases of 'actual' and 'constructive' knowledge (see *Belmont Finance Corpn Ltd v Williams Furniture Ltd (No 2)* [1980] 1 All ER 393; *International Sales and Agencies Ltd v Marcus* [1982] 3 All ER 551; *Westpac Banking Corpn v Savin* [1985] 2 NZLR 41 (NZCA); *Powell v Thompson* [1991] 1 NZLR 597 at 607–610; *Agip (Africa) Ltd v Jackson* [1990] Ch 265, dicta of Millett J; *El Ajou v Dollar Land Holdings plc* [1993] 3 All ER 717, per Millett J, noted by P Birks [1993] LMCLQ 248; revsd on other ground [1994] BCC 143). As the bank's *in personam* liability for 'knowing receipt' is closely analogous to its *in rem* liability to a tracing claim, it is submitted that constructive knowledge should be enough to establish liability under the former claim as it is with the latter (see C Harpum (1987) 50 MLR 217). In any event, it has recently been argued that there should be strict personal restitutionary liability (subject to the change of position defence) for having received property that was transferred without the equitable owner's knowledge (P Birks (1989) 105 LQR 528, [1989] LMCLQ 296; P Millett (1991) 107 LQR 71).

Finally, it should be noted that in cases of 'knowing receipt' and 'knowing assistance' the 'receiver' or 'assister' does not actually become a 'trustee' of any kind. Professor Birks has convincingly argued that the language of trusteeship is misplaced when applied to a person who has received property which was transferred without the equitable owner's knowledge (see P Birk's essay in *Commercial Aspects of Trusts and Fiduciary Obligations* (1993) (ed E McKendrick), pp 153–156). As we have seen, Professor Birks argues that the equitable owner has a personal restitutionary remedy against the receiver. While it is less certain that 'knowing assistance' leads to restitution, and the usual remedy is the equitable remedy of accounting for loss, it is certainly wrong to describe the assister as a 'trustee' when trust property may never come into his hands at all (Hanbury and Martin *Modern Equity* (14th ed, 1993), pp 300–301; A Burrows *The Law of Restitution* (1993), p 404).

QUESTION

What reason, if any, could there be for applying different standards of liability for 'knowing receipt' when the receipt arises under a commercial, as opposed to a non-commercial, transaction? See Hanbury and Martin, op cit, p 307; cf Burrows, op cit, p 153.

11 Bank's duty of confidentiality

Tournier v National Provincial and Union Bank of England [1924] 1 KB 461, Court of Appeal

Tournier was a customer of the bank and his account was overdrawn. A cheque was drawn by another customer of the bank in favour of Tournier who, instead of paying it into his own account, indorsed it over to a third party. When the cheque was presented for payment the bank contacted the indorsee's bank and was informed that the indorsee was a bookmaker. The bank subsequently telephoned Tournier's employer for his address and in the course of that conversation disclosed to the employer that Tournier was indebted to them and was sending money to a bookmaker. As a result of this disclosure Tournier lost his job. Tournier then sued the bank for slander and for breach of an implied contract that the bank would not disclose to third persons the state of his account or any transactions relating thereto. Tournier lost at first instance but appealed on the ground that the trial judge had failed to direct the jury as to the circumstances when it would be reasonable and proper for the bank to disclose information about their customer. The Court of Appeal upheld the appeal and ordered a new trial.

Bankes LJ: . . . At the present day I think it may be asserted with confidence that the duty is a legal one arising out of contract, and that the duty is not absolute but qualified. It is not possible to frame any exhaustive definition of the duty. The most that can be done is to classify the qualification, and to indicate its limits. . . . In my opinion it is necessary in a case like the present to direct the jury what are the limits, and what are the qualifications of the contractual duty of secrecy implied in the relation of banker and customer. There appears to be no authority on the point. On principle I think that the qualifications can be classified under four heads: (a) Where disclosure is under compulsion by law; (b) where there is a duty to the public to disclose; (c) where the interests of the bank require disclosure; (d) where the disclosure is made by the express or implied consent of the customer. An instance of the first class is the duty to obey an order under the Bankers' Books Evidence Act. Many instances of the second class might be given. They may be summed up in the language of Lord Finlay in *Weld-Blundell v Stephens* ([1920] AC 956 at 965), where he speaks of cases where a higher duty than the private duty is involved, as where 'danger to the State or public duty may supersede the duty of the agent to his principal'. A simple instance of the third class is where a bank issues a writ claiming payment of an overdraft stating on the face of the writ the amount of the overdraft. The familiar instance of the last class is where the customer authorizes a reference to his banker. It is more difficult to state what the limits of the duty are, either as to time or as to the nature of the disclosure. I certainly think that the duty does not cease the moment a customer closes his account. Information gained during the currency of the account remains confidential unless released under circumstances bringing the case within one of the classes of qualification I have already referred to. Again the confidence is not confined to the actual state of the customer's account. It extends to information derived from the account itself. A more doubtful question, but one vital to this case, is whether the confidence extends to information in reference to the customer and his affairs derived not from the customer's account but from other sources, as, for instance, from the account of another customer of the customer's bank. . . . The privilege of non-disclosure to which a client or a customer is entitled may vary according to the exact nature of the relationship between the client or the customer and the person on whom the duty rests. It need not be the same in the case of the counsel, the solicitor, the doctor, and the banker, though the underlying principle may be the same. The case of the banker and his customer appears to me to be one in which the confidential relationship between the parties is very marked. The credit of the customer depends very largely upon the strict observance of that confidence. I cannot think that the duty of non-disclosure is confined to information derived from the customer himself or from his account. To take a simple illustration. A police officer goes to a banker to make an inquiry about a customer of the bank. He goes to the bank, because he knows that the person about whom he wants information is a customer of the bank. The police officer is asked why he wants the information. He replies, because the customer is charged with a series of frauds. Is the banker entitled to publish that information? Surely not. He acquired the information in his character of banker. So in the present case Mr Fennell was put upon inquiry by a cheque drawn in the plaintiff's favour upon a customer's account. He acquired the information which he is said to have divulged in his character as the plaintiff's banker.

Scrutton LJ: . . . I have no doubt that it is an implied term of a banker's contract with his customer that the banker shall not disclose the account, or transactions relating thereto, of his customer except in certain circumstances. . . . I think it is clear that the bank may disclose the customer's account and affairs to an extent reasonable and proper for its own protection, as in collecting or suing for an overdraft; or to an extent reasonable and proper for carrying on the business of the account, as in giving a reason for declining to honour cheques drawn or bills accepted by the customer, when there are insufficient assets; or when ordered to answer questions in the law Courts; or to prevent frauds or crimes. I doubt whether it is sufficient excuse for disclosure, in the absence of the customer's consent, that it was in the interests of the customer, where the customer can be consulted in reasonable time and his consent or dissent obtained. I think also, in accordance with well-known authorities on the duties and privileges of legal advisers, that the implied legal duty towards the customer to keep secret his affairs does not apply to knowledge which the bank acquires before the relation of banker and customer was in contemplation, or after it ceased; or to knowledge derived from other sources during the continuance of the relation.

Atkin LJ: . . . In *Joachimson v Swiss Bank Corpn* ([1921] 3 KB 110) this Court had to consider what were the terms of the contract made between banker and customer in the ordinary course of business when a current account is opened by the bank. All the members of the Court were of opinion that the contract included several implied terms, some of which were then stated, so far as was necessary for the determination of that case, which turned upon the necessity of a demand before the customer could sue the bank for the amount of his credit balance. It is now necessary to consider whether there is any, and if so what, implied term as to an obligation of secrecy on the part of the bank. . . . I come to the conclusion that one of the implied terms of the contract is that the bank enter into a qualified obligation with their customer to abstain from disclosing information as to his affairs without his consent.

. . . To what information does the obligation of secrecy extend? It clearly goes beyond the state of the account, that is, whether there is a debit or a credit balance, and the amount of the balance. It must extend at least to all the transactions that go through the account, and to the securities, if any, given in respect of the account; and in respect of such matters it must, I think, extend beyond the period when the account is closed, or ceases to be an active account. It seems to me inconceivable that either party would contemplate that once the customer had closed his account the bank was to be at liberty to divulge as it pleased the particular transactions which it had conducted for the customer while he was such. I further think that the obligation extends to information obtained from other sources than the customer's actual account, if the occasion upon which the information was obtained arose out of the banking relations of the bank and its customers – for example, with a view to assisting the bank in conducting the customer's business, or in coming to decisions as to its treatment of its customers. . . . In this case, however, I should not extend the obligation to information as to the customer obtained after he had ceased to be customer. . . . I do not desire to express any final opinion on the practice of bankers to give one another information as to the affairs of their respective customers, except to say it appears to me that if it is justified it must be upon the basis of an implied consent of the customer.

NOTES

1. The ambit of a banker's duty of confidence is best stated by Bankes and Atkin LJJ in the *Tournier* case. Scrutton LJ's reluctance to extend the duty to information obtained from sources other than the customer's account has not found favour with the courts (eg *Lipkin Gorman v Karpnale Ltd* [1989] 1 WLR 1340 at 1357, per May LJ) or the commentators (eg Paget, p 255).

2. Although the duty would not appear to arise from agency, but to be implicit in the banker–customer relationship, the banker's duty to treat his customer's affairs as confidential is similar to the duty of good faith which an agent owes to his principal (Lord Chorley *Law of Banking* (6th ed, 1974), p 20; cf E P Ellinger *Modern Banking Law* (1987), pp 96–97). Even after *Tournier* the scope of the duty remains uncertain. Does it cover all information acquired by the banker, even if acquired when the banker provides non-banking, eg estate agency, services? If information from sources other than the customer's actual account is to be made subject to the duty of confidentiality, it must be acquired by the banker 'in his character of banker' (per Bankes LJ) or arise 'out of the banking relations of the bank and its customers' (per Atkin LJ). These dicta suggest that information acquired when the banker is providing a non-banking service would fall outside the *Tournier* duty. However, the issue remains undecided (see R M Goode [1989] JBL 269). In any event, even if the information is not covered by the *Tournier* duty, it may have been acquired in circumstances which give rise to a duty of confidence to a third party (see *A-G v Guardian Newspapers Ltd (No 2)* [1990] 1 AC 109, G Jones [1989] CLP 49).

3. In its Report, the Jack Committee recognised that the principle of confidentiality lay at the heart of the banker–customer relationship and warned of the danger of loss of customer confidence in the banking system if the principle was undermined by uncertainty as to the extent of its application in the light of modern banking practices. The Jack Committee recommended that the principle should be strengthened by statutory codification but this recommendation has since been rejected by the Government as unnecessary and likely to introduce new difficulties and confusion (White Paper (1990) Cm 1026, p 4). However, the Code of Banking Practice (2nd ed, 1994) has tried to strengthen the duty of confidentiality by stating that banks and building societies will observe a strict duty of confidentiality about their customers' (and former customers') personal financial affairs and will not disclose details of customer accounts or their names and addresses to any third party, including other companies in the same group, except in the four exceptional cases set out by Bankes LJ in *Tournier* (para 8.1). The Code further states that banks and building societies will not use the third *Tournier* exception to justify the disclosure for marketing purposes of their customers' details to third parties, including other companies within the same group (para 8.2). Except in response to a customer's specific request, banks and building societies must not pass customers' names and addresses to other companies in the same group for marketing purposes, in the absence of express written consent (para 10.1).

4. *Exception 1: compulsion by law.* In *Parry-Jones v Law Society* [1969] 1 Ch 1 at 9, Diplock LJ stated that:

> . . . a [contractual] duty of confidence is subject to, and overridden by, the duty of any party to that contract to comply with the law of the land. If it is the duty of such a party to a contract, whether at common law or under statute, to disclose in defined circumstances confidential information, then he must do so, and any express contract to the contrary would be illegal and void.

The Report of the Jack Committee identified 20 statutes under which disclosure could be compelled (see Appendix Q). These include the Bankers' Books Evidence Act 1879 (s 7), the Drug Trafficking Offences Act 1986 (ss 24 and 27), the Insolvency Act 1986 (s 236) and the Criminal Justice Act 1988 (s 98). Recent legislation which has made inroads into the confidentiality between banks and their customers is reviewed by M Chance in [1991] 12 JIBL 485. The bank owes no duty to its customer to oppose an application for the disclosure of confidential information made under a relevant statutory power (*Barclays Bank plc v Taylor* [1989] 3 All ER 563, CA, where the police applied for disclosure under s 9 of the Police and Criminal Evidence Act 1984).

Two increasingly common examples of the compulsion of law exception deserve special mention. The first is the *Shapira* order. This order takes its name from *Bankers Trust Co v Shapira* [1980] 1 WLR 1274 where the Court of Appeal ordered a bank to give discovery of confidential information concerning two customers who had defrauded the plaintiff and paid the proceeds into their account with the bank. The order assists the victim of fraud to trace his funds and often accompanies an order preventing the rogue dissipating his assets pending the outcome of the action (this order is called a *Mareva* injunction after *Mareva Cia Naviera SA v International Bulkcarriers SA, The Mareva* [1975] 2 Lloyd's Rep 509). As a general rule, the plaintiff may only use the information disclosed to him for the purposes of recovery of his money; exceptionally, the court will allow the plaintiff to disclose the information to a third party, as will be the case where the law of a foreign jurisdiction compels the plaintiff to make such disclosure (*Bank of Crete SA v Koskotas (No 2)* [1993] 1 All ER 748).

The second example arises under s 39 of the Banking Act 1987. Under s 39 the Bank of England can issue a notice requiring an authorised institution to disclose to it such information or documents as it might reasonably require for the performance of its supervisory functions under the Act. Any person who 'without reasonable excuse' fails to comply with a s 39 notice is guilty of an offence and liable to imprisonment or a fine (s 39(11)). The notice overrides the customer's right of confidentiality and even overrides a prior court injunction preventing disclosure (*A v B Bank* [1993] QB 311). It also appears to override a claim of legal professional privilege, except that s 39(13) allows the privilege to be asserted in a limited way by permitting a barrister, advocate or solicitor (but not, for example, an accountant) to refuse to produce a document containing a privileged communication (*Price Waterhouse v BCCI Holdings (Luxembourg) SA* [1992] BCLC 583 at 593, per Millett J, obiter). In *Bank of England v Riley* [1992] Ch 475, the Court of Appeal held that 'reasonable excuse', as used in s 42, did not cover privilege against self-incrimination but was restricted to such matters as 'physical inability to comply with a requirement for information or documents arising from illness or accidental destruction of papers etc' (at 482). In *A v B Bank*, above, at 324, Hirst J held that the situations envisaged by s 39(11) were 'well illustrated by *Bank of England v Riley*'.

5. *Exception 2: Duty to the public.* Given the serious inroads into the duty of confidentiality made by statute, the Jack Committee found it hard to see a role for the second exception and recommended its abolition (paras 5.30 and 5.41). The Government rejected this recommendation on the basis that the statutory route *requires* information from the banker, whereas the second exception *permits* him to disclose (White Paper (1990) Cm 1026, p 15). There have been few cases where the courts have had to adjudicate on the propriety of disclosure under the second exception. In *Libyan Arab Foreign Bank v Bankers Trust Co* [1988] 1 Lloyd's Rep 259, Bankers Trust in New York had discussions with the Federal Reserve Board about the plaintiff's accounts and relied, inter alia, on the second *Tournier* exception to justify this disclosure. Staughton J said:

> But presuming (as I must) the New York law on this point is the same as English law, it seems to me that the Federal Reserve Board, as the central banking system in the United States, may have a public duty to perform in obtaining information from banks. I accept the argument that higher public duty is one of the exceptions to a banker's duty of confidence, and I am prepared to reach a tentative conclusion that the exception applied in this case.

The existence of an independent ground of disclosure under the second exception has recently been highlighted by the judgment of Millett J in *Price Waterhouse v BCCI Holdings (Luxembourg) SA* [1992] BCLC 583. The case concerned disclosure of confidential information by Price Waterhouse to the Bingham Inquiry. The information concerned Price Waterhouse's client, the Bank of Credit and Commerce International Group ('BCCI'). While the case concerned the duty of confidentiality owed by accountants to their client, not a bank to its customer, the principles discussed by Millett J are of general relevance (see M Reed and R Chastney [1992] 2 JIBL 72). The Bingham Inquiry was a non-statutory inquiry set up by the Chancellor of the Exchequer and the Governor of the Bank of England to investigate the performance by the Bank of England of its statutory functions in relation to the supervision of BCCI. As a non-statutory inquiry it had no statutory power to order disclosure. However, Price Waterhouse wished to co-operate with the Inquiry and applied to the court for a declaration as to what they could and could not do. Millett J held that the public interest in maintaining confidentiality might be outweighed by some countervailing interest in disclosure and the latter was not limited to the public interest in detecting or preventing wrongdoing (citing *A-G v Guardian Newspapers Ltd (No 2)* [1990] 1 AC 109 at 214, 268, 282, HL). At 601 he stated:

The duty of confidentiality, whether contractual or equitable, is subject to a limiting principle. It is subject to the right, not merely the duty, to disclose information where there is a higher public interest in disclosure than in maintaining confidentiality.

In this case Millett J felt that the public interest in disclosure ought to prevail because there was an important public interest in the effective regulation and supervision of authorised banking institutions and the protection of depositors. He concluded that if it was in the public interest to require confidential information to be disclosed to the Bank of England under s 39 of the Banking Act 1987 to enable it to carry out its supervisory function, there was at least as great a public interest in the disclosure of such information to an inquiry set up to review the Bank's past performance of its statutory functions, provided the dissemination of such information was no wider in the latter case than would be authorised in the former case. See Part V of the Banking Act 1987 on preserving the confidentiality of supervisory information obtained under the Act.

6. *Exception 3: Interests of the bank.* In *Sutherland v Barclays Bank Ltd* (1938) 5 Legal Decisions Affecting Bankers 163 the bank dishonoured the plaintiff's cheque because there were insufficient funds in her account. The real reason for dishonour was that the bank knew she was betting. During the course of a telephone conversation between the plaintiff and the bank the plaintiff's husband interrupted and took up his wife's case. The bank then informed the husband that most of the cheques passing through the account were in favour of bookmakers. The plaintiff sued for breach of the duty of confidentiality. Du Parcq LJ thought that the bank was justified in disclosing the information to protect its own reputation. He also held that as the husband had joined the conversation, the bank had the plaintiff's implied consent to disclose the information to him. For criticism of this case, see E P Ellinger *Modern Banking Law* (1987), p 104. More recently, in *Hassneh Insurance Co of Israel v Mew* [1993] 2 Lloyd's Rep 243, a case on the extent of the duty of confidence arising under an agreement to arbitrate, Coleman J (at 249) observed with regard to the bank's duty of confidence that:

> . . . the bank should be able to disclose the information if to withhold it would or might prejudice the bank in the establishment or protection of its own legal rights vis-à-vis the customer or third parties. The essence of the matter is that it might need to disclose the information either as the foundation of a defence to a claim by a third party, or as the basis of a cause of action against a third party.

The Jack Committee noted two main areas of concern with regard to the interests of the bank exception. These were: (1) disclosure within the banking group; and (2) disclosure to credit reference agencies.

As to (1), the principle of separate corporate personality means that each company within the banking group must be viewed as a separate entity. Disclosure of confidential customer information by a bank to a parent or subsidiary company in the group will breach the bank's duty of confidentiality (*Bank of Tokyo v Karoon* [1987] AC 45n, CA). Yet it is arguable that disclosure of confidential information by a bank to a banking parent or subsidiary is 'in the interests of the bank' as it permits the banking group to be run in a cost-effective way and ensures that banks are able to fulfil their statutory obligations (under the Banking Act 1987) to report large exposures within the group. For these reasons, the Jack Committee recommended that the law should allow the passing of confidential information, without customer consent, between banking companies in the same group so long as what is disclosed is reasonably necessary for the specific purpose of protecting the bank and its banking subsidiaries against loss, in relation to the provision of normal banking services. However, the Jack Committee could see no justification for the transmission of such information, without customer consent, to non-banking subsidiaries in the same group. As we have seen, the Code of Banking Practice (2nd ed, 1994) falls somewhat short of the Jack Committee's proposals. Disclosure to other companies in the same group for marketing purposes is prohibited, unless it is made in response to the customer's specific request or with his express written consent (paras 8.2 and 10.1). Yet whilst the Code expressly prohibits the disclosure of confidential information to other companies in the same group, it subjects that prohibition to the *Tournier* exceptions. It is still possible for a bank to argue that disclosure of information for non-marketing purposes to banking and non-banking parent and subsidiary companies falls within the third, and possibly the fourth (by arguing implied customer consent to disclosure), *Tournier* exceptions. Furthermore, there is nothing in the Code to prohibit a bank using confidential customer information for its non-banking business (including for marketing purposes) so long as that business is conducted by a branch of the bank itself and not by a separately incorporated parent or subsidiary.

As to (2), there is some debate as to which *Tournier* exception applies when banks disclose confidential customer information to credit reference agencies. In its White Paper on Banking Services Law and Practice ((1990) Cm 1026, p 16), the Government considered that banks could already pass 'black' information (when the customer is in default) to credit reference agencies. This may be justified under the second or third *Tournier* exceptions (cf Goode [1989] JBL 269 at p 271). However, the Government proposed that the Code of Banking Practice should prohibit the transfer of 'white' information (when the customer is not in default) to credit reference agencies without the express consent of the customer. The first edition of the Code made no attempt to implement this proposal but the second edition provides that whilst 'black' information may be disclosed to credit reference agencies (subject to at least 28 days' notice of such disclosure to the customer), 'white' information will only be disclosed with the customer's consent (para 8.3).

7. *Exception 4: Customer's consent.* There is an established trade practice that bankers provide each other with credit references relating to their customers. Traditionally, customers have been held impliedly to consent to this practice unless they have instructed their bank not to supply such information. The Jack Committee recommended that such information should only be supplied with the customer's express consent but the Government rejected this recommendation (White Paper (1990) Cm 1026, p 16). The new edition of the Code of Banking Practice (2nd ed, 1994) now provides that a banker's reference or opinion as to a customer's ability to support or undertake a financial transaction or commitment should only be given with the express consent of the customer concerned (para 9.0 and 'Definitions').

8. *Other relevant legislation.*

(1) The Code of Banking Practice (2nd ed, 1994) states that banks and building societies will comply with the Data Protection Act 1984 and explain to their customers that under the Act they have rights of access to their personal records held on computer files (para 8.4).

(2) Banks and their employees must be careful not to fall foul of Part V of the Criminal Justice Act 1993, which came into force on 1 March 1994 (the Company Securities (Insider Dealing) Act 1985 is repealed in its entirety). Under s 52(1) of the 1993 Act an individual who has relevant non-public

information as an insider or tippee, from an inside source, is guilty of insider dealing, if he deals in the prohibited circumstances, in quoted securities that are price affected securities in relation to the information. Encouraging others to deal, knowing or having reasonable cause to believe that the other person would deal in securities in the circumstances covered by the dealing offence, or disclosing information to others, otherwise than in the proper performance of an employment, office or profession, is also prohibited (s 52(2)). The prohibited circumstances, in which it is an offence to deal, are where the transaction takes place on a regulated market, or where the person dealing relies on a professional intermediary or is himself acting as a professional intermediary (s 52(3)). For example, the mergers and acquisitions section of a bank may obtain information from a client company, which is then passed to its dealing arm, who proceed to trade in the shares on the bank's own account on the strength of that information. To avoid this possibility, and to comply with various regulatory requirements (eg the rules of the Securities Association which regulates investment banks and securities houses), banks have set up 'Chinese Walls' between their departments (ie systems designed to prohibit the transfer of information in the manner just described). However, doubt has arisen as to the effectiveness of these arrangements. In two recent cases concerning the effectiveness of Chinese Walls set up by firms of solicitors, the courts have viewed the efficiency of such arrangements with some scepticism (see *Lee (David) & Co (Lincoln) Ltd v Coward Chance (a firm)* [1991] Ch 259, Browne-Wilkinson V-C and *Re a Firm of Solicitors* [1992] QB 959, CA, noted by F M B Reynolds (1991) 107 LQR 536; see also J R Midgley (1992) 55 MLR 822). Ben Strong has noted that if this attitude were to be taken with multiple function fiduciaries in the City, the consequences could be severe for banks and stockbrokers, especially where a Self-Regulatory Organisation's rule book required a Chinese Wall (see (1991) 12 Co Law 180 at p 181). For further consideration of the problems facing multi-function fiduciaries in the financial services industry, see the Law Commission's Consultation Paper No 124 'Fiduciary Duties and Regulatory Rules' (1992) (above, p 174).

QUESTION

NE Credit Ltd operates a credit card business and is a wholly owned subsidiary of NE Bank plc. NE Credit Ltd receives an application from Adam to double the credit limit on his card. NE Credit Ltd is concerned that an increase in Adam's limit will make it difficult for him to pay his minimum monthly repayments on the card and so it asks NE Bank plc, where Adam holds a current and deposit account, for information relating to those accounts and, in particular, details of the levels of weekly expenditure from Adam's current account. The bank supplies the information to NE Credit Ltd and this results in Adam's application being rejected. Advise Adam as to his rights, if any, against the bank. Would your advice be different if (1) the bank believed that any increase in Adam's credit limit would mean that he would be unable to repay an existing loan made to him by the bank; or, alternatively, if (2) the credit card business was run by the bank itself and not by a separate company.

12 The customer's duty of care

Tai Hing Cotton Mill Ltd v Liu Chong Hing Bank Ltd [1986] AC 80, Privy Council

(The facts appear from Lord Scarman's judgment.)

The advice of the Judicial Committee of the Privy Council (Lords Scarman, Roskill, Brandon of Oakbrook, Brightman and Templeman) was delivered by **Lord Scarman:** This is an appeal by a company against a decision of the Court of Appeal in Hong Kong whereby its action to recover from three banks sums of money alleged to have been wrongfully debited against its current account with each was dismissed. The appeal raises a question of general principle in the law governing the relationship of banker and customer. Additionally, the appeal calls for consideration of a number of questions arising from the particular circumstances of the company's business relationship with each of the three banks.

The company was a customer of the banks, and maintained with each of them a current account. The banks honoured by payment on presentation some 300 cheques totalling approximately HK$5.5 million which on their face appeared to have been drawn by the company and to bear the signature of Mr Chen, the company's managing director who was one of the company's authorised signatories to its cheques. The banks in each instance debited the company's current account with the amount of the cheque. These cheques, however, were not the company's cheques. They were forgeries. On each the signature of Mr Chen had been forged by an accounts clerk employed by the company, Leung Wing Ling. The central issue in the appeal is upon whom the loss arising from Leung's forgeries is to fall, the company or the banks. The question of general principle is as to the nature and extent of the duty of care owed by a customer to his bank in the operation of a current account. . . .

The question of general principle
The question can be framed in two ways. If put in terms of the law's development, it is whether two House of Lords' decisions, one in 1918 and the other in 1933, represent the existing law. If put in terms of principle, the question is whether English law recognises today any duty of care owed by the customer to his bank in the operation of a current account beyond, first, a duty to refrain from drawing a cheque in such a manner as may facilitate fraud or forgery, and, secondly, a duty to inform the bank of any forgery of a cheque purportedly drawn on the account as soon as he, the customer, becomes aware of it. The first duty was clearly enunciated by the House of Lords in *London Joint Stock Bank Ltd v Macmillan* [1918] AC 777, and the second was laid down, also by the House of Lords, in *Greenwood v Martins Bank Ltd* [1933] AC 51.

The banks accept, of course, that both duties exist and have been recognised for many years to be part of English law. Their case is that English law recognises today, even if it did not in 1918 or 1933, an altogether wider duty of care. This is, they submit, a duty upon the customer to take reasonable precautions in the management of his business with the bank to prevent forged cheques being presented to it for payment. Further, and whether or not they establish the existence of this wider duty, they contend that the customer owes a duty to take such steps to check his periodic (in this case, monthly) bank statements as a reasonable customer in his position would take to enable him to notify the bank of any debit items in the account which he has not authorised. They submit that, given the relationship of banker and customer and the practice of rendering periodic bank statements, the two duties for which they contend are 'necessary incidents' of the relationship. The source of obligation, they say, is to be found both in the contract law as an implied term of the banking contract and in the tort law as a civil obligation arising from the relationship of banker and customer.

They accept that the reasoning to be found in *Macmillan's* case [1918] AC 777 appears at first sight to negative the existence of both the duties for which they contend: but they offer the explanation that the law of contract and the tort law were significantly different in 1918 from the state of the relevant modern law. In particular, they point to developments in the law relating to the circumstances in which the courts will now imply a term into a contract, and to the changes in tort law both as to the range of relationships giving rise to liability in tort and as to the circumstances in which loss or damage will be held to result from breach of a duty of care. Their implied term point they base on the decision of the House of Lords in *Liverpool City Council v Irwin* [1977] AC 239; and their two tort points on decisions of the Board in *Overseas Tankship (UK) Ltd v Morts Dock and Engineering Co Ltd, The Wagon Mound* [1961] AC 388 and of the House of Lords in *Anns v Merton London Borough Council* [1978] AC 728.

The Court of Appeal accepted the banks' submissions. Cons JA was led 'after a great deal of hesitation' to conclude:

> that, in the world in which we live today, it is a necessary condition of the relation of the banker and customer that the customer should take reasonable care to see that in the operation of the account the bank is not injured.

He, therefore, held that, in the absence of express agreement to the contrary, the duty would be implied into the banking contract as a necessary incident of the relationship between customer and banker. . . .

First, it is necessary to determine what *Macmillan's* case [1918] AC 777 decided. Upon this point their Lordships are in no doubt. The House held that the customer owes his bank a duty in drawing a cheque to take reasonable and ordinary precautions against forgery.

> The duty . . . is to draw the cheques with reasonable care to prevent forgery, and if, owing to neglect of this duty, forgery takes place, the customer is liable to the bank for the loss: per Lord Finlay LC at p 793.

In so formulating the duty the House excluded as a necessary incident of the banker–customer relationship any wider duty, though of course it is always open to a banker to refuse to do business save upon express terms including such a duty. Lord Finlay LC expressly excluded any such duty saying, at p 795:

> Of course the negligence must be in the transaction itself, that is, in the manner in which the cheque is drawn. It would be no defence to the banker, if the forgery had been that of a clerk of a customer, that the latter had taken the clerk into his service without sufficient inquiry as to his character.

And the House approved the judgment of Bray J in *Kepitigalla Rubber Estates Ltd v National Bank of India Ltd* [1909] 2 KB 1010. In that case the judge held that, while it is the duty of a customer in issuing his mandates (ie his cheques) to his bank to take reasonable care not to mislead the bank, there is no duty on the part of the customer to take precautions in the general course of carrying on his business to prevent forgeries on the part of his servants. Put in the terms of the banks' submission in this case, Bray J negatived the existence of the two duties for which the banks contend, and the House of Lords in *Macmillan's* case [1918] AC 777 agreed with him. . . .

Implied term

Their Lordships agree with Cons JA that the test of implication is necessity. As Lord Wilberforce put it in *Liverpool City Council v Irwin* [1977] AC 239, 254:

> such obligation should be read into the contract as the nature of the contract itself implicitly requires, no more, no less: a test, in other words, of necessity.

Cons JA went on to quote an observation by Lord Salmon in the *Liverpool* case to the effect that the term sought to be implied must be one without which the whole transaction would become 'inefficacious, futile and absurd' (p 262).

Their Lordships accept as correct the approach adopted by Cons JA. Their Lordships prefer it to that suggested by Hunter J which was to ask the question: does the law impose the term? Implication is the way in which necessary incidents come to be recognised in the absence of express agreement in a contractual relationship. Imposition is apt to describe a duty arising in tort, but inept to describe the necessary incident arising from a contractual relationship.

Their Lordships, however, part company with Cons JA in his conclusion (reached only after great hesitation, he said) that it is necessary to imply into the contract between banker and customer a wider duty than that formulated in *Macmillan's* case. *Macmillan's* case itself decisively illustrates that it is not a *necessary* incident of the banker–customer relationship that the customer should owe his banker the wider duty of care.

The relationship between banker and customer is a matter of contract. The classic, though not necessarily exhaustive, analysis of the incidents of the contract is to be found in the judgment of Atkin LJ in *Joachimson v Swiss Bank Corpn* [1921] 3 KB 110, 127: [see above, pp 558–559]. . . .

Atkin LJ clearly felt no difficulty in analysing the relationship upon the basis of the limited duty enunciated in *Macmillan's* case. And in *Macmillan's* case itself the protracted discussion, which is now only of historical interest, as to the true ratio decidendi of *Young v Grote* (1827) 4 Bing 253 reveals vividly that the House was aware of the possibility of a wider duty but rejected it.

The argument for the banks is, when analysed, no more than that the obligations of care placed upon banks in the management of a customer's account which the courts have recognised have become with the development of banking business so burdensome that they should be met by a reciprocal increase of responsibility imposed upon the customer: and they cite *Selangor United Rubber Estates Ltd v Cradock (No 3)* [1968] 1 WLR 1555 (Ungoed-Thomas J) and *Karak Rubber Co Ltd v Burden (No 2)* [1972] 1 WLR 602 (Brightman J). One can fully understand the comment of Cons JA that the banks must today look for protection. So be it. They can increase the severity of their terms of business, and they can use their influence, as they have in the past, to seek to persuade the legislature that they should be granted by statute further protection. But it does not follow that because they may need protection as their business expands the necessary incidents of their relationship with their customer must also change. The business of banking is the business not of the customer but of the bank. They offer a service, which is to honour their customer's cheques when drawn upon an account in credit or within an agreed overdraft limit. If they pay out upon cheques which are not his, they are acting outside their mandate and cannot plead his authority in justification of their debit to his account. This is a risk of the service which it is their business to offer. The limits set to the risk in the *Macmillan* [1918] AC 777 and *Greenwood* [1933] AC 51 cases can be seen to be plainly necessary incidents of the relationship. Offered such a service, a customer must obviously take care in the way he draws his cheque, and must obviously warn his bank as soon as he knows that a forger is operating the account. Counsel for the banks asked rhetorically why, once a duty of care was recognised, should it stop at the *Macmillan* and *Greenwood* limits. They submitted that there was no rational stopping place short of the wider duty for which they contended. With very great respect to the ingenious argument addressed to the Board their Lordships find in certain observations of Bray J in *Kepitigalla's* case [1909] 2 KB 1010 a convincing statement of the formidable difficulties in the way of this submission. Bray J said, at pp 1025–1026:

> I think Mr Scrutton's contention equally fails when it is considered apart from authority. It amounts to a contention on the part of the bank that its customers impliedly agreed to take precautions in the general course of carrying on their business to prevent forgeries on the part of their servants. Upon what is that based? It cannot be said to be necessary to make the contract effective. It cannot be said to have really been in the mind of the customer, or, indeed, of the bank, when the relationship of banker and customer was created. What is to be the standard of the extent or number of the precautions to be taken? Applying it to this case, can it be said to have been in the minds of the directors of the company that they were promising to have the pass-book and the cash-book examined at every board meeting, and to have a sufficient number of board meetings to prevent forgeries, or that the secretary should be supervised or watched by the chairman? If the bank desire that their customers should make these promises they must expressly stipulate that they shall. I am inclined to think that a banker who required such a stipulation would soon lose a number of his customers. The truth is that the number of cases where bankers sustain losses of this kind are infinitesimal in comparison with the large business they do, and the profits of banking are sufficient to compensate them for this very small risk. To the individual customer the loss would often be very serious; to the banker it is negligible.

Their Lordships reject, therefore, the implied term submission.

Tort

Their Lordships do not believe that there is anything to the advantage of the law's development in searching for a liability in tort where the parties are in a contractual relationship. This is particularly so in a commercial relationship. Though it is possible as a matter of legal semantics to conduct an analysis of the rights and duties inherent in some contractual relationships including that of banker and customer either as a matter of contract law when the question will be what, if any, terms are to be implied or as a matter of tort law when the task will be to identify a duty arising from the proximity and character of the relationship between the parties, their Lordships believe it to be correct in principle and necessary for the avoidance of confusion in the law to adhere to the contractual analysis: on principle because it is a relationship in which the parties have, subject to a few exceptions, the right to determine their obligations to each other, and for the avoidance of confusion because different consequences do follow according to whether liability arises from contract or tort, eg in the limitation of action. . . .

Their Lordships do not, therefore, embark on an investigation as to whether in the relationship of banker and customer it is possible to identify tort as well as contract as a source of the obligations owed by the one to the other. Their Lordships do not, however, accept that the parties' mutual obligations in tort can be any greater than those to be found expressly or by necessary implication in their contract. If, therefore, as their Lordships have concluded, no duty wider than that recognised in *Macmillan* [1918] AC 777 and *Greenwood* [1933] AC 51 can be implied into the banking contract in the absence of express terms to that effect, the banks cannot rely on the law of tort to provide them with greater protection than that for which they have contracted.

For these reasons their Lordships answer the general question by accepting the submission of the company that in the absence of express terms to the contrary the customer's duty is in English law as laid down in *Macmillan* and *Greenwood*. The customer's duty in relation to forged cheques is, therefore, twofold: he must exercise due care in drawing his cheques so as not to facilitate fraud or forgery and he must inform his bank at once of any unauthorised cheques of which he becomes aware. . . .

Estoppel

Their Lordships having held that the company was not in breach of any duty owed by it to the banks, it is not possible to establish in this case an estoppel arising from mere silence, omission, or failure to act.

Mere silence or inaction cannot amount to a representation unless there be a duty to disclose or act: *Greenwood's* case [1933] AC 51, 57. And their Lordships would reiterate that unless conduct can be interpreted as amounting to an implied representation, it cannot constitute an estoppel: for the essence of estoppel is a representation (express or implied) intended to induce the person to whom it is made to adopt a course of conduct which results in detriment or loss: *Greenwood's* case, per Lord Tomlin, at p 57.

Appeal allowed.

NOTES

1. How can banks 'increase the severity of their terms of business'? In *Tai Hing* the banks relied on clauses in their contracts with the plaintiff customer which included a requirement that the customer should notify the bank within a specified time of any errors in the monthly bank statements, which would otherwise be deemed correct. Lord Scarman accepted that these clauses were contractual in effect but went on to hold that (at 709–710):

> . . . in no case do they constitute what has come to be called 'conclusive evidence clauses.' Their terms are not such as to bring home to the customer either 'the intended importance of the inspection he is being expressly or impliedly invited to make,' or that they are intended to have conclusive effect against him if he raises no query, or fails to raise a query in time, upon his bank statements. If banks wish to impose upon their

customers an express obligation to examine their monthly statements and to make those statements, in the absence of query, unchallengeable by the customer after expiry of a time limit, the burden of the objection and of the sanction imposed must be brought home to the customer. . . . The test is rigorous because the bankers would have their terms of business so construed as to exclude the rights which the customer would enjoy if they were not excluded by express agreement. It must be borne in mind that, in their Lordships' view, the true nature of the obligations of the customer to his bank where there is not express agreement is limited to the *Macmillan* and *Greenwood* duties. Clear and unambiguous provision is needed if the banks are to introduce into the contract a binding obligation upon the customer who does not query his bank statement to accept the statement as accurately setting out the debit items in the accounts.

2. The verification clauses in *Tai Hing* failed on grounds of construction. Such clauses will be strictly construed against the bank ie the courts will apply the *contra proferentem* rule. However, some doubt has been expressed as to whether the clauses in *Tai Hing* really did fall short of the standard demanded by Lord Scarman (E P Ellinger [1986] LMCLQ 8 at p 11) and verification clauses using language similar to that found in *Tai Hing*, have been upheld by the Canadian Courts (eg *Arrow Transfer Co Ltd v Royal Bank of Canada* (1972) 27 DLR (3d) 81, Supreme Court of Canada). Verification clauses may also fail for other reasons. They may not have been incorporated into the contract (on failure to incorporate terms, though in a different context, see *Burnett v Westminster Bank Ltd* [1966] 1 QB 742). In *Tai Hing* this was not an issue as the customer had signed the bank's conditions. Further, the clauses may be held to be unreasonable, and, therefore, ineffective, under ss 2 and 3 of the Unfair Contract Terms Act 1977. Under s 13(1)(c) of the 1977 Act, clauses which exclude or restrict rules of evidence or procedure are treated in the same way as those which exclude or restrict liability. See also the new EC Directive on Unfair Contract Terms (93/13), considered above at p 564.

3. It is clear from *Tai Hing* that unless an effective verification clause is incorporated into the bank–customer contract, the customer is under no duty to examine his bank statements. Reviewing *Tai Hing*, the Supreme Court of Canada in *Canadian Pacific Hotels Ltd v Bank of Montreal* (1987) 40 DLR (4th) 385 reached the same conclusion. Cf s 4–406 of the Uniform Commercial Code (US) which places an obligation on the customer to check his statements (see E P Ellinger *Modern Banking Law* (1987), p 134). In *Wealden Woodlands (Kent) Ltd v National Westminster Bank Ltd* (1983) 133 NLJ 719, McNeill J rejected the suggestion that he should bring the law into line with that operating in the USA. For criticism of the general rule, see Pollock (1910) 26 LQR 4 and Holden (1954) 17 MLR 41.

4. Three points may be made in support of the Privy Council's decision in *Tai Hing* to restrict the duties owed by a customer to those set out in *Macmillan* (to exercise reasonable care in executing his written orders so as not to mislead the bank by ambiguities or to facilitate forgery) and *Greenwood* (promptly to notify the bank of forgery). These are that:

(1) the bank is usually in a far better position to absorb the loss than its customer;
(2) the present law is clear and certain; and
(3) the bank can always incorporate a verification clause into the bank–customer contract if it requires protection.

However, the chorus of disapproval against *Tai Hing* has been loud (see, for example, the forceful criticism of the case made by M H Ogilvie in (1986) 11 CBLJ

220). The main complaint against the decision is that it fails to bring the law into line with modern banking practices (E P Ellinger [1986] LMCLQ 8). The Jack Committee noted in its Report that:

> **6.11** In the light of that case, banks in their evidence to us have argued strongly that the present law is unjust on bankers. One consultee representing certain banking interests, who is in favour of a statutory duty on customers to examine their bank statements, asks eloquently: 'Where is the justice . . . that a bank, which could probably only detect the fraud by instituting elaborate, and certainly expensive, procedures – for which the customer would resent paying – should be held wholly to blame when their substantial corporate customer with ample resources could have prevented such fraud by the institution of elementary precautions?' Another, in principle sympathetic to this approach, doubts if it would be acceptable under the Unfair Contract Terms Act 1977, and argues instead for a more limited statutory provision allowing the courts to take into account contributory negligence on the part of the customer, in the case of actions against his bank for loss through fraud. On this view, the defence should be available to the banker having regard to the customer's share in the responsibility for such loss or damage, and the legislation should enumerate the circumstances that the court should take into account in assessing contributory negligence. The same consultee would go further in the case of business customers (only), and require a 'settled account system' by which, once a stated period has elapsed, neither party could reopen transactions across the account save in the most exceptional circumstances.

The Jack Committee concluded that:

> **6.13** On balance, we are impressed by the case for some reform of the law. It does seem most unfair that customers who exhibit the degree of negligence shown by the plaintiff in the Tai Hing case should, in the eyes of the law, be entitled to sue their bank with impunity. But we join the opposition of the majority of our consultees to a statutory duty on customers to examine bank statements, which seems an unreasonable imposition. *A fortiori*, we also go along with the majority in rejecting a 'settled account system', even for business customers. In the case of both these options, we see force in Lord Scarman's contention that banking is not the customer's business. In other words, customers are entitled to rely on banks performing their own functions to the highest professional standards. Yet the bank is surely entitled to some protection against the most reprehensible negligence on its customer's part.

> **6.14** We therefore favour a statutory provision whereby, in an action against a bank in debt or for damages, arising from an unauthorised payment, contributory negligence may be raised as a defence, but only if the court is satisfied that the degree of negligence shown by the plaintiff is sufficiently serious for it to be inequitable that the bank should be liable for the whole amount of the debt or damages. The effect of this provision would be to permit a bank to plead contributory negligence to a limited extent in an action brought against it in debt arising out of unauthorised payment, but to restrict, subject to the same limitation, its ability to use that defence in a similar action for damages.

5. In its White Paper on Banking Services Law and Practice ((1990) Cm 1026, p 30), the Government agreed that the law at present was unfair to banks and stated that it was disposed to make it more evenly balanced between banks and their customers. However, before proposing any changes in the law in this area the Government stated its intention to await the forthcoming Law Commission Report on contributory negligence as a defence in contract. The Law Commission produced its Report in December 1993: 'Contributory Negligence as a Defence in Contract' (Law Com No 219). The Law Commission's main recommendation is that 'apportionment of the plaintiff's damages on the ground of contributory negligence should be available in actions in contract where the defendant is in breach of an express or implied contractual duty to take reasonable care or exercise reasonable skill or both, but not where he is in breach of a contractual term which imposes a higher level of duty' (para 4.1). In the context of banking, the Law Commission notes that:

> **5.20** Under our recommendations, the customer's contributory negligence could be raised as a defence by a bank where the bank is liable for damages for breach of a contractual duty of care, but not where the bank owed a strict duty to the customer, for example, in an action in debt. Banks are subject to an implied contractual duty to carry out the banking service with reasonable care and skill. The customer's contributory negligence will be relevant where the bank is in breach of that duty. However, for the most part actions against banks concern breach of mandate by the bank, for example, where third party fraud has resulted in an unauthorised payment which the bank has debited against the customer's account. The duty of a bank to adhere to the terms of its mandate is strict. Apportionment on the grounds of the customer's contributory negligence will not be available in respect of breach of this duty.

The Law Commission go on to accept that their recommendations do not deal with the problem of customers sharing in the responsibility for payment under a forged mandate. The Law Commission, like the Privy Council in the *Tai Hing* case, believe that the banks are best placed to protect themselves against the consequences of paying on a forged mandate through the use of contract terms such as verification clauses. We have already considered the limitations of that approach (above, p 593).

6. Many of the common law obligations of the customer exemplified in *Macmillan* are, so far as they relate to the use of plastic cards, now set out in the Code of Banking Practice (2nd ed, 1994). Dr R Lawson has submitted that the customer's obligation to advise their card issuer when the card has been lost or stolen, when someone else knows their PIN (the personal identity number necessary to use the card) and when their account includes an apparently incorrect item (paras 19.1 and 22.2), probably all fall within the ambit of *Macmillan* ((1992) 142 NLJ 346 at p 354). The Code states that the customer's liability for unauthorised use of the card is limited to £50 (para 20.3). This provision extends to users of every type of card the protection previously given only to users of credit-tokens (which can include a cash card and a bank guarantee card) under ss 83 and 84 of the Consumer Credit Act 1974. However, para 20.4 of the Code goes further and states that the customer 'will' be liable for all losses if he acted fraudulently and 'may' be held liable for all losses if he acted 'with gross negligence' (which is defined to include the customer's failure to comply with any of the requirements of para 18.2 – see below, p 632 – if such failure has caused those losses).

7. What happens if the customer benefits from an incorrect entry on his bank statement through, for example, the bank's error in crediting the customer's account with the same sum twice over? If the bank acts within a reasonable time it can rectify the statement to show the true facts. If the wrongly credited sum has actually been paid out, the bank can seek to recover it as money paid under a mistake of fact. However, if in reliance on an erroneous credit entry the customer has changed his position and it would be inequitable to require him to effect reimbursement, the bank will be estopped from asserting the mistake and prevented from recovering the sum (*United Overseas Bank v Jiwani* [1976] 1 WLR 964). Alternatively, the customer could raise a defence of change of position against the bank's restitutionary claim (see above, p 540). Furthermore, a bank is not entitled to dishonour cheques drawn bona fide and without negligence on the faith of an incorrect entry in the customer's bank statement: *Holland v Manchester and Liverpool District Banking Co Ltd* (1909) 25 TLR 386, 14 Com Cas 241.

QUESTIONS

1. A leaves his cheque book with B knowing that B has previously been convicted of forgery. B forges A's signature on the cheques and cashes them at A's bank. Can the bank debit A's account?

2. A employs B as his wages clerk. B presents a cheque for £10,000 to A for his signature. B tells A that the cheque is in payment of B's annual bonus of £1,000 (which B has in fact earned). As A is in a hurry he signs the cheque without noticing the discrepancy. If A's bank honours the cheque, can it debit A's account with £10,000? If B had simply forged A's signature on the cheque would A's bank be entitled to debit A's account with £1,000? See *B Liggett (Liverpool) Ltd v Barclays Bank Ltd* [1928] 1 KB 48; E P Ellinger and C Y Lee [1984] LMCLQ 459.

3. A employs B as his wages clerk. B forges A's signature on one of A's cheques and cashes it at A's bank. A's bank sues B in deceit. Could the bank hold A vicariously liable for B's fraud? See E P Ellinger *Modern Banking Law* (1987), p 296; Fridman *The Law of Agency*, p 331; cf *National Commercial Banking Corpn of Australia Ltd v Batty* (1986) 65 ALR 385 (Aust).

4. A and B are directors of C Ltd. C Ltd has instructed its bank that A is authorised to draw on the company's account jointly with B. In fact A draws a cheque for £1,000 without obtaining B's signature and this is honoured by the bank. Subsequently, B hears of this and makes an entry into the company's books recording that a loan of £1,000 has been made to A. Six months later the new board of directors of C Ltd resolve to bring an action against the bank for breach of mandate. Advise the bank. See *London Intercontinental Trust Ltd v Barclays Bank Ltd* [1980] 1 Lloyd's Rep 241; *Limpgrange Ltd v BCCI SA* [1986] FLR 36.

5. Despite an instruction printed in his cheque book which states that a line should be drawn after the payee's name, A draws a cheque leaving a space between the payee's name and the printed words 'or order'. A hands the cheque to his friend B for delivery to the payee but B inserts 'per B' in the space after the payee's name, indorses it 'B' and obtains payment from A's bank. Can the bank debit A's account? See *Slingsby v District Bank Ltd* [1931] 2 KB 588, affd [1932] 1 KB 544; cf *Lumsden & Co v London Trustee Savings Bank* [1971] 1 Lloyd's Rep 114 at 121.

13 Termination of banker–customer relationship

Fixed term accounts will mature at the agreed time so that neither bank nor customer may unilaterally terminate their relationship before then. Customers with cheque accounts or ordinary savings accounts may unilaterally terminate the relationship at any time by drawing out the remaining funds and asking for the account to be closed. Banks must give reasonable notice before closing such accounts and terminating the relationship (*Joachimson v Swiss Bank Corpn*, see above, p 557, per Warrington LJ at 125, and per Atkin LJ at 127; the Code of Banking Practice (2nd ed, 1994), para 4.5). Reasonable notice must be long enough in the circumstances to enable the customer to make alternative banking arrangements (*Prosperity Ltd v Lloyd's Bank Ltd* (1923) 39 TLR 372). The bank need not give reasonable notice if merely calling in an overdraft and the bank does not terminate the relationship by demanding repayment (*National Bank of Greece SA v Pinios Shipping Co No 1, The Maira* [1990] 1 AC 637, HL).

A bank may close an account without reasonable notice if it combines two accounts. This will have the effect of closing one of the accounts without notice. In *Garnett v McKewan* (1872) LR 8 Exch 10 the court did not regard the right of combination as subject to notice. However, in *National Westminster Bank Ltd v Halesowen Presswork & Assemblies Ltd* [1972] AC 785 at 807, 810, 820, HL, the question of notice was left open, although there are strong dicta suggesting that notice, even though with immediate effect, is required.

As the relationship between bank and customer is regarded as a personal one, it will automatically terminate on the customer's death, bankruptcy, dissolution (if a partnership) or liquidation (if a company). On liquidation of the bank the relationship terminates and the balance standing to the customer's account becomes payable at once without the need of a demand (*Re Russian Commercial & Industrial Bank* [1955] Ch 148).

14 Dispute resolution

'Good Banking': Code of Banking Practice (2nd ed, 1994), paras 7.0–7.4

7.0 HANDLING CUSTOMERS' COMPLAINTS

7.1 Each bank and building society will have its own internal procedures for handling customers' complaints fairly and expeditiously.

7.2 Banks and building societies will inform their customers that they have a complaints procedure. Customers who wish to make a complaint will be told how to do so and what further steps are available if they believe that the complaint has not been dealt with satisfactorily either at branch or more senior level within the bank or building society.

7.3 Banks and building societies will ensure that all their staff who deal directly with customers are made aware of their institution's internal complaints procedure and are able to help customers by giving correct information about it.

7.4 Banks subscribing to the Code will be expected to belong to one or other of the following:

The Banking Ombudsman Scheme;
The Finance and Leasing Association Conciliation and Arbitration Schemes; or
The Consumer Credit Trade Association Arbitration Scheme.

Building societies have to belong to the Building Societies Ombudsman Scheme or another authorised scheme.

Banks and building societies will provide details of the applicable scheme to customers using such methods as leaflets, notices in branches or in appropriate literature, showing their current addresses and telephone numbers.

NOTES

1. The Building Societies Ombudsman scheme was established under Part IX of the Building Society Act 1986 and membership of the scheme is compulsory (although awards made by the Building Societies Ombudsman are not binding on member societies). The Banking Ombudsman Scheme (BOS), which became operational in 1986, is non-statutory and membership is on a voluntary basis (although awards made by the Banking Ombudsman are binding on member banks). The scheme covers 26 participating banks and 21 of their designated associates (usually banking subsidiary companies providing credit card, insurance and trustee services). This means that some 99 per cent of individuals holding a personal bank account fall within the scheme.

2. In its Report on Banking Services Law and Practice, the Jack Committee recommended that the voluntary BOS should be placed on a statutory basis (paras 15.24–15.26). This recommendation was opposed by the Banking Ombudsman and the Council of the Banking Ombudsman who claimed the present scheme was working well and that the proposed scheme would entail both the loss of the Ombudsman's power to make an award binding and a loss of flexibility which the voluntary scheme had maintained (*The Report of the Review Committee on Banking Services: A Response from the Council of the Banking Ombudsman*, April 1989). The Government also felt the present scheme worked well in practice and rejected the Jack Committee's proposal (White Paper (1990) Cm 1026, Annex 3, para 3.7).

3. For a critical analysis of the BOS, see P E Morris [1987] JBL 131 at 199. For a review of the first five years of the scheme, see P E Morris [1992] LMCLQ 227.

CHAPTER 18

Cheques and other instruments

1 Cheques

A cheque is defined by s 73 of the Bills of Exchange Act 1882 as 'a bill of exchange drawn on a banker payable on demand'. Section 73 also states that except as otherwise provided in the part of the Bills of Exchange Act 1882 relating to cheques (ss 73–82), the provisions of that Act applicable to bills of exchange payable on demand apply to cheques.

A cheque is, therefore, a negotiable instrument. But it is also a mandate from a customer to his bank to pay according to the customer's order. These two separate characteristics must be kept in mind when reading this chapter.

(a) Crossed cheques

General crossing

FIGURE 1   **CHEQUE CROSSED GENERALLY**

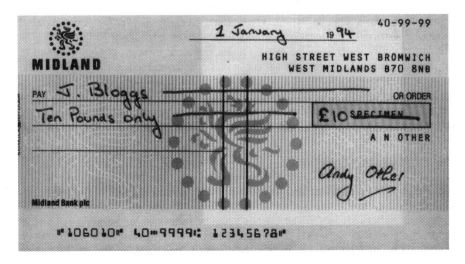

Figure 1 shows a cheque which is crossed generally (s 76(1)). Sometimes the words 'and company', or an abbreviation of those words, appear between the two parallel transverse lines. These words add nothing to the cheque which is crossed generally so long as two parallel transverse lines appear across its face. If the cheque is crossed generally it must be presented for payment through a bank account; the holder cannot present it in person for cash. However, following a recommendation contained in the Report of the Review Committee on Banking Services Law and Practice (the 'Jack Committee') ((1989) Cm 622, rec 7(4)), the Government intends to introduce legislation to make a cheque crossed generally 'non-negotiable', ie transferable but the transferee will not acquire a better title than his transferor had (White Paper (1990) Cm 1026, Annex 5, para 5.5). A crossed cheque will still have to be paid to a bank.

Special crossing

FIGURE 2   CHEQUE CROSSED SPECIALLY

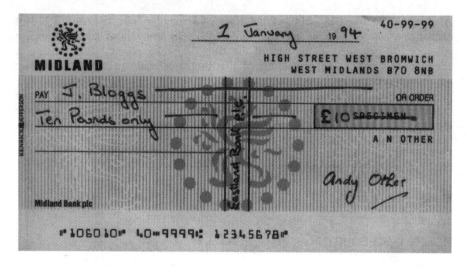

Figure 2 shows a cheque which is crossed specially (s 76(2)). Two parallel transverse lines are unnecessary, although they may be added. If the cheque is crossed specially it can only be presented for payment through the bank named in the cheque. However, following a recommendation contained in the Report of the Jack Committee (rec 7(3)), the Government intends to introduce legislation to abolish the special crossing (White Paper (1990) Cm 1026, Annex 5, para 5.5). The special crossing is now hardly ever used and the Government regards it as no longer necessary.

'Not negotiable' crossing

Figure 3 shows a crossed cheque marked 'not negotiable'. By s 81 of the 1882 Act, the transferee of such a cheque cannot acquire, and cannot give, a better title than his transferor had. However, the cheque remains transferable. To prevent transfer the cheque must contain words prohibiting transfer, or indicating an intention that it should not be transferable (eg it must be marked 'not transferable', or be drawn

FIGURE 3   CHEQUE CROSSED 'NOT NEGOTIABLE'

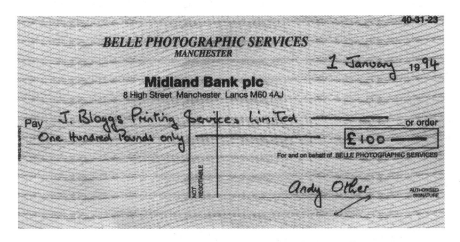

'Pay X only'): see s 8(1) of the 1882 Act and above, p 498. When the Government introduces legislation making a cheque crossed generally 'non-negotiable' (see above, p 600), the express marking of such a cheque 'not negotiable', will become otiose (although it will not be prohibited). If an *uncrossed* cheque is marked 'not negotiable' it is probably not transferable: *Hibernian Bank Ltd v Gysin and Hanson* [1939] 1 KB 483; cf *National Bank v Silke* [1891] 1 QB 435 at 438; and see above, p 499.

'Account payee' crossing

FIGURE 4   CHEQUE CROSSED 'ACCOUNT PAYEE'

Figure 4 shows a crossed cheque marked 'account payee'. Under s 1 of the Cheques Act 1992 (introducing a new s 81A(1) into the Bills of Exchange Act 1882; see below, p 611), the marking of a crossed cheque in this way (or marking it 'a/c payee', with or without the word 'only') makes the cheque non-transferable and only valid as between the parties to it (criticised by E P Ellinger (1992) 108 LQR 15 at p 19). The enactment of the Cheques Act 1992 (which came into force on 16 June 1992) altered the law in that previously the addition of the words 'account payee' to the crossing did not affect the transferability of the cheque but merely constituted a warning to the collecting bank that the cheque should not be collected for an account other than that of the named payee: *National Bank v Silke*, above; *Importers Co Ltd v Westminster Bank Ltd* [1927] 2 KB 297; *Universal Guarantee Pty Ltd v National Bank of Australasia Ltd* [1965] 1 WLR 691; see also *Standard Bank of South Africa Ltd v Sham Magazine Centre* 1977 (1) SA 484. For the effect of such a crossing on the statutory defences of the paying and collecting banks, see below, p 621 and p 624.

Who can cross a cheque? By s 77 of the 1882 Act only the drawer, holder and certain bankers may cross a cheque. A holder may cross an uncrossed cheque or alter a previous crossing by making it more restrictive eg turning a general crossing into a special crossing (s 77(2), (3) and (4)). A banker to whom a cheque is specially crossed may cross it to another banker for collection (s 77(5)). If an uncrossed cheque, or a cheque crossed generally, is sent to a banker for collection, he may cross it specially to himself (s 77(6)).

What is the effect of the drawee bank ignoring a crossing? Under s 79(2) of the 1882 Act, if the bank pays otherwise than in accordance with the crossing it may be liable to the true owner (see above, p 500) for any loss caused to him. The only exception to this rule is when the cheque on presentation for payment does not appear to be crossed or to have a crossing which has been obliterated or have been added to or altered in a way not authorised by the 1882 Act. In these circumstances the bank will not be held liable to either the true owner or the drawer if it pays the cheque in good faith and without negligence (s 79(2)). Save in so far as the bank is protected by the proviso to s 79(2) just referred to, the bank may not debit its customer's account if it pays otherwise than in accordance with the crossing because it will have exceeded its mandate (*Bobbett v Pinkett* (1876) 1 Ex D 368 at 372, 374). Save for an alteration to the crossing authorised by s 77 (see above), as the crossing is a material part of the cheque, if it is altered after the cheque is issued by the drawer, and the alteration is apparent, the cheque may be avoided (ss 78 and 64).

QUESTIONS

1. What are the benefits of crossing a cheque?
2. Are any of the following cheques transferable:

(1) An uncrossed cheque marked 'account payee only'. See Penn, Shea, Arora *The Law Relating to Domestic Banking* (1987), Vol 1, para 8.12?
(2) A crossed cheque drawn 'Pay X or bearer' and marked 'account payee only'?
(3) A crossed cheque drawn by X 'Pay Y or order', which is delivered to Y and marked by him 'account payee only'? See *Byles on Bills of Exchange* (26th ed, 1988) ('Byles'), p 86 and compare it with *Akrokerri (Atlantic) Mines Ltd v Economic Bank* [1904] 2 KB 465 which, obviously, predates the changes introduced by the Cheques Act 1992.

(b) The clearing system

Barclays Bank plc v Bank of England [1985] 1 All ER 385, Bingham J sitting as judge-arbitrator

Bingham J: . . . 8. The origins of the clearing house as it exists today can be traced back to a device adopted by bank employees in the eighteenth century, largely (as it would seem) for their own convenience. During the early years of the eighteenth century the banks employed walk clerks whose task it was to call at other banks in the City and the West End of London to present cheques for payment and obtain cash in exchange. As the use of cheques increased so this task became increasingly laborious. As a result a practice grew whereby, instead of visiting other banks on foot, the clerks would meet at a central point, exchange cheques and settle the difference between the total exchanged. To begin with, the meeting place was unofficial and unrecognised, but the advantages of this central exchange were obvious and in due course a room was hired and, in 1833, a building erected on the present site. The respondent entered the clearing house in 1864.

9. The clearing house is only one part, although a central part, of the complex and sophisticated clearing system which now operates in this country. This arbitration was concerned with debit clearing only, and effectively with the general clearing and the town clearing . . . Because the operation of these clearings is extremely familiar to all parties to this arbitration, I need not attempt to give any comprehensive account of the system in practice, nor need I identify the differences between the procedures of the various claimants where these exist. I shall confine myself to the bare summary needed to make sense of the discussion which follows.

10. I start with the case where a customer of a bank (the presenting or collecting bank) delivers to the presenting bank for collection and credit to his account a cheque drawn on another bank (the paying bank) by a person having an account at a branch of the paying bank, the cheque being eligible for handling through the general clearing but ineligible for handling through the town clearing. The steps which will normally follow are these. (1) The cheque will be stamped (crossed) on receipt by the branch which receives it. The amount will normally be credited to the customer's account forthwith. The customer will not, however, receive value for the cheque on that date: thus the customer cannot without agreement withdraw the sum prior to clearance, he will not earn interest or (if overdrawn) be relieved of his obligation to pay interest and it will not rank as a credit for purposes of calculating bank charges. The credit is provisional in the sense that it will be reversed if the cheque is dishonoured or not satisfactorily cleared and there is in any event a delay before it will become fully effective. (2) The branch which receives the cheque will in most cases encode it, by adding the sum payable under it in magnetisible ink to the cheque number, branch reference number and account number which are already printed on the bottom of it. At the end of the banking day the branch will sort out the cheques received during the day into bundles, one bundle for each bank whose cheques have been received. (3) These bundles will be collected from the branch during the evening of that day or early in the morning of the following day and taken to the clearing department of the presenting bank. If the encoding has not for any reason been done at the branch it will be done there, early on the day following receipt of the cheque at the branch. All the bundles received by the presenting bank from all its branches will then be amalgamated and placed in boxes labelled with the name of the bank on which they are drawn, the paying bank. They will also be checked to ensure that the cheques are all facing the same way, have the magnetisable ink characters at the bottom, are free of staples and are unfolded. They will be subject to no other inspection. (4) The cheques so sorted will then be taken in closed boxes to the clearing house [10 Lombard St, London], where they are either handed over to employees of the various paying banks or placed in racks reserved for those banks. The boxes are not opened and the cheques themselves are not the subject of consideration or inspection, which would be quite impracticable given that the cheques so handled run to several millions each day. (Sometimes the exchange or delivery may take place not at the clearing house but at the

clearing department of the paying bank, but it is not suggested that this variation of practice gives rise to any difference of principle). (5) From the clearing house the cheques will be taken to the clearing department of the paying bank, whose employees then feed all the cheques received for payment into reader-sorter machines. This process performs a number of functions. First, it sorts the cheques received into bundles for each of the paying bank's branches on which cheques have been drawn (and, for some branches, further sorts the cheques according to account number of customer's name). Second, it checks the totals charged against the paying bank in the clearing by the various presenting banks which have delivered cheques for payment, making necessary corrections. Third, it records the magnetisable references on the cheques sorted, so that this information can be transmitted to the computer centre where branch accounts are maintained. From this information a computer projection is (or is in some cases) made showing the state of customer's accounts at the end of the next day if the cheques are paid and no further transactions occur, but no alteration is made to the accounts themselves. No consideration is given to the validity or payability of a cheque at this stage. Thus a cheque obviously defective, for example because unsigned, will not be weeded out but will be treated in the same way as all other cheques. (6) Having been sorted, the cheques drawn on each branch will be delivered to that branch, so as to arrive during the night of the day on which they were received from the presenting bank or early the following morning. On the opening of the branch each cheque received overnight for payment will be inspected and considered by an officer of the branch to determine whether the cheque is technically in order (properly signed and dated, with numbers and figures corresponding, without unsigned alteration, and so on) and whether there is any reason (such as lack of funds, countermand or injunction) why the cheque should not be honoured. In the case of cheques for small amounts, or large and respected customers issuing large numbers of cheques, the process of inspection and consideration may be abbreviated, but the process described is the norm. If the cheque is to be paid, it is cancelled and the drawer's account is debited at the end of that working day. The debit projected by the computer will then take effect. If the cheque is not to be paid, it will be sent by first class post at the end of that working day to the branch at which it was delivered for collection and the computer projection entry will be reversed. Under rules agreed between the banks with seats in the clearing house, to which I must return, this step must be taken on the day the cheque is received at the branch, save in the case of inadvertence, when a delay until the next day is permitted. A telephone call will in that case be made to the branch at which the cheque was received for collection. (7) At the end of each working day the claimants settle between themselves by paying net balances between them. This is done by means of daily transfers to and from accounts maintained by each of them with the respondent. Such settlements comprise differences established in the general clearing carried out by their clearing departments on the preceding day and in the town clearing on that day, in each case on the assumption that all the cheques received for payment will be honoured. Dishonoured or unpaid cheques are the subject of later adjustment.

NOTES

1. There are two different cheque clearing systems operating under the control of the Association for Payment Clearing Services. To take advantage of one of the clearing systems a financial institution must be a member of it. If a financial institution is not a member of a particular system it can employ a member institution to act as its agent. The system described by Bingham J is the general cheque clearing system. In addition there is a similar town clearing system which handles cheques for more than £10,000 drawn on a City branch of a participating bank and received for collection by another such branch. The town clearing system is a streamlined version of the general clearing system and generally allows orders to be cleared in one day. It is used for only 1 per cent of cheques handled, but this relatively small number of cheques accounts for more than 90 per cent in value of all cheques drawn.

2. By s 45 of the Bills of Exchange Act 1882 a cheque must be presented for payment at the branch of the bank on which it is drawn. However, by s 46(2)(e) the drawer, and any indorser, of the cheque may expressly or impliedly waive, as regards himself, the holder's duty to present the bill for payment. For the consequences of failure to make presentation when it has not been waived, see above, p 516.

3. In *Barclays Bank plc v Bank of England*, above, at 387, Bingham J held that, where bank A (the presenting bank) receives from a customer for collection a cheque drawn on bank B (the paying bank) by a person having an account at a branch of the paying bank, and the cheque is dealt with through the inter-bank system for clearing cheques, the presenting bank's responsibility to its customer in respect of the collection of the cheque is discharged only when the cheque is physically delivered to that branch of the paying bank for decision whether it should be paid or not. He regarded the paying bank 'as being, from the time of receiving the cheque [in the clearing house] until the time of presenting it, a sub-agent of the presenting bank, which is itself an agent of the payee' (at 392).

4. The necessity of physical presentation of the cheque to the paying bank means that it is not possible for the bank collecting the cheque for its customer to present it for payment by electronic means. Electronic presentation, or truncation, of a cheque would entail passing details from the magnetic codeline on the cheque by computer from the collecting to the paying bank, with the cheque remaining in the possession of the collecting bank. Cheque truncation would bring to an end the daily movement of up to 10 million cheques between banks and different branches of banks as physical presentation is made. The commercial advantages of eliminating this time consuming process have led the Jack Committee to recommend (rec 7(8)), and the Government to agree to (White Paper (1990) Cm 1026, Annex 5, para 5.13), a change in the law to allow presentation of cheques by electronic means. However, the Government has been quick to point out that when the law is changed to allow for cheque truncation it will be necessary to ensure that the interests of customers are fully protected. The Government proposes that there should be provision in the Code of Banking Practice that, unless the evidence to resolve a dispute about a truncated cheque is produced within a specific number of working days of the complaint, the bank should recredit the customer's account that has been debited. The Government further proposes that under the Code the customer should have a right to receive a copy (or the original) of any cheque which has been truncated. For further discussion of the legal implications of cheque truncation, see J Vroegop [1990] LMCLQ 244.

(c) Protection of the paying bank

'Bank's liability for paying fraudulently issued cheques' by E P Ellinger (1985) 5 Ox JLS 293, pp 293–294

1. *Introduction*

In recent years there has been an abundance of cases in which dishonest employees have perpetrated frauds by misusing their employer's cheque book. By now some well defined patterns have emerged. There are cases in which the employee obtains a signature executed on a blank or on a partly completed cheque and then fills the instrument in improperly or changes a 'material detail' (within s 64 of the Bills of Exchange Act 1882, the 'BEA') by making the instrument payable to himself or by raising its amount.

Other frauds include the theft of instruments payable to the employer and their payment into the employee's personal account either under a forged indorsement (see, eg *Orbit Mining and Trading Co v Westminster Bank Ltd* [1963] 1 QB 794) or by the imaginative means of opening an account under a suitable fictitious name. By the same token, the employee may steal cheques issued by his employer to a genuine client and pay them to the credit of an account surreptitiously opened by him in the true payee's name. (See, eg *Marfani & Co Ltd v Midland Bank Ltd* [1968] 1 WLR 956; *Lumsden & Co v London Trustee Savings Bank* [1971] 1 Lloyd's Rep 114). The last and most crude type of fraud is the forgery of the employer's signature as drawer by the employee (for a remarkable case in recent years see *National Bank of New Zealand v Walpole & Patterson Ltd* [1975] 2 NZLR 7).

In all three types of case, the drawee bank honours the instrument in breach of its authority. In the first type of case, the cheque is vitiated when the material detail is altered (s 64 BEA). In addition, the bank pays an excessive amount or meets the demand of a person other than the intended payee. In the second case, it pays a cheque under a forged indorsement of the payee, which does not transfer the instrument (*Lacave v Crédit Lyonnais* [1897] 1 QB 148). The bank therefore does not comply with the drawer's instruction to pay the instrument to the 'holder' (given when the cheque is drawn to order: BEA, s 8).

It is clear that bankers are unable to recognize a fraud involving a forged indorsement. The signature of the payee or of the holder is unknown to them. A protection was conferred on them for the first time under s 19 of the Stamp Act 1853, which provided the model for the current provision: s 60 of the BEA. (Section 19 is still in force in respect of instruments which, being outside the scope of the BEA, are not governed by s 60; the bankers' draft – drawn on himself – is an example; *Capital and Counties Bank Ltd v Gordon* [1903] AC 240, 250–1; *Charles v Blackwell* (1877) 2 CPD 151, 159.) In cases of this type, the best advice that can be given to the customer (or 'true owner') is to sue the collecting bank. That bank is liable in conversion, unless it has collected the cheque in good faith, without negligence and for a customer (in which case it is protected by s 4 of the Cheques Act 1957.) (That he could also sue the collecting bank, see Chitty on Contracts (25th ed, 1983) $2463 and authorities there cited.)

In the other two types of fraud, the customer's rights against his own bank depend on common law doctrines. His argument would usually be that the bank paid the cheque without having the mandate to do so. This is particularly so where the customer's signature as drawer was forged. (That the bank's liability is not based on its failure to recognize the customer's signature has been clear since *Cocks v Masterman* (1858) 18 CB 273.) (That he could also sue the collecting bank, see *Chitty on Contracts* (25th ed, 1983) § 2463 and authorities there cited.)

The customer's action against his own bank usually assumes the form of an application for a declaration that the bank is not entitled to debit his account with the forged items. The bank has two possible defences. The one is based on negligence and on estoppel. Fundamentally, it asserts that the frauds or forgeries were occasioned by the customer's own carelessness, which involved a breach of a duty of care owed by him to the bank. It is said that he is, accordingly, precluded from disputing the debits involved. The other, frequently related defence, is based on the customer's failure to detect the frauds through his periodic statements. In some cases these statements include counterfoils which the customer is expected to return to the bank with an indication of any unwarranted debits.

Both defences have been considered by English and Commonwealth authorities. Traditionally, the first defence has been upheld only where the customer's carelessness was directly related to the drawing of the cheque. The second defence has been unsuccessful in England. It has been held consistently that the customer does not owe a contractual duty to peruse his statements or, in earlier days, his passbook. In Canada, where such a duty is undertaken by the customer at the time of the opening of the account, the law has taken a different course.

NOTES

1. In the circumstances identified by Professor Ellinger the drawee or paying bank (the 'paying bank') cannot debit its customer's account if it honours the cheque.

Furthermore, the paying bank may also be liable to the true owner of the cheque in conversion for the face value of the cheque (*Smith v Union Bank of London* (1875) LR 10 QB 291 (affd 1 QBD 31); *Bavins Junior and Sims v London and South Western Bank Ltd* [1900] 1 QB 270 at 278; cf *Charles v Blackwell* (1877) 2 CPD 151 at 162–163. See also R M Goode *Commercial Law* (1982), pp 517–518; E P Ellinger *Modern Banking Law* (1987), pp 286–289; R Bradgate and N Savage *Commercial Law* (1991), para 27.2.1). If the bank can trace the recipient of the money wrongfully paid, it may have a remedy against him for money paid under a mistake (*National Westminster Bank Ltd v Barclays Bank International Ltd* [1975] QB 654). If the money is paid to a collecting bank and that bank has already paid it over to its principal, the collecting bank will have a defence to the paying bank's restitutionary claim (see above, p 541).

2. *Common law defences of the paying bank.* Even if the bank has paid a cheque in the circumstances outlined by Professor Ellinger, it may still debit its customer's account in the following circumstances:

(1) the customer may be estopped by representation or negligence from relying on a forged or unauthorised signature (see above, pp 527 ff); if it is his own signature which is forged or unauthorised, he may also be held to have adopted or ratified it (see above, p 530);

(2) if there is a forged or unauthorised indorsement of a cheque payable to bearer (either because it was drawn payable to bearer, or because it has been indorsed in blank, or because it was drawn payable to a fictitious or non-existent payee) the bank can pay the bearer and debit the customer's account, if payment was made in good faith and without notice of any defect of the bearer's title to the cheque, because payment to the bearer of such a cheque is payment in due course which discharges the instrument (s 59 of the 1882 Act);

(3) if the cheque has been materially altered after issue by a person other than the drawer and without his authority or consent, the paying bank cannot take advantage of the proviso to s 64(1) of the Bills of Exchange Act 1882 as it is not a holder in due course (*Slingsby v District Bank Ltd* [1931] 2 KB 588 at 600; affd [1932] 1 KB 544) but it may be able to debit its customer's account when the amount of the cheque has been fraudulently raised on the basis that the customer's mandate is still good for the original amount, ie the customer can only require his account to be reinstated to the extent of the increase (*Chalmers and Guest on Bills of Exchange, Cheques and Promissory Notes* (14th ed, 1991) ('Chalmers and Guest'), p 539) – in any event the bank may be able to argue that the customer is estopped by his negligence from questioning the debit if the alteration is due to the customer's failure to take usual and reasonable precautions when drawing the cheque (*London Joint Stock Bank Ltd v Macmillan* [1918] AC 777);

(4) if the payment discharges the customer's prior indebtedness to the recipient of the payment, the bank can be subrogated to the rights of that recipient and debit its customer's account accordingly (*B Liggett (Liverpool) Ltd v Barclays Bank Ltd* [1928] 1 KB 48; Ellinger and Lee [1984] LMCLQ 459; but see also Goff and Jones *The Law of Restitution* (4th ed, 1993), pp 114 ff.

3. *Statutory defences.* There are three statutory defences available to the paying bank:

(1) Section 60 of the Bills of Exchange Act 1882 provides that a banker who pays in good faith and in the ordinary course of business a cheque (crossed or

uncrossed) drawn on him payable to order on which the indorsement of the payee or any subsequent indorsement is forged or unauthorised is deemed to have paid it in due course.

(2) Section 80 of the Bills of Exchange Act 1882 provides that where a banker upon whom a crossed cheque is drawn (or, by s 5 of the Cheques Act 1957, certain other crossed instruments) pays the cheque to another banker in good faith and without negligence and in accordance with the terms of the crossing, the banker paying the cheque, and, if the cheque has come into the hands of the payee, the drawer, are respectively entitled to the same rights and are placed in the same position as if payment had been made to the true owner thereof. The section will apply if the cheque bears a forged or unauthorised indorsement but it will not protect the paying bank if the drawer's signature has been forged or made without his authority as the instrument is not then a cheque at all (see R M Goode *Commercial Law* (1982), p 509).

(3) Section 1 of the Cheques Act 1957 provides that, if in good faith and in the ordinary course of business the bank pays a cheque drawn on it but which is not indorsed or is irregularly indorsed, it does not in doing so incur any liability by reason only of the absence of, or irregularity in, indorsement, and is deemed to have paid in due course. However, in its memorandum of 23 September 1957, the Committee of London Clearing Bankers stated that paying banks should require indorsement of cheques cashed over the counter and of cheques with receipt forms attached to them. If a bank pays a cheque without an indorsement as required by the Committee of London Clearing Bankers' memorandum, it would not be acting in the ordinary course of business and would forfeit the protection of s 1 of the Cheques Act 1957.

If the paying bank can bring itself within the protection of any of these statutory provisions it may debit its customer's account with the sum paid. If the bank can rely on s 80 of the 1882 Act or s 1 of the 1957 Act it will also have a defence against any action brought against it by the true owner. Whether the bank will have a defence against an action by the true owner if it can only bring itself within s 60 of the 1882 Act remains unclear (R M Goode *Commercial Law* (1982), p 511 and Chalmers and Guest, p 521 recognise the defence; E P Ellinger *Modern Banking Law* (1987), p 288 and R Bradgate and N Savage *Commercial Law* (1991), p 459 appear to reject the defence).

Carpenters' Co v British Mutual Banking Co Ltd [1938] 1 KB 511, Court of Appeal

The plaintiffs kept an account with the defendant bank. The plaintiffs' clerk (B) also held an account with the defendant bank. Over a period of time B misappropriated cheques drawn by the plaintiffs payable to the order of various tradesmen who had supplied goods to them. He also procured cheques to be drawn by the plaintiffs in favour of tradesmen who had not supplied goods. In both cases B forged the indorsement of the payees and paid the cheques into his account. The plaintiffs brought an action against the defendant bank for the amount of the cheques. Branson J found as a fact that the defendant bank did not act without negligence and so had lost the protection of s 82 of the Bills of Exchange Act 1882 (now s 4 of the Cheques Act 1957), but that they had paid the cheques in good faith and in the ordinary course of business and, notwithstanding their negligence, they were protected by s 60 of the 1882 Act. The plaintiffs appealed.

Greer LJ: . . . In the present case what happened was that when the cheques were presented to the defendant bank they had never ceased to be the property of the drawers, the Carpenters' Company, as they had never in fact been indorsed by the payees. The defendant bank was then asked by Blackborow to receive the cheques, and to place the amounts to the credit of his private account with it. This the bank did, and by so doing it in my judgment converted the cheques to its own use and became liable to the Carpenters' Company, the drawers of the cheques, for the face value of the cheques.

In my judgment s 60 of the Bills of Exchange Act 1882 only protects a bank when that bank is merely a paying bank, and is not a bank which receives the cheque for collection. In my judgment the learned judge was wrong in treating the defendant bank as if the bank had merely been a paying bank, and in failing to apply the law of conversion to the facts proved before him. The sole question which he had to decide was whether the bank was protected by s 82 of the Bills of Exchange Act from its liability for conversion of the cheques. He treated s 82 as applicable to the defendant bank, but decided that it had not proved that it received payment without negligence, but on the contrary he decided that it was negligent. . . .

It remains to say something with reference to the questions discussed in the judgment as to the effect of s 19 of the Stamp Act 1853. I agree with the view to which Slesser LJ called attention in the course of the argument that s 60 of the Bills of Exchange Act 1882 must be treated as inconsistent, so far as cheques are concerned, with the provisions of s 19 of the Stamp Act 1853 and the sole duty of the Court after the passing of the Bills of Exchange Act is to apply s 60 of that Act. The observations of Stirling LJ in *Gordon v London, City & Midland Bank* ([1902] 1 KB 242) were made per incuriam, as they refer to s 19 of the Stamp Act as if it had been part of the Bills of Exchange Act.

I have just referred to the mistake made by Stirling LJ in *Gordon's* case, but the case calls for consideration from another point of view. The cheques in that case belonged to various classes, but they were all crossed cheques. Class No 4 related to crossed cheques drawn on one branch of the defendant bank and handed to another branch for collection. As to these cheques it was held by the Master of the Rolls, Sir Richard Henn Collins, though with some difficulty, that though the defendant bank was a collecting bank as well as a paying bank, it was protected from liability by reason of s 60 of the Bills of Exchange Act. I find it a little difficult to follow the logic of this reasoning, because the bank was no less a collecting bank because it was collecting from one of its branches for the customer and paying the money so collected for the benefit of the fraudulent presenter of the cheque; but, be this as it may, it seems to me that the actual decision does not bind me in the present case inasmuch as there was an express finding of the jury on which the Court of Appeal acted that the bank acted without negligence. It seems to me impossible to say in the present case that the bank acted without negligence. Branson J has expressly found that it acted negligently, and it cannot, therefore, in my judgment, be heard to say when acting negligently that it was acting in the ordinary course of business within the meaning of s 60 of the Bills of Exchange Act 1882. The finding in this case that the bank acted negligently in my judgment distinguishes this case from *Gordon's* case. I note that by para 7 of the statement of claim the action was based alternatively on negligence. I think on this ground the decision in *Gordon's* case is not an authority on which we are bound to decide that the bank having acted negligently is excused by reason of s 60 of the Bills of Exchange Act 1882 from the consequences of its negligence. . . .

For the reasons above stated I am of opinion, though with some hesitation, that the learned judge was wrong in holding that the bank was entitled to the protection of s 60 of the Bills of Exchange Act, and the appeal will be allowed with costs, and judgment entered for the Carpenters' Company for the face value of all the cheques received by the bank and passed to the credit of Blackborow during the six years preceding the issue of the writ.

Slesser LJ: In this case the critical question arises whether or not the defendants have wrongfully received the proceeds of the plaintiffs' cheques and converted them. In so far as they received the plaintiffs' cheques at Blackborow's request and credited their customer Blackborow with the proceeds, which were at all times the property of the plaintiffs, they appear to me to have acted, albeit wrongly, as a receiving bank as well as in the capacity of a paying bank.

As paying banker they may well be protected by s 60 of the Bills of Exchange Act 1882 in so far as they acted in good faith, which is not disputed, and in the ordinary course of business. Branson J has come to the conclusion that in all the facts of this case, which I do not repeat, they did so act in the ordinary course of business. It was argued by Mr Schiller that in so far as the learned judge has held that they failed to show that they acted without negligence within the meaning of s 82 of the Bills of Exchange Act that therefore they cannot be held to have acted in the ordinary course of business. I do not agree; negligence does not necessarily preclude the protection of s 60, a view made clear in the case of the other requirement, of good faith, by s 90 of the same Act, which in terms provides that 'a thing is deemed to be done in good faith, within the meaning of this Act, where it is in fact done honestly, whether it is done negligently or not.' This provision is helpful, I think, in deciding whether an admittedly negligent act can be done in the ordinary course of business. In *Vagliano's* case ([1891] AC 107 at 117) Lord Halsbury LC, speaking of the alleged negligence of bankers evidenced by the pursuit of an unusual course of business, says: 'I should doubt whether . . . it would be possible to affirm that any particular course was either usual or unusual in the sense that there is some particular course to be pursued when circumstances occur, necessarily giving rise to suspicion.' Branson J points out in his judgment in the present case that there was nothing in the steps taken by the bank which was not in the ordinary course of business, and I agree with him.

Bissell & Co v Fox Bros & Co ((1885) 53 LT 193), which the learned judge cites, was a case decided under s 19 of the Stamp Act 1853, which section has no limitation of reference to payments in the ordinary course of business and therefore is of no assistance on that question in the present case. (See also the dicta of Stirling LJ in *Gordon's* case ([1902] 1 KB 242), which also can only refer to s 19 of the Stamp Act 1853.) That section, I think, is impliedly repealed by s 60 of the Bills of Exchange Act 1882, in the case of bills of exchange and cheques: see Lord Lindley in *Capital & Counties Bank v Gordon* ([1903] AC 240 at 251). But though I am of opinion that the Stamp Act 1853 is not here applicable, I think that the judge was entitled to hold on the facts that s 60 of the Bills of Exchange Act 1882, applied to this case, and therefore it follows that the bankers as payers are to be deemed to have paid the bill in due course notwithstanding that the indorsement has been forged, and I so treat them.

As receiving bank, however, unless protected by statute, they were guilty of conversion and liable in trover or for money had and received, for they dealt with the cheques which, for the want of a payee, were still the property of the plaintiffs in a manner inconsistent with the plaintiffs' rights as the true owners. See Lord Lindley in *Capital & Counties Bank v Gordon* ([1903] AC 240); Collins MR in the same case ([1902] 1 KB 242); *Morison v London County & Westminster Bank Ltd* ([1914] 3 KB 356 at 365 and 379), per Lord Reading CJ and per Phillimore LJ; *Lloyds Bank Ltd v E B Savory & Co* ([1933] AC 201 at 228), per Lord Wright.

As to the protection of the Bills of Exchange Act 1882, s 82; I think that the judge was entitled as a question of fact to find that the bank had failed to show that they had acted without negligence. . . .

I agree with Greer LJ that in so far as Collins MR and the rest of the Court in *Gordon's* case held that s 82 of the Bills of Exchange Act 1882 applied, and that there was no negligence, the observations of the Master of the Rolls and those of Stirling LJ as to the effect of s 60 or s 82 were obiter and are not binding in this case on a finding that there was negligence, and the protection of s 82 cannot be invoked by the bank at all.

It follows, therefore, that, on the finding of the learned judge that the bank have failed to prove that they acted without negligence, they are liable to the true owner in conversion, and that this appeal succeeds.

MacKinnon LJ (dissenting): . . . It is said that in paying them they acted negligently, and for that reason they cannot be said to have paid in the ordinary course of business. I do not agree with that contention. A thing that is done not in the ordinary course of business may be done negligently; but I do not think the converse is necessarily true. A thing may be done negligently and yet be done in the ordinary course of business. . . .

[His Lordship felt bound to follow *Gordon v Capital & Counties Bank* [1902] 1 KB 242 and, therefore, dismissed the appeal.]

NOTES

1. When does the bank pay in the ordinary course of business? The general rule is that the payment must accord with the mode of transacting business which is adopted by the banking community at large (*Australian Mutual Provident Society v Derham* (1979) 39 FLR 165 at 173). For example, if the bank closes at 3.00 pm and yet pays a cheque at 3.05 pm, it still acts in the ordinary course of business, as banks may pay cheques within a reasonable margin of time after their advertised time for closing (*Baines v National Provincial Bank Ltd* (1927) 96 LJKB 801). But payment will not be in the ordinary course of business if, for example, the bank pays a crossed cheque over the counter (*Smith v Union Bank of London* (1875) LR 10 QB 291; affd 1 QBD 31 at 35) or pays an order cheque bearing an irregular indorsement (*Slingsby v District Bank Ltd* [1932] 1 KB 544 at 565–566) although, because of s 1 of the Cheques Act 1957, the irregularity in the indorsement will no longer render the paying bank liable.

2. Chalmers and Guest prefer the view taken by Slesser and Mackinnon LJJ to that of Greer LJ on the question of whether the bank can pay in the ordinary course of business when it acts negligently (p 519). The same view has been taken by courts in Australia (*Smith v Commercial Banking Co of Sydney Ltd* (1910) 11 CLR 667 at 677, 688) and in South Africa (*Stapleberg v Barclays Bank* 1963 (3) SA 120). However, the opposite view is taken by Lord Chorley (*Law of Banking* (6th ed, 1974), p 93) and by Professor Holden (*The History of Negotiable Instruments in English Law* (1955), pp 227–228). Professor Holden even goes so far as to say that 'any suggestion that bankers who act negligently are (or can be) acting within "the ordinary course of business" is a gratuitous insult to the very fine body of men and women who are responsible for the day-to-day conduct of British banking' (op cit, p 228)! The Jack Committee have also gone against the view of Slesser and MacKinnon LJJ. Following criticism that the various statutory defences available to the paying banker 'overlap in considerable measure and in some respects their interrelationship is unclear' (R M Goode *Commercial Law* (1982), p 512), the Jack Committee recommended that these various statutory protections should be brought together and each should be made subject to the condition that the bank has acted 'in good faith and without negligence' (Report, rec 7(5)). The Government has accepted this recommendation (White Paper (1990) Cm 1026, Annex 5, para 5.9).

Cheques Act 1992

1. After s 81 of the Bills of Exchange Act 1882 there shall be inserted the following section—

81A.(1) Where a cheque is crossed and bears across its face the words 'account payee' or 'a/c payee', either with or without the word 'only', the cheque shall not be transferable, but shall only be valid as between the parties thereto.

(2) A banker is not to be treated for the purposes of s 80 above as having been negligent by reason only of his failure to concern himself with any purported indorsement of a cheque which under sub-s (1) above or otherwise is not transferable.

NOTES

1. The protection afforded by s 80 only extends to the payment of crossed cheques but s 2 of the Cheques Act 1992 states that, for the purposes of s 80, a 'crossed cheque' includes a cheque which under s 81A(1) or otherwise is not transferable. This probably means that the payment of a non-transferable uncrossed cheque now falls within s 80 but this is not the only possible interpretation of s 2 of the 1992 Act (see R Hooley [1992] CLJ 432).

2. As s 80 also affords protection to the drawer, if the cheque has come into the hands of the payee, he will indirectly benefit from the new s 81A(2). If s 80 applies the paying bank and the drawer are placed in the same position they would have been in if payment had actually been made to the true owner. The paying bank cannot be sued in conversion by the true owner and the drawer will be deemed to have paid any underlying indebtedness for which the cheque was given by him as conditional payment.

QUESTIONS

1. How does the protection offered to the paying bank by s 60 of the Bills of Exchange Act 1882 differ, if at all, from that offered by s 80 of the 1882 Act?
2. A draws an uncrossed cheque on his bank payable to 'B or order'. By accident B throws the cheque into his dustbin where it is found by C, a tramp, who takes it and forges B's indorsement on the cheque. C then presents the cheque to A's bank and obtains payment over the counter. Can A's bank debit A's account? See *Bank of England v Vagliano Bros* [1891] AC 107 at 117–118, HL; *Auchteroni & Co v Midland Bank Ltd* [1928] 2 KB 294 at 304.

(d) Protection of the collecting bank

In *Rhostar (Pvt) Ltd v Netherlands Bank of Rhodesia Ltd* 1972 (2) SA 703 at 715 Goldin J defined the term 'collecting banker' when he said:

> The collecting banker acts on behalf of his customer to collect the proceeds of the cheque from the paying banker.

The collecting bank owes its customer a duty to present the cheque for payment within a reasonable time of receiving it. Traditionally, where the branch of the collecting bank obliged to collect the cheque and the branch of the paying bank on which it is drawn are in the same place, the cheque has to be presented at the latest on the day following its receipt (*Forman v Bank of England* (1902) 18 TLR 339). If the two branches are in different places, the cheque has to be presented or forwarded for clearing by the next day (*Prideaux v Criddle* (1869) LR 4 QB 455). When a cheque is presented through the clearing system, presentation takes effect when the cheque is delivered to the branch on which it was drawn (*Barclays Bank plc v Bank of England*, see above, p 605).

If the collecting bank collects a cheque for anyone other than the true owner, the bank may be liable to the true owner in conversion for the face value of the cheque (criticised by E P Ellinger in *Modern Banking Law* (1987), pp 414–415) or for money had and received. As the collecting bank will have a defence to the restitutionary claim if it has already paid the proceeds of the cheque over to its principal, the most common form of action brought by the true owner against the bank is an action in conversion. What defences can the collecting bank raise to such a claim?

(i) *Holder in due course*

Westminster Bank Ltd v Zang [1966] AC 182, House of Lords

Tilley was the managing director and controlling shareholder of Tilley's Autos Ltd. Zang asked him to finance his gambling. Tilley gave Zang £1,000 in cash, which belonged to the company, and received from Zang a cheque for £1,000 drawn in favour of 'J Tilley or order'. Without indorsing the cheque, Tilley paid it into the company's account at the bank. The paying-in slip used by Tilley reserved the right of the bank, at its discretion, to postpone payment of cheques drawn against uncleared effects. When presented the cheque was dishonoured. The bank returned the cheque to Tilley who commenced an action on the cheque against Zang but that action was later dismissed for procedural reasons. The cheque was then returned to the bank which commenced its own action for dishonour against Zang. The bank claimed as holder in due course and holder for value. Roskill J gave judgment for the bank but this was reversed by the Court of Appeal. The bank appealed to the House of Lords.

Viscount Dilhorne: . . . 'Holder' is defined by s 2 of the Bills of Exchange Act 1882, as meaning 'the payee or indorsee of a bill or note who is in possession of it, or the bearer thereof.' As the appellants had received the cheque from Mr Tilley without indorsement by him, they did not become holders of the cheque within the meaning of s 2 of the Bills of Exchange Act 1882.

In 1957 the Cheques Act was passed with the object of reducing the labour involved and the time taken by collecting and paying banks in ensuring not only that each cheque was indorsed but also that the indorsement corresponded with the name of the payee on the face of the cheque. Section 2 deals with the rights of collecting banks in respect of cheques not indorsed by holders and reads as follows:

> A banker who gives value for, or has a lien on, a cheque payable to order which the holder delivers to him for collection without indorsing it, has such (if any) rights as he would have had if, upon delivery, the holder had indorsed it in blank.

The appellants relied upon this section and sought to establish (1) that the holder had delivered the cheque to them, (2) that it had been delivered to them for collection and (3) that they had given value for it or had a lien upon it. . . .

The first question, namely, whether the holder of the cheque had delivered it to the bank, was answered by the Court of Appeal in the affirmative. In my opinion, it is clear that Mr Tilley was, when he delivered the cheque to the bank, the holder of it within the meaning of s 2 of the Bills of Exchange Act 1882.

Much argument was directed to the second question, namely: was the cheque delivered to the bank for collection? It was argued for the respondent that 'collection' in s 2 of the Cheques Act was to be interpreted as meaning collection for payment into the payee's account when the payee is named on the cheque; and that as the appellants had received the cheque unindorsed with the direction that it was to be paid into the account of Tilley's Autos Ltd, they could not rely upon s 2. . . .

Production of a paid cheque indorsed by the payee is very strong evidence of receipt by the payee. By dispensing with the requirement of indorsement on all 'order' cheques, the Cheques Act deprived the drawer of ability to establish receipt by the payee in this way. He might, it is true, be able to secure evidence from the payee's bank if it had been credited to the payee's account, but, if it was credited to the account of some other person, it appears that it would be very difficult, if not impossible, for the drawer to establish into whose account it had gone and that it had been credited to that account on the instructions of the payee. So if 'collection' in s 2 is confined to meaning collection for the payee's account only, the drawer of the cheque not indorsed by the payee may still be able to prove receipt by the payee.

It can safely be assumed that it was not the intention of Parliament, when providing for relief from the need for indorsement, materially to prejudice the position and rights of the collecting and paying banks and of drawers of cheques. Section 1 provides protection for the paying banks. If the prescribed conditions are satisfied, s 2 gives the collecting banks the same rights in respect of an unindorsed cheque as in respect of an indorsed one. Section 4 provides protection for collecting banks and s 3 gives some protection to the drawer. That section provides that an unindorsed cheque which appears to have been paid by the banker on whom it is drawn is evidence of the receipt by the payee of the sum payable by the cheque.

The acceptance of a paid unindorsed cheque as evidence of its receipt by the payee of the sum payable by the cheque does not appear to be as cogent evidence of receipt by the payee as production of a paid cheque indorsed by him. But this is, in my opinion, no ground on which one would be entitled to construe s 2 in the way contended for by the respondent. I regard the language of that section as clear and unambiguous. I can see nothing in the section nor in the other sections of the Act from which it is to be inferred that 'collection' in s 2 means collection only for the payee's account. If that had been the intention of Parliament, it could easily have been expressed. If the protection given to the drawer by s 3 is inadequate, that is a matter for Parliament to rectify.

It is apparently the practice of the banks, which inadvertently was not followed in this case, to require the indorsement of a cheque by the payee when it is to be credited to some account other than that of the payee.

In my view, Mr Tilley handed in the cheque for collection and the appellants received it for collection. To bring themselves within s 2 it is not necessary for the appellants to show that it was after collection to be credited to the payee's account. In my opinion, the second question should be answered in favour of the appellants in the affirmative.

The next question for consideration is whether the appellants gave value for the cheque. They claimed in their statement of claim that by crediting the cheque to the account of Tilley's Autos Ltd, and by reducing the company's overdraft by £1,000 they had done so. Alternatively, they claimed that it was to be implied from the course of dealing between them and Tilley's Autos Ltd, that there was an agreement whereby Tilley's Autos Ltd were entitled to draw against uncleared effects and they alleged that this agreement amounted to their giving value for the cheque.

The claim that they gave value by crediting the cheque to the account of Tilley's Autos Ltd does not appear to have been pursued before Roskill J or in the Court of Appeal. The evidence was to the effect that although the cheque was credited to the account of Tilley's Autos Ltd with the result that the overdraft was reduced by £1,000, nonetheless the bank charged interest on the amount of the uncleared cheque for four days pending its clearance. They thus did not charge interest on £1,000 on the overdraft but charged it on the cheque. In these circumstances, it is hard to see that by crediting it to the account and reducing the overdraft the bank gave value for it. . . .

The account of Tilley's Autos Ltd was described as a 'swinging' account, sometimes substantially in credit and sometimes heavily overdrawn. In 1960 the limit on the overdraft was £2,000. In January, 1962, it was raised to £3,500. Tilley's Autos Ltd were, however, allowed to overdraw considerably in excess of this limit; for instance, the bank statements show that the overdraft on April 5 of £2,978 15s 10d rose to £4,902 15s 9d at the close of business on April 26, and throughout most of April the overdraft was in excess of the limit.

Mr Silburn [the branch manager] was asked whether, if the overdraft was near the limit of £3,500 and a cheque for £1,000 came in drawn by Tilley's Autos Ltd, he would have paid it, if the only thing to meet it was uncleared effects. His answer was that if the account was in bad odour, he would not.

If there had been an agreement of the character alleged, then Mr Silburn would have been bound to meet a cheque for £1,000 drawn by Tilley's Autos Ltd if there was an uncleared cheque of that amount credited to the account, even though the account at the time of the presentation of the cheque drawn by Tilley's Autos Ltd was overdrawn to the limit which Mr Silburn was prepared to allow. The words printed on the paying-in slip also negative the existence of any such implied agreement.

Danckwerts LJ expressed the view that, if the bank did in fact allow the customer to draw against the uncleared cheque for £1,000 before it was cleared, this amounted to giving value for it. Salmon LJ expressed the same opinion. He pointed out that there was no finding that the bank did honour any cheque drawn against the uncleared cheque for £1,000 and said that on the evidence of the bank manager and of the ledger sheet it was difficult to see how any such finding could have been made. Danckwerts LJ said that he felt some doubt as to the right deduction to be made from the accounts. . . .

Evidence was not given that cheques drawn by the company and presented between April 27 and May 2 were only honoured in consequence of the uncleared effects.

In the circumstances, I agree with the opinion of Salmon LJ. In my opinion, the bank did not establish that they had in fact allowed Tilley's Autos Ltd to draw against the cheque for £1,000.

It follows that the bank has failed to establish the facts necessary to support their contentions that they had given value. No such agreement as alleged is to be implied and no cheque was shown to have been honoured in consequence of the payment in of the cheque for £1,000. . . .

For these reasons, in my opinion, the appeal fails and should be dismissed.

[Lord Reid delivered a concurring judgment.
Lords Hodson, Upjohn and Wilberforce concurred.]

NOTES

1. When the case was before the Court of Appeal, Zang successfully argued that by returning the cheque to Tilley the bank had lost both its lien over the cheque, which arose because of an existing overdraft, and also its status as 'holder'. When Tilley returned the cheque to the bank after his abortive attempt to sue Zang, the bank did not take the cheque as a 'holder' as it was not indorsed by Tilley and s 2 of the 1957 Act no longer applied as the bank did not receive the cheque for collection, nor did the bank give value for it, when it took the cheque from Tilley for the second time: [1966] AC 182 at 202–203, 207, 211. This point was not considered by the House of Lords.

2. If the bank collects as agent for its customer, can it ever collect as a holder for value on its own account? The question was answered by Milmo J in *Barclays Bank Ltd v Astley Industrial Trust Ltd* [1970] 2 QB 527 at 538, when he said:

> I am unable to accept the contention that a banker cannot at one and the same time be an agent for collection of a cheque and a holder of that cheque for value. It seems to me that the language of s 2 of the Cheques Act 1957 negatives this proposition since it presupposes that a banker who has been given a cheque for collection may nevertheless have given value for it. It is, moreover, a commonplace occurrence for a banker to allow credit to a customer against an uncleared cheque. A banker who permits his customer to draw £5 against an uncleared cheque for £100 has given value for it but is it to be said that in consequence he is no longer the customer's agent for the collection of that cheque? I readily accept that if a banker holds a cheque merely – and I emphasise the word 'merely' – as his customer's agent for collection he cannot be a holder for value and still less a holder in due course; but that is an entirely different proposition.

In this case the bank successfully argued that it had a lien on five cheques paid into the bank because of the payee's existing overdraft. Milmo J held that 'the holder of a cheque who has a lien on it is by virtue of s 27(3) [of the 1882 Act] deemed to have taken that cheque for value within the meaning of s 29(1)(b) to the extent of the sum for which he has a lien' (at 539). As the bank had acted in good faith and without notice of any defect in the payee's title, it held the cheques as a holder in due course.

3. If the collecting bank can establish itself as a holder for value, or holder in due course, it can sue the drawer in its own name should the cheques be dishonoured on presentation for payment (as happened in *Midland Bank Ltd v R V Harris Ltd* [1963] 1 WLR 1021). If the bank is a holder in due course of a stolen or misappropriated cheque it has a defence to any claim in conversion because it is the true owner of the cheque. But a bank cannot be a holder in due course of a crossed cheque marked 'not negotiable' (s 81 of the 1882 Act). Neither can it be a holder in due course, nor any other type of holder, of a non-transferable cheque paid in for collection. As to the effect of the Cheques Act 1992 on the collecting bank's status as 'holder', see R Hooley [1992] CLJ 432. Furthermore, the bank cannot be a holder in due course if its customer's title depends on a forged signature or indorsement (s 24 of the 1882 Act).

(ii) *Cheques Act 1957, s 4*

Lloyds Bank Ltd v E B Savory & Co [1933] AC 201, House of Lords

The respondents were a firm of stockbrokers which drew cheques in favour of jobbers. In accordance with a rule of the Stock Exchange the cheques were crossed and made payable to bearer. The respondents had in their employment two clerks, P and S. P had an account at the Wallington branch of the bank. S's wife had an account, first at the Redhill branch, and subsequently at the Weybridge branch, of the same bank. Although the Wallington branch knew P was a stockbroker's clerk, enquiries were never made as to the name of his employer. Neither branch which Mrs S dealt with ever asked about her husband's occupation. On opening their accounts both P and Mrs S gave satisfactory references. Over a period of six years, first P, then S, stole a number of their employer's cheques and these were paid into the bank. P paid cheques directly into his account and S gave cheques to his wife who paid them into her account. Most cheques were paid into the bank using the 'branch credit' system. This meant that the cheques were paid into city branches of the bank using credit slips and these slips were forwarded to the country branches to be credited against the relevant accounts. The credit slips contained no particulars of the cheques so that the country branches did not know the name of the drawer of the cheques being credited. On discovering the fraud the respondents sued the bank in conversion. The case turned on whether the bank could prove that it acted without negligence so as to fall within the protection of s 4 of the Cheques Act 1957 (then s 82 of the Bills of Exchange Act 1882). Save with regard to one cheque which had been collected for Mrs S before she was a customer, Roche J found for the bank. The Court of Appeal reversed that decision mainly on the ground that it found the branch credit system to be defective. The House of Lords (by a majority) dismissed the bank's appeal.

Lord Wright: . . . Unless the appellants can establish that they acted without negligence, they, like other bankers in a similar position, are responsible in damages for conversion if their customers had no title or a defective title. In an ordinary action in conversion, once the true owner proves his title and the act of taking by the defendants, absence of negligence or of intention or knowledge are alike immaterial as defences. Section 82 is therefore not the imposition of a new burden or duty on the collecting banker, but is a concession affording him the means of avoiding a liability in conversion to which otherwise there would be no defence. As it is for the banker to show that he is entitled to this defence, the onus is on him to disprove negligence. . . .

As the defence of the section is invoked against the true owner, it is as against him that the absence of negligence is to be proved, and hence the case is put as a duty towards the true owner. But in the vast majority of cases the true owner is the customer. That the true owner is someone else is generally not apparent until the act of conversion has been done and the claim is made. A banker can safely assume that most cheques which he receives for collection are honestly come by, but as the risk of converting cheques in the course of collection cannot be eliminated there are certain well recognized circumstances which should put the banker on his guard, and there are certain well known precautions which a banker should adopt in connection with a customer's account. The most obvious circumstances which should put the banker on his guard (apart from manifest irregularities in the indorsement and such like) are where a cheque is presented for collection which bears on its face a warning that the customer may have misappropriated it, as for instance where a customer known to be a servant or agent pays in for collection a cheque drawn by third parties in favour of his employer or principal. Such a case carries even a clearer warning if the cheque is indorsed per pro. the employer or principal by the servant or agent. Such cases are illustrated by *Bissell v Fox* ((1885) 53 LT 193) and other authorities, of which I may refer to *Lloyds Bank v Chartered Bank of India, Australia and China* ([1929] 1 KB 40). Similarly if a cheque payable to a one-man company is paid in by the 'one man,' who is also managing director, to his private account: *A L Underwood Ltd v Bank of Liverpool and Martins* ([1924] 1 KB 775). A second type of case is where a servant steals cheques drawn by his employers and pays them or procures their payment into his own account. Such a case is illustrated by *Morison v London County and Westminster Bank* ([1914] 3 KB 356). In all these cases the cheque in itself, apart from knowledge possessed of the customer's position, indicates a possibility or even probability that the servant or agent may have misappropriated it and hence the bank may be converting it. . . . It is true that the question of absence of negligence must be considered separately in regard to each cheque, but it is also true that the matter must be considered, as Lord Dunedin says in *Taxation Comrs v English, Scottish and Australian Bank* ([1920] AC 683 at 689), in view also of all the circumstances antecedent and present. There may thus be relevant negligence in connection with the opening of the customer's account by the banker. It is now recognized to be the usual practice of bankers not to open an account for a customer without obtaining a reference and without inquiry as to the customer's standing; a failure to do so at the opening of the account might well prevent the banker from establishing his defence under s 82 if a cheque were converted subsequently in the history of the account: this rule was applied by Bailhache J in *Ladbroke v Todd* ((1914) 111 LT 43), who on that ground held that the banker had not made out his defence under s 82. The matter is now so well appreciated by bankers that the appellants have a printed rule saying that no new current account is to be opened without knowledge of or full inquiry into the circumstances and character of the customer. The crucial question which arises in connection with that part of this action which deals with the cheques collected for Perkins is whether on opening his account the appellants did not neglect a proper precaution – that, knowing him to be a stockbroker's clerk, they did not inquire who his employers were, and are therefore guilty of negligence within the meaning of s 82. In my judgment they were.

I think, agreeing herein with the unanimous opinion of the Lords Justices, and I think also of Roche J, on this point, that at least where the new customer is employed in some position which involves his handling, and having the opportunity of stealing, his employers' cheques, the bankers fail in taking adequate precautions if they do not ask the name of his employers, and fail even in carrying out the rule which I have just quoted, because they fail to ascertain a most relevant fact as to the intending customer's circumstances. This is specially true of a stockbroker's clerk; it may be different in the case of an employee whose work does not involve such opportunities, as, for instance, a technical employee in a factory. But in the case of a stockbroker's clerk or other similar employment, the bank are dealing with something which involves a risk fully known to them. . . .

It is argued that this is not the ordinary practice of bankers, and that a bank is not negligent if it takes all precautions usually taken by bankers. I do not accept that latter proposition as true in cases where the ordinary practice of bankers fails in making due provision for a risk fully known to those experienced in the business of banking. But as to the actual practice of banks in such cases, I am far from satisfied from the evidence in this case that it is not the usual practice. . . .

The onus throughout in these cases is on the banker to establish that he was not negligent, and in so far as reliance is placed on it being the usual practice of bankers not to ask the name of the employer, I do not think the appellants have here established that allegation. This very obvious piece of information, which could be obtained easily and without reflecting in any way on the customer, enables them to avoid the danger: all the cashier, with this information, has to do is in the case of each cheque to look at the drawer's name. The idea that the Bank can justify under s 82 their failure to do this, simply because they have a good reference – if indeed that idea be really held – appears to me to involve a confusion of ideas. Such a reference or introduction merely speaks to the general reputation of the man: knowledge of who are his employers is aimed at an entirely different purpose, that is to arm the Bank against the known, even if problematical, risk: it is unfortunately common knowledge that persons of respectability, well introduced, may still commit frauds. The reference may be fairly regarded as very sketchy in this case, and I think it was far from enough to dispense the manager from 'bothering' any further. Nor is it any reason why this information should not be obtained that the man may give a false answer or may thereafter change his employment. The former is not likely; as to the latter, in the present case there was no change in Perkins' employment, and it is useless to consider what might be the position if something had happened which did not happen. Nor is it any answer to a charge under s 82 of neglecting a proper precaution, that if it had been taken it might have been fruitless. Nor does a precaution cease to be proper for purposes of s 82 merely because, though generally effective, it may in special circumstances be ineffectual.

In each case negligence must be a question of fact in the particular circumstances, which may modify the general rule. In such a case, however, as that of Perkins I do not find any special circumstances to modify the rule, or justify the appellants in not seeking the information obviously proper.

[His Lordship considered the bank's position with regard to one cheque sent by P direct to the Wallington branch and continued:]

It is, however, necessary to deal with a further point as to the remainder of the cheques; there is a complication by reason that they were paid in at City offices of the Bank for immediate clearance as Town cheques: all the information then sent to the Wallington branch was the name of the account to be credited, of the payer-in and the amount. Banks keep no record of drawers' names. Under that system the fraud would not have been detected even if the Wallington branch had known the name of Perkins' employers, because they would never have known who drew the cheque. The system involves a division of knowledge, which in fact necessarily prevents the Bank from detecting any such fraud as the present. This system has been invoked by both sides: by the respondents as constituting a separate head of negligence, by the appellants as excusing them for failure to be put on inquiry or to detect the fraud. In my judgment, as a matter of law, the system can in this case be disregarded, because I hold that the Bank cannot in virtue of that system which it voluntarily adopts, no doubt for general convenience and in the general interest of its customers, put itself in any better position than if the cheques had all been paid into the one branch: the Bank cannot in that way claim to have split up its knowledge.

The appellants, however, strenuously contended that the system is very convenient, as it clearly is, because it enables cheques to be cleared and credited without delays of post; they also contended that it has been in use for forty years or more and, so far as the three witnesses called as experts in banking know, had never involved trouble; and they claimed that they were free from liability simply on the ground that, even if the name of Perkins' employers had been known at the Wallington branch, the fraud could not have been detected, because the branch which knew the drawer's name did not know the customer's name, and equally the branch which knew the customer's name did not know the drawer's name; and they claim that this regrettable consequence resulted from their following the ordinary practice of bankers, sanctified by long and successful usage. I do not think this is a sound argument. The practice, on its very face, is inconsistent with provident precautions against a known risk, and the mere fact that it is usual and long established is not a sufficient justification. It cannot be justified as an excuse simply because in the past by good fortune no harm seems to have happened. But for reasons already stated, I regard it as not material in this case: otherwise I should regard it as a separate head of negligence.

[His Lordship then turned to the cheques collected for the account of Mrs S. He continued:]

In my opinion, the appellants were guilty of negligence within s 82, or at least have not proved that they were not negligent, and cannot claim the protection of the section in regard to the cheques collected for Mrs Smith. For the reasons I have already discussed I shall treat the case as if the whole of the transaction in regard to the opening of the account had taken place at the Redhill branch. . . . I think the appellants' manager opened the account 'without knowledge or of full inquiry into the circumstances and character of the customer,' to quote again the appellants' own rule – and simply on that ground the appellants cannot be acquitted of negligence in opening the account. . . . So to hold is not to impose on the appellants the duty of being amateur detectives, or of making unnecessary or impertinent inquiries, nor to judge their acts in the light of what has since become known. . . . I do not wish to lay down any general rules as to what inquiries a manager ought to make when opening the account of a married woman. The evidence indicates to me that he would generally inquire or somehow learn about her means and circumstances, and, if she was living with her husband, something about him and his occupation or position in life. At no stage of this account was anything known or ascertained about Mrs Smith or her husband, either at Redhill or Weybridge. It does not appear that any one in the different branches even noticed all through the long course of the account how peculiar the account was, or troubled at all in the matter. . . . Proper inquiries at Redhill might or might not have led to the fraud being nipped in the bud. But in any case no such inquiries were made, and here also by a somewhat different route I reach the same conclusion as in regard to the Perkins cheques – namely, that the defence under s 82 is not made out.

I think the appeal fails on all points.

Lord Warrington of Clyffe: . . . There is here no special duty, contractual or otherwise, towards the true owners of the cheques. The standard by which the absence, or otherwise, of negligence is to be determined must in my opinion be ascertained by reference to the practice of reasonable men carrying on the business of bankers, and endeavouring to do so in such a manner as may be calculated to protect themselves and others against fraud. . . .

I have carefully read and considered the evidence as to the practice of bankers when applied to by a person who is in employment such as that of Perkins and Smith, and I am satisfied that it comes to this, that it is usual to inquire the name of the employer, unless there is such a thoroughly satisfactory reference as to make such an inquiry superfluous.

Lord Buckmaster: . . . a prudent bank manager, opening an account with a stockbroker's clerk, would ascertain who his employer was, unless the character of the reference was so satisfactory, or given by a customer so highly valued that the quality of the reference might be taken as dispensing with the need for the inquiry. . . .

In the present case the reference that was taken was that of a customer who had banked with them for nearly four years, who was also a stockbroker's clerk. His account was subsequently closed, but when, the manager could not say, and it was not known with what firm he was a clerk. He played football, and his name was constantly in the local papers as a football player. There is no evidence whatever as to what he was asked or what information he gave. That was the whole of the reference which was taken as a substitute for inquiring with what firm Perkins was working. I cannot regard it as proved to be a reference of such value as to dispense with the primary necessity of making the inquiry. . . .

The position with regard to Mrs Smith stands on a different footing. It is not clear what are the customary inquiries that are made when a married woman opens an account. Assuming that she is treated in that respect as in exactly the same position as a man, some information ought to be obtained from her or from her reference as to her occupation, unless the character of the reference is such as to dispense with the necessity for such inquiry. She also may be an employee of a firm, and again, in the absence of special conditions the name of the firm should be known. If there is nothing whatever in the reference, or in information afforded, the Bank ought, in my opinion, to inquire as to the occupation of her husband, for it is obvious that the rules of the Bank, dictated by common prudence in the conduct of their business, can be entirely avoided if such knowledge is not obtained. In this case no information whatever was forthcoming.

Lord Blanesburgh (dissenting): . . . the critical question, much reduced as a result of the argument at your Lordships' Bar, is now, I think, no more than this: whether in the case of Perkins the appellants were negligent in that their manager at Wallington, when informed on his application to open an account that he was a stockbroker's clerk, made no inquiry as to the name of his employer; and whether in the case of Mrs Smith they were negligent in that their manager at Redhill, before receiving her as a customer, refrained from inquiring, so that, in the result, both he and the appellants remained in ignorance, both as to the occupation of her husband, in fact also a stockbroker's clerk, and the name of his employers. Was the failure of the appellants, through their respective representatives, to obtain the information specified sufficient to deprive them in both cases, or in one, of the benefit of s 82 of the Bills of Exchange Act 1882?

My Lords, as the matter presents itself to my mind it is very necessary not to place this failure outside its proper perspective by dwelling upon the accident – for it is, I think, little more – that the employment as it was when each account was opened remained unchanged throughout its continuance. That circumstance in its relation to such frauds as those now in question is calculated to emphasize the relevance and to enhance the importance of the unasked question to an extent not admissible. For it is not suggested that the appellants would here have exposed themselves to any imputation of negligence if, having been given their name, they had refrained from making any inquiry of the employers as to the respectability of their clerk, or if, later, they had omitted to keep any record or otherwise to inform themselves of his employment for the time being. This being understood . . . it becomes to my mind clear that at least before the wider wisdom disclosed by these successful frauds had been acquired, inquiry as to the name of a customer's employer, when in fact it was made, had no reference at all to the possible perpetration of frauds within the reach of a clerk as such. It was neither designed nor in its imperfect range was it calculated to be a check upon these. Made, as according to the evidence the inquiry was made, only where the other references seemed to call for confirmation, its only purpose, I am satisfied, was to test the proposing customer's respectability by reference to the status and position of the employer who had so far trusted him as to receive him into his service – information whose value for that purpose was in no way lessened by a mere change in that employment subsequently effected – information, therefore, which called for no later inquiries on the subject – its end, when it was given, being fully attained. . . .

I find it difficult to see any negligence in relation to this matter in the Bank's failure to inform itself by inquiry as to the occupation of Mrs Smith's husband, so that, in an appropriate case, it might be followed by a further inquiry as to the name of his employer. In these days of emancipation when female clerks, married as well as single, abound, a decision to the contrary is in danger of being invoked as authority for the proposition that when a man known to be married applies to a bank to open an account, the bank is negligent if it refrains from making similar inquiry with reference to his wife – a proposition which still strikes me as extravagant.

With these additional reasons in support of it – if indeed they are additional – I find myself in accord with my noble and learned friend, Lord Russell of Killowen, whose opinion, about to be given, I have had the advantage of reading. With him, I would allow the appeal.

Lord Russell of Killowen (dissenting): . . . It seems, however, a very long step to take to say that, because if banks know that a customer is employed by a firm, whose cheque in favour of a third party he is paying in to his own credit, they should make inquiries before receiving payment of it, therefore banks are bound at the outset to ascertain the names of their customer's employers and are guilty of negligence if they do not.

I know of no authority before the present case justifying that proposition, and I can conceive no logical basis on which one can rest an obligation on A to make an inquiry for the purpose of regulating and guiding his future action during an indefinite period of time, the answer to which may c .se to be correct immediately after it is given.

Marfani & Co Ltd v Midland Bank Ltd [1968] 1 WLR 956, Court of Appeal

K, a Pakistani, was employed by the plaintiff company as a clerk. He was given a crossed cheque for £3,000 drawn by the plaintiffs on their bank payable to 'Eliaszade', a firm with which the plaintiffs did business. Instead of posting the cheque to the payee as instructed, K requested the defendant bank to open an account for him in the name of 'Eliaszade'. Appearing to be a person of substance, he made a deposit of £80 and stated that he intended to open a restaurant business and that the rest of the funds would be deposited later. K gave the name of another Pakistani customer of the defendant bank, a Mr Ali, as one of his two referees. Mr Ali was a good customer of the defendant bank who had introduced a number of satisfactory Pakistani customers to the bank on previous occasions. K was not asked for any identification, nor about his occupation, nor whether he had any other bank account. The next day K paid the cheque for £3,000 into his account. The following day, the bank obtained a favourable reference from Mr Ali (the other referee did not reply to the bank's request for a reference) and allowed K to withdraw the money credited to his account. The plaintiff brought an action against the defendant bank for conversion and the bank relied on s 4 of the Cheques Act 1957. Nield J held that the bank had not been negligent and the Court of Appeal dismissed the plaintiffs' appeal.

Diplock LJ set out s 4 of the Cheques Act 1957 and continued: . . . A pettifogger might be tempted to thwart the obvious intention of Parliament by treating the immunity of the banker as limited to actions based upon the receipt of payment as constituting the only act of conversion or as the cause of action for money had and received, and, had the matter first come before the courts in the heyday of literal interpretation, it might well have been so construed. Fortunately, however, the interpretation of s [82] of the Bills of Exchange Act 1882 [predecessor to s 4 of the Cheques Act 1957], was exposed to the robust common sense of Lord Macnaghten in *Gordon v Capital & Countries Bank* ([1903] AC 240 at 244), where he construed the section as extending the immunity 'to cover every step taken in the ordinary course of business and intended to lead up to that result,' ie, the receipt of payment of the cheque.

A purist might also comment (and some have) on the use of the expression 'negligence,' a term of art appropriate to a cause of action different in its legal characteristics from that of conversion or money had and received in respect of which the qualified immunity is conferred. It is, however, in my view, clear that the intention of the subsection and its statutory predecessors is to substitute for the absolute duty owed at common law by a banker to the true owner of a cheque not to take any steps in the ordinary course of business leading up to and including the receipt of payment of the cheque, and the crediting of the amount of the cheque to the account of his customer, in usurpation of the true owner's title thereto a qualified duty to take reasonable care to refrain from taking any such step which he foresees is, or ought reasonably to have foreseen was, likely to cause loss or damage to the true owner.

The only respect in which this substituted statutory duty differs from a common law cause of action in negligence is that, since it takes the form of a qualified immunity from a strict liability at common law, the onus of showing that he did take such reasonable care lies upon the defendant banker. Granted good faith in the banker (the other condition of the immunity), the usual matter with respect to which the banker must take reasonable care is to satisfy himself that his own customer's title to the cheque delivered to him for collection is not defective, ie, that no other person is the true owner of it. Where the customer is in possession of the cheque at the time of delivery for collection and appears upon the face of it to be the 'holder,' ie, the payee or indorsee or the bearer, the banker is, in my view, entitled to assume that the customer is the owner of the cheque unless there are facts which are, or ought to be, known to him which would cause a reasonable banker to suspect that the customer was not the true owner.

What facts ought to be known to the banker, ie, what inquiries he should make, and what facts are sufficient to cause him reasonably to suspect that the customer is not the true owner, must depend upon current banking practice, and change as that practice changes. Cases decided 30 years ago, when the use by the general public of banking facilities was much less widespread, may not be a reliable guide to what the duty of a careful banker in relation to inquiries, and as to facts which should give rise to suspicion, is today.

The duty of care owed by the banker to the true owner of the cheque does not arise until the cheque is delivered to him by his customer. It is then, and then only, that any duty to make inquiries can arise. Any antecedent inquiries which he may have made are relevant only in so far as they have already brought to his knowledge facts which a careful banker ought to ascertain about his customers before accepting for collection the cheque which is the subject-matter of the action and so relieved him of any need to ascertain them again when the cheque which is the subject-matter of the action is delivered to him.

What the court has to do is to look at all the circumstances at the time of the acts complained of and to ask itself: were those circumstances such as would cause a reasonable banker possessed of such information about his customer as a reasonable banker would possess, to suspect that his customer was not the true owner of the cheque? . . .

From the practical point of view of foreseeable loss to the true owner, it seems to me to make no difference whether the banker has received payment of the cheque or not, so long as he retains the payment in his own hands and it is capable of being followed and recovered from him by the true owner. The relevant time for determining whether the banker has complied with his duty of care towards the true owner of the cheque is, in my opinion, the time at which he pays out the proceeds of the cheque to his own customer, so depriving the true owner of his right to follow the money into the banker's hands. . . .

It seems a reasonable inference that what the defendants did in the present case was in accordance with current banking practice. Nield J accepted that it was, and Mr Lloyd [counsel for the plaintiffs] has not sought to argue the contrary. What he contends is that this court is entitled to examine that practice and to form its own opinion as to whether it does comply with the standard of care which a prudent banker should adopt. That is quite right, but I venture to think that this court should be hesitant before condemning as negligent a practice generally adopted by those engaged in banking business.

Mr Lloyd has developed before this court the same criticisms of the defendants' conduct, both as to the inquiries made of Kureshy and as to the reference given by Ali, as were developed before Nield J and dealt with in his judgment. This relieves me of the necessity of discussing them in detail. Suffice it to say that, as respects the inquiries made of Kureshy, he submits that the defendant bank, before opening the account, ought to have required Kureshy to produce some document to identify himself and to have inquired as to the name of his previous employer (he had told them that he was not employed) and about previous banking accounts held by him.

The defendant bank's answer was that they regarded a trustworthy reference as more reliable than inquiries made of the customer himself. It is to be borne in mind that, whatever inquiries it might be prudent for the bank to make for their own purposes, the only inquiries which they were under any duty to the plaintiff to make were inquiries directed to discovering whether their new customer might use the account for the fraudulent purpose of cashing cheques belonging to other people. The purpose of such inquiries would be (a) to find out whether the customer was a fraudulent rogue, and, if so, (b) whether he would be likely to have opportunities of dishonestly obtaining other people's cheques, in particular those of the plaintiff company. As a matter of commonsense, a person who is opening a bank account for a dishonest purpose is unlikely himself wittingly to give any information calculated to disclose his dishonest purpose. He will be prepared with appropriate answers to lull suspicion. It may be that a searching interrogation would reveal inconsistencies or improbabilities in his story, but a bank cannot reasonably be expected to subject *all* prospective customers to a cross-examination which cannot fail to give the impression that the bank doubts their honesty and which would be understandably resented by the 999 honest potential customers, on the off-chance of detecting the thousandth dishonest one. If there is some other independent and apparently trustworthy source from which the honesty of the potential customer may be verified, then to rely upon that source of information is not only less likely than interrogation of the customer himself to damage the bank's own business by driving away honest customers but is also more likely to result in the successful detection of the occasional dishonest one.

Mr Lloyd placed great reliance upon the speech of Lord Wright in *Lloyds Bank Ltd v E B Savory & Co* ([1933] AC 201) as authority for the proposition that it is the duty of a banker, when opening a new account, to ascertain the name of the customer's, or customer's spouse's, employers in addition to obtaining suitable references. Lord Wright went further than the other members of the three to two majority in that case, Lord Buckmaster and Lord Warrington, both of whom considered that such inquiries might be dispensed with if an apparently reliable and trustworthy reference were obtained. That case, as all other cases, depended on its own particular facts. The frauds had gone on for a very long time. There were many other matters calculated to arouse suspicion in the social conditions of the 1920s. The case was decided upon expert evidence, not of what is now current banking practice, but of what it was nearly 40 years ago. I find in it no more than an illustration of the application of the general principle that a banker must exercise reasonable care in all the circumstances of the case.

Mr Hodgson [counsel for the defendants] has argued that, in any event, upon the facts now known to us, none of the proposed inquiries would have resulted in any suspicion of Kureshy's honesty. He had prepared his scheme too well. Failure to make the inquiries was not causative of the loss. There are dicta, which can be found collected in *Baker v Barclays Bank Ltd* ([1955] 1 WLR 822 at 836–839), which suggest that, even if it could be proved that a failure to make a particular inquiry which a prudent banker would have made had had no causative effect upon the loss sustained by the true owner, the banker would nevertheless be disentitled to the protection of s 4 of the Cheques Act 1957. For my part, I think that those dicta are wrong. It is, however, obviously difficult to prove something so speculative as what would have happened if inquiries had been made which were not made, and I do not think that the defendant bank has sustained the onus of proving it here. I prefer to put it in the alternative way which I have already indicated. It does not constitute any lack of reasonable care to refrain from making inquiries which it is improbable will lead to detection of the potential customer's dishonest purpose if he is dishonest, and which are calculated to offend him and maybe drive away his custom if he is honest.

Cairns J: . . . I have felt great doubt as to whether the bank have discharged the onus which lies upon them with regard to those matters, but, in the end, I have reached the conclusion that they have discharged it. . . .

I wish to add this. It may be that competition between banks for customers tempts them to some extent to relax precautions taken on opening a new account. We have heard that former decisions of the courts adverse to banks have had the effect of causing them to tighten their rules about the inquiries to be made when an account is opened. I should be sorry if the effect of our decision in this case were to encourage any loosening of those rules. If the defendant bank here exercised sufficient care, it was in my view only just sufficient.

I agree that the appeal should be dismissed.

[Danckwerts LJ delivered a concurring judgment.]

Thackwell v Barclays Bank plc [1986] 1 All ER 676, Queen's Bench Division

Hutchison J: . . . I would hold that as a matter of law it is no answer for a bank who have been guilty of negligence in the collection of a cheque to prove that, even had the question the omission to ask which constitutes such negligence been asked, a reassuring answer would have been given. In support of the opposite view, counsel for the defendants cites the well-known passages in the judgments of the Court of Appeal, particularly that of Diplock LJ, in *Marfani & Co Ltd v Midland Bank Ltd* [1968] 2 All ER 573, [1968] 1 WLR 956. However, on a careful consideration of the judgments in that case, he felt compelled to concede that the statements on which he relied were obiter, and there are authorities pointing strongly the other way (see in particular *Selangor United Rubber Estates v Cradock (a bankrupt) (No 3)* [1968] 2 All ER 1073 at 1118, [1968] 1 WLR 1555 at 1607 and *Lloyds Bank Ltd v E B Savory & Co* [1932] 2 KB 122 at 148 per Greer LJ in the Court of Appeal; [1933] AC 201 at 233, [1932] All ER Rep 106 at 118 per Lord Wright in the House of Lords).

NOTES

1. As to the opening of an account, the Code of Banking Practice (2nd ed, 1994) (see above, p 562) states:

> 2.1 Banks and building societies are required by law to satisfy themselves about the identity of a person seeking to open an account to assist in protecting their customers, members of the public and themselves against fraud and other misuse of the banking system.

> 2.2 Banks and building societies will provide to prospective customers details of the identification needed.

The usual form of identity requested by the bank is a passport or a driving licence but as Cairns J emphasised in *Marfani* (at 980):

> . . . there is no hint in any of the decided cases of any such means of identification being considered necessary. If an apparently respectable referee, well known to the bank, identified the customer as a person known to him by the name which he claimed to be his, I cannot think that any further inquiry as to his identity would be necessary.

2. 'It would now be unlawful discrimination to require only women to state their partner's employment; given the change in work patterns in recent years it would probably be necessary for the bank to obtain such information from both male and female customers': R Bradgate and N Savage *Commercial Law* (1991), pp 465ff. In any event, the answer given in response to any inquiry about the customer's occupation, or that of his or her spouse, may cease to be accurate immediately it is given (see G Borrie (1960) 23 MLR 16 at 19). In *Orbit Mining & Trading Co Ltd v Westminster Bank Ltd* [1963] 1 QB 794 at 825 Harman LJ stated that: 'It cannot at any rate be the duty of the bank continually to keep itself up to date as to the identity of a customer's employer'.

3. As Lord Wright made clear in the *Savory* case (see above, p 617), the bank may be negligent in the manner it collects the cheque if it ignores a warning 'from manifest irregularities in the indorsement and such like' or where the cheque 'bears on its face a warning that the customer may have misappropriated it'. The bank will not be negligent if it makes inquiries after receiving such a warning and those inquiries show that the situation is perfectly innocent. But note that since the Cheques Act 1992 introduced a new s 81A(1) into the Bills of Exchange Act 1882, the collecting bank will be negligent if it collects a cheque crossed 'a/c payee only' for someone who is clearly not the named payee as such cheques are not transferable. On the other hand, if the bank collects such a cheque for the account of someone who has the same name as the named payee (but is a different person) it will not be negligent on this ground alone. Although, what if the cheque is for a sum significantly larger than has ever before been credited to that account? For a general discussion of the problems associated with the collection of a cheque drawn in favour of a third party, see G Borrie (1960) 23 MLR 16.

4. Section 4(2) of the 1957 Act extends the protection afforded by s 4(1) to the collection of cheques and certain other instruments eg conditional orders for payment, instruments drawn payable to 'cash or order', interest and dividend warrants, 'cheques' requiring a receipt, bankers' drafts. Section 3 of the Cheques Act 1992 has amended s 4(2) to include within the definition of 'cheques' those cheques which under s 81A(1) of the Bills of Exchange Act 1882 (see above, p 611) or otherwise are not transferable. The Cheques Act 1992 has cleared up any doubts which may have existed as to whether a non-transferable 'cheque' really fell within the definition of a cheque at all (see D Wheatley (1992) 142 NLJ 607). However, it appears that an instrument in the form of a cheque to which the drawer's signature is a forgery is not a cheque and is not within s 4 (*Paget's Law of Banking* (10th ed, 1989), p 472; cf *First Sport Ltd v Barclays Bank plc* [1993] 1 WLR 1229, where a majority of the Court of Appeal (Kennedy J dissenting) held such an instrument to be a 'cheque' within the terms of a cheque guarantee card), although the true owner (the drawer) of the instrument may still be able to recover substantial damages for conversion from the collecting bank (*Midland Bank Ltd v Reckitt* [1933] AC 1; criticised by Chalmers and Guest, p 181).

5. By s 4(3) of the 1957 Act the collecting bank will not be treated for the purposes of s 4(1) as having been negligent by reason only of its failure to concern itself with absence of, or irregularity in, indorsement of a cheque or other instrument specified in s 4(2). However, a memorandum of the Committee of London Clearing Bankers (23 September 1957) states that indorsement will still be required if (1) the instrument is tendered for an account other than that of the ostensible payee (unless it is specially indorsed to the customer for whose account it is tendered), or if (2) the payee's name is mis-spelt or he is incorrectly designated and there are circumstances to suggest that the customer is not the person to whom payment is intended to be made, or if (3) an instrument payable to joint payees is tendered for credit of an account to which all are not parties. If a collecting bank does not comply with the memorandum, and that failure is material, it will be unable to establish that it acted without negligence as it will have failed to comply with standard banking practice.

(iii) *Banking Act 1979, s 47*

In any circumstances in which proof of absence of negligence on the part of a banker would be a defence in proceedings by reason of s 4 of the Cheques Act 1957, a defence of contributory negligence shall also be available to the banker notwithstanding the provisions of s 11(1) of the Torts (Interference with Goods) Act 1977.

NOTES

1. It is also open to the collecting bank to plead in its defence to an action in conversion that (1) the proceeds actually reached the true owner, the payment discharged a debt of the true owner or the true owner benefitted from the payment in some other way (*B Liggett (Liverpool) Ltd v Barclays Bank Ltd* [1928] 1 KB 48); or (2) the true owner ratified the unauthorised transaction or is estopped from alleging the conversion (*Bank of Montreal v Dominion Gresham Guarantee and Casualty Co Ltd* [1930] AC 659, 666); or (3) the true owner's claim was itself tainted with illegality (*Thackwell v Barclays Bank plc* [1986] 1 All ER 676).

2. If the collecting bank innocently converts a cheque, it may be able to debit the account of its customer (who delivered the cheque to the bank for collection) with the amount it must pay to the true owner in settlement of its liability (*Redmond v Allied Irish Banks plc* [1987] FLR 307, where concessions were made).

QUESTIONS

1. Alan banked with the Cambridge branch of NE Bank plc. Using a cheque book supplied by the Cambridge branch, Alan drew a crossed cheque in favour of Bill or order. Bill indorsed the cheque specially to Chris for value. Daniel stole the cheque from Chris, forged Chris's signature on the bank and delivered it to Ethel in payment of a debt. Ethel took it to her bank, the Oxford branch of NE Bank plc, who obtained payment of the cheque from Alan's branch and credited Ethel's account with the proceeds. Advise the parties.
2. What would have been the position in the preceeding question if the cheque has been crossed 'not negotiable'? Or if it had been crossed 'account payee'?

2 Promissory notes

FIGURE 5   **PROMISSORY NOTE**

PROMISSORY NOTE

LAWYERS' COURT
TEMPLE
LONDON EC4

1 JANUARY 1994

£500   *TV Smith*

THREE MONTHS AFTER DATE I PROMISE TO PAY JOE
BLOGGS THE SUM OF FIVE HUNDRED POUNDS.

(SIGNED)

(T V SMITH)

Akbar Khan v Attar Singh [1936] 2 All ER 545, Privy Council

The plaintiff deposited the sum of Rs43,900 with the defendants and received a deposit receipt which stated that 'this amount to be payable after two years. Interest at the rate of Rs5.4.0 per cent per year to be charged'. The document was stamped as a receipt. The issue before the Privy Council was whether this document was a deposit receipt or a promissory note.

Lord Atkin, delivering the advice of the Board, stated: . . . It is indeed doubtful whether a document can properly be styled a promissory note which does not contain an undertaking to pay, not merely an undertaking which has to be inferred from the words used. It is plain that the implied promise to pay arising from an acknowledgment of a debt will not suffice, for . . . an IOU is not a promissory note, though of the implied promise to pay there can be no doubt. . . .

Their Lordships prefer to decide this point on the broad ground that such a document as this is not and could not be intended to be brought within a definition relating to documents which are to be negotiable instruments. Such documents must come into existence for the purpose only of recording an agreement to pay money and nothing more, though of course they may state the consideration. Receipts and agreements generally are not intended to be negotiable, and serious embarrassment would be caused in commerce if the negotiable net were cast too wide. This document plainly is a receipt for money containing the terms on which it is to be repaid. It is not without significance that the defendants who drew it, and who were experienced moneylenders did not draw it on paper with an impressed stamp as they would have to if the document were a promissory note, and that they affixed a stamp which is sufficient if the document is a simple receipt. Being primarily a receipt even if coupled with a promise to pay it is not a promissory note.

NOTES

1. This ruling of Lord Atkin has been applied by the Court of Appeal in *Claydon v Bradley* [1987] 1 WLR 521 at 526, 528.

2. By s 89(1) of the Bills of Exchange Act 1882, subject to certain qualifications contained in ss 83–89, the provisions of the 1882 Act relating to bills of exchange apply, with the necessary modifications, to promissory notes. By s 89(2), the maker of a promissory note is deemed to correspond with the acceptor of a bill, and the first indorser with the drawer of an accepted bill payable to his own order. As the maker is deemed the acceptor, s 89(3) states that the provisions of the Act relating to presentment for acceptance and to acceptance do not apply.

3. What are promissory notes used for? In international trade they are mainly used in forfaiting transactions where the importer will make a promissory note (supported by bank guarantees) which the exporter will indorse (without recourse) to a forfaiter at a discount. The forfaiter bears the credit risk, and economic and political risks, and must obtain payment of the instrument, or rediscount it in the secondary market (see R M Goode *Commercial Law* (1982), p 691). In domestic trade promissory notes serve two functions. First, they provide added security if they are made by a debtor or hirer. They give the creditor or lessor the advantage of being able to bring an action by summary procedure and prevent the maker of the note raising certain defences which would be available if an action was brought on the underlying transaction. As this may place the debtor or hirer in a worse position if sued on the note than if sued on the underlying transaction, ss 123 and 124 of the Consumer Credit Act 1974 precludes the taking of promissory notes in respect of regulated consumer credit and consumer hire agreements (see above, p 513). Secondly, as with international trade, they facilitate the refinancing of transactions in that the notes may be discounted to a financial institution. Unlike the assignment of a chose in action which is made subject to equities, the negotiation of a promissory note can pass a title free from any defects in the title of previous parties. This is what makes promissory notes the main negotiable instruments used as security for inland transactions (*Chitty on Contracts* (26th ed, 1989) ('Chitty'), Vol 2, para 2753).

4. As to the use of promissory notes as sterling commercial paper, see R MacVicar (1986) 2 JIBFL 40. Note also that bank notes are promissory notes payable to bearer on demand.

3 Travellers' cheques

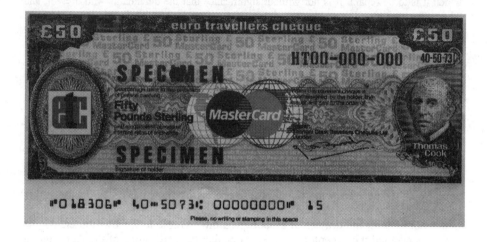

For a detailed analysis of the law relating to travellers' cheques, see Ellinger (1969) 19 Univ of Toronto LJ 132; Stassen (1978) 95 SALJ 180; Frohlich (1980) 54 ALJ 388.

QUESTIONS

1. Is the travellers' cheque shown in Figure 6 a bill of exchange? Compare the view expressed in Chitty, Vol 2, para 2842, with that found in R M Goode's *Commercial Law* (1982), at pp 522–523.

2. Adam purchased a number of travellers' cheques from B Bank. He did not sign or countersign the cheques when he collected them as he was in a hurry to get to the airport. At the airport Adam found that his plane had been delayed and so he decided to do some last minute shopping. Despite a number of notices warning passengers not to leave their baggage unattended, Adam left his rucksack on a seat in the departure lounge while he went to browse in a nearby bookshop. Adam spent nearly an hour in the bookshop and on his return to the departure lounge he found that the rucksack had been opened and his travellers' cheques taken. Adam immediately cancelled his holiday and returned to B Bank demanding a refund for the stolen travellers' cheques. B Bank refused to give a refund relying on a clause printed on the inside of the plastic wallet, which had contained his travellers' cheques, which stated that the traveller had a right to a refund so long as he 'properly safeguarded each cheque against loss or theft'. Advise Adam. Compare *Braithwaite v Thomas Cook Travellers Cheques Ltd* [1989] QB 553, with *Fellus v National Westminster Bank plc* (1983) 133 NLJ 766 and *El Awadi v Bank of Credit and Commerce International SA Ltd* [1990] 1 QB 606.

3. In fact it was Chris who had stolen Adam's travellers' cheques. After stealing the cheques, Chris immediately signed them in his own name. He then went to a local department store where he used the cheques to pay for some jewellery. Before tendering the cheques in payment, Chris countersigned them in the presence of the shop assistant. The department store now seeks payment of the cheques from B Bank. Advise the bank. Compare *City National Bank of Galveston v American Express Co* 7 SW 2d 886 (1928); affd 16 SW 2d 278 (1929), with *American Express Co v Anadarko Bank and Trust Co* 67 P 2d 55 (1937). See also Chitty, Vol 2, para 2850.

4 Bank giro system

'The Evolving Law of Payment by Wire Transfer – An Outsider's View of Draft UCC Article 4A' by B Geva (1988) 14 CBLJ 186, pp 187–188

'GIRO' is derived from the Greek word for circle. It denotes the cyclic operation involved in the transfer of credit balances from one bank account into another. Giro payments are either credit or debit transfers. In the former, the paying party's instructions are communicated by him directly to his bank so as to 'push' funds from his account to that of the payee. In the latter, the paying party's instructions are communicated to his bank by the payee *via* his own bank so as to 'pull' or 'draw' funds from the paying party's account into that of the payee.

Banking Services: Law and Practice Report by the Review Committee (1989) Cm 622, paras 7.74–7.76

7.74 What exactly is the status of a BGC [Bank Giro Credit]? The late Lord Chorley argued, as we said in our consultation paper . . ., that the transfer is probably made by way of equitable assignment. He maintained that the debtor who, in respect of the transaction is the paying customer, assigns part of the credit balance at his bank to his creditor (the assignee). We have some difficulty with this, not least because Scots law does not recognise equitable assignment and therefore, since the identical system operates throughout the UK, the legal position in Scotland must be subject to different analysis.

7.75 Others argue that there is probably no assignment in most instances and cite in evidence a good deal of case law. It is Chitty who best provides an exposition of the case against transfer by assignment. It is not a statutory assignment, because it does not meet the requirements of s 136 of the Law of Property Act 1925. That does not rule out an equitable assignment but Chitty goes on '. . . to attribute to the transferor an intention to effect an assignment militates against the true nature of the transaction. The one and only object of all the different type of giro forms is to instruct the paying banker to perform a service on behalf of his principal, who is the transferor'.

7.76 We therefore incline to the view that BGCs are a matter of contract. There appear to be typically three separate contracts: that between the transferor and paying bank (as principal and agent respectively), that between paying bank and receiving bank, and that between the latter and the transferee. That the receiving banker is also an agent is not disputed, though there are differences of view on the identity of his principal. . . .

NOTES

1. In its White Paper on Banking Services Law and Practice, the Government accepted the Jack Committee's recommendation that it should legislate to make clear that a transfer instruction by BGC does not constitute a legal assignment of the funds involved (White Paper (1990) Cm 1026, Annex 5, paras 5.21 and 5.22).

2. It is not clear when payment made through the giro system is complete. If payment is complete it is too late for the transferor to countermand his order to the paying bank to make payment. The Jack Committee recommended that banks should set a mutually acceptable point in the payment cycle after which countermand will no longer be effective and that they should advise their customers accordingly (rec 7(16)). In fact, the issues of countermand and completion of payment, with regard to both paper-based and electronic funds transfer systems, were considered separately by the Jack Committee in Chapter 12 of its Report (see also J Vroegop [1990] LMCLQ 64). The Jack Committee recommended a legislative definition of completion of payment (rec 12(2)) but as the issue is currently being investigated by the United Nations Commission on International Trade Law (UNCITRAL), the Government has decided to await UNCITRAL's findings before reviewing the need for legislation (White Paper (1990) Cm 1026, Annex 7, paras 7.13–7.16).

3. For a detailed analysis of the giro system, see E P Ellinger *Modern Banking Law* (1987), Ch 12; Chitty, Vol 2, paras 2950–2965; R R Pennington and A H Hudson *Commercial Banking Law* (1978), pp 275ff.

QUESTION

A is B's landlord. A claims that B is in breach of the terms of the lease and serves him with a notice to quit. B refuses to leave the property and continues to pay rent through the bank giro. For several weeks A does not notice these payments but when he does he immediately instructs his bank to pay the money back to B through the bank giro. B now argues that A has waived his right of forfeiture by reason of having accepted the rent. Advise A. See *Mardorf Peach & Co Ltd v Attica Sea Carriers Corpn of Liberia, The Laconia* [1977] AC 850, HL; *HMV Fields Properties Ltd v Bracken Self Selection Fabrics Ltd* 1991 SLT 31 and G Gretton [1992] JBL 335.

5 Electronic Funds Transfer (EFT)

(a) Definitions of EFT

Banking Services: Law and Practice Report by the Review Committee (1989) Cm 622, p x and para 9.03

EFT (Electronic Funds Transfer). Funds transfer effected through the banking system by electronic techniques, with input and output methods being largely or completely in electronic form.

9.03 For practical purposes, what this Report means by EFT's are payment messages transmitted either through magnetic material such as magnetic tapes, disks, and cassettes; or through purely electronic media such as telephones, telex, and electronic transmission between computers, or between a terminal and a computer.

US (Federal) Electronic Fund Transfer Act of 1978

903. (6) The term 'electronic fund transfer' means any transfer of funds, other than a transaction originated by check, draft, or similar paper instruments, which is initiated through an electronic terminal, telephonic instrument, or computer or magnetic tape so as to order, instruct, or authorise a financial institution to debit or credit an account. Such term includes, but is not limited to, point of sale transfers, automated teller machine transactions, direct deposits or withdrawals of funds, and transfers initiated by telephone.

UNCITRAL Legal Guide on Electronic Funds Transfer

A funds transfer in which one or more of the steps in the process that were previously done by paper-based techniques are now done by electronic techniques.

Royal Products Ltd v Midland Bank Ltd [1981] 2 Lloyd's Rep 194 at 198

Webster J described a customer's instruction to its bank to make an EFT to another bank: '. . . simply as an authority and instruction, from a customer to its bank, to transfer an amount standing to the credit of that customer with that bank to the credit of its account with another bank. . . .'

NOTE

In its Report on Banking Services Law and Practice, the Jack Committee identified six EFT systems in use in the UK (para 9.04). These are:

(1) CHAPS (Clearing House Automated Payment System), which is an electronic sterling credit transfer system allowing same day settlement of individual orders to pay sums in excess of £10,000.
(2) BACS (Bankers Automated Clearing Services), which provides a high volume, low value, automated batch clearing service for payment and collection transactions, including direct debits, standing orders, salaries, wages and pensions.

(3) SWIFT (Society for Worldwide Interbank Financial Telecommunications), which is not strictly a funds transfer system but an international network for members to pass rapid instructions relating to financial transactions between each other.

(4) ATMs (Automated Teller Machines), which are cash dispensing machines operated by the customer inserting his plastic card into the machine, followed by his Personal Identification Number (PIN).

(5) EFT-POS (Electronic Funds Transfer at Point of Sale), which is a payment system allowing retail payments to be made by transferring funds electronically from customers' to retailers' accounts. The customer's card is passed through a reader terminal at the retailer's point of sale and information encoded on the card, and that relating to the transaction, is sent through one of the independent EFT–POS processing systems, eg the Switch system. The customer authorises the transaction either by signing a receipt slip produced by the terminal or entering his PIN into a special terminal.

(6) Home and office banking systems, which provide a connection with a bank's central computer direct from the home or office, using either a television or telephone, together with a special keypad, or a personal computer. The service enables the customer to make balance enquiries and obtain other account information, transmit funds between his own accounts and instruct that payment be made to the accounts of an agreed range of third parties.

(b) Characteristics distinguishing EFT from other payment systems

Editor's Introduction to *Electronic Banking – The Legal Implications*, edited by R M Goode, pp v–vi

. . . payment messages are usually transmitted through one or more of three types of medium: paper, eg bills of exchange, cheques, bankers' payments, written direct debits and credit transfers; magnetic material, eg magnetic tapes, disks, cassettes; and purely electronic media, eg telephone, telex, electronic transmission between computers or between a terminal and a computer. Not infrequently such media will be employed in combination, as in the case of cheque truncation, where a cheque is issued and given to the payee's bank for collection but is retained by that bank, the data being transmitted electronically to the paying bank.

The characteristics of paper-based instructions and undertakings are that they embody a transaction in permanent form, are typically expressed in words and figures and are authenticated by a signature identifying the party giving the payment message. Paper-based message cannot readily be altered without this fact appearing on the face of the document. Finally, delivery of the payment message usually takes a significant period of time – hours, days or even weeks.

Magnetic material shares with paper-based items the characteristic that the transfer medium is tangible and movable, so that messages stored on it cannot only be located but can be recalled prior to their delivery to the intended recipient. There, however, the resemblance ends. The payment message is expressed in computer code, the handwritten signature is replaced by an electronic key designed to authenticate the message and, in contrast to a paper message where the message itself is permanent and is retained on the original paper, the message on tape, disk, etc, may, in the absence of security measures, be altered, erased or transferred to other magnetic material without this fact being discoverable from an examination of the medium.

In the case of pure electronic funds transfer, the message is not carried in permanent form, though it is possible to have it logged during transmission. The time taken for delivery of the message depends on whether it is a purely bilateral transmission – as in the case of CHAPS, where a message sent by or through a participating bank is transmitted electronically direct to the recipient bank – or is routed through a clearing house or batching centre, as in BACS, where the messages have to be sorted and then batched by addressee before being sent forward, a process which even in a purely automated clearing system will take at least some hours. The delay resulting from the batching process is significant in at least two respects. First, it allows of an opportunity to recall a payment message which may be denied in a near-instantaneous system. Secondly, until the batching process is complete a clearing participant sending a payment message will not know its net position in relation to other participants.

(c) What are the main problems relating to EFT law and practice?

In its Report on Banking Law and Practice, the Jack Committee grouped these problems under four headings (para 9.11):

Authentication of instructions. The passage quoted . . . [from Professor Goode's Introduction to *Electronic Banking – The Legal Implications*, above] . . . underlined the difference between paper-based systems, authenticated by signature, and EFT where the signature is replaced by an electronic key. Because this less reliable means of authenticating a customer's instructions provides new scope for error or fraud, issues arise about the standards of security that should be applied at the design stage to customer-activated EFT systems.

Operational security on existing systems. A variety of problems under this heading begins with the standards of care that should be applied to the safeguarding of payment card and Personal Identification Number (PIN). A privacy problem may arise from the customer's need to key data into some form of computer terminal; the data may be read by somebody else and used to that person's fraudulent advantage. The ease with which messages on magnetic material may be altered or erased, and the lack of written records in the case of some types of EFT, may also create security problems.

Liability for loss in case of fraud or technical failure is, as a general rule, more difficult to pinpoint in electronic than in paper-based systems. Issues are as to how losses should be allocated between the parties, and where the burden of proof should rest if the authority for a given transaction is in question.

Countermand or reversal of instructions. While this type of issue, unlike the other three, is not confined to EFT, it remains true that it is more difficult with an EFT, than with a paper-based, system to determine the point up to which an instruction can be countermanded or reversed. EFT has therefore highlighted a spectrum of problems that was there already, and which ranges from mere inconvenience to the customer at one end, to the priority of claims in insolvency at the other.

(d) Does the Code of Banking Practice address these problems?

(See above, p 562).

'Good Banking': Code of Banking Practice (2nd ed, 1994)

17.0 ISSUE OF CARDS

17.1 Card issuers will issue cards to customers only when they have been requested in writing or to replace or renew cards that have already been issued.

17.2 Card issuers will tell customers if a card issued by them has more than one function. Card issuers will comply with requests from customers not to use Personal Identification Numbers (PINs) where customers do not wish to use the functions operated by a PIN.

18.0 SECURITY OF CARDS

18.1 Card issuers will issue PINs separately from cards and will advise the PIN only to the customer.

18.2 Card issuers will tell customers of their responsibility to take care of their cards and PINs in order to prevent fraud. Card issuers will emphasise to customers that:

(a) they should not allow anyone else to use their card and PIN;
(b) they should take all reasonable steps to keep the card safe and the PIN secret at all times;
(c) they should never write the PIN on the card or on anything usually kept with it;
(d) they should never write the PIN down without making a reasonable attempt to disguise it.
(e) they should destroy any PIN advice promptly on receipt.

18.3 When customers are provided with an opportunity to select their own PIN, card issuers should encourage them to do so to help them remember the PIN.

19.0 LOST CARDS

19.1 Card issuers will inform customers that they must tell their card issuers as soon as reasonably practicable after they find that:

(a) their card has been lost or stolen;
(b) someone else knows their PIN;

. . .

20.0 LIABILITY FOR LOSS

20.1 Card issuers will bear the full losses incurred:

(a) in the event of misuse when the card has not been received by the customer;
(b) for all transactions not authorised by the customer after the card issuer has been told that the card has been lost or stolen or that someone else knows or may know the PIN (subject to 20.4 below);
(c) if faults have occurred in the machines, or other systems used, which cause customers to suffer direct loss unless the fault was obvious or advised by a message or notice on display.

20.2 Card issuers' liability will be limited to those amounts wrongly charged to customers' accounts and any interest on those amounts.

20.3 Customers' liability for transactions not authorised by them will be limited to a maximum of £50 in the event of misuse before the card issuer has been notified that a card has been lost or stolen or that someone else knows the PIN (subject to 20.4 below).

20.4 Customers will be held liable for all losses if they have acted fraudulently. They may be held liable for all losses if they have acted with gross negligence. Gross negligence may be construed as including failures to comply with any of the requirements of paragraph 18.2 if such failures have caused those losses.

20.5 In cases of disputed transactions the burden of proving fraud or gross negligence or that a card has been received by a customer will lie with the card issuer. In such cases card issuers will expect customers to co-operate with them in their investigations.

NOTES

1. The relationship between the card issuer and the customer is governed by contract. The Code is an attempt, on a voluntary basis, to standardise the contractual terms of the various card issuers and provide a more equitable relationship between them and their customers. This approach is comparable to that adopted in Australia and New Zealand which have codes of practice (see D Harland (1989) 15 CBLJ 259 and J Vroegop [1990] JBL 88 respectively), but can be contrasted with that taken in the United States where legislation has been used in an attempt to supersede contractual terms between card holders and card issuers (US (Federal) Electronic Fund Transfer Act 1978).

2. At present, the only UK legislation specifically directed to EFT is s 89 of the Banking Act 1987. Section 89 amends s 187 of the Consumer Credit Act 1974 and provides, in essence, that 'arrangements for the electronic transfer of funds from a current account at a bank . . .' are not to be treated as debtor–creditor–supplier agreements under s 12(b) and (c) of the 1974 Act. It follows that connected lender liability under s 75 of the 1974 Act does not extend to payment made with a pure debit card.

3. In its White Paper on Banking Services Law and Practice the Government stated its intention to legislate to ban the unsolicited mailing of *all* payment cards (including ATM and EFT-POS cards) except for card renewal for existing customers, to ensure that the customer is only liable up to a maximum of £50 for loss incurred as a result of loss or theft of *all* payment cards (including ATM and EFT-POS cards) up to the point where he notifies the card issuer, and to ensure that in the case of customer-activated EFT systems banks should not be permitted to exclude their liability for loss incurred through equipment failure and that the customer should be compensated for forseeable losses (and specially contemplated losses) due to failure of such equipment despite any contract term which restricts the bank's liability (White Paper (1990) Cm 1026, Annex 4, paras 4.5–4.7). As can be seen from paras 17.1, 20.1(c) and 20.3 of the Code of Banking Practice (2nd ed, 1994), the banks have tried to pre-empt these changes by bringing them into their voluntary Code (although note that the card issuer's liability for loss under paras 20.1(c) and 20.2 of the Code appears to be narrower than that proposed by the Government). Furthermore, these changes fall in line with various initiatives of the European Commission to promote the 'interoperability' of card payment systems in the member states of the European Community (see Commission Recommendation of 8 December on a European Code relating to Electronic Payment (87/598/EEC), OJ No 365/72, 24 December 1987; Commission Recommendation concerning Payment Cards (88/590/EEC), OJ L317/55, 24 November 1988; and the new EC Directive on Unfair Contract Terms (Directive 93/13 EEC, OJ 95, 21/4/93, p 29) is also relevant in this context: R Cranston (1992) 66 ALJ 225).

4. Since 1986, some 10–13 per cent of all complaints received each year by the Office of the Banking Ombudsman have concerned customer complaints over ATM transactions. A substantial proportion of these concern so-called 'phantom withdrawals' which, broadly speaking, refers to the situation where a customer has allegedly used a credit or debit card at an ATM, had his account debited by the bank and later claimed that the card was not used by him nor by a third party (as defined by P E Morris [1992] LMCLQ 227 at 242). The Banking Ombudsman's practice has been to place the burden of proving that the machine was not at fault on the card issuer and, if the card issuer can prove that there was no technical breakdown, then shift the burden to the customer to prove that he definitely did not use the card and that a third party has not gained access to the card and the PIN (see P E Morris, above, p 243). In the overwhelming majority of cases the customer is unable to discharge this heavy burden (although in *Judd v Citibank* 435 NYS 2d 210 (NY City Civ Ct, 1980) the court was prepared to believe the customer in the face of computer evidence of cash withdrawals; cf *Feldman v Citibank* 443 NYS 2d 43 (NY City Cit Ct, 1981) where the customer's evidence as to the circumstances surrounding the use of the card was not accepted). To avoid such a 'winner-take-all' or 'loser-lose-all' outcome based on the burden of proof, the Jack Committee recommended that there should be an apportionment of loss on an equitable basis between the card issuer and the customer in these cases (rec 10(12)). However, the Government rejected this proposal believing that under the existing procedure the customer had ample opportunity to establish his case (White Paper (1990) Cm 1026, Annex 4, para 4.11). Many customers would disagree and will welcome the way the Code of Banking Practice (1991) has extended the £50 limit of customer liability for card misuse to all ATM cards (para 18.3) and placed the burden of proving fraud or gross negligence or that a card has been received by the customer on the card issuer (para 18.4). It could be argued, however, that the Code merely substitutes unfairness to the customer with unfairness to the card issuer (see P E Morris, above, p 243).

Further reading on EFT should include: *Electronic Banking – The Legal Implications*, edited by R M Goode (1985); D Chorafas *Electronic Funds Transfer* (1988); B Geva [1988] LMCLQ 477 (on CHAPS); B Geva (1989) 15 CBLJ 406 (on debit cards); J Vroegop [1990] LMCLQ 547 (on the role of correspondent banks in direct funds transfer).

Part VI

The financing of international trade

CHAPTER 19

The financing of international trade

The price of goods sold under an international sales contract may be paid in various ways. The method chosen for any particular transaction will greatly depend on the seller's confidence in the integrity and solvency of the overseas buyer, as well as on the bargaining strengths of the respective parties. Where the seller has such confidence in the buyer, he may be prepared to accept direct payment from him. Direct payment may be made by mail transfer or by telegraphic or telecommunicated transfer of funds, by means of a banker's draft, or by a bill of exchange drawn by the seller on the buyer. Where the seller lacks confidence in the honesty or solvency of the buyer, he may insist that payment is made through the intervention of one or more banks. In fob and cif contracts, payment is usually effected through a bank. The two most common methods of payment which involve banks are the collection of documentary bills and payment under documentary credits.

1 Documentary bills

A 'documentary bill' is a bill of exchange to which the bill of lading (or other document of title) is attached. The seller will send a documentary bill to the buyer to ensure that the buyer does not take up the bill of lading, which gives him a right of disposal of the goods, without first accepting or paying the bill of exchange as previously agreed between the parties. If the buyer fails to accept or pay the bill of exchange (depending on whether it is a term or sight bill), he is bound to return the bill of lading to the seller and, if he wrongfully retains the bill of lading, the property in the goods does not pass to him (Sale of Goods Act 1979, s 19(3)). However, this method of payment does not prevent a buyer, who has dishonoured the bill of exchange, from passing title to the goods to a third party under one of the exceptions to the *nemo dat* rule: in particular, under s 9 of the Factors Act 1889 or s 25 of the Sale of Goods Act 1979 (*Cahn & Mayer v Pockett's Bristol Channel Steam Packet Co Ltd* [1899] 1 QB 643).

To avoid the risk of a fraudulent buyer passing title to the goods to a third party, the seller may instruct his own bank (the 'remitting bank') to deliver the bill of lading, and other shipping documents, to the buyer in his own country and, as a precondition to the release of those documents, collect the price from him, ie by acceptance or payment of the bill of exchange. If the remitting bank does not have an office in the buyer's country, it may instruct a local bank (the 'collecting bank') to perform this task as its agent (see *Calico Printer's Association Ltd v Barclays Bank Ltd* (1931) 145 LT 51: above, p 183). The relations between the seller and the remitting bank, and etween the remitting and collecting banks, will usually be governed by the *Uniform Rules for Collections* (1978 Revision), sponsored by the International Chamber of Commerce. The Uniform Rules only apply if incorporated into the contracts by the parties.

In most cases the remitting bank will discount the bill of exchange before acceptance or payment by the buyer. A bill of exchange is discounted when the bank credits the seller's account with the full amount of the bill (less banking charges) or when the bank agrees to advance to the seller a percentage of the face value of the bill. This has the advantage of releasing funds to the seller at an earlier date than if he waited for the bill of exchange to mature. But the remitting bank will usually retain a right of recourse against the seller: if the buyer dishonours the bill of exchange by non-acceptance or non-payment, the bank can sue the seller on the bill. This highlights the real disadvantage, from the seller's point of view, of payment under a documentary bill which is collected by, or discounted to, a bank: the buyer may accept the bill of exchange so that the bill of lading will be released to him, yet the seller has no assurance that the buyer will pay when the bill matures. Documentary credits provide a solution to this problem.

QUESTIONS

1. From the buyer's point of view, what are the advantages of payment by means of a documentary bill?
2. Does the remitting bank become a party to the bill of exchange by discounting it for the seller? What would be the practical significance of the remitting bank becoming a party to the bill? See *Barclays Bank Ltd v Aschaffenburger Zellstoffwerke AG* [1967] 1 Lloyd's Rep 387; *Barclays Bank Ltd v Astley Industrial Trust Ltd* [1970] 2 QB 527 at 538–539.

2 Documentary credits[1]

(a) The concept and function of documentary credits

Documentary Credits **by R Jack (2nd ed, 1993), para 1.3**

The general concept and function of documentary credits   In simple transactions of sale such as may take place in a shop the buyer pays the seller in exchange for the goods. In commercial transactions where buyer and seller are in different countries and the goods must be transported by sea or road or air by a third party carrier, something more sophisticated is required. A documentary credit is a means of providing payment first by substituting a bank for the buyer as the party which will make payment to the seller. Secondly, payment is made not against the transfer of the goods but against the documents which represent the goods after they have been shipped and are in transit. In broad terms a documentary credit provides the

---

1 The leading textbooks on this subject are H C Gutteridge and M Megrah *The Law of Bankers' Commercial Credits* (7th ed, 1984) ('Gutteridge and Megrah'); E P Ellinger *Documentary Letters of Credit – A Comparative Study* (1970) ('Ellinger'); R Jack *Documentary Credits* (2nd ed, 1993) ('Jack'). See also *Benjamin's Sale of Goods* (4th ed, 1992), Ch 23 ('Benjamin'); R M Goode *Commercial Law* (1982) ('Goode'), Ch 24; R R Pennington, A H Hudson and J E Mann *Commercial Banking Law* (1978), Part 4. For an excellent comparative study, see B Kozolchyk 'Letters of Credit' in *International Encyclopedia of Comparative Law*, Vol 9 ('Kozolchyk'), Ch 5.

promise by a bank of immediate or future payment against the presentation of documents to the bank or its agent, most commonly in connection with sale of goods. It is normally used in international transactions and it utilises the international banking system. The first advantage of credits as they are commonly operated is that they provide a seller with a promise of payment, often immediate payment, given by a bank in the seller's own country. Subject to the solvency of the bank, certainty of payment is achieved provided that the seller is able to meet the terms of the credit. That means in essence that he must be able to present the documents required by the credit within the time required by the credit. Credits may be used in different ways to achieve different results, in particular as to when the seller is paid and when the buyer has to provide reimbursement to the bank responsible for the payment. They may also be used, by the mechanism of transfer, to provide for payment to a party from whom the seller is himself acquiring the goods. The function of a credit may be thus not only to provide security of payment to the seller, but to arrange for the financing of the transaction.

NOTE

A documentary credit transaction normally operates as follows (assuming the underlying transaction is one of sale). The exporter and the overseas buyer agree in the contract of sale that payment shall be made under a documentary credit. The buyer then requests a bank in his own country (the 'issuing' bank) to open a documentary credit in favour of the seller on the terms specified by the buyer in his instructions (for an example of a request to open a documentary credit, see below, p 935). The issuing bank then opens the credit (which may be revocable or irrevocable: see below, p 642) and by its terms undertakes to pay the contract price or to pay, accept or negotiate a bill of exchange drawn for the price, provided that the specified transport documents (usually a bill of lading, an insurance policy and an invoice) are duly tendered and any other terms and conditions of the credit are complied with. The issuing bank may open the credit by sending it direct to the seller. Alternatively, as happens in most cases, the issuing bank may arrange for a bank in the seller's country (the 'advising' or 'correspondent' bank) to advise the seller that the credit has been opened. The issuing bank may also ask the advising bank to add its 'confirmation' to the credit. If it agrees to do so, the advising bank (now called the 'confirming' bank) gives the seller a separate payment undertaking in terms similar to that given by the issuing bank. The seller then ships the goods and tenders the required documents to the advising (or confirming) bank. If the documents conform to the terms of the credit, the advising (or confirming) bank will pay the contract price, or pay, accept, or negotiate a bill of exchange drawn for the price, and seek reimbursement from the issuing bank. Before releasing the documents to the buyer, the issuing bank will in turn seek payment from him. If the buyer is not in a position to pay, the issuing bank may release the documents to him under a 'trust receipt' (see below, p 963).

(b) Documentary credit defined

Uniform Customs and Practice for Documentary Credits (1993 Revision, ICC Publication No 500)

Article 2

Meaning of credit

For the purposes of these Articles, the expressions 'Documentary Credit(s)' and 'Standby

Letter(s) of Credit' (hereinafter referred to as 'Credit(s)'), mean any arrangement, however named or described, whereby a bank (the 'Issuing Bank') acting at the request and on the instructions of a customer (the 'Applicant') or on its own behalf,

i. is to make a payment to or to the order of a third party (the 'Beneficiary'), or is to accept and pay bills of exchange (Draft(s)) drawn by the Beneficiary,

or

ii. authorises another bank to effect such payment, or to accept and pay such bills of exchange (Draft(s)),

or

iii. authorises another bank to negotiate,

against stipulated document(s), provided that the terms and conditions of the Credit are complied with.

For the purposes of these Articles, branches of a bank in different countries are considered another bank.

NOTES

1. The terms 'documentary credit', 'banker's commercial credit' and 'commercial letter of credit' are synonymous. But documentary credits are only one type of letter of credit. Letters of credit may also be used in transactions which do not involve payment against the presentation of documents. Such letters of credit are called 'open' or 'clean' credits. Open credits do not fall within the scope of the Uniform Customs and Practice for Documentary Credits and so we shall not be concerned with them in this chapter.

2. Hereafter, the Uniform Customs and Practice for Documentary Credits will be referred to as the 'UCP'. Unless otherwise stated, all references in this chapter will be to the 1993 revision of the UCP. For discussion of the legal nature and standing of the UCP, see below, pp 646–647.

(c) Types of credit

(i) *Revocable and irrevocable credits*

Cape Asbestos Co Ltd v Lloyds Bank Ltd [1921] WN 274, King's Bench Division

Cape Asbestos Co Ltd (the sellers) agreed to sell 30 tons of asbestos sheets to buyers in Warsaw. The buyers, through their own bank, instructed Lloyds Bank Ltd to open a credit in favour of the sellers. Lloyds Bank informed the sellers 'This is merely an advice for the opening of the above-mentioned credit, and is not a confirmation of the same.' The first shipment of 17 tons was paid for through the credit. Lloyds Bank were then informed that the credit was cancelled. The sellers, not having had notice of the cancellation of the credit, shipped the remaining 13 tons to the buyers. When the sellers presented the shipping documents to Lloyds Bank in London, the bank refused to pay them. The sellers then sued Lloyds Bank for the balance of the credit.

Bailhache J: . . . The crucial question is whether the defendants are under any legal duty to inform the plaintiffs when the credit is withdrawn of the fact of its withdrawal. It is clear from the evidence that it is the practice of the defendants to inform persons to whom credits of this kind are given of the withdrawal of the credit, and that they would have done so in this instance but that under pressure of business they forgot to do so. What has to be considered, however, is not the practice of the defendants, but whether any legal duty is laid upon them to give notice. It is to be observed that the letter of June 14, 1920, from the defendants to the plaintiffs announced the opening of a revocable and not of a confirmed credit. A letter in that form intimates to the person in whose favour the credit is opened that he might find that the credit is revoked at any time. That being the representation by the defendants to the plaintiffs, are the defendants under any legal duty to give notice to the plaintiffs when the credit is revoked? . . . I have come to the conclusion that there is no legal obligation on the defendants to give notice in the circumstances. In a case of this kind the wise course for the seller to take before making a shipment of the goods would certainly be to inquire of the bank whether or not the credit had been withdrawn. The practice of the defendants to give notice in such cases is a most prudent, reasonable and business-like practice, and I hope that nothing I have said in this case leads banks to alter that practice; but at the same time it does not seem to be based upon any legal obligation or duty. It has been said that the defendants regard the giving of notice as an act of courtesy which they always perform except when, as in this case, it is unfortunately forgotten. That is the true view of the proceeding. It is an act of courtesy which it is very desirable should be performed, but it is not founded upon any legal obligation. If that conclusion is right it disposes of the case.

NOTES

1. A credit may be either revocable or irrevocable (UCP, art 6(a)). The credit should clearly indicate whether it is revocable or irrevocable (UCP, art 6(b)). In the absence of such indication the credit will be deemed to be irrevocable (UCP, art 6(c)).

2. A revocable credit may be amended and cancelled by the issuing bank at any moment and without prior notice to the beneficiary (UCP, art 8(a)). However, the issuing bank must reimburse any advising bank, or other authorised bank, which has paid, accepted, or negotiated a revocable credit before receiving notice of amendment or cancellation (UCP, art 8(b)).

3. An irrevocable credit (for a specimen, see below, p 938) constitutes a definite undertaking of the issuing bank that it will honour the credit, provided that the documents specified in the credit are presented and that the terms and conditions of the credit are complied with (UCP, art 9(a)). Except as otherwise provided by article 48 of the UCP (transferable credits), an irrevocable credit cannot be amended or cancelled without the consent of the issuing bank, the confirming bank, if any, and the beneficiary (UCP, art 9(d)). For rules governing the preliminary advice of the issue of an irrevocable credit, see UCP, art 11(c).

(ii) *Unconfirmed and confirmed credits*

A confirmed credit (for a specimen, see below, p 940) is one to which the advising bank has added its own definite undertaking to honour the credit, provided the specified documents are presented to it, or another authorised bank, and the terms and conditions of the credit are complied with (UCP, art 9(b)). The credit is unconfirmed when the advising bank has not provided such an undertaking (for an example of an unconfirmed credit, see below, p 942). The advising bank does not incur any liability to the beneficiary if the credit is unconfirmed (see UCP, art 10(c)). The issuing bank may ask the advising bank to confirm the credit but, subject to prior agreement between them, the advising bank is under no obligation to do so (UCP, art 7(a)). To avoid the risk of being held liable to pay the beneficiary, with no right of reimbursement from the issuing bank, an advising bank will, in practice, only confirm an irrevocable credit. If the advising bank reserves a right of recourse against the seller, its undertaking does not constitute a confirmation: *Wahbe Tamari & Sons Ltd v Colprogeca-Sociedada Geral de Fibras, Cafes e Products Colonias Lda* [1969] 2 Lloyd's Rep 18 at 21.

QUESTION

From both the seller's and the buyer's point of view, what are the advantages and disadvantages of an unconfirmed credit? See C M Schmitthoff [1957] JBL 17 at p 18.

(iii) *Sight and acceptance credits*

A sight credit provides for payment by the issuing bank, advising bank, or other bank on presentation of the specified documents. An acceptance credit provides for the beneficiary to present a time bill of exchange to the issuing bank, advising bank or other bank for acceptance against documents and payment by the accepting bank on maturity. After acceptance, and before maturity, the beneficiary may discount the bill for cash.

(iv) *Deferred payment credits*

Under this type of credit, payment is to be made a fixed time from the date of presentation of the documents, or from the date of shipment, as specified in the credit.

(v) *Straight and negotiation credits*

A straight credit is one where the undertakings of the issuing and confirming banks are directed to a named beneficiary and only he may rely on them. Under a negotiation credit the undertakings are directed to any bank, or any bank as described in the credit, which purchases and becomes a bona fide holder of a bill of exchange drawn by the seller under the credit, provided it is accompanied by the specified documents (UCP, art 10(b)). The bank which has purchased the documents from the beneficiary can then present them under the credit and receive payment in due course (UCP, art 10(d)). For a case where the court had to construe the words of an ambiguously worded credit to ascertain whether it was a straight or negotiation credit, see *European Asian Bank AG v Punjab and Sind Bank (No 2)* [1983] 1 WLR 642, CA; see also E P Ellinger [1984] JBL 379.

(vi) *'Red clause' and 'green clause' credits*

A red clause credit calls for payment in advance of shipment of the goods, often against a warehouseman's receipt. A green clause credit operates in the same way, save that the goods must be stored in the bank's name. Red clause and green clause credits are sometimes called anticipatory credits.

(vii) *Revolving credits*

A revolving credit allows the beneficiary to present documents and obtain payment as often as he wants during a credit period, so long as the overall financial limit specified in the credit is not exceeded. As each payment is made, the buyer automatically replenishes the sum that has been drawn down under the credit. A revolving credit is particularly useful when the contract of sale contemplates delivery of goods by instalments.

(viii) *Transferable and back-to-back credits*

Article 48(a) of the UCP defines a transferable credit as 'a credit under which the beneficiary (First Beneficiary) may request the bank authorised to pay, incur a deferred payment undertaking, accept or negotiate (the 'Transferring Bank'), or in the case of a freely negotiable Credit, the bank specifically authorised in the Credit as a Transferring Bank, to make the Credit available in whole or in part to one or more other Beneficiary(ies) (Second Beneficiary(ies)).' Article 48 sets out a number of conditions which must be met if the credit is to be transferable. Chief amongst these are the requirements that the credit must be expressly designated as 'transferable' by the issuing bank (art 48(b)), and that the transferring bank must expressly consent to the extent and manner of the transfer (art 48(c)). In *Bank Negara Indonesia 1946 v Lariza (Singapore) Pte Ltd* [1988] AC 583, the Privy Council held that, for the purposes of what is now art 48(c), the transferring bank's consent 'has to be an express consent made after the request [for transfer] and it has to cover both the extent and manner of the transfer requested' (per Lord Brandon at 599). This means that a bank may issue a transferable credit and later refuse to allow the transfer at will. For this reason the Privy Council's decision has been criticised as seriously impairing the usefulness of transferable credits (C M Schmitthoff [1988] JBL 49 at p 53; W Godwin [1990] JBL 48; Benjamin, para 23-040; cf Jack, paras 10.6–10.7). Unless otherwise stated in the credit, a transferable credit can be transferred only once (UCP, art 48(g)).

When a credit is transferred the second beneficiary (usually the seller's own supplier) is substituted to the rights and obligations of the first beneficiary (the seller) under the credit. This means that the second beneficiary can obtain payment under the credit by tendering the specified documents in his own name. This distinguishes transfer from assignment (see below, Chapter 20). The proceeds of a credit can be assigned to a third party even though the credit is not stated to be transferable (UCP, art 49). But assignment does not transfer the right of performance. This means that even after assignment of the proceeds of the credit, the seller must still present the specified documents to the bank, or the assignee must do so on the seller's behalf.

For detailed discussion of the legal nature of transfer, see, eg, Gutteridge and Megrah, pp 103–105; Jack, paras 10.19–10.26; Benjamin, para 23-041; Goode, pp 686–688; see also M J Smith [1991] JBL 447.

Under a back-to-back credit arrangement the seller will use the credit opened in his favour by the buyer as security for the issue of a second credit (the back-to-back credit) in favour of the seller's own supplier. Save for those terms relating to price and time for presentation of documents, the two credits will be identical in their terms. If the seller banks with the bank which advised him of the opening of the buyer's credit, he will usually ask that bank to issue the back-to-back credit in favour of his own supplier.

QUESTIONS

1. Are documentary credits negotiable instruments?
2. What are the commercial functions of transferable credits and back-to-back credits? See *Ian Stach Ltd v Baker Bosley Ltd* [1958] 2 QB 130 at 138.
3. Distinguish a transferable credit from a negotiation credit. See Goode, p 688.

(ix) *Standby credits*

See below, p 682.

(d) Fundamental principles

(i) *The legal nature and standing of the UCP*

The UCP is a set of rules governing the use of documentary credits. It was first published by the International Chamber of Commerce in 1933 and has been revised five times since then. The latest revision was published in 1993 (ICC Publication No 500), and came into effect on 1 January 1994. The UCP has been adopted by bankers and traders throughout the world. It has been described as 'the most successful harmonizing measure in the history of international commerce' (R M Goode [1992] LMCLQ 190).

The UCP must be incorporated into the text of the documentary credit to be effective to bind the parties to the credit (UCP, art 1). Incorporation is usually by express wording of the credit, but it may also be implied from the previous course of dealings between the parties. However, as the UCP is so widely used, even if it has not been incorporated into the credit, the courts are likely to treat it as evidencing current trade practices and decide any issue relating to the credit according to its terms (see, eg, Jack, para 1.26; Goode, p 657). But the UCP may be expressly excluded by the terms of the credit (UCP, art 1). In cases where there is no such express exclusion, the courts will endeavour to construe the express terms of the credit so as to avoid conflict with the rules of the UCP (*Forestal Mimosa Ltd v Oriental Credit Ltd* [1986] 1 WLR 631, CA). If there is conflict between the express terms of the credit and the UCP, the former will probably prevail over the latter (*Royal Bank of Scotland plc v Cassa di Risparmio Delle Provincie Lombard* [1992] 1 Bank LR 251, CA). The UCP will usually be construed in a purposive sense (*Sumitomo Bank Ltd v Co-operative Centrale Raiffeisen-Boerenleenbank BA, The Royan* [1988] 2 Lloyd's Rep 250, CA; *Rafsanjan Pistachio Producers Co-operative v Bank Leumi (UK) plc* [1992] 1 Lloyd's Rep 513; cf *Bankers Trust Co v State Bank of India* [1991] 2 Lloyd's Rep 443, CA).

For detailed discussion of the legal nature and standing of the UCP, see E P Ellinger [1984] LMCLQ 578 at pp 583–585; Kozolchyk, paras 21–31.

(ii) *The nature of the banks' undertakings*

When the credit is irrevocable and confirmed, the issuing and confirming banks each give *contractual* undertakings to the beneficiary to pay (or pay, accept or negotiate bills of exchange) according to the terms of the credit (*United City Merchants (Investments) Ltd v Royal Bank of Canada* [1983] 1 AC 168, below, p 653). It is generally agreed that these undertakings bind the respective banks as soon as the documentary credit reaches the hands of the beneficiary (dicta of Greer J in *Dexters Ltd v Schenker & Co* (1923) 14 Ll L Rep 586 at 588, being preferred to that of Rowlatt J in *Urquhart, Lindsay & Co Ltd v Eastern Bank Ltd* [1922] 1 KB 318 at 321–322; see generally, P N Todd [1983] JBL 468). But it is far from clear as to what, if any, consideration is provided by the beneficiary in support of these contractual undertakings. Various attempts have been made to find consideration moving from the beneficiary, or otherwise explain the legal basis of the banks' undertakings. These theories are reviewed in some detail by Gutteridge and Megrah, Ch 4 and Ellinger, Chs III–V. However, it is submitted that none of these theories stand up to rigorous analysis (see R M Goode 'Abstract Payment Undertakings', Ch 9 of P Crane and J Stapleton (eds), *Essays for Patrick Atiyah* (1991), p 218). Probably the best explanation is that the undertakings are binding through mercantile usage (*Hamzeh Malas & Sons v British Imex Industries Ltd* [1958] 2 QB 127 at 129 (below, p 648); see also Goode, op cit, pp 222–225). It would appear, therefore, that documentary credits are an exception to the doctrine of consideration (as is expressly recognised by the American Uniform Commercial Code, ss 5–105).

(iii) *The autonomy of the credit*

Urquhart, Lindsay & Co Ltd v Eastern Bank Ltd [1922] 1 KB 318, King's Bench Division

English manufacturers agreed with Indian buyers to manufacture and ship to them, by instalments, a quantity of machinery, at agreed prices. It was a term of the contract that the manufacturer's prices were subject to increase should the cost of labour or materials increase. Pursuant to the terms of the contract, the buyers opened a confirmed irrevocable credit with the defendant bank (the bank). The manufacturers then shipped two instalments of machinery, drew bills of exchange for the price and were paid under the credit. The buyers, finding that the manufacturers were including in their invoices an addition to the prices originally quoted, in respect of increases in the cost of labour or materials, instructed the bank only to pay so much of the next invoices as represented the original prices. The bank advised the manufacturers of this and refused to pay the bill of exchange drawn in respect of the third shipment. The manufacturers sued the bank for breach of contract.

Rowlatt J: In my view the defendants committed a breach of their contract with the plaintiffs when they refused to pay the amount of the invoices as presented. Mr Stuart Bevan [counsel for the defendants] contended that the letter of credit must be taken to incorporate the contract between the plaintiffs and their buyers; and that according to the true meaning of that contract the amount of any increase claimed in respect of an alleged advance in manufacturing costs was not to be included in any invoice to be presented under the letter of credit, but was to be the subject of subsequent independent adjustment. The answer to this is that the defendants undertook to pay the amount of invoices for machinery without qualification, the basis of this form of banking facility being that the buyer is taken for the purposes of all questions between himself and his banker or between his banker and the seller to be content to accept the invoices of the seller as correct. It seems to me that so far from the letter of credit being qualified by the contract of sale, the latter must accommodate itself to the letter of credit. The buyer having authorized his banker to undertake to pay the amount of the invoice as presented, it follows that any adjustment must be made by way of refund by the seller, and not by way of retention by the buyer.

Hamzeh Malas & Sons v British Imex Industries Ltd [1958] 2 QB 127, Court of Appeal

Jordanian buyers (the plaintiffs) agreed to purchase from British sellers (the defendants) a quantity of steel rods, to be delivered in two instalments. Payment for each instalment was to be by two confirmed letters of credit. The buyers duly opened the two credits with the Midland Bank Ltd. The sellers delivered the first instalment and were paid under the first credit. The buyers then complained that that instalment was defective and sought an injunction to restrain the sellers from drawing on the second credit. Donovan J refused to grant the injunction and the buyers appealed against that order.

Jenkins LJ: stated the facts and continued: It appears that when the first consignment of steel rods arrived they were, according to the plaintiffs, by no means up to contract quality and many criticisms were made on that score. That is a matter in issue between the parties. In the meantime the plaintiffs wish to secure themselves in respect of any damages they may be found to be entitled to when this dispute is ultimately tried out, by preventing the defendants from dealing with this outstanding letter of credit. Mr Gardiner [counsel for the plaintiffs], in effect, treats this as no more than part of the price, a sum earmarked to pay for the goods bought under the contract, which the plaintiffs have become entitled to repudiate; and he says that the defendants ought, acordingly, to be restrained from dealing with the amount of this letter of credit. He points out that he is not seeking any order against the bank, but merely against the defendants.

We have been referred to a number of authorities, and it seems to be plain enough that the opening of a confirmed letter of credit constitutes a bargain between the banker and the vendor of the goods, which imposes upon the banker an absolute obligation to pay, irrespective of any dispute there may be between the parties as to whether the goods are up to contract or not. An elaborate commercial system has been built up on the footing that bankers' confirmed credits are of that character, and, in my judgment, it would be wrong for this court in the present case to interfere with that established practice.

There is this to be remembered too. A vendor of goods selling against a confirmed letter of credit is selling under the assurance that nothing will prevent him from receiving the price. That is of no mean advantage when goods manufactured in one country are being sold in another. It is, furthermore, to be observed that vendors are often reselling goods bought from third parties. When they are doing that, and when they are being paid by a confirmed letter of credit, their practice is – and I think it was followed by the defendants in this case – to finance the payments necessary to be made to their suppliers against the letter of credit. That system of financing these operations, as I see it, would break down completely if a dispute as between the vendor and the purchaser was to have the effect of 'freezing,' if I may use that expression, the sum in respect of which the letter of credit was opened.

I agree with Mr Gardiner that this is not a case where it can be said that the court has no jurisdiction to interfere. The court's jurisdiction to grant injunctions is wide, but, in my judgment, this is not a case in which the court ought, in the exercise of its discretion, to grant an injunction. Accordingly, I think this application should be refused.

Sellers LJ: I agree, but I would repeat what my Lord has said on jurisdiction. I would not like it to be taken that I accept, or that the court accepts, the submission if it was made, as I think it was, that the court has no jurisdiction. There may well be cases where the court would exercise jurisdiction as in a case where there is a fraudulent transaction.

Pearce LJ: I agree.

NOTES

1. The UCP upholds the principle of the autonomy of the credit. The articles provide:

Article 3

Credits v. Contracts
a. Credits, by their nature, are separate transactions from the sales or other contract(s) on which they may be based and banks are in no way concerned with or bound by such contract(s), even if any reference whatsoever to such contract(s) is included in the Credit. Consequently, the undertaking of a bank to pay, accept and pay Draft(s) or negotiate and/or to fulfil any other obligation under the Credit, is not subject to claims or defences by the Applicant resulting from his relationships with the Issuing Bank or the Beneficiary.

b. A Beneficiary can in no case avail himself of the contractual relationships existing between the banks or between the Applicant and the Issuing Bank.

Article 4

Documents v. Goods/Services/Performances
In Credit operations all parties concerned deal with documents, and not with goods, services and/or other performances to which the documents may relate.

2. The courts have consistently emphasised the importance to international commerce of the principle of the autonomy of the credit: see, for example, *Discount Records Ltd v Barclays Bank Ltd* [1975] 1 WLR 315 at 320, per Megarry J; *Edward Owen Engineering Ltd v Barclays Bank International Ltd* [1978] QB 159 at 169, per Lord Denning MR (below, p 683); *United City Merchants (Investments) Ltd v Royal Bank of Canada* [1983] 1 AC 168 at 183, per Lord Diplock (below, p 654). See also *Power Curber International Ltd v National Bank of Kuwait SAK* [1981] 1 WLR 1233, where the Court of Appeal, emphasising the importance of the autonomy of the credit, enforced payment of the credit despite an order of a foreign court prohibiting payment.

3. For detailed discussion of the fraud exception to the principle of the autonomy of the credit, see below, pp 653 ff.

(iv) *Strict compliance*

Equitable Trust Co of New York v Dawson Partners Ltd (1927) 27 Ll L Rep 49, House of Lords

Dawson Partners Ltd of London agreed to purchase a quantity of vanilla beans from a seller in Batavia, payment to be by confirmed credit. The credit was issued by Equitable Trust Company of New York and advised through a branch of the Hong Kong and Shanghai Bank in Batavia. The credit called for payment against certain documents including 'a certificate of quality to be issued by experts'. Due to a mistake of the advising bank, the seller tendered a certificate of quality issued by a single expert. The seller was paid. When the issuing bank tendered the certificate to the buyers, they refused to pay on grounds of non-compliance with the credit. In fact, the seller had been fraudulent and shipped mainly rubbish to the buyers. Upholding a decision of the Court of Appeal, the House of Lords (by a majority of 4 to 1) ruled in favour of the buyers.

Viscount Sumner (who was one of the majority): The contract sued on – a confirmed credit of an ordinary kind – was made in writing in London between the parties to the action themselves. By its terms reimbursement is to be made on presentation of 'the documents,' and 'the documents,' in terms of the credit as ultimately agreed, include 'a certificate of quality to be issued by experts who are sworn brokers.' What the plaintiffs tendered, as one of the documents and as the only certificate of quality, was one issued by only one expert who was a sworn broker, and by nobody else. There is really no question here of waiver or of estoppel or of diligence or of negligence or of breach of a contract of employment to use reasonable care and skill. The case rests entirely on performance of the conditions precedent to the right of indemnity, which is provided for in the letter of credit.

It is both common ground and common sense that in such a transaction the accepting bank can only claim indemnity if the conditions on which it is authorised to accept are in the matter of the accompanying documents strictly observed. There is no room for documents which are almost the same, or which will do just as well. Business could not proceed securely on any other lines. The bank's branch abroad, which knows nothing officially of the details of the transaction thus financed, cannot take upon itself to decide what will do well enough and what will not. If it does as it is told, it is safe; if it declines to do anything else, it is safe; if it departs from the conditions laid down, it acts at its own risk. The documents tendered were not exactly the documents which the defendants had promised to take up, and *prima facie* they were right in refusing to take them.

NOTES

1. The documents must comply strictly to the terms of the credit. The principle of strict compliance applies to all contracts arising in a documentary credit transaction, ie the contract of sale, the contract between the buyer and the issuing bank, the contract between the banker and the seller, and the contract between the issuing and advising (or confirming) banks. But the degree of strictness varies according to the particular contract in issue: for example, it is higher in respect of the contract between banker and seller than it is in respect of the contract between banker and buyer. Why should this be so? See Kozolchyk, pp 82–83; Goode, pp 663–664; and Benjamin, para 23-154, fn 87. See also *Bunge Corpn v Vegetable Vitamin Foods (Private) Ltd* [1985] 1 Lloyd's Rep 613, below, p 651.

2. The principle of strict compliance is best illustrated by the following cases:

J H Rayner & Co Ltd v Hambro's Bank Ltd [1943] KB 37

The credit referred to the shipment of 'Coromandel groundnuts' but the seller tendered a bill of lading for 'machine-shelled groundnut kernels' and an invoice for 'Coromandel groundnuts'. Although it was well known in the trade that 'Coromandel groundnuts' were the same thing as 'machine-shelled groundnut kernels', the Court of Appeal held the bank entitled to reject the bill of lading for non-compliance with the terms of credit. Mackinnon LJ stated (at p 41) that '. . . it is quite impossible to suggest that a banker is to be affected with knowledge of the customs and customary terms of every one of the thousands of trades for whose dealings he may issue a letter of credit'.

Bank Melli Iran v Barclays Bank DCO [1951] 2 Lloyd's Rep 367

Bank Melli opened an irrevocable credit which was confirmed by Barclays Bank. The credit called for the tender of documents evidencing shipment of 'sixty new Chevrolet trucks'. The documents tendered by the seller included an invoice which described the trucks as 'in new condition', a certificate which described them as 'new, good, Chevrolet . . . trucks' and a delivery order describing them as 'new (hyphen) good'. Barclays Bank accepted the documents, paid the seller and debited Bank Melli's account accordingly. Bank Melli claimed Barclays were in breach of mandate by paying against non-conforming documents. McNair J held that the descriptions in the tendered documents were inconsistent with each other and that the tender was bad. However, he went on to hold that Bank Melli had subsequently ratified the actions of its agent, Barclays Bank, who were entitled to reimbursement. [For the position where inconsistent documents are tendered under a credit which incorporates the UCP, see art 13(a) of the UCP (below, p 671).]

Moralice (London) Ltd v E D and F Man [1954] 2 Lloyd's Rep 526

The seller tendered documents to the bank showing shipment of 499.7 metric tons of sugar. The credit called for documents showing shipment of 500 metric tons. McNair J held that the bank was entitled to reject the documents as the rule *de minimis non curat lex* did not apply as between the bank and the beneficiary seller, nor did it apply as between the buyer and his bank. The case would today be decided differently under art 39(b) of the UCP (see below, p 652).

In *Bunge Corpn v Vegetable Vitamin Foods (Private) Ltd* [1985] 1 Lloyd's Rep 613 at 616, Neill J held that while the *de minimis* rule did not apply as between a bank and a beneficiary of a letter of credit, the rule did apply as between the buyer and the seller. He held that there was no breach of contract by the buyers when there were minor differences between the credit as opened and that stipulated in the contract of sale. There had been 'substantial compliance' with the contract of sale.

Seaconsar Far East Ltd v Bank Markazi Jomhouri Islami Iran [1993] 1 Lloyd's Rep 236, CA and [1993] 3 WLR 756, HL

A confirmed irrevocable credit stipulated that all documents presented to the bank should bear the letter of credit number and the buyer's name. The seller presented documents to the advising bank and claimed payment. The advising bank refused to pay relying on the fact that one of the documents, the list of the goods shipped, did not carry the letter of credit number nor the buyer's name. On the seller's application for leave to serve proceedings on the issuing bank out of the jurisdiction, the Court of Appeal, by a majority, held that the tender was clearly bad and refused leave. Lloyd and Beldam LJJ rejected submissions that the omission was trivial and that, in any event, it could be cured by reference to the other tendered documents which all carried the necessary particulars. Their Lordships emphasised that neither of these arguments could apply when the credit clearly and expressly required each document to contain the necessary particulars. Stuart-Smith LJ, dissenting, thought that the seller's case was not 'unworthy of consideration'. The House of Lords later reversed the Court of Appeal and gave the seller leave to serve out of the jurisdiction. Their Lordships did not find it necessary to consider whether the tendered documents conformed to the credit, holding that there were other 'serious issues to be tried' in the case.

3. The harshness of the principle of strict compliance is mitigated in the following respects:

(1) Article 39 of the UCP provides for various tolerances. Sub-art (b) states that, save where the credit stipulates that the quantity of goods is not to be exceeded or reduced, the quantity of goods specified in the documents may be 5 per cent more or less than that specified in the credit, so long as the credit does not specify the quantity in terms of a stated number of packing units or individual items. Sub-art (c) provides for a tolerance of plus or minus 5 per cent in the invoice value, so long as sub-arts (a) or (b) do not apply. Under sub-art (a), the words 'about', 'approximately', 'circa' or similar expressions used in connection with the amount of the credit or the quantity or unit price of the goods are to be construed as allowing a difference not to exceed 10 per cent more or 10 per cent less than the amount or quantity or price to which they refer.

(2) The credit must be interpreted as a whole. This means that an isolated technical requirement may be construed flexibly in the light of the other terms of the credit (*Elder Dempster Lines Ltd v Ionic Shipping Agency Inc* [1968] 1 Lloyd's Rep 529 at 535–536).

(3) Article 37(c) of the UCP provides that the *description* of the goods contained in the commercial invoice must correspond with the description in the credit. In all other documents the goods may be described in general terms not inconsistent with the description of the goods in the credit. See also *Midland Bank Ltd v Seymour* [1955] 2 Lloyd's Rep 147 (below, p 667). But the goods must be properly *identified* in each document (*Banque de l'Indochine et de Suez SA v J H Rayner (Mincing Lane) Ltd* [1983] QB 711, CA).

(4) A mere typographical error, or other obvious slip or omission, does not constitute a discrepancy in the document (Gutteridge and Megrah, p 120). For example, in *Hing Yip Hing Fat Co Ltd v Daiwa Bank Ltd* [1991] 2 HKLR 35, Hong Kong Supreme Court, Kaplan J held that there had been a patent typographical error, and no discrepancy, when a document tendered to the issuing bank by the beneficiary gave the name of the applicant for the credit as 'Cheergoal *Industrial* Limited', when it should have been 'Cheergoal *Industries* Limited'. But where it is not clear whether the departure from the detail set out in the credit was deliberate or a mistake, the discrepancy justifies the rejection of the documents (Benjamin, para 23-156, citing *Beyene v Irving Trust Co* 762 F 2d 4 (1985)).

4. As well as complying strictly with the terms of the credit, each document tendered must also be regular on its face, ie it must be effective and legal (*Arnhold Karberg & Co v Blythe Green Jourdain & Co* [1916] 1 KB 495, where the tender of bill of lading which had become void because of the outbreak of war was held to have been a bad tender). The documents should also be of a type current in the trade and should not invite further enquiry (*M Golodetz & Co v Czarnikow-Rionda Co Inc* [1980] 1 WLR 495, CA). But this principle is of only limited application as a bank is not expected to have knowledge of particular trade practices (*J H Rayner & Co Ltd v Hambro's Bank Ltd*, above, p 651, per Mackinnon LJ).

5. A bank may reject conforming documents in cases of fraud (see below).

QUESTION

Would *J H Rayner & Co Ltd v Hambro's Bank Ltd* (above, p 651) be decided the same way today under art 37(c) of the UCP?

(v) *The fraud exception*

United City Merchants (Investments) Ltd v Royal Bank of Canada, The American Accord [1983] 1 AC 168, House of Lords

English sellers sold manufacturing equipment to Peruvian buyers and agreed to invoice for the order at twice the correct price, to enable the buyers to evade Peruvian exchange control regulations. Payment was to be made by confirmed irrevocable credit, and this was issued by the buyers' bank and confirmed by Royal Bank of Canada. The goods were shipped on 16 December 1976. However, the credit specified that the last day for shipment was 15 December 1976 and so the carriers' agent fraudulently issued a bill of lading showing shipment to have been made on 15 December. The sellers knew nothing of this fraud. On presentation of the documents the confirming bank refused to pay on the ground that it had information suggesting that shipment had not taken place on the day stated in the bill of lading. The sellers (strictly, the assignees of their rights under the credit) sued the confirming bank under the credit.

Mocatta J held that, as the sellers were innocent of the fraud of the carriers' agent, the bank was wrong to refuse payment of documents which, on their face, appeared to be in order. But, in a second judgment, he held that, because of the breach of Peruvian exchange control regulations, the credit was rendered unenforceable under the Bretton Woods Agreements Order in Council 1946. The Court of Appeal dismissed the sellers' appeal on the ground that whilst it was possible to divide the credit and allow payment for that half of the invoice price which did not infringe the exchange control regulations, the bank had been entitled to rely on the fraud of the carriers' agent and refuse payment of any sum. The sellers appealed.

Lord Diplock:

The documentary credit point
My Lords, for the proposition upon the documentary credit point, both in the broad form for which counsel for the confirming bank have strenuously argued at all stages of this appeal and in the narrower form or 'halfway house' that commended itself to the Court of Appeal,

there is no direct authority to be found either in English or Privy Council cases or among the numerous decisions of courts in the United States of America to which reference is made in the judgments of the Court of Appeal in the instant case. So the point falls to be decided by reference to first principles as to the legal nature of the contractual obligations assumed by the various parties to a transaction consisting of an international sale of goods to be financed by means of a confirmed irrevocable documentary credit. It is trite law that there are four autonomous though interconnected contractual relationships involved. (1) The underlying contract for the sale of goods, to which the only parties are the buyer and the seller; (2) the contract between the buyer and the issuing bank under which the latter agrees to issue the credit and either itself or through a confirming bank to notify the credit to the seller and to make payments to or to the order of the seller (or to pay, accept or negotiate bills of exchange drawn by the seller) against presentation of stipulated documents; and the buyer agrees to reimburse the issuing bank for payments made under the credit. For such reimbursement the stipulated documents, if they include a document of title such as a bill of lading, constitute a security available to the issuing bank; (3) if payment is to be made through a confirming bank the contract between the issuing bank and the confirming bank authorising and requiring the latter to make such payments and to remit the stipulated documents to the issuing bank when they are received, the issuing bank in turn agreeing to reimburse the confirming bank for payments made under the credit; (4) the contract between the confirming bank and the seller under which the confirming bank undertakes to pay to the seller (or to accept or negotiate without recourse to drawer bills of exchange drawn by him) up to the amount of the credit against presentation of the stipulated documents.

Again, it is trite law that in contract (4), with which alone the instant appeal is directly concerned, the parties to it, the seller and the confirming bank, 'deal in documents and not in goods,' as art 8 of the Uniform Customs [1974 Revision; now art 4, UCP 1993 Revision] puts it. If, on their face, the documents presented to the confirming bank by the seller conform with the requirements of the credit as notified to him by the confirming bank, that bank is under a contractual obligation to the seller to honour the credit, notwithstanding that the bank has knowledge that the seller at the time of presentation of the conforming documents is alleged by the buyer to have, and in fact has already, commited a breach of his contract with the buyer for the sale of the goods to which the documents appear on their face to relate, that would have entitled the buyer to treat the contract of sale as rescinded and to reject the goods and refuse to pay the seller the purchase price. The whole commercial purpose for which the system of confirmed irrevocable documentary credits has been developed in international trade is to give to the seller an assured right to be paid before he parts with control of the goods that does not permit of any dispute with the buyer as to the performance of the contract of sale being used as a ground for non-payment or reduction or deferment of payment.

To this general statement of principle as to the contractual obligations of the confirming bank to the seller; there is one established exception: that is, where the seller, for the purpose of drawing on the credit, fraudulently presents to the confirming bank documents that contain, expressly or by implication, material representations of fact that to his knowledge are untrue. Although there does not appear among the English authorities any case in which this exception has been applied, it is well established in the American cases of which the leading or 'landmark' case is *Sztejn v J Henry Schroder Banking Corpn* 31 NYS 2d 631 (1941). This judgment of the New York Court of Appeals was referred to with approval by the English Court of Appeal in *Edward Owen Engineering Ltd v Barclays Bank International Ltd* [1978] QB 159 [below, p 683], though this was actually a case about a peformance bond under which a bank assumes obligations to a buyer analogous to those assumed by a confirming bank to the seller under a documentary credit. The exception for fraud on the part of the beneficiary seeking to avail himself of the credit is a clear application of the maxim ex turpi causa non oritur actio or, if plain English is to be preferred, 'fraud unravels all.' The courts will not allow their process to be used by a dishonest person to carry out a fraud.

The instant case, however, does not fall within the fraud exception. Mocatta J found the sellers to have been unaware of the inaccuracy of Mr Baker's notation of the date at which the goods were actually on board *American Accord*. They believed that it was true and that the goods had actually been loaded on or before December 15 1976, as required by the documentary credit.

Faced by this finding, the argument for the confirming bank before Mocatta J was directed to supporting the broad proposition: that a confirming bank is not under any obligation, legally enforceable against it by the seller/beneficiary of a documentary credit, to pay to him the sum stipulated in the credit against presentation of documents, if the documents presented, although conforming on their face with the terms of the credit, nevertheless contain some statement of material fact that is not accurate. This proposition which does not call for knowledge on the part of the seller/beneficiary of the existence of any inaccuracy would embrace the fraud exception and render it superfluous.

My Lords, the more closely this bold proposition is subjected to legal analysis, the more implausible it becomes; to assent to it would, in my view, undermine the whole system of financing international trade by means of documentary credits.

It has, so far as I know, never been disputed that as betwen confirming bank and issuing bank and as between issuing bank and the buyer the contractual duty of each bank under a confirmed irrevocable credit is to examine with reasonable care all documents presented in order to ascertain that they appear *on their face* to be in accordance with the terms and conditions of the credit, and, if they do so appear, to pay to the seller/beneficiary by whom the documents have been presented the sum stipulated by the credit, or to accept or negotiate without recourse to drawer drafts drawn by the seller/beneficiary if the credit so provides. It is so stated in the latest edition of the Uniform Customs. It is equally clear law, and is so provided by art 9 of the Uniform Customs [1974 Revision; now UCP 1993 Revision, art 15], that confirming banks and issuing banks assume no liability or responsibility to one another or to the buyer 'for the form, sufficiency, accuracy, genuineness, falsification or legal effect of any documents.' This is well illustrated by the Privy Council case of *Gian Singh & Co Ltd v Banque de l'Indochine* [1974] 1 WLR 1234 [below, p 670], where the customer was held liable to reimburse the issuing bank for honouring a documentary credit upon presentation of an apparently conforming document which was an ingenious forgery, a fact that the bank had not been negligent in failing to detect upon examination of the document.

It would be strange from the commercial point of view, although not theoretically impossible in law, if the contractual duty owed by confirming and issuing banks to the buyer to honour the credit on presentation of apparently conforming documents despite the fact that they contain inaccuracies or even are forged, were not matched by a corresponding contractual liability of the confirming bank to the seller/beneficiary (in the absence, of course, of any fraud on his part) to pay the sum stipulated in the credit upon presentation of apparently confirming documents. Yet, as is conceded by counsel for the confirming bank in the instant case, if the broad proposition for which he argues is correct, the contractual duties do not match. As respects the confirming bank's contractual duty to the seller to honour the credit, the bank, it is submitted, is only bound to pay upon presentation of documents which not only appear on their face to be in accordance with the terms and conditions of the credit but also do not in fact contain any material statement that is inaccurate. If this submission be correct, the bank's contractual right to refuse to honour the documentary credit cannot, as a matter of legal analysis, depend upon whether *at the time of the refusal* the bank was virtually certain from information obtained by means other than reasonably careful examination of the documents themselves that they contained some material statement that was inaccurate or whether the bank merely suspected this or even had no suspicion that apparently conforming documents contained any inaccuracies at all. If there be any such right of refusal it must depend upon whether the bank, when sued by the seller/beneficiary for breach of its contract to honour the credit, is able to prove that one of the documents did in fact contain what was a material misstatement.

It is conceded that to justify refusal the misstatement must be 'material' but this invites the query: 'material to what?' The suggested answer to this query was: a misstatement of a fact which if the true fact had been disclosed would have entitled the buyer to reject the goods; date of shipment (as in the instant case) or misdescription of the goods are examples. But this is to destroy the autonomy of the documentary credit which is its raison d'être; it is to make the seller's right to payment by the confirming bank dependent upon the buyer's rights against the seller under the terms of the contract for the sale of goods, of which the confirming bank will have no knowledge.

Counsel sought to evade the difficulties disclosed by an analysis of the legal consequences of his broad proposition by praying in aid the practical consideration that a bank, desirous as it would be of protecting its reputation in the competitive business of providing documentary credits, would never exercise its right against a seller/beneficiary to refuse to honour the credit except in cases where at the time of the refusal it already was in possession of irrefutable evidence of the inaccuracy in the documents presented. I must confess that the argument that a seller should be content to rely upon the exercise by banks of business expediency, unbacked by any legal liability, to ensure prompt payment by a foreign buyer does not impress me; but the assumption that underlies reliance upon expediency does not, in my view, itself stand up to legal analysis. Business expediency would not induce the bank to pay the seller/beneficiary against presentation of documents which it was not legally liable to accept as complying with the documentary credit unless, in doing so, it acquired a right legally enforceable against the buyer, to require him to take up the documents himself and reimburse the bank for the amount paid. So any reliance upon business expediency to make the system work if the broad proposition contended for by counsel is correct, must involve that as against the buyer, the bank, when presented with apparently conforming documents by the seller, is legally entitled to the option, *exercisable at its own discretion and regardless of any instructions to the contrary from the buyer*, either (1) to take up the documents and pay the credit and claim reimbursement from the buyer, notwithstanding that the bank has been provided with information that makes it virtually certain that the existence of such inaccuracies can be proved, or (2) to reject the documents and to refuse to pay the credit.

The legal justification for the existence of such an independently exercisable option, it is suggested, lies in the bank's own interest in the goods to which the documents relate, as security for the advance made by the bank to the buyer, when it pays the seller under the documentary credit. But if this were so, the answer to the question: 'to what must the misstatement in the documents be material?' should be: 'material to the price which the goods to which the document relate would fetch on sale if, failing reimbursement by the buyer, the bank should be driven to realise its security.' But this would not justify the confirming bank's refusal to honour the credit in the instant case; the realisable value on arrival at Callao of a glass fibre manufacturing plant made to the specification of the buyers could not be in any way affected by its having been loaded on board a ship at Felixstowe on December 16, instead of December 15, 1976. . . .

The proposition accepted by the Court of Appeal as constituting a complete defence available to the confirming bank on the documentary credit point has been referred to as a 'half-way house' because it lies not only half way between the unqualified liability of the confirming bank to honour a documentary credit on presentation of documents which upon reasonably careful examination appear to conform to the terms and conditions of the credit, and what I have referred to as the fraud exception to this unqualified liability which is available to the confirming bank where the seller/beneficiary presents to the confirming bank documents that contain, expressly or by implication, material representations of fact that to his own knowledge are untrue; but it also lies half way between the fraud exception and the broad proposition favoured by the confirming bank with which I have hitherto been dealing. The half-way house is erected upon the narrower proposition that if any of the documents presented under the credit by the seller/beneficiary contain a material misrepresentation of fact that was *false to the knowledge of the person who issued the document* and intended by him to deceive persons into whose hands the document might come, the confirming bank is under no liability to honour the credit, even though, as in the instant case, the persons whom the issuer of the document intended to, and did, deceive included the seller/beneficiary himself.

My Lords, if the broad proposition for which the confirming bank has argued is unacceptable for the reasons that I have already discussed, what rational ground can there be for drawing any distinction between apparently conforming documents that, unknown to the seller, in fact contain a statement of fact that is inaccurate where the inaccuracy was due to inadvertence by the maker of the document, and the like documents where the same inaccuracy had been inserted by the maker of the document with intent to deceive, among others, the seller/beneficiary himself? Ex hypothesi we are dealing only with a case in which the seller/beneficiary claiming under the credit *has* been deceived, for if he presented documents to the confirming bank with knowledge that this apparent conformity with the terms and conditions of the credit was due to the fact that the documents told a lie, the seller/beneficiary would himself be a party to the misrepresentation made to the confirming bank by the lie in the documents and the case would come within the fraud exception, as did all the American cases referred to as persuasive authority in the judgments of the Court of Appeal in the instant case.

The American cases refer indifferently to documents that are 'forged or fraudulent,' as does the Uniform Commercial Code that has been adopted in nearly all states of the United States of America. The Court of Appeal reached their half-way house in the instant case by starting from the premiss that a confirming bank could refuse to pay against a document that it knew to be forged, even though the seller/beneficiary had no knowledge of that fact. From this premiss they reasoned that if forgery by a third party relieves the confirming bank of liability to pay the seller/beneficiary, fraud by a third party ought to have the same consequence.

I would not wish to be taken as accepting that the premiss as to forged documents is correct, even where the fact that the document is forged deprives it of all legal effect and makes it a nullity, and so worthless to the confirming bank as security for its advances to the buyer. This is certainly not so under the Uniform Commercial Code as against a person who has taken a draft drawn under the credit in circumstances that would make him a holder in due course, and I see no reason why, and there is nothing in the Uniform Commercial Code to suggest that a seller/beneficiary who is ignorant of the forgery should be in any worse position because he has not negotiated the draft before presentation. I would prefer to leave open the question of the rights of an innocent seller/beneficiary against the confirming bank when a document presented by him is a nullity because unknown to him it was forged by some third party; for that question does not arise in the instant case. The bill of lading with the wrong date of loading placed on it by the carrier's agent was far from being a nullity. It was a valid transferable receipt for the goods giving the holder a right to claim them at their destination, Callao, and was evidence of the terms of the contract under which they were being carried.

But even assuming the correctness of the Court of Appeal's premiss as respects forgery by a third party of a kind that makes a document a nullity for which at least a rational case can be made out, to say that this leads to the conclusion that fraud by a third party which does not render the document a nullity has the same consequence appears to me, with respect, to be a non sequitur, and I am not persuaded by the reasoning in any of the judgments of the Court of Appeal that it is not.

Upon the documentary credit point I think that Mocatta J was right in deciding it in favour of the sellers and that the Court of Appeal were wrong in reversing him on this point.

The Bretton Woods point
The Bretton Woods point arises out of the agreement between the buyers and the seller collateral to the contract of sale of the goods between the same parties that out of the payments in US dollars received by the sellers under the documentary credit in respect of each instalment of the invoice price of the goods, they would transmit to the account of the buyers in America one half of the US dollars received.

The Bretton Woods Agreements Order in Council 1946, made under the Bretton Woods Agreements Act 1945, gives the force of law in England to art VIII s 2(b) of the Bretton Woods Agreement, which is in the following terms:

> Exchange contracts which involve the currency of any member and which are contrary to the exchange control regulations of that member maintained or imposed consistently with this agreement shall be unenforceable in the territories of any member . . .

My Lords, I accept as correct the narrow interpretation that was placed upon the expression 'exchange contracts' in this provision of the Bretton Woods Agreement by the Court of Appeal in *Wilson, Smithett & Cope Ltd v Terruzzi* [1976] QB 683. It is confined to contracts to exchange the currency of one country for the currency of another; it does not include contracts entered into in connection with sales of goods which require the conversion by the buyer of one currency into another in order to enable him to pay the purchase price. As was said by Lord Denning MR in his judgment in the *Terruzzi* case at p 714, the court in considering the application of the provision should look at the substance of the contracts and not at the form. It should not enforce a contract that is a mere 'monetary transaction in disguise.'

I also accept as accurate what was said by Lord Denning MR in a subsequent case as to the effect that should be given by English courts to the word 'unenforceable.' The case, *Batra v Ebrahim*, is unreported, but the relevant passage from Lord Denning's judgment is helpfully cited by Ackner LJ in his own judgment in the instant case: [1982] QB 208, 241F–242B. If in the course of the hearing of an action the court becomes aware that the contract on which a party is suing is one that this country has accepted an international obligation to treat as unenforceable, the court must take the point itself, even though the defendant has not pleaded it, and must refuse to lend its aid to enforce the contract. But this does not have the effect of making an exchange contract that is contrary to the exchange control regulations of a member state other than the United Kingdom into a contract that is 'illegal' under English law or render acts undertaken in this country in performance of such a contract unlawful. Like a contract of guarantee of which there is no note or memorandum in writing it is unenforceable by the courts and nothing more.

Mocatta J, professing to follow the guidance given in the *Terruzzi* case [1976] QB 683, took the view that the contract of sale between the buyers and the sellers at the inflated invoice price was a monetary transaction in disguise and that despite the autonomous character of the contract between the sellers and the confirming bank under the documentary credit, this too was tarred with the same brush and was a monetary transaction in disguise and therefore one which the court should not enforce. He rejected out of hand what he described as a 'rather remarkable submission' that the sellers could recover that half of the invoice price which represented the true sale price of the goods, even if they could not recover that other half of the invoice price which they would receive as trustees for the buyers on trust to transmit it to the buyer's American company in Florida. He held that it was impossible to sever the contract constituted by the documentary credit; it was either enforceable in full or not at all.

In refusing to treat the sellers' claim under the documentary credit for that part of the invoice price that they were to retain for themselves as the sale price of the goods in a different way from that in which he treated their claim to that part of the invoice price which they would receive as trustees for the buyers, I agree with all three members of the Court of Appeal the learned judge fell into error.

I avoid speaking of 'severability,' for this expression is appropriate where the task upon which the court is engaged is construing the language that the parties have used in a written contract. The question whether and to what extent a contract is unenforceable under the Bretton Woods Agreement Order in Council 1946 because it is a monetary transaction in disguise is *not* a question of construction of the contract, but a question of th substance of the transaction to which enforcement of the contract will give effect. If the matter were to be determined simply as a question of construction, the contract between the sellers and the confirming bank constituted by the documentary credit fell altogether outside the Bretton Woods Agreement; it was not a contract to exchange one currency for another currency but a contract to pay currency for documents which included documents of title to goods. On the contrary, the task on which the court is engaged is to penetrate any disguise presented by the actual words the parties have used, to identify any monetary transaction (in the narrow sense of that expression as used in the *Terruzzi* case [1976] QB 683) which those words were intended to conceal and to refuse to enforce the contract to the extent that to do so would give effect to the monetary transaction.

In the instant case there is no difficulty in identifying the monetary transaction that was sought to be concealed by the actual words used in the documentary credit and in the underlying contract of sale. It was to exchange Peruvian currency provided by the buyers in Peru for US $331,043 to be made available to them in Florida; and to do this was contrary to the exchange control regulations of Peru. Payment under the documentary credit by the confirming bank to the sellers of that half of the invoice price (viz $331,043) that the sellers would receive as trustees for the buyers on trust to remit it to the account of the buyer's

American company in Florida, was an essential part of that monetary transaction and therefore unenforceable; but payment of the other half of the invoice price and of the freight was not; the sellers would receive that part of the payment under the documentary credit on their own behalf and retain it as the genuine purchase price of goods sold by them to the buyers. I agree with the Court of Appeal that there is nothing in the Bretton Woods Agreements Order in Council 1946 that prevents the payment under the documentary credit being enforceable to this extent.

[Lords Fraser of Tullybelton, Russell of Killowen, Scarman and Bridge of Harwich concurred.]

NOTES

1. Although Lord Diplock confined his remarks to fraud in relation to the tendered documents, the fraud exception also applies to fraud in the underlying transaction (see Goode, p 660; see also the decision of the Supreme Court of Canada in *Bank of Nova Scotia v Angelica-Whitewear Ltd* (1987) 36 DLR (4th) 161; cf Gutteridge and Megrah, p 183). But the reasoning behind Lord Diplock's ruling on the documentary credit point has been strongly criticised: see Roy Goode 'Abstract Payment Undertakings', Ch 9 of P Crane and J Stapleton (eds) *Essays for Patrick Atiyah* (1991), at pp 229–232. As Professor Ellinger has observed (Benjamin, para 23-105):

> It is disturbing that whilst a document stating the true loading date could have been rejected by the bank in the light of the doctrine of strict compliance, a document in which the loading date was fraudulently misrepresented by its maker constituted a valid tender in the beneficiary's hands.

See also E P Ellinger (1983) 11 ABLR 118 at pp 123–130; cf Jack, para 9.23. For a recent case where the issuing bank was held to be justified, on grounds of fraud, in its refusal to pay under the credit, see *Rafsanjan Pistachio Producers Co-operation v Bank Leumi (UK) plc* [1992] 1 Lloyd's Rep 513 (Hirst J). But the bank must plead and establish actual fraud. It is not enough for the bank to refuse to pay on the ground that it had evidence from which a reasonable banker would think that there had been fraud by the beneficiary, whether or not fraud actually existed in fact: *Society of Lloyd's v Canadian Imperial Bank of Commerce* [1993] 2 Lloyd's Rep 579 (Saville J).

2. In practice it is notoriously difficult for a buyer to prevent payment of an irrevocable credit on grounds of fraud. The burden of proving fraud is high and the courts have shown a marked reluctance to interfere with the smooth running of the system of documentary credits. As Sir John Donaldson MR stated in *Bolivinter Oil SA v Chase Manhattan Bank* [1984] 1 Lloyd's Rep 251 at 257:

> The wholly exceptional case where an injunction may be granted is where it is proved that the bank knows that any demand for payment already made or which may thereafter be made will clearly be fraudulent. But the evidence must be clear, both as to the fact of fraud and as to the bank's knowledge. It would certainly not normally be sufficient that this rests upon the uncorroborated statement of the customer, for irreparable damage can be done to a bank's credit in the relatively brief time which must elapse between the granting of such an injunction and an application by the bank to have it discharged.

3. But the standard of proof of fraud must not be overstated. In *United Trading Corpn SA v Allied Arab Bank Ltd* [1985] 2 Lloyd's Rep 554n, a case concerning the alleged fraudulent calling of a performance bond, the Court of Appeal rejected a submission that fraud was only established if every possibility of an innocent explanation could be excluded. As Ackner LJ stated at 561:

> We would expect the court to require strong corroborative evidence of the allegation, usually in the form of contemporary documents, particularly those emanating from the buyer. In general, for the evidence of fraud to be clear, we would also expect the buyer to have been given an opportunity to answer the allegation and to have failed to provide any, or any adequate answer in circumstances where one could properly be expected. If the Court considers that on the material before it the only realistic inference to draw is that of fraud, then the seller would have made out a sufficient case of fraud.
>
> While accepting that letters of credit and performance bonds are part of the essential machinery of international commerce (and to delay payment under such documents strikes not only at the proper working of international commerce but also at the reputation and standing of the international banking community), the strength of this proposition can be over-emphasized. As Mr Justice Neill observed in the judgment under appeal, it cannot be in the interests of international commerce or of the banking community as a whole that this important machinery that is provided for traders should be misused for the purposes of fraud. It is interesting to observe that in America, where concern to avoid irreparable damage to international commerce is hardly likely to be lacking, interlocutory relief appears to be more easily obtainable. A temporary restraining order is made essentially on the basis of suspicion of fraud, followed some months later by a further hearing, during which time the applicant has an opportunity of adding to the material which he first put before the Court. Moreover, their conception of fraud is far wider than ours and would appear to include ordinary breach of contract. (See *Dynamics Corpn of America v Citizens and Southern National Bank* 356 F Supp 991 (1973); *Harris Corpn v NIRT* 691 F 2d 1344 (1982); and *Itek Corpn v F N Bank of Boston* 566 F Supp 1210 (1983)). These cases appear to indicate that, for the purpose of obtaining relief in such cases, it is not necessary for an American plaintiff to demonstrate a cause of action against a bank, whereas it is, as previously stated, common ground that a plaintiff must in this country show a cause of action. There is no suggestion that this more liberal approach has resulted in the commercial dislocation which has, by implication at least, been suggested would result from rejecting the respondent's submissions as to the standard of proof required from the plaintiffs. Moreover, we would find it an unsatisfactory position if, having established an important exception to what had previously been thought an absolute rule, the Courts in practice were to adopt so restrictive an approach to the evidence required as to prevent themselves from intervening. Were this to be the case, impressive and high-sounding phrases such as 'fraud unravels all' would become meaningless.
>
> The learned Judge concluded that the test to be applied by the Courts is the standard of the hypothetical reasonable banker in possession of all the relevant facts. Unless he can say 'this is plainly fraudulent; there cannot be any other explanation', the Courts cannot intervene. We respectfully disagree. The corroborated evidence of a plaintiff and the unexplained failure of a beneficiary to respond to the attack, although given a fair and proper opportunity, may well make the only realistic inference that of fraud, although the possibility that he may ultimately come forward with an explanation cannot be ruled out. The claim before us is a claim for an interlocutory judgment. The first question is therefore – following the principles laid down in *American Cyanamid Co v Ethicon Ltd* [1975] AC 396 – Have the plaintiffs established that it is seriously arguable that, on the material available, the only realistic inference is that Agromark [the beneficiary] could not honestly have believed in the validity of its demands on the performance bonds?

In fact, the Court of Appeal went on to answer this question in the negative. The beneficiary's failure to defend the claim of fraud could be explained on the ground that it was contesting the jurisdiction of the English courts and did not wish to take any steps which might be interpreted as a submission to the jurisdiction. See also *Tukan Timber Ltd v Barclays Bank plc* [1987] 1 Lloyd's Rep 171 at 176, where Hirst J held that 'this was one of those very, very rare cases where the strict burden of proof [of fraud] was satisfied' but, nevertheless, refused to grant an injunction on the ground that the bank had already refrained from paying under the credit.

For arguments in favour of a more flexible application of the fraud exception on American lines, see E P Ellinger 'Documentary Credits and Fraudulent Documents' in C M Chinkin, P J Davidson and W J M Ricquier (eds) *Current Problems of International Trade Financing* (1983), p 185ff; and also S H van Houten (1984) 62 Can B Rev 385.

4. A buyer with insufficient evidence to prevent payment of the credit on grounds of fraud may still be able to obtain an order to restrain the seller from removing the proceeds of the credit from the jurisdiction or otherwise dealing with them within the jurisdiction (called a Mareva injunction). A Mareva injunction will be available where the buyer can show that there is a risk of assets being removed from the jurisdiction or otherwise dissipated. Although a Mareva injunction may be made to extend to assets outside the jurisdiction (*Derby & Co Ltd v Weldon (No 3 and 4)* [1990] Ch 65), it is thought unlikely that an English court would use one to prevent the dissipation of money paid under a credit by a bank abroad (see Jack, para 9.38).

As well as cases of fraud, there are other circumstances when the court will allow the bank to withhold payment to the beneficiary under the credit. These circumstances arise when:

(1) payment under the credit is illegal or unenforceable according to the law of the place where the bank's performance is due (*The American Accord*, above);

(2) the credit is procurred by misrepresentation of the beneficiary enabling the bank to rescind the credit *ab initio* (misrepresentation by the applicant for the credit would not vitiate the credit, but if the misrepresentation was fraudulent, and the beneficiary was an accomplice to that fraud, the bank can refuse payment: *Rafsanjan Pistachio Producers Co-operative v Bank Leumi (UK) Ltd* [1992] 1 Lloyd's Rep 513);

(3) there is a fundamental mistake which renders the credit void *ab initio*;

(4) the bank's duty to pay is frustrated or suspended through supervening illegality or governmental action;

(5) the bank has a right of set-off against the sum due to the beneficiary (*Hongkong and Shanghai Banking Corpn v Kloeckner & Co AG* [1990] 2 QB 514);

(6) the tendered documents are non-conforming.

These circumstances are considered further by Professor Goode in 'Abstract Payment Undertakings', Ch 9 of P Crane and J Stapleton (eds) *Essays for Patrick Atiyah* (1991), at pp 225–234.

QUESTION

Sid, a Liverpool manufacturer, agrees to sell a quantity of radios to Bill in Australia, payment to be by confirmed irrevocable documentary credit. The credit is opened and confirmed by Eastland Bank in Liverpool. Sid purports to ship the radios in sealed boxes and later presents the specified shipment documents to Eastland Bank, together with two term bills of exchange each drawn for one half of the agreed price. As the documents appear to be in order, the bank accepts the bills and returns them to Sid. Sid then sells one of the bills to his own bank, National Bank, at a discount. He retains the other bill. When the bills mature, Sid and National Bank each present their respective bills to Eastland Bank for payment. But

Eastland Bank, which has just heard from Bill that the boxes shipped by Sid were found on delivery to contain waste paper, seeks your advice as to whether it may refuse payment. See *Discount Records Ltd v Barclays Bank Ltd* [1975] 1 WLR 315.

(e) The contracts arising out of a documentary credit transaction

The contractual relationships arising out of a confirmed irrevocable documentary credit transaction are set out by Lord Diplock in *United City Merchants (Investments) Ltd v Royal Bank of Canada, The American Accord* [1983] 1 AC 168 at 181–183 (above, p 654). It should be noted, however, that Lord Diplock omitted to refer to the contract between the issuing bank and the seller. A diagrammatic representation of these contractual relationships appears as Figure 1.

FIGURE 1   **THE PARTIES TO A CONFIRMED IRREVOCABLE CREDIT**

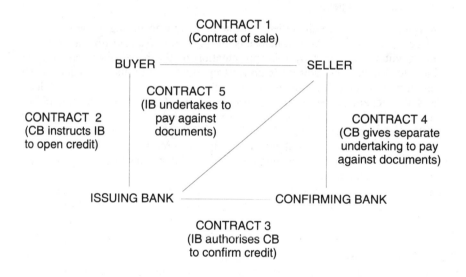

(i) *The contract of sale*

The credit to comply with the contract of sale

Garcia v Page & Co Ltd (1936) 55 Ll L Rep 391, King's Bench Division

By a contract dated 27 May 1935, Page & Co sold 2000 tons of ammonium sulphate to Garcia in Spain, shipment to be during the first half of September 1935. The contract required Garcia 'to open immediately a confirmed credit in London' in favour of Page & Co. There was considerable delay before the credit was opened. On 22 August Page & Co wrote to Garcia stating that if the credit was not received in London by 24 August the contract would be cancelled. The credit was opened on

24 August but not notified to Page & Co until 26 August. Further, the credit did not comply with that provided for in the contract of sale. Page & Co repudiated the contract. A satisfactory credit was opened on 3 September but Page & Co maintained their repudiation. The dispute came before Porter J on a case stated from the arbitrator.

During the course of counsels' submissions, Porter J stated that he was satisfied that the provision with regard to the opening of the credit was a condition precedent in the sense that the sellers would not ship unless it was arranged.

Porter J (when giving judgment): . . . In my view, under the original contract there was a contract by which a confirmed credit in the terms specified was a condition precedent, and it had to be opened immediately. That means that the buyer must have such time as is needed by a person of reasonable diligence to get that credit established. I cannot myself believe that to get that credit established a reasonable time would be from May 27 until Aug 22 or Aug 27 – whichever date you like to take. But just as I think that that was a condition precedent, so I think it is open to either of the parties, with the consent of the other, to prolong the time; and once you have put an end to the reasonable or particular time you have to allow another reasonable time from the moment you say: 'Now I demand you to fulfil that condition.'

To me it is clear, as at present advised, that up to Aug 22 the sellers were not demanding that the stipulation with regard to the confirmed credit should be immediately fulfilled. On the other hand, they were constantly urging that the matter should be taken in hand and I think making it quite plain that the step ought to be taken as speedily as possible. Then, on Aug 22, they did demand that the matter should be put in hand by the 24th. Whether Aug 24 was a reasonable time does not matter for this purpose. Starting from Aug 22, the buyer ought to have a reasonable time, having regard to all the circumstances of the case, to fulfil it.

To decide whether he had may involve a certain amount of evidence, which the arbitrator may take, of surrounding facts and circumstances – such as the difficulty Spaniards have in creating credits in this country by a particular date. I am not particularly impressed, though it is a matter for the arbitrator, with the difficulties, because some sort of credit was established by Aug 26. However, that is a matter to be taken into account. I think that is all the arbitrator has to find.

I say that because it has been urged upon me that I should take into consideration the fact that when the proper credit was finally established, three days of the time the sellers had for shipment had already elapsed. That is quite true, but I do not think that that seriously helps the case, because the delay that took place up to Aug 22 was with their consent; and if with their consent there were two or three days lost it would be part of their consent that that delay should take place.

For these reasons, I think the case should go back to the arbitrator in order that he may determine whether after Aug 22 the buyer had a reasonable time; and, as I say, the costs will be reserved.

NOTES

1. *Garcia v Page & Co Ltd* illustrates that the buyer's obligation to have a documentary credit opened in favour of the seller is usually a condition precedent to the seller's obligation to deliver the goods (cf M Clarke [1974] CLJ 260 at pp 264–269). But the opening of the credit may be construed as a condition precedent to the contract of sale itself (*Trans Trust SPRL v Danubian Trading Co Ltd* [1952] 2 QB 297 at 304, CA), or the contract of sale may impose an obligation on the seller which is a condition precedent to the opening of the credit (*Knotz v Fairclough Dodd and Jones Ltd* [1952] 1 Lloyd's Rep 226).

2. If the buyer opens a credit which does not comply with the terms of the contract of sale, he may remedy the defect if there is still time before the credit is required (*Kronman & Co v Steinberger* (1922) 10 Ll L Rep 39). But if the buyer fails to open the credit in time, or does not remedy a defective credit in time, he commits a repudiatory breach which entitles the seller to treat the contract of sale as discharged (*Dix v Grainger* (1922) 10 Ll L Rep 496) and claim damages for breach of contract (on the basis of *Hadley v Baxendale* (1854) 9 Exch 341). The seller will be able to claim damages for loss of profit on the transaction if, at the time the contract was made, such loss was within the reasonable contemplation of the parties as the probable consequence of the breach (*Trans Trust SPRL v Danubian Trading Co Ltd*, above; *Ian Stach Ltd v Baker Bosley Ltd* [1958] 2 QB 130 at 145).

3. The seller may decide to ship the goods despite the buyer's failure to open the credit on the due date or in its specified form. In *Panoutsos v Raymond Hadley Corpn of New York* [1917] 2 KB 473, a series of shipments of flour was to be paid for by confirmed bankers' credit. The buyer opened an unconfirmed credit. The sellers knew of this defect but still made some shipments before repudiating the contract. The Court of Appeal held that the non-conformity of the credit had been waived by the sellers and that the waiver could only be revoked if reasonable notice was given to the buyer. But in other cases the seller may be deemed to have agreed to a variation of the contract thus preventing him from changing his mind, even on reasonable notice. Variation, unlike waiver, will only be valid if supported by consideration. Identifying whether a contractual requirement has been waived or varied may prove difficult and will depend on the circumstances of each case. See, for example, *W J Alan & Co Ltd v El Nasr Export and Import Co* [1972] 2 QB 189, where Lord Denning MR decided the case on grounds of waiver of the seller's strict rights under the contract, whereas Megaw and Stephenson LJJ decided it on grounds of variation of the contract. The case is exhaustively examined by Malcolm Clarke, [1974] CLJ 260. For general discussion of variation and waiver, see G H Treitel *The Law of Contract* (8th ed, 1991), pp 96ff.

The time of opening of the credit

Where the contract of sale provides a date for the opening of the credit, the buyer must open the credit by that date. If the contract of sale stipulates that the credit must be opened 'immediately', the buyer has such time as is needed by a person of reasonable diligence to open such a credit (*Garcia v Page & Co Ltd*, above, p 662). But what if no time is stipulated?

Pavia & Co SpA v Thurmann-Nielsen [1952] 2 QB 84, Court of Appeal

A cif contract for the sale of shelled Brazilian groundnuts provided for payment by confirmed irrevocable credit and for shipment in the period from 1 February to 30 April 1949 at the sellers' option. The buyers did not open the credit until 22 April. The sellers claimed damages for breach of contract by delay in opening the credit. Affirming the decision of McNair J, the Court of Appeal upheld the sellers' claim.

Somervell LJ: . . . Speaking for myself, I would have no doubt, apart from any question arising with regard to export licences, that under this contract the obligation of the buyers was prima facie to open the credit on February 1 and to have it opened and available as from that date. . . .

The argument, which was very clearly put by Mr Widgery [counsel for the buyers], was on these lines: Normally, delivery and payment are concurrent conditions. You do not really need the credit until you are ready to deliver and have got your bills of lading, when you can go round to the bank and get your money. That is the object of it, to see that the seller can get immediate payment. He read to us, as he read to the learned judge below, certain cases in which Scrutton LJ pointed out (as, of course, I accept) that the main object of the credit system is that the seller may get his money when he has shipped his goods and, at any rate, in some forms of credit the buyer gets an interval of time before he has to meet bills. Whether under this particular form of credit there would be any interval of time between the time of its operation and the time when the buyer had to put his bank in credit I do not know, and to my mind it does not matter. I am quite clear that Scrutton LJ was not addressing himself to the problem which is at present before us. My view is that the contract would be unworkable if, as suggested by Mr Widgery, the buyer under it was under no obligation until a date, which he could not possibly know, and which there is no machinery for his finding out, namely, when the seller actually has the goods down at the port ready to be put on to the ship. There are no words in the contract which would justify us in arriving at that result and there is no reason why we should imply any such term into this contract. I do not think it is a question of implication. I think when a seller is given a right to ship over a period and there is machinery for payment, that machinery must be available over the whole of that period. If the buyer is anxious, as he might be if the period of shipment is a long one, not to have to put the credit machinery in motion until shortly before the seller is likely to want to ship, then he must put in some provision by which the credit shall be provided 14 days after a cable received from the seller, or the like. In the absence of any provision of that kind, I think the answer which the judge gave to the question posed is plainly right, and the appeal should be dismissed.

Denning LJ: The sale of goods across the world is now usually arranged by means of confirmed credits. The buyer requests his banker to open a credit in favour of the seller, and in pursuance of that request the banker, or his foreign agent, issues a confirmed credit in favour of the seller. This credit is a promise by the banker to pay money to the seller in return for the shipping documents. Then the seller, when he presents the documents, gets paid the contract price. The conditions of the credit must be strictly fulfilled, otherwise the seller would not be entitled to draw on it.

The question in this case is this: In a contract which provides for payment by confirmed credit, when must the buyer open the credit? In the absence of express stipulation, I think the credit must be made available to the seller at the beginning of the shipment period. The reason is because the seller is entitled, before he ships the goods, to be assured that, on shipment, he will get paid. The seller is not bound to tell the buyer the precise date when he is going to ship; and whenever he does ship the goods, he must be able to draw on the credit. He may ship on the very first day of the shipment period. If, therefore, the buyer is to fulfil his obligations he must make the credit available to the seller at the very first date when the goods may be lawfully shipped in compliance with the contract. I agree with the answer given by McNair J. The appeal should be dismissed.

Roxburgh J: I agree.

NOTES

1. In *Sinason-Teicher Inter-American Grain Corpn v Oilcakes and Oilseeds Trading Co Ltd* [1954] 1 WLR 1394, a cif contract for the sale of barley provided for shipment during October–November 1952. The buyers agreed to give the sellers a guarantee that the bank would take up the shipping documents on first presentation. The contract did not stipulate a time when the buyers should give the guarantee but when the buyers had failed to provide it by 10 September the sellers cancelled the contract. Affirming the decision of Devlin J, the Court of Appeal held that the sellers had been wrong to cancel the contract as the buyers had not been in default at that time. In an obiter dictum Denning LJ stated:

We were referred to *Pavia & Co SpA v Thurmann-Nielsen*. I agree with what Devlin J said about that case. It does not decide that the buyer can delay right up to the first date for shipment. It only decides that he must provide the letter of credit at latest by that date. The correct view is that, if nothing is said about time in the contract, the buyer must provide the letter of credit within a reasonable time before the first date for shipment. The same applies to a bank guarantee: for it stands on a similar footing.

2. In *Ian Stach Ltd v Baker Bosley Ltd* [1958] 2 QB 130, an fob contract for the sale of steel plates provided for payment by confirmed irrevocable credit and for shipment during August–September 1956 at the buyers' option. The buyers failed to open the credit by 1 August and Diplock J held them to be in breach of contract. It was argued that as the buyer stipulates the shipping date under a 'classic fob contract' (see above, p 447), the credit need only be opened a reasonable time before the date of shipment fixed by the buyer. Diplock J rejected that argument on grounds of uncertainty and held that the prima facie rule was that credit must be opened at the latest by the earliest shipping date. Diplock LJ observed (at 141) that Denning LJ's statement in the *Sinason-Teicher* case, that the credit must be provided a reasonable time before the first date for shipment, was obiter and that the other Lord Justices in that case did not express any view on the matter.

3. If the contract of sale specifies a shipment date, and not a period of shipment, the buyer must open the credit a reasonable time before that date (*Plasticmoda SpA v Davidsons (Manchester) Ltd* [1952] 1 Lloyd's Rep 527 at 538, per Denning LJ).

4. A documentary credit is regarded as 'opened' when it has been received by the seller or his agent (*Bunge Corpn v Vegetable Vitamin Foods (Private) Ltd* [1985] 1 Lloyd's Rep 613 at 617, per Neill J). The buyer will be liable for any delay in opening the credit, even if it was caused by circumstances beyond his control (*A E Lindsay & Co Ltd v Cook* [1953] 1 Lloyd's Rep 328).

QUESTION

Where an fob or cif contract does not specify the date by which the credit must be opened, but does specify a period of shipment, when must the buyer open the credit? Contrast Goode, pp 667–668 and Jack, para 3.21.

The expiry date of the credit

Article 42(a) of the UCP provides that all credits must stipulate an expiry date and a place for presentation of documents for payment, acceptance or, with the exception of freely negotiable credits, a place for presentation of documents for negotiation. An expiry date stipulated for payment, acceptance or negotiation will be construed as the expiry date for presentation of documents. Further, art 43(a) provides that every credit which calls for transport documents should also stipulate a specified period of time after the date of shipment during which presentation must be made. If no such period of time is stipulated, banks will not accept documents presented to them later than 21 days after the date of shipment. In all cases, documents must be presented not later than the expiry date of the credit.

The credit as payment

Unless otherwise agreed, payment by documentary credit constitutes conditional payment of the price. As Lord Denning MR stated (obiter) in *W J Alan & Co Ltd v El Nasr Export and Import Co* [1972] 2 QB 189 at 212:

> ... I am of the opinion that in the ordinary way, when the contract of sale stipulates for payment to be made by confirmed irrevocable letter of credit, then, when the letter of credit is issued and accepted by the seller, it operates as conditional payment of the price. It does not operate as absolute payment.
>
> It is analogous to the case where, under a contract of sale, the buyer gives a bill of exchange or a cheque for the price. It is presumed to be given, not as absolute payment, nor as collateral security, but as conditional payment. If the letter of credit is honoured by the bank when the documents are presented to it, the debt is discharged. If it is not honoured, the debt is not discharged: and the seller has a remedy in damages against both banker and buyer.

For reasons supporting this view, see M Clarke [1974] CLJ 260 at 274–276. See also *E D & F Man Ltd v Nigerian Sweets & Confectionery Co Ltd* [1977] 2 Lloyd's Rep 50; *Maran Road Saw Mill v Austin Taylor & Co Ltd* [1975] 1 Lloyd's Rep 156 (noted (1977) 40 MLR 91); and *Re Charge Card Services Ltd* [1989] Ch 497 at 516.

When the contract of sale specifies that payment is to be by documentary credit the seller must present the documents to the bank. He cannot 'short-circuit' the credit and present documents directly to the buyer and claim payment from him (*Soproma SpA v Marine & Animal By-Products Corpn* [1966] 1 Lloyd's Rep 367 at 385–386, McNair J). However, if the bank defaults, eg by becoming insolvent, the seller can normally claim payment from the buyer by tendering documents directly to him (*Soproma*, at 386; *Schmitthoff's Export Trade* (9th ed, 1990), p 438). This stems from the fact that in most cases the credit only operates as conditional payment. As Ackner J said in *E D & F Man Ltd v Nigerian Sweets & Confectionery Co Ltd*, above, at 56: 'The [buyers'] liability to the sellers was a primary liability. This liability was suspended during the period available to the issuing bank to honour the drafts and was activated when the issuing bank failed'. Alternatively, the seller can sue the buyer for damages for breach of contract.

(ii) *The contract between buyer and issuing bank*

Midland Bank Ltd v Seymour [1955] 2 Lloyd's Rep 147, Queen's Bench Division

Seymour contracted to purchase a large quantity of feathers from Hong Kong sellers. Payment was to be by confirmed irrevocable credit. The credit was issued by the Midland Bank after receiving instructions from Seymour given on the bank's pro forma application forms. Seymour had instructed the bank to make the credit 'available in Hong Kong'. On presentation of the shipping documents, the Midland Bank accepted, and later paid, various bills of exchange drawn by the sellers. But the sellers were fraudulent and had shipped rubbish. Seymour refused to reimburse the bank, raising various defences to the bank's claim for payment. One defence was that the documents tendered did not conform to the credit as the bill of lading did not state the description, quantity and price of the goods (although such information was contained in other tendered documents, eg the invoice, which were consistent with the bill of lading). Another defence was that the bank had not complied with its mandate by issuing a credit which provided for acceptance of drafts in London instead of Hong Kong. Devlin J gave judgment for the bank on its claim.

Devlin J held that the sellers had presented conforming documents as the credit was to be construed as requiring the presentation of a set of documents which were consistent between themselves, and which, when read together, provided a statement of the description, quantity and price of the goods. He held that the credit did not require each individual document to provide such information.

Devlin J continued: But if I had not reached that conclusion . . . I should have arrived at the same result on another ground. In my judgment, no principle is better established than that when a banker or anyone else is given instructions or a mandate of this sort, they must be given to him with reasonable clearness. The banker is obliged to act upon them precisely. He may act at his peril if he disobeys them or does not conform with them. In those circumstances there is a corresponding duty cast on the giver of instructions to see that he puts them in a clear form. Perhaps it is putting it too high for this purpose to say that it is a duty cast upon him. The true view of the matter, I think, is that when an agent acts upon ambiguous instructions he is not in default if he can show that he adopted what was a reasonable meaning. It is not enough to say afterwards that if he had construed the documents properly he would on the whole have arrived at the conclusion that in an ambiguous document the meaning which he did not give to it could be better supported than the meaning which he did give to it. If I am wrong in adopting the construction that Mr Diplock gives to this document, I am quite clear that at the best it is ambiguous. It is impossible to say that the document specifies in reasonably clear terms that the bill of lading has to contain the description and quantity.

That argument is met to some extent by Mr Mocatta when he points out that the form which was filled up is not Mr Seymour's own form but is the bank's form; and he relies upon what I think may be called the *contra proferentes* principle on which a person who prepares a form is responsible for any ambiguities that it contains, or must suffer for it. In my judgment, that principle does not apply in this case. It applies (or would apply) if there were some exception, as for example in one of the conditions or clauses on the back of the document which was inserted for the benefit of the bank. If there were some exception there, no doubt the principle would apply.

But this is not a case of that type. This is a printed document which shows the sort of thing that the bank wants, but it is left to the applicant for the credit to fill it up in what way he wants; and if he thinks there is some ambiguity in it there is no difficulty, so far as I can see, in his filling it up in a way to make it clear. For example, if he wanted plainly to specify that the bill of lading should contain the full description, I cannot see that there would be any difficulty in his doing so, or that the bank could conceivably object if he did so. The bank do not care what the bill of lading is or is not required to contain. It cannot matter to them so long as they are told clearly what it is that they have to look for.

[On the issue whether the bank had exceeded its mandate Devlin J continued:]

I have not to determine whether the Midland Bank is in breach by failing to create facilities in Hongkong. If they did so fail, and if it was in breach, it has caused no damage, because the seller has never tried to make use of that. The point is whether the bank is authorized to pay or accept only in Hongkong. . . . If it was authorized so to pay, then although the place of payment may be commercially immaterial, the bank has exceeded its mandate and cannot recover. It is a hard law sometimes which deprives an agent of the right to reimbursement if he has exceeded his authority, even though the excess does not damage his principal's interests. The corollary, which I have already noted in the judgment I delivered earlier, is that the instruction to the agent must be clear and unambiguous.

The mandate to the bank in this case does not make the place of availability expressly exclusive, and I do not think it ought lightly to be assumed that it was intended to be expressly exclusive. Let me take a simple example, uncomplicated by a letter of credit. A, who does business in London, arranges that his debt to X at Edinburgh will be discharged by his agent B, whose place of business is also in London. If matters were left there, X would, in accordance with the ordinary rule, have to come to London to collect his money. But it might well be that A would tell his agent B that he was to travel to Edinburgh to pay X there. If he did, and if before B went to Edinburgh X happened to come to London and call for the money and B paid it, it would be a strong thing to say that B could not debit A. It would be held in such a case as that, I think, that the naming of Edinburgh was merely an additional convenience made for the benefit of X, if he wanted to take advantage of it. So here I think the naming of Hongkong is additional and not exclusive. If it were not named, the drafts would have to be presented at the Midland Bank's place of business in London. That might not be convenient to the seller, and so there is a request for additional facilities in the place where the seller does business.

In the example which I took, the Court would ask chiefly whether there was any business reason why A should mind where X was paid so long as he was paid. The same is true of the buyers in this case, if the sellers do not want Hongkong and there is no reason why the buyers should. Mr Mocatta suggested that if the buyers were not interested in the place of payment, they still might be interested in the place where the documents were delivered to the bank, but this seems to me to be a separate matter. The buyers' right to receive the documents from the bank is not dealt with in the request for credit. That right must be, presumably, the subject of a separate arrangement whereunder the buyers can make what stipulations they want about bringing the documents to the place where they can be collected, and in the ordinary course of business such an arrangement would no doubt provide for advances to be made by the bank on the security of the documents. The fact that the buyer never objected to acceptance in London and always collected the documents from there suggests that London was the place where he wanted them.

In my judgment, acceptance in London was within the terms of the mandate to the bank in this case.

An alternative plea was raised that if the bank accepted the bill in the wrong place, then their conduct was ratified or adopted by the buyer in this case. Having regard to the conclusion which I have already expressed, I do not need to determine that matter. . . .

NOTES

1. The reason for the rule relating to ambiguous or unclear instructions given by the buyer to his bank is best stated by Lord Diplock in *Commercial Banking Co of Sydney Ltd v Jalsard Pty Ltd* [1973] AC 279 at 286, PC:

By issuing the credit, the banker does not only enter into a contractual obligation to his own customer, the buyer, to honour the seller's drafts if they are accompanied by the specified documents. By confirming the credit to the seller through his correspondent at the place of shipment he assumes a contractual obligation to the seller that his drafts on the correspondent bank will be accepted if accompanied by the specified documents, and a contractual obligation to his correspondent bank to reimburse it for accepting the seller's drafts. The banker is not concerned as to whether the documents for which the buyer has stipulated serve any useful commercial purpose or as to why the customer called for tender of a document of a particular description. Both the issuing banker and his correspondent bank have to make quick decisions as to whether a document which has been tendered by the seller complies with the requirements of a credit at the risk of incurring liability to one or other of the parties to the transaction if the decision is wrong. Delay in deciding may in itself result in a breach of his contractual obligations to the buyer or to the seller. This is the reason for the rule that where the banker's instructions from his customer are ambiguous or unclear he commits no breach of his contract with the buyer if he has construed them in a reasonable sense, even though upon the closer consideration which can be given to questions of construction in an action in a court of law, it is possible to say that some other meaning is to be preferred.

2. But the rule has its limits. In *European Asian Bank AG v Punjab and Sind Bank (No 2)* [1983] 1 WLR 642 at 656, Goff LJ said that 'a party relying on his own interpretation of the relevant document must have acted reasonably in all the circumstances in so doing. If instructions are given to an agent, it is understandable that he should expect to act on those instructions without more; but if, for example, the ambiguity is patent on the face of the document it may well be right (especially with the facilities of modern communication available to him) to have his instructions clarified by his principal, if time permits, before acting upon them'. See also, above at pp 87–88.

3. Article 5(a) of the UCP provides, inter alia, that the instructions for the issue of a credit, the credit itself, instructions for any amendment thereto, and the amendment itself, must be complete and precise. Further, art 5(b) provides that all instructions for the issue of a credit, the credit itself, all instructions for any amendment thereto, and the amendment itself, must state precisely the documents against which payment, acceptance or negotiation is to be made. See also arts 12 (incomplete or unclear instructions to advise, confirm or amend a credit) and 20 (ambiguity as to the issuers of documents).

4. In *European Asian Bank AG v Punjab and Sind Bank (No 2)*, above, Goff LJ pointed out that it was not strictly correct to refer to the issuing bank as the agent of the buyer, as Devlin J had done in *Midland Bank Ltd v Seymour*. Goff LJ was right, for the issuing bank does not contract with the seller on the buyer's behalf: the bank enters into a separate contract with the seller as principal. This does not alter the rule that the issuing bank, like an agent, is entitled to give ambiguous instructions a reasonable construction, but it does mean that it is probably more accurate to refer to the buyer's informed acceptance of an unauthorised act of the issuing bank (eg acceptance of non-conforming documents) as waiver of the bank's breach of mandate rather than as ratification of the act itself.

Gian Singh & Co Ltd v Banque de l'Indochine [1974] 1 WLR 1234, Privy Council

Banque de l'Indochine opened an irrevocable documentary credit on the instructions of Gian Singh & Co Ltd (the customer) to finance the purchase of a fishing vessel. The credit required the tender of a certificate signed by Balwant Singh, holder of Malaysian Passport E-13276, certifying that the vessel had been correctly built and was in a condition to sail. The certificate was tendered but the signature of Balwant Singh was a forgery, as was the passport presented to the bank for inspection. The bank accepted the documents and debited its customer's account with the sum paid to the beneficiary. The customer sued the bank claiming that its account had been wrongly debited. The Court of Appeal in Singapore gave judgment for the bank. The Privy Council dismissed the customer's appeal against that decision.

Lord Diplock delivered the judgment of the Privy Council (Lords Wilberforce, Diplock, Cross of Chelsea, and Kilbrandon and Sir Harry Gibbs): The fact that a document presented by the beneficiary under a documentary credit, which otherwise conforms to the requirements of the credit, is in fact a forgery does not, of itself, prevent the issuing bank from recovering from its customer money paid under the credit. The duty of the issuing bank, which it may perform either by itself, or by its agent, the notifying bank, is to examine documents with reasonable care to ascertain that they appear on their face to be in accordance with the terms and conditions of the credit. The express provision to this effect in article 7 of the Uniform Customs and Practice for Documentary Credits [1962 Revision; now UCP 1993 Revision, art 13(a)] does no more than re-state the duty of the bank at common law. In business transactions financed by documentary credits banks must be able to act promptly on presentation of the documents. In the ordinary case visual inspection of the actual documents presented is all that is called for. The bank is under no duty to take any further steps to investigate the genuineness of a signature which, on the face of it, purports to be the signature of the person named or described in the letter of credit.

The instant case differs from the ordinary case in that there was a special requirement that the signature on the certificate should be that of a person called Balwant Singh, and that that person should also be the holder of Malaysian passport no. E-13276. This requirement imposed upon the bank the additional duty to take reasonable care to see that the signature on the certificate appeared to correspond with the signature on an additional document prsented by the beneficiary which, on the face of it, appeared to be a Malaysian passport No E-13276 issued in the name of Balwant Singh. The evidence was that that is what the notifying bank had done when the certificate was presented. The onus of proving lack of reasonable care in failing to detect the forgery of the certificate lies upon the customer. In their Lordships' view, in agreement with all the members of the Court of Appeal, the customer did not succeed in making out any case of negligence against the issuing bank or the notifying bank which acted as its agent, in failing to detect the forgery.

NOTES

1. Article 13 of the UCP provides as follows:

Standard for examination of documents

a Banks must examine all documents stipulated in the Credit with reasonable care, to ascertain whether or not they appear, on their face, to be in compliance with the terms and conditions of the Credit. Compliance of the stipulated documents on their face with the terms and conditions of the Credit, shall be determined by international standard banking practice as reflected in these Articles. Documents which appear on their face to be inconsistent with one another will be considered as not appearing on their face to be in compliance with the terms and conditions of the Credit.

> Documents not stipulated in the Credit will not be examined by banks. If they receive such documents, they shall return them to the presenter or pass them on without responsibility.

b The Issuing Bank, the Confirming Bank, if any, or a Nominated Bank acting on their behalf, shall each have a reasonable time, not to exceed seven banking days following the day of receipt of the documents, to examine the documents and determine whether to take up or refuse the documents and to inform the party from which it received the documents accordingly.

c If a Credit contains conditions without stating the document(s) to be presented in compliance therewith, banks will deem such conditions as not stated and will disregard them.

Article 13(b) is considered further below at pp 674 ff. See also art 14(b) (issuing bank and/or confirming bank, or other bank acting on their behalf, must determine on the basis of the documents alone whether or not they appear on their face to comply with the terms of the credit and, if they do not comply, such banks have the right to reject the documents) and art 14(e) (issuing bank and/or confirming bank shall be precluded from claiming that documents are not in compliance with the credit where they fail to act according to the requirements of art 14 – see below, pp 674–679 and/or fail to hold the documents at the disposal of, or return them to, the presenter).

2. But it is important to note that so long as the issuing bank has exercised reasonable care to ascertain that the tendered documents, on their face, comply with the applicant's instructions and the terms of credit, it is not liable or responsible for the form, sufficiency, accuracy, genuineness, falsification or legal effect of any such documents (UCP, art 15). Article 15 applies to all banks involved in a documentary credit transaction.

3. Where the buyer has been the victim of a fraud of the seller, eg the seller ships rubbish, tenders complying documents and receives payment, the buyer's only claim against the issuing bank may be in negligence for failing to advise on the transaction, eg as to the need for an inspection certificate from a reliable third party. Such a claim will only succeed where the facts show that the bank has undertaken a duty to advise, which will be rare, or the bank has actually given misleading advice. In *Midland Bank Ltd v Seymour*, above at p 667, the bank was held liable on Seymour's counterclaim for contractual negligence because it failed to pass on certain adverse information about the Hong Kong sellers after being instructed by Seymour to make inquiries. However, the bank was only ordered to pay nominal damages as Seymour had suffered no loss as a result of this breach. See also *Commercial Banking Co of Sydney Ltd v Jalsard Pty Ltd* [1973] AC 279, PC.

General comments:

(1) If the issuing bank fails to comply with the buyer's instructions with regard to the opening of the credit or as to the acceptance or rejection of documents presented to it, the buyer is under no obligation to accept the documents from the bank and is not obliged to reimburse the bank for any payment made to the beneficiary. Further, the bank may be liable to the buyer for any loss sustained by him as a result of the bank's breach of contract.

(2) The issuing bank may always try to exclude its own liability for breach of contract. Such clauses may prove to be ineffective on grounds of construction or by reason of s 3 of the Unfair Contract Terms Act 1977. But the UCP does exonerate the issuing bank from liability for matters beyond its control. Article 16 protects the bank against liability for the consequences arising out of delay and/or loss in transit of messages and for errors in the translation and/or interpretation of messages. But it is submitted that art 16 does not exempt the issuing bank from liability for its own negligence (Jack, para 4.15). Article 17 excludes liability for force majeure events. Article 18 is particularly important because it exonerates the issuing bank from all liability for the errors of the advising bank (which acts as the issuing bank's agent), whether this bank has been chosen by the issuing bank or the beneficiary. But again it is submitted that this immunity does not extend to the issuing bank's own negligence (Jack, para 4.18; see also *Bank Leumi v M G Brin & Sons* [1992] LMLN 342, Israeli Supreme Court, noted [1993] LMCLQ 28). Article 18 may prove harsh on the buyer when the advising bank has been negligent, for there is no clear way to make the advising bank directly liable to him. In practice art 18 tends not to be relied upon by issuing banks.

QUESTION

Does acceptance of conforming documents by the issuing bank preclude the buyer from rejecting the goods if they prove defective on arrival? What if the defect was apparent on the face of the documents? See Goode, p 668.

(iii) *The contract between the issuing bank and the advising or confirming bank*

Bank Melli Iran v Barclays Bank DCO [1951] 2 Lloyd's Rep 367, King's Bench Division

(The facts appear above at p 651.)

McNair J: In my judgment, both on the construction of the documents under which the credit was established and in principle, the relationship between Bank Melli, the instructing bank, and Barclays Bank, the confirming bank, was that of principal and agent. This relationship was held to exist in substantially similar circumstances in *Equitable Trust Co of New York v Dawson Partners Ltd* ((1927) 27 Ll L Rep 49) (see per Viscount Cave LC at p 52, Lord Sumner at p 53, and Lord Shaw of Dunfermline at p 57), and the existence of this relationship is implicit in the judgments of the Court of Appeal in *J H Rayner & Co Ltd v Hambro's Bank Ltd* ([1943] KB 37). I accept as accurate the statement of Professor Gutteridge KC in his book on *Bankers' Commercial Credits*, at p 51, that 'as between the issuing banker' (in this case Bank Melli) 'and the correspondent' (in this case Barclays Bank) 'the relationship is, unless otherwise agreed, that of principal and agent . . .' On the facts of this case I find no agreement to the contrary.

NOTE

The advising bank will advise the beneficiary of the opening of the credit, collect the documents and make payment as the agent of the issuing bank (cf A Ward and R Wight [1993] 10 JIBL 432). But the confirming bank acts in a dual capacity. It acts as agent for the issuing bank with regard to the obligations of the issuing bank, and it acts as principal in relation to its own obligations, as confirming bank, to the beneficiary. An advising or confirming bank which pays the beneficiary against the tender of conforming documents may claim reimbursement from the issuing bank (UCP, arts 10(d) and 14(a)). So long as the tendered documents are regular on their face, the advising or confirming bank will be entitled to reimbursement even if the documents turn out to be forged or false (UCP, art 15).

Sometimes one bank ('the instructing bank') may ask another bank ('the correspondent issuer') to issue a credit in its own name. In such a case, only the correspondent issuer gives a payment undertaking to the beneficiary; there is no relationship between the instructing bank and the beneficiary. The correspondent issuer is entitled to reimbursement from the instructing bank. For cases of this type see *National Bank of Egypt v Hannevig's Bank Ltd* (1919) 1 Ll L Rep 69 and *Scandinaviska Akt v Barclays Bank* (1925) 22 Ll L Rep 523.

QUESTION

Intra Bank issues an irrevocable documentary credit in favour of Slicker. The credit is advised through Agro Bank. Agro Bank advises Slicker that payment will be made on the tender of certain documents to Intra Bank. Contrary to Intra Bank's instructions, Agro Bank omits to inform Slicker that the tendered documents must include a certificate of origin of the goods shipped. Slicker tenders documents, but not a certificate of origin, to Intra Bank. Relying on this omission, Intra Bank refuses to pay Slicker. Advise Slicker as to his rights, if any, against Intra Bank.

Slicker, hearing that Intra Bank is almost insolvent, also seeks your advice as to any rights he may have against Agro Bank.

We have already seen that the issuing bank, the confirming bank and any other bank acting on their behalf (including an advising bank) each has a reasonable time, not exceeding seven banking days following receipt of the documents, to examine the documents and determine whether to accept or reject them and to inform the party from which it received the documents accordingly (UCP, art 13(b): above, p 671). A reasonable time may be less than seven days. How is it determined? The issue was considered in the next case.

Bankers Trust Co v State Bank of India [1991] 2 Lloyd's Rep 443, Court of Appeal

Buyers (B) purchased 22,000 tons of steel plates from sellers (S), to be shipped from India to the United States. Payment was to be by confirmed irrevocable documentary credit. The credit was issued by Bankers Trust (BT) and confirmed by State Bank of India (SBI). The credit was subject to the UCP, 1983 Revision. On presentation of documents by S to SBI, S was paid over £10 million under the credit. Pursuant to the terms of the credit, SBI was immediately reimbursed that sum by BT. SBI forwarded the documents, comprising 967 sheets of paper, to BT, which received them on Wednesday 21 September. BT finished checking the documents by midday on Monday 26 September. Having discovered certain discrepancies BT sent the documents to B. On Wednesday 28 September BT telexed SBI asserting non-compliance and stating that details would follow. The telex concluded with the statement that 'Documents held at your risk and will be at your disposal after payment to us'. B returned the documents to BT on Thursday 29 September, identifying additional discrepancies not previously discovered by BT. On Friday 30 September BT telexed SBI rejecting the documents and listing 23 discrepancies. The telex concluded with the same statement that concluded the telex of 28 September. BT sought to recover the money paid to SBI on grounds of non-compliance of the documents. SBI did not dispute the existence of the discrepancies but alleged that BT was barred from rejecting the documents on the grounds that the notice of rejection (telex of 30 September) was too late under art 16(c) (now UCP 1993, art 13(b): above, p 671) and was not in a proper form as required by art 16(d) (now UCP 1993, art 14(d)(ii)). Hirst J and the Court of Appeal gave judgment in favour of SBI on both grounds.

Lloyd LJ: Weighing up all this evidence, and taking all the circumstances of this particular transaction into account, I am bound to regard a period of eight working days for examining these documents and determining whether to accept them or not as much too long. I regard it as irrelevant that the defendants did not themselves complain of delay until a meeting on Nov 7, 1988. It may be that eight days would not be regarded as excessive in other financial centres. Mr Barlow [a banking expert] made the valid point that what is reasonable will depend, not only on the number and complexity of the documents, but also on the level of sophistication in dealing with documents in the particular country. I say nothing of other countries. I speak only of London. In London, a major bank, such as the plaintiffs, should have been able to complete its examination of the documents, and reach a determination, in substantially less than eight working days. Approaching the case, therefore, in the way that Mr Goldsmith [counsel for BT] invited the Judge, as a straightforward question of fact, I would have no hesitation in dismissing the appeal.

But we cannot leave the question there, if only because the Judge took the view that there was an important question of principle to be decided in this case, and it is that question of principle that has occupied the greater part of the argument before us. The question can be stated thus: when art 16(c) [now UCP 1993 Revision, art 13(b)] speaks of the issuing bank having a 'reasonable time' to examine the documents and reach a determination, does that include time for the issuing bank to consult its customer? Does it in particular include time for the customer to examine the documents, as happened here, in order to discover further discrepancies which may have been missed by the issuing bank? Put even more shortly, the question is 'a reasonable time for what?'

In *Co-operative Centrale Raiffeisen-Boereleenbank BA v Sumitomo Bank Ltd, The Royan* [1987] 1 Lloyd's Rep 345 Mr Justice Gatehouse at first instance held that words must be read into art 16(b) [now UCP 1993 Revision, art 14(b)] entitling the bank to consult its customer, and that therefore the reasonable time under art 16(c) must be extended to cover the period of consultation. Mr Justice Hirst, in the present case, declined to follow Mr Justice Gatehouse (see [1991] 1 Lloyds Rep 587). This is the issue we now have to decide.

It is convenient to start at the easy end. As we know from their telex of Sept 28, the buyers spent nearly 72 hours combing through the documents in the hope of finding as many discrepancies as possible. Their stated purpose was 'to make an objection hold with the Indian bank'. This is quite plainly contrary to the spirit of the Code. It is also contrary to the letter of arts 15 [now UCP 1993 Revision, art 13(a)] and 16. Under art 15, it is the bank which is given the task of examining documents to ascertain whether they appear on their face to be in accordance with the terms and conditions of the credit. Nothing in art 15 suggests that it was ever intended that the task of examining the documents should fall on the customer as well as the bank. So when, in art 16(c), it is provided that the issuing bank shall have a reasonable time in which to examine the documents, these words mean what they say. A reasonable time for the bank to examine the documents cannot be extended by a further period of time to enable the customer to examine the documents. So what happened in the present case was not only the cause of an excessive time being taken overall; it was also clearly wrong in principle.

The next question is much more difficult. It is said that even if time is not to be allowed for the customer to examine the documents, there should at least be time for the customer to be consulted. There is much commercial sense in this part of Mr Goldsmith's argument. Thus the evidence was that discrepancies are found in nearly half of all credits. Mr Procter [a banking expert] described it, with pardonable exaggeration, as a national scandal. Yet in the vast majority of these cases the buyers are prepared to waive the discrepancy. It must be in the interests of all parties, therefore, that the issuing bank should consult with its customer before rejecting the documents, in case the customer is willing to waive the discrepancy.

It was the evidence of the expert witnesses on both sides that consultation between the issuing bank and its customer is not only common in practice, but also highly desirable. The Judge stressed in more than one place in his judgment that there is nothing in the Code to prevent such consultation. Nor could there be any objection to the customer seeing the document or documents in which there appears to be a discrepancy in order to decide whether to waive the discrepancy or not. But should the issuing bank be allowed extra time for such consultation? . . .

I start with the language of art 16(c) itself. The reasonable time allowed to the issuing bank is composed of two components, namely, (i) the time for the bank to examine the documents and (ii) time for the bank to determine whether to accept or reject the documents. Clearly the time taken to consult the buyers cannot be included under (i). Can it be included under (ii)? Mr Goldsmith submits that it can. He relies on two main arguments, and a third which was suggested to him by the Court. I take them in descending order of merit.

[His Lordship then considered counsel's arguments and continued:]

I am not persuaded by any of these three arguments to depart from what seems to me to be the plain meaning of the Code, namely, that the reasonable time allowed under art 16(c) is a reasonable time for the *bank* to examine the documents, and for the *bank* to determine, on the basis of the documents alone, whether to accept them or not. If it had been intended that the bank should also be allowed time to consult its customer whether the customer was willing to waive any discrepancies, it would have been easy enough to say so, by the insertion of 'after consulting the applicant' in art 16(b). But I see no reason to read in those words, whether as a matter of construction, or, as Mr Justice Gatehouse thought, as a matter of implication. . . .

I have taken the opportunity of reading the judgments of Lord Justice Farquharson and Sir John Megaw in advance. I naturally regret finding myself in a minority on this point. But I am comforted that it is only on the very narrow point whether the bank should be entitled to extra time for consulting its customer that there is any disagreement. On all other points of principle we are agreed. In particular we are agreed that on no view should a bank be allowed time to enable the buyers to examine the documents for the purpose of discovering further discrepancies. . . .

I turn to the second major question of principle, which I have already foreshadowed. I can deal with it very briefly. Article 16(d) [now UCP 1993 Revision, art 14(b)(ii)] provides that the notice of refusal –

. . . must state the discrepancies in respect of which the issuing bank refuses the documents and must also state whether it is holding the documents at the disposal of, or is returning them to, the presentor.

The telex of Sept 30, on which the plaintiffs rely, does not say 'The documents are at your disposal'. It says, 'The documents will be at your disposal when you have paid'. I do not see how such a telex can possibly be a good notice under art 16(d). The whole purpose of art 16(d) is that, as soon as the documents have been rejected, they should be put back in circulation. As Sir John Megaw pointed out in the course of argument, the effect of the plaintiffs' telex of Sept 30 was, on the contrary, to place the documents in purdah. They were not at the buyers' disposal. Nor were they are the sellers' disposal until the plaintiffs had been paid.

Mr Goldsmith argued that the only purpose of art 16(d) was to inform the defendants whether the bank was holding the documents for collection by the customer, or whether it would send them back by post or messenger. I cannot accept this argument as a matter of construction of art 16(d). But even if it were the correct construction of the article, the plaintiffs would still fall foul of art 16(e), since the plaintiffs did not in fact hold the documents at the disposal of the defendants. How could the documents be at the defendants' disposal, if the defendants could not collect them without first having paid?

In *The Royan*, the issuing bank sent a telex:

Please consider these documents at your disposal until we receive our Principal's instructions concerning the discrepancies mentioned in your schedules.

Mr Justice Gatehouse held that the telex was only a holding telex. He was reversed on this point in the Court of Appeal. I said at [1988] 2 Lloyd's Rep 250 at p 254:

. . . While the Judge was clearly right to regard Banque Misr's first telex of Oct 27, 1982 as a 'holding telex', I would respectfully disagree with his view that the same is true of the telex of Nov 6. The effect of that telex . . . was that the documents were being held unconditionally at the disposal of the sellers. The reference to 'until we receive our Principal's instructions' was no doubt reflecting the hope that the buyers and sellers might come to some agreement . . . I cannot read that expression of hope as meaning that the documents were not at the disposal of the sellers.

The difference between a telex saying that documents are being held at the disposal of the sellers *until* something happens, and a telex saying that documents will be at the disposal of the sellers *when* something happens may seem narrow. But the difference is critical. In the one case the documents are held unconditionally at the disposal of the sellers. In the other case, not. So I do not regard the decision in *The Royan* as supporting Mr Goldsmith's argument.

Mr Goldsmith's final argument depends on what he calls the underlying policy of the Code. By requiring the plaintiffs to part with the documents before receiving payment, one would be thwarting that policy. There are two answers to this submission. First, neither art

16 itself, nor the special terms of this credit, entitled the issuing bank to retain the documents as security for repayment by the defendants. Secondly, the argument runs counter to the final sentence of art 16(d). That sentence shows that the issuing bank must give notice that it *is* holding the documents at the disposal of the confirming bank *before* being entitled to claim any refund from the confirming bank.

Farquharson LJ: Article 16, paras (b) and (c) provide for the issuing bank to have a reasonable time to complete two tasks: (1) to examine the documents submitted by the presenting bank, (2) where the documents are not in accordance with the terms and conditions of the credit, to determine on the basis of the documents alone whether to take them up or to refuse them and claim that on their face they appear to be discrepant.

The question is: what steps may be taken by the bank within the time limit in arriving at its determination? If the task of the issuing bank is restricted to the examination of the documents, there is no room for it to make any 'determination'. If it discovers any discrepancies its function is simply to reject the documents. The making of a determination in my judgment implies something more. As Sir John Megaw pointed out in argument, it may be that one or more of the documents presented is in a foreign language in which none of the bank's staff is versed; or the technical nature of other documents may require an explanation from an expert. When a task has to be completed in a reasonable time that must mean reasonable in all the circumstances, and the circumstances would include the need for consultations of that nature. Similarly, if it is the custom among bankers, as the evidence disclosed, to enquire of the applicant for a letter of credit whether it wished the bank to reject the documents in reliance on the discrepancies it has found, it should be permitted to do so within the ambit of the reasonable time required to make its determination: I would hold that an issuing bank is acting within a reasonable time in making its determination if it consults where necessary a translator, an expert in the commodity being sold, or its applicant for the purposes described. Other circumstances which will no doubt be taken into account in determining what is a reasonable time, are the complication of the transaction, the number and complexity of the documents involved and, for example, the fact that the documents are being considered by the staff of a large bank at a busy financial centre. In the vast majority of cases where an applicant is consulted about discrepancies found in the documents, it can be done shortly by a telephone call or fax transmission. On the evidence it would be unusual to submit the documentation to the applicant for its inspection. If such a submission were made it could only be for the purpose of seeking the applicant's opinion on the correct course to take in the light of discrepancies already found. Article 16 does not, in my judgment, contemplate a period of time for the applicant to go through the documents, as in the present case, to see if it could find further discrepancies. While the bank may consult the customer for the limited purpose set out, it is still the bank which has to make the decision whether to reject.

The provision that the bank should arrive at its decision on the basis of the documents alone does not, in my judgment, prohibit consultations of this kind. It is merely to emphasize that the decision must be based on the discrepancies in the documents and not on any defect in the goods. . . .

A further point was taken by the respondent that the rejection telex sent by the appellant on Sept 30 was in breach of art 16(d) of UCP. I agree with the finding and reasoning of Lord Justice Lloyd in relation to that issue.

I would dismiss the appeal.

Sir John Megaw: I agree that this appeal should be dismissed.

As regards the question of construction of the provision of art 16(d) of the Code, as to 'holding documents at the disposal of . . . the presentor', I agree with the reasons given by Lord Justice Lloyd for rejecting the submissions of the plaintiffs.

I also agree that, on the facts, the plaintiffs' notice of rejection of the documents was not given within a reasnable time, and hence the appeal fails on that issue also. But, with diffidence, I have found myself unable to agree with Lord Justice Lloyd's opinion as to the question of principle which has been argued before us. I agree with the view expressed by Lord Justice Farquharson.

NOTES

1. This case is noted by R Jack [1991] 10 JIBFL 484, H Bennett [1992] LMCLQ 169 and M Sneddon (1992) 20 ABLR 175. See also *Hing Yip Hing Fat Co Ltd v Daiwa Bank Ltd* [1991] 2 HKLR 35 at 57–59, Supreme Court of Hong Kong, where Kaplan J took account of such factors as the smaller size of the bank, and the fact that checkers in Hong Kong did not have English as their mother language, when assessing what was a reasonable time for examination of the documents and determination of the bank's position with regard to them (noted by J D Murphy [1992] LMCLQ 26).

2. In *Bankers Trust Co v State Bank of India* all three members of the Court of Appeal held that the documents must not be sent to the applicant to enable him to examine them himself for further discrepancies. Their Lordships were also unanimous when holding that the issuing bank could consult the applicant as to whether he was willing to waive any discrepancies. But whereas Farquharson LJ and Sir John Megaw thought that time for consultation fell within what was to be considered as a reasonable time for determination by the bank, Lloyd LJ thought that any consultation period fell outside it. The 1993 revision of the UCP follows Lloyd LJ on this point. Article 14(c) of that revision provides that if the issuing bank determines that the documents appear on their face not to be in compliance with the terms of the credit, the bank may in its sole discretion approach the applicant for a waiver of the discrepancies, but that this does not extend what is a reasonable time for examination, determination and notification under art 13(b). It should be noted that the absolute limit of seven banking days, as set out in art 13(b), did not appear in earlier versions of the UCP.

3. Article 14(d)(i) of the UCP states that if the issuing bank and/or confirming bank, or other bank acting on their behalf, decides to reject the documents, it must give notice by telecommunication or, if that is not possible, by other expeditious means, without delay but no later than the close of the seventh banking day following receipt of the documents. Notice is to be given to the bank from which it received the documents, or to the beneficiary if it received the documents directly from him. In *Rafsanjan Pistachio Producers Co-operative v Bank Leumi (UK) plc* [1992] 1 Lloyd's Rep 513 at 531, Hirst J interpreted 'without delay' as meaning 'without unreasonable delay'. He held that whilst a telephone rejection might be called for in some cases, rejection by telex would usually be sufficiently expeditious. See also *Hing Yip Hing Fat Co Ltd v Daiwa Bank Ltd*, above, at 59–60, where Kaplan J held that notice given by mail or courier did not comply with what is now art 14(d)(i). He stated that if notice by phone, fax or telex was possible, as it was in the case before him, it should be used.

4. The notice of rejection must state the discrepancies in respect of which the document is being rejected. There has been some doubt as to whether a bank would be estopped from later raising further discrepancies not identified in the original rejection notice. The position at common law is that, absent special circumstances raising a true estoppel, the bank will not be prevented from relying upon discrepancies which were not listed in the original rejection notice (*Kydon Compania Naviera SA v National Westminster Bank Ltd, The Lena* [1981] 1 Lloyd's Rep 68). But the position was thought to be different under the UCP (see *Hing Yip Hing Fat Co Ltd v Daiwa Bank Ltd*, above, at 45–51). The 1993 revision of the UCP clarifies the issue by stating, for the first time, that the notice must specify *all* discrepancies in respect of which the bank refuses the documents (art 14(d)(ii)). This seems to lay the foundation for an estoppel (see M Sneddon (1992) 20 ABLR 174 at p 179). It is also consistent with the established principle that the beneficiary may cure the defects and retender the documents before the credit expires.

5. If the issuing bank and/or confirming bank fails to comply with art 14(d)(i) and (ii), or any other requirement of art 14, it will be precluded from claiming that the documents did not comply with the terms of the credit (UCP, art 14(e): see above, p 671).

(iv) *The contract between the banks and the seller*

Banque de l'Indochine et de Suez SA v J H Rayner (Mincing Lane) Ltd [1983] QB 711, Court of Appeal

An irrevocable credit was opened by a Djibouti bank and confirmed by the plaintiff bank (the confirming bank). The defendant sellers tendered documents to the confirming bank but the bank considered them to be defective for various reasons which the sellers were informed of. However, the confirming bank agreed to pay the sellers 'under reserve'. When the issuing bank, on the buyer's instructions, rejected the documents, the confirming bank demanded repayment from the sellers. The Court of Appeal affirmed Parker J's decision that the documents were defective but disagreed with his analysis of the effect of a payment under reserve.

Sir John Donaldson MR:
. . .

Payment under reserve
It seems that it is not unusual for a confirming bank to be asked to pay on documents which in its view do not fully comply with the terms of the letter of credit. The bank then has to decide whether (a) to refuse payment, (b) to pay, taking an indemnity from the beneficiary in respect of any loss or damage resulting from the deficiency in the documentation or (c) to pay the beneficiary 'under reserve.' Which course is adopted depends upon the extent and importance of the deficiencies as perceived by the confirming bank, the likelihood of the bank at whose request the credit was opened ('the issuing bank') and that bank's customer refusing to accept the correctness of any payment to the beneficiary and the credit worthiness, and value attached by the paying bank to the goodwill, of the person seeking to draw on the letter of credit. It is a tribute to the standing of J H Rayner (Mincing Lane) Ltd, the defendants, in the City of London that, notwithstanding the bank's conviction that the documents were seriously defective, they paid them 'under reserve.'

The use of the expression 'payment under reserve,' as denoting the character of a payment, is, we were told, widespread and would undoubtedly serve a very useful purpose if it had a defined and generally accepted meaning. Unfortunately it seems that it has not. If this is correct, banks will be most unwise to use it without at the same time stating precisely what they mean by it. In the longer term the International Chamber of Commerce, who are the authors and guardians of the Uniform Customs and Practice for Documentary Credits might like to turn their minds to this problem when undertaking the next revision. Meanwhile we have to determine what the parties meant by the expression when they used it on this occasion.

It is common ground that it relates to the circumstances in which the beneficiary can be called upon to repay the money which he has been paid under the letter of credit. The competing submissions are that (1) the money is repayable on demand if the issuing bank, in reliance upon some or all of the deficiencies alleged by the confirming bank, declines to reimburse the confirming bank or to ratify the payment, the beneficiary then being left to sue the confirming bank; (2) money is repayable if, but only if, the circumstances in (1) exist and the beneficiary accepts that the documentation was defective or this is established in a suit brought by the confirming bank against the beneficiary. If (2) is correct, the only effect of the qualification upon the payment, albeit an important effect, is that the beneficiary cannot resist an order for repayment on the basis that the payment itself had been made under a mistake of law. This was the submission accepted by the judge and his reasons appear in his judgment ante, pp 716D–717E; [1982] 2 Lloyd's Rep 476, 479.

The point is clearly one of difficulty. Mr Saville [counsel for the plaintiffs] characterised the view of the judge as 'a lawyer's view' as contrasted with 'a commercial view' and I think that this is right. It depends for its validity upon the parties having had it well in mind that money payable under a mistake of law is irrecoverable and wishing to do no more than eliminate this defence. This seems to me to be an improbable premise, when the parties are a commercial bank and a commodity merchant. As I see it, the dialogue to be imputed to the parties goes something like this:

Merchant: 'These documents are sufficient to satisfy the terms of the letter of credit and certainly will be accepted by my buyer. I am entitled to the money and need it.'
Bank: 'If we thought that the documents satisfied the terms of the letter of credit, we would pay you at once. However, we do not think that they do and we cannot risk paying you and not being paid ourselves. We are not sure that your buyer will authorise payment, but we can of course ask.'
Merchant: 'But that will take time and meanwhile we shall have a cash flow problem.'
Bank: 'Well the alternative is for you to sue us and that will also take time.'
Merchant: 'What about your paying us without prejudice to whether we are entitled to payment and then your seeing what is the reaction of your correspondent bank and our buyer?'
Bank: 'That is all right, but if we are told that we should not have paid, how do we get our money back?'
Merchant: 'You sue us.'
Bank: 'Oh no, that would leave us out of our money for a substantial time. Furthermore it would involve us in facing in two directions. We should not only have to sue you, but also to sue the issuing bank in order to cover the possibility that you might be right. We cannot afford to pay on those terms.'
Merchant: 'All right. I am quite confident that the issuing bank and my buyer will be content that you should pay, particularly since the documents are in fact in order. You pay me and if the issuing bank refuses to reimburse you for the same reason that you are unwilling to pay, we will repay you on demand and then sue you. But we do not think that this will happen.'
Bank: 'We agree. Here is the money "under reserve." '

Kerr LJ: . . . What the parties meant, I think, was that payment was to be made under reserve in the sense that the beneficiary would be bound to repay the money on demand if the issuing bank should reject the documents, whether on its own initiative or on the buyer's instructions. I would regard this as a binding agreement made between the confirming bank and the beneficiary by way of a compromise to resolve the impasse created by the uncertainty of their respective legal obligations and rights. For present purposes it is then unnecessary to go further and decide whether such a demand would only be effective if the grounds of the rejection included at least one of the grounds on which the confirming bank had relied in refusing to pay otherwise than under reserve. But I incline to the view that this should be implied, since the agreement to pay and accept the money under reserve will have been made against the background of these grounds of objection.

In the present case the issuing bank in fact rejected the documents on grounds which included at least one of the grounds of objection which had been raised by the plaintiffs. It therefore follows that the judgment in favour of the plaintiffs must in any event be upheld.

Sir Sebag Shaw: I agree.

NOTES

1. The 1993 revision of the UCP, like previous revisions, does not define what is meant by the expression 'payment under reserve'. But payment under reserve, or against an indemnity from the seller in respect of any discrepancies in the documents, is expressly recognised by the UCP (art 14(f)).

2. What are the seller's rights against an issuing bank or confirming bank which wrongfully refuses to accept conforming documents, or otherwise fails to honour the credit? So long as the seller remains able to tender conforming documents, he may bring an action against the bank for the amount of the credit together with interest. Alternatively, the seller may accept the bank's repudiatory breach and sue for damages, which will be assessed on a similar basis to those awarded for breach of the buyer's obligation to accept delivery under the contract of sale (*Urquhart, Lindsay & Co Ltd v Eastern Bank Ltd* [1922] 1 KB 318 at 324–325). If the seller sues for damages he is under a duty to mitigate his loss. Where the seller suffers loss because the bank has delayed in making payment, he may recover that loss from the bank so long as it is not too remote (*Ozalid Group (Export) Ltd v African Continental Bank* [1979] 2 Lloyd's Rep 231). If the bank fails to honour a bill of exchange which it has previously accepted, the seller will sue the bank on the bill of exchange itself.

3. Can the bank recover money paid to the seller against non-conforming documents? Where the bank has paid against forged or fraudulent documents it may either claim damages from the seller for the tort of deceit or look to recover the money paid to him as money paid under a mistake of fact (*Bank Russo-Iran v Gordon Woodroffe & Co Ltd* (1972) 116 Sol Jo 921, per Browne J, cited with apparent approval by Lord Denning MR in *Edward Owen Engineering Ltd v Barclays Bank International Ltd* [1978] QB 159 at 169–170). Where the bank has paid against non-conforming documents because of its own mistake it is unlikely to be able to recover the money so paid. Any restitutionary claim would probably be defeated by defences of change of position or estoppel (at least as against claims made by the issuing or confirming banks: claims by those banks would also be barred by UCP, art 14(e) – see above, p 679). If the bank negotiates a bill of exchange drawn by the seller on the buyer, who later dishonours the bill, it might be possible for the bank, as holder or indorser, to claim a right of recourse against the seller under ss 43(2) or 47(2) of the Bills of Exchange Act 1882. But there is considerable doubt whether such a right of recourse applies to a bill drawn under a credit (see, eg, Benjamin, para 23-122; Jack, para 5.71). Where the credit incorporates the UCP there is certainly no right of recourse for either the issuing bank or the confirming bank (UCP, art 9(a)(iv), 9(b)(iv)). However, an advising bank which negotiates a bill of exchange will have a right of recourse against the seller if the buyer defaults (under ss 43(2) or 47(2) of the Bills of Exchange Act 1882). Otherwise, the advising bank probably has no better claim to recover money paid by mistake than does an issuing or confirming bank (Benjamin, para 23-142; Jack, para 6.31). Where the bank has itself accepted a bill of exchange it has no right of recourse against the drawer (seller).

It should be noted that in the United States a bank may have a right of action against the seller for breach of warranty relating to the genuineness or regularity of the tendered documents (s 5-111(1) of the Uniform Commercial Code). English law does not appear to recognise such a warranty (Pennington, Hudson & Mann *Commercial Banking Law* (1978), pp 357–358; Benjamin, para 23-123 fn 4; Jack, para 5.74; cf Goode, pp 679–680 and [1980] JBL 443 at pp 445–446).

3 Standby credits, performance bonds and guarantees

Standby credits, performance bonds and guarantees have a different function to that of documentary credits. Whereas the function of documentary credits is to provide payment for goods and services against documents, the function of the instruments considered in this section is to provide security against default in performance of the underlying contract. Although standby credits, performance bonds and guarantees may be used to secure the performance of the buyer and (more usually) the seller under an international sale contract (see, eg, *State Trading Corpn of India Ltd v M Golodetz Ltd* [1989] 2 Lloyd's Rep 277), they are more often found in international construction contracts where the overseas employer requires financial security from a reputable third party (usually a bank) against the contractor defaulting in his performance of the contract.

(a) Standby credits

A standby letter of credit is similar to an ordinary documentary credit in that it is issued by a bank and embodies an undertaking to make payment to a third party (the beneficiary) or to accept bills of exchange drawn by him, provided the beneficiary tenders conforming documents. But, whereas a documentary credit is a primary payment mechanism for discharge of the payment obligation contained in the underlying contract (ie the issuing or confirming bank is the first port of call for payment), the standby credit is given by way of security with the intention that it should only be drawn on if the party by whom the work should be done, or the goods or services provided, (the principal) defaults in the performance of his contractual obligations to the beneficiary (see R M Goode 'Abstract Payment Undertakings', Ch 9 of P Cane and J Stapleton (eds) *Essays for Patrick Atiyah* (1991), at pp 212–213, 220; and also R M Goode [1992] LMCLQ 190 at pp 192–193).

The liability of a bank under a standby credit is intended to be secondary to that of the principal (although, technically, the form of the credit makes the bank's liability primary) and the credit performs the same security function as would be provided by a bank guarantee (see R M Goode *Commercial Law* (1982), pp 696–697). But, unlike a guarantee, a standby credit may be called upon by tendering any specified documents without the beneficiary having to prove actual default by the principal, eg the specified document may be simply a demand from the beneficiary or a statement from him that the principal is in default. Fraudulent calling on the credit is prohibited but, as we have already seen with regard to documentary credits (above, p 659), this is notoriously difficult to establish.

Standby credits are covered by the UCP (subject to its incorporation by the parties), and the principles of autonomy of the credit and strict compliance apply to standby credits as they do to documentary credits.

(b) Performance bonds and guarantees

Edward Owen Engineering Ltd v Barclays Bank International Ltd [1978] QB 159, Court of Appeal

The plaintiffs, English suppliers, contracted with Libyan buyers to supply and erect glasshouses in Libya. The plaintiffs agreed to provide the buyers with a performance bond for 10 per cent of the contract price and the buyers agreed to open a confirmed irrevocable credit in their favour. The plaintiffs instructed an English bank, the defendants, to provide the bond against their counter guarantee. The defendants instructed the Umma Bank in Libya to issue the bond, undertaking to pay the amount 'on demand without proof or conditions'. Umma Bank then issued the bond. But the buyers failed to open a confirmed irrevocable documentary credit as agreed and so the plaintiffs terminated the supply contract. Nevertheless, the buyers went on to claim payment under the performance bond from Umma Bank, who in turn claimed payment from the defendants. The plaintiffs sought an injunction to restrain the defendants from paying. An interim injunction was granted by Boreham J but later discharged by Kerr J. The plaintiffs appealed.

Lord Denning MR:

The law as to performance bonds
A performance bond is a new creature so far as we are concerned. It has many similarities to a letter of credit, with which of course we are very familiar. It has been long established that when a letter of credit is issued and confirmed by a bank, the bank must pay it if the documents are in order and the terms of the credit are satisfied. Any dispute between buyer and seller must be settled between themselves. The bank must honour the credit. That was clearly stated in *Hamzeh Malas & Sons v British Imex Industries Ltd* [1958] 2 QB 127. Jenkins LJ, giving the judgment of this court, said, at p 129: . . . [see above, p 648].

To this general principle there is an exception in the case of what is called established or obvious fraud to the knowledge of the bank. The most illuminating case is of *Sztejn v J Henry Schroder Banking Corpn* 31 NYS 2d 631 (1941) which was heard in the New York Court of Appeals. After citing many cases Shientag J said, at p 633:

It is well established that a letter of credit is independent of the primary contract of sale between the buyer and the seller. The issuing bank agrees to pay upon presentation of documents, not goods. This rule is necessary to preserve the efficiency of the letter of credit as an instrument for the financing of trade.

He said, at p 634, that in that particular case it was different because:

on the present motion, it must be assumed that the seller has intentionally failed to ship any goods ordered by the buyer. In such a situation, where the seller's fraud has been called to the bank's attention before the drafts and documents have been presented for payment, the principle of the independence of the bank's obligation under the letter of credit should not be extended to protect the unscrupulous seller.

That case shows that there is this exception to the strict rule: the bank ought not to pay under the credit if it knows that the documents are forged or that the request for payment is made fraudulently in circumstances when there is no right to payment.

I would in this regard quote the words of Browne J in an unreported case when he was sitting at first instance. It is *Bank Russo-Iran v Gordon Woodroffe & Co Ltd* ((1972) 116 Sol Jo 921). He said:

In my judgment, if the documents are presented by the beneficiary himself, and are forged or fraudulent, the bank is entitled to refuse payment if it finds out before payment, and is entitled to recover the money as paid under a mistake of fact if it finds out after payment.

But as Kerr J said in this present case:

In cases of obvious fraud to the knowledge of the banks, the courts may prevent banks from fulfilling their obligation to third parties.

Such is the law as to a confirmed letter of credit. How does it stand with regard to a performance bond or a performance guarantee? Seeing that it is a guarantee of performance – that is, a guarantee that the supplier will perform his contracted obligations – one would expect that it would be enforced in such a case as this: suppose the English supplier had been paid for the goods and had delivered them, but that the Libyan customer then discovered that they were defective and not up to contract or that they had been delayed. The Libyan customer could then claim damages for the breach. But instead of coming to England to sue for the breach, his remedy would be to claim payment under the guarantee – of the 10 per cent or the 5 per cent of the price – as liquidated damage, so to speak. He claims payment from the Umma Bank. The Umma Bank pay him 'on first request.' They claim on Barclays Bank International. Then Barclays pay 'on first demand without proof or conditions.' And Barclays claim against the English suppliers, the payment being 'conclusive evidence.'

It is obvious that that course of action can be followed, not only when there are substantial breaches of contract, but also when the breaches are insubstantial or trivial, in which case they bear the colour of a penalty rather than liquidated damages: or even when the breaches are merely allegations by the customer without any proof at all: or even when the breaches are non-existent. The performance guarantee then bears the colour of a discount on the price of 10 per cent or 5 per cent, or as the case may be. The customer can always enforce payment by making a claim on the guarantee and it will then be passed down the line to the English supplier. This possibility is so real that the English supplier, if he is wise, will take it into account when quoting his price for the contract.

Take the case one stage further. The English supplier is not in default at all. He has not shipped the goods because he has not been paid. The Libyan customer has not provided the confirmed letter of credit. It is still open to the Libyan customer to make some allegation of default against the English supplier – as for instance not doing the preliminary work or not being ready and willing – and on that allegation to claim payment under the performance guarantee. On that request being made, payment will be made by the banks down the line: and be made by them 'on demand without proof or conditions.'

So, as one takes instance after instance, these performance guarantees are virtually promissory notes payable on demand. So long as the Libyan customers make an honest demand, the banks are bound to pay: and the banks will rarely, if ever, be in a position to know whether the demand is honest or not. At any rate they will not be able to prove it to be dishonest. So they will have to pay.

All this leads to the conclusion that the performance guarantee stands on a similar footing to a letter of credit. A bank which gives a performance guarantee must honour that guarantee according to its terms. It is not concerned in the least with the relations between the supplier and the customer; nor with the question whether the supplier has performed his contracted obligation or not; nor with the question whether the supplier is in default or not. The bank must pay according to its guarantee, on demand, if so stipulated, without proof or conditions. The only exception is when there is a clear fraud of which the bank has notice.

Such has been the course of decision in all the cases there have been this year in our courts here in England. First of all, there was *R D Harbottle (Mercantile) Ltd v National Westminster Bank Ltd* [1978] QB 146 before Kerr J. The judge considered the position in principle. I would like to adopt a passage from his judgment, p 761E–G.

> It is only in exceptional cases that the courts will interfere with the machinery of irrevocable obligations assumed by banks. They are the life-blood of international commerce. Such obligations are regarded as collateral to the underlying rights and obligations between the merchants at either end of the banking chain. Except possibly in clear cases of fraud of which the banks have notice, the courts will leave the merchants to settle their disputes under the contracts by litigation or arbitration. . . . The courts are not concerned with their difficulties to enforce such claims; these are risks which the merchants take. In this case the plaintiffs took the risk of the unconditional wording of the guarantees. The machinery and commitments of banks are on a different level. They must be allowed to be honoured, free from interference by the courts. Otherwise, trust in international commerce could be irreparably damaged.

Since that time there has been before Donaldson J and afterwards in this court *Howe Richardson Scale Co Ltd v Polimex-Cekop and National Westminster Bank Ltd* ([1978] 1 Lloyd's Rep 161). In that case Roskill LJ spoke to the same effect. He said [at p 165]:

> Whether the obligation arises under a letter of credit or under a guarantee, the obligation of the bank is to perform that which it is required to perform by that particular contract, and that obligation does not in the ordinary way depend on the correct resolution of a dispute as

to the sufficiency of performance by the seller to the buyer or by the buyer to the seller as the case may be under the sale and purchase contract; the bank here is simply concerned to see whether the event has happened upon which its obligation to pay has risen.

So there it is: Barclays Bank International has given its guarantee – I might almost say its promise to pay – to Umma Bank on demand without proof or conditions. They gave that promise, the demand was made. The bank must honour it. This court cannot interfere with the obligations of the bank. . . .

I would therefore dismiss this appeal.

Browne LJ: I agree that this appeal should be dismissed for the reasons given by Lord Denning MR. Kerr J in *Harbottle (Mercantile) Ltd v National Westminster Bank Ltd* [1978] QB 146 and this court in the *Howe Richardson* case ([1978] 1 Lloyd's Rep 161) treated a bank's position under a guarantee or performance bond of the type given by Barclays Bank to the Umma Bank as being very similar to the position of a bank which has opened a confirmed irrevocable credit, and I have no doubt that this is right.

Geoffrey Lane LJ: The law applicable in these circumstances is conveniently set out, as Lord Denning MR and Browne LJ have indicated, by Roskill LJ in the recent decision in *Howe Richardson Scale Co Ltd v Polimex-Cekop and National Westminster Bank Ltd* ([1978] 1 Lloyd's Rep 161). The passage already cited by my brethren is followed by these words of Roskill LJ:

> The bank takes the view that that time has come and that it is compelled to pay; in my view it would be quite wrong for the court to interfere with Polimex's apparent right under this guarantee to seek payment from the bank, because to do so would involve putting upon the bank an obligation to inquire whether or not there had been timeous performance of the sellers' obligations under the sale contract.

In the present case Mr Ross-Munro [counsel for the suppliers] submits that, since this document between the two banks is expressed to be a guarantee, the bank is under no liability to pay prima facie unless, first of all, there is a principal debtor and, secondly, some default by the principal debtor in his obligations under his contract with the seller. Since, he submits, no such default on the part of the sellers is suggested, the guarantee does not come into effect. The answer to that appears to me to be this. Although this agreement is expressed to be a guarantee, it is not in truth such a contract. It has much more of the characteristics of a promissory note than the characteristics of a guarantee. . . .

The only circumstances which would justify the bank not complying with a demand made under that agreement would be those which would exonerate them under similar circumstances if they had entered into a letter of credit, and that is this, if it had been clear and obvious to the bank that the buyers had been guilty of fraud. Mr Ross-Munro, conceding that that is the situation, endeavours to show that indeed fraud is clear and obvious here, that the bank knew about it, and accordingly he is entitled to succeed.

The way he seeks to establish fraud is this. He points to the undoubted fact that the buyers in Libya have failed to reply to any of the requests for a proper confirmed letter of credit according, Mr Ross-Munro submits, to the terms of the contract and, moreover, have failed to produce any suggestion of any default or breach of contract on the part of the sellers in England which would possibly justify a demand that the peformance guarantee be implemented.

I disagree that that amounts to any proof or evidence of fraud. It may be suspicious, it may indicate the possibility of sharp practice, but there is nothing in those facts remotely approaching true evidence of fraud or anything which makes fraud obvious or clear to the bank. Thus there is nothing, it seems to me, which casts any doubt upon the bank's prima facie obligation to fulfil its duty under the two tests which I have set out.

It may be harsh in the result, but the sellers must have been aware of the dangers involved or, if they were not, they should have been aware of them, and either they should have declined to accept the terms of the performance bond or else they should have allowed for the possibility of the present situation arising by making some adjustment in the price.

I agree that the appeal should be dismissed.

NOTES

1. In legal terms, as opposed to matters of terminology and business usage, there may be no difference at all between a performance bond or guarantee and a standby credit. Much depends on the nature of the specified 'event' upon which payment under the bond or guarantee is to be made. For example, if payment is to be made on production of a written demand by the beneficiary, or his written declaration that the principal has defaulted, then the performance bond or guarantee (called an 'on demand' or 'first demand' bond or guarantee) is, in law, identical to a standby credit. At the other end of the scale, if payment is only to be made on actual proof of default by the principal, then the performance bond or guarantee (called a 'conditional' bond or guarantee) is a form of common law guarantee and not like a standby credit at all. Between these two extremes it is open to the parties to specify other 'events' which trigger payment under the bond or guarantee, eg production of a certificate from an independent third party attesting that the principal has defaulted (such a bond or guarantee is likely to be treated as of the 'on demand' type: *Gur Corpn v Trust Bank of Africa Ltd* (28 October 1986, unreported), a decision of Leggatt J, cited by R Jack *Documentary Credits* (2nd ed, 1993), para 12.28). In each case it is a question of construction of the terms of the instrument to ascertain precisely what the bank has undertaken to do (see, eg, *Wardens and Commonalty of the Mystery of Mercers of the City of London v New Hampshire Insurance Co* [1992] 2 Lloyd's Rep 365, CA).

2. Since the *Edward Owen* case, the courts have continued to treat 'on demand' performance bonds or guarantees (hereafter collectively referred to as 'demand guarantees') on a similar footing to documentary credits: see, eg, *Intraco Ltd v Notis Shipping Corpn, The Bhoja Trader* [1981] 2 Lloyd's Rep 256; *Bolivinter Oil SA v Chase Manhattan Bank* [1984] 1 WLR 392; cf *Potton Homes Ltd v Coleman Contractors (Overseas) Ltd* (1984) 28 BLR 19; and generally M Coleman [1990] LMCLQ 223. As Professor Goode has stated ([1992] LMCLQ 190 at p 192):

> Demand guarantees share with documentary credits the characteristic of being abstract payment undertakings, that is to say, they are promises of payment which are considered binding upon communication to the beneficiary without the need for acceptance, consideration, reliance, or solemnity of form, and are separate from and independent of the underlying contract.

The fact that a documentary credit is a primary payment mechanism, whereas a demand guarantee is intended as a secondary obligation, must not, of course, be overlooked (Goode, op cit, p 193).

3. The autonomous nature of a demand guarantee makes it vulnerable to abusive calling. Although the fraud exception applies, it is notoriously difficult to establish: see, eg *Harbottle (Mercantile) Ltd v National Westminster Bank* [1978] QB 146; *State Trading Corpn of India Ltd v E D & F Man (Sugar) Ltd* [1981] Com LR 235; *GKN Contractors Ltd v Lloyd's Bank plc* (1985) 30 BLR 48; and, generally, see above, pp 659–661. Nevertheless, the issuing bank will not be obliged to pay on a demand guarantee if it is tainted by initial illegality or some other vitiating factor (see R M Goode 'Abstract Payment Undertakings', Ch 9 of P Cane and J Stapleton (eds) *Essays for Patrick Atiyah* (1991), at pp 225–234). In cases of abusive calling, the principal probably stands a better chance of obtaining a *Mareva* injunction restraining the beneficiary from using the funds he has received in payment of the demand guarantee, than he does of obtaining an injunction to prevent payment in the first place (*Intraco Ltd v Notis Shipping Corpn, The Bhoja Trader* [1981] 2

Lloyd's Rep 256). In exceptional circumstances a *Mareva* injunction may be made to extend to assets beyond the jurisdiction (but see above, p 661).

4. The principle of strict compliance applies to demand guarantees. But there has been uncertainty as to whether it applies with the same rigour to demand guarantees as it does to documentary credits: in *Siporex Trade SA v Banque Indosuez* [1986] 2 Lloyd's Rep 146 at 159, Hirst J thought not, whereas in *IE Contractors Ltd v Lloyds Bank plc* [1989] 2 Lloyd's Rep 205 at 207, Leggatt J thought that it did. The true position would seem to be that outlined by Staughton LJ on appeal in the *IE Contractors* case [1990] 2 Lloyd's Rep 496 at 500–501 (noted by H Bennett [1991] 5 JIBL 207), namely, that while there may be more scope for interpreting the demand guarantee as not requiring the demand to follow any particular form, it is in all cases a question of construction of the terms of the guarantee and that, once construed, the requirements of the instrument must be strictly complied with.

5. The International Chamber of Commerce (ICC) has promulgated rules designed to provide a fair balance between the competing interests of the principal, beneficiary and those banks involved in the issue of demand guarantees: see the ICC's Uniform Rules for Demand Guarantees (1992), which, in due course, are likely to replace the ICC's Uniform Rules for Contract Guarantees (1978) – for the time being parties can choose beween either set of rules. The Uniform Rules only apply if adopted by the parties concerned. See generally, R Goode [1992] LMCLQ 190.

4 Other financing methods

There are a number of other methods of financing international trade. They include the following.

(a) Forfaiting

Forfaiting is a type of non-recourse finance which assists the export seller's cash flow whilst giving the buyer a period of credit. The seller draws a term bill of exchange on the buyer, the bill being drawn 'without recourse' to himself. The bill is accepted by the buyer and backed by the buyer's bank, which may either execute an aval on the bill (see above, p 531) or give a separate guarantee. The seller may then indorse the bill 'without recourse' and discount it to his own bank (the forfaiter). Alternatively, the buyer may make a promissory note which is guaranteed by his bank before being indorsed 'without recourse' by the seller and sold to the forfaiter. The advantage of this form of finance from the seller's point of view is that he receives an immediate payment of the cash value of the bill or note (less the usual charges and a discount fee) without recourse should the buyer default on payment. However, the forfaiter has the aval or guarantee of the buyer's bank to fall back on if the bill or note is dishonoured by non-payment. Usually, the forfaiter will itself sell the bill or note on into the *à forfait* market.

(b) International factoring

See below, pp 783–786.

(c) International financial leasing

A financial leasing arrangement is a three-party transaction. The lessee negotiates with a supplier to supply goods (usually capital items such as ships, aircraft or heavy equipment). The lessee also negotiates with a lessor (a bank or finance house) which purchases the goods from the supplier and leases them to the lessee. The lease is for the period of the anticipated working life of the asset and rentals are structured so as to amortise the capital cost of the equipment and give the lessor a return on capital (R M Goode [1987] JBL 318 and 399).

The Ottawa Convention on International Financial Leasing (1988), when in force, will govern certain types of financial leasing arrangements, namely those where:

(1) the lessee selects the goods and the supplier without relying primarily on the skill and judgment of the lessor;
(2) the supplier knows that the equipment is being acquired by the lessor in connection with a leasing arrangement; and
(3) the rentals are calculated to amortise the capital cost of the equipment (art 1(2)).

The Convention will only apply where the lessor and the lessee have places of business in different States and either all three parties (lessor, lessee and supplier) have places of business in Contracting States, or both the supply contract and the lease arrangement are governed by the law of a Contracting State (art 3(1)). The most important feature of the Convention is that it shifts responsibility for the non-delivery, late delivery or delivery of non-conforming equipment from the lessor to the supplier (see arts 8, 10 and 12(5)). This reflects the fact that the lessor has only a financial interest in the transaction. For further details, see *Schmitthoff's Export Trade* (9th ed, 1990), pp 464–466; R M Goode [1988] JBL 347.

(d) Confirming houses

Where an overseas buyer uses the services of a confirming house in the seller's country, and the confirming house makes itself liable to the seller for the price, the confirming house provides, in effect, non-recourse finance to the seller (see above, p 79).

5 Export credit guarantees

The seller may insure himself against loss arising from the overseas buyer's failure to pay the price. He can do this by taking out an export credit guarantee (available from government and private agencies). An export guarantee covers such risks as the buyer's insolvency (commercial risk) and his inability to accept the goods or pay the price due to circumstances beyond his control, eg government orders (political risk). Export guarantees may also assist the seller to secure finance from his bank. For detailed discussion, see *Benjamin's Sale of Goods* (4th ed, 1992), Ch 24.

Part VII
Assignment and receivables financing

CHAPTER 20

Assignment of choses in action

1 Introduction*

(a) Chose in action defined

'The History of the Treatment of Choses in Action by the Common Law' by W S Holdsworth (1920) 33 Harvard LR 967, pp 967–968

'All personal things are either in possession or action. The law knows no *tertium quid* between the two.'[1] It follows from this that the category of *choses* in action is in English law enormously wide, and that it can only be defined in very general terms. This is clear from the terms of the definition given by Channell J in *Torkington v Magee*,[2] which is generally accepted as correct. It runs as follows: ' "Chose in action" is a known legal expression used to describe all personal rights of property which can only be claimed or enforced by action, and not by taking physical possession.' In fact the list of *choses* in action known to English law includes a large number of things which differ widely from one another in their essential characteristics. In its primary sense the term '*chose* in action' includes all rights which are enforceable by action – rights to debts of all kinds, and rights of action on a contract or a right to damages for its breach; rights arising by reason of the commission of tort or other wrong; and rights to recover the ownership or possession of property real or personal. It was extended to cover the documents, such as bonds, which evidenced or proved the existence of such rights of action. This led to the inclusion in this class of things of such instruments as bills, notes, cheques, shares in companies, stock in the public funds, bills of lading, and policies of insurance. But many of these documents were in effect documents of title to what was in substance an incorporeal right of property. Hence it was not difficult to include in this category things which were even more obviously property of an incorporeal type, such as patent rights and copyrights. Further accessions to this long list were made by the peculiar division of English law into common law and equity. Uses, trusts, and other equitable interests in property, though regarded by equity as conferring proprietary rights analogous to

* See generally, O R Marshall *The Assignment of Choses in Action* (1950); Crossley Vaines *Personal Property* (5th ed, 1973), Ch 11; Cheshire, Fifoot and Furmston *Law of Contract* (12th ed, 1991), Chs 16 and 17; G H Treitel *The Law of Contract* (8th ed, 1991), Ch 16; A P Bell *Modern Law of Personal Property in England and Ireland* (1989), Ch 15; P V Baker and P St J Langan *Snell's Equity* (29th ed, 1990), Ch 5. For further detail, see A G Guest and others (eds) *Chitty on Contracts* (26th ed, 1989), Ch 19; R P Meagher, W M C Gummow and J R F Lehane *Equity Doctrines and Remedies* (3rd ed, 1992), Chs 6–8.

the rights recognised by law in hereditaments or in chattels, were regarded by the common law as being merely *choses* in action.

1 *Colonial Bank v Whinney* (1885) 30 Ch D 261, 285, per Fry LJ, whose dissenting judgment was upheld by the House of Lords (1886) 11 App Cas 426.
2 [1902] 2 KB 427, 430.

NOTES

1. Choses in action are usually divided into legal choses in action on the one hand and equitable choses in action on the other. Legal choses in action are those which before the coming into force of the Supreme Court of Judicature Act 1873 could be enforced by action at law and equitable choses in action are those which were enforceable only by a suit in equity.

2. The distinction between legal and equitable choses in action is made in *Snell's Equity* (29th ed, 1990) at p 71:

A chose may be legal (ie enforceable in a court of law), such as a debt, bill of exchange, policy of insurance, sweepstake ticket or share in a company; or it may be equitable, such as a legacy, a legatee's rights in an unadministered estate, a share in a trust fund, surplus proceeds of sale in the hands of a mortgagee, or a right to relief against forfeiture of a lease for non-payment of rent.

3. For criticism of this form of classification, see *Halsbury's Laws of England* (4th ed (reissue), 1991), Vol 6, para 5.

(b) Assignment defined

Norman v Federal Comr of Taxation (1963) 109 CLR 9, High Court of Australia

By a deed dated 21 December 1956 the taxpayer assigned to his wife as a gift all the interest derived from the sum of £3,000 which was part of a sum deposited by him on loan at interest with a named firm. The loan was not for a fixed term and the firm was free to pay it or any part of it at any time without notice. By the same deed the taxpayer also assigned dividends to which he might be entitled arising from estates in which he had a beneficial interest. In 1957 the trustees of these estates transferred to the taxpayer his proportion of certain shares and he was registered as the shareholder. During the year ending 30 June 1958, £450 was paid by way of interest on the loan of £3,000 and dividends amounting to £460 were paid on the shares. The Commissioner claimed that these sums remained the income of the taxpayer and assessable to tax in his hands. The taxpayer argued that because of the deed of assignment the interest and dividend payments were part of his wife's income and not his own. By a majority (McTiernan and Windeyer JJ dissenting) the High Court of Australia held that the assignment of the interest and the dividend payments was ineffective.

Menzies J: . . . It is common ground that the assignment did not operate as a legal assignment of interest or the taxpayer's right to it, and the real question is whether there was an effectual equitable assignment of a right to interest. I do not think there was because what was assigned was not an existing right but was no more than a right which might thereafter come into existence and so could not be effectually assigned in equity without consideration.

In general future property was not assignable at common law: *Lunn v Thornton* ((1845) 1 CB 379) but in equity after-acquired property was assignable for value according to the principles stated by Lord Macnaghten in *Tailby v Official Receiver* ((1888) 13 App Cas 523) but only for value notwithstanding the assignment was by deed: *Re Ellenborough* ([1903] 1 Ch 697). If then interest that may arise under a contract has the character of a future rather than an existing right, the deed, lacking consideration, was not effective to entitle the assignee to the interest in question as and when it became due and payable. I regard interest which may accrue in the future upon an existing loan repayable without notice as having the character of a right to come into existence rather than of a right already in existence and I do not regard *G & T Earle (1925) Ltd v Hemsworth RDS* ((1928) 44 TLR 758), upon which Mr Bright for the taxpayer relied, as any authority to the contrary. In that case no more was decided than that an assignment of a specific fund retained under a building contract which did not become payable until an architect's certificate was given, which happened after the date of the assignment, was a good legal assignment of a chose in action. As Wright J, the learned trial judge, said in a judgment fully approved by the Court of Appeal:— 'I find there was a specific fund . . . In my judgment the retention moneys represented moneys actually earned at the date of the certificate, though in fact these retention moneys, as their name indicates, were to be held as a sort of security and in any case subject to having set off against them any cross-claims, which would reduce the amount when the final settlement came and the final certificate was issued. The retention moneys, therefore, were only future in the sense that they were not payable until some future date' ((1928) 44 TLR 605 at 609). An accruing debt arising out of contract, though not payable at the date of the assignment, was, it was held, assignable at law. One other observation upon the applicability of that case to the present may be made, that is, it is not to be assumed that every right that can now be assigned at law without consideration pursuant to s 25(6) of the Judicature Act and corresponding legislation can also be assigned in equity voluntarily. Thus if, as seems to be generally accepted, (see *Halsbury's Laws of England* 3rd ed, vol 4, para 1003), the section extends to future debts and not merely debts not presently payable, in equity as distinct from the Judicature Act, the effectiveness of voluntary assignment remains limited to existing rights and interests. See *Tailby v Official Receiver* and *Re McArdle* ([1951] Ch 669 at 676), per Jenkins LJ.

[For the same reason as that given by Windeyer J (below, p 695) and because of a specific provision of Australian tax legislation, Menzies J held that the dividend payments remained assessable to tax in the hands of the taxpayer.]

Windeyer J (dissenting): . . . In *Lampet's Case* ((1612) 10 Co Rep 46b at 48a), Coke spoke of 'the great wisdom and policy of the sages and founders of our law, who have provided that no possibility, right, title, nor thing in action, shall be granted or assigned to strangers, for that would be the occasion of multiplying of contentions and suits'. It was a somewhat unsophisticated view of legal rights that led the common lawyers to classify choses in action and debts with mere possibilities, and to condemn all assignments of them as leading to maintenance.

Assignment means the immediate transfer of an existing proprietary right, vested or contingent, from the assignor to the assignee. Anything that in the eye of the law can be regarded as an existing subject of ownership, whether it be a chose in possession or a chose in action, can to-day be assigned, unless it be excepted from the general rule on some ground of public policy or by statute. But a mere expectancy or possibility of becoming entitled in the future to a proprietary right is not an existing chose in action. It is not assignable, except in the inexact sense into which, again to use Maitland's words, lawyers slipped when it is said to be assignable in equity for value.

The distinction between a chose in action, which is an existing legal right, and a mere expectancy or possibility of a future right is of cardinal importance in this case, as will appear. It does not, in my view, depend on whether or not there is a debt presently recoverable by action because presently due and payable. A legal right to be paid money at a future date is, I consider, a present chose in action, at all events when it depends upon an existing contract on the repudiation of which an action could be brought for anticipatory breach.

The common law doctrine that debts and other choses in action were not assignable never applied to Crown debts; and, by the influence of the law merchant, bills of exchange and promissory notes were outside it. And it was never accepted in equity. 'Courts of equity from the earliest times thought the doctrine too absurd for them to adopt' said Buller J in 1791 in the course of a vigorous condemnation of it: *Master v Miller* ((1791) 4 Term Rep 320 at 340). Furthermore he said that already at common law it had been 'so explained away that it remains only an objection to the form of the action in any case'. Blackstone had said 'this nicety is now disregarded': *Commentaries*, ii, 442. In *Balfour v Sea Fire Life Assurance Co* ((1857) 3 CBNS 300 at 308), Willes J said that the doctrine had long been exploded 'as everyone must know'. What had happened was that the common law rule came to be circumvented in various ways. One was by novation. Another was by the assignor giving a power of attorney to the assignee to sue the debtor at law in the assignor's name, without having to render an account: the history of this has been narrated at length by Mr Bailey in learned articles in the *Law Quarterly Review* vols 47 and 48. And courts of equity would come to the assistance of the assignee if the assignor refused to do whatever was necessary to enable the assignee to get the benefit of the assignment. Thus a recalcitrant assignor would be required, on having an indemnity for his costs, to permit his name to be used in an action to recover the debt; or an assignor would be restrained from receiving the debt for himself, as for example in *L'Estrange v L'Estrange* ((1850) 13 Beav 281). Because the assistance of equity was available, it was generally not needed. The common law courts recognized that an assignee might sue in the assignor's name. So that in 1849 it could be said that 'the courts of law have adopted the doctrines of the court of chancery in regard to assignments of choses in action'; so much so that 'In ordinary cases, where the plaintiff has an easy remedy by suing in the name of the assignor, the court (scil. the Court of Chancery) will not entertain jurisdiction, but leave the party to his remedy at law': *Spence, Equitable Jurisdiction of the Court of Chancery*, vol 2, pp 853, 854; and see *Roxburghe v Cox* ((1881) 17 Ch D 520), Dicey, *Parties to an Action* (1870) pp 66–72. Therefore, as the Chief Justice observed during the hearing of this case, it is somewhat misleading to say, as is often said, that before the Judicature Act the common law would not allow assignments of legal choses in action. Long before 1873 the development of common law processes and the impact of equity had pushed the common law prohibition of the assignment of choses in action back into history. Nevertheless the original doctrine survived, to this extent that, until the Judicature Act 1873, s 25(6), and the corresponding statutory provisions in Australia and elsewhere came into operation, an assignee of a legal debt could not in his own name bring an action against the debtor to recover the debt. The original creditor must be the plaintiff on the record. He remained in law the owner of the chose in action. What the provision of the Judicature Act 1873, did was to render unnecessary the previous circumlocutions. Debts and other legal choses in action were made directly assignable by the statutory method. But this, while it simplified assignments, has not simplified the law surrounding them, as the argument in this case showed. . . .

[I]t was said a thing which is not yet in existence cannot be the subject of an equitable assignment except for consideration. That, as I have said, is undoubtedly so. It is true too that the interest, to the extent of £450, that the deed assigned was not due and payable at the date of the deed. But a contract to pay a sum of money on a future day, call it interest or what you will, calculable in amount according to conditions presently agreed, is in my view a presently existing chose in action. As between the parties to a contract of money lent at interest the borrower is simply a debtor who must pay a sum or sums (called interest) that he has, for good consideration (the forbearance of the creditor) contracted to pay to his creditor at the time or times stipulated. Why should not the creditor before the date when this debt becomes due and payable, assign his right to receive payment on the due date? He could assign the whole under the statute: *Walker v Bradford Old Bank Ltd* ((1884) 12 QBD 511). Why not part in equity? What he assigns is not, it seems to me, a right to arise in the future but a present contractual right to be paid at a future date a sum of money, to be calculated in the agreed manner: cf *Lett v Morris* ((1831) 4 Sim 607). In *Brice v Bannister* ((1878) 3 QBD 569 at 573), Lord Coleridge CJ said 'that a debt to become due is a chose in action, is clear'. Interest on money lent is recoverable by action at law as a debt separate from the principal, as the common indebitatus count for interest shows: . . .

But it was urged this case is not like a case of a loan for a fixed term. What was owing might, it is pointed out, have been repaid by the partnership, or reduced below £3,000, after the date of the deed of assignment and before 1st July 1957. As a matter of law, no doubt that is so. But it does not, I think, follow that the taxpayer had for that reason no assignable right. He had a present right to be paid interest at a future date on the money he had lent, unless in the meantime the loan was repaid. The taxpayer assigned the benefit of this contract, to the extent of £450 to become due conditionally in 1958, to his wife by the deed of 1956. I consider that the deed was an effectual equitable assignment. . . .

I turn now to the second matter, the sum of £460. . . .

Is a dividend that may become payable in the future upon shares presently held something that can be assigned in equity? Is it a present chose in action or a mere possibility? Is it property in existence, or something not in existence and therefore not capable of being assigned in the absence of consideration? I think it is the latter. The court will not compel directors to declare a dividend: *Bond v Barrow Haematite Steel Co* [1902] 1 Ch 353. A dividend is not a debt until it is declared. Until then it is in the eye of the law a possibility only. When it is declared it becomes a debt for which a shareholder who is on the register at the date of the declaration may sue. The companies paid the dividends to the registered holder of the shares, the taxpayer. They knew nothing of the purported assignment. Depending perhaps in some cases on their articles of association, they might have paid the dividends directly to the taxpayer's wife had they been directed by him to do so. But, in the absence of consideration, such a direction would have been merely a revocable mandate, not an assignment. Dividends that may be declared are to my mind quite unlike the interest that will become due according to an existing contract of loan if the loan be not repaid.

[McTiernan J (dissenting) gave a similar judgment to that of Windeyer J.
Dixon CJ delivered a judgment similar to that of Menzies J.
Owen J concurred with Menzies J.]

NOTES

1. Section 25(6) of the Supreme Court of Judicature Act 1873 provided in general terms for the assignment of choses in action at law. It was repealed and substantially re-enacted by s 136 of the Law of Property Act 1925. An assignment under s 136 is called a 'statutory' or 'legal' assignment and it will pass the legal right to the chose in action. If there is a legal assignment of a legal or equitable chose in action the assignee may bring an action to enforce the chose in his own name. Exceptionally, assignment at law is also possible in the following cases, namely (1) assignments by and to the Crown, (2) assignment of annuities, (3) assignment of certain negotiable instruments under the law merchant (now mostly regulated by statute), and (4) assignment of particular choses in action in accordance with the provisions of special statutory enactments (eg assignment of shares in a company under s 182(1) of the Companies Act 1985 and s 1 of the Stock Transfer Act 1963 (as amended); assignment of policies of life insurance under s 1 of the Policies of Assurance Act 1867; assignment of copyright under s 90 of the Copyright, Designs and Patents Act 1988).

2. Since the seventeenth century the courts of equity have always permitted and given effect to assignments of choses in action. Such an assignment is called an 'equitable assignment' and it will pass an equitable, though not a legal, right to the chose in action. In the case of an *absolute* equitable assignment of an equitable chose in action the assignee can bring an action to enforce the chose in his own name. However, if the assignor retains an interest in the chose, the equitable assignee of an equitable chose in action must join the assignor to the action. In the case of an equitable assignment of a legal choses in action (absolute or non-absolute) the action had to be brought in the name of the assignor (see Windeyer J, above, as to how equity would compel the assignor to lend his name to the action), although the modern practice is simply for the assignee to join the assignor to the action as co-plaintiff if he is willing to co-operate, and as co-defendant if he is not (G H Treitel *The Law of Contract* (8th ed, 1991) ('Treitel'), pp 578–579). Today, equitable assignments will be given effect to in all courts to the same extent and in the same manner as formerly in a court of equity (s 49 of the Supreme Court Act 1981).

3. Whether at law or in equity, only existing proprietary rights (including existing choses in action) can be assigned. Future choses in action (including a mere expectancy or *spes successionis*) cannot be assigned, although the purported assignment for value of a future chose in action will be given effect in equity as a contract to assign the chose if and when it comes into existence and comes into the hands of the assignor. The law is best summarised by Windeyer J in *Norman v Federal Comr of Taxation* when he said that (at 24):

> . . . in equity a would-be present assignment of something to be acquired in the future is, when made for value, construed as an agreement to assign the thing when it is acquired. A court of equity will ensure that the would-be assignor performs this agreement, his conscience being bound by the consideration. The purported assignee thus gets an equitable interest in the property immediately the legal ownership of it is acquired by the assignor, assuming it to have been sufficiently described to be then identifiable. The prospective interest of the assignee is in the meantime protected by equity. These principles, which now govern assignments for value of property to be acquired in the future, have been developed and established by a line of well-known cases, of which *Holroyd v Marshall* (1862) 10 HL Cas 191; *Collyer v Isaacs* (1881) 19 Ch D 342; *Tailby v Official Receiver* (1888) 13 App Cas 523; and *Re Lind, Industrials Finance Syndicate v Lind* [1915] 2 Ch 345, are the most important.

4. As can be seen from *Norman v Federal Comr of Taxation*, it may be extremely difficult to distinguish between existing and future choses in action. Compare that case with the following cases:

G & T Earle Ltd v Hemsworth RDC (1928) 44 TLR 758, Court of Appeal

A firm of contractors agreed to build certain cottages for Hemsworth RDC. By the terms of the building contract, as subsequently varied, each month the contractors were to be paid 90 per cent of the value of all work completed by them as certified by the architects. The remaining 10 per cent of the value of the work completed was to be held in a retention fund which was to be paid to the contractors on the issue of the architects' final certificate. During the course of the building work the contractors purported to assign to the plaintiffs 'all moneys now or hereafter to become due to us from the Hemsworth Rural District Council for retention money'. At the time of the assignment all the retention fund had accrued but the architects had not issued their final certificate. The issue before the Court of Appeal was whether the money standing to the credit of the retention fund was an existing chose in action or a mere expectancy at the time of the purported assignment. Affirming the decision of Wright J, the Court of Appeal held that it was an existing chose. In the only reasoned judgment delivered in the Court of Appeal, Scrutton LJ stated that 'where the thing assigned arises out of an existing contract, although it may not become payable until a later date than the assignment, it is a debt or other legal thing in action which can be assigned and sued for without joining the assignor as a party'. As the retention money had already been earned when the assignment took place it represented an existing chose in action, even though the time of actual payment had yet to accrue.

Shepherd v Federal Taxation Comr (1965) 113 CLR 385, High Court of Australia

The taxpayer was the grantee of certain letters patent relating to castors. He granted to C a licence to manufacture the castors and, in return, C agreed to pay him royalties directly in proportion to the number of castors manufactured. By deed the taxpayer then purported to assign by way of gift absolutely and unconditionally to certain named persons all his 'right title and interest in and to an amount equal to ninety per cent of the income which' might accrue during a period of three years under the licence agreement. The High Court of Australia (Barwick CJ and Kitto J; Owen J dissenting) held that on its true construction the deed constituted a present assignment of an existing chose in action. The majority accepted that the taxpayer had assigned his existing contractual right to future royalties, even though the quantum of the royalties had yet to be ascertained. As Kitto J said (at 396): 'The tree, though not the fruit, existed at the date of the assignment as a proprietary right of the appellant of which he was competent to dispose; and he assigned ninety per centum of the tree.' The majority distinguished *Norman v Federal Comr of Taxation* as a case where the taxpayer had no existing right to future interest payments because interest would only be payable if the loan remained in existence and the taxpayer had no right to keep it in existence in the future as the debtor firm had the right to repay the loan whenever it wished. By contrast, in *Shepherd's* case there was certainty at the time of the assignment that the contractual relationship between the patentee and the licensee was not terminable at the whim of the obligor during the period for which the assignment was to operate (see M C Cullity and H A J Ford (1966) 30 Conv 286).

5. Treitel attempts to reconcile these cases as follows (pp 586–587):

> If the contingency on which the money is payable is essentially within the control of the creditor, there is no difficulty in holding that the disposition is an assignment: thus a builder can assign instalments to become due to him under a building contract as the work progresses, for here the contingency on which the money will become due is simply his own performance. If, however, the contingency is not within his control, the disposition is prima facie an agreement to assign: this would be the position where a person purported to assign future dividends in a company which was not under any obligation to him to declare any dividends. But even where the rights of the assignor depend on a contingency outside his control, he may purport to assign *either* his present right to future income from a specified source *or* the future income itself. A disposition of the first kind may be regarded as an assignment and a disposition of the second kind as an agreement to assign. The question into which category it falls turns on the construction of the document purporting to effect the disposition.

6. For a detailed history of the law relating to the assignment of choses in action, see S J Bailey (1931) 47 LQR 516, (1932) 48 LQR 248 and 547.

(c) Assignment distinguished from novation, acknowledgment and power of attorney

Chitty on Contracts (26th ed, 1989), Vol 2, para 1436 states that novation takes place 'where the two contracting parties agree that a third shall stand in the relation of either of them to the other'. Unlike an assignment, which does not require the debtor's consent, a novation requires the consent of all parties (*Rasbora Ltd v JCL Marine Ltd* [1977] 1 Lloyd's Rep 645). Furthermore, unlike an assignment, which merely transfers a right, the effect of a novation is to extinguish the original contract and replace it with a new contract. This new contract must be supported by consideration moving from the new promisee (*Tatlock v Harris* (1789) 3 Term Rep 174, 180).

Since the middle of the nineteenth century, it has been possible for a transferee to bring an action against a fundholder for money had and received if the transferor instructs a person (the fundholder) holding a fund for him to pay it to the transferee and the fundholder agrees to do so (*Griffin v Weatherby* (1868) LR 3 QB 753). The transferee need not provide consideration for the fundholder's promise as his remedy is restitutionary and not contractual. It was always accepted that only a fundholder could attorn in this way; a transferee could only enforce a promise made by a mere debtor (ie not holding a fund) if the transferee had supplied consideration for the promise to pay (*Liversidge v Broadbent* (1859) 4 H & N 603). However, in *Shamia v Joory* [1958] 1 QB 448 Barry J rejected this limitation (*Liversidge v Broadbent* not being cited to him) holding that if a creditor asks his debtor to pay a third party, and the debtor agrees to do so, and informs the third party of his agreement, then the third party is entitled to sue the debtor even though he supplied no consideration for the debtor's promise. The decision has been described as 'unsound' and has been subjected to sustained criticism (see, Goff and Jones *The Law of Restitution* (4th ed, 1993), at pp 573–575; J D Davies (1959) 75 LQR 220 at pp 231–233; cf Treitel, at p 577). Even if *Shamia v Joory* is correct, the principle of *acknowledgment* (as it has been called) differs from assignment in that it requires the consent of the debtor.

The creditor may give a third party a power of attorney to sue the debtor in the creditor's name without having to account to the creditor (see, for example, *Gerard v Lewis* (1867) LR 2 CP 305). Unlike an assignment, which is irrevocable, the creditor may generally revoke his power of attorney.

QUESTIONS

1. Why was the common law against the assignment of choses in action? See *Fitzroy v Cave* [1905] 2 KB 364 at 372, CA.

2. In the case of an equitable assignment of a legal chose in action or the non-absolute equitable assignment of an equitable chose in action, why must the assignee join the assignor to the action against the debtor? See Treitel at p 578; *Weddell v J A Pearce & Major* [1988] Ch 26 at 40–41. Can this requirement ever be dispensed with? See *William Brandt's Sons & Co v Dunlop Rubber Co Ltd* [1905] AC 454 at 462, per Lord Macnaghten.

3. Can all existing choses in action be assigned? See below, pp 724 ff.

4. Can a debtor assign his payment obligation to a third party? See *Tolhurst v Associated Portland Cement Manufacturers (1900) Ltd* [1902] 2 KB 660 at 668, CA, and Treitel at pp 603–607.

2 Statutory assignment

Law of Property Act 1925, s 136(1)

136. (1) Any absolute assignment by writing under the hand of the assignor (not purporting to be by way of charge only) of any debt or other legal thing in action, of which express notice in writing has been given to the debtor, trustee or other person from whom the assignor would have been entitled to claim such debt or thing in action, is effectual in law (subject to equities having priority over the right of the assignee) to pass and transfer from the date of such notice—
(a) the legal right to such debt or thing in action;
(b) all legal and other remedies for the same; and
(c) the power to give a good discharge for the same without the concurrence of the assignor:
    Provided that, if the debtor, trustee or other person liable in respect of such debt or thing in action has notice—
(a) that the assignment is disputed by the assignor or any person claiming under him; or
(b) of any other opposing or conflicting claims to such debt or thing in action;
he may, if he thinks fit, either call upon the persons making claim thereto to interplead concerning the same, or pay the debt or other thing in action into court under the provisions of the Trustee Act 1925.

Requirements

(i) *Legal and equitable choses may be assigned*

Torkington v Magee [1902] 2 KB 427, Divisional Court

Magee contracted with Rayner to sell him a reversionary interest in certain funds under a settlement. Rayner by deed assigned his interest in the contract to Torkington and notice in writing of the assignment was given to Magee. Torkington alleged that Magee had broken the contract and brought an action for damages, as assignee, in his own name. The issue before Channell J was whether the executory contract of purchase of the reversionary interest was assignable under s 25 of the Judicature Act 1873 as a 'legal chose in action' (now a 'legal thing in action' in s 136 of the Law of Property Act 1925).

Channell J: . . . We have, therefore, to consider the meaning of the expression 'other legal chose in action' in sub-s 6 of s 25 of the Judicature Act 1873. In order to arrive at this meaning, I think it necessary to consider what is the object of the Act, and of the particular section of the Act in which the words are to be found. The Act provided for the amalgamation of the then existing superior Courts of Law and Equity with a view to the administration in the new Court of one system of law in place of the two systems previously known as Law and Equity, and the general scope of the Act was to enable a suitor to obtain by one proceeding in one Court the same ultimate result as he would previously have obtained either by having selected the right Court, as to which there frequently was a difficulty, or after having been to two Courts in succession, which in some cases he had to do under the old system. The 25th section provided what was to be the rule in future in cases where previously the two systems differed. . . . 'Chose in action' is a known legal expression used to describe all personal rights of property which can only be claimed or enforced by action, and not by taking physical possession. It is an expression large enough to include rights which it can hardly have been intended should be assignable by virtue of the sub-section in question, as, for instance, shares, which can only be transferred as provided by the Companies Acts. It is probably necessary, therefore, to put some limit upon the generality of the words; . . . I think the words 'debt or other legal chose in action' mean 'debt or right which the common law looks on as not assignable by reason of its being a chose in action, but which a Court of Equity deals with as being assignable.' That is the point of difference or variance between the rules of equity and common law which it is intended to deal with by this sub-section. Further, by the words of the sub-section itself the assignment is to be effectual in law, subject to all the equities which would have been entitled to priority over the rights of the assignee if this Act had not been passed. This seems to mean that the cases dealt with are cases where the assignee had some right before the Act – that is to say, where the right of the assignee had previously been recognised by a Court of Equity. . . . Now, the question we have to consider in the present case is whether an executory contract of purchase under which each party has rights and responsibilities, but of which there had been no breach at the date of the assignment, so that at that date no action could be brought upon the contract, but which, if occasion should ever arise to enforce it, must of necessity be enforced by action, is assignable by this sub-section as a 'legal chose in action.' That it is a legal chose in action, and was so at the date of the assignment, cannot be denied; but the question is whether it is so within the meaning of the words as used in the sub-section. I think it is, because it is a case in which the assignee would, at any rate after giving notice of the assignment, have had rights if the Act had not been passed. The Court of Equity would undoubtedly have recognised his right, and would have treated the assignor as being trustee for his assignee, and they would have given to the assignee all the rights and remedies as against his assignor which they gave to a cestui que trust against his trustee, and would have given to him as against the other party to the contract all the rights and remedies which they gave to a cestui que trust against a third person dealing with his trustee in reference to the subject of the trust after notice of the trust. . . . I may mention, not as an authority, but in explanation of the view I take, that I myself in *Marchant v Morton, Down & Co* ([1901] 2 KB 829 at 832) have held that this sub-section is merely machinery; that it enables an action to be brought by the assignee in his own name in cases where previously he would have sued in the assignor's name, but only where he could so sue. I think that in the present case, where there was a contract of sale which gave the purchaser an equitable interest in the property contracted to be sold, the assignment and notice gave the assignee a legal right to sue, not only for specific performance if he had a case for it, but also for damages if he either was driven or elected to take that remedy. I think, therefore, that the appeal should be allowed, and judgment be entered for the plaintiff for £100. The Chief Justice and Mr Justice Darling concur in this judgment.

[The decision of the Divisional Court was reversed on other grounds by the Court of Appeal in [1903] 1 KB 644.]

NOTES

1. Also see *Re Pain, Gustavson v Haviland* [1919] 1 Ch 38 where Younger J (at 44) held that 'the expression in the section [s 25 of the Judicature Act 1873] "legal choses in action" includes choses in equity within its scope'.

2. Although both equitable and legal choses in action can be assigned under s 136, they also remain assignable in equity. As Lord Macnaghten stated in *William Brandt's Sons & Co v Dunlop Rubber Co Ltd* [1905] AC 454 at 461: 'The statute does not forbid or destroy equitable assignments or impair their efficacy in the slightest degree.'

3. Whether equitable choses can be assigned under s 136 becomes, therefore, a somewhat academic question since absolute equitable assignments of equitable choses (which alone fall within s 136) already enabled the assignee to sue in his own name without joining the assignor and did not need consideration.

(ii) *Absolute assignment*

Durham Bros v Robertson [1898] 1 QB 765, Court of Appeal

Under the terms of a building contract building contractors agreed to build certain houses for Robertson and take a lease of them. The contract also gave the contractors the option of paying an increased ground rent in consideration of which they were to receive from Robertson a sum of £1080. Later the contractors purported to assign the £1080 to the plaintiffs by letter in the following terms: 'In consideration of money advanced from time to time we hereby charge the sum of £1080, being the agreed price for £60 per annum ground-rent which will become due to us from John Robertson . . . on the completion of the above buildings as security for the advances, and we hereby assign our interest in the above-named sum until the money with added interest be repaid to you.' The plaintiffs gave notice of the assignment to Robertson and an action was started by them to recover the sum due. Robertson claimed that there had not been a valid assignment under s 25(6) of the Judicature Act 1873 (now s 136 of the Law of Property Act 1925). The Court of Appeal agreed with him.

Chitty LJ: . . . To bring a case within the sub-section transferring the legal right to sue for the debt and empowering the assignee to give a good discharge for the debt, there must be (in the language of the sub-section) an absolute assignment not purporting to be by way of charge only. It is requisite that the assignment should be, or at all events purport to be, absolute, but it will not suffice if the assignment purport to be by way of charge only. It is plain that every equitable assignment in the wide sense of the term as used in equity is not within the enactment. As the enactment requires that the assignment should be absolute, the question arose whether a mortgage, in the proper sense of the term, and as now generally understood, was within the enactment. In *Tancred v Delagoa Bay and East Africa Rly Co* ((1889) 23 QBD 239) there was an assignment of the debt to secure advances with a proviso for redemption and reassignment upon repayment. It was there held by the Divisional Court (disapproving of a decision in *National Provincial Bank v Harle* ((1881) 6 QBD 626), that such a mortgage fell within the enactment. It appears to me that the decision of the Divisional Court was quite right. The assignment of the debt was absolute: it purported to pass the entire interest of the assignor in the debt to the mortgagee, and it was not an assignment purporting to be by way of charge only. The mortgagor-assignor had a right to redeem, and on repayment of the advances a right to have the assigned debt reassigned to him. Notice of the reassignment pursuant to the sub-section would be given to the original debtor, and he would thus know with certainty in whom the legal right to sue him was vested. I think that the principle of the decision ought not to be confined to the case where there is an express provision for reassignment. Where there is an absolute assignment of the debt, but by way of security, equity would imply a right to a reassignment on redemption, and the sub-section would apply to the case of such an absolute assignment. In a well-known judgment of the Exchequer Chamber in *Halliday v Holgate* ((1868) LR 3 Exch 299: see below, p 801), the late Willes J, in delivering the judgment of the Court, distinguished between lien, pledge, and mortgage, and spoke of a mortgage as passing the property out and out. A mortgage is not mentioned in the enactment; but where there is an absolute assignment of the debt, the limiting words as to a charge only are not sufficient to exclude a mortgage. . . .

The assignment before us complies with all the terms of the enactment save one, which is essential: it is not an absolute but a conditional assignment. The commonest and most familiar instance of a conditional assurance is an assurance until JS shall return from Rome. The repayment of the money advanced is an uncertain event, and makes the assignment conditional. Where the Act applies it does not leave the original debtor in uncertainty as to the person to whom the legal right is transferred; it does not involve him in any question as to the state of the accounts between the mortgagor and the mortgagee. The legal right is transferred, and is vested in the assignee. There is no machinery provided by the Act for the reverter of the legal right to the assignor dependent on the performance of a condition; the only method within the provisions of the Act for revesting in the assignor the legal right is by a retransfer to the assignor followed by a notice in writing to the debtor, as in the case of the first transfer of the right. The question is not one of mere technicality or of form: it is one of substance, relating to the protection of the original debtor and placing him in an assured position.

It is necessary to refer to *Brice v Bannister* ((1878) 3 QBD 569). In that case there was an assignment of £100 out of money due or to become due to the assignor under a contract to build a ship, with an express power to give a good discharge to the debtor. Lord Coleridge CJ held that the assignment was within the 25th section. The Court of Appeal decided the case quite apart from the Act. Cotton LJ expressly decided the case on the ground of equitable assignment. That is shewn by the opening sentence of his judgment, where he says that the letter was a good equitable assignment. Bramwell LJ reluctantly assented to this view. Brett LJ dissented, but on general principles. So soon as it was ascertained that there was a good equitable assignment, with power to give a discharge, it became unnecessary to consider whether it fell within the Act or not. In *Ex p Nichols* ((1883) 22 Ch D 782 at 787) the present Master of the Rolls, referring to this decision, treated the assignment as an equitable assignment. He said that the decision was founded on the principle that the right of an equitable assignment of a debt cannot be defeated by a voluntary payment by the debtor to the assignor. The decision of Lord Coleridge CJ in *Brice v Bannister*, that the case fell within the 25th section, appears to me to be open to question. The assignment purported to be by way of charge only. It was a direction to pay the £100 out of money due or to become due. No doubt it purported to be a charge of an unredeemable sum of £100; but still it was a charge. The section speaks of an absolute assignment of any debt or other chose in action. It does not say 'or any part of a debt or chose in action.' It appears to me as at present advised to be questionable whether an assignment of part of an entire debt is within the enactment. If it be, it would seem to leave it in the power of the original creditor to split up the single legal cause of action for the debt into as many separate legal causes of action as he might think fit. However, it is not necessary to decide the point in the present case, and I leave it open for future consideration.

[A L Smith and Collins LJJ concurred.]

Hughes v Pump House Hotel Co Ltd [1902] 2 KB 190, Court of Appeal

Hughes, a building contractor, assigned to his bank all moneys due or to become due under a building contract with the defendants. The assignment stated that it was '[i]n consideration of [the bank] continuing a bank account with [Hughes] . . . and by way of continuing security to [the bank] for all moneys due or to become due to [the bank] from [Hughes]'. Notice of the assignment was given to the defendants. Subsequently, Hughes brought an action against the defendants to recover sums due under the building contract. On a preliminary issue, Wright J held that the assignment was not absolute but by way of charge only. The defendants appealed.

Mathew LJ: . . . In every case of this kind, all the terms of the instrument must be considered; and, whatever may be the phraseology adopted in some particular part of it, if, on consideration of the whole instrument, it is clear that the intention was to give a charge only, then the action must be in the name of the assignor; while, on the other hand, if it is clear from the instrument as a whole that the intention was to pass all the rights of the assignor in the debt or chose in action to the assignee, then the case will come within s 25, and the action must be brought in the name of the assignee. . . . What, then, is the effect of the assignment? It seems to me clear from its terms that the intention was to pass to the assignees complete control of all moneys payable under the building contract, and to put them for all purposes in the position of the assignor with regard to those moneys. That being so, I think, unless there be some difficulty created by the decisions on the subject, this instrument may be properly described as an absolute assignment, because it is one under which all the rights of the assignor in respect of the moneys payable under the building contract were intended to pass to the assignees, and not one which purports to be by way of charge only. The learned judge appears to have been of opinion that the assignment was not absolute, but purported to be by way of charge only, because the object was that it should be a continuing security for such amount as might from time to time be due from the assignor to the assignees. But, if that were the true criterion, it might equally well be argued that a mortgage is not an absolute assignment, because under a mortgage it may become necessary to take an account in order to ascertain how much is due; but, though a mortgage is only a security for the amount which may be due, it is nevertheless an absolute assignment because the whole right of the mortgagor in the estate passes to the mortgagee.

Cozens-Hardy LJ: . . . If, on the construction of the document, it appears to be an absolute assignment, though subject to an equity of redemption, express or implied, it cannot in my opinion be material to consider what was the consideration for the assignment, or whether the security was for a fixed and definite sum, or for a current account. In either case the debtor can safely pay the assignee, and he is not concerned to inquire into the state of the accounts between the assignor and the assignee: nor does it matter that the assignee has obtained a power of attorney, and a covenant for further assurance from the assignor. Both these elements were found in *Burlinson v Hall* ((1884) 12 QBD 347). The real question, and, in my opinion, the only question, is this: Does the instrument purport to be by way of charge only? It remains to apply these principles to the document of March 7, 1901. In my opinion that document is an absolute assignment, and does not purport to be by way of charge only. It assigns all moneys due or to become due under the contract. It follows that the plaintiff, Hughes, has no right of action, and that the order of Wright J must be discharged.

NOTES

1. Where an assignment is not absolute it will still be an effective assignment, but effective only in equity and not under the statute, ie the assignor must be joined as a party to the action to enforce the chose.

2. Assignment by way of security for a debt can be absolute. In *Burlinson v Hall* (1884) 12 QBD 347, DC, debts were assigned to the plaintiff on trust that he should receive them and out of them pay himself a sum due to him from the assignor, and pay the surplus to the assignor. Day J stated:

> I think this is an 'absolute assignment.' It is said that it is an assignment of a security for payment of the debt, and that the moment that purpose is answered the surplus will belong to the assignee. But still the assignment is, in terms, absolute. Not indeed absolute as a sale, but absolute as contradistinguished from conditional, an assignment giving a title there and then. This deed does so. True, if the debt due from the assignor were paid off, the assignor might be entitled to have the subject-matter of the assignment re-assigned to him. But the right of the assignee to whom it is assigned is absolute. No person can control him in dealing as he thinks fit with that which was assigned to him.

3. But an assignment by way of charge is not absolute as the title to the chose in action is not transferred to the assignee. As Denman J stated in *Trancred v Delagoa Bay and East Africa Rly Co* (1889) 23 QBD 239 at 239, DC: '. . . a document given "by way of charge" is not one which absolutely transfers the property with a condition for re-conveyance, but is a document which only gives a right to payment out of a particular fund or particular property, without transferring that fund or property'.

4. An assignment which is absolute under s 136 of the Law of Property Act 1925 may nevertheless be registrable as a charge under Part XII of the Companies Act 1985. See below, p 766.

(iii) *By writing under the hand of the assignor*

No particular form of words is necessary. However, the following points should be borne in mind:

(1) The assignment cannot be executed by an agent of the assignor (*Wilson v Wallani* (1880) 5 Ex D 155 – a case on s 23 of the Bankruptcy Act 1869; now s 178 of the Insolvency Act 1986); save that a partner who has authority to deal with a chose in action belonging to the firm, when acting in relation to the business of the firm, may bind the firm and all the partners to the assignment of that chose, even though the other partners had not signed the deed of assignment and were unaware that the assignment had been executed (*Re Briggs & Co, ex p Wright* [1906] 2 KB 209).
(2) In *Curran v Newpark Cinemas Ltd* [1951] 1 All ER 295, below, at p 708, the Court of Appeal appears to have accepted that the written notice to the debtor could also constitute the assignment in writing itself. For another decision to the same effect, see *Cossill v Strangman* [1963] NSWR 1695 (Supreme Court of New South Wales).
(3) It may be necessary to register the assignment. Under s 344 of the Insolvency Act 1986, where a person engaged in any business makes a general assignment of existing or future book debts, or any class of them, and is subsequently adjudged bankrupt, the assignment will be void against the trustee of the bankrupt's estate as regards book debts which were not paid before the presentation of the bankruptcy petition, unless the assignment had been registered under the Bills of Sale Act 1878. As to registration of a charge on the book debts of a company, see below, p 768.

(iv) *Notice to the debtor*

W F Harrison & Co Ltd v Burke [1956] 2 All ER 169, Court of Appeal

Mrs Burke entered into a hire-purchase agreement with a finance company whereby she hired a refrigerated counter on immediate payment of £30 and 24 instalments of £8 9s 6d a month, until a total of £233 8s was paid. Only the £30 was paid. By an assignment dated 7 December 1954, the finance company purported to assign to the plaintiffs the sum of £203 8s as 'now legally due and owing' to them from Mrs Burke. On 6 December 1954, the day before the assignment was executed, a letter, purporting to be a notice of assignment, was drawn up by the plaintiffs, dated 6 December 1954 and addressed to Mrs Burke. The letter stated that 'We hereby give you notice that by an indenture dated Dec 6, 1954, the debt amounting to £203 8s owing by you to [the finance company] has been assigned to us absolutely and the debt is now due and owing to us'. The letter was posted on 8 December and received by Mrs Burke on 9 December.

Denning LJ: . . . The question is whether that is a valid notice of assignment such as to transfer to the plaintiffs the legal right to sue for the debt. The sum owing at Dec 7, 1954, was not £203 8s, as stated in the assignment, but only the instalments which had then accrued due – £33 18s, and, therefore, the notice of assignment did not give the right figure for the debt. Further, it gave the wrong date of the assignment; it said that the indenture was dated Dec 6, 1954, whereas the only assignment produced to the court is one dated Dec 7, 1954. The question is whether that error in giving the date of the assignment makes the notice bad.

In *Stanley v English Fibres Industries Ltd* ((1899) 68 LJQB 839), it was held by Ridley J that, if the date given for the assignment was bad, the notice did not comply with the requirements of the Supreme Court of Judicature Act 1873, s 25(6). I find myself in agreement with that decision. Section 136(1) of the Law of Property Act 1925, shows that the written notice of the assignment is an essential part of the transfer of title to the debt, and the requirements of the sub-section must be strictly complied with. I think that the notice itself must be strictly accurate, in particular, in regard to the date which is given for the assignment. Even though it is only one day out, as in this case, the notice of assignment is bad.

I need not say anything about the amount of the debt, which in this case was put at £203 8s, when it was, in fact, only £33 18s; but, as at present advised, I should have thought that a notice of assignment ought to state the amount of the debt correctly, because it concerns a transfer of title and the statutory requirements must be strictly complied with. I find myself in agreement with the judgment of the county court judge that the plaintiffs did not prove a right or title in themselves to this debt in accordance with s 136(1) of the Act of 1925, and I think that the appeal must fail.

Morris LJ: I agree. A question might be raised in regard to the assignment itself, which is an assignment of the debts or sums of money referred to in the schedule. The schedule refers to a debt of £203 8s owing by the first defendant. At the date of the assignment there was not a debt of £203 8s. But we have not had argument in regard to the validity of the assignment itself, and, therefore, I express no opinion in regard to it. We have been concerned with the question whether there has been a valid notice in writing of the assignment. Section 136(1) of the Law of Property Act 1925, requires express notice in writing and provides that if that is given the assignment

> is effectual in law . . . to pass and transfer from the date of such notice – (a) the legal right to such debt or thing in action . . .

The notice in writing in this case refers to a debt amounting to £203 8s. If this were a good notice, it would seem to be a notice that, as from the date thereof, the plaintiffs had a 'legal right to such debt', namely, a debt of £203 8s. There was no debt of £203 8s, but I do not think it necessary to decide this case on that point. I think that the case can be decided on the question of the date. The notice is dated Dec 6. Whether the purported assignment was good or not, it was not in existence on Dec 6. It came into existence on Dec 7. It seems to me that s 136(1) of the Act of 1925, must be complied with; and I think that the notice dated Dec 6 which purported to be a notice relating to an assignment dated Dec 6, when there was no such assignment in existence, was not a good notice enabling the assignment which came into existence on the following day to pass the legal right to the debt assigned. I therefore agree that the learned judge came to a correct conclusion.

Parker LJ: I also agree.

Van Lynn Developments Ltd v Pelias Construction Co Ltd [1969] 1 QB 607, Court of Appeal

The defendants were overdrawn at their bank. The plaintiffs paid off that indebtedness and took an assignment of the debt from the bank. The plaintiffs' solicitors then sent a letter to the defendants in the following terms: 'We have been instructed by our above-named clients to apply to you for the payment of a sum of

£5,296 19s 5d outstanding to them following the assignment of the debt to them by National Provincial Bank Ltd. Notice of this assignment has already been given to you . . . .' In fact, no such notice had been given and the question arose whether the solicitors' letter was itself a notice of assignment such as to satisfy the statute.

Lord Denning MR: . . . What is a sufficient notice of assignment? There are only two or three cases on the subject. There is the case of *Stanley v English Fibres Industries Ltd* ((1899) 68 LJQB 839), which was accepted and applied by this court in *W F Harrison & Co Ltd v Burke* ([1956] 1 WLR 419). Those cases show that, if a notice of assignment purports to identify the assignment by giving the date of the assignment, and that date is a wrong date, then the notice is bad. The short ground of those decisions was that the notice with a wrong date was a notice of a non-existing document. Assuming those cases to be correct, they leave open the question whether it is necessary to give the date of the assignment. Test it this way: Suppose the mistaken sentence were omitted in this letter so that it ran: 'We have been instructed by our above-named clients to apply to you for the payment of a sum of £5,296 19s 5d outstanding to them following the assignment of the debt to them by the National Provincial Bank Limited.' Would that be a good notice, even though it gives no date for the assignment? I think it would. I think the correct interpretation of this statute was given by Atkin J in *Denney, Gasquet and Metcalfe v Conklin* ([1913] 3 KB 177 at 180). It is quite plain from his judgment that no formal requirements are required for a notice of assignment. It is sufficient if it brings

> to the notice of the debtor with reasonable certainty the fact that the deed does assign the debt due from the debtor so as to bind the debt in his hands and prevent him from paying the debt to the original creditor.

It seems to me to be unnecessary that it should give the date of the assignment so long as it makes it plain that there has in fact been an assignment so that the debtor knows to whom he has to pay the debt in the future. After receiving the notice, the debtor will be entitled, of course, to require a sight of the assignment so as to be satisfied that it is valid, and that the assignee can give him a good discharge. But the notice itself is good, even though it gives no date.

This notice does, however, go on to make an inaccurate statement. It says that, 'Notice of this assignment has already been given to you.' But, as Davies LJ said in the course of the argument, that is merely an inaccurate surplusage. It can be ignored.

Davies LJ: . . . it is very interesting to notice . . . what was the unsuccessful argument by Mr Croom-Johnson for the defendants [in *Denney, Gasquet and Metcalfe v Conlin* [1913] 3 KB 177]. According to the report, he submitted (at 179) that:

> In order to be valid the notice must expressly state (1) that there has been an assignment; (2) the names and addresses of the assignees so that the debtor may be in a position to seek out the new creditors created by the assignment for the purpose of paying the debt; and (3) what has been assigned.

The present document does show all that. It sets out the amount of the debt assigned by the bank to the plaintiffs and claims that that should be paid forthwith. It seems to me that, leaving out of consideration the last sentence of the first paragraph of that letter, it is a perfectly satisfactory notice of assignment in every respect, and that its validity cannot be destroyed by the inaccurate statement in the second sentence of that paragraph.

I agree, for the reasons which my Lord has given, that this appeal should be dismissed.

Widgery LJ: . . . The statute only requires that information relative to the assignment shall be conveyed to the debtor, and that it shall be conveyed in writing. That fact is fully demonstrated by the judgment of Atkin J to which reference has already been made. Once it is appreciated that the section requires no more, it becomes obvious that the objection to the notice in this case, that it was not intended as a notice but merely to record the fact that notice had already been given, must fail. The letter of June 27 in my judgment undoubtedly contains the necessary particulars and it matters not in the slightest that the writer did not think when he wrote the letter that he was performing the function of giving notice under the section.

So far as the argument based on failure to give the date of the assignment is concerned, it seems to me it would be very undesirable to attach to this procedure technicalities which are not mentioned in the statute and which are not necessary to give effect to it. The notice is a notice given by the assignee for his own protection. It is given by the assignee in order to prevent the debtor continuing to deal with the assignor. It is clearly necessary that the debtor should be given information which tells him that an assignment has been made, which identifies the debt, and which sufficiently identifies the assignee. I see no reason at all why other and irrelevant information should be required as a feature of the notice. It is said that in some instances the debtor would want to know the date of the assignment. For my part I find it very difficult to visualise a case in which the date would have any relevance at all so far as the debtor was concerned, and I would certainly regard it as a retrograde step to require, as a general rule, that the notice should specify the date of the assignment. I would therefore dismiss this appeal.

NOTES

1. In *Harrison v Burke*, Morris LJ appears to have adopted a less restrictive interpretation of s 136 than does Denning LJ. Denning LJ considered that any inaccuracy in the notice would vitiate it, whereas Morris LJ's judgment rests on the narrower ground that the notice is only vitiated if the date of the assignment recorded on the notice antedates the actual date of the assignment. See R E Megarry in (1956) 72 LQR 321 who submits that '[t]here is something to be said for the view that an error as to date should not be fatal *per se*, but should invalidate the assignment only if it induces uncertainty' (p 322).

2. Further criticism of Denning LJ's literal interpretation of the notice requirements of s 136 is made by Dr Roderick Munday in (1981) 131 NLJ 607 at p 608, who states:

> If there is, then, consensus that an assignee is under no obligation whatever to furnish the debtor with the date of the assignment, it is puzzling that the assignee's notice is held invalid under s 136(1) where he provides superfluous information, even if it happens to be inaccurate. It is not easy to maintain the proposition that a misinformed debtor (at least, on this score) will always be at a greater disadvantage than a debtor who is kept entirely in the dark as to the date upon which his creditor assigned the right to the debtor. Indeed, it might be more logical to argue that, if the wrong date referring the debtor to a non-existent document invalidates the notice of assignment, a notice which affords the debtor no clue to the date and, hence, to the document is at least equally pernicious (see, eg, *International Leasing Corpn (Vic) Ltd v Aiken* [1967] 2 NSWLR 427 at 449–50, per Asprey JA).

3. The strict rules relating to statutory assignments are in marked contrast to the more liberal regime for equitable assignments where any informal notice will secure an equitable assignment provided the fact of the assignment is clearly brought to the attention of the debtor, trustee or fundholder (see, for example, *Whittingstall v King* (1882) 46 LT 520).

4. In *Holt v Heatherfield Trust Ltd* [1942] 2 KB 1 at 6, Atkinson J held that:

> . . . 'such notice' [in s 136] is the date of a notice which has been given to the debtor, and refers back to the express notice in writing mentioned earlier in the section. It is express notice in writing given to the debtor, and, in my judgment, the date of that notice is the date on which it is received by or on behalf of the debtor.

This dictum applies when there is a dispute between the assignor and the assignee but there is some doubt as to whether it also applies when the dispute is between successive assignees. See Treitel, at p 584.

(v) *Notice to assignee?*

Curran v Newpark Cinemas Ltd [1951] 1 All ER 295, Court of Appeal

Curran obtained judgment against Newpark Cinemas for a debt and costs. The debt was paid but the costs remained outstanding so Curran procured the issue of a garnishee summons against a debtor of Newpark Cinemas. The debtor opposed the summons claiming that, before being served with the summons, Newpark Cinemas had already given the debtor written notice that '. . . pursuant to the arrangements for valuable consideration which we, Newpark Cinemas Ltd, have made with Barclays Bank Ltd, we give you irrevocable directions, instructions and authority to pay to the said Barclays Bank Ltd . . . all moneys payable to us. . . . This authority and instructions can be varied or cancelled only by a document duly signed on behalf of Barclays Bank Ltd . . .'. No notice of assignment had been given by the bank to the debtor and there was no evidence that the bank had been given notice of the document sent by Newpark Cinemas to the debtor. The County Court judge held there had been no valid assignment of the debt to the bank. The debtor appealed to the Court of Appeal (Somervell, Jenkins and Birkett LJJ).

Jenkins LJ read the judgment of the court: . . . It is, no doubt, true that s 136(1) does not require any particular form of assignment, or that the notice given to the debtor should necessarily have been given by the assignee. The sub-section does, however, clearly postulate that, whatever its form, there should be a document amounting to an absolute assignment by writing under the hand of the assignor. Given such an assignment, and given the requisite notice to the debtor, the assignment (to put it shortly) is to operate as a legal assignment of the debt in question. Section 136(1), however, does not provide that a document which would not, independently of the sub-section or its predecessor (Supreme Court of Judicature Act 1873, s 25(6)), have operated as an absolute assignment at law or in equity is to have the force of an absolute assignment for the purposes of the sub-section. The document here relied on is the direction and authority, which in point of form is not an assignment to the bank of the debt in question but merely a direction to the garnishees to pay the debt in question to the bank. On the footing that there had, in fact, been no prior agreement with the bank to give such a direction, and that the bank had not been notified of the fact that such a direction had been given, we think the result would follow that the direction and authority, though expressed to be irrevocable except with the consent of the bank, could in fact have been revoked by the judgment debtors at any time as amounting to no more than an arrangement between the judgment debtors and the garnishees in which they alone were concerned and which, in the absence of any such agreement or notification, conferred no interest in the debt on the bank. If that is right, then we think that the contention of counsel for the garnishees to the effect that the mere production by the garnishees of the direction and authority, without proof of any agreement with, or notice to, the bank, sufficed in itself to establish an absolute assignment of which express notice had been given to the garnishees, and hence a legal assignment by virtue of s 136(1), necessarily fails.

[The Court of Appeal held that whilst there was no evidence that the bank had not been given notice of the direction and authority, there was prima facie evidence of an asignment in that the notice to the debtor referred to prior arrangements with the bank. The garnishee order was set aside and the case remitted to the County Court with a view to the bank being ordered to appear and state its claim.]

But the requirement of notice to, or consent of, the assignee has been rejected in Australia.

Grey v Australian Motorists & General Insurance Co Pty Ltd [1976] 1 NSWLR 669, Court of Appeal of New South Wales

Grey was a car repairer. The defendant was an insurance company which indemnified motorists against the costs of having their vehicles repaired. Grey claimed the cost of repair of six vehicles from the defendant. The defendant claimed that Grey was not the proper plaintiff as he had previously assigned the debts in question to a finance company. It was alleged that Grey had assigned the debts by completing a number of standard forms of assignment supplied by the finance company which stated that Grey 'irrevocably directs payment of this account direct to the absolute assignee thereof [the finance company]'. The completed forms had been sent to the defendant to obtain payment but there was no evidence that the finance company had notice of or assented to the assignments. A central issue before the Court of Appeal was whether there could be a statutory assignment under s 136 (or rather its Australian equivalent) when no notice of the assignment had been given to the assignee. The Court of Appeal (Samuels and Mahoney JJA; Glass JA dissenting) held that there had been a statutory assignment of the debts.

Glass JA (dissenting): . . . There is little authority on the question whether the operation of the section depends on the assent of the purposed assignee. It is clear that a transfer of property made in proper form vests the title in the transferee at once, notwithstanding his lack of knowledge: *Standing v Bowring* ((1885) 31 Ch D 282). His remedy, if he wishes to reject the gift, is to transfer it back. Accordingly, the absence of consent cannot invalidate the assignment. His Honour ruled, however, that an assignment uncommunicated to the assignee cannot be absolute within the meaning of the section. He relied in this respect upon the following passage in the judgment of Asprey JA in *International Leasing Corpn (Vic) Ltd v Aiken* ((1967) 85 WNNSW 766 at 793): '. . . there can be no effective *absolute* assignment of a debt as between an assignor and an assignee within the meaning of s 12 unless and until the assignee has had notice of the assignment executed by the assignor and has assented to it (see *Rekstin v Severo Sibirsko etc and Bank of Russian Trade Ltd* ([1933] 1 KB 47); Jenks' *English Civil Law*, 4th ed, vol 2, para 1626, pp 890–892; see also *Curran v Newpark Cinemas Ltd* ([1951] 1 All ER 295), where both the last-mentioned case and *Standing v Bowring* were referred to; and cf *Norman v Federal Comr of Taxation* ((1963) 109 CLR 9 at 29), per Windeyer J. An assignment of a debt uncommunicated to the assignee can only be a conditional assignment, that is to say, predicated upon the condition that if the assignee repudiates it when it is brought to his notice, there would be without more, an automatic revesting of the legal ownership of the debt in the assignor.'

With great respect to his Honour, I cannot agree that his proposition is supported by authority in the general terms in which it is formulated. *Rekstin's* case depends upon the special rules governing the relationship of banker and customer. Jenks quoted *Rekstin's* case; and *Curran's* case, to which I shall later refer, stands upon different ground. An absolute assignment is to be contrasted with a conditional assignment. A conditional assignment is an assignment which becomes operative or ceases to be operative upon the happening of an event: *Durham Bros v Robertson* ([1898] 1 QB 765 at 773). Accordingly, an assignment of a chose in action, until a loan is repaid is conditional: ibid. But an assignment of a debt with a proviso for redemption and reassignment upon repayment of a loan is absolute: *Tancred v Delagoa Bay and East Africa Rly Co* ((1889) 23 QBD 239). A distinction is clearly drawn between a reassignment occurring by force of the original transaction (conditional), and a reassignment which depends upon a further assurance (absolute). These authorities, as well as *Standing v Bowring* and the language of the section, and, in my view, inconsistent with the general proposition that an assignment, otherwise absolute in its terms, must operate conditionally where the assignee, not having been consulted, has the right to reassign. . . .

In *Curran v Newpark Cinemas Ltd* the court had before it a direction to a second party to pay money to a bank which had not been communicated to the bank. It was held that the document relied on failed to establish an absolute assignment to the bank, because the direction to pay recorded in it could have been revoked at any time by the party giving it, in the absence of evidence that the bank had been notified or had agreed to the arrangement. The document before us takes a different form. . . . In *Curran's* case the assignment was subject to a condition subsequent.

[However, Glass JA went on to hold that the assignments were conditional on other grounds and, therefore, outside the statute.]

Samuels JA: . . . *Curran's* case is distinguishable from the present one. There, Jenkins LJ, as he then was, emphasized that the document in question was not in form an assignment, but 'merely a direction to the garnishees to pay a third party (ie the bank) . . .' and could only answer the description of an assignment 'if and when communicated to the bank, as, until so communicated, it was revocable by the judgment debtors at any time and, therefore, not absolute'. The authority referred to is *Rekstin's* case. His Lordship went on to say that, although s 136(1) of the Law of Property Act 1925 (the equivalent of s 12 of the Conveyancing Act) did not require any particular form of assignment, it did however 'clearly postulate that, whatever its form, there should be a document amounting to an absolute assignment by writing under the hand of the assignor. Given such an assignment, and given the requisite notice to the debtor, the assignment (to put it shortly) is to operate as a legal assignment of the debt in question'. Accordingly, I would read that judgment (which was the judgment of the court) as having no application to a case where the document relied on is in form an assignment which would, independently of statute, have operated as an absolute assignment at law or in equity. The distinction relevant for present purposes is really that between an assignment and a mere revocable mandate or authority. . . .

Finally, and perhaps most importantly, s 12 sets out the requirements of an effective statutory assignment. It provides that the assignment must be absolute and in writing and stipulates for express notice to the debtor. But it does not mention notice to the assignee, much less the necessity for his consent; nor are either of these stipulations to be found in s 136 of the Law of Property Act 1925 (Imp.). And they did not appear in s 25(6) of the Judicature Act 1873 (Imp.) which s 136 replaced. According to s 12, the conditions to be satisfied if an assignment is to derive validity from the statute are that it must be absolute, in writing and written notice must be given to the debtor. If, in addition, notice to the assignee were required, one would have expected the statute to prescribe it.

[Mahoney JA decided the case on the basis that Grey had admitted that the debts had been assigned.]

NOTES

1. If there is no prior agreement between the assignor and the assignee, the assignment must be communicated to the assignee by the assignor, or by someone with his authority. The debtor can act as the assignor's agent for this purpose (*Burn v Carvalho* (1839) 4 My & Cr 690). If the debtor is acting without authority he may nevertheless bind himself to pay the 'assignee' on grounds of 'attornment' or 'acknowledgment' (Goff and Jones, at p 575).

2. It could be argued that notice to the assignee only provides evidence of the assignor's intention to assign the chose, as opposed to giving his debtor a revocable mandate to pay the purported assignee. If so, notice to the assignee would be irrelevant if clear evidence of an intention to assign could be supplied from some other source (eg the assignor had executed a deed of assignment). But see Treitel, at pp 583–584, for alternative theories as to why the assignor must give notice to the assignee.

(vi) *Consideration?*

Re Westerton, Public Trustee v Gray [1919] 2 Ch 104, Chancery Division

After Mr Westerton's death there was found in his despatch box an envelope containing (1) a deposit receipt for £500 deposited with his bank; (2) an order in writing signed by Mr Westerton directing his bank to pay Mrs Gray the £500 then on deposit; and (3) a letter to Mrs Gray in which Mr Westerton informed her that he wished to give her the £500 in return for all her kindness to him. The deposit receipt was not indorsed by Mr Westerton and no notice was given to the bank of any assignment until after Mr Westerton's death.

Sargant J: . . . I now turn to the principal difficulty in the case, and that is the absence of valuable consideration. It seems to me, though I am not sure that it was completely admitted by Mr Gover, that apart from the Judicature Act 1873, s 25, sub-s 6, the want of consideration would have been fatal to Mrs Gray's claim. Prior to the Judicature Act 1873, a legal chose in action such as this debt could not be transferred at law, and the assignee of the debt could only have sued in the name of the assignor, and in the absence of consent by the assignor or of a binding contract by the assignor to allow the use of his name, the use of the assignor's name could only have been enforced by filing a bill in equity and so obtaining an injunction in personam to allow the use of the name, and equity would not have granted that relief unless the assignment had been for valuable consideration. But to my mind the effect of s 25, sub-s 6, of the Judicature Act 1873, has been to improve the position of the assignee of a chose in action who satisfies the words of the sub-section, that is to say, an assignee under an absolute assignment by writing under the hand of the assignor nor purporting to be by way of charge only, by enabling that assignee to dispense at law with the use of the name of the assignor and so to dispense with the circuitous process of compelling the assignor in equity to allow his name to be used in proceedings by the assignee. The result of the sub-section is that an assignee who takes under such an absolute assignment as is there mentioned can now sue at law in his own name, and I see no reason why in the present case the assignee should not do so. . . .

It does seem to me that the aim of the sub-section was to reform procedure and to make it unnecessary for an assignee who had an out and out assignment to go through the double process that was formerly necessary in the case of an unwilling assignor. . . . To that extent, as I have said, the position of the assignee as a question of procedure was improved; he could come at once at law, and come not in the name of the assignor but in his own name as assignee. But if that is so and by means of that simplification of procedure the assignee has been relieved from taking preliminary proceedings in equity, there seems to me to be nothing very startling in the further conclusion, that the assignee has also been relieved from the terms which equity imposed as a condition of assisting him in obtaining the legal right, if at law the question of consideration was regarded as wholly immaterial; and I think that it must have been so regarded for this reason, that at law the action was brought in the name of the assignor, so that there was no question at all of any transaction between the assignor and the assignee under which the question of consideration could arise. If that be so and if since the Judicature Act 1873, the assignee can come directly in his own name and sue as effectually as he could have done in the name of the assignor, it appears to me that there is no reason for continuing against the assignee those terms which were imposed by equity as a condition of granting relief. The position of the assignee has in this respect been improved once and for all by the sub-section of the Judicature Act in question, which has conferred on him a legal right to sue, and in my judgment I ought not to consider that legal right as being in any way dependent upon the question whether the assignment was made for valuable consideration or not, provided it complies with the express conditions of that sub-section. In my judgment, therefore, Mrs Gray is entitled to the sum of £500 in question with interest from the date of the death of the testator.

NOTES

1. The dicta in *Re Westerton* to the effect that consideration is always required for equitable assignment of an existing legal chose in action is wrong (at least where the assignor has done everything which is necessary according to the nature of the property to transfer the title to it: see below, pp 720 ff).

2. In *Re Westerton* notice to the debtor was not given until after the death of the assignor. Sargant J, at 111, held that the mere omission to give notice at the time of the assignment was of no consequence so long as notice was given before the action was brought. However, Sargant J did go on to point out that if, without notice of the assignment, the bank had paid the money to the assignor, the payment would have been good payment as against the donee. Notice may also be given after the assignee's death (*Bateman v Hunt* [1904] 2 KB 530 at 538, CA).

QUESTIONS

1. The tentative view of Chitty LJ in *Durham Bros v Robertson* that an assignment of part of a debt falls outside s 136 has since been confirmed by the courts (see, for example, *Williams v Atlantic Assurance Co* [1933] 1 KB 81 at 100, CA). What are the reasons for excluding such an assignment from the statute? See *Durham Bros v Robertson*, above, at p 702; and *Re Steel Wing Co* [1921] 1 Ch 349 at 357).

2. Bevin, a builder, who was erecting some houses for Smart, executed a written document addressed to his bankers which stated: 'In consideration of your allowing me an overdraft of £1000, I hereby assign to you my interest in that amount (ie £1000) out of the monies which will become due to me from Smart, until my overdraft has been fully repaid'. Advise the bankers:

(1) of the effect of this document;
(2) of the steps they should take to secure and enforce their rights.

3 Equitable assignment

(a) Introduction

An assignment not falling within s 136 may nevertheless be effective as an equitable assignment. This may occur where:

(1) the assignment is not in writing signed by the assignor;
(2) the assignment is not absolute because it is by way of charge, or conditional, or of only part of a debt;
(3) no notice of the assignment has been received by the debtor; or
(4) the assignment is of future property, expectancies or bare possibilities.

(b) Methods of assignment

Timpson's Executors v Yerbury [1936] 1 KB 645, Court of Appeal

Romer LJ: . . . Now the equitable interest in property in the hands of a trustee can be disposed of by the person entitled to it in favour of a third party in any one of four different ways. The person entitled to it (1) can assign it to the third party directly; (2) can direct the trustees to hold the property in trust for the third party (see per Sargant J in *Re Chrimes* ([1917] 1 Ch 30)); (3) can contract for valuable consideration to assign the equitable interest to him; or (4) can declare himself to be a trustee for him of such interest. . . . 'For a man to make himself a trustee', said Sir George Jessel MR in *Richards v Delbridge* ((1874) LR 18 Eq 11 at 15), 'there must be an expression of intention to become a trustee.' 'It is true', he had said in an earlier part of his judgment, 'he need not use the words "I declare myself a trustee" but he must do something which is equivalent to it, and use expressions which have that meaning.' In *Milroy v Lord* ((1862) 4 De GF & J 264 at 274) Turner LJ, after referring to two methods of making a voluntary settlement valid, namely, by assignment or declaration of trust, added: 'The cases I think go further to this extent, that if the settlement is intended to be effectuated by one of the modes to which I have referred, the Court will not give effect to it by applying another of those modes. If it is intended to take effect by transfer, the Court will not hold the intended transfer to operate as a declaration of trust, for then every imperfect instrument would be made effectual by being converted into a perfect trust.'

NOTES

1. Method (1) equally applies for the assignment of legal choses in action. Also, the assignor can directly assign his legal or equitable title to trustees to hold on trust for the assignee.

2. Method (2) only applies if the chose is equitable and probably operates by way of trust rather than assignment (*Halsbury's Laws of England* (4th ed, 1991), Vol 6, para 27 fn; *Grey v IRC* [1958] Ch 375 at 381, per Upjohn J; on appeal [1958] Ch 690 at 710–711, CA, per Lord Evershed MR, and at 722, per Ormerod LJ; affd [1960] AC 1 at 16, HL, per Lord Radcliffe). However, a creditor (as legal owner) may instruct his debtor to hold a debt on trust for a third person (*M'Fadden v Jenkyns* (1842) 1 Hare 458; 1 Ph 153 (on appeal); criticised by J C Hall [1959] CLJ 99 at pp 108–109).

3. Method (3) can also apply to legal choses in action. An express contract to assign property then ascertained itself constitutes an equitable assignment (if supported by consideration). A contract to assign will be implied in equity where the assignor purports to transfer the chose direct to the assignee for value. See *Holroyd v Marshall* (1862) 10 HL Cas 191; *Tailby v Official Receiver* (1888) 13 App Cas 523 (see below, pp 754 ff).

4. If the assignor declares himself trustee of his equitable interest there is some doubt as to whether this method operates as an assignment or the creation of a sub-trust (see PVB (1958) 74 LQR 180 at 182). Again, the assignor may declare himself trustee of his legal interest for the assignee.

(c) Requirements

(i) *Intention*

William Brandt's Sons & Co v Dunlop Rubber Co Ltd [1905] AC 454, House of Lords

Merchants agreed with a bank, by whom they were financed, that buyers of goods sold by the merchants should pay the price directly to the bank. When goods had been sold, the bank forwarded to the buyers notice in writing that the merchants had made over to the bank the right to receive the purchase money and requested the buyers to sign an undertaking to remit the purchase-money to the bank. The buyers returned the acknowledgment to the bank but then paid a third party by mistake. The bank sued the buyers and the question arose whether there had been an equitable assignment.

Lord Macnaghten held that even without consideration of the notice sent to the buyers there was clear evidence of an equitable assignment between the merchants and the bank (at 460) and continued: The statute [s 25(6) of the Judicature Act 1873; now s 136 of the Law of Property Act 1925] does not forbid or destroy equitable assignments or impair their efficacy in the slightest degree. Where the rules of equity and the rules of the common law conflict, the rules of equity are to prevail. Before the statute there was a conflict as regards assignments of debts and other choses in action. At law it was considered necessary that the debtor should enter into some engagement with the assignee. That was never the rule in equity. It 'is certainly not the doctrine of this Court,' said Lord Eldon, sitting in Chancery in *Ex p South* ((1818) 3 Swan 392). In certain cases the Judicature Act places the assignee in a better position than he was before. Whether the present case falls within the favoured class may perhaps be doubted. At any rate, it is wholly immaterial for the plaintiffs' success in this action. But, says the Lord Chief Justice, 'the document does not, on the face of it, purport to be an assignment nor use the language of an assignment.' An equitable assignment does not always take that form. It may be addressed to the debtor. It may be couched in the language of command. It may be a courteous request. It may assume the form of mere permission. The language is immaterial if the meaning is plain. All that is necessary is that the debtor should be given to understand that the debt has been made over by the creditor to some third person. If the debtor ignores such a notice, he does so at his peril. If the assignment be for valuable consideration and communicated to the third person, it cannot be revoked by the creditor or safely disregarded by the debtor. I think that the documents which passed between Brandts [the Bank] and the company [the buyers] would of themselves . . . have constituted a good equitable assignment.

[Lord James delivered a concurring judgment.
The Earl of Halsbury LC and Lord Lindley concurred.]

NOTES

1. An assignment must be distinguished from a revocable mandate to a third party authorising him to collect payment from the debtor and also from a revocable mandate to the debtor directing him to pay the third party. For example, a cheque is only a revocable mandate and not the assignment of any money standing to the credit of the drawer in his bank account (*Hopkinson v Forster* (1874) LR 19 Eq 74). For discussion of when the assignor's mandate will be revocable and when it will be irrevocable, see A P Bell *Modern Law of Personal Property in England and Ireland* (1989) ('Bell'), at pp 370–371.

2. In *Elders Pastoral Ltd v Bank of New Zealand (No 2)* [1990] 1 WLR 1478, PC, Lord Templeman emphasised that 'The simplest form of an equitable assignment of a debt is an agreement by a debtor with a creditor that a debt due or to become due to the debtor from a third party shall be paid by the third party to the creditor.' To avoid confusion, it should be noted that Lord Templeman refers to the assignee as the 'creditor', whereas in the extract from Lord Macnaghten's speech in *William Brandt's Sons & Co v Dunlop Rubber Co Ltd*, and also in Note 1 above, the assignee is referred to as the 'third party'.

(ii) *Writing*

An equitable assignment can be oral. However, writing is sometimes required.

Law of Property Act 1925, s 53(1)

53. (1) Subject to the provisions hereinafter contained with respect to the creation of interests in land by parol— . . .
(c) a disposition of an equitable interest or trust subsisting at the time of the disposition, must be in writing signed by the person disposing of the same, or by his agent thereunto lawfully authorised in writing or by will.

NOTES

1. When is there a 'disposition' under s 53(1)(c)? It occurs (and writing is required) in the following circumstances; namely, when:

(1) A assigns an equitable interest to B;
(2) A assigns his equitable interest to trustees to hold on trust for B;
(3) A directs his own trustees to hold on trust for B (*Grey v IRC* [1960] AC 1, HL);
(4) A declares himself a bare trustee of his equitable interest for B, ie A drops out and the existing trustees hold for B instead of A (Underhill and Hayton *Law of Trusts and Trustees* (14th ed, 1987), pp 179–180; cf B Green (1984) 47 MLR 385 at pp 396–399). But writing is not required if the sub-trust creates a new interest, ie if the declaration of trust splits the benefit between A and B, or if it imposes active duties on A as trustee (see PVB (1958) 74 LQR 180 at p 182).

It remains doubtful whether when A contracts for value to assign his equitable interest to B it is a 'disposition' or whether it creates a constructive trust under s 53(2) of the Law of Property Act 1925, which can be oral. See *Oughtred v IRC* [1960] AC 206 (noted by J W A Thornely [1960] CLJ 31) and *Re Holt's Settlement* [1969] 1 Ch 100 at 116. Also see Hanbury and Martin *Modern Equity* (14th ed, 1993), pp 89–92.

2. Under s 2 of the Law of Property (Miscellaneous Provisions) Act 1989, a contract for the sale or other disposition of a chose in action which constitutes an interest in land can only be made in writing and only by incorporating all the terms which the parties have expressly agreed in one document or, where contracts are exchanged, in each.

(iii)   *Notice to assignee*

Giving notice of the equitable assignment to the assignee, or obtaining his prior agreement, has been held necessary if there is a direct assignment of a legal chose in action (*Morrell v Wootten* (1852) 16 Beav 197 at 203, per Sir John Romilly MR) but not if the assignment is by way of a declaration of a trust (*Middleton v Pollock* (1876) 2 Ch D 104). Notice to, or agreement of, the assignee has been held necessary if there is an equitable assignment of an equitable chose in action, whether directly or by declaration of a trust (*Re Hamilton, FitzGeorge v FitzGeorge* (1921) 124 LT 737 at 739, per Lord Sterndale MR). Without such notice or agreement, the assignment is deemed to be revocable (*Re Hamilton*, above). For criticism of the anomaly between the different notice rules for the declaration of a trust of equitable as opposed to legal choses, see J C Hall [1959] CLJ 99 at 105. Furthermore, if the assignment is by way of deed (and, therefore, irrevocable) it is difficult to see why notice to the assignee should be necessary (although see Treitel at pp 583–584). The High Court of Australia has gone even further. In *Comptroller of Stamps (Victoria) v Howard-Smith* (1936) 54 CLR 614 at 622, Dixon J said:

> Nor does it appear necessary that the intention to pass the equitable property shall be communicated to the assignee. What is necessary is that there shall be an expression of intention then and there to set over the equitable interest, and, perhaps, it should be communicated to someone who does not receive the communication under confidence or in the capacity only of an agent for the donor.

When notice of the assignment is given to the debtor by letter it is effective only when received by him (*Holt v Heatherfield Trust Ltd* [1942] 2 KB 1). However, it has been held that when notice of the assignment is given to the assignee by letter it is effective when posted (*Alexander v Steinhardt, Walker & Co* [1903] 2 KB 208; but this has been doubted in *Timpson's Executors v Yerbury* [1936] 1 KB 645 at 657–658, per Lord Wright MR).

(iv)   *Notice to debtor*

Gorringe v Irwell India Rubber and Gutta Percha Works (1886) 34 Ch D 128, Court of Appeal

As the defendants were indebted to H & Co, they wrote to them agreeing to hold a sum due from C & Co to H & Co's disposal until the balance of their indebtedness to H & Co was repaid. Before notice of this equitable assignment was given to C & Co, a petition was presented to wind up the defendants, who were subsequently put into liquidation. The liquidator took out a summons to determine whether the money due from C & Co belonged to the defendants or to H & Co. Bacon V-C held that there had been no assignment to H & Co as there had been no notice given to the debtor before the commencement of the winding up. H & Co appealed to the Court of Appeal which allowed the appeal.

Cotton LJ: . . . It is contended that in order to make an assignment of a *chose in action*, such as a debt, a complete charge, notice must be given to the debtor. It is true that there must be such a notice to enable the title of the assignee to prevail against a subsequent assignee. That is established by *Dearle v Hall* ((1823) 3 Russ 1: below, p 737), but there is no authority for holding this rule to apply as against the assignor of the debt. Though there is no notice to the debtor the title of the assignee is complete as against the assignor.

[Bowen and Fry LJJ delivered concurring judgments.]

NOTES

1. In *Warner Bros Records Inc v Rollgreen Ltd* [1976] QB 430, the Court of Appeal held that an equitable assignee of an option to renew a contract for services (a legal chose), who had not given notice of his assignment to the other contracting party, could not exercise the option. This decision has been criticised and is probably best confined to equitable assignments of contractual options (see D M Kloss (1975) 39 Conv (NS) 261).

2. Notice *should* be given to the debtor (or to the trustee) for the following reasons:

(1) If the debtor pays his original creditor, or gives him a negotiable instrument, before he receives notice of the assignment he will be under no obligation to pay the assignee (*Bence v Shearman* [1898] 2 Ch 582). If the debtor disregards the notice and pays the wrong person he remains liable to pay the assignee (*Brice v Bannister* (1878) 3 QBD 569).
(2) Notice prevents further 'equities' arising between the debtor and the assignor which might bind the assignee (see below, p 733).
(3) Notice is necessary to preserve the assignee's priority against subsequent assignees under the rule in *Dearle v Hall* (1823) 3 Russ 1 (see below, p 737).
(4) Notice, if in writing, may turn the assignment into a statutory assignment.

3. Under a contract to assign future property the assignee cannot give notice of the assignment until he has a vested interest in the property. For the problems that this may cause the assignee, see below, p 757.

James Talcott Ltd v John Lewis & Co Ltd [1940] 3 All ER 592, Court of Appeal

A creditor (the North American Dress Co Ltd) placed the following notice on its invoices by means of a rubber stamp: 'To facilitate our accountancy and banking arrangements, it has been agreed that this invoice be transferred to and payment in London funds should be made to James Talcott Ltd . . .'. The defendant debtor ignored the notice and paid the creditor. The plaintiff (as assignee) sued the debtor for payment of the sum alleged to be assigned. Macnaghten J dismissed the claim. The plaintiff appealed but the Court of Appeal, by a majority, dismissed the appeal.

MacKinnon LJ: . . . One may have a notice to a debtor from his creditor asking him to pay the money to a third party. The terms of it may be such as to indicate that it is to be paid to that third party because that third party has, by virtue of an assignment, become the person entitled to receive it. On the other hand, it may be a request to pay the debt to a third party, not because that third party has a right to it, but because, as a matter of convenience, the creditor desires that it shall be paid to that third party as his agent to receive it in respect of the right of the creditor still surviving to receive the debt himself. Plainness of meaning is necessary in order that the debtor who has received a notice to pay a third party shall be rendered liable to pay the money over again if he disregards the notice. The language is immaterial if the meaning is plain, but that plain meaning must be that the debt and the right to receive it have been transferred to the third party. It is not merely that I have made some arrangement by which I request another to pay this money to the third party as my agent. The question is whether this stamped clause put upon the invoices did amount to a plain intimation to the first defendants that the right to receive this money had been transferred to the plaintiffs.

First of all, it is not a notice sent by the plaintiffs at all. If it were sent direct by the plaintiffs to the first defendants, the mere fact that it emanated from them would go some little way to indicate that they were doing so pursuant to a right of theirs. I do not say that there is very much in that, but the fact that it is stamped on their own invoice by the North American Dress Co Ltd makes it a communication from them, and not a communication from John Lewis & Co Ltd to the plaintiffs. The words are these:

> To facilitate our accountancy and banking arrangements, it has been agreed that this invoice be transferred to and payment in London funds should be made to James Talcott, Ltd. . . . Errors in this invoice must be notified to James Talcott, Ltd immediately.

It would have been so simple for James Talcott Ltd to give a correct notice, 'This debt has been assigned to us,' or to insist that the North American Dress Co Ltd should in clear terms give that intimation, that it is a matter of extreme wonder and speculation why this stamp should have been couched in this extremely vague and obscure language.

We have been told (I think that it appears from one of the letters) that the wording of this extraordinary sentence was actually settled by counsel. I can only conceive that it was couched in this obscure language to conceal the fact that the North American Dress Co Ltd were carrying on their business with borrowed money, and had assigned to the plaintiffs the money to which they themselves were entitled.

The words begin – and they are the first words to be read by anybody who did read them – 'To facilitate our accountancy and banking arrangements . . .'. The word 'our' suggests that it is still a debt due to the North American Dress Co Ltd and that it is only a matter of their internal business arrangements. It is true that the words go on 'it has been agreed,' and it is suggested that that must mean an agreement between the North American Dress Co Ltd and the plaintiffs, though I do not know why it should. There is nothing to show that it has been agreed between those parties. There are the vague, uncertain words 'it has been agreed.' Then it goes on to say 'that this invoice be transferred to.' It is suggested that those words in themselves ought to be taken to mean that the debt due upon this invoice shall be assigned, but they do not say so. The invoice is transferred:

> . . . and payment in London funds should be made to James Talcott Ltd. . . . Errors in this invoice must be notified to James Talcott Ltd immediately.

As I have said, it is not enough to make the debtor liable to pay over again if he has creditors, if he has merely received a notice that he is to pay to some other party merely as agent for his creditor. He is not bound to pay over again unless he has received a sufficiently plain notice that the right to receive the money has been transferred to the third party, so that he will at his peril neglect that notice and neglect the right of the third party. I think that this notice stamped on the invoice was ambiguous. I think that it is equally consistent with being merely a request to pay to the plaintiffs, as agents of the creditor to receive the money, and it does not indicate sufficiently clearly that there has been an assignment of the debt to the plaintiffs so that they should become the real creditors of the first defendants, be the only persons entitled to be paid the money. That was the view taken by Macnaghten J, with the result that he dismissed the claim. I think that his decision was right, and that this appeal fails.

Goddard LJ (dissenting): I have the misfortune to differ from MacKinnon LJ and Macnaghten J. I do so only with great hesitation, but, as I have formed a very clear opinion, assisted, I may say, by the very clear and forcible argument of counsel for the appellants, I think that I must express my opinion of dissent. The law of this country allows a creditor to assign his debt to a third party. If the debtor receives notice of that assignment, he must pay the assignee. If he pays the assignor, he does so at his peril. If the assignor does not account to the assignee for the money, the debtor will have to pay a second time. Notice may be given by the assignor or by the assignee. For myself, I think that the fact that the notice is given by the assignor may strengthen the position, as far as the debtor is concerned, in this way. I should not draw any inference which is adverse by reason of the fact that it is given by the assignor, because, if the debtor gets a notice from B telling him to pay B the money he owes to A, he will naturally want to know if he is safe in doing so, and he will apply to A, the assignor. If he gets a notice from the assignor, then, of course, he can safely pay, because he will be paying in accordance with the directions of his creditor.

I do not say that this is an easy case, and I think that much clearer words could have been used, but, in my opinion, the words are clear enough to indicate the position to John Lewis & Co Ltd, if they ever thought about it. Probably the reason why they did not pay the plaintiffs was that they ignored the notice and never thought about it. I think that it is enough to tell them that the plaintiffs had a charge on, or were interested in, the money, and, therefore, for my part, I would allow this appeal.

Du Parcq LJ: . . . A notice to pay a debt to a third person may be given in words which show that there has been an assignment of the debt. It may be given in words which show that there has not been an assignment of the debt. It may be given in words which leave it in doubt whether or not there has been an assignment of the debt. If those words are in the first category, the plaintiffs succeed. If the words are in either of the other categories, the plaintiffs fail. I say either of the other categories, because it is not enough that the notice should be capable of being understood to mean that the debt is assigned. It must be plain and unambiguous, and not reasonably capable, when read by an intelligent business man, of a contrary construction.

NOTES

1. In *Herkules Piling Ltd v Tilbury Construction Ltd* (1992) 32 Con LR 112, Hirst J held that the debtor did not receive notice of assignment when he received a copy of the contract of assignment from the assignor on discovery in arbitration proceedings. His Lordship held that in order to constitute notice there must be some kind of formal notification by the assignee, or possibly by the assignor on his behalf. Hirst J rejected as wrong a submission that the debtor must or may pay the assignee where he learns by some other credible means that the money does not or may not belong to the assignor but to the assignee. As to when notice to the debtor becomes effective, see above, p 716.

2. For a comparison between the more relaxed rules of construction applicable to notice of equitable assignments, as opposed to the stricter rules applicable to notice of statutory assignments, see Roderick Munday (1981) 131 NLJ 607 at p 608; and above, p 707.

3. Notice of an equitable assignment may be oral. However, the following statutory provisions may make it necessary to give notice in writing.

Law of Property Act 1925, s 137(3), (10)

137. . . . . (3) A notice, otherwise than in writing, given to, or received by, a trustee after the commencement of this Act as respects any dealing with an equitable interest in real or personal property, shall not affect the priority of competing claims of purchasers in that equitable interest.

. . .

(10) This section does not apply until a trust has been created, and in this section 'dealing' includes a disposition by operation of law.

(v) *Consideration?*

Snell's Equity (29th ed, 1990), p 79

(e) *Value sometimes required.* Value is necessary for an equitable assignment of rights of property not yet in existence, or for the creation of a mere charge (as distinct from a complete transfer),[88] for such assignments are based on there being a contract that the property in question shall be assigned or stand charged.[89] But value does not appear to be required for other equitable assignments, whether the chose is legal or equitable,[90] provided the assignor has done everything required to be done by him in order to transfer the chose in action.[91] There are difficulties in this doctrine of 'every effort,' as it may be called.[92] It produces the result that a voluntary assignment of a legal chose in action may be a valid equitable assignment if it is in writing, even if no notice of it has been given,[93] but not if it is oral[94]; for an assignor has not done all that he must do to assign the chose at law if he fails to put the assignment in writing, whereas others besides him may give the notice.[95] Value also seems to be unnecessary for an assignment of an equitable thing in action, such as a legacy or an interest in trust funds,[96] provided that the assignment is complete and perfect[97]; for there is no reason why a man should not be able to give away an equitable interest as freely as he can give away a legal interest.[98]

88 *Re Earl Lucan* (1890) 45 Ch D 470.
89 See *Matthews v Goodday* (1861) 31 LJ Ch 282.
90 *Pulley v Public Trustee* [1956] NZLR 771.
91 *Re Patrick* [1891] 1 Ch 82; *Re Griffin* [1899] 1 Ch 408; and see *Blakely v Brady* (1839) 2 Dr & Wal 311.
92 See (1943) 59 LQR 61.
93 *Holt v Heatherfield Trust Ltd* [1942] 2 KB 1, an unsatisfactory decision, where value in fact seems to have been given: see (1943) 59 LQR 58, 508; H A Hollond, ibid, 129. *Holt's* case was followed in *Pulley v Public Trustee* [1956] NZLR 771. Consider also *German v Yates* (1915) 32 TLR 52; *Glegg v Bromley* [1912] 3 KB 474 at 491; *Norman v Federal Comr of Taxation* (1963) 109 CLR 9.
94 *Olsson v Dyson* (1969) 120 CLR 365.
95 *Olsson v Dyson*, supra, at pp 386, 387 (a dissenting judgment but not on this point); cf *Re Fry* [1946] Ch 312.
96 See *Re Wale* [1956] 1 WLR 1346.
97 *Bentley v Mackay* (1851) 15 Beav 12; *Voyle v Hughes* (1854) 2 Sm & G 18; *Nanney v Morgan* (1887) 37 ChD 346; and see *Re McArdle* [1951] Ch 669 (a difficult case: see (1951) 67 LQR 295).
98 See the full survey by L A Sheridan (1955) 33 Can BR 284.

Norman v Federal Comr of Taxation (1963) 109 CLR 9, High Court of Australia

(The facts appear above at p 692.)

Windeyer J: . . . It is settled that any assignment that satisfies the requirements of the statute is valid and fully effectual although it be voluntary. That is to say the law now provides a means whereby the legal owner of a chose in action may make a complete and perfect gift of it. That being so, and as equity does not perfect an imperfect gift, can there ever now be an effectual voluntary assignment unless all the statutory requirements are met? The question is not an easy one if a purely logical answer be sought. Equity intervened to assist the assignments of choses in action because they were not assignable at law. Now that they are, why, it may be asked, should equity aid imperfect attempts at voluntary assignments of them. On the other hand, it can be urged that the statute provides a method or machinery whereby assignment may be effected, but that it does not detract from the validity of any transaction that would have been effective in equity if it had occurred before the statute came into operation. There is some authority for the latter proposition: see eg *German v Yates* ((1915) 32 TLR 52). And Lord Macnaghten's well-known words in *William Brandt's Sons & Co v Dunlop Rubber Co* ([1905] AC 454 at 461), are sometimes invoked in support of it: 'Why that which would have been a good equitable assignment before the statute should now be invalid and inoperative because it fails to come up to the requirements of the statute, I confess I do not understand. The statute does not forbid or destroy equitable assignments or impair their efficacy in the slightest degree'. But this was said in reference to an assignment for value. I do not think that his Lordship's remarks should be read as qualifying the principle that equity does not perfect imperfect voluntary assignments. If an attempt is made to assign, by way of gift, a chose in action assignable under the statute, then, as I see the matter, the requirements of the statute cannot be ignored; for the general rule of equity is that an effective assignment occurs only if the donor does all that, according to the nature of the property, he must do to transfer the property to the donee. But the weight of authority is, I think in favour of the view that in equity there is a valid gift of property transferable at law if the donor, intending to make, then and there, a complete disposition and transfer to the donee, does all that *on his part* is necessary to give effect to his intention and arms the donee with the means of competing the gift according to the requirements of the law: see *Brunker v Perpetual Trustee Co Ltd* ((1937) 57 CLR 555 at 600–602) per Dixon J; *Re Smith* ((1901) 84 LT 835); *Re Rose* ([1949] Ch 78); *Re Rose* ([1952] Ch 499). I think therefore that, if a man, meaning to make an immediate gift of a chose in action that is his, executes an instrument that meets the requirements of the statute and delivers it to the donee, actually or constructively, he has put it out of his power to recall his gift. It is true that until notice is given to the debtor or person against whom the chose is enforceable at law, all the requirements of the statute have not been complied with. But the notice can be given by the donee; and, if the donee has express or implied authority to give it, I think that equity would now allow the donor to deny the right of the donee to do so and so intercept his gift. I reach this conclusion with some hesitation, for it involves some departure from the majority view in *Anning v Anning* ((1907) 4 CLR 1049). But it accords, it seems to me with general principle. For these reasons I consider that, if the debt that the deed in this case purported to assign had been an existing chose in action assignable by the statutory procedure, the only question would be whether the assignor had purported to make an absolute assignment of it, and whether he did all that on his part had to be done to that end. The difficulty is that, as will appear, what it was sought to assign was part only of a prospectively larger debt. . . .

As to whether consideration is required for the equitable assignment of a chose in action not assignable at law:

One might have expected that this would long ago have been authoritatively settled. But the question is, according to *Halsbury*, 3rd ed, vol 4, p 495, 'uncertain'. Lord Evershed said in *Re McArdle* ([1951] Ch 669 at 673) that the problem is 'vexed and difficult'. . . .

If the interest to be assigned is a creature of equity, such as the beneficial interest of a cestui que trust, then, apart from any statutory provisions, an assignment of it can, of course, only be effected in equity; for the common law does not know it. Any present assignment of such an interest, that is to say of a chose in equity, is therefore necessarily an equitable assignment. Such an assignment can be by way of gift; and, except that writing is required by s 9 of the Statute of Frauds [now s 53(1)(c) of the Law of Property Act 1925], no formality is necessary beyond a clear expression of an intention to make an immediate disposition. In short, there is no reason at all why a person should not give away any beneficial interest that is his: the classic statement is that of Knight Bruce LJ in *Kekewich v Manning* ((1851) 1 De GM & G 176); see too *In re McArdle (dec'd)*. It is, of course, necessary that the transaction should take the form of, and be intended as, an immediate transfer of the beneficial interest of the assignor, as distinct from an agreement to assign it. The distinction is critical, for consideration is always necessary to attract the support of equity to a transaction that is a contract rather than a conveyance. The judgment of Stuart VC in *Voyle v Hughes* ((1854) 2 Sm & G 18), puts all this clearly.

Turning, from assignments that are equitable because the property assigned is a chose in equity, to assignments that are equitable because the property assigned is a legal chose in action not assignable except by the aid of equity: It has been said that historically there could be no equitable assignment of a debt except for value. Whether this be correct or not as a general proposition, it never meant that there must be consideration as now understood in the law of contract. An assignment in satisfaction, or part satisfaction, of an antecedent debt was taken in equity as made for value. And this was what had happened in case after case appearing in the reports in which assignments were upheld in equity before the Judicature Act. Whether equity would then give any aid to an assignment of a chose in action made for no value at all, but as a pure gift, is less clear. There are in the reports categorical statements each way, extending over two centuries or more. . . .

[His Lordship briefly reviewed the cases and continued:]

It seems to me that, in principle, so far as a deed has any efficacy in connexion with equitable assignments, it is not that a deed takes the place of valuable consideration where that is needed to attract the aid of equity. Rather it is that, in cases where value is not so required but a clear expression of intention is, the delivery of a deed couched in terms of present gift manifests, in the best possible way, the intention of the assignor to make an immediate and irrevocable transfer.

The intervention of equity in support of assignments of choses in action has been ascribed historically, in the main, to one or other of two grounds. One is to hold men to agreements and promises which they have made for value; the other is the analogy of a trust. Story put the two somewhat together when, adopting Butler's note to *Coke on Littleton* (232 b), he said: 'Every such assignment is considered in equity as in its nature amounting to a declaration of trust, and to an agreement to permit the assignee to make use of the name of the assignor to recover the debt, or to reduce the property into possession': Story, *Equity Jurisprudence* 7th ed (1857) para 1040. An assignment, of course, differs from a declaration of trust. And it is trite to say that an ineffectual attempt to assign property will not be rescued by equity by being construed as a valid declaration of trust: *Milroy v Lord* ((1862) 4 De GF & J 264). Nevertheless, the analogy between the creation of a trust and an equitable assignment of a chose in action, which creates an equitable interest in the assignee, is significant.

An agreement to assign will be effective as an equitable assignment if it be for value; for then equity looks on that as done which ought to be done. But this does not mean that there cannot be in equity an actual assignment of a chose in action as distinct from an agreement to assign. I think there can, and that it can be by way of gift. In such a case equity enforces the assignment, not by compelling the assignor to do something, but by refusing to allow him to act in a way inconsistent with what he has done, that is by restraining him from derogating from his gift. His conscience becomes bound, not by value received, but because, as between him and the assignee, his gift was complete.

This view of the matter is in accordance with the decision of the Court of Appeal in *Re Patrick* ([1891] 1 Ch 82), a case concerning a voluntary settlement by which the settlor assigned certain debts to trustees before the Judicature Act 1873, came into operation. The Court, consisting of Lindley, Bowen and Fry LJJ, held that there had been a complete assignment of the debts. The decision has been somewhat depreciated by text-writers, because Lindley LJ said that the assignment of the debts was complete 'within the principle of *Kekewich v Manning* ((1851) 1 De GM & G 176) which is the leading case on this subject'; and it has been pointed out that *Kekewich v Manning* was a case of the assignment of an equitable chose, not of a legal chose in action. But, as between assignor and assignee, does that make any difference? Why should consideration be said to be necessary to bind the conscience in the one case when it is not necessary in the other? Before 1873 a chose in equity and a chose in action were both transferable in equity and only in equity. The assignments were alike made effective because of the remedies that a court of equity could provide. To speak of equity not perfecting an imperfect gift seems beside the point where no gift could be made except in equity. To say that the donor must do everything that according to the nature of the property is necessary to transfer it means little when it is in law not transferable; for equity looks to the intent not the form. These considerations have added weight in the case of part of a debt; for a part of a debt never was assignable so as to be recoverable at law even in an indirect way. It being necessary for the decision of this case to come to a conclusion on a vexed question, my conclusion is that the deed that the taxpayer executed did not fail because it was voluntary. The whole of a debt being now voluntarily assignable under the statute, it would be a strange anomaly if a part could not be the subject of voluntary equitable assignment. To say, 'you can give away the whole, but you cannot give away a part, for a part you must get a price' would seem to contradict common sense. And I do not think it necessary to do so.

NOTES

1. There has been much debate as to whether failure to comply with the requirements of s 136 of the Law of Property Act 1925 prevents the gratuitous equitable assignment of a legal chose in action (when the chose could be assigned under the section) on the basis that the assignor has not done everything in his power to complete the gift. The issue does not arise with the assignment of part of a debt, which could not be assigned under the statute in any event.

2. In *Norman v Federal Comr of Taxation*, Windeyer J held that failure by the assignor to give notice to the debtor did not make the gift imperfect as such notice could be given by the assignee. But what if the assignment is oral? This question was not addressed by Windeyer J in *Norman v Federal Comr of Taxation* but was subsequently answered in *Olsson v Dyson* (1969) 120 CLR 365 where the High Court of Australia held that a voluntary oral assignment of a debt was ineffective. In the passage set out above, Snell submits that a voluntary assignment of a legal chose cannot be oral, but only *Olsson v Dyson* is cited in support of that statement. J C Hall makes a similar statement in [1959] CLJ 99 at p 1125. But contrast Treitel, at p 591, who submits that the oral voluntary assignments of a legal choses can be valid so long as they are perfect gifts and that they are not imperfect *merely* for want of writing. Citing *German v Yates* (1915) 32 TLR 52, Treitel submits that before the Judicature Act 1873 equity allowed the gift of a chose by equitable assignment without formal requirements and that the 1873 Act did not impair the validity of such assignments but merely provided a second means of making such a gift. Also see Cheshire, Fifoot and Furmston's *Law of Contract* (12th ed, 1991), at p 512 fn, where it is submitted that *Olsson v Dyson* 'clearly does not represent English law', and at pp 513–514. For criticism of Treitel's thesis, see Bell, at p 373. The issue remains unresolved.

3. Consideration is only a relevant issue as between the assignor (or his successors in title) and the assignee. So far as the debtor is concerned he cannot refuse to pay the assignee merely on the ground that there has been no consideration: *Walker v Bradford Old Bank* (1884) 12 QBD 511.

4. A voluntary promise under seal, though unenforceable in equity, may entitle the assignee to sue the assignor for damages for breach of contract (*Cannon v Hartley* [1949] Ch 213) and may later constitute an irrevocable assignment of any such property to which the promisor does become entitled and which is in fact paid to or vested in the promisee (*Re Bowden, Hulbert v Bowden* [1936] Ch 71; and *Re Adlard* [1954] Ch 29).

5. For detailed discussion as to how far consideration is necessary for an equitable assignment, see R E Megarry (1943) 59 LQR 58 and 208; Professor Hollond

(1943) 59 LQR 129; Sheridan (1955) 33 Can Bar Rev 284; and, especially, J C Hall [1959] CLJ 99.

QUESTIONS

1. A purports to assign shares to B, but uses the wrong transfer form. B gives no consideration but does receive notice of the assignment. Has there been a valid equitable assignment of the shares? See *Milroy v Lord* (1862) 4 De GF & J 264.

2. Under their father's will, A and his brothers and sister were entitled to a house after the death of their mother. A's wife, B, carried out certain improvements to the house. After the improvements were completed, A and his brothers and sister wrote to B promising to pay her £500 from the estate when distributed 'in consideration of you carrying out certain alterations and improvements to the house'. Was there a valid equitable assignment of the £500? See *Re McArdle* [1951] Ch 669; REM (1951) 67 LQR 295.

4 Principles applicable to both statutory and equitable assignments

(a) Non-assignable choses in action

Trendtex Trading Corpn v Crédit Suisse [1982] AC 679, House of Lords

The plaintiffs, Trendtex (T), sold cement to an English company (cif Lagos) with payment to be made under a letter of credit issued by the Central Bank of Nigeria (CBN). CBN failed to honour the letter of credit and T sued them for breach of contract. The defendants, Crédit Suisse (CS), who had provided T with financial assistance in connection with the cement contract, guaranteed T's legal costs of the proceedings against CBN. CS saw the proceedings as providing its only prospect of recovering the money owed to it by T. In return, T assigned to CS by way of security its right of action against CBN. T was successful before the Court of Appeal but CBN obtained leave to appeal to the House of Lords. At this juncture, T (now owing US $1.5 million to CS) entered into an agreement with CS whereby T assigned outright to CS any residual interest in its claim against CBN and agreed that CS could re-assign the right of action to a purchaser of its choice (the agreement recited that CS had received an offer from a third party to buy the right of action for US $800,000). Five days later CS re-assigned the right of action to a third party for US $1.1 million and five weeks after that the third party settled with CBN for US $8 million. T was suspicious of these arrangements and claimed that the agreement and assignment were void as they savoured of maintenance and champerty. The Court of Appeal (Lord Denning MR, Bridge and Oliver LJJ) upheld the assignment. T appealed.

Lord Wilberforce: . . . If no party had been involved in the agreement of January 4, 1978, but Trendtex and Credit Suisse, I think that it would have been difficult to contend that the agreement, even if it involved (as I think it did) an assignment of Trendtex's residual interest in the CBN case, offended against the law of maintenance or champerty. As I have already shown, Crédit Suisse had a genuine and substantial interest in the success of the CBN litigation. It had, and I do not think that the legitimacy of its action was challenged, guaranteed the previous costs. It had by the documents of September 6 and November 26, 1976, taken a security interest in the litigation or its proceeds. To carry this a stage further by a surrender of Trendtex's residual interest (if this was the effect of the agreement of January 4, 1978) would, in my view, have been lawful, though a question might have arisen (and indeed may arise) whether, after Crédit Suisse had been satisfied as creditors, Trendtex could claim the return to it of any surplus. The possibility of this could not invalidate the agreement; it would arise under it, and clearly fall within the exclusive jurisdiction clause.

The vice, if any, of the agreement lies in the introduction of the third party. It appears from the face of the agreement not as an obligation, but as a contemplated possibility, that the cause of action against CBN might be sold by Crédit Suisse to a third party, for a sum of US $800,000. This manifestly involved the possibility, and indeed the likelihood, of a profit being made, either by the third party or possibly also by Crédit Suisse, out of the cause of action. In my opinion this manifestly 'savours of champerty,' since it involves trafficking in litigation – a type of transaction which, under English law, is contrary to public policy.

Lord Roskill: . . . My Lords, before considering these submissions in any detail it is necessary to recall that the Criminal Law Act 1967 by s 13(1) abolished the crimes of maintenance and champerty and by s 14(1) provided that neither should any longer be actionable as a tort. But s 14(2) further provided that these provisions should not affect any rule of law as to the cases in which a contract was to be treated as contrary to public policy or otherwise illegal. It therefore seems plain that Parliament intended to leave the law as to the effect of maintenance and champerty upon contracts unaffected by the abolition of them as crimes and torts.

My Lords, it is clear, when one looks at the cases upon maintenance in this century and indeed towards the end of the last, that the courts have adopted an infinitely more liberal attitude towards the supporting of litigation by a third party than had previously been the case. One has only to read the classic judgment of Danckwerts J affirmed by the Court of Appeal, in *Martell v Consett Iron Co Ltd* [1955] Ch 363 to see how this branch of the law has developed and how the modern view of sufficiency of interest has come about. My Lords, learned counsel cited to your Lordships many of the cases on maintenance which are there discussed. For my part I think no further review of them is necessary today. I would only emphasise the importance when reading them of distinguishing between the use of the word maintenance to denote *lawful* maintenance and the use of that word to denote what was then both a crime and a tort.

My Lords, one of the reasons why equity would not permit the assignment of what became known as a bare cause of action, whether legal or equitable, was because it savoured of maintenance. If one reads the well known judgment of Parker J in *Glegg v Bromley* [1912] 3 KB 474, 490, one can see how the relevant law has developed. Though in general choses in action were assignable, yet causes of action which were essentially personal in their character, such as claims for defamation or personal injury, were incapable of assignment for the reason already given. But even so, no objection was raised to assignments of the proceeds of an action for defamation as in *Glegg v Bromley*, for such an assignment would in no way give the assignee the right to intervene in the action and so be contrary to public policy: see Fletcher Moulton LJ, at pp 488–489.

My Lords, just as the law became more liberal in its approach to what was *lawful* maintenance, so it became more liberal in its approach to the circumstances in which it would recognise the validity of an assignment of a cause of action and not strike down such an assignment as one only of a bare cause of action. Where the assignee has by the assignment acquired a property right and the cause of action was incidental to that right, the assignment was held effective. *Ellis v Torrington* [1920] 1 KB 399 is an example of such a case. Scrutton LJ stated, at pp 412–413, that the assignee was not guilty of maintenance or champerty by reason of the assignment he took because he was buying not in order to obtain a cause of action but in order to protect the property which he had bought. But, my Lords, as I read the cases it was not necessary for the assignee always to show a property right to support his assignment. He could take an assignment to support and enlarge that which he had already acquired as, for example, an underwriter by subrogation: see *Compania*

Colombiana de Seguros v Pacific Steam Navigation Co [1965] 1 QB 101. My Lords, I am afraid that, with respect, I cannot agree with the learned Master of the Rolls [1980] QB 629, 657 when he said in the instant case that 'The old saying that you cannot assign a "bare right to litigate" is gone.' I venture to think that that still remains a fundamental principle of our law. But it is today true to say that in English law an assignee who can show that he has a genuine commercial interest in the enforcement of the claim of another and to that extent takes an assignment of that claim to himself is entitled to enforce that assignment unless by the terms of that assignment he falls foul of our law of champerty, which, as has often been said, is a branch of our law of maintenance. For my part I can see no reason in English law why Crédit Suisse should not have taken an assignment to themselves of Trendtex's claim against CBN for the purpose of recouping themselves for their own substantial losses arising out of CBN's repudiation of the letter of credit upon which Credit Suisse were relying to refinance their financing of the purchases by Trendtex of this cement from their German suppliers.

My Lords, I do not therefore think that Mr Brodie [counsel for Trendtex] is correct in criticising the judgment of Oliver LJ [[1980] QB 629] on the ground that the learned Lord Justice failed to distinguish between the interest necessary to support an assignment of a cause of action and the interest which would justify the maintenance of an action by a third party. I think, with respect, that this submission involves over-analysis of the position. The court should look at the totality of the transaction. If the assignment is of a property right or interest and the cause of action is ancillary to that right or interest, or if the assignee had a genuine commercial interest in taking the assignment and in enforcing it for his own benefit, I see no reason why the assignment should be struck down as an assignment of a bare cause of action or as savouring of maintenance.

But, my Lords, to reach that conclusion and thus to reject a substantial part of Mr Brodie's argument for substantially the same reasons as did Oliver LJ does not mean that at least article 1 of the agreement of January 4, 1978, is not objectionable as being champertous, for it is not an assignment designed to enable Crédit Suisse to recoup their own losses by enforcing Trendtex's claim against CBN to the maximum amount recoverable. Though your Lordships do not have the agreement between Crédit Suisse and the anonymous third party, it seems to me obvious, as already stated, that the purpose of article 1 of the agreement of January 4, 1978, was to enable the claim against CBN to be sold on to the anonymous third party for that anonymous third party to obtain what profit he could from it, apart from paying to Crédit Suisse the purchase price of US $1,100,000. In other words, the 'spoils,' whatever they might be, to be got from CBN were in effect being divided, the first US $1,100,000 going to Crédit Suisse and the balance, whatever it might ultimately prove to be, to the anonymous third party. Such an agreement, in my opinion, offends for it was a step towards the sale of a bare cause of action to a third party who had no genuine commercial interest in the claim in return for a division of the spoils, Crédit Suisse taking the fixed amount which I have already mentioned. To this extent I find myself in respectful disagreement with Oliver LJ.

[Lord Fraser of Tullybelton delivered a concurring judgment.
Lords Edmund-Davies and Keith of Kinkel concurred.]

[Their Lordships went on to order the action be stayed. Their Lordships held that as the agreement was governed by Swiss law it was for the Swiss courts to decide what effect the invalidity of the assignment under English law had on the agreement as a whole.]

NOTES

1. Snell (pp 84–85) defines maintenance as 'the supply of pecuniary assistance to the plaintiff or the defendant in an action by a stranger without lawful excuse' and champerty as 'maintenance coupled with an agreement to divide the spoils'. Both are contrary to public policy (see generally *Giles v Thompson* [1994] 1 AC 142, HL).

2. In *Trendtex*, Lord Roskill held that although the assignment from T to CS did not savour of maintenance, because CS had a genuine commercial interest in the enforcement of T's claim, the assignment was champertous, because it facilitated the sale of a bare cause of action to a third party who had no genuine commercial interest in the claim in return for a division of the 'spoils' between CS and the third party. This leaves open the question whether an assignee of a right to sue, who *has* a genuine commercial interest in the claim, may nevertheless profit from the assignment. In *Brownton Ltd v Edward Moore Inbucon Ltd* [1985] 3 All ER 499 the Court of Appeal (Sir John Donaldson MR, Lloyd LJ and Sir John Megaw) held that if the assignee has a genuine commercial interest it was not fatal to the validity of the assignment that he may be better off as a result of it, or that he might make a profit out of it (although an excessive level of profit may indicate that the commercial interest was not genuine: per Sir John Megaw at 506 – see also *Advanced Technology Structures Ltd v Cray Valley Products Ltd* [1993] BCLC 723, CA). Lloyd LJ left open the question whether any profit would be returnable by the assignee to the assignor (at 509). In answer to that question, Chitty submits that if the assignment is out and out and not by way of security it is difficult to see why the assignee should return any profit to the assignor (Vol 1, para 1176 fn). For further comment on *Trendtex*, see J W A Thornely [1982] CLJ 29. On champertous contracts and assignments generally, see Y L Tan (1990) 106 LQR 656.

3. When does an assignee have a 'commercial interest'? In *Brownton Ltd v Edward Moore Inbucon Ltd*, above, the plaintiff sued the first defendant alleging that it had negligently advised the plaintiff to purchase an unsuitable computer. The second defendant supplied the computer and the plaintiff sued it for breach of contract. The first defendant settled with the plaintiff and took an assignment of the plaintiff's right of action against the second defendant. The Court of Appeal held that the first defendant had a genuine commercial interest in taking the assignment as (1) the contracts between the plaintiff and the first and second defendants arose out of same transaction; and (2) the first and second defendants had been sued in respect of the same damage to the plaintiff so that any sum recovered from the second defendant would have gone to reduce the sum recoverable from the first defendant. But compare this case with *Bourne v Colodense Ltd* [1985] ICR 291 where the Court of Appeal held the defendant had a 'commercial interest' in the enforcement of the plaintiff's rights against his union when those rights did not arise in a trade or commercial context (see Y L Tan (1990) 106 LQR 656 at 664). The plaintiff unsuccessfully sued the defendant for personal injuries caused by negligence. As the plaintiff's union had agreed to pay the plaintiff's costs, the trial judge ordered the plaintiff to pay the defendant's costs. When the union refused to pay the costs the defendant applied to the court for the appointment of a receiver to take proceedings in the plaintiff's name to realise the plaintiff's claim towards the satisfaction of the costs due to the defendant. The Court of Appeal held that the defendant clearly had a commercial interest in the enforcement of such rights as the plaintiff had against his union, for without the enforcement of those rights the defendant would have had a worthless order for costs. In effect, the Court of Appeal regarded the defendant's 'financial interest' as its 'commercial interest' to satisfy the *Trendtex* test.

4. Although a right to sue (in contract or tort) for unliquidated damages cannot be assigned unless the assignee has a legitimate interest in the cause of action (but see Y L Tan (1990) 106 LQR 656 at 664–668 as to whether tort claims may be assigned at all), a claim to a simple debt can be assigned even if the assignee has no interest in the cause of action (*County Hotel and Wine Co v London and North Western Rly Co* [1918] 2 KB 251 at 258, per McCardie J; affd [1919] 2 KB 29, [1921] 1 AC 85). If it were otherwise, the 'factoring' of debts could not take place (see below, p 753).

5. An assignment of a bare right to litigate is valid if made by a trustee in bankruptcy or by the liquidator of a company under their statutory powers (Insolvency Act 1986, s 314(1) (bankruptcy); ibid, s 167(1)(b), Sch 4, Pt III, para 6 (liquidation). See *Ramsey v Hartley* [1977] 1 WLR 686 where the Court of Appeal allowed the trustee in bankruptcy to sell the bankrupt's right of action back to the bankrupt himself. See also, *Weddell v J A Pearce & Major* [1988] Ch 26.

6. If the assignee has a sufficient proprietary right, or a genuine commercial interest, in the assignment of a claim for unliquidated damages, the assignee can recover no more as damages than the assignor could have recovered (*GUS Property Management Ltd v Littlewoods Mail Order Stores Ltd* 1982 SLT 533 at 538, per Lord Keith of Kinkel). The limits to this principle have recently been explored by the Court of Appeal and House of Lords in *Linden Gardens Trust Ltd v Lenesta Sludge Disposals Ltd* (1992) 57 BLR 57, CA; revsd [1994] AC 85, HL. In this case, a building contractor contracted with the assignor to work on the assignor's building. When executing the work, the contractor committed various breaches of contract. The assignor spent some £22,000 to remedy one breach but was unaware of the full extent of the other breaches. The assignor then sold its proprietary interest in the building for its full market value and, shortly afterwards, assigned its rights of action arising under the building contract to the assignee. The full extent of the contractor's breaches then became apparent and the assignee spent some £236,000 on remedying them. The assignee sought to recover that sum from the contractor as damages for breach of contract. The contractor claimed that the assignee could not recover more than the assignor could have recovered. The contractor argued that the assignee's loss was limited to £22,000. The Court of Appeal (Staughton LJ, Nourse LJ and Sir Michael Kerr) rejected that argument holding that as the breaches had all occurred before the assignment, a right of action had vested in the assignor which was the subject of a valid assignment. It was irrelevant that the assignor had been paid the full market value for its proprietary interest (see J Cartwright (1990) 6 Const LJ 14 on this point). The House of Lords, reversing the Court of Appeal, held that the assignee had no right of action against the contractor because the assignment was ineffective under a non-assignment clause in the building contract (see below, p 732). By deciding the case on this ground, their Lordships did not have to consider the issue of the measure of damages recoverable by the assignee. But compare this case with *St Martin's Property Corpn Ltd v Sir Robert McAlpine & Sons Ltd* (an appeal heard concurrently with the *Linden Gardens'* appeal and reported in the same report). The facts were similar to those found in the *Linden Gardens* case, save that there had been no breach of the building contract before the assignment, all breaches occurring after that date. In this case both the Court of Appeal and the House of Lords held (for different reasons) that the attempted assignment of the assignor's rights under the building contract was ineffective because of a non-assignment clause in that contract (see below, p 732). The question then arose as to whether the assignor could claim substantial damages from the contractor for breach of the building contract. The problem facing the assignor was that at the time of the breaches of contract the assignor no longer owned the property and had suffered no financial loss. It was the purported assignee who had suffered the loss. The Court of

Appeal allowed the assignor to recover from the contractor a sum equal to the assignee's loss by holding the assignor liable to indemnify the assignee. But the House of Lords rejected that argument on the ground that the damage claimed was too remote. Their Lordships held that the assignor was entitled to claim substantial damages on the ground that it was contemplated by the parties to the building contract that the assignor would be entitled to enforce contractual rights on behalf of subsequent occupiers or purchasers of the property who would suffer from defective performance but were unable to acquire rights under the building contract because of the non-assignment clause (by analogy with the rule in *Dunlop v Lambert* (1839) 6 Cl & Fin 600, HL). As Lord Browne-Wilkinson said (at 430):

> In my judgment the present case falls within the rationale of the exceptions to the general rule that a plaintiff can only recover damages for his own loss. The contract was for a large development of property which, to the knowledge of both Corporation and McAlpine, was going to be occupied, and possibly purchased, by third parties and not by Corporation itself. Therefore it could be foreseen that damage caused by a breach would cause loss to a later owner and not merely to the original contracting party, Corporation. As in contracts for the carriage of goods by land, there would be no automatic vesting in the occupier or owners of the property for the time being who sustained the loss of any right of suit against McAlpine. On the contrary, McAlpine had specifically contracted that the rights of action under the building contract *could* not without McAlpine's consent be transferred to third parties who became owners or occupiers and might suffer loss. In such a case, it seems to me proper, as in the case of the carriage of goods by land, to treat the parties as having entered into the contract on the footing that Corporation would be entitled to enforce contractual rights for the benefit of those who suffered from defective performance but who, under the terms of the contract, could not acquire any right to hold McAlpine liable for breach. It is truly a case in which the rule provides 'a remedy where no other would be available to a person sustaining loss which under a rational legal system ought to be compensated by the person who has caused it.'

[Lords Keith of Kinkel, Bridge of Harwich and Ackner all accepted Lord Browne-Wilkinson's reasoning on this point. Lord Griffith agreed with the result but based his decision on somewhat broader grounds.]

Other non-assignable choses in action

(1) The benefit of the *performance* of a contract is only assignable in 'cases where it can make no difference to the person on whom the obligation lies to which of two persons he is to discharge it' (*Tolhurst v Associated Portland Cement Manufacturers (1900) Ltd* [1902] 2 KB 660 at 668, per Sir R Collins MR). Therefore, the benefit of the performance of a contract which involves personal skill or confidence cannot be assigned. For example, the right to employ a person under a contract of employment is not assignable (*Nokes v Doncaster Amalgamated Collieries Ltd* [1940] AC 1014); or if a seller of goods has personal confidence in his buyer's ability to keep his business going and pay the seller for goods sold on credit, the contractual right to the seller's performance cannot be assigned (*Cooper v Micklefield Coal and Lime Co Ltd* (1912) 107 LT 457). This restriction does not prevent the assignment of any benefit *arising under* the contract, eg wages or salary due to an employee are normally (subject to Note 2 below) assignable by him (*Shaw & Co v Moss Empires Ltd and Boston* (1908) 25 TLR 190). As Professor Goode has stated in (1979) 42 MLR 553 at 555: 'What is non-transferable is the duty to perform, not the fruits of performance'.

(2) An assignment may be void on grounds of public policy (other than

maintenance and champerty). For example, an assignment of the salary of a public officer, paid from central (not local) funds, is void on this ground (eg *Arbuthnot v Norton* (1846) 5 Moo PCC 219, where it was held that a judge could not assign his salary). See D W Logan (1945) 61 LQR 240 for the policy reasons against the assignment of the salary of public officers and Treitel, at p 601, for criticism of those reasons.

(3) An assignment may be prohibited by statute, eg social security benefit and child benefit is not assignable (Social Security Administration Act 1992, s 187).

(4) An assignment may be prohibited by contract. See the next case.

Helstan Securities Ltd v Hertfordshire County Council [1978] 3 All ER 262, Queen's Bench Division

(The facts appear from the judgment.)

Croom-Johnson J read the following judgment: This case asks what is the effect, where there is a purported assignment of a chose in action, of a condition in the contract which forbids assignment without consent?

The Hertfordshire County Council ('the county council') contracted with Renhold Road Surfacing Ltd ('Renholds') for road-works to be carried out. There were a number of these agreements. They were all in the form of the Institution of Civil Engineers Conditions of Contract (known as the ICE Conditions of Contract) (4th Edn). Renholds got into very severe financial difficulties. They are now as good as penniless. They said that they were owed, in one way or another, £46,437 by the county council under the contracts. They sold these debts to the plaintiffs. The plaintiffs gave notice of these assignments to the county council, who did not consent to the assignments. The plaintiffs as assignees of the debts have sued the county council claiming that sum of £46,437.

The county council say that they are under no obligation to pay, for two reasons. The first is that each contract contained a condition prohibiting the assignment of the debts. It read as follows: '(3) The contractor [that is to say Renholds] shall not assign the contract or any part thereof or any benefit or interest therein or thereunder without the written consent of the employer [that is to say the county council].' Condition 4 of the contract forbids subletting the whole of the works and deals with subcontracting parts of the works.

[The second reason concerned allegations of fraud during the execution of the works. His Lordship was not asked to decide this issue. He continued:]

Issue 1 incorporates an ambiguity. There are two points here. One, is the transaction valid as between assignor and assignee on the one hand, but void as between assignee and debtor on the other? Two, is it valid at all, even between the assignor and the assignee? Both points are taken in the defence. . . .

The way in which the plaintiffs put their case is this, that there is a distinction to be drawn between debts and other choses in action, and they say the decided cases lean towards that distinction. On the basis that there is such a distinction, the plaintiffs go on to say that condition 3 prohibits the assignment of the contract and certain choses in action arising from it, but on its construction does not prohibit the assignment of debts. Is there any such general distinction? In my view, No. A debt is but one instance of a chose in action, though it may be a common one. Do the authorities support such an argument?

[His Lordship reviewed all the cases which had considered (obiter) the legal effect of such a prohibition and continued:]

The plaintiffs submit that there is here a good assignment of the debts, notwithstanding the prohibition in condition 3, even if it purports to bar the assignment of debts. They cite

Williams v Earle ((1868) LR 3 QB 739) which deals with a covenant by a lessee not to assign the lease. There was an assignment in breach of that covenant, which Blackburn J held to be a good assignment so as to entitle the lessor to sue the 'assignee' on other covenants. The plaintiffs say that by parity of reasoning the same should apply here, and that the assignment of these debts to them should be held a good assignment. But the law concerning covenants running with the land is not something which is readily adaptable to choses in action.

If the reported cases are not a sure guide, one is thrown back in this case on the agreement. There are certain kinds of choses in action which, for one reason or another, are not assignable and there is no reason why the parties to an agreement may not contract to give its subject-matter the quality of unassignability. In these circumstances, one has to look at the clause itself. The words 'benefit or interest therein or thereunder' do cover the debts which result from the performance of the contract. I cannot draw the distinction which the plaintiffs' counsel asked me to draw, namely that there is a difference between a right to payment on an engineer's certificate and the resulting debts. If there is such a difference, both are caught by this clause. It is the contract which creates the entitlement to be paid, and that is a benefit or interest under the contract.

I find no ambiguity such as would lead me to consider the background against which the contract was made as an aid to interpretation. If I did, the background would not help the plaintiffs. The clause is obviously there to let the employer retain control of who does the work. Condition 4, which deals with subletting, has the same object. But closely associated with the right to control who does the work, is the right at the end of the day to balance claims for money due on the one hand against counterclaims, for example, for bad workmanship on the other. The plaintiffs say that such a counterclaim may be made against the assignees instead of against the assignors. But the debtors may only use it as a shield by way of set-off and cannot enforce it against the assignees if it is greater than the amount of the debt: *Young v Kitchin* ((1878) 3 Ex D 127). And why should they have to make it against people whom they may not want to make it against, in circumstances not of their choosing, when they have contracted that they shall not?

Although arguments showing potential hardship cannot prevail over the construction of the clause, I should mention two which have been advanced. It is said by the plaintiffs that if the assignment is void, the debtor can take the benefit of the work done by the assignor and avoid paying the assignee. The defendants reply that the assignee must make proper enquiries before he buys a debt, and these enquiries may go to the likelihood of the debtor having the money with which to pay, or the prospect of a counterclaim which would extinguish the debt, or the existence of a prohibitory condition such as the present. On all these things depends the price he is prepared to pay. There is no injustice in expecting the purchasers of debts to make these enquiries.

My decision on issue 1 is that condition 3 does in this case make the assignment invalid, and in those circumstances the defendants are entitled to judgment against the plaintiffs and this action fails.

NOTES

1. Commenting on *Helstan Securities Ltd v Hertfordshire County Council* in (1979) 42 MLR 553, Professor Goode states (p 553, pp 554–555):

> . . . in so far as the case decided that the assignment was ineffective as between the plaintiffs and the defendant it is unexceptional. . . . But the defendants in that case went further and asserted that the effect of the prohibition against assignment was to render the purported assignment ineffective even as between assignor and assignee; and though such a contention was not necessary for their success, the learned judge appeared to have considered it well founded and to have treated the assignment as totally void. If this is indeed the purport of his judgment, it is open to serious objection both as a matter of law and on grounds of policy.

Why? See pp 555–557 of Professor Goode's note (above).

Professor Goode's conclusions on the affect of non-assignment clauses have recently been approved by the House of Lords in *Linden Gardens Trust Ltd v Lenesta Sludge Disposals Ltd* and *St Martin's Property Corpn Ltd v Sir Robert McAlpine & Sons Ltd* [1994] 1 AC 85 at 104. As Lord Browne-Wilkinson said (at 108):

> . . . a prohibition on assignment normally only invalidates the assignment as against the other party to the contract so as to prevent a transfer of the chose in action: in the absence of the clearest words it cannot operate to invalidate the contract as between the assignor and the assignee and even then it may be ineffective on the grounds of public policy.

2. There are good arguments for and against the effectiveness of non-assignment clauses (they are set out by B Allcock [1983] CLJ 328 at pp 344–345). But note that the United States has come out firmly in favour of the free assignability of debts. Article 9-318(4) of the Uniform Commercial Code states that: 'A term in any contract between an account debtor and an assignor is ineffective if it prohibits assignment of an account or prohibits creation of a security interest in a general intangible for money due or to become due or requires the account debtor's consent to such assignment or security interest'. See also art 6(1) of the UNIDROIT Convention on International Factoring 1988 which provides that the assignment of receivables by the supplier to the factor is to be effective notwithstanding any agreement between the supplier and the debtor prohibiting such assignment.

3. The effectiveness of a non-assignment clause depends on its construction. In *Helstan Securities Ltd v Hertfordshire County Council* the clause in question was construed liberally so as to include within it a prohibition on the assignment of debts. In *Linden Gardens Trust Ltd v Lenesta Sludge Disposals Ltd* and *St Martin's Property Corpn Ltd v Sir Robert McAlpine & Sons Ltd* [1994] AC 85, the House of Lords has recently adopted a similarly liberal approach to the construction of non-assignment clauses. In that case their Lordships held that a clause in a building contract which prohibited the employer or the contractor assigning 'this contract' without the other's consent, prevented the assignment of a claim for damages for breach of contract. A majority of the Court of Appeal ((1992) 57 BLR 57) had held that the prohibition only extended to assigning the benefit of performance of the contract and not to an assignment of the benefits arising under the contract, ie a claim for damages under the contract. Although the House of Lords accepted that it was hypothetically possible to draft a non-assignment clause in such a way as to achieve this result, their Lordships held that the clause in question did not do this. As Lord Browne-Wilkinson said (at 105–106):

> The question is to what extent does clause 17 on its true construction restrict rights of assignment which would otherwise exist? In the context of a complicated building contract, I find it impossible to construe clause 17 as prohibiting only the assignment of rights to future performance, leaving each party free to assign the fruits of the contract. The reason for including the contractual prohibition viewed from the contractor's point of view must be that the contractor wishes to ensure that he deals, and deals only, with the particular employer with whom he has chosen to enter into a contract. Building contracts are pregnant with disputes: some employers are much more reasonable than others in dealing with such disputes. The disputes frequently arise in the context of the contractor suing for the price and being met by a claim for abatement of the price or cross-claims founded on an allegation that the performance of the contract has been defective. Say that, before the final instalment of the price has been paid, the employer has assigned the benefits under the contract to a third party, there being at the time existing rights of action for defective work. On the Court of Appeal's view, those rights of action would have

vested in the assignee. Would the original employer be entitled to an abatement of the price, even though the cross-claims would be vested in the assignee? If so, would the assignee be a necessary party to any settlement or litigation of the claims for defective work, thereby requiring the contractor to deal with two parties (one not of his choice) in order to recover the price for the works from the employer? I cannot believe that the parties ever intended to permit such a confused position to arise.

Again, say that before completion of the works the employers assigned the land, together with the existing causes of action against the contractor, to a third party and shortly thereafter the contractor committed a repudiatory breach? On the construction preferred by the Court of Appeal, the right to insist on further performance, being unassignable, would have remained with the original employers whereas the other causes of action and the land would belong to the assignee. Who could decide whether to accept the repudiation, the assignor or the assignee?

These possibilities of confusion (and many others which could be postulated) persuade me that parties who have specifically contracted to prohibit the assignment of the contract cannot have intended to draw a distinction between the right to peformance of the contract and the right to the fruits of the contract. In my view they cannot have contemplated a position in which the right to future performance and the right to benefits accrued under the contract should become vested in two separate people. I say again that that result could have been achieved by careful and intricate drafting, spelling out the parties' intentions if they had them. But in the absence of such a clearly expressed intention, it would be wrong to attribute such a perverse intention to the parties. In my judgment, clause 17 clearly prohibits the assignment of any benefit of or under the contract.

The liberal approach to construction evidenced in *Helstan Securities* and *Linden Gardens* can be contrasted with the restrictive approach to construction of non-assignment clauses adopted by the courts in the United States (B Allcock, above, pp 340–341).

(b) Assignee takes subject to equities

Business Computers Ltd v Anglo-African Leasing Ltd [1977] 1 WLR 578, Chancery Division

The plaintiffs sold two computers to the defendants under two separate transactions. At 29 May 1974, £10,587.50 remained owing by the defendants to the plaintiffs under these transactions. By a third transaction, the plaintiffs sold another computer to the defendants and then leased it back from them under a hire purchase agreement. Under the terms of the hire purchase agreement, the plaintiffs were to pay the defendants monthly instalments payable on the 18th of each month. The 13th instalment due on the 18 May was not paid, nor were any subsequent instalments. On 13 June 1974, debenture holders appointed a receiver over the plaintiffs under the terms of a floating charge. This crystallised the charge which had the effect of assigning the sums owed by the defendants to the debenture holders. Notice of the assignment was given to the defendants on 17 June. The receiver claimed the debt of £10,587.50 from the defendants who tried to set off against it (1) the 13th instalment due on 18 May (which the receiver conceded) and (2) damages of £30,000 under the terms of the hire purchase agreement which the receiver had repudiated on 31 July and which repudiation was accepted by the defendants on 8 August.

Templeman J: . . . Set off has been allowed against an assignee in a variety of circumstances. In *Biggerstaff v Rowatt's Wharf Ltd* [1896] 2 Ch 93 a debtor who became entitled to a liquidated claim against a company before a floating charge crystallised was allowed to set off the liquidated claim against the debt after the debenture crystallised. This decision does not assist the defendants because in the present case no claim liquidated or otherwise for £30,000 arose on or before June 17 when the defendants received notice that the debentures had crystallised.

In *Christie v Taunton, Delmard, Lane and Co* [1893] 2 Ch 175 a debtor was allowed to set off against an assignee a debt from the assignor which accrued due before the date of the assignment but was not payable until after the assignment. In the present case the defendants on June 17, 1974, when they received notice of the assignment completed by the appointment of the receiver did not possess a claim for £30,000 payable then or on any subsequent date. That claim only arose in August 1974.

In *Government of Newfoundland v Newfoundland Rly Co* (1888) 13 App Cas 199 a debtor sued by an assignee for a sum payable pursuant to a contract between the debtor and the assignor was allowed to set off a claim for unliquidated damages made by the debtor against the assignor for breach of the same contract by the assignor. This case also does not assist the defendants because the debt owed by the defendants for £10,587.50 arose under different and separate contracts from the hire purchase agreement under which the defendants' claim for £30,000 has now arisen.

In *Watson v Mid Wales Rly Co* (1867) LR 2 CP 593 a debtor sued on a bond by the assignee of the bond was not allowed to set off arrears of rent which accrued due from the assignor to the debtor after the assignment under a lease made before notice of the assignment. Bovill CJ said, at p 598:

> No case has been cited to us where equity has allowed against the assignee of an equitable chose in action a set off of a debt arising between the original parties subsequently to the notice of assignment, out of matters not connected with the debt claimed, nor in any way referring to it. . . . In all the cases cited . . . some qualification occurred in the original contract, or the two transactions were in some way connected together, so as to lead the court to the conclusion that they were made with reference to one another.

In the present case, the claim of the defendants under the hire purchase agreement for £30,000 arose subsequently to notice of the assignment of the debt of £10,587.50 and the transactions out of which the claim and the debt arose respectively were separate and not connected in any way. Set off is therefore not available by the defendants against the assignees, the debenture holders.

In *Re Pinto Leite and Nephews, ex p Visconde des Olivaes* [1929] 1 Ch 221 a debtor owed £100,000 payable in January 1932 and the original creditor, after assigning the debt on March 2, 1926, became liable to the debtor for £15,000 as a result of a contract entered into between the debtor and the creditor prior to the assignment. There was no connection between the debt of £100,000 and the contract under which the £15,000 became owing. The debtor was not allowed to set off the £15,000 liability against the debt of £100,000 claimed by the assignee. Clauson J said, at p 233:

> It is, of course, well settled that the assignee of a chose in action . . . takes subject to all rights of set off which were available against the assignor, subject only to the exception that, after notice of an equitable assignment of a chose in action, a debtor cannot set off against the assignee a debt which accrues due subsequently to the date of notice, even though that debt may arise out of a liability which existed at or before the date of the notice; but the debtor may set off as against the assignee a debt which accrues due before notice of the assignment, although it is not payable until after that date:

and, at p 236:

> when the debt assigned is at the date of notice of the assignment payable in future, the debtor can set off against the assignee a debt which becomes payable by the assignor to the debtor after notice of assignment, but before the assigned debt becomes payable, if, but only if, the debt so to be set off was debitum in praesenti at the date of notice of assignment.

In the present case the £30,000 claim did not accrue due until after the date of notice of the assignment and cannot therefore be set off.

I was referred to *Bankes v Jarvis* [1903] 1 KB 549, but that case only decided that a debtor could set off against a trustee for the creditor all claims which at the date of the action could have founded a set off against the creditor beneficiary. See also *Hanak v Green* [1958] 2 QB 9, 24 where the decision in *Bankes v Jarvis* was supported on the ground that 'There was a close relationship between the dealings and transactions which gave rise to the respective claims.' No such close relationship was put forward in the present case.

I was referred to *N W Robbie & Co Ltd v Witney Warehouse Co Ltd* [1963] 1 WLR 1324, but that case only decided that a debtor cannot after notice of an assignment of his debt by his creditor improve his position as regards set off by acquiring debts incurred by the assignor creditor to a third party. I have already referred to *George Barker (Transport) Ltd v Eynon* [1974] 1 WLR 462, but that case only decided that if a receiver after his appointment took the benefit of a contract entered into before his appointment, he could not dispute a lien conferred by that contract but not exercised until after the appointment. The defendants in the present case cannot invoke this principle. The contracts under which the debt of £10,587.50 became payable were completed before the receiver was appointed, apart from the payment now sought against the defendants. I was also referred to *Rother Iron Works Ltd v Canterbury Precision Engineers Ltd* [1974] QB 1. In that case, pursuant to a contract made before the appointment of a receiver, a debtor delivered goods to the company and the goods were accepted by the receiver. The debtor was allowed to set off the price of the goods against his debt to the company because the receiver could not take the benefit of the contract without the burden. He was not entitled to the debt and to the goods and to keep the purchase price. A similar point does not arise in the present case.

The result of the relevant authorities is that a debt which accrues due before notice of an assignment is received, whether or not it is payable before that date, or a debt which arises out of the same contract as that which gives rise to the assigned debt, or is closely connected with that contract, may be set off against the assignee. But a debt which is neither accrued nor connected may not be set off even though it arises from a contract made before the assignment. In the present case the claim for £30,000 did not accrue before June 17, 1974, when the defendants received notice of the appointment of the receiver and thus notice of the completed assignment of the debt of £10,587.50 to the debenture holders and there was no relevant connection between the transactions which gave rise to the claim and to the debt respectively.

NOTES

1. The assignee takes 'subject to equities' having priority over his right, whether or not he knew of their existence when he took his assignment (*Athenaeum Life Assurance Society v Pooley* (1858) 3 De G & J 294).

2. Certain 'equities' can be set up by the debtor against the assignee whether they arise before or after the debtor receives notice of the assignment. Defences which the debtor could have raised against the assignor, and cross-claims arising out of, or closely connected with, the transaction which gave rise to the chose being assigned, are 'equities' of this type. Defences include any claim that the original transaction giving rise to the chose has been vitiated by illegality, mistake, fraud, or other misrepresentation (*Graham v Johnson* (1869) LR 8 Eq 36). Such cross-claims may be liquidated or unliquidated (*Government of Newfoundland v Newfoundland Rly Co* (1888) 13 App Cas 199). However, it appears that at least one category of tort claim is not to be regarded as closely connected with the transaction giving rise to the chose assigned. In *Stoddart v Union Trust Ltd* [1912] 1 KB 181, the Court of Appeal held that the debtor's claim to damages for deceit, which induced the contract giving rise to the chose assigned, could not be set off against the assignee (criticised by A Tettenborn [1987] Conv 385 and F Oditah *Legal Aspects of Receivables Financing* (1991) ('Oditah'), pp 234–235).

3. Liquidated cross-claims arising out of some other transaction which is independent of that which gave rise to the chose being assigned may be set off by the debtor against the assignee only if they accrue before notice of assignment is given to the debtor (compare *Roxburghe v Cox* (1881) 17 Ch D 520, where set-off was allowed, with *Watson v Mid-Wales Rly Co* (1867) LR 2 CP 593, where set-off was denied). Unless there is contrary agreement between the assignor and the debtor, unliquidated cross-claims cannot be set off if they are not inseparably connected with the contract giving rise to the chose assigned (*Aboussafy v Abacus Cities Ltd* [1981] 4 WWR 660).

4. A debtor can never recover from the assignee if his cross-claim exceeds the assigned debt. He must claim against the assignor (*Young v Kitchin* (1878) 3 Ex D 127). Furthermore, a debtor cannot recover back his payment made to the assignee on the ground that the payment was made for a consideration that had totally failed (*Pan Ocean Shipping Ltd v Creditcorp Ltd, The Trident Beauty* [1994] 1 All ER 470, HL).

5. If the assigned debt is created by contract, the contract may provide, by an express or implied term, that the assignee takes free of equities (*Re Blakely Ordnance Co* (1867) 3 Ch App 154 at 159–160). If the debt is embodied in a negotiable instrument, a person who purchases the instrument in good faith, before its maturity, and without notice of any defect in the title of the holder or of previous dishonour, will take it free from equities (Bills of Exchange Act 1882, ss 29(1) and 38(2)). Furthermore, the assignee is only liable to equities available against the original assignor, not to those available against an intermediate assignee (*Re Milan Tramways Co* (1884) 25 Ch D 587 at 593, CA; cf Treitel at p 594; S R Derham *Set-Off* (1987) ('Derham'), at p 253).

6. Further reading: Derham, Ch 12; Oditah, Ch 8; and R Derham (1991) 107 LQR 126. For reference: P R Wood *English and International Set-Off* (1989), Ch 16.

QUESTIONS

1. Under separate contracts Owen owed Piper, a builder and decorator, sums of £1000 for painting and decorating his house and £400 for installing a boiler. Piper assigned the £1000 in writing to Rigby for value. Piper also wrote to Owen telling him to pay the £400 to Slate (to whom Piper was indebted), and then told Slate by telephone of his instruction to Owen. Soon afterwards, owing to its defective installation, the boiler burst, causing £500 worth of damage to Owen's house. Piper has since been adjudged bankrupt. Advise Tyler (Piper's trustee in bankruptcy), Owen, Rigby and Slate as to the legal position.

2. Adam owes money to Bill (debt 1) and also to Cathy (debt 2). Dave owes money to Adam (debt 3). Adam assigns Dave's debt (debt 3) in writing to Eric for value. Before he has notice of the assignment of debt 3 to Eric, Dave takes an assignment of Adam's debt to Bill (debt 1). After he has notice of the assignment of debt 3 to Eric, Dave takes an assignment of Adam's debt to Cathy (debt 2). If Eric sues Dave for debt 3, can he set off debt 1 and/or debt 2 against the claim? See *Bennett v White* [1910] 2 KB 643, CA; *N W Robbie & Co Ltd v Witney Warehouse Co Ltd* [1963] 1 WLR 1324, CA.

(c) Priorities – the rule in *Dearle v Hall*

Dearle v Hall (1823) 3 Russ 1, Court of Chancery

Brown, a beneficiary, assigned his interest by way of security first to Dearle and then to Sherring. The trustees were not given notice of the assignments. Some years later Brown assigned his interest to Hall. Before purchasing the interest, Hall made enquiries of the trustees and they indicated that the interest was unencumbered. Hall gave the trustees notice of his assignment. Subsequently, Dearle and Sherring gave the trustees notice of their assignments.

Sir Thomas Plumer MR: . . . The ground of this claim is priority of title. They [Dearle and Sherring] rely upon the known maxim, borrowed from the civil law, which in many cases regulates equities – '*qui prior est in tempore, potior est in jure.*' If, by the first contract, all the thing is given, there remains nothing to be the subject of the second contract, and priority must decide. But it cannot be contended that priority in time must decide, where the legal estate is outstanding. For the maxim, as an equitable rule, admits of exception, and gives way, when the question does not lie between bare and equal equities. If there appears to be, in respect of any circumstance independent of priority of time, a better title in the *puisne* purchaser to call for the legal estate, than in the purchaser who precedes him in date, the case ceases to be a balance of equal equities, and the preference, which priority of date might otherwise have given, is done away with and counteracted. The question here is, – not which assignment is first in date, – but whether there is not, on the part of Hall, a better title to call for the legal estate than Dearle or Sherring can set up? or rather, the question is, Shall these Plaintiffs now have equitable relief to the injury of Hall?

What title have they shown to call on a court of justice to interpose on their behalf, in order to obviate the consequences of their own misconduct? All that has happened is owing to their negligence (a negligence not accounted for) in forbearing to do what they ought to have done, what would have been attended with no difficulty, and what would have effectually prevented all the mischief which has followed. Is a Plaintiff to be heard in a court of equity, who asks its interposition on his behoof, to indemnify him against the effects of his own negligence at the expense of another who has used all due diligence, and who, if he is to suffer loss, will suffer it by reason of the negligence of the very person who prays relief against him? The question here is not, as in *Evans v Bicknell*, whether a court of equity is to deprive the Plaintiffs of any right – whether it is to take from them, for instance, a legal estate, or to impose any charge upon them. It is simply, whether they are entitled to relief against their own negligence. They did not perfect their securities; a third party has innocently advanced his money, and has perfected his security as far as the nature of the subject permitted him: is this Court to interfere to postpone him to them?

They say, that they were not bound to give notice to the trustees; for that notice does not form part of the necessary conveyance of an equitable interest. I admit, that, if you mean to rely on contract with the individual, you do not need to give notice; from the moment of the contract, he, with whom you are dealing, is personally bound. But if you mean to go further, and to make your right attach upon the thing which is the subject of the contract, it is necessary to give notice; and, unless notice is given, you do not do that which is essential in all cases of transfer of personal property. The law of *England* has always been, that personal property passes by delivery of possession; and it is possession which determines the apparent ownership. If, therefore, an individual, who in the way of purchase or mortgage contracts with another for the transfer of his interest, does not divest the vendor or mortgagor of possession, but permits him to remain the ostensible owner as before, he must take the consequences which may ensue from such a mode of dealing. That doctrine was explained in *Ryall v Rowles* ((1750) 1 Ves Sen 348, 1 Atk 165), before Lord Hardwicke and three of the Judges. If you, having the right of possession, do not exercise that right, but leave another in actual possession, you enable that person to gain a false and delusive credit, and put it in his power to obtain money from innocent parties on the hypothesis of his being the owner of that which in fact belongs to you. The principle has been long recognised, even in courts of law. In *Twyne's* case ((1602) 3 Co Rep 80), one of the badges of fraud was, that the possession had remained in the vendor. Possession must follow right; and if you, who have the right, do not take posession, you do not follow up the title, and are responsible for the consequences.

'When a man,' says Lord Bacon (*Maxims of the Law*, max 16), 'is author and mover to another to commit an unlawful act, then he shall not excuse himself by circumstances not pursued.'

It is true that a chose in action does not admit of tangible actual possession, and that neither Zachariah Brown nor any person claiming under him were entitled to possess themselves of the fund which yielded the £93 a year. But in *Ryall v Rowles* the Judges held, that, in the case of a chose in action, you must do every thing towards having possession which the subject admits; you must do that which is tantamount to obtaining possession, by placing every person, who has an equitable or legal interest in the matter, under an obligation to treat it as your property. For this purpose, you must give notice to the legal holder of the fund; in the case of a debt, for instance, notice to the debtor is, for many purposes, tantamount to possession. If you omit to give that notice, you are guilty of the same degree and species of neglect as he who leaves a personal chattel, to which he has acquired a title, in the actual possession, and under the absolute control, of another person.

Is there the least doubt, that, if Zacharian Brown had been a trader, all that was done by Dearle and Sherring would not have been in the least effectual against his assignees; but that, according to the doctrine of *Ryall and Rowles*, his assignees would have taken the fund, because there was no notice to those in whom the legal interest was vested? In that case it was the opinion of all the Judges, that he who contracts for a chose in action, and does not follow up his title by notice, gives personal credit to the individual with whom he deals. Notice, then, is necessary to perfect the title, – to give a complete right *in rem*, and not merely a right as against him who conveys his interest. If you are willing to trust the personal credit of the man, and are satisfied that he will make no improper use of the possession in which you allow him to remain, notice is not necessary; for against him the title is perfect without notice. But if he, availing himself of the possession as a means of obtaining credit, induces third persons to purchase from him as the actual owner, and they part with their money before your pocket-conveyance is notified to them, you must be postponed. In being postponed, your security is not invalidated: you had priority, but that priority has not been followed up; and you have permitted another to acquire a better title to the legal possession. What was done by Dearle and Sherring did not exhaust the thing (to borrow the principle of the civil law) but left it still open to traffic. These are the principles on which I think it to be very old law, that possession, or what is tantamount to possession, is the criterion of perfect title to personal chattels, and that he, who does not obtain such possession, must take his chance.

I do not go through the cases which constitute exceptions to the rule, that priority in time shall prevail. A man may lose that priority by actual fraud or constructive fraud; by being silent, for instance, when he ought to speak; by standing by, and keeping his own security concealed. By such conduct, even the advantage of possessing the legal estate may be lost. . . .

On these grounds, I think that the plaintiffs have not shewn a title to call on a court of equity to interpose in their behalf, and to take the fund from an individual who has used due diligence, in order to give it to those whose negligence has occasioned all the mischief. There is no equality of equities between the defendant Hall, and the plaintiffs. . . .

The bill, therefore, must be dismissed, but, as against Hall, without costs. I do not make the plaintiffs pay costs to Hall, because they may have been losers without any intention to commit a fraud, and I am unwilling to add to their loss. Constructive fraud is the utmost that can be imputed to them.

[On appeal, Lord Lyndhurst LC affirmed the Master of the Rolls' judgment.]

NOTES

1. Sir Thomas Plumer MR sought to justify his decision on two grounds: the conduct of the competing assignees and the need for notice to perfect an equitable assignment. Today, neither ground can be used to justify the rule in *Dearle v Hall*. In *Foster v Cockerell* (1835) 3 Cl & Fin 456 the House of Lords disregarded the conduct of the competing assignees and gave priority to the assignee who was the first to give notice to the trustees. In *Ward and Pemberton v Duncombe* [1893] AC 369 at 392, Lord Macnaghten stressed that notice was not needed to perfect the title of an equitable assignee. As Lord Macnaghten said in that case (p 391): 'I am not sure that the doctrine rests upon any very satisfactory principle.'

2. In the light of subsequent cases, the rule in *Dearle v Hall* can be said to give priority to the assignee who is the first to give notice to the debtor or trustees, with the proviso that the subsequent assignee does not have actual or constructive notice of the earlier assignment at the time when he takes his assignment (*Re Holmes* (1885) 29 Ch D 786). The rule has been described as a 'mechanical rule of thumb' (G McCormack [1990] JBL 314 at p 320). By ignoring the reasons for failure to give notice, it can cause considerable injustice (as in *Re Dallas* [1904] 2 Ch 385). Furthermore, it is an arbitrary rule in that it can be relied on by an assignee who has given value but not by a volunteer (Bell, at p 531; cf Snell, pp 65–66). See also, F Oditah (1989) 9 OJLS 521 at pp 525–527 for further criticism of the rule.

3. By s 137(3) of the Law of Property Act 1925, notice of the assignment of an 'equitable interest' must be in writing to preserve priority (see above, p 719).

Compaq Computer Ltd v Abercorn Group Ltd [1991] BCC 484, Chancery Division

Compaq, a manufacturer of computers and computer products, appointed Abercorn as an authorised dealer and supplied it with computer products on standard terms which reserved title in the products to Compaq until payment of the price. It was further provided that Abercorn would hold the goods as 'bailee and agent' for Compaq and would strictly account to Compaq for the full proceeds thereof received from third parties and keep a separate account of all such proceeds or monies. Abercorn then entered into a written invoice discounting agreement with Kellock, pursuant to which it assigned to Kellock nearly £400,000 owed by customers under sub-sales of Compaq products. Notice in writing of each of these assignments was given by Kellock to the relevant debtor. On Abercorn's subsequent receivership, a dispute arose between Compaq and Kellock as to which of them was entitled to be paid the proceeds of the sub-sales.

Mummery J held that on its true construction the terms of the agreement between Compaq and Abercorn operated by way of a charge over the proceeds of the sub-sales and that charge was void for non-registration under Part XII of the Companies Act 1985 (see above, p 423). On that ground alone, Kellock were entitled to the proceeds of the sub-sales. However, on the assumption that he was wrong on that issue, his Lordship then considered whether Kellock's rights as assignee took priority over Compaq's equitable interest in the proceeds of the sub-sales.

Mummery J: I deal first with the arguments on the rule in *Dearle v Hall*. It was accepted by Compaq that if the rule did apply, Kellock would enjoy priority. Two arguments were advanced on behalf of Compaq as to why the rule in *Dearle v Hall* did not apply.

The first argument was that the rule did not apply because the subject-matter in question consisted of legal choses in action, ie debts owing to Abercorn by subpurchasers of Compaq products. It was contended that the rule is confined to equitable choses in action and to other equitable interests including, after 1926, equitable interests in land – see s 137(1) of the Law of Property Act 1925. . . .

In brief, Compaq's submission was that it is the equitable nature of the property dealt with and not the equitable nature of the dealing with it – for example, by way of assignment – which attracts the rule.

It is, however, established on the authorities that the rule in *Dearle v Hall* applies to equitable assignments of legal choses in action. In *Pfeiffer* [*E Pfeiffer Weinkellerei-Weineinkauf GmbH & Co v Arbuthnot Factors Ltd* [1988] 1 WLR 150] at p 163 Phillips J said:

> The rule in *Dearle v Hall* is an exception to the general principle that equitable interests take priority in the order in which they are created. The rule applies to dealings with equitable interests in any property and, in particular, to equitable assignments of legal choses in action. Under the rule, priority depends upon the order in which notice of the interest created by the dealing is given to the person affected by it, ie, in the case of assignments of a debt, the debtor.

He went on to note that counsel conceded that if the rights asserted by the plaintiff were rights conferred by equitable assignment, the rule in *Dearle v Hall* must apply. The judge applied the rule because he held that such security rights as were conferred upon the plaintiff by the agreement were conferred by equitable assignment.

That passage in the judgment of Phillips J was criticised in argument before me. It was submitted that counsel had wrongly made a concession. I disagree. In my judgment, the view of Phillips J and the concession made by counsel receives full support from earlier authorities, including *Dearle v Hall* itself at p 58; 495.

[His Lordship then referred to the following cases, namely: *Gorringe v Irwell India Rubber & Gutta Percha Works* (1886) 34 Ch D 128 at 132, per Cotton LJ (see above, p 716) and, at 135, per Bowen J; *Ward and Pemberton v Duncombe* [1893] AC 369 at 383ff, per Lord Macnaghten; *Marchant v Morton, Down & Co* [1901] 2 KB 829 at 831, per Channell J; and *B S Lyle Ltd v Rosher* [1959] 1 WLR 8 at 16, per Lord Morton and, at 14, per Viscount Kilmuir LC.]

Those formulations of the rule both appear to accept its applicability to an equitable assignment of a legal chose in action, such as a debt. I therefore reject the submission that the rule in *Dearle v Hall* cannot apply to this case because the relevant dealings were with debts.

The second argument advanced on behalf of Compaq against the application of the rule in *Dearle v Hall* was that the rule only applies in the case of successive assignments of equitable interests already created and not to the case of the creation of a new equitable interest – for example, by way of a declaration of trust. For this proposition reliance was placed on *Hill v Peters* [1918] 2 Ch 273 at p 279, where Eve J referred to the observations of Lord Macnaghten [in *Ward and Pemberton v Duncombe* [1893] AC 369 at 383] as to the undesirability of doing anything to extend the doctrine of *Dearle v Hall* to cases which were not already covered by it, and stated:

> The principle on which the rule in *Dearle v Hall* is founded, which regards the giving of notice by the assignee as the nearest approach to the taking of possession, has no application, in my opinion, to the beneficiary who has no right to possession himself, and who can only assert his claim to receive through his trustee.

In *Lyle v Rosher* there was argument about the correctness of the opinion expressed by Eve J on the distinction between a declaration of trust and an equitable assignment. No opinion on that question was expressed by four members of the House of Lords. Lord Reid, however, discussed the point and expressed the view at p 22 that, to apply the rule in *Dearle v Hall* to defeat the rights of a cestui que trust would introduce an exception to the general law.

– and he concluded at p 23:

> I think that it would be an innovation in the law of England to require a cestui que trust for his own protection to give notice of the trust in his favour to the person who holds the fund.

On the basis of those observations it was submitted on behalf of Compaq that the rule in *Dearle v Hall* did not apply because, as already submitted in argument on the charge point, Abercorn never became beneficially entitled to the proceeds of sale of Compaq products; by virtue of Abercorn's fiduciary obligations, the beneficial interest in those proceeds vested automatically in Compaq. There was, therefore, no assignment by Abercorn, by way of charge or otherwise, of the proceeds of sale. They were the subject of a trust in favour of Compaq which determined when the price of the Compaq products and other sums owing were paid. There was no equitable assignment of a chose in action to compete with the assignment made by Abercorn in favour of Kellock and, if there was only one assignment, there was no room for the application of *Dearle v Hall*.

In my judgment, assuming that there is a distinction between the creation of a trust and an equitable assignment, Compaq's argument fails on the construction of the terms and conditions of the dealer agreement. No bare trust of the proceeds of sale was created in favour of Compaq. An equitable assignment may be effected by an agreement between a debtor and a creditor that the debt owing shall be paid out of a specific fund coming to the debtor – see the speech of Lord Wilberforce in *Swiss Bank Corpn v Lloyds Bank Ltd* [1982] AC 584 at p 613A–E.

In my view, there was such an agreement in this case. In cl 8.3 and cl 8.3.2 Abercorn and Compaq in substance agreed that the debts owing by Abercorn to Compaq would be paid out of a specific fund coming to Abercorn, namely the proceeds of the subsales of Compaq products to Abercorn's customers. That was an equitable assignment of the proceeds of sale. I have held on the charge point that that assignment was by way of charge, registrable and void for want of registration. If I am wrong on that point and the assignment was not by way of charge, it was nevertheless an equitable assignment to which the rule in *Dearle v Hall* can apply when determining whether or not it enjoys priority over another equitable assignment of the same debt or fund. . . . Kellock had by virtue of the discounting agreement and assignments made pursuant to it priority over Compaq in respect of the proceeds of sale of the Compaq products supplied on the terms and conditions of the dealer agreement.

I should, however, briefly deal with the other argument advanced by Kellock: that it was a purchaser for value of the legal title to the debts without notice of any prior equitable interest of Compaq and therefore took free of any such interest. Paragraph (3) of the schedule requires me to assume that Kellock did not have notice or knowledge of Compaq's terms and conditions. . . .

Kellock's submission was that it was a bona fide purchaser for value of the debts without notice of Compaq's interest at the time of the purchase and that it therefore enjoyed priority over any interest that Compaq might have by way of retention of title, charge or equitable interest. Reliance was placed on *Pilcher v Rawlins* (1872) 7 Ch App 259 at pp 268–269 where James LJ said:

> . . . according to my view of the established law of this Court, such a purchaser's plea of a purchase for valuable consideration without notice is an absolute, unqualified, unanswerable defence, and an unanswerable plea to the jurisdiction of this Court.

Taylor v Blakelock (1886) 32 Ch D 560 was also cited along with *Thorndike v Hunt* (1859) 3 De GF & J 563, 44 ER 1386 to demonstrate the strength of the position of a purchaser for value in contrast to the position of a volunteer.

The paramount plea of the bona fide purchaser for value without notice of an equitable interest in a debt or other legal thing in action has to be considered, however, in the context of s 136(1) of the Law of Property Act 1925 which provides: . . . [see above, p 699]. . . .

The effect of that section was considered by Phillips J in *Pfeiffer* at p 162. He accepted the submission that the effect of s 136(1) and of the earlier section which it replaced (s 25(6) of the Supreme Court of Judicature Act 1873) was that it enabled the assignee to acquire a title which has all the procedural advantages of legal title, but so far as priorities are concerned his position is no better than if the assignment had been effected prior to those Acts. Phillips J said at p 162:

> It follows that, even if the assignment is effected for value without notice of a prior equity, priorities fall to be determined as if the assignment had been effected in equity, not in law.

That view was challenged but the judge held that it was supported by the views expressed by Channell J on s 25(6) of the 1873 Act in *Marchant v Morton, Down & Co* at p 832. No distinction was drawn in that case or in *Pfeiffer* between an assignment for value and a voluntary assignment.

It was submitted on behalf of Kellock that the conclusion of Phillips J on this point was wrong, particularly in not recognising a distinction between an assignee for value and a volunteer. I was referred to *Read v Brown* (1888) 22 QBD 128, a case not cited in *Pfeiffer*, for the proposition that s 25(6) of the 1873 Act gave to the assignee of a debt more than the mere right to sue for it. Lord Esher MR said at 131:

> . . . it gives him the debt and the legal right to the debt . . .

He rejected the contention that the provision only affected procedure and confirmed that the words meant what they said, ie they transferred the legal right to the debt as well as the legal remedies for its recovery. He said at p 132:

> The debt is transferred to the assignee and becomes as though it has been his from the beginning; it is no longer to be the debt of the assignor at all, who cannot sue for it, the right to sue being taken from him; the assignee becomes the assignee of a legal debt and is not merely an assignee in equity, and the debt being his, he can sue for it, and sue in his own name.

It was submitted that if this is correct, the matter of priorities is not as stated by Phillips J in *Pfeiffer*. I was referred to obiter comments of Robert Goff J in *Ellerman Lines Ltd v Lancaster Maritime Co Ltd* [1980] 2 Lloyd's Rep 497 at p 503 that:

> . . . a legal assignment . . . ranks before any equitable interest, even a prior equitable interest, unless the assignee had actual or constructive notice of the equitable interest at the time of the assignment.

I was also referred to obiter remarks of Viscount Finlay in *Performing Right Society Ltd v London Theatre of Varieties Ltd* [1924] AC 1 at p 19 to the effect that:

> There may possibly be cases in which a person who has made an equitable assignment might by a subsequent assignment have transferred the legal interest in the same work to a purchaser for value without notice, whose title would prevail over the merely equitable right, and such a possibility is one reason for the rule of making the legal owner a party.

Those authorities were not cited to Phillips J in *Pfeiffer* but I have not been convinced by the arguments advanced on behalf of Kellock that he came to the wrong conclusion in holding that, even if there is a legal assignment for value without notice of a prior equity, priorities fall to be determined as if the assignment had been effected in equity. Section 136(1) provides that the assignment is 'subject to equities having priority over the right of the assignee'. The effect of those words is to create, in the case of a statutory assignment of a chose in action, an exception to the general rule that an equity will not prevail against a bona fide purchaser of a legal estate for value without notice of the prior equity. If that is so, in the hands of Abercorn, the assignor to Kellock, the rights of action against the subpurchasers which it assigned to Kellock were subject to an earlier equitable assignment of those same rights to Compaq and Kellock therefore took subject to that prior equity. Unless the rule in *Dearle v Hall* were applicable, the result would be determined by the ordinary rule as to priorities, ie the basic rule of the order of creation where the merits are equal. The rule in *Dearle v Hall* apart, Kellock could not put itself in a stronger position than Abercorn as against Compaq by giving notice of the assignment from Abercorn to the subpurchasers and by then seeking to rely on the statutory assignment thereby completed to take in priority to the equity of Compaq.

As I have mentioned, it is not necessary to form a final view on this point in order to answer the points of law raised by way of preliminary issue. As at present advised, however, I would follow the decision of Phillips J in *Pfeiffer*.

NOTES

1. The case is noted by L S Sealy in [1992] CLJ 19.

2. For a strongly argued case in favour of the bona fide purchaser rule when there is competition between a statutory assignee and an equitable assignee, see F Oditah (1989) 9 OJLS 521. But recent cases (*E Pfeiffer Weinkellerei-Weinenkauf GmbH & Co v Arbuthnot Factors Ltd* [1988] 1 WLR 150; *Compaq Computer Ltd v Abercorn Group Ltd*) and academic opinion generally (D W McLauchlan (1980) 96 LQR 90 at pp 92–93, R M Goode *Commercial Law* (1982), pp 872–873) are against Dr Oditah.

3. Assuming that a seller's reservation of title clause gives him an equitable right to trace into the proceeds of sub-sales held by the buyer, is priority between the seller and an assignee of the buyer's book debts governed by the rule in *Dearle v Hall*? There is no clear answer to this question. It has been argued by D W McLauchlan that there is no room for the rule when the buyer holds the proceeds on trust for the seller. He argues that the rule in *Dearle v Hall* is restricted to competing assignments and does not apply in a situation when one of the interests is an equitable tracing right arising by operation of law (above, at 95ff). But Professor Goode counters that argument by stating that as it is the seller who chooses the form of his interest, by imposing an accounting obligation in the sale contract, and as he knows that the buyer may sell the debts arising from sub-sales to a bona fide purchaser, then the seller has no cause to complain if the rule in *Dearle v Hall* is applied against him (above, at 873). In *Compaq Computer Ltd v Abercorn Group Ltd*, Mummery J avoided this difficult question by holding that the accounting obligation in the sale contract gave rise to an equitable assignment and not a bare trust. However, the case does point the way to the likely construction of similarly worded reservation of title clauses which are not void as unregistered charges. On this basis, a seller who wishes to obtain priority over the proceeds of a sub-sale must either give notice to the sub-buyer (which, in practice, is extremely difficult), or ensure that any subsequent purchaser of the buyer's receivables is on notice as to the seller's interest (under the new s 416(2) of the Companies Act 1985, inserted by the Companies Act 1989, a factoring company taking an assignment of book debts, and not a charge over them, is not deemed to have notice of the seller's charge over his buyer's book debts simply because the charge is already registered). For a general discussion of reservation of title clauses and priorities, see G McCormack *Reservation of Title* (1990), Ch 9; and F Oditah *Legal Aspects of Receivables Financing* (1991), pp 149–154.

4. For criticism of the application of the rule in *Dearle v Hall* when determining priority in the context of stock-in-trade and receivables financing, see below, p 781. Proposals for reform of the priority rules are considered below at pp 782–783.

QUESTIONS

1. In *Ward and Pemberton v Duncombe* (1893) Lord Macnaghten expressed fears that the rule in *Dearle v Hall* might have been 'established at the expense of principles at least as important as those to which (the rule) has been referred'. Identify and critically examine the principles to which Lord Macnaghten referred.

2. A Ltd is owed money by B Ltd for goods supplied. A Ltd assigns (orally) the debt to C Factors Ltd for value. C Factors Ltd immediately gives notice of the assignment to B Ltd. Two weeks later A Ltd assigns (in writing) the same debt to D Factors Ltd for value. D Factors Ltd, which has no knowledge of the previous assignment, gives notice of its assignment to B Ltd. Which assignee has priority to the debt? Would it make any difference to your answer if D Factors Ltd had actually been paid the debt by B Ltd? See *E Pfeiffer Weinkellerei-Weineinkauf GmbH & Co v Arbuthnot Factors Ltd* [1988] 1 WLR 150 at 163.

CHAPTER 21

Receivables financing

1 General introduction*

(a) 'Receivables financing' defined

***Legal Aspects of Receivables Financing* by F Oditah (1991), p 2**

The expression 'receivables financing' is ambiguous.[1] In this book, however, the expression is used to denote any arrangement by which money is raised on the strength of contractual receivables. Receivables form an integral part of the assets of every trading company. Mortgage and charge debts, car loans, insurance premiums, credit card debts, secured consumer loans, equipment loans, freights (including sub-freights), rentals from real and personal property, debts for goods sold or services rendered, are all receivables. So important is this category of liquid assets that Macleod was compelled to write over a hundred years ago:

> . . . if we were asked – who made the discovery which has most deeply affected the fortunes of the human race? We think, after full consideration we might safely answer – the man who first discovered that a debt is a saleable commodity.[2] When Daniel Webster said that credit has done more a thousand times to enrich nations than all the mines of the world, he meant discovery that a debt is a saleable chattel.[3]

A hundred years on, nothing has diminished the importance of receivables as a basis for raising money. If anything, the indications are to the contrary. In developed economies the bulk of corporate wealth is locked up in debts. The recycling of these valuable assets as well as their utilisation in the provision of working capital is the primary focus of this book. As would be expected both the recycling and utilisation take a variety of forms. Receivables could be, and frequently are, discounted either privately or in the money markets. Also they may be, and often are, assigned or charged as security for a loan, or an overdraft or other revolving credit facility. Between discounting and security lies a third possibility – outright assignment in discharge or reduction of a pre-existing debt, very little known and almost completely ignored in discussions of forms and patterns of receivables financing. There could also be more complex combinations of these. Normative arguments as to which form

---

* See generally, R M Goode *Commercial Law* (1982), pp 856–876; R M Goode *Legal Problems of Credit and Security* (2nd ed, 1988), Ch V; I R Davies *Textbook on Commercial Law* (1992), Ch 11. For detailed analysis, see P M Briscoe *Law and Practice of Credit Factoring* (1975); F Oditah *Legal Aspects of Receivables Financing* (1991); F Salinger *Factoring Law and Practice* (1991).

is better are not useful because there is no absolute, universal objective criterion by reference to which their relative merits may be ascertained. A number of considerations are relevant to the choice of any one form. The technique chosen will normally reflect the desire to give the company a financing package tailored to meet its own particular circumstances and needs.

1 In one sense receivables financing means financing the creation of contractual receivables. This is usually the sense in which the related expression 'stock-in-trade financing' is used. Since every going concern necessarily generates receivables, the financing of receivables would in this sense be the financing of an enterprise. The expression, however, has a narrower meaning, namely, the raising of money on the strength of receivables.
2 Macleod *Principles of Economical Philosophy* (2nd ed, 1872), p 481, cited in I Gilmore *Security Interests in Personal Property* (1965), p 213, n 7.
3 Macleod *Elements of Economics* (1881), p 327, cited in I Gilmore, op cit, p 213, n 7.

NOTES

1. Like Dr Oditah's book, this chapter is concerned with the raising of money on the strength of receivables.

2. The term 'receivable' is not defined in English law. In this chapter it will be used to mean 'account receivable' which is 'the right to payment of a sum of money, whether presently or in the future, for goods supplied, services rendered or facilities made available' (R M Goode *Legal Problems of Credit and Security* (2nd ed, 1988), p 106). The terms 'receivables' and 'book debts' are often used interchangeably. Unlike 'receivables', the term 'book debts' has been the subject of legal definition (see below, p 768). However, as Dr Oditah has pointed out, the term 'receivables' is wider than 'book debts' and whilst it includes book debts, it is not limited to them (op cit, p 19).

3. A simple contract debt is a *pure* receivable. If the debtor tenders a bill of exchange or promissory note in payment of the debt then the negotiable instrument is a *documentary* receivable. This is because the negotiable instrument contains an independent payment obligation which, at least in a general sense, acts in substitution for the payment obligation arising out of the underlying pure receivable (see Chapter 15). In consequence, a security over receivables would cover both pure receivables and negotiable instruments tendered in payment by the obligor (*Siebe Gorman & Co Ltd v Barclays Bank Ltd* [1979] 2 Lloyd's Rep 142; see below, p 773). On the other hand, negotiable instruments tendered as *security* for payment, but not as payment, in no sense act as a substitute for the underlying pure receivable and are not to be classified as documentary receivables (see Oditah, op cit, pp 26–27).

(b) Financing techniques: sale or charge

If a trader wants to convert his receivables into cash he can either sell them or mortgage (or charge) them as security for a loan, overdraft or other form of revolving credit. Outright assignment in discharge or reduction of a pre-existing debt is a species of sale (Oditah, op cit, p 33). Technically, there is no sale when receivables are assigned in repayment of an advance made under a financing agreement. The advance is not the purchase price of the receivables and does not provide the consideration necessary for a sale (Oditah, op cit, p 71).

The sale of receivables often takes the form of an assignment of a trader's book debts to the financier ('factor') under a factoring agreement (see below, p 753). It could also involve the block discounting of hire-purchase or credit sale agreements (see below, p 758). However, other 'sale' mechanisms may also be used (eg a sale and agency agreement, as used in *Welsh Development Agency v Export Finance Co Ltd* [1992] BCLC 148, see below).

A financier who advances cash to a trader may take a mortgage of, or charge over, the trader's receivables as security. A mortgage of a debt is an assignment (statutory or equitable) of it upon terms, express or implied, that it is to be reassigned to the transferor when the obligation which it secures has been discharged. Before reassignment the mortgagee has a proprietary interest in the debt. A charge on a debt (which can only be an *equitable* charge) is a mere incumbrance giving the chargee a preferential right to, but not ownership of, the debt. However, the default provisions in the charge usually confer on the chargee (1) a power of attorney to convert the charge into a mortgage by executing an assignment in the name of the chargor, and (2) a power to appoint a receiver. According to Dr Oditah, '[t]hese powers diminish to vanishing point, any remaining distinction between a charge and a mortgage' (op cit, at p 96). For further consideration of the distinction between a mortgage and a charge, see R M Goode [1984] JBL 172; and Chapter 24.

Securitisation of receivables has become an important source of finance for institutional investors. It can be contrasted with factoring which is mainly used to provide finance for the manufacturing sector. Securitisation involves raising finance by packaging together pools of receivables (eg home mortgages, finance leases, hire purchase agreements, conditional sale agreements and trade receivables) and then selling them to a special-purpose company. Typically, the special-purpose company raises the purchase price through loan notes issued in the securities market. The loan notes are secured on the receivables. The difference between the interest rate paid to the noteholders and that paid on the original loan by the borrower represents the transferor's profit margin. As securitisation involves either an outright sale or a sale coupled with a sub-charge, it will not be given separate consideration in this chapter. For further details, see *Securitisation* (1990) (ed D C Bonsall); and E Ferran *Mortgage Securitisation – Legal Aspects* (1992).

(c) How do you distinguish between a sale and a security transaction?

Welsh Development Agency v Export Finance Co Ltd [1992] BCLC 148, Court of Appeal

The defendant (Exfinco) provided finance to a company called Parrot Corp Ltd (Parrot) which sold computer floppy discs to overseas buyers. The finance was provided under the terms of a Master Agreement whereby Parrot first sold the floppy discs to Exfinco and then resold the same discs to overseas buyers as Exfinco's agent. The sale to Exfinco was at a discount to the resale price as Exfinco would pay Parrot in advance of receiving payment from the overseas buyers. Later Parrot created a charge over its book debts in favour of the plaintiff (WDA). When Parrot went into receivership WDA claimed that moneys owed by the overseas buyers to Parrot were subject to its charge (which had been duly registered). Exfinco claimed to be entitled to these moneys as payment for the goods which it owned and which had been sold on its behalf by Parrot as its agent. One of the main issues was whether the Master Agreement had created a charge on the assets of Parrot which was void for non-registration under s 395 of the Companies Act 1985 (see below, p 766). Exfinco claimed that the Agreement effected a sale of goods and not a charge on the goods. Reversing Browne-Wilkinson V-C, the Court of Appeal held the Master Agreement to have effected a sale of goods and gave judgment for Exfinco.

Dillon LJ: I turn then to issue 2: were the transactions under the master agreement by way of sale or secured loan?

It is not suggested that the master agreement was in any sense a sham or that its terms did not represent the true agreement between the parties. Moreover it is not suggested in this case, as it was in *Lloyds & Scottish Finance Ltd v Cyril Lord Carpet Sales Ltd* ([1992] BCLC 609), that in what they actually did the parties had departed from what was provided for by the master agreement, and that therefore they ought to be treated as having made some fresh agreement by conduct in the place of the master agreement.

What is said is that in determining the legal categorisation of an agreement and its legal consequences the court looks at the substance of the transaction and not at the labels which the parties have chosen to put on it.

This is trite law, but it is law which has fallen to be applied in different types of cases where different factors are the relevant factors for consideration. It is therefore not surprising that the words used by eminent judges in different cases in applying the principle do not all fit very harmoniously together.

Thus the task of looking for the substance of the parties' agreement and disregarding the labels they have used may arise in a case where their written agreement is a sham intended to mask their true agreement. The task of the courts there is to discover by extrinsic evidence what their true agreement was and to disregard, if inconsistent with the true agreement, the written words of the sham agreement. This is discussed in the judgments of Diplock and Russell LJJ in *Snook v London and West Riding Investments Ltd* [1967] 1 All ER 518, [1967] 2 QB 786 and is exemplified by some of the cases cited in *Street v Mountford* [1985] 2 All ER 289, [1985] AC 809 and *AG Securities v Vaughan* [1988] 3 All ER 1058, [1990] 1 AC 417 where in an endeavour to set up a licence to occupy, rather than a tenancy of, residential accommodation the landlord had introduced into the agreement terms purportedly reserving to himself a right to introduce further occupants which were plainly inconsistent with the real intention.

But the question can also arise where, without any question of sham, there is some objective criterion in law by which the court can test whether the agreement the parties have made does or does not fall into the legal category in which the parties have sought to place their agreement. One can see that in the comments of Lord Templeman in *Street v Mountford* [1985] 2 All ER 289 at 298, [1985] AC 809 at 824 on the case of *Shell-Mex and BP Ltd v Manchester Garages Ltd* [1971] 1 All ER 841, [1971] 1 WLR 612, where the defendant had been allowed to use a petrol company's filling station for the purposes of selling petrol, and the question was whether the transaction was a licence or a tenancy. Lord Templeman said that the agreement was only personal in its nature and therefore a licence if it did not confer the right to exclusive occupation of the filling station, since no other test for distinguishing between a contractual tenancy and a contractual licence appeared to be understandable or workable.

In the present case Mr Moss QC asserts for WDA that there are, on the authorities, clearly laid down criteria for what is a charge, that all those criteria are present in the present case in the master agreement, and that the master agreement is therefore necessarily as a matter of law a charge, whatever the parties may have called it or thought it was.

He relies in particular on the passage in the judgment of Romer LJ in *Re George Inglefield Ltd* [1933] Ch 1 at 27–28, [1932] All ER Rep 244 at 256–257 where Romer LJ sets out what he regarded as the essential differences between a transaction of sale and a transaction of mortgage or charge. These were three, viz:

[i] In a transaction of sale the vendor is not entitled to get back the subject-matter of the

sale by returning to the purchaser the money that has passed between them. In the case of a mortgage or charge, the mortgagor is entitled, until he has been foreclosed, to get back the subject-matter of the mortgage or charge by returning to the mortgagee the money that has passed between them. [ii] . . . if the mortgagee realises the subject-matter of the mortgage for a sum more than sufficient to repay him, with interest and the costs, the money that has passed between him and the mortgagor he has to account to the mortgagor for the surplus. If the purchaser sells the subject-matter of the purchase, and realizes a profit, of course he has not got to account to the vendor for the profit. [iii] . . . if the mortgagee realizes the mortgaged property for a sum that is insufficient to repay him the money that [has been] paid to the mortgagor, together with interest and costs, then the mortgagee is entitled to recover from the mortgagor the balance of the money . . . If the purchaser were to resell the purchased property at a price which was insufficient to recoup him the money that he had paid to the vendor . . . he would not be entitled to recover the balance from the vendor.

But these indicia do not have the clarity of the distinction between a tenancy and a licence to occupy, viz that it must be a tenancy if the grantee has been given exclusive occupation of the property in question. In particular it is clear from *Re George Inglefield Ltd*, and the *Lloyds & Scottish* case, (a) that there may be a sale of book debts, and not a charge, even though the purchaser has recourse against the vendor to recover the shortfall if the debtor fails to pay the debt in full and (b) that there may be a sale of book debts, even though the purchaser may have to make adjustments and payments to the vendor after the full amounts of the debts have been got in from the debtors. As to the latter see especially the judgment of Lord Hanworth MR in *Re George Inglefield Ltd* [1933] Ch 1 at 20.

In my judgment there is no one clear touchstone by which it can necessarily and inevitably be said that a document which is not a sham and which is expressed as an agreement for sale must necessarily, as a matter of law, amount to no more than the creation of a mortgage or charge on the property expressed to be sold. It is necessary therefore to look at the provisions in the master agreement as a whole to decide whether in substance it amounts to an agreement for the sale of goods or only to a mortgage or charge on goods and their proceeds.

[Ralph Gibson LJ delivered a similar judgment.]

Staughton LJ:

Sale or charge?
(a) *The test*
We were referred to a bewildering array of authority on this topic, some of it by no means easy to reconcile. The problem is not made any easier by the variety of language that has been used: substance, truth, reality, genuine are good words; disguise, cloak, mask, colourable device, label, form, artificial, sham, stratagem and pretence are 'bad names', to adopt the phrase quoted by Dixon J in *Palette Shoes Pty Ltd v Krohn* (1937) 58 CLR 1 at 28. It is necessary to discover, if one can, the ideas which these words are intended to convey.

One can start from the position that statute law in this country, when it enacts rules to be applied to particular transactions, is in general referring to the legal nature of a transaction and not to its economic effect. The leading authority on this point, albeit in a case from Malaya, is the advice of Lord Devlin in *Chow Yoong Hong v Choong Fah Rubber Manufactory Ltd* [1961] 3 All ER 1163 at 1167, [1962] AC 209 at 216:

> There are many ways of raising cash besides borrowing . . . If in form it is not a loan, it is not to the point to say that its object was to raise money for one of them or that the parties could have produced the same result more conveniently by borrowing and lending money.

See too the *Crowther Committee's Report on Consumer Credit* (Cmnd 4596 (1971)) para 1.3.6, where it was said that the existing law was deficient because:

> It lacks any functional basis: distinctions between one type of transaction and another are drawn on the basis of legal abstractions rather than on the basis of commercial reality.

There are in my opinion two routes by which this principle can be overcome. The first, which I will call the external route, is to show that the written document does not represent the agreement of the parties. It may, if one wishes, then be called a sham, a cloak or a device. The second is the internal route, when one looks only at the written agreement, in order to ascertain from its terms whether it amounts to a transaction of the legal nature which the parties ascribe to it. These two routes are described, for example, by Lord Hanworth MR in *Re George Inglefield Ltd* [1933] Ch 1 at 19, 23, [1932] All ER Rep 244 at 252, 254, by Maugham LJ in *Re Lovegrove* [1935] Ch 464 at 496, [1935] All ER Rep 749 at 759, and by Knox J in *Re Curtain Dream plc* [1990] BCLC 925 at 937. (I express no view on the way that Knox J described the second route or the result which he reached; an appeal is pending.)

The Welsh Agency do not rely on the external route in this case. They disclaim any argument that the master agreement was a sham. It is not therefore necessary for me to consider the external route in any detail, except for the purpose of showing what this appeal is *not* about. One can show that the written document does not reflect the agreement of the parties by proving a collateral agreement, or at least a common intention, to that effect. Or there may be proof of a subsequent variation, as was argued in *Lloyds & Scottish Finance Ltd v Cyril Lord Carpets Sales Ltd* ([1992] BCLC 609). . . .

There was here no sham, no collateral agreement or common intention to be bound by different terms, and no subsequent variation to that effect. So I can leave the external route, and turn to an internal consideration of the master agreement itself. This must be carried out on the basis that the parties intended to be bound by its terms, and by nothing else.

If one part of the agreement purports to create a particular legal transaction, it may happen that other provisions are inconsistent with such a transaction. The task of the court is then to ascertain which is the substance, the truth, the reality. That was plainly the approach of Lord Herschell LC in *McEntire v Crossley Bros Ltd* [1895] AC 457 at 463–466, [1895–9] All ER Rep 829 at 832–833, where there are repeated references to inconsistency. See also the speech of Lord Watson where he said ([1895] AC 457 at 467, [1895–9] All ER Rep 829 at 834):

> The duty of a Court is to examine every part of the agreement, every stipulation which it contains, and to consider their mutual bearing upon each other; but it is entirely beyond the function of a Court to discard the plain meaning of any term in the agreement unless there can be found within its four corners other language and other stipulations which necessarily deprive such term of its primary significance.

Mr Moss argued that the court is free to disregard the label which the parties have attached to a transaction. If by label one means the description which is found on the backsheet, or even in a preamble or a recital, I can see that it should be given little if any weight. A label can also be found elsewhere. Thus in *Street v Mountford* [1985] 2 All ER 289, [1985] AC 809, Mrs Mountford agreed to 'to take' a furnished room; the references to 'licence' in the agreement were in truth labels and nothing more. 'Licence' was the name by which the agreement described itself. And in *AG Securities v Vaughan* [1988] 2 All ER 309 at 315, [1990] 1 AC 417 at 444 Bingham LJ said that:

> . . . the true legal nature of a transaction is not to be altered by the description the parties choose to give it.

In my judgment the correct process, when one is following the internal route, is to look at the operative parts of the document, in order to discover what legal transaction they provide for. If some parts appear to be inconsistent with others in this respect, a decision must be made between the two. This is what I understand by ascertaining the substance of the transaction. The cases on whether an agreement provides for a licence or tenancy – *Street v Mountford, AG Securities v Vaughan* and *Aslan v Murphy (Nos 1 and 2)* [1989] 3 All ER 130, [1990] 1 WLR 766 – do not in my opinion overturn this well-established doctrine. Nor does the decision of the majority of this court in *Gisborne v Burton* [1988] 3 All ER 760, [1989] QB 390. There it was held, with reference to the Agricultural Holdings Act 1948, that one must look at the scheme of a pre-ordained series of transactions as a whole, instead of concentrating on each pre-ordained step individually. The doctrine of revenue law, derived from *W T Ramsay Ltd v IRC* [1981] 1 All ER 865, [1982] AC 300 and other cases, was thus extended to private transactions. I do not need to consider whether it should also be extended to this case; there is no series of transactions here, but only the one master agreement.

It can be said that Exfinco have adopted their method of business because their customers wished to avoid the registration provisions of the Companies Act, and the appearance of loans in their balance sheets. But one should not, from sympathy for creditors or rather for a debenture holder, overthrow both established law and recognised methods of providing finance for trade and industry.

NOTES

1. For commentary on this case, see E Ferran [1992] CLJ 434; and F Oditah [1992] JBL 541.

2. In *Re Curtain Dream plc* [1990] BCLC 925, a company obtained a credit line from a financier. Under the terms of the financing agreement, the company was to sell goods to the financier and then repurchase those goods at an increased price. The financier would pay for the goods as soon as it received a bill of exchange, accepted by the company, which provided for payment of the increased sum at the end of a credit period. Until payment had been made, the financier retained title to the goods under the terms of the resale contract. Knox J held the transaction to be one of loan secured by a charge over the goods and not one of sale and resale with a retention of title clause being part of the resale. He held that the most important factor indicating a charge was that the financier was obliged to retransfer the goods back to the company, as this gave the company an equity of redemption in the goods.

3. In *Re Curtain Dream plc*, the company was under an *obligation* to repurchase. The fact that the 'vendor' has a *right* to repurchase the subject matter of the sale when and if the 'purchaser' has received payment in full from the third party is not fatal to a claim that the transaction is one of sale (*Welsh Development Agency v Export Finance Co Ltd* [1991] BCLC 936 at 949, per Browne-Wilkinson V-C). But in factoring and block discount agreements the vendor will usually be placed under an obligation to repurchase the factored or discounted receivables in certain circumstances, eg the third party debtor's insolvency or bankruptcy. Such repurchase or recourse arrangements do not create an equity of redemption. See Oditah, op cit, at pp 38–39, as to why not.

4. For a recent example of an assignment being held to be absolute and not by way of charge, see *Re Marwalt Ltd* [1992] BCC 32.

QUESTIONS

1. If the financing agreement provides that the 'purchaser' of receivables has a right of recourse against the 'vendor' in the event of the debtor's non-payment, does this indicate a charge? See *Olds Discount Co Ltd v John Playfair Ltd* [1938] 3 All ER 275.

2. If the terms of the financing agreement consistently indicate a sale and this is not a sham, will the courts take into account that a financier's real function is the lending of money when assessing whether the transaction is really one of loan secured by a charge? See *Olds Discount Co Ltd v Cohen* [1938] 3 All ER 281n.

3. If the financing agreement provides for the sale of receivables, will the courts hold the agreement to be a sham if it can be shown that the parties operated the agreement in a manner different from that envisaged in it? See *Lloyds and Scottish Finance Ltd v Cyril Lord Carpets Sales Ltd* [1992] BCLC 609, HL.

(d) Why is the distinction important?

See the extract from Romer LJ's judgment in *Re George Inglefield Ltd* [1933] Ch 1, which appears above at pp 748–749. In addition:

(1) a sale of receivables need not be registered (but see s 344 of the Insolvency Act 1986, below, p 765); a 'charge' over a company's receivables must generally be registered (below, p 766);

(2) even if registered, a mortgage of, or charge over, a company's receivables may be set aside on the company's receivership, administration or liquidation because it is deemed a preference, transaction at an undervalue, extortionate credit bargain, floating charge created during the relevant time, or an attempt to defraud creditors (see Insolvency Act 1986, ss 238, 239, 244, 245, 423–425; considered below, pp 919 ff); a sale is unlikely to be avoided on any of these grounds, save that it could be reopened if the level of 'discount' given to the financier is deemed to be extortionate (see Oditah, op cit, p 43);

(3) a sale of receivables is liable to *ad valorem* duty on the instruments by which the sale is effected and VAT; a loan secured by a mortgage or charge is not liable to stamp duty and is exempt from VAT;

(4) the creation of additional debt or security may be prohibited by the terms of an existing debenture but a sale would fall outside such a restriction (although it is now usual for the terms of a prohibition to extend to *all* forms of dealing with the company's receivables).

Under prevailing accountancy practice, receivables which have been sold to a financier are removed from a vendor company's balance sheet and are replaced with the proceeds of sale (this process is described as 'off balance sheet financing'). By contrast, money advanced under a loan is entered as a liability in the accounts of a corporate borrower (which could weaken its balance sheet) and the mortgaged or charged receivables continue to be shown as assets of the company. But when receivables are sold to a financier under a financing arrangement, the financier is usually given, inter alia, a right of recourse against the vendor. This means that the commercial effect of a financing sale is similar to that of a secured loan. Accounts which simply record the consideration for the sale as an asset of the vendor will give, therefore, a misleading picture of the vendor's financial position. With this in mind, the Accounting Standards Board propose that accounts should reflect the economic substance of a transaction and it is in the process of drawing up accounting standards to that effect (see Financial Reporting Exposure Draft No 4 'Reporting the Substance of Financial Transactions', February 1993). But see E Ferran [1992] CLJ 434 at p 436 for the problems that this approach may cause.

2 Financing by sale

(a) Factoring

'Some Aspects of Factoring Law – I: The Acquisition of Rights in the Receivables' by R M Goode [1982] JBL 240, pp 240–241

Structure of a factoring transaction
Factoring is a transaction by which one person (the supplier or 'client') supplying goods or services to trade customers on short-term credit assigns the resulting receivables to another, the factor, upon terms that the assignment is to be notified to the debtors[1] and the factor is to collect in the receivables direct, assume responsibility for the maintenance of the relevant accounts and, within agreed limits, bear the risk of default in payment by customers. Factoring is thus a useful method of improving the supplier's liquidity. This could be done either by selling the receivables outright, or by mortgaging or charging them. Hitherto, factoring has almost invariably been carried out by way of outright sale, thus avoiding the need to register an assignment of receivables as a charge on book debts.[2]

Receivables which the factor is prepared to purchase without recourse are termed 'approved' receivables. These are receivables arising from transactions specifically approved by the factor or falling within an agreed limit authorised to be given to a particular customer. It is usual for factoring to be conducted on a 'whole turnover' basis, that is to say, the client offers or assigns all his receivables to the factor. Those which are not approved (termed 'unapproved' receivables) are purchased on a recourse basis. The factor thus provides a collection and accounting service and, as regards approved receivables, credit protection. In addition, instead of deferring payment for the receivables until the date they mature[3] ('maturity factoring') the factor will normally agree to allow the client to draw up to 80 per cent of the price in advance, charging the client a discount for the period the factor is out of his money.

Relations between the factor and the client are governed by a master agreement, the factoring agreement, which incorporates detailed undertakings and warranties by the client in relation to the receivables and the underlying contracts. Breach of these in relation to any receivable will usually render that receivable unapproved and entitle the factor to debit back the price.

1 Usually by a notice of assignment stamped on the invoice. Notification is what distinguishes full factoring from invoice discounting (or non-notification factoring). The latter is a pure financial facility.
2 Under s[s 395–399] of the Companies Act 19[85]. Where the client is a sole trader or partnership firm, the assignment will usually be registrable [under s 344 of the Insolvency Act 1986].
3 Or, in the case of approved receivables, the date of the customer's insolvency, if this occurs before maturity.

NOTES

1. Assignment lies at the heart of factoring. It is important, therefore, to keep in mind the general law relating to the assignment of choses in action when considering factoring arrangements (see above, Chapter 20). However, when negotiable paper is discounted before maturity, the discounting is by negotiation and not by assignment.

2. There are two types of agreement commonly used by factors. Factoring may take place under a 'whole turnover' agreement whereby the client agrees to sell, and the factor agrees to buy, all the client's receivables. The receivables vest in the factor as they come into existence. By contrast, factoring can also take place under a 'facultative' agreement which provides for the client to offer receivables for sale to the factor at agreed intervals and for acceptance of each offer by the factor as regards those receivables he is willing to purchase. The factor is under no obligation to purchase such receivables as are offered to him. The facultative agreement simply provides a set of putative terms which will govern specific transactions as and when they are entered into (R M Goode [1982] JBL 240 at p 241). Under a facultative agreement, receivables vest in the factor only when he has accepted the client's offer to sell (see below, p 757).

3. The whole turnover and facultative agreements just described are valid only as equitable assignments. As such, they convey or transfer property (ie debts) from the client to the factor. This may make the agreements subject to *ad valorem* stamp duty which is payable on any instrument evidencing such a conveyance or transfer by way of sale (Stamp Act 1891 as amended). The rate of duty is 1 per cent of the consideration, subject to an exemption which relates to any independent transaction whereof the consideration does not exceed £30,000. In principle, a whole turnover agreement will be subject to the tax because the agreement is the instrument by which equitable assignment of existing and future receivables is effected. However, the tax can be avoided if at the time of execution of the agreement the consideration is uncertain so that it is not possible to calculate the *ad valorem* duty. A facultative agreement will not be taxable if the factor's acceptance of the client's offer to sell is evidenced by conduct and not by a written instrument. Stamp duty is a tax on instruments, not on transactions. It remains undecided as to whether duty will be payable on any written notice of vested receivables sent by the client to the factor after assignment has taken place (see Oditah, op cit, p 49). Individual transactions under master factoring agreements are unlikely to qualify for small transaction relief, even if the transaction itself is for less than £30,000. This is because the individual transaction will be grouped together with all the other sales which have taken place under the master agreement when calculating whether relief is due (see Finance Act 1958, s 34(4); *A-G v Cohen* [1937] 1 KB 478). On stamp duty generally, see F R Salinger *Factoring Law and Practice* (1991), paras 7-07 to 7-11; Oditah, op cit, pp 47–50.

4. A copy of a master 'factoring agreement' appears below at p 944 (hereafter referred to as the 'MFA'). Is it a 'whole turnover' or a 'facultative' agreement?

Can future receivables be factored?

Holroyd v Marshall (1862) 10 HL Cas 191, House of Lords

Lord Westbury LC: . . . a contract which engages to transfer property, which is not in existence, cannot operate as an immediate alienation merely because there is nothing to transfer.

But if a vendor or mortgagor agrees to sell or mortgage property, real or personal, of which he is not possessed at the time, and he receives the consideration for the contract, and afterwards becomes possessed of property answering the description in the contract, there is no doubt that a Court of Equity would compel him to perform the contract, and that the contract would, in equity, transfer the beneficial interest to the mortgagee or purchaser immediately on the property being acquired. This, of course, assumes that the supposed contract is one of that class of which a Court of Equity would decree the specific performance. If it be so, then immediately on the acquisition of the property described the vendor or mortgagor would hold it in trust for the purchaser or mortgagee, according to the terms of the contract. For if a contract be in other respects good and fit to be performed, and the consideration has been received, incapacity to perform it at the time of its execution will be no answer when the means of doing so are afterwards obtained.

Tailby v Official Receiver (1888) 13 App Cas 523, House of Lords

I compounded with his creditors. At I's request, T signed promissory notes in favour of those creditors and paid a large sum to them. T took from I a bill of sale as counter-security. The bill of sale assigned (inter alia) 'all the book debts due and owing or which may during the continuance of this security become due and owing to the said mortgagor'. The bill also contained a power of attorney and a proviso that if the mortgagor on demand failed to pay the amount due, the mortgagee could take possession and sell the mortgaged property. On I's bankruptcy an issue arose as to whether the assignment of future book debts generally, without any delimitation as to time, place, or amount, was too vague to be upheld. Reversing the judgment of the Court of Appeal, the House of Lords upheld the validity of the assignment.

Lord Watson: The rule of equity which applies to the assignment of future choses in action is, as I understand it, a very simple one. Choses in action do not come within the scope of the Bills of Sale Acts, and though not yet existing, may nevertheless be the subject of present assignment. As soon as they come into existence, assignees who have given valuable consideration will, if the new chose in action is in the disposal of their assignor, take precisely the same right and interest as if it had actually belonged to him, or had been within his disposition and control at the time when the assignment was made. There is but one condition which must be fulfilled in order to make the assignee's right attach to a future chose in action, which is, that, on its coming into existence, it shall answer the description in the assignment or, in other words, that it shall be capable of being identified as the thing, or as one of the very things assigned. When there is no uncertainty as to its identification, the beneficial interest will immediately vest in the assignee. . . .

It is unnecessary for the purposes of this case to consider how far a general assignment of all after-acquired property can receive effect, because the assignment in question relates to one species of property only. I have been unable to discover any principle upon which the decision of the Court of Appeal can be supported, unless it is to be found in *Belding v Read* ((1865) 3 H & C 955). That case arose in a Court of Common Law, and, with all deference to the very learned judges who decided it, I am bound to say that, in my opinion, they misapprehended the doctrine laid down by Lord Westbury in *Holroyd v Marshall* ((1862) 10 HL Cas 191), which was not new doctrine, but, as the noble Lord explicitly stated, was the mere enunciation of elementary principles long settled in Courts of Equity. It is possible that the learned judges were misled by the reference which the noble Lord makes to specific performance, an illustration not selected with his usual felicity. Not a single decision by an Equity Court was cited to us, prior in date to *Belding v Read*, which gives the least support to the opinions expressed in that case, and I venture to doubt whether any such decision exists. It is true that judges on the equity side of the Court have, in one or two instances, deferred to the views expressed in *Belding v Read*, which they assumed to be an authoritative exposition of the law applied by this House in *Holroyd v Marshall*; but these views conflict with the previous cases in equity, to which Lord Westbury referred as establishing a well-known and elementary principle. In *Bennett v Cooper* ((1846) 9 Beav 252), Lord Langdale MR gave effect to an equitable mortgage by a debtor of 'all sums of money then or thereafter to become due to him, and all legacies or bequests which had already or might thereafter be given or bequeathed to him or his wife, by any person whomsoever.' I cannot understand upon what principle an assignment of all legacies which may be bequeathed by any person to the assignor is to stand good, and effect is to be denied to a general assignment of all future book debts. As Cotton LJ said, in *Re Clarke* ((1887) 36 Ch D 348 at 353): 'Vagueness comes to nothing if the property is definite at the time when the Court is asked to enforce the contract.' A future book debt is quite as capable of being identified as a legacy; and in this case the identity of the debt, with the subjects assigned, is not matter of dispute. When the consideration has been given, and the debt has been clearly identified as one of those in respect of which it was given, a Court of Equity will enforce the covenant of the parties, and will not permit the assignor, or those in his right, to defeat the assignment upon the plea that it is too comprehensive.

I am accordingly of opinion that the order appealed from ought to be reversed, and the judgment of the Divisional Court restored.

Lord Macnaghten: The claim of the purchaser was rested on well-known principles. It has long been settled that future property, possibilities and expectancies are assignable in equity for value. The mode or form of assignment is absolutely immaterial provided the intention of the parties is clear. To effectuate the intention an assignment for value, in terms present and immediate, has always been regarded in equity as a contract binding on the conscience of the assignor and so binding the subject-matter of the contract when it comes into existence, if it is of such a nature and so described as to be capable of being ascertained and identified. . . .

My Lords, I should wish to say a few words about *Holroyd v Marshall* ((1862) 10 HL Cas 191), because I am inclined to think that *Belding v Read* ((1865) 3 H & C 955) is not the only case in which Lord Westbury's observations have been misunderstood. To understand Lord Westbury's judgment aright, I think it is necessary to bear in mind the state of the law at the time, and the point to which his Lordship was addressing himself. *Holroyd v Marshall* laid down no new law, nor did it extend the principles of equity in the slightest degree. Long before *Holroyd v Marshall* was determined it was well settled that an assignment of future property for value operates in equity by way of agreement, binding the conscience of the assignor, and so binding the property from the moment when the contract becomes capable of being performed, on the principle that equity considers as done that which ought to be done, and in accordance with the maxim which Lord Thurlow said he took to be universal, 'that whenever persons agree concerning any particular subject, that, in a Court of Equity, as against the party himself, and any claiming under him, voluntary or with notice, raises a trust:' *Legard v Hodges* ((1792) 1 Ves 477). It had also been determined by the highest tribunals in the country, short of this House – by Lord Lyndhurst as Lord Chancellor in England, and by Sir Edward Sugden as Lord Chancellor in Ireland – that an agreement binding property for valuable consideration had precedence over the claim of a judgment creditor. Some confusion, however, had recently been introduced by a decision of a most eminent judge, who was naturally less familiar with the doctrines of equity than with the principles of common law. In that state of things, in *Holroyd v Marshall*, in a contest between an equitable assignee and an execution creditor, Stuart VC decided in favour of the equitable assignee. His decision was reversed by Lord Campbell LC in a judgment which seemed to strike at the root of all equitable titles. Lord Campbell did not hold that the equitable assignee obtained no interest in the property the subject of the contract when it came into existence. He held that the equitable assignee did obtain an interest in equity. But at the same time he held that the interest was of such a fugitive character, so shadowy, and so precarious, that it could not stand against the legal title of the execution creditor, without the help of some new act to give it substance and strength. It was to this view, I think, that Lord Westbury addressed himself; and by way of shewing how real and substantial were equitable interests springing from agreements based on valuable consideration, he referred to the doctrines of specific performance, illustrating his argument by examples. One of the examples, perhaps, requires some qualification. That, however, does not affect the argument. The argument is clear and convincing; but it must not be wrested from its purpose. It is difficult to suppose that Lord Westbury intended to lay down as a rule to guide or perplex the Court, that considerations applicable to cases of specific performance, properly so-called, where the contract is executory, are to be applied to every case of equitable assignment dealing with future property. Lord Selborne has, I think, done good service in pointing out that confusion is sometimes caused by transferring such considerations to questions which arise as to the propriety of the Court requiring something or other to be done in specie (*Wolverhampton and Walsall Rly Co v London and North Western Rly Co* ((1873) LR 16 Eq 433)). His Lordship observes that there is some fallacy and ambiguity in the way in which in cases of that kind those words 'specific performance,' are very frequently used. Greater confusion still, I think, would be caused by transferring considerations applicable to suits for specific performance – involving, as they do, some of the nicest distinctions and most difficult questions that come before the Court – to cases of equitable assignment or specific lien where nothing remains to be done in order to define the rights of the parties, but the Court is merely asked to protect rights completely defined as between the parties to the contract, or to give effect to such rights either by granting an injunction or by appointing a receiver, or by adjudicating on questions between rival claimants.

The truth is that cases of equitable assignment or specific lien, where the consideration has passed, depend on the real meaning of the agreement between the parties. The difficulty, generally speaking, is to ascertain the true scope and effect of the agreement. When that is ascertained you have only to apply the principle that equity considers that done which ought to be done if that principle is applicable under the circumstances of the case. The doctrines relating to specific performance do not, I think, afford a test or a measure of the rights created.

[Lord Herschell delivered a concurring judgment.
Lord FitzGerald upheld the appeal on different grounds.]

NOTES

1. Both Lord Westbury and Lord Macnaghten stressed that the assignor must have actually received the consideration if the contract to assign was to constitute an 'equitable assignment' of future choses in action. In the context of the factoring of receivables, future receivables can only be factored under a whole turnover agreement. Under the terms of such an agreement, the factor is obliged to purchase future receivables and, thereby, provides the consideration necessary to support a contract to assign them. The contract to assign constitutes an equitable assignment from the date the consideration is executed. This will be the date that the factor first makes a credit or payment under the agreement. As Professor Goode has noted: '. . . a single credit or payment suffices, as this type of factoring agreement is an indivisible contract for the global sale of receivables, not a series of separate transactions' ([1982] JBL 240 at p 242).

2. Future receivables cannot be factored under a facultative agreement. This is because the factor is under no obligation to purchase the receivables offered to him and so provides no consideration to support a valid assignment of future receivables. Only after the receivables have come into existence can the client offer them to the factor. If the factor purchases any receivable offered to him an equitable assignment will take place at that stage.

3. However, the factor faces a number of disadvantages if future receivables are assigned to him and those receivables have not yet come into existence:

(1) he cannot intervene in actions concerning the property to which he is not yet entitled;
(2) he cannot give notice of his assignment to secure his priority against other assignees until there is some debtor to whom effective notice can be given (*Re Dallas* [1904] 2 Ch 385);
(3) he cannot give notice of his assignment to the debtor so as to stop the debtor's equities enforceable against the assignor until the debt has come into existence

(Oditah, op cit, pp 239–240; compare Salinger, op cit, paras 9-19–9-21);

(4) even if he is the first to give notice to the debtor, he may be defeated by a statutory assignee who has actually been paid the debt on the grounds that the statutory assignee is a bona fide purchaser for value of the legal title in the payments received without notice of the factor's equitable assignment (*E Pfeiffer Weinkellerei-Weineinkauf GmbH & Co v Arbuthnot Factors Ltd* [1988] 1 WLR 150 at 163);

(5) if the receivable comes into existence as a result of post-liquidation performance of an underlying contract by the client or its liquidator, the 'disposition' of the receivable under the terms of a pre-liquidation factoring agreement will be void unless the court orders otherwise (Insolvency Act 1986, s 127).

QUESTION

A whole turnover agreement provides that the client is to sell, and the factor is to purchase, 50 per cent of the client's turnover. Is this agreement capable of constituting an equitable assignment?

(b) Block discounting

Lloyds & Scottish Finance Ltd v Cyril Lord Carpets Sales Ltd [1992] BCLC 609, House of Lords (the case was decided in 1979)

(The facts are irrelevant.)

Lord Scarman: Block discounting is a well-known service offered by certain finance houses to traders who do a substantial business by way of hire-purchase or credit-sale agreements with their customers. Though there are variations of detail, the essential feature of the service is that in return for an immediate advance the trader sells to the finance house at a discount his interest in the agreements he has with his customers. The trader gives the house his guarantee of due performance by his customers of their obligations. He includes a number, often a very large number, of hire-purchase or credit-sale agreements in each discounting transaction: hence the City's name 'block discounting' for this type of transaction. The service is similar to many other financial services offered in the City of London and elsewhere – an immediate advance of money against documents, which are purchased at a discount. It is an adaptation of the historic business of discounting bills and notes to the particular circumstances of the hire-purchase and credit-sale trade. The finance house looks only to the discount for its profit. Once the trader has met his commitment for the advance and the discount charge (out of the moneys received or receivable from his customers whose debts he has sold), the finance house is content that the trader should keep for himself whatever else is collected from the customers.

Of course the facility offered is money. The finance house advances money in reliance upon obligations which have not yet matured. But is it the lending of money? The question was answered (at first instance) 40 years ago. If the transaction be genuine and not a sham to cover something different, the judges held it to be a sale, not a loan. The three cases in which this answer was given have stood over the years unchallenged – and are, no doubt, the basis of City practice. They are *Re George Inglefield Ltd* [1933] Ch 1, [1932] All ER Rep 244; *Olds Discount Co Ltd v Cohen* [1938] 3 All ER 281n and *Olds Discount Co Ltd v Playfair Ltd* [1938] 3 All ER 275.

NOTES

1. A copy of a master 'block discounting' agreement appears below at p 957 (hereafter referred to as the 'MBDA').

2. A block discounting agreement is essentially facultative. It provides a set of terms upon which blocks of receivables may later be sold by a dealer to the finance company. Each sale constitutes a separate transaction by which blocks of debt are equitably assigned to the finance company. Under the terms of the master agreement the dealer gives the finance company a power of attorney to execute a legal assignment, should this prove necessary.

3. With a block discounting agreement it is usual not to give notice of the assignment of the debt to the dealer's customers. The dealer collects the debt as agent of the finance company. From the dealer's point of view, this has the advantage of allowing the dealer to retain control over his debts and maintain a relationship with his customers. From the finance company's point of view, block discounting saves it the costs associated with debt collection.

4. Yet block discounting is inherently more risky for the finance company than notification factoring. The main reasons for this are:

(1) if a customer pays the dealer he is discharged from his debt whether or not the dealer pays the finance company;
(2) the dealer is under no obligation to account to the finance company for payments received from its customers, nor is he obliged to segregate such payments from his other resources (although under the terms of the master agreement the dealer will have guaranteed payment by the hirers or credit buyers and will have secured that guarantee by accepting a series of bills of exchange, or issuing promissory notes, payable to the finance company); contrast this with factoring where the client receives the proceeds on trust for the factor (*GE Crane Sales Pty Ltd v Comr of Taxation* (1971) 46 ALJR 15, High Court of Australia) and where the client will be liable for conversion if he misappropriates any cheque, or other negotiable instrument, paid to him (*International Factors Ltd v Rodriguez* [1979] QB 351);
(3) the finance company is at risk of loss of priority to another assignee who gives notice to the hirer or credit buyer (although under the terms of the master agreement the dealer usually undertakes not to assign, charge or otherwise encumber any receivable assigned to the finance company);
(4) if the finance company does collect the debt itself, it takes the debt subject to all defences and rights of set-off which have accrued between the customer and the dealer in the period up to when the customer receives notice of the assignment.

(c) The financier's discount is not an interest charge

Welsh Development Agency v Export Finance Co Ltd [1992] BCLC 148, Court of Appeal

(The facts appear above at p 747.)

Dillon LJ: The essence of the transaction when a trader raises finance by factoring book debts or block discounting hire-purchase agreements is that the trader sells the book debts to a finance company for a price which is necessarily discounted from the full aggregate face value of the debts. It is discounted, primarily, because the trader will be getting an immediate payment, while the finance company will have to wait for the debts to come in from the debtors and they may well not be presently payable. Indeed with hire-purchase agreements the debt will be payable by the hirer by instalments over what may be a considerable period. The rate of discount will also no doubt take into account the risk the finance company is assuming that the debtor will fail to pay the debts. . . .

It is normal, therefore, that the rate of discount for the finance company will be calculated by reference to the appropriate rate of interest for the period for which the finance company is out of its money. It has been normal for the amount of discount to be calculated once and for all; it will be actually received by the finance company when the finance company receives payment of the book debt from the debtor, or from the vendor under rights of recourse for the finance company against the vendor. If the vendor has guaranteed to the finance company that the debtor will pay the debt punctually, and the debtor does not pay punctually, it may well be that the finance company could claim damages from the vendor, to be measured by a computation of interest over the period for which it has been kept out of its money in excess of the period on which the calculation of the amount of the finance company's discount was based.

The classic exposition by Lord Devlin in *Chow Yoong Hong v Choong Fah Rubber Manufactory Ltd* [1961] 3 All ER 1163 at 1167, [1962] AC 209 at 217, of the difference between interest and discounts is as follows:

> When payment is made before due date at a discount, the amount of the discount is no doubt often calculated by reference to the amount of interest which the payer calculates his money would have earned if he had deferred payment to the due date. But that does not mean that discount is the same as interest. Interest postulates the making of a loan and then it runs from day to day until repayment of the loan, its total depending on the length of the loan. Discount is a deduction from the price *fixed once and for all at the time of payment*. (My emphasis.)

Lord Wilberforce made a statement to the same effect – that discount is fixed and paid once and for all whereas interest accrues from day-to-day – in the *Lloyds & Scottish* case after citing from Lord Devlin's opinion in *Chow Yoong Hong*. Lord Wilberforce also referred to statements in *Willingale (Inspector of Taxes) v International Commercial Bank Ltd* [1978] 1 All ER 754 at 756, 760, [1978] AC 834 at 841, 843 by Lord Salmon and by Lord Fraser of Tullybelton to the effect that, unlike interest, discount is not earned and does not accrue from day-to-day.

NOTES

1. In *Welsh Development Agency* the discount was not fixed but fluctuating. It was closely tied to the average period taken by all overseas buyers to pay. However, Dillon LJ held that this did not convert the discount into interest on a loan and did not negate the transaction as being one of sale and purchase.

2. Factors may also make an 'administration charge' if they provide administrative services such as ledger administration, debt collection and credit protection. However, there is evidence that some factors make this charge even when these additional services are not provided (eg *Re Charge Card Services Ltd* [1987] Ch 150 at 171).

(d) The financier's security

Whether finance is provided under a factoring or block discount agreement, the financier usually obtains one or more of the following types of security against the client/dealer (hereafter collectively referred to as the 'client').

(i) *Guarantees and indemnities*

These appear in the MFA at clause 11 (and in the Schedule), and in the MBDA at clause 9. Dr Oditah has noted that these guarantees and indemnities 'afford personal security to the factor [and block discounter] although when combined with a right to set off damages and loss against the retention fund, could, no doubt, prove powerful' (op cit, p 51).

(ii) *A right of recourse*

Such a right appears in the MFA at clause 12, and in the MBDA at clause 9. The right of recourse found in a factoring or block discounting agreement does not create an equity of redemption giving rise to a mortgage of, or charge over, a debt (see above, p 751; and below, p 782).

(iii) *A right of retention*

Such a right appears in the MBDA at clause 3, and in the case next cited.

Does the financier's right of retention create a registrable charge on the book debts of the client?

Re Charge Card Services Ltd [1987] Ch 150, Chancery Division

Charge Card Services Ltd (the company) entered into an invoice discounting agreement by which it agreed to factor its receivables to Commercial Credit Services Ltd (the factor). The relevant provisions of the agreement were as follows:

- By clause 3(a) the factor could require the company to repurchase any receivable in certain specified circumstances (eg if the debtor disputed liability).
- By clause 3(c) the company guaranteed payment by every debtor and agreed to indemnify the factor against loss caused by the debtor's failure to pay.
- By clause 4 the purchase price payable by the factor to the company was the gross amount payable by the debtor less any discount allowable and less a discount charge calculated in the manner prescribed by standard condition 3.
- By clause 6 the factor's obligation to pay was made subject to the right of debits and right of retention set out in standard condition 3.
- By clause 10 (read with clause 11) the factor had the option of determining the agreement on the company going into insolvent liquidation, whereupon the company was obliged to repurchase at face value so much of any receivable purchased by the factor as then remained outstanding. At the date of the trial the factor had not exercised this option.

- By standard condition 3A the factor had to maintain a current account which would be credited with (inter alia) the purchase price of each receivable and which would be debited with (inter alia) the amount of any receivables which the factor had required the company to repurchase, inter alia, under clause 3(a) (but not under clause 10).
- By standard condition 3B the factor was to remit to the company or its order any balance for the time being standing to the credit of the current account less any amount which the factor in its absolute discretion decided to retain as security for:
  (i) any claims or defences against the company,
  (ii) any risk of non-payment by a debtor, and
  (iii) any amount prospectively chargeable to the company as a debit under standard condition 3A.

The company went into insolvent liquidation and a dispute arose between its liquidator and the factor as to the validity of the factor's right of retention under standard condition 3B. Millett J upheld the validity of the factor's right.

Millett J: It was submitted on behalf of the company that the right of retention was expressly reserved by Commercial Credit as security for its prospective rights of set off, and that in consequence it constituted a charge on book debts created by the company which was void against the liquidator for want of registration under s 95 of the Companies Act 1948 (now s 395 of the Companies Act 1985). . . .

In my judgment, and leaving aside for the moment the possible claim under clause 10, the short answer to these submissions is that Commercial Credit's right of retention under standard condition 3B(iii) in respect of any amount prospectively chargeable to the company as a debit to the current account is a matter not of set off but of account. In *Halesowen Presswork & Assemblies Ltd v National Westminster Bank Ltd* [1971] 1 QB 1, Buckley LJ said, at p 46:

> Where the relationship of the banker and customer is a single relationship such as I have already mentioned, albeit embodied in a number of accounts, the situation is not, in my judgment, a situation of lien at all. A lien postulates property of the debtor in the possession or under the control of the creditor. Nor is it a set-off situation, which postulates mutual but independent obligations between the two parties. It is an accounting situation, in which the existence and amount of one party's liability to the other can only be ascertained by discovering the ultimate balance of their mutual dealings.

Counsel for the company put forward a sophisticated analysis of the various provisions of the agreement to show that, despite the wording of clause 4, the discounting charge was not integral to the ascertainment of the purchase price but, like the administration charge, a true contra item. In my judgment, however, the crucial factor is not the definition of the purchase price, but the extent of Commercial Credit's obligation to pay. This is to be found in clause 6, and it is an obligation to pay, not the purchase price, which is merely a credit in the current account, but the balance shown on the current account subject to the right of retention. The right of retention thus constitutes a contractual limitation on the company's right to require payment of the balance on the current account. It is an essential safeguard against overpayment since, except at the end of the month when the discounting and administration charges are debited, and in the unlikely event of there being no bad debts at all, the balance on the current account can never represent the true amount owing by Commercial Credit. The sum made payable by clause 6, therefore, is in effect a provisional payment only and represents the best estimate that can be made at the time of the true state of account between the parties.

In my judgment, this is not a case of set off at all, for there are no mutual but independent obligations capable of being quantified and set off against each other. There are reciprocal obligations giving rise to credits and debits in a single running account, a single liability to pay the ultimate balance found due on taking the account, and provisions for retention and provisional payment in the meantime.

If this analysis is correct, it also provides an answer to the company's claim that the right of retention in standard condition 3B(iii) constitutes a registrable charge, for there is no relevant property capable of forming the subject matter of the charge. The only asset which the company could charge is its chose in action, ie the right to sue Commercial Credit for the sum due under the agreement, but this already contains within it the liability to suffer a retention. Counsel for the company naturally stressed the fact that the right of retention is expressed to be by way of security, but that is of no avail if, as I hold, it secures Commercial Credit, not against default by the company in the performance of its obligations, but against overpayment by itself.

This still leaves the company's liability to repurchase outstanding receivables at face value if Commercial Credit serves a notice of termination under clause 10. The purchase price payable by the company in this event is not available to be debited to the current account under standard condition 3A(ii), but Commercial Credit has the right to retain money to meet it under standard condition 3B(i). It has been conceded before me that this is a true right of set off. Accordingly, as well as in case I am wrong in my analysis of the other rights of retention, I must deal with the company's contentions that the right of retention in standard condition 3B is a registrable charge on the company's book debts and that in so far as it gives a right of set off in respect of sums only contingently due from the company at the date of liquidation it goes beyond what is permitted by s 31 of the Bankruptcy Act 1914 [now s 323 of the Insolvency Act 1986; and r 4.90 of the Insolvency Rules 1986].

If the right of retention constitutes a charge, there is no doubt that it is a charge on book debts and is a charge created by the company. But is it a charge at all? The sum due from Commercial Credit to the company under the agreement is, of course, a book debt of the company which the company can charge to a third party. In my judgment, however, it cannot be charged in favour of Commercial Credit itself, for the simple reason that a charge in favour of a debtor of his own indebtedness to the chargor is conceptually impossible.

Counsel for the company conceded that a debt cannot be assigned in whole or in part to the debtor, since such an assignment operates wholly or partially as a release. Likewise, it was conceded, it cannot be made the subject of a legal or equitable mortgage in favour of the debtor, since this requires a conveyance or assignment by way of security, and this operates as a conditional release. But, it was submitted, an equitable charge need involve no conveyance or assignment of property, so that any objection on this ground falls away.

[His Lordship then examined the requirements for the creation of an equitable charge as set out in *Palmer v Carey* [1926] AC 703 at 706–707 and in *National Provincial and Union Bank of England v Charnley* [1924] 1 KB 431 at 449–450 and continued:]

Thus the essence of an equitable charge is that, without any conveyance or assignment to the chargee, specific property of the chargor is expressly or constructively appropriated to or made answerable for payment of a debt, and the chargee is given the right to resort to the property for the purpose of having it realised and applied in or towards payment of the debt. The availability of equitable remedies has the effect of giving the chargee a proprietary interest by way of security in the property charged.

It is true, therefore, that no conveyance or assignment is involved in the creation of an equitable charge, but in my judgment the benefit of a debt can no more be appropriated or made available to the debtor than it can be conveyed or assigned to him. The objection to a charge in these circumstances is not to the process by which it is created, but to the result. A debt is a chose in action; it is the right to sue the debtor. This can be assigned or made available to a third party, but not to the debtor, who cannot sue himself. Once any assignment or appropriation to the debtor becomes unconditional, the debt is wholly or partially released. The debtor cannot, and does not need to, resort to the creditor's claim against him in order to obtain the benefit of the security; his own liability to the creditor is automatically discharged or reduced.

In *Halesowen Presswork & Assemblies Ltd v National Westminster Bank Ltd* [1971] 1 QB 1, 46 Buckley LJ, in a passage subsequently approved in the House of Lords [1972] AC 785 by Viscount Dilhorne, at p 802, Lord Simon of Glaisdale at p 808, and Lord Cross of Chelsea, at p 810, stated that he could not understand how it could be said with any kind of accuracy that the bank had a lien upon its own indebtedness to its customer. It is true that this comment was made in relation to a lien rather than a charge, and a lien unlike a charge can only attach to tangible property. But the reason why it was said that the bank did not have a lien on the credit balance in its customer's current account was clearly based on the identity of the parties rather than the particular character of the security given.

Counsel for the company relied on *Ex p Caldicott* (1884) 25 Ch D 716, in which a partner deposited money with a bank by way of security for the indebtedness of his firm. The Court of Appeal held that the bank was not required to value its security before proving for its debt against the firm. It was, however, not necessary to decide whether the deposit created a charge; it was sufficient that it did not create a security on the joint estate.

It does not, of course, follow that an attempt to create an express mortgage or charge of a debt in favour of the debtor would be ineffective to create a security. Equity looks to the substance, not the form; and while in my judgment this would not create a mortgage or charge, it would no doubt give a right of set off which would be effective against the creditor's liquidator or trustee in bankruptcy, provided that it did not purport to go beyond what is permitted by s 31 of the Bankruptcy Act 1914 [now s 323 of the Insolvency Act 1986; and r 4.90 of the Insolvency Rules 1986.]

[Although the case went to the Court of Appeal ([1988] 3 All ER 702), there was no appeal on this part of Millett J's judgment.]

NOTES

1. Millett J's decision has generated both judicial and academic criticism. In *Welsh Development Agency v Export Finance Co Ltd* [1991] BCLC 936 at 953, Browne-Wilkinson V-C said:

> I am satisfied that this case is indistinguishable from *Re Charge Card Services Ltd (No 2)* [1987] BCLC 17, [1986] 3 All ER 289, [1987] Ch 150, where Millett J held that very similar provisions did not create a charge. His grounds for decision, as I understand them, were twofold. First, where by contract parties have agreed that credits and debits in relation to a number of different liabilities are to be made to a running account and the obligation is to pay only the balance due on that account, that cannot constitute a charge on any sum due which is to be credited to that account. I have considerable doubts whether, in the absence of that decision, I would have reached the same conclusion. But in the interests of preserving consistency in matters which have an important general commercial impact, I follow that decision. Millett J's second ground of decision was that it is conceptually impossible to have a charge in favour of X over a debt owed by X. This view has been trenchantly attacked by an article in International Financial Law Review (1988) p 26. I have real doubts on that issue also, but I propose to follow Millett J's decision.

On appeal in the same case, Dillon LJ echoed these doubts when he stated (obiter) that: '. . . I have considerable difficulty with the view expressed by Millett J that a book debt due to the company (Charge Card Services Ltd) from Commercial Credit could not be charged in favour of Commercial Credit itself because a charge in favour of a debtor of his own indebtedness to the chargor is conceptually impossible' ([1992] BCLC 148 at 166–167). Ralph Gibson and Staughton LJJ did not consider this issue and Millett J's decision cannot be considered as overruled (see C Mayo [1992] 7 JIBL 257).

2. The main reason why it is argued that such a charge is 'conceptually impossible' has been explained, and supported, by Professor Goode as follows:

> . . . a debt is a species of property only as between the creditor and a third party taking an assignment or charge. In the relationship between creditor and debtor the debt is merely an obligation. As creditor I do not *own* the debt, I am *owed* it. Accordingly as against the debtor I have nothing to assign or charge back to him. [(1989) 15 Mon LR 361 at 368.]

See also, R M Goode *Legal Problems of Credit and Security* (2nd ed, 1988), pp 124–129); P Millett (1991) 107 LQR 679 at p 680.

3. But Millett J's decision has been subjected to severe criticism by the majority of academic writers: see, in particular, P R Wood *English and International Set-Off* (1989), paras 5-179 to 5-181; D E Allan (1989) 15 Mon LR 337; and F Oditah [1992] JBL 541 at pp 555–562. The critics argue, inter alia, that a debt can be 'property' as between the creditor and the debtor, at least when it is charged back to the debtor as security. Furthermore, to support their submission that it is indeed conceptually possible for a creditor to charge a debt back to the debtor by way of security, the critics point to *Re Jeavons, ex p Mackay, ex p Brown* (1873) 8 Ch App 643 (better reported in (1873) 42 LJ(NS) Bankruptcy 68), where an argument that a debtor cannot have a charge on royalties due from him was advanced and rejected by the Court of Appeal. The Legal Risk Review Committee, appointed by the Bank of England in 1991 to consider legal uncertainties affecting the wholesale financial markets in the United Kingdom, recommended that there should be legislation to make it clear that charge backs are permitted under English law (*Final Report of the Legal Risk Review Committee*, October 1992).

QUESTIONS

1. In *Re Charge Card Services Ltd*, Millett J held that the factor's right of retention did not constitute a security against default by the company in the performance of its obligations, but against overpayment by itself. Do you agree?
2. Would you have expected factors and block discounters to have welcomed, or opposed, this part of Millett J's decision in *Re Charge Card Services Ltd*? Why?

(e) Registration

Insolvency Act 1986, s 344

344. (1) The following applies where a person engaged in any business makes a general assignment to another person of his existing or future book debts, or any class of them, and is subsequently adjudged bankrupt.
(2) The assignment is void against the trustee of the bankrupt's estate as regards book debts which were not paid before the presentation of the bankruptcy petition, unless the assignment has been registered under the Bills of Sale Act 1878.
(3) For the purposes of subsections (1) and (2)—
(a) 'assignment' includes an assignment by way of security or charge on book debts, and
(b) 'general assignment' does not include—
    (i) an assignment of book debts due at the date of the assignment from specified debtors or of debts becoming due under specified contracts or
    (ii) an assignment of book debts included either in a transfer of a business made in good faith and for value or in an assignment of assets for the benefit of creditors generally.
(4) For the purposes of registration under the Act of 1878 an assignment of book debts is to be treated as if it were a bill of sale given otherwise than by way of security for the payment of a sum of money; and the provisions of that Act with respect to the registration of bills of sale apply accordingly with such necessary modifications as may be made by rules under that Act.

NOTES

1. What are 'book debts'? See below, at p 768.

2. Section 344 only applies to a general assignment of book debts by a person who is subsequently adjudged bankrupt. It does not apply, therefore, to any such assignment made by a company. A company cannot be adjudged bankrupt!

3. Registration does not constitute notice to the debtor and does not guarantee the priority of the assignment over subsequent interests (R M Goode *Legal Problems of Credit and Security* (2nd ed, 1988), pp 113–114).

3 Financing by secured transactions

(a) Generally

A factor may secure the financing transaction in a number of ways; for example, negotiable paper may be pledged with the factor, title may be retained by the factor in a sale and resale agreement and the factor may even claim a right to trace the proceeds of authorised sub-sales (see above, p 747), and the client's debtor may even attorn to the factor (see above, p 698). However, the most common forms of security taken by the factor are mortgages and equitable charges (see above, p 747). Problems related to taking a mortgage of, or equitable charge over, a debt will be considered further in this section.

(b) Registration of 'charges' on a company's property

Part XII of the Companies Act 1985 on the registration of charges has been completely overhauled by Part IV of the Companies Act 1989. Part IV of the 1989 Act inserts new sections to replace the earlier Act. Although these changes have not yet been brought into effect, the following text anticipates the new law as originally enacted and the references are to sections of the Companies Act 1985 as amended by the Companies Act 1989.

Companies Act 1985, ss 395 and 396

395. (1) The purpose of this Part is to secure the registration of charges on a company's property.
(2) In this Part—
    'charge' means any form of security interest (fixed or floating) over property, other than
        an interest arising by operation of law; and
    'property', in the context of what is the subject of a charge, includes future property.
(3) It is immaterial for the purposes of this Part where the property subject to a charge is situated.
. . .
396. (1) The charges requiring registration under this Part are—
. . .

(c) a charge on intangible movable property (in Scotland, incorporeal moveable property) of any of the following descriptions—

. . .

    (iii) book debts (whether book debts of the company or assigned to the company),

. . .

(e) a floating charge on the whole or part of the company's property.

(2) The descriptions of charge mentioned in subsection (1) shall be construed as follows—

. . .

(f) the deposit by way of security of a negotiable instrument given to secure the payment of book debts shall not be treated for the purposes of paragraph (c)(iii) as a charge on book debts;

(g) a shipowner's lien on subfreights shall not be treated as a charge on book debts for the purposes of paragraph (c)(iii) or as a floating charge for the purposes of paragraph (e).

NOTES

1. We have already seen in the previous chapter that for an assignment to be effective under s 136 of the Law of Property Act 1925 it must be 'absolute' and 'not purporting to be by way of charge only'. However, an assignment may be absolute for the purposes of s 136 and still operate by way of security for a debt (see *Burlinson v Hall* (1884) 12 QBD 347, per Day J; above, p 703). Whether an assignment is absolute under s 136 turns on whether the assignor has unconditionally transferred to the assignee for the time being the sole right to the debt in question as against the debtor. By contrast, a corporate assignor will have executed a 'charge' over its property for the purposes of Part XII of the Companies Act 1985 if it retains any interest in the nature of an equity of redemption as against the assignee. Thus, an assignment of a debt to secure advances with a proviso for redemption and reassignment upon repayment (ie a mortgage of the debt) would be absolute under s 136 (see *Trancred v Delagoa Bay and East Africa Rly Co* (1889) 23 QBD 239) but registrable as a 'charge' under the Companies Act 1985 if the assignor is a company. As a 'charge' is defined in s 395(2) of the Companies Act 1985 to mean 'any form of security interest (fixed or floating) over property . . .' it encompasses both a mortgage of, and an equitable charge over, a debt.

2. Section 399(1) of the Companies Act 1985 declares that failure to deliver particulars of the charge to the Registrar of Companies within the stipulated period renders the charge void against (a) an administrator or liquidator of the company, and (b) any person who for value acquires an interest in or right over property subject to the charge (unless the acquisition is expressly subject to the charge: s 405(1)). Therefore, the main consequence of non-registration is that the charge-holder will lose his priority in an insolvency.

QUESTION

A deposit of negotiable instruments by way of pledge is exempt from registration (s 396(2)(f) of the Companies Act 1985). What justifies this exemption?

(i) What is a 'book debt'?

Independent Automatic Sales Ltd v Knowles & Foster [1962] 1 WLR 974, Chancery Division

The plaintiff company carried on a business of manufacturing and dealing in automatic machines. For that purpose it obtained finance from the defendant merchant banking firm whereby it was agreed that bills of exchange and other documents belonging to the plaintiff and deposited with the defendant should be pledged to the defendant as continuing security for the payment of all liabilities of the plaintiff to the defendant. The plaintiff then deposited 53 hire purchase agreements with the defendant as security for a loan. Each agreement included a provision whereby the hirer, on exercising his option to terminate or return the machine, was liable for not less than one half of the purchase price. On the plaintiff's liquidation, the liquidator claimed delivery of the hire purchase agreements and an account of all money received under them on the ground that the charge created by the deposit of the agreements was void against him for non-registration under s 95 of the Companies Act 1948 (an earlier version of ss 395–399 of the Companies Act 1985), since the debts arising under the agreements were 'book debts' within s 95(2)(e) of the 1948 Act.

Buckley J: In my judgment, the charge constituted by the deposit of one of these agreements was a charge upon each and all of the benefits of the company under that agreement. If those benefits included any rights which can properly be described as 'book-debts' the charge was, in part at least, a charge on book-debts and therefore registrable under the section.

Nearly 100 years ago in *Shipley v Marshall* ((1863) 14 CBNS 566) the Court of Common Pleas considered the meaning of the term 'book-debts' as used in s 137 of the Bankruptcy Act 1861. Erle CJ said (at 570): 'By "book-debts," the legislature doubtless intended to describe debts in some way connected with the trade of the bankrupt: and I am inclined to give the term a wider range. But it is enough to say that this was a debt connected with and growing out of the plaintiff's trade.' Williams J said (at 571): 'The words of s 137 are no doubt as Mr Griffits has pointed out, authorising the assignees to sell the "book-debts due or growing due to the bankrupt, and the books relating thereto." This, it is said, can only mean debts which are actually entered in some book kept by the bankrupt in the course of his trade. I cannot, however, accede to that construction. I think the meaning of the statute is, that the assignees shall dispose of all debts due to the bankrupt in respect of which entries could be made in the ordinary course of his business: otherwise, a debt by accident omitted to be entered would not pass by the assignment.' Byles J said (at 573): 'It is said that "book-debts" must mean debts which are entered in the trade-books of the bankrupt. I agree with my Brother Williams that they must be such debts as are commonly entered in books.' And a little later he said: 'Suppose the trader kept no books, or was blind and could not write, and did not choose to incur the expense of keeping a clerk or book-keeper, – upon the construction contended for by the defendant, there could be no book-debts which could be made the subject of sale and assignment under s 137 of the Bankruptcy Act 1861. That surely would not be a very sensible construction to put upon the statute.'

So far as I am aware, no more precise definition of the meaning of the term 'book-debts' has ever been attempted judicially and I shall not attempt one. *Shipley v Marshall*, I think, establishes that, if it can be said of a debt arising in the course of a business and due or growing due to the proprietor of that business that such a debt would or could in the ordinary course of such a business be entered in well-kept books relating to that business, that debt can properly be called a book-debt whether it is in fact entered in the books of the business or not. . . .

Mr Bagnall [counsel for the defendants] has further argued that any debts which could arise under the agreements could only have come into existence after the date of the deposit.

I will assume, as seems probable, that at that date all the amounts payable on the signing of the agreements had been paid and that no instalments of hire rent were in arrear. Mr Bagnall's submission was that in these circumstances there would at the date of the deposit have been no book-debts in existence and that, since he says one cannot charge what does not exist, the deposits did not per se constitute any charge on book-debts, although he conceded that if and when a book-debt came into existence under any of the agreements that book-debt would immediately become charged by reason of the deposit. He contends that s 95 does not on its true construction require a charge on future book-debts to be registered and that 'book-debts' in sub-s (2)(e) means only existing book-debts. . . .

I think that there are two answers to this argument. First, for reason I have already given, I am of opinion that upon the true interpretation of the form of agreement used in this case the hirer became liable immediately upon the agreement coming into operation to the extent of his minimum liability under it notwithstanding that some part of that liability was to be discharged by future payments and that the debts so constituted were existing book-debts at the date of the deposit. The proposition that when the agreements were deposited there were no book-debts in existence which could be charged is, in my judgment, untenable.

Secondly, in my judgment, a charge on future book-debts of a company is registrable under s 95. That it is competent for anyone to whom book-debts may accrue in the future to create an equitable charge upon those book-debts which will attach to them as soon as they come into existence is not disputed. (See *Tailby v Official Receiver* ((1888) 13 App Cas 523).) That such a charge can accurately be described as a charge on book-debts does not appear to me to be open to question. Such a charge would not, of course, be effective until a book-debt came into existence upon which it could operate. Nevertheless, I think it would be accurate to speak of the charge being created at the date of the instrument, deposit or other act giving rise to it, for no further action on the part of the grantor would be required to bring the charge to life. A charge on book-debts, present and future, is not an unusual form of security in the commercial world, and it would seem to me strange if such a charge were registrable (as it undoubtedly is) and a charge confined to future book-debts were not. I find nothing in the language of s 95 requiring me to read sub-s (2)(e) in so restricted a way as to confine it to a charge on existing book-debts. . . .

Accordingly, in my judgment, the charges created by the deposit of 53 agreements were registrable under s 95, and, not having been registered, they are void as against the plaintiff liquidator. There will be a declaration that the charges are void as against the plaintiff liquidator, and an order for the delivery up of the agreements.

NOTES

1. There has been much debate as to whether a company's 'cash at bank' is a book debt of that company. The relationship between the bank and the company is that of debtor and creditor so long as the company's account is in credit. But the debt owing to the company will not have arisen in the course of its business, unless the company ran an investment business and the deposit was made by way of investment. For this reason 'cash at bank' should not be regarded as a book debt of the company (unless the company's business is investment) and general accounting practice reflects this. However, the cases do not provide any clear guidance on this issue, see *Re Brightlife Ltd* [1987] Ch 200; *Re Permanent Houses (Holdings) Ltd* (1988) 5 BCC 151 at 154; *Northern Bank Ltd v Ross* [1990] BCC 883 (NICA). For further discussion, see R M Goode *Legal Problems of Credit and Security* (2nd ed, 1988), pp 114–115; Oditah, op cit, pp 23–24; E Ferran *Mortgage Securitisation – Legal Aspects* (1992), pp 76–77, whose prudent advice is that a fixed charge on the company's bank accounts should be registered in any event.

2. In his report, *A Review of Security Interests in Property* (published in 1989: see below, p 791), Professor Diamond recommended an expanded definition of what are now called 'book debts' (see below, at p 772). However, Professor Diamond concluded that it was not necessary to make charges on bank accounts registrable (para 23.4.12). He reasoned that:

> Given the way in which bank accounts are conducted in secrecy, the amounts a company has to its credit in its bank accounts are not generally known, and since this is not a visible asset it is unlikely that any creditors are misled by the existence of an unknown charge. The assumption is in many cases that, so far from having credit balances at the bank, a company has an overdraft. [Para 23.4.10.]

3. The Legal Risk Review Committee (above, p 765) has recently recommended that it should be provided by statute that charges over bank deposits and other non-trading debts are not registrable (*Final Report of the Legal Risk Review Committee*, October 1992).

Paul and Frank Ltd v Discount Bank (Overseas) Ltd [1967] Ch 348, Chancery Division

The plaintiff company had completed a letter of authority to an export credit guarantee organisation (ECG) authorising it to pay the defendant discount bank any moneys which might become payable under an exchange insurance policy. On the plaintiff's liquidation, the liquidator claimed that the letter of authority was void under s 95 of the Companies Act 1948 (an earlier version of ss 395–399 of the Companies Act 1985), as an unregistered charge on a book debt of the company.

After hearing the accountancy evidence Pennycuick J held that even after ECG had accepted liability for a claim and the amount of the claim had been ascertained the right to payment under the ECG policy would not in practice have been entered in the books of the plaintiff company.

Pennycuick J continued: I turn now to s 95 of the Companies Act 1948. . . .

Looking at the matter for a moment apart from authority, I do not think that in ordinary speech one would describe as a 'book-debt' the right under a contingency contract before the contingency happens. By 'contingency contract' in this connection I mean contracts of insurance, guarantee, indemnity and the like. However, this point is not free from authority, and I have been referred to two cases as to what is meant by a 'book-debt.' . . .

Counsel on both sides have addressed their arguments in great part to the nature of the company's right at the date when the contingency under the policy occurred, or alternatively the date when the liability of ECG was accepted and the amount ascertained. Even if this is the true test, the findings on accountancy practice which I have made would conclude the case in favour of the defendants. But I do not think that this is the true test. Section 95 requires registration of a charge on book-debts within 21 days of creation. It seems to me that, in order to ascertain whether any particular charge is a charge on book-debts within the meaning of the section, one must look at the items of property which form the subject matter of the charge at the date of its creation and consider whether any of those items is a book-debt. In the case of an existing item of property, this question can only be answered by reference to its character at the date of creation. Where the item of property is the benefit of a contract and at the date of the charge the benefit of the contract does not comprehend any book-debt, I do not see how that contract can be brought within the section as being a book-debt merely by reason that the contract may ultimately result in a book-debt. Here the ECG policy admittedly did not comprehend any book-debt at the date of the letter of authority, and that seems to me to be an end of the matter.

Mr Sutcliffe, for the plaintiffs, contended that a contract requires registration under paragraph (e) if at any time it may result in a book-debt. If this were right, the section would be of wide scope and would cover a charge on any possible contract which might produce a money obligation unless it could be shown that the obligation, even when admitted and quantified, was such as would not commonly be entered in the books of a company.

Mr Sutcliffe relied on another principle laid down by Buckley J in *Independent Automatic Sales Ltd v Knowles & Foster* ([1962] 1 WLR 974). After holding that upon the true interpretation of the hire-purchase agreement 'the hirer became immediately liable to the extent of his minimum liability under it notwithstanding that some part of that liability is to be discharged by future payments,' Buckley J went on as follows . . .

[His Lordship quoted the passage cited above at p 769, and continued:]

Mr Wheeler, for the first defendant, and Mr Bateson, for the second defendant, unless I misunderstood them, found it difficult to resist Mr Sutcliffe's contention on this point, except by saying that the second proposition of Buckley J is wrong. I confess that I do not share that difficulty. If a charge upon its proper construction covers future debts, in the sense of debts under a future contract which, when that contract comes to be made, will constitute book-debts, eg, an ordinary contract for the sale of goods on credit, I see no reason why paragraph (e) should not be fairly applicable to the charge; and that, I think, is all that Buckley J says. It by no means follows, it seems to me, that paragraph (e) applies to an existing contract which does not comprehend a book-debt merely by reason that that contract may result in a book-debt in the future. Nor did Buckley J say so.

I prefer to rest my decision on the ground which I have indicated. But, as I have said, if indeed the test were the character of ECG's obligation when liability is admitted and the amount ascertained, then the plaintiffs' claim would fail on the facts, namely, the evidence of accountancy practice.

NOTES

1. Fixed charges over future book debts are registrable (*Independent Automatic Sales*), whereas fixed charges over contingent debts are not (*Paul and Frank*). This means that a book debt which arises from an existing contract will be non-registrable if the debt is contingent, whereas a book debt arising from a non-existent contract will be registrable if the debt is not contingent. However, this distinction, as drawn by Pennycuick J in *Paul and Frank*, has been the subject of considerable criticism, see Oditah, op cit, pp 30–32; Ferran, op cit, pp 77–80. Furthermore, in *Contemporary Cottages (NZ) Ltd v Margin Traders Ltd* [1981] 2 NZLR 114 (High Court of New Zealand), Thorp J has held (at 126) that:

> There seems to me to be a basic conflict between the proposition that registration may be required in respect of a debt not existing at the time of the charge, and the concept that the test is to be the character of the property assigned and charged at the date of the creation of the charge. I prefer the proposition which lies behind the judgment of Buckley J, ie, that the charge over future book debts is created at the time of the execution of an appropriate assignment pursuant to *Tailby's* case, to distinguishing between book debts which arise from existing contracts and book debts which arise from non-existent contracts on any basis which makes charges over the latter registrable but charges over the former not registrable. That consequence, which is necessarily involved in the proposal by Pennycuick J, is one which seems to me, with respect, to indicate the illogicality of the distinction.

2. In *Re Brush Aggregates Ltd* [1983] BCLC 320, R A K Wright QC, sitting as a deputy judge, held that a charge on future debts which might arise under a contract already in existence at the date of the charge would be registrable as a fixed charge on book debts. As a matter of construction of the terms of the assignment, the deputy judge distinguished *Paul and Frank* as a case involving the assignment by way of security of a contingent contractual right (non-registrable), as opposed to an assignment by way of security of any money which might become due under that contract (registrable). However, considerable doubt has been expressed as to whether the distinction drawn by the deputy judge has any substance to it (see E Ferran, op cit, p 79).

3. In his report, Professor Diamond recommended that charges on insurance policies should become registrable charges (Diamond Report, para 23.5.4). He had no proposals as regard other contingent debts (para 23.9.24). However, it should be noted that under the existing law a *floating* charge over debts (book debts or otherwise) is registrable and this includes a floating charge taken over contingent debts (s 396(1)(e) of the Companies Act 1985). Whether a floating charge over book debts can be registered under s 396(1)(c)(iii) remains in issue. In *The Annangel Glory* [1988] 1 Lloyd's Rep 45, Saville J (at 50) raised the question but did not find it necessary to decide the point.

A Review of Security Interests in Property by Professor A L Diamond, paras 23.9.22 and 23.9.25

23.9.22   . . . As I understand the concept of 'book debts', what is meant is debts due or to become due to the company in respect of goods supplied or to be supplied or services rendered or to be rendered by the company in the course of the company's business. It is usual to add to such a definition 'whether entered in a book or not', since although such debts do normally appear in a company's books, it would be strange if a failure to enter certain debts in the books prevented those debts from being book debts (see *Shipley v Marshall* (1863) 14 CBNS 566, 571, per Williams J). These days, of course, the company's books may be kept on a computer rather than on paper in 'books'. The added phrase, however, does raise the question whether 'book debts' is still the appropriate label, and the expression does have a slightly antique air.

23.9.25   It would in my view be an improvement if the expression 'book debts' were in future legislation to be replaced by a more modern term, such as 'receivables', but a possible disadvantage is that 'book debts' is used in s 344 of the Insolvency Act 1986. In any event, whichever term is used, it should be defined on the lines indicated in paragraph 23.9.22 above.

(ii) *Distinguishing a fixed charge from a floating charge*

Tailby v Official Receiver (1888) 13 App Cas 523, House of Lords

The facts appear above at p 755.

Lord Macnaghten: I pause for a moment to point out the nature and effect of the security created by the bill of sale of 1879. It belongs to a class of securities of which perhaps the most familiar example is to be found in the debentures of trading companies. It is a floating security reaching over all the trade assets of the mortgagor for the time being, and intended to fasten upon and bind the assets in existence at the time when the mortgagee intervenes. In other words, the mortgagor makes himself trustee of his business for the purpose of the security. But the trust is to remain dormant until the mortgagee calls it into operation.

NOTES

1. For further discussion of the characteristics of a floating charge, see below, at pp 838 ff.

2. But is it possible to have a fixed charge over all present and future book debts? See the next case.

Siebe Gorman & Co Ltd v Barclays Bank Ltd [1979] 2 Lloyd's Rep 142, Chancery Division

In 1971, R H McDonald Ltd executed a debenture in favour of Barclays Bank, secured by charges over various categories of property listed in clause 3 of the debenture. Clause 3 read:

> The Company as beneficial owner hereby charges with the payment or discharge of all monies and liabilities hereby covenanted to be paid or discharged by the Company: . . . (d) by way of first fixed charge all book debts now and from time to time due and owing to the Company.

Clause 5 provided:

> . . . During the continuance of this security the Company . . . (c) shall pay into the Company's account with the Bank all monies which it may receive in respect of the book debts and other debts hereby charged and shall not without the prior consent of the Bank in writing purport to charge or assign the same in favour of any other person and shall if called upon to do so by the Bank execute a legal assignment of such book debts and other debts to the Bank.

Slade J held that a fixed charge had been created.

Slade J: . . . if I had accepted the premise that R H McDonald Ltd would have had the unrestricted right to deal with the proceeds of any of the relevant books debts paid into its account, so long as that account remained in credit, I would have been inclined to accept the conclusion that the charge on such book debts could be no more than a floating charge. I refer to the respective definitions of a floating charge and a specific charge given by Lord Macnaghten in *Illingworth v Houldsworth* [1904] AC 355 at p 358:

> A specific charge, I think, is one that without more fastens on ascertained and definite property or property capable of being ascertained and defined; a floating charge, on the other hand, is ambulatory and shifting in its nature, hovering over and so to speak floating with the property which it is intended to affect until some event occurs or some act is done which causes it to settle and fasten on the subject of the charge within its reach and grasp.

If the debenture on its true construction had given the bank no rights whatsoever, at a time when the account of R H McDonald Ltd was in credit, to prevent the company from spending in the ordinary course of business all or any of the proceeds of book debts paid into its account, I would have been inclined to regard the charge, for all the wording of the debenture, as doing no more than 'hovering over and so to speak floating with' the book debts, within the words of Lord Macnaghten. Such, I would conceive, is the effect of a charge on future book debts in the form more usually employed. Commonly it is intended, by both creditor and debtor, that the debtor shall have the free disposal of the proceeds of future book debts which may come into his hands, so long as the creditor takes no steps to enforce his security, or the charge has not otherwise crystallised.

In my judgment, however, it is perfectly possible in law for a mortgagor, by way of continuing security for future advances, to grant to a mortgagee a charge on future book debts in a form which creates in equity a specific charge on the proceeds of such debts as soon as they are received and consequently prevents the mortgagor from disposing of an unencumbered title to the subject matter of such charge without the mortgagee's consent, even before the mortgagee has taken steps to enforce its security. . . . This in my judgment was the effect of the debenture in the present case. I see no reason why the Court should not give effect to the intention of the parties, as stated in cl 3(d), that the charge should be a first fixed charge on book debts. I do not accept the argument that the provisions of cl 5(c) negative the existence of a specific charge. All that they do, in my judgment, is to reinforce the specific charge given by cl 3. The mere fact that there may exist certain forms of dealing with book debts which are not specifically prohibited by cl 5(c) does not in my judgment turn the specific charge into a floating charge.

NOTES

1. In the Irish case *Re Armagh Shoes Ltd* [1984] BCLC 405, Hutton J held that the fact that a document by its express words purports to create a fixed or specific charge does not prevent the court from construing the charge as a floating one. The learned judge in that case was also prepared to infer from the terms of the charge as a whole that the company had a licence to deal with the assets charged in the ordinary course of its business, even though it was not stated.

2. In *Re Brightlife Ltd* [1987] Ch 200, Hoffmann J held that a charge over book debts which was expressed to be a fixed charge was in reality a floating charge. He said (at 209):

> ... although clause 3(A)(ii)(a) speaks of a 'first specific charge over the book debts and other debts, the rights over the debts created by the debenture were in my judgment such as to be categorised in law as a floating charge. ...
>
> It is true that clause 5(ii) does not allow Brightlife to sell, factor or discount debts without the written consent of Norandex. But a floating charge is consistent with some restriction upon the company's freedom to deal with its assets. For example, floating charges commonly contain a prohibition upon the creation of other charges ranking prior to or pari passu with the floating charge. Such dealings would otherwise be open to a company in the ordinary course of its business. In this debenture, the significant feature is that Brightlife was free to collect its debts and pay the proceeds into its bank account. Once in the account, they would be outside the charge over debts and at the free disposal of the company. In my judgment a right to deal in this way with the charged assets for its own account is a badge of a floating charge and is inconsistent with a fixed charge.

Hoffmann J (at 210) explained *Siebe Gorman* as a case where the bank under the terms of the charge had an implied right to control drawings on the account. A similar implied right of control was found to exist in *Re a Company (No 005009 of 1987), ex p Copp* [1989] BCLC 13. The right of control can also be made express, as it was in *Re Keenan Bros Ltd* [1986] BCLC 242 (Irish Supreme Court). See further, R Pennington (1985) 6 Co Law 9; G McCormack (1987) 8 Co Law 3; R Pearce [1987] JBL 18; Oditah, op cit, pp 96–103.

3. More recently, in *Re Atlantic Computer Systems plc* [1992] Ch 505 the Court of Appeal has held that a funder's charge on book debts due to the chargor company under existing equipment leases was a fixed charge, even though there were no stated controls over the proceeds of the charged book debts and those proceeds were paid direct to the chargor company and used by it in the ordinary course of its business. The Court of Appeal decided the issue as a 'short point of law' and did not examine any of the cases dealing with attempts to take fixed charges over present and future book debts. This is unfortunate as *Re Atlantic Computer Systems plc* appears to remove the need for any express or implied control over the chargor's dealings with debts and their proceeds if the charge is to be fixed.

4. However, as *Re Atlantic Computer Systems plc* was a case where the equipment leases were in existence at the time the charge was taken, it may be possible to confine the decision to charges over the money proceeds of trading agreements in existence at the date the charge was taken. This would leave the control test undisturbed in the case of general assignments of existing and future book debts (see M G Bridge (1991) 107 LQR 397). Yet in *Re Atlantic Medical Ltd* [1992] BCC 653, Vinelott J held, following *Re Atlantic Computer Systems plc*, that an assignment by way of charge over existing *and future* equipment leases was a fixed charge, even though there was no express or implied control over the chargor's dealings with the proceeds due under the leases. The distinction drawn between existing and future leases was specifically rejected by Vinelott J (at 658).

5. The theory that a fixed chargee must control the book debts *and* the proceeds of the debts has recently been dealt a further blow by the Court of Appeal in *Re New Bullas Trading Ltd* [1994] BCC 36. The debenture in that case purported to create a fixed charge over the chargor company's present and future book debts. The debenture expressly provided that (a) the chargor was to pay the proceeds of the book debts into a specified bank account; (b) the chargor was to deal with such proceeds as directed by the chargee; and (c) in the absence of directions, the proceeds of the book debts were to be released from the fixed charge and stand subject to a floating charge. No directions were given by the chargee. At first instance, Knox J treated the book debts and their proceeds as indivisible and, following *Re Brightlife Ltd,* held the charge to be floating as the chargor company (in the absence of directions) was free to deal with the proceeds as it wished. Reversing Knox J, the Court of Appeal held that the book debts were subject to a fixed charge while they were uncollected and a floating charge on realisation. Nourse LJ, giving the leading judgment, stated that the matter was governed by the clear agreement of the parties that the book debts and their proceeds were divisible and should be treated separately. By this reasoning the Court of Appeal avoided consideration of whether Knox J was right to apply the control test when the debts and proceeds are not divisible. Leaving aside *Re Atlantic Computer Systems plc* and *Re Atlantic Medical Ltd*, cases of doubtful authority on this point, the decided cases indicate that the control test should be applied in such circumstances (see also *William Gaskell Group Ltd v Highley* [1993] BCC 200).

(iii) *What benefits accrue to the chargee if he takes a fixed, as opposed to a floating, charge over the chargor company's book debts or other receivables?*

The main benefits are:

(1) A fixed charge takes effect on its creation so that the chargor's control over the charged assets is restricted; a floating charge only takes effect on crystallisation (see below, p 842) so that the chargor can deal with the charged assets up until then (see *Re Keenan Bros Ltd* [1986] BCLC 242 at 245, per Henchy J).

(2) A floating charge is incomplete until crystallisation so that up until then the chargor's unsecured creditors may set off debts due by the company against sums they owe to it (*Biggerstaff v Rowatt's Wharf Ltd* [1896] 2 Ch 93); a fixed charge is not subject to set-off after the unsecured creditors have received notice of the assignment (Oditah, op cit, at p 95; cf R M Goode [1984] JBL 172 at p 174).

(3) The expenses of a liquidation rank in priority to the claims of a floating charge holder, whereas those expenses always rank behind the claims of a holder of a

fixed charge (Insolvency Act 1986, ss 115 and 156; Insolvency Rules, SI 1986/1925, rr 4.180, 4.218 and 12.2; Ferran, op cit, p 191, fn).

(4) A fixed charge takes priority over preferential creditors (*Re Lewis Merthyr Consolidated Collieries Ltd* [1929] 1 Ch 498); a floating charge is ranked after preferential creditors on the chargor's receivership or liquidation (Insolvency Act 1986, ss 40 and 175; also see Companies Act 1985, s 196) and this applies even when the holder of a prior fixed charge agrees with the holder of a subsequent floating charge that the fixed charge 'shall be postponed to and rank in priority immediately after' the floating charge (*Re Portbase (Clothing) Ltd; Mond v Taylor* [1993] BCC 96, per Chadwick J).

(5) A company administrator needs court approval to dispose of property subject to a fixed charge but property subject to a floating charge may be freely disposed of, subject to the chargee's priority being transferred to the proceeds acquired from the disposition of the charged property (Insolvency Act 1986, s 15).

(6) A floating charge, but not a fixed charge, may be declared invalid under s 245 of the Insolvency Act 1986 (see below, p 919).

(NB The references to 'floating charge' in ss 15, 40, 175 and 245 of the Insolvency Act 1986 means a charge which *as created* was a floating charge: Insolvency Act 1986, ss 15(3), 40 and 251.)

(iv) *Do any benefits accrue to the chargee if he takes a floating, as opposed to a fixed, charge over the chargor company's book debts or other receivables?*

Only a floating charge holder can appoint an administrative receiver (Insolvency Act 1986, s 29(2)). The advantages which result from this power of appointment are highlighted in the following extract.

'Lightweight Floating Charges' by F Oditah [1991] JBL 49, pp 49–50

Despite the relatively modest ranking of floating charges in the pecking order, the Insolvency Act 1986, has made the floating charge an attractive security once again. First, only a person entitled to appoint an administrative receiver[1] may receive notice of a petition for an administration order.[2] Secondly, only such a creditor can 'block' the making of an administration order, provided he appoints an administrative receiver by the time the petition is heard.[3] Also, the duty of the administrator is to carry out proposals aimed at achieving the purpose of his appointment. Since the administrator has a potentially unlimited tenure, his appointment removes two vital rights from the chargee, namely, the ability to control the timing and conduct of realisation of his security. The property may have depreciated when the administrator vacates office. Worse still, the administrator may not even sell the property at all, or for some time. For these reasons, a first mortgagee may insist on taking a first floating charge over the company's undertaking, even where his specific security fully secures his exposure. Such floating charges intended only for protection against the insolvency procedure are called lightweight charges, since they need not contain all the covenants and restrictions typically found in floating charges, but only restrictions on the creation of other floating charges ranking ahead of or *pari passu* with them.[4] Another reason for taking lightweight floating charges is the new powers given to an administrative receiver.[5] Under the new law, an administrative receiver may apply to Court for leave to sell assets subject to a specific charge.[6] Thus, a lender with only a fixed charge may find that another lender has this potential ability to dispose of property subject to his security. In the event he will lose control over the timing and conduct of realisation of his security.

1 Administrative receiver is defined in s 29(2) of the Insolvency Act 1986.
2 Insolvency Act 1986, s 9(2)(a).
3 Insolvency Act 1986, ss 9(3), 10(2)(b).
4 Rumbelow [1989] LS Gaz, March, 32 at 33.
5 *Corporate Recovery: The Immediate Impact of the Administrator Scheme, A Report by City University Department of Law*, April 1988, p 8.
6 Insolvency Act 1986, s 43.

(v) *Can a receivables financier take both a fixed and a floating charge over a company's book debts and other receivables?*

Re Croftbell Ltd [1990] BCC 781, Chancery Division

To secure a loan Croftbell Ltd ('the company') gave the bank a floating charge over its present and future property and a fixed charge over its only substantial asset (shares in another company). Under the terms of the floating charge the bank had power to appoint a receiver on the presentation of a petition for an administration order. When the company later presented such a petition the bank appointed joint receivers and applied to dismiss the petition pursuant to s 9(3) of the Insolvency Act 1986. Vinelott J acceded to the bank's application.

Vinelott J: Mr Bannister's [Counsel for the company] alternative submission was that even if the debenture did operate to create a floating charge on the assets of the company, other than the shares of Toller's Garage Ltd, it should nonetheless be disregarded for the purposes of s 9 of the 1986 Act because it is mere artifice aimed at circumventing the purpose of Pt II of the Act. He submitted that the legislature intended that the court should have power to appoint an administrator if satisfied that the requirements of s 8 have been satisfied, save only where all or substantially all the assets of the company are comprised in a floating charge and the holder of the charge has power to appoint a receiver who by virtue of his powers under the debenture as enlarged by the 1986 Act will be in a position to continue the company's business. The power of the court should not be stultified, he said, by the device of tacking a floating charge on to a fixed charge over the company's sole or principal asset.

I do not find it necessary and it would not I think be appropriate to venture into the question what legislative purpose is to be inferred from precluding a court from appointing an administrator against the wishes of a debenture holder who has power to appoint an administrative receiver. As I understand Mr Bannister's argument it is not suggested that a debenture creating a floating charge (which I think this debenture did) falls outside s 29(2) merely because at the time when the receivers are appointed substantially the only asset of the company is subject to a fixed charge, securing a sum in excess of the likely value of that asset – for instance, a factory in the possession of the company and used for the purposes of its business. The property of the company would then comprise the interest of the company as mortgagor and the question whether the holder of a floating charge has power to appoint a receiver over substantially the whole of the company's property cannot depend on the amount of the debt secured by the fixed charge relative to the value of the company's uncharged assets. Equally it cannot have been intended to exclude a floating charge which when created extended to future assets merely because at the creation of the charge the company had no assets or no assets which were not the subject of a fixed charge; for that would exclude the obvious and common case where the floating charge was created to finance the commencement of a company's intended business. Mr Bannister submitted that it is otherwise if it was contemplated when the charge was created that the company would not carry on any active business but would continue as a passive receptacle of an asset which was subject to a fixed charge in favour of the same debenture holder. In such circumstances, he said, the floating charge serves no purpose except to enable the debenture holder to frustrate the court's power to appoint an administrator.

I do not think that the answer to the question whether the holder of a debenture, which on its face creates a floating charge, has power to appoint an administrative receiver can turn on the intention of the company when the debenture was executed or the knowledge by the debenture holder of those intentions. The intentions of the company might change and the company might have substantial assets outside the scope of the fixed charge when the power to appoint a receiver is exercised.

NOTES

1. In *Re Atlantic Computer Systems plc* [1992] Ch 505, two banks leased computer equipment to a company as part of a financing package. As security, the banks took an assignment of sub-leases of the same equipment and of rents due under those sub-leases. As we have already seen (above, p 774), the assignment was by way of a fixed charge. Later an administrator was appointed to secure a better break-up value of the company's assets than would have been effected on a winding up (Insolvency Act 1986, s 8(3)(d)). The administrator continued to receive rents from the sub-lessees but he did not remit those rents to the banks, even though considerable sums were due to the banks under the terms of the head leases. By virtue of s 11(3)(c) of the Insolvency Act 1986, the consent of the administrator or leave of the court was required before steps could be taken to enforce the banks' security over the company's property or repossess the equipment in the company's possession under the head leases. The banks applied to the court for directions. Reversing Ferris J, the Court of Appeal refused to order the administrator to pay rent to the banks under the head leases. The Court of Appeal held that there was no 'expenses of the administration' principle whereby an owner of property suffering loss because of s 11 of the 1986 Act could recover compensation for such loss by some other remedy (although the banks were given leave to recover their equipment from the sub-lessees). On the other hand, if administrators wrongly retain goods otherwise than for the proper purpose of the administration then, so long as they have not been released as administrators, they remain liable at the direction of the court to pay not only for the use of the goods of another, but also for compensation for having wrongfully refused leave (under s 11(3)(c)) to the owner to retake the goods (*Barclays Mercantile Business Finance Ltd v Sibec Developments Ltd* [1992] 1 WLR 1253, Millct J). Administrators who wrongfully retain goods may also be held personally liable for the tort of conversion.

2. *Re Atlantic Computer Systems plc* illustrates that even the holder of a fixed charge may suffer at the hands of a company administrator. To avoid this happening a funder would be well advised to take both a fixed and a floating charge over such of the company's assets as its book debts or other receivables. The funder could then use his power, as a floating charge holder, to appoint an administrative receiver and block the appointment of an administrator (see M G Bridge (1991) 107 LQR 395 at 397).

4 Equities affecting assigned receivables

Unlike a mortgagee of a debt, a chargee does not own the charged debt. This has led Professor Goode to submit that giving notice of the charge to the debtor does not prevent the debtor's right of set-off building up against the debt ([1984] JBL 172 at p 174). Cf Oditah, op cit, pp 95–96, 245–246. If Professor Goode is correct, the chargee would be placed in a worse position than that of an assignee, who can stop equities accumulating by giving the debtor notice of assignment (see above, pp 733 ff). But in practice this distinction is rarely encountered. This is because a charge over receivables usually contains a power to convert it into a mortgage through execution of an assignment by the chargee in the name of the chargor (see above, p 747). Therefore, for the purposes of set-off, a charge may be equated with an assignment (R M Goode *Legal Problems of Credit and Security* (2nd ed, 1988), p 117).

Business Computers Ltd v Anglo-African Leasing Ltd

(See above, p 733.)

NOTES

1. See notes above, pp 735–736.
2. For non-assignable receivables, see above, pp 729 ff.

QUESTION

Can a customer recover payment from his supplier's factor when the customer has prepaid for goods which are never supplied, or which, if delivered, are lawfully rejected by him? See *Pan Ocean Shipping Co Ltd v Creditcorp Ltd* [1993] 1 Lloyd's Rep 443, CA (noted by A Tettenborn [1993] CLJ 220); affd [1994] 1 All ER 470, HL. See also art 10 of the UNIDROIT Convention on International Factoring 1988 (see below, p 785).

5 Priorities

(a) Generally

Dearle v Hall

(See above, p 737.)

NOTES

See notes above, p 739.

Compaq Computer Ltd v Abercorn Group Ltd

(See above, p 739.)

NOTES

See notes above, pp 743–744.

(b) Registration and the rule in *Dearle v Hall*

Companies Act 1985, ss 416 and 711A

416. (1) A person taking a charge over a company's property shall be taken to have notice of any matter requiring registration and disclosed on the register at the time the charge is created.
(2) Otherwise, a person shall not be taken to have notice of any matter by reason of its being disclosed on the register or by reason of his having failed to search the register in the course of making such inquiries as ought reasonably to be made.
(3) The above provisions have effect subject to any other statutory provision as to whether a person is to be taken to have notice of any matter disclosed on the register.

711A. (1) A person shall not be taken to have notice of any matter merely because of its being disclosed in any document kept by the registrar of companies (and thus available for inspection) or made available by the company for inspection.
(2) This does not affect the question whether a person is affected by notice of any matter by reason of a failure to make such inquiries as ought reasonably to be made.
(3) In this section 'document' includes any material which contains information.
(4) Nothing in this section affects the operation of—
(a) s 416 of this Act (under which a person taking a charge over a company's property is deemed to have notice of matters disclosed on the companies charges register), or
(b) s 198 of the Law of Property Act 1925 as it applies by virtue of s 3(7) of the Land Charges Act 1972 (under which the registration of certain land charges under Part XII, or Chapter III of Part XXIII, of this Act is deemed to constitute actual notice for all purposes connected with the land affected).

NOTES

1. Registration of an assignment as a charge under the Companies Act 1985, ss 395ff, does not constitute notice to the debtor so as to give the assignee priority under the first limb of the rule in *Dearle v Hall* (see Oditah, op cit, p 133).

2. However, under s 416(1), if the factor takes a charge over a company's property (quaere, whether this means a charge as defined generally by s 395(2) of the Companies Act 1985, or a *registrable* charge falling within s 396), he will be deemed to have notice of any matter requiring registration and already disclosed on the register at the time the factor's charge is created. Such notice would prevent the factor taking priority over the prior chargee, even if the factor was the first to give notice to the debtor. In these circumstances, the prior chargee would take priority under the general rule that estates and interests rank according to their date of creation. But if the factor is not a chargee, registration of a prior charge will not of itself put him on notice and prevent him obtaining priority under the rule in *Dearle v Hall* (s 416(2)). However, the rule in *Dearle v Hall* will not apply if the non-chargee factor has actual notice of the prior charge. Nor will it apply if the non-chargee factor has 'inferred knowledge' of the charge arising out of his deliberate failure to make such enquiries as he ought reasonably to have made (see s 711A(2) of the Companies Act 1985, as amended); although failure to check the register will not of itself infer such knowledge (s 416(2)). It is certainly arguable that as the question of prior charges will generally be of importance to the factor, the enquiries which he ought to have made (for the purposes of s 711A(2)) before entering into the factoring agreement should include enquiries as to prior charges created by his client (Salinger, op cit, para 8-12).

3. Registration of a general assignment by a trader of existing or future book debts, for the purposes of s 344 of the Insolvency Act 1986, constitutes neither notice to the debtor nor notice to third parties (see R M Goode *Legal Problems of Credit and Security* (2nd ed, 1988), p 114).

(c) Criticism

The rule in *Dearle v Hall* is generally acknowledged to be an unsatisfactory determinant of priority in situations of stock-in-trade and receivables financing (per D M McLauchlan (1980) 96 LQR 90 at p 98).

Report of the Committee on Consumer Credit (Chairman: Lord Crowther) (1971, Cmnd 4596), Vol 2, p 579

It is doubtful whether any system of priorities can be provided which will do justice in all situations. Certainly existing rules of law fall far short of the ideal. For example, if a debt is assigned to A and afterwards the assignor fraudulently assigns the same debt to B who takes in good faith then if B is the first to give notice to the debtor he gains priority under the rule in *Dearle v Hall*. This rule implicitly assumes that notice to the debtor is equivalent to notice to the second assignee. But this will not in fact be the case unless the second assignee, before giving value, makes enquiries of the debtor to see whether he has had notice of a prior assignment. In the financing of receivables such enquiries would be quite impracticable and the second assignee would not give notice to the debtors, or indeed have occasion to communicate with them, until after he had taken his assignment and paid the price. Moreover the rule in *Dearle v Hall* does not provide a secured party with any machinery for protecting a security interest in future receivables due from future debtors.

NOTES

1. The problems associated with the factoring of future receivables are highlighted at p 757 above.

2. For further criticism of the use the rule in *Dearle v Hall* to determine priority in the context of receivables financing, see J S Ziegel (1963) 41 Can Bar Rev 54, 109–110; and R M Goode (1976) 92 LQR 528 at 566.

QUESTION

A Bank plc lends money to B Ltd and takes as security a floating charge over the company's existing and future assets, including its receivables. As is usual with such charge instruments, the instrument restricts the company's right to factor or discount its receivables. Prescribed particulars of the charge are duly registered with the Registrar of Companies but these particulars do not include details of the restrictive covenant on factoring or discounting. B Ltd then purports to assign all its existing and future receivables to C Factors Ltd under a whole turnover agreement which contains a warranty from B Ltd that it has the unencumbered right to factor its receivables. Having searched the register C Factors Ltd are at all times aware of the bank's floating charge, but they do not know of the restrictive covenant. Will C Factors Ltd acquire the receivables unencumbered by the bank's charge? See R M Goode *Commercial Law* (1982), pp 774–775; and Salinger, op cit, para 8-12.

6 Reform

As Professor Goode has noted: 'In economic terms, a sale of receivables with recourse is virtually indistinguishable from a loan on the security of the receivables, for in both cases the trader receives money now and has to repay it himself, or ensure payments by debtors, later' (*Commercial Law* (1982), p 856). As we have already seen, a major distinction between a sale and a loan secured on a company's book debts is that only the latter must be registered under the Companies Act 1985, s 395ff (see above, p 752). Registration protects any third party who subsequently deals with the company and who would otherwise be unaware that the company's book debts were encumbered. However, if the financing arrangement is structured as a sale with a right of recourse, the finance company is fully secured and yet others dealing with the company are ignorant of the fact. This anomaly has been criticised: see, for example, *Gough on Company Charges* (1978), pp 259–260; the *Report of the Committee on Consumer Credit* (Chairman Lord Crowther) (Cmnd 4596 (1971)) Chs 4 and 5.

Most recently, Professor Diamond has recommended reform.

A Review of Security Interests in Property by Professor A L Diamond, paras 18.2.3 and 18.2.4

18.2.3   Both Article 9 of the Uniform Commercial Code and the Canadian Uniform Personal Property Security Act apply not only to transactions creating security interests, including those in debts ('accounts' in the North American Acts), but also to sales or assignments of accounts. These do not have to be by way of security, and are covered even if they are sales for cash. The explanation for this given by the Uniform Commercial Code, Official Comment to Section 9-102, is: 'Commercial financing on the basis of accounts . . . is often so conducted that the distinction between a security transfer and a sale is blurred, and a sale of such property is therefore covered . . . whether intended for security or not. . . . The buyer then is treated as a secured party, and his interest as a security interest.'

18.2.4   Thus the factoring contract would be treated as if it created a security interest. One can see the affinity between an assignment of accounts receivable and a loan on the security of accounts receivable by contemplating an outright assignment for cash coupled with an obligation to repurchase the account (tantamount to repaying the cash) if the debtor whose debt was assigned fails to pay the assignee. An attempt to distinguish between assignments with recourse from those without would probably not be profitable. Moreover, although in one sense an assignment of a debt where notice or intimation is given to the debtor whose debt is assigned is being made public, it is not a public fact that can be readily discovered by a single search, but would require expensive and time-consuming enquiries of individual debtors. In the light of the North American experience it would seem to be a sound decision to include the assignment of accounts as if they were security interests.

NOTE

In Part II of his report, Professor Diamond recommends that a new register of security interests should be set up. He proposes that the date of filing would in many cases be the relevant date for determining the priority of competing security interests and that it would be possible to file an entry before the security interest was actually created and to cover future dealings in a single filing. The new law would apply to security interests created by companies, partnerships and individuals in the course of their business. These recommendations are considered in detail below, at pp 798–799.

7 International factoring

A factoring agreement is considered as 'international' when the factor's client (as supplier of goods or services) and the person responsible for the payment of goods and services are situated in different States (Salinger, op cit, p 115). In these circumstances, factoring is used to finance international trade. A common practice is for the supplier to enter into a factoring agreement with a factor in his own country (the 'export factor'). The export factor then enters into an arrangement with correspondent factors (the 'import factors') in the countries of the supplier's customers. The import factors accept the credit risk of the debtors situated in their own country and are responsible for collection. The export factor sub-assigns the purchased debt to the import factors. At all times, the import factor is responsible to the export factor and the export factor is responsible to the supplier. Rights of recourse may be exercised along that chain. This method of international factoring is known as a 'two factor' system.

Other methods of international factoring include:

(1) the 'single factor' system, where the export factor does not use an import factor for routine collections but only for the collection of seriously overdue debts or on the debtor's insolvency;
(2) 'direct import factoring', where the supplier simply factors the debt to a factor in the importing country;
(3) 'direct export factoring' where the export factor handles the functions of the import factor using correspondents to assist with collections in the debtor's country.

Reflecting the growing importance of international factoring, the International Institute for the Unification of Private Law (UNIDROIT) adopted a draft Convention on international factoring in May 1988. The Convention, known as 'The Unidroit Convention on International Factoring', aims to 'facilitate international factoring, while maintaining a fair balance of interests between the different parties involved in factoring transactions' (in the words of the Preamble to the Convention). The Convention is confined to international factoring. It will only apply if:

(1) the parties to the contract of sale have places of business in different States and
   (a) those States and the State in which the factor has its place of business are Contracting States; or
   (b) both the contract of sale of goods and the factoring contract are governed by the law of a Contracting State (art 2(1)); *and*
(2) the factoring contract is one under which the supplier may or will assign to the

factor receivables arising from contracts of sale of goods (including the supply of services) made between the supplier and its customers (debtors) other than those for the sale of goods bought primarily for their personal, family or household use (art 1(2)(a)); *and*

(3) the factor performs at least two of the functions listed, namely, finance for the supplier, including loans and advance payments, maintenance of accounts (ledgering) relating to the receivables, collection of receivables and protection against default in payment of debtors (art 1(2)(b)); *and*

(4) notice of the assignment of the receivables is given to the debtors.

The Convention may be excluded in whole (but not in part)

(1) by the parties to the factoring agreement; or

(2) by the parties to the contract of sale, as regards receivables arising at or after the time the factor has been given written notice of such exclusion (art 3(1) and (2)).

The substantive provisions of the Convention are set out below. They should be interpreted having regard to the object and purpose of the Convention as well as to its international character and the need to promote uniformity in its application and the observance of good faith in international trade (art 4(1)). Questions concerning matters governed by the Convention which are not expressly settled by it are to be settled in conformity with the general principles on which it is based or, in the absence of such principles, in conformity with the law applicable by virtue of the rules of private international law (art 4(2)).

Unidroit Convention on International Factoring (Ottawa, 28 May 1988), Chapters II–IV

CHAPTER II—RIGHTS AND DUTIES OF THE PARTIES

Article 5

As between the parties to the factoring contract:
(a) a provision in the factoring contract for the assignment of existing or future receivables shall not be rendered invalid by the fact that the contract does not specify them individually, if at the time of conclusion of the contract or when they come into existence they can be identified to the contract;
(b) a provision in the factoring contract by which future receivables are assigned operates to transfer the receivables to the factor when they come into existence without the need for any new act of transfer.

Article 6

1.—The assignment of a receivable by the supplier to the factor shall be effective notwithstanding any agreement between the supplier and the debtor prohibiting such assignment.
2.—However, such assignment shall not be effective against the debtor when, at the time of conclusion of the contract of sale of goods, it has its place of business in a Contracting State which has made a declaration under Article 18 of this Convention.
3.—Nothing in paragraph 1 shall affect any obligation of good faith owed by the supplier to the debtor or any liability of the supplier to the debtor in respect of an asignment made in breach of the terms of the contract of sale of goods.

Article 7

A factoring contract may validly provide as between the parties thereto for the transfer, with or without a new act of transfer, of all or any of the supplier's rights deriving from the contract of sale of goods, including the benefit of any provision in the contract of sale of goods reserving to the supplier title to the goods or creating any security interest.

Article 8

1.—The debtor is under a duty to pay the factor if, and only if, the debtor does not have knowledge of any other person's superior right to payment and notice in writing of the assignment:
(a) is given to the debtor by the supplier or by the factor with the supplier's authority;
(b) reasonably identifies the receivables which have been assigned and the factor to whom or for whose account the debtor is required to make payment; and
(c) relates to receivables arising under a contract of sale of goods made at or before the time the notice is given.
2.—Irrespective of any other ground on which payment by the debtor to the factor discharges the debtor from liability, payment shall be effective for this purpose if made in accordance with the previous paragraph.

Article 9

1.—In a claim by the factor against the debtor for payment of a receivable arising under a contract of sale of goods the debtor may set up against the factor all defences arising under that contract of which the debtor could have availed itself if such claim had been made by the supplier.
2.—The debtor may also assert against the factor any right of set-off in respect of claims existing against the supplier in whose favour the receivable arose and available to the debtor at the time a notice in writing of assignment conforming to Articles 8(1) was given to the debtor.

Article 10

1.—Without prejudice to the debtor's rights under Article 9, non-performance or defective or late performance of the contract of sale of goods shall not by itself entitle the debtor to recover a sum paid by the debtor to the factor if the debtor has a right to recover that sum from the supplier.
2.—The debtor who has such a right to recover from the supplier a sum paid to the factor in respect of a receivable shall nevertheless be entitled to recover that sum from the factor to the extent that:
(a) the factor has not discharged an obligation to make payment to the supplier in respect of that receivable; or
(b) the factor made such payment at a time when it knew of the supplier's non-performance or defective or late performance as regards the goods to which the debtor's payment relates.

CHAPTER III—SUBSEQUENT ASSIGNMENTS

Article 11

1.—Where a receivable is assigned by a supplier to a factor pursuant to a factoring contract governed by this Convention:
(a) the rules set out in Articles 5 to 10 shall, subject to sub-paragraph (b) of this paragraph, apply to any subsequent assignment of the receivable by the factor or by a subsequent assignee;
(b) the provisions of Articles 8 to 10 shall apply as if the subsequent assignee were the factor.
2.—For the purposes of this Convention, notice to the debtor of the subsequent assignment also constitutes notice of the assignment to the factor.

Article 12

This Convention shall not apply to a subsequent assignment which is prohibited by the terms of the factoring contract.

CHAPTER IV—FINAL PROVISIONS

. . .

Article 17

1.—Two or more Contracting States which have the same or closely related legal rules on matters governed by this Convention may at any time declare that the Convention is not to apply where the supplier, the factor and the debtor have their places of business in those States. Such declarations may be made jointly or by reciprocal unilateral declarations.
2.—A Contracting State which has the same or closely related legal rules on matters governed by this Convention as one or more non-Contracting States may at any time declare that the Convention is not to apply where the supplier, the factor and the debtor have their places of business in those States.
3.—If a State which is the object of a declaration under the previous paragraph subsequently becomes a Contracting State, the declaration made will, as from the date on which the Convention enters into force in respect of the new Contracting State, have the effect of a declaration made under paragraph 1, provided that the new Contracting State joins in such declaration or makes a reciprocal unilateral declaration.

Article 18

A Contracting State may at any time make a declaration in accordance with Article 6(2) that an assignment under Article 6(1) shall not be effective against the debtor when, at the time of conclusion of the contract of sale of goods, it has its place of business in that State.

NOTES

1. The Convention comes into force six months after the date of deposit of the third instrument of ratification, acceptance, approval or accession (art 14(1)).

2. The Convention has been criticised for its limited scope. In particular, it has been criticised for failing to deal with the relationship between the factor and the supplier (which is governed by domestic law) and also its failure to address the questions of priority of competing claims to receivables. Furthermore, although international factoring raises a number of difficult questions of conflict of laws (see Salinger, op cit, paras 12-02–12-15; and M Moshinsky (1992) 108 LQR 591), the Convention may be criticised for avoiding the issue. See Salinger, op cit, para 12-28. However, if the Convention had been any wider in its scope there must be some doubt as to whether it would have received the broad welcome it did (it secured the approval of delegates representing 55 States when it was adopted).

3. For further details, see Salinger, op cit, Chs 6 and 12 (which are heavily relied upon in the commentary to this section); and R M Goode [1988] JBL 347 at p 510.

Part VIII

Commercial credit and security

CHAPTER 22

Introduction

1 Commercial credit

Credit plays an important role in the world of commerce. Let us take the sale of goods as an example. The seller may have to borrow money from his bank to finance the expansion of his business so that he can obtain the buyer's order and supply the goods as required. The bank loan is a form of credit. On the other hand, the buyer may be unwilling or unable to pay for the goods in advance or on delivery and require a period of credit from the seller. The buyer may even need to sell the goods himself before he can pay his supplier. In these circumstances, the seller may provide the credit himself by deferring payment, or he may accept payment by means of a bill of exchange payable at a future date. The extent to which the seller is willing to accommodate the buyer will greatly depend on the bargaining strengths of the parties. But a seller who has accommodated the buyer by allowing him credit may be unwilling or unable to wait until the credit period expires before receiving funds locked up in the debt he is owed. In such circumstances, he may sell the debt to a factoring company, or discount the bill of exchange to a bank or discount house, for immediate cash. Alternatively, he may borrow on the strength of those receivables (see above, Chapter 21).

So far we have considered the means by which the seller provides credit to the buyer. However, the seller may be unwilling to do this. The seller may prefer to sell the goods to a third party, such as a finance house, and leave it to the third party to supply the goods to the buyer on credit terms, eg through hire-purchase, conditional sale, credit sale or finance leasing. Alternatively, the buyer may simply borrow money from a commercial lender and use the loan to pay the seller.

But no matter who provides credit, or how, the creditor will usually require some form of security. For example, the seller may reserve title in the goods or demand that payment is made by irrevocable documentary credit; the bank or factoring company may require security over other property belonging to the borrower; the finance house may ask for a third party guarantee. In all these cases the creditor is trying to ensure that he is not left high and dry should the debtor fail before making payment. In certain cases, the creditor may even insure himself against such loss (see above, p 688).

(a) Credit defined

The term 'credit' is used in many different senses. For example, it may be used to describe someone's financial standing (eg 'his credit is good'); alternatively, it may be used in a legal sense, such as to describe some form of financial accommodation. In this chapter, we shall be concerned with credit in the sense of financial accommodation, that is, 'the provision of a benefit (cash, land, goods, services or facilities) for which payment is to be made by the recipient in money at a later date' (R M Goode *Commercial Law* (1982), p 707; cf the Consumer Credit Act 1974, s 9(1) which defines credit as including 'a cash loan, and any other form of financial accommodation').

(b) The forms of credit

There are two forms of credit: loan credit and sale credit. *Loan credit* is granted where money is lent to the debtor on terms that it must be repaid to the creditor, together with interest, in due course, eg as with a bank loan or overdraft. *Sale credit* is granted where the debtor is allowed to defer payment of the price of goods and services supplied, eg as with conditional sale, hire-purchase, and credit sale agreements. It used to be important to distinguish between loan credit and sale credit because of the different regulatory regimes which applied to each (eg the Moneylenders Acts never applied to instalment selling and hire-purchase). However, in so far as a transaction is now caught by the Consumer Credit Act 1974 the distinction between the two forms of credit has become irrelevant in this context. But the distinction remains relevant in other contexts, eg a company's borrowing powers may be restricted by its Memorandum or Articles of Association, or it may breach the terms of a debenture given to its bankers by further borrowing, yet in both cases the company remains free to purchase goods and service on sale credit.

A distinction must also be made between *fixed-sum credit* and *revolving credit*. Fixed-sum credit is granted where the debtor receives a fixed amount of credit which must be repaid in a lump sum or by instalments over a period of time. Non-instalment loans, hire-purchase agreements and conditional sale agreements are all examples of fixed-sum credit. By contrast, revolving credit is granted where the debtor is allowed a credit facility which he may draw on as and when he pleases, up to an overall credit limit. The debtor may then restore the facility in whole or in part as he repays the creditor. A bank overdraft provides a good example of revolving credit: as cheques are drawn by the customer and paid by the bank, the available balance of the overdraft decreases; as amounts are paid to the credit of the account, the available balance of the overdraft increases. In strict legal terms, the overdraft facility is a standing offer for a loan made by the bank which the customer accepts each time he draws upon that facility, so that a series of unilateral contracts come into existence. In contrast, where the bank provides the customer with a bank loan of a fixed amount, the customer enters into a single bilateral contract with the bank. Both fixed-sum credit and revolving credit may be purchase-money (eg where a customer purchases a car for cash advanced direct from the finance house to the car dealer and where goods and services are purchased by credit card) or non-purchase money (eg a bank loan for general purposes and an overdraft).

(c) The Consumer Credit Act 1974

In general, the Consumer Credit Act 1974 applies to any agreement whereby credit of £15,000 or less (secured or unsecured) is supplied to an individual, including an unincorporated trader (but not when the credit is supplied to a company): ss 8(1)–(2) and 189(1). Such an agreement is called a 'regulated consumer credit agreement' (s 8(3)). However, regulated consumer credit agreements between private individuals are exempt from most of the provisions of the Act.

Where the Act applies it regulates such matters as the form, contents, terms and enforcement of a regulated consumer credit agreement. Wherever credit of £15,000 or less is provided to an unincorporated trader it will be important to consider the impact of the Consumer Credit Act 1974 on that transaction. However, as the Act is a general consumer protection statute, and is not designed for the protection of commercial debtors, we do not intend to consider its provisions any further at this stage. (For further discussion, see below, pp 853–854.)

QUESTIONS

1. List the principal institutions granting commercial credit. See R M Goode *Consumer Credit Law* (1989), p 25.
2. 'The provision of credit for trade and industry stimulates production and encourages enterprise. Credit also tides individuals and companies over difficult times' (F Oditah *Legal Aspects of Receivables Financing* (1991), p 1). Can you think of any other motives for demanding credit? Is the provision of credit always a good thing?

2 Security

(a) The nature and purpose of security

In 1985 Professor Diamond was asked by the Minister for Corporate and Consumer Affairs to examine the need for alteration of the law relating to security over property other than land. His report was published by the Department of Trade and Industry in 1989 and is entitled *A Review of Security Interests in Property*. In the extract which follows, Professor Diamond considers the nature and purpose of security.

A Review of Security Interests in Property **by Professor A L Diamond (1989), paras 3.1–3.3**

The nature of security
3.1   There are two types of security. One type is often known as personal security. This is where a person who is not otherwise liable under a contract between the debtor and the creditor enters into a separate contract with the creditor under which he assumes some form of liability to ensure that the creditor does not lose (or loses less than he otherwise might) if the debtor fails to perform his contractual obligations. The debtor's contractual obligations may involve the payment of money, but this is not necessarily the case: they may require the performance of any kind of act. Personal security may take the form of a guarantee, caution

or indemnity, or may be known as a performance bond. This report is not concerned with this form of security.

3.2   The other type of security is security over property. This is a right relating to property, the purpose of which is to improve the creditor's chance of getting paid or of receiving whatever else the debtor is required to do by way of performance of the contract. It is this type of security – security over property other than land – which is the subject matter of this report. Such security may be possessory, where the creditor takes possession of the subject matter of the security, or non-possessory.

The purpose of security
3.3   As stated in the last paragraph, the purpose of security is to improve the creditor's chance of obtaining performance of the contract with the debtor. In particular, the taking of security may have any one or more of the following effects:

(a)   *Coercion*
In most situations the last thing the creditor wants is to have to enforce his security. His prime objective is that the contract he has entered into with the debtor should be performed. The debtor's fear that the security may be enforced, or a threat by the creditor to enforce the security, will often be enough to ensure that a debtor who is having difficulty in fulfilling all his contracts will give priority to performance in favour of the secured creditor.

(b)   *Insolvency*
If the debtor is unable to meet all his obligations, the creditor with security will usually be in a better position than unsecured creditors, for he will be able to look to the security which, if it has sufficient value, will enable him to receive money on its disposal. In some situations the agreement creating the right by way of security will enable the creditor to appoint a receiver in specified circumstances.

(c)   *Execution or diligence*
Another creditor may, usually after obtaining a judgment against the debtor, attempt to seize the debtor's property by way of execution or diligence, or a landlord may, without obtaining a judgment, distrain on the debtor's goods or sequestrate the debtor's goods for rent. The holder of security will hope to exercise his rights against the property subject to the security and to prevent seizure by or on behalf of the other creditor.

(d)   *Sale*
If the debtor purports to sell the subject matter of the security interest, the question arises whether the holder of the security interest can assert his rights as against the buyer or whether he can, in the alternative or in addition, lay claim to the proceeds of the sale in the debtor's hands.

(e)   *General*
The above may be summed up in Professor Goode's words: 'All forms of real security . . . confer on the secured creditor at least two basic real rights: the right of pursuit, and the right of preference. The secured party can follow his asset, and its products and proceeds, into the hands of any third party other than one acquiring an overriding title by virtue of some exception to the *nemo dat* rule; and the secured party is entitled to look to the proceeds of the asset to satisfy the debt due to him in priority to the claims of other creditors.' (R M Goode *Commercial Law*, p 733.) Professor Goode continues: 'Other real rights are available for the enforcement of the security, depending on the nature of the security interest. These are: the retention or recovery of possession of the asset; sale of the asset; foreclosure; and an order vesting legal title in the secured creditor.'

NOTES

1. A creditor holding personal security has merely a personal claim against the third party guarantor (as well as against the original debtor). The weakness of personal security is that its value depends on the continued solvency of the third party. If the third party is made bankrupt, or goes into liquidation, the creditor is only left with a right to prove for a dividend in competition with other unsecured creditors.

2. By contrast, a creditor holding real security (or 'security over property' as Professor Diamond describes it) can rely on his right of preference to ensure priority over other creditors in the event of the debtor's bankruptcy or liquidation. As Professor D E Allan has observed ((1989) 15 Mon LR 337 at p 343):

> ... the principal value of traditional security is to give the creditor a preferred position in the insolvency or liquidation of the debtor. The major fear of creditors is the insolvency of the debtor and the risk that the creditor will have to line up and share *pari passu* with all other creditors. Security provides a means whereby, in the event of this catastrophe, the secured party can make off with the assets against which he is secured and satisfy his claim in full outside the bankruptcy.

3. But what is of benefit to a creditor holding real security (hereafter referred to as 'a secured creditor') may be of detriment to the debtor and to unsecured creditors generally. Professor Allan continues (op cit, p 343):

> This privileged position [ie of the secured creditor] ... is at variance with a legal policy manifested in the bankruptcy and winding-up legislation of seeking the rehabilitation of the debtor and, where that is not possible, of providing an even-handed distribution among creditors of all types. It concedes to any secured creditor the right to withdraw the assets against which he is secured and virtually to determine unilaterally that the debtor shall be put into bankruptcy or liquidation without reference to whether the situation of the debtor is salvageable and without regard to the interests of other creditors. The position is particularly acute so far as the unsecured creditors are concerned. ...

Some of Professor Allan's concerns have been met by statutory intervention. In particular, the Insolvency Act 1986, ss 10(1) and 11(3), imposes restrictions on the secured creditor's right to enforce his security where a petition has been presented for an administration order or an administration order has been made (see *Bristol Airport plc v Powdrill* [1990] Ch 744, CA and *Re Atlantic Computer Systems plc* [1992] Ch 505, CA). Such intervention evidences a modest shift of balance away from secured creditors and back towards the principle of *pari passu* distribution (M G Bridge [1992] JBL 1 at p 17). However, the extent to which insolvency law should generally look to redistribute assets from secured to unsecured creditors, in the interests of equality, raises important policy questions (as to which, see F Oditah *Legal Aspects of Receivables Financing* (1991), p 18; and F Oditah (1992) 108 LQR 459 at p 472).

4. So what justifies placing a secured creditor in such a privileged position? A number of theories have been advanced which seek to justify the privilege on grounds of economic efficiency (see A Schwartz (1981) 10 Journal of Legal Studies 1 for a general review; see also T H Jackson and A T Kronman (1979) 88 Yale LJ 1143). None of these theories is entirely convincing (Schwartz, op cit, p 33). By contrast, the most convincing explanation is probably that which turns on the premiss that the priority given to real security makes credit accessible to many debtors who, in the absence of such security, may be unable to obtain unsecured finance. As Dr Oditah submits (op cit, p 18):

... the law recognises and gives effect to the priority of secured creditors because security makes available funds which may otherwise be employed elsewhere, or made available only on terms which the average debtor can ill afford. This may or may not be perceived as detrimental to unsecured creditors of a common debtor, but it can scarcely be shown to be at their expense.[73] Indeed a secured creditor has already paid for his priority through receipt of a lower return on his investment. On the other hand, unsecured creditors have already been paid for allowing this priority and they receive a higher rate of return because of their lower priority position. Since most creditors are free to select the terms on which they would lend, there is no compelling argument based on considerations of fairness for adopting one legal rule rather than the other.[74]

73 See Goode (1983) 8 Can Bus LJ 53 (the priority of secured creditors is justified by the concepts of bargain, value and notice). Some forms of value recognised by law may appear to be rather shadowy, eg where the first in, first out rule applies. But this is not in fact so as a banker who honours cheques drawn on an overdrawn account gives value.
74 Jackson (1982) 91 Yale LJ 857 at 871.

See also F Oditah (1992) 108 LQR 459 at p 472.

Whatever the justification for it, there can be little doubt that the system of secured credit is here to stay, at least for the foreseeable future (M Bridge (1992) 12 OJLS 333 at p 341). To abolish the system would be futile for, as Professors Jackson and Kronman have pointed out (op cit, p 1157), '. . . if the law denied debtors the power to prefer some creditors over others through a system of security agreements, a similar network of priority relationships could be expected to emerge by consensual arrangement between creditors'.

QUESTION

Is a secured creditor always ensured priority over other creditors on the debtor's bankruptcy or liquidation? What if two creditors hold security over the same property?

(b) Real security and security interest

Real security means security in a *res* (or asset). It involves the grant to the creditor of an interest in one or more assets of the debtor (or a third party) to secure the debtor's obligations. The interest conferred may be full legal ownership or some lesser property right in the asset. A creditor granted an interest in such circumstances is described as having a 'security interest' (R M Goode *Legal Problems of Credit and Security* (2nd ed, 1988), p 1; see also *Bristol Airport plc v Powdrill* [1990] Ch 744 at 760, where Browne-Wilkinson V-C, without claiming it was comprehensive, adopted a similar definition of 'security' when interpreting s 248 of the Insolvency Act 1986). As a consequence of the grant of his interest the creditor acquires those rights which inhere in the asset and which, therefore, can be exercised against third parties generally. Such 'real' rights include the rights of pursuit and preference. However, these real rights must be distinguished from rights of pursuit and preference conferred on the creditor by agreement with the debtor (or third party) independently of the creation of any property interest in the asset. In such circumstances, the rights of pursuit and preference will only bind the parties to the particular agreement and not third parties generally (see R M Goode (1989) 15 Mon LR 361 at 363–364, replying to the contrary argument presented by D E Allan (1989) 15 Mon LR 337 at p 346). However, equity blurs the distinction between rights *in* an asset (real rights) and rights *to* an asset (personal rights). Because equity treats as done that which ought to be done, most agreements to give security in an asset will be treated as proprietary in nature, ie as if the agreements were actual transfers (R M Goode (1987) 103 LQR 433 at pp 437–438; and F Oditah (1992) 108 LQR 459 at pp 469–470).

Only four types of consensual security (ie created by agreement between the parties) give a creditor a security interest: pledge, contractual lien, mortgage and charge (R M Goode *Legal Problems of Credit and Security* (2nd ed, 1988), pp 10–15; and (1989) 15 Mon LR 361 at p 362; contra, Oditah, op cit, pp 5–11; and D E Allan (1989) 15 Mon LR 337 at p 348). Other types of consensual security are regarded as quasi-security (see below). Furthermore, in certain circumstances real security may arise automatically by operation of law. The main category of real security arising by operation of law is the lien (other than the contractual lien). Pledges, common law liens (including contractual liens) and the principal statutory lien (the unpaid seller's lien) are all possessory securities, ie the creditor takes possession of the subject matter of the security (see below, Chapter 23). Mortgages, charges, equitable liens and maritime liens are non-possessory securities (see below, Chapter 24).

(c) Quasi-security

Real security can be contrasted with quasi-security. Although quasi-security is intended to fulfil a security function, it does not give the creditor a security interest because it does not involve rights *in* an asset which bind third parties generally (R M Goode (1989) 15 Mon LR 361 at p 362). Examples of such quasi-security include: contractual set-off, subordination agreements, flawed assets, and negative pledge clauses in unsecured financing (see R M Goode *Commercial Law* (1982), pp 719–727, and *Legal Problems of Credit and Security* (2nd ed, 1988), pp 4–5, 17–24).

Hire purchase agreements, conditional sale agreements and retention of title clauses (although again fulfilling security functions) are also regarded as quasi-securities. Although in the case of these security devices the creditor does have a right in the asset, it is a right which he retains and not one which the debtor grants to him. Only real rights created by the debtor (not retained by the creditor) are regarded as rights by way of security. This distinction was established by the House of Lords in *McEntire v Crossley Bros Ltd* [1895] AC 457, and has recently been restated by their Lordships House in *Armour v Thyssen Edelstahlwerke AG* [1991] 2 AC 339 (on appeal from the Inner House of the Court of Session (Scotland)). In *Armour v Thyssen*, sellers claimed redelivery of steel supplied under a contract of sale containing an 'all monies' reservation of title clause. Receivers of the buyers resisted the claim arguing that the clause constituted an attempt, ineffective under Scottish law, to create a right of security over corporeal movables without transfer of possession, and that the property in the steel passed to the buyers on delivery. The House of Lords upheld the seller's claim on the ground that the buyers had not created a security over the goods in favour of the seller. Lord Jauncey of Tullichettle stated that '[i]t is of the essence of a right of security that the debtor possesses in relation to the property a right which he can transfer to the creditor, which right must be retransferred to him on payment of the debt'. As the contract of sale reserved property in the seller until payment of all debts due, the buyers 'had no interest of any kind whatsoever in the particular goods . . . [and] . . . were never in a position to confer on the [sellers] any subordinate right over the steel . . .' (per

Lord Keith of Kinkel). See also, R M Goode (1989) 15 Mon LR 360 at p 362 (who argues that if the debtor has neither an interest in the asset *nor the power to dispose of it* he cannot give it in security); contra Oditah, op cit, pp 5–8, and Allan, op cit, pp 348–349).

An important consequence of distinguishing between real security and quasi-security is that whereas most types of consensual non-possessory real security must be registered under the Bills of Sale Acts 1878–1891, or Part XII of the Companies Act 1985 (as amended by Part IV of the Companies Act 1989), or possibly some other Act (eg as with land, shares, ships etc), quasi-security is not registrable (but see s 344 of the Insolvency Act 1986; above, p 765). Whether a security is registrable or not can affect its validity and priority in the event of the debtor's bankruptcy or insolvency (see below, Chapter 27).

(d) How is the creation of real security to be determined?

Professor Goode answers the question as follows:

> . . . two elements must be conjoined, an intention to create security and an agreement in a form which effectuates this intention . . . mere intention is not sufficient. The parties must by their agreement have given effect to that intention in accordance with legal requirements. . . . [(1989) Mon LR 360 at p 364.]

But it is sometimes difficult to ascertain the precise legal form of an agreement which fulfills a security function. To identify the legal nature of the transaction the court must examine its substance and ascertain the real intention of the parties.

Welsh Development Agency v Export Finance Co Ltd [1992] BCLC 148, Court of Appeal

(See above, p 747.)

NOTES

See notes above, p 751.

(e) Reform

A Review of Security Interests in Property by **Professor A L Diamond (1989), paras 8.2.1–8.2.11**

8.2 Defects in the present law

8.2.1 *(a) Obstacles to security*. Having concluded that legal obstacles to the creation of security interests where both parties are contracting in the course of a business should be kept to the minimum necessary, how far does the present law reflect this policy? In England and Wales I can sum up the present position as being one where a security interest can be taken in almost anything, provided an appropriate method is used, but that it is not always clear what the most appropriate method is. . . .

8.2.3 For reasons I am coming to, I think English law is in urgent need of reform. . . .

8.2.4   *(b) The law lacks a functional basis.* The English law of security is divided into rigid compartments, making the law fragmented and incoherent. Transactions essentially similar in nature are treated in very different ways. This has the effect of complicating the legal issues quite unnecessarily. . . .

8.2.5   This can cause problems when an attempt is made to create a security interest, for a method must be chosen appropriate to the property concerned and the effect that is desired. There are, for example, many cases in the law reports where the parties adopted the form of a sale followed by a hire-purchase agreement only to find that, perhaps for reasons of timing, perhaps for other reasons, it totally failed to take effect – in England and Wales because the Bills of Sale Acts had not been complied with. . . .

8.2.6   It can also cause problems at the stage of enforcement, for different forms of security interest may have very different consequences. In England and Wales the difference between the equitable rules governing mortgages and the common law or statutory rules governing hire-purchase agreements, for example, can be striking. If goods subject to a mortgage or charge are seized and sold, and fetch more than the amount owed by the debtor to repay the loan with interest and costs, the excess belongs to the debtor. If the goods were subject to a hire-purchase agreement, however, the creditor can keep the excess.

8.2.7   *(c) Complexity.* The compartmentalisation of the law just referred to inevitably gives rise to a law that is complex and uncertain. In England and Wales the old division between common law and equity, parallel systems administered in separate courts before 1876, still looms large in the field of security law. For example, an innocent purchaser, who buys goods not knowing of any security interest in them, may be in a radically different position according to whether the security interest of which he is unaware was equitable or legal. In a case concerning charterparties (*Re Welsh Irish Ferries Ltd* [1986] Ch 471) the judge had to consider whether a contractual 'lien' was a charge registrable under the Companies Act and for this purpose had to explore the effect in equity of a non-statutory assignment of contractual rights. (See too *The Annangel Glory* [1988] 1 Lloyd's Rep 45.)

8.2.8   The complexity of the law leads to difficulty, and perfectly legitimate business activities are in consequence attended with unnecessary expense and delay. The complications may be disastrous for a party who gets it wrong. What should and could be a routine business activity may involve complicated documentation or uncertainty. Particularly difficult are the rules relating to the secured creditor's right to the proceeds of the subject matter of the security if it is sold.

8.2.9   Because issues are decided by reference to rules that evolved for different purposes, the law is capable of acting unfairly and may fail to hold a just balance as between the parties. In some cases creditors have found that they lose the protection that they intended to obtain, and sometimes debtors are harshly treated because of the failure of the law to recognise their true position as a party who has given security. Although any legal rule is capable of producing the wrong result in a particular fact situation, the present law is notably defective. The rules vary widely according to distinctions which have no commercial or rational significance.

8.2.10   *(d) Priorities.* Because there are so many different ways of achieving similar economic ends, it is difficult to reconcile competing interests. This causes problems in determining priorities and leads to fortuitous differences in insolvency. There is no logical plan for ranking conflicting claims, though Scotland has some statements of principle in s 464 of the Companies Act 1985. The uncertainty of the effect of some clauses in contracts for the sale of goods seeking to retain title can make it difficult for a receiver or liquidator to discover what are in effect security interests.

8.2.11   *(e) Purchasers.* Particularly unfortunate is that the effect of security interests on purchasers may be difficult to ascertain. I have already referred to the effect of the differences between legal and equitable rules in the law of England and Wales. In addition, there is inadequate protection for the purchaser of property subject to a security interest of which he was unaware, and perhaps could not discover. Such purchasers are put at risk and inadequately protected by the law. It may even be difficult for them to secure speedy legal advice because of the fragmentation of the law and the varieties of security interest that are possible.

NOTES

1. At present, the law regulates transactions according to their form rather than their substance or function. Real security and quasi-security fulfil the same security function but they are regulated differently because of their form. The problems which the 'form over substance' approach can lead to are highlighted by Professor Diamond in this extract from his report. See also, R M Goode (1984) 100 LQR 234.

2. For a recent example of some of the problems caused by the present law, see *Compaq Computer Ltd v Abercorn Group Ltd* (above, p 739). In particular, see Note 3 above, at p 743; and L S Sealy [1992] CLJ 19 at p 21.

The main recommendation made by Professor Diamond in his report is to replace the present law relating to security interests with new legislation containing a simpler and unified system, with similar rules applying to all types of consensual security interests, but excluding interests arising by operation of law (Report, paras 1.9, 9.2.1 and 9.3.1). The new unified system proposed by Professor Diamond is based closely on art 9 of the American Uniform Commercial Code (UCC) and the Personal Property Security Acts introduced in several Canadian provinces (Report, para 9.2.2).

The new legislation would have two key characteristics. First, it would give the term 'security interest' a functional definition. The term would cover 'not only mortgages, charges and security interests in the strict sense but also any other transfer or retention of any interest in or rights over property other than land which secures the payment of money or the performance of any other obligation' (Report, para 9.3.2). Secondly, it would establish a new register of security interests to replace the bills of sale registers and the registration of charges under the Companies Act 1985 (although security interests in land would continue to be registered with the Registrar of Companies). Under the new system the date of filing a 'financing statement' (with minimum particulars) would be the relevant date for determining the priority of competing security interests (except for possessory security interests, security interests in consumer goods and purchase money security interests). The first to file would win the priority race. However, it would be possible to file an entry before the security interest was actually created so that, for example, a financing statement could be filed in the course of negotiations for a loan. It would also be possible to cover a series of security agreements between the same parties over a period of time by making a single filing at the start of the period.

The detailed recommendations made by Professor Diamond appear in Part II of his report. See also, A Diamond (1989) 42 CLP 231; and M Lawson [1989] JBL 287. For a critical assessment of art 9 of the UCC and a summary of the Canadian personal property legislation, see I Davies *Textbook on Commercial Law* (1992), pp 365–373.

However, it appears that Professor Diamond's proposals are unlikely to be implemented in the short or medium-term. This was the fate of similar proposals made in Part V of the Report of the Crowther Committee on Consumer Credit (HMSO, 1971, Cmnd 4596), even though those proposals were later supported by the Cork Committee when reviewing insolvency law and practice (1982, Cmnd 8558, para 1623). In a written answer in April 1991, the Secretary of State for Trade and Industry stated that, because of the complexity and potential cost of the Diamond proposals, he had 'decided not to accept the recommendations in Part II of the [Diamond] report for England and Wales' (189 HC Official Report (5th series) col 482, 24 April 1991). The Secretary of State's decision is to be regretted for there is a clear case for reform of the present law relating to security interests. But see M G Bridge [1992] JBL 1, who concludes that, whatever happens to the Diamond Report, reform is already taking place at both the case law and statutory levels (op cit, p 25).

CHAPTER 23

Possessory security

1 Pledge

(a) What is a pledge?

Coggs v Bernard (1703) 2 Ld Raym 909, Court of King's Bench

Holt CJ (describing various types of bailment): The fourth sort is, when goods or chattels are delivered to another as a pawn, to be a security to him for money borrowed of him by the bailor; and this is called in Latin vadium, and in English a pawn or a pledge. . . .

As to the fourth sort of bailment, viz vadium or a pawn, in this I shall consider two things; first, what property the pawnee has in the pawn or pledge, and secondly for what neglects he shall make satisfaction. As to the first, he has a special property, for the pawn is a securing to the pawnee, that he shall be repaid his debt, and to compel the pawner to pay him. But if the pawn be such as it will be the worse for using, the pawnee cannot use it, as cloaths, etc but if it be such, as will be never the worse, as if jewels for the purpose were pawn'd to a lady, she might use them. But then she must do it at her peril, for whereas, if she keeps them lock'd up in her cabinet, if her cabinet should be broke open, and the jewels taken from thence, she would be excused; if she wears them abroad, and is there robb'd of them, she will be answerable. And the reason is, because the pawn is in the nature of a deposit, and as such is not liable to be used. And to this effect is Ow 123. But if the pawn be of such a nature, as the pawnee is at any charge about the thing pawn'd, to maintain it, as a horse, cow, etc then the pawnee may use the horse in a reasonable manner, or milk the cow, etc in recompense for the meat. As to the second point Bracton 99 b gives you the answer. Creditor, qui pignus accepit, re obligatur, et ad illam restituendam tenetur; et cum hujusmodi res in pignus data sit utriusque gratia, scilicet debitoris, quo magis ei pecunia crederetur, et creditoris quo magis ei in tuto sit creditum, sufficit ad ejus rei custodiam diligentiam exactam adhibere, quam si praestiterit, et rem casu amiserit, securus esse possit, nec impedietur creditum petere. In effect, if a creditor takes a pawn, he is bound to restore it upon the payment of the debt; but yet it is sufficient, if the pawnee use true diligence, and he will be indemnified in so doing, and notwithstanding the loss, yet he shall resort to the pawnor for his debt. Agreeable to this is 29 Ass 28, and *Southcote's* case is. But indeed the reason given in *Southcote's* case is, because the pawnee has a special property in the pawn. But that is not the reason of the case; and there is another reason given for it in the Book of Assize, which is indeed the true reason of all these cases, that the law requires nothing extraordinary of the pawnee, but only that he shall use an ordinary care for restoring the goods. But indeed, if the money for which the goods were pawn'd, be tender'd to the pawnee before they are lost, then the pawnee shall be answerable for them; because the pawnee, by detaining them after the tender of the money, is a wrong doer, and it is a wrongful detainer of the goods, and the special property of the pawnee is determined. And a man that keeps goods by wrong, must be answerable for them at all events, for the detaining of them by him, is the reason of the loss. Upon the same difference as the law is in relation to pawns, it will be found to stand in relation to goods found.

Halliday v Holgate (1868) LR 3 Exch 299, Exchequer Chamber

Willes J: . . . There are three kinds of security: the first, a simple lien; the second, a mortgage, passing the property out and out; the third, a security intermediate between a lien and a mortgage – viz, a pledge – where by contract a deposit of goods is made a security for a debt, and the right to the property vests in the pledge so far as is necessary to secure the debt. It is true the pledgor has such a property in the article pledged as he can convey to a third person, but he has no right to the goods without paying off the debt, and until the debt is paid off the pledgee has the whole present interest.

NOTES

1. The essential characteristics of a pledge are that: (a) it is created by contract, (b) the property pledged must be actually or constructively delivered to the pledgee, and (c) the pledgee is given a 'special property' in the subject matter of the pledge. Usually, a pledge secures repayment of a debt but, in principle, there is no reason why it should not secure the performance by the pledgor of some other obligation (*Halsbury's Laws of England* (4th ed), Vol 36, para 101).

2. Although the pledgee is given special property in the goods pledged, he does not become the general owner of the goods. This led Lord Mersey in *The Odessa* [1916] 1 AC 145 at 158–159, to question whether it was appropriate to describe the pledgee's 'interest' in the goods as a form of property at all. However, even if the pledgee is described as having merely 'a special interest' in the pledged goods, it is, nevertheless, an interest of proprietary significance. As Professor N E Palmer has observed in his treatise on bailment (*Bailment* (2nd ed, 1991), pp 1382–1383):

> The pledgee, eg, has an inherent right of sale; and the interests distributed by the pledge (to wit, the pledgor's reversion and the pledgee's special property) are capable of surviving both a sale of the chattel by the pledgor, and its repledge by the pledgee, respectively. Further, in common with other varieties of bailment, the pledgee's possession entitles him to exercise the proprietary and possessory remedies against a third party wrongdoer, and to recover at common law damages calculated according to the full value of the goods (or the full cost of their depreciation) as if he were the owner.

3. At common law, the terms 'pledge' and 'pawn' were used interchangeably, although the pledge of a bill of lading was never described as a 'pawn' (*Halsbury's Laws of England* (4th ed), Vol 36, para 101n). Under the Pawnbrokers Acts 1872–1960 (now repealed), the term 'pledge' referred to the goods and 'pawn' to the act of delivery or receipt of the goods. Under s 189(1) of the Consumer Credit Act 1974, the term 'pawn' means any article subject to a pledge and 'pledge' means the pawnee's rights over an article taken in pawn. The 'pawnee' is the recipient of the goods and the 'pawnor' is the person who delivered them to the pawnee.

(b) Delivery

Official Assignee of Madras v Mercantile Bank of India Ltd [1935] AC 53, Privy Council

A firm of merchants (the merchants) purchased groundnuts and transported them to Madras by rail. For each consignment of groundnuts the merchants obtained a railway receipt from the railway companies. The receipt entitled the named consignee, or indorsee, to obtain delivery of the groundnuts from the railway companies. The merchants then raised loans against the consignments by sending, inter alia, the railway receipts, duly indorsed in blank, to the respondent bank. On the insolvency of the merchants, the Official Assignee of Madras, in whom their property vested by reason of the insolvency, disputed whether the bank had taken a valid pledge of the groundnuts. The issue before the Privy Council was whether the pledging of railway receipts was a pledge of the goods represented by them or merely a pledge of the actual documents. The Privy Council held that under the relevant Indian legislation the railway receipts were documents of title to the goods and that the owner of the goods could pledge the goods by pledging the documents of title. The Privy Council affirmed the judgment of the High Court of Madras in favour of the bank. But the Privy Council also emphasised that if the case had been governed by English law the result would have been different.

Lord Wright (delivering the advice of the Privy Council): But the arguments advanced on behalf of the appellant have sought to treat the matter as concluded by the history and present state of the relevant law in England, which will now be briefly summarized. At the common law a pledge could not be created except by a delivery of possession of the thing pledged, either actual or constructive. It involved a bailment. If the pledgor had the actual goods in his physical possession, he could effect the pledge by actual delivery; in other cases he could give possession by some symbolic act, such as handing over the key of the store in which they were. If, however, the goods were in the custody of a third person, who held for the bailor so that in law his possession was that of the bailor, the pledge could be effected by a change of the possession of the third party, that is by an order to him from the pledgor to hold for the pledgee, the change being perfected by the third party attorning to the pledgee, that is acknowledging that he thereupon held for him; there was thus a change of possession and a constructive delivery: the goods in the hands of the third party became by this process in the possession constructively of the pledgee. But where goods were represented by documents the transfer of the documents did not change the possession of the goods, save for one exception, unless the custodier (carrier, warehouseman or such) was notified of the transfer and agreed to hold in future as bailee for the pledgee. The one exception was the case of bills of lading, the transfer of which by the law merchant operated as a transfer of the possession of, as well as the property in, the goods. This exception has been explained on the ground that the goods being at sea the master could not be notified; the true explanation may be that it was a rule of the law merchant, developed in order to facilitate mercantile transactions, whereas the process of pledging goods on land was regulated by the narrower rule of the common law and the matter remained stereotyped in the form which it had taken before the importance of documents of title in mercantile transactions was realized. So things have remained in the English law: a pledge of documents is not in general to be deemed a pledge of the goods; a pledge of the documents (always excepting a bill of lading) is merely a pledge of the *ipsa corpora* of them; the common law continued to regard them as merely tokens of an authority to receive possession. . . .

The common law rule was stated by the House of Lords in *William McEwan & Sons v Smith* ((1849) 2 HL Cas 309). The position of the English law has been fully explained also more recently in *Inglis v Robertson* ([1898] AC 616) and in *Dublin City Distillery Ltd v Doherty* ([1914] AC 823). But there also grew up that legislation which is compendiously described as the Factors Acts, the first in 1823, then an Act in 1825, then an Act in 1842, then an Act in 1877, and finally, the Act in 1889 now in force. The purpose of these Acts was to protect bankers who made advances to mercantile agents: that purpose was effected by means of an inroad on the common law rule that no one could give a better title to goods than he himself had. The persons to whom the Acts applied were defined as agents who had in the customary course of their business as such authority to sell goods or to consign goods for sale or raise money on the security of goods; in the case of such persons thus intrusted with possession of the goods or the documents of title to the goods, the possession of the goods or documents of title to the goods was treated in effect as evidence of a right to pledge them, so that parties bona fide and without notice of any irregularity advancing money to such mercantile agents on the goods or documents were held entitled to a good pledge, even though such mercantile agents were acting in fraud of the true owner. Section 3 of the Factors Act 1889, provides that 'a pledge of document of title to goods shall be deemed to be a pledge of the goods.' It has been held that this section only applies to transactions within the Factors Act: *Inglis v Robertson*.

Thus the curious and anomalous position was established that a mercantile agent, acting it may be in fraud of the true owner, can do that which the real owner cannot do, that is, obtain a loan on the security of a pledge of the goods by a pledge of the documents, without the further process being necessary of giving notice of the pledge to the warehouseman or other custodier and obtaining the latter's attornment to the change of possession. But it is obvious that the ordinary process of financing transactions in goods is much facilitated by ability to pledge the goods by the simple process of pledging the documents of title. It need not be repeated that bills of lading stand apart, nor need it be observed here that some warehousing companies have, by means of private Acts, assimilated their warrants or delivery orders to bills of lading for this purpose.

NOTES

1. As delivery lies at the heart of a pledge, only chattels which are capable of actual or constructive delivery can be pledged. This means, for example, that bearer bonds may be pledged (*Carter v Wake* (1877) 4 Ch D 605) but not the choses in action (the shares) represented by share certificates (*Harrold v Plenty* [1901] 2 Ch 314). For reasons of public policy, certain other chattels may not be pledged, eg firearms, ammunition, military, naval and airforce equipment, equipment issued to those in the territorial army reserve or Royal Auxiliary Air Force, and Social Security cards or used stamps therefor. In each case the prohibition arises under statute.

2. In *Meyerstein v Barber* ((1866) LR 2 CP 38; affd *sub nom Barber v Meyerstein* (1870) LR 4 HL 317) it was argued that delivery of an exhausted bill of lading only operated as an agreement to pledge goods and not as the symbolic delivery of the goods themselves. The Court of Common Pleas held that the bill of lading was not exhausted and delivery of the goods represented by the document had been made to complete the pledge. However, Willes J stated obiter that: '. . . a mere contract to pledge even specific goods, and even if money is actually advanced upon the faith of the contract, is not sufficient to carry the legal property in the goods . . . such a transaction amounts only to an authority to take possession of the goods. . . .'. As to exhaustion of a bill of lading, see A H Hudson (1963) 26 MLR 442.

3. Contrast Willes J's dictum in *Meyerstein v Barber* with the decision of Kekewich J in *Hilton v Tucker* (1888) 39 Ch D 669, where money was lent pursuant to an agreement that the borrower would deliver certain goods into the lender's possession. The goods were not delivered until a month after the loan had been made. Kekewich J held that with a pledge of goods it was not essential that the loan and delivery of possession should be contemporaneous. He held that it was enough if possession was delivered within a reasonable time of the loan in pursuance of the contract to pledge. But if delivery does not take place, Willes J's dictum would apply.

4. In *Official Assignee of Madras v Mercantile Bank of India Ltd*, Lord Wright stated that there would be constructive delivery of goods held by a third person on behalf of the pledgor if that third person attorned to the pledgee. Constructive delivery will also take place when the goods are in the possession of the pledgor and he contracts to continue to hold them as bailee for the pledgee and not on his own account as owner (*Meyerstein v Barber* (1866) LR 2 CP 38 at 52, per Willes J). In *Dublin City Distillery Ltd v Doherty* [1914] AC 823 at 852, Lord Parker of Waddington stated that the pledgor's agreement to hold the goods on behalf of the pledgee '. . . operates as a delivery of the goods to the pledgee and a redelivery of the goods by the pledgee to the pledger (*sic*) as bailee for the purposes mentioned in the agreement'. The delivery/redelivery theory can also be used to explain what happens when a third person attorns to the pledgee. But the theory only works if specific goods are pledged. If the goods are part of an undivided bulk, then according to Hope JA in *Maynegrain Pty Ltd v Compafina Bank* [1982] 2 NSWLR 141 at 149 (reversed on another ground (1984) 58 ALJR 389, PC):

> . . . an attornment in respect of an undifferentiated portion of a larger quantity of goods does not operate as a delivery of some severed portion of the goods and a redelivery of that portion to the attornor; it operates as if such a delivery and redelivery had been effected, the attornor being estopped from denying the necessary severance and appropriation by virtue of the attornment itself, and no doubt in many cases because the attornee has acted to his prejudice on the basis of the attornment. It is, however, irrelevant that the attornee knows that in fact no severance or appropriation has taken place.

See also *Re London Wine Co (Shippers) Ltd* [1986] PCC 121 (above, p 260).

Wrightson v McArthur and Hutchisons (1919) Ltd [1921] 2 KB 807, King's Bench Division

In consideration of the plaintiff allowing the first defendant more time to pay for goods, the second defendant (the company) set aside certain specified goods in two rooms on its premises which were locked up and the keys handed to the plaintiff, no other goods being in those rooms. In a subsequent letter to the plaintiff, the company stated that: 'The goods to be locked up, the keys in your possession, and you to have the right to remove same as desired.' On the company's liquidation, an issue arose as to whether the letter evidenced a charge. If so, the security, being unregistered, was void against the liquidator. On the other hand, if the security was a pledge completed by delivery of possession of the goods without reference to the letter, then it was valid as not requiring registration (see below, p 813). Rowlatt J upheld the validity of the security.

Rowlatt J: The point to which this case is now reduced is whether the circumstance that the rooms, the keys of which were delivered, were within the defendants' premises, prevents the delivery of the keys conferring possession of the contents of the rooms. If the keys delivered had been the outside key of the whole warehouse containing these goods I should have felt no difficulty, nor should I have felt any difficulty had the key been of an apartment or receptacle in the premises of a third party as was the case in *Hilton v Tucker* ((1888) 39 Ch D 669). On the other hand if, the rooms being in the defendants' premises, the keys had been given without the licence to go and remove the goods at any time I should have thought it clear that possession of the goods did not pass. It would be merely a case of the goods remaining in the defendants' possession with the security that they should not be interfered with, but without any power of affirmative control at the free will of the plaintiff. It would be like the case of furniture left in a locked room in a house that is let furnished, where the lessor has no right to enter except upon reasonable notice and at reasonable times. The actual question has to be considered in the light of the principle that delivery of a key has effect not as symbolic delivery, but as giving the actual control. This was the view expressed by Lord Hardwicke in *Ward v Turner* ((1752) 2 Ves Sen 431), where he says the key is the means of coming at the possession. The matter was fully discussed in the light of all the cases in *Pollock and Wright on Possession in the Common Law*, p 61 and following pages. In *Hilton v Tucker*, already referred to, in a judgment delivered since the date of that work, Kekewich J observes 'that the delivery of the key in order to make constructive possession must be under such circumstances that it really does pass the full control of the place to which admission is to be gained by means of the key.' If I might criticise that statement my criticism would only be as to the propriety of the use of the word 'constructive' in the connection in question.

I think therefore there can be no doubt as to the true principle, and the difficulty is in its application. There are two cases in which delivery of the key of a box in a house has been held to confer possession of the contents. The first was *Jones v Selby* ((1710) Prec Ch 300), referred to by Lord Hardwicke in *Ward v Turner* above mentioned, the other was *Mustapha v Wedlake* ([1891] WN 201), but in both those cases both parties were living in the house and therefore the person receiving the delivery could not be expected to take away the box, but could hold possession of it in the house. It has never been held, so far as I know, that delivery of the key of a box which the deliverer retains in his own house, where the other party does not live, passes possession of the contents. Upon the whole, however, I think that in the case before me the possession was transferred, having regard to the fact that a licence to come and make the necessary entry to use the key was also conferred, a licence which it seems to me could not be revoked. The door into the building would be open in business hours, and the mere fact that the plaintiff might wrongfully be excluded from the whole building does not, I think, affect the matter. If the key had been given him with the intention to pass to him the possession of the room itself upon a demise of it, I cannot doubt that possession would pass. I see no difference when the key is given to pass possession not of the room, but of the chattels. The key guards both in the same way.

NOTES

1. In *Hilton v Tucker* (1888) 39 Ch D 669, pursuant to an agreement with the pledgee, the pledgor hired a room in a building belonging to a third party and stored certain prints and engravings there. The pledgor then wrote to the pledgee informing him that the third party held the key to the room 'which I place entirely at your disposal'. Kekewich J held that the prints and engravings had been constructively delivered to the pledgee even though the pledgor continued to have access to the room (via a duplicate key). Although the pledgee must usually be given exclusive control of the pledged chattels, Kekewich J stressed that in this case the 'laxity in the control of the room' was irrelevant as the pledgor had only a limited right of access (to clean the room and list the chattels) and at all times had acknowledged that his right was subject to the pledgee's paramount control. The issue appears to turn on whether the deliveror really intends to relinquish possession of the chattels to the deliveree. It should also be noted that the question of whether the pledgee needed the third party's permission to pass through the building (to gain access to the room) was not raised in *Hilton v Tucker*. The question was also ignored by Rowlatt J in *Wrightson v McArthur and Hutchisons (1919) Ltd*. As Andrew Bell has observed: 'In general, a key will not confer possession if the third party has not agreed to grant access to persons other than the deliveror' (A P Bell *Modern Law of Personal Property in England and Ireland* (1989), pp 47–48).

2. In *Dublin City Distillery Ltd v Doherty* [1914] AC 823 whisky was kept in a bonded warehouse over which the distillery company and the Inland Revenue had joint control. In particular, the warehouse had two locks; the distillery company held the key to one lock and the Revenue held the key to the other. The distillery company purported to pledge the whisky to the respondent by entering the transaction into its books and by issuing invoices and warrants to the respondent. The House of Lords held that there had been no constructive delivery of the whisky and, therefore, no pledge. Lord Atkinson held that the warrants issued by the distillery company did not entitle the respondent to delivery of the whisky without further attornment to him (at 847–848; and Lord Sumner at 862–865; cf Lord Parker of Waddington at 853). When reviewing the law relating to constructive delivery, Lord Atkinson accepted that it could take place by delivery of the key to a store or house but doubted 'whether, owing to the dual control over this whisky exercised by the distillers and the Revenue officer, it would not be necessary in the present case that both keys should be delivered' (at 843–844). Lord Parker of Waddington viewed the question of dual control somewhat differently. He held that dual control meant that the distillery company and the Revenue had joint possession of the whisky so that the respondent could not take delivery from either one of them without the consent of the other (at 857–858).

QUESTIONS

1. Why was the pledgee's licence to enter the pledgor's premises held to be irrevocable in *Wrightson v McArthur and Hutchinson (1919) Ltd* (above, p 805)? See Bell, op cit, pp 48–49.
2. On the issue of 'exclusive control', how can *Hilton v Tucker* be distinguished from *Dublin City Distillery Ltd v Doherty*?
3. Does transfer of a key constitute actual, constructive or symbolic delivery of the chattels to which it gives access? Compare A C H Barlow (1956) 19 MLR 394 with Bell, op cit, p 58.

(c) Re-delivery

Reeves v Capper (1838) 5 Bing NC 136, Court of Common Pleas

W, the master of a ship, pledged his chronometer to C as security for a loan. Pursuant to the terms of the loan agreement, C returned the chronometer to W for use on a specific voyage. After the voyage W pledged the chronometer to R. R claimed that the original pledge had been destroyed when C had parted with possession of the chronometer by redelivering it to W. Tindal CJ held that this redelivery did not destroy the pledge.

Tindal CJ: . . . we agree entirely with the doctrine laid down in *Ryall v Rolle* ((1750) 1 Atk 165), that in the case of a simple pawn of a personal chattel, if the creditor parts with the possession he loses his property in the pledge: but we think the delivery of the chronometer to Wilson under the terms of the agreement itself was not a parting with the possession, but that the possession of Captain Wilson was still the possession of Messrs Capper. The terms of the agreement were, that 'they would allow him the use of it for the voyage:' words that gave him no interest in the chronometer, but only a licence or permission to use it, for a limited time, whilst he continued as their servant, and employed it for the purpose of navigating their ship. During the continuance of the voyage, and when the voyage terminated, the possession of Captain Wilson was the possession of Messrs Capper; just as the possession of plate by a butler is the possession of the master; and the delivery over to the Plaintiff was, as between Captain Wilson and the Defendants a wrongful act, just as the delivery over of the plate by the butler to a stranger would have been; and could give no more right to the bailee than Captain Wilson had himself. We therefore think the property belonged to the Defendants, and that the rule must be made absolute for entering the verdict for the Defendants.

NOTES

1. Whether the pledgor holds as owner or as bailee after the goods are redelivered to him turns on the intention of the parties. An agreement to hold the goods for a special purpose indicates such an intention. This type of agreement is commonly found in international trade finance. After the importing buyer has pledged the bill of lading and other shipping documents as security for an advance from his bank, he may later be allowed to take back those documents to enable him to sell the goods and pay off the bank. To ensure that the bank maintains its constructive possession of the goods represented by the documents, it will only release the documents to the buyer under a letter of trust or a trust receipt (an example of which appears below at p 963). By the terms of such a letter or receipt, the buyer undertakes that in consideration of the release of the documents to him he will hold them on trust for the bank, will use them to sell the goods as the bank's agent and will hold the goods themselves until sale, and the proceeds after sale, on trust for the bank (see R M Goode *Commercial Law* (1982), pp 692–695).

2. The pledge will be preserved if the pledgor takes the goods without permission or obtains redelivery by fraud (*Mocatta v Bell* (1857) 24 Beav 585). However, when redelivery is obtained by fraud the pledgee's rights may be lost against a subsequent pledgee or purchaser who takes the pledged chattels bona fide, for value and without notice. In *Babcock v Lawson* (1880) 5 QBD 284, the pledgors, who were merchants, obtained redelivery of the pledged goods by fraudulently misrepresenting to the pledgees that they had sold the goods and that the pledgees would be paid from the proceeds of sale. Upon redelivery, the pledgors obtained an advance from the defendants and deposited the goods with them. The Court of Appeal held that as the pledgees had parted with their special property in the goods to the pledgors, they could not recover the goods from the defendants who had obtained them bona fide and for good consideration. An important feature of this case was that, because of the fraud, the pledgees intended to divest themselves of their special property in the pledged goods. But what if the goods, or documents of title to the goods, are redelivered to the pledgor for a special purpose other than sale? Should the pledgee be bound by any subsequent sale or pledge, or should the *nemo dat* rule apply?

3. A similar problem to that noted at 2 above arises when the pledgee redelivers goods to the pledgor under the terms of a trust receipt. In *Lloyds Bank Ltd v Bank of America* [1938] 2 KB 147, the pledgee bank returned bills of lading to the pledgor, against a trust receipt, so that the pledgor could sell the goods and pay the bank off out of the proceeds. Instead of selling the goods, the pledgor repledged them to a second bank. It was held that the second bank got a good title as against the first bank by virtue of s 2 of the Factors Act 1889 (see above, p 312). The Court of Appeal held that for the purposes of s 2, the pledgee was deemed the (joint) 'owner' of the goods. But s 2 will only apply if, inter alia, the pledgor is a mercantile agent and the goods, or documents of title to the goods, were entrusted to him in that capacity (*Astley Industrial Trust Ltd v Miller* [1968] 2 All ER 36).

4. Both *Babcock v Lawson* and *Lloyds Bank v Bank of America* can be distinguished as cases where the pledgees intended to divest themselves of their special property in the goods and redelivered the goods to the pledgor for that purpose. But where a pledgee intends to retain his special property, and redelivers the goods, or the documents of title to the goods, to the pledgor for a purpose other than disposition, his rights are not to be defeated by an unauthorised disposition by the pledgor, so long as the pledgee has not in some other way lent himself to the transaction (*Mercantile Bank of India Ltd v Central Bank of India Ltd* [1938] AC 287, PC). This may seem harsh on a third party who buys, or takes a pledge, from the pledgor in good faith and without notice. However, if legislation is enacted to implement Professor Diamond's recommendation that redelivery to the pledgor must be registered, the third party will be protected in such circumstances (Professor A L Diamond *A Review of Security Interests in Property* (DTI, 1989), para 11.5.7).

QUESTION

Swell agrees to lend £1,000 to Tight, an artist, on the security of some of Tight's pictures, and Tight accordingly places these in an empty shed in his garden, locks the shed, and sends the only key to Swell with a letter stating that Swell can enter and remove the pictures whenever he wishes. Consider the rights of the parties in the following alternative circumstances:

(1) Tight, pretending that he wishes to show the pictures to an admirer, obtains the key from Swell for an hour. Tight removes a picture and sells it to Swap.
(2) The roof of the shed springs a leak and Swell, on learning of this, hands Tight the key and asks him to cover up the pictures. Tight takes the opportunity to remove a picture and sell it to Flint.
(3) Tight had previously stolen the pictures from Otto, who now looks to recover them from Swell. See the Torts (Interference with Goods) Act 1977, s 11(2).

(d) Re-pledge by the pledgee

Donald v Suckling (1866) LR 1 QB 585, Court of Queen's Bench

The pledgor deposited debentures with Simpson as security for the payment, at maturity, of a bill of exchange indorsed by the pledgor and discounted by Simpson. *Before* maturity of the bill, Simpson pledged the debentures to the defendant to secure a loan which exceeded the amount secured by the original pledge. The pledgor sought to recover the debentures from the defendant, by a claim in detinue, without tendering the amount of the original debt. The Court of Queen's Bench (Shee J dissenting) held that he was not entitled to do so.

Mellor J: . . . The question thus raised by this plea is, whether a pawnee of debentures, deposited with him as a security for the due payment of money, at a certain time, does, by repledging such debentures and depositing them with a third person as a security for a larger amount, before any default in payment by the pawnor, make void the contract upon which they were deposited with the pawnee, so as to vest in the pawnor an immediate right to the possession thereof, notwithstanding that the debt due by him to the original pawnee remains unpaid. . . .

In a contract of pledge for securing the payment of money, we have seen that the pawnee may sell and transfer the thing pledged on condition broken; but what implied condition is there that the pledgee shall not in the meantime part with the possession thereof to the extent of his interest? It may be that upon a deposit by way of pledge, the express contract between the parties may operate so as to make a parting with the possession, even to the extent of his interest, before condition broken, so essential a violation of it as to revest the right of possession in the pawnor; but in the absence of such terms, why are they to be implied? There may possibly be cases in which the very nature of the thing deposited might induce a jury to believe and find that it was deposited on the understanding that the possession should not be parted with; but in the case before us we have only to deal with the agreement which is stated in the plea. The object of the deposit is to secure the repayment of a loan, and the effect is to create an interest and a right of property in the pawnee, to the extent of the loan, in the goods deposited; but what is the authority for saying that until condition broken the pawnee has only a personal right to retain the goods in his own possession?

In *Johnson v Stear* ((1863) 15 CBNS 330), one Cumming, a bankrupt, had deposited, with the defendant 243 cases of brandy, to be held by him as a security for the payment of an acceptance of the bankrupt for £62 10s, discounted by the defendant, and which would become due January 29, 1863, and in case such acceptance was not paid at maturity, the defendant was to be at liberty to sell the brandy and apply the proceeds in payment of the acceptance. On the 28th January, before the acceptance became due, the defendant contracted to sell the brandy to a third person, and on the 29th delivered to him the dock warrant, and on the 30th such third person obtained actual possession of the brandy. In an action of *trover*, brought by the assignee of the bankrupt, the Court of Common Pleas held that the plaintiff was entitled to recover, on the ground that the defendant wrongfully assumed to be owner, in selling; and although that alone might not be a conversion, yet, by delivering over the dock warrant to the vendee in pursuance of such sale, he 'interfered with the right which the bankrupt had on the 29th if he repaid the loan'; but the majority of the Court (Erle CJ, Byles and Keating JJ) held that the plaintiff was only entitled to nominal damages, on the express ground, 'that the deposit of the goods in question with the defendant to secure repayment of a loan on a given day, with a power to sell in case of default on that day, created *"an interest and a right of property in the goods, which was more than a mere lien*; and the wrongful act of the pawnee *did not annihilate the contract between the parties nor the interest of the pawnee in the goods* under that contract." ' From that view of the law, as applied to the circumstances of that case, Mr Justice Williams dissented, on the ground 'that the bailment was terminated by the sale before the stipulated time, and consequently that the title of the plaintiff to the goods became as free as if the bailment had never taken place.' Although the dissent of that most learned judge diminishes the authority of that case as a decision on the point, and although it may be open to doubt whether in an action of *trover* the defendant ought not to have succeeded on the plea of not possessed, and whether the plaintiff's only remedy for damages was not by action on the contract, I am nevertheless of opinion that the substantial ground upon which the majority of the Court proceeded, viz that the 'act of the pawnee did not annihilate the contract, nor the interest of the pawnee in the goods,' is the more consistent with the nature and incidents of a deposit by way of pledge. I think that when the true distinction between the case of a deposit, by way of pledge, of goods, for securing the payment of money, and all cases of *lien*, correctly so described, is considered, it will be seen that in the former there is no implication, in general, of a contract by the pledgee to retain the personal possession of the goods deposited; and I think that, although he cannot confer upon any third person a better title or a greater interest than he possesses, yet, if nevertheless he does pledge the goods to a third person for a greater interest than he possesses, such an act does not *annihilate the contract of pledge* between himself and the pawnor; but that the transaction is simply inoperative as against the original pawnor, *who upon tender of the sum secured immediately becomes entitled to the possession of the goods*, and can recover in an action for any special damage which he may have sustained by reason of the act of the pawnee in repledging the goods; and I think that such is the true effect of Lord Holt's definition of a 'vadium or pawn' in *Coggs v Bernard* (above, p 800); although he was of opinion that the pawnee could in no case use the pledge if it would thereby be damaged, and must use due diligence in the keeping of it, and says that the creditor is bound to restore the pledge upon payment of the debt, because, by detaining it after the tender of the money, he is a wrongdoer, his special property being determined; yet he nowhere says that the misuse or abuse of the pledge before payment or tender annihilates the contract upon which the deposit took place.

If the true distinction between cases of lien and cases of deposit by way of pledge be kept in mind, it will, I think, suffice to determine this case in favour of the defendant, seeing that no tender of the sum secured by the original deposit is alleged to have been made by the plaintiff; and considering the nature of the things deposited, I think that the plaintiff can have sustained no real damage by the repledging of them, and that he cannot successfully claim the immediate right to the possession of the debentures in question.

I am therefore of opinion that our judgment should be for the defendant.

Blackburn J: . . . Now I think that the subpledging of goods, held in security for money, before the money is due, is not in general so inconsistent with the contract, as to amount to a renunciation of that contract. There may be cases in which the pledgor has a special personal confidence in the pawnee, and therefore stipulates that the pledge shall be kept by him alone, but no such terms are stated here, and I do not think that any such term is implied by law. In general all that the pledgor requires is the personal contract of the pledgee that on bringing the money the pawn shall be given up to him, and that in the meantime the pledgee shall be responsible for due care being taken for its safe custody. This may very well be done though there has been a subpledge; at least the plaintiff should try the experiment whether, on bringing the money for which he pledged those debentures to Simpson, he cannot get them. And the assignment of the pawn for the purpose of raising money (so long at least as it purports to transfer no more than the pledgee's interest against the pledgor) is so far from being found in practice to be inconsistent with or repugnant to the contract, that it has been introduced into the Factors Acts, and is in the civil law (and according to *Mores v Conham* ((1610) Owen 123) in our own law also) a regular incident in a pledge. If it is done too soon, or to too great an extent, it is doubtless unlawful, but not so repugnant to the contract as to be justly held equivalent to a renunciation of it.

Cockburn CJ: I think it unnecessary to the decision in the present case to determine whether a party, with whom an article has been pledged as a security for the payment of money, has a right to transfer his interest in the thing pledged (subject to the right of redemption in the pawnor) to a third party. I should certainly hesitate to lay down the affirmative of that proposition. Such a right in the pawnee seems quite inconsistent with the undoubted right of the pledgor to have the thing pledged returned to him immediately on the tender of the amount for which the pledge was given. In some instances it may well be inferred from the nature of the thing pledged, – as in the case of a valuable work of art, – that the pawnor, though perfectly willing that the article should be intrusted to the custody of the pawnee, would not have parted with it on the terms that it should be passed on to others and committed to the custody of strangers. It is not, however, necessary to decide this question in the present case. The question here is, whether the transfer of the pledge is not only a breach of the contract on the part of the pawnee, but operates to put an end to the contract altogether, so as to entitle the pawnor to have back the thing pledged without payment of the debt. I am of opinion that the transfer of the pledge does not put an end to the contract, but amounts only to a breach of contract, upon which the owner may bring an action, – for nominal damages if he has sustained no substantial damage; for substantial damages, if the thing pledged is damaged in the hands of the third party, or the owner is prejudiced by delay in not having the thing delivered to him on tendering the amount for which it was pledged.

NOTES

1. Subject to Mellor J's caveat that a prohibition on repledge may be imposed by an express term in the contract, or might be implied by virtue of the special character of the goods in exceptional cases, the Court of Queen's Bench held in *Donald v Suckling* that a repledge by the pledgee does not destroy the original pledge, even if made before the pledgor's default and for a sum exceeding that secured by the original pledge. It was not the *ratio* of the case that a pledgee has the right to repledge in such circumstances. Mellor J appears to have proceeded on the basis that a repledge was not a breach of contract, but Cockburn CJ did not feel it necessary to decide whether a pledgee had a general right to repledge. The issue was also left open by Willes J in *Halliday v Holgate* (1868) LR 3 Exch 299 at 302.

2. If the pledgor tenders payment to the pledgee he may demand the return of the pledged chattels. The pledgee is thereby divested of his special property in the chattels and the pledgor is given an immediate right to possess them. This right allows the pledgor to bring an action in conversion against the subsequent pledgee should he refuse to return the chattel to him. He can also sue the original pledgee for breach of the contract of pledge in these circumstances. But for so long as the original pledgee has a special property in the pledged chattel the pledgor has no immediate right to possession and so cannot bring an action in detinue or conversion (*Halliday v Holgate*, above, at 302–303). This explains why it was so important for the pledgor in *Donald v Suckling*, who had not tendered payment, to establish that the original pledgee had been divested of his special property in the debentures.

3. If the pledgor sells the goods while they are still subject to the pledge, the buyer can sue the re-pledgee in conversion if he refuses to deliver up the goods after the buyer has tendered the amount owed, under the original pledge, to the original pledgee (*Franklin v Neate* (1844) 13 M & W 481). The buyer cannot sue the original pledgee for breach of the contract of pledge as he is not privy to that contract.

4. Save for circumstances described by Mellor J in the caveat referred to above, when will the pledgee's disposition of the subject matter of the pledge 'annihilate' the contract of pledge? Sale of the subject matter would not appear to be enough (*Johnson v Stear* (1863) 15 CBNS 330, 143 ER 812), although its deliberate destruction would (*Cooke v Haddon* (1862) 3 F & F 229, 176 ER 103, where pledgee had drunk wine). As to the pledgee's duty of care and safekeeping of the subject matter of the pledge, see *Coggs v Bernard*, per Holt CJ, above, at pp 800–801.

5. The modes of terminating the pledge are:

(1) tender of the amount due;
(2) pledgee redelivering possession of the chattel to the pledgor without reservation (see above, p 806);
(3) pledgee accepting some alternative security or other discharge of the debt;
(4) 'annihilation' of the contract of pledge (see above).

Sale of the subject matter of the pledge on the pledgor's default is also a form of termination.

(e) Realisation

Re Hardwick, ex p Hubbard (1886) 17 QBD 690, Court of Appeal

(The facts are irrelevant.)

Bowen LJ: . . . A special property in the goods passes to the pledgee in order that he may be able – if his right to sell arises – to sell them. In all such cases there is at Common Law an authority to the pledgee to sell the goods on the default of the pledgor to repay the money, either at the time originally appointed, or after notice by the pledgee.

The Odessa [1916] 1 AC 145, Privy Council

(The facts are irrelevant.)

Lord Mersey: . . . If the pledgee sells he does so by virtue and to the extent of the pledgor's ownership, and not with a new title of his own. He must appropriate the proceeds of the sale to the payment of the pledgor's debt, for the money resulting from the sale is the pledgor's money to be so applied. The pledgee must account to the pledgor for any surplus after paying the debt. He must take care that the sale is a provident sale, and if the goods are in bulk he must not sell more than is reasonably sufficient to pay off the debt, for he only holds possession for the purpose of securing himself the advance which he has made. He cannot use the goods as his own. These considerations show that the right of sale is exercisable by virtue of an implied authority from the pledgor and for the benefit of both parties. It creates no jus in re in favour of the pledgee; it gives him no more than a jus in rem such as a lienholder possesses, but with this added incident, that he can sell the property motu proprio and without any assistance from the Court.

NOTES

1. Unlike a mortgagee, a pledgee has no right of foreclosure (*Carter v Wake* (1877) 4 Ch D 605). Unless contract or statute otherwise provides, the pledgee has no right to become the owner of the pledged goods on default by the pledgor. The pledged goods must either be redeemed or sold.

2. As the pledge is only collateral security for the pledgor's debt, if sale of the pledged chattel does not realise the amount lent on it the pledgee may bring an action for the deficit (*Jones v Marshall* (1889) 24 QBD 269, per Lord Coleridge CJ).

3. If a pledge or pawn is caught by the terms of the Consumer Credit Act 1974, redemption and sale are strictly controlled by the terms of that Act (see below).

(f) Statutory control

(i) *Consumer Credit Act 1974*

A 'pawn' (see above, p 801) made by an 'individual' (ie not a body corporate), and which secures an advance of £15,000 or less, is regulated by the Consumer Credit

Act 1974 (see s 8(1) and (2)). This means that:

(1) the pawnee must be licensed if he takes pawns by way of business (or else he commits an offence and cannot rely on his rights as pledgee (ss 21, 39 and 40);
(2) a pawn-receipt must be given in the prescribed form, informing the pawnor of his rights (or else the pawnee commits an offence, but he can still rely on his rights as pledgee) (ss 114(1), 115 and 170);
(3) the pawnee cannot sell the pawn within six months of the pawning (s 116(1)) and even then he must give the pawnor notice of his intention to sell and inform him of the asking price (s 121(1));
(4) *ownership* of an unredeemed pawn passes to the pawnee automatically at the end of a six months redemption period where the pawn is security for fixed sum credit not exceeding £25, or running account credit on which the credit limit does not exceed £25 (s 120(1)(a)).

For further details of the special procedures for the redemption and sale of a pawn caught by the Consumer Credit Act 1974, see ss 114–122 of that Act. But note that ss 114–122 do not apply to pledges of documents of title to goods, nor to pledges of bearer bonds (s 114(3)(a)). Neither do they apply to non-commercial agreements (s 114(3)(b)). A non-commercial agreement is a consumer credit agreement (or consumer hire agreement) not made by the creditor or owner in the course of a business carried on by him (s 189(1)).

(ii) *Registration*

A pledge which takes effect on delivery of a chattel or a bill of lading does not require registration under the Bills of Sale Acts 1878–1891 (*Re Hardwick, ex p Hubbard* (1886) 17 QBD 690) or the Companies Act 1985, as amended by the Companies Act 1989 (s 396(1)(b); and, previously, *Wrightson v McArthur and Hutchisons (1919) Ltd* [1921] 2 KB 807). The possessory nature of a pledge means that third parties are put on notice of the pledgee's rights without the need for registration (see R M Goode *Commercial Law* (1982), p 713). On the other hand, a mere agreement to make a pledge, without any delivery of the chattel or bill of lading, is registrable (*Dublin City Distillery Ltd v Doherty* [1914] AC 823 at 854, per Lord Parker of Waddington).

(iii) *Insolvency Act 1986*

Although there has yet to be a case on the point, it is submitted that a pledge would fall within the definition of 'security' contained in s 248(b) of the Insolvency Act 1986. This is of particular significance when a pledge is taken over a company's property and that company is subsequently made the subject of an administration order (explained below, p 901). In these circumstances, no steps could be taken to enforce the pledge except with the consent of the administrator or the leave of the court (Insolvency Act 1986, s 11(3)(c); see also s 10(1)(b) of the same Act). For the application of s 11(3)(c) to a possessory lien, see below, p 825.

2 Lien

(a) What is a lien?

Hammonds v Barclay (1802) 2 East 227, Court of King's Bench

Grose J: . . . A lien is a right in one man to retain that which is in his possession belonging to another, till certain demands of him the person in possession are satisfied.

Tappenden v Artus [1964] 2 QB 185, Court of Appeal

(The facts appear below, at p 821.)

Diplock LJ: The common law remedy of a possessory lien, like other primitive remedies such as abatement of nuisance, self-defence or ejection of trespassers to land, is one of self-help. It is a remedy in rem exercisable upon the goods, and its exercise requires no intervention by the courts, for it is exercisable only by an artificer who has actual possession of the goods subject to the lien. Since, however, the remedy is the exercise of a right to continue an existing actual possession of the goods, it necessarily involves a right of possession adverse to the right of the person who, but for the lien, would be entitled to immediate possession of the goods. A common law lien, although not enforceable by action, thus affords a defence to an action for recovery of the goods by a person who, but for the lien, would be entitled to immediate possession.

NOTES

1. Grose J has provided the classic definition of a common law (or possessory) lien. Like a pledge, a common law lien depends on possession (although a lien depends on the lienee *already* having possession, whereas a pledge is a *delivery* of possession). Unlike a pledge, a common law lien merely gives a personal right of retention to the person (the lienee) in possession of goods belonging to another (the lienor) (*Legg v Evans* (1840) 6 M & W 36 at 42, per Parke B). This means that the lienee, in contrast to the pledgee, cannot dispose of his interest and, at common law, he has no implied right to sell the goods which are the subject matter of the lien (*Donald v Suckling* (1866) LR 1 QB 585 at 604, 610, 612; see above, p 808).

2. There are four main types of lien: (a) common law; (b) statutory; (c) equitable; and (d) maritime. The most important statutory lien is the unpaid seller's lien (ss 41–43 of the Sale of Goods Act 1979; above, p 394). Like the common law lien, a statutory lien such as the unpaid seller's lien is a possessory lien. (For other examples of statutory liens, see the Consumer Credit Act 1974, ss 70(2), 73(5). Statute may create rights similar to a lien, eg under s 88 of the Civil Aviation Act 1982 an airport has the right to detain an aircraft for unpaid airport charges and aviation fuel supplied: *Bristol Airport plc v Powdrill* [1990] Ch 744.) By contrast, equitable and maritime liens are non-possessory liens. An equitable lien is analogous to an equitable charge. The lien of the unpaid vendor of land is the most common example of this type of lien (see L A Sheridan *Rights in Security* (1974), pp 228–231). A maritime lien is a right of action in rem against a ship and freight for payment due under a contract, for the cost of salvage or for damage caused by a ship (see L A Sheridan, op cit, pp 194–198).

3. The remainder of this chapter will concentrate on the common law lien. Unless expressly stated otherwise, all references in this chapter to a 'lien' should be read as references to that type of lien.

(b) Possession

Forth v Simpson (1849) 13 QB 680, Court of Queen's Bench

The owner of race horses stabled them with a trainer to be trained and kept. From time to time the horses, by order of the owner, were sent to run at different races, where the owner selected and paid the rider. The trainer claimed a lien over the horses for the cost of training and keep.

Lord Denman CJ: I have little doubt that the care and skill employed by a trainer upon a race horse are of such a nature as would, on general principles, give a right of lien. But it is essential to a lien that the party claiming it should have had the right of continued possession. In the present case there was no right of continued possession; for the owner of the horses might, at his own pleasure, have sent them to any race, and to be ridden by any jockey of his own selection. The circumstances of this case, therefore, make it like the case of a livery stable keeper; for it is immaterial whether the owner's possession be more or less, if he has a right to assert it at all, and to interrupt the possession of the party claiming the lien.

Coleridge J: I also have no doubt that the skill and labour of a trainer are a good foundation for a lien; because he educates an untaught animal, and otherwise adapts it for a particular purpose, and thereby greatly improves its value. But it is a well established principle that, without the right of continuing possession, there can be no right of lien. Now a good test of the existence of such right of possession is to consider in whose possession the race horse is when it is employed in doing that for which it has been trained. The evidence shewed that the horse, during the race, was in the owner's possession, and in his possession rightfully and according to usage or contract. The horse, before the race, is placed for convenience in the stable of the trainer; but during the race it is in the care of the jockey nominated by the owner. It appears too that, if, on any occasion, the jockey were selected by the trainer, the trainer, pro hac vice, would have only the delegated authority of the owner. I think it is part of the understanding that the owner shall have the possession and control of the horse to run at any race. This is quite inconsistent with the trainer's continuing right of possession.

[Patteson and Erle JJ delivered concurring judgments.]

NOTES

1. *Forth v Simpson* was followed by Rose J in *Ward v Fielden* [1985] CLY 2000. See also *Hatton v Car Maintenance Co Ltd* [1915] 1 Ch 621 at 624 (below, pp 816–817).

2. In *Forth v Simpson*, Coleridge J stated that it was part of the 'understanding' that the owner was to have possession of the horses. This illustrates that the terms of any agreement between the creditor and the debtor can prevent a lien arising. Another example of the parties' agreement being inconsistent with the existence of a lien is where the creditor extends a period of credit to the debtor (*Wilson v Lombank Ltd* [1963] 1 WLR 1294). In such cases the intention of the parties prevents a lien arising.

3. For a valid lien to arise the creditor's possession must be lawful as against the debtor. Possession must not be obtained by force or other tortious means (*Bernal v Pim* (1835) 1 Gale 17), nor must it arise as a result of fraud or any other kind of misrepresentation (*Madden v Kempster* (1807) 1 Camp 12). Furthermore, as a general rule no lien will arise from wrongful possession resulting from the act of a debtor who is not the owner of the goods (see below, pp 821 ff, for the rule and its exceptions).

4. For cases on loss of possession, see below, pp 826 ff.

(c) How does a lien arise?

A common law lien generally arises by operation of law (*Re Bond Worth Ltd* [1980] Ch 228 at 250, per Slade J). Unlike a pledge, it does not depend upon the express or implied agreement of the parties. However, it is also possible to create a common law possessory lien by agreement (Crossley Vaines *Personal Property* (5th ed, 1973), p 137; Bell, op cit, p 137). If the agreement also gives the lienee a power of sale, the lien is in reality a pledge (R M Goode *Legal Problems of Credit and Security* (2nd ed, 1988), p 14).

This section will concentrate on particular liens arising by operation of law (ie by judicially recognised usage). A particular lien gives the lienee the right to retain a chattel until all charges *incurred in respect of that chattel* have been paid. By contrast, a general lien gives the lienee the right to retain a chattel until all claims against the lienor are satisfied, *whether or not those claims arise in respect of the retained chattel*. General liens are considered below, at pp 818 ff.

Hatton v Car Maintenance Co Ltd [1915] 1 Ch 621, Chancery Division

The owner of a motor car entered into an agreement with the defendant company whereby the company agreed to maintain the vehicle, supply a driver and do any necessary repairs. An amount having become due by the owner under the agreement, the company took possession of the car and claimed a lien on it for the amount due. Sargant J rejected the company's claim.

Sargant J: Now it is clear that the amount to be paid is not merely for the repair of the car, but is for the wages of the chauffeur and the supply of petrol and oil, and that kind of thing, and therefore it is an inclusive lump sum.

It was said by Mr Crossfield [Counsel for the defendant] that whenever an article is repaired, the repairer gets a lien on the article for the amount of his charges. Well, I do not dissent at all from that view of the law, assuming that the repairer gets the article in his shop for the purpose of repair and by that repair improves it, as he would ordinarily do. But certainly I cannot find anything in the authorities which have been cited to me to show that, if what the contractor does is not to improve the article but merely to maintain it in its former condition, he gets a lien for the amount spent upon it for that maintenance. The cases with regard to horses seem to point entirely the other way, because it is clear that a jobmaster has no lien at all for the amount of his bill in respect of feeding and keeping a horse at his stable, whereas, on the other hand, a trainer does get a lien upon a horse for the improvement which he effects to the horse in the course of training it for a race. A case was cited to me by Mr Crossfield with regard to the extent of the lien of an innkeeper, but I do not think that has really any application to the present case. Here all that was to be done by the contractor was for the purpose of maintaining the car in the condition in which it was sent to him, and in my judgment he would have no lien, that is no common law lien, in respect of the amount owing to him for that service.

That really would be sufficient to dispose of the case, but I think I ought also to express my opinion that, on the cases cited to me, even if he had such a lien originally, that lien would be lost by virtue of the arrangement under which the owner was to be at liberty to take the car away, and did take the car away, as and when she pleased. The existence of a lien seems to me to be inconsistent with an arrangement under which the article is from time to time taken entirely out of the possession and control of the contractor, for I cannot think that the fact that the chauffeur was to be deemed to be the servant of the company was intended to have the effect, or had the effect, of leaving the car in the possession of the company. I think that clause was inserted for quite other and fairly obvious reasons.

Re Southern Livestock Producers Ltd [1964] 1 WLR 24, Chancery Division

By an agreement with a pig company, a farmer agreed to 'care for' a herd of pigs and supervise the breeding of the herd. The company supplied boars for the latter purpose. On the company's liquidation, the farmer claimed a lien over the pigs to cover outstanding sums expended in feeding and caring for the herd. Pennycuick J rejected the farmer's claim.

Pennycuick J: The authorities which I have cited bind me in this court. It is perfectly clear that unless the bailee can establish improvement he has no lien. If this matter were free from authority it would, I think, be tempting to draw the line in rather a different place so as to cover the case where a person by the exercise of labour and skill prevents a chattel from deteriorating in contradistinction to improving it. The obvious example is feeding of animals which would otherwise die; but other examples come to mind. It seems to me to be illogical that a kennel keeper should have a lien for the expense of stripping a dog, but not for that of boarding it. However, it is quite impossible for me at this time of day to introduce that sort of modification into a well-established principle.

Turning now to the facts of the present case, the first step is to look again at the agreement. What the farmer undertakes to do under that agreement is to care for a specified number of pigs and piglets. The word 'care' received a definition in the recital. The word means 'house feed care for and arrange for the proper servicing and farrowing of' the sows and gilts concerned, and also the piglets farrowed by the sows and gilts. Mr Figgis, who appears for the liquidator, accepts the position that under that agreement the farmer was required to employ, and did employ, labour and skill. . . . But, says Mr Figgis, the agreement does not provide for any improvement upon the subject-matter of the agreement, namely, the pigs and their litters. I have come to the conclusion that I must accept this argument. The operations comprised in the definition of 'care' add up precisely to 'care' in the ordinary sense of that word and do not seem to me to go in any respect beyond it. It is of great importance to observe in this connection that the company is under obligation to supply the boars for the service of the sows. The position would be different if the farmer had to supply the boars. In that case it appears from *Scarfe v Morgan* ((1838) 4 M & W 270) that the farmer would have a lien in respect of service charge, provided he could identify this item.

Mr Sunnucks, for the farmer, contends that one must look at the herd of pigs as a whole and that the agreement provides for the improvement of the herd as a whole by the production of litters. I agree that one must look at the herd as a whole and not pig by pig, and that is, indeed, accepted by Mr Figgis. But when one does look at the herd as a whole, one finds that the production of litters results from the natural properties of the sows in co-operation with the boars supplied by the company, and I do not think this production of litters could fairly be described as an improvement effected by the farmer. What the farmer does is merely to look after the herd as it increases from other causes.

I say again that I am not altogether attracted by the argument on behalf of the liquidator, and I should be glad if I were able to draw the line in a manner rather more generous to the person claiming a lien. But it seems to me that to do so in the way in which I am asked so to do by Mr Sunnucks would be to make an unjustifiable inroad upon well-established principles. I do not think it is legitimate to say that a person improves a flock or herd of animals merely by supervising its natural increase, however much skill and care is involved in that process.

I would add that, even if there were an element of improvement in this respect – that is, supervising the production of litters – the farmer would find himself in this difficulty because under the terms of the agreement it would be impossible to apportion the sums expended by him between the ordinary upkeep on the one hand and the improvement on the other hand.

NOTES

1. Where goods are entrusted to a person to do work on them, that person will have a lien for the work done, provided that he improves the goods. The lien is called an improver's (or artificer's) lien and it is a particular lien (although, exceptionally, an improver may be able to assert a lien over a part of a composite chattel, or one of a group of chattels, even though he has not worked on that part or on that particular chattel in the group, eg 'a car repairer could exercise a lien on the spare tyre for work carried out on the engine' per Lloyd J in *The Ijaola* [1979] 1 Lloyd's Rep 103 at 116; much depends on whether the contract was entire: see Palmer, op cit, p 944 and p 955). The lien only arises when the work is complete (*Pinnock v Harrison* (1838) 3 M & W 532). However, if the owner of the goods prevents completion by withdrawing his instructions, the improver is entitled to a lien for his charges in respect of that part which is actually completed (*Lilley v Barnsley* (1844) 1 Car & Kir 344).

2. A particular lien can also arise where a person is under a legal obligation to perform services, eg a common carrier or an innkeeper. A common carrier (not a private carrier) has a lien for his carriage charges as they become due, ie when the goods arrive at their destination. An innkeeper's lien extends over the belongings the guest brings into the inn (which includes a hotel: s 1(1) of the Hotel Proprietors Act 1956) and secures the amount of his bill for food and lodging (*Matsuda v Waldorf Hotel Co Ltd* (1910) 27 TLR 153). However, the lien does not affect the clothes the guest is wearing at any particular moment (*Sunbolf v Alford* (1838) 3 M & W 248), neither does it extend to any vehicle (or any property left therein) or any horse or other live animal or its harness or other equipment (s 2(2) of the Hotel Proprietors Act 1956).

QUESTIONS

1. Does a warehouseman enjoy a common lien (general or particular) in respect of his storage charges? See N E Palmer *Bailment* (2nd ed, 1991), pp 873–877.
2. B agrees to restore A's painting for £100. A delivers the painting to B's studio. Before the restoration is complete A demands the return of his picture. Advise B as to whether (a) he may keep the painting until A pays for the work actually done; and (b) he may ignore the demand, complete the restoration and claim the £100. See *Hounslow London Borough Council v Twickenham Garden Developments Ltd* [1971] Ch 233 at 253; and contrast *Bolwell Fibreglass Pty Ltd v Foley* [1984] VR 97 at 111.

(d) General liens

General liens may arise by express or implied agreement. In certain cases an agreement for a general lien may be established by well established trade usage.

Rushforth v Hadfield (1805) 6 East 519, Court of King's Bench

A common carrier retained a bankrupt's goods, after the cost of carriage of those goods had been paid, on the ground that he had a right to retain the goods until the cost of carriage of other goods was paid. The assignee of the estate of the bankrupt brought an action in trover against the carrier to recover the value of his goods. The common carrier claimed a general lien arising from a general usage of the trade. At the trial the jury gave a verdict for the carrier; which was moved to be set aside as a verdict against the law and evidence.

Lawrence J: I agree that there ought to be a new trial. Common carriers are every day attempting to alter the situation in which they have been placed by the law. At common law they are bound to receive and carry the goods of the subject for a reasonable reward, to take due care of them in their passage, and to deliver them in the same condition as when they were received: but they are not bound to deliver them without being paid for the carriage of the particular article, and therefore they have a lien to that extent. Of late years however they have been continually attempting to alter their general character by special notices on the one hand to diminish their liability, and on the other hand by extending their lien. But what evidence have we in this case to say that their common law situation is altered? To do that it must be shewn that both parties have consented to the alteration: the carrier cannot alter his situation by his own act alone. It is said that a general lien is convenient to the parties concerned: I do not say that it may not be so, but it must arise out of the contract of the parties. It may be convenient enough for the customer to say, that in consideration that you, the carrier, will give up your right to stop each particular parcel of goods for the price of the carriage, I will agree that you may stop any one parcel of my goods for the carriage price of all together. But still this must be by contract between them; and usage of trade is evidence of such a contract. And where such a usage is general, and has been long established so as to afford a presumption of its being commonly known, it is fair to conclude that the particular parties contracted with reference to it. Then, if in this case there had been evidence of a usage so uniform and frequent as to warrant an inference that the parties contracted with reference to it, it should have been left to the jury to infer that it was part of their contract.

Le Blanc J: . . . General liens are a great inconvenience to the generality of traders, because they give a particular advantage to certain individuals who claim to themselves a special privilege against the body at large of the creditors instead of coming in with them for an equal share of the insolvent's estate. All these general liens infringe upon the system of the bankrupt laws, the object of which is to distribute the debtor's estate proportionably amongst all the creditors, and they ought not to be encouraged. But I do not mean to say that a usage in trade may not be so general and well established as to induce a jury to believe that the parties acted upon it in their particular agreement; and I cannot say that such an agreement would not be good in law. . . . The instances of detainer by carriers for their general balance which were proved at the trial were very few and recent with a view to found so extensive a claim. . . . Without saying therefore that there may not be such a usage as that insisted on, I am clearly of opinion that there should be a new trial in order to have the case submitted to the jury on its true ground, which it does not appear to have been upon the last trial.

[Lord Ellenborough CJ and Grose J delivered concurring judgments.]

[At the new trial the jury gave a verdict for the plaintiff; which was moved to be set aside.]

Rushforth v Hadfield (1806) 7 East 224, Court of King's Bench

Lord Ellenborough CJ: It is too much to say that there has been a general acquiescence in this claim of the carriers since 1775, merely because there was a particular instance of it at that time. Other instances were only about 10 or 12 years back, and several of them of very recent date. The question however results to this, what was the particular contract of these parties? And as the evidence is silent as to any express agreement between them, it must be collected either from the mode of dealing before practised between the same parties, or from the general dealings of other persons engaged in the same employment, of such notoriety as that they might fairly be presumed to be known to the bankrupt at the time of his dealing with the defendants, from whence the inference was to be drawn that these parties dealt upon the same footing as all others did, with reference to the known usage of the trade. But at least it must be admitted that the claim now set up by the carriers is against the general law of the land, and the proof of it is therefore to be regarded with jealousy. In many cases it would happen that parties would be glad to pay small sums due for the carriage of former goods, rather than incur the risk of a great loss by the detention of goods of value. Much of the evidence is of that description. Other instances again were in the case of solvent persons, who were at all events liable to answer for their general balance. And little or no stress could be laid on some of the more recent instances not brought home to the knowledge of the bankrupt at the time. Most of the evidence therefore is open to observation. If indeed there had been evidence of prior dealings between these parties upon the footing of such an extended lien, that would have furnished good evidence for the jury to have found that they continued to deal upon the same terms. But the question for the jury here was, whether the evidence of a usage for the carriers to retain for their balance were so general as that the bankrupt must be taken to have known and acted upon it? And they have in effect found either that the bankrupt knew of no such usage as that which was given in evidence, or knowing, did not adopt it. And growing liens are always to be looked at with jealousy, and require stronger proof. They are encroachments upon the common law. If they are encouraged the practice will be continually extending to other traders and other matters. The farrier will be claiming a lien upon a horse sent to him to be shod. Carriages and other things which require frequent repair will be detained on the same claim; and there is no saying where it is to stop. It is not for the convenience of the public that these liens should be extended further than they are already established by law. But if any particular inconvenience arise in the course of trade, the parties may, if they think proper, stipulate with their customers for the introduction of such a lien into their dealings. But in the absence of any evidence of that sort to affect the bankrupt, I think the jury have done right in negativing the lien claimed by the defendants on the score of general usage.

Le Blanc J: This is a case where a jury might well be jealous of a general lien attempted to be set up against the policy of the common law, which has given to carriers only a lien for the carriage price of the particular goods. The party therefore who sets up such a claim ought to make out a very strong case. But upon weighing the evidence which was given at the trial, I do not think that this is a case in which the Court are called upon to hold out any encouragement to the claim set up, by overturning what the jury have done, after having the whole matter properly submitted to them.

[Grose and Lawrence JJ delivered concurring judgments.]

NOTE

The following have been held to have general liens as a matter of usage: solicitors (*Stevenson v Blakelock* (1813) 1 M & S 535); bankers (*Brandao v Barnett* (1846) 3 CB 519); factors (*Baring v Corrie* (1818) 2 B & Ald 137); stockbrokers (*Re London & Globe Finance Corpn* [1902] 2 Ch 416); and insurance brokers (*Hewison v Guthrie* (1836) 2 Bing NC 755).

QUESTIONS

1. Why was there such hostility to general liens in *Rushforth v Hadfield*?

2. How may a general lien be 'convenient to the parties concerned' (per Lawrence J, above, p 819)? See Bell, op cit, pp 142–143.

(e) Liens and third parties

Tappenden v Artus [1964] 2 QB 185, Court of Appeal

T allowed A to use a van pending completion of a hire-purchase agreement between them. It was a condition of the bailment that A should tax and insure the vehicle at his own expense. The van broke down and A took it to the defendants' garage for repair. Shortly afterwards T withdrew his permission for A to use the van and demanded its return. The defendants refused to deliver up the van until paid for their work. At first instance, T succeeded in his action against the defendants for the return of the van and damages for its retention. The defendants appealed to the Court of Appeal (Willmer and Diplock LJJ).

Diplock LJ (delivering the judgment of the court): Since a common law lien is a right to continue an existing actual possession of goods (that is to say, to refuse to put an end to a bailment) it can only be exercised by an artificer if his possession was lawful at the time at which the lien first attached. To entitle him to exercise a right of possession under his common law lien adverse to the owner of the goods, he must thus show that his possession under the original delivery of the goods to him was lawful – *Bowmaker Ltd v Wycombe Motors Ltd* ([1946] KB 505) – and continued to be lawful until some work was done by him upon the goods. Where, therefore, as in the present case, possession of the goods was originally given to the artificer not by the owner himself, but by a bailee of the owner, the test whether the artificer can rely upon his common law lien as a defence in an action for detinue brought against him by the owner is whether the owner authorised (or is estopped as against the artificer from denying that he authorised) the bailee to give possession of the goods to the artificer. This, it seems to us, is the test which, after some vacillation, is laid down by the modern authorities. It is as a result of applying this test that the cases which have been cited to us fall upon one side or other of the line. . . .

These cases, all of which fall upon one side of the line, seem to us to do no more than support the propositions that where no question of ostensible authority arises, (1) the mere fact of delivery of possession of goods by an owner to a bailee does not of itself give the bailee authority to deliver possession of the goods to a third party; and (2) that whether the bailee has such authority depends in each case upon the purpose of the bailment and terms of the contract (if any) under which the goods are bailed to him.

The latter proposition was most clearly stated in the judgment of Collins J in the Divisional Court case of *Singer Manufacturing Co v London & South Western Rly Co* ([1894] 1 QB 833), a case which falls on the other side of the line. This passage, although it was not the ratio decidendi of the other member of the court, has been repeatedly cited with approval, and is the foundation of the modern law on this topic. In that case a man who was in possession under a hire-purchase agreement of a Singer sewing machine placed it in a railway cloakroom during the time that the hiring was in existence and, the hiring having come to an end, the owners of the machine claimed it from the railway company, who set up a warehouseman's lien. In his judgment Collins J said this: 'I think in this case the lien may also be rested on another ground; and that is, that the person who deposited this machine was, as between himself and the owner of it, entitled to the possession of it at the time he deposited it. He was entitled to it under a contract of hire, which gave him the right to use it, I presume, for all reasonable purposes incident to such a contract, and among them, I take it, he acquired the right to take the machine with him if he travelled, and to deposit it in a cloakroom if he required to do so. In the course of that reasonable user of the machine, and before the contract of bailment was determined, he gave rights to the railway company in respect of the custody of it. I think those rights must be good against the owners of the machine, who had not determined the hire-purchase agreement at the time that those rights were acquired by the railway company.'

This, in our view, lays down the correct test for determining what authority is conferred by the owner of goods upon the bailee to part with possession of the goods when the purpose of the bailment is the use of the goods by the bailee. He is entitled to make reasonable use of the goods, and if it is reasonably incidental to such use for the bailee to give possession of them to a third person in circumstances which may result in such person acquiring the common law remedy of lien against the goods, the bailee has the authority of the owner to give lawful possession of the goods to the third person. This is not strictly an 'implied term' in *The Moorcock* ((1889) 14 PD 64) sense of the contract between the bailor and the bailee. The grant of authority to use goods is itself to be construed as authority to do in relation to the goods all things that are reasonably incidental to their reasonable use. If the bailor desires to exclude the right of the bailee to do in relation to the goods some particular thing which is reasonably incidental to their reasonable use, he can, of course, do so, but he must do so expressly.

In the case of a bailment for use, therefore, where there is no express prohibition upon his parting with possession of the goods (and no question of ostensible authority arises), the relevant inquiry is whether the giving of actual possession of the goods by the bailee to the person asserting the common law lien was an act which was reasonably incidental to the bailee's reasonable use of the goods. This was the inquiry in *Williams v Allsup* ((1861) 10 CBNS 417) a ship's mortgage case where there was no express provision requiring the mortgagor to keep the ship in repair. Willes J there said (at 427): 'By the permission of the mortgagees the mortgagor has the use of the vessel. He has, therefore, a right to use her in the way in which vessels are ordinarily used. Upon the facts which appear on this case, this vessel could not be so used unless these repairs had been done to her. The state of things, therefore, seems to involve the right of the mortgagor to get the vessel repaired, – not on the credit of the mortgagees, but upon the ordinary terms, subject to the shipwright's lien. It seems to me that the case is the same as if the mortgagees had been present when the order for the repairs was given. To that extent I think the property of the mortgagees is impliedly modified.' It was also the inquiry in *Keene v Thomas* ([1905] 1 KB 136) a hire-purchase case, in which there was an express provision requiring the hirer to keep a dog-cart in repair, and in *Green v All Motors Ltd* ([1917] 1 KB 625), another hire-purchase case, in which there was a similar obligation on the hirer to keep a car in repair. But Scrutton LJ, citing *Williams v Allsup* and *Singer Manufacturing Co v London & South Western Rly Co*, put the decision upon the broader ground with which we concur (at 633): 'The law is clear. The hirer of a chattel is entitled to have it repaired so as to enable him to use it in the way in which such a chattel is ordinarily used. The hirer was therefore entitled, without any express authority from the owner, to have the motor car repaired so as to enable him to use it as a motor car is ordinarily used.'

Albemarle Supply Co v Hind & Co ([1928] 1 KB 307), which was also cited, is on a different point, namely, the ostensible authority of the bailee. It was another case of a hire-purchase agreement, but the agreement contained a term which expressly excluded the hirer's right to create a lien on the vehicles in respect of repairs. The artificer to whom possession of the vehicles was delivered for the purpose of repair was aware that the vehicles were bailed to the hirer under a hire-purchase agreement, but was not aware of the express exclusion of his right to create a lien. It was held that vis-à-vis the artificer the owner had given the hirer ostensible authority to give possession of the vehicles to the artificer for the purpose of effecting repairs, and could not rely upon a secret limitation upon the terms upon which the hirer was authorised to do so, that is, upon terms excluding the artificer's common law remedy of lien. It was a case where the owner was estopped from denying that he had conferred on his bailee authority to give up possession of the vehicles to the artificer on the ordinary terms, and thus subject to the ordinary remedy of lien.

The actual decision in that case is not germane to the present appeal, for the artificer here relies solely upon the actual authority conferred by the bailor on the bailee, and not upon any ostensible authority in excess of that actual authority. . . .

Finally, there is *Bowmaker Ltd v Wycombe Motors Ltd*. It was another hire purchase case in which, however, the bailment to the hirer had been lawfully determined before he delivered possession of the vehicle to the artificer. Since the hirer's possession of the vehicle was itself unlawful, it followed that he could not then confer any lawful possession upon the artificer upon which the artificer could base his claim to a lien. But there is a passage in the judgment of Goddard LJ which summarises with his usual accuracy and clarity the true ratio decidendi of the cases. He said this ([1946] KB 505 at 509): 'So, too, it has been held in the cases to which our attention has been called, more especially *Green v All Motors Ltd* and *Albemarle Supply Co Ltd v Hind & Co* that in the case of a motor car where it is necessary that the motor car should be kept in running condition and repair during the time the hire-purchase agreement is current and valid, the hirer has a right to take it and get it repaired and, if he does so the repairer can exercise an artificer's lien on it, because at the time when the motor car was left with him he, the hirer, had the right, whether you call it by implied authority or by legitimate authority, to use that car in all reasonable ways, and among those ways was a right to get the car repaired and kept in running order. Therefore he was placing it with the repairer with the implied consent of the owner and the artificer's lien on that account will prevail against the owner. These cases have also held, and quite understandably, that an arrangement between the owner and the hirer that the hirer shall not be entitled to create a lien, does not affect the repairer. A repairer has a lien although the owner has purported to limit the hirer's authority to create a lien in that way. That seems to me to depend upon this: Once an artificer exercises his art upon a chattel, the law gives the artificer a lien upon that chattel which he can exercise against the owner of the chattel if the owner of the chattel has placed it with him or has authorised another person to place it with him. If I send my servant with my chattel to get it repaired, the artificer will get the lien which the law gives him on that chattel although I may have told my servant that he is not to create a lien. The fact is that the lien arises by operation of law because the work has been done on the chattel.'

To this statement of principle we would only add the rider that the latter part of it which deals with ostensible authority should be understood as restricted to cases where the artificer has no express notice of the limit upon the authority of the person to whom the owner has given possession of the chattel.

Mr Forbes [Counsel for the plaintiff] has argued that this principle is limited to bailments under contracts of hire purchase where there is a liability on the hirer to keep the goods in repair. We cannot accept this. *Williams v Allsup* was not a hire purchase case at all; the *Singer Company's* case was concerned with a warehousemen's lien, not with an artificer's lien. We think that Mr Hammerton [Counsel for the defendants] is right in his contention that, at any rate if there is consideration for the bailment, the principle applies to all cases where the purpose of the bailment of goods is their use by the bailee.

In the present case the purpose of the bailment of the Dormobile van was clearly for use on the roads by the bailee. Mr Forbes has submitted that it was a gratuitous bailment, made in anticipation of the bailee's entering into a hire-purchase agreement in respect of the van. We do not think this is right. It was a term of the bailment that the bailee, not the bailor, should license the van at his own expense and insure it upon comprehensive terms. This was in fact done in the bailee's own name although it does not appear whether or not this was a term of the prior arrangement as to licensing and insurance. There was thus good consideration in law for the bailment, and it is unnecessary to consider what the position would have been if the bailment had been purely gratuitous.

It is a statutory offence to use a motor vehicle on the highway which is in an unroadworthy condition. If the van should become unroadworthy during the period of the bailment the bailee could not use it for the purposes of the bailment unless he were to have it repaired. In the ordinary way, save in the case of minor adjustments, a motor vehicle can be repaired only by delivering possession of it to an expert mechanic to effect the repairs; and in our view the giving of actual possession of a motor vehicle to an artificer for the purpose of effecting repairs necessary to render it roadworthy is an act reasonably incidental to the bailee's reasonable use of the vehicle. If the bailor desires to exclude the bailee's authority to do this, he must do so expressly. . . .

Different considerations would apply to repairs which were not necessary to make the van roadworthy, for the execution of such repairs might not be reasonably necessary to the reasonable use of the van by the bailee, which was the purpose of the bailment; but there is no suggestion in the evidence that any of the repairs in respect of which the lien was claimed were not necessary to make the van roadworthy.

We are, therefore, of opinion that the artificer was entitled to a common law lien upon the van in respect of the repairs which he effected, and he is entitled to assert that lien against the bailor because the bailor gave the bailee authority to give lawful possession of the van to the artificer for the purpose of effecting such repairs as were necessary to make the van roadworthy.

For these reasons we allow this appeal.

NOTES

1. Why did the hire-purchaser have ostensible or apparent authority to bind the owner with a lien in *Albemarle Supply Co Ltd v Hind & Co* [1928] 1 KB 307 (below, p 826) but not in *Bowmaker Ltd v Wycombe Motors Ltd* [1946] KB 505? Merely allowing the hirer to have possession of the vehicle would not of itself be enough to bring into operation the doctrine of estoppel (see above, p 306). However, in *Albemarle* the hire-purchaser had garaged the vehicles with the defendants over a long period with the apparent sanction of the owner (at least the owner did not interfere with this arrangement). Although not explicit in their Lordships' reasoning, it is probable that the Court of Appeal found the necessary representation in this conduct of the owner (this is how the case was explained by Isaacs and Higgins JJ in *Fisher v Automobile Finance Co of Australia Ltd* (1928) 41 CLR 167 at 177 and 180, High Court of Australia). On the other hand, in the *Bowmaker* case the hire-purchaser took the vehicle to the garage for a one-off repair. There was no representation of authority by the owner.

2. There are other exceptional cases when wrongful possession resulting from the act of a third party may nevertheless bind the owner. Such cases are set out in *Crossley Vaines* at p 137 as follows:

(1) A mercantile agent, seller or buyer in possession of goods may by wrongful disposition bind the owner (ss 2, 8 and 9 of the Factors Act 1889, and ss 24 and 25 of the Sale of Goods Act 1979).
(2) If the person claiming the lien is obliged by law to receive the goods, eg a common carrier or an innkeeper, he is not affected by the wrongful disposition by the depositor, unless he has knowledge of the wrongdoing (see, for example, *Marsh v Police Comr* [1945] KB 43, where the Court of Appeal held the Ritz Hotel entitled to exercise a lien over stolen goods brought onto its premises by a guest).
(3) The lien is claimed in respect of a negotiable instrument received in good faith and without notice of any dishonour (s 27(3) of the Bills of Exchange Act 1882).

QUESTION

Rook hired a car from Bishop, stole a quantity of jewellery from King's shop and drove off in the car, which he then negligently damaged against a wall. He left the car at Queen's garage for repair, pledged one necklace to Pawn for £60 and took the rest of the stolen jewellery to Castle's hotel, where he stayed until he was arrested three weeks later. Queen, Pawn and Castle now refuse to surrender the car and the jewellery unless they are paid, respectively, £80 for repairing the car, £60 for the necklace and £200 for hotel charges. Advise Bishop and King. What is the position if Bishop had originally bought the car from Queen and still owes Queen £50 of the purchase price?

(f) Enforcement

(i) *Generally*

We have already established that, as a general rule, a common law lien cannot be enforced by sale (above, p 814). However, a lienee may be given a power of sale in the following circumstances:

(1) by contract;
(2) by trade usage (see *Re Tate, ex p Moffatt* (1841) 2 Mont D & De G 170);
(3) by statute, eg Innkeepers Act 1878, s 1 (innkeeper's right of sale); Torts (Interference with Goods) Act 1977, ss 12 and 13 (bailee's right of sale of uncollected goods); Sale of Goods Act 1979, s 48 (unpaid seller's right of resale).

Additionally, on the application of any party to a cause or matter, a court has power under the Rules of the Supreme Court, Order 29, r 4(1) to order the sale, in such manner and on such terms (if any) as it may specify, of any property (other than land) which is the subject matter of the cause or matter or as to which any question arises therein and which is of a perishable nature or likely to deteriorate if kept or which for any other good reason it is desirable to sell forthwith. In *Larner v Fawcett* [1950] 2 All ER 727, the Court of Appeal exercised this power on the interocutory application of a race horse trainer claiming a lien over the respondent's horse to cover outstanding charges. The Court emphasised that the power of sale under Order 29, r 4 could be exercised even though the common law lienee has no power of sale at law or in equity. The Court went on to hold that it was proper to make such an order for sale in this case on the grounds that (1) the horse was 'eating its head off' at the trainer's expense; and (2) the owner had unreasonably delayed in requesting its return. The proceeds of sale were ordered to be paid into court to abide the result of the action.

(ii) *Insolvency Act 1986*

In *Bristol Airport plc v Powdrill* [1990] Ch 744, the Court of Appeal held (obiter) that the exercise of a possessory lien over a company's property was included within the statutory definition of 'security' contained in s 248(b) of the Insolvency Act 1986 and, therefore, was caught by s 11(3)(c) of that Act. When an administration order is made in respect of a company (see below, p 901), 'no . . . steps may be taken to enforce any security over the company's property . . . except with the consent of the administrator or the leave of the court' (Insolvency Act 1986, s 11(3)(c)). This could create a number of practical problems for someone claiming a lien over the company's property when an administrator has been appointed, eg is the lien holder liable to damages in conversion if he refuses to hand over the goods to the administrator pending an application to the court for leave? Woolf LJ attempted to deal with a number of these problems when he said:

> You are not taking steps to enforce a security unless by relying on the security you are preventing the administrator doing something to . . . [a] chattel in which he has an interest which he would otherwise be entitled to do. Taking first the case of the ordinary repairer who is entitled to retain goods until his charges are paid. Unless and until someone who is entitled to possession of those goods seeks to obtain possession of the goods, the lien holder does not take steps to enforce his lien. The security which is given to the lien

holder entitles him to refuse to hand over the possession of the goods, but until he makes an unqualified refusal to hand over the goods he has not in my judgment taken steps to enforce the security for the purposes of s 11(3)(c) of the Act of 1986 . . . I would not regard a person who is otherwise entitled to a lien as enforcing that lien if he does not make an unqualified refusal to hand over the goods to an administrator but instead indicates to the administrator that unless the administrator consents to his exercising his right to detain, he will apply promptly to the court for leave and does so. In my view such conduct would not amount to taking steps to enforce the lien within the meaning of s 11(3)(c) of the Act of 1986.

Browne-Wilkinson V-C agreed with Woolf LJ; Staughton LJ did not express an opinion as to the correctness of Woolf LJ's dicta.

(g) Termination of lien

Albemarle Supply Co Ltd v Hind and Co [1928] 1 KB 307, Court of Appeal

B hired three taxicabs from the plaintiffs under hire-purchase agreements. The agreements required B to keep the cabs and their equipment in good repair but prohibited him from selling, pledging or parting with possession of them without the plaintiffs' consent, and from creating a lien on them in respect of repairs. For a number of years B garaged the cabs, and two other cabs, with the defendants who serviced them and carried out necessary repairs. The defendants knew of the hire-purchase agreements but were not aware of their terms. B's account then fell into arrears, but the defendants allowed him to take the cabs from their garage each day on condition that the cabs continued 'in pawn' and were returned to the garage each night. B then fell into arrear with his hire-purchase instalments and the plaintiffs terminated the agreements and demanded the three cabs from the defendants. The defendants claimed a lien over the three cabs for the balance of their general account for all five cabs due from B. The balance of account included the cost of rent, washing, oil and petrol, which would not be the subject of a repairing lien.

Scrutton LJ: The plaintiffs' first line of attack on the lien claim was a clause in their hire-purchase agreement providing that 'the hirer shall not have or be deemed to have any authority to pledge the credit of the owners for repairs to the vehicle or to create a lien upon the same in respect of such repairs.' This Court in *Green v All Motors Ltd* ([1917] 1 KB 625) has held that the mere knowledge by the repairer that there is a hire-purchase agreement without knowledge of its exact terms relating to the car which he repairs does not deprive him of his lien. The owner leaving the cab in the hands of a man who is entitled to use it gives him an implied authority to have it repaired with the resulting lien for repairs. Rowlatt J had held in a previous case, and the judge below in the present case followed his decision, that a contractual limitation of authority not communicated to the repairer does not limit the implied authority derived from the hirer's being allowed to possess and use the car. I agree with this view; if a man is put in a position which holds him out as having a certain authority, people who act on that holding out are not affected by a secret limitation, of which they are ignorant, of the apparent authority. The owners can easily protect themselves by requiring information as to the garage where the cab is kept, and notifying the garage owner that the hirer has no power to create a lien for repairs. They will thus escape the lien, though they may not get their cab repaired.

The plaintiffs next contended that any lien was lost because the cabs went out of the possession of the garage each day to ply for hire. The defendant proved an agreement with Botfield at a time when the lien existed, that the cabs should go out for hire each day on the terms that they should be returned to the garage each night, the lien continuing while the cabs were in possession of the garage. I do not think any plying for hire under this agreement prevented the lien, if any, from continuing, and in my view repair of a damaged cab, though it may be described as 'maintenance,' gave rise to a repairer's lien.

It was next said that the lien for repairs was lost inasmuch as it was originally claimed for a larger amount and a different cause than the right one. I have considered the numerous authorities cited, and in my view the law stands as follows: A person claiming a lien must either claim it for a definite amount, or give the owner particulars from which he himself can calculate the amount for which a lien is due. The owner must then in the absence of express agreement tender an amount covering the lien really existing. If he does not, unless excused, he has no answer to a claim of lien. He may be excused from tendering (1) if he has no knowledge or means of knowledge of the right amount; (2) if the person claiming the lien for a wrong cause or amount makes it clear that he will not release the goods unless his full claim is satisfied, and that claim is wrongful. The fact that the claim is made for more than the right amount does not matter unless the claimant gives no particulars from which the right amount can be calculated, or makes it clear that he insists on the full amount of the right claimed: see *Scarfe v Morgan* ((1838) 4 M & W 270); *Dirks v Richards* ((1842) 4 Man & G 574); *Huth & Co v Lamport* ((1886) 16 QBD 735 at 736), per Lord Esher; and *Rumsey v North Eastern Rly Co* ((1863) 14 CBNS 641 at 651 and 654), per Erle CJ and Willes J.

In the present case the accounts handed to the plaintiffs show the items relating to the repairs to each cab, and the plaintiffs did not tender because they thought their agreement prevented the creation of a lien, not because they could not ascertain what repairs were done. I do not think the defendants ever pinned themselves definitely to a demand for the whole sum.

[Lord Hanworth MR and Sargant J delivered concurring judgments (although Sargant J did not address the issue of loss of possession).]

NOTES

1. Professor N E Palmer notes that '[t]he loss of possession is a question of fact but the effect upon the lien itself is one of law . . . the question is whether the change of circumstances, and the intentions accompanying it, are inconsistent with the further continuance of the lien' (*Bailment* (2nd ed, 1991), p 949). In *Albemarle Supply Co Ltd v Hind and Co*, the intention of the parties was expressed in the terms of their agreement for the release of the cabs. An intention to maintain the lien may also be implied (see *Allen v Smith* (1862) 12 CBNS 638, where the lien was not lost when a guest took a horse out of an innkeeper's stable intending to return it). But where there is no evidence of a contrary intention (as in the great majority of cases), loss of possession will terminate the lien (see, for example, *Pennington v Reliance Motor Works Ltd* [1923] 1 KB 127).

2. In *Pennington v Reliance Motor Works Ltd*, E agreed with the plaintiff to rebuild his car. Without the plaintiff's authority, E sub-contracted the work to the defendants. The defendants completed the work and returned the car to E, who delivered it back to the plaintiff. The defendants were not paid by E. When the plaintiff later delivered his car to the defendants for further repairs the defendant claimed a lien on it for the earlier work done for E. McCardie J held that there was no lien as the plaintiff gave no authority, express or implied, to E to create one and no custom of the trade was proved. He also held, in the alternative, that even if there had been a lien it had been lost when the defendants parted with possession of the car to E. As McCardie J stated: '. . . the defendants allowed E to take possession of the car not for any limited purpose, but in the belief that he would get payment from [the plaintiff], and would pay them as soon as he could'. Cf s 44 of the Sale of Goods Act 1979.

3. Therefore, a lien may be terminated by the following means:

(1) a loss of possession to the lienor (or to a third party, as the lienee then losses his immediate right to possession and will be unable to redeliver to the lienor: *Mulliner v Florence* (1878) 3 QBD 484 at 489; cf s 48(2) of the Sale of Goods Act 1979);

(2) waiver of the necessity of making a tender (as outlined by Scrutton LJ in *Albemarle Supply Co Ltd v Hind and Co* (above, p 827);

(3) payment or tender of the amount due.

It may also be lost by:

(4) accepting alternative security in substitution for the lien (save that taking bills of exchange as alternative security usually only suspends the lien so that it will revive on dishonour – *Stevenson v Blakelock* (1813) 1 M & S 535);

(5) a wrongful sale (*Mulliner v Florence* (1878) 3 QBD 484) or other act of conversion (eg using the goods subject to the lien: *Rust v McNaught and Co Ltd* (1918) 144 LT Jo 440, CA).

Furthermore, the holder of a general lien will be held to have abandoned it if he agrees to release the goods merely on payment of sums due in respect of those goods alone (*Morley v Hay* (1828) 3 Man & Ry KB 396).

QUESTIONS

1. Distinguish *Forth v Simpson* (above, p 815) from *Albemarle Supply Co Ltd v Hind and Co.*

2. Would the decision in *Pennington v Reliance Motor Works Ltd* have been different if (a) E had obtained delivery from the defendants by stating (untruthfully) that he had instructed the plaintiff to pay the defendants directly (see *Wallace v Woodgate* (1824) 1 C & P 575); or, alternatively, (b) when returning the car to E, the defendants had expressly reserved a right to retake the goods? (see Bell, op cit, p 147).

(h) Registration

As a lien is a possessory security it does not require registration by virtue of the Bills of Sale Acts 1878–1891 (unless the right to exercise the lien arises by virtue of a written agreement: above, p 816), nor by virtue of the Companies Act 1985, as amended by the Companies Act 1989 (s 396(1)(b)).

3 Reform

We have already noted that Professor Diamond has proposed a complete overhaul of the law relating to security interests (above, p 798). He recommends that pledges are brought within the proposed unified scheme for security interests and governed by the same rules as other security interests, eg as to rights and methods of enforcement and effectiveness in insolvency (Diamond Report, paras 9.5.1–9.5.6). However, he would exempt pledges from the proposed registration requirements, so long as the pledged goods remain in the possession of the pledgee (Diamond Report, para 11.5.7). When pledged goods are released to the pledgor for a temporary purpose (as in *Reeves v Capper*) the pledge would have to be registered if it was to remain effective against third parties. Finally, it should be noted that Professor Diamond recommends that it should be possible to create a security interest over intangible moveable property (eg a debt or other chose in action) by taking a pledge of 'chattel paper' (ie a document not consisting of a document of title) representing or relating to that property (para 10.4.22).

As the new legislation proposed by Professor Diamond would only extend to security interests created by agreement, it would not apply to security interests arising without the need for express agreement (ie any type of non-contractual lien): Diamond Report, para 9.3.1. Although Professor Diamond does not specifically deal with contractual liens, they are likely to be treated in the same way as pledges.

CHAPTER 24
Non-possessory security

---

1 Mortgage

(a) Mortgage defined

Santley v Wilde [1899] 2 Ch 474, Court of Appeal

Lindley MR: . . . a mortgage is a conveyance of land or an assignment of chattels as a security for the payment of a debt or the discharge of some other obligation for which it is given. This is the idea of a mortgage: and the security is redeemable on the payment or discharge of such debt or obligation, any provision to the contrary notwithstanding.

Downsview Nominees Ltd v First City Corpn Ltd [1993] AC 295, Privy Council

Lord Templeman: A mortgage, whether legal or equitable, is security for repayment of a debt. The security may be constituted by a conveyance, assignment or demise or by a charge on any interest in real or personal property. An equitable mortgage is a contract which creates a charge on property but does not pass a legal estate to the creditor. Its operation is that of an executory assurance, which, as between the parties, and so far as equitable rights and remedies are concerned, is equivalent to an actual assurance, and is enforceable under the equitable jurisdiction of the court. All this is well settled law and is to be found in more detail in the textbooks on the subject. . . .

NOTES

1. A mortgage involves the transfer of ownership of property from the mortgagor (the debtor or a third party) to the mortgagee (the creditor) as security for a debt or other obligation (although this no longer remains true for a legal mortgage of land which, since 1926, must be made either by demise for a term of years or by charge by way of legal mortgage: Law of Property Act 1925, ss 85, 86). A mortgage may be either legal or equitable. It may be of real or personal property.[1] As a mortgage

---

1 As the mortgage of land is dealt with in the casebooks on land law, we shall concentrate on the mortgage of personal property (defined above at p 32).

does not require the delivery of possession of the mortgaged property, that property can be tangible or intangible (ie choses in action can be mortgaged).

2. A legal mortgage of personal property is a transfer of legal title to the mortgagee with an express or implied proviso for retransfer on redemption.[2] As future property cannot generally be transferred at common law, a legal mortgage usually involves the present transfer of property to which the transferor holds the legal title at the date of the transfer (*Halsbury's Laws of England* (4th ed reissue, 1992), para 658). A legal mortgage of tangible personal property may be oral (*Newlove v Shrewsbury* (1888) 21 QBD 41, CA) but the general rule for intangible personal property is that the assignment must be in writing with notice to the obligee (s 136(1) of the Law of Property Act 1925).

3. The nature of an equitable mortgage was considered in the next case.

Swiss Bank Corpn v Lloyds Bank Ltd [1982] AC 584, Court of Appeal

The plaintiff bank agreed to lend foreign currency to IFT to enable it to buy shares and loan stock in FIBI, an Israeli bank. Under clause 3(b) of the loan agreement, IFT agreed to observe all the conditions attached to the Bank of England consent which had been obtained for the loan under the Exchange Control Act 1947. The conditions were, inter alia, that on acquisition the FIBI securities should be held in a separate account and that repayment of the loan was to be made from the proceeds of sale of those securities. The plaintiff bank claimed to be an equitable chargee of the FIBI securities or the proceeds of sale thereof. Browne-Wilkinson J upheld the claim but was reversed on appeal.

Buckley LJ: We are not concerned here with a charge on an equitable interest in property but with an equitable charge upon property in the legal ownership of the party creating the charge.

An equitable charge may, it is said, take the form either of an equitable mortgage or of an equitable charge not by way of mortgage. An equitable mortgage is created when the legal owner of the property constituting the security enters into some instrument or does some act which, though insufficient to confer a legal estate or title in the subject matter upon the mortgagee, nevertheless demonstrates a binding intention to create a security in favour of the mortgagee, or in other words evidences a contract to do so. . . . From the way in which the judge dealt with the matter in his judgment it is, I think, clear that he was applying his mind to the question whether the circumstances of the case gave rise to an equitable charge by way of mortgage. The argument in this court has also proceeded upon the same lines, but I must not overlook the possibility of the existence of an equitable charge which is not of the nature of a mortgage.

The essence of any transaction by way of mortgage is that a debtor confers upon his creditor a proprietary interest in property of the debtor, or undertakes in a binding manner to do so, by the realisation or appropriation of which the creditor can procure the discharge of the debtor's liability to him, and that the proprietary interest is redeemable, or the obligation to create it is defeasible, in the event of the debtor discharging his liability. If there has been no legal transfer of a proprietary interest but merely a binding undertaking to confer such an interest, that obligation, if specifically enforceable, will confer a proprietary interest in the subject matter in equity. The obligation will be specifically enforceable if it is an obligation for the breach of which damages would be an inadequate remedy. A contract to mortgage

---

2 A mortgagor is said to have an 'equity of redemption' entitling him to redeem or recover the property even though he has failed to pay at the appointed time. The equity of redemption may be determined by release, lapse of time, sale and foreclosure (Fisher and Lightwood *Law of Mortgages* (10th ed, 1988), pp 8–9).

property, real or personal, will, normally at least, be specifically enforceable, for a mere claim to damages or repayment is obviously less valuable than a security in the event of the debtor's insolvency. If it is specifically enforceable, the obligation to confer the proprietary interest will give rise to an equitable charge upon the subject matter by way of mortgage.

It follows that whether a particular transaction gives rise to an equitable charge of this nature must depend upon the intention of the parties ascertained from what they have done in the then existing circumstances. The intention may be expressed or it may be inferred. If the debtor undertakes to segregate a particular fund or asset and to pay the debt out of that fund or asset, the inference may be drawn, in the absence of any contra indication, that the parties' intention is that the creditor should have such a proprietary interest in the segregated fund or asset as will enable him to realise out of it the amount owed to him by the debtor: compare *Re Nanwa Gold Mines Ltd* [1955] 1 WLR 1080 and contrast *Moseley v Cressey's Co* (1865) LR 1 Eq 405 where there was no obligation to segregate the deposits. But notwithstanding that the matter depends upon the intention of the parties, if upon the true construction of the relevant documents in the light of any admissible evidence as to surrounding circumstances the parties have entered into a transaction the legal effect of which is to give rise to an equitable charge in favour of one of them over property of the other, the fact that they may not have realised this consequence will not mean that there is no charge. They must be presumed to intend the consequence of their acts.

In the present case the loan agreement contained no express requirement that IFT should charge the FIBI securities or the fruits of the borrowing by way of mortgage to secure repayment of the loan. Such intention must be found, if at all, by implication.

A binding obligation that a particular fund shall be applied in a particular manner may found no more than an injunction to restrain its application in another way, but if the obligation be to pay out of the fund a debt due by one party to the transaction to the other, the fund belonging to or being due to the debtor, this amounts to an equitable assignment pro tanto of the fund: see *Rodick v Gandell* (1852) 1 De GM & G 763, 777 and *Palmer v Carey* [1926] AC 703, 706–707:

> This is but an instance of a familiar doctrine of equity that a contract for valuable consideration to transfer or charge a subject matter passes a beneficial interest by way of property in that subject matter if the contract is one of which a court of equity will decree specific performance.

With this in mind I address myself to the construction and effect of clause 3(b) of the loan agreement. It is said that by that subclause IFT covenanted with the plaintiff that all the requirements of the Bank of England from time to time would be observed by IFT during the continuance of the agreement. Accordingly, it is said that IFT covenanted that the loan should be repaid out of the sale proceeds of the securities in the 'relative loan portfolio' (see condition (vii)) and out of no other source save in so far as those sale proceeds should fall short of being sufficient. So, it is said, the relevant loan portfolio, which by the terms of the Bank of England permission was required to be kept as a separate fund distinct from any other foreign currency securities owned by IFT, should be the primary source for repayment of the loan. Therefore, it is contended, the parties have manifested an intention that the plaintiff should have such a proprietary interest in the FIBI securities or any other fruits of the borrowing into which they might be converted from time to time as would enable the plaintiff to realise out of that property, so far as it should suffice, any amount required to repay the loan.

Mr Parker has conceded that IFT was only obliged by clause 3(b) of the loan agreement to observe such requirements of the Bank of England as might be in force from time to time. The Bank of England could have waived or rescinded condition (vii) at any time. He accepts that the equitable charge which the plaintiff claims was consequently a precarious one. The fact that an equitable charge may be precarious, however, is not in my view necessarily a sufficient ground for holding that there is no such charge. A mortgage of a terminable lease would be a precarious security, vulnerable to determination of the lease by the landlord, but I can see no reason why such a lease should not be capable of being the subject matter of a mortgage, if a mortgagee of it could be found. In the present case, however, it is not the continued existence of the subject matter which is precarious; it is those very terms of the contract which are alleged to give rise to the equitable charge, that is to say, the Bank of England conditions requiring segregation of the fruits of the borrowing and repayment of the loan thereout, which might have been terminated or waived by the Bank of England at any time during the continuance of the agreement. The Bank of England might at any time have permitted repayment of the loan out of some other fund, and in that event the plaintiff could have had no ground of complaint about the loan being so discharged. A security of this kind, if capable of constituting a security at all, would, it seems to me, be so precarious that one would need very clear indications that the parties intended, or must be taken to have intended, to enter into such an arrangement by way of security, particularly where the relevant agreement contains an express charge on another subject matter. In my judgment, however, clause 3(b) of the agreement was incapable, upon its true construction, of constituting any security or creating any equitable charge. So far as it consisted of a covenant, it required IFT to observe the requirements of the Bank of England during the continuance of the agreement. It was directed to ensuring that the loan should not become tainted with any illegality by reason of any failure to comply with those requirements, such as they might be from time to time. In this respect it is, I think, significant that the covenant is linked with the warranty contained in the same sub-clause, which is obviously directed to the legality of the transaction at the date of the agreement. The covenant is, in my opinion, in substance a negative one, viz not to do anything which might invalidate the bargain between the parties; but, although some argument was addressed to us based upon this negative quality, it is not that which weighs with me. What is to my mind important is that there is here no obligation to repay the loan out of the fruits of the borrowing in any event; the covenant merely requires IFT to repay the loan in a manner approved by the Bank of England. No doubt the plaintiff could have objected to repayment in any manner not so approved and could have obtained an injunction restraining such repayment, if this would have served any useful purpose; but the covenant does not, in my judgment, confer upon the plaintiff any specifically enforceable right to have the loan repaid out of the FIBI securities or out of any other fruits of the borrowing. It consequently did not, in my judgment, give rise to an equitable charge by way of mortgage.

[Brandon and Brightman LJJ concurred.]

[The decision of the Court of Appeal was affirmed by the House of Lords [1982] AC 584, 604.]

NOTES

1. An equitable mortgage of personal property is a transfer of an equitable title to the mortgagee, or a declaration of trust in his favour, with an express or implied proviso for retransfer or termination of the trust on redemption (*Halsbury's Laws of England* (4th ed reissue, 1992), Vol 4 (1), para 659).

2. An equitable mortgage can arise as follows:

(1) by a present mortgage of an equitable interest (eg a second mortgage of goods when the first mortgage is legal – the second mortgage will be equitable as the owner divests himself of his legal title by the first mortgage thereby leaving himself only with an equity of redemption); or

(2) by an agreement to give a legal or equitable mortgage, so long as it is supported by consideration (or made by deed) and can be specifically enforced (see *Swiss Bank Corpn v Lloyds Bank Ltd*, above, p 831; *Thames Guaranty Ltd v Campbell* [1985] QB 210 at 218; affd [1985] QB 210, CA).

3. An agreement to mortgage after-acquired property can only operate as a contract to assign the property when it is acquired. A debtor's agreement to mortgage his after-acquired property will give the creditor an equitable interest in the property as soon as it is acquired by the debtor, so long as the creditor has actually advanced the money (ie the consideration is executed) and the property is described sufficiently to be identifiable when acquired (*Holroyd v Marshall* (1862) 10 HL Cas 191, above, p 754; as explained in *Tailby v Official Receiver* (1888) 13 App Cas 523, HL, above, p 755). The consideration must be executed because equity will not decree specific performance of a contract to borrow and lend money (*Roger v Challis* (1859) 27 Beav 175). Once the consideration is executed the requirement that the contract be specifically enforceable becomes irrelevant (see generally Meagher, Gummow and Lehane *Equity Doctrine and Remedies* (3rd ed, 1992), Ch 6).

4. An equitable mortgage of personal property, not being of an equitable interest in such property (which must be in writing under the Law of Property Act 1925, s 53(1)(c)), can be oral. However, writing will be necessary if a mortgage (or other security) relates to a regulated agreement under the Consumer Credit Act 1974 (see below, p 853) and the security is not given by the debtor himself (Consumer Credit Act 1974, s 105(6)).

(b) Enforcement

Harrold v Plenty [1901] 2 Ch 314, Chancery Division

D deposited a certificate of shares with P as security for a debt. P claimed an order for transfer of the shares to himself by foreclosure or, in the alternative, sale.

Cozens-Hardy J: . . . Now, it is plain that a pledgee is in a very different position from an ordinary mortgagee. He has only a special property in the thing pledged. He may obtain a sale, but he cannot obtain a foreclosure. I do not think that this is properly a case of pledge. A share is a chose in action. The certificate is merely evidence of title, and whatever may be the result of the deposit of a bearer bond, such as that which Sir George Jessel dealt with in *Carter v Wake* ((1877) 4 Ch D 605), I think I cannot treat the plaintiff as a mere pledgee. The deposit of the certificate by way of security for the debt, which is admitted, seems to me to amount to an equitable mortgage, or, in other words, to an agreement to execute a transfer of the shares by way of mortgage. The result is that the plaintiff is entitled to a judgment substantially in the form which would be given if, instead of the certificate of shares, the document had been a title-deed of real estate or a policy of assurance. . . .

NOTES

1. Foreclosure extinguishes the equity of redemption of the mortgagor, and all persons claiming through him, and vests the mortgaged property absolutely in the mortgagee (although see A P Bell *Personal Property in England and Ireland* (1989), p 186, as to the precise mechanism by which this takes place).

2. Unlike the remedy of sale under a power of sale, foreclosure generally requires a court order.

Stubbs v Slater [1910] 1 Ch 632, Court of Appeal

P, being indebted to the defendant stockbrokers, deposited with them as security a certificate for 390 shares, and signed a blank transfer of the same. After sending P repeated notices that they would have to sell the shares if the debt was not paid, the defendants sold the shares. P sued the defendants for wrongful conversion of the shares, alleging inter alia that the sale was bad because the notices demanded more than was owed. The Court of Appeal held that in the circumstances the defendants had reasonably exercised their implied power of sale as mortgagees.

Cozens-Hardy MR referred to his own judgment in *Harrold v Plenty* and continued: . . . This then was a transaction of mortgage and not a transaction of pledge. It was a transaction of mortgage, in which there was no express power of sale given, but which by law involves and implies a right in the mortgagee to sell after giving reasonable notice. I need scarcely pause to say that the notice here was reasonable, if ever there was reasonable notice. Then the matter came before the Court of Appeal in 1902 in *Deverges v Sandeman, Clark & Co* ([1902] 1 Ch 579). There it was laid down that in the case of a mortgage by deposit of shares there is an implied power to sell, if no time is fixed, upon giving reasonable notice, and the only point decided in that case was whether or not the notice was reasonable. Nothing else was there decided except that the general principle applicable to transactions of this kind was for the first time laid down by the Court of Appeal. In the course of my judgment, which I refer to only because I see no reason to change the view which I there expressed, I say this: 'Although a mistake as to the amount due may destroy the effect of the notice, as between pledgor and pledgee – *Pigot v Cubley* ((1864) 15 CBNS 701) – I think that is not the law as between mortgagor and mortgagee. In order to restrain a mortgagee from selling in the absence of fraud, it is not sufficient to contest the amount due on the mortgage. The mortgagor must pay into Court, or tender to the mortgagee, the amount claimed to be due.' I there referred to *Pigot v Cubley*, saying that a mistake as to the amount due might destroy the effect of the notice as between pledgor and pledgee. I have looked at that case again and as at present advised I can find nothing in the judgment in the Court which bears out the last sentence in the head-note, which says that 'a notice that he' – ie, the pledgee – 'will sell unless an excessive sum be paid immediately, is not such a notice as will justify the sale.' But, however that may be, it seems to me that in a mortgage as distinguished from a pledge that head-note affords no ground for the contention that a mortgagee has not a power of sale after giving reasonable notice unless the notice specifies with precise accuracy the amount due on the mortgage. I see no ground for making any exception from the general law in this particular class of mortgage. There was here alleged to be due on the mortgage the sum of £69 odd. That being so, and there having been abundant applications for payment, I am clearly of opinion that the mortgagee had a perfect right to sell these shares.

[Buckley J delivered a concurring judgment.
Joyce J concurred.]

NOTES

1. By the Law of Property Act 1925, s 101(1), where the mortgage is made by deed, a mortgagee is given a statutory power to sell the mortgaged property when the mortgage money has become due. This power applies to any mortgage of any property made by deed, save those to which the Bills of Sale Acts apply (see Bell, op cit, p 187; and below, p 852). However, in *Re Morritt, ex p Official Receiver* (1886) 18 QBD 222 at 241–242, Lopes LJ held (Lord Esher MR concurring) that a power of sale was to be implied into a mortgage within the Bills of Sale Act (1878) Amendment Act 1882, by virtue of s 7 of that Act.

2. *Stubbs v Slater* is a case where a mortgagee of intangible property was held to have a common law power of sale. Whether a mortgagee of tangible property has such a common law power of sale is not clear. In *Re Morritt, ex p Official Receiver* (1886) 18 QBD 222 at 233, Cotton LJ held that a mortgagee of personal chattels, which are in his possession, had a common law power of sale (Lindley and Bowen LJJ concurred). But in the same case Fry LJ, dissenting, held that a power of sale was not to be implied by law into a mortgage of chattels (at 235). See also *Deverges v Sandeman, Clark & Co* [1902] 1 Ch 579 at 589, where Vaughan Williams LJ questioned whether a mortgagee of personal chattels had a common law power of sale. For contrasting treatment of this issue compare Crossley Vaines *Personal Property* (5th ed, 1973), p 447, with Bell, op cit, p 187.

3. An express power of sale may be inserted in the mortgage. A well drafted mortgage of real or personal property will contain such a provision.

4. Even if the mortgagee has no express or implied power of sale, he may apply to the court for an order for sale (Law of Property Act 1925, s 91). When a mortgage is made by deed a court also has power to appoint a receiver (Law of Property Act 1925, ss 101, 109). However, in most cases the mortgage contains an express power of appointment.

QUESTION

In *Stubbs v Slater* (above, p 835) the sale of the mortgaged shares realised more than the sum owed by the mortgagor to the mortgagee. What do you think happened to the balance? How, if at all, would your answer be different if the mortgagee had obtained an order for foreclosure before selling the shares?

2 Equitable charge

(a) Equitable charge defined

Swiss Bank Corpn v Lloyds Bank Ltd [1982] AC 584, Court of Appeal

(The facts appear above at p 831.)

Buckley LJ: An equitable charge which is not an equitable mortgage is said to be created when property is expressly or constructively made liable, or specially appropriated, to the discharge of a debt or some other obligation, and confers on the chargee a right of realisation by judicial process, that is to say, by the appointment of a receiver or an order for sale. . . .

[His Lordship then considered whether clause 3(b) of the loan agreement constituted an equitable charge by way of mortgage – as quoted above at pp 831–833 – and continued:]

Nor, in my opinion, can it [clause 3(b)] have given rise to a charge of a kind to which the remedies of a mortgagee would not have attached but which would have been enforceable by the appointment of a receiver or an order for sale. In *National Provincial and Union Bank of England v Charnley* [1924] 1 KB 431 it seems that Atkin LJ may have had a charge of this nature in mind. He said, at pp 449–450:

. . . I think there can be no doubt that where in a transaction for value both parties evince an intention that property, existing or future, shall be made available as security for the payment of a debt, and that the creditor shall have a present right to have it made available, there is a charge, even though the present legal right which is contemplated can only be enforced at some future date, and though the creditor gets no legal right of property, either absolute or special, or any legal right to possession, but only gets a right to have the security made available by an order of the court.

In the present case I do not consider that it can properly be said that the parties evinced an intention that the FIBI securities or any other fruits of the borrowing should be made available as security for repayment of the loan. The only intention which they evinced was that the loan should be repaid in a manner approved by the Bank of England.

Accordingly, in my judgment, the loan agreement did not give rise to any equitable charge in favour of the plaintiff.

NOTES

1. In *Re Bond Worth Ltd* [1980] Ch 228 at 250, Slade J stated that: 'The technical difference between a "mortgage" or "charge", though in practice the phrases are often used interchangeably, is that a mortgage involves a conveyance of property subject to a right of redemption, whereas a charge conveys nothing and merely gives the chargee certain rights over the property as security for the loan'. As a charge is a mere encumbrance and does not convey ownership of property, it can only arise in equity (and so is called an 'equitable charge') or by statute (as is the case with a charge by way of legal mortgage over land: Law of Property Act 1925, ss 85–87). A charge over personal property must be equitable, it cannot be legal.

2. Unlike a mortgagee, a chargee has no right to foreclosure (*Tennant v Trenchard* (1869) 4 Ch App 537). If a mortgage is foreclosed the equity of redemption is extinguished and the mortgaged property vests absolutely in the mortgagee. However, this cannot happen with a charge as there is no transfer of ownership (in law or in equity) to be given full effect by extinguishing the equity of redemption.

3. In practice, there is little difference between a mortgage and a charge as it is usual for the instrument creating the charge to provide expressly that the chargee has the rights of a mortgagee: see Fisher and Lightwood, op cit, p 5; and above, p 747. In any event, if the charge is by deed, the chargee will have statutory powers of sale and of appointment of a receiver (Law of Property Act 1925, ss 101(1), 205(1)(xvi)).

4. In general, a charge must be created by agreement which, if not made by deed, must be supported by consideration. An agreement for value, or by deed, for an equitable charge will be treated as an equitable charge (*Tailby v Official Receiver* (1888) 13 App Cas 523 at 549, per Lord Macnaghten). As a charge creates an equitable interest, and does not transfer such an interest, it falls outside s 53(1)(c) of the Law of Property Act 1925 and so may be oral. If the charge extends to future property it must be given for value (a deed is not enough) and the property must be sufficiently described to be identifiable when acquired (*Holroyd v Marshall*, above, p 754; *Tailby v Official Receiver*, above, p 755). However, there is no need to demonstrate an intention, in the sense of a positive knowledge and wish, to create a charge: 'the existence of the contract, the obligation and the specified fund are sufficient for the law to create such a charge' (*Kingscroft Insurance Co Ltd v HS Weavers (Underwriting) Agencies Ltd* [1993] 1 Lloyd's Rep 187 at 193, per

Harman J). For the creation of an equitable charge by declaration of trust, see *Re Bond Worth Ltd* [1980] Ch 228 at p 250; cf *Carreras Rothman Ltd v Freeman Mathews Treasure Ltd* [1985] Ch 207 at 227.

(b) Fixed and floating charges

(i) *Nature of fixed charge*

A fixed (or specific) charge attaches as soon as the charge is created or the debtor acquires an interest in the property to be charged, whichever is the later. Once attached, the charge prevents the debtor dealing with the property without first paying off the indebtedness secured by the charge or obtaining the chargee's consent. If the debtor does not do this before transferring the property, the transferee will take the property subject to the charge, unless he is a bona fide purchaser for value without notice. On the other hand, if the charge allows the debtor to deal with the charged property at his will, it cannot be a fixed charge.

Siebe Gorman & Co Ltd v Barclays Bank Ltd [1979] 2 Lloyd's Rep 142, Chancery Division

(See above, pp 773–774.)

NOTES

(See above, pp 774–775.)

(ii) *Nature of floating charge*

A floating charge hovers over a changing fund of assets, including assets acquired by the debtor after the creation of the charge. Under a floating charge the debtor is at liberty to deal with the charged assets in the ordinary course of the debtor's business, and does so free from the charge. Only upon the happening of certain events, such as the appointment of a receiver or insolvency, is the floating charge said to 'crystallise' and become fixed on the assets then comprising the fund or subsequently acquired by the debtor. At that point, the debtor has no further right to deal with the charged assets.

It is not possible in English law for individual borrowers to give a floating charge over their assets, because to do so would infringe the Bills of Sale Acts of 1878 and 1882 (and in particular it would be impossible to meet the requirement that the goods affected be specifically described in a schedule to the instrument). But the Bills of Sale Acts do not apply to a company, and so it is possible for a company to grant a floating charge over all its assets both present and future. This appears from the next case, which was the first to establish the validity of the floating charge.

Re Panama, New Zealand and Australian Royal Mail Co (1870) 5 Ch App 318, Court of Appeal in Chancery

The question in this case was whether the debentures given by the company were effective to give the holders a charge upon the proceeds of sale of the company's ships and other assets, in priority to the claims of its general creditors, in the winding up. The court held that they were.

The debentures were in the following form:

The *Panama, New Zealand, and Australian Mail Co Ltd*
Mortgage Debenture
No 404   £100

> By virtue of the powers contained in our articles of association we, the *Panama, New Zealand, and Australian Royal Mail Co Ltd*, in consideration of the sum of £100 paid to us by *J E Naylor*, of, etc, and the Rev *T H Stokoe* of, etc, are held and firmly bound, and do hereby for ourselves, our successors and assigns, charge the said undertaking, and all sums of money arising therefrom, and all the estate, right, title, and interest of the company therein, with the payment to the said *J E Naylor* and *T H Stokoe*, their executors, administrators, or assigns, of the said sum of £100, together with interest for the same at the rate of £6 per cent by the year, the principal sum to be repaid on the 2nd of January, 1870, and the interest to be payable in the meantime half-yearly, on the 1st of January and the 1st of July in each year, until the repayment thereof. Given under our common seal.

Giffard LJ: This is an appeal from an order of Vice-Chancellor Malins by which he has declared that the mortgage debentures issued under the seal of the company are a charge upon the proceeds of the sale of the vessels and other property of the company. . . .

What I have to decide in the present case is simply this: What are the rights of the debenture holders, the state of things being that the concern is being wound up, and that the whole of its property is being realized? I confess that I can have no doubt whatever as to what the effect of the debenture is. In the first place, as regards the powers that were given to the company, there was a power given to mortgage, and a power given to raise money by debentures; but, of course, they might include in one and the same instrument a mortgage and a debenture, that is to say, a mortgage and a bond. Accordingly they did issue what they called a mortgage debenture, which was, in substance, a bond, and a charge upon their property for the sum borrowed on bond. The form of the instrument is not an assignment but a charge; the company charge the undertaking, and all sums of money arising therefrom, and all estate, right, title, and interest of the company therein, with payment of the principal sum and interest. I asked in the course of the argument what could be the subject matter of that charge, and the answer given was, that there were valuable contracts, and that all that the charge was meant to cover was the income arising from the business being carried on, and that it would not extend to property, such as the ships and other property of that nature, which were absolutely essential to the carrying on of the concern. I cannot accede to any such proposition as that. I have no hesitation in saying that in this particular case, and having regard to the state of this particular company, the word 'undertaking' had reference to all the property of the company, not only which existed at the date of the debenture, but which might afterwards become the property of the company. And I take the object and meaning of the debenture to be this, that the word 'undertaking' necessarily infers that the company will go on, and that the debenture holder could not interfere until either the interest which was due was unpaid, or until the period had arrived for the payment of his principal, and that principal was unpaid. I think the meaning and object of the security was this, that the company might go on during that interval, and, furthermore, that during the interval the debenture holder would not be entitled to any account of mesne profits, or of any dealing with the property of the company in the ordinary course of carrying on their business. I do not refer to such things as sales or mortgages of property, but to the ordinary application of funds which came into the hands of the company in the usual course of business. I see no difficulty or inconvenience in giving that effect to this instrument. But the moment the company comes to be wound up, and the property has to be realized, that moment the rights of these parties, beyond all question, attach. My opinion is, that even if the company had not stopped the debenture holders might have filed a bill to realize their security. I hold that under these debentures they have a charge upon all property of the company, past and future, by the term 'undertaking,' and that they stand in a position superior to that of the general creditors, who can touch nothing until they are paid. The appeal, therefore, must be dismissed with costs.

The essential characteristics of the floating charge appear from the cases which follow. For an example of a debenture creating a floating charge, see below, p 965.

Illingworth v Houldsworth [1904] AC 355, House of Lords

(The facts are irrelevant.)

Lord Macnaghten: I should have thought there was not much difficulty in defining what a floating charge is in contrast to what is called a specific charge. A specific charge, I think, is one that without more fastens on ascertained and definite property or property capable of being ascertained and defined; a floating charge, on the other hand, is ambulatory and shifting in its nature, hovering over and so to speak floating with the property which it is intended to affect until some event occurs or some act is done which causes it to settle and fasten on the subject of the charge within its reach and grasp. . . .

[Parts of the judgments of the members of the Court of Appeal in this case, reported sub nom *Re Yorkshire Woolcombers' Association Ltd* [1903] 2 Ch 284, are cited by Slade J in *Re Bond Worth Ltd*, above at pp 416–417.]

Evans v Rival Granite Quarries Ltd [1910] 2 KB 979, Court of Appeal

(The facts are irrelevant.)

Buckley LJ: . . . A floating security is not a future security; it is a present security, which presently affects all the assets of the company expressed to be included in it. On the other hand, it is not a specific security; the holder cannot affirm that the assets are specifically mortgaged to him. The assets are mortgaged in such a way that the mortgagor can deal with them without the concurrence of the mortgagee. A floating security is not a specific mortgage of the assets, plus a licence to the mortgagor to dispose of them in the course of his business, but is a floating mortgage applying to every item comprised in the security, but not specifically affecting any item until some event occurs or some act on the part of the mortgagee is done which causes it to crystallize into a fixed security.

Re Bond Worth Ltd [1980] Ch 228, Chancery Division

(See above, pp 414–417.)

NOTES

1. In *Re Yorkshire Woolcombers' Association Ltd* [1903] 2 Ch 284 at 295, Romer LJ was careful to make it clear that he was not attempting an exact definition of a floating charge. In *Re Croftbell Ltd* [1990] BCC 781 at 784, Vinelott J stated that Romer LJ was concerned not to define a floating charge for all purposes but to indicate the features which are material in distinguishing a specific charge extending to future assets from a floating charge (Vinelott J said much the same thing again in *Re Atlantic Medical Ltd* [1992] BCC 653 at 658).

2. It is clear from the cases above that a vital feature of the floating charge is that it authorises the company to deal with those assets in the ordinary course of business. It follows that the company may not only sell and buy such property during the currency of a floating charge, but – at least where the charge is expressed in conventional terms – may also create mortgages and charges, ranking in priority to the floating charge itself. However, a company may not create a second floating charge over the same assets to rank in priority to an existing charge (*Re Benjamin Cope & Sons Ltd* [1914] 1 Ch 800), although it may create a second floating charge over part of its assets ranking in priority to an existing floating charge, if the power to create such a charge was reserved in the earlier charge (*Re Automatic Bottle Makers Ltd* [1926] Ch 412, CA). Even where, by what is commonly termed a 'negative pledge clause', the creation of later charges is forbidden by the terms of the original charge, the claim of a subsequent chargee will prevail if he took the charge without notice of the clause, even though he had notice of the floating charge itself (*English and Scottish Mercantile Investment Co v Brunton* [1892] 2 QB 700, CA – although the subsequent chargee will be deemed to have notice of a negative pledge clause when s 416(1) of the Companies Act 1985, as amended by the Companies Act 1989, is brought into force and regulations are made to effect s 415(2)(a) of the 1985 Act, as amended: see below, p 850).

3. The fact that a floating charge merely 'hovers' over a changing fund of assets has raised a question as to whether the chargee has a present equitable proprietary interest before crystallisation. The question has generated considerable academic debate: for example, contrast the view taken by Dr W J Gough in his *Company Charges* (no proprietary interest until crystallisation) with that of Professor J H Farrar in (1980) 1 Co Lawyer 83 (equitable interest even before crystallisation). On balance, the cases support the view expressed by Buckley LJ in *Evans v Rival Granite Quarries* (above, p 840) that the chargee has a present equitable interest before crystallisation but that the interest is defeasible by a transaction in the ordinary course of business (see, in particular, *Re Margart Pty Ltd, Hamilton v Westpac Banking Corpn* [1985] BCLC 314, a decision of the Supreme Court of New South Wales; followed by Vinelott J in *Re French's (Wine Bar) Ltd* [1987] BCLC 499 and *Re Atlantic Medical Ltd* [1992] BCC 653). This is important, for as Dr E V Ferran explains: 'it is only because a floating charge constitutes a present proprietary interest that, first, a floating charge has priority over a second co-extensive floating charge and secondly, that third parties who have notice of a negative pledge contained in a floating charge are postponed to that charge' ([1988] CLJ 213 at p 237). See also R M Goode *Legal Problems of Credit and Security* (2nd ed, 1988), p 50.

QUESTION

To secure further borrowing facilities, X Ltd creates a floating charge over its present and future assets in favour of A Bank. The charge contains a negative pledge clause. Later, wishing to purchase a new factory, X Ltd approaches B Bank for a loan. B Bank agrees to make the loan, subject to it taking a mortgage (ie legal charge) over the factory to rank in priority to any other security. X Ltd agrees to this and the loan is made, factory purchased and mortgage executed all within a couple of days. At all material times B Bank was aware of A Bank's floating charge and had actual knowledge of the negative pledge clause. Shortly afterwards X Ltd went into liquidation and the floating charge 'crystallised'. Advise the liquidator as to whether A Bank's charge or B Bank's mortgage has priority. See *Abbey National Building Society v Cann* [1991] 1 AC 56, HL; noted by R Gregory (1990) 106 LQR 550; J de Lacy [1991] LMCLQ 531; G Goldberg (1992) 108 LQR 380.

(iii) *Crystallisation of a floating charge*

A floating charge will crystallise, and become a fixed charge attaching to the assets of the company at that time, (1) when a receiver is appointed; (2) when the company goes into liquidation (since the licence to deal with the assets in the ordinary course of business will then necessarily terminate); (3) when the company ceases to carry on business; (4) in the case where the debenture empowers the charge-holder to convert the floating charge into a fixed charge by giving the company 'notice of conversion', and such a notice is given; and (5) where an event occurs which under the terms of the debenture causes 'automatic' crystallisation. This depends upon there being a provision in the document creating the charge which states that the charge will crystallise on the happening of some particular event – eg if a creditor of the company levies execution against its property, or if the company gives security over assets covered by the charge to a third party without the charge-holder's consent. There has been much controversy over automatic crystallisation clauses, both as to their legality and as to whether, as a matter of policy, their use should be prohibited or subjected to restrictions by law. Of course, it is reasonable to provide that the charge-holder shall have the right to *appoint a receiver* in such an event, since this is an overt act of which everyone can be aware; but the position is different where crystallisation is automatic, since this can take place without any act on the part of anyone. There are two schools of thought on the question. One takes the view that the floating charge is not an established phenomenon having fixed characteristics, but is simply the creature of the draftsman and that a creditor is free to strengthen his security in this way if he wants to. The other looks at the effect of such an arrangement on third parties and contends that it must be against public policy to have a charge crystallise in circumstances which may be unknown (and perhaps even unknowable) at the time, so that a company could not give a buyer a good title even though everyone was acting in good faith. (This is, however, pressing the argument too far, for the company would have ostensible authority to continue to deal with its property in such circumstances.[1]) There is clear authority upholding the effectiveness of an automatic crystallisation clause in New Zealand: *Re Manurewa Transport Ltd* [1971] NZLR 909; *Dovey Enterprises v Guardian Assurance Publiations* [1993] 1 NZLR 540. In the Australian decision *Stein v Saywell* (1969) 121 CLR 529, [1969] ALR 481, the High Court was divided in its opinion. In Canada, opposition to automatic crystallisation clauses can be found in *R v Consolidated Churchill Copper Corpn Ltd* [1978] 5 WWR 652. In *Re Woodroffes (Musical Instruments) Ltd* [1986] Ch 366, Nourse J expressed the view, obiter, that 'the general body of informed opinion is of the view that automatic crystallisation is undesirable'. This may be contrasted with the remarks, also obiter, of Hoffmann J in *Re Brightlife Ltd*

---

1 Goode *Commercial Law* (London, 1982) at 799; cf D E Allan (1989) 15 Mon LR 337 at pp 354–356 and Professor Goode's reply (1989) 15 Mon LR 361 at pp 366–367.

[1987] Ch 200 at 214–215, [1986] 3 All ER 673 at 680–681.[2] He said:

[Counsel] said that public policy required restrictions upon what the parties could stipulate as crystallising events. A winding up or the appointment of a receiver would have to be noted on the register. But a notice [of conversion] need not be registered and a provision for automatic crystallisation might take effect without the knowledge of either the company or the debenture holder. The result might be prejudicial to third parties who gave credit to the company. Considerations of this kind impressed Berger J in the Canadian case of *R v Consolidated Churchill Copper Corpn Ltd* where the concept of 'self-generating crystallisation' was rejected.

I do not think that it is open to the courts to restrict the contractual freedom of parties to a floating charge on such grounds. The floating charge was invented by Victorian lawyers to enable manufacturing and trading companies to raise loan capital on debentures. It could offer the security of a charge over the whole of the company's undertaking without inhibiting its ability to trade. But the mirror image of these advantages was the potential prejudice to the general body of creditors, who might know nothing of the floating charge but find that all the company's assets, including the very goods which they had just delivered on credit, had been swept up by the debentureholder. The public interest requires a balancing of the advantages to the economy of facilitating the borrowing of money against the possibility of injustice to unsecured creditors. These arguments for and against the floating charge are matters for Parliament rather than the courts and have been the subject of public debate in and out of Parliament for more than a century.

Parliament has responded, first, by restricting the rights of the holder of a floating charge and secondly, by requiring public notice of the existence and enforcement of the charge. For example, priority was given to preferential debts in 1897 and the Companies Act 1907 invalidated floating charges created within three months before the commencement of the winding up. This period has since been extended and is now one year. The registration of floating and other charges was introduced by the Companies Act 1900. The Companies Act 1907 required registration of the appointment of a receiver and the Companies Act 1929 required notice of such appointment to be given on the company's letters and invoices.

These limited and pragmatic interventions by the legislature make it in my judgment wholly inappropriate for the courts to impose additional restrictive rules on grounds of public policy. It is certainly not for a judge of first instance to proclaim a new head of public policy which no appellate court has even hinted at before. I would therefore respectfully prefer the decision of the New Zealand Supreme Court in *Re Manurewa Transport Ltd*, recognising the validity of a provision for automatic crystallisation, to the contrary dicta in the Canadian case I have cited.

The Cork Committee (1982, Cmnd 8558, paras 1578–79) considered that automatic crystallisation was 'not merely inconvenient', but that there was 'no place for it in a modern insolvency law'. The Committee recommended that the circumstances in which a floating charge crystallised should be defined by statute, and that all other ways (including automatic crystallisation) should be banned. But Parliament appears to have decided that automatic crystallisation should be allowed to stay, subject to safeguards which should remove any risks flowing from the possibility that it may occur without the knowledge of one or more of the parties concerned. Under s 410(3) of CA 1985, as amended, the Secretary of State is empowered to make regulations requiring registration of an event causing a floating charge to crystallise, and it is contemplated that the regulations will declare ineffective such a crystallising event until registration has been effected.

The floating charge was unknown in Scots common law, as was the institution of

2 Hoffmann J reasserted this view in *Re Permanent Houses (Holdings) Ltd* [1988] BCLC 563 at 567: 'provided the language of the debentures was sufficiently clear, there was no conceptual reason why the parties should not agree that any specified event should cause the charge to crystallise'. The Northern Irish High Court has recently upheld the effectiveness of an automatic crystallisation clause in *Re Sperrin Textiles Ltd* (1992) 10 Bull of NI Law 12.

receivership. Legislation making both possible was passed in 1961 and 1972 (see now Part XVIII of CA 1985 and IA 1986, ss 50–71). These statutory provisions do not allow for automatic crystallisation in Scotland.

Re Woodroffes (Musical Instruments) Ltd [1986] Ch 366, Chancery Division

The company had given a first floating charge to its bank and a second floating charge to Mrs Woodroffe. A provision in the latter instrument empowered Mrs Woodroffe by giving notice to the company to convert the charge into a fixed charge, and this she did on 27 August 1982. The bank appointed receivers on 1 September 1982. In this action, which was brought to establish the priorities as between the two debentureholders and the company's other creditors, Nourse J held that Mrs Woodroffe's notice did not have the effect of crystallising the bank's charge, as well as her own, on 27 August. He also ruled that the bank's charge would have crystallised if the company had ceased to carry on business at any time between 27 August and 1 September, but that there was no sufficient evidence that this had happened.

Nourse J: On what date did the bank's floating charge crystallise? Mr Jarvis, for the bank, supported by Mr Marks, for Mrs Woodroffe, arguing in favour of 27 August, submit in the first instance that the effect of Mrs Woodroffe's notice of conversion was to crystallise not only her own charge, but also the bank's. They say that the notice, by determining Mrs Woodroffe's licence to the company to employ the assets subject to the charge in the ordinary course of its business, rendered any further use of those assets unlawful and impracticable, with the result that the company's business must be taken to have ceased at that time. Consequently, they submit that there was a crystallisation of both charges.

I find myself quite unable to accept that submission, which appears to me to run contrary to fundamental principles of the law of contract. I do not see how the determination of Mrs Woodroffe's licence can in some way work a determination of the bank's, or produce the effect that the bank has had its charge crystallised over its head and possibly contrary to its own wishes. The relationship between the company and the bank was governed by the [bank's] debenture, which, although it contained a prohibition against creating any subsequent charge without consent – see clause 5 – did not provide for the bank's floating charge to crystallise either on the creation or crystallisation of a subsequent charge.

On analysis it appears to me that the arguments of Mr Jarvis on this point are founded, and can only be founded, on an implied term in the [bank's] debenture. . . . It does not seem to me to be at all clear that a term to the effect contended for by Mr Jarvis must be implied. Why should it be assumed that the bank and the company, in particular the bank, intended that the crystallisation of a subsequent charge should in all circumstances cause a crystallisation of the bank's? No doubt it might suit the bank's interests in the great majority of circumstances, but that does not mean that it can be assumed in all. For example, the bank might have taken the view that it was in its own interests that the business of the company should continue. Unless Mrs Woodroffe had either appointed her own receiver, or had applied for an injunction restraining it from dealing with its assets in contravention of her own fixed charge, I can see no reason why the company could not have continued to carry on its business. True it could only have done so in breach of its contract with Mrs Woodroffe, but the bank might have been prepared to indemnify it against that liability or even to pay off Mrs Woodroffe. I can see no ground for any species of implication to the effect contended for. . . .

The question whether the cessation of the company's business causes an automatic crystallisation of a floating charge is one of general importance upon which there appears to be no decision directly in point. Such authorities as there are disclose a uniform assumption in favour of crystallisation. There is a valuable discussion of them in *Picarda on The Law Relating to Receivers and Managers*, pp 16–18. One of the questions there raised is whether there is any distinction for this purpose between a company ceasing to carry on business on the one hand and ceasing to be a going concern on the other. My own impression is that these phrases are used interchangeably in the authorities . . . but whether that be right or wrong, I think it clear that the material event is a cessation of business and not, if that is something different, ceasing to be a going concern.

[His Lordship referred to a number of authorities, and continued:]

It is unnecessary for me to examine any of those cases in detail, or to quote extracts from the judgments of the many judges who decided them. They all, to a greater or lesser extent, assume that crystallisation takes place on a cessation of business. . . .

Although the general body of informed opinion is of the view that automatic crystallisation is undesirable (see in particular the Report of the Review Committee on Insolvency Law and Practice (Cmnd 8558) 30 April 1981, paras 1570–1582) I have not been referred to any case in which the assumption in favour of automatic crystallisation on cessation of business has been questioned. On that state of the authorities it would be very difficult for me to question it, even if I could see a good ground for doing so. On the contrary, it seems to me that it is in accordance with the essential nature of a floating charge. The thinking behind the creation of such charges has always been a recognition that a fixed charge on the whole undertaking and assets of the company would paralyse it and prevent it from carrying on its business: see, eg *Re Florence Land and Public Works Co, ex p Moor* ((1878) 10 Ch D 53). On the other hand it is a mistake to think that the chargee has no remedy while the charge is still floating. He can always intervene and obtain an injunction to prevent the company from dealing with its assets otherwise than in the ordinary course of its business. That no doubt is one reason why it is preferable to describe the charge as 'hovering', a word which can bear an undertone of menace, rather than as 'dormant'. A cessation of business necessarily puts an end to the company's dealings with its assets. That which kept the charge hovering has now been released and the force of gravity causes it to settle and fasten on the subject of the charge within its reach and grasp. The paralysis, while it may still be unwelcome, can no longer be resisted. . . .

[His Lordship then held that the evidence did not support the view that the company had ceased business before 1 September.]

NOTE

In *William Gaskell Group Ltd v Highley* [1993] BCC 200, Morritt J followed the decision of Nourse J in *Re Woodroffes (Musical Instruments) Ltd* to the effect that the cessation of business necessarily put an end to a company's capacity to deal with its assets and, therefore, automatically caused a floating charge to crystallise.

QUESTION

Does the making of an administration order (see below, p 901) crystallise a floating charge? See L C B Gower *Principles of Modern Company Law* (5th ed, 1992), p 419; cf *Palmer's Company Law* (25th ed, 1992), para 13.129.

(iv) *What benefits accrue to a creditor by taking a fixed charge, as opposed to a floating charge, over a debtor company's assets?*

(See above, pp 775–776.)

(v) *What benefits accrue to a creditor by taking a floating charge, as opposed to a fixed charge, over a debtor company's assets?*

(See above, pp 776–777.)

(vi) *Can a creditor take both a fixed and floating charge over the same assets?*

Re Croftbell Ltd [1990] BCC 781, Chancery Division

(See above, pp 777–778.)

NOTES

(See above, p 778.)

3 Equitable lien

An equitable lien is a non-possessory security which arises by operation of law.[1] The lien of the unpaid seller of land is the most common example of this type of lien, although unpaid vendors of intangible personal property have also been held to have such a lien (eg *Re Stucley* [1906] 1 Ch 67; *Langen and Wind Ltd v Bell* [1972] Ch 685). In *Lord Napier and Ettrick v Hunter* [1993] AC 713 (noted by N H Andrews [1993] CLJ 223; J Martin (1993) 143 NLJ 1061), the House of Lords recently held that an insurer's right of subrogation gave the insurer an equitable proprietary interest in a fund recovered by the assured from the wrongdoer and that the insurer's proprietary interest was to be supported by an equitable lien over the fund held by the assured. However, the unpaid seller of goods has no equitable lien (*Re Wait* [1927] 1 Ch 606 at 639, per Atkin LJ; *Transport and General Credit Corpn v Morgan* [1939] Ch 531 at 546, per Simonds J). The holder of an equitable lien has the same remedies as docs a chargee, namely an order for sale and the appointment of a receiver. For further details of this type of security, see L A Sheridan *Rights in Security* (1974), pp 228–232; A P Bell *Modern Law of Personal Property in England and Ireland* (1989), pp 180–183, 186. See also J Phillips 'Equitable Liens – A Search for a Unifying Principle' in N Palmer and E McKendrick (eds) *Interests in Goods* (1993), Ch 25.

---

1 A maritime lien is also a non-possessory security arising by operation of law. It is a right of action in rem against a ship and freight for payment due under a contract, for the cost of salvage or for damage caused by a ship. For details, see L A Sheridan *Rights in Security* (1974), pp 194–198.

4 Statutory control

(a) Protection of third parties

The statutory requirement that non-possessory security interests must be registered provides a prospective creditor (ie a third party) with the opportunity to establish whether the debtor has already encumbered the property in his possession. Without registration the non-possessory security interest would be hidden and the prospective creditor could be misled as to the creditworthiness of the debtor (Diamond Report (HMSO, 1989), para 11.1.3; cf F Oditah [1992] JBL 541 at pp 542–543). Furthermore, registration may also benefit a creditor by enabling him to publicise his own non-possessory security interest and so reduce the chances of the encumbered asset being disposed of by the debtor to a bona fide third party purchaser without notice of it, and who might, therefore, take priority over it (R M Goode (1984) 100 LQR 234 at pp 238–239).

Non-possessory security interests may be registrable under the Bills of Sale Acts 1878 and 1882 (if given by individuals), or under the Companies Act 1985 (if given by companies). We shall concentrate on registration under these statutes, although it should be noted that registration may also be required for certain types of property (eg ships and aircraft) in other specialised registers (see Diamond Report, Ch 12).

(i) *Bills of Sale Acts*

The Bills of Sale Act 1878 and the Bills of Sale Act (1878) Amendment Act 1882 (as amended) control, inter alia, the registration of bills of sale. It should be noted at once that any security issued by a company is excluded from the operation of these Acts (s 17 of the 1882 Act; and *Richards v Kidderminster Overseers* [1896] 2 Ch 212).

According to Lord Esher MR in *Mills v Charlesworth* (1890) 25 QBD 421 at 424: 'A bill of sale, in its ordinary meaning, is the document which is given where the legal property in the goods passes to the person who lends money on them, but the possession does not pass'. This common law description of a bill of sale has been considerably extended by the Bills of Sale Acts 1878 and 1882. For the purposes of the 1878 and 1882 Acts, the term 'bill of sale' is defined to include a much broader class of documents relating to 'personal chattels' than is the case at common law (see s 4 of the 1878 Act, which lists the various documents; also s 3 of the 1882 Act). Those documents falling within the statutory definition divide into three broad categories: (1) instruments transferring legal or beneficial ownership of personal chattels; (2) instruments conferring a right to take possession of personal chattels as security for any debt; and (3) agreements by which a right in equity to any personal chattels, or to any charge or security thereon, is to be conferred (*Halsbury's Laws of England* (4th ed, 1992), Vol 4(1), para 619). In general, all written mortgages and charges relating to personal chattels fall within the statutory definition of a bill of sale and are caught by the Bills of Sale Acts (but not equitable liens, which arise by operation of law and not by agreement).

As a bill of sale is defined in terms of documents, oral transactions fall outside the definition and are not caught by the Bills of Sale Acts. The same applies to transactions whereby the transferee's rights are completed by delivery without reference to any document, eg a pledge or possessory lien (*Charlesworth v Mills*

[1892] AC 231 at 235, HL). Furthermore, s 4 of the 1878 Act excludes certain documents from the definition of 'bill of sale'. In particular, 'transfers of goods in the ordinary course of business of any trade or calling' and bills of lading are excluded from the statutory definition. Intangible property is excluded from the definition of 'personal chattels' (s 4 of the 1878 Act) so that, for example, an asignment of book debts would not be caught by the Bills of Sale Acts (although s 344 of the Insolvency Act 1986 makes a general assignment of book debts by way of security registrable under the 1878 Act; see above, p 765). After-acquired property has recently been held to constitute personal chattels for the purpose of the Bills of Sale Acts (*Welsh Development Agency v Export Finance Co Ltd* [1991] BCLC 936 at 956, per Browne-Wilkinson V-C (reversed by the Court of Appeal on another ground [1992] BCLC 148), disapproving Lord Macnaghten's dictum to the contrary in *Thomas v Kelly* (1888) 13 App Cas 506 at 521). This means that agreements conferring a right in equity over after-acquired goods, under the rule in *Holroyd v Marshall* (1862) 10 HL Cas 191 (above, p 754), are caught by the Bills of Sale Acts.

There are two types of bills of sale, namely, those given as security for the payment of money ('security bills') and those which are given otherwise than as security for the payment of money ('absolute bills'). The 1878 Act applies to both absolute and security bills so long as they confer on the holder or grantee a power to seize or take possession of any personal chattels comprised in or made subject to the bill (s 3 of the 1878 Act). However, with regard to security bills, the 1878 Act must be read together with the 1882 Act. The 1882 Act applies only to security bills and provides that any provisions in the 1878 Act which are inconsistent with the 1882 Act are repealed as to such bills of sale (s 15 of the 1882 Act).

The 1878 Act sets out a scheme for the registration of bills of sale of personal chattels which remain in the possession of the grantor. Under this scheme all such bills of sale must be attested and registered within seven days of their execution (s 8 of the 1878 Act). If a security bill is not attested and registered within seven days of its execution (and does not truly state the consideration for which it was given) the bill is rendered 'void in respect of the personal chattels comprised therein' (s 8 of the 1882 Act). This means that the security granted by the bill becomes unenforceable, although any other covenant in the bill remains enforceable, eg the grantor's covenant as to payment (*Heseltine v Simmons* [1892] 2 QB 547 at 553–554, CA). To maintain the registration, it must be renewed every five years (s 11 of the 1878 Act). A transfer or assignment of a registered bill of sale need not be registered (s 10 of the 1878 Act).

Registration is a cumbersome process. It is regulated by the 1878 Act which provides that the bill of sale, with every schedule or inventory thereto annexed or therein referred to, and a true copy of the bill and of every schedule or inventory and of every attestation of the execution of such bill, together with an affidavit containing certain required particulars, must be presented to the registrar (a master of the Supreme Court, Queen's Bench Division); and the copy of the bill of sale and the original affidavit must be filed with him (see *Halsbury's Laws of England* (4th ed reissue, 1992) Vol 4(1), para 739). Every security bill must have annexed to it a schedule containing an inventory of the personal chattels comprised in the bill of sale. To ensure that this schedule of chattels is accurate, and that no creditor consulting the registered copy of the bill of sale is misled, failure to include a specific description of an item in the schedule renders the bill void as regard to it, except as against the grantor himself (s 4 of the 1882 Act). The accuracy of the schedule annexed to a security bill is further maintained by s 5 of the 1882 Act which, in general, renders a bill of sale void, except as against the grantor, in respect of any chattels specifically described in the schedule of which the grantor was not the true owner at the time of the execution of the bill of sale (see *Lewis v Thomas* [1919] 1 KB 319, where a person who held goods on hire-purchase was held not to be their true owner). In practice, s 5 of the 1882 Act prevents an individual giving a floating charge over future property.

Registration does not of itself constitute notice to third parties (*Joseph v Lyons* (1884) 15 QBD 280 at 286, CA). It remains possible for a bona fide purchaser from the grantor, without notice of the prior bill of sale, to acquire a good title and override that of the grantee (although in the case of a security bill this will only be possible if the title acquired by the original grantee is purely equitable or the original grantee is estopped from asserting his legal title or there was a sale in market overt). If the subsequent disposition of the goods by the grantor is itself a registrable bill of sale, priority will generally be governed by s 10 of the 1878 Act. Under s 10 of the 1878 Act, the date of registration governs priority between two or more bills of sale comprising, in whole or in part, any of the same chattels. With regard to security bills, this general rule applies in the following cases: (1) as between two registered security bills; and (2) where an absolute bill is granted after the grant of a security bill. If a security bill is granted after an absolute bill (whether registered or not) the security bill will be void, except as against the grantor, under s 5 of the 1882 Act.

(ii) *Companies Act 1985 (as amended)*

Sections 395ff of the Companies Act 1985 contain important provisions about the registration of charges created by a company over its property. Particulars, in a prescribed statutory form, of most kinds of charge created by a company (but not all: for the list of transactions to which the Act applies, see s 396) must be delivered to the registrar within 21 days. Failing registration, s 399 declares that the security is void as against (1) an administrator or liquidator of the company, and (2) any person who for value acquires an interest in or right over property subject to the charge (unless the acquisition is expressly subject to the charge: s 405(1)). There are also criminal penalties for non-compliance.

The nature of this sanction of 'partial voidness' is curious. First it should be noted that it is the *security* that is avoided, and not the obligation, which remains good as an unsecured debt. Secondly, the charge is void only as against the persons mentioned and not, for instance, inter partes, nor against an execution creditor. And the chargee may dispose of the property in exercise of a power of sale and give a good title to the purchaser, even though the charge is 'void'; but there are statutory rules which postpone the claims of the charge-holder in the proceeds of sale to the holders of prior encumbrances, and nullify them altogether in an administration or liquidation (s 406).

As between the holders of successive charges over the same property, the position is complex. If particulars of both charges are duly registered within the respective 21-day periods, the ordinary rules of law apply and nothing turns on the time of registration; thus, broadly speaking, a legal charge will have priority over an equitable charge, a fixed charge over a floating charge and, as between two equitable charges, the earlier in time will prevail. Similar rules will apply if *neither* charge is registered. But if particulars (even defective particulars) of the later charge are registered either within the statutory 21 days or before *complete and accurate* particulars of the earlier charge are registered, the later charge will gain priority (s 404). Section 404(2) deals with the possibility that both sets of particulars may be incomplete or inaccurate – in effect it provides that, to the extent that the omission or inaccuracy is material, the first to have that vital element recorded prevails.

As between a charge-holder and an administrator or liquidator, omissions and errors in the registered particulars, if not corrected in time, will render a charge void to the extent that rights which ought to have been disclosed are not revealed; but the court has a discretion to order otherwise (s 402).

The *late delivery* of particulars does not render a charge void against an administrator or liquidator unless the company is insolvent at the date when particulars are delivered *and* the administration or liquidation proceedings begin within a specified period (varying from six months to two years) of that date: six months for a fixed charge, two years for a floating charge given to a person 'connected with' the company (as defined by the Insolvency Act 1986, s 249), and one year for any other floating charge (s 400).

The obligation to register particulars is placed by statute on the company, but any person interested in the charge may do so instead (s 398(1)). The registrar, after registration, sends a copy of the particulars to both the company and the chargee, with a note of the date when they were delivered (s 398(5)). This is a departure from the previous practice, under which it was necessary to send to the registrar the charge document itself along with the particulars and the registrar, after checking the particulars against the document, returned it to the person who had lodged it, together with a certificate of due registration which was conclusive evidence that the requirements of the Act had been complied with. This new regime, which relieves the registrar and his staff of the burdensome task of checking every charge document, streamlines the procedure but plainly gives the charge-holder far less protection.

Section 401 makes provision for the delivery of further particulars, in order to supplement or vary the registered particulars (eg where the sum secured by the charge has been increased), or even to correct them where those originally lodged were inaccurate; and s 403 allows for the registration of a memorandum that a charge has ceased to affect the company's property – a procedure which is purely optional and is not binding on an administrator or liquidator although, since the memorandum must be signed by both the company and the chargee, it would give rise to an estoppel in favour of a person who subsequently acquired an interest in the property in reliance on it.

The Act also provides for the registration of similar particulars when a company buys property which is already subject to a charge; but in this case the only sanction for non-registration is a fine, and the security itself is not struck down.

The *registered particulars* are those prescribed by regulation pursuant to s 415. Traditionally, the particulars have included the names and descriptions of the parties, the date and description of the instrument creating the charge, the amount due or owing on the charge, short particulars of all the property mortgaged or charged, and particulars of any commission or discount. But under the new legislation, significantly, s 415(2)(a) expressly authorises the inclusion in the prescribed particulars of a statement 'whether the company has undertaken not to create other charges ranking in priority to or pari passu with the charge', so that any 'negative pledge' clause will be disclosed, and a person wishing to take a subsequent charge will be deemed to have notice of it.

There is an obligation to give notice to the registrar of the appointment of a receiver (s 409), and power to extend this requirement by regulation (s 410) so as to include other events which operate to crystallise a floating charge (a 'notice of conversion' or the fact that the company had ceased to carry on business). More specifically, in relation to an 'automatic crystallisation' clause, the regulations may provide that the crystallisation will be ineffective until notice of the event has been registered (s 410(3)).

The *company itself* is required to keep a register of charges at its own office, together with a copy of every instrument creating or evidencing a charge over its property (s 411). Since this provision covers every kind of charge, and not only those of which particulars must be filed with the registrar, its obligations are potentially very burdensome indeed. But neither the validity of the charge nor any question relating to priority is affected by the failure to observe the requirements of this section, and in practice the criminal sanctions prescribed are never invoked.

Both the particulars of charges held by the registrar and the register of charges and copy charge instruments held by the company are open to public inspection (ss 709, 411). But whereas a person is not taken to have notice of the information at the company's own office (s 711A), the doctrine of constructive notice has been expressly preserved, *as against a person taking a charge on the company's property*, by s 416(1) (above, p 780). Other persons, such as a purchaser of property from the company, are not deemed to have notice, even where such a person has 'failed to search the register in the course of making such inquiries as ought reasonably to have been made' (s 416(2)). A purchaser could, however, be affected with notice of particulars of a charge held by the registrar by reason of some other statutory provision (s 416(3)) – eg a floating charge affecting a company's land, by virtue of the Law of Property Act 1925, s 198.

Foreign companies which have charges over property situated in this country are obliged to register particulars with the registrar under similar rules as apply to local companies (ss 703ff).

NOTES

1. The discussion in this section assumes that Part IV of the Companies Act 1989 is in force. However, it should be noted that the 1989 Act is not retrospective so that all existing charges will be governed by the old law. See also E Ferran and C Mayo [1991] JBL 152; G McCormack [1990] LMCLQ 520.

2. Under s 395(2) of the Companies Act 1985 (as amended) a 'charge' is defined as any form of security interest over property not arising by operation of law and property is defined as including future property (above, p 766). A 'security interest' is not defined by the Act but it is likely that the courts will define it in similar terms to that which appear above at p 794 (as did Browne-Wilkinson V-C in *Bristol Airport plc v Powdrill* [1990] Ch 744 at 760, when construing the term 'security' in the context of s 248 of the Insolvency Act 1986; cf Farrar, Furey and Hannigan *Company Law* (3rd ed, 1991), p 270).

QUESTIONS

1. Is a clause retaining title to goods sold, while they remain in their original state in the corporate buyer's possession, a registrable charge under s 396 of the Companies Act 1985 (as amended)? See M G Bridge [1991] JBL 1 at 21.

2. To be bound by s 416(1) of the Companies Act 1985 (as amended) must the subsequent chargee have taken a *registrable* charge?

(iii) *Insolvency Act 1986*

There are controls in the Insolvency Act to protect third parties in the event of any unlawful preference or transaction at an undervalue (ss 238–239, 339–340): see below, pp 919 ff.

(b) Protection of debtors

Where security is given by an individual (usually the principal debtor) there are statutory controls which protect him against harsh and unreasonable terms and oppressive enforcement of the security. Such protection is to be found in the Bills of Sale Act (1878) Amendment Act 1882 (as amended) and the Consumer Credit Act 1974. Neither statute affords protection to companies who are principal debtors or who have given security to secure the debt of another person. Companies are regarded as having sufficient bargaining strength to look after their own interests (although this must be doubted when the company is small and heavily indebted to a lender who demands further security).

(i) *Bills of Sale Acts*

Unlike the Bills of Sale Act 1878, which is concerned with the protection of creditors, the Bills of Sale Act (1878) Amendment Act 1882 is primarily concerned with the protection of the grantor of a security bill (*Manchester, Sheffield and Lincolnshire Rly Co v North Central Wagon Co* (1888) 13 App Cas 554 at 560, per Lord Herschell). Pursuant to s 9 of the 1882 Act, a bill of sale made or given by way of security for the payment of money by the grantor thereof is rendered void unless made in accordance with the form prescribed by the Act. Every bill of sale made or given in consideration of any sum under £30 is also rendered void (s 12 of the 1882 Act). In both cases the security itself, and any personal covenant contained in the bill, is rendered unenforceable (*Davies v Rees* (1886) 17 QBD 408, CA; contrast this sanction with that for non-registration under s 8 of the 1882 Act). A covenant in the bill for the repayment of principal and interest will be unenforceable but the money lent will be recoverable as money had and received, together with reasonable interest (*Bradford Advance Co Ltd v Ayers* [1924] WN 152).

The 1882 Act also prohibits the grantee of a security bill seizing the chattels to which it relates unless (1) the grantor is in default, or fails to comply with any obligation necessary for maintaining the security; (2) the grantor becomes bankrupt, or suffers the goods to be distrained for rent, rates or taxes; (3) the grantor fraudulently removes or allows the goods to be removed from the premises; (4) the grantor fails to comply with a written request for his last receipts for rents, rates and taxes; (5) execution has been levied against the grantor's goods. Even then the seizure may be made subject to the 'default notice' provisions of the Consumer Credit Act 1974 (s 7A of the 1882 Act; also see below, p 853). The goods may not be removed by the grantee within five days of seizure (s 13 of the 1882 Act) thereby giving the grantor the opportunity to apply to the court for relief (s 7 of the 1882 Act).

(ii) *Consumer Credit Act 1974*

The Consumer Credit Act 1974 is a general consumer protection statute. In general, it applies to any agreement whereby credit of £15,000 or less (secured or unsecured) is supplied to an individual, including an unincorporated trader (but not when credit is supplied to a company): ss 8(1)–(2) and 189(1). Such an agreement is called a 'regulated consumer credit agreement' (s 8(3)). However, regulated consumer credit agreements between private individuals (called 'non-commercial agreements': s 189(1)) are exempt from most of the provisions of the Act. Within these limits, the 1974 Act applies whether or not the individual debtor is also afforded protection by the Bills of Sale Acts. What follows is only a brief outline of some of the main provisions of the 1974 Act (for further details, see R Bradgate and N Savage *Commercial Law* (1991), Chs 21–23; R M Goode *Consumer Credit Law* (2nd ed, 1989)).

The 1974 Act protects the individual debtor in two ways. First, it regulates the business practices of the credit industry in general (eg by restricting advertising and canvassing). In particular, it requires those operating a consumer credit business to be licensed (s 21). The term 'consumer credit business' is defined so as to include within the licensing requirement not only those whose principal business is the provision of credit but also those who supply credit in the course of some other business carried on by them (s 189(1)). Operating a consumer credit business without a licence is a criminal offence (s 39) and any credit agreement entered into by an unlicensed creditor is unenforceable without an order from the Director General of Fair Trading (s 40). Secondly, the Act controls the form, content, terms and enforcement of a regulated consumer credit agreement. The form and content of a regulated agreement is prescribed by regulations made under s 60 of the Act (the Consumer Credit (Agreements) Regulations 1983, SI 1983/1553, as amended). The regulations prescribe that, inter alia, the agreement must identify any security provided. Failure to comply with these regulations renders the agreement unenforceable without a court order (s 65). Enforcement is further controlled by Part VII of the Act. If a creditor is in breach of any term of a regulated consumer credit agreement, no security can be enforced against the creditor without first serving on him a 'default notice' specifying the nature of the alleged breach and giving the debtor at least seven days to take remedial action or pay compensation as specified in the notice (ss 87–89). Seizure is not permitted under the Bills of Sale Act (1878) Amendment Act 1882 if the period of grace specified in the default notice has not expired or the debtor has taken the action specified in the notice (s 7A of the 1882 Act). If the creditor is not in breach of the agreement and the creditor wishes to exercise a contractual right to seize his goods, he must give the debtor at least seven days' notice of his intention to do so (s 76). The control on enforcement only applies where agreement is specified to be for a fixed period (s 76(2)(a)).

Finally, it should be noted that under s 137 of the 1974 Act a court may reopen a credit agreement when it finds the credit bargain extortionate. A credit bargain is defined as an agreement where *credit of any amount* is provided to an individual, together with any other transaction which must be taken into account in computing the total charge for credit (s 137(2)). A credit bargain is deemed extortionate if it (1) requires the debtor or a relative of his to make payments which are grossly exorbitant, or (2) otherwise grossly contravenes ordinary principles of fair dealing (s 138(1)). In determining whether a credit bargain is extortionate the court is to have regard to, inter alia, interest rates prevailing when the agreement was made, the debtor's age and experience, the degree to which the debtor was under financial pressure when he entered into the agreement, and the degree of risk accepted by the creditor having regard to the value of any security provided (s 138(2)–(5)). If the court reopens a credit agreement it may, inter alia, set aside any obligation imposed on the debtor or a surety by the credit bargain or alter the terms of the credit agreement or any security instrument (s 139(2)).

QUESTION

Chattel mortgages are rarely used in granting credit. Why?

5 Reform

We have already noted (see above, p 798) that in Part II of his report Professor Diamond recommended wholesale reform of the law relating to security in property (other than land) along the lines of art 9 of the US Commercial Code and the Personal Property Security Acts in force in many Canadian provinces. The new system proposed by Professor Diamond would extend to all types of consensual security interests, possessory and non-possessory, created by companies, partnerships, and individuals in the course of their business (Diamond Report, paras 1.9–1.15 for summary). A new register of security interests would be introduced together with a notice filing system. The Bills of Sale Acts would be repealed and charges would no longer be registrable under the Companies Act (save for charges over land). Floating charges would be brought within the new system and so become available to all business people whether incorporated or not (Diamond Report, paras 16.15).

Pending such wholesale reform, Professor Diamond recommended immediate reform of the system for the registration of company charges (Part III of his report). Part IV of the Companies Act 1989 implements some of Professor Diamond's proposals for reform but ignores his two main recommendations, namely: (1) to fix priority as between charges by reference to the date of registration, and (2) to give a person about to take security from a company provisional protection for the short period between his search of the register and the lodging of particulars of his charge (Diamond Report, Ch 26).

CHAPTER 25

Guarantees

1 The legal nature of a guarantee

(1) A contract of guarantee is a contract whereby the surety (or guarantor) promises the actual or potential creditor of a third person (the principal debtor) to be responsible to him, in addition to the principal debtor, for the due performance by the principal debtor of his existing or future obligations to the creditor, if the principal debtor fails to perform those obligations.[1] The contract may be constituted by the personal engagement of the surety, or by the surety providing real security without any personal liability, or by both (*Smith v Wood* [1929] 1 Ch 14; *Re Conley* [1938] 2 All ER 127).

(2) The most important feature of a guarantee is that it is an accessory, or secondary, contract. This means that for there to be a valid contract of guarantee, between surety and creditor, there has to be a valid principal obligation, between the principal debtor and the creditor. It follows from the secondary nature of the contract of guarantee that there is a general principle that a surety's liability is co-extensive with that of the principal debtor. In other words, the surety is generally only liable to the same extent that the principal debtor is liable to the creditor, and that there is usually no liability on the part of the surety if the underlying obligation is void or unenforceable, or if that obligation ceases to exist. However, this general principle may be modified or displaced by the terms of the guarantee (*Moschi v Lep Air Services Ltd* [1973] AC 331 at 349, per Lord Diplock: below, p 868). Furthermore, in exceptional cases, the courts may ignore the principle altogether and hold the surety liable notwithstanding that the principal obligation guaranteed never arises or becomes unenforceable or ceases to exist otherwise than by the consent or with the agreement of the creditor (eg see below, p 872). See generally, R E Mitchell (1947) 63 LQR 355; J Steyn (1974) 90 LQR 246; G Andrews and R Millett *Law of Guarantees* (1992), Ch 6.

---

1 See generally, R M Goode *Commercial Law* (1982), Ch 33; R M Goode *Legal Problems of Credit and Security* (2nd ed, 1988), Ch VII; I R Davies *Textbook on Commercial Law* (1992), Ch 17. For further detail, see D G M Marks and G Moss (eds) *Rowlatt on the Law of Principal and Surety* (4th ed, 1982); *Chitty on Contracts* (26th ed, 1989), Vol II, Ch 12; G Andrews and R Millett *Law of Guarantees* (1992).

2 Guarantee and indemnity distinguished

Yeoman Credit Ltd v Latter [1961] 1 WLR 828, Court of Appeal

The plaintiff finance company let a car on hire-purchase to the first defendant who was, as all the parties were aware, an infant (ie a minor). By a separate agreement headed 'Hire-purchase indemnity and undertaking' the second defendant undertook to indemnify the finance company against any loss resulting or arising out of the hire-purchase agreement. When the first defendant failed to pay the instalments due under the hire-purchase agreement, the finance company claimed against the second defendant under the terms of the indemnity. The county court judge tried the following questions as preliminary issues: (1) whether the hire-purchase agreement was void under the Infants Relief Act 1874; and (2) if so, whether the second defendant could be held liable under his agreement to indemnify the finance company for any loss arising out of or resulting from that void agreement with the first defendant. The judge held (1) that the hire-purchase agreement was void; and (2) that the undertaking by the second defendant was a guarantee and, therefore, as the principal agreement was void, the guarantee was also void. The Court of Appeal agreed with the judge on the first issue but reversed him on the second. The case was then sent back to the county court for the full trial.

Holroyd Pearce LJ: In the county court it was argued by the second defendant as a preliminary point that the indemnity, though so called, was really a guarantee, and that since it guaranteed a void contract it was itself void on the reasoning and authority of Oliver J, who held in *Coutts & Co v Browne-Lecky* ([1947] KB 104) that since a guarantee is by definition an obligation to answer for the debt, default or miscarriage of another, there cannot, in respect of a void contract, be any debt, default or miscarriage to answer for.

There are, therefore, two questions raised by this appeal. First, is the document in question a guarantee although styled an indemnity? And, if it is a guarantee, is it void? In its widest sense a contract of indemnity includes a contract of guarantee. But in the more precise sense used in various cases dealing with s 4 of the Statute of Frauds 1677 (and used in the arguments in this case), a contract of indemnity differs from a guarantee. An indemnity is a contract by one party to keep the other harmless against loss, but a contract of guarantee is a contract to answer for the debt, default or miscarriage of another who is to be primarily liable to the promisee.

Mr Laughton-Scott, for the second defendant, in an able argument, admits that if the so-called indemnity in this case is in truth a contract of indemnity, he cannot, on the authorities, claim that it was void. If, however, it is in essence a guarantee, then the judge was right in regarding himself as bound by *Coutts v Browne-Lecky*, and this court should hold likewise unless it takes the view (for which Mr Lawson contends) that that case was wrongly decided. Mr Lawson argues that it is out of accord with other authorities, and that we should accept the view taken in certain cases that the guarantor of a void contract may yet be liable, a view which is in accord with that taken by the civil law.

The document in question is headed and described as 'Hire-purchase indemnity and undertaking.' It is clear from the wording of the document and the surrounding circumstances that it was intended to be something more than a mere guarantee. This tells in favour of its being in truth an indemnity. However, I agree with Mr Laughton-Scott that we must have regard to its essential nature in order to decide whether or not it is really no more than a guarantee. Its ultimate object, of course, was to ensure that the plaintiffs received back with profit the money that they had laid out in the transaction; but that ultimate object is shared by guarantee and indemnity alike. It is the method by which that object is attained which decides the class to which the document belongs.

Its material words are as follows: 'I undertake and agree as follows: (1) To indemnify you against any loss resulting from or arising out of the agreement and to pay to you the amount of such loss on demand and whether or not at the time of demand you shall have exercised all or any of your remedies in respect of the hirer or the chattels but so that upon payment in full by me of my liabilities hereunder I shall obtain such of your rights as you may at your discretion assign to me.' Thus, under paragraph 1 the second defendant does not obtain the full rights of subrogation to which a guarantor is by law entitled, but only such rights of subrogation as the plaintiffs may choose to allow. The second defendant does, however, under clause 8 (as will be seen) get valuable rights of a nature different from subrogation. Clause 2 reads: 'The amount of your loss for the purpose of this indemnity whether or not the agreement shall have been terminated by any party thereto shall be the total amount which the hirer would have had to pay under the agreement to entitle him to exercise the option of purchasing the chattels plus all expenses you may incur in the exercise or enforcement of your rights under the agreement . . . less the amount actually paid to you under the agreement by the hirer.' By that clause the second defendant is assuring to the plaintiffs such amount as will make up the sums paid by the hirer to the total amount of hire payable under the agreement, and the price of the option together with any expenses incurred by the plaintiffs in enforcing the agreement. Clause 3 provides that if the car has come into the plaintiffs' possession, they shall either give the second defendant credit for any amount which the plaintiffs realise on the sale of it, or shall, after payment in full by the second defendant of the full sum due, transfer the car to the second defendant so that he can sell it and keep the proceeds.

One may sum up the effect of the document in question as this: It protects the plaintiffs against any loss they may suffer since it assures to them the full sum of the hire-purchase price, plus any costs incurred by them in enforcing the hire-purchase agreement. Thus the rights of the second defendant (if called upon to pay) are different from the rights of subrogation under a guarantee, rights which would, in such a case as this, be useless. Moreover, whereas the plaintiffs' rights against the hirer and the second defendant would, under a normal guarantee, be identical, the document in question gives to the plaintiffs wholly different rights from those which they have against the hirer under the hire-purchase agreement. In some circumstances the plaintiffs' rights against the hirer may be higher than those against the second defendant, and in some circumstances lower.

If, as happened in the present case, the plaintiffs seize the car on default and sell it for a good price, the hirer's liability will be greater than that of the second defendant. Against the hirer the plaintiffs can claim under clause 7 of the hire-purchase agreement such sum as will make up the sums already paid by the hirer to half the purchase-price as agreed compensation for depreciation; but they need not give any credit for the value or proceeds of the car which they have seized. Against the second defendant, however, they can claim the total hire-purchase price plus expenses of enforcement, but they must give credit for the whole proceeds of the car. Hence the substantial difference between the respective sums claimed in this action against the first and second defendants. This difference is caused solely by the difference between the plaintiffs' rights under the indemnity and the hire-purchase agreement.

If, however, the hirer had determined the agreement himself when he had paid sums amounting to half the hire-purchase price, and if the car had failed to fetch as much as half the hire-purchase price, falling short of it by, say, £100 (which it might have done) then the hirer would have had to pay nothing under the hire-purchase agreement, while the second defendant would have had to pay £100. Moreover, in the latter instance the hirer would have been guilty of no debt, default or miscarriage, yet the second defendant would have to pay £100 under the indemnity. Mr Laughton-Scott argues that the mere fact that in occasional circumstances such a result may be produced does not destroy the essential nature of the agreement in question, which is to answer for the debt, default or miscarriage of another. Nevertheless, it raises a strong suspicion that that may not really be its essential nature.

Further, the agreement does not provide that the second defendant shall make good the particular defaults of the hirer. If the hirer fails to pay the instalments, no recourse can be had to the second defendant for those instalments. None of the actual obligations of the hirer can, if he defaults, be enforced against the second defendant. Only if the totality of the transaction produces either a loss, or a profit less than that which the total hire-purchase price would have yielded can the second defendant be asked to pay. And, if he is asked to pay, the fact that the hirer has made no default is no defence. For it is irrelevant to the calculations on which the second defendant's liability is based. And that liability may well arise from a lawful return of the car by the hirer coupled with a fall in the price of secondhand cars. The agreement is in truth (as clause 1 states) an indemnity against 'any loss resulting from or arising out of the agreement,' and not a surety against loss resulting from particular breaches of the agreement.

All these considerations point strongly towards the agreement being what it claims to be, namely, an indemnity. The surrounding circumstances (so far as one can gather them in the absence of the evidence) also support that claim. The parties were, it would seem, all aware of the legal difficulty created by the hirer's infancy. Hence the necessity for this special form of indemnity. That circumstance, as well as the wording of the document, makes it improbable that the transaction was intended as a guarantee of particular obligations if, as appears, they were known not to be binding against the infant. These assumptions, however, may thereafter be shown by the evidence to be incorrect.

In the leading case of *Lakeman v Mountstephen* ((1874) LR 7 HL 17) the plaintiff, a contractor, was failing to do certain sewage work because he was not sure that the Board of Health would pay for it; and the defendant, who wanted the work to be done, said: 'Mountstephen, go and do the work, and I will see you paid.' The House held that these words did not constitute a promise to pay the debt of another, and that they were rightly left to the jury as evidence of a primary obligation on the defendant. Lord Selborne said (at 24–25): 'There can be no suretyship unless there be a principal debtor, who of course may be constituted in the course of the transaction by matters ex post facto, and need not be so at the time, but until there is a principal debtor there can be no suretyship. Nor can a man guarantee anybody else's debt unless there is a debt of some other person to be guaranteed. The tendency, therefore, of any view of this contract which would place it in the position of a guarantee for a future liability to be undertaken by the local board, would be absolutely to defeat the whole purpose of the communication, which was to remove a difficulty then pressing upon the mind of the contractor, as to whether or not he had sufficient authority from anyone to go on with the work; and the answer was given in terms de praesenti for the express purpose of inducing him at once to go on.' In the present case the agreement is more consistent with a primary obligation on the second defendant to secure the plaintiffs against loss if the transaction should turn out unremunerative rather than a secondary obligation to make good the particular defaults of the hirer.

In *Wauthier v Wilson* ((1912) 28 TLR 239) a father and infant son signed a joint and several promissory note, the father joining as guarantor. Pickford J had held that the debt against the infant was void, but that, nevertheless, a guarantor of it remained liable on the authority of a decision of Kay J in *Yorkshire Railway Wagon Co v Maclure* ((1881) 19 Ch D 478). The Court of Appeal (without expressly disagreeing with the trial judge) preferred to take a different view. Farwell LJ said: '. . . if Mr Newbolt's contention that this was a case of a guarantee were to prevail it would follow that these three parties deliberately sat down to enter into an arrangement under which money was to be advanced on a promissory note on which no one was liable at all, there being no one liable as principal and therefore no one liable as surety.' And later Farwell LJ said: 'That seemed to him [the Lord Justice] to be the plain meaning of the transaction, on the assumption that the plaintiff knew that the son was under age; and it followed that, in his [his Lordship's] opinion, the father acted as principal and incurred liability as principal.'

I would take a somewhat similar view of the transaction in the present case in the absence of any evidence to the contrary. The second defendant was in effect saying to the plaintiffs: 'Go on with the transaction, and I will see you make your profit and suffer no loss.' No doubt it was hoped that the hirer would fulfil his obligations, although not legally bound by them. But the second defendant was not purporting to guarantee or make good any particular obligation of the hirer. Under the terms of his agreement he had no liability to do so. His liability was to see that the plaintiffs made their intended profit even though the hirer lawfully, without any default, terminated the hiring. He was underwriting the profitable success of the transaction, he was not insuring against contractual breaches of it by the hirer.

For those reasons, the agreement was not a contract of guarantee, but a contract of indemnity.

Harman LJ: . . . I cannot but admire the courage with which the judge faced the real difficulties of the present situation. He preferred to let himself decide the question whether this contract was one of guarantee or indemnity. It seems to me a most barren controversy. It dates back, of course, to the Statute of Frauds, and has raised many hair-splitting distinctions of exactly that kind which brings the law into hatred, ridicule and contempt by the public. Nevertheless, this difficulty persists, and the decided cases on the subject are hardly to be reconciled.

Where all concerned know that the first promisor is an infant, so that as against him the promise cannot be enforced, the court should incline to construe the document signed by the adult (the second promisor) as an indemnity, for that must have been the intention of the promisee and the second promisor. Both know that the first promise has no legal validity; it may be that both hope that the first promisor will honour his engagement, but with the knowledge that he cannot be obliged to do so it must have been their intention that the promise of the adult promisor should have an independent validity. Otherwise the whole transaction is a sham. . . .

Starting from this premise I approach the document between the plaintiffs and the second defendant in the present case, and I find that upon its true construction this is clearly a document of indemnity.

Davies LJ: All through this case I have found myself in considerable doubt as to the true meaning of the contract with which we are concerned, and, despite the powerful reasons that have been given in the opinions expressed by my Lords, I find myself still in that unhappy position. But as the case involves no question of general law but concerns merely the transaction recorded in this particular document, I think that probably the less I say about it the better. I content myself, therefore, by saying that I am still extremely concerned as to whether the real meaning of this document is not that it sets up machinery to secure to the finance company in any event the receipt of the full amount of the money due under the hire-purchase agreement (if any) plus any expenses incurred – whether or not the contract is terminated by the finance company under clause 4 of the agreement in the event therein provided, or whether or not it is terminated by the hirer at his option under clause 5; but that throughout the primary liability under the whole transaction taken together falls on the hirer. But my Lords have formed a firm view about it.

I will only add that I am wholly unconvinced in this case by the argument that was mentioned by Farwell LJ in *Wauthier v Wilson* ((1912) 28 TLR 239) and is one of the arguments that have found favour with my Lords, namely, that all the parties to the transaction knew that the hirer here was an infant. For it is manifest on the facts of this case that, despite that fact, the finance company, both by correspondence and by the writ in this action, were pursuing the infant in order to try to recover moneys due under the agreement. That argument, therefore, does not prevail with me.

NOTES

1. By s 4 of the Statute of Frauds 1677 a guarantee is not enforceable unless evidenced by a note or memorandum in writing signed by the guarantor or by some other person authorised to sign it on his behalf (see below, p 862).

2. Under a guarantee the surety provides a secondary obligation to the creditor, under an indemnity his obligation is primary. The distinction between the two types of obligation is neatly explained in *Birkmyr v Darnell* (1704) 1 Salk 27 at 28 as follows:

> If two come in a shop, and one buys, and the other, to gain him credit, promises the seller, *if he does not pay you, I will*; this is a collateral undertaking, and void without writing, by the Statute of Frauds: but if he says, *Let him have the goods, I will be your paymaster*, or *I will see you paid*, this is an undertaking as for himself, and he shall be intended to be the very buyer, and the other to act but as his servant.

3. Whether a contract is one of guarantee or of indemnity is a matter of construction. As Holroyd-Pearce LJ said in *Yeoman Credit Ltd v Latter*: '. . . we must have regard to its essential nature in order to decide whether or not it is really no more than a guarantee'. Thus, the fact that a contract states that the surety is to be liable 'as principal debtor' does not necessarily turn what is in reality a guarantee into an indemnity (*Heald v O'Connor* [1971] 1 WLR 497 at 503, per Fisher J). But this does not mean that a principal debtor clause is meaningless when incorporated into a contract of guarantee. For example, such a clause may be effective to prevent the surety claiming that he is discharged by release of the principal debtor (*General Produce Co v United Bank Ltd* [1979] 2 Lloyd's Rep 255), or it may absolve the creditor from the usual requirement that he must first demand payment from the guarantor before commencing proceedings against him (*High Street Services Ltd v Bank of Credit & Commerce International SA* [1993] Ch 425, CA). The complex issues raised by the use of principal debtor clauses in guarantees are examined in detail by A Berg (1993) 6 JIBLF 283 at pp 286ff.

4. Why is it important to distinguish a guarantee from an indemnity? First, contracts of guarantee, but not contracts of indemnity, are prima facie unenforceable by the creditor if they do not comply with the requirements of s 4 of the Statute of Frauds 1677 (below, p 862). Secondly, as we have already noted, liability of a guarantor is normally co-extensive with the liability of the principal debtor. Thus, if the liability of the principal debtor to the creditor is unenforceable, or has been discharged, the liability of the surety may depend on whether the contract is one of guarantee or an indemnity (as in *Yeoman Credit Ltd v Latter*).

5. The Infants Relief Act 1874 has since been repealed by s 1 of the Minors' Contracts Act 1987. Section 2 of the 1987 Act now provides that where a guarantee is given in respect of an obligation of a party to a contract which is itself unenforceable against the other party because he is a minor, then the guarantee shall not for that reason alone be unenforceable against the guarantor. The age of majority is now 18 years (Family Law Reform Act 1969, s 1).

QUESTION

What distinguishes a contract of guarantee from (1) a performance bond or performance guarantee (see Chapter 19), and (2) a contract of insurance (see Chapter 26)?

3 Types of guarantees

There are various types of guarantee. The following are the most important.

Bipartite and tripartite guarantees. In all cases the creditor must be made a party to the contract of guarantee. After all, the creditor must be privy to the surety's promise if he is to enforce it. But it is not necessary for the principal debtor also to be made a party to that contract (although the guarantee must *involve* the principal debtor to the extent that the surety's liability is made accessory to his). In most cases, only the creditor and surety are party to the contract of guarantee. In some cases, the principal debtor may not even know that the surety has entered into the guarantee, eg where a dealer guarantees to a finance company that a hire-purchaser will pay his instalments as they fall due under a hire-purchase agreement. However, sometimes all three parties are joined to the contract.

Discrete and continuing guarantees. A guarantee is discrete where the surety guarantees the fixed indebtedness of the principal debtor arising from a specific transaction or transactions, eg where a finance company lets a car on hire-purchase and a surety guarantees that the hirer will pay the instalments as they fall due under the terms of the hire-purchase agreement. By contrast, a continuing guarantee extends over a series of transactions between the principal debtor and the creditor under the terms of a master agreement or facility agreed between them. In such cases, the surety's liability is not fixed but varies according to the principal debtor's outstanding indebtedness to the creditor at any one time, eg where a bank extends a general overdraft facility to a company and one of the company's directors guarantees any indebtedness that may accrue with use of that facility (eg see the guarantee which appears below at p 971). Whereas a discrete guarantee will be discharged on satisfaction of the fixed indebtedness, a continuing guarantee endures for as long as there is a debtor–creditor relationship between the principal debtor and the creditor, or until the surety gives notice of withdrawal of his guarantee as regards future transactions, or until the guarantee is terminated by operation of law, eg on the surety's insolvency (see generally, R M Goode *Commercial Law* (1982), pp 878–882).

On the termination of a continuing guarantee of a current account, the creditor should freeze the account and ensure that any future receipts from the principal debtor are paid into a separate account. This will avoid the effect of the rule in *Clayton's Case* (1816) 1 Mer 572 whereby receipts paid into the guaranteed account will reduce the earliest indebtedness first, ie the guaranteed indebtedness, whilst new drawings on the account will fall outside the guarantee. Alternatively, the guarantee can be worded so as to exclude the rule in *Clayton's* case.

Limited guarantees. Guarantees may be limited in duration or in amount, or both. It is important to distinguish between the guarantee of a fixed sum, or of part of an indebtedness, and the guarantee of the entire indebtedness with a fixed limit of liability. In the former case, the guaranteed part of the debt is treated as if it were a separate debt, so that on paying that sum the surety discharges that notional separate debt and, unless otherwise provided in the guarantee, becomes entitled to share rateably in securities held for the full indebtedness (per R M Goode *Legal Problems of Credit and Security* (2nd ed, 1988), pp 189–190, citing *Goodwin v Gray* (1874) 22 WR 312). If the principal debtor becomes insolvent, the creditor can only prove in the insolvency for the balance of the debt, while the surety can prove for the amount he has paid (*Re Sass* [1896] 2 QB 12). By contrast, where the surety has guaranteed the entire indebtedness with a fixed limit of liability, the guaranteed indebtedness remains indivisible and the surety cannot take over the securities held by the creditor, or prove in the principal debtor's insolvency, unless he pays off the entire indebtedness. Unless the surety discharges the entire indebtedness, the creditor can prove in the debtor's insolvency for the full indebtedness, even though the surety had paid under his guarantee (*Re Sass*, above).

4 The contract of guarantee

(a) Formation

A contract of guarantee must meet the basic requirements necessary for all contracts: agreement between the parties (through offer and acceptance), consideration (unless under seal), certainty as to terms, and intention to create legal relations.

A contract of guarantee may be unilateral or bilateral. If the guarantee is given in return for a promise by the creditor to enter into a transaction with the principal debtor, eg to make a loan to him, then the contract of guarantee will be bilateral and the creditor's promise is consideration for the surety's promise under the guarantee. Neither promise may be withdrawn without the consent of the other party. However, it is more often the case that the surety offers to guarantee the principal debtor's obligations in return for some act or forbearance by the creditor. The creditor does not promise to act or forbear but should the act be done or the forbearance given that in itself will constitute both an acceptance of the surety's offer and also consideration for the surety's promise under the guarantee. In these circumstances, the contract of guarantee will be unilateral in character. Furthermore, unless the surety has received separate consideration to hold his offer of a unilateral contract open, he may withdraw it at any time before it is accepted by the creditor. This explains why a continuing guarantee can normally be terminated by the surety as regards future indebtedness. The guarantee will usually be treated as a standing offer which is accepted *pro tanto* by part performance of the consideration, but remains revocable at all times as regards future liabilities (per *Chitty on Contracts* (26th ed, 1989), Vol II, para 5018).

Again, like all contracts, a contract of guarantee may be void or voidable on grounds of fraud, misrepresentation, mistake of fact (including *non est factum*), undue influence, duress or illegality (see the standard contract textbooks for detailed discussion of these vitiating factors). A contract of guarantee is not a contract *uberrimae fidei* and does not generally require the creditor to disclose all material facts to the surety (*Seaton v Heath* [1899] 1 QB 782 at 792, per Romer LJ; revsd on the facts [1900] AC 135). Exceptionally, where the creditor is aware of some unusual or extraordinary feature of the transaction which affects the risk the surety is about to undertake, he will be under a duty to disclose it to the surety (*Hamilton v Watson* (1845) 12 Cl & Fin 109 at 119, per Lord Campbell).

(b) Form

Statute of Frauds 1677, s 4

4. No action against executors, etc, upon a special promise, or upon any agreement, or contract for sale of lands, etc, unless agreement, etc, be in writing, and signed. . . . noe action shall be brought . . . whereby to charge the defendant upon any speciall promise to answere for the debt default or miscarriages of another person . . . unlesse the agreement upon which such action shall be brought or some memorandum or note thereof shall be in writeing and signed by the partie to be charged therewith or some other person thereunto by him lawfully authorized.

Mercantile Law Amendment Act 1856, s 3

3. Written guarantee not to be invalid by reason that the consideration does not appear in writing. No special promise to be made by any person . . . to answer for the debt, default, or miscarriage of another person, being in writing, and signed by the party to be charged therewith, or some other person by him thereunto lawfully authorised, shall be deemed invalid to support an action, suit, or other proceeding to charge the person by whom such promise shall have been made, by reason only that the consideration for such promise does not appear in writing, or by necessary inference from a written document.

NOTES

1. Although it is now rare, in a commercial context, for a guarantee to be unenforceable because of failure to comply with the requirements of s 4 of the Statute of Frauds, this can happen. In *Deutsche Bank AG v Ibrahim* (1992) Financial Times, 15 January, the principal debtor was required by the plaintiff bank to provide security for his overdraft facility. He deposited with the bank the title deeds to two flats which he had purchased but which were registered in the names of his daughters. The bank failed to obtain a declaration that there had been a valid equitable mortgage of the flats. D E Neuberger QC (sitting as a Deputy High Court Judge) held that the deposit was by way of guarantee of the repayment of the loan by the father and that, as there was no memorandum signed by the daughters complying with the requirements of s 4 of the Statute of Frauds, the bank's claim was unenforceable. It should be noted that failure to comply with the section renders the guarantee unenforceable only and not void (*Maddison v Alderson* (1883) 8 App Cas 467).

2. Section 4 prescribes two ways of achieving enforceability of a guarantee. Thus, in *Elpis Maritime Co Ltd v Marti Chartering Co Inc, The Maria D* [1992] 1 AC 21, the defendant brokers, who were acting for charterers during the negotiation of a charterparty, orally guaranteed payment of demurrage and freight by the charterers to the plaintiff shipowners. The guarantee was later embodied in the terms of the written charterparty made with the shipowners. The first page of the charterparty was signed by the brokers in such a way that indicated that they were acting as agents for the charterers, but all other pages, including the one containing the guarantee, were signed by them without any indication whether they were signing as the charterers' agents. The House of Lords held that the guarantee was enforceable against the brokers. On the assumption that the brokers signed the page of the charterparty containing the guarantee as a contracting party, the prior oral agreement of guarantee was subsumed in the later written agreement, and the written agreement, being signed by the brokers, complied with the first of the two ways of achieving enforceability prescribed by s 4 of the Statute of Frauds. Alternatively, on the assumption that the brokers signed the relevant page as agents for the charterers, so that they were not a contracting party, the relevant page of the charterparty nevertheless contained a sufficient memorandum or note of the prior oral agreement of guarantee signed by the party to be charged, so as to satisfy the second requirement for achieving enforceability prescribed by s 4. The intention with which, or the capacity in which, the brokers signed the relevant page of the charterparty was wholly irrelevant to the question whether there had been compliance with s 4 (per Lord Brandon, at 32–33). What would have been the result of this case if there had been no prior oral agreement, the brokers' guarantee had been contained solely in the written charterparty, and the brokers had signed the charterparty as agents of the charterers?

3. A subsequent agreement to vary the terms of a contract of guarantee must also comply with s 4 if the variation is to be enforceable. If the variation does not comply with s 4, the original contract of guarantee remains enforceable, assuming it complies with s 4, as if it had not been varied (*Morris v Baron & Co* [1918] AC 1 at 16). But an oral variation may be set up by the surety as a defence to a claim brought on the original contract (*Re A Debtor (No 517 of 1991)* (1991) Times, 25 November). Section 4 does not apply to a subsequent agreement to terminate or avoid a contract of guarantee (*Morris v Baron & Co*, above).

Other statutory requirements

Section 105(1) of the Consumer Credit Act 1974 provides that any security (including a guarantee or indemnity) provided in relation to a consumer credit or consumer hire agreement must be in writing (unless it is provided by the debtor or hirer: sub-s (6)). Any contract of guarantee or indemnity caught by sub-s (1) must contain all the express terms of the contract, be signed by or on behalf of the surety, and be in a readily legible form when it is presented to or sent to the surety for his signature (sub-s (4)). If the creditor fails to comply with any of these requirements he must obtain a court order before he can enforce the security against the surety (sub-s (7)). The form and contents of contracts of guarantee and indemnity caught by s 105(1) are regulated by statutory instrument (see generally, Andrews and Millett, op cit, Ch 17).

(c) Construction

As a general rule, contracts of guarantee are strictly construed in favour of the surety. As Lord Campbell said in *Blest v Brown* (1862) 4 De GF & J 367 at 376:

> It must always be recollected in what manner a surety is bound. You bind him to the letter of his engagement. Beyond the proper interpretation of that engagement you have no hold upon him. He receives no benefit and no consideration. He is bound, therefore, according to the proper meaning and effect of the written agreement he has entered into.

In most cases the terms of the guarantee will have been drafted by the creditor, often relying on a standard form contract, and, in cases of ambiguity, the *contra proferentem* rule will be applied.

But the principle of strict construction does not prevent the court, in appropriate circumstances, from relying on extrinsic evidence to construe the contract of guarantee. Thus, in *Perrylease Ltd v Imecar AG* [1988] 1 WLR 463, Scott J had to consider whether to allow extrinsic evidence to be adduced to explain an ambiguously worded guarantee. The surety objected on the ground that this was precluded by s 4 of the Statute of Frauds. Scott J held that s 4 did not prevent the admission of extrinsic evidence to identify the true name of the surety who had been misdescribed in the guarantee, and also to identify the liability being guaranteed, regardless of whether it was a present or future liability. He concluded (at 472–473):

> Where there is a written contract of guarantee objective extrinsic evidence is, in my judgment, admissible to explain the meaning of the terms used by the parties whether the terms relate to a present liability or to a future liability. There is no difference, in my judgment, between the rules governing the admissibility of evidence in order to construe written contracts in general, and those governing the admissibility of evidence to construe written contracts that are subject to the Statute of Frauds.

However, extrinsic evidence cannot be used to explain an incomplete written contract of guarantee or incomplete memorandum (*Holmes v Mitchell* (1859) 7 CBNS 361).

Finally, it should be noted that in contracts of guarantee there is a strong prima facie rule of construction that the surety's obligations are to be interpreted as co-extensive with those of the principal debtor (see above, p 855).

5 Relations between creditor and surety

(a) The nature and extent of the surety's liability

Moschi v Lep Air Services Ltd [1973] AC 331, House of Lords

The respondent creditors agreed to give up liens held by them over goods supplied to the principal debtor in consideration of the principal debtor's agreement to pay £40,000 to the creditors by weekly instalments. The appellant guaranteed the obligations of the principal debtor under the agreement. The principal debtor repeatedly failed to pay any of the instalments. The creditors treated these breaches of contract as a repudiation and accepted it. They then sued the guarantor for the full amount of the weekly instalments, ie for those instalments which had become due and those which would have become due if the principal debtor's repudiation had not been accepted. The House of Lords, affirming the decision of the Court of Appeal, upheld the creditors' claim.

Lord Reid: The first contention of the appellant is that he is under no liability to pay anything because his obligation under clause (XIII) was discharged by the action of the respondents in accepting the company's repudiation and so bringing the contract to an end. He supports this startling contention by relying on the principle that if a creditor agrees to a variation of the debtor's contract he thereby discharges a guarantor from liability. He argues that acceptance of a repudiation should be regarded as equivalent to a variation of the contract. I agree with your Lordships that there is no substance in this argument and I reject it.

His next argument is more formidable. He says, look at clause (XIII). It merely guarantees that each instalment of £6,000 shall be duly paid. But by reason of the accepted repudiation the contract was brought to an end before the later instalments became payable. So they never did become payable. All that remained after the contract was terminated was a claim for damages. But I never guaranteed to pay damages. If the creditor chooses to act so that future instalments are not payable by the debtor he cannot recover them from me.

To meet that argument I think that it is necessary to see what in fact the appellant did undertake to do. I would not proceed by saying this is a contract of guarantee and there is a general rule applicable to all guarantees. Parties are free to make any agreement they like and we must I think determine just what this agreement means.

With regard to making good to the creditor payments of instalments by the principal debtor there are at least two possible forms of agreement. A person might undertake no more than that if the principal debtor fails to pay any instalment he will pay it. That would be a conditional agreement. There would be no prestable obligation unless and until the debtor failed to pay. There would then on the debtor's failure arise an obligation to pay. If for any reason the debtor ceased to have any obligation to pay the instalment on the due date then he could not fail to pay it on that date. The condition attached to the undertaking would never be purified and the subsidiary obligation would never arise.

On the other hand, the guarantor's obligation might be of a different kind. He might undertake that the principal debtor will carry out his contract. Then if at any time and for any reason the principal debtor acts or fails to act as required by his contract, he not only breaks his own contract but he also puts the guarantor in breach of his contract of guarantee. Then the creditor can sue the guarantor, not for the unpaid instalment but for damages. His contract being that the principal debtor would carry out the principal contract, the damages payable by the guarantor must then be the loss suffered by the creditor due to the principal debtor having failed to do what the guarantor undertook that he would do.

In my view, the appellant's contract is of the latter type. He 'personally guaranteed the performance' by the company 'of its obligation to make the payments at the rate of £6,000 per week.' The rest of the clause does not alter that obligation. So he was in breach of his contract as soon as the company fell into arrears with its payment of the instalments. The guarantor, the appellant, then became liable to the creditor, the respondents, in damages. Those damages were the loss suffered by the creditor by reason of the company's breach. It is not and could not be suggested that by accepting the company's repudiation the creditor in any way increased his loss. The creditor lost more than the maximum which the appellant guaranteed and it appears to me that the whole loss was caused by the debtor having failed to carry out his contract. That being so, the appellant became liable to pay as damages for his breach of contract of guarantee the whole loss up to the maximum of £40,000.

Lord Diplock: The law of guarantee is part of the law of contract. The law of contract is part of the law of obligations. The English law of obligations is about their sources and the remedies which the court can grant to the obligee for a failure by the obligor to perform his obligation voluntarily. Obligations which are performed voluntarily require no intervention by a court of law. They do not give rise to any cause of action.

English law is thus concerned with contracts as a source of obligations. The basic principle which the law of contract seeks to enforce is that a person who makes a promise to another ought to keep his promise. This basic principle is subject to an historical exception that English law does not give the promisee a remedy for the failure by a promisor to perform his promise unless either the promise was made in a particular form, eg, under seal, or the promisee in return promises to do something for the promisor which he would not otherwise be obliged to do, ie, gives consideration for the promise. The contract which gives rise to the instant appeal does not fall within this exception. In return for the guarantor's promise to the creditor the latter promised to extend credit to the debtor and to release his lien upon the debtor's goods.

Each promise that a promisor makes to a promisee by entering into a contract with him creates an obligation to perform it owed by the promisor as obligor to the promisee as obligee. If he does not do so voluntarily there are two kinds of remedies which the court can grant to the promisee. It can compel the obligor to pay to the obligee a sum of money to compensate him for the loss that he has sustained as a result of the obligee's failure to perform his obligation. This is the remedy at common law in damages for breach of contract. But there are some kinds of obligation which the court is able to compel the obligor actually to perform. In some cases, such as obligations to transfer title or possession of property to the obligee or to refrain from doing something to the detriment of the obligee, a remedy to compel performance by a decree of specific performance or by injunction is also available. It was formerly obtainable only in a court of equity. In these cases it was an alternative remedy to that of damages for breach of contract obtainable only in a court of common law. But, since a court of common law could make and enforce orders for payment of a sum of money, where the obligation was itself an obligation to pay a sum of money, even a court of common law could compel the obligor to perform it. Historically this was the only remedy which the court would grant at common law when an obligor failed to perform this kind of obligation. The remedy of damages for non-performance of the obligation was not available as an alternative.

It ceased to be important to identify an obligation which the obligor had failed to perform as being an obligation to pay a sum of money after the Judicature Act of 1875 had abolished the necessity for a plaintiff to select the form of action appropriate to his claim. But before the Common Law Procedure Acts 1852 to 1860 there were important procedural differences between an action brought to compel performance of the obligation arising from a promise to pay a sum of money for which the form of action was indebitatus assumpsit, and an action brought to recover compensation for the loss sustained as a result of the obligor's failure to perform any other kind of obligation arising out of contractual promises – for which the form of action was a special assumpsit.

In the absence of modern authority it becomes necessary to go back a century or more to see whether a contractual promise by the guarantor to guarantee to the creditor that the debtor would perform his own obligations to the creditor to pay a sum of money to him was itself classified as giving rise to an obligation on the part of the guarantor to pay that sum of money to the creditor if the debtor did not do so, or as an obligation to see to it that the debtor did perform his own obligations to the creditor.

In s 4 of the Statute of Frauds 1677 a contract of guarantee is described in the language of the 17th century as 'any special promise to answer for the debt, default or miscarriage of another person.' Translated into modern legal terminology 'to answer for' is 'to accept liability for,' and 'debt, default or miscarriage' is descriptive of failure to perform legal obligations, existing and future, arising from any source, not only from contractual promises but in any other factual situations capable of giving rise to legal obligations such as those resulting from bailment, tort, or unsatisfied judgments. These words were so construed by Abbott CJ in *Kirkham v Marter* (1819) 2 B & Ald 613, 616.

By the beginning of the 19th century it appears to have been taken for granted, without need for any citation of authority, that the contractual promise of a guarantor to guarantee the performance by a debtor of his obligations to a creditor arising out of contract gave rise to an obligation on the part of the guarantor to see to it that the debtor performed his own obligations to the creditor. Statements to this effect are to be found in *Wright v Simpson* (1802) 6 Ves 714, 734, per Lord Eldon and in *Re Lockey* (1845) 1 Ph 509, 511, per Lord Lyndhurst. These are the two cases which are cited as authority for this proposition by Sir Sidney Rowlatt in his authoritative work on *Principal and Surety*. They can be supplemented by other similar statements, including one in your Lordships' House, which confirm that it was taken for granted that this was the legal nature of the guarantor's obligation arising out of a contract of guarantee: *Mactaggart v Watson* (1836) 3 Cl & F in 525, 540, per Lord Brougham.

It is because the obligation of the guarantor is to see to it that the debtor performed his own obligations to the creditor that the guarantor is not entitled to notice from the creditor of the debtor's failure to perform an obligation which is the subject of the guarantee, and that the creditor's cause of action against the guarantor arises at the moment of the debtor's default and the limitation period then starts to run. It is also why, where the contract of guarantee was entered into by the guarantor at the debtor's request, the guarantor has a right in equity to compel the debtor to perform his own obligation to the creditor if it is of a kind in which a court of equity is able to compel performance: see *Ascherson v Tredegar Dry Dock and Wharf Co Ltd* [1909] 2 Ch 401. It is the existence of this right on the part of the guarantor that accounts for the rule laid down by Lord Eldon in *Samuell v Howarth* (1817) 3 Mer 272, 278 and approved by your Lordships' House in *Creighton v Rankin* (1840) 7 Cl & F 325, 346 that where the creditor, after the guarantee has been entered into, gives a contractual promise to the debtor to allow him time to pay the guaranteed debt, the guarantor is discharged from his obligation to the creditor. This is because the creditor by altering the debtor's obligation to him has deprived the guarantor of his equitable right to compel the debtor to perform his original obligation to the creditor, which was all that the guarantor had guaranteed. In contrast, the guarantor is not discharged by the mere voluntary forbearance of the creditor to take steps to obtain timeous performance by the debtor of the obligation which is the subject of the guarantee; for this does not affect the guarantor's equitable right to compel the debtor to perform it.

It follows from the legal nature of the obligation of the guarantor to which a contract of guarantee gives rise that it is not an obligation himself to pay a sum of money to the creditor, but an obligation to see to it that another person, the debtor, does something; and that the creditor's remedy for the guarantor's failure to perform it lies in damages for breach of contract only. That this was so, even where the debtor's own obligation that was the subject of the guarantee was to pay a sum of money, is clear from the fact that formerly the form of action against the guarantor which was available to the creditor was in special assumpsit and not in indebitatus assumpsit: *Mines v Sculthorpe* (1809) 2 Camp 215.

The legal consequence of this is that whenever the debtor has failed voluntarily to perform an obligation which is the subject of the guarantee the creditor can recover from the guarantor as damages for breach of his contract of guarantee whatever sum the creditor could have recovered from the debtor himself as a consequence of that failure. The debtor's liability to the creditor is also the measure of the guarantor's.

Whether any particular contractual promise is to be classified as a guarantee so as to attract all or any of the legal consequences to which I have referred depends upon the words in which the parties have expressed the promise. Even the use of the word 'guarantee' is not in itself conclusive. It is often used loosely in commercial dealings to mean an ordinary warranty. It is sometimes used to mis-describe what is in law a contract of indemnity and not of guarantee. Where the contractual promise can be correctly classified as a guarantee it is open to the parties expressly to exclude or vary any of their mutual rights or obligations which would otherwise result from its being classifiable as a guarantee. Every case must depend upon the true construction of the actual words in which the promise is expressed.

In the instant appeal, however, the actual words used are simple, unambiguous, and contain no qualification except to impose a limit upon the guarantor's maximum liability under the guarantee.

The particular obligation of the debtor of which performance was guaranteed was to satisfy an existing debt to the creditor by instalments to be paid in the future. It arose from one of a number of inter-related mutual promises made by the debtor to the creditor and by the creditor to the debtor all of which were contained in a single contract; but the guarantor did not guarantee performance by the debtor of any obligations arising from any of his other promises. As between the debtor and the creditor all their obligations to one another to which their mutual promises gave rise, including the particular obligation of which performance was guaranteed by the guarantor, possessed the characteristics which the law ascribes to obligations whose common source is the same contract.

The debtor failed to perform voluntarily many of his obligations under the contract – both the obligation of which performance was guaranteed and other obligations. The cumulative effect of these failures by December 22, 1967, was to deprive the creditor of substantially the whole benefit which it was the intention of the parties that he should obtain from the contract. The creditor accordingly became entitled, although not bound, to treat the contract as rescinded: see *Hongkong Fir Shipping Co v Kawasaki Kisen Kaisha Ltd* [1962] 2 QB 26. He elected to do so on that date. It was held by the official referee and by the Court of Appeal, in my view rightly, that the debtor's failures to pay the instalments of the existing debt were in themselves sufficient to deprive the creditor of substantially the whole benefit which it was the intention of the parties that he should obtain from the contract, even if his failures to perform other obligations were left out of account.

My Lords, it has become usual to speak of the exercise by one party to a contract of his right to treat the contract as rescinded in circumstances such as these, as an 'acceptance' of the wrongful repudiation of the contract by the other party as a rescission of the contract. But it would be quite erroneous to suppose that any fresh agreement between the parties or any variation of the terms of the original contract is involved when the party who is not in default elects to exercise his right to treat the contract as rescinded because of a repudiatory breach of the contract by the other party. He is exercising a right conferred upon him by law of which the sole source is the original contract. He is not varying that contract; he is enforcing it.

It is no doubt convenient to speak of a contract as being terminated or coming to an end when the party who is not in default exercises his right to treat it as rescinded. But the law is concerned with the effect of that election upon those obligations of the parties of which the contract was the source, and this depends upon the nature of the particular obligation and upon which party promised to perform it.

Generally speaking, the rescission of the contract puts an end to the primary obligations of the party not in default to perform any of his contractual promises which he has not already performed by the time of the rescission. It deprives him of any right as against the other party to continue to perform them. It does not give rise to any secondary obligation in substitution for a primary obligation which has come to an end. The primary obligations of the party in default to perform any of the promises made by him and remaining unperformed likewise come to an end as does his right to continue to perform them. But for his primary obligations there is substituted by operation of law a secondary obligation to pay to the other party a sum of money to compensate him for the loss he has sustained as a result of the failure to perform the primary obligations. This secondary obligation is just as much an obligation arising from the contract as are the primary obligations that it replaces: see *R V Ward Ltd v Bignall* [1967] 1 QB 534, 548.

Although this is the general rule as to the effect of rescission of the contract upon obligations of which it was the source, there may be exceptional primary obligations which continue to exist notwithstanding that the contract has been rescinded. These are obligations that are ancillary to the main purpose of the contract – which is, of course, that the parties should perform their primary obligations voluntarily. Mutual promises to submit to arbitration disputes arising as to the performance by the parties of their other obligations arising from the contract may be expressed in terms which make it clear that it was the common intention of the parties that their primary obligation to continue to perform these promises should continue notwithstanding that their other primary obligations had come to an end: *Heyman v Darwins Ltd* [1942] AC 356.

But this is the exception. Although in the instant appeal the Court of Appeal came to the right decision, I cannot accept entirely that part of their reasoning in support of it in which they suggest that the primary obligation of the debtor to continue to pay the instalments which he had promised under clause (IX) of the contract was not ended by the rescission of the contract but remained in existence although the law no longer permitted him to pay them. A legal obligation to continue to perform is inconsistent with the withdrawal of any legal right to do so. The better explanation is that which I have already given, viz, that upon rescission of the contract the primary obligation of the debtor to pay the instalments was converted by operation of law into a secondary obligation either to pay damages for failure to perform it; or, as these were instalments of a debt existing at the date of the contract, it may be a revived obligation to pay the balance of the whole debt immediately.

The guarantor's obligation under his contract of guarantee does not, as the Court of Appeal appear to suggest, depend upon the debtor's primary obligation continuing to exist after the contract had been rescinded. Nor is it affected by whether the debtor's secondary obligation which was substituted for it by operation of law is classified as an obligation to pay damages or as an obligation to pay the debt. It was the debtor's failure to perform his primary obligation to pay the instalments in circumstances which put an end to it that constituted a failure by the guarantor to perform his own primary obligation to the creditor to see that the instalments were paid by the debtor, and substituted for it a secondary obligation of the guarantor to pay to the creditor a sum of money for the loss he thereby sustained. It is the guarantor's own secondary obligation, not that of the debtor, that the creditor is enforcing in his claim for damages for breach of his contract of guarantee.

Lord Simon of Glaisdale: . . . I have had the advantage of reading the speeches prepared by my noble and learned friends, Lord Reid and Lord Diplock; and I agree with their comments on the judgment of the Court of Appeal. I also agree with the historical analysis made by my noble and learned friend, Lord Diplock: it is important as showing that the liability of a surety at common law always sounded in damages rather than in debt, even when he was guaranteeing a debt. . . .

The accrued instalments . . .

It was argued for the appellant that the respondents' acceptance of the company's repudiation effected a substantial alteration in the contractual relationship of the parties; that this was clearly prejudicial to the appellant's interest as guarantor; that he should, therefore, have been consulted before, and his consent obtained to, the alteration; and that, since he was not so consulted and never consented, he was discharged from liability.

This seems to me to be, with all respect, an impossible argument. It is only in the jurisprudence of Humpty-Dumpty that the rescission of a contract can be equated with its variation. The acceptance of the repudiation of an agreement does not alter its terms in any way – it merely transmutes the primary obligation of the promisor to perform the terms contractually into a secondary obligation, imposed by law, to pay damages for their breach.

Moreover, the suggested rule would make nonsense of the whole commercial purpose of suretyship: you would lose your guarantor at the very moment you most need him – namely, at the moment of fundamental breach by the principal promisor. Take a usual case giving rise to suretyship – that of a trader with a bank overdraft. The bank forbears to close the account (so as to put the trader into bankruptcy or liquidation) in consideration of the trader finding a guarantor of the overdraft and agreeing to pay it off by instalments. The trader thereafter repudiates his obligation to pay off the overdraft by instalments; whereupon the bank closes the account, so terminating the contractual relationship of banker and customer. It would be absurd to suppose that the guarantor of the overdraft was thereby discharged from his liability as surety.

Finally, if authority were needed *Chatterton v Maclean* [1951] 1 All ER 761 is against the appellant's proposition (see the passage from Parker J's judgment cited below).

The outstanding instalments

It was on this part of the case that counsel for the appellant mounted his most formidable argument. In outline this ran as follows. What the appellant was guaranteeing was that the company would make weekly payments on dates most of which fell after December 22, 1967. When, on December 22, the respondents accepted the company's repudiation, the contract was rescinded by agreement between them; and the company had thereafter no duty (or, indeed, right) to make the stipulated payments which the appellant had guaranteed. It follows that the subject-matter of the appellant's guarantee entirely disappeared after December 22, so that he was pro tanto exonerated from all liability in relation thereto. The company admittedly become immediately liable to pay damages for breach of its contract to make payments; but the appellant had guaranteed the later payments, not the immediate damages.

It was argued for the respondents, on the other hand, that the contractual duty assumed by the appellant was to ensure the performance by the company of such of its contractual obligations as were guaranteed; and that, when the company evinced an intention not to perform its guaranteed contractual obligations, and when such repudiation was accepted by the respondents, the appellant became in breach of his own obligation, so as himself to be liable in damages.

In my judgment, the argument for the respondents is the correct legal analysis, for the following reasons:

(1) The contention of the appellant is, in my view, both in principle and in practice impossible to reconcile with the rule in *Hochster v De la Tour* (1853) 2 E & B 678 – namely, that if a promisor under a contract, even before the time for its performance has arrived, evinces an intention not to perform it, the promisee may treat this as an immediate breach of contract and bring his action accordingly. . . . In the instant case, therefore, it was accepted that the respondents could, on December 22, treat the company's conduct as a refusal to perform the executory part of the contract, and sue the company at once for damages for breach of contract, notwithstanding that the company might notionally have changed its mind before the time for performance had arrived and decided to comply with its executory obligations. The measure of damages in such an action would be the totality of the outstanding debt with a discount for accelerated payment: cf *Frost v Knight* (1872) LR 7 Exch 111, 117. It would be very strange and hardly workable if the promisee had to wait until the time for the promisor's performance had arrived before having his remedy against the surety. Indeed, it is difficult to see how the promisee would even then have any remedy against the surety unless he had himself in the meantime performed his own obligations under the contract or (if those obligations were still executory) held himself ready and willing to perform them. The instant case provides a striking example of the absurdity of any such requirement. Both conceptually and practically, I find it impossible to reconcile the appellant's proposition with the policy of the law exemplified in the doctrine of what is conveniently though perhaps misleadingly called acceptance of anticipatory breach. If the appellant is right, the promisee is still, vis-à-vis the surety, impaled on that same Morton's fork from which the rule in *Hochster v De la Tour* (1853) 2 E & B 678 enabled him to escape vis-à-vis the principal promisor.

(2) The appellant's contention becomes even more unworkable if the obligation the performance of which is guaranteed is not one to pay money, but to deliver goods or to perform services.

(3) The appellant's argument, again in this part of the case, involves that the promisee would lose the benefit of the guarantee at the very moment he most needs it – namely, on a repudiation by the principal promisor of his obligations under the contract.

(4) The respondents' proposition is supported by the high authority of Rowlatt, *The Law of Principal and Surety*, 3rd ed (1936), p 144. The learned author was discussing the rule that on default of the principal promisor causing damage to the promisee the surety is, apart from special stipulation, immediately liable to the full extent of his obligation, without being entitled to require either notice of the default, or previous recourse against the principal, or simultaneous recourse against co-sureties. 'The reason for the rule,' wrote Rowlatt, 'is that it is the surety's duty to see that the principal pays or performs his duty as the case may be. . . .' No other reason for the rule was proposed in argument before your Lordships, nor was the rule itself questioned; which suggests that Rowlatt's proposed reason is the correct one, which his own high standing would in any case vouch. It is true that the authorities which Rowlatt cited for the proposition: *Wright v Simpson* (1802) 6 Ves 714 and *Re Lockey* (1845) 1 Ph 509 are not direct decisions on the point, in the sense of its being their ratio decidendi. But, more significantly, both Lord Eldon in the former case and Lord Lyndhurst in the latter seem to assume without question that the law is as stated by Rowlatt.

(5) That it is the surety's duty to see that the principal pays, or performs his other duty, as the case may be (so that non-payment or other non-performance by the principal is a breach of the surety's contract, sounding in damages), is further suggested by the wording of s 4 of the Statute of Frauds 1677: 'any special promise to answer for the debt, default or miscarriages of another person.' The teutonic 'answer for' is used here in a sense more accurately connoted in modern English by its romance equivalent 'be responsible for' (see *Oxford English Dictionary*, s.v. *answer*, *v.* I. 3). A further shade of meaning as indicating the nature of the surety's common law obligation may be seen in Shakespeare's 'Let his neck answer for it, if there be any martial law.'

(6) The point is still further reinforced by the historical analysis of my noble and learned friend, Lord Diplock, which shows that the liability of the surety gave rise to an action of special assumpsit not of indebitatus assumpsit, breach therefore sounding in damages and not in debt, even if it was a debt which was guaranteed. . . . This is only consistent with the surety's obligation, even when guaranteeing a payment, being not to pay a sum of money in default but to ensure performance of the principal promisor's obligation.

(7) Although not a direct decision on the point, *Chatterton v Maclean* [1951] 1 All ER 761 supports the respondents' proposition. Parker J is reported as saying, at pp 764–765:

> Counsel for the defendant urges, first, that the very acceptance, the very treating of the hirer's conduct as a repudiation of the contract, amounts to a new contract. That leads to the rather startling conclusion that a guarantor of the performance of a contract is always released where the creditor does what he is lawfully entitled to do, namely, to treat the principal debtor's breach as a repudiation. It would mean that whenever a creditor exercised his ordinary rights a guarantor was released, not merely in respect of future liabilities, but in respect of accrued liabilities.

Parker J treats it as self-evident that, where the principal creditor lawfully accepts the principal debtor's breach as a repudiation of the contract, the surety is *not* released either in respect of accrued or of future liabilities.

It follows, in my judgment, therefore, that when on December 22, 1967, the respondents accepted the company's fundamental breach of the terms of the contract, including those guaranteed, as a repudiation of the contract, the respondents were entitled to sue the appellant for the total sum guaranteed (except in so far as already satisfied by payment made by the company), and that the measure of damages would be such net sum with an appropriate discount for accelerated payment (though in the instant case there is no question of any discount). I would therefore dismiss the appeal on this ground.

Lord Kilbrandon: The appellant argued that the repudiation of the contract had the effect of discharging the guarantor. But this position is inconsistent with what was said in *Chatterton v Maclean* [1951] 1 All ER 761. It appears to depend on a misunderstanding of *Holme v Brunskill* (1878) 3 QBD 495, in which it was held that an agreement between the principals to vary the terms of the contract guaranteed may discharge the guarantor. But repudiation is not variation.

In the present case what the appellant guaranteed was 'the performance by Rolloswin Investments Ltd of its obligations to make payments at the rate of £6,000 per week.' This is the class of undertaking referred to in *Rowlatt on the Law of Principal and Surety*, 3rd ed (1936) at p 143. The learned author points out that as soon as a breach is committed of the duty, performance of which is guaranteed, the surety is immediately liable to the full extent of his obligation, and gives as 'the reason for the rule that it is the surety's duty to see that the principal pays or performs his duty as the case may be.' This would be very clear where A had undertaken to deliver a valuable object to B twelve months thence, the performance being guaranteed by C. B having on the following day sold the object to D, he immediately (see *Hochster v De la Tour* (1853) 2 E & B 678) becomes liable in damages to B (specific performance being impossible) and C becomes liable under the guarantee accordingly.

[Lord Gardiner concurred.]

NOTE

Moschi v Lep Air Services Ltd illustrates the principle of co-extensiveness (above, p 855). The fact that the payments were to be by instalments did not cause any difficulty because the surety had guaranteed *complete performance* of the contract by the principal debtor. But contrast *Moschi* with *Hyundai Heavy Industries Co Ltd v Papadopoulos* [1980] 1 WLR 1129 (above, p 235), where the surety guaranteed payment of instalments due under a shipbuilding contract. In *Hyundai*, a shipbuilding contract provided for payment of five instalments by the buyer. A clause in the contract permitted the builders to cancel the contract where the buyers were in default in payment of any instalment. The buyers failed to pay the second instalment. The builders cancelled the contract and sued the surety for the unpaid instalment. The surety argued that since the first instalment was recoverable on cancellation, and the second instalment would likewise have been recoverable if it had been paid (applying *Dies v British and International Mining and Finance Corpn Ltd* [1939] 1 KB 724, where prepayments were recoverable because there had been a total failure of consideration in relation thereto: as explained by Kerr LJ in *Rover International Ltd v Cannon Film Sales Ltd (No 3)* [1989] 3 All ER 423 at 439–440), there was no claim for the second instalment as against the principal debtor or the surety, even though it was unpaid at the date of cancellation. By a majority of 3:2, the House of Lords held that the cancellation did not destroy the builders' accrued right to recover the second instalment. The majority distinguished *Dies* by holding in effect that there had not been a total failure of consideration by the builders (see *Rover v Cannon*, above, at 439). Furthermore, their Lordships emphasised that the commercial purpose of the guarantee was to enable the builders to recover from the surety when the principal debtor failed to pay.

However, Viscount Dilhorne went on to state (obiter, at 1137) that the surety would have been liable for the accrued but unpaid second instalment even if the cancellation had deprived the builders of their accrued right to that instalment. In that event, the principal debtor would still be liable to pay damages to the creditor for breach of contract, but his liability in damages may be for less than the surety is liable to pay. If Viscount Dilhorne is right, this provides a major exception to the principle of co-extensiveness. But, save for some obiter dicta of Roskill LJ in *Hyundai Shipbuilding and Heavy Industries Co Ltd v Pournaras* [1978] 2 Lloyd's

Rep 502 (a case on similar facts), Viscount Dilhorne's dictum has little to support
or commend it. As Andrews and Millett, op cit, submit (at p 160):

> . . . there can be no justification for creating a situation in which the surety remains liable
> for the instalments in circumstances in which the principal is not, unless the contract on its
> true construction is to be regarded as one of indemnity rather than one of guarantee. It is
> submitted, with the greatest respect, that the suggestion that the surety may be liable for
> accrued instalments in circumstances in which the principal is not, is plainly wrong and
> should not be followed.

(b) Discharge of the surety

Holme v Brunskill (1878) 3 QBD 495, Court of Appeal

Holme let Riggindale farm, and a flock of sheep, to George Brunskill. Robert
Brunskill, the defendant, guaranteed redelivery of the farm and the flock in good
order and condition at the end of the tenancy. Holme later accepted the surrender of
one field from George in return for a reduction in rent, without the knowledge or
consent of Robert. At the end of the tenancy the flock was reduced in number and
quality and so Holme claimed against Robert under the terms of his guarantee.
Although the trial jury found that the variation of the terms of the tenancy
agreement had not made a material difference to the tenancy, the Court of Appeal
held by a majority that the variation had discharged Robert from his liability on the
guarantee.

Cotton LJ: It was contended by the defendant, that even if there was a continuance of the
old tenancy the effect of the surrender of the Bog Field was to discharge him as surety from
all liability. The Bog Field contained about seven acres, and the jury, in answer to a question
left to them, at the trial, found that the new agreement with the tenant had not made any
substantial or material difference in the relation between the parties, as regards the tenant's
capacity to do the things mentioned in the condition of the bond, and for the breaches of
which the action was brought. The plaintiff's contention was that this must be treated as a
finding that the alteration was immaterial, and that, except in the case of an agreement to
give time to the principal debtor, a surety was not discharged by an agreement between the
principals made without his assent, unless it materially varied his liability or altered what
was in express terms a condition of the contract.

In my opinion this contention on behalf of the plaintiff cannot be sustained. No doubt,
there is a distinction between the cases, which have turned on the creditor agreeing to give
time to the principal debtor, and the other cases. Where a creditor does bind himself to give
time to the principal debtor, he with an exception hereafter referred to, does deprive the
surety of a right which he has, that is to say of the right at once to pay off the debt which he
has guaranteed, and to sue the principal debtor, and without inquiry whether the surety has,
by being deprived of this right, in fact suffered any loss, the Courts have held that he is
discharged. The exception to which I have referred is, where the creditor on making the
agreement with the principal debtor expressly reserves his right against the surety, but this
reservation is held to preserve to the surety the right above referred to, of which he would be
otherwise deprived. The cases as to discharge of a surety by an agreement made by the
creditor, to give time to the principal debtor, are only an exemplification of the rule stated by
Lord Loughborough in the case of *Rees v Berrington* ((1795) 2 Ves 540): 'It is the clearest
and most evident equity not to carry on any transaction without the knowledge of him [the
surety], who must necessarily, have a concern in every transaction with the principal debtor.
You cannot keep him bound and transact his affairs (for they are as much his as your own)
without consulting him.'

The true rule in my opinion is, that if there is any agreement between the principals with reference to the contract guaranteed, the surety ought to be consulted, and that if he has not consented to the alteration, although in cases where it is without inquiry evident that the alteration is unsubstantial, or that it cannot be otherwise than beneficial to the surety, the surety may not be discharged; yet, that if it is not self-evident that the alteration is unsubstantial, or one which cannot be prejudicial to the surety, the Court, will not, in an action against the surety, go into an inquiry as to the effect of the alteration, or allow the question, whether the surety is discharged or not, to be determined by the finding of a jury as to the materiality of the alteration or on the question whether it is to the prejudice of the surety, but will hold that in such a case the surety himself must be the sole judge whether or not he will consent to remain liable notwithstanding the alteration, and that if he has not so consented he will be discharged. . . .

In the present case, although the Bog Field contained seven acres only, yet it cannot be said to be evident that the surrender of it could not prejudicially affect the surety. Some of the witnesses for the plaintiff admitted that it was occasionally used for pasturing, that its loss would be appreciable in the spring, and that it might make a difference of fifteen in the number of the sheep which the farm would carry.

The case may also be considered in another point of view. The bond given by the defendant the surety, was to guarantee the delivery up of the flock of sheep therein referred to at the determination of the tenancy of the Riggindale Farm, which in our opinion, must mean Riggindale Farm as then demised to George Brunskill, and the bond certainly implied that he should continue to hold the farm as then demised till the flock was given up. The contention of the plaintiff, if it could be supported, would make a variation in this contract, as to the materiality of which there is at least a doubt, and would make the defendant liable for a deterioration of the flock during the time when the tenant held a smaller farm than that contemplated by the contract of the surety.

The plaintiff's counsel relied on some observations made by Lord Cottenham in the case of *Hollier v Eyre* ((1840) 9 Cl & Fin 1). But, in fact, those observations are in favour of the defendant and not of the plaintiff. What Lord Cottenham says is, 'the surety will be left to judge for himself between his original undertaking and another substituted for it, but that is not the case where the contract remains the same, though part of the subject-matter is withdrawn from its operation.' In this case, as already pointed out, the original contract of the surety was that the flock should be delivered up in good condition, together with the farm, as then demised to the tenant. No part of that which was guaranteed was ever withdrawn from the operation of the bond. But the plaintiff attempts to substitute for the contract that the flock should be given up in good condition, with the farm, as then demised, a contract that it should be delivered up in like condition with a farm of different extent. In my opinion the surety ought to have been asked to decide whether he would assent to the variation. He never did so assent, and in my opinion was discharged from liability, notwithstanding the finding of the jury, inasmuch as in my opinion the question was not one which ought to have been submitted to them.

[Thesiger LJ concurred in this judgment.
Brett LJ dissented from this judgment, holding that the variation, when not violating a specific condition of the surety's contract, must be proved to be material.]

NOTES

1. The surety has the benefit of implied rights of indemnity and subrogation against the principal debtor, as well as rights of contribution against his co-sureties (see below, p 876 and p 877). It is an implied condition of the contract of guarantee that those rights must be preserved, the surety having accepted the risk of liability under his guarantee on that basis. Anything which alters or extinguishes those rights is a breach of condition, unless the guarantee provides otherwise or the surety consents to the act or omission in question. The effect of a breach of condition is to entitle the surety to full discharge from liability, whether or not the surety can show he is prejudiced by the breach. Thus, the surety will be discharged from liability where the creditor releases the principal debtor (*Commercial Bank of Tasmania v Jones* [1893] AC 313) or a co-surety (*Mercantile Bank of Sydney v Taylor* [1893] AC 317), releases a security, wholly or in part (*Pledge v Buss* (1860) John 663), binds himself to give time to the principal debtor without reserving his rights against the surety (*Webb v Hewett* (1857) 3 K & J 438), or otherwise varies the terms of the principal contract without the surety's consent in a manner which is not self-evidently non-prejudicial (*Holme v Brunskill*, above).

2. But contrast the effect of an act or omission by the creditor which is a breach of condition with one that is merely a breach of the creditor's equitable obligation to respect the surety's interests, eg where the creditor causes the surety loss by careless failure to register a security (*Wulff v Jay* (1872) LR 7 QB 756). Where there is a breach of this equitable obligation the surety is only discharged from liability under his guarantee to the extent that he is actually prejudiced by the breach. It has even been suggested that where the creditor causes the surety loss by failing to realise a security at the best price he is in breach of a tortious duty of care owed to the surety (*Standard Chartered Bank Ltd v Walker* [1982] 3 All ER 938 at 942, per Lord Denning MR; followed in *American Express International Banking Corpn v Hurley* [1985] 3 All ER 564). However, in *China and South Sea Bank Ltd v Tan Soon Gin* [1990] 1 AC 536, Lord Templeman, delivering the advice of the Privy Council, held that a creditor owed the surety no duty to exercise his power of sale over mortgaged securities, which meant that the surety was not discharged from liability by a reduction in the value of the securities which resulted from the creditor's delay in selling them (but note that under s 91(2) of the Law of Property Act 1925 a mortgagor may apply to the court for an order directing the sale of mortgaged property notwithstanding the mortgagee's wishes to delay the sale: *Palk v Mortgage Services Funding plc* [1993] Ch 330, CA). Lord Templeman decided the case on the basis of equitable principles holding (at 543–544) that:

> . . . the tort of negligence . . . does not supplant the principles of equity or contradict contractual rights or complement the remedy of judicial review or supplement statutory rights.

But his Lordship also held that once the creditor does decide to sell he must obtain the current market price. In the light of Lord Templeman's overall emphasis on equitable principles, that obligation must arise in equity rather than in tort (*Cuckmere Brick Co Ltd v Mutual Finance Ltd* [1971] Ch 949, where the Court of Appeal held that a mortgagee who decides to sell must take reasonable care to obtain a proper price, would have to be explained on that basis). Similarly, the Court of Appeal in *Parker-Tweedale v Dunbar Bank plc* [1991] Ch 12 and the Privy Council in *Downsview Nominees Ltd v First City Corpn Ltd* [1993] AC 295 (Lord Templeman again delivering the advice of the Judicial Committee) have both held that a mortgagee's duties arise in equity and not in tort (see A Berg [1993] JBL 213). Considerable doubt must now be cast on the common law approach of Lord Denning in *Standard Chartered Bank v Walker*.

3. In most commercial contracts of guarantee the surety's rights to full or *pro tanto* discharge from liability (on the grounds set out above) are expressly excluded by the terms of the guarantee (see, eg, *Continental Illinois National Bank v Papanicolaou* [1986] 2 Lloyd's Rep 441). Any such clause probably falls outside the ambit of the Unfair Contract Terms Act 1977 (R M Goode *Legal Problems of Credit and Security* (2nd ed, 1988), pp 193–196).

Finally, it should be noted that the surety's liability may be discharged for other reasons. Payment or performance by the principal debtor will discharge the surety. Part payment or performance will discharge the surety *pro tanto*. The surety's liability to pay may also be discharged by operation of law. Furthermore, where the creditor commits a repudiatory breach of the principal contract, and the principal debtor accepts it, the surety is also discharged (as he would be if the creditor commits a repudiatory breach of the contract of guarantee). Where the creditor commits a non-repudiatory breach of the principal contract the surety will not be discharged unless the breach involves a 'not unsubstantial' departure from the terms of the principal contract which has itself been expressly or by implication incorporated into the guarantee (*National Westminster Bank plc v Riley* [1986] BCLC 268 at 275–276; *The Wardens and Commonality of the Mystery of Mercers of the City of London v New Hampshire Insurance Co* [1992] 2 Lloyd's Rep 365).

6 Relations between surety and principal debtor

(a) Indemnity

Where the guarantee was given at the request, express or implied, of the principal debtor, the surety has a right to be indemnified by him for liability incurred and payments made under the guarantee. The surety's right to be indemnified arises from an implied contract between the surety and the debtor, although it may alternatively be said to have a restitutionary basis arising from the fact that the surety has been compelled by law to discharge the debt of the principal debtor (*Re a Debtor* [1937] Ch 156; *Anson v Anson* [1953] 1 QB 636 at 641–643). The surety's right to an indemnity does not usually arise until he has paid the creditor. However, as soon as the surety's liability becomes enforceable, even though not yet discharged, equity allows him to bring an action for a declaration that he is entitled to be indemnified and obtain an order that the principal debtor pay to the creditor what is due to him (*Wolmershausen v Gullick* [1893] 2 Ch 514).

So far we have considered the position where the guarantee was requested by the principal debtor. Where no such request was made, and yet a guarantee was given, it is much harder to establish a firm legal basis for the surety's right of indemnity. Without such a request there can be no contractual right. Furthermore, unless the surety acts in circumstances of necessity (which is unlikely), there is no clear restitutionary basis for the surety's claim. This is because the Court of Appeal ruled in *Owen v Tate* [1976] QB 402 that the surety has no right of recourse against the principal debtor where he voluntarily assumed his obligations under the guarantee without the prior request of the principal debtor. However, *Owen v Tate* has been the subject of much criticism and it may well have been wrongly decided (see P Birks and J Beatson (1976) 92 LQR 188; A Burrows *The Law of Restitution* (1993), pp 213–216).

The surety may modify or waive his right to an indemnity by the terms of his guarantee.

(b) Subrogation

Where a surety pays the full amount of the indebtedness to which his guarantee relates, he is entitled to be subrogated to the creditor's rights against the principal debtor and any security held by the creditor, whether that security was taken before or after he gave his guarantee and whether or not he was aware of its existence (*Forbes v Jackson* (1882) 19 Ch D 615). The right of subrogation arises to prevent unjust enrichment of the debtor who would otherwise obtain release of his securities without payment. The right does not depend on the debtor having requested the surety to provide the guarantee (see generally, A Burrows *The Law of Restitution* (1993), pp 82–83, 215; cf Andrews and Millett, op cit, pp 304–305).

The surety's right of subrogation is now reinforced by s 5 of the Mercantile Law Amendment Act 1856 which provides that the surety is entitled to have assigned to him 'every judgment, specialty or other security which shall be held by the creditor' in respect of the debt.

7 Relations between co-sureties

Where a surety pays more than his proportionate share of the indebtedness he has an equitable right to recover the excess from any other surety of the same debt, ie from a co-surety. In *Dering v Earl of Winchelsea* (1787) 2 Bos & P 270 at 273, Eyre CB said:

> In the particular case of sureties, it is admitted that one surety may compel another to contribute to the debt for which they are jointly bound. On what principle? Can it be because they are jointly bound? What if they are jointly and severally bound? What if severally bound by the same or different instruments? In every one of those cases sureties have a common interest and a common burthen. They are bound as effectually quoad contribution, as if bound in one instrument, with this difference only that the sums in each instrument ascertain the proportions, whereas if they were all joined in the same engagement they must all contribute equally.

As the right to contribution arises in equity and not in contract, the surety is entitled to contribution from a co-surety even though they were unaware of each other's existence. But the right to contribution may be modified or excluded by express contract with the co-surety (*Craythorne v Swinburne* (1807) 14 Ves 160). Where a surety receives any security from the principal debtor, or takes over security from the creditor on discharging his liability, the security must, as between his co-sureties, be brought into account (*Steel v Dixon* (1881) 17 Ch D 825; *Berridge v Berridge* (1890) 44 Ch D 168). This is known as the principle of hotchpot.

The surety may also have statutory rights to contribution under the Civil Liability (Contribution) Act 1978 where he can bring himself within its requirements.

QUESTION

Alan, Bert and Chris are directors of Datacare Ltd. Each director provides Datacare's bank with a guarantee of the company's overdraft. The guarantees given by Alan and Bert are without limit, but the one given by Chris is limited to £10,000. Datacare's overdraft increases to £60,000 and the bank demands repayment. When the company fails to make repayment, the bank claims £60,000 from Alan under his guarantee. Alan pays the indebtedness in full and seeks your advice as to what amounts, if anything, he may claim from Bert and Chris by way of contribution. Advise Alan. See *Ellesmere Brewery Co v Cooper* [1896] 1 QB 75.

Part IX
Principles of insurance law

CHAPTER 26

Insurance

---

1 Introduction[1]

Broadly speaking, in a contract of insurance one party undertakes, in return for a consideration paid by the other, to pay a sum of money to the other *if* a specified event should happen, or *when* such an event should happen, or to make payments to the other *until* such an event should happen, the essence of the arrangement being that it is either uncertain whether, or uncertain when, the event will occur. The contract is commonly known as a 'policy' (at least if it is in writing), the parties are called respectively 'the insurer' (or 'underwriter') and 'the insured' (or 'assured'), and the consideration is referred to as 'the premium'.

Contracts of insurance may be subdivided into two categories: (1) *indemnity insurance*, where the undertaking is to provide the insured with an indemnity against a possible future loss or liability – eg, damage to property caused by fire, or a motorist's liability in tort to a third party who may be injured by his driving, and (2) *contingency insurance*, where the promise is to pay a specified sum on the happening of a named event – eg a personal injury policy or a life policy. In the latter case, the insurer contracts to pay a predetermined sum when the person whose life is assured dies, and the sum is payable irrespective of the value of the life that is lost. In the same way, if an insurer in a personal injury policy promises to pay the insured £10,000 if he should lose the sight of an eye, he must pay that sum without regard to the loss to the insured that that injury actually represents. Another form of contingency insurance is a contract of annuity, where the premium is a lump sum paid in advance and the insurer agrees to make regular periodic payments of a fixed amount until the death of the person concerned.

It is of the essence of a contract of insurance that the event insured against must be uncertain, either in the sense that it may or may not occur, or that the time of the occurrence is uncertain. Thus, a policy of insurance on goods will not normally protect the insured against depreciation or fair wear and tear, or against losses arising from some internal or inherent cause, such as the deterioration of perishable goods (commonly referred to technically as 'inherent vice'). Nor will it be construed as covering events brought about by the deliberate act of the insured himself (eg loss caused by fraud or arson on his part). There is, in addition, a further reason why an

---

1 Specialist textbooks include J R Birds *Modern Insurance Law* (3rd ed, 1993); M A Clarke *The Law of Insurance Contracts* (2nd ed, 1994); E R Hardy Ivamy *General Principles of Insurance Law* (6th ed, 1993).

insured is debarred from recovering on an insurance in events such as his own fraud or arson, namely the general constraints of public policy.

Gray v Barr [1971] 2 QB 554, Court of Appeal

Barr took a loaded shotgun to Gray's house to look for his wife, who had been committing adultery with Gray. During an altercation with Gray the shotgun went off and Gray was killed. His dependants claimed damages from Barr under the Fatal Accidents Act, and Barr sought an indemnity against the Prudential Assurance Co under an insurance policy which covered him against his legal liability to pay damages in respect of injuries to third parties caused by accidents. It was held that his conduct amounted to manslaughter (although a jury had in fact acquitted him when he was charged with this offence in a criminal trial) and that it would be against public policy to allow him to claim on the policy.

Salmon LJ: . . . *Is the defendant precluded on grounds of public policy from enforcing the contract of insurance?*
It is well settled that if a man commits murder or committed felo de se in the days when suicide was still a crime, neither he nor his personal representatives could be entitled to reap any financial benefit from such an act: *Re Crippen's Estate* [1911] P 108; *Beresford v Royal Insurance Co Ltd* [1938] AC 586. This was because the law recognised that, in the public interest, such acts should be deterred and moreover that it would shock the public conscience if a man could use the courts to enforce a money claim either under a contract or a will by reason of his having committed such acts.
　Crimes of violence, particularly when committed with loaded guns, are amongst the worst curses of this age. It is very much in the public interest that they should be deterred. A man, covered by a 'hearth and home' policy such as the present, walks into a bank with a loaded gun. He intends only to frighten and not to shoot the cashier. He slips and accidentally shoots a customer standing by the counter. It would be strange indeed if he could enforce the policy in respect of his liability to that customer. Once you threaten violence with a loaded gun and it goes off it is so easy to plead accident. Evidently it is very difficult for the prosecution to prove the contrary. Although public policy is rightly regarded as an unruly steed which should be cautiously ridden, I am confident that public policy undoubtedly requires that no one who threatens unlawful violence with a loaded gun should be allowed to enforce a claim for indemnity against any liability he may incur as a result of having so acted. I do not intend to lay down any wider proposition. In particular, I am not deciding that a man who has committed manslaughter would, in any circumstances, be prevented from enforcing a contract of indemnity in respect of any liability he may have incurred for causing death or from inheriting under a will or upon the intestacy of anyone whom he has killed. Manslaughter is a crime which varies infinitely in its seriousness. It may come very near to murder or amount to little more than inadvertence, although in the latter class of case the jury only rarely convicts. . . .
　The cases of *Tinline* [1921] 3 KB 327 and *James* [1927] 2 KB 311, in which it was held that persons convicted of manslaughter for reckless and drunken driving could nevertheless recover indemnity from their insurers, were doubted in *Haseldine v Hosken* [1933] 1 KB 822 but approved by this court in *Marles v Philip Trant & Sons Ltd* [1954] 1 QB 29. It seems now to be settled law that a motorist can rely on his policy of insurance to indemnify him in respect of his liability for any injuries which he has caused otherwise than on purpose: *Hardy v Motor Insurers' Bureau* [1964] 2 QB 745. These road traffic cases may be sui generis. In any event, although motor cars have sometimes been called lethal weapons, these cases are not in my view akin to the cases in which injuries are caused in the course of unlawfully threatening a man with a loaded gun. Public policy is not static. Even if the crime of suicide had not been abolished by statute, it may be that today *Beresford's* case would have been differently decided. In any event, threatening violence with a loaded gun would, I am sure, now be generally regarded as much more shocking and necessary to be deterred

than what the unfortunate Major Rowlandson [the suicide] did in *Beresford's* case. I am confident that, in any civilised society, public policy requires that anyone who inflicts injuries in the course of such an act shall not be allowed to use the courts of justice for the purpose of enforcing any contract of indemnity in respect of his liability in damages for causing injury by accident. . . .

[Lord Denning MR and Phillimore LJ delivered concurring judgments.]

There is one further element which is an essential requirement of a contract of insurance, and which distinguishes it from a wagering contract: the event upon which the insurer's liability depends must be one in which the insured has an *insurable interest* – that is to say, the event must, at least prima facie, be one which is adverse to the insured's interests. I cannot, as a rule, insure a stranger's house against fire, because I do not stand to lose anything if it is burnt down; but if I am a mortgagee of the property, this gives me an insurable interest. In the same way, one person normally cannot take out a life policy on the life of someone else, but he could if the latter is a key employee in his business.

Macaura v Northern Assurance Co [1925] AC 619, House of Lords

Macaura, who owned an estate in Ireland, sold all the timber on the estate to a newly-formed company, Irish Canadian Sawmills Ltd, in which Macaura effectively owned all of the shares. He had insured the timber in his own name with the respondent company. When the timber was destroyed in a fire, it was held that he could not claim on the policy because he had no insurable interest in it.

Lord Sumner: My Lords, this appeal relates to an insurance on goods against loss by fire. It is clear that the appellant had no insurable interest in the timber described. It was not his. It belonged to the Irish Canadian Sawmills, Ltd, of Skibbereen, co. Cork. He had no lien or security over it and, though it lay on his land by his permission, he had no responsibility to its owner for its safety, nor was it there under any contract that enabled him to hold it for his debt. He owned almost all the shares in the company, and the company owed him a good deal of money, but, neither as creditor nor as shareholder, could he insure the company's assets. The debt was not exposed to fire nor were the shares, and the fact that he was virtually the company's only creditor, while the timber was its only asset, seems to me to make no difference. He stood in no 'legal or equitable relation to' the timber at all. He had no 'concern in' the subject insured. His relation was to the company, not to its goods, and after the fire he was directly prejudiced by the paucity of the company's assets, not by the fire.

[Lords Buckmaster and Wrenbury delivered concurring opinions.
Lords Atkinson and Phillimore concurred.]

Parts of the law governing contracts of insurance are governed by statute. Thus, the Life Assurance Act 1774 (which is not in fact confined in its application to life insurance) defines an insurable interest for some purposes, and the Third Parties (Rights against Insurers) Act 1930 allows claims to be made directly against an insurer (eg by the victim of a motoring accident) where the insured is insolvent. The law of *marine insurance* (ie the insurance of ships and their cargoes and freight) is largely codified by the Marine Insurance Act 1906. But for the purposes of the present study, we shall concentrate on the general principles of insurance law, which are based mainly on the common law.

Persons wishing to carry on business as insurers must be authorised to do so by the Secretary of State under the Insurance Companies Act 1982.

The insurance industry is also regulated in practice, but only in regard to contracts of insurance taken out by private individuals, by Statements of Insurance Practice, first introduced in 1986. The rulings of the Insurance Ombudsman are also influential in affecting the conduct of business.

2 Formation of the contract

(a) Insurance a contract *uberrimae fidei*

A contract of insurance is the paradigm case of a contract *uberrimae fidei* – a contract of the utmost good faith. The insurer is unlikely to know anything about the insured or the nature of the risk for which cover is sought, apart from such information as he is given by the insured. Accordingly, the insured is required by law to disclose to the insurer in advance of the contract all material facts known to him. A fact is material for this purpose if it is one which would influence the judgment of a reasonable and prudent insurer in deciding whether to undertake the risk and, if so, at what premium: *Lambert v Co-operative Insurance Society* [1975] 2 Lloyd's Rep 485, CA. And if there is a change of cover during the currency of the policy, all relevant facts must again be disclosed. (The insurer is under similar obligations: *Banque Financière de la Cité SA v Westgate Insurance Co Ltd* [1991] 2 AC 249.) If any material information is withheld, the contract may be avoided.

Glicksman v Lancashire & General Assurance Co Ltd [1927] AC 139, House of Lords

Glicksman and his partner had insured the stock of their tailoring business against burglary with the respondent company; but the company declined liability when a burglary happened, on the ground that Glicksman had not disclosed at the time when he applied for the cover that another insurance company had once declined to grant him insurance. An arbitrator found as a fact that this information was material, and in consequence the House of Lords (albeit with reluctance) held that the insurer's refusal to accept liability was justified.

Viscount Dunedin: . . . The law has often been stated, but perhaps it is just as well to state it again. A contract of insurance is denominated a contract uberrimae fidei. It is possible for persons to stipulate that answers to certain questions shall be the basis of the insurance, and if that is done then there is no question as to materiality left, because the persons have contracted that there should be materiality in those questions; but quite apart from that, and alongside of that, there is the duty of no concealment of any consideration which would affect the mind of the ordinary prudent man in accepting the risk. . . .

The fact that a question of this sort was put showed that the insurance company thought it was material whether a proposal had been refused or not, and that that was brought to the knowledge of the claimant. My Lords, under the circumstances I have considerable doubts, but then I am not entitled to take any view of my own on that, because that is a fact and the arbitrator has found it as a fact and I cannot get beyond the arbitrator's finding. I think that the reasoning of the learned judges in the Court of Appeal is impeccable. This was brought to the knowledge of the claimant that it was a material fact, and he certainly did not disclose it, and, therefore, the policy is void. . . .

[Lords Atkinson, Shaw of Dunfermline, Wrenbury and Carson concurred.]

Woolcott v Sun Alliance and London Insurance Ltd [1978] 1 WLR 493, Queen's Bench Division

Woolcott's house, which was insured with the Sun Alliance, was destroyed in a fire. The company refused payment because when he had applied for the insurance cover he had not disclosed the fact that he had convictions for robbery and other offences some 12 years previously. He did not volunteer this information to the building society through which the insurance was taken out, and he was not asked any question about his character on the application form, although the judge accepted that he would have answered such a question truthfully if he had been asked it. Caulfield J held that the company was entitled to deny liability.

Caulfield J: I come now to the issues in this case. They are these: (1) [Discussion of this issue is omitted] . . . (2) Was there a duty on the plaintiff to disclose his criminal record to the building society in his application for an advance? (3) As there was no disclosure by the plaintiff, was this non-disclosure material?

These are my findings. . . .

On the second issue in this action I refer to the judgment of MacKenna J in *Lambert v Co-operative Insurance Society Ltd* [1975] 2 Lloyd's Rep 485. This judgment I have found the most comprehensive and the most helpful, and I have followed the principles which are fully explained in it. The relevant passage begins where MacKenna J, giving the first judgment of the Court of Appeal, said, at p 487:

> Everyone agrees that the assured is under a duty of disclosure and that the duty is the same when he is applying for a renewal as it is when he is applying for the original policy. The extent of that duty is the matter in controversy. There are, at least in theory, four possible rules or tests which I shall state. (1) The duty is to disclose such facts only as the particular assured believes to be material. (2) It is to disclose such facts as a reasonable man would believe to be material. (3) It is to disclose such facts as the particular insurer would regard as material. (4) It is to disclose such facts as a reasonable or prudent insurer might have treated as material.

Ultimately, in a most comprehensive judgment, he went on to conclude that the proper test was the fourth test, and the principles which he has explained in that case I have followed in reaching my judgment on this particular issue. The duty, in my judgment, rested on the plaintiff, when he completed his application form for a loan, to disclose his criminal record, for, by that application, he was accepting that the society would effect insurance of his property on his behalf as well as on their own behalf. I do not think the absence of a proposal form for insurance modifies in any degree the duty of disclosure on the plaintiff. The plaintiff knew the society would be effecting a policy of insurance on their own behalf and on his behalf, and accordingly, in my judgment, there was a duty upon the plaintiff to disclose such facts as a reasonable or prudent insurer might have treated as material.

On the third issue, I have accepted the evidence of the underwriters who have given evidence. I accept that the criminal record of an assured can effect the moral hazard which insurers have to assess; indeed this is almost self-evident. I therefore hold that on the particular facts of this case the non-disclosure of a serious criminal offence like robbery by the plaintiff was a material non-disclosure.

For these reasons the defendants, in my judgment, are entitled to avoid the policy in so far as that policy affects the plaintiff's separate interest. There will be judgment accordingly.

Many contracts of insurance are effected on the basis of a proposal form which the insured is required to complete beforehand, and in this he will usually be asked a number – often a considerable number – of questions. The fact that specific questions are put to the insured in this way does not displace his obligation to make disclosure under the doctrine of *uberrima fides*. Thus, in *Glicksman's* case, a question on the proposal form asked whether other insurers had at any time refused to give cover to the insured. No insurer had ever refused cover to the *partnership*, and so it was possible for Glicksman and his partner to answer this question truthfully in the negative; but even so, they remained under their common law duty to disclose the fact that Glicksman himself had once been refused insurance.

The fact that a specific question has been put to the insured in a proposal is usually sufficient to satisfy the court that the matter that it deals with is material.

The obligation to make disclosure of material facts under the doctrine of *uberrima fides* is limited to facts of which the insured is aware. In *Joel v Law Union & Crown Insurance Co* [1908] 2 KB 863, CA, Miss Morrison had taken out insurance on her life without disclosing that she had suffered from mental illness; but this was a fact of which she was unaware because she believed that she had only had depression following influenza. Fletcher Moulton LJ said (at 884): 'The duty is a duty to disclose, and you cannot disclose what you do not know.'

However, the common law doctrine may be supplemented by a provision in the contract of insurance which makes the *accuracy* of replies to the questions in the proposal form a condition of the validity of the policy. If this is the case, the policy can be avoided if untrue information is given, however honestly, by the insured because he is unaware of the true facts. It can also be avoided if inaccurate information is given on a matter which would not otherwise be regarded as material.

Dawsons Ltd v Bonnin [1922] 2 AC 413, House of Lords

Dawsons insured a lorry with Bonnin and others, underwriters at Lloyd's, under a policy which recited that the proposal which Dawsons had completed should be the basis of the contract and be held as incorporated in it. In reply to a question in the proposal, they stated that the lorry would usually be garaged at their ordinary place of business in Glasgow; but in fact it was normally garaged at a farm on the outskirts of the city. The lorry was destroyed by a fire at the latter address. The House of Lords held that, although the misstatement was not material, the insurers were entitled to rely on the 'basis of the contract' provision to avoid liability.

Viscount Cave: My Lords, it is common ground that the proposal for the policy of insurance issued by the respondents to the appellants contained a misstatement as to the place where the lorry to be insured would usually be garaged; and the only question is whether this misstatement avoids the policy.

The policy commences with a recital of the proposal (a full copy of which is annexed to the policy), and proceeds 'which proposal shall be the basis of this contract and be held as incorporated therein.'. . .

Upon the whole, it appears to me, both on principle and on authority, that the meaning and effect of the 'basis' clause, taken by itself, is that any untrue statement in the proposal, or any breach of its promissory clauses, shall avoid the policy; and if that be the contract of the parties, it is fully established, by decisions of your Lordships' House, that the question of materiality has not to be considered. . . .

In these circumstances it appears to me to be irrelevant to consider the conflicting evidence in the case as to whether a misstatement as to the place of garage is, in the ordinary sense, material or not. The parties have agreed that it shall be deemed material, and that concludes the matter.

I must confess that I have little sympathy with the respondents, who seek to profit by a mistake to which their agent contributed; but the case must be decided according to law, and I think that the law is on their side.

[Viscount Haldane and Lord Dunedin delivered concurring opinions.
Viscount Finlay and Lord Wrenbury dissented.]

The above rules, if applied strictly, can operate very harshly, especially where the insured is a lay person. This has caused considerable disquiet, which has led to recommendations for reform of the law on two occasions: first, by the Law Reform Committee in its Fifth Report in 1957 (*Conditions and Exceptions in Insurance Policies*, Cmnd 62, 1957) and more recently by the Law Commission in 1980 (*Insurance Law – Non-disclosure and Breach of Warranty* (L Com Rep No 104, Cmnd 8064, 1980)). However, there has not so far been any legislative reform. Instead, the insurance industry has put into operation a system of self-regulation in the form of Statements of Insurance Practice. These state that an insurer will not repudiate liability as against a policyholder who is a private individual on grounds of non-disclosure of a material fact which he could not reasonably be expected to disclose. (See further on this topic, J R Birds 'Self-Regulation and Insurance Contracts' in F D Rose (ed) *New Foundations for Insurance Law* (1987), and A D M Forte (1986) 49 MLR 754, I Cadogan and R Lewis (1992) 2 *Insurance Laws & Practice* 107.) The Insurance Ombudsman has also intervened in a number of rulings to ensure that the worst effects of the doctrine of non-disclosure are mitigated.

In addition to the special rules of the doctrine of *uberrima fides*, the normal principles of misrepresentation and fraud may, of course, also be invoked to invalidate a contract of insurance.

(b) Agency

A contract of insurance is commonly effected through an insurance broker or other agent, or a salesman employed by the insurer. Difficult questions may arise here if, as is common, the intermediary is in law the agent of the insured but is remunerated by a commission paid by the insurer. In addition to the obvious risk of conflicts of interest, there may be uncertainty as to the scope of the intermediary's authority to make representations and to receive information on behalf of the insurer. For instance, in *Dawsons Ltd v Bonnins* (above), the inaccurate reply to the question on the proposal was written down by an 'insurance agent' who was the insurers' local representative and the mistake was not noticed by the insured when the proposal was signed; but this fact did not bar the insurers from disowning liability under the policy.

3 Content and interpretation of the contract

(a) The risk, and exceptions

It is obviously of central importance in any contract of insurance to identify the nature and scope of the risk which the policy covers. Although this is purely a matter of construction of the particular contract, many standard terms have, over time, been the subject of judicial rulings which allow the task of construction to be approached with a reasonable degree of certainty. Thus, the meanings of words such as 'accident', 'all risks', 'damage by fire', 'loss' (and 'consequential loss'), 'natural causes' and 'perils of the seas' have been discussed in many authoritative cases, which are cited in some detail in the leading manuals of insurance law. Even so, such words may admit of different shades of meaning which have to be examined in the particular case: in *Gray v Barr*, for instance (above, p 882), there was a difference of opinion among the judges on the question whether Gray's death had been caused by an 'accident'. The trial judge thought that it had; a majority of the members of the Court of Appeal that it had not; while Salmon LJ thought that it *was* caused by accident, but not by the kind of 'accident' intended to be covered by the policy.

One well-known rule of construction which may be of particular relevance in relation to insurance contracts is the *contra proferentem* rule – that any ambiguity in a document is to be construed in the sense least favourable to the person who has drawn it up. This is illustrated by *Houghton v Trafalgar Insurance Co Ltd*, below. But the *contra proferentem* presumption will not invariably prevail: in *Gray v Barr* (above), Barr was not given the benefit of the doubt over the meaning of the word 'accident'.

Houghton v Trafalgar Insurance Co Ltd [1954] 1 QB 247, Court of Appeal

Six people were being carried in a car designed to seat five when it was involved in an accident. The insurance policy contained a provision excluding liability for damage 'arising whilst the car is conveying any load in excess of that for which it was constructed'. The insurer sought to deny liability, but the court held that the clause was ambiguous and should be construed as referring only to a *weight* load.

Somervell LJ: It is said that . . . there is no liability under the policy, and that the car was not covered because of a provision in a group of clauses which are headed 'Exclusions.' The first part of the clause which contains the provision relied on reads, '(d) Loss, damage and/or liability caused or arising whilst any such car is engaged in racing, pace-making, in any reliability trials, speed testing, or is conveying any load in excess of that for which it was constructed.' It is argued that the load here was in excess of that for which the car was constructed, in that one passenger was seated on the knees of another and the seating accommodation was all occupied. The judge decided against that contention, adversely to the defendants, who now appeal.

If there is any ambiguity, since it is the defendants' clause, the ambiguity will be resolved in favour of the assured. In my opinion, the words relied on, 'any load in excess of that for which it was constructed,' only clearly cover cases where there is a weight load specified in respect of the motor-vehicle, be it lorry or van. I agree that the earlier words in the clause obviously are applicable to an ordinary private car in respect of which there is no such specified weight load. But there was – and I think that it would have been inadmissible – no evidence whether this was a form which was used for lorries as well as for ordinary private motor-cars. I do not think that that matters. We have to construe the words in their ordinary meaning, and I think that those words only clearly cover the case which I have put. If that is right, they cannot avail the insurance company in the present case.

Denning LJ: It would surprise most motor-car owners to be told that if they squeezed in an extra passenger, one more than the ordinary seating capacity, thereby they lost the benefit of the insurance policy. But that is what the insurance company are contending here. They say that by reason of this exclusion clause they are under no liability. If the clause had such an interpretation I would regard it almost as a trap. I am glad to find that the clause does not bear that extended interpretation. It is only applicable to cases where there is a specified weight which must not be exceeded, as in the case of lorries. I agree that the appeal should be dismissed.

[Romer LJ delivered a concurring judgment.]

The risk may be defined both affirmatively by words such as 'fire' or 'accident' which specifically describe it, and also by words of *exception* or limitation which exclude liability in particular cases. The provision in *Houghton's* case is an example of such an exception.

(b) Conditions and warranties

The law of insurance, anomalously, has traditionally used the term 'warranty' in a sense rather different from its use in the general law of contract. A warranty in this sense is an undertaking given by the insured which forms the very basis of the contract, one the breach of which releases the insurer from liability, rather than merely giving rise to a claim in damages. In other words, it is used in a way which to some extent resembles the term 'condition' in other branches of the law. However, the recent decision of the House of Lords in *Bank of Nova Scotia v Hellenic Mutual War Risks Association (Bermuda) Ltd, The Good Luck* [1992] 1 AC 233, HL has pointed up a subtle but important distinction: the breach of a condition in the general law of contract does not of itself avoid or terminate the contract, but merely gives the party who is not in breach the right to determine it if he so elects; in contrast, in insurance law, if the insured gives a warranty and this is broken, the insurer is *automatically* discharged from liability unless the insurer decides to waive the breach. So if an insured warrants the accuracy of a statement in the proposal, and it proves not to have been true, the insurer is discharged from liability under the policy *ab initio*. Alternatively, if circumstances change *during* the currency of the policy which cause the warranty to be breached, the insurer is discharged from liability under the policy from that time onwards.

However, the word 'condition' also has a role to play in insurance contracts. Thus, the policy may make it a condition of the insurer's liability in respect of a particular loss that he is given notice of the relevant event within 14 days of its occurrence. In a context such as this, the term 'condition' is used in much the same way (or ways!) as in the general law of contract.

Where a warranty is not complied with, the insurer can avoid liability even though the breach of warranty has no connection with the loss which has occurred, as the following case shows.

Conn v Westminster Motor Insurance Association Ltd [1966] 1 Lloyd's Rep 407, Court of Appeal

Conn's nine-year-old taxi was badly damaged when it ran off the road as he was driving it at 2 am – probably because he had fallen asleep at the wheel. The defendant insurance company declined liability on the ground that he had failed to comply with a term of the policy which required him to take reasonable steps to maintain the vehicle in an efficient condition. In particular, the taxi's two front tyres were entirely bald – the canvas was showing through in places – and there was also some evidence that the brakes were defective. However, the defective state of the vehicle had not caused or contributed to the accident. The Court of Appeal, reversing the trial judge, held that the company could disown liability.

Willmer LJ: . . . The [trial judge] went on to point out that when the accident happened it was not associated with the smoothness of either of the front tyres or with their condition in combination with the brakes. With all respect, as I have already stated, and as I think is accepted by both sides, that is an entirely irrelevant consideration. We are not concerned with the question whether any breach of the condition (if there was one) caused or contributed to the accident. The only question is whether there was in fact a breach of the condition in the policy. . . .

[Davies and Salmon LJJ delivered concurring judgments.]

The strict legal position in regard to warranties is mitigated for insured persons who are private individuals by the current Statements of Insurance Practice, by virtue of which (1) statements in proposal forms may not be elevated to the status of warranties in relation to matters not material to the risk, and (2) insurers will not normally (in the absence of fraud) repudiate liability on the grounds of breach of warranty where the circumstances of the loss are unconnected with the breach.

It is often a difficult question of construction for the court to determine whether a term in a policy which is expressed to be a warranty is to be given its full technical meaning (ie a promissory warranty on the accuracy or fulfilment of which the validity of the contract depends), or is to be read simply as defining the risk which is covered. The distinction is important, for in the former case a breach will invalidate the contract and allow the insurer to disclaim liability even in respect of a risk which is not affected by the breach, while a breach in the second case will excuse the insurer only if it is causally connected with the loss which is the basis of the claim. This point is illustrated by the following case.

Farr v Motor Traders' Mutual Insurance Society [1920] 3 KB 669, Court of Appeal

Farr owned two taxis, which he insured with the defendant company, on the basis of a proposal in which he stated that the vehicles were to be driven in only one shift per 24 hours. Six months later, one of the taxis was driven for two shifts in 24 hours for one or two days while the other was being repaired. Thereafter each cab was once again used for only one shift per day. When a claim was made in respect of an accident to the former of these taxis, the insurer claimed that its use on a double-shift basis during August was a breach of warranty which discharged it from liability. The Court held that the statement was not a warranty but was merely descriptive of the risk, and that the insurer was liable.

Bankes LJ: The question in this appeal relates to the construction of a contract of insurance into which the parties have entered. The assured answered certain questions in a proposal form, and those questions and the answers thereto were made the basis of the contract and were incorporated therein. The only question for decision by the learned judge, and by us, is whether the answer to one of the questions constitutes a warranty by the assured. If, as a matter of construction, it can properly be held that the question and answer amount to a warranty, then, however absurd it may appear, the parties have made a bargain to that effect, and if the warranty is broken, the policy comes to an end.

The position is very clearly and accurately put in *Macgillivray on Insurance Law*, p 360, to which Scrutton LJ has called my attention. In the section dealing with representations and warranties in fire policies he says: 'It is a little doubtful how much is to be inferred from the mere description in a fire or burglary policy of the premises or goods insured. It may be put in three ways: (i) that the description is a representation of the state of the premises or goods; (ii) that the description is a definition of risk; (iii) that the description is a warranty that the premies or goods shall correspond thereto.' In this case the question which we have to decide is whether the particular statement in the proposal form is a definition of the risk or a warranty. Then he says: 'But if the description is embodied in the policy' – which is the case here – 'whether actually or by reference, it has at least the force of a limitation of the risk to be run. In this view the premises or goods will be covered by the policy so long, but only so long, as they comply with the description, and if the description is considered merely as a limitation of the risk and not a warranty the insurer will not be wholly discharged, but the policy will merely cease to attach until the property once more corresponds to the description.' In the present case the proposal form contains the following: 'Is the vehicle driven solely by the proposer?' – 'No.' 'If not, state whether driven in one or more shifts per 24 hours.' – 'Just one.' That was a true statement at the time it was made, and it remained a true description of the risk down to August. In that month one of the two taxi-cabs which the assured owned required some repairs, and it was sent away for that purpose. When it was away the assured gave the driver of that cab permission to take out the other cab, as the assured said, in order to earn a few shillings. As a consequence that taxi-cab was for a day or a little longer driven in more than one shift each 24 hours; but apparently that took place for a very short time. Then the practice of driving these two cabs separately by separate drivers in one shift per day each was resumed, and continued down to and including the date when the second accident happened.

The question is whether we are to construe the question and answer, as the defendants contend, as a warranty, the effect of which would be that in August, when the cab was driven in two shifts per day, the policy came to an end; or whether we are to construe them, as Rowlatt J has construed them, as words descriptive of the risk, indicating that whilst the cab is driven in one shift per 24 hours the risk will be covered, but that if in any one day of 24 hours the cab is driven in more than one shift, the risk will no longer be covered and will cease to attach until the owner resumes the practice of driving the cab in one shift only. In my opinion, having regard to the nature of the question, it is impossible to construe the answer thereto as a warranty.

On these short grounds I think that the view taken by Rowlatt J upon the construction of this contract is the correct one, and that the appeal fails.

[Warrington and Scrutton LJJ concurred.]

Another difficult question which has arisen in many cases is whether the insured warrants only that a state of facts *is* true at the time he makes it, or that it *will continue to be true* throughout the currency of the cover. Again, this is basically a question of construction, but the task of the court is made easier by the existence of a wealth of relevant precedents.

4 Liability of the insurer

(a) Notice

In principle, the insured is entitled to payment of the sum assured on the happening of the event that has been insured against. But in practice most policies stipulate that he should give notice of the event and details of his loss within a specified time, and it may be a condition of the insurer's liability that this requirement is strictly adhered to.

(b) The onus of proof

The burden of proving that the event which has occurred is covered by the policy and, in a policy of indemnity, that he has suffered loss or damage is on the insured; but where the insurer seeks to avoid liability on the ground that the claim is covered by an exception the onus is normally shifted to him. This will be the case also where he claims to be entitled to avoid liability on the ground that the insured caused the loss deliberately, or that the claim is fraudulent.

The standard of proof is the civil one of the balance of probabilities. The insured is required to show that the event was the 'proximate' or 'operative' cause of his loss – often a difficult issue, but of course one which is not confined to this branch of the law. The court takes a broad approach: thus, where loss or damage is caused to goods by water as a result of action taken to prevent a fire from spreading, the loss is treated as caused by the fire (*Symington & Co v Union Insurance Society of Canton* (1928) 97 LJKB 646, CA). In contrast, in *Winicofsky v Army & Navy General Assurance Association Ltd* (1919) 88 LJKB 1111, where goods were stolen during an air raid, it was held that it was not the air raid but the theft which was the cause of the loss – the air raid had merely facilitated it.

In indemnity insurance, the onus is also on the insured to prove the quantum of his loss, except where the parties have agreed the value of the insured property under the terms of the policy. It may also be agreed as a term of the contract that the insurer will pay only for any loss in excess of a specified sum; or that the insured will bear a proportionate part of the loss if the property is insured for less than its full value (sometimes called an 'average' clause – a term which is implied by law in contracts of marine insurance); or that a person who has insured the same risk with more than one insurer will claim only a rateable proportion of his loss.

A claim under a contract of indemnity insurance is, by definition, limited to the amount of the insured's actual loss.

Castellain v Preston (1883) 11 QBD 380, Court of Appeal

In July 1878 Preston and others, who owned certain land and buildings in Liverpool, contracted to sell the property to their tenants, Rayners. Two weeks later part of the buildings was damaged by a fire. The owners claimed for their loss from their insurers and, after negotiation, were paid a sum of £330. They also completed the sale of the land and received the full purchase price from the buyers. In this action the court held that, since the owners had sustained no loss, they were bound to repay the £330 to their insurers.

Cotton LJ: In this case the appellant's company insured a house belonging to the defendants, and before there was any loss by fire the defendants sold the house to certain purchasers. Afterwards there was a fire, and an agreed sum was paid by the insurance office to the defendants in respect of the loss. . . .

The company seek to obtain the benefit either wholly or partly of the amount paid by them out of the purchase-money which the defendants have received since the fire from the purchasers. In my opinion, the plaintiff is right in that contention. I think that the question turns on the consideration of what a policy of insurance against fire is, and on that the right of the plaintiff depends. The policy is really a contract to indemnify the person insured for the loss which he has sustained in consequence of the peril insured against which has happened, and from that it follows, of course, that as it is only a contract of indemnity, it is only to pay that loss which the assured may have sustained by reason of the fire which has occurred. In order to ascertain what that loss is, everything must be taken into account which is received by and comes to the hand of the assured, and which diminishes that loss. It is only the amount of the loss, when it is considered as a contract of indemnity, which is to be paid after taking into account and estimating those benefits or sums of money which the assured may have received in diminution of the loss. . . .

Brett LJ: . . . The very foundation, in my opinion, of every rule which has been applied to insurance law is this, namely, that the contract of insurance contained in a marine or fire policy is a contract of indemnity, and of indemnity only, and that this contract means that the assured, in case of a loss against which the policy has been made, shall be fully indemnified, but shall never be more than fully indemnified. That is the fundamental principle of insurance, and if ever a proposition is brought forward which is at variance with it, that is to say, which either will prevent the assured from obtaining a full indemnity, or which will give to the assured more than a full indemnity, that proposition must certainly be wrong.

[Bowen LJ delivered a concurring judgment.]

(c) Reinstatement

Although the insurer's liability is normally to pay the insured a sum of money to reimburse him for his loss, the contract may give the insurer the option of reinstating the property. Thus, if a building is wholly or partly destroyed by fire, the insurer may have it rebuilt or repaired instead of paying the value of the loss. If the insurer does so elect, he must then reinstate the property whether the cost to him is greater or less than the sum insured. Under the old Fires Prevention (Metropolis) Act 1774, s 83 – which, incidentally, is not confined in its application to 'the metropolis' – an insured or other interested person is entitled to *require* an insurance company to apply the policy monies towards reinstating an insured building which is destroyed or damaged by fire, but this statutory obligation extends only to expending the amount of the policy monies and no more.

5 Rights of the insurer

An insurer who has reimbursed the insured for his loss under an indemnity policy has three rights: of salvage, of subrogation and of contribution.

(a) Salvage

Where an insurer has compensated an insured for the total loss of the insured property, all rights to the property are ceded by operation of law to the insurer, who thereby becomes their owner. So, if a car or ship is so damaged that it is uneconomic to repair it (a 'constructive total loss') and the insurer pays its owner its full value, the insurer can exercise this right of salvage in respect of the wrecked property and sell it for what it will fetch. In *Holmes v Payne* [1930] 2 KB 301, Mrs Payne lost a pearl necklace which she had insured for an agreed value of £600. The insurers agreed to settle her claim by allowing her to buy other articles of jewellery to a total value of £600. After this, when she had bought only £264 worth of replacement jewellery, the necklace was found. Roche J held that the agreement was equivalent to the payment of a full indemnity, with the consequence that the insurers had become the owners of the necklace and were bound to allow her to buy the other £336 worth of jewellery.

(b) Subrogation

The doctrine of subrogation has its basis in the principle of unjust enrichment. It has two aspects. One, illustrated by the case of *Castellain v Preston* (above, p 892) is the rule that an insured cannot ever receive more than a full indemnity for his loss, and if he does receive more, he is accountable to the insurer for it. The second is that an insurer who has indemnified his assured is entitled to succeed to all the rights of the latter – as it is commonly put, to 'stand in his shoes' – and so he may, for instance, sue any third party who is liable to the insured for the loss in an action of tort or contract. For this purpose, he may use the insured's name in the litigation. In the well-known case of *Lister v Romford Ice & Cold Storage Co Ltd* [1957] AC 555, HL, Lister, a lorry driver employed by the Romford Ice company, had negligently injured his father when reversing his lorry. The company's insurers paid damages to the father and then brought this action in the company's name to recoup the money from Lister. It was held that the insurers were entitled to do so for, standing in the company's shoes, they could (1) allege that he was in breach of a term in his contract of employment that he would drive with reasonable care and skill, and (2) alternatively, claim contribution from him as a joint tortfeasor under what is now the Civil Liability (Contribution) Act 1978.

The insured, for his part, may not do anything which prejudices the insurer's right of subrogation, eg grant a release to a tortfeasor or compromise his claim without the insurer's consent.

(c) Contribution

Where an insured has taken out more than one policy of indemnity insurance in respect of the same risk, any one insurer who has met a claim for the loss in full is entitled to claim contribution in equity on a rateable basis from the other insurers.

6 Marine insurance

The law of insurance has its origins in the early days of seafaring, and most of its principles were worked out first in relation to the risks associated with ships and their cargoes and the loss of freight which the carrier would sustain if a ship should fail to complete its voyage. The law governing contracts of marine insurance was codified by statute in the Marine Insurance Act 1906 – the last of the great codification exercises carried out by Sir Mackenzie Chalmers, following his successful work with the Bills of Exchange Act 1882 and the Sale of Goods Act 1893. In some special respects, marine insurance law has developed its own rules; but, broadly speaking, its principles are indicative of those of insurance law generally, and judges in non-marine cases do quite often refer to marine insurance decisions and even to the Act itself for guidance. In this chapter, no special attention has been paid to those topics where marine insurance law has different rules – eg that a contract of marine insurance must be recorded in writing. It is thought sufficient in a work of this nature to deal with the subject of insurance generally, and to add the warning that if an issue of marine insurance is involved, a specialist work should be consulted.

Part X

Insolvency law

CHAPTER 27

Insolvency

1 Introduction

The law relating to the bankruptcy of individuals goes back to a statute of Henry VIII in 1542. The concern of this early legislation (which applied only to persons engaged in trade) was to establish a procedure for the realisation and orderly distribution of the debtor's property among his creditors generally: the fate of the person himself – and still less the question of his rehabilitation into the world of commerce – was not thought to be important. We do not need to look further than the pages of Dickens to discover that in as late as Victorian times people who could not pay their debts were treated little better than criminals, even when their insolvency was due purely to misfortune. There were, it is true, major steps taken to ameliorate the position by the Bankruptcy Acts of 1883 and 1914, but the regime remained a fairly harsh one and the 'stigma of bankruptcy' something that it was never easy to shake off.

Corporate insolvency law, by comparison, dates only from the first companies legislation of 1844. And in stark contrast with the position in bankruptcy, the individuals concerned have traditionally been able to escape with relative impunity by taking advantage of the principle of limited liability.

Until the reforms of 1985–86 there was separate legislation for bankruptcies and corporate insolvencies, although some of the principles of bankruptcy law were extended to companies by the operation of a general 'incorporation' provision in the Companies Act.

The initiative for change came from the report of the Review Committee on Insolvency Law and Practice (Cmnd 8558, 1982), commonly known as the 'Cork Committee' after its chairman, Sir Kenneth Cork. This committee recommended that the law should be streamlined and modernised and that bankruptcy law and corporate insolvency law should be integrated and brought rather more into line. This would involve a relaxation of the harsher aspects of bankruptcy law, with a much greater emphasis on the restoration of the debtor to a normal role in the community, and at the same time a tightening up in those areas of corporate insolvency law which had formerly lent themselves to abuse. These recommendations were largely implemented by the Insolvency Act 1985; but very little of this Act was brought into force. Instead, it was almost immediately superseded by the Insolvency Act 1986 – a consolidating measure which brought together the new legislation of 1985 and large parts of the Companies Act. In the remainder of this chapter, the Insolvency Act 1986 is referred to as 'IA 1986'.

2 The basic objectives of insolvency law

We may summarise the basic objectives of insolvency law as follows.
    In the bankruptcy of individuals:

(1) to protect the insolvent from harassment by his creditors;
(2) to enable him to make a fresh start, especially in less blameworthy cases;
(3) to have him reduce his indebtedness by making such contribution from his present resources and future earnings as is just, taking into account his personal circumstances and the claims and needs of his family.

In corporate insolvency:

(1) where possible, to preserve the business, or the viable parts of it (but not necessarily the *company*);
(2) where it is considered that the principle of limited liability has been abused, to impose personal liability and other sanctions on those responsible.

In both forms of insolvency:

(1) to ensure that all creditors participate *pari passu* (ie on an equal footing) in the estate, except in so far as they may have priority as secured creditors or a statutory right to preference;
(2) to ensure that secured creditors deal fairly in realising and enforcing their security, vis-à-vis both the debtor and the other creditors;
(3) to investigate impartially the reasons for failure and to see that such disabilities and penalties as are appropriate are imposed, in the interests of society;
(4) where the assets of the insolvent have been improperly dealt with prior to the onset of insolvency (eg so as to remove them from the estate, or give a preference to some creditors at the expense of others), to recoup the assets for the benefit of the general estate.

The importance of the *pari passu* principle is shown by the following case.

British Eagle International Airlines Ltd v Cie Nationale Air France [1975] 1 WLR 758, House of Lords

Many of the world's airlines are members of IATA (the International Air Transport Association). A 'clearing house' scheme was set up under which the debts and credits between one airline and another arising from carrying each other's passengers and cargo were not settled directly but were pooled through IATA. A balance was struck each month and the net sum due was then paid by IATA to each airline or vice versa, as appropriate. British Eagle went into liquidation at a time when it was a net debtor to the scheme as a whole, but if the scheme was ignored it was a net creditor as between itself and Air France. The House of Lords, by a majority, held that the clearing house arrangement was contrary to public policy, in that the parties to it were contracting out of the statutory regime which would apply in a liquidation.

Lord Cross of Chelsea: . . . What the respondents are saying here is that the parties to the 'clearing house' arrangements by agreeing that simple contract debts are to be satisfied in a particular way have succeeded in 'contracting out' of the provisions contained in s [107] for the payment of unsecured debts 'pari passu.' In such a context it is to my mind irrelevant that the parties to the 'clearing house' arrangements had good business reasons for entering into them and did not direct their minds to the question how the arrangements might be affected by the insolvency of one or more of the parties. Such a 'contracting out' must, to my mind, be contrary to public policy. The question is, in essence, whether what was called in argument the 'mini liquidation' flowing from the clearing house arrangements is to yield to or to prevail over the general liquidation. I cannot doubt that on principle the rules of the general liquidation should prevail. I would therefore hold that notwithstanding the clearing house arrangements, British Eagle on its liquidation became entitled to recover payment of the sums payable to it by other airlines for services rendered by it during that period and that airlines which had rendered services to it during that period became on the liquidation entitled to prove for the sums payable to them. . . .

[Lords Diplock and Edmund-Davies concurred.
Lords Morris of Borth-y-Gest and Simon of Glaisdale dissented.]

3 The various definitions of insolvency

There is no single meaning of the term 'insolvent'. It is important to distinguish between three different definitions of this unhappy state – or, rather, at least three, since these are broad-brush distinctions and any one of them may have variations on points of detail.

'Balance-sheet' insolvency. The first test of insolvency has regard to the person's assets and liabilities, and looks to see whether there is, overall, a net surplus or a deficit. If there is a deficit, that person is insolvent. A company with investments which have fallen in value may become 'insolvent' within this definition, even though it is currently trading satisfactorily and paying its way.

'Commercial' insolvency. This test is not concerned with the asset position, but with liquidity. It is sometimes also called 'practical' insolvency or insolvency on a 'cash-flow' basis. The person concerned may have substantial assets, but is unable to pay his debts as they fall due. This could be so of a company, for instance, which has its wealth tied up in property that is not readily realisable (eg in out-of-season stock, or half-finished products), or which has over-spent on research and development for a new project which is still on the drawing-board.

'Ultimate' insolvency. Here we are concerned with the final outcome of events. The debtor's assets have been sold for what they will fetch – perhaps in a forced sale, on a break-up basis – and the costs of realisation and of administering the estate are brought into account. If his creditors have received less than 100p in the pound, we can say that the estate was insolvent. Many a person who could very reasonably have claimed to be solvent if his assets were valued on a going-concern basis may prove, in the event, to be insolvent in this sense if the worst happens.

Insolvency, as such, has very few legal consequences. So, for instance, the fact that a person who is a party to a contract becomes insolvent does not amount to a repudiation of the contract or entitle the other party to terminate it, unless the contract so provides. Occasionally, however, rights may be affected by *statute* because a party has become insolvent – eg, in a sale of goods, an unpaid seller is given the right to stop the goods in transit if the buyer has become insolvent (see above, p 398). But it is usually only as a consequence of some *insolvency procedure* that the legal position changes – eg when an individual has been declared bankrupt, or a company has gone into liquidation or receivership.

Where 'insolvency' is a precondition for the operation of a provision in a statute or a contract or other document, it is obviously important to determine in which of the various senses the term is to be construed. Thus, in the Sale of Goods Act 1979, a person is deemed to be insolvent 'if he has either ceased to pay his debts in the ordinary course of business or he cannot pay his debts as they become due' (s 61(4)); and so the seller's right of stoppage in transit referred to above will arise if the buyer is 'insolvent' in a 'commercial' sense. In contrast, the question whether a director can be held liable for 'wrongful trading' (see below, p 924) depends in part on whether there was a 'reasonable prospect that the company would avoid going into insolvent liquidation'; and for this purpose IA 1986 prescribes a 'balance sheet' test (s 214(6)). Plainly, the relevant definition must be examined closely in each case.

4 Insolvency procedures

(a) Individual insolvency

When an individual becomes insolvent, a choice of statutory procedures is available.

County court administration orders made under the County Courts Act 1984, Part VI. (These orders should not be confused with administration orders made in relation to insolvent companies under Part II of the Insolvency Act 1986 (see below, p 901).) An order may be made against a person who cannot pay the whole of a judgment debt and whose total indebtedness is not more than £5000. A moratorium comes into effect and an officer of the court supervises the payment of the debts of such creditors as are known by instalments out of the debtor's income.

Individual voluntary arrangements (IA 1986, Part VIII). This is a scheme of voluntary arrangement of a fairly informal kind, supervised by a professional insolvency practitioner. A moratorium can be sought from the court, staying all enforcement proceedings while the supervisor of the scheme and the creditors consider proposals to resolve the position, eg by a compromise, which can be made binding on all creditors if supported by a sufficient majority.

Bankruptcy orders (IA 1986, Part IX). A bankruptcy order may be made against a person on his own petition, or that of one or more creditors whose debts total at least £750, on the ground that he is unable to pay his debts (or, in the case of a creditor's petition, that he 'appears to have no reasonable prospect' of paying his debts). A 'commercial' rather than a 'balance-sheet' test of insolvency is thus applied. A debtor will be deemed unable to pay his debts if he has failed to pay a debt within three weeks after being served with a statutory demand for payment, or if execution has been issued against him and has been returned unsatisfied. An order will not be made on the basis of a debt which is the subject of a bona fide dispute; nor will the court resolve such a dispute in the bankruptcy proceedings – the parties must litigate the matter elsewhere in the normal way.

The Official Receiver (a government officer attached to the court) takes charge of the bankrupt's assets until an independent insolvency practitioner is appointed trustee. On his appointment, the bankrupt's assets vest in the trustee. He has the responsibility of administering the bankrupt's estate, realising the available assets and applying them, so far as they will go, towards satisfying the creditors. Certain creditors are entitled to be paid in priority: the Crown, for up to twelve month's PAYE and National Insurance contributions and six months' VAT, and employees, for up to £800 unpaid wages. (For full details, see IA 1986, Sch 6.) The rules in this respect are identical, or nearly so, to those which apply in a company liquidation, as are those relating to transactions at an undervalue, preferences and transactions defrauding creditors which are discussed below, at pp 919–922. The bankrupt is entitled to keep tools, books, vehicles, etc necessary for his employment and furniture, clothing and household equipment necessary for use by him and his family.

During the currency of a bankruptcy order, the bankrupt is subject to a number of disabilities – eg he may not be a company director – and there are restrictions upon his obtaining credit. But it is now the policy of the law that this situation should not continue for any long period: unless there has been some impropriety, or the person has been bankrupt more than once, a *discharge in bankruptcy* becomes effective automatically after three years (or in cases where the debts are less than £20,000, two years). Once a bankrupt is discharged, all his pre-bankruptcy debts are deemed to have been satisfied, and he is free to live a normal life again.

For further reading, see I F Fletcher *The Law of Insolvency* (1990), R Gregory *Bankruptcy of Individuals* (2nd ed, 1992).

(b) Corporate insolvency

Again, a range of procedures is available.

Voluntary arrangements (IA 1986, Part I; note also Companies Act 1985, ss 425–427A). This is a new procedure introduced by the Act of 1986. It is similar in many respects to the individual voluntary arrangement, except that the legislation contains no provision for a moratorium while the scheme is formulated and the arrangement put in place. This is a weakness of the law as it stands at present: the only way to avoid it is the rather costly option of combining a voluntary arrangement with a petition for an administration order (see below). Once again, a qualified insolvency practitioner is brought in to put proposals to a meeting of the company's creditors and, if they agree to its terms, to supervise the scheme.

Administration orders (IA 1986, Part II). This is another innovation dating from the 1986 reforms. An administration order is an order of the court putting the company under the control of an insolvency practitioner, which may be made when the court is satisfied that the company is, or is likely to be, unable to pay its debts, and also considers that one or more of the following objects is likely to be achieved (IA 1986, s 8):

(1) the survival of the company, and the whole or any part of its undertaking, as a going concern;
(2) the approval of a voluntary arrangement (see above);
(3) the sanctioning of a compromise or arrangement between the company and its creditors and others under s 425 of the Companies Act 1985;
(4) a more advantageous realisation of the company's assets than would be effected on a winding up.

If the court makes an order, it is binding on all the company's creditors. However, administration is regarded as being incompatible with a receivership (or, rather, with an *administrative* receivership, that is, a receivership for the enforcement of a floating charge created over all, or substantially all, of the company's assets: see below, p 906). So, if an administrative receiver is already in office, the court will not make an administration order; and the holder of a floating charge can block the making of an administration order by appointing a receiver before the petition comes on for hearing.

Most administration orders are made on ground (1) or ground (4) above. Under ground (1), a company which is insolvent or nearly so may gain sufficient time to trade its way back into solvency, or to find new financial support. The administrator will then hand control back to the directors and shareholders. Under ground (4), the administrator is likely to allow the company to continue trading under his supervision, in the hope of finding someone who is willing to buy the company's business or the viable parts of it as a going concern. This may be easier to achieve in an administration than in a liquidation, since a liquidator must realise the company's assets with reasonable expedition, and his trading powers are constrained by that requirement.

An administrator has wide statutory powers, which are set out in IA 1986, Sch 1. In addition he may, with the leave of the court, dispose of assets which are in the company's possession but which are owned by others (eg, machines which the company has on lease or hire-purchase, or goods which it has contracted to buy on 'retention of title' terms) or which are subject to security interests in favour of other parties (IA 1986, s 15). This provision plainly makes it easier for an administrator to sell the business on a going-concern basis, and prevents the owner or security-holder from being obstructive if such a sale is proposed. Any order which the court makes under s 15 will, of course, make provision for the person concerned to be paid the value of his interest out of the proceeds of sale of the property.

If the administrator decides that the purpose for which the order was made cannot be achieved, he may apply to the court to have the order discharged, and in most cases liquidation will then follow. The administrator will very likely in such a case be appointed liquidator – a convenient step which short-circuits some statutory procedures.

The administration procedure is elaborate and rather costly, and when the legislation was first introduced doubts were expressed whether much use would be made of it. However, it has proved to have a useful role to play, and orders are being made at the rate of about 200 per year. The Cork Committee thought that there was a need to institute a procedure similar to receivership to meet the case where a receiver could not be appointed because the company had not given a floating charge over its assets. The administration regime does, of course, meet this need. But it has also been invoked in circumstances where there has been a floating charge but the holder has chosen not to exercise his powers: sometimes, because this might attract unwelcome publicity (eg in the case of an insolvent football club); at other times, because there have been overriding considerations of public interest, as in the affairs of Maxwell Communications plc and the Polly Peck group.

The case of *Re Cavco Floors Ltd* illustrates the operation of the administration procedure in practice: it also shows the remarkable willingness of the judges in the Companies Court to make the new procedure a workable one, even to the point of bending the rules to accommodate a deserving case.

Re Cavco Floors Ltd [1990] BCLC 940, Chancery Division

(The facts appear from the judgment.)

Harman J: In this matter counsel (Mr Dicker) appears before me, on the instructions of well-known solicitors in the matter of an intended petition. He offers me an undertaking by the solicitors to present a petition forthwith (whether tonight or tomorrow morning is not important, but very very speedily) and he invites me to make an order now on that intended petition. The petition is the petition of Cavco Floors Ltd (the company) for the making of an administration order in respect of the company; the purposes are for the more advantageous realisation of the company's assets than would be effected on a winding up.

The evidence, which is impressively marshalled in the affidavit of Mrs Harvey, a director and substantial shareholder in the company, sets out the company's business, shows that for the year to July 1989, on what appear to be very well-compiled accounts, the company was trading profitably and had a credit balance on its profit-and-loss account, deposes to the well-known fact that the building trade is currently undergoing severe cash-flow difficulties and finally avers that the company is, on the basis that it is unable to pay its debts as they fall due, insolvent. All that I find impressive and I accept that evidence completely.

Mrs Harvey goes on to depose that there are none the less substantial assets of the company in current contracts which are profitable, a statement which appears to be well warranted by the material before the court, and that if an administrator is appointed who can carry on the business over the next comparatively short time there are various offers for the assets and goodwill of the company which may realise substantially better sums than could conceivably be expected if the company has to go into creditors' voluntary liquidation. She also shows that there is a creditor who has obtained a judgment against the company, although the company has a very substantial claim by way of offset against that creditor, that that creditor has served a statutory demand and may be in a position to present a winding-up petition at any time in the course of this week.

Further, she shows that the National Westminster Bank plc, as the company's bankers, are in a position to appoint an administrative receiver, have a comparatively small secured debt, some £13,000-odd, but have refused the directors' request so to appoint. Quite why they have chosen to take that course I do not understand, since it was advised by the licensed insolvency practitioner now proposed to be appointed as administrator. The bank has, however, written a letter, which it is undertaken will be put in evidence. That letter was written this morning by the insolvency and debt recovery department of the bank to the solicitors acting for the company. It sets out very clearly that the bank has had the draft petition, the affidavit of Mrs Harvey and the draft report of the proposed administrator. By the letter the bank consents to the abridgment of time between presentation of the petition and the hearing and to an administration order to be made forthwith. The bank by that letter therefore entirely accedes to the petition and presumably waives any possibility of objection by the bank as the person entitled to appoint an administrative receiver.

I have been concerned whether it is right for the court to appoint an administrator in this pell-mell way, it being clear that the whole design of ss 8, 9, 10 and 11 of the Insolvency Act 1986 is that Parliament expected that petitions would be presented, notice given of the presentation and the petition should then come on for hearing after a short interim, during which s 10 is designed to assure that nothing whatever can happen to the assets or business of the company. The Insolvency Rules 1986, SI 1986/1925, provide in r 2.1 for the procedure on the making of an administration order. By r 2.2 a report is required, which is satisfied by the report in this case of Mr David Gilbert, the insolvency practitioner, and other procedural requirements are set out. It is quite plain that r 2.5 expects that the petition and affidavits shall be filed, that copies for service shall be provided and that the petition is to be served on various people including the proposed administrator. In this case Mr Gilbert consents to the waiver of that requirement, which I can waive. The 1986 rules provide further by r 2.7(1) that the service of the petition shall be not less than five days before the date fixed for hearing. Again, it is plain that the whole of the rules proceed on a basis that there will be an interval between presentation and hearing.

However, in this case the directors (having been warned of the dangers of trading while insolvent) have said that they are not prepared to carry on the business of the company even for some two or three days during which, the evidence of Mrs Harvey makes it plain, it is vital that the company continue to perform its building contracts, that the bank has withdrawn support and will not finance the business for that short time, and therefore that unless an administrator is appointed forthwith there is a serious risk that the company will suffer the substantial difficulties that arise in the building trade, which it is notorious are quick to be snatched by prime contractors when a sub-contractor fails to perform according to his contract.

I have vacillated for some time whether it is right to abridge the time quite so drastically, but in the end I have concluded under counsel's persuasion that this is a case where the preparation of the petition, the affidavit in support and the r 2.2 statement give me such confidence that the only possible result after hearing representations must be that the court would make an administration order and that no injustice can possibly be caused to any person by my abridging time, not permitting any notice to be given to the creditor who has presented a statutory demand and not giving any time to the bank to have second thoughts on the consent which it gave this morning.

It is, in my view, an undesirable procedure for the court to act before presentation in this way, but it is a procedure which may need to be adopted in some cases and I am convinced by the evidence I have had that it is appropriate in this case. I shall therefore make an administration order and appoint Mr Gilbert as the administrator for the purposes set out in the petition.

Receivership, and in particular administrative receivership (IA 1986, Part III). The term *receiver* is a word that is used in a number of contexts, some of which have no necessary connection with insolvency. The court, for instance, has an inherent jurisdiction to appoint a person to act as a receiver in order to protect and preserve property which is the subject of litigation – eg in relation to partnership property pending the resolution of a partnership dispute. It may also appoint a receiver to enforce a charge or other security by taking control of the charged assets and, if appropriate, selling them.

We shall not be concerned in this section with the special rules that apply to receivers appointed by the court, but will look only at the type of receiver who is appointed *out of court*, by the holder of a charge, to enforce the security by taking control of the charged assets and realising them for the benefit of the charge-holder. It has been customary for a century or more for the instrument which creates a charge to include among its terms a power for the charge-holder to appoint a receiver in this way. The power will normally be exercisable if there is some default on the part of the debtor or if an event occurs which puts the security in jeopardy. A receiver may be appointed to enforce either a fixed charge or a floating charge – or, for that matter, a security which combines both; but our interest will be centred mainly on the receiver who is appointed to enforce a floating charge which has been granted by a company over its undertaking and all of its assets, present and future.

Shamji v Johnson Matthey Bankers Ltd shows that the holder of a charge is entitled to have regard to his own interests in deciding whether to appoint a receiver: he owes no duty of care to the chargor or his guarantors.

Shamji v Johnson Matthey Bankers Ltd [1986] BCLC 278, [1991] BCLC 36, Chancery Division and Court of Appeal

A group of companies owed the defendant bank (JMB) £21 million, secured by mortgage debentures. JMB was pressing for the loan to be repaid, but had allowed the group 21 days to try to obtain alternative finance, and had agreed to extend this period by a further 14 days if it was satisfied that the refinancing negotiations were proceeding in a proper and expeditious manner. JMB appointed receivers within this 14-day period. The plaintiff alleged that JMB in taking this step had been in breach of a duty of care towards the group and its guarantors, but the court held that no such duty was recognised in law.

Hoffmann J: Counsel for the defendants said under the terms of the security documents as pleaded in the statement of claim, JMB had a contractual right to appoint a receiver at any time after demanding payment. In the absence of bad faith, the bank could not owe the mortgagors or guarantors a duty of care in deciding whether to exercise that right. It might owe some duty in the way in which the right was exercised (eg it might owe a duty to take reasonable care not to appoint an incompetent) but not as to whether it was exercised or not. Counsel for the plaintiffs relied on *Cuckmere Brick Co Ltd v Mutual Finance Ltd* [1971] 2 All ER 633, [1971] Ch 949; *Standard Chartered Bank Ltd v Walker* [1982] 3 All ER 938, [1982] 1 WLR 1410 and *Tse Kwong Lam v Wong Chit Sen* [1983] 3 All ER 54, [1983] BCLC 88. These cases demonstrate that a mortgagee or receiver exercising a power to sell the mortgaged property owes a duty to the mortgagor or the guarantor to take reasonable care to obtain the fair value. It is important however to observe that in this matter there can be no real conflict of interest between mortgagor and mortgagee. As Lord Denning MR said in the *Standard Chartered Bank* case ([1982] 3 All ER 938 at 942, [1982] 1 WLR 1410 at 1415):

> He owes this duty not only to himself, to clear off as much of the debt as he can, but also to the mortgagor so as to reduce the balance owing as much as possible, and also to the guarantor so that he is made liable for as little as possible on the guarantee.

Lord Moulton in *McHugh v Union Bank of Canada* [1913] AC 299 at 311, in a passage quoted in the *Tse Kwong Lam* case described the duty as –

> to behave in conducting such realisation as a reasonable man would behave in the realisation of his own property.

It is clear, however, that in the case of a conflict between the interests of the mortgagor and mortgagee, any duty of care which the mortgagee owes to the mortgagor is subordinated to his right to act in the protection of his own interests. As Salmon LJ said in the *Cuckmere Brick Co* case ([1971] 2 All ER 633 at 643, [1971] Ch 949 at 965):

> If the mortgagee's interests, as he sees them, conflict with those of the mortgagor, the mortgagee can give preference to his own interests. . . .

The appointment of a receiver seems to me to involve an inherent conflict of interest. The purpose of the power is to enable the mortgagee to take the management of the company's property out of the hands of the directors and entrust it to a person of the mortgagee's choice. That power is granted to the mortgagee by the security documents in completely unqualified terms. It seems to me that a decision by the mortgagee to exercise the power cannot be challenged except perhaps on grounds of bad faith. There is no room for the implication of a term that the mortgagee shall be under a duty to the mortgagor to 'consider all relevant matters' before exercising the power. If no such qualification can be read into the security documents, I do not think that a wider duty can exist in tort. . . .

[The Court of Appeal affirmed this judgment, [1991] BCLC 36.]

NOTE

The *Cuckmere Brick* case and other decisions referred to by Hoffmann J in relation to the receiver's duties when realising the security must now be read as laying down a very restricted duty of care, in the light of the decision of the Privy Council in *Downsview Nominees Ltd v First City Corpn Ltd*. See the extract from this case cited below, p 909.

The term 'receiver' was originally used to describe a person appointed to receive the *income* (eg rents) yielded by the property in question – hence the name. When the receiver's function was extended to include taking charge of the property itself, and perhaps selling it, the name was not changed. But where the property included a business which it was important to keep on foot as a going concern, it was necessary to ensure also that there was continuity of management while the receiver was in office; and so (whether the appointment was made by the court or by the charge-holder) in these cases a *manager* as well as a receiver would be appointed – or, more commonly, the same individual would be appointed a *receiver and manager*. It is evident that such an appointment will invariably be appropriate where the charge extends to the whole or part of the debtor company's undertaking.

Against this background, it is possible to understand the statutory definitions of 'receiver' and 'administrative receiver' (IA 1986, s 29). A 'receiver' includes a receiver or manager of the property of a company, and also a receiver or manager of part of the property of a company (s 29(1)), while an 'administrative receiver' means (s 29(2)):

(a) a receiver or manager of the whole (or substantially the whole) of a company's property appointed by or on behalf of [the holder(s) of a floating charge], or
(b) a person who would be such a receiver or manager but for the appointment of some other person as the receiver of part of the company's property.

The law relating to a receiver who is not an administrative receiver is left to be governed largely by the common law (and by other statutes which may be relevant, such as the Law of Property Act 1925): the Insolvency Act 1986 contains only a few rules, eg a prohibition on a body corporate (s 30) or an undischarged bankrupt (s 31) from acting as a receiver. But there are now extensive statutory provisions relating to administrative receivers (ss 42–49 and Sch 1).

An administrative receiver has statutory powers similar to those of an administrator: indeed, the provisions of Sch 1 apply to both office-holders alike. There is also a power (s 43) for an administrative receiver to dispose of charged property, which is similar to, but rather more limited than, the power conferred on an administrator by s 15 (see above). The Act provides that, in general, an administrative receiver, in the exercise of his powers, is deemed to be the agent of the company (and not of the charge-holder who appointed him); but this deemed agency ceases if the company goes into liquidation (s 44). Section 44 in fact simply gives statutory force to the situation which would normally arise in any case as a result of provisions in the charge instrument. This is, however, an anomalous form of 'agency'. It does have the effect of ensuring that liabilities incurred by the receiver are met from the company's assets and not from those of the security-holder, but the company has few, if any, of the normal rights and powers of a principal – eg the power to give directions to the agent, or to remove him from office.

An administrative receiver must be an appropriately qualified insolvency practitioner, and he is required to observe a number of statutory reporting obligations and obliged to follow prescribed procedures. But, of all the insolvency procedures, receivership remains relatively one of the speediest, cheapest and most informal, because there is no court involvement.

The receiver's responsibilities are focused primarily on the interests of the charge-holder whom he represents. His function may be simply to sell up some or all of the company's assets and apply them towards clearing the charge-holder's debt, with little or no regard to the consequences for the other creditors, employees, shareholders and, indeed, the business itself. But he may, alternatively, be charged with the responsibility of managing the business for a time, in the hope that the company will trade its way out of a bad patch, or will find a new source of finance, or at the very least that its undertaking can be sold on a going-concern rather than a break-up basis, in whole or in part, and so fetch a better price. Whatever his function, however, the interests of the charge-holder who has appointed him come first, as the following cases illustrate.

Gomba Holdings UK Ltd v Homan [1986] 1 WLR 1301, Chancery Division

This case was a sequel to *Shamji v Johnson Matthey Bankers Ltd* (above, p 904). After the receivers had sold assets realising some £11 million, and while negotiations were taking place to make further sales, Shamji claimed to have entered into an agreement with an undisclosed third party which would provide funds to pay off the remainder of the debt owed by his group of companies to the bank. In these proceedings, the companies sought an order requiring the receivers not to dispose of further assets without first giving the companies five days' notice, and a further order compelling the receivers to disclose information about actual and pending sales. Hoffmann J refused both orders.

Hoffmann J: . . . I shall consider first motion 3 to restrain the receivers from entering into any commitments to dispose of assets unless they have first given the plaintiffs five working days' written notice of the details of any such proposed commitment. Mr Cullen submitted that pending the proposed redemption, the balance of convenience favoured such an order because the sale of an asset without notice to the plaintiffs might upset the arrangements with the unknown third party. This may be true, although I think there are other matters which also enter into the balance of convenience. But the primary difficulty is that I can see no arguable cause of action which could entitle the plaintiffs to such relief. The security documents give the receivers an unrestricted right to sell at any time. Until actual redemption or at least a valid tender of the redemption price, these powers continue to exist. The fact that the plaintiffs claim that they will shortly be able to redeem cannot give them a right in law to restrict the powers granted to the receivers.

Even if there were a cause of action, I do not think that the balance of convenience would favour an injunction. The receivers are entitled to take the view that they should continue with realisations on the assumption that redemption may not take place. The circumstances of Mr Shamji's secret arrangements with the anonymous purchaser are to say the least unusual and the receivers, while no doubt hoping that he will come up with the money, could hardly be blamed for retaining some scepticism. It is not the first occasion on which Mr Shamji has assured them or the bank that repayment is imminent. It does not follow that unless restrained in this way the receivers will take any opportunity to sell. It is in the interests of the debenture holder as well as the plaintiffs that the receivers should not unnecessarily jeopardise a bona fide and realistic proposal to discharge the indebtedness in full. No doubt the receivers will exercise a commercial judgment in the matter. But an enforced delay of five working days or even the need to reveal the proposed transaction to the plaintiffs may cause the loss of an advantageous sale. As against this possibility of loss, the plaintiffs are unable to offer anything in support of a cross-undertaking in damages. I therefore dismiss motion 3.

Most of the three-day hearing of these motions was taken up with discussion of motion 1 for information. The cases do not provide very much guidance on the extent of the duty of a receiver and manager of the property of a company to provide information to the directors during the currency of the receivership. A receiver is an agent of the company and an agent ordinarily has a duty to be ready with his accounts and to provide his principal with information relating to the conduct of his agency. But these generalisations are of limited assistance because a receiver and manager is no ordinary agent. Although nominally the agent of the company, his primary duty is to realise the assets in the interests of the debenture holder and his powers of management are really ancillary to that duty: *Re B Johnson & Co (Builders) Ltd* [1955] Ch 634, 644–645. . . .

There are, I think, certain principles which can be deduced from what the parties may be supposed to have contemplated as the commercial purpose of the power to appoint a receiver and manager. The first is that the receiver and manager should have the power to carry on the day to day process of realisation and management of the company's property without interference from the board. As Lord Atkinson said in *Moss SS Co Ltd v Whinney* [1912] AC 254, 263, the appointment of a receiver:

entirely supersedes the company in the conduct of its business, deprives it of all power to enter into contracts in relation to that business, or to sell, pledge, or otherwise dispose of the property put into the possession, or under the control of the receiver and manager. Its powers in these respects are entirely in abeyance.

This relationship between the receivers and the company would suggest that the board may be entitled to periodic accounts but cannot, merely because it is the board and the receivers are agents of the company, demand current information about the conduct of the business. . . .

The second principle which can be deduced from the nature of receivership is that, in the absence of express contrary provision made by statute or the terms of the debenture, any right which the company may have to be supplied with information must be qualified by the receiver's primary duty to the debenture holder. If the receiver considers that disclosure of information would be contrary to the interests of the debenture holder in realising the security, I think he must be entitled to withhold it and probably owes a duty to the debenture holder to do so. The company may be able to challenge the receiver's decision on the ground of bad faith or possibly that it was a decision which no reasonable receiver could have made, but otherwise I think that the receiver is the best judge of the commercial consequences of disclosing information about his activities.

All these considerations, which in my view tend to negate a general obligation upon a receiver to provide information to the company, are valid only during the currency of the receivership. Once the receivership has ended, the case is altered. There is no longer any right to manage the property or duty to the debenture holder which can conflict with a receiver's duty to account as agent to the company. It is not necessary for me to express a view on whether provision of the statutory accounts on the termination of the receivership should be assumed prima facie to be a proper accounting or whether, even in the absence of some challenge to the figures provided, the company can ask for something more. I only wish to emphasise that *Smiths Ltd v Middleton* [1979] 3 All ER 842, in which Blackett-Ord V-C decided that a company was entitled to a general order for an account against a receiver, was a case in which the receivership had come to an end.

During the receivership, the company's right to information . . . must in my judgment depend upon demonstrating a 'need to know' for the purpose of enabling the board to exercise its residual rights or peform its duties. I do not want to explore the question of what this might entail further than is necessary for the purposes of this case. An instance given in some of the cases is that the board may need information from the receivers in order to comply with its statutory obligation to render accounts. There has not yet been any suggestion in these proceedings that information is required for this purpose. More relevant in this case is the fact that the board may need information in order to exercise the company's right to redeem. It seems to me at least arguable that the right to redeem gives rise to a right on the part of the company to ask for sufficient information to make it effective. If the company has no way of finding out which assets have been sold and which remain to be redeemed, the right may in practice be incapable of exercise.

For the purposes of this motion I therefore propose to assume that a board which demonstrates a bona fide intention and ability to redeem is entitled not merely to a redemption statement showing how much is still owing but also to reasonable information about the nature of the assets remaining in the hands of the receivers. On the other hand, conformably with the principles I have discussed, I think that the receiver's duty to provide such information must be subordinated to his primary duty not to do anything which may prejudice the interests of the debenture holder.

[His Lordship discussed the evidence, and concluded:]

The history of this case, both before and after the appointment of the receivers, is a chronicle of unfulfilled assurances by Mr Shamji that someone was just about to provide the money to pay his debts to the bank. In my judgment the receivers were under no obligation to provide any information until they had firmer evidence that there was a realistic prospect of redemption. . . .

NOTE

Under the Companies Act 1985, which applied when the *Gomba Holdings* case was decided, there were no express provisions obliging a receiver to provide information about the progress of the receivership, either to the company or the other creditors. It is now provided, however, by IA 1986, s 48, that an *administrative* receiver must make a report to the company's creditors and others, normally within three months from his appointment, giving specified information. But, significantly, the decision in *Gomba Holdings* is echoed in s 48(6), which states that information need not be disclosed which would seriously prejudice the carrying out of his functions by the administrative receiver.

Downsview Nominees Ltd v First City Corpn Ltd [1993] AC 295, Privy Council

Glen Eden Motors Ltd (GEM) had executed a debenture creating a first charge in favour of the Westpac bank and a debenture creating a second charge to First City Corporation (FCC). GEM had been trading at a loss when the debt due to FCC became payable, and FCC appointed receivers, who decided that it was necessary to sell GEM's assets. They removed Pedersen, the manager of GEM, from office. Pedersen consulted Russell, who controlled Downsview, a finance company, and as a result (1) Downsview took an assignment of the Westpac debenture, (2) it appointed Russell receiver under that debenture, (3) Russell then took control of GEM's assets, displacing the FCC receivers, and (4) Pedersen was reinstated as manager. Russell announced that it was his intention that GEM should trade its way out of its difficulties. FCC and its receivers warned Russell that in their view this course was likely to result in further losses, which would damage the company and FCC as the lower-ranking debentureholder, and offered to pay off the whole of the money owed under the Westpac debenture. But Downsview refused this offer, and Russell and Pedersen continued to run the company, which lost a further $500,000. The Privy Council held Downsview and Russell liable in damages for breaches of their duty to use their powers as chargee and receiver for proper purposes; but they also confirmed two important points: (1) that a receiver's duties are owed primarily, if not exclusively, to the security holder who has appointed him, and this is inconsistent with the existence of a duty of care in law owed to the company or other creditors; and also (2) that his powers are conferred upon him solely for the purpose of securing the repayment of his appointor's debt, so that if either the company or any other interested party offers to pay off the debt, he must accept that offer and discharge this, his only, function.

The opinion of the Privy Council was delivered by **Lord Templeman**, who dealt with a number of points and continued: The next question is the nature and extent of the duties owed by a mortgagee and a receiver and manager respectively to subsequent encumbrancers and the mortgagor.

Several centuries ago equity evolved principles for the enforcement of mortgages and the protection of borrowers. The most basic principles were, first, that a mortgagee is security for the repayment of a debt and, secondly, that a security for repayment of a debt is only a mortgage. From these principles flowed two rules, first, that powers conferred on a mortgagee must be exercised in good faith for the purpose of obtaining repayment and secondly that, subject to the first rule, powers conferred on a mortgagee may be exercised although the consequences may be disadvantageous to the borrower. These principles and rules apply also to a receiver and manager appointed by the mortgagee.

It does not follow that a receiver and manager must immediately upon appointment seize all the cash in the coffers of the company and sell all the company's assets or so much of the assets as he chooses and considers sufficient to complete the redemption of the mortgage. He is entitled, but not bound, to allow the company's business to be continued by himself or by the existing or other executives. The decisions of the receiver and manager whether to continue the business or close down the business and sell assets chosen by him cannot be impeached if those decisions are taken in good faith while protecting the interests of the debenture holder in recovering the moneys due under the debenture, even though the decisions of the receiver and manager may be disadvantageous for the company.

The nature of the duties owed by a receiver and manager appointed by a debenture holder were authoritatively defined by Jenkins LJ in a characteristically learned and comprehensive judgment in *Re B Johnson & Co (Builders) Ltd* [1955] Ch 634, 661–663. Jenkins LJ said:

> the phrase 'manager of the company,' prima facie, according to the ordinary meaning of the words, connotes a person holding, whether de jure or de facto, a post in or with the company of a nature charging him with the duty of managing the affairs of the company for the company's benefit; whereas a receiver and manager for debenture holders is a person appointed by the debenture holders to whom the company has given powers of management pursuant to the contract of loan constituted by the debenture, and, as a condition of obtaining the loan, to enable him to preserve and realise the assets comprised in the security for the benefit of the debenture holders. The company gets the loan on terms that the lenders shall be entitled, for the purpose of making their security effective, to appoint a receiver with powers of sale and of management pending sale, and with full discretion as to the exercise and mode of exercising those powers. The primary duty of the receiver is to the debenture holders and not to the company. He is receiver and manager of the property of the company for the debenture holders, not manager of the company. The company is entitled to any surplus of assets remaining after the debenture debt has been discharged, and is entitled to proper accounts. But the whole purpose of the receiver and manager's appointment would obviously be stultified if the company could claim that a receiver and manager owes it any duty comparable to the duty owed to a company by its own directors or managers.
>
> In determining whether a receiver and manager for the debenture holders of a company has broken any duty owed by him to the company, regard must be had to the fact that he is a receiver and manager – that is to say, a receiver, with ancillary powers of management – for the debenture holders, and not simply a person appointed to manage the company's affairs for the benefit of the company. . . . The duties of a receiver and manager for debenture holders are widely different from those of a manager of the company. He is under no obligation to carry on the company's business at the expense of the debenture holders. Therefore he commits no breach of duty to the company by refusing to do so, even though his discontinuance of the business may be detrimental from the company's point of view. Again, his power of sale is, in effect, that of a mortgagee, and he therefore commits no breach of duty to the company by a bona fide sale, even though he might have obtained a higher price and even though, from the point of view of the company, as distinct from the debenture holders, the terms might be regarded as disadvantageous.
>
> In a word, in the absence of fraud or mala fides . . . the company cannot complain of any act or omission of the receiver and manager, provided that he does nothing that he is not empowered to do, and omits nothing that he is enjoined to do by the terms of his appointment. If the company conceives that it has any claim against the receiver and manager for breach of some duty owed by him to the company, the issue is not whether the receiver and manager has done or omitted to do anything which it would be wrongful in a manager of a company to do or omit, but whether he has exceeded or abused or wrongfully omitted to use the special powers and discretions vested in him pursuant to the contract of loan constituted by the debenture for the special purpose of enabling the assets comprised in the debenture holders' security to be preserved and realised.

The duties owed by a receiver and manager do not compel him to adopt any particular course of action, by selling the whole or part of the mortgaged property or by carrying on the business of the company or by exercising any other powers and discretions vested in him. But since a mortgage is only security for a debt, a receiver and manager commits a breach of his duty if he abuses his powers by exercising them otherwise than 'for the special purpose of enabling the assets comprised in the debenture holders' security to be preserved and realised' for the benefit of the debenture holder. In the present case the evidence of the second defendant himself and the clear emphatic findings of Gault J [1989] 3 NZLR 710, 749, which have already been cited, show that the second defendant accepted appointment and acted as receiver and manager

> not for the purpose of enforcing the security under the Westpac debenture but for the purpose of preventing the enforcement by the plaintiffs of the [FCC] debenture.

This and other findings to similar effect establish that, ab initio and throughout his receivership, the second defendant did not exercise his powers for proper purposes. He was at all times in breach of the duty, which was pleaded against him, to exercise his powers in good faith for proper purposes.

Gault J rested his judgment not on breach of a duty to act in good faith for proper purposes but on negligence. He said, at pp 744, 747:

> on an application of negligence principles, a receiver owes a duty to the debenture holders to take reasonable care in dealing with the assets of the company . . . [The first defendant's] position is merely a specific example of the duty a mortgagee has to subsequent chargeholders to exercise its powers with reasonable care . . .

Richardson J, delivering the judgment of the Court of Appeal [1990] 3 NZLR 265, 278–280, agreed that duties of care in negligence as defined by Gault J were owed by the second defendant as receiver and manager and by the first defendant as first debenture holder to the plaintiffs as second debenture holders. Richardson J agreed that the second defendant was in breach of his duty but, differing from Gault J, held that the first defendant had committed no breach.

The general duty of care said to be owed by a mortgagee to subsequent encumbrancers and the mortgagor in negligence is inconsistent with the right of the mortgagee and the duties which the courts applying equitable principles have imposed on the mortgagee. If a mortgagee enters into possession he is liable to account for rent on the basis of wilful default; he must keep mortgage premises in repair; he is liable for waste. Those duties were imposed to ensure that a mortgagee is diligent in discharging his mortgage and returning the property to the mortgagor. If a mortgagee exercises his power of sale in good faith for the purpose of protecting his security, he is not liable to the mortgagor even though he might have obtained a higher price and even though the terms might be regarded as disadvantageous to the mortgagor. *Cuckmere Brick Co Ltd v Mutual Finance Ltd* [1971] Ch 949 is Court of Appeal authority for the proposition that, if the mortgagee decides to sell, he must take reasonable care to obtain a proper price but is no authority for any wider proposition. A receiver exercising his power of sale also owes the same specific duties as the mortgagee. But that apart, the general duty of a receiver and manager appointed by a debenture holder, as defined by Jenkins LJ in *Re B Johnson & Co (Builders) Ltd* [1955] Ch 634, 661, leaves no room for the imposition of a general duty to use reasonable care in dealing with the assets of the company. The duties imposed by equity on a mortgagee and on a receiver and manager would be quite unnecessary if there existed a general duty in negligence to take reasonable care in the exercise of powers and to take reasonable care in dealing with the assets of the mortgagor company. . . .

The liability of the second defendant in the present case is firmly based not on negligence but on the breach of duty. There was overwhelming evidence that the receivership of the second defendant was inspired by him for improper purposes and carried on in bad faith, ultimately verging on fraud. The liability of the first defendant does not arise under negligence but as a result of the first defendant's breach of duty in failing to transfer the Westpac debenture to the first plaintiff at the end of March 1987. It is well settled that the mortgagor and all persons having any interest in the property subject to the mortgage or liable to pay the mortgage debt can redeem. It is now conceded that the first plaintiff was entitled to require the first defendant to assign the Westpac debenture to the first plaintiff on payment of all moneys due to the first defendant under the Westpac debenture. . . .

The first defendant was from the end of March 1987 in breach of its duty to assign the Westpac debenture to the first plaintiff. If that debenture had been assigned, the second defendant would have ceased to be the receiver and manager and none of the avoidable losses caused by the second defendant would have been sustained. . . .

NOTE

Prior to the ruling in this case, it was accepted as a result of several decisions that a secured creditor and any receiver acting on his behalf was under a duty of care towards the debtor and others interested (eg a guarantor of the debt) when exercising a power of sale, and perhaps more generally: *Cuckmere Brick Co Ltd v Mutual Finance Ltd* [1971] Ch 949, CA; *Standard Chartered Bank Ltd v Walker* [1982] 1 WLR 1410, CA. It is plain from the Privy Council's ruling in *Downsview* that any such duty of care is now to be restricted to taking reasonable care to obtain a proper price, if it has been decided to sell the property, and that otherwise the receiver has only a duty to act in good faith.

The above cases emphasise the essential difference between a receivership and other forms of insolvency procedure, such as administration or liquidation. An administrator or liquidator is appointed to act in the interests of all the parties who are concerned in the insolvency, and to hold the balance between the various competing interests. A receiver, in contrast, is concerned only with the enforcement of his appointor's security. It is not his role to see to the payment of any other creditors – indeed, if there is a surplus in his hands after realising the security he must hand it over to the company (*Re GL Saunders Ltd* [1986] 1 WLR 215). There is one exception to this rule: s 40 of IA 1986 requires a receiver appointed to enforce a *floating* charge to pay the debts which would be entitled to preference in a liquidation (eg certain debts owed to the Crown and employees, see below, p 926) in priority to the charge-holder. A receiver who fails to do so is personally liable to the creditors concerned (*IRC v Goldblatt* [1972] Ch 498).

Winding up (IA 1986, Part IV). Winding up, or liquidation, is a procedure which anticipates the dissolution of a company – its ceasing to exist as a corporate entity. An insolvency practitioner is appointed to act as *liquidator*, with the task of closing down or selling off the company's business, realising all of its assets, paying off its creditors and, if there is a surplus remaining, distributing it amongst those who are entitled to it under the company's constitution. It is possible that he may keep the business going for a while, but he will do this only with a view to its ultimate sale – rehabilitation is not within a liquidator's terms of reference! The company need not, of course, be insolvent, but the legislation treats every liquidation as a form of insolvency procedure and deals with the whole subject in the Insolvency Act. There are two ways of bringing a liquidation about: by resolution of the company itself (called a 'voluntary' liquidation), and by court order (a 'compulsory' liquidation). We shall deal with each of these in turn.

A *voluntary winding up* may take two forms. If the directors of the company are able to certify that all of its creditors will be paid in full, the liquidation proceeds under the control of the members and is called a 'members' voluntary winding up'. If they cannot do this, control of the liquidation passes to the creditors and it is known as a 'creditors' voluntary winding up'. Either way, a qualified insolvency practitioner is appointed liquidator to administer the winding up. He has very wide powers, which are set out in IA 1986, Sch 4. The court is not normally involved, but it does have advisory and back-up powers which can be invoked if necessary. When he has completed his administration and distributed all the moneys in his hands, the liquidator makes his final account to the members or the creditors, and sends a return to the Registrar of Companies. The company is automatically dissolved three months later.

A *winding up by the court*, or 'compulsory' winding up, results from a court order, which is normally made on the petition of the company itself or one or more of its members or creditors. One of the grounds on which an order may be made is that the company is unable to pay its debts (IA 1986, s 122(1)(f)). For this purpose, a 'commercial' test of insolvency is prima facie the appropriate one, but the Act provides, alternatively, that a company may be deemed to be unable to pay its debts if it is insolvent on a 'balance-sheet' basis (s 123(2)). A company will also be deemed insolvent (as is the case in bankruptcy) if it has failed to comply with a statutory demand for payment of a debt of £750 or more, or if execution against it has been returned unsatisfied (s 123(1)). The Official Receiver takes charge of the company's assets and affairs until a liquidator is agreed on by the members and/or the creditors, and the administration then proceeds on a basis largely similar to a voluntary liquidation, except that the liquidator is responsible to the court and more immediately under its control.

Assets in the liquidation. In contrast with the position in bankruptcy, the assets in a liquidation are not vested in the liquidator but remain vested in the company. But all control passes from the directors and shareholders to the liquidator.

The assets available to the liquidator include all the property which is beneficially owned by the company at the time when it goes into liquidation. This will exclude assets in the possession of the company which belong to someone else (eg goods which have been supplied to it on 'retention of title' terms: see above, p 407). It will also exclude property which the company holds on trust for another person. Rather surprisingly, the courts have, on occasion, found a trust to exist in circumstances which would ordinarily be regarded as having created a debtor–creditor relationship and not a trust. We look at two examples in the cases which follow.

Re Kayford Ltd [1975] 1 WLR 279, Chancery Division

Kayfords carried on a mail-order business. Its directors were worried about the financial position of its principal supplier, and consulted the company's accountants. They advised the directors to open a separate bank account and to pay all pre-payments made by Kayford's customers from then on into this new account, and to draw money from it only as the relevant goods were delivered to the customer. When the suppliers became insolvent Kayfords' own financial position became impossible and it also went into liquidation. The court held that the money in the account did not belong to the company but was held on trust for Kayfords' customers.

Megarry J: . . . The question for me is whether the money in the bank account . . . is held on trust for those who paid it, or whether it forms part of the general assets of the company. Mr Heyman appears for the joint liquidators, . . . and he has contended that there is no trust, so that the money forms part of the general assets of the company and thus will be available for the creditors generally. On the other hand, Mr Kennedy appears for a Mr Joels, who on December 12 paid the company £32.20 for goods which have not been delivered; and a representation order is sought on behalf of all others whose moneys have been paid into the bank account, some 700 or 800 in number. I make that order. Mr Kennedy, of course, argued for the existence of an effective trust. I may say at the outset that on the facts of the case Mr Heyman was unable to contend that any question of a fraudulent preference arose. If one leaves on one side any case in which an insolvent company seeks to declare a trust in favour of creditors, one is concerned here with the question not of preferring creditors but of preventing those who pay money from becoming creditors, by making them beneficiaries under a trust. . . .

Now there are clearly some loose ends in the case. Nevertheless, despite the loose ends, when I take as a whole the affidavits of Mr Wainwright, Mr Kay and Mr Hall (the bank manager) I feel no doubt that the intention was that there should be a trust. There are no formal difficulties. The property concerned is pure personalty, and so writing, though desirable, is not an essential. There is no doubt about the so-called 'three certainties' of a trust. The subject-matter to be held on trust is clear, and so are the beneficial interests therein, as well as the beneficiaries. As for the requisite certainty of words, it is well settled that a trust can be created without using the words 'trust' or 'confidence' or the like: the question is whether in substance a sufficient intention to create a trust has been manifested.

In *Re Nanwa Gold Mines Ltd* [1955] 1 WLR 1080 the money was sent on the faith of a promise to keep it in a separate account, but there is nothing in that case or in any other authority that I know of to suggest that this is essential. I feel no doubt that here a trust was created. From the outset the advice (which was accepted) was to establish a trust account at the bank. The whole purpose of what was done was to ensure that the moneys remained in the beneficial ownership of those who sent them, and a trust is the obvious means of achieving this. No doubt the general rule is that if you send money to a company for goods which are not delivered, you are merely a creditor of the company unless a trust has been created. The sender may create a trust by using appropriate words when he sends the money (though I wonder how many do this, even if they are equity lawyers), or the company may do it by taking suitable steps on or before receiving the money. If either is done, the obligations in respect of the money are transformed from contract to property, from debt to trust. Payment into a separate bank account is a useful (though by no means conclusive) indication of an intention to create a trust, but of course there is nothing to prevent the company from binding itself by a trust even if there are no effective banking arrangements.

Accordingly, of the alternative declarations sought by the summons, the second, to the effect that the money is held in trust for those who paid it, is in my judgment the declaration that should be made. I understand that questions may be raised as to resorting to the interest on the moneys as a means of discharging the costs of the summons; on that I will, of course, hear argument. I should, however, add one thing. Different considerations may perhaps arise in relation to trade creditors; but here I am concerned only with members of the public, some of whom can ill afford to exchange their money for a claim to a dividend in the liquidation, and all of whom are likely to be anxious to avoid this. In cases concerning the public, it seems to me that where money in advance is being paid to a company in return for the future supply of goods or services, it is an entirely proper and honourable thing for a company to do what this company did, upon skilled advice, namely, to start to pay the money into a trust account as soon as there begin to be doubts as to the company's ability to fulfil its obligations to deliver the goods or provide the services. I wish that, sitting in this court, I had heard of this occurring more frequently; and I can only hope that I shall hear more of it in the future.

NOTE

In this case, Megarry J accepted that there was no question of a fraudulent preference, under the law as it then stood. This was undoubtedly correct, for fraudulent preference required proof of a *dishonest* intention on the part of the company that the creditor or creditors concerned would have an advantage in a subsequent liquidation. Under IA 1986, s 239 however, the concept of 'fraudulent preference' has been replaced by 'preference', and the requirement to show dishonesty has been eliminated: see below, p 919. It is likely that this point would need reconsideration under the new law if the facts of *Re Kayford Ltd* were to occur again.

Barclays Bank Ltd v Quistclose Investments Ltd [1970] AC 567, House of Lords

Rolls Razor Ltd was in serious financial difficulties. It had declared a dividend on its ordinary shares, but did not have the funds to pay it. With the knowledge of its bank, it agreed to borrow some £209,000 from Quistclose (the respondents) on the understanding that the money would be used only for the purpose of paying the dividend. The loan was made and the money paid in to the bank, but before the shareholders had been paid their dividend Rolls Razor went into liquidation. The House of Lords held that the bank held the £209,000 on a resulting trust for Quistclose.

Lord Wilberforce: . . . Two questions arise, both of which must be answered favourably to the respondents if they are to recover the money from the bank. The first is whether as between the respondents and Rolls Razor Ltd the terms upon which the loan was made were such as to impress upon the sum of £209,719 8s 6d a trust in their favour in the event of the dividend not being paid. The second is whether, in that event, the bank had such notice of the trust or of the circumstances giving rise to it as to make the trust binding upon them.

It is not difficult to establish precisely upon what terms the money was advanced by the respondents to Rolls Razor Ltd. There is no doubt that the loan was made specifically in order to enable Rolls Razor Ltd to pay the dividend. There is equally, in my opinion, no doubt that the loan was made only so as to enable Rolls Razor Ltd to pay the dividend and for no other purpose. This follows quite clearly from the terms of the letter of Rolls Razor Ltd to the bank of July 15, 1964, which letter, before transmission to the bank, was sent to the respondents under open cover in order that the cheque might be (as it was) enclosed in it. The mutual intention of the respondents and of Rolls Razor Ltd, and the essence of the bargain, was that the sum advanced should not become part of the assets of Rolls Razor Ltd, but should be used exclusively for payment of a particular class of its creditors, namely, those entitled to the dividend. A necessary consequence from this, by process simply of interpretation, must be that if, for any reason, the dividend could not be paid, the money was to be returned to the respondents: the word 'only' or 'exclusively' can have no other meaning or effect.

That arrangements of this character for the payment of a person's creditors by a third person, give rise to a relationship of a fiduciary character or trust, in favour, as a primary trust, of the creditors, and secondarily, if the primary trust fails, of the third person, has been recognised in a series of cases over some 150 years.

[His Lordship referred to a number of authorities and continued:]

These cases have the support of longevity, authority, consistency and, I would add, good sense. But they are not binding on your Lordships and it is necessary to consider such arguments as have been put why they should be departed from or distinguished.

It is said, first, that the line of authorities mentioned above stands on its own and is inconsistent with other, more modern, decisions. Those are cases in which money has been paid to a company for the purpose of obtaining an allotment of shares (see *Moseley v Cressey's Co* (1865) LR 1 Eq 405; *Stewart v Austin* (1866) LR 3 Eq 299; *Re Nanwa Gold Mines Ltd* [1955] 1 WLR 1080). I do not think it necessary to examine these cases in detail, nor to comment on them, for I am satisfied that they do not affect the principle on which this appeal should be decided. They are merely examples which show that, in the absence of some special arrangement creating a trust (as was shown to exist in *Re Nanwa Gold Mines Ltd*), payments of this kind are made upon the basis that they are to be included in the company's assets. They do not negative the proposition that a trust may exist where the mutual intention is that they should not.

The second, and main, argument for the appellant was of a more sophisticated character. The transaction, it was said, between the respondents and Rolls Razor Ltd, was one of loan, giving rise to a legal action of debt. This necessarily excluded the implication of any trust, enforceable in equity, in the respondents' favour: a transaction may attract one action or the other, it could not admit of both.

My Lords, I must say that I find this argument unattractive. Let us see what it involves. It means that the law does not permit an arrangement to be made by which one person agrees to advance money to another, on terms that the money is to be used exclusively to pay debts of the latter, and if, and so far as not so used, rather than becoming a general asset of the latter available to his creditors at large, is to be returned to the lender. The lender is obliged, in such a case, because he is a lender, to accept, whatever the mutual wishes of lender and borrower may be, that the money he was willing to make available for one purpose only shall be freely available for others of the borrower's creditors for whom he has not the slightest desire to provide.

I should be surprised if an argument of this kind – so conceptualist in character – had ever been accepted. In truth it has plainly been rejected by the eminent judges who from 1819 onwards have permitted arrangements of this type to be enforced, and have approved them as being for the benefit of creditors and all concerned. There is surely no difficulty in recognising the co-existence in one transaction of legal and equitable rights and remedies: when the money is advanced, the lender acquires an equitable right to see that it is applied for the primary designated purpose (see *Re Rogers* (1891) 8 Morr 243 where both Lindley LJ and Kay LJ recognised this): when the purpose has been carried out (ie the debt paid) the lender has his remedy against the borrower in debt: if the primary purpose cannot be carried out, the question arises if a secondary purpose (ie, repayment to the lender) has been agreed, expressly or by implication: it if has, the remedies of equity may be invoked to give effect to it, if it has not (and the money is intended to fall within the general fund of the debtor's assets) then there is the appropriate remedy for recovery of a loan. I can appreciate no reason why the flexible interplay of law and equity cannot let in these practical arrangements, and other variations if desired: it would be to the discredit of both systems if they could not. In the present case the intention to create a secondary trust for the benefit of the lender, to arise if the primary trust, to pay the dividend, could not be carried out, is clear and I can find no reason why the law should not give effect to it.

I pass to the second question, that of notice. I can deal with this briefly because I am in agreement with the manner in which it has been disposed of by all three members of the Court of Appeal. I am prepared, for this purpose, to accept, by way of assumption, the position most favourable to the bank, ie, that it is necessary to show that the bank had notice of the trust or of the circumstances giving rise to the trust, at the time when they received the money, viz, on July 15, 1964, and that notice on a later date, even though they had not in any real sense given value when they received the money or thereafter changed their position, will not do. It is common ground, and I think right, that a mere request to put the money into a separate account is not sufficient to constitute notice. But on July 15, 1964, the bank, when it received the cheque, also received the covering letter of that date which I have set out above: previously there had been the telephone conversation between Mr Goldbart and Mr Parker, to which I have also referred. From these there is no doubt that the bank was told that the money had been provided on loan by a third person and was to be used only for the purpose of paying the dividend. This was sufficient to give them notice that it was trust money and not assets of Rolls Razor Ltd: the fact, if it be so, that they were unaware of the lender's identity (though the respondent's name as drawer was on the cheque) is of no significance. I may add to this, as having some bearing on the merits of the case, that it is quite apparent from earlier documents that the bank were aware that Rolls Razor Ltd could not provide the money for the dividend and that this would have to come from an outside source and that they never contemplated that the money so provided could be used to reduce the existing overdraft. They were in fact insisting that other or additional arrangements should be made for that purpose. As was appropriately said by Russell LJ [in the Court of Appeal], it would be giving a complete windfall to the bank if they had established a right to retain the money.

In my opinion, the decision of the Court of Appeal was correct on all points and the appeal should be dismissed.

[Lords Reid, Morris of Borth-y-Gest, Guest and Pearce concurred.]

Other cases in which a relationship was held not to be that of debtor and creditor but to involve a trust include *Carreras Rothmans Ltd v Freeman Mathews Treasure Ltd* [1985] Ch 207; *Chase Manhattan Bank NA v Israel-British Bank (London) Ltd* [1981] Ch 105 and *Neste Oy v Lloyds Bank plc* [1983] 2 Lloyd's Rep 658; contrast *Swiss Bank Corpn v Lloyd's Bank Ltd* [1982] AC 584, HL, where the opposite conclusion was reached.

The liquidator may *disclaim* any asset which is unsaleable or fettered with onerous liabilities, and any unprofitable contract (IA 1986, ss 178ff). A person who is disadvantaged by a disclaimer may prove for his losses as a creditor in the liquidation.

Avoidance of antecedent transactions. The assets available for distribution by the liquidator may be augmented as a result of the operation of a number of special statutory provisions, under which transactions that have taken place in the period immediately prior to the liquidation may be set aside. The language of each of these provisions is complex and calls for careful study; in the present chapter we can only describe them in outline.

First, s 127 of IA 1986 provides that, in a winding up by the court, any disposition of the company's property made after the commencement of the winding up is void, unless the court otherwise orders. This means that if a company has paid off a debt, given security over its property to a creditor, or sold an asset (even for full value) during this 'twilight' period before it goes into liquidation, it is automatically avoided unless the court agrees that it should be upheld. The leading case of *Re Gray's Inn Construction Co Ltd* (below) sets out some of the factors which the court will take into account in deciding whether to exercise this discretion. It also demonstrates, perhaps surprisingly, that both payments by a company *into* its bank account and drawings made by the company *out* of its account are 'dispositions' within the meaning of the section.

In a similar provision, executions issued against the property of a company after the commencement of the winding up are declared to be void by IA 1986, s 128.

Re Gray's Inn Construction Co Ltd [1980] 1 WLR 711, Court of Appeal

An order was made to wind up the company on 9 October 1972, on the basis of a petition which had been presented on 3 August. The bank allowed the company to continue to use its bank account while the hearing of the petition was pending. The court, varying the judgment of Templeman J in the court below, ruled (1) that both payments into and payments out of the account were 'dispositions' of the company's property within s 127 and (2) that the bank ought to have become aware of the fact that a petition had been presented at some date before 15 August. In the exercise of its discretion, it allowed transactions made before that date to stand, but declined to validate those which had been effected later. The extract cited below indicates the factors which the court is likely to take into account in exercising its discretion under the statute.

Buckley LJ: . . . It is a basic concept of our law governing the liquidation of insolvent estates, whether in bankruptcy or under the Companies Acts, that the free assets of the insolvent at the commencement of the liquidation shall be distributed rateably amongst the insolvent's unsecured creditors as at that date. In bankruptcy this is achieved by the relation of the trustee's title to the bankrupt's assets back to the commencement of the bankruptcy. In a company's compulsory winding up it is achieved by s 227 [of the Companies Act 1948, equivalent to IA 1986, s 127]. There may be occasions, however, when it would be beneficial, not only for the company but also for its unsecured creditors, that the company should be enabled to dispose of some of its property during the period after the petition has been presented but before a winding up order has been made. An obvious example is if the company has an opportunity by acting speedily to dispose of some piece of property at an exceptionally good price. Many applications for validation under the section relate to specific transactions of this kind or analogous kinds. It may sometimes be beneficial to the company and its creditors that the company should be enabled to complete a particular contract or project, or to continue to carry on its business generally in its ordinary course with a view to a sale of the business as a going concern. In any such case the court has power under s 227 of the Companies Act 1948 to validate the particular transaction, or the completion of the particular contract or project, or the continuance of the company's business in its ordinary course, as the case may be. In considering whether to make a validating order the court must always, in my opinion, do its best to ensure that the interests of the unsecured creditors will not be prejudiced. Where the application relates to a specific transaction this may be susceptible of positive proof. In a case of completion of a contract or project the proof may perhaps be less positive but nevertheless be cogent enough to satisfy the court that in the interests of the creditors the company should be enabled to proceed, or at any rate that proceeding in the manner proposed would not prejudice them in any respect. The desirability of the company being enabled to carry on its business generally is likely to be more speculative and will be likely to depend on whether a sale of the business as a going concern will probably be more beneficial than a break-up realisation of the company's assets. In each case, I think, the court must necessarily carry out a balancing exercise. . . . Each case must depend upon its own particular facts.

Since the policy of the law is to procure so far as practicable rateable payments of the unsecured creditors' claims, it is, in my opinion, clear that the court should not validate any transaction or series of transactions which might result in one or more pre-liquidation creditors being paid in full at the expense of other creditors, who will only receive a dividend, in the absence of special circumstances making such a course desirable in the interests of the unsecured creditors as a body. If, for example, it were in the interests of the creditors generally that the company's business should be carried on, and this could only be achieved by paying for goods already supplied to the company when the petition is presented but not yet paid for, the court might think fit in the exercise of its discretion to validate payment for those goods.

Where a third party proposes to enter into a transaction with a company which is liable to be invalidated under s 227 of the Companies Act 1948, the third party can decline to do so until the company has obtained a validating order, or it might itself seek a validating order, or it can enter into the transaction in anticipation of the court making a retroactive validating order at a later date. In the present case the bank adopted the last course. A third party who does that takes the risk of the court refusing to make the order.

It may not always be feasible, or desirable, that a validating order should be sought before the transaction in question is carried out. The parties may be unaware at the time when the transaction is entered into that a petition has been presented; or the need for speedy action may be such as to preclude an anticipatory application; or the beneficial character of the transaction may be so obvious that there is no real prospect of a liquidator seeking to set it aside, so that an application to the court would waste time, money and effort. But in any case in which the transaction is carried out without an anticipatory validating order the disponee is at risk of the court declining to validate the transaction. It follows, in my view, that the parties when entering into the transaction, if they are aware that it is liable to be invalidated by the section, should have in mind the sort of considerations which would influence the court's decision.

A disposition carried out in good faith in the ordinary course of business at a time when the parties are unaware that a petition has been presented may, it seems, normally be validated by the court . . . unless there is any ground for thinking that the transaction may involve an attempt to prefer the disponee, in which case the transaction would probably not be validated. In a number of cases reference has been made to the relevance of the policy of ensuring rateable distribution of the assets. . . .

But although that policy might disincline the court to ratify any transaction which involved preferring a pre-liquidation creditor, it has no relevance to a transaction which is entirely post-liquidation, as for instance a sale of an asset at its full market value after presentation of a petition. Such a transaction involves no dissipation of the company's assets, for it does not reduce the value of those assets. It cannot harm the creditors and there would seem to be no reason why the court should not in the exercise of its discretion validate it. A fortioti, the court would be inclined to validate a transaction which would increase or has increased, the value of the company's assets, or which would preserve, or has preserved, the value of the company's assets from harm which would result from the company's business being paralysed. . . .

[Goff LJ and Sir David Cairns concurred.]

It should be noted that ss 127 and 128 are applicable in all compulsory liquidations, whether or not the company is insolvent.

A second set of statutory provisions (which apply in liquidations of all types) allows the court to order the avoidance of transactions which have taken place prior to the commencement of the winding up – that is, even before the petition is presented or the resolution for winding up is passed. Some of these provisions apply also in an administration. They include:

- *Transactions at an undervalue* (IA 1986, s 238). Where a company has made a gift of property or has parted with property for an inadequate consideration, within two years of the commencement of the winding up, at a time when the company was unable to pay its debts, the court may make an order annulling the transaction.
- *Preferences* (IA 1986, s 239). Where a company has given a preference to a particular creditor (that is, paid his debt or done some other act which would put him in a better position in the event of the company's insolvency) within six months (or, in certain cases, two years) prior to the commencement of the liquidation, at a time when the company was unable to pay its debts, the court may order that it be struck down. It is necessary to show that the company was influenced by a desire to prefer the creditor.
- *Transactions defrauding creditors* (IA 1986, s 423). If a company has entered into a transaction at an undervalue *at any time* for the purpose of putting assets beyond the reach of a creditor or potential creditor, it may be avoided by order of the court.
- *Extortionate credit transactions* (IA 1986, s 244). A transaction involving the giving of credit to the company which was entered into within three years prior to the winding up may be set aside or varied by the court if its terms are deemed extortionate.
- *Floating charges* (IA 1986, s 245). No order of the court is required in this case. A floating charge created by a company within the period of twelve months (or, where the chargee is a person 'connected with' the company, such as a director or another company in the same group, two years) prior to the commencement of its winding up is declared by this section to be invalid, unless (1) 'new value', in the form of money paid or goods or services supplied, was given to the company in consideration of the charge or (2) where the chargee is not a 'connected person', the company was solvent at the relevant time. In other words, where the statutory conditions apply, a *floating*

charge may not be taken during the period immediately prior to an insolvent liquidation to secure an *existing* debt. A fixed charge is not caught by s 245, although it may be struck down as a preference if the requirements of ss 239–240 are satisfied.

The operation of some of these provisions is illustrated by the cases which follow.

Re MC Bacon Ltd [1990] BCLC 324, Chancery Division

The company had carried on business profitably as an importer and wholesaler of bacon until it lost its main customer. Its fortunes then rapidly dwindled and it soon had to be wound up. This action was brought to challenge a debenture which had been given to its bank on the alternative grounds that it was a transaction at an undervalue (IA 1986, s 238), or a preference (s 239); but Millett J held that it was neither. It was not a transaction at an undervalue because the giving of security had neither depleted the company's assets nor diminished their value, and it was not a preference because the directors' motive in giving the charge had not been to prefer the bank but to keep the company trading.

Millett J: . . .

Voidable preference

So far as I am aware, this is the first case under the section and its meaning has been the subject of some debate before me. I shall therefore attempt to provide some guidance.

The section replaces s 44(1) of the Bankruptcy Act 1914, which in certain circumstances deemed fraudulent and avoided payments made and other transactions entered into in favour of a creditor 'with a view of giving such creditor . . . a preference over the other creditors'. Section 44(1) and its predecessors had been construed by the courts as requiring the person seeking to avoid the payment or other transaction to establish that it had been made 'with the dominant intention to prefer' the creditor.

Section 44(1) has been replaced and its language has been entirely recast. Every single word of significance, whether in the form of statutory definition or in its judicial expression, has been jettisoned. 'View', 'dominant', 'intention' and even 'to prefer' have all been discarded. These are replaced by 'influenced', 'desire', and 'to produce in relation to that person the effect mentioned in sub-s (4)(b)'.

I therefore emphatically protest against the citation of cases decided under the old law. They cannot be of any assistance when the language of the statute has been so completely and deliberately changed. It may be that many of the cases which will come before the courts in future will be decided in the same way that they would have been decided under the old law. That may be so, but the grounds of decision will be different. What the court has to do is to interpret the language of the statute and apply it. It will no longer inquire whether there was 'a dominant intention to prefer' the creditor, but whether the company's decision was 'influenced by a desire to produce the effect mentioned in sub-s (4)(b)'.

This is a completely different test. It involves at least two radical departures from the old law. It is no longer necessary to establish a *dominant* intention to prefer. It is sufficient that the decision was *influenced* by the requisite desire. That is the first change. The second is that it is no longer sufficient to establish an *intention* to prefer. There must be a *desire* to produce the effect mentioned in the subsection.

This second change is made necessary by the first, for without it it would be virtually impossible to uphold the validity of a security taken in exchange for the injection of fresh funds into a company in financial difficulties. A man is taken to intend the necessary consequences of his actions, so that an intention to grant a security to a creditor necessarily involves an intention to prefer that creditor in the event of insolvency. The need to establish that such intention was dominant was essential under the old law to prevent perfectly proper transactions from being struck down. With the abolition of that requirement intention could not remain the relevant test. Desire has been substituted. That is a very different matter. Intention is objective, desire is subjective. A man can choose the lesser of two evils without desiring either.

It is not, however, sufficient to establish a desire to make the payment or grant the security which it is sought to avoid. There must have been a desire to produce the effect mentioned in the subsection, that is to say, to improve the creditor's position in the event of an insolvent liquidation. A man is not to be taken as *desiring* all the necessary consequences of his actions. Some consequences may be of advantage to him and be desired by him; others may not affect him and be matters of indifference to him; while still others may be positively disadvantageous to him and not be desired by him, but be regarded by him as the unavoidable price of obtaining the desired advantages. It will still be possible to provide assistance to a company in financial difficulties provided that the company is actuated only by proper commercial considerations. Under the new regime a transaction will not be set aside as a voidable preference unless the company positively wished to improve the creditor's position in the event of its own insolvent liquidation.

There is, of course, no need for there to be direct evidence of the requisite desire. Its existence may be inferred from the circumstances of the case just as the dominant intention could be inferred under the old law. But the mere presence of the requisite desire will not be sufficient by itself. It must have influenced the decision to enter into the transaction. It was submitted on behalf of the bank that it must have been the factor which 'tipped the scales'. I disagree. That is not what sub-s (5) says; it requires only that the desire should have influenced the decision. That requirement is satisfied if it was one of the factors which operated on the minds of those who made the decision. It need not have been the only factor or even the decisive one. In my judgment, it is not necessary to prove that, if the requisite desire had not been present, the company would not have entered into the transaction. That would be too high a test.

It was also submitted that the relevant time was the time when the debenture was created. That cannot be right. The relevant time was the time when the decision to grant it was made. In the present case that is not known with certainty. . . . But it does not matter. If the requisite desire was operating at all, it was operating throughout.

[His Lordship then ruled that the directors' motive had not been a desire to prefer the bank in the event of a liquidation, but to keep the company trading. He continued:]

Transaction at an undervalue
Section 238 of the 1986 Act is concerned with the depletion of a company's assets by transactions at an undervalue.

[His Lordship read s 238(4) and continued:]

The granting of the debenture was not a gift, nor was it without consideration. The consideration consisted of the bank's forbearance from calling in the overdraft and its honouring of cheques and making of fresh advances to the company during the continuance of the facility. The applicant relies therefore on para (b).

To come within that paragraph the transaction must be (i) entered into by the company; (ii) for a consideration; (iii) the value of which measured in money or money's worth; (iv) is significantly less than the value; (v) also measured in money or money's worth; (vi) of the consideration provided by the company. It requires a comparison to be made between the value obtained by the company for the transaction and the value of consideration provided by the company. Both values must be measurable in money or money's worth and both must be considered from the company's point of view.

In my judgment, the applicant's claim to characterise the granting of the bank's debenture as a transaction at an undervalue is misconceived. The mere creation of a security over a company's assets does not deplete them and does not come within the paragraph. By charging its assets the company appropriates them to meet the liabilities due to the secured creditor and adversely affects the rights of other creditors in the event of insolvency. But it does not deplete its assets or diminish their value. It retains the right to redeem and the right to sell or remortgage the charged assets. All it loses is the ability to apply the proceeds otherwise than in satisfaction of the secured debt. That is not something capable of valuation in monetary terms and is not customarily disposed of for value.

In the present case the company did not suffer that loss by reason of the grant of the debenture. Once the bank had demanded a debenture the company could not have sold or charged its assets without applying the proceeds in reduction of the overdraft; had it attempted to do so, the bank would at once have called in the overdraft. By granting the debenture the company parted with nothing of value, and the value of the consideration which it received in return was incapable of being measured in money or money's worth.

Counsel for the applicant (Mr Vos) submitted that the consideration which the company received was, with hindsight, of no value. It merely granted time and with it the opportunity to lose more money. But he could not and did not claim that the company ought to have received a fee or other capital sum in return for the debenture. That gives the game away. The applicant's real complaint is not that the company entered into the transaction at an undervalue but that it entered into it at all.

In my judgment, the transaction does not fall within sub-s (4), and it is unnecessary to consider the application of sub-s (5) which provides a defence to the claim in certain circumstances.

Conclusion
In my judgment, the granting of the debenture to the bank was neither a voidable preference nor a transaction at an undervalue and I dismiss the application.

Re Yeovil Glove Co Ltd [1965] Ch 148, Court of Appeal

The company had given its bank security by way of a floating charge less than 12 months before going into liquidation. At the time, it had an overdraft of £65,000. In the period between the creation of the charge and the liquidation the bank had met cheques drawn by the company totalling £110,000 and had received about the same sum in credits paid into the account by the company. It owed £67,000 to the bank and had other debts of some £94,000 when it went into liquidation. The Court of Appeal, applying the rule in *Clayton's* case (1816) 1 Mer 572, held that the whole of the £67,000 was cash advanced to the company subsequently to creation of the charge, so that the security was not caught by s 322 of the Companies Act 1948 (equivalent to IA 1986, s 245).

Harman LJ: . . . The only question which arises is whether there was cash paid to the company at the time of or subsequently to the creation of, and in consideration for, the charge. It was admittedly created within 12 months of the winding up at a time when the company was insolvent. It is further agreed that so far as the overdraft was incurred before the date of the floating charge, the charge would not be a valid security for it. The liquidator's claim is a simple one, namely, that as neither cash nor a covenant to pay cash was made at the time of the execution of the document, there was no consideration for it in the legal sense of that term except the bank's immediate forbearance. This seemed to me, I confess, an attractive argument. . . .

It was argued that consideration in law is a well-known term and ought to receive its ordinary meaning, and that subsequent payments provided by the bank to defray the company's day-to-day outgoings or wages or salaries or indebtedness to its suppliers by cheque would not be consideration in law for the execution of a charge bearing an earlier date unless those payments were made in pursuance of a promise contained in, or made at or before the date of, the charge itself. It was, however, pointed out that such subsequent payments would in fact not be made in consideration for the charge, but in consideration for the promise.

Now it is apparent on the face of the section that cash subsequently paid to the company may be within the exception if so paid in consideration for the anterior charge, and the argument is that the words 'in consideration for' in this section cannot, therefore, be used in the technical sense, but mean 'by reason of' or 'having regard to the existence of' the charge. Oddly enough, there is no reported decision on these words, nor are they discussed in any of the well-known textbooks. There has, however, come to light a decision of Lord Romer, when a judge of first instance, in *Re Thomas Mortimer Ltd* ([1965] Ch 186n) in 1925, a decision on the corresponding section of the Companies (Consolidation) Act 1908, which was in the same terms as the present section except that the period was three instead of 12 months. A transcript of this judgment was before us. The facts of that case were, I think, indistinguishable from those of the present, and Romer J held that payments by the bank after the date of the charge were made in consideration for the charge. . . .

That decision, if right, is enough to cover the present question, and Plowman J so held. . . .

In the instant case some £111,000, representing its trading receipts, was paid into the No 1 account by the company between the date of the charge and the appointment of the receiver, and the bank paid out during the same period about £110,000. Those payments were either made directly to or to the order of the company, or were transfers to the No 3 or No 4 accounts against advances previously made to the company to defray wages or salaries. All the company's accounts were at all times overdrawn, so that every payment was a provision of new money by means of which, on the figures, it is overwhelmingly probable that all the creditors existing at the date of the charge were in fact paid off.

There arises at this point the consideration which has given me most trouble in this case, namely, that as the No 1 account was carried on after as well as before the charge in precisely the same way, the bank would be entitled in accordance with the rule in *Clayton's Case* ((1816) 1 Mer 572), to treat payments in as being in satisfaction of the earliest advances made. The result is startling, for thus the bank pays itself out of moneys received subsequent to the charge for the whole of the company's indebtedness to it prior to the charge, and which was admittedly not covered by it. The result is that the whole of the pre-charge indebtedness is treated as paid off, and the bank is left bound to set off against its post-charge advances only the excess received after satisfying the company's pre-charge indebtedness. This would seem largely to nullify the effect of the section in the case of a company having at the date of the charge a largely overdrawn account with its bank, and which continues to trade subsequently. Of course, if at the date of the charge a line were drawn in the bank's books and a new account opened, then the company could successfully argue that payments out by the bank subsequent to the charge were, within a few hundred pounds, wholly repaid by the company from its trading receipts, with the result that no substantial sum would be due on the charge. It was, however, held by Romer J in *Re Thomas Mortimer Ltd* that *Clayton's Case* applied with the result stated, and I can see no escape from it, nor in spite of frequent pressing by the court did the appellant's counsel put forward any alternative. . . .

It follows, if the decision in *Re Thomas Mortimer Ltd* be right, that there is admittedly nothing left for the unsecured creditors. In my judgment Romer J's decision was right, and was rightly followed by Plowman J in the present case.

The fallacy in the appellant's argument lies, in my opinion, in the theory that, because the company's payments in to the bank after the date of the charge were more or less equal to the payments out by the bank during the same period, no 'new money' was provided by the bank. This is not the fact. Every such payment was in fact new money having regard to the state of the company's accounts, and it was in fact used to pay the company's creditors. That the indebtedness remained approximately at the same level was due to the fact that this was the limit set by the bank to the company's overdraft. I can find no reason to compel the bank to treat all payments in after the charge as devoted to post-charge indebtedness. The law is in fact the other way. . . .

[Willmer and Russell LJJ delivered concurring judgments.]

The third broad head under which the company's assets may be augmented in a liquidation is by making personal claims against the company's former officers and others for compensation for breach of duty or for contribution on some other ground. The relevant sections of IA 1986 are s 212 (misfeasance), s 213 (fraudulent trading) and s 214 (wrongful trading).

- *Misfeasance* (IA 1986, s 212). This provision does not create a new head of liability but simply provides a summary procedure by which the liquidator may recover property or claim compensation from the company's former officers on the grounds of accountability, misfeasance or breach of duty.
- *Fraudulent trading* (IA 1986, s 213). If, in the course of winding up, it is found that any business of the company has been carried on with intent to defraud creditors or for any fraudulent purpose, the court may order that those who were knowingly parties to this wrongdoing should contribute such sums as it thinks proper to the company's assets. For the purposes of this provision, actual dishonesty must be shown (*Re Patrick & Lyon Ltd* [1933] Ch 786).
- *Wrongful trading* (IA 1986, s 214). A director or former director of a company in insolvent liquidation may be ordered to contribute personally to the assets in the hands of the liquidator if he knew, or ought to have concluded, that there was no reasonable prospect that it would avoid going into insolvent liquidation and failed to take every step with a view to minimising the potential loss to the company's creditors that he ought to have taken. The case next cited illustrates the working of this section.

Re Produce Marketing Consortium Ltd (No 2) [1989] BCLC 520, Chancery Division

The company (PMC) was in the business of fruit importers and distributors. Its directors, David and Murphy, had continued to run the business when they ought to have known that it was insolvent and heading inevitably towards liquidation. They were ordered to make a payment of £75,000 to the liquidator.

Knox J: . . . Section 214 of the 1986 Act . . . reads, so far as is material, as follows:

(1) Subject to subsection (3) below, if in the course of the winding up of a company it appears that subsection (2) of this section applies in relation to a person who is or has been a director of the company, the court, on the application of the liquidator, may declare that the person is to be liable to make such contribution (if any) to the company's assets as the court thinks proper.

(2) This subsection applies in relation to a person if – (a) the company has gone into insolvent liquidation, (b) at some time before the commencement of the winding up of the company, that person knew or ought to have concluded that there was no reasonable prospect that the company would avoid going into insolvent liquidation, and (c) that person was a director of the company at that time. . . .

(3) The court shall not make a declaration under this section with respect to any person if it is satisfied that after the condition specified in subsection (2)(b) was first satisfied in relation to him that person took every step with a view to minimising the potential loss to the company's creditors as (assuming him to have known that there was no reasonable prospect that the company would avoid going into insolvent liquidation) he ought to have taken.

(4) For the purposes of subsections (2) and (3), the facts which a director of a company ought to know or ascertain, the conclusions which he ought to reach and the steps which he ought to take are those which would be known or ascertained, or reached or taken, by a reasonably diligent person having both – (a) the general knowledge, skill and experience that may reasonably be expected of a person carrying out the same functions as are carried out by that director in relation to the company, and (b) the general knowledge, skill and experience that that director has.

(5) The reference in subsection (4) to the functions carried out in relation to a company by a director of the company includes any functions which he does not carry out but which have been entrusted to him . . .

The first question is whether it appears that sub-s (2) applies to Mr David and Mr Murphy. There is no question but that they were directors at all material times and that PMC has gone into insolvent liquidation. The issue is whether at some time after 27 April 1986 and before 2 October 1987, when it went into insolvent liquidation, they knew or ought to have concluded that there was no reasonable prospect that PMC would avoid going into insolvent liquidation. It was inevitably conceded by counsel for the first respondent that this question has to be answered by the standards postulated by sub-s (4), so that the facts which Mr David and Mr Murphy ought to have known or ascertained and the conclusions that they ought to have reached are not limited to those which they themselves showing reasonable diligence and having the general knowledge, skill and experience which they respectively had, would have known, ascertained or reached but also those that a person with the general knowledge, skill and experience of someone carrying out their functions would have known, ascertained or reached.

The 1986 Act now has two separate provisions; s 213 dealing with fraudulent trading . . . and s 214 which deals with what the sidenote calls 'wrongful trading'. It is evident that Parliament intended to widen the scope of the legislation under which directors who trade on when the company is insolvent may, in appropriate circumstances, be required to make a contribution to the assets of the company which, in practical terms, means its creditors.

Two steps in particular were taken in the legislative enlargement of the court's jurisdiction. First, the requirement for an intent to defraud and fraudulent purpose was not retained as an essential. . . .

I pause here to observe that at no stage before me has it been suggested that either Mr David or Mr Murphy fell into this category.

The second enlargement is that the test to be applied by the court has become one under which the director in question is to be judged by the standards of what can reasonably be expected of a person fulfilling his functions, and showing reasonable diligence in doing so. I accept the submission of counsel for the first respondent in this connection, that the requirement to have regard to the functions to be carried out by the director in question, in relation to the company in question, involves having regard to the particular company and its business. It follows that the general knowledge, skill and experience postulated will be much less extensive in a small company in a modest way of business, with simple accounting procedures and equipment, than it will be in a large company with sophisticated procedures.

Nevertheless, certain minimum standards are to be assumed to be attained. Notably there is an obligation laid on companies to cause accounting records to be kept which are such as to disclose with reasonable accuracy at any time the financial position of the company at that time: see the Companies Act 1985, s 221(1) and (2)(a). . . .

As I have already mentioned, the liquidator gave evidence that the accounting records of PMC were adequate for the purposes of its business. The preparation of accounts was woefully late, more especially in relation to those dealing with the year ending 30 September 1985 which should have been laid and delivered by the end of July 1986.

The knowledge to be imputed in testing whether or not directors knew or ought to have concluded that there was no reasonable prospect of the company avoiding insolvent liquidation is not limited to the documentary material actually available at the given time. This appears from s 214(4) which includes a reference to facts which a director of a company ought not only to know but those which he ought to ascertain, a word which does not appear in sub-s (2)(b). In my judgment this indicates that there is to be included by way of factual information not only what was actually there but what, given reasonable diligence and an appropriate level of general knowledge, skill and experience, was ascertainable. This leads me to the conclusion in this case that I should assume, for the purposes of applying the test in s 214(2), that the financial results for the year ending 30 September 1985 were known at the end of July 1986 at least to the extent of the size of the deficiency of assets over liabilities.

Mr David and Mr Murphy, although they did not have the accounts in their hands until January 1987, did, I find, know that the previous trading year had been a very bad one. They had a close and intimate knowledge of the business and they had a shrewd idea whether the turnover was up or down. In fact it was badly down in that year to £526,459 and although I have no doubt that they did not know in July 1986 that it was that precise figure, I have no doubt that they had a good rough idea of what it was and in particular that it was well down on the previous year. A major drop in turnover meant almost as night follows day that there was a substantial loss incurred, as indeed there was. That in turn meant again, as surely as night follows day, a substantial increase in the deficit of assets over liabilities.

That deals with their actual knowledge but in addition I have to have regard to what they have to be treated as having known or ascertained and that includes the actual deficit of assets over liabilities of £132,870. This was £80,000 over Mr David's personal guarantee. It was a deficit that, for an indefinite period in the future could not be made good even if the optimistic prognostications of level of turnover entertained by Mr David and Mr Murphy were achieved.

Counsel for the first respondent was not able to advance any particular calculation as constituting a basis for concluding that there was a prospect of insolvent liquidation being avoided. He is not to be criticised for that for in my judgment there was none available. Once the loss in the year ending 30 September 1985 was incurred PMC was in irreversible decline, assuming (as I must) that the respondents had no plans for altering the company's business and proposed to go on drawing the level of reasonable remuneration that they were currently receiving. . . .

The next question which arises is whether there is a case under s 214(3) for saying that after the end of July 1986 the respondents took every step with a view to minimising the potential loss to the creditors of PMC as, assuming them to have known that there was no reasonable prospect of PMC avoiding insolvent liquidation, they ought to have taken. This clearly has to be answered No, since they went on trading for another year. . . .

I am therefore driven to the conclusion that the court's discretion arises under s 214(1). . . .

In my judgment the jurisdiction under s 214 is primarily compensatory rather than penal. Prima facie the appropriate amount that a director is declared to be liable to contribute is the amount by which the company's assets can be discerned to have been depleted by the director's conduct which caused the discretion under sub-s (1) to arise. But Parliament has indeed chosen very wide words of discretion and it would be undesirable to seek to spell out limits on that discretion.

[His Lordship reviewed the facts, and ordered David and Murphy to make a contribution of £75,000.]

Administration of the estate. The company's creditors 'prove' for their debts in the liquidation by submitting a claim in a prescribed form to the liquidator, which he may admit in whole or in part or reject, subject to an appeal to the court. Contingent and future liabilities are admitted at an estimated or discounted value. A creditor who is also indebted to the company normally has the right to *set off* his indebtedness against his claim and either prove for the balance or account for it to the liquidator: thus, to the extent that he can exercise this right, his claim is paid off in full. The House of Lords, in *National Westminster Bank Ltd v Halesowen Presswork & Assemblies Ltd* [1972] AC 785, HL held that the right of set-off is a mandatory feature of insolvency law which is not capable of being waived or varied by contract.

A *secured creditor* may exercise his right to have recourse to the security independently of the liquidation. If there is a surplus after realising the security, he must account for it to the liquidator; if a shortfall, he may prove for the outstanding balance. Alternatively, he may elect to surrender his security and prove for the whole of his debt as an unsecured creditor.

The Act provides that certain debts, such as claims (within prescribed limits) by the Crown in respect of unpaid PAYE, National Insurance contributions and VAT and by employees for unpaid wages and salaries, shall be entitled to be paid in priority to other those of creditors (including the holder of any floating charge) in a winding up (IA 1986, ss 175, 386 and Sch 6). The list of preferential debts is the same as applies in bankruptcy and in receivership.

The *order of application of assets* is as follows: (1) expenses of the liquidation, (2) preferential debts, (3) debts secured by a floating charge, (4) unsecured debts, (5) debts payable to members of the company in their capacity as members (eg unpaid dividends): IA 1986, s 74(2)(f)). Any surplus remaining after satisfaction of all the company's liabilities is payable to the members in accordance with their respective rights and liabilities. If the assets are insufficient to pay the debts of any category of creditor in full, the claims of all those in that category abate proportionately.

Forms

The forms which follow are reproduced by permission of the persons and bodies mentioned on pp ix–xi, to whom acknowledgment is again made.

Forms

1 Commercial invoice

INVOICE TO

M/S BONGAH TOSE MACHINALET KESHAVARZI
TEHRAN
I.R.O. IRAN.

DELIVER TO

INVOICE   ES No.   1484/4

STANDEN ENGINEERING LIMITED
HEREWARD WORKS,
STATION ROAD, ELY,
CAMBRIDGESHIRE CB7 4BP
ENGLAND

Telephone: 0353 661111   Telex: 81486
Fax: 0353 662370

DATE	ORDER NO.	DATE DESPATCHED
5.6.91		

QTY.	DESCRIPTION	AMOUNT
		PDS.
	AS PER L/C NO 69/005/002983	
168 PAIRS	CONSISTING OF PART SHIPMENT OF:	
	1000 PAIRS OF NARROW WHEELS TO FIT UNIVERSAL 650 M.	
	AT PDS.679/77 PER PAIR COST	114201/36
	AT PDS. 78/75 PER PAIR FREIGHT	13230/00
	AT PDS.115/6743 PER PAIR USANCE	19433/28

	TOTAL C & F TEHRAN	146864/64

WE HEREBY STATE THAT THE MERCHANDISE IS AS PER PROFORMA
INVOICE NO. 1375 DD 8.11.89

IRANIAN CUSTOMS TARIFF NO. 87/06 B5

WE CERTIFY THIS INVOICE TO BE TRUE AND CORRECT AND IN
ACCORDANCE WITH OUR BOOKS, ALSO THAT THE GOODS ARE OF
ENGLAND ORIGIN.

WE HEREBY CERTIFY THAT THE PRICES STATED IN THIS INVOICE
ARE THE CURRENT EXPORT MARKET PRICES FOR THE MERCHANDISE
DESCRIBED THEREIN AND WE ACCEPT FULL RESPONSIBILITY FOR
ANY INACCURACIES OR ERRORS THEREIN.

TOTAL NETT AND GROSS WEIGHT 53760 KGS.

FOR AND ON BEHALF OF STANDEN ENGINEERING LIMITED

....
K. J. T. LINCOLN, SALES MANAGER

	C & F TEHRAN	TOTAL	PDS. 146864/64

NOTES

1. This invoice relates to the same transaction as the combined transport bill of lading which appears as Form 2, below. Accompanying it also were a certificate of origin, signed by the local Chamber of Commerce, and an international inspection certificate, confirming that the goods shipped complied strictly in quality and quantity with the specification of the goods in this invoice. These documents were all listed in the letter of credit as required to be produced as conditions of payment.

2. The contract was on C & F terms (see above, p 461), and so the sellers were not obliged to make arrangements regarding insurance, or to produce a policy or certificate of insurance.

3. 'Usance' is here used by the parties to refer to the cost of obtaining the letter of credit and other banking charges. In its more usual meaning, 'usance' is the period of time allowed for the payment of a bill of exchange, especially a foreign bill (see the Bills of Exchange Act 1882, s 4). It would normally be the buyer's obligation to arrange for the letter of credit directly with his own bank.

2 Combined transport bill of lading

Consignor		

Consignor
M/S STANDEN ENGINEERING LIMITED
HEREWARD WORKS. STATION ROAD
ELY CAMBRIDGESHIRE CB7 4BP ENGLAND
TEL: 0353 661111.

FBL

B I F A

FBL No.   844

Customs Reference/Status

G
B

Shipper's Reference

Forwarder's Reference
616 9106 844 01

Consigned to order of
TO THE ORDER OF
BANK SADERAT IRAN

NEGOTIABLE FIATA
COMBINED TRANSPORT
BILL OF LADING

issued subject to ICC Uniform Rules for a Combined
Transport Document (ICC publication 298)

I C C

Notify address
"NOTIFY PARTY"   APPLICANT
M/S BONGAH TOSE MACHINALET KESHAVARZI
TEHRAN I.R.O. IRAN.

TRANS CARGO

Link House, 62/66 High Street,
Billericay, Essex CM12 9BS
Phone: 0277 633 666
Fax No: 0277 626643
Tlx: 995878 TCARGO

Place of Receipt	
Ocean Vessel TRUCK	Port of Loading ELY, ENGLAND
Port of Discharge TEHRAN	Place of Delivery TEHRAN

Marks and Numbers	Number and Kind of Packages	Description of Goods	Gross Weight	Measurement
	168 (ONE HUNDRED AND SIXTY EIGHT) PAIRS - S.T.B. ---------------------------------- 168 PAIRS CONSISTING OF PART SHIPMENT OF: 1000 PAIRS OF NARROW WHEELS TO FIT UNIVERSAL 650 M. MERCHANDISE IS AS PER PROFORMA INVOICE NO.1375 DD 8.11.89.		GRS WT. 53760 KGS NET WT. 53760 KGS	

GOODS EN ROUTE
FREIGHT PREPAID
IRANIAN CUSTOMS TARIFF NO. 87/06 B5
SHIPMENT:FROM ENGLAND TO TEHRAN BY TRUCK
INSURANCE EFFECTED IN IRAN
IRAN INSURANCE CO, TLX NO.214154
BANK SADERAT IRAN, MEIDAN ESTEGHLAL BRANCH, L/C NO. 69/005/002983
BANK SADERAT IRAN, LONDON -REF. DC 41175

according to the declaration of the consignor.

The goods and instructions are accepted and dealt with subject to the Standard Conditions printed overleaf.

COPY

Taken in charge in apparent good order and condition, unless otherwise noted herein, at the place of receipt for transport and delivery as mentioned above.

One of these Combined Transport Bills of Lading must be surrendered duly endorsed in exchange for the goods. In Witness whereof the original Combined Transport Bills of Lading all of this tenor and date have been signed in the number stated below, one of which being accomplished the other(s) to be void.

Freight Amount £13230.00	Freight Payable at BILLERICAY	Place and date of issue; Stamp and signature BILLERICAY, 28.06.1991.
Cargo Insurance through the undersigned ☐ not covered ☐ Covered according to attached Policy	Number of Original FBL's THREE (3).	**TRANSCARGO** International UK Ltd., Link House, 62-66 High Street, BILLERICAY, ESSEX, CM12 9BS
For delivery of goods please apply to TIZPAR INTERNATIONAL TRANSPORT (PRIVATE CO LTD) NO. 447 SAADI AVENUE, TEHRAN-11, IRAN. PHONE: 021 304931/5 - TELEX: 212464		

Standard Conditions (1984) governing
FIATA COMBINED TRANSPORT BILLS OF LADING

Definitions Merchant means and includes the Shipper, the Consignor, the Consignee, the Holder of this Bill of Lading, the Receiver and the Owner of the Goods. The Freight Forwarder means the issuer of this Bill of Lading as named on the face of it.

The headings set forth below are for easy reference only.

CONDITIONS

1. Applicability
Notwithstanding the heading "Combined Transport Bill of Lading", the provisions set out and referred to in this document shall also apply if the transport as described on the face of the Bill of Lading is performed by one mode of transport only.

2. Issuance of the "Combined Transport Bill of Lading".
2.1 By the issuance of this "Combined Transport Bill of Lading" the Freight Forwarder:
a) undertakes to perform and or in his own name to procure the performance of the entire transport, from the place at which the goods are taken in charge to the place designated for delivery in this Bill of Lading.
b) assumes liability as set out in these Conditions.
2.2 For the purposes and subject to the provisions of this Bill of Lading, the Freight Forwarder shall be responsible for the acts and omissions of any person of whose services he makes use for the performance of the contract evidenced by this Bill of Lading.

3. Negotiability and title to the goods
3.1 By accepting this Bill of Lading the Merchant and his transferees agree with the Freight Forwarder that unless it is marked "non-negotiable", it shall constitute title to the goods and the holder, by endorsement of this Bill of Lading, shall be entitled to receive or to transfer the goods herein mentioned.
3.2 This Bill of Lading shall be prima facie evidence of the taking in charge by the Freight Forwarder of the goods as herein described. However, proof to the contrary shall not be admissible when this Bill of Lading has been negotiated or transferred for valuable consideration to a third party acting in good faith.

4. Dangerous Goods and Indemnity
4.1 The Merchant shall comply with rules which are mandatory according to the national law or by reason of international Convention, relating to the carriage of goods of a dangerous nature, and shall in any case inform the Freight Forwarder in writing of the exact nature of the danger, before goods of a dangerous nature are taken in charge by the Freight Forwarder and indicate to him, if need be, the precautions to be taken.
4.2 If the Merchant fails to provide such information and the Freight Forwarder is unaware of the dangerous nature of the goods and the necessary precautions to be taken and if, at any time, they are deemed to be a hazard to life or property, they may at any place be unloaded, destroyed or rendered harmless, as circumstances may require, without compensation, and the Merchant shall be liable for all loss, damage, delay or expenses arising out of their being taken in charge, or their carriage, or of any service incidental thereto.
The burden of proving the Freight Forwarder knew the exact nature of the danger constituted by the carriage of the said goods shall rest upon the person entitled to the goods.
4.3 If any goods shipped with the knowledge of the Freight Forwarder as to their dangerous nature shall become a danger to the vehicle or cargo, they may in like manner be unloaded or landed at any place or destroyed or rendered innocuous by the Freight Forwarder, without liability on the part of the Freight Forwarder, except to General Average, if any.

5. Description of Goods and Merchant's Packing
5.1 The Consignor shall be deemed to have guaranteed to the Freight Forwarder the accuracy, at the time the goods were taken in charge by the Freight Forwarder, of the description of the goods, marks, number, quantity, weight and/or volume as furnished by him, and the Consignor shall indemnify the Freight Forwarder against all loss, damage and expenses arising or resulting from inaccuracies in or inadequacy of such particulars. The right of the Freight Forwarder to such indemnity shall in no way limit his responsibility and liability under this Bill of Lading to any person other than the Consignor.
5.2 Without prejudice to Clause 6 (A) (2) (c), the Merchant shall be liable for any loss, damage or injury caused by faulty or insufficient packing of goods or by faulty loading or packing within containers and trailers and on his behalf or packing has been performed by the Merchant or on behalf of the Merchant by a person other than the Freight Forwarder, or by the defect or unsuitability of the containers, trailers or flats, when supplied by the Merchant, and shall indemnify the Freight Forwarder against any additional expenses so caused.

6. Extent of Liability
A. 1) The Freight Forwarder shall be liable for loss of or damage to the goods occurring between the time when he takes the goods into his charge and the time of delivery.
2) The Freight Forwarder shall, however, be relieved of liability for any loss or damage if such loss or damage was caused by:
a) an act or omission of the Merchant, or person other than the Freight Forwarder acting on behalf of the Merchant or from whom the Freight Forwarder took the goods in charge;
b) insufficiency or defective condition of the packaging or marks and/or numbers;
c) handling, loading, stowage or unloading of the goods by the Merchant or any person acting on behalf of the Merchant;
d) inherent vice of the goods;
e) strike, lockout, stoppage or restraint of labour, the consequences of which the Freight Forwarder could not avoid by the exercise of reasonable diligence.
f) any cause or event which the Freight Forwarder could not avoid and the consequences whereof he could not prevent by the exercise of reasonable diligence;
g) a nuclear incident if the operator of a nuclear installation or a person acting for him is liable for this damage under an applicable International Convention or national law governing liability in respect of nuclear energy.
3) The burden of proving that the loss or damage was due to one or more of the above causes or events shall rest upon the Freight Forwarder.
When the Freight Forwarder establishes that, in the circumstances of the case, the loss or damage could be attributed to one or more of the causes or events specified in b) to d) above, it shall be presumed that it was so caused. The claimant shall, however, be entitled to prove that the loss or damage was not, in fact, caused wholly or partly by one or more of these causes or events.
B When in accordance with clause 6, A.1 the Freight Forwarder is liable to pay compensation in respect of loss or damage to the goods and the stage of transport where the loss or damage occurred is known, the liability of the Freight Forwarder in respect of such loss or damage shall be determined by the provisions contained in any international Convention or national law, which provisions
(i) cannot be departed from by private contract, to the detriment of the claimant, and
(ii) would have applied if the Claimant had made a separate and direct contract with the Freight Forwarder in respect of the particular stage of transport where the loss or damage occurred and received as evidence thereof any particular document which must be issued in order to make such international convention or national law applicable

7. Paramount Clause
The Hague Rules contained in the International Convention for the unification of certain rules relating to Bills of Lading dated Brussels 25th August 1924, or in those countries where they are already in force the Hague-Visby Rules contained in the Protocol of Brussels dated February 23rd 1968, as enacted in the Country of Shipment shall apply to all carriage of goods by sea and where no mandatory international or national law applies to the carriage of goods by inland waterways also, and such provisions shall apply to all goods whether carried on deck or under deck.

8. Limitation Amount
8.1 When the Freight Forwarder is liable for compensation in respect of loss of or damage

to the goods, such compensation shall be calculated by reference to the value of such goods at the place and time they are delivered to the Consignee in accordance with the contract or should have been so delivered.
8.2 The value of the goods shall be fixed according to the current commodity exchange price, or, if there be no such price, according to the current market price, or if there be no commodity exchange price or current market price, by reference to the normal value of goods of the same kind and quality.
8.3 Compensation shall not, however, exceed 2 SDR (SDR = Special Drawing Right units per kilo of gross weight of the goods lost or damaged, unless, with the consent of the Freight Forwarder, the Merchant has declared a higher value for the goods and such higher value has been stated in the CT Bill of Lading, in which case such higher value shall be the limit. However, the Freight Forwarder shall not, in any case, be liable for an amount greater than the actual loss to the person entitled to make the claim.

9. Delay, Consequential Loss, etc.
Arrival times are not guaranteed by the Freight Forwarder. If the Freight Forwarder is held liable in respect of delay, consequential loss or damage other than loss of or damage to the goods, the liability of the Freight Forwarder shall be limited to double the freight for the transport covered by this Bill of Lading, or the value of the goods as determined in Clause 8, whichever is the less.

10. Defences
10.1 The defences and limits of liability provided for in these Conditions shall apply in any action against the Freight Forwarder for loss of or damage or delay to the goods whether the action be founded in contract or in tort.
10.2 The Freight Forwarder shall not be entitled to the benefit of the limitation of liability provided for in paragraph 3 of Clause 8 if it is proved that the loss or damage resulted from an act or omission of the Freight Forwarder done with intent to cause damage or recklessly and with knowledge that damage would probably result.

11. Liability of Servants and Sub-contractors
11.1 If an action for loss of or damage to the goods is brought against a person referred to in paragraph 2 of Clause 2, such person shall be entitled to avail himself of the defences and limits of liability which the Freight Forwarder is entitled to invoke under these Conditions.
11.2 However, if it is proved that the loss or damage resulted from an act or omission of this person, done with intent to cause damage or recklessly and with knowledge that damage would probably result, such person shall not be entitled to benefit of limitation of liability provided for in paragraph 3 of Clause 8.
11.3 Subject to the provisions of paragraph 2 of Clause 10 and paragraph 2 of this Clause the aggregate of the amounts recoverable from the Freight Forwarder and the persons referred to in paragraph 2 of Clause 2 shall in no case exceed the limits provided for in these Conditions.

12. Method and Route of Transportation
The Freight Forwarder reserves to himself a reasonable liberty as to the means, route and procedure to be followed in the handling, storage and transportation of goods.

13. Delivery
If delivery of the goods or any part thereof is not taken by the Merchant, at the time and place when and where the Freight Forwarder is entitled to call upon the Merchant to take delivery thereof, the Freight Forwarder shall be entitled to store the goods or the part thereof at the sole risk of the Merchant, where upon the liability of the Freight Forwarder in respect of the goods or that part thereof stored as aforesaid (as the case may be) shall wholly cease and the cost of such storage (if paid by the Freight Forwarder) shall forthwith upon demand be paid by the Merchant to the Freight Forwarder.

14. Freight and Charges
14.1 Freight shall be paid in cash without discount and, whether prepayable or payable at destination, shall be considered as earned on receipt of the goods and not to be returned or relinquished in any event.
14.2 Freight and all other amounts mentioned in this Bill of Lading are to be paid in the currency named in the Bill of Lading or, at the Freight Forwarder's option in the currency of the country of dispatch or destination at the highest rate of exchange for bankers sight bills current for prepayable freight on the day of dispatch and for freight payable at destination on the day when the Merchant is notified of arrival of the goods there or on the date of withdrawal of the delivery order, whichever rate is the higher, or at the option of the Freight Forwarder on the date of the Bill of Lading.
14.3 All dues, taxes and charges or other expenses in connection with the goods shall be paid by the Merchant.
14.4 The Merchant shall reimburse the Freight Forwarder in proportion to the amount of freight for any costs for deviation or delay or any other increase of costs of whatever nature caused by war, warlike operations, epidemics, strikes, government directions or force majeure.
14.5 The Merchant warrants the correctness of the declaration of contents, insurance, weight, measurements or value of the goods but the Freight Forwarder reserves the right to have the contents inspected and the weight, measurements or value verified. If on such inspection it is found the declaration is not correct it is agreed that a sum equal either to five times the difference between the correct figure and the freight charged, or to double the correct freight less the freight charged, whichever sum is the smaller, shall be payable as liquidated damage to the Freight Forwarder for his inspection costs and losses of freight on other goods notwithstanding any other sum having been stated on the Bill of Lading as freight payable.

15. Lien
The Freight Forwarder shall have a lien on the goods for any amount due under this Bill of Lading including storage fees and for the cost of recovering same and may enforce such lien in any reasonable manner which he may think fit.

16. General Average
The Merchant shall indemnify the Freight Forwarder in respect of any claims of a General Average nature which may be made on him and shall provide such security as may be required by the Freight Forwarder in this connection.

17. Notice
Unless notice of loss of or damage to the goods and the general nature of it be given in writing to the Freight Forwarder or the persons referred to in paragraph 2 of Clause 2, at the place of delivery before or at the time of the removal of the goods into the custody of the person entitled to delivery thereof under this Bill of Lading, or if the loss or damage be not apparent, within seven consecutive days thereafter, such removal shall be prima facie evidence of the delivery by the Freight Forwarder of the goods as described in this Bill of Lading.

18. Non-delivery
Failure to effect delivery within 90 days after the expiry of a time limit agreed and expressed in a CT Bill of Lading, or, where no time limit is agreed and so expressed, failure to effect delivery within 90 days after the time it would be reasonable to allow for diligent completion of the combined transport operation shall, in the absence of evidence to the contrary, give to the party entitled to receive delivery, the right to treat the goods as lost.

19. Time Bar
The Freight Forwarder shall be discharged of all liability under the rules of these Conditions, unless suit is brought within nine months after
(i) the delivery of the goods, or
(ii) the date when the goods should have been delivered, or
(iii) the date when in accordance with Clause 18, failure to deliver the goods would in the absence of evidence to the contrary, give to the party entitled to receive delivery, the right to treat the goods as lost.

20. Jurisdiction
Actions against the Freight Forwarder may only be instituted in the country where the Freight Forwarder has his principal place of business and shall be decided according to the law of such country.

NOTE

This is not a bill of lading in the traditional form used for the carriage of goods by sea, but a modification of that form used for 'combined transport' (see above, p 464). (The standard conditions have since been revised.)

3 Application to open documentary credit

Request to Open an Irrevocable Documentary Credit

MIDLAND
TRADE & INTERNATIONAL
BANKING SERVICES

TO: **Midland Bank plc** _____ Branch/IBC

Date: _____

For Bank Use
L/C No. _____ D/T No. _____ CID No. _____

INDICATE CHOICE WITH [X] **REMAINDER TO BE TYPED OR COMPLETED IN BLACK INK IN BLOCK CAPITALS**

**APPLICANT'S NAME
& ADDRESS**

Applicant's reference *(Not transmitted)*

**BENEFICIARY'S NAME
& ADDRESS**

METHOD OF ADVICE [ ] Teletransmission (Swift or Telex)　　[ ] Mail　　[ ] Courier

TRANSFERABILITY　　This credit is transferable [ ]　　To _____ only

EXPIRY DATE　　　　　　　**PLACE** _____

LATEST DATE FOR SHIPMENT _____

PERIOD FOR PRESENTATION　Documents to be presented within _____ days of the date of the transport document but in any event within the credit validity.

AMOUNT Currency _____ Figures _____

　　　　Words _____

AMOUNT VARIATION +/- _____ %

Available by [ ] Payment　　[ ] Acceptance　　[ ] Negotiation　　[ ] Deferred Payment

With drafts *(if applicable)* **drawn at** _____

PARTSHIPMENTS [ ] Allowed　　[ ] Prohibited

TRANSHIPMENTS [ ] Allowed　　[ ] Prohibited

SHIPMENT/DESPATCH/TAKING IN CHARGE

From _____ To _____

INCOTERMS _____ (ie EXW / FCA / FAS / FOB / CFR / CIF / CPT / CIP / DAF / DES / DEQ / DDU / DDP)

PLACE _____

QUANTITY & DESCRIPTION OF GOODS *(avoiding excessive detail)*

1016-8 (12/93 - UOI = 1 x PD25)　　　　　*member* HSBC ⬣ *group*

DOCUMENTS REQUIRED	[X]	Invoice in _____ copies

TRANSPORT DOCUMENT [ ] **Full set "on board" Marine Bills of Lading**

EITHER: [ ] to order & blank endorsed   [ ] to order of Applicant

OR: [ ] **Non-Negotiable Sea Waybill** evidencing goods consigned to Applicant

OR: [ ] **Full set Multimodal Transport Document**

[ ] to order & blank endorsed   [ ] to order of Applicant

OR: [ ] **Air Waybill** evidencing goods consigned to Applicant

[ ] Air Waybill to show actual flight number & date

OR: [ ] **CMR** (Road Transport)

OR: [ ] **Rail** Consignment Note   } evidencing goods consigned to Applicant

OTHER: (specify) [ ] _____

TRANSPORT DOCUMENT TO BE MARKED [ ] **Freight paid**   [ ] **Freight payable at destination**

NOTIFY PARTY (if any)

INSURANCE DOCUMENT

EITHER: [ ] **Insurance Certificate**   [ ] **Insurance Policy**   [ ] **Insurance document not required**

RISKS TO BE COVERED

[ ] Institute Marine Cargo Clauses (A)   [ ] Institute Air Cargo Clauses (A)   [X] War Risks

[ ] Other Risks (specify) _____

INSURED AMOUNT

[ ] Gross Invoice Amount Plus 10%   [ ] Other Amount (specify)

[ ] **Packing List** in ___ copies   [ ] **Certificate of** _____ **Origin** in ___ copies

[ ] **Weight List** in ___ copies   [ ] **GSP Certificate of Origin Form 'A'** in ___ copies

OTHER DOCUMENTS (if any)

ADDITIONAL CONDITIONS (if any)

CHARGES
Unless otherwise stipulated all charges will be for the account of the applicant and will be taken in Sterling

Midland charges payable by: [ ] Applicant   [ ] Beneficiary

Other charges payable by: [ ] Applicant   [ ] Beneficiary

DRAWINGS under this credit are to be debited to our   [ ] Sterling   [ ] _____ Currency   Account No. _____

Please convert currency drawings utilising   [ ] Spot rate   [ ] Forward Contract   [ ] Currency Option No. _____

Please open for our account a documentary credit in accordance with the above mentioned particulars, and except so far as otherwise expressly stated, subject to the Uniform Customs & Practice for Documentary Credits in operation at the time of issuance.

SIGNED For and on behalf of the Company _____ as Applicant

Guidance Notes for Documentary Credit Applicants

GENERAL

All documentary Credits (D/Cs) will be issued subject to the Uniform Customs and Practice for Documentary Credits (UCP) applicable at the time of issuance as published by the International Chamber of Commerce (ICC). The issuance of any credit will be at the discretion of the bank and subject to availability of a banking facility sanctioned for this purpose. It is emphasised that in documentary credit operations, banks deal exclusively with documents and not with the underlying goods or services (UCP Article 4). The bank is not directly concerned with the proper fulfilment of the contract between buyer and seller.

Advising Bank	Wherever possible, offices of the HSBC Group will be utilised unless otherwise stipulated in 'additional conditions'.
Documents	All D/C terms and conditions should be covered by the documents called for in the credit; otherwise they will be disregarded. Documents which appear on their face to comply with the D/C terms and conditions will be accepted as due presentation under the credit.
UCP	As an applicant of a Documentary Credit you should be familiar with the requirements of UCP. Copies of the current publication may be obtained directly from the ICC upon payment of a fee.

Expiry

Date of Expiry	The latest date that documents may be presented by the beneficiary at the place of expiry. This should be less than or equal to the latest shipment date plus the period for presentation.
Period for Presentation	The number of days between the shipment and expiry dates. Usually 21 days, but may depend upon how quickly the documents need to be available to you.
Place of Expiry	D/Cs will usually expire at the counters of the advising bank in the country of the beneficiary.

Availability

Negotiation	Used primarily for D/Cs in currencies different from that of the beneficiary's country. If you select this option, the D/C will be available for negotiation at the counters of the advising bank in the country of the beneficiary until the D/C expiry date. Your account will be debited upon presentation to us of conforming documents (D/C payable at sight) or on the maturity date (D/C payable at usance). You should allow up to 21 days after expiry for the transmission of documents to the UK.
Acceptance/ Deferred Payment	Select this option where you have agreed with your supplier extended terms of payment (usance period). In the case of acceptances, drafts will be drawn on the advising bank and settled by them at maturity. Deferred Payment credits have the same effect but drafts are not drawn. This can help to reduce the beneficiary's liability to stamp duty in countries where this is still levied on this type of transaction. In both cases your account is debited on the maturity date. (See also "Settlement in Foreign Currency")
Payment	The D/C will be available at the counters of the advising bank for payment of sight drafts drawn on them until the expiry date. Your account will be debited upon presentation to us of conforming documents. Allow up to 21 days after expiry for the transmission of documents to the UK. Please note that you are responsible for any interest costs between the date payment is effected in the foreign centre to the value date of our remittance in settlement of the presentation. Any such interest will be charged at the bank's current overdraft rate for the currency concerned.
	Alternatively, you may permit the advising bank to claim from us telegraphically with value date three working days after presentation of documents to them. In this case your account will be debited on the value date and you will not pay any interest cost. However, it is most unlikely that the documents will have arrived at the time your account is debited.
Other D/C Types	Appropriate advice will be provided upon request.
Transferability	Any further instructions and/or restrictions on transfer should be incorporated in "Additional Conditions".
Transhipment	We interpret instructions to prohibit transhipment as denying the applicability of UCP500 sub-articles 23d, 24d, 27c, 28d, as appropriate. Otherwise transhipment should be allowed.
Settlement in Foreign Currency	In order to effect timely settlement of drawings, your settlement instructions should appear on the application form. In any event, for maturing payments, we require your settlement instructions at least two working days prior to the due date. If you require advice on currency hedging products please contact your local International Banking Centre.
Beneficiaries in the UK	All such credits will be advised directly to the beneficiary. We believe this to be in the best interests of all parties.
Charges	Unless otherwise stipulated, all bank charges will be for account of the applicant. The most common commercial practice is for issuing bank charges to be borne by the applicant with foreign bank charges being for account of the beneficiary. Please ensure that your application form is correctly marked. Please note that Midland Bank charges will be calculated in Sterling.

Amendments to the D/C Terms and Conditions

Forms are available upon request for the provision of your amendment instructions to the bank.

Any amendment must be agreed by all parties to the credit. It should be noted that an amendment may be rejected by the beneficiary at any time prior to presentation of documents.

Any increase or reduction in the value of the credit should be fully explained. For example, an increase may reflect an increase in the quantity of goods or in the unit price.

Please ensure that any alterations made to the terms and conditions of the credit are fully reflected in amendments to the documents called for by the credit.

4 Irrevocable documentary credit

```
OUR REFERENCE 09L/999478
-----------------------
```

```
DOCUMENTARY CREDITS DEPARTMENT
P.O.BOX 181
27-32 POULTRY
LONDON EC2P 2BX
```

```
IRREVOCABLE DOCUMENTARY CREDIT
------------------------------
```

```
TO:
```

```
HONGKONG AND SHANGHAI BANKING CORPORATION LTD
P O BOX 10118
1 QUEENS ROAD CENTRAL
HONG KONG
```

WE ARE PLEASED HEREBY TO ISSUE OUR IRREVOCABLE DOCUMENTARY CREDIT
09L/999478 AS DETAILED BELOW:

BENEFICIARY: APPLICANT:

INTERNATIONAL SELLERS LIMITED   BUYERS (UK) LIMITED
35TH FLOOR, TWO EXCHANGE SQUARE   LOWER STREET
CONNAUGHT PLACE, HONG KONG   LONDON SE1

DATE OF EXPIRY: SEPTEMBER 30, 1994   PLACE OF EXPIRY: HONG KONG

AMOUNT: USD 202,500.00 PLUS OR MINUS 5%
(TWO HUNDRED TWO THOUSAND FIVE HUNDRED AND 00/00`S UNITED STATES DOLLARS
PLUS OR MINUS 5%)

PARTIAL SHIPMENT: NOT ALLOWED   TRANSHIPMENTS: ALLOWED

SHIPMENT FROM: HONG KONG PORT
FOR TRANSPORTATION TO: ANY UK PORT
NO LATER THAN: SEPTEMBER 15, 1994

THIS CREDIT IS AVAILABLE WITH ANY BANK BY NEGOTIATION OF DRAFTS DRAWN BY
THE BENEFICIARY AT SIGHT ON MIDLAND BANK PLC P.O. BOX 181 27-32 POULTRY
LONDON EC2P 2BX (AND NO OTHER ADDRESS) FOR 100% OF INVOICE VALUE MARKED
"DRAWN UNDER DOCUMENTARY CREDIT NUMBER 09L/999478 OF MIDLAND BANK PLC."

ACCOMPANIED BY THE FOLLOWING DOCUMENTS:

member HSBC **X** *group*

Registered in England (No. 14259)
Registered Office: Poultry London EC2P 2BX

OUR REFERENCE 09L/999478

SIGNED COMMERCIAL INVOICE IN ORIGINAL AND TWO COPIES

FULL SET CLEAN ON BOARD BILLS OF LADING ISSUED TO ORDER AND BLANK ENDORSED
MARKED FREIGHT PAID

G.S.P. CERTIFICATE OF ORIGIN IN ORIGINAL AND ONE COPY

PACKING LIST IN ORIGINAL AND THREE COPIES

GOODS DESCRIPTION :
SPARE PARTS FOR ELECTRICAL APPLIANCES
AS PER ORDER NUMBER JE1994
TERMS OF DELIVERY: CFR ANY UK PORT

DOCUMENTS TO BE PRESENTED WITHIN 21 DAYS AFTER THE DATE OF SHIPMENT BUT IN
ANY EVENT WITHIN THE VALIDITY OF THE CREDIT.

ALL BANKING CHARGES OTHER THAN OUR OWN ARE FOR ACCOUNT OF THE
BENEFICIARY.

WE HEREBY ENGAGE WITH DRAWERS AND/OR BONA FIDE HOLDERS THAT DRAFTS DRAWN
AND NEGOTIATED IN CONFORMITY WITH THE TERMS OF THIS CREDIT WILL BE
HONOURED ON PRESENTATION, AND THAT DRAFTS ACCEPTED WITHIN THE TERMS OF
THIS CREDIT WILL BE HONOURED AT MATURITY.

EXCEPT SO FAR AS OTHERWISE EXPRESSLY STATED THIS CREDIT IS SUBJECT TO THE
UNIFORM CUSTOMS AND PRACTICE FOR DOCUMENTARY CREDITS, 1993 REVISION. I.C.C.
PUBLICATION NO. 500

BANK TO BANK INSTRUCTIONS:

PLEASE ADVISE THIS CREDIT WITHOUT ADDING YOUR CONFIRMATION.

REMIT ALL DOCUMENTS TO OURSELVES IN TWO REGISTERED AIRMAILS.

COMMUNICATIONS REGARDING THIS CREDIT SHOULD BE SENT TO OUR ABOVE ADDRESS.
TELEPHONE: 071-260 5978 TELEX: 888401 MIDBKN G FAX: 071-260 4640
KINDLY ENSURE THAT YOU ALWAYS QUOTE OUR REFERENCE NUMBER FOR THIS CREDIT.

OUR ADDRESS FOR PERSONAL CALLERS ONLY IS: MIDLAND BANK PLC,
DOCUMENTARY CREDITS DEPARTMENT, 62-76 PARK STREET, SOUTHWARK,
LONDON, SE1. (THIS ADDRESS IS NOT TO BE USED FOR CORRESPONDENCE).

                    AUTHORISED SIGNATURE(S)

        THIS DOCUMENT CONSISTS OF 2 PAGE(S)

Registered in England (No. 14259)
Registered Office: Poultry London EC2P 2BX

member HSBC **(X)** *group*

5 Advice to beneficiary of in-coming confirmed credit

OUR REFERENCE: 09L/103734   PAGE: 1

DOCUMENTARY CREDITS DEPARTMENT   MARCH 14, 1994
PO BOX 181
27-32   POULTRY
LONDON EC2P 2BX

ADVICE OF CONFIRMED IRREVOCABLE DOCUMENTARY CREDIT

BENEFICIARY: ISSUING BANK:

INTERNATIONAL SELLERS LTD   ANY BANK
LOWER STREET   ANY TOWN
LONDON   ANYWHERE
SE1

                                      THEIR REFERENCE: EXP/LC/1
                                      ISSUE DATE: MARCH 10. 1994

APPLICANT:
INTERNATIONAL BUYERS LIMITED
38TH FLOOR, TWO EXCHANGE SQUARE
CONNAUGHT PLACE
HONG KONG

                         AMOUNT; GBP 50.000.00
                         (FIFTY THOUSAND AND 00/000'S POUNDS
                         STERLING)

                         DATE OF EXPIRY: April 20, 1994
                         PLACE OF EXPIRY: UK

WE ARE PLEASED TO ADVISE YOU OF AN IRREVOCABLE CREDIT OPENED IN YOUR
FAVOUR. DETAILS OF WHICH ARE ATTACHED.

THIS ADVICE, TOGETHER WITH ITS ATTACHMENTS, (AND ANY SUBSEQUENT
AMENDMENTS) WILL MAKE UP THE IRREVOCABLE CREDIT IN YOUR FAVOUR AND MUST
ACCOMPANY ALL PRESENTATIONS. PLEASE READ CAREFULLY ALL THE TERMS AND
CONDITIONS OF THE CREDIT AND, IF YOU DO NOT FULLY AGREE WITH ANY OF THEM,
CONTACT INTERNATIONAL BUYERS LTD 35TH FLOOR, TWO EXCHANGE SQUARE CONNAUGHT
PLACE HONG KONG IMMEDIATELY.

THIS CREDIT BEARS THE CONFIRMATION OF MIDLAND BANK PLC AND WE UNDERTAKE
THAT PRESENTATIONS TO US IN COMPLIANCE WITH THE CREDIT TERMS AND
CONDITIONS WILL BE HONOURED.

THE CREDIT IS AVAILABLE WITH MIDLAND BANK PLC BY PAYMENT OF YOUR DRAFTS
AT SIGHT ON MIDLAND BANK PLC ACCOMPANIED BY DOCUMENTS AS STIPULATED BY
THE CREDIT.

DOCUMENTS FOR THIS CREDIT MAY BE PRESENTED AT THIS OFFICE OR AT ANY OF OUR
AUTHORISED BRANCHES, WHEN PRESENTING DOCUMENTS KINDLY QUOTE OUR REFERENCE
NUMBER AND INCLUDE ONE ADDITIONAL COPY OF YOUR INVOICE FOR OUR RECORDS.

Registered in England (No. 14259)
Registered Office Poultry London EC2P 2BX
4183-8L (09/92) IS

```
OUR REFERENCE  09L/103734                          PAGE: 2
```

THE DESCRIPTION OF THE MERCHANDISE ON THE INVOICE(S) MUST APPEAR EXACTLY
AS SHOWN IN THE DOCUMENTARY CREDIT.

IF, DUE TO DISCREPANCIES, WE ARE UANBLE TO HONOUR DOCUMENTS WHEN
PRESENTED, WE RESERVE THE RIGHT TO MAKE A HANDLING CHARGE FOR THE
ADDITIONAL COSTS INVOLVED IN DEALING WITH SUCH PRESENTATIONS.

CHARGES ARE FOR YOUR ACCOUNT INCLUDING:-

```
ADVISING COMMISSION          GBP     40.00
CONFIRMATION COMMISSION      GBP     62.50
```

PAYMENT COMMISSION OF 0.1% MINIMUM GBP 50.00 PER PAYMENT.

WE SHALL BE PLEASED TO RECEIVE YOUR REMITTANCE IN SETTLEMENT OF THE ABOVE
CHARGES, ALTERNATIVELY THEY WILL BE DEDUCTED FROM THE PROCEEDS FOLLOWING
PRESENTATION OF DOCUMENTS.

EXCEPT SO FAR AS OTHERWISE EXPRESSLY STATED THIS CREDIT IS SUBJECT TO THE
UNIFORM CUSTOMS AND PRACTICE FOR DOCUMENTARY CREDITS, 1993 REVISION.
I.C.C. PUBLICATION NO. 500.

COMMUNICATIONS REGARDING THIS CREDIT SHOULD BE SENT TO OUR ABOVE ADDRESS.
TELEPHONE : 071 260 5978 TELEX: 8814463 MIDCCR G FAX 071 260 4640
KINDLY ENSURE THAT YOU ALWAYS QUOTE OUR REFERENCE NUMBER FOR THIS CREDIT.

AUTHORISED SIGNATURE(S)

THIS DOCUMENT CONSISTS OF 2 (PAGE)S

Registered in England (No. 14259)
Registered Office Poultry London EC2P 2BX
4183-8L (09/92) IS

member HSBC ⟨X⟩ *group*

NOTE

Details of the credit itself are provided by means of a photocopy of the credit as
issued to the bank.

6 Advice to beneficiary of in-coming unconfirmed credit

OUR REFERENCE : 09L/528267

DOCUMENTARY CREDITS DEPARTMENT   APRIL 14, 1994
P.O.BOX 181
27-32 POULTRY
LONDON EC2P 2BX

OUR ADDRESS FOR PERSONAL CALLERS - SEE BELOW

ADVICE OF AN IRREVOCABLE UNCONFIRMED DOCUMENTARY CREDIT

TO: ISSUING BANK:

SELLERS (UK) LIMITED   HONGKONG AND SHANGHAI BKG CORP LTD
LOWER STREET   LEVEL 19 PO BOX 64
LONDON SE1   1 QUEENS ROAD CENTRAL
                                   HONG KONG

                                   THEIR REFERENCE: HSBC1/94
                                   ISSUE DATE: 14/04/1994
APPLICANT:
INTERNATIONAL BUYERS LIMITED
CONNAUGHT PLACE, HONG KONG   AMOUNT: GBP 10,000.00
                                   (SAY GBP TEN THOUSAND AND 00/100'S)

                                   DATE OF EXPIRY: SEPTEMBER 30, 1994

WE ARE PLEASED TO ADVISE YOU OF AN IRREVOCABLE CREDIT OPENED IN YOUR
FAVOUR, DETAILS OF WHICH ARE ATTACHED. WE HAVE AUTHENTICATED THE
COMMUNICATION IN ACCORDANCE WITH ARTICLE 7(A) UCP 500.

THIS ADVICE, TOGETHER WITH ITS ATTACHMENTS (AND ANY SUBSEQUENT
AMENDMENTS), MAKE UP THE IRREVOCABLE CREDIT IN YOUR FAVOUR AND MUST
ACCOMPANY ALL PRESENTATIONS. PLEASE READ THE TERMS AND CONDITIONS OF THE
CREDIT CAREFULLY, AND IF YOU DO NOT FULLY AGREE WITH ANY OF THEM, CONTACT
INTERNATIONAL BUYERS LIMITED IMMEDIATELY.

THIS CREDIT DOES NOT BEAR THE CONFIRMATION OF MIDLAND BANK PLC AND THIS
ADVICE CONVEYS NO ENGAGEMENT ON OUR PART.

THIS CREDIT IS AVAILABLE WITH MIDLAND BANK PLC BY NEGOTIATION OF YOUR
DRAFTS AT SIGHT DRAWN ON THE ISSUING BANK(NAME AND ADDRESS AS STATED IN
THE ATTACHED) ACCOMPANIED BY DOCUMENTS AS STIPULATED IN THE CREDIT.ANY
NEGOTIATION EFFECTED BY US WILL BE WITH RECOURSE TO YOURSELVES.

DOCUMENTS MAY BE PRESENTED AT THIS OFFICE OR AT ANY OF OUR AUTHORISED
BRANCHES AS INDICATED ON THE ATTACHED LIST. WHEN PRESENTING DOCUMENTS
KINDLY QUOTE OUR REFERENCE NUMBER AND PROVIDE ONE ADDITIONAL COPY OF YOUR
INVOICE FOR OUR RECORDS.

THE DESCRIPTION OF THE MERCHANDISE ON THE INVOICE(S) MUST APPEAR EXACTLY
AS SHOWN IN THE DOCUMENTARY CREDIT.

IF, DUE TO DISCREPANCIES, WE ARE UNABLE TO HONOUR DOCUMENTS WHEN
PRESENTED, WE RESERVE THE RIGHT TO MAKE A HANDLING CHARGE FOR THE

member HSBC **(X)** *group*

Registered in England (No. 14259)
Registered Office: Poultry London EC2P 2BX

ADDITIONAL COSTS INVOLVED IN DEALING WITH SUCH PRESENTATIONS.

CHARGES ARE FOR YOUR ACCOUNT, INCLUDING:-

ADVISING COMMISSION	GBP	40.00
POSTAGES	GBP	6.50

CABLE CHARGES, IF APPLICABLE.

NEGOTIATION COMMISSION OF 0.1% ON EACH DRAFT MINIMUM GBP 50.00 PER
NEGOTIATION.

WE SHALL BE PLEASED TO RECEIVE YOUR REMITTANCE IN SETTLEMENT OF THE ABOVE
CHARGES, ALTERNATIVELY THEY WILL BE DEDUCTED FROM THE PROCEEDS FOLLOWING
PRESENTATION OF DOCUMENTS.

WHEN PRESENTING DOCUMENTS PLEASE PROVIDE US WITH YOUR FULL BANKING
DETAILS, TOGETHER WITH ANY OTHER INSTRUCTIONS, ON THE ATTACHED FORM.

EXCEPT SO FAR AS OTHERWISE EXPRESSLY STATED THIS CREDIT IS SUBJECT TO
UNIFORM CUSTOMS AND PRACTICE FOR DOCUMENTARY CREDITS, 1993 REVISION, I.C.C
PUBLICATION NO. 500.

COMMUNICATIONS REGARDING THIS CREDIT SHOULD BE SENT TO OUR ABOVE ADDRESS.
TELEPHONE: 071-260 5978 TELEX: 888401 MIDBKN G FAX: 071-260 4640
KINDLY ENSURE THAT YOU ALWAYS QUOTE OUR REFERENCE NUMBER FOR THIS CREDIT.

OUR ADDRESS FOR PERSONAL CALLERS ONLY IS: MIDLAND BANK PLC,
DOCUMENTARY CREDITS DEPARTMENT, 62-76 PARK STREET, SOUTHWARK,
LONDON, SE1. (THIS ADDRESS IS NOT TO BE USED FOR CORRESPONDENCE).

AUTHORISED SIGNATURE(S)

member HSBC **XD** *group*

Registered in England (No. 14259)
Registered Office: Poultry London EC2P 2BX

NOTE

Details of the credit itself are provided by means of a photocopy of the credit as
issued to the bank.

7 Factoring agreement

:   ■   Venture Factors PLC.

     ■   Subsidiary of IFN Factors
          The Netherlands
          Part of the ABN AMRO Group

     ■   Sussex House
          Perrymount Road
          Haywards Heath
          West Sussex RH16 1DN

     ■   Telephone 0444 441717
          Fax 0444 415982

AGREEMENT FOR THE FACTORING OR DISCOUNTING OF DEBTS

1. PARTIES:
(1)   VENTURE FACTORS PLC. of Sussex House Perrymount Road Haywards Heath West Sussex ("the Factor") whose registered office Sussex House Perrymount Road Haywards Heath West Sussex RH16 1DN;

(2)   The person ("the Client") named in section 1 of the schedule ("the Schedule") annexed to and forming part of this Agreement.

2. DATE:
          This agreement shall be deemed to be made (i) if the Client is a body corporate on the date on which it is executed by or on behalf of the Client or (ii) if the Client is not a body corporate on the date on which it is executed by the Factor.

3. DEFINITIONS AND INTERPRETATION:
(1)   In this Agreement except where the context otherwise requires:
 (i) The singular shall include the plural and vice versa and any of the three genders shall include the other two;

 (ii) references to "the Factor" shall include the Factor's successors and assigns; references to clauses (except where otherwise specified) are to clauses of this Agreement; references to any statute shall be deemed to include any statutory modification or re-enactment thereof or any part thereof;

 (iii) the expressions specified in the appendix annexed to and forming part of this Agreement shall have the meanings assigned to them therein;

 (iv) the headings to clauses are for ease of reference only and shall not affect or limit the meaning or extent of any clause; and

 (v) expressions which in or for the purpose of proceedings outside England and Wales have no precise counterpart in the jurisdiction in which those proceedings are to take place shall have the meaning of the closest equivalent expression in such jurisdiction.

(2)   This Agreement shall be construed and take effect according to English law and the Client submits to the jurisdiction of the English courts without prejudice to the right of the Factor to take proceedings in the courts of any state in which the Client carries on business or has assets.

4. TRANSFER OF OWNERSHIP OF DEBTS:
(1)   The Client shall sell and the Factor shall purchase all Debts incurred or to be incurred by any Debtor of the class or description specified in section 2 of the Schedule which shall be in existence at the Commencement or which shall come into existence at any time thereafter before termination of this Agreement. The ownership of every such Debt in existence at the Commencement shall vest in the Factor at the Commencement and of every such Debt coming into existence thereafter shall vest in the Factor upon such Debt coming into existence.

(2)   Upon the vesting in the Factor of any Debt pursuant to clause 4(1) there shall also vest in the Factor the ownership of all the Related Rights pertaining to such Debt and the Factor shall at any time after such sale also have the right to have transferred to it any Goods included in the Sale Contract giving rise to such Debt (otherwise than when the ownership of such Goods is vested in the Debtor).

5. PERFECTION OF FACTOR'S TITLE:
          The Client shall at any time at the request of the Factor and at the expense of the Client execute and deliver to the Factor a formal written assignment (with the applicable stamp duty endorsed thereon) of any Debt or Related Rights purchased by the Factor. The Client shall hold in trust for the Factor and separately from the Client's own property any Debt or Related Rights or Transferred Goods purchased by the Factor of which the ownership shall fail to vest in the Factor for any reason.

6. PURCHASE PRICE AND NOTIFICATION OF DEBTS:
(1)   The Purchase Price of each Debt (together with its Related Rights and any Transferred Goods pertaining to such Debt) purchased by the Factor shall be equivalent to the amount (including any tax or duty) payable by the Debtor in respect of such Debt according to the relevant Sale Contract after there has been deducted therefrom (i) any discount allowance or other deduction allowed or allowable by the Client to the Debtor and (ii) the factoring fee and discount charge in respect of such Debt (as provided for in clause 9(1) and (iii) in the case of a Currency Debt bank and other charges incurred by the Factor in collecting and converting the proceeds into Sterling.

     ■   Registered in England No 2281768

     ■   Registered office as above

2

(2)The Client shall promptly notify the Factor of each Debt sold to the Factor in such manner and with such particulars and documents evidencing the Debt as the Factor may from time to time require as soon as the relevant Goods have been Delivered or if so required by the Factor at any other time. No Notification shall include any Debt previously notified.

(3)If in relation to any Debt the Client is unable to give to the Factor every one of the warranties and undertakings contained in this Agreement then the Client shall notify such Debt to the Factor separately from other Debts and clearly mark the relevant Notification to that effect.

7. CLIENT ACCOUNTS; CREDIT OF PURCHASE PRICE; PAYMENT BY THE FACTOR:
(1)Upon receipt by the Factor of a Notification relating to any Debt the Factor shall credit its Purchase Price to the Debts Purchased Account. For administrative convenience the Factor may in its absolute discretion make any such credit before deduction of any of the items to be deducted in computing such purchase price as provided for in clause 6(1) and may consequently debit such item to any account of the Client at any time thereafter.

(2)The Factor shall transfer the amount credited to the Debts Purchased Account pursuant to clause 7(1) in respect of each Debt to the credit of the Current Account on the Transfer Date. The Factor may debit to the Current Account all amounts payable by the Client to the Factor (whether arising under this Agreement or otherwise) including any contingent or prospective liability of the Client to the Factor in accordance with clause 10.

(3)At any time after twenty four hours following receipt of a Notification by the Factor relating to any Approved Debt (subject to the provisions of clauses 7(5) to 7(7) inclusive) the Factor shall at the request of the Client make a Prepayment to the Client in respect of such Debt. The Factor may at any time in its absolute discretion make a Prepayment in respect of any notified Debt. The amounts of all such Prepayments shall be debited to the Current Account. Solely for the purposes of this clause a Debt shall be deemed to be an Approved Debt notwithstanding that it is of the nature or description specified in section 4 of the Schedule if it otherwise would rank as an Approved Debt.

(4)Subject to the provisions of clause 7(5) within one working day of receiving a request from the Client so to do the Factor shall pay to the Client the whole or any part of the balance standing to the credit of the Client on the Current Account.

(5)The Factor shall not be obliged to make any payment (including any Prepayment) to the Client:

(a) whilst any petition for the bankruptcy or winding up of the Client or for an administration order in relation to the Client pursuant to the Act or any proposal for a voluntary arrangement in relation to the Client pursuant to the Act is pending; or

(b) if the effect of that payment would be to make the credit balance in favour of the Client after a combination of all the accounts in the Client's name in the Factor's records less than the Minimum Balance whether or not such accounts have been so combined.

(6)The Factor shall not be obliged to make any Prepayment if the effect of it would be that the aggregate amount of all Prepayments made in respect of Debts owing by any one Debtor would be in excess of the percentage specified in section 6 of the Schedule of the aggregate amount of all Outstanding Debts.

(7)At any time when the Factor shall have the Right of Immediate Termination the Factor may withhold all Prepayments and shall have the right to the repayment by the Client of any Prepayments previously made and unrecovered promptly on the demand of the Factor.

(8)Any payment (including any Prepayment) to be made by the Factor hereunder shall be made by cheque sent by post to the Client or to any bank account of the Client or by such other means of transmission as the parties may agree in writing.

(9)The Factor shall send to the Client a statement of its accounts with the Client once in each month or at such other intervals as may be agreed. Such statement shall be deemed correct and shall be binding on the Client except for manifest errors or errors in law or any error notified by the Client to the Factor within fourteen days of its despatch.

8. DEBTS PAYABLE OTHERWISE THAN IN STERLING:
(1)Unless otherwise agreed by the Factor at the request of the Client the Purchase Price of every Currency Debt shall be paid in Sterling and shall be computed by reference to the spot selling rate of the relevant currency quoted in London by Barclays Bank PLC on the date when payment for such Debt is received by the Factor.

(2)For the purpose of calculating the Factoring Fee in respect of any Currency Debt and for making a provisional credit of the Purchase Price the Factor may apply such selling rate ruling on the date when the Notification relating to the Debt is received by the Factor and thereafter make such adjustment as may be necessary to accord with clause 8(1).

(3)On Recourse of any Currency Debt the repurchase price shall be computed by reference to the rate applied in crediting the Purchase Price to the Current Account.

9. FACTORING FEES AND DISCOUNT CHARGES:
(1)The Factoring Fees and Discount Charges to be deducted in computing the purchase price of Debts shall be as follows:

(a) in respect of every Debt purchased by the Factor a Factoring Fee equivalent to such percentage as is specified in section 7 of the Schedule (or such other percentage as may be agreed by the parties in writing) of the notified value of such Debt before

3

the deduction of any discount or other allowance allowed or allowable at any time to the Debtor; and

(b) in respect of each Debt in relation to which a Prepayment is made, a Discount Charge equivalent to the rate per annum specified in section 8 of the Schedule calculated daily with monthly rests on the amount of such Prepayment from the date on which it is made until it has been fully recovered by the Factor.

(2)   For the purposes of clause 9(1)(b) any amount debited to the Current Account (except by reason of Recourse) shall be deemed to be and shall be treated as a Prepayment and for administrative convenience the Factor may calculate and debit such Discount Charges in aggregate each month by applying the rate referred to in clause 9(1)(b) to the total of Outstanding Debts at the end of each day after deducting therefrom the aggregate of the amounts of credit balances on Debtor accounts in the Factor's records and (i) after further deducting any credit balance in favour of the Client on a combination of the accounts of the client in the Factor's records or (ii) after adding any debit balance therein.

(3)   In respect of each Unapproved Debt which remains outstanding after the number of days specified in section 9(a) of the Schedule following the last day of the month in which the relevant invoice is dated there shall be payable by the Client to the Factor a supplementary fee equivalent to such percentage as is specified in section 9(b) of the Schedule of the notified value of such Debt (or the amount thereof unpaid) on the last day of each month on which it remains outstanding. Any such supplementary fee shall be debited to the Current Account on the date on which it becomes payable.

(4)   If the aggregate amount of Factoring Fees in respect of Debts of which Notifications shall be received by the Factor in any year commencing on the Commencement or any anniversary thereof shall be less than the minimum sum specified in section 10 of the Schedule then the Client shall pay to the Factor an additional factoring fee equivalent to the difference between the sum so specified and the said aggregate amount. Such additional factoring fee shall be calculated provisionally for each period of three months and debited to the current account at the end of each such period with any necessary adjustment at the end of each year. In the event of termination of this agreement otherwise than on an anniversary of the Commencement the minimum amount to be so applied to the final period shall be such proportion of the amount specified in section 10 of the Schedule as the final period bears to one year.

(5)   If the aggregate amount of factoring fees in respect of Debts notified during any period of three months starting on the first day of the month next following the occurrence of any of the events specified to in sub-clause (6) of this clause (notwithstanding the termination of this Agreement before the end of such period) shall be less than such aggregate amount in respect of Debts notified during the period of three months ended immediately before such event then (in addition to and without prejudice to any other rights of the Factor on the occurrence of any such event) the Client shall pay to the Factor a sum equal to the difference between such two aggregate amounts.

(6)   The events referred to in sub-clause (5) of this clause are as follows:

(a) The Client's insolvency;

(b) The dissolution of any partnership comprising the Client; or

(c) The end of a period of four weeks during which no Notifications shall have been received by the Factor from the Client.

10. SET-OFF AND COMBINATION OF ACCOUNTS:
(1)   The Factor shall be entitled to set off, against any amount payable by the Factor to the Client, the amount of any actual or contingent liability or prospective liability of the Client to the Factor (whether arising in or by contract tort restitution assignment or breach of statutory duty and whether arising under this Agreement or otherwise) and where the amount of any such liability cannot be immediately ascertained the Factor shall be entitled to make a reasonable estimate thereof.

(2)   The Factor may in its absolute discretion without notice or other formality combine any two or all the accounts maintained in the Factor's records in the name of the Client. At any time when the Factor shall have Right to Immediate Termination all such accounts shall be deemed to have been combined. Any balance owing to the Factor as a result of such combination of accounts shall be paid by the Client to the Factor in sterling forthwith upon demand.

11. WARRANTIES AND UNDERTAKINGS OF THE CLIENT:
(1)   In addition to and without prejudice to any other undertaking given elsewhere in this agreement the Client warrants and undertakes (as applicable):

(a) that save as disclosed by the Client to the Factor in writing no disposition charge trust or other encumbrance (whether created by the Client or otherwise) affects or may affect any of the Debts or Related Rights or Transferred Goods sold to the Factor and that no supplier to the Client has or may have any claim to any such Debt or Related Rights whether by equitable tracing right or otherwise;

(b) that prior to entry into this Agreement the Client has disclosed to the Factor every fact or matter known to the Client which the Client knew or should reasonably have known might influence the Factor in its decision whether or not to enter into this Agreement or to accept any person as surety for the Client's obligations to the Factor or as to the terms of the Agreement or as to the making of any Prepayment or the designation of any Debt as an Approved Debt and to disclose promptly to the Factor any such fact or matter of which the Client becomes aware during the currency of this Agreement including (without prejudice to the generality of the foregoing) any change or prospective change in the constitution or control of the Client or of any such surety or any prospective security right to be created by the Client affecting any of its assets;

(c) immediately after the sale of any Debt to the Factor to make an appropriate entry in the Client's records of account regarding such sale and in all cases in which the Client acts as agent of the Factor pursuant to clause 13(3) to ensure that all

4

accounts and records relating to Debtors are clearly marked that the Debts so recorded thereon have been sold to the Factor;

(d) to indemnify the Factor against all costs and expenses (including legal costs and fees) incurred by the Factor in enforcing or attempting to enforce payment and collection of all Unapproved Debts and in settling or compromising any disagreement with a Debtor (whether justified or not); and

(e) to pay to the Factor all costs and expenses incurred by the Factor (except the Factor's own administrative costs) in entering into this Agreement and in enforcing the terms thereof.

(2) The inclusion of any Debt in a Notification (other than a Notification pursuant to clause 6(3)) or any report made to the Factor pursuant to clause 13(3) shall be deemed to constitute a warranty by the Client that:

(a) the Client has the unqualified right to sell the Debt and its Related Rights to the Factor;

(b) the Goods have been Delivered and the Debt is a legally binding obligation of the Debtor to the extent of the amount notified and has arisen from a Sale Contract made in the ordinary course of the Client's business as specified in section 11 of the Schedule which:

(i) provides for the invoice to be expressed and payment to be made in a currency specified in section 12 of the Schedule on terms not more liberal than those specified therein;

(ii) is subject to the law of a country specified therein; and

(iii) is otherwise as approved by the Factor;

and the Client will not vary or attempt to vary any of the terms of any such Sale Contract without the prior written consent of the Factor;

(c) the client has no obligations to the Debtor other than under any Sale Contract and there exists no agreement between the Client and the Debtor for set-off or for abatement or whereby otherwise the amount of the Debt specified in the Notification may be reduced except in accordance with the terms of the Sale Contract as approved by the Factor herein;

(d) the Client is not in breach of any of its obligations under the relevant Sale Contract and that the Debtor will accept the goods and the invoice therefor (or if the Debtor is or shall become insolvent that the person having the duty to administer the estate of the Debtor will accept proof of Debt for the unpaid balance thereof) without any dispute or claim whatsoever including claims for release of liability (or of inability to pay) because of force majeure or because of the requirements of any law or of rules orders or regulations having the force of law; and

(e) the Debtor has an established place of business and is not an Associate.

12. DISAGREEMENTS, CREDIT NOTES AND RECOURSE:

(1) If (notwithstanding the warranties and undertakings given by the Client in relation to any Debt) a disagreement should arise between the Client and the Debtor relating to the Debtor's liability to pay in full the notified amount of any Debt (less any discount or allowance approved by the Factor herein) the Client shall forthwith notify the Factor of such disagreement.

(2) The Client undertakes:

(a) to use its best endeavours promptly to settle every such disagreement subject to the right of the Factor itself to settle or compromise any such disagreement or to require that the Client should settle or compromise it on such terms as the Factor may in its absolute discretion think fit; and

(b) promptly to perform all further and continuing obligations of the Client to the Debtor under any Sale Contract giving rise to a Debt sold to the Factor and to give evidence to the Factor of such performance and to agree that in the event of the failure of such performance the Factor may itself perform such obligations at the expense of the Client; and the Client shall be bound by anything done by or at the direction of the Factor pursuant to this clause.

(3) The Client shall promptly advise the Factor in such manner and with such documents as the Factor may require of all credit notes issued to Debtors. The Factor shall have the right by notice to the Client to require that:

(a) as from the date of such notice no credit note for any Debtor should be authorised or issued by the Client without the Factor's consent and

(b) for this purpose the originals of all credit notes which the Client wishes to issue shall be sent to the Factor for despatch to the Debtors after the giving of such consent.

(4) The Factor shall have Recourse:

(a) in respect of every Debt which ranks as an Unapproved Debt by reason of a breach of warranty or undertaking given by the Client to the Factor as soon as such breach occurs;

(b) in respect of every Debt which is the subject of a separate Notification pursuant to clause 6(3) at any time after receipt by the Factor of such Notification;

5

(c) in respect of every Debt which comprises solely discount or any other deduction wrongly claimed or deducted by the Debtor or which is the subject of such disagreement as is described in clause 12(1) on the sixtieth day after the making of such deduction or claim or the arising of such disagreement;

(d) in respect of every other Unapproved Debt on the day next following that on which it is due for payment by the Debtor; and

(e) in respect of every Debt which the Debtor (or if the Debtor is insolvent the person who has the duty to administer the Debtor's estate) claims to be unable to pay by reason of any law or rules or regulations having the force of law (other than arising solely from the Debtor's insolvency) as soon as such claim is made.

The ownership of every Debt (together with any Related Rights and Transferred Goods pertaining thereto) the subject of Recourse shall remain vested in the Factor until the repurchase price has been fully discharged.

(5) With every advice of a credit note pursuant to clause 12(3) and immediately on notice of any Recourse the Client shall furnish the Factor with a cheque drawn on a London clearing bank in favour of the Factor for the amount of the credit note or the repurchase price of the Debt the subject of the Recourse as the case may be. On receipt of advice of any credit note or the notice of any Recourse the amount thereof shall be debited to the Current Account and on collection of any such cheque from the drawee the amount of the cheque shall be credited to the Current Account.

(6) Following the vesting of the ownership of any Debt in the Client by reason of Recourse the Factor shall credit to the Current Account the amount of any recovery made by the Factor arising from the enforcement or realisation of any Related Rights or Transferred Goods pertaining to such Debt.

13. NOTICES TO AND COLLECTION FROM DEBTORS:
(1) Whilst the ownership of any Debt remains vested in the Factor the Factor shall have the sole right to enforce payment of and collect such Debt and to institute defend or compromise proceedings in its own name or the name of the Client in such manner and upon such terms as it may in its absolute discretion think fit. The Client shall cooperate in such enforcement collection or proceedings and in the recovery of any Goods the ownership of which shall not have passed to the Debtor.

(2) The Client undertakes:

(a) to give each Debtor and prospective Debtor notice in the form prescribed by the Factor and in the manner specified in section 13 of the Schedule (or as otherwise required by the Factor) that each Debt owing by such Debtor has been purchased by and assigned to the Factor; and

(b) in any case in which such notice includes directions to the Debtor to make payment to the Factor to use its best endeavours to ensure that payment by the Debtor is made solely to the Factor.

(3) Where it is specified in section 13 of the Schedule that no notices shall be given or if reference to "Agent" is made in the said section:

(a) without prejudice to the Factor's rights pursuant to clause 13(1) the Factor hereby appoints the Client as agent of the Factor for the purpose of administering the accounts of Debtors and enforcing payment of and collecting Debts and the Client accepts such appointment and undertakes:

(i) to act promptly and efficiently in carrying out such tasks; and

(ii) not to hold itself out as agent of the Factor except while the provisions of clause 13(3) apply and while such provisions apply not to hold itself out as an agent for the Factor for any purpose other than those specified in clause 13(3); and

(b) the Client shall furnish the Factor by such date in each month as the Factor may direct with such copies of the records and such reports and statements showing the position of the accounts of Debtors as the Factor may require.

(4) The Factor may at any time by notice to the Client withdraw any such agency in which event the Client shall forthwith give the notices prescribed in clause 13(2) in such form and manner as the Factor may direct and the provisions of clause 13(1) shall thereafter apply in full.

(5) The Client shall forthwith deliver to the Factor (or if so required by the Factor direct to a bank account designated by the Factor) the identical monies cheque or other instrument comprising any payment received by the Client in or on account of the discharge of any Debt purchased by the Factor and shall meanwhile hold the said monies cheque or instrument in trust for the Factor.

14. CREDIT LIMITS AND ALLOCATION OF PAYMENTS:
(1) Any Credit Limit may in the Factor's absolute discretion be increased reduced or cancelled by the Factor by oral or written notice to the Client at any time and any such change shall take immediate effect except that no reduction or cancellation shall affect any Debt arising from Goods Delivered before the receipt by the Client of notice of such cancellation or reduction.

(2) Where two or more Debts are owing by the same Debtor they shall be treated as falling within any Credit Limit relating to that Debtor in the order in which they are respectively due for payment by the Debtor.

(3) If the aggregate of Outstanding Debts owing by any Debtor exceeds the Credit Limit relating to that Debtor at any time before cancellation of such Credit Limit then to the extent that any Debt within the Credit Limit shall be paid or

6

otherwise satisfied then the next Debt in the order referred to in clause 14(2) shall fall within it.

(4)When Approved and Unapproved Debts are owing by the same Debtor (except as provided in clause 14(5)) the Factor shall have the right to appropriate any payment by the Debtor or any credit or allowance granted by the Client to the Debtor in satisfaction of any Approved Debt in priority to any Unapproved Debt owing by that Debtor notwithstanding any contrary appropriation by the Debtor.

(5)Following the Onset of Insolvency of any Debtor any dividend or other benefit received by either the Factor or the Client in reduction of any Debt owed by such Debtor shall be divided between the Factor and the Client. The Factor shall be entitled to such proportion of the dividend or benefit as the total of Approved Debts owed by the Debtor bears to the total of all such Debts as at the Onset of Insolvency. The Client's share of any such dividend or other benefit received by the Factor shall be credited to the Current Account.

(6)The Client shall not disclose to the Debtor or any third party the amount of or absence of any credit limit or reasons therefor and shall indemnify the Factor for all losses costs claims and demands arising out of breach of this requirement.

15. CREDIT BALANCES:
The Client hereby irrevocably authorises the Factor to make payment on account of or in settlement of any credit balance appearing on the account of any Debtor in the records of the Factor whether such credit balance arises from the issue of a credit note by the Client or otherwise.

16. RECOVERY OF VALUE ADDED TAX:
(1)For the purpose of recovering any value added tax included in any Debt owing by a Debtor as at the Onset of Insolvency of that Debtor the Client shall (if so required by the Factor) repurchase such Debt and use its best endeavours to recover such tax. The Client irrevocably authorises the Factor in the name of the Client

    (a) to submit proof of debt in the estate of such Debtor and/or

    (b) to obtain from the person who has the duty to administer the estate of the Debtor any certificate that may be necessary for the purpose of such recovery.

(2)If any Debt repurchased pursuant to clause 16(1) shall be an Approved Debt then the repurchase price shall be nil and the Client shall hold in trust for the Factor and immediately pay to the Factor (or in the Factor's absolute discretion the Factor may debit the Current Account with) the amount of any such tax recoverable and of any dividend or other benefit received in reduction of such Debt.

(3)If any such repurchased Debt shall be an Unapproved Debt then the repurchase price shall be the amount specified in the Notification relating thereto or the unpaid balance thereof.

17. CLIENT'S ACCOUNTS AND RECORDS:
(1)Whether or not the Client is a body corporate it shall provide for the Factor:

    (a) a signed copy of its audited balance sheet and accounts for each year or accounting reference period (as defined in the Companies Act 1985) ending during the currency of this Agreement within six months of the end of such period; and

    (b) such other accounts or statements of its financial position or affairs as the Factor may at any time require.

(2)The Client shall promptly furnish the Factor (at the Client's expense) with such of the books records or documents included in the Related Rights or copies of them and copies of any other records or documents of the Client as the Factor may at any time require.

(3)Any official or duly authorised representative or agent of the Factor may at any time enter upon any premises at which the Client carries on business and inspect and/or take copies of any such records or documents (at the Client's expense) and/or remove any books records or documents included in the Related Rights.

18. POWER OF ATTORNEY:
The Client hereby irrevocably appoints the Factor and the Directors and the Company Secretary and every other officer for the time being of the Factor jointly and each of them severally to be the Client's attorney in the name of the Client to execute such deeds or documents and to complete and indorse such instruments and to institute or defend such proceedings and to perform such other acts as the Factor may consider requisite in order to perfect the Factor's title to any Debt Related Rights or Transferred Goods and to secure performance of any of the Client's obligations under this Agreement or under any Sale Contract.

19. COMMENCEMENT AND TERMINATION:
(1)This Agreement shall commence on the Commencement and unless it is terminated pursuant to clause 19(2) shall continue for the minimum period prescribed in section 15 of the Schedule and thereafter until the expiry of the period (specified in section 16 of the Schedule) of notice of termination given by either party to the other.

(2)On the occurrence of any of the following events the Factor shall have the right by notice to the Client to terminate this Agreement forthwith or at any time thereafter:

    (a) The Client's Insolvency or its calling any meeting of its creditors;
    (b) A petition for an administration order pursuant to the Act in relation to the Client (being a body corporate) or a resolution of its members for its winding up;

7

(c) The dissolution of any partnership comprising the Client;

(d) The Client's income or assets or any part thereof being seized under any execution legal process or distress for rent or the making or threat of a garnishee order on any person indebted to the Client;

(e) The occurrence of any of the events referred to in paragraphs (a) to (d) inclusive of this clause in relation to any person who has given a guarantee or indemnity in respect of the Client's obligations under this Agreement or the death of any such person or the termination or attempted termination of any such guarantee or indemnity;

(f) Any breach of any covenant or undertaking given by any person in reliance upon which the Factor entered into or continued this Agreement or the withdrawal or attempted withdrawal of any waiver or release given to the Factor in relation to any security right affecting any asset of the Client;

(g) The cessation or threatened cessation of the Client's business; or

(h) Any material or persistent breach of any of the Client's obligations under this Agreement.

(3)   On the giving of notice by the Factor pursuant to clause 19(2) the Factor shall have immediate Recourse in respect of all Outstanding Debts but so that the ownership of none of such Debts shall vest in the Client until the repurchase price of all such Debts has been received by the Factor.

(4)   Subject to the provisions of clauses 7(6) and 19(3) termination of this Agreement shall not affect the rights and obligations of either party in relation to Debts which are in existence on the date of termination or the obligations of the Client pursuant to clauses 9(5) and 9(6) and such rights and obligations shall remain in full force and effect until duly extinguished.

20. EXCLUSION OF OTHER TERMS AND PRESERVATION OF THE FACTOR'S RIGHTS:
(1)   This Agreement (including the Appendix thereto and the Schedule and any special conditions set out therein) contains all the terms agreed between the Factor and the Client to the exclusion of any agreement statement or representation made by or on behalf of the Factor prior to the making of this Agreement whether orally or in writing. Except to the extent provided for herein no variation of this Agreement or of any term thereof shall be valid unless it is in writing and signed on behalf of the Factor by a Director or the Company Secretary and on behalf of the Client (being a body corporate) by a Director or the Company Secretary of the Client or (not being a body corporate) by every person named as Client herein.

(2)   The Factor's rights under this Agreement shall not be affected in any way by the granting of time or indulgence by the Factor to the Client or to any other person nor by any failure or delay in the exercise of any right or option under this Agreement or otherwise.

(3)   The Factor shall be entitled to rely upon any act done or document signed or any telex or facsimile or oral communication sent by any person purporting to act sign or send or make on behalf of the Client notwithstanding any defect in or absence of authority vested in such person.

21. CONSTITUTION AND PLURALITY OF CLIENT:
(1)   If the Client comprises two or more persons:

(a) references to the Client in clauses 7(5) and 19(2) shall be deemed to be references to any one or more of them;
(b) all undertakings and warranties given herein shall be deemed to have been given by every one of them;
(c) their liability hereunder shall be joint and several and the Factor may release or compromise with any one or more of them without affecting its rights against the others; and
(d) the Factor may in its absolute discretion treat any notice to or demand on any one or more of them as notice to or demand on them all and any notice to the Factor by any one or more of them as notice by them all.

(2)   If the Client comprises a partnership all the persons who have executed this Agreement warrant that all the present partners of such partnership are named herein.

(3)   Except as provided in clause 19(2) this Agreement and all the terms thereof shall remain in full force and effect notwithstanding any change in the constitution of the Client whether by death retirement addition or otherwise.

22. ASSIGNMENT OR DELEGATION BY CLIENT:
     The Client shall not be entitled to assign any of its rights or delegate any of its obligations under this Agreement without the prior written consent of the Factor.

23. NOTICES:
     Any notice or demand required or permitted to be served or made by the Factor shall be validly served or made if handed (in the case of a body corporate) to any officer of the Client (or if the Client is not a body corporate) to any of the persons comprising the Client or if sent by telex or facsimile transmission or by post or delivered to the registered office of the Client or to its address stated herein or to its address last known to the Factor or to any address at which the Client carries on business. Notices and demands served personally shall take effect upon such service and notices sent and demands made by post shall be conclusively deemed to have been received within seventy-two hours of the time of posting and notices sent and demands made by telex or facsimile shall be deemed to have been received upon their transmission.

APPENDIX

DEFINITIONS:

"the Act"
The Insolvency Act 1986;

"Approved Debt"
Any Debt which is (when aggregated with all other Outstanding Debts owing by the same Debtor) for the time being within a Credit Limit established in accordance with clause 14 and in relation to which the Client is not in breach of any obligation under this Agreement and which is not a Debt of the nature or description contained in section 4 of the Schedule;

"Associate"
An associate as defined in section 184 of the Consumer Credit Act 1974 of the Client or a director or shareholder or employee of the Client;

"Commencement"
The date of Commencement of this Agreement as specified in section 14 of the Schedule;

"Credit Limit"
A limit established by the Factor in its absolute discretion in relation to any Debtor for the purpose of determining which Debts owing by such Debtor may be classified as Approved Debts;

"Currency Debt"
Any Debt which is represented by an invoice expressed otherwise than in sterling or is payable otherwise than in sterling in the United Kingdom in accordance with the Sale Contract giving rise to it;

"Current Account"
An account maintained by the Factor in the name of the Client for the recording of transactions between the Factor and the Client pursuant to this Agreement;

"Debt"
Any obligation incurred by a Debtor under a Sale Contract and where the context so admits a part of a Debt;

"Debtor"
Any person who incurs any obligation to the Client under a Sale Contract or who may incur such an obligation under a prospective Sale Contract;

"Debts Purchased Account"
An account maintained in the records of the Factor in the name of the Client for the purpose of recording the Purchase Price of Debts (together with any Related Rights and Transferred Goods pertaining thereto);

"Delivered"
In the case of goods, despatched to or to the order of the Debtor from a place in the United Kingdom and, in the case of services, completed;

"Discount Charge"
The discount charge (if any) to be deducted in computing a Purchase Price in accordance with clause 9(1)(b) and dealt with in accordance with clause 9(2);

"Factoring Fee"
The fee to be deducted in computing the Purchase Price of every Debt purchased by the Factor in accordance with clause 9(1)(a);

"Goods"
Any goods (and where the context so admits any services) the subject of a Sale Contract;

"Insolvency"
(i) In the case of an individual: bankruptcy or sequestration;
(ii) in the case of a partnership: winding up by the court or bankruptcy or sequestration;
(iii) in the case of a corporate body: winding up by the court or voluntary winding up by reason of its inability to pay its debts or the appointment of an administrator pursuant to the Act or of a receiver of any part or all of its income or assets; and
(iv) in any case: any informal or voluntary arrangement (whether or not in accordance with the Act) with or for the benefit of the general body of creditors of the individual partnership or body corporate;

"Minimum Balance"
The amount which at any time is equivalent to the aggregate of the amounts of the following:
(i) all outstanding Unapproved Debts as shown in the records of the Factor;
(ii) all liabilities of the Client to the Factor which may be debited to the Current Account pursuant to clause 7(2) but which have not been so debited; and
(iii) such percentage of the outstanding Approved Debts (as shown in the records of the Factor) as is the remainder after deducting from 100 per cent the percentage specified in section 5 of the Schedule;

"Notification"
    A notification of a Debt by the Client to the Factor pursuant to clause 6(2) and "notified" shall be construed accordingly;

"Onset of Insolvency"
    (i) In the case of sequestration or bankruptcy or winding up by the court: the date of the sequestration award or the bankruptcy or winding up order respectively;
    (ii) in the case of voluntary winding up: the date of the effective resolution for winding up by members of the body corporate;
    (iii) in the case of the appointment of a receiver or administrator: the date of his appointment; and
    (iv) in the case of an arrangement the date when it is made;

"Outstanding Debt"
    Any Debt which has been included in a Notification and which remains vested in the Factor and unpaid and "outstanding" shall be construed accordingly;

"Prepayment"
    A payment made by the Factor to the Client on account of any Purchase Price (before the Transfer Date thereof) up to the percentage specified in section 5 of the Schedule of the amount of such Debt as notified;

"Purchase Price"
    The amount payable by the Factor to the Client pursuant to clause 6(1) for each Debt (together with any Related Rights and Transferred Goods pertaining thereto) purchased by the Factor;

"Recourse"
    The right of the Factor to require the Client to repurchase a Debt (together with any Related Rights and Transferred Goods relating thereto) purchased by the Factor at a repurchase price equivalent to the amount of such Debt as notified;

"Related Rights"
    (i) All the Client's rights under the Sale Contract giving rise to a Debt;
    (ii) the benefit of all guarantees indemnities insurances and securities given to or held by the Client in relation to such Debt;
    (iii) all cheques bills of exchange and other instruments held by or available to the Client in relation to such Debt; and
    (iv) the ledgers computer data records and documents on or by which such Debt is recorded or evidenced;

"Right of Immediate Termination"
    The right of the Factor to terminate this Agreement forthwith by notice in the circumstances described in clause 19(2) whether or not the Factor shall have exercised that right;

"Sale Contract"
    A contract for the supply of Goods by the Client;

"Transfer Date"
    The day specified in section 3 of the Schedule on which any Purchase Price is to be transferred to the Current Account pursuant to clause 7(2);

"Transferred Goods"
    Any Goods in respect of which the Factor shall have exercised its right pursuant to clause 4(2)

"Unapproved Debt"
    A debt which is not an Approved Debt.

THE SCHEDULE

(forming part of an agreement for the factoring or discounting of Debts between Venture Factors PLC. and the person named in section 1 hereof)

1   (a)   Name and trading address
            of Client :

     (b)   Place of incorporation :   England
            Registered number :
            (clause 1)

2   Debtors for inclusion   All United Kingdom based debtors
     (clause 4(1)) :

3   Transfer Date (clause 7(2)) :   One working day after receipt of
                                                    notification from the bankers for
                                                    the time being to the Factor of
                                                    receipt of cleared funds

4   Debts within Credit Limits which
     are not Approved Debts (clause 7(3)
     and Definition of Approved Debt) :   ALL

5   Prepayment percentage (clause 7(3)   % on debts less than
     and definition of Prepayment) :   days from end of month of
                                                    invoice date

6   Prepayment concentration on single
     Debtor - percentage (clause 7(6)):   Up to % on agreed names

7   Factoring Fee (exclusive of value
     added tax) (clause 9(1)(a)):   %

8   Discount Charge (clause 9(1)(b)):   % over the Base Rate of Midland
                                                    Bank Plc for the time being in
                                                    force

9   Supplementary Fee (exclusive of value
     added tax)(clause 9(3)):

     (a)   Number of days :   N/A
     (b)   Percentage rate: N/A

10   Additional Factoring Fee (exclusive
     of value added tax) - minimum
     (clause 9(4))   :   N/A

....
Initial Initial   Initial Initial

11   Nature of Client's Business
        (clause 11(2)(b)):

12   Client's Sale Contract
        (clause 11(2)(b)):
        (a)   Currency: Sterling
        (b)   Terms of payment: Up to 60 days with maximum
                                                   settlement discount of 5%
        (c)   Governing law: English

13   Notices to Debtors and Collection
        Arrangements (clauses 13(2) and
        13(3)):   On all Invoices

14   Commencement (clause 19(1)):

15   Minimum Period (clause 19(1)):   Twelve Calendar Months

16   Period of Notice of Termination
        (clause 19(1)):   Three Calendar Months

17   Special Conditions:

        1   Prepayments (Clause 7(3)) will not normally be available on the following
                classes of sales:

                -       Sales to customers from whom you also buy and for whom you are
                        therefore unable to give the Warranty under Clause 11.

                -       Sales to related and group companies (if any).

                -       Sales to private individuals. For the avoidance of misunderstanding the
                        words "private individuals" shall mean individuals who do not purchase
                        goods or services for the purpose of trading on their own account.

                -       Debts at commencement which are in Solicitors hands or similar.

                Sales to the above classes of Debtors are to be separately notified.

        2   The Agreement is to be supported by the Personal Guarantee and Indemnities
                of

        3   Prior to the commencement of prepayments a release of the book debts will be
                required from any Debenture which exists or may come into existence in the
                future.

....
Initial Initial   Initial Initial

4   Audited accounts to be provided as soon as signed each year. Monthly management accounts will be required within 21 days of each month end. Should these not be received within the agreed timescale, Venture Factors PLC. reserves the right to reduce the prepayment level.

....
Initial Initial

....
Initial Initial

IN WITNESS whereof such of the parties as are bodies corporate have caused their respective Common Seals to be affixed to this Deed and such of the parties as are not bodies corporate have executed this Deed in the presence of the persons named below.

The Common Seal of VENTURE FACTORS PLC.)
was hereunto affixed to this Deed on the)
)
        day of   19)
)

in the presence of:

(Full Name)...Director) ....
)
(Full Name).......................................Director/Secretary) ....

The Common Seal of)
was hereunto affixed to this Deed on the)
        day of   19)
)

in the presence of:
)
)

(Full Name)...Director) ....
)
(Full Name).......................................Director/Secretary) ....
)

8 Master block discounting agreement

THIS AGREEMENT is made the . . . . . day of . . . .

BETWEEN:

(1) *(name of finance company)* whose registered office is at *(address)* Company registration no . . . ('the Company') and
(2) *(name of dealer)* [of *(address) or* whose registered office is at *(address)*] [Company Registration no . . .] ('the Dealer').

IT IS AGREED as follows:

1 Discounting of Agreements

The Company will at the request of the Dealer and if the Company thinks fit purchase from the Dealer the rights of the Dealer ('the Contract Rights') under the hire-purchase and credit sale agreements ('the Agreements') entered into by the Dealer as owner or seller with the hirers or buyers named in the Agreements together with the goods comprised in such of the Agreements as are hire-purchase agreements.

2 Documents to accompany request to purchase

When submitting requests to purchase to the Company [(which requests shall be submitted at [weekly *or* monthly] intervals and shall relate to not less than . . . agreements at a time)] the Dealer shall forward to the Company the following documents:

2.1 A schedule of the Agreements to which the request relates such schedule being in the Company's standard form for the time being or in such other form as may be approved by the Company;
2.2 The original agreements referred to in the schedule;
2.3 A satisfaction note signed by the hirer or buyer under each of the Agreements recording the acknowledgment of the hirer or buyer that he received the goods in proper condition.

3 Payment to Dealer

If the Company accepts the Dealer's request to purchase it shall notify the Dealer accordingly and then the Contract Rights and in the case of hire-purchase agreements the property in the goods comprised in those agreements shall vest in the Company which shall pay to the Dealer a sum representing the total balances outstanding under the Agreements ('the Collection Value') less:

3.1 a retention of . . .% of the Collection Value by way of security for performance of the Dealer's obligations under this agreement;
3.2 a discount charge of . . .% (or such other percentage as may from time to time be agreed) of the difference between the Collection Value and the retention.

4 Release of retention

So long as the Dealer is not in default under this agreement and none of the hirers or buyers is in default under any of the Agreements the Company will release to the Dealer every [month] or with the written consent of the Company the Dealer may every [month] deduct from the instalments collected by him an aliquot portion of the retention spread over the period (or if there are differing periods the average period) for which the sums representing the Collection Value of the discounted agreements are payable. If any hirer or buyer under any of the Agreements is in default or if the Dealer has incurred any liability to the Company whether under this agreement or under any other agreement or in any manner whatsoever and whether such liability shall be by way of debt or damages the Company may apply in discharge of the Dealer's liability so much of the retention as shall be necessary for that purpose.

5 Duties of Dealer

The Dealer undertakes at his own expense:

5.1 Agreement to assign
To execute an assignment of all or any of the Contract Rights in the form required by the Company and until such assignment to hold the Contract Rights and the Agreements as trustee for the Company.

5.2 Legal charges and stamp duty
To pay to the Company the amount of all legal charges and all stamp duties paid or incurred by the Company on any such assignment the Company being at liberty to recoup itself for such charges and duties out of the retention referred to in clause 3 above.

5.3 Dealer to keep accounts
To maintain proper accounts on behalf of the Company in the names of the hirers and buyers showing the amounts paid by and due from the hirers and buyers both before and after purchase of the Agreements by the Company under this agreement and to permit the Company and its agents full facilities to inspect and audit such accounts and take copies of and extracts from them whenever the Company shall require.

5.4 Dealings with other companies
To notify the Company of all dealings of the Dealer with any other person firm or company with whom the Dealer has an agreement or arrangement to discount hire-purchase credit sale or hiring agreements or rentals or to sell goods to be let by such person firm or company under hire-purchase or credit sale agreements and the Dealer shall at the request of the Company supply full details of all transactions entered into by the Dealer with such person firm or company.

5.5 Dealer's accounts
To provide the Company on request with audited and other accounts and balance sheets relating to the Dealer's business.

5.6 Bills of exchange and notes
By way of collateral security for the due performance of the Dealer's obligations under this agreement to accept or indorse such bills of exchange and make or indorse such promissory notes as may from time to time be required by the Company for sums not exceeding in the aggregate the total balances remaining due from the hirers or buyers under the Agreements. The Company shall have the right to transfer or negotiate any such bills or notes whether or not the Dealer is in default under the terms of this agreement and any transferee or holder of such bills or notes shall take them as a holder in due course free from any equities or defences of the Dealer.

5.7   Collection of instalments as agent
To collect punctually as agent for the Company all sums due under the Agreements and remit such sums without any deduction save as authorised by clause 4 above to the Company at such intervals as the Company may require holding them meanwhile on trust for the Company and if the Company so requires paying such sums into a bank account to be opened in the name of the Company or as the Company shall direct provided that the Company may at any time terminate the Dealer's authority and agency to collect sums from hirers or buyers under the Agreements and the Dealer shall then cease to collect or engage in collecting them.

5.8   Repossess goods on request
At the Dealer's own expense to repossess any goods comprised in any of the Agreements if required so to do but not otherwise provided that the Dealer shall not repossess any goods contrary to law or in an illegal manner and shall indemnify the Company against all claims arising from repossession and shall hold all repossessed goods on trust for the Company and deal with them as the Company shall direct.

6 Waiver of presentment and notice of dishonour

In respect of any bills of exchange or promissory notes taken by the Company from the Dealer pursuant to the provisions of this agreement the Dealer shall be deemed to have waived presentment for acceptance or payment and notice of dishonour and such waiver shall operate in favour of the Company and all other parties to whom the Company shall negotiate or otherwise transfer such bills or notes.

7 Power of attorney

The Dealer irrevocably appoints the Company the Dealer's attorney for the execution of any assignment required to be executed by the Dealer in favour of the Company under the provisions of this agreement and for the purpose of executing all other documents necessary to vest title in the Company to any of the Agreements or any goods comprised in the Agreements and further irrevocably appoints the Company the attorney of the Dealer for the purpose of accepting and indorsing all bills of exchange and making and indorsing all promissory notes which the Dealer is obliged to accept make or indorse pursuant to the provisions of this agreement.

8 Representations by Dealer

Every request to purchase sent by the Dealer to the Company pursuant to the provisions of this agreement shall be deemed to incorporate representations by the Dealer that:
8.1   the deposit shown in each of the Agreements as paid has in fact been paid in the manner stated and that any allowance given to the hirer or buyer for goods taken in part exchange is reasonable in relation to the value of such goods;
8.2   the Dealer is the owner of the goods specified in such of the Agreements as are hire-purchase agreements and that such goods are free from charges or incumbrances;
8.3   the details of the hirer or buyer and the particulars of the goods and other information set out in the Agreements are correct in every respect;
8.4   none of the goods comprised in any of the hire-purchase agreements was previously the property of the hirer or was previously held by the hirer under

any other hire-purchase agreement except as stated in the hire-purchase agreement submitted by the Dealer;

8.5 the goods described in each of the Agreements are in existence and have been duly delivered to the hirer or buyer named in that agreement;

8.6 all the requirements of the Consumer Credit Act 1974 any regulations made under that Act and all other relevant Acts and regulations have been complied with in relation to each of the Agreements and that in particular such agreements comply with the formal requirements of the Consumer Credit Act 1974 and regulations made under that Act and the hirers or buyers have been supplied with all requisite copies of the Agreements;

8.7 the provisions of any of the Agreements excluding conditions of fitness or merchantable quality in relation to the goods were brought to the notice of the hirer or buyer and their effect made clear to him;

8.8 no right of action is vested in any hirer or buyer in respect of any representation breach of condition breach of warranty or other express or implied term relating to the goods comprised in any of the Agreements;

8.9 the goods specified in the Agreements are in good order repair and condition and comply in all respects with the requirements of the law and with all terms of the Agreements express or implied;

8.10 all the Agreements are fully valid and enforceable against and are not disputed or subject to cancellation or rescission by the hirers and buyers named in the Agreements and all contracts of guarantee or indemnity given in connection with the Agreements are fully valid enforceable and undisputed and the Dealer has no knowledge of any fact which would or might invalidate any such agreement or contract or affect any right to enforce them.

In the event of any of the above representations being false (whether the falsity was known to the Dealer or not) a loss to the Company shall be deemed to have occurred for the purpose of clause 9 below on the date upon which the company purchased the contract Rights under the Agreement or Agreements in respect of which such representations have been made and the Company may then avail itself of any or all of the remedies provided by clause 9 below.

9 Recourse provisions

9.1 The Dealer shall on demand indemnify the Company against all loss or damage which the Company may sustain as a result of purchasing from the Dealer any contract rights or any goods comprised in any of the Agreements whether or not such loss or damage results from the commission of any breach by the hirer or buyer under such agreement and whether or not the Company has any legal right to claim against such hirer or buyer or against any guarantor or indemnifier in respect of any associated contract of guarantee or indemnity for such loss or damage or has availed itself of its legal remedies against such hirer buyer guarantor or indemnifier or against the goods and the Dealer shall be liable to pay the amount of such loss or damage to the Company immediately it occurs.

9.2 For the purpose of this agreement the Company's loss in relation to any hire-purchase or credit sale agreement shall be deemed to have occurred as provided by clause 8 above or upon termination of the hire-purchase or credit sale agreement or of the hiring of the goods comprised in any such hire-purchase agreement or upon the hirer or buyer making default for 14 days in payment of any sum due under the agreement whichever of the above events shall first occur. Such loss shall be computed as:

9.2.1 the unpaid balance of the total price or total purchase price payable under the hire-purchase or credit sale agreement including interest on overdue instalments payments made by the Company to third parties pursuant to powers contained in the agreement all legal and other expenses incurred by the Company in relation to the agreement and all other sums for which the hirer or buyer is liable under the hire-purchase or credit sale agreement (or would be liable if the hire-purchase or credit sale agreement were binding on him) and has not paid to the Company **less**

9.2.2 such rebate for the acceleration of payment as the Company would have been obliged to allow the hirer or buyer under the terms of the hire-purchase or credit sale agreement if the hirer or the buyer had completed his payments on the date of the deemed loss;

provided that where in the case of a hire-purchase agreement the Company has repossessed and sold the goods comprised in the agreement credit shall be given for the net proceeds of sale (after deducting the costs and expenses of repossession storage insurance and sale) in computing such loss.

9.3 Where the Dealer has indemnified the Company as provided in this agreement (and in the case of a hire-purchase agreement the goods have not been sold by the Company) the Company shall at the Dealer's request and at his expense reassign to the Dealer the benefit of the hire-purchase or credit sale agreement (if such agreement is still subsisting and the rights of the owner under that agreement were assigned to the Company and are still vested in the Company) together with the Company's interest in the goods provided that:

9.3.1 the Company shall not be under any liability to the Dealer to deliver to him the goods comprised in any such hire-purchase agreement or to take any steps for the recovery of such goods nor shall the Company incur any liability to the Dealer if the goods are no longer in existence or available to be repossessed or are in a defective damaged or useless state;

9.3.2 where the Dealer has incurred other liabilities to the Company whether under this agreement or otherwise the Company shall be entitled to dispose of the goods and to assign its rights under the hire-purchase or credit sale agreement and any associated contract of guarantee or indemnity as it thinks fit and to apply the proceeds of sale and of the assignment in reduction of such liabilities of the Dealer.

10 Interest on overdue payments

In the event of the Dealer failing to pay on demand the sums due under clause 9 above the Dealer shall be liable to pay interest on such sums at the rate of . . .% per year from the date of demand for payment to the date when payment is made. Such interest shall accrue from day to day and shall run after as well as before any judgment obtained against the Dealer.

11 Rights under the Sale of Goods Act 1979

The terms and conditions in favour of the Company under this agreement shall be in addition to and not in substitution for any terms conditions or warranties implied in favour of a purchaser of goods under the Sale of Goods Act 1979.

12 No waiver

The liability of the Dealer under this agreement shall not be discharged diminished or affected by the granting of any time or indulgence to the Dealer or any hirer buyer guarantor or indemnifier or by the effecting of any compromise with or any agreement not to sue any hirer buyer guarantor or indemnifier or by any variation of the terms of any of the Agreements or by the failure of the Company to institute or pursue any legal proceedings against any hirer buyer guarantor or indemnifier or to take any steps of any kind for recovery of the goods or to take hold unimpaired or enforce any security or securities for payment from any hirer buyer guarantor or indemnifier and no waiver by the Company of any branch of the Dealer's obligations under this agreement shall operate as a waiver of any future or continuing breach.

13 Dealer not agent

Save as expressly provided by this agreement the Dealer is not the agent of nor shall be be deemed to have authority from the Company for any purpose and in particular he is not the agent of and shall not be deemed to have authority from the Company to vary terminate or accept notice of termination of any of the Agreements or to accept the return of any goods by any hirer or buyer under any such agreement or to institute any legal proceedings against any hirer buyer guarantor or indemnifier and if the Dealer collects any instalment from any hirer or buyer after the Dealer's authority to collect such instalments has been terminated pursuant to the provisions of clause 5.7 above the sum so collected shall be held in trust for the Company.

14 Right of set-off

Where the Dealer has incurred any liability to the Company whether under this agreement or otherwise and whether such liability is liquidated or unliquidated the Company may set off the amount of such liability against any sum that would otherwise be due to the Dealer under this agreement.

15 Notices

All notices demands and statements required or permitted to be given to the Dealer under the provisions of this agreement shall be validly given if served personally on the Dealer or sent by prepaid post to or left at the address of the Dealer stated in this agreement or at the Dealer's present or last known business or private address or where the Dealer is a registered company to or at its registered office or any present or the last known business address. Any such notice demand or statement sent to the Dealer by post shall be conclusively deemed to have been received by the Dealer within 48 hours after the time of posting.

16 Termination of agreement

This agreement may be terminated by either party by [one month's] notice in writing given at any time but such termination shall be without prejudice to the liabilities of either party accrued before the date of termination.

AS WITNESS etc

(signatures of both parties)

9 Trust receipt

To *(name of bank)*
of *(address)*

(date)

1 Acknowledgment of receipt

[I *or* We] acknowledge that [I *or* we] have received from you, upon and subject to the terms and conditions set out below, the documents of title described in the schedule below ('the Documents') relating to the goods described in it ('the Goods'), which are now pledged to you as security upon the terms of (*specify details of memorandum of pledge, letter of hypothecation etc as appropriate*).

2 Documents etc to be held as trustee

[I *or* We] acknowledge that [I *or* we] have received the Documents and will hold them, the Goods, the proceeds of any sale of the Goods and all insurance money arising from them, as trustee[s] for you.

3 Purpose and terms

[I *or* We] hold the Documents and will deal with them only for the following purpose and on the following terms that is to say in order to obtain delivery of and to warehouse the Goods. The Goods will be warehoused in your name or otherwise as directed by you but at [my *or* our] expense, and [I *or* we] shall hand to you the relative warrants immediately on receipt. [I *or* We] undertake to keep the Goods duly covered by insurance as agreed between us pursuant to (*specify details as above*) and in case of loss to pay the insurance money immediately and specifically to you without any deduction [*or* in order to deliver the Goods to the buyer[s] named in the schedule below. [I *or* We] agree to pay to you immediately and specifically on receipt the whole proceeds of sale and each part of the proceeds (whatever form they may take) without any deduction. Pending the sale, [I *or* we] undertake to keep the Goods duly covered by insurance as agreed between us in (*specify details as above*) and in case of loss to pay the insurance money immediately and specifically to you without any deduction. [I *or* We] confirm that [I am *or* we are] not indebted to the buyer[s].]

4 Transaction to be kept separate

[I *or* We] undertake that this transaction will be kept separate from any other transaction and that the Documents, the Goods, the proceeds of any sale and all insurance money shall be kept separate and distinct from any other documents, goods, proceeds of sale or insurance money relating to or arising from any other transaction.

5 Documents returnable on demand

[I *or* We] undertake to return to you immediately on demand at any time (whether or not the purpose set out above shall have been completed) the Documents and/or any other documents received by us in exchange or substitution for them and to comply promptly and fully with any instructions which you may give as to the manner of dealing with the Goods or any of them or the removal of them to, or storage of them at, any place.

6 Governing law and jurisdiction

[Details omitted.]

SCHEDULE

Reference Number: ....

Particulars of the Documents: ....

Description of the Goods: ....

Marks and Numbers: ....

Vessel: ....

Name[s] of buyer[s]: ....

Invoice price: ....

(signature(s) of customer(s))

10 Debenture (fixed and floating charge)

3i PLC

DEBENTURE

dated the   day of   19

Payment Covenant

1. THE Company named in the Second Schedule hereto (hereinafter called 'the Company') HEREBY COVENANTS with 3i plc whose registered office is at 91 Waterloo Road London SE1 8XP (hereinafter called '3i') . . . that it will on such date or dates as provided by Clause 2 hereof PAY or DISCHARGE to 3i all moneys and liabilities now or at any time or times hereafter due or owing or incurred by the Company to 3i in any manner whatever whether actually or contingently and whether as principal or surety including interest thereon at such rate as may be agreed in writing from time to time between the Company and 3i whether before or after the execution of this Debenture and together also with all commission charges costs and expenses payable in connection therewith.

Payment Date
2. ALL or any moneys and liabilities due or owing or incurred by the Company to 3i shall be repaid or discharged by the Company on demand unless otherwise agreed in writing from time to time between the Company and 3i whether before or after the execution of this Debenture (such agreement or agreements in writing being hereinafter together referred to as 'the Agreement').

Charging Clause
3. THE Company as beneficial owner HEREBY CHARGES with the payment and discharge to 3i of all moneys and liabilities . . . hereby covenanted to be paid and discharged by the Company and all other sums intended to be hereby secured:—

FIRST—THE property described in the Third Schedule hereto together with all buildings and fixtures (including trade fixtures) and fixed plant and machinery from time to time thereon and therein;

SECOND—ALL other freehold and leasehold property of the Company both present and future together with all buildings and fixtures (including trade fixtures) and fixed plant and machinery from time to time thereon and therein;

THIRD—ALL the plant machinery chattels or other equipment described in the Fourth Schedule hereto . . .

FOURTH—THE goodwill and the uncalled capital of the Company both present and future;

FIFTH—THE book debts and other debts due or owing to the Company both present and future;

SIXTH—THE stock-in-trade work-in-progress pre-payments investments quoted on a recognised Stock Exchange and cash of the Company both present and future;

SEVENTH—ALL other the undertaking and all other property and assets of the Company both present and future.

Nature of Charges

4. THE charges on the property and assets FIRST SECOND THIRD FOURTH and FIFTH described are created as fixed charges and constitute charges by way of legal mortgage on the property FIRST and SECOND described which is now vested in the company . . .

The charges on the property and assets SIXTH and SEVENTH described (and also on such other property and assets of the Company both present and future as 3i may have agreed in writing to exclude from the fixed charge or are otherwise not charged hereunder by way of fixed charge) are created as floating charges until a demand has been made under Condition 8 set out in the First Schedule hereto or until the provisions of Condition 9 set out in the First Schedule hereto become operative when the floating charges shall crystallise and become fixed charges.

The charges created hereby shall be a continuing security and shall unless otherwise agreed in writing by 3i be first charges. The Company shall not without the previous written consent of 3i:—

(i) create or continue any mortgage or charge upon the mortgaged chattels or any part thereof or allow any lien to arise on or affect the mortgaged chattels or any part thereof;
(ii) create or continue any mortgage or charge upon any part of the other property or assets hereby charged which would rank either in priority to or pari passu with the charges hereby created;
(iii) allow any lien to arise on or affect any part of the other property or assets hereby charged except in the case of a lien arising by operation of law in the ordinary course of business.

Warranty

5. THE Company HEREBY WARRANTS to 3i that it is the absolute beneficial owner free from all liens charges and encumbrances of all the mortgaged chattels.

Incorporation of Conditions

6. THIS Debenture is issued subject to and with the benefit of the conditions set out in the First Schedule hereto. The property and assets FIRST and SECOND above described are therein referred to as 'the specifically mortgaged property'. The specifically mortgaged property and the property and assets THIRD FOURTH FIFTH SIXTH and SEVENTH described are therein together referred to as 'the mortgaged property'. The bank specified in the Fifth Schedule hereto (or such other bank as 3i may agree to in writing) is therein referred to as 'the Bank'.

EXECUTED as a Deed by the Company and delivered the day and year first above written.

THE FIRST SCHEDULE hereinbefore referred to

CONDITIONS

Deposit of deeds and documents of title

1. Subject to the rights of any prior mortgagee the Company shall deposit with 3i and 3i shall during the continuance of this security be entitled to hold and retain all deeds and documents of title relating to the specifically mortgaged property and all invoices documents of title guarantees and maintenance agreements relating to the mortgaged chattels.

Further charges
2. The Company shall forthwith if and when called upon by 3i so to do execute in favour of 3i or as 3i shall direct such further legal or other mortgages or charges as 3i shall require . . .

Leases
3. The Company shall pay the rents reserved by and perform and observe all the covenants agreements and stipulations on the part of the lessee contained in any lease or leases of the specifically mortgaged property . . .

Payments
4. The Company shall as and when the same shall become payable pay all taxes rates duties charges assessments and outgoings whatsoever . . . which shall be assessed charged or imposed upon or payable in respect of the specifically mortgaged property or any part thereof . . .

After-acquired property
5. Upon the acquisition or purchase by the Company from time to time of any freehold or leasehold property the Company shall forthwith notify 3i in writing.

Use of premises
6. (A) The Company shall use the specifically mortgaged property only for such purpose or purposes as may for the time being be authorised as the permitted use or user thereof under or by virtue of the Planning Acts (as hereinafter defined) . . .

Use of chattels
(B) The Company shall not use or permit the mortgaged chattels to be used in contravention of any legislation (as hereinafter defined) or otherwise in any way contrary to law . . .

Development
7. The Company shall not carry out any development within the meaning of the Planning Acts in or upon the specifically mortgaged property or any part thereof without first obtaining such permission as may be required under or by virtue of the Planning Acts . . .

Crystallisation of security subject to demand for repayment
8. In respect of any moneys or liabilities due owing or incurred by the Company to 3i which by virtue of the Agreement are to be discharged otherwise than on demand 3i shall nevertheless be entitled by notice to the Company to demand the immediate payment and discharge thereof (or any part thereof) together with all interest and any other sums forthwith (or otherwise as 3i may require) at any time after the happening of any of the following events:—

(A) if the Company makes default in the payment on due date of any money which may have become due hereunder or under the Agreement or under any deed or document supplemental hereto or thereto;

(B) if any distress execution sequestration or other process is threatened levied or enforced upon or sued out against all or any of the property of the Company or any company or individual who has guaranteed or become surety for repayment of all or any part of the moneys and liabilities hereby secured (hereinafter referred to as 'a Guarantor') or 3i is of the opinion that such property is otherwise in jeopardy;

(C) if the Company or a Guarantor is unable to pay its debts within the meaning of section 123 of the Insolvency Act 1986 or certifies that it is unable to pay its debts as and when they fall due;

(D) if the Company or a Guarantor fails to comply with any of the covenants conditions or provisions contained herein or in the Agreement or in any deed or document supplemental hereto or thereto or if any warranty given by the Company or a Guarantor or any Director (as defined in the Agreement or in any deed or document supplemental thereto) to 3i proves to be materially untrue;

(E) if the specifically mortgaged property or the mortgaged chattels (both as defined herein or in any deed or document supplemental hereto or to the Agreement) or any part thereof is compulsorily acquired by or by order of any local or other authority and as a result the business of the Company or a Guarantor is seriously affected;

(F) if a proposal is made to the Company or a Guarantor and its creditors for a voluntary arrangement pursuant to section 1 of the Insolvency Act 1986;

(G) if a meeting of the Company or a Guarantor is convened for the purpose of considering a resolution for the winding up of the Company or a Guarantor;

(H) if an application is made to the Court for an order for the winding up of the Company or a Guarantor.

If any of the aforementioned events occurs 3i shall be under no obligation to advance any moneys under the Agreement.

Upon any demand being made for payment of any moneys hereby secured such moneys shall become payable immediately and all rights of the Company to deal for any purpose whatever with the mortgaged property or any part thereof shall forthwith cease and any floating charge shall forthwith crystallise and become a fixed charge.

Crystallisation of security without demand
9. The moneys hereby secured shall become immediately payable and all rights of the Company to deal for any purpose whatever with the mortgaged property or any part thereof shall forthwith cease and the floating charges shall forthwith crystallise and become fixed charges on the happening of any of the following events:—

(A) if an order is made for the winding up of the Company or a Guarantor by the court or if an effective resolution is passed for the members' or creditors' voluntary winding up of the Company or a Guarantor;

(B) if a petition is presented for an administration order to be made in relation to the Company or a Guarantor pursuant to the Insolvency Act 1986;

(C) if the Company or a Guarantor stops payment or ceases to carry on its business or substantially the whole of its business or threatens to cease to carry on the same or substantially changes the nature of its business;

(D) if the Company without the previous consent of 3i shall sell transfer lease dispose of or deal with the mortgaged chattels or any part thereof or purport so to do;

(E) if any encumbrancer takes possession or a receiver (as hereinafter defined) is appointed of all or any part of the property and assets of the Company or a Guarantor;

(F) if a Guarantor (being an individual) makes application to the court for a voluntary arrangement pursuant to section 253 of the Insolvency Act 1986 or enters into some other scheme of arrangement with creditors or is unable to pay his debts within the meaning of section 268 of the Insolvency Act 1986 or presents a debtor's petition to the court pursuant to the Insolvency Act 1986.

If any of the aforementioned events occurs 3i shall be under no obligation to advance any moneys under the Agreement.

In this Debenture 'receiver' shall mean both a receiver or receiver and manager of part only of the mortgaged property and an administrative receiver as defined by the Insolvency Act 1986.

Receiver Appointment
10. (A) At any time after the moneys hereby secured shall have become payable or at the request of the Company 3i may without further notice appoint in writing under its hand any person or persons to be a receiver or receivers (hereinafter called a 'Receiver' which expression shall include any substituted receiver or receivers) of all or any part of the mortgaged property in like manner in every respect as if 3i had become entitled under the Law of Property Act 1925 to exercise the power of sale thereby conferred and every Receiver so appointed shall have and be entitled to exercise all powers conferred by the said Act as if such Receiver had been duly appointed thereunder and in particular by way of addition to but without hereby limiting any general powers hereinbefore referred to every such Receiver so appointed shall have the powers hereinafter referred to.

Removal
(B) 3i may from time to time by writing under its hand remove any Receiver appointed by it (but in the case of an administrative receiver such removal shall only be with the sanction of the court) and may whenever it may deem it expedient appoint a new Receiver in the place of any Receiver whose appointment may for any reason have terminated and may from time to time fix the remuneration of any Receiver appointed by it.

Powers
(C) At any time after the moneys hereby secured shall have become payable any Receiver appointed hereunder may without further notice exercise all or any of the following powers:—

 (i) take immediate possession of get in and collect the mortgaged property or any part thereof . . .;
 (ii) carry on the business of the Company . . .;
 (iii) make and effect all repairs and insurances and do all other acts which the Company might do in the ordinary conduct of its business as well for the protection as for the improvement of the mortgaged property;
 (iv) sell convert into money and realise all or any part of the mortgaged property . . .;

[Remaining powers omitted.]
In addition to the above powers an administrative receiver may exercise all the powers conferred upon him by Schedule 1 to the Insolvency Act 1986.

Sale
11. Section 103 of the Law of Property Act 1925 shall not apply to this Debenture
. . .

Book Debts

12. During the continuance of this security the Company shall:—

(A) pay into a current account or a separate designated account (as 3i may require) of the Company with the Bank all moneys which it may receive in respect of the book debts and other debts hereby charged and (subject to any rights of the Bank in respect thereof) pay or otherwise deal with such moneys standing in such account in accordance with any directions from time to time given in writing by 3i . . .;

(B) if called upon to do so by 3i execute a legal assignment of such book debts and other debts to 3i in such terms as 3i may require and give notice thereof to the debtors from whom the debts are owing or incurred and take such other steps as 3i may require to perfect such legal assignment;

(c) deal with such book debts and other debts in accordance with any directions from time to time given in writing by 3i (subject to any rights of the Bank in respect thereof) and in default of and subject to any such directions deal with the same only in the ordinary course of getting in and realising the same (but not sell assign factor or discount the same in any way) . . .

[Clauses 13–29, dealing with obligations of the company to repair, insure, etc are omitted.]

THE SECOND SCHEDULE hereinbefore referred to

Name Registered Office and Registered Number of the Company

THE THIRD SCHEDULE hereinbefore referred to

Description of Freehold or Leasehold property specifically charged

THE FOURTH SCHEDULE hereinbefore referred to

Description of Plant Machinery or Equipment mortgaged

THE FIFTH SCHEDULE hereinbefore referred to

Name and Address of Branch of the Bank

EXECUTED as a DEED for
and on behalf of THE COMPANY by:—

Director

Director/Secretary

11 'All monies' continuing bank guarantee

Dated _____ 19 ____

to

Midland Bank plc

Guarantee

re:

5231-6 (03/93) **Guarantee**   **A13**

IMPORTANT - PLEASE READ THE FOLLOWING NOTE BEFORE SIGNING THIS DOCUMENT

This document is a guarantee.

You should sign the guarantee form in front of a witness, who should be your solicitor or a Bank official.

The Bank will hold the guarantee as security for all the debts to the Bank of the person, persons or company named as "the Principal" in this document, but only up to the Guarantee Limit, where applicable.

These debts may be overdrafts, loans or money due under other facilities that the Bank has granted the Principal or grants the Principal in the future. Or the debts may arise from guarantees that the Principal has given the Bank or gives the Bank in the future. Normally the Bank will not notify you of future loans or guarantees.

If two or more people are named as "the Principal", the guarantee will be held as security for the debts described above which each of them owes as well as for the debts which both or all of them owe.

If any of the Principal's debts are not paid when due, the Bank may require you to pay the total amount of the overdue debts, up to the guarantee limit, where applicable. You will also be charged interest if you pay late.

The guarantee is separate from and not limited by any other mortgage or guarantee which you may already have given the Bank or which you may give in the future.

The guarantee contains other terms which affect you.

The guarantee is an important legal document. The Bank recommends that before signing it you should seek the advice of your own solicitor, or other professional adviser.

Checker's Initials	

TO **Midland Bank plc**

Guarantee

1.　In consideration of Midland Bank plc ("the Bank") granting continuing or otherwise affording to

("the Principal")

banking facilities credit accommodation or other financial assistance

("the Guarantor")

hereby agrees and undertakes to pay and satisfy the Bank on demand (but subject to the limit if any of the aggregate amount recoverable under this Guarantee as provided below) the whole and each and every part of the monies and liabilities defined in clause 2.

Provided that the aggregate amount recoverable from the Guarantor under this Guarantee shall be limited to the sum of

£　　　　　　　　(　　　　　　　　　　　　　　　　pounds sterling)

together with interest on that sum as provided in clause 4.

"Monies and Liabilities"

2.　　(i)　The words "monies and liabilities" mean all monies and liabilities which now are or shall at any time hereafter be due owing or incurred to the Bank by the Principal whether actually or contingently and whether presently or in the future and whether solely or jointly with any other person and whether as principal or surety or in any way whatsoever including (as well after as before any demand made or judgment obtained) interest discount commission and other lawful charges and expenses but shall not include any monies and liabilities arising under a regulated consumer credit agreement falling within Part V of the Consumer Credit Act 1974, unless specifically agreed between the Principal and the Bank.

　　　(ii)　Where there are two or more persons comprised in the expression "the Principal" the monies and liabilities hereby secured shall include the monies and liabilities due owing or incurred to the Bank by any of such persons whether solely or jointly with one or more of the others and the expression "the Principal" shall be construed accordingly.

　　　(iii)　Where the persons comprised in the expression "the Principal" are carrying on business in partnership under a firm name the monies and liabilities hereby secured shall (notwithstanding any change in the composition of the partnership) include the monies and liabilities which shall at any time hereafter be due owing or incurred to the Bank by the person or persons from time to time carrying on the partnership business under that name or under any name in succession thereto and the expression "the Principal" shall be construed accordingly.

Provision of facilities for the Principal

3.　The Bank may at any time or times without notice to the Guarantor (but without being under any obligation to the Guarantor to do so) grant continue or otherwise afford to the Principal (whether solely or jointly with any other person) banking facilities credit accommodation or other financial assistance in such amount upon such terms and subject to such conditions as may from time to time be agreed between the Bank and the Principal.

Interest after demand

4.　Any sum or sums demanded from the Guarantor under this Guarantee (including any sums demanded pursuant to Clause 14 hereof) shall bear simple interest (as well after as before any judgment) at the daily rate of 3 per centum per annum over the Bank's base rate from time to time from the date of demand until the date of payment thereof.

Independence of this security

5.　This Guarantee shall be in addition to and shall be independent of every other security (including any other guarantee given by the Guarantor) which the Bank may at any time hold for any of the monies and liabilities.

Determination

6.　This Guarantee shall be a continuing security and shall remain in full force and effect until release by the Bank. Provided always that if the Guarantor shall give to the Bank a written notice of determination the monies and liabilities secured by this Guarantee shall be the monies and liabilities owing (whether actually or contingently and whether or not demand shall have been made therefor) to the Bank by the Principal at the expiration of three months after actual receipt of such notice by the Bank.

Currency Conversion

7. For the purpose of or pending the discharge of any of the monies and liabilities the Bank may convert any monies received recovered or realised by the Bank under this Guarantee (including the proceeds of any previous conversion under this Clause) from their existing currency of denomination into such other currency of denomination as the Bank may think fit and any such conversion shall be effected at the Bank's then prevailing spot selling rate of exchange for such other currency against the existing currency. Each previous reference in this Clause to a currency extends to funds of that currency and for the avoidance of doubt funds of one currency may be converted into different funds of the same currency.

Suspense Account

8. All monies received recovered or realised by the Bank under this Guarantee (including the proceeds of any conversion pursuant to Clause 7 above) may in the discretion of the Bank be credited to any suspense or impersonal account and shall bear interest at such rate if any as may be agreed in writing between the Bank and the Guarantor (and in default of agreement shall bear simple interest at the daily rate paid by the Bank on deposit accounts subject to 7 days notice of withdrawal from time to time) and may be held in such account for so long as the Bank may think fit pending the application from time to time (as the Bank shall be entitled to do as it may think fit) of such monies and any accrued interest thereon in or towards the discharge of any of the monies and liabilities.

Restrictions on recovery by the Guarantor

9. This Guarantee shall secure the full amount of the monies and liabilities from time to time and (notwithstanding that the aggregate amount recoverable from the Guarantor under this Guarantee may be subject to the limit if any in Clause 1 of this Guarantee) so long as this Guarantee remains in effect the Guarantor shall not unless the monies and liabilities have been paid and discharged in full be entitled to share in or succeed to or benefit from (by subrogation or otherwise) any rights the Bank may have or any security (whether by way of mortgage guarantee or otherwise) the Bank may hold (over all or any of the assets of the Principal or the proceeds of sale thereof) nor until the monies and liabilities have been so paid and discharged shall the Guarantor exercise enforce or seek to enforce without the prior written consent of the Bank any rights which the Guarantor may have against the Principal or any other person and arising by reason of the payment of any part of the monies and liabilities provided that any monies received recovered or realised by the Guarantor in or as a result of the exercise (whether with or without the Bank's consent) of such rights shall be held by the Guarantor as trustee upon trust to apply the same as if they were monies received recovered or realised by the Bank under this Guarantee.

Variation of terms and release of securities

10. The Bank may at any time without discharging or otherwise affecting this Guarantee vary the terms of or renew or determine any credit or other facilities made or to be made available to the Principal by the Bank take such security (whether by way of mortgage guarantee or otherwise) in respect of all or any of the monies and liabilities as it may from time to time think fit exchange release modify refrain from perfecting or enforcing or otherwise deal with any such security it may hold grant time or indulgence to or compound with the Principal or any other person and do or omit to do any act or thing which but for this provision might discharge or otherwise affect the liability of the Guarantor under this Guarantee.

Irregularities in other securities: incapacity of Principal

11. This Guarantee shall not be discharged or otherwise affected by the total or partial invalidity or unenforceability of or any irregularity or defect in any security (whether by way of mortgage guarantee or otherwise) the Bank may now or at any time hold in respect of all or any of the monies and liabilities and the Guarantor hereby indemnifies (subject to the limit if any provided in Clause 1 of this Guarantee) the Bank against all loss occasioned by or arising from any legal limitation disability or want of capacity of or affecting the Principal or any person acting or purporting to act on behalf of the Principal (including any want of authority in such person) in respect of all or any of the monies and liabilities.

Negligence in realisations

12. Provided that the Bank shall exercise reasonable care in selecting any receiver the amount recoverable from the Guarantor under this Guarantee shall not be affected by any neglect by the Bank or by any agent of or receiver appointed by the Bank in connection with the realisation of any security which the Bank may from time to time hold from the Principal or from any other person and the Bank shall not be liable at the suit of the Guarantor in respect of any such neglect.

Certificate of sum due

13. A certificate of a manager or officer of the Bank as to the amount for the time being of the monies and liabilities shall (apart from obvious mistakes) be for all purposes conclusive against the Guarantor.

Costs of enforcement

14. The Guarantor shall on demand pay on a full indemnity basis all costs charges and expenses in any way incurred by the Bank in relation to the enforcement of this Guarantee (including the costs of any proceedings in relation to this Guarantee or the monies and liabilities).

Appropriation after notice of determination

15. If the Guarantor shall give to the Bank a written notice of determination pursuant to Clause 6 of this Guarantee the Bank may open a new account or accounts for the Principal in its books and if the Bank does not do so then unless the Bank gives express written notice to the contrary to the Principal as from the time of receipt of such notice of determination by the Bank all payments made by the Principal to the Bank in the absence of any express appropriation by the Principal to the contrary shall be treated as having been

credited to a new account of the Principal and not as having been applied in reduction of the amount due owing or incurred from the Principal to the Bank at the time when it received such notice of determination.

Retention of Guarantee

16. Notwithstanding that the monies and liabilities shall have been paid in full the Bank may decline to release this Guarantee for such period as the Bank in its absolute discretion thinks fit to the intent that the Bank shall be entitled before releasing this Guarantee or any security held to secure the liability arising under it to satisfy itself that any payment will not be challenged whether as a preference given by the Principal or otherwise howsoever and in the event of any such challenge the Bank shall retain the benefit of this Guarantee and any security held to secure liability hereunder.

Service of demand

17. Any demand or notice under this Guarantee may be made or given by any manager or officer of the Bank or of any branch thereof by letter addressed to the Guarantor and delivered to the Guarantor (or any officer of the Guarantor if a body corporate) or sent by first class post to or left at the address of the Guarantor last known to the Bank (or at the registered office of the Guarantor if a body corporate) and if sent by post shall be deemed to have been made or given at noon on the day following the day the letter was posted and shall be effective notwithstanding that it be undelivered or be returned undelivered.

Liability of Guarantor before recovery from the Principal

18. The Bank shall be entitled to make demand under this Guarantee and to enforce all or any of the obligations of the Guarantor hereunder notwithstanding that it may not at the time of such demand or thereafter have sought to enforce any rights or remedies which it may have in respect of the monies and liabilities against the Principal or against any other surety or otherwise in relation to any security thereafter.

Set-off

19. In addition to all rights of set-off conferred by law the Bank shall be entitled to set-off against monies due from the Guarantor under this Guarantee all or any monies from time to time standing to the credit of the Guarantor with the Bank whether on current or any other account whatsoever.

Acquisition of shares in the Guarantor

20. A Guarantor which is a body corporate shall not be liable under this Guarantee in respect of such part (if any) of the monies and liabilities as may have been incurred by the Principal directly or indirectly in connection with the acquisition of shares of the Guarantor (or of any holding company of the Guarantor) unless and to the extent that the provision of financial assistance by this Guarantee in connection with such acquisition is not unlawful.

Governing law

21. This Guarantee shall be executed governed and construed in accordance with English law.

Interpretation

22. (a) Where the context so admits:

    (i) the expression "the Bank" shall include its successors and assigns

    (ii) any reference herein to a person shall include a body corporate

    (iii) reference to the singular shall include the plural and vice versa and the use of the masculine pronoun shall include the feminine.

  (b) Where there are two or more persons comprised in the expression "the Guarantor" the obligations of the Guarantor under this Guarantee shall be the obligations of such persons jointly and severally.

  (c) Any of the persons comprised in the expression the Guarantor may give notice under clause 6 of this Guarantee to determine the continuing nature of his joint and several liability hereunder but any such notice shall not affect or determine the obligations of the other persons so comprised and this Guarantee shall continue to affect those persons as if they had been the only persons originally so comprised.

  (d) The Bank shall be at liberty at any time to release or discharge any person comprised in the expression the Guarantor from his liability hereunder (to the intent that such release or discharge shall unless it provides otherwise also release or discharge that person from all rights of contribution whether accrued or inchoate which are then or might afterwards become enforceable by any of the other persons so comprised) and to give time for payment to accept any composition from or make any other arrangements with any such person without in any such case thereby releasing or discharging the others in whole or in part or otherwise prejudicing or affecting the rights and remedies of the Bank against those others.

IN WITNESS whereof the Guarantor has duly entered into this Guarantee on the

day of   19

This is an important legal document. The Bank recommends that before signing it you should seriously consider seeking the advice of a solicitor or other professional adviser.

Signed by ———————————————   Signed by ———————————————

in the presence of:-   in the presence of:-

Witness Signature ————————————   Witness Signature ————————————

Name   Name

Address   Address

Occupation   Occupation

Signed by——————————————————— Director

Signed by——————————————————— Director/Secretary

duly authorised on behalf of   Limited/Public Limited
Company by virtue of a Resolution of the Board passed on or before the execution of this Guarantee.

Index